WHERE CHEFS EAT

—

A GUIDE TO CHEFS' FAVORITE RESTAURANTS

WHERE CHEFS EAT

—

A GUIDE TO CHEFS' FAVORITE RESTAURANTS

Chef selection by
Joe Warwick

CONTENTS

Key
Preface
Chefs' Biographies

KEY

Breakfast
Whether it's a lazy or a snatched one, the chef couldn't start the day without breakfast here.

Late night
Service is over but the night is still young, this is where the chef satisfies any late-night hunger pangs.

Regular neighbourhood
Around the corner from the chef's work or home, this restaurant serves up food good enough to eat regularly.

Local favourite
This is the restaurant that best expresses the cuisine of the chef's home town.

Bargain
When money is limited but their appetite for good food isn't, this is where the chef goes when they're on a budget.

High end
For a special occasion or when money is no object, this is where the chef goes to splash out.

Wish I'd opened
Professional respect and admiration make this the restaurant that the chef wishes they'd opened.

Worth the travel
Across the country or on the other side of the world, there's no distance the chef wouldn't travel to eat at this restaurant.

PREFACE

Not so long ago the idea of a restaurant guide based on chefs' recommendations would have seemed fanciful: chefs cooked and a cabal of restaurant critics and inspectors told us where to eat. Although that's still true, chefs have become empowered beyond their kitchens, while traditional restaurant criticism struggles to be heard over the din of an online world where everyone has a voice.

When it comes to searching for trusted restaurant recommendations amidst so much noise and chatter, turning to accomplished chefs makes perfect sense. Modern chefs are no longer chained to their stoves. In many ways they're better attuned to their local restaurant scenes than the average critic, and rarely travel abroad without where they're going to eat being top of the agenda.

When crowdsourcing, why not return to the source? That was the original logic behind *Where Chefs Eat*. In this new book, we surveyed 630 leading international chefs who gave us recommendations in over 70 different countries – both where we've been before and new destinations. We've also found more space for the chefs' comments.

As before, the chefs surveyed were asked to recommend places to fulfil specific needs: be it breakfast or late-night venues; cheap or lavish thrills; reliable locals or once-in-a-lifetime destinations. The result is an eclectic, chef-curated compilation of 3,250 guaranteed good meals – an essential travel companion for anyone who loves eating.

I'd like to thank all the chefs who kindly took the time to take part. This book really wouldn't have been possible without their help. – Joe Warwick

THE CHEFS

Participating chefs and their restaurant recommendations

ADAM AAMANN
Aamanns
Øster Farimagsgade 12, Copenhagen
Copenhagen-based re-inventor of the smørrebrød, or open sandwich, who has since taken the idea to New York.

1.th **286**..High end
Acme **865**..............................Worth the travel
Damindra **288**.............Regular neighbourhood
Krummen & Kagen **297**...................Breakfast
Noma **289**...........................Wish I'd opened
Torvehallerne **291**..............................Bargain

CARLES ABELLAN
Comerç 24
Carrer Comerç 24, Barcelona
elBulli graduate with multiple tapas bars to his name, his most recent being Bravo 24 in the W Hotel.

The Bazaar by José Andrés **728**.......Worth the
travel
Can Jubany **492**..............................High end
Dos Palillos **518**.....................Wish I'd opened
Mosquito **520**....................................Bargain
El Quim de la Boqueria **519**..............Breakfast
Tlaxcal **513**....................................Late night

MATT ABERGEL
Yardbird
33–35 Bridges Street, Hong Kong
Calgary born, he trained under Japanese chef Masayoshi Takayama at Masa in New York, before taking the helm at Hong Kong's Zuma. Runs yakitori gastropub Yardbird (2011) and Rōnin (2013).

Amber **182**......................................High end
Cafe Pushkin **623**..................Worth the travel
The Chairman **183**....................Local favourite
Chicken HOF & SOJU **190**................Late night
One Harbour Road **181**.....................Regular
neighbourhood
One Harbour Road **181**...............Wish I'd opened
Tori + Salon **218**....................Wish I'd opened
Tsim Chai Kee Noodle **187**..................Bargain

MATTHEW ACCARRINO
SPQR
1911 Fillmore Street, San Francisco
New Jersey-raised, Culinary Institute of America-educated head chef of Italian-inspired SPQR in San Francisco.

Ciccio **708**......................................Bargain
The French Laundry **709**...................High end
Grace **833**.............................Worth the travel
Manresa **703**..........................Local favourite
Nopa **754**.....................................Late night
Out the Door **755**.......Regular neighbourhood
The Restaurant at Meadowood **708**.......Local
favourite
Tartine Bakery **752**...........................Breakfast

DANIEL ACHILLES
Reinstoff
Schlegelstrasse 26c, Berlin
German trained, he settled in Berlin as head chef at Reinstoff, winning plaudits for his avant-garde German cuisine including a Michelin star within a year of opening.

Cocolo Ramen **553**......Regular neighbourhood
Henne **551**..............................Local favourite
Monsieur Vuong **554**..........................Bargain
Monsieur Vuong **554**..........Wish I'd opened
El Poblet **507**.........................Worth the travel
Vendôme **544**................................High end
Yumcha Heroes **554**........................Late night
Zur letzten Instanz **554**............Local favourite

GASTÓN ACURIO
Astrid & Gastón
Avenida Paz Soldan 290, Lima
Founder of an impressive Lima-based restaurant empire that began with Astrid & Gastón in 1994.

El Celler de Can Roca **493**.....Worth the travel
Central **906**...........................Local favourite
Eggo **907**.......................................Breakfast
Maido **907**.................Regular neighbourhood
La Picantería **909**.............................Bargain
OSSO Carnicería & Salumeria **908**..........Wish
I'd opened

IVO ADAM
Seven
Via Moscia 2, Ascona
Swiss head chef of award-winning Seven and Seven Seas Lounge in the lakeside town of Ascona, Adam manages several restaurants and businesses in the Seven Group.

Aifach **560**...........................Worth the travel
Anne-Sophie Pic **565**.......................High end
L'Atelier de Joël Robuchon **459**.......Worth the
travel
Chez Vrony **564**..............................Breakfast
Eden Roc **563**.................................Breakfast
Grotto Baldoria **563**...........................Bargain
Tentazioni **563**............Regular neighbourhood

TOM ADAMS
Pitt Cue Co.
1 Newburgh Street, London
From a meat-peddling truck on London's Southbank, he has gone on to open his first bricks 'n' mortar barbeque outpost in 2012.

The Black Rat Restaurant **310**...........Wish I'd
opened
The Breslin Bar & Dining Room **843**......Worth
the travel
The Clove Club **371**...........................High end
Leila's Café **372**..............................Breakfast
Patty & Bun **329**...............................Bargain
Quo Vadis **350**.......................Local favourite
St. John Bread & Wine **374**.................Regular
neighbourhood
Tas Firin **373**.................................Late night

ALBERT ADRIÀ
Tickets
Avinguda Paral-lel 164, Barcelona
Younger brother of Ferran who's recently branched out from pastry to open Tickets and 41 Grados Experience.

El Celler de Can Roca **493**.......Local favourite
Dos Palillos **518**...............................Late night
Granja Viader **518**..........................Breakfast
Rafa's **495**...........................Wish I'd opened
Suculent **519**.............Regular neighbourhood
Umi **218**................................Worth the travel
Umi **218**.......................................High end
Viena **512**.......................................Bargain

FERRAN ADRIÀ
elBulli Foundation
Cala Montjoi, Roses
From 1984 to 2011 he changed the course of haute cuisine with elBulli. He plans to continue that work with his foundation.

Bar Pinotxo 517...............................Breakfast
Bras 436.............................Worth the travel
Dos Palillos 518.........Regular neighbourhood
Rias de Galicia 517...........................High end

ANDONI LUIS ADURIZ
Mugaritz
Aldura Aldea 20, Errenteria
With credentials that read like a checklist of Spanish haute cuisine it's not surprising Aduriz opened award-winning Mugaritz at just twenty-six.

Akelarre 483.....................................High end
Arzak 483...High end
Asador Etxebarri 479.........................High end
Bar Txepetxa 484.................................Bargain
La Bodega Donostiarra 485................Bargain
Bodegón Alejandro 485.....................Regular
neighbourhood
El Celler de Can Roca 493....Worth the travel
Elkano 481...........................Local favourite
Kabuki Wellington 500.....................Late night
La Mar 908....................Wish I'd opened
Nerua 480.......................................Late night
Quique Dacosta Restaurante 505....Worth the
travel
Restaurante ni neu 489.....................Bargain

TOM AIKENS
Tom's Kitchen
27 Cale Street, London
Koffmann and Robuchon trained, he made his name as head chef at Pied à Terre before opening his own restaurants, including Tom's Kitchen, in London and Istanbul.

Brasserie Chavot 340............Wish I'd opened
Colbert 321..................Regular neighbourhood
The Dairy 323.....................................Bargain
Daylesford 320................................Breakfast
The Elm 873..........................Worth the travel
Granger & Co 330...........................Breakfast
Hélène Darroze 342.........................High end
The Orange 320................................Breakfast
Soho Kitchen & Bar 351.................Late night
The Wolseley 345....................Local favourite

RAHUL AKERKAR
Indigo
4 Mandlik Road, Mumbai
In 1999 he opened Indigo, a restaurant with a European-meets-Indian menu. Branches and a new grill restaurant followed.

L'Arpège 458.........................Worth the travel
Bade Miya 154.................................Late night
Imàgo 581............................Worth the travel
Royal China India 156.........................Regular
neighbourhood
Shree Thaker Bhojanalay 157...Local favourite
Wasabi by Morimoto 152.................High end

MASSIMILIANO ALAJMO
Le Calandre
Via Liguria 1, Sarmeola di Rubano
After training in France under Veyrat and Guérard he returned home to Italy and his family's esteemed restaurant Le Calandre in 1983.

Dario Doc 598..Bargain
Enoiteca Mascareta 600.................Late night
Harry's Bar 601...............Wish I'd opened
Maison Troisgros 445.........................High end
Ristorante da Giovanni 599......Local favourite
Ristorante Duomo 596........Worth the travel
Ristorante Quadri 601.........................Regular
neighbourhood

JOSEAN ALIJA
Nerua
Avenida Abandoibarra 2, Bilbao
Following spells at hotels, elBulli and Martín Berasategui he opened Nerua and a more casual bistro in the Guggenheim in 2011.

Asador Etxebarri 479................Local favourite
Asador Indusi 479.....Regular neighbourhood
Baita Gaminiz 479......Regular neighbourhood
Bras 436.........................Wish I'd opened
El Celler de Can Roca 493..................High end
Elkano 481.................Regular neighbourhood
Masa 846...Late night
Noma 289...High end
Quique Dacosta Restaurante 505.........High end
Sukiyabashi Jiro 212............Worth the travel
Txakoli Simón 480......Regular neighbourhood

YANNICK ALLÉNO
Le 1947
Hôtel Le Cheval Blanc, Le Jardin Alpin, Courchevel
After twenty-five years working in haute hotel kitchens, multi-Michelin-starred Alléno left Le Meurice in 2013 to concentrate on 'Le 1947' at Le Cheval Blanc hotel in Courchevel.

Julien 465......................................Late night
Les Orchidées 452...........................Breakfast
Restaurant Edouard Loubet 438.......High end
Le Stresa 464............Regular neighbourhood
Ultraviolet 166.........................Worth the travel
Zen 452..Bargain

OMAR ALLIBHOY
Tapas Revolution
Westfield, Ariel Way, London
With elBulli and Maze on his résumé Madrid-born Allibhoy joined El Pirata de Tapas in 2008, launching the popular Tapas Revolution shortly after.

Bistrot de Luxe 327....Regular neighbourhood
Busaba Eathai 347.....................Local favourite
Dinner by Heston Blumenthal 326....High end
La Fromagerie 328...........................Breakfast
Ibu Oka 244............................Worth the travel
Khans 319..........................Wish I'd opened
Locale 324...Late night
Taberna de la Daniela 503.......Local favourite
Tickets 515...........................Worth the travel

DAVID ALMANY
Osteria Mozza
42–46, 2 Bayfront Avenue, Singapore
Los Angeles chef who worked his way up at Mario Batali's Osteria Mozza, taking the Italian-American fare on its first venture abroad, as executive chef of its Singapore outpost.

Burnt Ends 238.................Wish I'd opened
chi SPACCA 739.....................Worth the travel
CUT 234.....................Regular neighbourhood
DB Bistro Moderne 234.........................Regular
neighbourhood
DB Bistro Moderne 234...................Breakfast
Kake Da Dhaba 234............................Bargain
Lavender Food Square Centre 234...Late night
No Signboard Seafood 233......Local favourite
Otowa 236.................Regular neighbourhood
Waku Ghin 235...................................High end

MAOZ ALONIM
HaBasta
4 Hashomer Street, Tel Aviv
Tel Aviv's HaBasta, a bistro serving food from the nearby market and a chefs' favourite, was the brainchild of oenophile Alonim and Itay Hargil. Alonim co-owns nearby Café Europa.

Chanan Margilan 142...........................Bargain
Lucifer 143.......................................Late night
Mati Bar 143....................................Breakfast
The Minzar 143......................Local favourite
Shrabic 141...........................Worth the travel
Thai House 145..........Regular neighbourhood
Yakimono 145...................................High end

BRUNO OTEIZA & MIKEL ALONSO
Biko
Avenida Presidente Masaryk 407, Mexico City
With a shared Basque culinary heritage,
and training under luminaries such as Juan
Mari Arzak, they showcase their unique
Basque-Mexican fusion cuisine at Biko's in
Mexico City.
Arzak 483................................Wish I'd opened
Azurmendi 482................................High end
El Bajío 882...................................Bargain
Laja 881............................Worth the travel
Patisserie Dominique 884.................Breakfast
Quintonil 884..............................Late night
Raíz 889.....................Regular neighbourhood

WOJCIECH MODEST AMARO
Atelier Amaro
Ulica Agrykola 1, Warsaw
Polish chef who, after honing his skills in the
kitchens of elBulli and Noma, opened Atelier
Amaro in Warsaw (2012), the only Polish
restaurant to hold a Michelin star.
Bodega 1900 513...............Wish I'd opened
El Celler de Can Roca 493.....Worth the travel
Mąka i Woda 614................................Bargain
Noma 289....................................High end
Stary Dom 615...................Local favourite

GAGGAN ANAND
Gaggan
68/1 Soi Langsuan, Ploenchit Road, Bangkok
Kolkata born, he trained with Ferran Adrià
and now presents 'progressive Indian'
cuisine at his celebrated Bangkok restaurant,
Gaggan.
Bird Land 210...................................High end
Chairoj 224.................Regular neighbourhood
Gai Tawn Pratunam 224.....................Bargain
Kewpie's 159......................Local favourite
Nodaiwa 216...................................High end
Osteria Francescana 577.......Worth the travel
Soi 38 Night Market 226..................Late night
Sukiyabashi Jiro 212.........................High end
Talat Don Wai 227............................Breakfast
Tickets 515.........................Wish I'd opened

PRAVEEN ANAND
Dakshin
Sheraton Park Hotel, T.T.K. Road, Chennai
Executive chef at Dakshin (Chennai), Anand
trained in Western cuisine, later becoming a
culinary ambassador for South Indian food.
He also launched On the Rocks at Chennai's
Sheraton Park.
Bentley Restaurant & Bar 87.Worth the travel
Iggy's 236.........................Worth the travel
M on the Bund 171...............Worth the travel
Madurai Arulanandam 157.................Regular
neighbourhood
Mathsya 157...............................Late night
Murugan Idli Kadai 158..........Local favourite
Mylai Karpagambal Mess 158.........Breakfast
Royal Vega 158.................Wish I'd opened
Shiraz Art Cafe 158........................High end

NICK ANDERER
Maialino
2 Lexington Avenue, New York City
Indiana-born executive chef and partner
at Maialino, he worked with Mario Batali,
apprenticed in Italy and cooked at Gramercy
Tavern before joining Danny Meyer's Union
Hospitality Group.
Bar Tartine 750..................Worth the travel
Battersby 871....................Wish I'd opened
Congee Village 864............................Bargain
David's Bagels 863.........................Breakfast
Dover 873....................Wish I'd opened
Eisenberg's Sandwich Shop 862............Local
favourite
Gramercy Tavern 863......................High end
Mayahuel 850.............Regular neighbourhood
Swift Hibernian Lounge 867............Late night

JOSÉ ANDRÉS
Minibar
855 East Street Northwest, Washington D.C.
Spanish chef-owner of ThinkFoodGroup,
with a dozen restaurants across the US,
including Minibar, Zaytinya, Oyamel, Jaleo,
China Poblano and Mi Casa at Dorado Beach
in Puerto Rico.
2 Amys 762................Regular neighbourhood
800 Degrees 743...................Wish I'd opened
El Bajío 882.................................Breakfast
Bar Pinotxo 517................................Breakfast
El Capricho 490....................Worth the travel
Daikaya 763.................Regular neighbourhood
The Inn at Little Washington 811.......High end
Makoto 763.................Regular neighbourhood
La Mar 908......................Worth the travel
Restaurant Nora 764.............Local favourite
Toki Underground 764......................Regular
neighbourhood

IZU ANI
La Serre
Mohammed Bin Rashid Boulevard, Dubai
Nigerian executive chef of La Serre, with
a glittering résumé featuring L'Auberge
de L'Ill, The Square, Arzak and Akelarre;
brought French cuisine to Dubai with La
Petite Maison.
L'Auberge de L'Ill 428........Wish I'd opened
Baker & Spice 145..........................Breakfast
Eataly 146....................................Bargain
Koya 349.........................Worth the travel
Qbara 146.................Regular neighbourhood
Reflets by Pierre Gagnaire 147........High end

MICHAEL ANTHONY
Gramercy Tavern
42 East 20th Street, New York City
Moved from Cincinnati to Paris where he
worked at L'Arpège and L'Astrance. After
a stint at Blue Hill at Stone Barns he joined
Gramercy Tavern.
Kikunoi 201......................Worth the travel
Maialino 863.................................Breakfast
McCrady's 802....................Worth the travel
Momofuku Ssäm Bar 851..............Late night
Per Se 846....................................High end
Yakitori Totto 842............................Bargain

GONZALO ARAMBURU
Aramburu
Salta 1050, Buenos Aires
Learnt his trade in Europe and the US, under
culinary giants including Charlie Trotter, Martín
Berasategui and Joël Robuchon, returning to
Buenos Aires to open experimental tasting-
menu-only Aramburu.
Astor 936....................................Bargain
Brindillas 931.....................Worth the travel
Café San Juan 942...............Local favourite
Caseros 942....................Wish I'd opened
Paraje Arévalo 938.........................High end
Las Pizarras 937........Regular neighbourhood
El Refuerzo Bar Almacen 943.........Late night

VÍCTOR ARGUINZÓNIZ
Asador Etxebarri
Plaza de San Juan 1, Atxondo
Chef-owner of Asador Etxebarri, a Basque
Country farmhouse he took over in 1989 and
turned into a gastronomic destination.
Akelarre 483......................Wish I'd opened
Arzak 483...........................Wish I'd opened
Ibai 488.................Regular neighbourhood
Mugaritz 480....................Worth the travel
Nerua 480.........................Wish I'd opened
Nihonryori Ryugin 216.........Worth the travel
Zuberoa 482.....................Wish I'd opened

CATHAL ARMSTRONG
Restaurant Eve
110 South Pitt Street, Alexandria
Championing Ireland's culinary culture, the native Dubliner headed across the pond to Washington, D.C., opening Virginia's Restaurant Eve in 2004.

Capital Grille 811	Local favourite
Central Michel Richard 763	Wish I'd opened
Dining Room 383	Worth the travel
Elsie's Magic Skillet 810	Breakfast
Gamasot 811	Regular neighbourhood
Lotte Plaza 810	Bargain
Per Se 846	High end

JUAN MARI & ELENA ARZAK
Arzak
Avenida Alcalde José Elósegui 273, San Sebastián
Father and daughter behind the three-Michelin-starred Arzak, owned and run by the family since 1897.

Akelarre 483	Wish I'd opened
Alameda 481	Worth the travel
Asador Etxebarri 479	High end
Bernardina Vinoteca 485	Regular neighbourhood
Biko 882	Worth the travel
Borda Berri 486	Bargain
El Celler de Can Roca 493	Worth the travel
Elkano 481	High end
A Fuego Negro 486	Bargain
Ganbara Jatetxea 487	Regular neighbourhood
Geltoki 487	Breakfast
Haizea Bar 487	Breakfast
Iggy's 236	Worth the travel
Mugaritz 480	Worth the travel
Nerua 480	Wish I'd opened
Tamboril 489	Bargain
Zuberoa 482	Worth the travel

CORRADO ASSENZA
Caffè Sicilia
Corso Vittorio Emanuele III 125, Noto
A champion pastry chef and owner of Caffè Sicilia, a pastry-coffee-ice cream bar in Noto, southeastern Sicily.

Antica Osteria Cera 600	Wish I'd opened
I Sapori del Val di Noto 596	Local favourite
I Sapori del Val di Noto 596	Bargain
La Madia 595	Local favourite
La Madia 595	High end
Ristorante Crocifisso 596	Local favourite
Ristorante da Tuccino 595	Worth the travel
Ristorante Dammuso 597	Local favourite
Ristorante Duomo 596	Local favourite
Ristorante Duomo 596	High end

ALEX ATALA
D.O.M. Restaurante
Rua Barão de Capanema 549, São Paulo
Chef-proprietor of D.O.M. in São Paulo, Atala is famous for combining unusual indigenous ingredients with European technique.

Epice 923	High end
Maní 925	High end
Mocotó 929	Bargain
Padaria Jardim Brasil 928	Breakfast
Restaurante Vito 928	Regular neighbourhood
Spot 921	Wish I'd opened
Sushi Sawada 213	Worth the travel
Umi 218	Worth the travel

JASON ATHERTON
Pollen Street Social
8–10 Pollen Street, London
Created Maze for Gordon Ramsay before going it alone with Pollen Street Social, Little Social, Social Eating House, Berners Tavern and outposts in the Far East.

Baozi Inn 336	Bargain
Barrafina 346	Regular neighbourhood
Chiswick 103	Worth the travel
The French Laundry 709	Wish I'd opened
Goodman 341	Late night
The Ledbury 331	High end
Mercato 171	Worth the travel
Momofuku Seiõbo 98	Worth the travel
Quintessence 219	Worth the travel
Restaurant Sat Bains 312	High end
Restaurant Sat Bains 312	Worth the travel
The Wolseley 345	Breakfast

PASCAL AUSSIGNAC
Club Gascon
57 West Smithfield, London
Born in Toulouse, trained across France, he has founded a London empire based around gutsy foie gras-loving Gascon cooking.

The Breakfast Club 366	Breakfast
Busaba Eathai 347	Bargain
Colbert 321	Wish I'd opened
The Gallery 341	Late night
J Sheekey 338	Regular neighbourhood
The Modern Pantry 359	Local favourite
Noma 289	High end
La Tupina 430	Worth the travel

JOSÉ AVILLEZ
Belcanto
Largo de São Carlos 10, Lisbon
Worked for Adrià, Ducasse and Frechon before returning home to Portugal and launching Cantinho do Avillez and Belcanto.

El Celler de Can Roca 493	Wish I'd opened
Cervejaria Ramiro 532	Regular neighbourhood
Grande Palácio Hong Kong 536	Bargain
Mugaritz 480	Worth the travel
Ocean 524	Worth the travel
Pastelaria Bénard 536	Breakfast
A Taberna da Rua das Flores 536	Local favourite

LUÍS BAENA
Notting Hill Kitchen
92 Kensington Park Road, London
Legendary Portuguese chef with a career spanning three decades and several continents. Left the kitchens at Tivoli Hotels to join London's Notting Hill Kitchen in 2013.

Cervejaria Ramiro 532	Late night
EMO Gourmet Restaurant 525	High end
Machne Yuda 141	Worth the travel
O Talho 534	Wish I'd opened
Tasca da Esquina 535	Local favourite

SAT BAINS
Restaurant Sat Bains
Lenton Lane, Nottingham
Chef-proprietor of a cutting-edge culinary destination in the somewhat unlikely setting of Nottingham, England.

Casamia 305	Worth the travel
The Fat Duck 304	Wish I'd opened
The Hand & Flowers 305	Regular neighbourhood
Maroush 328	Late night

STEFANO BAIOCCO
Villa Feltrinelli
Via Rimembranza 38–40, Gargnano
Following spells with Ducasse, Gagnaire and Adrià he worked at Florence's Enoteca Pinchiorri before joining Villa Feltrinelli.

Geranium 296	Worth the travel
Ikarus 604	Wish I'd opened
De Kas 401	Wish I'd opened
Le Louis XV 447	High end
Al Mandracchio 590	Local favourite
Osteria Teatro Strabacco 590	Late night
Pasticceria Veneto 586	Breakfast
Ristorante Pizzeria Nablus 586	Late night
La Sosta 586	Bargain
La Tortuga 586	Regular neighbourhood

DAN BARBER
Blue Hill at Stone Barns
630 Bedford Road, Pocantico Hills
A perennial chefs' favourite and the original culinary brains behind field-to-fork destinations, Blue Hill in New York and Hudson Valley's Blue Hill at Stone Barns.
Aponiente **476**........................Wish I'd opened
Jackson Diner **852**....................Local favourite

PASCAL BARBOT
L'Astrance
4 Rue Beethoven, Paris
A protégé of Alain Passard, whom he worked under for five years, prior to opening the celebrated L'Astrance in 2000.
Asador Etxebarri **479**.......................Late night
L'Atelier de Joël Robuchon **459**.........High end
Azurmendi **482**...................Worth the travel
Bras **436**............................Wish I'd opened
Maison Decoret **432**...............Worth the travel
La Pâtisserie des Rêves **470**....Local favourite
Restaurant André **239**...........Worth the travel
SaQuaNa **436**.............Regular neighbourhood

JUAN MANUEL BARRIENTOS
El Cielo
Carrera 40 N 10a–22, Medellin
The celebrated Latin American chef opened Medellin's El Cielo, a multi-award-winning shrine to molecular gastronomy, in his twenties.
Alinea **827**............................Wish I'd opened
Alinea **827**......................Worth the travel
Donde Juancho **904**............................Bargain
Sancho Paisa **904**.......Regular neighbourhood
Sancho Paisa **904**...................Local favourite

DARIO BARRIO
Dassa Bassa
Calle de Villalar 7, Madrid
Madrilenian who cut his teeth in kitchens in Las Palmas, London, Bordeaux, Zurich and Madrid before opening Dassa Bassa.
During the making of this book, Dario was in a fatal accident. Phaidon have retained his recommendations as a mark of respect for his contribution to the industry.
Atrio **498**...............................Worth the travel
El Chaflán **499**............Regular neighbourhood
Corral de la Moreria **499**.................Late night
Corral de la Moreria **499**.......Wish I'd opened
Estado Puro **500**......................Local favourite
Isaac Salido **500**...............................Breakfast
Ramón Freixa Madrid **502**................High end
Restaurante MEATing **502**...................Bargain

ITALO BASSI
Enoteca Pinchiorri
Via Ghibellina 87, Florence
Runs the kitchen at Enoteca Pinchiorri in partnership with Riccardo Monco, whom he has worked alongside for close to twenty years.
L'Atelier de Joel Robuchon Étoile **462**.....Wish I'd opened
Celadon **224**...........................Worth the travel
Le Louis XV **447**................................High end
Tapasotto **601**.................................Late night
Trattoria Fratelli Briganti **598**............Bargain

EMMANUEL BASSOLEIL
Skye Restaurant & Bar
Hotel Unique, Avenida Brigadeiro Luis Antonio 4700, São Paulo
Born in Burgundy and trained under Troisgros, Bassoleil moved to Brazil in 1987 and currently oversees Skye restaurant.
D.O.M. Restaurante **921**........Worth the travel
Mani **925**.......................................High end
Marie-Madeleine **922**.......................Breakfast
Restaurante Vito **928**...........Wish I'd opened
Rex Restaurante **924**......................Late night
Tian **922**...Bargain
Tordesilhas **924**......................Local favourite
Tre Bicchieri **925**........Regular neighbourhood

BEN BATTERBURY
True South Dining Room
The Rees Hotel, 377 Frankton Road, Queenstown
Born in England, executive chef Batterbury is now based in Central Otago, where he heads up the kitchen at True South Dining Room.
Atlas Beer Café **121**.............Wish I'd opened
Fergburger **122**...............................Late night
Fleurs Place **121**...................Local favourite
Kappa Sushi Cafe **122**.........................Regular neighbourhood
Merediths **131**.................................High end
Vudu Café & Larder **123**.................Breakfast
Yama Express **123**.............................Bargain

JEAN-MARIE BAUDIC
Youpala Bistrot
5 Rue Palasne de Champeaux, Saint-Brieuc
A proud Breton who credits Jeffroy and Gagnaire as his two culinary fathers, Baudic cooks market-driven food at Youpala Bistrot.
Le Bacaretto **436**..................Wish I'd opened
Le Bon Sens **433**..............................Bargain
Bras **436**..High end
Char à Bancs **433**.......Regular neighbourhood
Hotel Torre Martí **497**............Worth the travel
Manoir Montmorency **665**................Breakfast
Restaurant Patrick Jeffroy **433** Local favourite
La Tour de Montlhéry **451**.................Late night

BENJAMIN BAYLY
The Grove Restaurant
Saint Patrick's Square, Auckland
Stints at London's The Square and The Ledbury laid the ground for Bayly's Auckland homecoming and his position at The Grove.
Bracu **118**............................Wish I'd opened
Île de France **132**...............................Bargain
Merediths **131**.................................High end
New Flavour **131**..............................Late night
The Refreshment Room **133**...............Regular neighbourhood
SIDART **133**...........................Local favourite
SPQR **755**..........................Worth the travel
Vevo Foodstore **131**.........................Breakfast

BO BECH
Geist
Kongens Nytorv 8, Copenhagen
Culinary alchemist Bech, ex-Paustian head chef, opened Geist in Copenhagen in 2010, where he serves experimental New Nordic grazing dishes.
L'Atelier de Joël Robuchon **337**.........Wish I'd opened
Atelier September **287**.....................Breakfast
Kebabistan **292**..............................Late night
Mocotó **929**....................................Bargain
Relæ **293**................Regular neighbourhood
Saison **756**.....................................High end
Schønnemann **290**................Local favourite
Sushi Sawada **213**................Worth the travel

HEINZ BECK
La Pergola
Via Alberto Cadlolo 101, Rome
Born in Germany, he worked under Winkler before moving to La Pergola in 1994. Since 2009 he's also overseen the menu at Apsleys.
Antico Forno Roscioli **581**................Breakfast
L'Atelier de Joël Robuchon **337**........High end
The Botanist **320**...........................Breakfast
Charleston **596**....................Wish I'd opened
The Jerry Thomas Project **581**........Worth the travel
Residenz Heinz Winkler **541**....Local favourite
Il Ristorante Bulgari **212**.......Worth the travel
Romeo **583**......................................Bargain
Il San Lorenzo **584**.....Regular neighbourhood
Zuma **327**....................Regular neighbourhood

RAINER BECKER
Zuma
5 Raphael Street, London
In 2013, eleven years after opening Asian-inspired Zuma (now with outlets worldwide) and Roka with Arjun Waney, Becker launched Oblix, in London's Shard.

The Chairman 183..................Worth the travel
Daquise 333.................................Late night
The Fat Duck 304.............................High end
Noma 289.............................Worth the travel
Riding House Café 364......................Breakfast
Riva 318.................Regular neighbourhood
The River Café 325..................Local favourite
Sonny's Kitchen 318....Regular neighbourhood
Wright Brothers 352...Regular neighbourhood

JEAN BEDDINGTON
English-born Beddington opened her own eponymous restaurant in Amsterdam before going freelance as a 'culinary creative'.

Beyrouth 402.............Regular neighbourhood
Conservatorium Brasserie 403.........Breakfast
Eetsalon Van Dobben 398........Local favourite
Magnolia Ristorante 576.......Worth the travel
Mi Ka 407..Bargain
La Rive 402.........................Worth the travel
Tetsuya's 92..........................Wish I'd opened
Tunes Restaurant 405.......................High end
Uliassi 591.........................Worth the travel
Yamazato 405....................................High end

AKRAME BENALLAL
Restaurant Akrame
19 Rue Lauriston, Paris
Pierre Gagnaire protégé, the Parisian chef and owner of Akrame (2011) won his second Michelin star in 2014, and recently launched an Akrame outpost in Hong Kong.

Allard 455............................Local favourite
À la Goutte d'Or 471...Regular neighbourhood
L'Atelier de Joël Robuchon 459..........Wish I'd opened
Carette 470.....................................Breakfast
D.O.M. Restaurante 921........Worth the travel
Neva Cuisine 463...............................Bargain
Pierre Gagnaire 463...........................High end
Terroir Parisien 455.................Local favourite

MARTIN BENN
Sepia
201 Sussex Street, Sydney
Began his career in London before relocating to Sydney in 1996. After a stint at the acclaimed Tetsuya's he opened the Japanese-inspired Sepia.

Attica 113..High end
Attica 113.........................Worth the travel
Berta 87.................Regular neighbourhood
Bird Land 210......................Wish I'd opened
Golden Fields 114...................Local favourite
Momofuku Seiōbo 98............Wish I'd opened
Mr. Wong 90......................................Bargain
Quay 102..High end
Rosso Pomodoro Pizzeria 86...........Late night
Spice Temple 91....................Local favourite
Takazawa 218.......................Worth the travel

SHANNON BENNETT
Vue de Monde
525 Collins Street, Melbourne
Melbourne-born chef who worked with Albert Roux, Marco Pierre White and Alain Ducasse before heading home to open Vue de Monde at the tender age of twenty-four.

Bar Di Stasio 114.......Regular neighbourhood
Cookie 106...........................Local favourite
Federal Doma Café 74.......................Bargain
Harvest Café 74................Wish I'd opened
Mamasita 108....................................Late night
Sixpenny 95.......................................High end
Three Blue Ducks 102......................Breakfast
Ultraviolet 166....................Worth the travel

MARTÍN BERASATEGUI
Martín Berasategui
Loidi Kalea 4, Lasarte-Oria
At only twenty Berasategui became head chef of Bodegón Alejandro, which cemented his reputation as a Basque culinary heavyweight.

Akelarre 483..........................Local favourite
Arzak 483............................Local favourite
Chila 939..........................Worth the travel
Kaia Kaipe 481............Regular neighbourhood
Masa 846.............................Worth the travel
Muguruza 483..................................Breakfast
Va Bene Disco Burger 489..............Late night
Xarma Jatetxea 489...........................Bargain
Zuberoa 482.......................................High end
Zuberoa 482........................Wish I'd opened

DONALD BERGER
Don's
16 Quang An, Hanoi
Raised in Montreal, he explored three continents before settling in Hanoi to offer a globally inspired menu at Don's Tay Ho.

8½ Otto e Mezzo Bombana 182......Worth the travel
Le Beaulieu 227...............................High end
Bún Bò Nam Bộ 227.........................Bargain
Chả Cá Lã Vọng 227.........................Bargain
El Gaucho 228.......................Wish I'd opened
Lake View Food Centre 228.............Late night
Ming 228....................Regular neighbourhood
Phở Học Gia Truyền 228...................Breakfast
Quán Ăn Ngon 229..................Local favourite

GUILLERMO GONZÁLEZ BERISTÁIN
Pangea
Bosques del Valle 110–20, San Pedro Garza García
Culinary Institute of America-trained Beristáin worked the line at Michelin-starred restaurants across Europe, opening Pangea in Monterrey in 1998, the flagship of his burgeoning group of high-end Mexican restaurants.

Chef Herrera 886.............................Late night
La Nacional 886....................Local favourite
Neuquen 887.....................................Bargain
Restaurant Cafe Capri 886.............Breakfast
Romero y Azahar 887.........................Regular neighbourhood
Rosetta 885........................Worth the travel
Yamasan Ramen House 887...Wish I'd opened

DANIEL BERLIN
Daniel Berlin Krog
Diligensvägen 21, Tomelilla
Left the Swedish city of Malmö behind to open a restaurant in the heart of the Österlen countryside, where uber-local produce is king.

Bastard 262................Regular neighbourhood
Bastard 262........................Local favourite
Fäviken Magasinet 261.....................High end
Frantzén 270.....................................High end
Hedone 322........................Worth the travel
Noma 289..High end
Spooneny 265....................................Bargain

JOHN BESH
August
301 Tchoupitoulas Street, New Orleans
This busy executive chef at August in New Orleans has seven other restaurants in and around the city, and another in San Antonio, Texas.

Ba Mien 820................Regular neighbourhood
Bon Ton Café 817....................Local favourite
Camellia Grill 821............................Late night
Galatoire's Restaurant 818...............High end
Momofuku Ssäm Bar 851......Wish I'd opened
RedFarm 856..........................Worth the travel
Satsuma 816.....................................Breakfast

MARK BEST
Marque
4/5 355 Crown Street, Sydney
Quitting his job as an electrician to become a kitchen apprentice, he discovered a passion for French food and trained in Europe, opening Sydney's Marque – a bastion of New Australian cuisine – in 1999.

Chat Thai 88	Bargain
The Fish Shop 96	Regular neighbourhood
Golden Century Seafood 89	Late night
Kitchen by Mike 99	Breakfast
Mr. Wong 90	Local favourite
Narisawa 216	Worth the travel
Quay 102	High end

TOMI BJÖRCK
Gaijin
Bulevardi 6, Helsinki
Opened his first Asian-inspired restaurant, Stockholm's Farang, in 2009 followed by three restaurants in Helsinki. His fifth venture, Bronda, opened in 2014.

Brown Sugar 86	Breakfast
Chat Thai 88	Late night
Cholo 298	Regular neighbourhood
Dinner by Heston Blumenthal 326	Worth the travel
Mama San 240	Bargain
Quay 102	High end
Sturehof 276	Local favourite

ANTON BJUHR
Gastrologik
Artillerigatan 14, Stockholm
Runs Gastrologik in Stockholm with Jacob Holmström where the focus is pastry and baking, and Speceriet, a casual offshoot.

Ekstedt 273	High end
Eriks Bakficka 274	Regular neighbourhood
Max Hamngatan 272	Late night
Petite France 271	Breakfast
Roberta's 875	Worth the travel
Sturehof 276	Local favourite
Taylors & Jones with the Twist 271	Bargain

GALTON BLACKISTON
Morston Hall Restaurant
Morston Hall Hotel, The Street, Holt
Self-taught chef and owner of Norfolk's Morston Hall hotel for over twenty years, he recently opened a fish-and-chip shop in Cromer.

Balthazar 868	Breakfast
Hakkasan 342	Late night
The Ledbury 331	Worth the travel
The Waterside Inn 304	High end

RAYMOND BLANC
Le Manoir aux Quat'Saisons
Church Road, Great Milton
Self-taught Gallic culinary legend and chef-patron at two-Michelin-starred Le Manoir aux Quat'Saisons in Oxfordshire. Founded the Brasserie Blanc chain in 2012.

Shaun Dickens at The Boathouse 312	Local favourite
Texture 330	Regular neighbourhood

APRIL BLOOMFIELD
The Spotted Pig
314 West 11th Street, New York City
From Birmingham, UK, to New York via London, April made her name at The Spotted Pig before opening The Breslin and The John Dory Oyster Bar.

Eleven Madison Park 862	High end
Husk 801	Worth the travel
Jing Fong 861	Bargain
Keens Steakhouse 841	Local favourite
Maialino 863	Regular neighbourhood
Noma 289	Worth the travel
Rose Bakery 838	Breakfast

JONNIE BOER
Restaurant De Librije
Broerenkerkplein 13–15, Zwolle
Acclaimed Dutch chef with a collection of restaurants and related businesses in the Netherlands, built around his Zwolle flagship, De Librije.

Bistro Bonne Femme 394	Regular neighbourhood
Ron Gastrobar 404	Local favourite
Thaise Snackbar Bird 400	Bargain
Yardbird 188	Wish I'd opened
Yardbird 188	Worth the travel

SAUL BOLTON
Saul
200 Eastern Parkway, New York City
Opened the produce-championing Saul in Brooklyn in 1999, which has since been joined by The Vanderbilt, Botanica and Red Gravy.

Antonio's 779	Worth the travel
The Bagel Hole 871	Breakfast
Brooklyn Fare 872	High end
Café Grumpy 872	Breakfast
Fonda 873	Regular neighbourhood
Gorilla Coffee 874	Breakfast
Peter Luger Steakhouse 875	Local favourite
Tacos Matamoros 876	Late night
Al di Là Trattoria 873	Wish I'd opened
White Bear 877	Bargain

UMBERTO BOMBANA
8½ Otto e Mezzo Bombana
18 Chater Road, Hong Kong
Arguably Asia's most famous Italian chef who operates 8½ Otto e Mezzo Bombana in Hong Kong and Shanghai, and Opera Bombana in Beijing.

Daigo 215	High end
Lei Garden 185	Local favourite
Pierre Gagnaire 463	Wish I'd opened
Tasty Congee & Noodle Wantun Shop 187	Bargain
Wagyu Takumi 181	Regular neighbourhood
Yardbird 188	Late night

NEIL BORTHWICK
Merchants Tavern
36 Charlotte Road, London
Former Michel Bras sous chef, Edinburgh-born Borthwick honed his skills at The Square, opening Merchants Tavern in 2013 with Murano's Angela Hartnett.

Cafe Murano 352	Late night
The Kitchin 377	Worth the travel
Leila's Café 372	Bargain
Rochelle Canteen 372	Regular neighbourhood
The Square 344	High end
St. John Bread & Wine 374	Local favourite

MARTIN BOSLEY
Since becoming head chef at Grain of Salt at the age of just twenty, Bosley has been a fixture on Wellington's restaurant scene for over two decades.

Central Kitchen 750	Worth the travel
Dragons Chinese Restaurant 123	Bargain
Floriditas 124	Breakfast
The French Café 129	High end
Havana Bar & Restaurant 124	Late night
Nikau Café 125	Regular neighbourhood
Rich Table 749	Wish I'd opened

ETTORE BOTRINI
Botrini's
Vasileos Georgiou 24, Athens
Holds the reins of his family's long-running restaurant in Corfu and also oversees Botrini's in Athens, and ArtO2 in Thessaloniki.

Bodegón Alejandro 485	Bargain
Le Chateaubriand 466	Wish I'd opened
The Gallery 341	High end
Klimataria 629	Local favourite
Martín Berasategui 482	Regular neighbourhood
Zanettos 629	Worth the travel

MASSIMO BOTTURA
Osteria Francescana
Via Stella 22, Modena
Culinary traditions are not easily challenged
in Italy but Bottura has succeeded with
Modena's avant-garde Osteria Francescana.
A-Frame 731..Bargain
Astrid & Gastón 906...............Worth the travel
Blue Hill at Stone Barns 790..Wish I'd opened
Central 906............................Worth the travel
Le Chateaubriand 466.........................Bargain
The Clove Club 371...............................Bargain
D.O.M. Restaurante 921........Worth the travel
Dal Pescatore 589...................Local favourite
Daniel 844.............................Worth the travel
Eleven Madison Park 862.................High end
L'Erba del Re 576........Regular neighbourhood
Little Serow 763....................................Bargain
Má Pêche 841.......................................Bargain
Momofuku Ssäm Bar 851......................Bargain
Mon Café 577......................................Breakfast
Mugaritz 480........................Worth the travel
Noma 289.............................Worth the travel
Pasticceria Bar Dondi 577.................Breakfast
Piazza Duomo 591..............................High end
Pizzeria Mozza 235..............................Bargain
Del Posto 860.......................Worth the travel
Pujol 884..............................Worth the travel

LOUIS BOUCHARD TRUDEAU
Le Bouchon du Pied Bleu
179 Saint-Vallier Ouest, Québec
Runs Le Bouchon du Pied Bleu, offering a
laid-back Lyonnais-inspired take on Quebec
cuisine, with his partner, Thania Goyette.
L'Affaire Est Ketchup 664........Local favourite
Bar Isabel 682......................Worth the travel
Le Buffet de l'Antiquaire 664..............Bargain
Chez Gaston 664...............................Late night
Le Clocher Penché 664.......................Breakfast
Le Moine Échanson 665.........Wish I'd opened
Patente et Machin 665......................Regular
                                                  neighbourhood
La Tanière 665....................................High end

MEYJITTE BOUGHENOUT
Absynthe
Surfers Paradise Boulevard, Gold Coast
Worked in France for Pic, Blanc and Gagnaire,
before moving to Australia in 1995 and open-
ing Absynthe in 2005.
Noma 289.............................Worth the travel
Ocean Seafood 77............................Late night
Pigs and Pints 77........Regular neighbourhood
Sushi on James 77................................Bargain
Vie Bar & Restaurant 78..........Local favourite
Vintage Espresso 78.........................Breakfast

DANIEL BOULUD
Daniel
60 East 65th Street, New York City
After training in France he moved to
New York in the 1980s, founding his own
Manhattan-based empire, starting with the
opening of Daniel in 1993.
Blue Hill at Stone Barns 790.............High end
Crif Dogs 848.......................................Bargain
Four Seasons 319...................Local favourite
La Grenouille 839...................Local favourite
The Regency Bar & Grill 844............Breakfast
Roberta's 875......................Wish I'd opened
Rotisserie Georgette 844....................Regular
                                                  neighbourhood
Sorella 865..Late night
State Bird Provisions 750.....Worth the travel

SEAN BROCK
McCrady's
2 Unity Alley, Charleston
Since leading the charge to reinvent Southern
cooking after opening McCrady's in 2006,
Brock has opened two incarnations of
more casual Husk.
El Amigo Taqueria 803.........................Bargain
Arnold's Country Kitchen 803...Local favourite
The Barn 804..High end
Big Bad Breakfast 788......................Breakfast
Hermitage Cafe 803...........................Late night
Noma 289.............................Worth the travel
Rolf and Daughters 804......................Regular
                                                  neighbourhood
Two Boroughs Larder 802...................Regular
                                                  neighbourhood

BRUCE BROMBERG
Blue Ribbon Brasserie
97 Sullivan Street, New York City
Along with his brother Eric, Bruce founded
the New York-based Blue Ribbon group,
which takes in everything from high-end
sushi to late-night comfort food.
L'Atelier de Joël Robuchon 712........High end
Barbuto 854..........................Local favourite
Camellia Grill 821.............................Breakfast
Congee Village 864..............................Bargain
Keens Steakhouse 841..........Wish I'd opened
Sage 713.....................Regular neighbourhood
Sage 713..............................Worth the travel
Sushi Sho 221.......................Worth the travel
Wo Hop 862..Late night

FELIPE BRONZE
ORO
Rua Frei Leandro 20, Rio de Janeiro
Began working in Rio de Janeiro restaurants
at sixteen, before leaving to study in the US.
In 2011 he opened his latest restaurant ORO.
Aconchego Carioca 914...........Local favourite
Azumi 914...Late night
Cervantes 915......................................Bargain
Irajá Gastrô 915...................Wish I'd opened
Olympe 916..High end
Satyricon 917............Regular neighbourhood
Talho Capixaba 917...........................Breakfast
Tickets 515...........................Worth the travel

AL BROWN
Depot Eatery
86 Federal Street, Auckland
A familiar face across New Zealand thanks to
TV, he has been the co-owner of Wellington's
heavily garlanded Logan Brown since 1996.
Barilla Dumpling 131...........................Bargain
Coco's Cantina 128................Wish I'd opened
The French Café 129...........................High end
Little and Friday 132.........................Breakfast
Masu 129.....................Regular neighbourhood
State Bird Provisions 750.....Worth the travel

THOMAS BÜHNER
Restaurant La Vie
Krahnstrasse 1, Osnabrück
Strongly influenced by his time under Harald
Wohlfahrt at Restaurant Schwarzwaldstube,
Bühner opened multi-Michelin-starred
Restaurant La Vie in Osnabrück's Old Town
in 2006.
11A Küche mit Garten 543...................Bargain
11A Küche mit Garten 543...................Regular
                                                  neighbourhood
LT Grill 150..........................Worth the travel
Per Se 846............................Worth the travel
Poppenborg 545....................Local favourite
Restaurant De Librije 394..................High end
Seesteg 544.......................................Breakfast
Zuma 327............................Wish I'd opened

JUSTIN BURDETT
Ruka's Table
163 Main Street, Highlands
Waving the flag for farm-to-table 'gourmet
Southern cuisine', executive chef Burdett
– previously of the beloved Miller Union in
Atlanta – joined the team at Ruka's Table,
North Carolina, in 2012.
Bacchanalia 769.................................High end
The Breslin Bar & Dining Room 843......Worth
                                                        the travel
King James Public House 791............Wish I'd
                                                          opened
Madison's Restaurant 793.......Local favourite
Octopus Bar 770...............................Late night
Thai Paradise 793.......Regular neighbourhood
Waffle House 772.............................Breakfast

LUKE BURGESS
Garagistes
103 Murray Street, Hobart
Following training at Tetsuya's and Noma, Burgess returned to Tasmania to open Pecora Café (2006), then Garagistes (2009), where he showcases foraged ingredients and natural wines.

The Agrarian Kitchen **81**	Local favourite
Brae **81**	Worth the travel
Jasmin One **97**	Bargain
Kondo **212**	High end
Mary's **95**	Late night
Pigeon Hole **80**	Breakfast
Relæ **293**	Wish I'd opened
Tricycle Cafe & Bar **81**	Regular neighbourhood

PIER BUSSETTI
Aragvi
1 Ulofa Palme ulica, Moscow
A baker's son, Bussetti took Turin's Locanda Mongreno to Castello di Govone in 2010, before taking the helm at Aragvi in Moscow.

41 Grados Experience **513**	Worth the travel
Libery **594**	Regular neighbourhood
Il Pagliaccio **582**	High end
Paul **624**	Breakfast
Ragout **624**	Bargain
Ragout **624**	Late night
Tickets **515**	Wish I'd opened

JORDI BUTRÓN MELERO
Espai Sucre
Carrer de Sant Pere Més Alt 72, Barcelona
A graduate of elBulli who worked with pastry for Gagnaire and Bras, Melero opened the dessert-only Espai Sucre in 2000.

Bacoa **517**	Bargain
El Celler de Can Roca **493**	Local favourite
Coure **513**	Late night
Espai Kru **516**	High end
Forn Mistral **518**	Breakfast
La Mar Salada **512**	Wish I'd opened
Suculent **519**	Regular neighbourhood

KATIE BUTTON
Cúrate
11 Biltmore Avenue, Asheville
One-time science student, a change in course led to a seven-month internship at elBulli. Button moved to North Carolina and opened award-winning Cúrate tapas bar (2011) and sister bar Nightbell (2014).

Chai Pani **790**	Bargain
Cucina24 **791**	High end
D.O.M. Restaurante **921**	Worth the travel
FIG Bistro **791**	Regular neighbourhood
The Junction **791**	Breakfast
Storm Rhum Bar & Bistro **792**	Late night
Table **792**	Local favourite
Wicked Weed Brewing **792**	Wish I'd opened

ADAM BYATT
Trinity
4 The Polygon, London
Formerly at The Square, Byatt now has two London restaurants of his own: Trinity and Bistro Union.

Bone Daddies Ramen Bar **346**	Bargain
Brew **319**	Breakfast
The Foyer & Reading Room **340**	Local favourite
Meat Liquor **328**	Wish I'd opened
The Sportsman **310**	Worth the travel
Spuntino **351**	Late night
The Square **344**	High end
Zucca **355**	Regular neighbourhood

JO BØE KLAKEGG
Fauna
Solligata 2, Oslo
Returned to his native Norway, having added chef de partie at Noma to his impressive résumé, to be head chef and co-owner of Oslo's Fauna.

Åpent Bakeri **258**	Breakfast
Café Sara **258**	Late night
Hai Café **259**	Bargain
Noma **289**	Worth the travel
Olympen **260**	Local favourite
Pjoltergeist **260**	Regular neighbourhood

MICHAEL CABALLO
Edulis
169 Niagara Street, Toronto
Bringing his Spanish heritage to Canada, having cooked at revolutionary Basque restaurant Mugaritz, he opened Edulis in 2012 with his wife Tobey Nemeth.

Cisne Azul **499**	Wish I'd opened
Kaiseki Yu-zen Hashimoto **679**	High end
Pantheon **679**	Bargain
Rhum Corner **685**	Late night
Le Sélect Bistro **680**	Regular neighbourhood

GABRIELA CÁMARA BARGELLINI
Contramar
Durango 200, Mexico City
Self-taught Slow Food champion Bargellini founded five modern restaurants in Mexico City, starting with fish restaurant Contramar (1998), famous for its raw tuna tostada.

El Bajío **882**	Breakfast
Biko **882**	High end
Duo Salado y Dulce **883**	Breakfast
El Farolito **889**	Late night
Itanoni **881**	Wish I'd opened
Néctar **889**	Worth the travel
Restaurante Bar Montejo **884**	Regular neighbourhood
Tacos Hola **885**	Regular neighbourhood
Tori Tori **886**	Regular neighbourhood

RICARD CAMARENA
Ricard Camarena
Calle Doctor Sumsi 4, Valencia
Studied in Valencia, going on to build a modern Valencian restaurant empire, including fine-dining flagship Ricard Camarena Restaurant, Mercat Central de Valencia, Central Bar and Scoundrel Bistro.

Askua **507**	Regular neighbourhood
Casa Carmela **507**	Local favourite
Culler de Pau **498**	Worth the travel
Moltto **507**	Breakfast
Quique Dacosta Restaurante **505**	High end
Rausell **508**	Wish I'd opened
Restaurante Parpalló **506**	Bargain

YVES CAMDEBORDE
Le Comptoir du Relais
9 Carrefour de l'Odéon, Paris
A Paris veteran at the helm of Relais Saint-Germain and bistro Le Comptoir since 2005.

L'Astrance **469**	Bargain
L'Auberge des Glazicks **433**	High end
Café de Flore **456**	Breakfast
Cap e Tot **431**	Wish I'd opened
Le Chateaubriand **466**	Local favourite
La Grenouillère **437**	Worth the travel
Le Repaire de Cartouche **467**	Bargain

ANDREAS CAMINADA
Schloss Schauenstein
Schlossgasse 1, Fürstenau
The new star of Swiss gastronomy who plies his trade in Schauenstein castle in the heart of the Alps.

Alain Ducasse au Plaza Athénée **462**	High end
B12 **561**	Breakfast
Kronenhalle **567**	Local favourite
De Leest **394**	Worth the travel
Tibits **568**	Late night
Waldheim **561**	Regular neighbourhood
Zuma **327**	Wish I'd opened

FRANK CAMORRA
MoVida Bar de Tapas Y Vino
1 Hosier Lane, Melbourne
Barcelona-born Camorra, aka 'The MoVida guy' has had Melbournians swooning over his interpretation of Spanish tapas since 2003, leading to another five MoVida outposts, the latest in Sydney.

Aponiente **476**	Worth the travel
Borek **110**	Bargain
Brae **81**	High end
Grossi Florentino **108**	Local favourite
Ling Nam **108**	Late night
Da Noi **113**	Wish I'd opened
Pellegrini's Espresso Bar **109**	Breakfast
Sapa Hills **111**	Regular neighbourhood

ALEJANDRO CANCINO
Urbane
181 Mary Street, Brisbane
Argentinian executive chef at Brisbane's Urbane and The Euro brasserie, trained at Mugaritz and Le Manoir aux Quat'Saisons, winning Tokyo's Bulgari Hotel a Michelin star aged twenty-eight.

Attica 113..High end
Miel Container 75.................................Bargain
Moda 76.....................Regular neighbourhood
Mugaritz 480........................Wish I'd opened
New Farm Deli 76............................Breakfast
Nihonryori Ryugin 216..........Worth the travel
Public 76...Late night
Restaurant Two 76...............Local favourite

GUILLAUME CANTIN
Les 400 Coups
400 Rue Notre-Dame Est, Montreal
Head chef at Les 400 Coups in Old Montreal and a Quebec native, Cantin earned his stripes at the Leaning Bell (Quebec), Panache (Quebec) and Maison Boulud.

Dominion Square Tavern 690...............Regular neighbourhood
Flocons de Sel 445................Worth the travel
Lawrence Restaurant 693.................Breakfast
Mangiafoco 696...............................Late night
Racines 690............................Local favourite
Toqué! 697...High end
Le Vin Papillon 696................Wish I'd opened

HOMARO CANTU
Moto
945 West Fulton Market, Chicago
Divides his time between cooking at the cutting-edge restaurants Moto and iNG, and running Cantu Designs, his food technology company.

Al's Beef 382...........................Local favourite
The Bristol 826.....................................High end
Freddy's Pizza 826.....Regular neighbourhood
Jam 828...Breakfast
La Pasadita 835..................................Late night
Publican Quality Meats 834....Wish I'd opened
Le Taillevent 464...................Worth the travel

ANDREA CARLSON
Burdock & Co.
2702 Main Street, Vancouver
Vancouver's Burdock & Co., Carlson's latest venture, epitomizes her locavore, vegetable-focused philosophy. She honed her skills at Vancouver's Raincity Grill and Bishop's.

Beaucoup Bakery 668......................Breakfast
Blue Hill at Stone Barns 790..Worth the travel
East Van Roasters 670..........Wish I'd opened
Hawksworth Restaurant 668....Local favourite
Hawksworth Restaurant 668............High end
Hy's Encore 668.....................Local favourite
Maenam 671...........................Local favourite
Pho Tan 673...Bargain
Pidgin 670.................Regular neighbourhood
Suika 669...Late night
Thomas Haas 672.............................Breakfast
Tojo's 669.................................Local favourite
Vij's 669..High end
Wildebeest 671......................Local favourite

ANDREW CARMELLINI
Locanda Verde
377 Greenwich Street, New York City
Born in Ohio, Carmellini made his name in New York as head chef at Café Boulud. Currently chef-partner at Locanda Verde, The Dutch and Lafayette.

L'Arpège 458..........................Worth the travel
Le Bernardin 839................................High end
Daniel 844..High end
Gahm Mi Oak 840.............................Late night
Great NY Noodletown 861...............Late night
Ippudo NY 849.....................................Bargain
Motorino 851.......................................Bargain
The Willows Inn 720.............Worth the travel

MATEU CASAÑAS
Compartir
Riera Sant Vicenç, Cadaqués
Longtime chef de cuisine at elBulli, Casañas left to launch Compartir in Cadaqués with fellow elBulli chefs Oriol Castro and Eduard Xatruch. Continues to work with the elBulli Foundation.

Almadraba Restaurant 495......Local favourite
Cal Campaner 495......Regular neighbourhood
El Celler de Can Roca 493......Worth the travel
La Cosa Nostra 495.............................Bargain
els Brancs 495...................................Late night
Emporium Restaurant 492................High end
Mercado de San Miguel 501..Wish I'd opened
Raspa & Wine 496....................Local favourite
Si Us Plau 496.....................................Breakfast

ORIOL CASTRO
Compartir
Riera Sant Vicenç, Cadaqués
elBulli chef for over fifteen years with Mateu Casañas and Eduard Xatruch. When it closed, they opened the informal Compartir in Cadaqués, though remain committed to the elBulli Foundation.

Bar Pinotxo 517................................Breakfast
Bar Sport 498.....................................Bargain
El Boquerón de Plata 520.................Late night
Bras 436...............................Worth the travel
Cal Pep 513............................Local favourite
Cal Pep 513..Late night
Casa de Tapas Cañota 516..............Late night
El Celler de Can Roca 493................High end
Le Louis XV 447...................Wish I'd opened
La Nansa 497.............Regular neighbourhood
Pic Nic 497.................Regular neighbourhood
Quimet i Quimet 517.........................Late night

MIGUEL CASTRO E SILVA
Largo
Rua Serpa Pinto 10a, Lisbon
Respected Portuguese culinary authority whose latest restaurant Largo is housed in a former convent.

Belcanto 535........................Wish I'd opened
Cabana da Estrela 536........................Bargain
Marítima de Xabregas 533.................Bargain
Pastelaria Cristal 537........................Breakfast
Restaurante Doca Peixe 532..............Regular neighbourhood
Restaurante São Gabriel 524..........Worth the travel
Restaurante XL 537...........................Late night
Robalo 525............................Worth the travel
Vale do Gaio 528....................Local favourite

MORENO CEDRONI
La Madonnina del Pescatore
Via Lungomare Italia 11, Senigallia
Owns La Madonnina del Pescatore, opened in 1984, and also runs Il Clandestino Susci Bar, opened in 2000, on the beach in Portonovo, and Baglioni in London.

Le Boudoir 590.................................Breakfast
Le Chateaubriand 466...........Wish I'd opened
Al Convento 575...................Worth the travel
Il Laghetto 590..........Regular neighbourhood
Luna Rossa 591...................................Late night
Ristorante Zass 575.............................High end
Trattoria Cibo e Vino 591....................Bargain
Uliassi 591................................Local favourite

JOSEF CENTENO

Bäco Mercat
408 South Main Street, Los Angeles
Leaving Los Angeles's Lazy Ox Canteen in 2012, Centeno opened wildly popular flatbread sandwich outlet Bāco Mercat, followed by Bar Amá and Japanese-Italian Orsa & Winston.

Blanca 872	Worth the travel
Cole's 732	Late night
Daikokuya 735	Late night
Gjelina 738	Local favourite
Guisados 730	Bargain
Hui Tou Xiang 736	Breakfast
KaGaYa 735	High end
Night + Market 740	Regular neighbourhood
Rustic Canyon 737	Local favourite
Terroni Downtown LA 732	Breakfast
ZZ's Clam Bar 853	Wish I'd opened

CHAKALL

Blend
Rua do Norte 24, Lisbon
Born in Buenos Aires, he's made turban-wearing his trademark while running multiple restaurants in Portugal and Germany.

Kymbu 646	Worth the travel
Marítima de Xabregas 533	Regular neighbourhood
Restaurante dos Bons Amigos 533	Late night
Restaurante O Poleiro 533	Local favourite
Solar dos Presuntos 533	High end

DAVID CHANG

Momofuku Noodle Bar
171 1st Avenue, New York City
Since opening the Momofuku Noodle Bar in 2004, Chang now has five very different New York City outposts, plus restaurants in Sydney and Toronto.

Balthazar 868	Wish I'd opened
Benu 756	Worth the travel
Golden Century Seafood 89	Bargain
Great NY Noodletown 861	Late night
Locanda Verde 870	Breakfast
Del Posto 860	Regular neighbourhood
Sushi Sawada 213	Worth the travel
Torrisi Italian Specialties 868	Local favourite

JOANNE CHANG

Myers + Chang
1145 Washington Street, Boston
Harvard graduate Chang swapped management consultancy for the heat of the kitchen, working at New York's Payard Patisserie and Boston's Mistral before launching Flour bakery and café chain in 2000.

O Ya 777	High end
Sam's 777	Regular neighbourhood
Sorellina 777	Wish I'd opened
Taiwan Café 777	Bargain
Winsor Dim Sum Café 777	Breakfast

DOMINIC CHAPMAN

The Royal Oak
Paley Street, Maidenhead
Head chef at The Royal Oak, he previously ran the kitchen at Heston Blumenthal's Hinds Head.

Agnadio 629	Worth the travel
The Ivy 338	Local favourite
Racine 327	Regular neighbourhood
The Red Fort 351	Late night
The Seafood Restaurant 305	Wish I'd opened
The Waterside Inn 304	High end
The Wolseley 345	Breakfast

JEREMY CHARLES

Raymonds
95 Water Street, St. John's
Native Newfoundlander and co-owner of Raymonds in St John's, Charles champions regional Newfoundland cuisine.

Duke of Duckworth 662	Local favourite
Fabulous Foods Limited 662	Bargain
Fäviken Magasinet 261	Worth the travel
Fixed Coffee & Baking 663	Breakfast
Fogo Island Inn 662	High end
Hartwood 888	Wish I'd opened
Mallard Cottage 663	Regular neighbourhood
The UnderBelly 663	Late night

SVEN CHARTIER

Saturne
17 Rue Notre-Dame des Victoires, Paris
French with Swedish roots, Chartier creates clean Nordic-like flavours at Saturne, in the Bourse in Paris.

Le Baratin 472	Regular neighbourhood
L'Entrée des Artistes 467	Late night
Starvin' Joe 468	Bargain

LANSHU CHEN

Le Moût Restaurant
59 Cunzhong Street, Taichung City
Trained at the Cordon Bleu and then with Pierre Hermé and Thomas Keller before moving back to her native Taiwan to become head chef at French-influenced Le Moût.

Din Tai Fung 174	Regular neighbourhood
Keelung Miaokou Night Market 173	Bargain
Shi Yang Shan Fang 177	Local favourite
Shi Yang Shan Fang 177	Wish I'd opened
Shoraku 176	High end
Tripod King 173	Late night

ANDRÉ CHIANG

Restaurant André
41 Bukit Pasoh Road, Singapore
Taiwan-born Chiang cooked at Jaan par André in Singapore's Swissotel, before opening Restaurant André in a 1920s townhouse.

Burnt Ends 238	Regular neighbourhood
Commis 705	Wish I'd opened
Narisawa 216	High end
Relæ 293	Worth the travel
Sasa 176	Local favourite
Sungei Road Laksa 233	Breakfast

CARMELO CHIARAMONTE

Born in Modica, Sicilian chef Chiaramonte, former executive chef at restaurant Il Cuciniere in Catania, now consults as the 'Cuciniere Errante' ('Nomadic Chef').

Pakta 516	Worth the travel
A Putia Do Calabrisi 595	Regular neighbourhood
Restaurante da Adraga 526	Wish I'd opened
Ristorante Mm 595	Breakfast
Torre del Saracino 575	High end
Trattoria del Gallo 597	Local favourite

ALBERTO CHICOTE

NODO
Calle de Velázquez 150, Madrid
Madrilenian born and bred, his restaurants Nodo and Pan de Lujo in the Spanish capital fuse Asian and Mediterranean flavours.

Alinea 827	Worth the travel
Asador Etxebarri 479	Local favourite
El Celler de Can Roca 493	High end
Hakkasan 342	Worth the travel
El Hórreo 477	Wish I'd opened
Momofuku Ko 850	Worth the travel
L'Orangerie 940	Breakfast
Per Se 846	Worth the travel
Sacha 503	Regular neighbourhood
La Terraza 504	High end

MANGO TSANG CHIU LIT

Ming Court
555 Shanghai Street, Hong Kong
With forty years of experience in Hong Kong's hotel and Michelin-starred restaurants, he took the reins at Hong Kong's prestigious Ming Court in 2013.

Kau Kee 184	Regular neighbourhood
The Place 191	High end

LAU CHIU SHING

Fook Lam Moon
43–45 Johnston Road, Hong Kong
Chui Fook Chuen's disciple, the Executive Chef at Hong Kong's Fook Lam Moon was recently recognized as one of Asia's best Cantonese cooks in Asia's 50 Best Restaurant Awards.

Chiu Chow Chuen 180	Late night
Kwong Kee 189	Regular neighbourhood
Sang Kee Congee Shop 186	Breakfast
Wing Wah Noodle Shop 188	Bargain

ASHLEY CHRISTENSEN
Poole's Diner
426 South McDowell Street, Raleigh
A North Carolina native and self-taught cook, she settled in Raleigh, opening Poole's Diner in 2007, now one of seven neighbourhood bars, restaurants and cafés in her Southern food empire.

Ăn **792**	High end
Asador Etxebarri **479**	Worth the travel
Bida Manda **794**	Regular neighbourhood
Centro **794**	Bargain
The Mecca Restaurant **794**	Breakfast
The Players' Retreat **794**	Late night
The Players' Retreat **794**	Local favourite

SAIPIN CHUTIMA
Lotus of Siam
953 East Sahara Avenue, Las Vegas
After spells in Northridge and Norwalk, James Beard Award-winning chef Chutima brought Northern Thai cuisine to Las Vegas, opening Lotus of Siam in 1999.

L'Atelier de Joël Robuchon **712**	High end
Blueberry Hill **712**	Breakfast
Casa di Amore **712**	Late night
Le Cirque **713**	High end
eat **713**	Breakfast
In-N-Out Burger **728**	Bargain
Joyful House **713**	Regular neighbourhood
Restaurant Guy Savoy **471**	High end

FILIP CLAEYS
De Jonkman
Maalsesteenweg 438, Bruges
Following five years at De Karmeliet and four years with Sergio Herman at Oud Sluis, he opened De Jonkman on the outskirts of Bruges.

Bistro Christophe **420**	Late night
Casa Fito **489**	Bargain
Het Gebaar **410**	Worth the travel
Hof van Cleve **417**	High end
Kabuki **490**	Worth the travel
Restaurant Es Torrent **478**	Wish I'd opened
Le Siphon **421**	Regular neighbourhood

SAMANTHA & SAMUEL CLARK
Moro
34–36 Exmouth Market, London
The husband-and-wife team who opened the Moorish-influenced Moro in 1997. Morito, a bijou tapas bar next door, followed.

El Campero **476**	Worth the travel
Dock Kitchen **325**	Regular neighbourhood
Koya **436**	Bargain
The Ledbury **331**	High end
The River Café **325**	Wish I'd opened
Sōmine **361**	Late night
St. John Bread & Wine **374**	Breakfast
The Towpath Café **367**	Local favourite

SHAUN CLOUSTON
Logan Brown
192 Cuba Street, Wellington
Executive chef and partner of Wellington's Logan Brown where he began his career and returned in 2006, after years spent working in Sydney.

Attica **113**	High end
Huxtable **111**	Worth the travel
Little Penang **124**	Bargain
Nikau Café **125**	Breakfast
Ortega Fish Shack & Bar **125**	Regular neighbourhood

BEL COELHO
Clandestino
Rua Medeiros de Albuquerque, São Paulo
Alex Atala protégé and São Paulo native, Coelho studied at the prestigious Culinary Institute of America before returning to Brazil to open Dui. Now consulting and exploring Brazil.

Bar da Dona Onça **920**	Local favourite
Coffee Lab **926**	Breakfast
Maní **925**	High end
Martin Fierro **928**	Bargain
Mocotó **929**	Bargain
Tanuki **928**	Local favourite
Virada's do Largo **912**	Worth the travel

JUSTIN COGLEY
Aubergine
Monte Verde at 7th Street, Carmel-by-the-Sea
Professional figure skater turned award-winning chef, Cogley worked for mentor Charlie Trotter for five years before taking the reins at seafood restaurant Aubergine in Carmel, California in 2011.

Le Bernardin **839**	Wish I'd opened
Big Sur Bakery **702**	Local favourite
Carmel Belle **702**	Breakfast
Compagno's Market and Deli **703**	Regular neighbourhood
In De Wulf **421**	Worth the travel
Manresa **703**	High end
Red's Donuts **703**	Bargain

MAURO COLAGRECO
Mirazur
30 Avenue Aristide Briand, Menton
The Argentine-born protégé of Passard and the late Loiseau opened the handsome Côte d'Azur-based Mirazur in 2006.

Hostellerie Jérôme **442**	High end
Maní **925**	Worth the travel
La Merenda **441**	Local favourite
L'O à la Bouche **441**	Regular neighbourhood
La Spiaggetta **585**	Breakfast

TYSON COLE
Uchi
801 South Lamar Boulevard, Austin
Cole made his name in Austin, training under Takehiko Fuse, before opening his own Japanese-inspired restaurants Uchi and Uchiko.

Baguette et Chocolat **807**	Breakfast
Bartlett's **804**	Regular neighbourhood
Contigo **805**	Local favourite
Hopdoddy Burger Bar **805**	Wish I'd opened
Soto **856**	Worth the travel

YOANN CONTE
Restaurant Yoann Conte
13 Vieille Route des Pensières, Veyrier-Du-Lac
Raised in Brittany, Conte apprenticed with Marc Veyrat before developing his own 'mountain cuisine' in evidence at Restaurant Yoann Conte overlooking Lake Annecy.

Café Brunet **442**	Regular neighbourhood
La Chèvre d'Or **438**	Wish I'd opened
Chez Luigi **442**	Bargain
Epicure **462**	High end
Le Kintessence **442**	Worth the travel
La Scierie **442**	Local favourite

ULTAN COOKE
Aniar
53 Dominick Street Lower, Galway
Head chef at Galway's Michelin-starred Aniar Restaurant since 2013, Ireland-born Cooke previously ran the kitchen at Smiths of Smithfield.

Asian Tea House **388**	Late night
The Greenhouse Dublin **386**	Worth the travel
Kai Café + Restaurant **388**	Regular neighbourhood
Kappa-ya **389**	Bargain
Owenmore Restaurant **388**	High end
Upstairs@McCambridge's **389**	Breakfast
Wild Honey Inn **383**	Wish I'd opened

LEE COOPER
L'Abattoir
217 Carrall Street, Vancouver
After thirteen years and a résumé that includes spells with Blumenthal and Vongerichten, he opened his first restaurant, L'Abattoir, in 2010.

Chambar **670**	Wish I'd opened
Le Crocodile **674**	High end
Kingyo **674**	Late night
Maison Publique **693**	Worth the travel
Peaceful Restaurant **669**	Bargain
Peaceful Restaurant **669**	Regular neighbourhood
Tomahawk Barbeque **673**	Breakfast
Waterfront Restaurant **660**	Local favourite

JOSÉ CORDEIRO

Restaurante Chefe Cordeiro
Praça do Comércio 20–23, Lisbon
Winning recognition at Feitoria with creative interpretations of traditional Portuguese dishes, Angola-born Cordeiro opened his eponymous restaurant in 2013.

Alma 537...................Regular neighbourhood
Arzak 483..............................Worth the travel
Belcanto 535.................................High end
Bica Do Sapato 532.................Local favourite
Café de São Bento 534....................Late night
Cantinho do Avillez 535....................Regular
neighbourhood
Casa da Guia 525.........................Breakfast
Confeitaria Tavi 526......................Breakfast
Fortaleza do Guincho 525..................High end
Il Gallo d'Oro 526.................Worth the travel
Largo 536................Regular neighbourhood
Maçã Verde 532.............................Bargain
Martín Berasategui 482........Worth the travel
Ocean 524.....................................High end
ODE Porto Wine House 527.....Local favourite
Porto Santa Maria 525.......Wish I'd opened
Restaurante DOP 527.............Local favourite
Restaurante Eleven 532...................Regular
neighbourhood
Restaurante Henrique Leis 524........High end
Restaurante O Gaio 528......................Bargain
Restaurante O Sapo 526......................Bargain
Restaurante Pajú 527......................Late night
Restaurante Rio's 526.......................Regular
neighbourhood
Restaurante São Gabriel 524............High end
Restaurante Sao Valentim 526...........Regular
neighbourhood
Shis 527...............................Wish I'd opened
Spazio Buondi – Nobre 534.....Local favourite
O Talho 534............................Local favourite
Tasca da Esquina 535.......................Regular
neighbourhood
Tavares Rico 535.............................High end
Vila Joya 524.................................High end
The Yeatman 527.............................High end

IGLES CORELLI

Ristorante Atman
Via Roma 4, Pescia
Author, teacher and chef recognized for his avant-garde approach to Italian cuisine which sees him merge different cuisines and flavours.

Il Caffè Sotto I Portici 599.................Regular
neighbourhood
La Capanna di Eraclio 576........Local favourite
Povero Diavolo 579...............Wish I'd opened
San Domenico 575.............................High end
Villa Feltrinelli 586................Worth the travel

RAÚL CORREA

Zest
2 Tartak Street, San Juan
Most recently took over San Juan Water Beach Club Hotel's culinary operations as executive chef at Zest, serving modern Puerto Rican cuisine.

1919 Restaurant 890.......................High end
Bouchon 712........................Worth the travel
La Cueva del Mar 891.......................Bargain
En Boga 891...............Regular neighbourhood
The English Rose 890.....................Breakfast
La Jaquita Baya 891..............Local favourite
Jose Enrique 891..................Wish I'd opened
Pizzeria de Pirilo 892.....................Late night

CHRIS COSENTINO

Porcellino
550 Church Street, San Francisco
Cosentino, aka @OffalChris – a leading expert in offal cookery – took up executive chef position at San Francisco's Incanto in 2003, reopening as Porcellino in 2014.

Commis 705....................................High end
Father's Office 736.................Wish I'd opened
Kingdom of Noodles 757....................Bargain
Maison Publique 693.............Worth the travel
Nopa 754.....................................Late night
Swan Oyster Depot 753...........Local favourite
Yank Sing 757...............................Breakfast
Yummy Yummy 757.....Regular neighbourhood

DANIEL COSTA

Corso 32
10345 Jasper Avenue, Edmonton
Canadian Costa, following a spell in private catering, paid homage to his Italian heritage, opening thirty-four-seat Corso 32 in 2010 and expanding with a spuntini bar next door in 2014.

Duchess Bake Shop 659...................Breakfast
Izakaya Tomo 659...........................Late night
Leva 659.................Regular neighbourhood
Red Ox Inn 659..............................High end
Roscioli 584......................Worth the travel
Thanh-Thanh 660............................Bargain
Tres Carnales Taquería 660................Regular
neighbourhood

OLLIE COUILLAUD

The Lawn Bistro
67 High Street, London
Stints with Bruce Poole and Philip Howard led to Couillaud running the kitchen at La Trompette and Lawn Bistro, joining Peyton & Byrne as the Royal Academy's executive chef in 2014.

Arzak 483............................Worth the travel
Brew 334....................................Breakfast
Hoo Hing Supermarket 314................Bargain
The Little Bar 334................Wish I'd opened
Michel Trama 431................Worth the travel
Le Relais des Salines 438.......Local favourite
The Square 344...............................High end
Sticks'n'Sushi 334......Regular neighbourhood
Wong Kei 337................................Late night

MATTHEW CRABBE

Two Rooms
3-11-7 Kita-Aoyama, Tokyo
Worked at Sydney's Tetsuya's, then in London, the US and Mexico before moving to Tokyo where he is chef-director of Two Rooms and Ruby Jack's Steakhouse.

Akanoren 214................................Late night
Hyotei 203..................................Breakfast
Kyubey 212..................................High end
Maru 219...................Regular neighbourhood
Shiba Tofuya-Ukai 217............Local favourite
Table 468...........................Worth the travel
Toriyoshi 218...............................Bargain

GERARD CRAFT

Niche
7734 Forsyth Boulevard, St. Louis
Raised in Washington, D.C., Craft came to dominate the St. Louis food scene, following up on his first fine-dining establishment, Niche (2005), with Taste by Niche, Brasserie by Niche and Pastaria.

Blood and Sand 785........................Late night
Five Star Burgers 786......................Bargain
Gringo 786.................Regular neighbourhood
Half & Half 786............................Breakfast
Mission Taco Joint 786....................Regular
neighbourhood
Olio 787....................Regular neighbourhood
Pappy's Smokehouse 787......Wish I'd opened
Sidney Street Cafe 787.....................High end
Southwest Diner 787.......................Breakfast
Tony's 788...............................Local favourite

CARLO CRISCI

Restaurant du Cerf
Rue du Temple 10, Cossonay
From a family of restaurateurs, Crisci's been behind the stove at Le Cerf in Switzerland for thirty-five years winning two Michelin stars in the process.

Auberge de la Veveyse 565	Regular neighbourhood
La Brasserie du Grand Chêne 565	Late night
L'Écu Vaudois 564	Bargain
Pierre Gagnaire 463	Worth the travel
Les Prés d'Eugénie 430	High end
Restaurant du Jorat 565	Regular neighbourhood
Rôtisserie Au Gaulois 564	Regular neighbourhood

JORDI CRUZ

ABaC
Avinguda del Tibidabo 1, Barcelona
Worked at Estany Clar in Cercs where he became the youngest ever Spaniard to win a Michelin star. He's now ABaC's head chef.

El Celler de Can Roca 493	High end

PAUL CUNNINGHAM

Henne Kirkeby Kro
Strandvejen 234, Henne
Head chef at Henne Kirkeby Kro, the renowned restaurant-with-rooms on Jutland's 'wild West Coast', Essex-born Cunningham won his previous restaurant, The Paul in Copenhagen, a Michelin star.

Aamanns Deli & Take Away 296	Local favourite
L'Arpège 458	Worth the travel
Balthazar 868	Wish I'd opened
Blue Hill at Stone Barns 790	Worth the travel
The Coffee Factory 288	Regular neighbourhood
Granola 279	Breakfast
ISSA 295	Bargain
John's Hotdog Deli 295	Late night
Mielcke & Hurtigkarl 279	High end
Paté Paté 296	Regular neighbourhood

TIM CUSHMAN

O Ya
9 East Street, Boston
After travelling the world with US restaurant group Lettuce Entertain You, he now owns O Ya where modern Japanese meets New England.

Charlie's Sandwich Shoppe 774	Breakfast
Di Fara Pizza 873	Wish I'd opened
Kiin Kiin 292	Worth the travel
Nebo 775	Regular neighbourhood
No. 9 Park 776	Local favourite
Oleana 778	High end
Peach Farm 776	Late night
Regina Pizza 776	Bargain

OLLIE DABBOUS

Dabbous
39 Whitfield Street, London
Trained at Le Manoir aux Quat'Saisons, then became head chef of Texture in London before opening Dabbous (2012) and Barnyard (2014).

Hereford Road 331	Local favourite
The Modern Pantry 359	Breakfast
Le Relais de Venise 329	Regular neighbourhood
Tayyabs 375	Bargain
Trattoria Cammillo 598	Worth the travel
Umu 344	High end

QUIQUE DACOSTA

Quique Dacosta Restaurante
Carretera Las Marinas, Dénia
Began working at El Poblet in 1989. A decade later, having worked his way to head chef, he took over and renamed it.

41 Grados Experience 513	Wish I'd opened
ABaC 520	Worth the travel
Akelarre 483	High end
Arzak 483	High end
Askua 507	Late night
Atrio 498	Worth the travel
Azurmendi 482	High end
Bodega 1900 513	Wish I'd opened
Casa Federico 505	Regular neighbourhood
Casa Gerardo 477	Worth the travel
Casa Marcial 477	Worth the travel
El Celler de Can Roca 493	High end
Les Cols 494	Worth the travel
DiverXo 499	Worth the travel
Dos Cielos 515	Worth the travel
L'Escaleta 504	Local favourite
El Faralló 505	Regular neighbourhood
La Finca 506	Local favourite
Garnacha Tinta 507	Breakfast
El Marino 505	Regular neighbourhood
Martín Berasategui 482	High end
Minibar 764	Wish I'd opened
Miramar 494	Worth the travel
Mugaritz 480	High end
Nerua 480	Worth the travel
Pakta 516	Wish I'd opened
Peix & Brases 505	Regular neighbourhood
Ramón Freixa Madrid 502	Worth the travel
Restaurante Casa Pepa 506	Regular neighbourhood
Restaurante La Cuina 506	Regular neighbourhood
Restaurante Las Rejas 490	Worth the travel
Restaurante Riff 508	Local favourite
Ricard Camarena 508	Local favourite
La Salita 508	Local favourite
Sant Pau 497	High end
Santceloni 503	Worth the travel
Sergi Arola Gastro 503	Worth the travel
La Sirena Restaurante 506	Local favourite
La Taberna Del Gourmet 504	Local favourite
Tastem 508	Late night
La Terraza 504	Worth the travel
Tickets 515	Wish I'd opened
Torreblanca 508	Breakfast

ANDREAS DAHLBERG

Bastard
Mäster Johansgatan 11, Malmö
The head chef and owner of Bastard in Malmö, who also goes by the rock 'n' roll moniker of Andy Bastard.

Amass 286	High end
Le Baratin 472	Worth the travel
Casual Street Food 263	Regular neighbourhood
Casual Street Food 263	Late night
Casual Street Food 263	Bargain
Chez Panisse 701	Wish I'd opened
Le Comptoir du Relais 457	Worth the travel
Daniel Berlin Krog 266	Local favourite
La Gazzetta 468	Worth the travel
Momofuku Ssäm Bar 851	Worth the travel
Relæ 293	High end
The River Café 325	Worth the travel
Roberta's 875	Worth the travel
Saltimporten Canteen 264	Bargain
Saltimporten Canteen 264	Local favourite
Solde Kaffebar 265	Breakfast
St. John Bar and Restaurant 362	Worth the travel

MATHIAS DAHLGREN

Mathias Dahlgren Matbaren
Grand Hôtel, Södra Blasieholmshamnen 8, Stockholm
Multiple winner of Swedish chef of the year, he opened Matsalen in the Grand Hotel in 2007 where he also has Matbaren.

Amida Kolgrill 277	Bargain
Gott's Roadside 704	Wish I'd opened
Ramen Ki Mama 278	Regular neighbourhood
Rosendals Trädgård 270	Local favourite
Saison 756	High end
Taverna Brillo 276	Late night
Urban Deli 266	Breakfast

LUKE DALE-ROBERTS

The Test Kitchen
375 Albert Road, Cape Town
British-born Dale-Roberts worked in Asia before moving to South Africa where he now owns The Test Kitchen and The Pot Luck Club.

95 Keerom 646	Local favourite
Burrata 647	Bargain
Four & Twenty 647	Breakfast
Jordan Restaurant 651	Regular neighbourhood
Osteria Francescana 577	Worth the travel
Royale Eatery 648	Late night
Rust en Vrede 651	High end

PAUL DAY
Sansho
Petrská 1170/25, Prague
London Chinatown-trained butcher-chef-
owner of Sansho in Prague, and owner of
The Real Meat Society (Prague's only whole
animal butchers).
Las Adelitas **610**.............................Late night
Café Savoy **609**.........................Local favourite
Cuckoo's Den **150**.................Worth the travel
La Degustation Bohême Bourgeoise **609**........
High end
Kastrol **610**.................Regular neighbourhood
Katsura **610**...............Regular neighbourhood
Lokál **611**....................Regular neighbourhood
Můj šálek kávy **611**.........................Breakfast
Sapa Market **612**.................................Bargain
Smokehouse **369**...................Wish I'd opened
The Tavern **612**...........Regular neighbourhood

GERT DE MANGELEER
Hertog Jan
Torhoutse Steenweg 479, Bruges
Runs Hertog Jan with sommelier Joachim
Boudens whom he met while working at
Molentje in the Netherlands.
Bistro Christophe **420**......................Late night
Bistro de Kruiden Molen **417**....Local favourite
Frituur Bosrand **420**............................Bargain
Hakkasan **342**......................Wish I'd opened
Lam en Yin **410**..................Worth the travel
Le Pain Quotidien **413**......................Breakfast
Restaurant De Librije **394**.................High end
Rock Fort **421**..............Regular neighbourhood
Zuma **327**..........................Worth the travel

NICOLAS DE VISCH
Belgium-born chef who's carved out a
culinary career in restaurants and hotel
groups in Europe, the Middle East and most
recently, Asia.
L'Atelier de Joël Robuchon **176**........High end
Belgian Beer Café Liège **173**....Local favourite
FiFi **175**.......................Regular neighbourhood
Hachibei **175**......................Wish I'd opened
Jiang Tai Lang **175**............................Late night
Ju-Ding Shabu Shabu **175**..................Bargain
La Rive **402**.........................Worth the travel

MICHAEL DEANE
Deanes
36–40 Howard Street, Belfast
Belfast chef-restaurateur who, aside from his
flagship Deanes, now runs six other outposts
across the city.
L'Atelier de Joël Robuchon **459**.......Worth the
travel
Meat Liquor **328**...................Wish I'd opened
The Raj **382**................Regular neighbourhood
The Sphinx **382**...............................Late night
Vila Joya **524**..................................High end

SANG-HOON DEGEIMBRE
L'Air du Temps
Rue de la Croix Monet 2, Eghezee
Korean-Belgian, who opened L'Air du Temps
in Namur, Wallonia, where he grew up, in
1997. Praised for using super-local produce.
Brasserie François **419**......................Bargain
Le Cabestan **412**..............................Late night
Mission Chinese Food **751**....Wish I'd opened
Le Pain Quotidien **419**......................Breakfast
La Paix **412**.................Regular neighbourhood
Aux Petits Oignons **420**...........Local favourite
Quique Dacosta Restaurante **505**.....High end
Saturne **453**.........................Worth the travel

ŞEMSA DENIZSEL
Kantin
Akkavak Sokağı 30, Istanbul
Opened Kantin, a restaurant that focuses on
serving healthy, seasonal Turkish soul food, in
Istanbul in 2000.
L'Arcangelo **581**....................Worth the travel
Bay Nihat Lale **630**................Worth the travel
Kaymakçi Pando **634**........................Breakfast
Kizilkayalar **635**................................Late night
Lale İşkembecisi **635**.........................Late night
Meşhur Filibe Köftecisi **636**..................Bargain
Metanet Lokantasi **630**.........Worth the travel
Mikla **635**..High end
Roscioli **584**........................Worth the travel
St. John Bar and Restaurant **362**.........Worth
the travel

GREG & GABRIELLE QUIÑÓNEZ DENTON
Ox Restaurant
2225 Northeast Martin Luther King Jr
Boulevard, Portland
Greg and his wife and fellow chef Gabrielle,
co-owners of Portland's Argentine grill-
inspired Ox Restaurant, met in 1999, cooking
at Hiro Sone's Michelin-starred Terra.
Asador Etxebarri **479**...........Worth the travel
Barwares **714**...................................Late night
Little Bird Bistro **716**.............Wish I'd opened
Lovely's Fifty Fifty **716**.......................Regular
neighbourhood
Ned Ludd **717**........................Local favourite
Olympic Provisions Southeast **718**...Breakfast
PaaDee **718**......................................Bargain
Roe **719**..High end

KOBE DESRAMAULTS
In De Wulf
Wulvestraat 1, Dranouter
In the Belgian countryside close to the
French border, Desramaults runs In De Wulf
in the area which was his childhood home.
Attica **113**...............................Worth the travel
l'Auberge In De Zon **421**........Local favourite
Bon Bon **412**.....................................High end
La Grenouillère **437**.................Local favourite
J.E.F. **415**....................Regular neighbourhood
De Lieve **416**.....................................Bargain
Martino **416**....................................Late night
Roberta's **875**....................Wish I'd opened
Simon Says **416**..............................Breakfast
The Sportsman **310**..............Worth the travel
Volta **417**....................Regular neighbourhood

JUSTIN DEVILLIER
La Petite Grocery
4238 Magazine Street, New Orleans
California-raised chef-owner of acclaimed
New Orleans bistro La Petite Grocery, Devillier
joined the team in 2004, taking over ownership
in 2010.
The Admiral **790**..................Worth the travel
Le Bernardin **839**..............................High end
Brigtsen's **821**......................Local favourite
Cooter Brown's **822**.........................Late night
Dong Phuong Bakery **820**.................Bargain
Gracious Bakery **820**.......................Breakfast
Nora Gray **690**....................Wish I'd opened

ESTEFANÍA DI BENEDETTO
Paraje Arévalo
Arévalo 1502, Buenos Aires
Followed stints at Mugaritz and The Fat Duck
by returning to her native Argentina where
she now co-runs restaurants Paraje Arévalo
and Local.
Cassis **931**...........................Worth the travel
Doppelgänger Bar **943**....................Late night
L'épi Boulangerie **944**.....................Breakfast
Guido's Bar **935**........Regular neighbourhood
Puratierra **934**.....................Local favourite
Siamo Nel Forno **938**........................Bargain
Sol de Mayo **931**................Wish I'd opened
Tegui **938**..High end

HAROLD DIETERLE
Perilla
9 Jones Street, New York
A graduate of the Culinary Institute of America,
Dieterle opened his first restaurant, Perilla,
in 2007 and followed with the Thai Kin Shop
and German-Italian The Marrow in 2012.
Beacon **790**...........................Local favourite
Brooklyn Fare **872**............................High end
Chelsea Bagel & Cafe **859**...............Breakfast
Daddy-O **855**..................................Late night
Gramercy Tavern **863**.............Local favourite
Grand Sichuan **855**...........................Bargain
Park Side Restaurant **877**......Wish I'd opened
da Umberto **860**.........Regular neighbourhood

XABIER DIEZ ESTEIBAR
Xarma Jatetxea
Avenida de Tolosa 123, San Sebastián
A San Sebastián native, heavily influenced by his time at Arzak who has since gone on to create hugely inventive plates at Xarma.
Agorregi 483...Bargain
Arzak 483...High end
Château de Brindos 429.........Worth the travel
A Fuego Negro 486.........................Late night
Martín Berasategui 482...........Local favourite
Mirador de Ulía 488....Regular neighbourhood
Pasteleria Gaztelo 488.....................Breakfast
La Rampa 488.......................Wish I'd opened

MATT DILLON
Sitka & Spruce
1531 Melrose Avenue, Seattle
Runs five restaurants, one of which, The Old Chaser Farm outside Seattle, is his home, where he farms and forages.
Asador Etxebarri 479.............Wish I'd opened
Boulette's Larder 747......................Breakfast
Canon 721..Late night
Maneki 722...Bargain
Poppy 724.................Regular neighbourhood
Prunier 470.......................................High end
Una Pizza Napoletana 757.....Worth the travel

VLADISLAV DJATSUK
Tchaikovsky
Hotel Telegraaf, Vene 9, Tallinn
Executive chef at Tallinn's Hotel Telegraaf, Djatsuk has represented Estonia at the Bocuse d'Or.
Alexander 622.................................High end
Chedi 620...Late night
Chedi 620...................Regular neighbourhood
Kohvik Moon 620........Regular neighbourhood
Kolm Sibulat 621.............................Bargain
Leib Resto ja Aed 621.......................Regular
neighbourhood
Olo 300............................Worth the travel
Põhjaka Mõis 621....................Local favourite
Põhjaka Mõis 621..............................Bargain

ÜRYAN DOĞMUŞ
Gile Restaurant
Şair Nedim Caddesi Akaretler, Istanbul
Co-owner of fine-dining Gile Restaurant with Cihan Kipçak, Culinary Institute of America-trained Doğmuş previously held executive chef posts at Istanbul's Mikla and La Mouette, and Argos in Cappadocia.
Beyti 634....................................Local favourite
Bleu Lounge & Grill 637...................Late night
Karaköy Lokantası 637.......................Regular
neighbourhood
Mikla 635..High end
Safi Meyhane 635..................Wish I'd opened
Sütlüce Kokoreçcisi 638.......................Bargain
Van Kahvalti Evi 636........................Breakfast
Yüzevler Kebap 630..............Worth the travel

CHRISTIAN DOMSCHITZ
Vestibül
Doktor-Karl-Lueger-Ring 2, Vienna
A veteran of Vienna's restaurant scene, he's currently behind the stove at Vestibül in the Burgtheater.
Balthazar 868.....................Wish I'd opened
Café Anzengruber 605....................Late night
Dinner by Heston Blumenthal 326....Worth the travel
Holy Moly! 606.......................Local favourite
Meixner's Gastwirtschaft 606.............Regular
neighbourhood
Mraz & Sohn 606..................Worth the travel
Steirereck 607..................................High end
Stomach 607..............Regular neighbourhood

VINNY DOTOLO
Animal
435 North Fairfax Avenue, Los Angeles
One half of the dynamic duo who co-own Los Angeles hotspots Animal, Son of a Gun, Trois Mec (with Ludo Lefebvre) and run a successful catering business, Caramelized Productions.
Honor Bar 729..........Regular neighbourhood
In-N-Out Burger 733.............Local favourite
Papa Cristo's 734...............................Bargain
Red Medicine 729............................Late night
Relæ 293..........................Worth the travel
Sqirl 733...Breakfast
Sushi Zo 731....................................High end
Tsujita Annex 737.................Wish I'd opened

PETER DOYLE
Est.
252 George Street, Sydney
With a career spanning three decades, the owner of Est. could be described as a founding father of modern Australian cooking.
Hugo's Manly 93.....................Local favourite
Monopole 97.......................Wish I'd opened
Mr. Wong 90....................................Late night
Ormeggio at The Spit 94.....................Regular
neighbourhood
Pilu at Freshwater 92.........................High end
Pizza Pesce Birra 94............................Bargain
Semilla 457.......................Worth the travel
The Swimmers Club 99....................Breakfast

JULIEN DUBOUÉ
Afaria
15 Rue Desnouettes, Paris
Basque-born Duboué trained with Dutournier in Paris and Boulud in New York and has gone on to open two Paris bistros inspired by the cuisine of southwest France.
Le 114 Faubourg 462.............Worth the travel
Alain Ducasse au Plaza Athénée 462 High end
L'Ami Jean 458.......................Wish I'd opened
Art Macaron 456..............................Breakfast
L'Auberge du Pas de Vent 431..Local favourite
L'Avant Comptoir 456...........................Regular
neighbourhood
Au Bon Coin les Pieds de Cochon 431 Breakfast
Daniel 844.......................................High end
Les Fables de la Fontaine 459............Regular
neighbourhood
La Ferme d'Orthe 431..........................Bargain
A Fuego Negro 486..............Worth the travel
Marismo 929..........................Worth the travel
Mercado Municipal 920.....................Bargain
Mocotó 929..........................Worth the travel
La Régalade 469..............................Late night
Le Relais de la Poste 430.....................High end
La Réserve Rimbaud 435.......Worth the travel
Square One 229.....................Worth the travel

WYLIE DUFRESNE
Owner of wd~50, the envelope-pushing Manhattan restaurant he opened with the backing of former boss Jean-Georges Vongerichten, which sadly closed it's doors in late 2014.
Asador Portuetxe 484...........Worth the travel
Bar Veloce 848.................................Late night
Empellón Cocina 849...........Worth the travel
Katz's Delicatessen 865..........Local favourite
Momofuku Ssäm Bar 851......................Regular
neighbourhood
Mugaritz 480.......................Wish I'd opened

THIERRY DUHR
Le Bouquet Garni
32 Rue de l'Eau, Luxembourg
Veteran Duhr travelled extensively throughout Europe before taking the helm at Le Bouquet Garni twenty years ago, where in 2013 he was awarded the Gault Millau Luxembourg Chef of the Year.
Restaurant L'Adresse 423...............Late night

RODNEY DUNN
The Agrarian Kitchen
650 Lachlan Road, Lachlan
Trading city life for verdant pastures in 2007, Dunn – former Australian Gourmet Traveller food editor and Tetsuya-trained chef – founded The Agrarian Kitchen farm-based cookery school in rural Tasmania.
Backdoor Fanny's 79......................Bargain
Berta 80...................Regular neighbourhood
The French Laundry 709...................High end
Garagistes 80.........................Local favourite
Mr. Wong 90....................Worth the travel
Pigeon Hole 80.............................Breakfast
Sidecar 80......................................Late night
Swan Oyster Depot 753........Wish I'd opened

MARCUS EAVES
Pied à Terre
34 Charlotte Street, London
Cooks at Pied à Terre in London. Eaves is a protégé of its previous chef Shane Osborn.
Frantzén 270....................Worth the travel
The Gallery 341...............................Late night
Hereford Road 331....Regular neighbourhood
Pitt Cue Co. 350.................................Bargain
Polpo 350.....................Wish I'd opened
Les Prés d'Eugénie 430....................High end
Social Eating House 351..........Local favourite
The Wolseley 345.............................Breakfast

MIKE EGGERT
Pinbone
3 Jersey Road, Sydney
Originally an experimental pop-up venture Eggert (ex-Duke and Billy Kwong) ran with Jemma Whiteman and Berri Eggert, Pinbone found a permanent Woollahra site in 2013.
10 William St 96..........Regular neighbourhood
121BC 99...........................Wish I'd opened
Chinese Noodle House 93...................Bargain
Fatima's 100.....................................Late night
Momofuku Seiōbo 98........................High end
Sean's Panaroma 86.................Local favourite
The Sportsman 310.............Worth the travel
Three Blue Ducks 102......................Breakfast

MIKAEL EINARSSON
Djuret
Lilla Nygatan 5, Stockholm
Oversees the menu at Djuret, Pubologi and Leijontornet in Stockholm having previously worked across Sweden and at London's The Square.
Chez Betty 278...........Regular neighbourhood
Fäviken Magasinet 261..........Wish I'd opened
Fäviken Magasinet 261..........Worth the travel
Frantzén 270.......................................High end
Nytorget 6 277..................................Breakfast
Råkultur 275..Bargain
Sturehof 276....................................Late night

MAGNUS EK
Oaxen Krog & Slip
Beckholmsvägen 26, Stockholm
Ek and his wife Agneta Green left Oaxen island, where they ran renowned Oaxen Skärgårdskrog, to open Oaxen Krog and casual sister restaurant Slip in Stockholm's Djurgården in 2013.
19 Glas 270...............Regular neighbourhood
Fäviken Magasinet 261.........Worth the travel
Frantzén 270.......................................High end
Lydmar Hotel 272.............................Breakfast
Palmyra Kebab 266.............................Bargain
Pubologi 270............................Local favourite
Sturehof 276....................................Late night

RICHARD EKKEBUS
Amber
The Landmark Hotel, 15 Queen's Road, Hong Kong
Gagnaire, Passard and Savoy-trained Dutchman who is Culinary Director at Hong Kong's Landmark Mandarin Oriental.
The Chairman 183...............Worth the travel
Dimdimsum Dimsum 190...................Bargain
Le Louis XV 447..................Wish I'd opened
Luk Yu Tea House 185..............Local favourite
Man Wah 186......................................High end
Nihonryori Ryugin 216...........Worth the travel
Sang Kee Congee Shop 186...........Breakfast
Under Bridge Spicy Crab 181..........Late night
Yardbird 188..............Regular neighbourhood

NIKLAS EKSTEDT
Ekstedt
Humlegårdsgatan 17, Stockholm
'New Nordic' wunderkind, whose résumé includes stints with Blumenthal and Ducasse, opened Ekstedt in 2011, eschewing electricity to cook only with fire and earning a Michelin star in the process.
Gastrologik 274.....................Wish I'd opened
La Gazelle 271.....................................Bargain
Mikla 635...............................Worth the travel
Operabaren 273.........................Local favourite
P.A. & Co 275...............Regular neighbourhood
Speceriet 276.......................Wish I'd opened
Sturehof 276....................................Late night
Urban Deli 266..................................Breakfast
Volt 276...High end

JOSE ENRIQUE
Jose Enrique
Calle Duffaut 176, San Juan
Puerto Rican Enrique returned to his homeland after cooking across the US to open his celebrated eponymous San Juan restaurant in 2007, followed by Capital and Miel.
Le Bernardin 839...................Wish I'd opened
Bodegas Compostela 890...................High end
Brooklyn Fare 872...............Worth the travel
La Casita Blanca 890...............Local favourite
La Comay 890..Bargain
Kasalta 892...Breakfast
New Taste of China 892..................Late night

FISUN ERCAN
Restaurant Su
5145 Rue Wellington, Montreal
Chef, cookbook author and culinary instructor Ercan moved to Montreal at sixteen from her native Turkey, whose traditions influence her informal, elegant cuisine.
Arts Café 691.....................................Breakfast
Big in Japan 691.................................Late night
Le Chien Fumant 692.......................Late night
Eleven Madison Park 862...................High end
Joe Beef 695.............................Local favourite
KanBai 697...Bargain
Lili Co. 693..Breakfast
Mikla 635..............................Worth the travel
Ottolenghi 369...................Wish I'd opened
Tripes & Caviar 697....Regular neighbourhood

RENEE ERICKSON
Boat Street Café
3131 Western Avenue, Seattle
After thirteen years at the helm of Seattle's Boat Street Café, seafood-loving Erickson opened highly acclaimed Walrus and the Carpenter, The Whale Wins and Barnacle wine bar.
Le Bernardin 839................................High end
La Cale 436............................Worth the travel
Il Corvo 721...Bargain
Delancey 722..............Regular neighbourhood
Luce 716...............................Wish I'd opened
Le Pichet 722.....................................Late night
Vif Wine and Coffee 725.................Breakfast

ANTONIO ESCALANTE
Antonio's
Purok 138, Tagaytay City
Born in the Philippines and educated in Australia, he opened his first restaurant in 2002 and now owns a celebrated grill, breakfast place and cocktail lounge in Manila.

Gloria Maris 247.................................Breakfast
Grace Park 246.......................Wish I'd opened
JT's Manukan 247..............................Late night
New Harlem Restaurant 247..............Bargain
El Quim de la Boqueria 519....Worth the travel
Ramen Yushoken 247...........................Regular
neighbourhood
Terry's 246...............................Local favourite
UMU 246...High end

SUMITO ESTÉVEZ SINGH
Mondeque Restaurante
Avenida Jovito Villalba, Margarita Island
Born in Caracas and raised in India, where he developed a taste for exotic flavours. Founded the Culinary Institute of Caracas.

Alto 902.......................Regular neighbourhood
Alto 902..High end
Astrid & Gastón 906..............Worth the travel
La Casa de Rubén 903..............Local favourite
Mokambo 903...................................Breakfast
Mokambo 903...................Wish I'd opened

ROB EVANS
Duckfat
43 Middle Street, Portland
A Californian based in Maine who honed his skills at the French Laundry. His restaurant Duckfat is named after the not-so-secret ingredient in its Belgian-style fries.

Akelarre 483...........................Worth the travel
Binkley's 700.........................Worth the travel
Boda 779..Late night
Fore Street 779......................Local favourite
Gorgeous Gelato 780............Wish I'd opened
Hot Suppa! 780...............................Breakfast
Otto Pizza 780.....................................Bargain
Pai Men Miyake 780....Regular neighbourhood
Piccolo 780...High end

JOHNNY FARAH
Lux
Al Gamarik Street, Lebanon
Accessory designer, organic farmer and restaurateur who owns two popular restaurants in Beirut: Casablanca and Lux.

L'Atelier de Joël Robuchon 459........Worth the travel
Burgundy 138.....................................High end
Falafel Sahyoun 138............................Bargain
Kunitoraya 450......................Worth the travel
Liza 138.................................Local favourite
Souk El Tayeb 139............................Breakfast
Sporting Club Beach 139....................Regular
neighbourhood

BRAD FARMERIE
Public
210 Elizabeth Street, New York City
Pittsburgher who worked in London with Peter Gordon. Opened Public in 2003 in New York, where he now also oversees Madam Geneva and American grill restaurant Saxon + Parole.

Blue Hill at Stone Barns 790..Wish I'd opened
Blue Ribbon Brasserie 869..............Late night
Cafe Pushkin 623....................Worth the travel
Caravan 359.......................................Breakfast
Depot Eatery 128....................Worth the travel
Keens Steakhouse 841...........Local favourite
Nong's Khao Man Gai 717.................Bargain
Pok Pok NY 875.................................Bargain
The Providores and Tapa Room 329.Breakfast
Prune 852..Breakfast
Publican Quality Meats 834.................Bargain
The Restaurant at Meadowood 708.........High end
Roberta's 875.........................Wish I'd opened
Speedy Romeo 876.....Regular neighbourhood
Uilliam's 624............................Worth the travel

YAIR FEINBERG
FeinCook Studio
84 Ben Zvi Road, Tel Aviv
Tel Aviv-based chef who trained in France and now cooks privately, teaches and runs culinary tours through FeinCook Studio.

Abu Hassan 141...............................Breakfast
Bertie 142...................Regular neighbourhood
The Bun 142.......................................Late night
Dolce Stil Novo 594................Worth the travel
Pinat Hashlosha 144...........................Bargain
Raphaël 144...........................Local favourite
Shila 144...............................Wish I'd opened
Taizu 144..High end

MICHAEL FERRARO
Delicatessen NYC
54 Prince Street, New York City
After stints at the Mercer Kitchen and the Biltmore Room, he became chef-partner of New York's Delicatessen and Macbar, its macaroni-and-cheese-serving annex.

Balthazar 868...................................Breakfast
Le Bernardin 839...................Wish I'd opened
DB Bistro Moderne 840......................High end
DiverXo 499...........................Worth the travel
Gray's Papaya 845..............................Bargain
Great NY Noodletown 861...............Late night
Grimaldi's Pizzeria 874............Local favourite
Minetta Tavern 853................Local favourite
Peter Luger Steakhouse 875....Local favourite
Ushiwakamaru 857.....Regular neighbourhood

FEDERICO FIALAYRE
Tomo 1
Carlos Pellegrini 521, Buenos Aires
Born into a family of cooks, Fialayre carries on the culinary legacy of his mother and aunt at Tomo 1, the restaurant famed for its take on Porteña cuisine.

Aramburu 941......................................High end
La Bourgogne 939..............................High end
Chila 939..High end
Florería Atlántico 939..........................Regular
neighbourhood
Florería Atlántico 939.........................Late night
La Picantería 909...................Wish I'd opened
Las Pizarras 937..................................Bargain
Las Pizarras 937...................Wish I'd opened
La Stampa 936..........Regular neighbourhood
Tegui 938...............................Local favourite
Tordesilhas 924.....................Wish I'd opened

KONSTANTIN FILIPPOU
Restaurant Konstantin Filippou
Dominikanerbastei 17, Vienna
Since 2013 Filippou has been bringing his Austrian and Greek heritage to bear at his self-named international restaurant in Vienna.

Agapé Substance 455.............Wish I'd opened
L'Ambroisie 454..................................High end
Atera 870.............................Worth the travel
Café Anzengruber 605....................Late night
Do & Co Restaurant 605.................Breakfast
Ergon 629..Bargain
Skopik & Lohn 607..................Local favourite
Tim Raue 552..........Regular neighbourhood

ROLF FLIEGAUF
Ecco
Via del Segnale 10, Ascona
The youngest European chef, at twenty-nine, to win two Michelin stars for his restaurant Ecco, German Fliegauf has since won two stars for its St. Moritz spin-off, Ecco on Snow.

Alinea 827.............................Worth the travel
Beefbar 446.........................Wish I'd opened
Grotto Baldoria 563................Local favourite
Pizzeria Caruso 562..........................Late night
Restaurant De Librije 394..................High end
Silberburg 540...................................Breakfast

PAUL FLYNN
The Tannery Restaurant
10 Quay Street, Dungarvan
Opened The Tannery in 1997, following a
distinguished London career that included
running Chez Nico.

L'Atmosphere 390	Bargain
Ballymaloe Restaurant 385	Local favourite
Bistrot de Luxe 327	Worth the travel
Chapter One 385	High end
Fishy Fishy Café 384	Wish I'd opened
Genoa's Takeaway 390	Late night
The Greenhouse Dublin 386	High end
The House Restaurant 389	Regular neighbourhood
Restaurant Patrick Guilbaud 386	High end
The Shamrock Restaurant 390	Breakfast

MARC FOSH
Simply Fosh
Carrer de la Missió 7, Palma
Having begun his career at the Greenhouse
in London, Fosh now lives in Spain where he's
owned Simply Fosh since 2009.

Avant-Garde van Groeninge 394	Worth the travel
The British Larder Suffolk 314	Worth the travel
Es Molí d'en Bou 478	High end
Fibonacci 478	Breakfast
Joan Marc Restaurant 478	Regular neighbourhood
Katz's Delicatessen 865	Breakfast
Sa Cuina de n'Aina 479	Local favourite

PAUL FOSTER
The Dining Room at Mallory
Mallory Court Hotel, Harbury Lane, Royal
Leamington Spa
Trained at Le Manoir aux Quat'Saisons and
Sat Bains, and headed up the kitchen at
Tuddenham Mill before recently taking up the
helm at Mallory Court Hotel's Dining Room.

Bar Boulud 326	Regular neighbourhood
Bubbledogs 363	Bargain
Duck & Waffle 358	Late night
The Fat Duck 304	High end
Kitchen Table 363	Wish I'd opened
Mugaritz 480	Worth the travel
Pea Porridge 314	Local favourite
St. John Bread & Wine 374	Breakfast

JASON FOX
Commonwealth
2224 Mission Street, San Francisco
Co-owner of Commonwealth, Fox opened
San Francisco's Mission Street in 2010, and
has a résumé that includes Bar Tartine and
Scott Howard.

Atelier Crenn 750	High end
Aziza 755	Local favourite
Bar Agricole 755	Local favourite
Benu 756	Local favourite
Bouche 746	Late night
Boulevard 747	Local favourite
Cal Pep 513	Worth the travel
Coi 754	Local favourite
Commis 705	Local favourite
Comstock Saloon 746	Late night
flour + water 751	Local favourite
Hisop 514	Worth the travel
Kajitsu 843	Worth the travel
Mission Banh Mi 751	Bargain
Nojo 748	Breakfast
El Quim de la Boqueria 519	Worth the travel
Quince 747	High end
The Restaurant at Meadowood 708	High end
S & T Hong Kong 755	Bargain
SPQR 755	Local favourite
State Bird Provisions 750	Wish I'd opened
The Willows Inn 720	Worth the travel
Yamo 753	Bargain

JASON FRANEY
Canlis
2576 Aurora Avenue North, Seattle
A protégé of Daniel Humm, whom he worked
under at Campton Place and Danny Meyer's
Eleven Madison Park, he left to become
executive chef of Seattle's landmark Canlis
restaurant.

Betony 839	Wish I'd opened
Canon 721	Late night
Castagna 715	Worth the travel
Monsoon 722	Breakfast
Pho Viet Anh 722	Bargain
Staple & Fancy 724	Regular neighbourhood
The Willows Inn 720	High end

BJÖRN FRANTZÉN
Frantzén
Lilla Nygatan 21, Stockholm
Frantzén met Daniel Lindeberg in 1998
while they were working at Edsbacka Krog.
A decade later they opened Frantzén/
Lindeberg, which later became Frantzén. He
opened the Flying Elk in 2013.

AG 271	Regular neighbourhood
Esperanto 274	High end
Fäviken Magasinet 261	Worth the travel
Max Hamngatan 272	Wish I'd opened
Råkultur 275	Bargain
Riche 275	Breakfast
Sturehof 276	Late night

NEAL FRASER
BLD
7450 Beverly Boulevard, Los Angeles
Worked in Los Angeles for Splichal, Puck
and Rockenwagner; ran Rix and his own restaurants, Grace and BLD, before launching
Fritzi Dog in 2012.

Bäco Mercat 731	Local favourite
Blue Hill at Stone Barns 790	High end
Blue Hill at Stone Barns 790	Wish I'd opened
Daikokuya 735	Bargain
Genwa Korean BBQ 733	Late night
Loteria Grill 734	Breakfast
Sushi Gen 735	Regular neighbourhood
The Restaurant in San Miguel de Allende 887	Worth the travel

RAMÓN FREIXA
Ramón Freixa Madrid
Calle Claudio Coello 67, Madrid
Barcelona-born Freixa trained in his family's
restaurant before going on to open three
restaurants of his own, in Barcelona, Madrid
and Colombia.

Atera 870	Wish I'd opened
Bar Pinotxo 517	Breakfast
El Celler de Can Roca 493	High end
La Gabinoteca 500	Late night
Mamá Framboise 501	Breakfast
Pierre Gagnaire 463	Worth the travel
Restaurante El Pescador 502	Regular neighbourhood
Santceloni 503	Local favourite
La Terraza 504	Local favourite
Tickets 515	Bargain

THRAINN FREYR VIGFÚSSON
Lava Restaurant
Blue Lagoon, 240 Grindavik
Head chef at Reykjavik's Kolabrautin until late 2013, Vigfússon now heads up Blue Lagoon's Lava Restaurant alongside Viktor Örn Andrésson.

Alinea **827**	Worth the travel
Bakarí Sandholt **252**	Breakfast
Bæjarins Beztu Pylsur **252**	Late night
Dabbous **363**	Worth the travel
Grillið **253**	Local favourite
Relæ **293**	Wish I'd opened
Svarta Kaffið **253**	Bargain
Vegamót **254**	Regular neighbourhood
Vox **254**	High end

FORD FRY
JCT. Kitchen & Bar
1198 Howell Mill Road, Atlanta
Chef and owner of Atlanta-based restaurant empire Rocket Fire Restaurants, whose ventures include JCT. Kitchen & Bar, No. 246, King + Duke, The Optimist and St. Cecilia.

Antico Pizza **769**	Wish I'd opened
Bacchanalia **769**	High end
Cakes & Ale **772**	Local favourite
Community Q BBQ **772**	Bargain
Fox Bros. Bar-B-Q **770**	Bargain
Goode Company Taqueria **809**	Breakfast
Nuevo Laredo Cantina **770**	Regular neighbourhood
Octopus Bar **770**	Late night
Son of a Gun **742**	Worth the travel

JUAN GAFFURI
Elena
Posadas 1086, Buenos Aires
From commis to executive chef, Gaffuri has spent over ten years working in Four Seasons hotel kitchens in Egypt, the US, Mexico and latterly in his home town of Buenos Aires, Argentina.

La Brigada **942**	Local favourite
Croque Madame **935**	Breakfast
El Cuartito **941**	Late night
DBGB Kitchen & Bar **848**	Worth the travel
La Rambla **940**	Bargain
Restaurante Oviedo **940**	Regular neighbourhood
Unik **938**	High end

PIERRE GAGNAIRE
Pierre Gagnaire
6 Rue Balzac, Paris
French toque star whose restaurant empire spans the globe from his eponymous Paris flagship all the way to South Korea and beyond.

Bras **436**	Wish I'd opened
Carette **470**	Breakfast
Kifuné **470**	Local favourite
Restaurant Akrame **470**	Regular neighbourhood
Le Stella **470**	Late night
La Tour d'Argent **455**	High end
Villa Feltrinelli **586**	Worth the travel

CHRIS GALVIN
Bistrot de Luxe
66 Baker Street, London
UK-born Michelin-starred chef, Francophile and co-owner of a string of award-winning restaurants based on modern French cuisine, he opened the flagship Bistro de Luxe in 2005.

Le 114 Faubourg **462**	Worth the travel
Bar Italia **345**	Bargain
Le Gavroche **341**	Local favourite
The Goring Dining Room **320**	High end
Ronnie Scott's **351**	Late night
The Square **344**	Wish I'd opened
The Wolseley **345**	Breakfast

JEFF GALVIN
Galvin at Windows
London Hilton, 22 Park Lane, London
British Michelin-starred chef and co-owner of seven family-run, French-inspired restaurants, which he runs with his brother Chris.

Balthazar **868**	Wish I'd opened
Chez Bruce **334**	Local favourite
The Foyer & Reading Room **340**	Breakfast
The Gallery **341**	Late night
Le Gavroche **341**	Local favourite
Le Manoir aux Quat'Saisons **312**	High end
The River Café **325**	Worth the travel

EMILIO GARIP
Restaurante Oviedo
Antonio Beruti 2602, Buenos Aires
Founder of Buenos Aires pioneer Oviedo, Garip has tirelessly sourced the best local produce for twenty-five years to maintain the restaurant's position at the top.

L'Assiette Champenoise **435**	Worth the travel
L'Atelier de Joël Robuchon **459**	High end
La Bourgogne **939**	High end
Brasserie Lutetia **456**	Breakfast
Chila **939**	Late night
Florería Atlántico **939**	Late night
Italpast **930**	Regular neighbourhood
Lobby Bar **931**	Breakfast
Magritte **944**	Bargain
Tomo 1 **935**	Local favourite

COLBY GARRELTS
Bluestem
900 Westport Road, Kansas City
James Beard Award-winning chef credited with invigorating the Kansas City dining scene with his progressive Midwestern fare. Co-owner of Bluestem (2004) and Rye (2012).

Genessee Royale **784**	Regular neighbourhood
Michael Smith **784**	High end
Oklahoma Joe's Bar-B-Que **773**	Local favourite
Oklahoma Joe's Bar-B-Que **773**	Wish I'd opened
El Pollo Rey **774**	Bargain
Port Fonda **784**	Late night
Room 39 **785**	Breakfast
Saison **756**	Worth the travel

ANDRÉ GARRETT
André Garrett at Cliveden
Cliveden House, Taplow
Classically trained in London's finest kitchens, including spells with Ladenis and Loubet, he ran the pass at Galvin at Windows before joining Cliveden House hotel as executive chef.

Arbutus **345**	Bargain
The Crown at Bray **304**	Regular neighbourhood
The French Laundry **709**	Wish I'd opened
Hakkasan **342**	High end
The Hand & Flowers **305**	Local favourite
Meat Liquor **328**	Late night
Noma **289**	Worth the travel
The Wolseley **345**	Breakfast

MATTHEW GAUDET
West Bridge
1 Kendall Square, Cambridge
Ten years working in New York in the likes of Eleven Madison, Jean Georges Park and Aquavit gave Gaudet the grounding to return home to Boston and open West Bridge in 2012.

Area Four **777**.............Regular neighbourhood
Bras **436**..Breakfast
Bras **436**.............................Worth the travel
Bubbledogs **363**.................Wish I'd opened
J. T. Farnhams **778**...................Local favourite
The Ledbury **331**.............Worth the travel
Mugaritz **480**.................................High end
Neptune Oyster **775**.................Local favourite
Peach Farm **776**..............................Late night
Pho Pasteur **776**.................................Bargain
Pho 'n Rice **779**..................................Bargain
Pierre Gagnaire **463**.......................High end

ALEXANDRE GAUTHIER
La Grenouillère
19 Rue de la Grenouillère, La Madelaine-sous-Montreuil
Discovered by Ducasse, rising star Gauthier took over his family's century-old restaurant La Grenouillère in 2003.

L'Arnsbourg **428**...............................High end
L'Avant Comptoir **456**.....................Late night
Le Caveau **437**.................................Bargain
Le Chateaubriand **466**.....................Late night
Le Chatillon **437**..............................Breakfast
La Colline du Colombier **434**..............Wish I'd opened
Combal.Zero **593**............................High end
Le Comptoir du Relais **457**..............Breakfast
La Cour de Rémi **437**..........................Regular neighbourhood
In De Wulf **421**......................Local favourite
Maison Troisgros **445**.....................High end
Manresa **703**....................Worth the travel
L'Olivo **573**.........................Worth the travel
Roberta's **875**...................Wish I'd opened
Silencio **453**.....................................Late night

ALEXIS GAUTHIER
Gauthier Soho
21 Romilly Street, London
French-born chef-patron at London's Michelin-starred Gauthier Soho, where the menu's emphasis on vegetables is distinctly un-French.

Le Bernardin **839**..............................High end
Cay Tre **347**..Bargain
Dean Street Townhouse **347**...........Breakfast
The Ivy **338**...........................Local favourite
New Mayflower **336**......................Late night
The River Café **325**...........Wish I'd opened
La Table de Tee **226**...............Worth the travel
Tendido Cuatro **332**.....Regular neighbourhood

ROBIN GILL
The Dairy
15 The Pavement, London
Having worked at Le Manoir aux Quat'Saisons, Dublin-born Gill's impressive résumé was further boosted by a stint at Noma. He opened The Dairy bistro in Clapham in 2013.

41 Grados Experience **513**................High end
Asador Etxebarri **479**...........Worth the travel
Barrafina **346**............Regular neighbourhood
Beigel Bake **370**..............................Late night
La Conca del Sogno **574**........Wish I'd opened
Hawksmoor **358**..............................Breakfast
Honest Burgers **357**..........................Bargain
Mien Tay **319**......................................Bargain
Upstairs at the Ten Bells **374**..................Local favourite

PETER GILMORE
Quay
5 Hickson Road, Sydney
Executive chef of Quay since 2001, Gilmore describes his market-driven style as 'a celebration of being a cook in Australia'.

Banana Blossom **93**...........................Bargain
Bras **436**..........................Wish I'd opened
Golden Century Seafood **89**.............Late night
In De Wulf **421**................Worth the travel
Marque **101**.....................................High end
Rockpool Bar & Grill **91**...........Local favourite
Spice Temple **91**.........Regular neighbourhood
Tastebuds **102**.................................Breakfast

HERNÁN GIPPONI
HG Restaurant
Fierro Hotel, Soler 5682, Buenos Aires
Training in double-Michelin-starred kitchens in Spain helped Gipponi elevate traditional Argentine dishes to the very height of gastronomy at his eponymous BA restaurant.

Aramburu **941**.................................Late night
La Cabrera **936**....................Local favourite
Chila **939**...............................Local favourite
Don Julio **937**.......................Local favourite
La Fachada **937**................................Bargain
Le Grill **939**............................Local favourite
La Lucha **907**....................Wish I'd opened
Mugaritz **480**...................Wish I'd opened
Au Pied de Cochon **694**.........Worth the travel
Las Pizarras **937**.........Regular neighbourhood
Quique Dacosta Restaurante **505**.......Wish I'd opened
Tegui **938**.......................................High end
Unik **938**.............................Local favourite
Vicente López **941**.........................Breakfast

GUNNAR KARL GÍSLASON
Dill Restaurant
Sturlugötu 5, Reykjavík
Opened Dill in 2009 where his Modern Nordic approach is influenced by his time spent with Lauterbach, Redzepi and Henriksen.

3 Frakkar **252**...........................Local favourite
Aska **871**.............................Worth the travel
Bæjarins Beztu Pylsur **252**...................Bargain
The Fremont Diner **707**........Wish I'd opened
Grái Kötturinn **253**............................Breakfast
K-Bar **253**.......................................Late night
Sæmundur í Sparifötunum **253**..........Regular neighbourhood
Slotskøkkenet **282**..........................High end

MANOJ GOEL
Varq
1 Mansingh Road, New Delhi
Runs the kitchen at legendary Indian chef Hemant Oberoi's Varq, which serves innovative takes on North Indian street food.

The Big Chill Cafe **150**...........Wish I'd opened
Chimney Sizzlers **150**........................Bargain
The China Kitchen **151**.......................High end
Karavalli **153**....................Worth the travel
Karim's **151**...........................Local favourite
Masala Art **152**..........Regular neighbourhood
Paranthe wali Gali **152**.................Breakfast

SUZANNE GOIN
Lucques
8474 Melrose Avenue, Los Angeles
Goin launched her Los Angeles empire with Lucques (1998). Eighteen years on, and with two James Beard Awards, she and business partner Caroline Styne co-own A.O.C., Tavern and The Larder.

Bar Isabel **682**.....................Worth the travel
Camino **704**........................Worth the travel
Canelé **728**.......................................Breakfast
Pizzeria Mozza **741**....Regular neighbourhood
Spago **730**.......................................High end

PETER GOOSSENS
Hof van Cleve
Riemegemstraat 1, Kruishoutem
Has run his rustic yet refined Flanders restaurant since 1987. Combines Belgian traditions with French haute technique and Asian influences.

L'Air du Temps 419................................High end
Alain Ducasse au Plaza Athénée 462.....Worth the travel
Aqua 544........................Worth the travel
Arabelle Meirlaen 418........................High end
L'Atelier de Joël Robuchon 459.......Worth the travel
Bartholomeus 422........................High end
Benoit & Bernard Dewitte 418.Local favourite
Berto 423........................Local favourite
Bistro de Kruiden Molen 417...............Bargain
Bon Bon 412........................High end
Boury 423........................High end
Brasserie Boulevard 417......Local favourite
Brasserie Latem 418................Local favourite
Le Chalet De La Forêt 415...............High end
Comme Chez Soi 413........................High end
Demaré 422........................Breakfast
La Durée 422........................High end
L'Eau Vive 420........................High end
Escabeche 423........................Local favourite
't Fornuis 410........................High end
Friture René 411........................Late night
De Hermelijn 415.......Regular neighbourhood
Hertog Jan 420........................High end
Het Gebaar 410........................High end
't Huis van Lede 415...Regular neighbourhood
In De Wulf 421........................High end
De Jonkman 420........................High end
Martino 416........................Late night
't Nieuw Stadion 416........................Bargain
Le Nouveau Blé d'Or 422........................Breakfast
Nuance 411........................High end
La Paix 412........................High end
Plein 25 415..........Regular neighbourhood
Pure C 395........................Worth the travel
De Schone van Boskoop 411..Worth the travel
Sel Gris 422........................High end
Le Siphon 421........................Bargain
Slagmolen 419........................High end
Volta 417........................Bargain
Vrijmoed 417........................Local favourite
't Zilte 411........................High end

PETER GORDON
The Providores and Tapa Room
109 Marylebone High Street, London
Fusion pioneer Gordon runs restaurants in Istanbul, London, and his native New Zealand, where he reopened the iconic Sugar Club in 2013.

Avondale Sunday Market 129..............Bargain
Depot Eatery 128.....................Local favourite
The French Café 129........................High end
Ponsonby Road Bistro 132................Regular neighbourhood
Ponsonby Social Club 132...............Late night
Rabbithole Cafe 130........................Breakfast
Takazawa 218........................Wish I'd opened

PATRICK GOUBIER
Chez Patrick
222 Queens Road East, Hong Kong
Lyonnaise globetrotter who has worked in London, the Caribbean, Vietnam and Rome, Goubier is now settled in Hong Kong.

L'Atelier de Joël Robuchon 185..........Regular neighbourhood
Cecconi's Italian 183..Regular neighbourhood
Georges Blanc 446...............Worth the travel

LUCA GOZZANI
Fasano
Rua Vitório Fasano 88, São Paulo
Head chef of Fasano in São Paulo since 2012, Italian-born Gozzani met restaurateur Rogério Fasano at Enoteca Pinchiorri in Florence, who lured him to Brazil.

Colher de Pau 922.....Regular neighbourhood
Enoteca Pinchiorri 598..........Worth the travel
Marie-Madeleine 922........................Breakfast
Peixaria Bar e Venda 928........Local favourite
Roberta Sudbrack 917...........Wish I'd opened
Terraço Itália 920........................High end

LORI GRANITO
Magnolia
17 Po Yan Street, Hong Kong
Her unconventional career has seen the New Orleans native's small Cajun-Creole private catering business flourish in Hong Kong, alongside American-style burrito joint, Little Burro.

208 Duecento Otto 189......................Regular neighbourhood
L'Auberge de L'Ill 428..........Worth the travel
Caprice 183........................High end
The Flying Pan 184........................Late night
Little Burro 180........................Bargain
Wagyu Kaiseki Den 190........................Breakfast
Wagyu Kaiseki Den 190.........Wish I'd opened
Yung Kee 188........................Local favourite

BERTRAND GRÉBAUT
Septime
80 Rue de Charonne, Paris
Trained at l'ESAG, one of France's best culinary schools, he came of culinary age with Passard before opening Septime in 2011.

Le Baratin 472............Regular neighbourhood
Café des Musées 454...............Local favourite
Kødbyens Fiskebar 295.........Wish I'd opened
Le Pacifique 472........................Late night
Le Pavillon de la Reine 454...............Breakfast
Sacha 503........................Worth the travel
Taing Song-Heng 454........................Bargain
Yam'Tcha 451........................High end

BEN GREENO
Momofuku Seiōbo
80 Pyrmont Street, Sydney
Runs the kitchen for David Chang in Sydney. Born in England, he's worked with Sat Bains and René Redzepi.

The Bridge Room 87...........................High end
The Bunker 122........................Breakfast
The Clove Club 371...............Worth the travel
Fratelli Paradiso 97.................Local favourite
Golden Century Seafood 89..............Late night
Marrickville Pork Roll 95...................Bargain
Momofuku Ssäm Bar 851......Wish I'd opened
Vincent 103.........Regular neighbourhood

MEHMET GÜRS
Mikla
Meşrutiyet Caddesi 15, Istanbul
Turkish toque star who, thanks to his Finnish-Swedish mother and a childhood partially spent in Stockholm, works some Nordic influences into his cooking at his Istanbul restaurant Mikla.

Amass 286........................Worth the travel
Kantin 638........................Local favourite
Kiyi 639.....................Regular neighbourhood
Manresa 703........................Wish I'd opened
Noma 289........................High end

RODOLFO GUZMÁN
Boragó
Avenue Nueva Costanera 3467, Santiago
Inspired by his time at Mugaritz with Andoni Luis Aduriz and his own study of chemical engineering and bioprocesses, he opened Boragó in Santiago in 2007.

Aquí Está Coco 947..................Local favourite
Mestizo 947........................Late night
Mestizo 947...........................Wish I'd opened
Mugaritz 480........................Worth the travel
El Quillay 947........................Bargain
Quinoa 947........................Breakfast
Rancho Doña María 946.....................Regular neighbourhood
The Singular Restaurant 946............High end

GABRIELLE HAMILTON
Prune
54 East 1st Street, New York City
Chef-owner of Prune in Manhattan, which gained cult status for its gutsy approach as outlined in her memoir *Blood, Bones and Butter*.
Balthazar 868...............................Breakfast
Barbuto 854...............Regular neighbourhood
Cotogna 747.......................Worth the travel
Daniel 844...................................High end
Kafana 849....................................Bargain
Marea 841...................................High end
OTTO Enoteca Pizzeria 853................Regular neighbourhood
Del Posto 860...............................High end
The River Café 325..............Worth the travel
Rochelle Canteen 372...........Worth the travel
Two Boroughs Larder 802.....Worth the travel

ANNA HANSEN
The Modern Pantry
47–48 St John's Square, London
Opened The Providores and Tapa Room with Peter Gordon in London's Marylebone in 2001. She launched her own restaurant, The Modern Pantry, in Clerkenwell in 2008.
The Clove Club 371.....Regular neighbourhood
Dishoom Shoreditch 371..................Late night
Dishoom Shoreditch 371....................Bargain
The Hand & Flowers 305........Worth the travel
Koya 349....................................Breakfast
Mugaritz 480...............................High end
Ottolenghi 369........................Local favourite
Public 868........................Wish I'd opened
Sunday 369..................................Breakfast

BRIAN MARK HANSEN
Søllerød Kro
Søllerødvej 35, Holte
After manning the stove at Christiansholm Slot, Hansen returned in 2013 to run the kitchen at Søllerød Kro, a 330-year-old inn where he was formerly sous chef.
Cofoco 295....................................Bargain
Dinner by Heston Blumenthal 326....Worth the travel
The French Laundry 709........Wish I'd opened
Geranium 296...............................High end
Marchal 289................................Breakfast
Pluto 290.................Regular neighbourhood
Restaurant Mêlée 279.....................Late night
Restaurant Rudolf Mathis 283...............Local favourite

STEFFEN HANSEN
Grefsenkollen
Grefsenkollveien 100, Oslo
In 2008 he took over the kitchen at Grefsenkollen, a timber ski lodge originally opened in 1927.
Aamanns Deli & Take Away 296.......Breakfast
Acme 865...................Regular neighbourhood
Arakataka 258................................Bargain
Arakataka 258...........Regular neighbourhood
L'Atelier de Joël Robuchon 712........High end
Atera 870...........................Worth the travel
Bagatelle 258........................Local favourite
Le Benjamin 258........Regular neighbourhood
Eleven Madison Park 862......Wish I'd opened
Jean-Georges 845................Worth the travel
Mathias Dahlgren 272..........Worth the travel
Le Meurice 450.............................High end
Le Mirazur 440....................Worth the travel
The Nighthawk Diner 259...............Breakfast
Norma's 841................................Breakfast
RyuGin 216........................Worth the travel
Saigon Lille Café 260.......................Bargain
Taco República 260.........................Late night
VQ 24 Hours 322............................Late night
The Wolseley 345...........................Breakfast

HENRY HARRIS
Racine
239 Brompton Road, London
Elder of the two Harris brothers, he owns Racine in London's Knightsbridge which celebrated a decade in business in 2012.
Le Gavroche 341........................Local favourite
North China 318.........Regular neighbourhood
Ranoush Juice 329..........................Late night
The Sportsman 310..............Worth the travel
Tayyabs 375..................................Bargain
Violet 365....................................Breakfast
Zuma 327....................................High end
Zuni Café 749.....................Wish I'd opened

MATTHEW HARRIS
Bibendum
81 Fulham Road, London
Has carved out a career at Terence Conran's Bibendum, in Michelin's former London HQ, where he began cooking in 1987.
The Begging Bowl 370...........Worth the travel
Bravi Ragazzi 375..........................Late night
The Ivy 338......................Wish I'd opened
Joy King Lau 336.............................Bargain
The Verandah 226.........................Breakfast
The Wolseley 345......................Local favourite
Yauatcha 352.............Regular neighbourhood
Zuma 327....................................High end

SAM HARRIS
Zucca
184 Bermondsey Street, London
The River Café-trained force behind Zucca, a Modern Italian opened in southeast London's Bermondsey Street in 2010.
Albion Cafe 370.............................Breakfast
Cafe Fast 354................................Bargain
Magdalen 356............Regular neighbourhood
Noma 289.........................Worth the travel
The Square 344.............................High end
St. John Bar and Restaurant 362.....Late night
St. John Bar and Restaurant 362........Local favourite
St. John Bar and Restaurant 362.......Wish I'd opened

STEPHEN HARRIS
The Sportsman
Faversham Road, Seasalter
In 1999 he took over a rundown pub in Seasalter, on a remote part of the Kentish coast, and built it up into one of the England's most exciting destination restaurants.
L'Arpège 458.........................Worth the travel
David Brown Delicatessen 311...........Regular neighbourhood
Elliott's Coffee Shop 311.................Breakfast
Frantzén 270.......................Worth the travel
The Goods Shed Restaurant 310............Local favourite
Hedone 322.................................High end
Le Mirazur 440....................Worth the travel

TOM HARRIS
Harris worked with the nose-to-tail St. John group for ten years where he won a Michelin star, then went on to retain the star at One Leicester Street, where he was chef-patron until 2013.
Baozi Inn 336................................Bargain
Barney Greengrass 845........Worth the travel
Beigel Bake 370.......................Local favourite
The Clove Club 371.................Wish I'd opened
Lardo 364..................Regular neighbourhood
Leila's Café 372.............................Breakfast
St. John Bar and Restaurant 362......High end
Umut 2000 361..............................Late night

ANGELA HARTNETT
Murano
20 Queen Street, London
Began her career with Gordon Ramsay
before going solo with Murano in 2010.
She now oversees several other casual and
less casual establishments in London and
Hampshire.
Barrafina 346......................................Bargain
Brawn 366................Regular neighbourhood
The Delaunay 337............................Late night
HIX 348...Late night
The Modern Pantry 359...................Breakfast
Momofuku Ko 850.................Worth the travel
Moro 360..................Regular neighbourhood
The Sportsman 310...............Wish I'd opened
The Square 344.................................High end
St. John Bread & Wine 374......Local favourite
Tramshed 373.............Regular neighbourhood
The Waterside Inn 304.......................High end
Zucca 355...................Regular neighbourhood

DAVID HAWKSWORTH
Hawksworth Restaurant
801 West Georgia Street, Vancouver
Worked in the UK at L'Escargot, Le Manoir
aux Qaut'Saisons and The Square before
making his name at West Restaurant in
Vancouver. Opened his eponymous restaurant
in 2011.
L'Abattoir 669.....................................High end
Atera 870.............................Worth the travel
Dan Japanese Restaurant 671...........Regular
                                      neighbourhood
Go Fish 668.........................Wish I'd opened
Gyoza King 674................................Late night
Kirin Restaurant 672............................Bargain
Thomas Haas 672.............................Breakfast
Vij's 669.................................Local favourite

NIGEL HAWORTH
Northcote
Northcote Road, Blackburn
Has run Northcote with Craig Bancroft since
1984. They also operate five food-led pubs
across the North of England, including The
Three Fishes at Milton, and The Highwayman
Inn at Burrow.
Bentley's Oyster Bar & Grill 339.........Regular
                                      neighbourhood
Clayton Street Chippy 311...................Bargain
The Fat Duck 304.................Wish I'd opened
The Inn at Whitewell 311..........Local favourite
Ocean 524............................Worth the travel
The Wolseley 345.............................Breakfast

FERGUS HENDERSON
St. John Bar and Restaurant
26 St John Street, London
Champion of using the bits of beast that Brit-
ish chefs tended to leave behind before St.
John arrived in 1994. Opened St. John Bread
& Wine in 2003.
Attica 113...............................Worth the travel
Chez Georges 452.................Wish I'd opened
Ciao Bella 355............Regular neighbourhood
Le Gavroche 341................................High end
London Jade Garden 336......................Bargain
The Sirloin 362...................................Breakfast
Sweetings 359.......................Local favourite

MARGOT HENDERSON
Rochelle Canteen
Arnold Circus, London
Wife of Fergus 'nose-to-tail' Henderson, she
is a culinary force in her own right running
the Rochelle Canteen in London's East End
and Arnold & Henderson with her business
partner Melanie Arnold.
Bar Italia 345.....................................Breakfast
Barrafina 346........................Wish I'd opened
Brawn 366..Bargain
Ducksoup 348............Regular neighbourhood
Hix Oyster & Fish House 308.................Worth
                                           the travel
Ikeda 343..High end
Red Rooster 838...................Worth the travel
Royal China 319................................Late night
St. John Bar and Restaurant 362....Breakfast
St. John Bar and Restaurant 362............Local
                                           favourite

CLAUS MØLLER HENRIKSEN
Slotskøkkenet
Dragsholm Allé, Hørve
Danish Noma graduate who oversees the
dining rooms — one formal, one casual — at
the striking Dragsholm Slot, a restored
thirteenth-century castle 75 km. south of
Copenhagen.
Amass 286...High end
Elmely Kro 283.......................Local favourite
Noma 289.............................Worth the travel
Pluto 290....................Regular neighbourhood
Schønnemann 290..............................Bargain
Sokkelund Café & Brasserie 280......Breakfast

JAMES HENRY
Bones
43 Rue Godefroy Cavaignac, Paris
Part of la nouvelle vague transforming Paris's
eating habits, Australian Henry trained with
Daniel Rose before opening the laid-back
Bones in 2013.
Asador Etxebarri 479............Worth the travel
Le Baratin 472............Regular neighbourhood
Le Chateaubriand 466..............Local favourite
Chez Panisse 701...................Wish I'd opened
Deux Fois Plus de Piment 467............Bargain
Moon Under Water 111.........Worth the travel
Saturne 453..High end
Ten Belles 465..................................Breakfast

SERGIO HERMAN
Pure C
Boulevard de Wielingen 49, Cadzand
Since closing the legendary Oud Sluis in 2013,
Sergio hasn't rested on his laurels, focusing
on Pure C, the Cadzand-Bad restaurant
he opened in 2010, and The Jane, his new
venture in Antwerp.
Auberge des Moules 395.........Local favourite
B&B Sofie Lachaert 418.....................Breakfast
Brasserie Bristol 422..Regular neighbourhood
Café Stanny 410...................................Bargain
Celsius 159...High end
Finjan 410..Late night
The Gallery 341....................Wish I'd opened
Restaurant Es Torrent 478.................High end

AGUS HERMAWAN
Restaurant Blauw
Amstelveenseweg 158, Amsterdam
Has been overseeing the Indonesian-inspired
kitchen at Amsterdam's Blauw since it
opened in 2008.
Anne&Max 403.................................Breakfast
Het Bosch 405.......................Wish I'd opened
Mama San 240......................Worth the travel
Oriental 128 404........Regular neighbourhood
Sarong 241...........................Worth the travel
Sie Joe 399...Bargain
Soho Sushi 404.................................Late night
Toscanini 401.........................Local favourite
Visaandeschelde 407..........................High end

DIEGO HERNÁNDEZ BAQUEDANO
Corazón de Tierra
La Villa del Valle, Ensenada
Opened Corazón de Tierra at a Guadalupe
hilltop farm and hacienda in 2011, notable for
its daily-changing tasting menu. Opened his
first restaurant, Uno, in Tijuana in 2008.
Amaranta 889....................................Breakfast
La Caza Club 881........Regular neighbourhood
Coi 754................................Worth the travel
Manzanilla 880........................Local favourite
Mariscos El Pizón 880..........................Bargain
Noma 289..............................Wish I'd opened
Quintonil 884.......................................High end
Sud 777 885.......................................Late night

GEORGIANNA HILIADAKI
Funky Gourmet
13 Paramithias Street, Athens
Athens-born Institute of Culinary Education-trained Hiliadaki completed an internship at elBulli, establishing Athens's Funky Gourmet Restaurant in 2009, winning a Michelin star in 2012.

Aleria **628**................Regular neighbourhood
Alinea **827**...........................Worth the travel
New Taste **628**................................Breakfast
Noma **289**......................................High end
PBox Eatery **628**................................Bargain

SHAUN HILL
The Walnut Tree
Llanddewi Skirrid, Abergavenny
British restaurant legend that put Gidleigh Park in Devon and the Merchant House in Ludlow on the map. Now runs The Walnut Tree Inn in Abergavenny, South Wales.

The Fountain **340**............................Breakfast
Gidleigh Park **307**.............................High end
The Hardwick **379**......Regular neighbourhood
Hiša Franko **615**....................Worth the travel
Polpo **350**............................Wish I'd opened
Spuntino **351**...................................Bargain

REON HOBSON
Pescatore
50 Park Terrace, Christchurch
The Kiwi-born chef worked all around the world, from Level 41, Sydney to Restaurant Gordon Ramsay and Marco Pierre White's L'Escargot in London, before returning home to run Pescatore in Christchurch.

Berowra Waters Inn **86**.........Wish I'd opened
Burger and Beers Inc. **118**................Regular neighbourhood
Fiddlesticks Restaurant & Bar **118**. Breakfast
Fine Fish **94**.....................................Bargain
Flying Fish **98**...............................Late night
The Monday Room **119**....................Late night
One Six Eight **102**......Regular neighbourhood
Pegasus Bay **119**..................Worth the travel
Saggio di Vino **119**...................Local favourite
Venuti **119**......................................Bargain

CHRISTOPHER HODGSON
Hodge's
668 Euclid Avenue, Cleveland
A food truck pioneer, bringing Cleveland its first ever food wagon, Hodgson opened the first of many bricks 'n' mortar outposts, Hodge's Cleveland, with Scott Kuhn in 2012.

L'Albatros **795**........................ Wish I'd opened
Bar Cento **795**...............................Late night
Chez François **798**...........................High end
Dante **795**.......................................High end
Eat at Joe's **796**..............................Breakfast
Edwins **796**...............Regular neighbourhood
Fire Food and Drink **796**.................Breakfast
Flour Restaurant **798**......................Regular neighbourhood
Happy Dog **796**................................Bargain
Lolita **796**.............................Local favourite
Lucky's Cafe **797**.............................Breakfast
Redd **709**...........................Worth the travel
The Tavern Company **797**................Late night

PETER HOFFMAN
Back Forty
190 Avenue B at 12th Street, New York
Best known for his farm-to-table ethics, the outspoken New York chef-restaurateur owns East Village's organic, environmentally responsible burger joint Back Forty, and Back Forty West, on the former Savoy site in SoHo.

ABC Kitchen **871**....................Wish I'd opened
Il Buco Alimentari e Vineria **866**.......High end
Clover Club **872**............................Late night
Cocoron **867**...................................Bargain
FIG **801**.............................Worth the travel
Grand Central Oyster Bar **838**.Local favourite
Soba-ya **852**...............Regular neighbourhood

ESBEN HOLMBOE BANG
Maaemo
Schweigaards Gate 15, Oslo
Danish chef of, and partner in, Maaemo in Oslo, who took inspiration from Copenhagen, notably Noma, before opening his successful take on Modern Nordic in 2011.

Arakataka **258**................................Bargain
The Ledbury **331**.................Worth the travel
Manfreds & Vin **293**....Regular neighbourhood
Noma **289**......................................High end
Relæ **293**...................Regular neighbourhood
Schønnemann **290**...................Local favourite

BRAD HOLMES
Ulla
509 Fisgard Street, Victoria
Owner of Ulla in Victoria, Holmes previously worked at Vancouver hotspots Feenies, West, Chow, Lumière and, lastly, Cibo before setting up with partner and front- of-house manager Sahara Tamarin.

Brasserie L'Ecole **661**.....................Late night
El Celler de Can Roca **493**......Worth the travel
Fol Epi **661**.....................................Breakfast
Hawksworth Restaurant **668**...............Worth the travel
Meat & Bread **670**................Wish I'd opened
Point-No-Point Resort **660**................High end
Relish Food and Coffee **661**...............Bargain
Sooke Harbour House **660**.......Local favourite
Tibetan Kitchen **661**....Regular neighbourhood
Uchida Eatery/Shokudo **661**...............Regular neighbourhood

JACOB HOLMSTRÖM
Gastrologik
Artillerigatan 14, Stockholm
The Swedish chef and co-founder of Gastrologik in Stockholm (2011) comes from a family of restaurateurs and honed his skills at Mathias Dahlgren's Matbaren and Matsalen.

Daniel Berlin Krog **266**..........Worth the travel
Mathias Dahlgren **272**......................High end
Mathias Dahlgren Matbaren **272**......High end
Östermalms Korvspecialist **275**..........Bargain
Sturehof **276**................................Late night
Volt **276**.............................Local favourite
Wienercaféet **273**............................Breakfast

DAN HONG
Ms. G's
155 Victoria Street, Sydney
Learning his trade in his family's Vietnamese restaurants and Sydney's Tetsuya, Hong went on to oversee four hit Merivale-group restaurants – Ms. G's, Papi Chulo, El Loco and Mr. Wong.

Chat Thai **88**.................................Late night
Din Tai Fung **88**.....................Wish I'd opened
Golden Century Seafood **89**....Local favourite
Husk **804**............................Worth the travel
Malay-Chinese Takeaway **89**...............Bargain
Palace Chinese Restaurant **90**.........Breakfast
Quay **102**.......................................High end
Sussex Centre Food Court **92**.............Regular neighbourhood

GEOFF HOPGOOD
Hopgood's Foodliner
325 Roncesvalles Avenue, Toronto
Brought his Nova Scotian roots and love of
the sea (he harvests his own salt) to Toronto
in the shape of seafood-focused Hopgood's
Foodliner in 2012.
Bar Isabel 682.....................................Late night
Barberian's Steakhouse 681..............High end
Electric Mud BBQ 683............Wish I'd opened
Farmhouse Tavern 682............Local favourite
Grand Electric 684................................Bargain
Japango 683..............Regular neighbourhood
Manfreds & Vin 293...............Worth the travel
The Senator 681.................................Breakfast

LINTON HOPKINS
Restaurant Eugene
2277 Peachtree Road, Atlanta
A native of Atlanta, where he owns Restaurant
Eugene (2004) and the pub Holeman & Finch
(2008). Worked at Washington's D.C. Coast,
and Mr. B's Bistro and Windsor Court in New
Orleans.
L'Arpège 458...................................High end
Blakely Chicken 772............................Bargain
Highlands Bar and Grill 762.....Local favourite
The Ordinary 802...................Wish I'd opened
The Restaurant at Meadowood 708.......Worth
the travel
White House 771.............................Breakfast

PHILIP HOWARD
The Square
6–10 Bruton Street, London
Chef and co-owner of The Square in London
since it opened in 1991, he's more recently
teamed up with restaurateur Rebecca
Mascarenhas at Kitchen W8 (2009) and
Sonny's Kitchen (2012).
Hakkasan 342....................................Late night
Hakkasan 342.....................................High end
Régis et Jacques Marcon 432.........Worth the
travel
The River Café 325..............Wish I'd opened
Scott's 344...............................Local favourite
The Wolseley 345................................Breakfast
Zucca 355..................Regular neighbourhood

GUNTHER HUBRECHSEN
Gunther's
36 Purvis Street, Singapore
Belgian-born Hubrechsen's training with
Alain Passard has certainly informed his
classical French cooking at his eponymous
Singapore restaurant.
L'Arpège 458.....................................High end
Le Bistrot Du Sommelier 232...............Regular
neighbourhood
Killiney Kopitiam 237........................Breakfast
Lau Pa Sat 236....................................Late night
Lau Pa Sat 236.....................................Bargain

DAN HUNTER
Brae
4285 Cape Otway Road, Birregurra
Having won accolades aplenty at Royal Mail
in Victoria, Aussie chef Hunter – former head
chef at Mugaritz – opened the destination
restaurant Brae in December 2013.
L'Arpège 458.....................................High end
Attica 113..High end
Birregurra General Store 81................Regular
neighbourhood
Chin Chin 106......................................Bargain
Cumulus Inc. 107.....................Local favourite
Golden Century Seafood 89.............Late night
Momofuku Seiōbo 98............Worth the travel
Mugaritz 480...........................Wish I'd opened
Sixpenny 95...........................Worth the travel
St Ali 112...Breakfast

MICHAEL HUNTER
Reds Wine Tavern
77 Adelaide Street West, Toronto
Hunter by name... An Ontario native,
outdoors man and keen forager and hunter,
he built his career on home soil, joining Reds
Wine Tavern as executive chef in 2013.
360 Restaurant 683..................Local favourite
Bar Isabel 682...........Regular neighbourhood
Buca 680.........................Wish I'd opened
Forestview Chinese 678..................Breakfast
Pasteur 90..Late night
Au Pied de Cochon 694.........Worth the travel
Sassafraz 686......................................High end

METTE HVARRE GASSNER
Ti Trin Ned
Norgesgade 3, Fredericia
Proclaiming 'we don't call our kitchen Nordic',
Mette and husband Rainer reach beyond
borders for inspiration at Ti Trin Ned, appeal-
ing to diners' senses with local ingredients
and innovative techniques.
Bubbledogs 363.................Wish I'd opened
Geist 288.................Regular neighbourhood
Geranium 296.....................................High end
Kok & Vin 283....................................Bargain
MASH 289..Late night
Svinkløv Badehotel Restaurant 282......Worth
the travel

ALFONSO & ERNESTO IACCARINO
Don Alfonso
Corso Sant'Agata 11–13, Sant'Agata sui
Due Golfi
Champions of tradition and innovation, they
run their family restaurant and hotel on an
organic farm, and restaurants in Macau and
Marrakech.
Indego by Vineet 146............Worth the travel
Pizzaria La Notizia 574....................Late night
Ristorante Tasso 574............................Bargain
Lo Scoglio da Tommaso 574.............Regular
neighbourhood
Tetsuya's 92.......................................High end
Zuma 327.............................Wish I'd opened

TAKASHI INOUE
Takashi
456 Hudson Street, New York City
A third-generation Korean immigrant born in
Japan, he's made his name in New York with
Takashi, his take on *yakiniku* (table-grilling).
Astrid & Gastón 906...............Worth the travel
Atera 870................................Local favourite
La Bonbonniere 845.........................Breakfast
Brushstroke 869..................................High end
Congee Village 864............................Breakfast
Coquette 819.........................Wish I'd opened
Ichimura at Brushstroke 870.............Regular
neighbourhood
Los Tacos No. 1 859............................Bargain

JOHN JACKSON & CONNIE DESOUSA
CHARCUT Roast House
899 Centre Street Southwest, Calgary
Meat-loving Jackson, together with co-chef
and co-owner Connie DeSousa, put Calgary
firmly on the food map with the 2010 launch
of CHARCUT Roast House's urban-rustic
cuisine.
Candela 656.............Regular neighbourhood
Cassis Bistro 656.............................Breakfast
Cibo 656.....................Regular neighbourhood
Downtownfood 657.....Regular neighbourhood
Mallard Cottage 663.......Worth the travel
Mercato 171.............Regular neighbourhood
Model Milk 657................................Late night
NOtaBLE 657.............Regular neighbourhood
River Café 658..................................Breakfast
Rouge 658.............................Local favourite
Shikiji 658.................Regular neighbourhood
Una Pizza + Wine 658......................Late night
Vintage Chophouse 659....................High end

ROBERT JACOBSSON

B.A.R naturlig krog & vinbar
Erik Dahlbergsgatan 3, Malmö
Former Noma sous chef and Tivoli Gardens head chef, Jacobsson joined forces with Besnik Gashi to open B.A.R 'bistro' in Malmö, serving New Nordic fare.

Bastard 262	Late night
Bastard 262	Wish I'd opened
Daniel Berlin Krog 266	Worth the travel
Hagen 263	Regular neighbourhood
Jalla Jalla 264	Local favourite
Nordic Street Food 264	Bargain
Rosen Bar & Dining 264	Breakfast
Vollmers 265	High end

ANDRÉ JAEGER

Die Fischerzunft
Rheinquai 8, Schaffhausen
Chef-owner of Die Fischerzunft, Jaeger has brought his unique East meets West cooking to the banks of the Rhine for over three decades.

Bouchon 708	Wish I'd opened
Coya 340	Worth the travel
Hummer- & Austernbar 566	Late night
Restaurant Adelboden 562	High end
Restaurant Gemeindehaus 562	Bargain
Restaurantschiff PATIO 557	Local favourite
Sala of Tokyo 568	Regular neighbourhood

JISOO JANG

Beal St.
363–28 Hongun-dong, Seoul
Passed through the kitchens of Michael Mina and Benu before returning to Seoul to open two American-style restaurants, Beal St. and Burger B.

Antibes 193	Wish I'd opened
Bim Bom 193	Breakfast
Congdu 193	Local favourite
Jeju sic-dang 194	Regular neighbourhood
O'neul 194	High end
Sanchez 194	Late night
Sisili 194	Bargain

MARGOT JANSE

The Tasting Room
9 Wilhelmina Street, Franschhoek
Trained by Johannesburg restaurateur Ciro Molinaro, Dutch-born Janse joined Le Quartier Francais in Franschoek in 1995, winning The Tasting Room dozens of accolades in her nineteen-year tenure.

Babel 649	Local favourite
Babel 649	Wish I'd opened
Bread & Wine 650	Regular neighbourhood
Café des Arts 650	Breakfast
Café des Arts 650	Bargain
Osteria Francescana 577	Worth the travel
Pierneef à La Motte 650	High end
Raan Jay Fai 226	Worth the travel

JENNIFER JASINSKI

Rioja
1431 Larimer Street, Denver
Executive chef and co-owner of Denver's Rioja, Bistro Vendôme and Euclid Hall, Culinary Institute of America-trained Jaskinski spent ten years working with Wolfgang Puck, her 'mentor and culinary role model'.

Colt & Gray 709	Regular neighbourhood
Dal Pescatore 589	Worth the travel
Frasca Food and Wine 709	High end
New Saigon 710	Bargain
Patzcuaro's 710	Regular neighbourhood
Pho Duy 710	Bargain
Sushi Sasa 710	Regular neighbourhood

JULIUS JASPERS

Julius Bar & Grill
Ceintuurbaan 256–260, Amsterdam
A judge on Dutch TV's Top Chef, Jaspers opened Julius Bar & Grill, a modern barbeque restaurant, in 2013.

Asador Etxebarri 479	High end
Colonnade 224	Breakfast
Compartir 491	Worth the travel
Le Garage 404	Local favourite
New King 398	Bargain
Restaurant De Librije 394	High end
Ron Gastrobar 404	Regular neighbourhood
Ron Gastrobar 404	Wish I'd opened
Taste of Culture 400	Late night
Visaandeschelde 407	Regular neighbourhood

MARCUS JERNMARK

Aquavit
65 East 55th Street, New York City
Jernmark headed Stateside to become executive chef at New York's Swedish Consulate, joining Aquavit in 2009 and winning it a Michelin star for its New Nordic cuisine in 2013.

Balthazar 868	Local favourite
Bouchon Bakery 845	Breakfast
Brooklyn Fare 872	High end
Brooklyn Fare 872	Wish I'd opened
Esquisse 211	Worth the travel
Felix 869	Regular neighbourhood
Per Se 846	High end
Sake Bar Hagi 842	Late night

DREW JOHNSON

Kincaid Grill
6700 Jewel Lake Road, Anchorage
Christopher 'Drew' Johnson worked at his family-owned restaurant, The Speedy Pig in Alabama, before moving to Alaska in 2005. He began his successful tenure at Kincaid Grill in 2008.

City Diner 700	Breakfast
Crow's Nest 700	High end
Palace Kitchen 722	Worth the travel
Spenard Roadhouse 700	Regular neighbourhood
Spenard Roadhouse 700	Local favourite
Taco King 700	Bargain
Whale's Tail 700	Late night
Whale's Tail 700	Wish I'd opened

TIMOTHY JOHNSON

Apicius
23 Stone Street, Cranbrook
A protégé of Nico Ladenis, Johnson opened Apicius in Kent in 2004, winning acclaim for his imaginative, French-influenced cooking.

Alinea 827	High end
Bouchon 708	Wish I'd opened
Bras 436	Worth the travel
Dinner by Heston Blumenthal 326	Worth the travel
Gary Danko 748	Wish I'd opened
The Landgate Bistro 308	Regular neighbourhood
The Pleasant Café 311	Breakfast

JEAN JOHO

Everest
440 South LaSalle Street, Chicago
Born in Alsace, Joho oversees the restaurant at Las Vegas's Eiffel Tower, Chicago's Everest and Paris Club and Boston's Brasserie Jo.

L'Atelier de Joël Robuchon 712	High end
L'Auberge de L'Ill 428	Worth the travel
Lawry's The Prime Rib 828	Local favourite
The Lobby 830	Breakfast
Slurping Turtle 830	Late night

HYWEL JONES

The Park Restaurant
Lucknam Park Hotel, Colerne, Chippenham
After training with Nico Ladenis and Marco Pierre White, he's been at Lucknam Park near Bath since 2004.

The Eastern Eye 313	Late night
Facil 557	Worth the travel
The Fig Tree 380	Regular neighbourhood
The Harbourmaster 379	Wish I'd opened
The Hardwick 379	Local favourite
Jika Jika 313	Breakfast
The Square 344	High end

JONATHAN JONES
The Anchor & Hope
36 The Cut, London
Co-owner of London's The Anchor & Hope and Great Queen Street, Jones is a graduate of Fergus Henderson's St. John.

The Abbeville Kitchen **323**	Breakfast
Franco Manca **356**	Wish I'd opened
Lahore Karahi **333**	Bargain
Otto's **360**	High end
Roti Joupa **324**	Late night
Le Saint Eutrope **432**	Worth the travel
St. John Bar and Restaurant **362**	Local favourite

DYLAN JONES & BO (DUANGPORN) SONGVISAVA
Bo.lan
Soi Sukhumvit 53, Klongteoy, Bangkok
Slow Food-championing husband-and-wife team who combine ethical ingredients with traditional Thai recipes.

Appia **224**	Regular neighbourhood
Arzak **483**	High end
Arzak **483**	Worth the travel
Bras **436**	High end
Gastro 1/6 **225**	Breakfast
Nahm **225**	Local favourite
Opposite Mess Hall **225**	Regular neighbourhood
Opposite Mess Hall **225**	Late night
Xia Duck Noodles **227**	Bargain

MIKAEL JONSSON
Hedone
301–303 Chiswick High Road, London
Self-taught chef and owner of Hedone who won a Michelin star in 2012, one year after opening the restaurant.

L'Arpège **458**	High end
Franco Manca **356**	Bargain
The Ledbury **331**	Local favourite
Medlar **321**	Regular neighbourhood
Le Mirazur **440**	Wish I'd opened
Monmouth Coffee Company **338**	Breakfast
Passage 53 **453**	Worth the travel

MARK JORDAN
Ocean Restaurant
The Atlantic Hotel, Le Mont de la Pulente, St Brelade
Welsh-born chef who got his first kitchen job with the late Keith Floyd and now heads up the kitchen at the two-Michelin-starred Ocean Restaurant in Jersey.

Big Vern's **376**	Breakfast
Noma **289**	Worth the travel
Siam Garden **376**	Regular neighbourhood

MARTIN JUNEAU
Pastaga
6389 Boulevard Saint Laurent, Montreal
Co-owner and chef of Montreal's celebrated wine bar and small-plate joint Pastaga, Juneau's culinary journey started in a hospital kitchen. He opened his first restaurant Montée de Lait in 2004.

Alep **697**	Regular neighbourhood
Le Chien Fumant **692**	Late night
Hôtel Herman **692**	Local favourite
Joe Beef **695**	High end
Lawrence Restaurant **693**	Bargain
Raymonds **663**	Worth the travel
Le Vieux Vélo **696**	Breakfast
Le Vin Papillon **696**	Wish I'd opened

TOMOYASU KAMO
Kamo
Avenue des Saisons 123, Brussels
Young Brussels-based Japanese sushi master who previously worked at the Tagawa Hotel. He opened Kamo in 2007.

Bissoh **434**	Wish I'd opened
Bon Bon **412**	Local favourite
Le Chalet De La Forêt **415**	Worth the travel
Le Chat Noir **413**	Late night
Het Kriekske **413**	Regular neighbourhood
Makimura **219**	Worth the travel
Nihonryori Ryugin **216**	High end
Orientalia **414**	Regular neighbourhood

TOMAŽ KAVČIČ
Gostilna pri Lojzetu
Dvorec Zemono, Vipava
Slovenian who cooks at Gostilna Pri Lojzetu near Ajdovščina, built in 1683 and run as a restaurant by his family since 1897.

Abram Tourist Farm **616**	Local favourite
Don Alfonso **574**	Wish I'd opened
Gostilnica Mandrija **616**	Bargain
La Pergola **582**	High end
Sur Mesure par Thierry Marx **451**	Worth the travel
Trattoria Sandra **579**	Regular neighbourhood

JACOB KENEDY
Bocca di Lupo
12 Archer Street, London
After a decade at Moro he opened Bocca di Lupo in 2008, followed by Gelupo, his gelateria and coffee bar that sits opposite.

A.Wong **334**	Breakfast
Antepliler **368**	Bargain
Bō Làng **333**	Breakfast
Koffmann's **326**	Wish I'd opened
Moro **360**	Regular neighbourhood
Roux at the Landau **330**	High end
Royal China **319**	Breakfast
Sweetings **359**	Local favourite
The Walnut Tree **380**	Worth the travel

TOM KERRIDGE
The Hand & Flowers
126 West Street, Marlow
Owner of The Hand & Flowers, the former rundown pub in Marlow, southeast England, which he took over in 2005 and turned into a destination.

The Fat Duck **304**	High end
The Hinds Head **304**	Regular neighbourhood
Meat Liquor **328**	Late night
Pollen Street Social **344**	Wish I'd opened
Restaurant André **239**	Worth the travel
Terroirs **375**	Bargain

DAVID KINCH
Manresa
320 Village Lane, Los Gatos
Opened Northern California's Manresa in 2002 having studied cooking in France, Spain, Germany, Japan and the US.

Benu **756**	High end
Brooklyn Fare **872**	Wish I'd opened
Cafe Delmarette **707**	Bargain
Carnitas Trejo **708**	Regular neighbourhood
Coi **754**	High end
Donostia **703**	Late night
Ginza Kojyu **211**	Worth the travel
Ishikawa **220**	Worth the travel
Soif **707**	Regular neighbourhood
Verve Coffee Roasters **707**	Breakfast

MUSTAFA CIHAN KIPÇAK
La Mouette
Tomtom Kaptan Sokak 18, Istanbul
In partnership with Üryan Doğmuş, he oversees the menu at Istanbul's La Mouette, located in a boutique hotel in a nineteenth-century building, and Gile in Akaretler.

Beyti **634**	Local favourite
Emirgan Sütiş **638**	Breakfast
Faros Kebap **634**	Regular neighbourhood
Kantin **638**	Wish I'd opened
Karadeniz Dönercisi **634**	Bargain
Mikla **635**	High end
Sardunya **630**	Worth the travel

MILES KIRBY

Caravan
11–13 Exmouth Market, London
Ran the kitchen at The Providores and Tapas
Room before launching Caravan with fellow
Kiwi Chris Ammermann in 2010. A second
branch in King's Cross followed in 2012.

Afghan Kitchen 367	Bargain
Bar Jules 748	Worth the travel
Blue Ribbon Sushi 869	Late night
Bone Daddies Ramen Bar 346	Late night
The Company Shed 308	Worth the travel
Ducksoup 348	Regular neighbourhood
Moro 360	Regular neighbourhood
The Oyster Inn 118	Worth the travel
Palm2 365	Local favourite
Palmera Oasis 369	Late night
Public 868	Worth the travel
Rochelle Canteen 372	Regular neighbourhood
Roka 364	High end
The Slanted Door 748	Worth the travel
St. John Bar and Restaurant 362	Local favourite
The Towpath Café 367	Breakfast
Trip Kitchen 367	Breakfast
Trullo 369	Regular neighbourhood
The Windsor Castle 366	Regular neighbourhood

REBECCA KIRHOFFER

Rebeccas
265 Glenville Road, Greenwich
Following an extended, successful spell
as a private chef-caterer, Kirhoffer opened
her eponymous restaurant in Greenwich,
Connecticut, in 1997, with husband and fellow
chef Reza Khorshidi.

The Barn at Bedford Post 789	Regular neighbourhood
Blue Ribbon Brasserie 869	Late night
The Dutch 869	Late night
The Four Seasons Restaurant 838	Wish I'd opened
Geist 288	Worth the travel
Glenville Pizza 762	Local favourite
Lakeside Diner 762	Breakfast
Marea 841	High end
Minetta Tavern 853	Late night
Le Pain Quotidien 762	Bargain

MATTHEW KIRKLEY

L2O
2300 North Lincoln Park West, Chicago
Prior to becoming executive chef and partner
at Chicago's two-Michelin-starred seafood
restaurant L2O, following the departure
of Laurent Gras, Kirkley worked at Joël
Robuchon (Las Vegas).

L'Ambroisie 454	High end
Avec 832	Local favourite
La Brasserie Georges 443	Wish I'd opened
Flocons de Sel 445	Worth the travel
Pizano's Pizza & Pasta 830	Regular neighbourhood
Three Happiness 832	Late night

SCOT KIRTON

La Colombe
Spaanschemat River Road, Cape Town
South African who took over at La Colombe
in 2010. Previously cooked at Constantia
Uitsig's River Café.

Banana Jam Café 646	Bargain
Carne SA 647	Wish I'd opened
The Ledbury 331	Worth the travel
Mzoli's Place 647	Local favourite
Olympia Café 648	Breakfast
Rafiki's 648	Late night
tashas 649	Regular neighbourhood
The Test Kitchen 649	High end

TOM KITCHIN

The Kitchin
78 Commercial Quay, Edinburgh
Trained with Koffmann, Ducasse and Savoy,
owner of The Kitchin (2006) and The Scran &
Scallie (2013) in his hometown of Edinburgh.

Anstruther Fish Bar 378	Bargain
Koffmann's 326	Regular neighbourhood
Noma 289	Worth the travel
Ondine Restaurant 378	Local favourite
The Peat Inn 378	High end
La Petite Maison 343	Wish I'd opened
Urban Angel 378	Breakfast

JAMES KNAPPETT

Kitchen Table
70 Charlotte Street, London
With a glittering résumé including stints at
The Ledbury, Noma and Per Se, Knappett settled in London as chef-patron of Bubbledogs,
a gourmet hot dog-Champagne concept with
a fine-dining annex, Kitchen Table.

Andrew Edmunds 345	Bargain
Fäviken Magasinet 261	Worth the travel
Parlour Kensal 325	Regular neighbourhood
Per Se 846	High end
St. John Bread & Wine 374	Local favourite
Sushi Tetsu 360	Wish I'd opened

PETER KNOGL

Cheval Blanc
Grand Hotel Les Trois Rois, Blumenrain 8, Basel
Swiss master of Mediterranean haute cuisine
which he serves up at his restaurant Cheval
Blanc in Basel.

Hotel Restaurant Mühle 540	Local favourite
De Leest 394	Worth the travel
Martín Berasategui 482	High end
Martín Berasategui 482	Wish I'd opened
Mercedes Spot 560	Breakfast
Restaurant Wiesengarten 560	Regular neighbourhood

ATUL KOCHHAR

Benares
Berkeley Square, London
Indian-born, British-based chef and owner of
Benares (2007), Kochhar is widely accepted
as the pioneer of modern Indian cuisine.

Busaba Eathai 347	Wish I'd opened
D.O.M. Restaurante 921	Worth the travel
Duck & Waffle 358	High end
HIX at the Albemarle 342	Late night
Lahore Kebab House 375	Bargain
Shoryu Ramen 352	Local favourite
The Wolseley 345	Breakfast

PIERRE KOFFMANN

Koffmann's
The Berkeley, Wilton Place, London
Gascon-born, he became a legend in London
at La Tante Claire, opened in 1977. Made his
comeback in 2010 with Koffmann's at The
Berkeley.

A.Wong 334	Bargain
Asador Etxebarri 479	Worth the travel
L'Auberge du Pont de Collonges 442	Wish I'd opened
Le Colombier 321	Regular neighbourhood
The Five Fields 321	High end
Le Gavroche 341	Local favourite
Raoul's 327	Breakfast
Royal China 319	Bargain

RASMUS KOFOED

Geranium
Per Henrik Lings Allé 4, Copenhagen
Danish gold medal winner at the 2011
Bocuse d'Or and the co-owner of Geranium,
he trained at Hotel d'Angleterre and at
Scholteshof.

41 Grados Experience 513	Wish I'd opened
Geist 288	Late night
Ipsen & Co. 279	Breakfast
Noma 289	Local favourite
Relæ 293	Local favourite
Safir Kebab 294	Bargain
Viet-Nam Nam 280	Regular neighbourhood

ONNO KOKMEIJER
Ciel Bleu Restaurant
Ferdinand Bolstraat 333, Amsterdam
Dutch born and trained, he has established Ciel Bleu as one of the city's best restaurants since his arrival there in 2003.

@7 **406**	Breakfast
Alinea **827**	Worth the travel
Brasserie Bark **403**	Late night
Café Loetje **403**	Wish I'd opened
Eetsalon Van Dobben **398**	Bargain
Orbit **406**	Regular neighbourhood
Salonboot Soeverein **405**	High end
Yamazato **405**	Local favourite

ANATOLY KOMM
Varvary
8a Strastnoy boulevard, Moscow
Russian who trained as a geophysicist before taking up cooking in 2000. He's won acclaim by reinventing traditional Russian dishes.

L'Astrance **469**	Worth the travel
Cassia **237**	Worth the travel
Mugaritz **480**	Worth the travel
Osteria Francescana **577**	Wish I'd opened
Osteria Francescana **577**	Worth the travel
Zuma **188**	Wish I'd opened

ROBERT KRANENBORG
The former executive chef of the Intercontinental Hotels Group, he currently consults for clients including Hotel De L'Europe.

Bolenius **406**	Local favourite
Bord'Eau **398**	High end
Izakaya **400**	Wish I'd opened
Julius Bar & Grill **400**	Late night
Toscanini **401**	Regular neighbourhood
Worst **400**	Breakfast
Yardbird **188**	Worth the travel

STUART BRIOZA & NICOLE KRASINSKI
State Bird Provisions
1529 Fillmore Street, San Francisco
Husband-and-wife team and chef-owners of San Francisco's State Bird Provisions, where they serve small plates on trolleys, dim-sum style, the alumni of Rubicon and Savarin opened Progress in 2013.

20th Century Café **748**	Breakfast
Ibai **488**	Worth the travel
Manresa **703**	High end
Nopa **754**	Late night
La Palma Mexicatessan **752**	Bargain
Swan Oyster Depot **753**	Wish I'd opened
Zuni Café **749**	Local favourite

THOMAS KURT
e.t.a. hoffmann
Yorckstrasse 83, Berlin
Baden-born Kurt has been a fixture on the Berlin restaurant scene since the mid-1980s, and has run the informal e.t.a. hoffman for over a decade.

Austeria Brasserie **557**	Regular neighbourhood
El Borriquito **550**	Late night
Curry 36 **551**	Bargain
The Grand **553**	Local favourite
Hugos **557**	High end
Rio Grande **552**	Wish I'd opened
Steirereck **607**	Worth the travel
van Loon Restaurantschiffe **552**	Breakfast

MATÍAS KYRIAZIS
Paraje Arévalo
Arévalo 1502, Buenos Aires
Buenos Aires-born Kyriazis is one half, with Estefanía Di Benedetto, of the chef duo behind the esteemed Paraje Arévalo and Local.

Aramburu **941**	Local favourite
Astor **936**	Bargain
Asturias **936**	Breakfast
Chila **939**	High end
Doppelgänger Bar **943**	Late night
Le Grill **939**	Wish I'd opened
Guido's Bar **935**	Regular neighbourhood
Maní **925**	Worth the travel

TIM LAI
Tim's Kitchen
84–90 Bonham Strand, Hong Kong
Born in Hong Kong in 1949, Lai started cooking at seventeen and worked under Cantonese cooking legend Choi Lee. He opened Tim's Kitchen in 2000.

Gaya **460**	Wish I'd opened
Lin Heung Tea House **185**	Local favourite
Paradise of King Asia **181**	Regular neighbourhood
Sang Kee Congee Shop **186**	Bargain
Sing Heung Yuen **187**	Bargain
Yuet Wah Hui **188**	Late night

FRANCK-ELIE LALOUM
Jade on 36
33 Fucheng Lu, Shanghai
Parisian chef who worked his way through some of France's best kitchens before moving to Shanghai to head up Jade on 36.

L'Astrance **469**	Worth the travel
The Commune Social **168**	Wish I'd opened
Cuivre **166**	Regular neighbourhood
Mr & Mrs Bund **171**	Late night
Sproutworks **170**	Bargain
Wagas **172**	Breakfast
Yongfoo Elite **168**	Local favourite

FLORIAN LAMELOT
Orient8
Jalan Asia Afrika, Jakarta
Apprenticed with Jean-Marie Gauthier among others before working at Daniel Boulud in New York and latterly, Orient8 in Jakarta.

Akelarre **483**	Worth the travel
Bandar Jakarta **245**	Local favourite
Bar-Roque Grill **238**	Worth the travel
Beautika **245**	Local favourite
Cuca **241**	Local favourite
Daniel **844**	Wish I'd opened
Ju-Ma-Na **244**	High end
KU DE TA **243**	Late night
Nyoman's Beer Garden **242**	Bargain
SKYE **245**	Late night
Teba Mega Café **241**	Local favourite
Union **245**	Local favourite
Vin+ **246**	Bargain

RETO LAMPART
Lampart's
Oltnerstrasse 19, Hägendorf
Swiss-born chef whose interest in architecture now informs his approach to food at the one-Michelin-starred Lampart's.

Flocons de Sel **445**	Worth the travel
Rathskeller Olten **563**	Local favourite
Restaurant Camino **568**	Regular neighbourhood
Restaurant de l'Hôtel de Ville **564**	High end
Restaurant Felsenburg **563**	Regular neighbourhood

ALBERTO LANDGRAF
Epice
Rua Haddock Lobo 1002, São Paulo
Runs São Paulo's Epice, opened in 2011, and trained in London, where he worked with Gordon Ramsay and Tom Aikens.

D.O.M. Restaurante **921**	High end
D.O.M. Restaurante **921**	Wish I'd opened
Lá da Venda **927**	Breakfast
Maní **925**	Local favourite
Mocotó **929**	Bargain
Nerua **480**	Worth the travel
Shinzushi **926**	Regular neighbourhood
Sujinho **922**	Late night

FILIP LANGHOFF
Restaurant Ask
Vironkatu 8, Helsinki
Former head chef at Chez Dominique, he is currently chef and partner in Restaurant Ask, opened in 2012, and owns food consultancy firm CIBUS.

Amass **286**	Worth the travel
Chef & Sommelier **298**	Regular neighbourhood
Fafa's **299**	Late night
Gran Delicato **299**	Breakfast
Maaemo **259**	High end
Olo **300**	Local favourite
Teurastamon Portti **301**	Bargain

NORMAND LAPRISE
Toqué!
900 Place Jean-Paul-Riopelle, Montreal
A former accountant turned chef, Laprise trained at Hotel de la Cloche near Dijon before returning home to Canada and opening his flagship Toqué! and sister restaurant Brasserie T!
Big in Japan **691**.................................Bargain
Bistro Isakaya **692**............................Bargain
Le Chique **888**....................Worth the travel
Joe Beef **695**.........................Local favourite
Maison Pic **446**.............................High end
Noma **289**........................Worth the travel
Au Pied de Cochon **694**....................Regular
                                                    neighbourhood
Au Pied de Cochon **694**..........Local favourite
Vila Joya **524**....................Wish I'd opened

MIKE LATA
FIG
232 Meeting Street, Charleston
Opened Charleston's FIG bistro in 2003 with Adam Nemirow, and The Ordinary oyster bar in 2012. Lata worked across the US and France before landing in Charleston.
Butcher & Bee **801**......Regular neighbourhood
Butcher & Bee **801**..........................Late night
Charleston Grill **801**.......................High end
EVO **802**...Bargain
Hominy Grill **801**............................Breakfast
Hominy Grill **801**....................Local favourite
Septime **468**......................Worth the travel

SASU LAUKKONEN
Chef & Sommelier
Huvilakatu 28, Helsinki
Having earned his stripes as head chef of La Petite Maison and Loft Restaurant & Lounge in Helsinki, in 2010 Laukkonen took the helm at his own restaurant. In 2014 it won it's first Michelin star.
Café Ekberg **298**............................Breakfast
Fafa's **299**...Late night
Kosmos **300**.........................Local favourite
Koya **349**..Bargain
Maaemo **259**.....................Wish I'd opened
Manfreds & Vin **293**....Regular neighbourhood
Le Mirazur **440**....................Worth the travel
Noma **289**..High end
Relæ **293**...........................Worth the travel
Sea Horse **301**......................Local favourite

YVES LE LAY
Alexander
Pädaste Manor, Muhu Island
Danish-born head chef at Estonia's acclaimed Alexander restaurant at Pädaste Manor and its bistro offshoot, Neh, in Tallinn.
Epicure **462**...........................Worth the travel
The French Laundry **709**........Wish I'd opened
Kohvik Moon **620**.......Regular neighbourhood
Au Pied de Cochon **694**....................Late night
Søllerød Kro **281**..............................High end

GWENDAL LE RUYET
Grand-Cru
Lodecká 4, Prague
Brittany-born executive chef at Grand-Cru, who trained under Ducasse and earned recognition at Prague's Céleste for his lighter, pared-down versions of French classics.
Café de Paris **608**............................Late night
Čerstvě pražená káva **609**.............Breakfast
Cukrkávalimonáda **609**.....................Bargain
La Degustation Bohême Bourgeoise **609** Local
                                                         favourite
Miura Restaurant **608**.......................High end
Restaurace Na Kopci **612**..................Regular
                                                    neighbourhood
Saturne **453**......................Wish I'd opened

JUSTIN LEBOE
Model Milk
308 17th Avenue Southwest, Calgary
Ex-French Laundry chef and VP of Concorde Group, Leboe ran fine-dining Rush before opening Model Milk in 2011, offering elevated comfort food in a converted 1930s dairy.
Carbone **852**.....................Wish I'd opened
Cassis Bistro **656**........Regular neighbourhood
CHARCUT Roast House **656**.....Local favourite
Diner Deluxe **657**............................Breakfast
Pho Hoai **657**...................................Bargain
Teatro **658**.......................................High end
Una Pizza + Wine **658**....................Late night

COREY LEE
Benu
22 Hawthorne Street, San Francisco
A James Beard Award-winning chef who trained at seven three-Michelin-starred restaurants in England, France and the US before opening two-Michelin-starred Benu in 2010.
L'Astrance **469**.....................Worth the travel
Blue Ribbon Brasserie **869**...............Late night
Coi **754**..............................Local favourite
Din Tai Fung **88**......................Wish I'd opened
Fook Lam Moon **184**...............Worth the travel
The French Laundry **709**....................High end
Joe Beef **695**......................Worth the travel
Peter Luger Steakhouse **875**..Wish I'd opened
R&G Lounge **746**........Regular neighbourhood
San Tung **749**....................................Bargain
Tartine Bakery **752**..........................Breakfast

EDWARD LEE
610 Magnolia
610 West Magnolia Avenue, Louisville
Hailing from Brooklyn before settling in Louisville, Lee's Asian-accented 'New Southern' cuisine at 610 Magnolia and MilkWood has earned him a loyal following.
Eleven Madison Park **862**..................High end
Hakata Tonton **855**.....Regular neighbourhood
Hawksworth Restaurant **668**.Worth the travel
Jack Fry's **774**.........................Local favourite
New Wonjo **841**...............................Late night
Peg Leg Porker **804**..............Wish I'd opened
Waffle House **774**.............................Bargain
The Wieners Circle **827**...................Breakfast

JEREMY LEE
Quo Vadis
26–29 Dean Street, London
Scottish-born chef who left the Blueprint Café in 2011 to take the reins at Quo Vadis, bringing his award-winning combination of French technique and British seasonality.
The Anchor & Hope **373**.....................Bargain
Antica Torre **592**...................Worth the travel
Bibendum **333**.................................High end
Koya **349**......................Regular neighbourhood
Maison Bertaux **349**.......................Breakfast
The River Café **325**.................Local favourite
St. John Bar and Restaurant **362**...........Wish
                                                        I'd opened

MAN-SING LEE
Man Wah
5 Connaught Road, Hong Kong
Behind the stove at Man Wah, in the last few years Lee has won the Cantonese restaurant a Michelin star with his careful attention to sourcing the finest ingredients.
Da Dong Roast Duck **162**........Wish I'd opened
Dragon Inn Seafood **192**...................High end
Jing Fong **861**....................Worth the travel
Kau Kee **184**....................................Bargain
Tim Ho Wan **190**.........Regular neighbourhood
Tsui Wah **189**.................................Breakfast
Wing Kee Noodle **182**....................Late night

SUSUR LEE
Lee
601 King Street West, Toronto
Critically acclaimed Asian-fusion chef, Hong Kong-born Lee's Toronto restaurants include Lotus, Lee and Bent, with outposts in Washington D.C. and Singapore.
Boom Breakfast & Co **683**................Breakfast
Buca **680**...High end
Jacob's & Co. Steakhouse **680**..........High end
King's Noodle Restaurant **678**.........Late night
Makoto **765**....................Worth the travel
Nota Bene **683**.................................High end
Pho Tien Thanh **684**..........................Bargain
Taste of China Restaurant **678**...........Regular
                                                    neighbourhood

ARMIN LEITGEB
Armin Leitgeb Consulting
Austrian-born chef who trained at Le Jardin des Sens, L'Auberge de L'Ill, Restaurant Tantris and The French Laundry. Now a consultant, he was head chef at Singapore's Les Amis until 2012.

Brasserie Les Haras 428	Wish I'd opened
Fisch Poseidon 541	Breakfast
Geisel's Vinothek 541	Late night
Der Metzgerwirt 605	Bargain
Rosengarten Simon Taxacher 604	Local favourite
Schwedenkapelle 605	Regular neighbourhood
Tantris 542	High end
Tippling Club 239	Worth the travel

ÁNGEL LEÓN
Aponiente
Calle Puerto Escondido 6, El Puerto de Santa María
TV favourite in his native Spain, León is as much inventor as chef: alongside running the Michelin-starred Aponiente he works with universities developing culinary gadgets.

El Faro de El Puerto 476	Late night
El Faro de El Puerto 476	Local favourite
Quique Dacosta Restaurante 505	High end
Quique Dacosta Restaurante 505	Wish I'd opened
Las Rejas 476	Bargain
Restaurante El Arriate 476	Regular neighbourhood
Restaurante Venta Pinto 477	Breakfast

SÉGUÉ LEPAGE
Le Comptoir
4807 Boulevard Saint-Laurent, Montreal
After immersing himself in charcuterie in France, Lepage opened Le Comptoir – a temple to meat and natural wines – in 2010.

Chez Sardine 854	Worth the travel
Le Club Chasse et Pêche 696	High end
Hôtel Herman 692	Regular neighbourhood
Icehouse 692	Late night
Joe Beef 695	Wish I'd opened
Liverpool House 695	Wish I'd opened
Maison Premiere 874	Bargain
Micro Resto La Famille 694	Breakfast
Le Vin Papillon 696	Wish I'd opened

SEBASTIEN LEPINOY
Les Amis
1 Scotts Road, Singapore
Robuchon protégé and former head chef at Macau's Michelin-starred Cépage, Lepinoy was lured to Singapore in 2013 to be executive chef at the celebrated Les Amis.

&Made 237	Regular neighbourhood
L'Atelier de Joël Robuchon 185	Wish I'd opened
Boon Tong Kee 237	Local favourite
Ice-Cold Beer 236	Late night
Killiney Kopitiam 237	Breakfast
Killiney Kopitiam 237	Bargain
Restaurant de l'Hôtel de Ville 564	High end
Tate Dining Room & Bar 187	Worth the travel

JEREME LEUNG
Jereme Leung Creative Concepts
Made his name with the Whampoa Club, before creating a culinary consultancy specializing in his 'new Chinese' style of cooking.

Bo Innovation 182	Wish I'd opened
Da-Wan Yakiniku 174	Worth the travel
Hai Ji 162	Worth the travel
Jesse 167	Local favourite
Jian Bing Guo Zhi Stall 169	Bargain
Kappo Yu 167	High end
The Stage 171	Breakfast
Stranger Hot Pot 167	Late night
Tables 169	Breakfast
Tetsuya's 92	Wish I'd opened
Top Chef 169	Regular neighbourhood
Yi Café 170	Breakfast

ROSS LEWIS
Chapter One
18–19 Parnell Square, Dublin
Son of a farmer, Irish-born Lewis found cooking while at university. He opened Chapter One in 1992.

Ballymaloe Restaurant 385	Breakfast
L'Ecrivain 386	High end
Farmgate Café 384	Local favourite
Fishy Fishy Café 384	Wish I'd opened
M & L Chinese Restaurant 386	Late night
Osteria Francescana 577	Worth the travel
That's Amore 387	Regular neighbourhood

PAUL LIEBRANDT
The Elm
160 North 12th Street, New York City
Worked for Marco Pierre White, Pierre Gagnaire and Raymond Blanc prior to moving Stateside where the 'Englishman in New York' earned multiple accolades. Opened The Elm in Brooklyn in 2013.

Balthazar 868	Breakfast
Balthazar 868	Late night
Blue Ribbon Sushi 869	Regular neighbourhood
Bonchon Chicken 840	Bargain
Gotham Bar and Grill 852	Local favourite
Masa 846	High end
Minetta Tavern 853	Wish I'd opened

OLIVIER LIMOUSIN
L'Atelier de Joël Robuchon
92 Narathiwas Ratchanakharin Road, Bangkok
Following stints at L'Amphyclès, under mentor Philippe Groult, and various Michelin-starred Paris establishments, he joined L'Atelier de Joël Robuchon in 2006.

Alain Ducasse 339	High end
Apicius 462	Worth the travel
Aubaine 339	Breakfast
Augustine Kitchen 318	Regular neighbourhood
Cafe Boheme 347	Late night
Casse-Croûte 354	Local favourite
La Petite Maison 343	Wish I'd opened

MARCUS LINDNER
The Alpina Gstaad
Alpinastrasse 23, Gstaad
Fine-dining veteran Lindner has over thirty years' experience in Europe's most renowned hotel kitchens, and now runs three at The Alpina in Gstaad.

Basta 560	Bargain
Globus 566	Wish I'd opened
Old Crow 567	Late night
The Restaurant 568	High end
Restaurant Les Saisons 562	Breakfast
Wasserngrat 560	Worth the travel
Wirtschaft Neumarkt 568	Local favourite

GEOFF LINDSAY
Dandelion
133 Ormond Road, Melbourne
Modern Vietnamese Dandelion (2011) was Lindsay's first new venture since selling the renowned Pearl. His modern Australian take on Asian cuisine won him plaudits from the outset.

Attica 113	High end
Café Di Stasio 114	Regular neighbourhood
I Love Pho 111	Breakfast
Icebergs Dining Room and Bar 86	Wish I'd opened
Melbourne Supper Club 108	Late night
Prune 852	Worth the travel
Thanh Nga Nine 112	Bargain

DONALD LINK
Herbsaint
701 Saint Charles Avenue, New Orleans
James Beard Award-winning chef-owner of Cochon, Cochon Butcher, Herbsaint and Pêche restaurants in New Orleans, which cover the trajectory of Southern food, from high-end to Cajun pork patties.

Asador Etxebarri 479	Worth the travel
Bayona 818	High end
La Boulangerie 821	Breakfast
Commander's Palace 819	Local favourite
The Company Burger 822	Wish I'd opened
Guy's Po-Boys 823	Bargain
Lilette 823	Regular neighbourhood
Taceaux Loceaux 816	Late night

ANITA LO

Annisa
13 Barrow Street, New York City
A second-generation Chinese-American who trained in Paris at L'Ecole Ritz-Escoffier, she opened Annisa in New York's Greenwich Village in 2000.

L'Artusi **853**	Regular neighbourhood
Bouley **869**	Local favourite
Jewel Bako **849**	High end
Lincoln Restaurant **716**	Worth the travel
Patisserie Claude **856**	Breakfast
The Spotted Pig **857**	Late night
Taïm **857**	Bargain

GIORGIO LOCATELLI

Locanda Locatelli
8 Seymour Street, London
Born into a family of chefs, Locatelli came to London at nineteen, working at the Savoy and winning Zafferano its first Michelin star before opening Locanda Locatelli in 2002.

Beijing Dumpling **336**	Late night
Caravan **369**	Wish I'd opened
Don Alfonso **574**	Worth the travel
Le Laurent **463**	High end
Oblix **356**	Local favourite
Taste of Siam **357**	Bargain
Tinello **320**	Regular neighbourhood

CHRISTIAN LOHSE

Fischers Fritz
Charlottenstrasse 49, Berlin
Formerly the personal chef to the Sultan of Brunei, Lohse has been creating French-inspired cuisine for more than a decade at Berlin's Fischers Fritz.

Café Einstein **556**	Breakfast
Dorint Söl'ring Hof **546**	Worth the travel
Hermanns Einkehr **556**	Local favourite
HORVÁTH **552**	High end
Hot Spot **556**	Regular neighbourhood
Paris Bar **550**	Wish I'd opened

CHONG CHEE LOONG

Hakkasan
Krystal, Waterfield Road, Mumbai
Malaysian chef who has been a firm fixture in Hakkasan the world over and now heads up the Mumbai branch.

Alinea **827**	Wish I'd opened
Bacchanalia **232**	Worth the travel
Bade Miya **154**	Bargain
Candies **154**	Regular neighbourhood
Le Cirque Signature **154**	High end
Imbiss **155**	Regular neighbourhood
Lemongrass **155**	Regular neighbourhood
Leopold Café **156**	Late night
Suzette **157**	Breakfast
Trishna **157**	Local favourite

DANIEL LÓPEZ

Kokotxa
Campanario 11, San Sebastián
Worked with Donostia doyens Arzak and Subijana before opening Kokotxa with his partner in 2002, winning it a Michelin star five years later.

Asador Ekaitz **484**	Regular neighbourhood
Casa Urola **486**	Local favourite
Elkano **481**	High end
Elosta **486**	Late night
A Fuego Negro **486**	Wish I'd opened
La Guinda **487**	Breakfast
Nihonryori Ryugin **216**	Worth the travel

JÉRÔME LORVELLEC

Nobu
12 Avenue des Spélugues, Monte Carlo
Returned to Nobu to oversee Matsuhisa in 2010 and Nobu's Monaco outpost in 2014, having launched Pershing Hall and Black Calavados in Paris.

L'Atelier de Joël Robuchon **459**	Wish I'd opened
Boulangerie Eric Kayser **440**	Breakfast
Fleur de Sel **440**	Bargain
Au Grand Inquisiteur **441**	Local favourite
Le Mirazur **440**	High end
Napul'è **585**	Regular neighbourhood
Silks **83**	Worth the travel
The Stables Bar **83**	Late night

JENN LOUIS

Lincoln Restaurant
3808 North Williams Avenue, Portland
Chef and co-owner of Portland's Lincoln Restaurant and Sunshine Tavern, Louis also launched a successful catering business, Culinary Artistry, in 2000.

Chen's Good Taste **715**	Bargain
Club 21 **715**	Late night
Hostaria del Rio **576**	Worth the travel
Jake's Famous Crawfish **715**	Local favourite
Nong's Khao Man Gai **717**	Wish I'd opened
Nostrana **717**	High end
Podnah's Pit **719**	Breakfast
Zilla Saké **719**	Regular neighbourhood

JAMES LOWE

Lyle's
56 Shoreditch High Street, London
Ran proceedings at Fergus Henderson's St. John Bread & Wine, worked at The Fat Duck and Noma, before forming chef-trio The Young Turks. Opened Lyle's in London in 2014.

40 Maltby Street **354**	Regular neighbourhood
The Clove Club **371**	Local favourite
Fäviken Magasinet **261**	Worth the travel
Koya Bar **349**	Breakfast
Pitt Cue Co. **350**	Bargain
The River Café **325**	High end
St. John Bread & Wine **374**	Wish I'd opened

TERRY LOWE

Black Barn Bistro
Black Barn Road, Havelock North
Lowe's training took in the New Zealand Navy, Spanish restaurants and British luxury hotels before he took the reins at the Black Barn Bistro in 2003.

Common Room **120**	Late night
Depot Eatery **128**	Wish I'd opened
The Farm at Cape Kidnappers **120**	High end
Flying Fish **133**	Worth the travel
Mamacita **120**	Regular neighbourhood
Pacifica **120**	Local favourite
Rose and Shamrock Village Inn **120**	Bargain
Taste Cornucopia **120**	Breakfast

ANTHONY LUI

Flower Drum
17 Market Lane, Melbourne
Partner in Melbourne's legendary Cantonese, Flower Drum, since 2003, where owner Gilbert Lau first enticed him to cook in 1981.

Brae **81**	Worth the travel
Dmarco Espresso Bar **107**	Breakfast
Grossi Florentino **108**	Local favourite
I Love Pho **111**	Bargain
Rockwell and Sons **109**	Regular neighbourhood
Saint Crispin **110**	Wish I'd opened
Waku Ghin **235**	High end

ROSS LUSTED

The Bridge Room
44 Bridge Street, Sydney
Ex-Rockpool head chef, Lusted spent a decade in Asia working for Aman Resorts, returning to open Asian-inspired The Bridge Room with John Fink (of Quay and Otto) in 2011.

The Apollo **96**	Regular neighbourhood
Cumulus Inc. **107**	Wish I'd opened
Golden Century Seafood **89**	Late night
Gyu Ho **203**	Worth the travel
Kepos Street Kitchen **100**	Breakfast
Mamak **90**	Bargain
Marque **101**	High end
Sean's Panaroma **86**	Local favourite

WILLIAM MAHI

Spondi Restaurant
Pyrronos 5, Athens
Basque-born Mahi worked with several Michelin-starred chefs including Ducasse and Nicolas Le Bec, taking in Asia and Istanbul on his travels, before settling at Athens's two-Michelin-starred Spondi.

Eleven Madison Park **862**	Wish I'd opened
Martín Berasategui **482**	Wish I'd opened
Mugaritz **480**	Wish I'd opened
Tickets **515**	Worth the travel
Tudor Hall Restaurant **628**	Breakfast

MAK KWAI PUI
Tim Ho Wan
18 Hoi Ting Road, Hong Kong
Former chef at the Four Seasons's prestigious Lung King Heen, Chef Mak has elevated steamed buns to the pinnacle of haute cuisine with his burgeoning dim sum empire.

Chung Chung Food Shop 189	Late night
Forum 180	Local favourite
Ho Choi Seafood Restaurant 191	Regular neighbourhood
Man Wah 186	High end
Metro Buffet and Grill 191	Breakfast
Shin Yeh 177	Worth the travel
Wing Hap Lung 192	Bargain

JAMIE MALONE
Sea Change
818 South 2nd Street, Minneapolis
Malone, head chef at Sea Change, travelled extensively in Hong Kong, Vietnam and Europe, before bringing her award-winning sustainable seafood menu to Minneapolis.

The Bachelor Farmer 781	Wish I'd opened
La Belle Vie 781	Local favourite
Chimborazo 781	Bargain
Left Handed Cook 782	Regular neighbourhood
NoMad 843	Worth the travel
Piccolo 782	High end
Tilia 782	Late night
Victor's 1959 Cafe 782	Breakfast

LUKE MANGAN
Glass
488 George Street, Sydney
Australian, trained in Melbourne under Herman Schneider and in the UK with Michel Roux, he owns and operates branches of his Salt Grill brand.

Bernasconi's 98	Breakfast
Catalina 99	Local favourite
China Doll 96	Regular neighbourhood
Est. 88	High end
Happy Chef 89	Bargain
Hinoki & The Bird 731	Wish I'd opened
Mr. Wong 90	Late night
Paichē 736	Worth the travel
Del Posto 860	High end
Sean's Panaroma 86	Regular neighbourhood

TONY MANTUANO
Spiaggia
980 North Michigan Avenue, Chicago
Chef-partner of Michelin-starred standard bearer for Italian food, Spiaggia, since 1984, and Lorenzo (Miami), Bar Toma and Terzo Piano (Chicago) and Mangia Trattoria in Kenosha.

Avec 832	Late night
Dinner by Heston Blumenthal 326	Worth the travel
Glunz Tavern 831	Regular neighbourhood
Keefer's 828	Local favourite
NoMad 843	Worth the travel
Nookies 831	Breakfast
Pizzarium 582	Wish I'd opened
Ristorante Quadri 601	High end
Spacca Napoli 831	Regular neighbourhood
White Bear 877	Bargain

GREG MARCHAND
Frenchie
5–6 Rue du Nil, Paris
The Nantes native travelled the globe, from New York to Hong Kong, before returning to his homeland to open Frenchie – the nickname Jamie Oliver gave him at Fifteen.

L'Ambroisie 454	Local favourite
L'Astrance 469	High end
Le Bal Café 471	Breakfast
Brasserie Thoumieux 459	Wish I'd opened
Candelaria 454	Late night
Le Coq Rico 471	Regular neighbourhood
Encore 464	Regular neighbourhood
Le Glass 465	Late night
La Poule au Pot 451	Late night
Ravioli Chinois Nord-Est 472	Bargain
Sông Quê Café 367	Bargain
La Tour de Montlhéry 451	Late night

GUALTIERO MARCHESI
Ristorante Teatro alla Scala
Piazza della Scala, Milan
Legendary Italian, widely credited as the father of modern Italian cooking, his current businesses include 'Il Marchesino', his flagship restaurant in Milan.

Ristorante Corale Verdi 577	Regular neighbourhood
Trattoria del Nuovo Macello 589	Local favourite
Zazà Ramen 589	Bargain

MARÍA MARTE
El Club Allard
Calle Ferraz 2, Madrid
Dominican Republic-born Marte moved to Spain to pursue culinary ambitions, realized in the shape of a second Michelin star at her restaurant El Club Allard in 2011.

Aroma de la Montaña 895	Worth the travel
Casa Lucio 498	Local favourite
La Gabinoteca 500	Bargain
Kabuki Wellington 500	High end
Matilda Café Cantina 501	Breakfast
Mercado San Antón 501	Regular neighbourhood
La Panamericana 501	Late night
Viridiana 504	Wish I'd opened

DAVID MARTIN
La Paix
Rue Ropsy-Chaudron 49, Anderlecht
One-time disciple of Passard, bought the Brussels brasserie, La Paix, in 2004, where butchers who visited the abattoir opposite began meeting in 1892.

Asador Etxebarri 479	Wish I'd opened
La Buvette 412	Bargain
Friture René 411	Local favourite
Hertog Jan 420	High end
Kigawa 205	Worth the travel
Pâtisserie Le Saint-Aulaye 413	Breakfast
La Table du Boucher 418	Regular neighbourhood

VIRGILIO MARTÍNEZ
Central
Calle Santa Isabel 376, Lima
Ran the kitchen at Gastón Acurio's seminal haute Peruvian Astrid & Gastón, before launching his own celebrated Lima restaurant Central in 2010, and Lima in London in 2013.

Astrid & Gastón 906	High end
Canta Rana 906	Bargain
Coi 754	Worth the travel
Eggo 907	Breakfast
Maido 907	Regular neighbourhood
La Mar 908	Local favourite
El Mercado 908	Wish I'd opened

RETO MATHIS
La Marmite
Mathis Food Affairs, Corviglia
Swiss chef who credits his time living in Togo and the Far East as inspiration for his high-end, high-altitude food: his six restaurants are under one roof at 8,000 feet.

L'Atelier de Joël Robuchon 459	Wish I'd opened
Eleven Madison Park 862	Worth the travel
La Padella 561	Regular neighbourhood
The Piz 561	Bargain
Restaurant Les Saisons 562	Breakfast
Da Vittorio – St Moritz 562	High end

TONY MAWS
Craigie on Main
853 Main Street, Cambridge
The owner of The Kirkland Tap & Trotter and Craigie on Main, which he originally ran in a different Cambridge location as the Craigie Street Bistrot (2003).

Belly Wine Bar 778.................Wish I'd opened
Chilli Garden 778.......Regular neighbourhood
Grill 23 775...High end
Neptune Oyster 775.................Local favourite
Peach Farm 776..............................Late night
Pho Viet 776...Bargain
Sofra 778...Breakfast
St. Anselm 876....................Worth the travel

FRANCESCO MAZZEI
L'Anima
1 Snowden Street, London
Opened L'Anima in London in 2008. Born in Calabria, he first arrived in the UK in 1996, working for restaurateurs Corbin and King and Alan Yau.

Bar Boulud 326................................Late night
Busaba Eathai 347.............................Bargain
Cipriani 145....................Worth the travel
CUT at 45 Park Lane 340.....................High end
The Duke of Cambridge 368.....Local favourite
Hakkasan 342............Regular neighbourhood
Lapprodo 573......................Worth the travel
The Wolseley 345...........................Breakfast
Zuma 327..............................Wish I'd opened

KEVIN MCCAFFERY
Banana Tree Grille
Bluebeard's Castle Resort, St Thomas
Baltimore-born McCaffery's culinary formation was in the kitchens of the American South before he took the reins at the Banana Tree Grille on St Thomas.

Bad Ass Coffee 895..........................Breakfast
Betsy's Bar 895................................Late night
Cuzzin's 895..............................Local favourite
Greengo's Caribbean Cantina 896.......Bargain
Hook Line & Sinker 896....................Breakfast
JK's Restaurant 794..............Worth the travel
Pie Whole 896....................Wish I'd opened
Thirteen 896..............Regular neighbourhood
Zozo's Ristorante 895.........................High end

MATT MCCALLISTER
FT33
1617 Hi Line Drive, Dallas
Learned his trade with some of the country's greatest chefs, including José Andrés, Sean Brock and Daniel Boulud, launching Dallas's FT33 in 2012, serving 'season-inspired modern cuisine'.

Crossroads Diner 807.....................Breakfast
Gemma 807..Late night
Houston's 807............Regular neighbourhood
Lucia 807.............................Wish I'd opened
Mansion Restaurant 808........................High end
McCrady's 802....................Worth the travel
Off-Site Kitchen 808............................Bargain
Patina Green 810....................Local favourite

ANDREW MCCONNELL
Cumulus Inc.
45 Flinders Lane, Melbourne
Melbourne-born, he worked his way through the city's restaurant scene before opening Cumulus Inc. in 2008, Cutler & Co. in Fitzroy in 2009, and most recently Moon Under Water at the Builders Arms Hotel.

Attica 113...High end
Bar Di Stasio 114.............................Late night
Bones 466.......................Wish I'd opened
Le Chateaubriand 466...........Worth the travel
Duchess of Spotswood 113.............Breakfast
I Love Pho 111.....................................Bargain
Momofuku Seiōbo 98............Worth the travel

BRAD MCDONALD
The Lockhart
22–24 Seymour Place, London
Formerly of Brooklyn's Colonie, Gran Eléctrica and Governor, acclaimed Mississippi-born McDonald brought Deep South-influenced cuisine to London in 2014 at The Lockhart.

Balthazar 868.................Wish I'd opened
Au Cheval 832......................Worth the travel
The Clove Club 371.....Regular neighbourhood
Franny's 874............................Local favourite
Minca 850...Bargain
Sake Bar Hagi 842............................Late night
St. John Bread & Wine 374..............Breakfast
Sushi Yasuda 839.............................High end
Veselka 852..Breakfast

CHRIS MCDONALD
Cava
1560 Yonge Street, Toronto
Canadian Slow Food and nose-to-tail devotee and executive chef and owner of Toronto's Cava, where he showcases inventive tapas. Career highlights include Chez Panisse and Santa Fe's Coyote Café.

Bairrada Churrasqueira 679...............Regular
neighbourhood
Barberian's Steakhouse 681.....Local favourite
Café Boulud 686................................High end
Fogo Island Inn 662..............Worth the travel
Mt. Everest Restaurant 682.................Bargain
SiChuan House Cuisine 678..............Late night
Trattoria della Posta 592.......Wish I'd opened

MURRAY MCDONALD
Fogo Island Inn
210 Main Road, Fogo Island
Globe-trotting McDonald returned to his native Newfoundland to become executive chef of the remote, architecturally stunning Fogo Island Inn in 2012.

Cava 682.................................Worth the travel
Chinched Bistro 662...........................Bargain
Fäviken Magasinet 261.........Wish I'd opened
Mallard Cottage 663........................Breakfast
Nicole's Café 662.......Regular neighbourhood
Noma 289.............................Wish I'd opened
Raymonds 663......................................High end

BRENDAN MCGILL
Hitchcock
133 Winslow Way East, Bainbridge Island
Alaskan-born chef and owner of Seattle's Hitchcock (2010), its little sister next door, the Hitchcock Deli & Charcuterie (2011) and German beer hall Altstadt (2013).

Beast 714...............................Wish I'd opened
Café Presse 721...............................Breakfast
Il Corvo 721..Bargain
Little Uncle 722.........Regular neighbourhood
Maekawa Bar 722............................Late night
O'o Farm 711......................Worth the travel
Sushi Kappo Tamura 724......................High end

ISAAC MCHALE
The Clove Club
380 Old Street, London
Co-founder of The Young Turks chef collective, Orkney-born McHale worked at The Ledbury, Noma and Momofuku before opening The Clove Club in East London in 2013.

Franco Manca 356..............................Bargain
Golden Century Seafood 89....Wish I'd opened
Hoi Polloi 371..................................Breakfast
Kêu Bánh Mì Deli 372..Regular neighbourhood
The Ledbury 331...................................High end
Pujol 884.............................Worth the travel
The Quality Chop House 360....Local favourite
Tava Restaurant 361.........................Late night

NIALL MCKENNA
James Street South Restaurant
21 James Street South, Belfast
The chef-owner of Belfast's James Street South, opened in 2003, and the Bar + Grill, launched in 2001, both located in a converted linen mill in the city centre.

Bistro at Balloo House 383.......Local favourite
Canteen at the MAC 380..................Breakfast
Chapter One 385...................Worth the travel
The Great Room Restaurant 381.......High end
Mourne Seafood Bar 382....................Bargain
The River Café 325.............Wish I'd opened
Shu 382.....................Regular neighbourhood

JP MCMAHON
Aniar
53 Lower Dominick Street, Galway
Heralded as 'the perfect ambassador of modern Irish cuisine', restaurateur and Culinary Director of the EatGalway Restaurant Group McMahon opened Cava tapas restaurant in 2008 and Aniar in 2011.
Ard Bia at Nimmos **388**....................Breakfast
The Fatted Calf **390**.................Local favourite
Galway Farmers Market **388**...............Bargain
The Greenhouse Dublin **386**...............High end
Kai Café + Restaurant **388**......................Regular
neighbourhood
Sheridans Cheesemongers **389**.......Late night
St. John Bar and Restaurant **362**.......Wish I'd
opened
Tickets **515**..............................Worth the travel

THOMAS MCNAUGHTON
flour + water
2401 Harrison Street, San Francisco
Worked in Michelin-starred restaurants across Europe, learning the finer arts of pasta-making. His first San Francisco venture, flour + water, was swiftly followed by Central Kitchen and Salumeria.
Bar Tartine **750**...........Regular neighbourhood
El Celler de Can Roca **493**.....Worth the travel
Chez Panisse **701**.....................Local favourite
Nopa **754**....................................Late night
The Restaurant at Meadowood **708**...High end
SanJalisco **752**.................................Breakfast
State Bird Provisions **750**......Wish I'd opened
Turtle Tower **758**..............................Bargain

TORY MCPHAIL
Commander's Palace
1403 Washington Avenue, New Orleans
Originally hailing from Washington State, he's been calling the shots in the kitchen of New Orleans's Commander's Palace since 2002.
Betony **839**............................Worth the travel
Café du Monde **818**..............Local favourite
La Cocinita **816**..........................Late night
Coulis **822**................................Breakfast
Emeril's New Orleans **817**.................High end
Mondo **819**.........................Wish I'd opened
Reginelli's **823**.................................Bargain
La Thai Uptown **823**....Regular neighbourhood

ARABELLE MEIRLAEN
Arabelle Meirlaen
Chemin de Bertrandfontaine 7, Marchin
Trained at Belgium's Libramont hotel school, opening her eponymous restaurant in 2013. Meirlaen is the only female chef in Belgium to hold a Michelin star.
El Celler de Can Roca **493**.....Worth the travel
Enoteca **418**.................................Bargain
Passage 53 **453**...........................High end

PAVEL MENCL
Kastrol
Ohradské Náměstí 1625/2, Prague
Prague-based chef and television personality who serves up classic Czech fare at the no-frills, produce-led Kastrol.
Café Imperial **608**........................Breakfast
La Degustation Bohême Bourgeoise **609**..High
end
Le Jules Verne **460**................Worth the travel
Lokál **611**...............................Local favourite
Noodles **611**...................................Bargain
SaSaZu **612**............Regular neighbourhood
U Sapíků **607**............................Local favourite

NUNO MENDES
Chiltern Firehouse
1 Chiltern Street, London
Portuguese-born Mendes worked at elBulli, Jean Georges and the Coyote Café before opening Viajante and Corner Room in London, then taking up residence at André Balazs's new hotel, the Chiltern Firehouse.
Beagle **366**.................................Breakfast
Bubbledogs **363**...............Wish I'd opened
Central **906**......................Worth the travel
Mangal Ocakbasi **361**...............Late night
Raw Duck **365**............Regular neighbourhood
St. John Bread & Wine **374**......Local favourite
Sushi Tetsu **360**..............................High end

JOSÉ MENDIN
Pubbelly
1418 20th Street, Miami
One third of the Pubbelly boys, entrepreneurs and chefs behind some of Miami's most popular kitchens, including Pubbelly, Pubbelly Sushi, L'Echon Brasserie and PB Steak.
DB Bistro Moderne **765**.....................High end
Enriqueta's Sandwich Shop **765**.......Breakfast
Harry's Pizzeria **765**....Regular neighbourhood
Joe's Stone Crab **767**...............Local favourite
Restaurante Tierra **490**.........Worth the travel
Sakaya Kitchen **766**.............................Bargain
Yakko-San **768**................................Late night
Zuma Miami **767**..................Wish I'd opened

MICHAEL MEREDITH
Merediths
365 Dominion Road, Auckland
Born in Samoa, moved to New Zealand at thirteen and made his name at Auckland's The Grove before opening Merediths in 2007.
Attica **113**................................Worth the travel
Banzai **131**...................................Bargain
Cocoro **132**.............Regular neighbourhood
Coco's Cantina **128**....Regular neighbourhood
Depot Eatery **128**............................Late night
The French Café **129**...............Local favourite
Little Bird Unbakery **130**...............Breakfast
Mugaritz **480**.......................Wish I'd opened
The Musket Room **867**..........Worth the travel
Noma **289**...........................Worth the travel
Restaurant Sat Bains **312**.....Wish I'd opened
SIDART **133**...................................High end

CLAUS MEYER
Meyers Bageri
Jægersborggade 9, Copenhagen
Shareholder in Noma, he has interests in other Copenhagen restaurants and owns a group of branded delis and bakeries.
AOC **286**...............................Local favourite
Blue Hill at Stone Barns **790**.............High end
Dill Restaurant **252**.........................Late night
Geist **288**............................Worth the travel
Maison Pic **446**................................High end
Maison Troisgros **445**.......................High end
Manfreds & Vin **293**............................Bargain
La Mar **908**......................Wish I'd opened
Noodle House **295**............................Bargain
Red Medicine **729**............................Bargain
Relæ **293**............................Local favourite
Restaurant Mêlée **279**.....................Late night
Den Røde Cottage **281**............Local favourite
Sáigón Quán **280**........Regular neighbourhood
Sin Huat Eating House **233**....Worth the travel
Søllerød Kro **281**.............................High end
Tinggården **280**..........Regular neighbourhood
Wee Nam Kee **235**.................Worth the travel

WILL MEYRICK
Sarong
Jalan Petitenget 19, Kerobokan, Bali
Scotsman Meyrick, aka 'The Street Food Chef', travelled extensively throughout Southeast Asia, settling in Bali to bring elevated pan-Asian street food to Sarong (2008), Mama San, and E&O in Jakarta.
Babi Guling Chandra **240**..........Local favourite
Burnt Ends **238**...................Worth the travel
Café Zucchini **242**......Regular neighbourhood
Gourmet Café **243**..............................Bargain
Locavore **244**.................................High end
Locavore **244**...........................Wish I'd opened
Petitenget **243**...........Regular neighbourhood
Sari Ratu Padang **242**.......................Late night
Watercress Cafe **241**.........................Breakfast

CHRISTOPHE MICHALAK
Michalak Masterclass
60 Rue du Faubourg Poissonnière, Paris
Picardy-born pastry chef who has overseen the dessert menu at Alain Ducasse au Plaza Athénée since 2000 and opened his own Parisian pâtisserie, Michalak Masterclass in 2013.

Big Fernand **464**	Regular neighbourhood
Brasserie Thoumieux **459**	High end
Mr & Mrs Bund **171**	Worth the travel
Pascade **452**	Bargain
Le Père Claude **469**	Late night
La Régalade **469**	Local favourite
Ze Kitchen Galerie **458**	Wish I'd opened

JAKOB MIELCKE
Mielcke & Hurtigkarl
Frederiksberg Runddel 1, Frederiksberg
Born in Aarhus, he left Denmark to work with Pierre Gagnaire, then opened Mielcke & Hurtigkarl with Jan Hurtigkarl in 2008.

L'Arpège **458**	High end
Banzai **294**	Bargain
Fäviken Magasinet **261**	Worth the travel
Geist **288**	Regular neighbourhood
Granola **279**	Breakfast
Hos Fischer **296**	Local favourite
Kaffebaren på Amager **286**	Breakfast
Relæ **293**	Local favourite

THOMASINA MIERS
Wahaca Covent Garden
66 Chandos Place, London
On the back of her 2005 success in BBC's Masterchef, she opened Wahaca in 2008. She now has twelve branches across London.

Bentley's Oyster Bar & Grill **339**	Late night
Bocca di Lupo **346**	Regular neighbourhood
Le Café Anglais **319**	Regular neighbourhood
Le Caprice **340**	Late night
Dock Kitchen **325**	Regular neighbourhood
Dock Kitchen **325**	Local favourite
Foxtrot Oscar **321**	Breakfast
Hereford Road **331**	Regular neighbourhood
HIX **348**	Late night
J Sheekey **338**	Late night
The Ledbury **331**	Wish I'd opened
Lucky 7 **331**	Bargain
MeroToro **883**	Worth the travel
Origen **888**	Worth the travel
The River Café **325**	Regular neighbourhood
The River Café **325**	High end
Royal China **319**	Bargain

FLORA MIKULA
Auberge Flora
44 Boulevard Richard Lenoir, Paris
Nîmes-born chef whose career has seen her work in London, New York and Paris's best kitchens, Mikula's Provençal roots are still evident at her hotel-restaurant, Auberge Flora.

L'AOC **455**	Local favourite
L'Arpège **458**	High end
Auberge du Pont d'Acigné **433**	High end
Bones **466**	Wish I'd opened
Boucherie des Provinces **468**	Bargain
La Buvette **466**	Regular neighbourhood
Candelaria **454**	Late night
Le Dauphin **467**	Local favourite
Dill Restaurant **252**	Worth the travel
Geranium **296**	Worth the travel
Lao Siam **471**	Regular neighbourhood
Le Mary Celeste **454**	Wish I'd opened
La Rotonde **457**	Late night

TORY MILLER
L'Etoile
1 South Pinckney Street, Madison
After stints at Eleven Madison Park and Judson Grill, James Beard Award-winning Miller, executive chef at L'Etoile and Graze, worked at L'Etoile as Odessa Piper's chef de cuisine.

4 & 20 Bakery and Cafe **811**	Breakfast
Blue Hill at Stone Barns **790**	High end
Culver's **811**	Local favourite
Forequarter **812**	Late night
Girl & the Goat **833**	Worth the travel
Ha Long Bay **812**	Regular neighbourhood
Hakata Tonton **855**	Bargain
Totto Ramen **842**	Wish I'd opened

MICHAEL MINA
Michael Mina
252 California Street, San Francisco
Born in Egypt, Mina presides over an extensive coast-to-coast empire of American restaurants.

Bouchon Bakery **845**	Breakfast
Brooklyn Fare **872**	Wish I'd opened
Hana **706**	Regular neighbourhood
Petrossian **842**	High end
R&G Lounge **746**	Late night
Roli Roti **747**	Bargain
Sushi Kanesaka **212**	Worth the travel
Zuni Café **749**	Local favourite

CARLO MIRARCHI
Roberta's
261 Moore Street, New York City
Co-owner of runaway Brooklyn hit Roberta's, which opened in 2008 as a no-nonsense, no-reservations, rock 'n' roll bar and pizza joint, and sister establishment Blanca.

Benu **756**	Worth the travel
The Brooklyn Star **872**	Late night
Le Comptoir du Relais **457**	Worth the travel
La Grenouillère **437**	Worth the travel
Gus's Fried Chicken **803**	Worth the travel
Hakata Tonton **855**	Late night
Katz's Delicatessen **865**	Local favourite
Peking Duck House **861**	Regular neighbourhood
Pok Pok NY **875**	Late night
St. John Bar and Restaurant **362**	Worth the travel
St. John Bread & Wine **374**	Worth the travel
Sushi Mizutani **213**	Worth the travel
Ushiwakamaru **857**	Regular neighbourhood

RIKI MIZUKAMI
Pasticceria Ikkouan
5-3-15 Koishikawa, Tokyo
Born into a family of confectioners, following his apprenticeship he opened his own shop that produces Kyoto-style tea sweets.

Asaba Ryokan **206**	Worth the travel
La Beccata **210**	Regular neighbourhood
Crescent **215**	High end
Iroha Sushi **201**	Local favourite
Kinjohro **200**	Worth the travel
Nakasei Kitaten **210**	Local favourite
Sant Pau **497**	Worth the travel
Shabu-shabu Zakuro Ginzaten **212**	Local favourite
Tenichi Ginza Honten **213**	Local favourite
Teuchisoba Yonosuke **214**	Bargain

NENAD MLINAREVIC
Focus
Seestrasse 18, Vitznau
Swiss chef with Serbian roots who staged in a host of Switzerland's starred kitchens now has two Michelin stars of his own at his restaurant, Focus.

Confiserie Sprüngli **566**	Breakfast
Kronenhalle **567**	Local favourite
Miracle **567**	Bargain
Nagasui **567**	Regular neighbourhood
Noma **289**	Wish I'd opened
Schloss Schauenstein **561**	High end

KHALID MOHAMMED
Chaud
2 Queen's Park West, Port of Spain
Trained at New York's French Culinary Institute before opening Chaud in Trinidad and Tobago's Port of Spain in 2008.
Blue Hill at Stone Barns **790**..Worth the travel
The Breakfast Shed **897**..................Breakfast
Me Asia **897**.................................Late night
Sugarcane Raw Bar Grill **766** Worth the travel
Wings Restaurant & Bar **897**....Local favourite

CYRIL MOLARD
Ma Langue Sourit
1 Rue de Remich, Moutfort
Molard's seasonal, ingredient-led cuisine has seen him win many plaudits, including a Michelin star at his restaurant Ma Langue Sourit, and Gault Millau's Luxembourg Chef of the Year 2014.
Bistronome **424**.........Regular neighbourhood
La Grenouillère **437**...............Wish I'd opened
Pure C **395**..........................Worth the travel
Restaurant Clairefontaine **423**.Local favourite
La Table du Pain **424**.......................Breakfast
Victor's **545**.................................High end
Wasabi **424**.....................................Bargain

MATT MOLINA
Pizzeria Mozza
641 North Highland Avenue, Los Angeles
Trained at the Los Angeles Culinary Institute and headed east to work at Del Posto, before returning to oversee the rapidly expanding Pizzeria Mozza and Osteria Mozza restaurant group.
Cactus Tacos **733**..............................Bargain
Esquina **238**.....................Worth the travel
Graffiti Sublime Coffee **733**..............Breakfast
Matsuhisa Restaurant **729**..............High end
Park's BBQ **734**.......................Local favourite
Son of a Gun **742**.................Wish I'd opened
SUGARFISH by Sushi Nozawa **730**......Regular neighbourhood
Uncle Boons **868**...................Worth the travel

MARTÍN MOLTENI
Puratierra
3 de Febrero 1167, Buenos Aires
Globe-trotting Molteni trained in Australia and France before returning to his native Argentina to showcase his homeland's produce at his restaurant Puratierra.
El Bistro **939**......................................High end
Le Blé **936**...................................Breakfast
Cassis **931**........................Wish I'd opened
El Cuartito **941**................................Bargain
La Mar **908**.......................Worth the travel
Paraje Arévalo **938**.........................Late night
Los Platitos **934**....................Local favourite
Restó **940**..................Regular neighbourhood

GUILLAUME MONJURÉ
Le Palégrié
8 Rue Palais Grillet, Lyon
Trained with Olivier Roellinger in Brittany and Jean-Pierre Vigato at Apicius in Paris, ahead of opening Le Palégrié in 2012.
La Boîte à Café **443**.........................Breakfast
La Cave de Cécile **444**........................Bargain
Chez Terra **444**.......Regular neighbourhood
Flocons de Sel **445**............................High end
In De Wulf **421**.....................Worth the travel
Noma **289**........................Wish I'd opened
Restaurant Daniel et Denise **444**...........Local favourite

RUSSELL MOORE
Camino
3917 Grand Avenue, Oakland
Worked for Alice Waters at Chez Panisse for twenty-one years, leaving in 2008 to open Camino where he cooks over a coal-fired grill.
Bar Agricole **755**..............................Late night
Ippuku **701**..............Regular neighbourhood
El Molino Central **707**.........Wish I'd opened
El Paisa **705**.....................................Bargain
The Restaurant at Meadowood **708**..High end
Spoon **701**..................................Breakfast
Town **711**.............................Worth the travel

ALEJANDRO MORALES
Parador La Huella
Calle de Los Cisnes, José Ignacio
Self-describing La Huella as a humble 'parador', the team, with Morales running the kitchen, belie the impact their sophisticated beachside grill has had on Latin America's gastronomic reputation.
Café Misterio **930**...................Local favourite
Camino **704**.........................Worth the travel
Elmo Resto Bar **930**..........................Bargain
Lucifer **929**...............Regular neighbourhood
Mistura Manantiales **930**.................High end
Santa Teresita **930**.........................Breakfast
Santas Negras **930**.........................Late night

MARTIN MORALES
Ceviche
17 Frith Street, London
Left Lima at twelve, worked as a Disney Media executive and helped launch iTunes in Europe before opening Peruvian restaurants Ceviche (2012) and Andina (2013) in London.
Bistrot de Luxe **327**..................Local favourite
Burro e Salvia **370**.....Regular neighbourhood
Crab House Café **308**......................High end
The Ethicurean **313**.............Wish I'd opened
Euro Café **332**.................................Breakfast
La Nueva Palomino **905**.........Worth the travel
Sagar **325**.......................................Bargain
Zhengzhong Lanzhou Lamian **338**.....Late night

EDUARDO MORENO
La Isabela
Los Chorros, Caracas
Quirky Venezuelan cook, who operates his arty Caracas restaurant, La Isabela, like a private club, with reservations by introduction only.
El Aranjuez **902**....................Local favourite
Arepera Amadani **902**....................Breakfast
Aska **871**.............................Worth the travel
Fugu **902**...................Regular neighbourhood
Mediterraneo **903**.............................Bargain
Perros Rulo **903**............................Late night
Recoveco **903**.................................High end

WILLY TRULLÁS MORENO
El Willy
22 Zhongshan Dong Er Lu, Shanghai
Left Barcelona behind to open tapas bar El Willy in Shanghai; he followed that with ElEfante and Bikini in 2012.
41 Grados Experience **513**....Wish I'd opened
Asador Etxebarri **479**.............Worth the travel
Bar Pinotxo **517**...............................Breakfast
Charmant **166**.................................Late night
Goga **167**...................Regular neighbourhood
Guyi **169**...Bargain
Quimet i Quimet **517**................Local favourite
Sushi Oyama **168**...........................High end

MASAHARU MORIMOTO
Wasabi by Morimoto
1 Mansingh Road, New Delhi
The sun never sets on the restaurant empire of the star of TV's Iron Chef – it stretches from the Napa Valley to Mexico City to Mumbai via his first, eponymous restaurant in Philadelphia.
Cagen **848**...................Regular neighbourhood
Eggs 'n Things **710**........................Breakfast
Gion Maruyama **201**.........................High end
Hassho **198**........................Local favourite
Kyubey **212**.........................Worth the travel
Seoul Garden **842**...........................Late night
Shirokiya **711**..................................Bargain
Takotsubo **198**.................Wish I'd opened

DAVID MCMILLAN & FRÉDÉRIC MORIN
Joe Beef
2491 Rue Notre-Dame Ouest, Montreal
Culinary 'enfants terribles' behind Montreal's Joe Beef and Liverpool House bistros, offering gutsy, decadent French-Canadian fare, and Le Vin Papillon wine bar.
The Cypress Room **765**..........Wish I'd opened
L'Express **692**........Regular neighbourhood
Maison Publique **693**.........................Breakfast
Moishes **694**........................Local favourite
MonNan **690**.................................Late night
Au Pied de Cochon **694**......................High end
Pubbelly **766**.........................Worth the travel
Rotisserie Panama **691**.......................Bargain
Schwartz's **695**...............................Breakfast

FREDERIC MORINEAU
The Ritz Carlton Grand Cayman
West Bay Road, Georgetown
A member of the prestigious Maîtres Cuisiniers de France, Morineau's career has seen him oversee several restaurants in Europe, the US and the Caribbean.
Le Bernardin **839**....................Worth the travel
Calypso Grill **893**........Regular neighbourhood
Gelato & Co. Cremeria Italiana **892**....Wish I'd
opened
Icoa Fine Foods **892**.....................Breakfast
Morgan's Harbour Restaurant **893**.........Local
favourite
Ragazzi **893**..................................Bargain

GAL BEN MOSHE
GLASS Berlin
Uhlandstrasse 195, Berlin
Born in Tel Aviv, Moshe did stints in London and Chicago under Gordon Ramsay and Grant Achatz before moving to his adoptive home of Berlin to open the envelope-pushing GLASS.
Aroma **550**.................................Late night
The Bird **555**.......................Local favourite
Le Chateaubriand **466**.............Wish I'd opened
La Crémerie **550**........Regular neighbourhood
Dolores **555**...............................Bargain
HARTMANNs **551**.............................High end
Osteria Francescana **577**......Worth the travel

KAMAL MOUZAWAK
Tawlet
12 Naher Street, Beirut
Founded Beirut's first farmers' market, Souk el Tayeb, and operates Tawlet, a farmers' kitchen that serves regional Lebanese dishes.
Boubouffe **138**...............................Late night
Caffè Al Bicerin **594**..............Worth the travel
Chez Maguy **141**.........Regular neighbourhood
Fadel **140**..........................Local favourite
Fäviken Magasinet **261**.........Wish I'd opened
Al Halabi **140**.....................Local favourite
Aux Lyonnais **452**................Worth the travel
Osteria da Gemma **593**.........Worth the travel
Le Professeur **139**..............................Bargain
Rafic Al Rashidi **139**.....................Breakfast
The Terrace **140**.............................Breakfast

MARKUS MRAZ
Mraz & Sohn
Wallensteinstrasse 59, Vienna
Cooking is a family affair for Vienna-based Mraz: he took over his restaurant, Mraz & Sohn, from his father, his own son is a chef there and his partner, Peggy Strobel, is the sommelier.
Alinea **827**........................Wish I'd opened
Der Floh **604**..................................Bargain
Mochi **606**...............Regular neighbourhood
Pure C **395**.......................Worth the travel
Servitenwirt **606**...................Local favourite
Steirereck **607**.............................High end

MARCO MÜLLER
Rutz
Chausseestrasse 8, Berlin
Arrived at Rutz in Berlin in 2004, where he has won praise for cooking that takes in German, Austrian and Swiss influences.
3 minutes sur mer **552**.......................Regular
neighbourhood
Atera **870**.......................Worth the travel
Bandol sur Mer **553**...............Local favourite
Café Einstein **556**.........................Breakfast
Chicago Williams BBQ **553**..................Bargain
Cookies Cream **553**..............Wish I'd opened
Facil **557**...................................High end
Rosenburger **554**...........................Late night

DHARSHAN MUNIDASA
Nihonbashi Honten
11 Galle Face Terrace, Colombo
Sri Lankan-Japanese founder of Nihonbashi Honten, originally opened in Colombo in 1995. The Ministry of Crab followed in 2012.
Bettei Senjyuan **198**..............Wish I'd opened
Galle Face Green Street Market **159**...Regular
neighbourhood
Inoue Ramen **211**.............................Bargain
Jubako **215**................................High end
Tsukiji Market **213**.......................Breakfast
Tsukiji Market **213**................Worth the travel

DAVID MUÑOZ
DiverXo
Calle Padre Damián 23, Madrid
A graduate of London's Nobu and Hakkasan's kitchens, Muños returned to his native Madrid in 2007 to open DiverXo, which garnered three Michelin stars in just six years.
El Celler de Can Roca **493**......Worth the travel
Don Lay **499**................................Late night
Mugaritz **480**.........................Wish I'd opened
Sacha **503**........................Local favourite
Sudestada **503**.............................High end
TriCiclo **504**.............Regular neighbourhood
Viridiana **504**......................Local favourite

JOSH MURPHY
Moon Under Water
211 Gertrude Street, Melbourne
Tasmanian Murphy, head chef and co-owner of the landmark Builders Arms Hotel public house and Moon Under Water, previously headed the kitchen at Cumulus Inc.
Attica **113**..................................High end
Bones **466**.......................Worth the travel
Bubbledogs **363**....................Wish I'd opened
Café Romantica **106**.......................Late night
Commercial Club Hotel **110**.................Bargain
The European **107**......Regular neighbourhood
France-Soir **113**...................Local favourite
Young Bloods Diner **111**...................Breakfast

KEVIN NADERI
Roost
1972 Fairview Street, Houston
After stages at Picoline, Madrona Manor and Brennan's, in 2011 twenty-six-year-old Naderi opened Houston's Roost, whose eclectic menu showcases the chef's Persian heritage.
Brennan's of Houston **808**...................High end
Darband Shishkabob **809**..................Bargain
Elizabeth Street Café **805**.....Worth the travel
Jeffrey's **806**....................Worth the travel
Josephine House **806**.........Worth the travel
Lamberts Downtown Barbecue **806**......Worth
the travel
The Pass & Provisions **809**..............Breakfast
Perla's **806**.......................Worth the travel

CARRIE NAHABEDIAN
Naha
500 North Clark Street, Chicago
A Chicagoan of Armenian extraction, began cooking at the city's Ritz Carlton at seventeen before opening Naha in 2000 and Brindille in 2013.
Bacchanalia **828**.........Regular neighbourhood
Çiya Sofrasi **636**.................Worth the travel
Gene and Georgetti **828**.........Local favourite
Grace **833**...................................High end
Köşebaşi **637**.....................Worth the travel
La Madia **830**.................................Bargain
Les Nomades **830**.................Wish I'd opened
La Sirena Clandestina **834**...............Late night
Walker Brothers Original Pancake House **773**
Breakfast
XOCO **831**...................................Bargain

HISATO NAKAHIGASHI
Miyamasou
375 Daihizan, Kyoto
The son of a famed Japanese chef who
trained in France then returned to his native
Kyoto to take over his family's restaurant,
Miyamasou.
Bellota 204..................Regular neighbourhood
Bellota 204.................................Late night

SOLEDAD NARDELLI
Chila
Alicia Moreau de Justo 1160, Buenos Aires
Itinerant Nardelli – a household name on
Argentinian television and head chef at Chila
in Buenos Aires – has been travelling around
her homeland for five years in search of
independent farmers.
Aramburu 941....................................High end
Cassis 931.........................Wish I'd opened
Chez Manu 931......................Wish I'd opened
Local 937....................Regular neighbourhood
Maní 925................................Worth the travel
El Obrero 934..........................Local favourite
Restaurante Casal de Catalunya 943...Regular
                                                    neighbourhood

YOSHIHIRO NARISAWA
Narisawa
2-6-15 Minami Aoyama, Tokyo
Trained in Switzerland with Girardet, in
France with Robuchon and in Italy at Antica
Osteria del Ponte, he opened Les Créations
de Narisawa (now called Narisawa) in 2003.
Chinese Tapas Renge 220.................Late night
Chinese Tapas Renge 220....................Bargain
HiRosofi 211............................Local favourite
Noma 289...............................Worth the travel
Shokuninkan 204...................Worth the travel
Ubuka 221....................Regular neighbourhood

PAUL NEWMAN
Coyaba
Grace Bay, Providenciales
Worked in five-star resorts across the
Caribbean, from Jamaica to Bermuda, and
Anguilla to the British Virgin Islands, opening
Coyaba in 1999.
5A5 Steak Lounge 746..........Worth the travel
Las Brisas 894................................Breakfast
Buccan 768............................Worth the travel
Café Boulud 686.....................Worth the travel
Da Conch Shack 893................Local favourite
DBGB Kitchen & Bar 848........Wish I'd opened
Fresh Catch 893.................................Bargain
Garam Masala 894..........................Late night
George Restaurant 681........Worth the travel
HMF 769...Late night
Jacala Beach Restaurant 896...........Wish I'd
                                                           opened
The Restaurant 894............................High end
Starfish Oyster Bed & Grill 681........Worth the
                                                              travel
Yoshi's Sushi Bar 894.Regular neighbourhood

HEIKO NIEDER
The Restaurant
The Dolder Grand, Kurhausstrasse 65, Zurich
Wherever this German-born veteran of haute
cuisine goes, awards follow: his restaurant
at Zurich's Dolder Grand currently holds two
Michelin stars.
Ah-Hua 566.................Regular neighbourhood
Chäsalp 566............................Local favourite
Dübi Imbiss 565.................................Bargain
Kafischnaps 567...............................Breakfast
Restaurant de l'Hôtel de Ville 564.....High end
Restaurant de l'Hôtel de Ville 564.....Wish I'd
                                                            opened

MAGNUS NILSSON
Fäviken Magasinet
Fäviken 216, Järpen
Swedish chef, trained in Paris at L'Astrance
and L'Arpège, he returned to Sweden in 2008,
to open the tiny twelve-seat restaurant,
Fäviken Magasinet.
Attica 113..............................Worth the travel
Bras 436..............................Wish I'd opened
Le Chateaubriand 466..........................High end
Gastrologik 274.....................Worth the travel
Natur Café at Kretsloppshuset 262.....Regular
                                                    neighbourhood
Natur Café at Kretsloppshuset 262........Local
                                                       favourite
Östermalms Korvspecialist 275..........Bargain

PETTER NILSSON
Spritmuseum Restaurant
Spritmuseum, Djurgårdsvägen 38, Stockholm
Swede who cooked at Les Trois Salons in
Uzès and went on to co-own and run La
Gazzetta in Paris. Now back in Stockholm to
head up the new Spritmuseum restaurant.
Babylon 277................Regular neighbourhood
Le Chateaubriand 466..............Local favourite
Mugaritz 480..........................Worth the travel
Noma 289..High end
Pom & Flora 278................................Breakfast
Restaurang Gandhi 278.......................Bargain
Roseval 472.....................................Late night

JUSTIN NORTH
Centennial Hotel
88 Oxford Street, Sydney
Kiwi who worked for Raymond Blanc then ran
the Becasse group until 2012, and now fronts
the kitchen at Sydney's Centennial Hotel.
Berardo's 78..........................Worth the travel
Café Le Monde 78..............................Breakfast
Chin Chin 106...................................Late night
Flower Drum 107...............................High end
Jugemu & Shimbashi Restaurant 94...Regular
                                                    neighbourhood
Mamak 90..Bargain
Spice Temple 91.......................Local favourite
Sushi Takumi Masa 217..........Wish I'd opened

BENNY NOVAK
ICI Bistro
Avenida Pará, São Paulo
Opened São Paulo's ICI Bistro with Renato
Ades in 2002, followed by 210 Diner, with
a reputation for serving the best burger in
town, and Tappo Trattoria.
Barcelona Doces e Pães 921...........Breakfast
Carbone 852.........................Worth the travel
Churrascaria Boi na Brasa 927...........Regular
                                                    neighbourhood
Churrascaria Boi na Brasa 927...........Bargain
Deliqatê 923....................................Breakfast
Filial 927...Late night
Maní 925..High end
Tanuki 928...................Regular neighbourhood
Ton Hoi 920..................Regular neighbourhood

SAMUEL NUTTER
Bror
Sankt Peders Stræde 24a, Copenhagen
County Durham-born Nutter opened restau-
rant Bror ('brother' in Danish) with fellow ex-
Noma sous chef and long-time friend Victor
Wågman in 2013 to great critical fanfare.
Atelier September 287....................Breakfast
Beyti 291...Late night
Casa D'Antino 288............................High end
Le Chateaubriand 466..........Worth the travel
Noma 289.............................Local favourite
Noodle House 295..............................Bargain
The Raby Hunt Restaurant 308..........Wish I'd
                                                              opened
Told & Snaps 291.......Regular neighbourhood

NICOLAI NØRREGAARD
Kadeau
Wildersgade 10, Copenhagen
In 2007 Nørregaard opened produce-based
restaurant Kadeau on the remote Danish is-
land of Bornholm. A second incarnation of the
Baltic-island venue opened in Copenhagen's
Christianshavn in 2012.
Atelier September 287....................Breakfast
Bento 294.....................Regular neighbourhood
Chicky Grill 294.................................Bargain
Frantzén 270.........................Worth the travel
Geist 288..Late night
In De Wulf 421......................Worth the travel
Kødbyens Fiskebar 295.........Wish I'd opened
Noma 289..High end
Pluto 290......................Regular neighbourhood
Restaurant Sankt Annæ 290.....Local favourite
Søllerød Kro 281................................High end
Le Verre Volé 465...................Worth the travel

PATRICK O'CONNELL
The Inn at Little Washington
Middle and Main Street, Washington
Owner of The Inn at Little Washington in
Virginia, a self-taught cook, he began cater-
ing business Blue Ridge Mountains in 1972,
opening The Inn in 1978.

2 Amys **762**		Regular neighbourhood
Eleven Madison Park **862**		Worth the travel
Johnny's Half Shell **763**		Local favourite
Maison Troisgros **445**		Wish I'd opened
Le Parc **435**		Worth the travel
Sushi Rock Café **764**		Bargain
Le Taillevent **464**		High end

SHUKO ODA
Koya
49 Frith Street, London
Learned the art and hard graft of udon-making
at Kunitoraya in Paris, opening London noodle
bar Koya in 2010 with John Devitt and Junya
Yamasaki, then Koya Bar in 2013.

Dinner by Heston Blumenthal **326**		High end
Franco Manca **356**		Regular neighbourhood
Noma **289**		Worth the travel
Silk Road **357**		Bargain
St. John Bread & Wine **374**		Local favourite

KIM ÖHMAN
Farang
Ainonkatu 3, Helsinki
Swedish chef and co-owner of Stockholm's
Farang (2013), sleek offshoot of the success-
ful Southeast Asian flagship restaurant in
Helsinki, which opened in 2009.

Amida Kolgrill **277**		Bargain
Cal Pep **513**		Wish I'd opened
Chat Thai **88**		Worth the travel
Gyrella **277**		Late night
Mathias Dahlgren Matbaren **272**		High end
Rolfs Kök **273**		Regular neighbourhood
Sosta Espresso Bar **273**		Breakfast
Sturehof **276**		Local favourite

AIZPEA OIHANEDER PEREZ
Xarma Jatetxea
Avenida de Tolosa 123, San Sebastián
Runs San Sebastián's avant-garde Xarma
Jatetxea with Xabier Diez, whom she met
at Arzak, before the two went on to work
for culinary heavyweights Michel Bras and
Martín Berasategui.

Akelarre **483**		High end
Bar Nestor **484**		Late night
Cocinandos **490**		Worth the travel
La Guinda **487**		Breakfast
Iriarte Jatetxea **489**		Bargain
Kokotxa **488**		Regular neighbourhood
Martín Berasategui **482**		Local favourite
Zuberoa **482**		Wish I'd opened

DAVIDE OLDANI
D'O
Via Magenta 18, Cornaredo
Born in Cornaredo, near Milan, he trained
with Marchesi at Le Gavroche in London
and at Louis XV in Monte Carlo, opening D'O
in 2003.

Le Chateaubriand **466**		Bargain
D.O.M. Restaurante **921**		High end
Dry **587**		Late night
Limonaia **573**		Breakfast
Le Louis XV **447**		Wish I'd opened
Noma **289**		Worth the travel
Osteria Francescana **577**		Worth the travel
Piazza Duomo **591**		Worth the travel
Ristorante Berton **588**		Local favourite
Ristorante Cracco **588**		Local favourite
ristorante20 **587**		Bargain
Zero **589**		Regular neighbourhood

TOM OLDROYD
Polpo
41 Beak Street, London
Oversees all of the restaurants in Russell
Norman's rapidly expanding, London-based,
Polpo group.

Alle Testiere **600**		High end
Bar Italia **345**		Late night
Corte Sconta **600**		High end
Dean Street Townhouse **347**		Breakfast
Govinda's Pure Vegetarian **348**		Bargain
Quo Vadis **350**		Regular neighbourhood
Le Relais des Maures **441**		Worth the travel
St. John Bar and Restaurant **362**		Local favourite
Tonkotsu **352**		Late night
The Wolseley **345**		Wish I'd opened

RODRIGO OLIVEIRA
Mocotó
Avenida Nossa Senhora do Loreto 1100,
São Paulo
Originally opened by his father, José Oliveira
de Almeida, São Paulo's Mocotó serves
authentic Amazonian cuisine.

As Véia **925**		Local favourite
Bar Número **923**		Late night
Carlinhos Restaurante **926**		Bargain
Casa Garabed **927**		Regular neighbourhood
Jun Sakamoto **927**		High end
Il Luogo di Aimo e Nadia **588**	Worth the travel
Padaria Jardim Brasil **928**		Breakfast
Roberta Sudbrack **917**		Wish I'd opened
Sushi Hiroshi **927**		Regular neighbourhood

ENRIQUE OLVERA
Pujol
Francisco Petrarca 254, Mexico City
One of a new wave of Mexican chefs
re-imagining indigenous cuisine by marrying
it with a fine dining setting, Olvera opened
Pujol in Mexico City in 2000.

Azul Histórico **882**		Local favourite
Blanca **872**		Wish I'd opened
El Farolito **889**		Late night
Manzanilla **880**		High end
Maximo Bistrot **883**		Bargain
Nicos **883**		Breakfast
Noma **289**		Worth the travel
Rosetta **885**		Regular neighbourhood

UWE OPOCENSKY
Mandarin Grill & Bar
The Mandarin Oriental, 5 Connaught Road,
Hong Kong
German, worked for Anton Mosimann in
London and did a stint with the Shangri-La
Hotel group, before joining The Mandarin
Oriental, Hong Kong.

8½ Otto e Mezzo Bombana **182**		High end
Din Tai Fung **191**		Bargain
Ebeneezer's Kebabs & Pizzeria **180**	Late night
Eleven Madison Park **862**		Worth the travel
Fäviken Magasinet **261**		Worth the travel
Kau Kee **184**		Local favourite
Rōnin **186**		Wish I'd opened
Tim Ho Wan **190**		Bargain
Yardbird **188**		Late night
Zuma **188**		Regular neighbourhood

KEN ORINGER
Clio
370a Commonwealth Avenue, Boston
Boston born, worked across the US before
returning home to open Clio, followed by
another four Boston restaurants, Earth in
Maine, and Toro tapas bar in New York City
in 2013.

Buvette **854**		Regular neighbourhood
Buvette **854**		Breakfast
Carbone **852**		High end
Daniel **844**		High end
Grand Central Oyster Bar **838**	Local favourite
Izakaya Ten **859**		Late night
Lobster Place **859**		Regular neighbourhood
Minetta Tavern **853**		Local favourite
Pearl & Ash **867**		Wish I'd opened
Del Posto **860**		Regular neighbourhood
RedFarm **856**		Regular neighbourhood
Septime **468**		Worth the travel
Shanghai Cafe **861**		Bargain
The Spotted Pig **857**		Late night
Los Tacos No. 1 **859**	Regular neighbourhood
ZZ's Clam Bar **853**		Regular neighbourhood

MATTHEW ORLANDO

Amass
Refshalevej 153, Copenhagen
Californian Orlando's résumé reads like a
Who's Who of the culinary world: he worked
under Eric Ripert, Raymond Blanc, Heston
Blumenthal and René Redzepi before opening
his own restaurant Amass in 2013.

Atelier September 287	....	Wish I'd opened
Bror 287	....	Regular neighbourhood
Forage 720	....	Worth the travel
Franny's 874	....	Bargain
Potato Shack Cafe 706	....	Breakfast
Relæ 293	....	Local favourite
Sake Bar Hagi 842	....	Late night
Slotskøkkenet 282	....	High end

RAFAEL OSTERLING

Rafael
San Martin 300, Lima
Left Lima to study and train in Europe, return-
ing to Peru and opening Rafael, where he
fuses Peruvian and Mediterranean flavours.
Lima's El Mercado and La Despensa in
Bogotá followed.

Canta Rana 906	....	Bargain
La Gloria 907	....	Late night
Momofuku Seiōbo 98	....	Worth the travel
El Pan de la Chola 908	....	Breakfast
La Picantería 909	....	Regular neighbourhood
The River Café 325	....	Wish I'd opened

REIF OTHMAN

Zuma
Gate Village 6, Sheikh Zayed Road, Dubai
Launched his culinary career in Singapore
before relocating to Dubai, working at Les
Amis before leading the charge at Dubai and
Abu Dhabi's Zuma as executive chef.

Adam Road Food Centre 232	....	Bargain
Boulevard Café 146	....	Breakfast
Geylang Serai Market 233	....	Bargain
Kozue 220	....	High end
Mercado de San Miguel 501	...	Wish I'd opened
Narisawa 216	....	Worth the travel
Ravi 147	....	Late night
Tekka Food Centre 234	....	Bargain
Violet Oon's Kitchen 233	....	Local favourite
Wok It 147	....	Regular neighbourhood
Wox 147	....	Regular neighbourhood

GUSTAV OTTERBERG

Ekstedt
Humlegårdsgatan 17, Stockholm
Head chef at Stockholm's Michelin-starred
Ekstedt, frequently ranked as one of the top
ten restaurants in the world, the 'Nordic
kitchen' brainchild of Niklas Ekstedt.

Chez Betty 278	....	Regular neighbourhood
Frantzén 270	....	High end
Frantzén 270	....	Worth the travel
Råkultur 275	....	Local favourite

YOTAM OTTOLENGHI

Ottolenghi
287 Upper Street, London
London-based Israeli chef and co-owner of
the eponymous group of sleek Middle Eastern-
Mediterranean deli-cafes with business
partner Sami Tamimi, and Nopi restaurant,
which opened in 2011.

Fernandez & Wells 348	....	Breakfast
Honey & Co. 363	....	Wish I'd opened
Locanda Locatelli 328	....	High end
Mangal Ocakbasi 361	....	Bargain
Mei Mei 775	....	Worth the travel
Morito 360	....	Local favourite
Randall & Aubin 350	..	Regular neighbourhood
Shoryu Ramen 352	....	Late night

NATHAN OUTLAW

Restaurant Nathan Outlaw
St Enodoc Hotel, Rock
Cornish-based seafood specialist, runs Res-
taurant Nathan Outlaw and Seafood & Grill,
a variation on the latter opened in London at
The Capital hotel in 2012.

Fresh from the Sea 306	....	Bargain
Le Louis XV 447	....	High end
Le Louis XV 447	....	Worth the travel
Porthminster Café and Restaurant 306	.....	
		Bargain
The Seafood Restaurant 305	..	Wish I'd opened
The Seahorse 307	......	Regular neighbourhood
The Seahorse 307	....	Local favourite

PAUL OWENS

The Cliff Restaurant
Derricks, St James
Liverpool-born Owens has lived in Barbados
for twenty-five years, where he now heads
up the kitchen at The Cliff Restaurant.

Le Bernardin 839	....	High end
Le Gavroche 341	....	High end
Marshalls 897	....	Regular neighbourhood
Marshalls 897	....	Bargain
On the Rocks 897	....	High end
Restaurant Gordon Ramsay 322	......	High end
Senderens 464	....	Worth the travel

CHRISTIAN PAGE

Short Order
6333 West 3rd Street, Los Angeles
Keeps an eye on proceedings at superior Los
Angeles's burger joint, Short Order, where he
arrived when it opened in late 2011.

Canelé 728	....	Worth the travel
Daikokuya 735	....	Bargain
Gramercy Tavern 863	....	Wish I'd opened
Isa 874	....	Worth the travel
Milo and Olive 737	...	Regular neighbourhood
Osteria Mozza 741	....	High end
Short Cake 742	....	Breakfast

PAUL PAIRET

Ultraviolet
Shanghai
Having worked across Asia, he arrived in
Shanghai to open Jade on 36 in 2005, follow-
ing that up with Mr & Mrs Bund in 2009 and
Ultraviolet in 2012.

Asador Etxebarri 479	....	Wish I'd opened
Auberge du Vieux Puits 435	...	Worth the travel
Le Baratin 472	....	Local favourite
Capo 170	....	Regular neighbourhood
Crystal Jade 172	....	Local favourite
Din Tai Fung 168	....	Bargain
Farine 167	....	Breakfast
Fook Lam Moon 184	....	Local favourite
Hôtel Costes 450	....	High end
Jean-Georges 845	....	Breakfast
Kabb 172	....	Bargain
Le Louis XV 447	....	High end
Lung King Heen 185	....	Worth the travel
Mercato 171	....	Regular neighbourhood
Mugaritz 480	....	Worth the travel
Tickets 515	....	Worth the travel
Unico 172	....	Regular neighbourhood

STEVIE PARLE

Dock Kitchen
342–344 Ladbroke Grove, London
Worked at Moro and the River Café,
before opening his own dining room, with a
globetrotting menu, in designer Tom Dixon's
showroom in 2009.

Baiwei 336	....	Bargain
Cay Tre 347	....	Regular neighbourhood
Çiya Sofrasi 636	....	Worth the travel
The Clove Club 371	....	Local favourite
Dishoom Shoreditch 371	....	Late night
Gymkhana 341	....	Wish I'd opened
Pavilion 365	....	Breakfast
The River Café 325	....	High end

JAMES PARRY

Sixpenny
83 Percival Road, Sydney
Impressive culinary heritage includes stints
at Mugaritz, Noma and Blue Hill at Stone
Barns. Launched Sixpenny in a sleepy Sydney
suburb in 2012 with Daniel Puskas.

Cafe Mint 100	....	Breakfast
Ester 89	....	Regular neighbourhood
Fatima's 100	....	Late night
Golden Century Seafood 89	....	Local favourite
Mugaritz 480	....	Worth the travel
Pasteur 90	....	Bargain
Rockpool 91	....	High end
Zuni Café 749	....	Wish I'd opened

DAVID PASTERNACK
ESCA
402 West 43rd Street, New York
The owner of ESCA, opened in partnership with Mario Batali in 2005, and Barchetta (2014). Once described by The New York Times as a 'fish whisperer'.

Astrid & Gastón **906**..............Worth the travel
Balthazar **868**...................................Breakfast
Daniel **844**...High end
Peasant **867**..........................Wish I'd opened
Sake Bar Hagi **842**............................Late night
Super Tacos **846**..................................Bargain
Tertulia **857**................Regular neighbourhood

DANIEL PATTERSON
Coi
373 Broadway Street, San Francisco
Born in Massachusetts, moved to California in 1989, the self-taught cook and brains behind San Francisco's Coi (2006), he's since opened Plum (2010), Haven (2012) and Alta CA (2013).

Benu **756**..High end
Boot and Shoe Service **704**.................Regular
neighbourhood
D.O.M. Restaurante **921**........Worth the travel
Hawker Fare **705**................................Bargain
Nopa **754**...Late night
Pizzaiolo **706**..............Regular neighbourhood
Zuni Café **749**.........................Local favourite

FRANCK PECOL
Franck
376 Wukang Lu, Shanghai
Grandson of a French bistro owner, the Marseille cookery-school graduate travelled the world before settling in Shanghai, where he opened his eponymous Parisian-style bistro in 2007.

Asador Etxebarri **479**............Wish I'd opened
Blanca **872**...........................Worth the travel
Din Tai Fung **168**.....................Local favourite
Fu 1088 **168**...............................Local favourite
Grand Brasserie **170**..........................High end
Pho Real **169**......................................Bargain

ZAKARY PELACCIO
Fish & Game
13 South 3rd Street, Hudson
Indiana-born, opened the Asian-tinged Fatty Crab in 2005, following this up with two additional branches, before leaving the Fatty group to focus on Fish & Game in Hudson, New York (2013).

A&A Bake & Doubles Shop **871**.......Breakfast
Baanrai Yarmyen **227**............Wish I'd opened
Il Buco **866**.................Regular neighbourhood
Il Buco Alimentari e Vineria **866**.........Regular
neighbourhood
Fruit n Spice **229**...................Worth the travel
Great NY Noodletown **861**...............Late night
Isa **874**....................................Worth the travel
Vinegar Hill House **876**............Local favourite

TOM PEMBERTON
Hereford Road
3 Hereford Road, London
Driving force behind Hereford Road, which he opened in West London in 2007 following his time running St. John Bread & Wine.

The Anchor & Hope **373**......................Regular
neighbourhood
Dabbous **363**.........................Wish I'd opened
Great Queen Street **337**....................Bargain
The Hand & Flowers **305**.......Worth the travel
Moro **360**..Late night
Pied à Terre **364**...............................High end
St. John Bar and Restaurant **362**...........Local
favourite
St. John Bread & Wine **374**.............Breakfast

KEVIN PEMOULIE
Thirty Acres
500 Jersey Avenue, Jersey City
New Jersey-born Pemoulie was David Chang's chef de cuisine at Momofuku Noodle Bar for five years before returning to his home state to open Thirty Acres.

Dozzino **788**............................Local favourite
Estela **867**...................Regular neighbourhood
Kenilworth Diner **789**.......................Breakfast
Mission Cantina **865**.........................Late night
Mission Cantina **865**...Regular neighbourhood
Del Posto **860**....................................High end
Razza **789**.................................Local favourite
Septime **468**...........................Worth the travel
Taqueria Downtown **789**.....................Bargain

IÑIGO PEÑA
Narru
Calle Zubieta 56, Donostia
Young rising star, who trained with Basque Country's best at Arzak, Martín Berasategui and Mugaritz before opening Narru in 2011.

Elkano **481**......................................Late night
Hotel Val de Ruda **491**.....................Breakfast
Ibai **488**.......................Regular neighbourhood
Ibai **488**.................................Local favourite
Kaia Kaipe **481**................................Late night
Va Bene Disco Burger **489**.................Bargain
Yamazato **405**........................Worth the travel
Zuberoa **482**.....................................High end

NEIL PERRY
Rockpool
11 Bridge Street, Sydney
Left hairdressing to cook, opened Rockpool in Sydney (1989), the more casual Rockpool Bar & Grill in Melbourne (2007) and Sydney (2009), where he also opened Spice Temple the same year.

Asador Etxebarri **479**...........Worth the travel
Azuma **87**....................Regular neighbourhood
The Bridge Room **87**...Regular neighbourhood
The Bridge Room **87**..............Worth the travel
Chairman Mao **98**........Regular neighbourhood
Chinatown Noodle King **88**..................Bargain
Flower Drum **107**................................High end
Golden Century Seafood **89**............Late night
Kiroram Silkwood Road **93**................Bargain
Mugaritz **480**.........................Worth the travel
Noma **289**..............................Worth the travel
Per Se **846**.............................Worth the travel
Reuben Hills **101**...................Wish I'd opened
Room 10 **97**....................................Breakfast
Sydney Madang **92**.....Regular neighbourhood

BJÖRN PERSSON
Koka
Viktoriagatan 12, Gothenburg
Owner of the French meets west coast Swedish brasserie, Familjen; the small hours bolthole, Björns Bar; Spisa; and modern Scandinavian Koka.

L'Ami Jean **458**.....................Worth the travel
Bhoga **266**...............................Local favourite
Bror **287**................................Worth the travel
Mr. P **267**......................Regular neighbourhood
Mr. P **267**..Late night
Sjömagasinet **267**....................Local favourite

BASILIO PESCE
Porzia
1314 Queen Street West, Toronto
Former head chef of Toronto's North 44 and Biff's Bistro, Pesce opened his first restaurant in 2013: an Italian eatery named after his mother.

Bar Buca **680**.........................Wish I'd opened
Buca **680**...High end
Food & Liquor **684**...........................Late night
Impasto **696**..........................Worth the travel
Phoenix Restaurant **682**....................Bargain
Pizzeria Libretto **685**...Regular neighbourhood
Sukhothai **678**..........................Local favourite

CAL PETERNELL
Chez Panisse
1517 Shattuck Avenue, Berkeley
Raised in New Jersey, he's been at Alice Water's Chez Panisse since 1995, before that he cooked at Biba, the Blue Room, Bix and Bizou.

Bar Pinotxo 517	Worth the travel
Cal Pep 513	Worth the travel
Camino 704	Local favourite
Franny's 874	Worth the travel
Little Saigon 701	Bargain
Turtle Tower 758	Bargain
Vik's Chaat Corner 702	Regular neighbourhood

JOCKY PETRIE
The Ledbury
127 Ledbury Road, London
Resident Scot at The Fat Duck from 2002 to 2013, where he became head of creative development in 2009, before departing to become head of development at The Ledbury.

L'Astrance 469	High end
Brasserie Léon de Lyon 443	Wish I'd opened
The Hawthorn Restaurant 377	Worth the travel
House Café 384	Bargain
Jackie Lennox Chip Shop 384	Late night
Koya 349	Regular neighbourhood
Paco Gandía 506	Worth the travel
Tetote Factory 324	Breakfast
The Walpole 324	Bargain

JEAN-FRANÇOIS PIÈGE
Brasserie Thoumieux
79 Rue Saint-Dominique, Paris
Worked with Cirino, Constant and Ducasse before taking charge at Les Ambassadeurs in Paris's Hôtel de Crillon. Left to launch Brasserie Thoumieux (2009), Jean-Francois Piège (2010), and Hotel Thoumieux (2011).

La Closerie des Lilas 456	Late night
Masa 846	High end
The Restaurant 741	Breakfast
Rino 467	Bargain
Son of a Gun 742	Worth the travel

PEETER PIHEL
Fäviken Magasinet
Fäviken 216, Järpen
Formerly oversaw the kitchen at Alexander, in the Pädaste Manor Hotel on Estonia's Muhu island and Neh, in Tallinn, and is now sous chef at Magnus Nilsson's destination restaurant Fäviken Magasinet.

Åre Bageri & Breadgarden 261	Breakfast
D.O.M. Restaurante 921	Worth the travel
Eleven Madison Park 862	High end
Leib Resto ja Aed 621	Local favourite
Ölbaren 261	Regular neighbourhood
Põhjaka Mõis 621	Bargain
Relæ 293	Wish I'd opened

JOSÉ PIZARRO
Pizarro
194 Bermondsey Street, London
Spaniard who's made London his home, worked with Spanish food purveyors Brindisa before, in 2011, opening José and Pizarro.

Arzak 483	Worth the travel
Elkano 481	Wish I'd opened
Hutong 356	Regular neighbourhood
The India Club 374	Bargain
Murano 343	High end
Quo Vadis 350	Late night
The Wolseley 345	Breakfast
Zucca 355	Local favourite

ZACH POLLACK
Sotto
9575 West Pico Boulevard, Los Angeles
Formerly of Pizzeria Ortica (2009) and now at Sotto (2010), he was studying architecture in Florence when he first fell in love with Italian food.

Canelé 728	Breakfast
Father's Office 736	Wish I'd opened
Night + Market 740	Bargain
Son of a Gun 742	Regular neighbourhood

BRUCE POOLE
Chez Bruce
2 Bellevue Road, London
Co-owner of Chez Bruce in suburban south-west London since 1995, he's also a partner in The Glasshouse and La Trompette.

The Old Spot 313	Local favourite
Red Lion Freehouse 315	Regular neighbourhood
The Square 344	High end
Sticky Walnut 305	Worth the travel
The Walnut Tree 380	Worth the travel
The Wolseley 345	Breakfast

MICHEL PORTOS
Le Malthazar
19 Rue Fortia, Marseille
Based in Bordeaux, and now Marseille where he runs Le Malthazar, he previously ran his own restaurant in Perpignan, having trained at Les Jardins de l'Opéra and Troisgros.

Brasserie OM 438	Breakfast
Chez Michel 439	Local favourite
Chez Sauveur 439	Bargain
Au Falafel 439	Regular neighbourhood
Maison Pic 446	Worth the travel
Le Mas de Lulli 439	Late night
Peron 440	Wish I'd opened
Le Petit Nice 440	High end

DAVID POSEY
Blackbird
619 West Randolph Street, Chicago
Culinary Institute of America-trained Posey's introduction to Chicago's restaurant scene came via a stint at Trio, then Alinea. Posey joined Blackbird in 2007, becoming chef de cuisine in 2011.

Avec 832	Regular neighbourhood
Au Cheval 832	Late night
Chicken Hut 826	Bargain
L2O 827	High end
Lula 828	Local favourite
Ramen Misoya 773	Wish I'd opened
Saison 756	Worth the travel

ALFRED PRASAD
Tamarind
20 Queen Street, London
Trained at Bukhara and Dum-Pukh, he arrived at Tamarind in London in 2001, becoming executive chef for The Tamarind Collection, which includes Imli Street and Zaika.

The Bangala Hotel 159	Worth the travel
Bar Italia 345	Late night
Brindisa Chorizo Grill 356	Bargain
Bukhara 150	Local favourite
The French Laundry 709	Wish I'd opened
Maxim Chinese Restaurant 324	Regular neighbourhood
Saravanaa Bhavan 158	Late night

DIETMAR PRIEWE
Sansibar
Hörnumer Strasse 80, Sylt
After stints in kitchens in Berlin, Priewe swapped the metropolis for the idyllic surroundings of the island of Sylt, where he runs the kitchen at the iconic Sansibar.

L'Auberge du Pont de Collonges 442	Worth the travel
Bullerei 542	Wish I'd opened
Café Wien 546	Breakfast
Carls an der Elbphilharmonie 542	Late night
Dorint Söl'ring Hof 546	Local favourite
Jim Block 543	Bargain
Restaurant Amador 540	High end
Strandhaus 546	Regular neighbourhood

CHRISTIAN F. PUGLISI
Relæ
Jægersborggade 41, Copenhagen
Sicilian, he worked at elBulli and at Taillevent before becoming sous chef at Noma, leaving to open Relæ in 2010, followed by Manfreds & Vin across the street a year later.
Attica 113.............................Worth the travel
The Coffee Collective 292.............Breakfast
Fu Wa 292................Regular neighbourhood
Kebabistan 292.................................Late night
Noma 289........................Local favourite
Pepe in Grani 573.................Worth the travel
Ranee's 293...................................Bargain
Rumi 106.........................Worth the travel
Selfish 294...............Regular neighbourhood
Søllerød Kro 281...............................High end
Tartine Bakery 752........................Breakfast

GLYNN PURNELL
Purnell's
55 Cornwall Street, Birmingham
The loud and proud Brummie did his training under Ramsay, Bosi and Alastair Little before opening the first of his now three establishments in Birmingham in 2007.
Adil 315......................................Local favourite
Arzak 483.............................Worth the travel
Bar Boulud 326.............................Late night
Cafe Alf Resco 307..........................Breakfast
The Fat Duck 304.............................High end
Al Frash 315.............................Local favourite
The Hand & Flowers 305........Wish I'd opened
Imrans 315............................Local favourite
Roka 364...................Regular neighbourhood

DANIEL PUSKAS
Sixpenny
83 Percival Road, Sydney
Apprenticed at Tetsuya's and travelled widely, returning to Sydney to work at Oscillate Wildly where he met fellow chef James Parry. They opened fine-dining restaurant Sixpenny in 2012.
10 William St 96..........Regular neighbourhood
L'Arpège 458...................................High end
L'Astrance 469................................High end
Attica 113..High end
Brae 81...High end
Chinese Noodle House 93..................Bargain
Ester 89.........................Wish I'd opened
Golden Century Seafood 89.............Late night
Via Tevere Pizzeria 671.........Worth the travel

PAUL QUI
Qui
1600 East 6th Street, Austin
Taken under sushi-master Tyson Cole's wing at Uchi, then Uchiko, went on to open Qui and a permanent spot for his East Side King fleet of food trucks in Austin, Texas (2013).
Franklin Barbecue 805...........Local favourite
JuiceLand 806................................Breakfast
The Restaurant at Meadowood 708......Worth the travel
Saison 756..High end
Saison 756...................Wish I'd opened
Tan Tan Restaurant 810.....................Bargain
Las Trancas 806.........Regular neighbourhood
Las Trancas 806.............................Late night

GULAM QURESHI
Dum Pukht
Sardar Patel Marg, New Delhi
With thirty-six years of service at ITC Maurya under his belt, Qureshi took the helm at New Delhi's Dum Pukht in 1988, offering superlative Awadhi clay pot fare in a fine-dining setting.
Bukhara 150........................Local favourite
Karim's 151..Bargain
Royal Indian 159................Worth the travel
Swagath 152.............Regular neighbourhood

ALEXANDRA RAIJ
El Quinto Pino
401 West 24th Street, New York City
Jewish-American with Argentine roots who runs four Iberian-focused New York outposts; El Quinto Pino, Txikito, El Comedor and La Vara.
Bar Corvo 871...............................Breakfast
Battersby 871.............Regular neighbourhood
Battersby 871...................................High end
El Castillo de Jagua 863..................Breakfast
Dim Sum Go Go 860.......................Late night
La Isla Café 864................................Bargain
M. Wells Dinette 877...Regular neighbourhood
Poole's Diner 795.................Worth the travel
Roberta's 875.......................Local favourite
Roberta's 875......................Wish I'd opened

THEO RANDALL
Theo Randall
1 Hamilton Place, London
English cook with an Italian bent, he ran the kitchen at the River Café for over a decade, leaving in 2007 to open Theo Randall at the InterContinental.
Cachao 332.......................................Breakfast
Caminetto d'Oro 575..............Worth the travel
Lemonia 332.......................................Bargain
Momo 343...Late night
La Petite Maison 343.............Wish I'd opened
Princess Garden of Mayfair 344.........Regular neighbourhood
The Tangerine Dream Café 322...............Local favourite
Zuma 327...High end

NEIL RANKIN
Smokehouse
63–69 Canonbury Road, London
Leaving the realms of fine dining after meeting his mentor Adam Perry Lang, barbeque maestro and ex-Pitt Cue Co. chef Rankin opened Smokehouse in 2013.
Apollo Banana Leaf 333......................Bargain
The Clove Club 371................Wish I'd opened
Duck & Waffle 358.............................Breakfast
L'Enclume 306.......................Worth the travel
Gymkhana 341..........Regular neighbourhood
Meat Liquor 328..............................Late night
Medlar 321...High end
The Quality Chop House 360....Local favourite

SHAUN RANKIN
Ormer
7–11 Don Street, St Helier
A passion for the local produce of his adoptive home of Jersey saw the County Durham-born chef win a Michelin star at his restaurant Ormer just four months after opening.
The Bass & Lobster 376.......................Regular neighbourhood
Cancale Oyster Stands 432.................Bargain
Green Island Restaurant 376...Local favourite
Le Jules Verne 460.............................High end
Le Manoir aux Quat'Saisons 312.....Wish I'd opened
El Tico Beach Cantina 376.............Breakfast
Zuma 327.......................................Late night

GIORGIO RAPICAVOLI
Eating House
804 Ponce de Leon Boulevard, Coral Gables
Miami-born Rapicavoli honed his skills at 660 at The Angler's on Miami Beach. Initially a pop-up, his Eating House restaurant (famous for its brunch) went permanent in 2012.
Blackbrick Chinese 764.........Wish I'd opened
Joe's Stone Crab 767..............Local favourite
Las Olas Cafe 768.............................Bargain
Ristorante Garden 592.........Worth the travel
El Tropico 766.................................Breakfast
Yakko-San 768..........Regular neighbourhood
Zuma Miami 767...............................High end

VICKY RATNANI

Aurus
Juhu Tara Road, Mumbai
Born and bred in Mumbai, he travelled the
world cooking on ocean liners before pursuing
a career as a TV cook and consultant.

Aswad 154	Breakfast
L'Atelier de Joël Robuchon 459	Worth the travel
Bade Miya 154	Late night
Bukhara 150	Worth the travel
Daniel 844	Worth the travel
Gajalee 155	Regular neighbourhood
Gunpowder 151	Worth the travel
Jean-Georges 845	Worth the travel
Jimmy Boy 155	Local favourite
Momofuku Ko 850	Worth the travel
Noor Mohammadi 156	Bargain
Olympia Coffee House 156	Breakfast
Peter Luger Steakhouse 875	Worth the travel
Sardar Refreshment 156	Bargain
Sergi Arola Gastro 503	Worth the travel
Tetsuya's 92	Worth the travel
Wasabi by Morimoto 152	High end
Wasabi by Morimoto 152	Wish I'd opened

TIM RAUE

Tim Raue
Rudi-Dutschke Strasse 26, Berlin
Berliner, who owns Restaurant Tim Raue,
Uma and Shochu Bar having previously won
acclaim for Ma Tim Raue.

Bar Masa 844	Wish I'd opened
Eleven Madison Park 862	High end
Eleven Madison Park 862	Worth the travel
GästeHaus Klaus Erfort 545	Worth the travel
Majore 596	Regular neighbourhood
Sets 551	Breakfast
Tim Ho Wan 190	Bargain

ALBERT RAURICH

Dos Palillos
Carrer d'Elisabets 9, Barcelona
Ferran Adrià's right-hand man at elBulli for
seven years, he left in 2007 to open the Asian
tapas bar, Dos Palillos.

41 Grados Experience 513	High end
Compartir 491	Worth the travel
Dos Cielos 515	Late night
Gresca 514	Local favourite
Lolita Tapería 514	Bargain
Pasteleria Escribà 519	Breakfast
Tapas 24 515	Wish I'd opened
Xiringuito Escribà 516	Regular neighbourhood

JORGE RAUSCH

Criterión
Calle 69a 5–75 Zona G, Bogotá
Rausch trained and cut his culinary teeth in
Britain and is now chef-owner of three Latin
American restaurants: Criterión, Bistronomy
and Rausch Restaurant.

Andres Carne de Res 905	Local favourite
Club Colombia 904	Breakfast
Crepes & Waffles 904	Wish I'd opened
DiverXo 499	Worth the travel
Gordo Brooklyn 904	Late night
Harry Sasson 904	High end
Julia 905	Bargain
Sushigozen 905	Regular neighbourhood

MARTÍN REBAUDINO

Roux
Peña 2300 y Azcuenaga, Buenos Aires
From a culinary family, Rebaudino trained
in some of Spain's best kitchens before
becoming head chef at Oviedo. After nineteen
years he decided it was time to open his own
place, Roux.

Akelarre 483	Worth the travel
Astrid & Gastón 906	High end
La Cabrera 936	Local favourite
Italpast 930	Regular neighbourhood
Nucha 938	Breakfast
El Sanjuanino 940	Late night
Sarkis 943	Bargain

RENÉ REDZEPI

Noma
Strandgade 93, Copenhagen
Macedonian-Dane behind Noma, opened in
2003, the Nordic-sourced agenda of which
has changed haute cuisine in Scandinavia and
beyond forever.

Amass 286	Wish I'd opened
Attica 113	Worth the travel
Benu 756	Worth the travel
Café Det Vide Hus 287	Breakfast
Le Chateaubriand 466	Wish I'd opened
The Clove Club 371	Worth the travel
Coi 754	Worth the travel
Frantzén 270	Worth the travel
Koi Palace 702	High end
Manfreds & Vin 293	Bargain
Relæ 293	Wish I'd opened
Roscioli 584	Bargain
Schønnemann 290	Local favourite
Tivolihallen 290	Local favourite
Toldbod Bodega 291	Local favourite

MADS REFSLUND

Acme
9 Great Jones Street, New York City
Co-founder of Noma, Refslund took New Nordic
cuisine to New York, becoming executive chef
at NoHo's Acme in 2012.

Blue Hill at Stone Barns 790	High end
Blue Ribbon Brasserie 869	Late night
BONDST 866	Local favourite
Contra 864	Regular neighbourhood
Gasoline Alley Coffee 866	Breakfast
Lil' Frankie's 850	Bargain
Noma 289	Worth the travel

ADAM REID

The French by Simon Rogan
The Midland Hotel, Peter Street, Manchester
Manchester born and bred, Reid now runs
the kitchen for Simon Rogan at Manchester's
century-old Midland Hotel.

La Degustation Bohême Bourgeoise 609	Worth the travel
Kitchen Table 363	Wish I'd opened
Mughli 309	Late night
The Parlour 309	Regular neighbourhood
Sugar Junction 309	Breakfast
The Wharf 309	Bargain
Yang Sing 310	Local favourite

EMMANUEL RENAUT

Flocons de Sel
1775 Route du Leutaz, Megève
Born in Soisy-sous-Montmorency, he trained
at London's Claridge's and worked for Marc
Veyrat, before opening Flocons de Sel in 1998.

L'Atelier de Joël Robuchon 459	Wish I'd opened
Piazza Duomo 591	High end
La Régalade 469	Bargain
La Sauvageonne 445	Late night
Le Sciozier 443	Local favourite

ANDREA REUSING

Lantern
423 West Franklin Street, Chapel Hill
Opened Lantern, in North Carolina, with her
brother in 2002, where she combines Asian
flavours with sustainable local ingredients.

Crook's Corner 793	Regular neighbourhood
Holeman & Finch Public House 770	Worth the travel
Neal's Deli 792	Breakfast
Panciuto 793	High end
Poole's Diner 795	Wish I'd opened
Scratch 793	Local favourite
Toast 793	Bargain

EVAN RICH
Rich Table
199 Gough Steet, San Francisco
Worked at a series of high-end culinary institutions in New York and San Francisco, including Quince and Coi, before opening Rich Table in 2012.

Alta CA 758.....................................Late night
Coi 754...High end
The House of Prime Rib 753....Local favourite
Koi Palace 702...............................Breakfast
Nopa 754...........................Wish I'd opened
Outerlands 754..........Regular neighbourhood
The Restaurant at Meadowood 708......Worth the travel

ANDY RICKER
Pok Pok
3226 Southeast Division Street, Portland
Began the Thai-inspired Pok Pok, in Oregon, in 2006, where he also opened Whiskey Soda Lounge, Pok Pok Noi and Sen Yai, followed by three New York outposts.

Ava Gene's 713..........Regular neighbourhood
Binh Minh Bakery and Deli 714..........Bargain
Del Posto 860...................................High end
Great NY Noodletown 861..............Late night
Nahm 225.............................Worth the travel
Le Pigeon 719.........................Local favourite
St. John Bread & Wine 374....Wish I'd opened

JACK RIEBEL
Following thirty years working the line at some of the Twin Cities' finest restaurants, Riebel most recently won accolades as executive chef and co-owner of meat-mecca Butcher & the Boar, before leaving in 2014.

L'Astrance 469......................Worth the travel
La Belle Vie 781...............................High end
Brasa 781.........................Wish I'd opened
Hmongtown Marketplace 783.............Bargain
Hong Kong Noodle 781.....................Regular neighbourhood
Keys Café & Bakery 783.................Breakfast
Matt's Bar 782.......................Local favourite
Mickey's Diner 783..........................Late night

LOUIS-PHILIPPE RIEL
6 Paul Bert
6 Rue Paul Bert, Paris
Self-taught, Quebec-born Riel is head chef at Bertrand Auboyneau's innovative take on 'bistronomy' at 6 Paul Bert in Paris's 11th Arrondissement.

Asador Etxebarri 479............Worth the travel
Beautys 691..................................Breakfast
Rino 467..High end
Rotisserie Romados 695....................Bargain
Schwartz's 695................................Late night
Toqué! 697.............................Local favourite
Le Verre Volé 465.......Regular neighbourhood

LIONEL RIGOLET
Comme Chez Soi
Place Rouppe 23, Brussels
Cooks at Brussels's Comme Chez Soi. He took over running its kitchen from his father-in-law, Pierre Wynants, who retired in 2006.

Al Piccolo Mondo 414.......................Late night
Pistolet Original 414......................Breakfast
Le Poechenellekelder 414.......Local favourite
Prego! 414.................Regular neighbourhood
Toucan sur Mer 414...........................Bargain

MARTINS RITINS
Restaurant Vincents
Elizabetes iela 19, Riga
Latvian, born in a British refugee camp, grew up in Corby in the English Midlands, worked in Toronto and opened Vincents, in Riga, in 1994.

Art Café Sienna 622.......................Breakfast
Foodbox 622......................................Bargain
Koks 297..........................Worth the travel
Koya 623.....................Regular neighbourhood
Kukšu Muiža 622.................Wish I'd opened
Vīna Studija 623...............................Late night

FERNANDO RIVAROLA
El Baqueano
Chile 495, Buenos Aires
Alligator, llama and chinchilla are on the menu at Spanish-trained Rivarola's indigenous-meat-focused restaurant El Baqueano.

Central 906..........................Worth the travel
D.O.M. Restaurante 921...................High end
Epice 923.............................Worth the travel
Kaeshi I + D Cocina 942...................Late night
Mocotó 929.......................Wish I'd opened
Moreneta 935.................................Breakfast
Pasaje Solar 943........Regular neighbourhood
Restó 940..Bargain
Tarquino 941..............................Local favourite

HELENA RIZZO
Maní
Rua Joaquim Antunes 210, São Paulo
Brazilian, who gave up modelling to cook, training at Fasano, Emmanuel Bassoleil and at El Celler de Can Roca. She opened Maní in 2006.

Le Chateaubriand 466...........Worth the travel
Chou 926...........................Wish I'd opened
Coffee Lab 926...............................Breakfast
D.O.M. Restaurante 921....................High end
Frevo 923..Late night
Goshala 926.......................................Bargain
Mercearia do Conde 924....................Regular neighbourhood
Tordesilhas 924......................Local favourite

CHAD ROBERTSON
Tartine Bakery
600 Guerrero Street, San Francisco
Baker and co-owner of Tartine Bakery and Bar Tartine whose legendary country bread has won him admirers not only in San Francisco but worldwide.

Alta CA 758......................................Late night
Boulette's Larder 747.Regular neighbourhood
Boulette's Larder 747......................Breakfast
Boulette's Larder 747...............Local favourite
Estela 867..........................Worth the travel
Foreign Cinema 751..................Local favourite
Gallardo's 751...................................Bargain
Manfreds & Vin 293..............Wish I'd opened
Outerlands 754......................Local favourite
Relæ 293.............................Worth the travel
Saison 756.......................................High end
La Taqueria 752.................................Bargain

JOAN, JORDI & JOSEP ROCA
El Celler de Can Roca
Can Sunyer 48, Girona
The band of talented Catalan brothers behind El Cellar de Can Roca; Joan, the eldest of the trio, runs the kitchen; middle brother Josep, is sommelier; and Jordi is pastry chef.

Roca, Joan
Astrid & Gastón 906..............Worth the travel
Cal Tet 491...............Regular neighbourhood
Can Marquès 493.........................Breakfast
Can Roca 493.............Regular neighbourhood
Eleven Madison Park 862...............High end
Es Xarcu 477...........................Local favourite
Koy Shunka 512....................Worth the travel
Pierre Gagnaire 463.........Wish I'd opened
Tapas 24 515.....................................Bargain
Toc Al Mar 491...............................Late night
Roca, Jordi
L'Atelier de Joël Robuchon 459..........Wish I'd opened
Can Roca 493..................................Breakfast
Central 906..........................Worth the travel
Compartir 491........................Local favourite
Ca l'Enric 498........................Local favourite
Le Louis XV 447...............................High end
Pujol 884.............................Worth the travel
Restaurant Can Xifra 492...................Regular neighbourhood
Tickets 515..........................Worth the travel
Umai 494...Late night
Roca, Josep
Le Baratin 472......................Worth the travel
Can Marquès 493..........................Breakfast
Can Roca 493.............Regular neighbourhood
Caves Madeleine 434....Wish I'd opened
Els Casals 496..................................Bargain
Maison Troisgros 445.......................High end
El Motel 493...........................Local favourite
Restaurant Villa Más 496......Worth the travel

THOMAS RODE ANDERSEN
Kong Hans Kælder
Vingårdstræde 6, Copenhagen
At Kong Hans Kælder since 1996, he's also the poster boy for the Palaeolithic movement, launching Palæo – healthy fast food – in 2012.
Amass **286**...High end
Bror **287**...High end
Cafe Europa 1989 **287**.....................Breakfast
Geist **288**......................Regular neighbourhood
Noma **289**............................Local favourite
Obauer **604**........................Worth the travel
Pluto **290**..............................Late night
Pony **296**................................High end
Sáigón Quán **280**.........................Bargain
Sauvage **555**...................Wish I'd opened
Tantris **542**.....................Worth the travel

RUTH ROGERS
The River Café
Rainville Road, London
Upstate New York-born co-founder of the River Café, which she opened in West London with the now sadly deceased Rose Gray, in 1987.
L'Ami Louis **453**............................High end
Maroush **328**.............................Late night
Shake Shack **863**..............................Bargain
St. John Bar and Restaurant **362**............Local
favourite
Trattoria Da Laura **585**..........Wish I'd opened
Trattoria Gianni Franzi **585**....Worth the travel
The Wolseley **345**..............................Breakfast

NIKO ROMITO
Ristorante Reale
Contrada Santa Liberata, Castel di Sangro
Runs the two-Michelin-starred Ristorante Reale and his own school of the culinary arts in the Valley of Castel di Sangro in the Abruzzan mountains.
L'Atelier de Joël Robuchon Étoile **462**.....Wish
I'd opened
Ristorante Al Metrò **572**.....................Regular
neighbourhood
Taverna 58 **572**..................................Bargain
Taverna de li Caldora **572**........Local favourite

ANTHONY ROSE
Rose and Sons
176 Dupont Street, Toronto
Chef and co-owner of Toronto's Rose and Sons smokehouse diner and Big Crow barbeque joint, his first projects since he left The Drake Hotel.
Allen's **679**.................Regular neighbourhood
Cheese Boutique **680**..........................Bargain
Commisso Bros. & Racco Italian Bakery **685**...
Late night
Favourites Dining Room **684**............High end
House of Chan **685**..................Local favourite
Sky Ranch **686**...............................Breakfast
Vesta Lunch **678**..................Wish I'd opened

DANIEL ROSE
Spring
6 Rue Bailleul, Paris
Chicago-born Rose has seemingly done the impossible and gained widespread acclaim as an American cooking in Paris at his restaurant Spring.
Le Bal Café **471**...............................Breakfast
Midory **450**...................................Bargain
Pierre Gagnaire **463**........................High end
Le Relais de l'Entrecôte **463**...Wish I'd opened
Roscioli **584**.....................Worth the travel
La Tour de Montlhéry **451**................Late night

FABIO ROSSI
Ristorante Vite
Via Montepirolo 7, Cerasolo
Former chef of the Michelin-starred Acero Rosso, Rossi has continued to be a champion of local produce and traditions at current restaurant Vite.
L'Atelier de Joël Robuchon **459**..........Wish I'd
opened
Barrumba **578**...............................Late night
Le Calandre **599**...............................High end
El Celler de Can Roca **493**.....Worth the travel
Osteria Francescana **577**....................High end
Il Piastrino **578**.......................Local favourite
Rose & Crown **578**..........................Late night
Scaccianoia Caffè **578**......................Breakfast
Trattoria Da Savino **578**.....................Bargain

NIKOS ROUSSOS
Funky Gourmet
13 Paramithias Street, Athens
New York-trained Athens native returned home via a stint at elBulli to open avant-garde Funky Gourmet with co-chef Georgi-anna Hiliadaki in 2009, winning it a second Michelin star in 2014.
Aleria **628**...................Regular neighbourhood
Bras **436**...........................Worth the travel
El Celler de Can Roca **493**................High end
Gramercy Tavern **863**............Wish I'd opened
New Taste **628**................................Breakfast
Psomi & Alati **628**..............................Bargain

JULIEN ROYER
Jaan
Swissôtel, 2 Stamford Road, Singapore
The latest culinary sensation to man the helm at Singapore's legendary Jaan, Frenchman Royer trained under Michel Bras and Bernard Andrieux among others.
Bar-Roque Grill **238**........................Late night
Bras **436**.......................Wish I'd opened
Brasserie Gavroche **238**....................Regular
neighbourhood
Din Tai Fung **235**.....................Local favourite
Esquisse **211**......................Worth the travel
Shinji by Kanesaka **232**....................High end
Tiong Bahru Bakery **239**.....................Breakfast
Wee Nam Kee **235**.............................Bargain

GABRIEL RUCKER
Le Pigeon
738 East Burnside Street, Portland
Grew up in Napa, moved to Oregon in 2003, worked at Paley's Place and the Gotham Building Tavern. He opened Le Pigeon in 2006 and Little Bird in 2010.
Bunk Sandwiches **715**........................Bargain
Caves Madeleine **434**...........Worth the travel
Noisette **717**..................................High end
Paley's Place **718**...................Local favourite

ALEJANDRO RUIZ
Casa Oaxaca
Constitución 104, Oaxaca
Famous for his contemporary take on Oaxacan cuisine at Casa Oaxaca – expect to find grasshoppers on the menu alongside myriad Mexican moles.
Itanoni **881**...................................Breakfast
Mezquite **887**...............................Late night
Origen **888**.................Regular neighbourhood
Pitiona **888**....................................High end
Quintonil **884**.....................Worth the travel

BEN RUSSELL
Aria
1 Eagle Street, Brisbane
Former sous chef at Matt Moran's Aria, Sydney, he landed the head chef position at Aria, Brisbane (sister of the Sydney flagship) in 2009, delivering modern Australian fare to eager Brisbanites.
Alfredo's Pizzeria **74**...Regular neighbourhood
L'Atelier de Joël Robuchon **185**.......Worth the
travel
Esquire **75**.....................................High end
Lefty's Old Time Music Hall **75**............Wish I'd
opened
Miel Container **75**..............................Bargain
Pearl Café **76**.................................Breakfast
WaraWara Izakaya **77**......................Late night

ALFREDO RUSSO
Dolce Stil Novo
Piazza della Repubblica 4, Turin
Born in Turin, he opened Dolce Stil Novo in the Venaria Palace in 1990, having worked in many of Piedmont's best kitchens.

5-Cinco **556**	High end
5-Cinco **556**	Wish I'd opened
Astor Grill **147**	High end
Astor Grill **147**	Wish I'd opened
La Barrique **593**	Local favourite
Combal.Zero **593**	Local favourite
La Credenza **593**	Local favourite
Flower Drum **107**	Worth the travel
Le Jules Verne **460**	High end
Le Jules Verne **460**	Wish I'd opened
Mr & Mrs Bund **171**	High end
Mr & Mrs Bund **171**	Wish I'd opened
Vintage 1997 **594**	Local favourite

PATRICK RYAN
Port Fonda
4141 Pennsylvania Avenue, Kansas City
The brains behind gleaming gourmet Mexican Airsteam trailer, Port Fonda, ex-Frontera Grill Ryan went permanent in Westport, Kansas City in 2012.

Gates Bar-B-Q **783**	Local favourite
Genessee Royale **784**	Breakfast
Happy Gillis **784**	Wish I'd opened
Johnny Jo's Pizzeria **784**	Bargain
Longman & Eagle **828**	Worth the travel
The Rieger Grill & Exchange **785**	Regular neighbourhood
Rye **774**	High end
Town Topic **785**	Late night

HENRIQUE SÁ PESSOA
Alma
Calçada Marquês de Abrantes 92, Lisbon
Owner of Alma, gained experience in London and Sydney before returning to Portugal to work at Bairro Alto and Sheraton hotels.

100 Maneiras **534**	Wish I'd opened
Belcanto **535**	High end
Cervejaria Ramiro **532**	Regular neighbourhood
Estado Líquido **537**	Late night
Osteria Cucina di Amici **537**	Bargain
Restaurante DOC **528**	Worth the travel
Tartine **536**	Breakfast
Tasca da Esquina **535**	Local favourite

OLDŘICH SAHAJDÁK
La Degustation Bohême Bourgeoise
Haštalská 18, Prague
With the ambitious aim to 'introduce classic Czech cuisine to the world', Sahajdák is head chef and owner of the one-Michelin-starred La Degustation in Prague's Old Town.

Café Savoy **609**	Breakfast
In De Wulf **421**	Worth the travel
Krystal Mozaika Bistro **610**	Regular neighbourhood
Lokál **611**	Local favourite
Polévkárna **611**	Bargain
Sansho **612**	Late night
Sansho **612**	Wish I'd opened
Le Terroir **613**	High end

CHRIS SALANS
Mozaic
Jalan Raya Sanggingan, Ubud, Bali
French-American chef-owner of Ubud's Mozaic Restaurant, where he attracts wide acclaim for fusing classic Cordon Bleu training with Balinese flavours, and Mozaic Beach Club in Seminyak.

Café Batu Jimbar **240**	Breakfast
Ibu Oka **244**	Regular neighbourhood
Kura Kura **240**	High end
Mama San **240**	Local favourite
Ryoshi **243**	Wish I'd opened
Warung Kolega **244**	Bargain

MARA SALLES
Tordesilhas
Alameda Tietê 489, São Paulo
Partner and chef at Tordesilhas, her restaurant in São Paulo, she's been researching Brazilian food for over twenty years.

Arturito **926**	Wish I'd opened
D.O.M. Restaurante **921**	High end
Jardim de Napoli **920**	Local favourite
Jiyuu Sushi **925**	Regular neighbourhood
Padaria Juliet **924**	Breakfast
Quina do Futuro **913**	Worth the travel
Riviera Bar **922**	Late night
Sujinho **922**	Bargain

STEVE SAMSON
Sotto
9575 West Pico Boulevard, Los Angeles
Son of a Bolognese mother and American father, Samson runs Southern Italian-inspired Sotto (2010) in partnership with fellow chef Zach Pollack.

La Cocina de Doña Esthela **880**	Worth the travel
Daily Dose Café **732**	Breakfast
Kokekokko **735**	Regular neighbourhood
Manhattan Beach Post **736**	Local favourite
Pollo a la Brasa **734**	Bargain
Red Medicine **729**	Late night
Trois Mec **743**	Wish I'd opened
Urasawa **730**	High end

MARCUS SAMUELSSON
Red Rooster
310 Lenox Avenue, New York City
Ethiopian-born, Swedish-raised Samuelsson made his name at New York's Aquavit, opening Red Rooster in 2011, followed by Ginny's Supper Club and American Table Cafe and Bar.

Barbuto **854**	Local favourite
Le Bernardin **839**	High end
Empire Diner **859**	Late night
Forgtmenot **864**	Regular neighbourhood
Gramercy Tavern **863**	Wish I'd opened
Mathias Dahlgren **272**	Worth the travel
Minetta Tavern **853**	Late night
Patisserie des Ambassadors **838**	Breakfast
The Red Cat **860**	Local favourite
Sushi Park **742**	Worth the travel
Totto Ramen **842**	Bargain

PABLO SAN ROMÁN
D.O.
Hegel 406, Mexico City
Basque executive chef and co-founder of Denominación de Origen, aka 'D.O.', with a reputation for serving and promoting world-class Spanish cuisine.

Asian Bay **881**	Regular neighbourhood
Asian Bay **881**	Late night
El Cardenal **883**	Local favourite
Ojo de Agua **888**	Breakfast
Pitiona **888**	High end

JOSÉ SANTAELLA
Santaella
219 Calle Canals, San Juan
Chef and CEO of gourmet catering company, JSB Cooking Group, elBulli-trained Santaella opened his eponymous Puerto Rican restaurant, small-plates joint Santaella, in 2011.

Le Bernardin **839**	High end
BLT Steak **889**	Regular neighbourhood
El Coco de Luis **891**	Bargain
Employees Only **855**	Late night
Kasalta **892**	Breakfast
Momofuku Noodle Bar **851**	Wish I'd opened
Tickets **515**	Worth the travel

CÉSAR SANTOS
Oficina do Sabor
Rua do Amparo, Olinda
Renowned Brazilian chef opened Oficina do Sabor ('flavour workshop') in the Pernambuco hilltop town of Olinda in 1992, pairing French technique with local ingredients. Also runs Kaamo at Kenoa Resort.

Anjo Solto Creperia & Bar **912**	Late night
L'Auberge du Pont de Collonges **442**	Worth the travel
Geraldo **913**	Bargain
Leite **913**	Local favourite
Maison do Bomfim **912**	Regular neighbourhood
Paraíso Tropical **912**	Wish I'd opened
Parraxaxá **913**	Breakfast
Wiella Bistrô **913**	High end

DAVID SASEK
Coda
Tržiště 368–9, Prague
After prolonged stints at Prague's five-star hotels, and a brief sojourn in Ireland, Sasek took up the executive chef post at Coda, Prague, in 2007.

L'Atelier de Joël Robuchon **459**	Worth the travel
Bakeshop Praha **608**	Breakfast
Bistro Santinka **608**	Bargain
La Degustation Bohême Bourgeoise **609**	Local favourite
La Degustation Bohême Bourgeoise **609**	High end
Divinis **610**	Regular neighbourhood
Divinis **610**	Wish I'd opened
Kalina **610**	Regular neighbourhood
Malý Buddha **611**	Bargain
Sansho **612**	Regular neighbourhood
Sansho **612**	Wish I'd opened
Yamato **613**	Late night

STEVEN SATTERFIELD
Miller Union
999 Brady Avenue Northwest, Atlanta
Satterfield – a Georgia native – renounced his music career for the heat of the kitchen, rapidly rising through the ranks to become chef and co-owner of Atlanta's farm-to-table Miller Union.

Bacchanalia **769**	High end
Cardamom Hill **769**	Regular neighbourhood
The General Muir **770**	Breakfast
Gramercy Tavern **863**	Worth the travel
Octopus Bar **770**	Late night
Ria's Bluebird **771**	Local favourite
Sotto Sotto **771**	Regular neighbourhood
Swan Oyster Depot **753**	Wish I'd opened
Taqueria del Sol **771**	Bargain

GUY SAVOY
Restaurant Guy Savoy
18 Rue Troyon, Paris
Bourgogne-born, trained with the Troisgros brothers, Savoy opened his eponymous Paris flagship in 1980. Today he has five international outposts.

L'Ami Louis **453**	Local favourite
Atelier Crenn **750**	Worth the travel
Hostellerie du Port de Groslée **443**	Bargain
Pouic Pouic **457**	Late night
Relais Bernard Loiseau **434**	Regular neighbourhood
Roberta's **875**	Breakfast

JONATHON SAWYER
The Greenhouse Tavern
2038 East 4th Street, Cleveland
Worked at New York's Kitchen 22 and Parea, and returned to his hometown of Cleveland, subsequently opening four restaurants including flagship The Greenhouse Tavern.

Big Star **835**	Late night
Café Brioso **798**	Breakfast
Locanda Margon **597**	High end
Lolita **796**	Local favourite
Miega Korean Barbeque **797**	Bargain
Sushi Sho **221**	Worth the travel
Vero Pizza Napoletana **797**	Regular neighbourhood

KEVIN SBRAGA
Sbraga
440 South Broad Street, Philadelphia
Two years after opening his eponymous modern American restaurant in Philadelphia (2011), South Jersey-born Sbraga launched Southern-inspired The Fat Ham.

Avance **798**	High end
Broad Street Diner **799**	Breakfast
The Cypress Room **765**	Worth the travel
High Street on Market **799**	Wish I'd opened
Pho Ha **800**	Bargain
Pizzeria Stella **800**	Regular neighbourhood
Pub & Kitchen **800**	Late night
Santucci's Original Square Pizza **800**	Local favourite

EMANUELE SCARELLO
Agli Amici
Via Liguria 252, Udine
The fifth generation of his family to run Ristorante Agli Amici in Udine, which the Scarellos first opened back in 1887.

Birreria Gambrinus **580**	Late night
Al Cacciatore **579**	Local favourite
Caffetteria Torinese **580**	Breakfast
Concordia **580**	Bargain
Don Alfonso **574**	Worth the travel
Gostilna pri Lojzetu **616**	Regular neighbourhood
Trattoria Ai Ciodi **579**	Wish I'd opened
Da Vittoria **585**	High end

JESSE SCHENKER
Recette
328 West 12th Street, New York
Florida native, he opened Recette in New York's Greenwich Village in 2010, following his success with his Recette Private Dining.

Barbuto **854**	Regular neighbourhood
Bus Stop Cafe **854**	Breakfast
Gramercy Tavern **863**	Local favourite
The Pass & Provisions **809**	Worth the travel
Per Se **846**	High end
Sake Bar Hagi **842**	Bargain

THORSTEN SCHMIDT
Ruths Gourmet
Hans Ruths Vej 1, Skagen
Having opened Malling & Schmidt in central Denmark (2005), Schmidt – now head chef at Ruths Gourmet in Skagen – is described by René Redzepi as 'one of the pioneers within Nordic regional cuisine'.

Emmerys **282**	Breakfast
Geranium **296**	Worth the travel
Molskroen **282**	High end
Restaurant Et **281**	Regular neighbourhood
St. Pauls Apothek **281**	Late night

MICHAEL SCHWARTZ
Michael's Genuine Food & Drink
130 Northeast 40th Street, Miami
Owns Michael's Genuine Food & Drink, a Grand Cayman outpost, Harry's Pizzeria and The Cypress Room in Miami, and runs Restaurant Michael Schwartz at Miami's Raleigh Hotel.

Bestia **732**	Worth the travel
The Broken Shaker **767**	Late night
Enriqueta's Sandwich Shop **765**	Bargain
Japanese Market Sushi Deli **765**	Wish I'd opened
Joe's Stone Crab **767**	Local favourite
Jugofresh **768**	Breakfast
Macchialina **768**	Regular neighbourhood
NAOE **766**	High end

SHAUN SEARLEY
The Quality Chop House
88–94 Farringdon Road, London
After honing his skills at the Paternoster Chop House and Bistroteque, Searley assumed cooking duties at the seasonal, ingredient-led Quality Chop House in 2013.

El Celler de Can Roca **493**	Worth the travel
Duck & Waffle **358**	Late night
The Hand & Flowers **305**	High end
Kitchen Table **363**	Wish I'd opened
Pavilion **365**	Breakfast
Smokehouse **369**	Regular neighbourhood
St. John Bar and Restaurant **362**	Local favourite

MINDY SEGAL
Mindy's Hot Chocolate
1747 North Damen Avenue, Chicago
Pastry chef trained in Chicago, where she worked with Charlie Trotter, ahead of opening her dessert bar Hot Chocolate in 2005.

Arturo's Tacos 826	.....Regular neighbourhood
Au Cheval 832	Late night
Chicken Hut 826	Bargain
Longman & Eagle 828	Breakfast
Maurice Pastry Luncheonette 717	.....Wish I'd opened
Vivant 466	Worth the travel

TOM SELLERS
Restaurant Story
201 Tooley Street, London
Within months of opening Story, at age twenty-six, Sellers received his first Michelin star. The London-based culinary wunderkind trained under luminaries including Thomas Keller, René Redzepi and Tom Aikens.

Dinner by Heston Blumenthal 326	.....High end
The Garrison 354	Breakfast
José 354	Regular neighbourhood
Meat Liquor 328	Late night
Meat Liquor 328	Bargain
St. John Bar and Restaurant 362	Local favourite
Sushi Zo 731	Worth the travel

DIDEM ŞENOL TIRYAKIOĞLU
Lokanta Maya
Kemankeş Caddessi 35a, Istanbul
Trained at New York's French Culinary Institute, returning to Istanbul in 2010 to open Lokanta Maya, a bistro with a line in modern Turkish cooking, and Gram café.

Asador Etxebarri 479	Worth the travel
Dönerci Şahin Usta 639	Bargain
Kantin 638	Regular neighbourhood
Mikla 635	High end
Yeni Lokanta 637	Local favourite

KARAM SETHI
Trishna
15–17 Blandford Street, London
Runs Gymkhana and the British branch of the legendary Mumbai seafood specialist Trishna, having worked at the original outpost, New Delhi's Bukhara and at London's Zuma.

The Delaunay 337	Breakfast
Electric Diner 330	Wish I'd opened
Mary's Fish Camp 856	Worth the travel
Meat Liquor 328	Late night
Patty & Bun 329	Bargain
La Petite Maison 343	High end
Roka 364	Regular neighbourhood
Spuntino 351	Worth the travel
The Wolseley 345	Local favourite

ILYA SHALEV
Ragout
Bolshaya Gruzinskaya Ulitsa 69, Moscow
A rising star on Moscow's foodie scene, the Israeli chef and co-owner of Ragout restaurant spent eighteen years overseas, under the tutelage of Alain Senderens in Paris among others.

Delicatessen 623	Local favourite
The Ivy 338	Late night
Miznon 143	Regular neighbourhood
The Wolseley 345	Breakfast

ESTHER SHAM
Ta Pantry
8 Watson Road, Hong Kong
Raised in Los Angeles, staged in restaurants across France, she returned to her native Hong Kong to open Ta Pantry in 2008.

Ada 180	Bargain
Ping Kee 192	Breakfast
RyuGin Hong Kong 192	High end
Sushi Hiro 181	Regular neighbourhood
Tai Ping Koon 187	Local favourite
Tsui Wah 189	Local favourite

ALON SHAYA
Domenica
123 Baronne Street, New Orleans
Tel Aviv-born, Philadelphia-raised chef-partner at New Orleans's Domenica, the Italian restaurant peppered with Israeli-Jewish culinary influences which he opened with Octavio Mantilla and John Besh in 2009.

August 816	High end
Bacchanal 816	Late night
The Company Burger 822	Wish I'd opened
Le Croissant d'Or 818	Breakfast
Emeril's New Orleans 817	Local favourite
Ideal Market 820	Bargain
Tan Dinh 819	Regular neighbourhood
Willie Mae's Scotch House 821	Local favourite

ALAN SHEN
28 HuBin Road
28 Hubin Road, Hangzhou
Joined Hyatt Regency Hangzhou in 2005, working his way up to sous chef by 2008, and now tasked with management of the hotel's culinary operations.

Fat Aunt Stinky Tofu 162	Bargain
Gold Chino 162	High end
Grandma's Kitchen 162	Wish I'd opened
Hai Di Lao Hotpot 163	Late night
Krishna Yuan Hall 163	Regular neighbourhood
No.8 Downing Street 163	Local favourite
Zhi Wei Guan 163	Breakfast

SARAH PILNER & JASPER SHEN
Aviary
1733 Northeast Alberta Street, Portland
The pair of chefs – alongside Kat Whitehead – behind Portland's omni-cultural Aviary restaurant met while working at Michelin-starred New Nordic institution Aquavit.

Le Bernardin 839	High end
Boxer Ramen 714	Wish I'd opened
Grain & Gristle 715	Late night
El Nutri Taco 718	Bargain
Overlook Family Restaurant 718	Breakfast
Le Pigeon 719	Local favourite
Pho Hung 718	Regular neighbourhood
Swan Oyster Depot 753	Worth the travel

CHRIS SHEPHERD
Underbelly
1100 Westheimer Road, Houston
Ex-Brennan's chef Shepherd, inspired by the ethnic diversity of Houston, left boundary-pushing Catalan restaurant in 2012 to take his own pioneering route, serving 'New American Creole' at Underbelly.

Andrew Michael Italian Kitchen 803	.....Worth the travel
Brothers Taco House 808	Breakfast
Cafe TH 808	Bargain
HK Dim Sum 809	Regular neighbourhood
NoMad 843	High end
The Ordinary 802	Wish I'd opened
Pho Binh by Night 809	Late night
Reef 810	Local favourite

OLIVER JAMES SHERIDAN
Le Bistrot du Boulanger
42 Rue de Zurich, Strasbourg
British-born Sheridan runs the kitchen at Le Bistrot du Boulanger, owned by Strasbourg's legendary father-and-son bakers Patrick and Bruno Denil.

Auberge de la Nachtweid 428	.Local favourite
Binchstub 428	Late night
La Casserole 429	High end
La Cuiller à Pot 429	Wish I'd opened
Hofbräuhaus 541	Worth the travel
Moustique et Frelon 429	Bargain
Le Penjab 429	Regular neighbourhood
La Villa Schmidt 540	Breakfast

BRUCE SHERMAN

North Pond
2610 North Cannon Drive, Chicago
Chicagoan who has run North Pond since 1999. Formally trained in Paris, he spent four years in India where he consulted for regional palace hotels.

Il Buco **866**	Worth the travel
El Chorrito **831**	Late night
Coalfire Pizza **833**	Bargain
Furama **832**	Breakfast
Spoon Thai **828**	Bargain
The Wieners Circle **827**	Local favourite

JAY SHERWOOD

Amisfield Bistro
10 Lake Hayes Road, Queenstown
Head chef at winery restaurant Amisfield Bistro, Los Angeles-born Sherwood staged in Michelin-starred restaurants across the US and Europe before being coaxed to New Zealand.

Atlas Beer Café **121**	Wish I'd opened
Bella Cucina **122**	Regular neighbourhood
The Bunker **122**	High end
Kappa Sushi Cafe **122**	Bargain
No5 Church Lane **122**	Late night
Riverstone Kitchen **121**	Worth the travel
Vudu Café & Larder **123**	Breakfast

MASATO SHIMIZU

15 East
15 East 15th Street, New York City
Following a seven-year apprenticeship at Sukeroku in Tokyo, he moved to New York where, after four years at Jewel Bako, he opened 15 East.

ABC Kitchen **871**	Wish I'd opened
Blue Hill at Stone Barns **790**	Local favourite
Il Buco **866**	Regular neighbourhood
Congee Village **864**	Bargain
Kunjip **841**	Late night
Panya **851**	Breakfast
Per Se **846**	High end

HIDEKI SHIMOGUCHI

Chikurin
21 Renge Uji, Kyoto
Trained at Kyoto's Kikunoi, and worked under his father at kaiseki restaurant Chikurin for six years. Handed the mantle of Chikurin's sister restaurant, Byodoin Omotesando Chikurin, in 2003.

Shuhaku **202**	Regular neighbourhood

JON SHOOK

Animal
435 North Fairfax Avenue, Los Angeles
Co-owner of Los Angeles's much-lauded Animal, Son of a Gun and Trois Mec with Vinny Dotolo. The 'Two Dudes' also run Caramelized Productions catering business.

The Apple Pan **743**	Late night
Ed's Coffee Shop **740**	Bargain
Fountain Coffee Room **729**	Breakfast
Matsuhisa Restaurant **729**	Regular neighbourhood
Mélisse **737**	High end
Del Posto **860**	Worth the travel
South Beverly Grill **730**	Wish I'd opened
Spago **730**	Local favourite

TIM SIADATAN

Trullo
300–302 St Paul's Road, London
Star graduate of the 2002 first-year intake of Jamie Oliver's Fifteen, he trained further at Moro and St. John, before opening Trullo in 2010.

Blue Hill at Stone Barns **790**	Worth the travel
Le Coq **368**	Late night
Le Coq **368**	Bargain
Herman Ze German **374**	Wish I'd opened
Maison d'être **368**	Breakfast
Moro **360**	Local favourite
The River Café **325**	High end
St. John Bread & Wine **374**	Regular neighbourhood

GEIR SKEIE

Brygga 11
Brygga 11, Sandefjord
Norwegian winner of the 2008 Bocuse d'Or and 2009 Bocuse d'Or world final, he worked at Mathuset Midtåsen Solvold before opening Brygga 11 restaurants in Sandefjord (2010) and Stord (2013).

Conradis **261**	Regular neighbourhood
The Elm **873**	Wish I'd opened
The French Laundry **709**	Worth the travel
Koka **266**	High end
Mathias Dahlgren **272**	High end

BRIAN SKINNER

The Acorn
3995 Main Street, Vancouver
Following spells at Noma and London's Viajante and Sketch, Skinner returned to Vancouver, opening The Acorn in 2012, drawing in carnivores and vegetarians alike for his award-winning vegetable-based cuisine.

Burdock & Co. **672**	High end
Hawkers Delight Deli **673**	Regular neighbourhood
The Juice Truck **670**	Wish I'd opened
The Naam **672**	Local favourite
Noma **289**	Worth the travel
Peaceful Restaurant **669**	Bargain
Slickity Jim's Chat 'n' Chew **673**	Breakfast

BEVAN SMITH

Riverstone Kitchen
1431 State Highway 1, Oamaru
New Zealander who in 2006 opened Riverstone Kitchen on his parents' North Otago farm, following spells in Brisbane and London.

Amisfield Bistro **121**	Local favourite
Clooney **130**	High end
Coda **106**	Late night
Depot Eatery **128**	Breakfast
Depot Eatery **128**	Bargain
Federal Diner **123**	Breakfast
The French Café **129**	High end
Midori **123**	Regular neighbourhood
MoVida Bar De Tapas Y Vino **109**	Worth the travel
Pegasus Bay **119**	Local favourite
Sean's Panorama **86**	Wish I'd opened

MICHAEL SMITH

The Three Chimneys
1 Colbost, Isle of Skye
A true Highlander who started his career in Inverness, Smith trained in London before returning north to run the much-garlanded Three Chimneys on the Isle of Skye.

Andrew Fairlie **379**	High end
Ballinluig Motor Grill **379**	Bargain
The Burger Joint **840**	Worth the travel
Citation Taverne & Restaurant **379**	Breakfast
Loch Bay **377**	Local favourite
Moro **360**	Wish I'd opened
Au Pied de Cochon **450**	Late night
Rocpool **377**	Regular neighbourhood

CLARE SMYTH

Restaurant Gordon Ramsay
68 Royal Hospital Road, London
Northern Irish, she worked at The Fat Duck, The Waterside Inn, Gidleigh Park and The French Laundry, before joining Restaurant Gordon Ramsay in 2002 and becoming chef-patron in 2013.

Alain Ducasse **339**	High end
Bar Boulud **326**	Late night
El Celler de Can Roca **493**	Worth the travel
Le Gavroche **341**	Wish I'd opened
Hibiscus **342**	Worth the travel
Scott's **344**	Regular neighbourhood
Scott's **344**	Local favourite
Tom's Kitchen **322**	Breakfast
Zucca **355**	Bargain

VÍTOR SOBRAL

Tasca da Esquina
Rua Domingos Sequeira 41c, Lisbon
Portuguese chef Sobral made his name
at 1990s Lisbon hotspot Alcantara before
relaunching Terreiro do Paço in 2004. He
opened Tasca Da Esquina in Lisbon in 2009
and a São Paulo branch followed in 2012.
100 Maneiras 534......Regular neighbourhood
Belcanto 535...............Regular neighbourhood
Brasil a gosto 923....................Local favourite
Kinoshita 925.........................Worth the travel
Restaurante Amadeus 921.......Local favourite
Restaurante Marcel 924..........Local favourite
Solar dos Presuntos 533........Local favourite

MICHAEL SOLOMONOV

Zahav
237 Saint James Place, Philadelphia
James Beard Award-winning chef and owner
of Philadelphia's acclaimed Zahav, serving
contemporary Israeli food since 2008.
Cafe 48 142..........................Worth the travel
Café Soho 799.............................Late night
The Farm and Fisherman 799...Local favourite
High Street on Market 799............Breakfast
Pho 75 799.................Regular neighbourhood
Sbraga 800.....................................Bargain
Vetri 800..High end

BJORN SOMLO

Nudel
37 Church Street, Lenox
A passionate locavore who bypassed formal
training to learn on the job in New Orleans
and New York, opening Nudel in Lenox,
Massachusetts, in 2009.
Area Four 777.......................Worth the travel
Ayelada 779.....................................Bargain
Community Table 762.............Wish I'd opened
CrossRoads Food Shop 789................Regular
                                          neighbourhood
Spoon 778.....................................Breakfast

HIRO SONE

Ame
689 Mission Street, San Francisco
His big break came at Wolfgang Puck's Spago
in Tokyo, which eventually brought him to the
Hollywood original. Subsequently opened
Terra in Napa and Ame in San Francisco.
Asador Etxebarri 479......................High end
Hagakure 219.................................Bargain
Hale Kai's 215................................Late night
Inoue Ramen 211............................Bargain
Iyasare 701.........................Worth the travel
Kitcho Arashiyama Honten 204.........High end
Lers Ros Thai 758...........................Late night
Manresa 703.......................Worth the travel
Miyagino 204...............................Breakfast
Osteria da Gemma 593..........Wish I'd opened
Pho Ao Sen 706..............................Bargain
RyuGin 216......................Local favourite
RyuGin 216....................................High end
Sangoan 217..............Regular neighbourhood
Sushi Takumi Masa 217....................High end

BEN SPALDING

Creative Belly Limited
Ran Simon Rogan's two-year London pop-up
Roganic in 2011, and after a brief stint at
John Salt, launched Creative Belly events,
offering experimental pop-up ventures
around the UK.
L'Autre Pied 327.....................Local favourite
The Ledbury 331......................Local favourite
Raj Bari 310................Regular neighbourhood
Restaurang 28 + 267............Worth the travel
Restaurant Gordon Ramsay 322.......High end
Street Feast 318............................Late night

SUSAN SPICER

Bayona
430 Dauphine Street, New Orleans
The grande dame of the New Orleans res-
taurant scene, Spicer began her career with
Daniel Bonnot at Louis XVI in 1979, launching
Bayona in 1990 and Mondo in 2010.
The Barn 804......................Worth the travel
Brigtsen's 821.......................Local favourite
Clancy's 822.........................Local favourite
Cochon Butcher 817......................Breakfast
La Condesa 805...................Wish I'd opened
El Crucero 504......................Worth the travel
Domenica 817.............Regular neighbourhood
Lost Love Lounge 820.....................Late night
Zimmer's Seafood 819......................Bargain

RYAN SQUIRES

Esquire
145 Eagle Street, Brisbane
Staged at Noma, elBulli and Per Se, returning
to Brisbane where he caused a stir with his
experimental cuisine at Urbane and Buffalo
Club, opening degustation-only restaurant
Esquire in 2011.
Beccofino 74.........................Local favourite
Harajuku Gyoza 75..........................Late night
Mizu 75.......................Regular neighbourhood
Pearl Café 76................................Breakfast
Taro's Ramen & Café 77....................Bargain
Town Restaurant and Café 74...............Worth
                                          the travel

LJUBOMIR STANISIC

100 Maneiras
Rua do Teixeira 35, Lisbon
Born in Bosnia, he moved Portuguese food
into avant-garde territory with his 100
Maneiras restaurants in Cascais.
La Boulangerie by Stef 537...........Breakfast
Café de São Bento 534......................Late night
Cervejaria Ramiro 532..............Local favourite
Les Hautes Roches 434.......Worth the travel
Jesus é Goês 533............................Bargain
Noma 289............................Worth the travel
Ocean 524..High end
Solar dos Presuntos 533.........Local favourite
Tasca da Esquina 535.Regular neighbourhood

ADAM STOKES

Adam's
21a Bennett's Hill, Birmingham
Success has come quickly for Lincolnshire-
born Stokes: he gained his first Michelin star
at twenty-nine, and his eponymous restau-
rant in Birmingham was awarded the same
honour just six months after opening.
Barrafina 346....................Wish I'd opened
The Breakfast Club 347.....................Breakfast
El Celler de Can Roca 493......Worth the travel
Duck & Waffle 358............................Late night
The Ledbury 331.............................High end
The Malt Shovel 314...Regular neighbourhood
Simpsons 315........................Local favourite
Wee Hurrie 377................................Bargain

CRAIG STOLL
Delfina Restaurant
3621 18th Street, San Francisco
A native New Yorker with a quartet of neighbourhood Italians in San Francisco: Delfina, two Pizzeria Delfinas and Locanda.
Chez Panisse **701**...............................High end
Foreign Cinema **751**....Regular neighbourhood
Nopa **754**...Late night
Swan Oyster Depot **753**...........Local favourite
Tartine Bakery **752**..........................Breakfast
Wing Lee Bakery **749**...........................Bargain
The Walrus and the Carpenter **725**......Worth the travel
Yuet Lee **754**.......................................Late night
Zuni Café **749**............Regular neighbourhood
Zuni Café **749**......................Local favourite

ETHAN STOWELL
How to Cook a Wolf
2208 Queen Anne Avenue North, Seattle
Seattle chef-restaurateur whose highly acclaimed and growing empire of establishments include Tavolàta, How to Cook a Wolf, Anchovies & Olives, Bar Cotto, and Mkt.
Ba Bar **720**...Late night
Café Besalu **720**...............................Breakfast
Canlis **721**...High end
Dick's Drive-In **722**..............................Bargain
Green Leaf **722**..........Regular neighbourhood
Ristorante Laganà **583**..........Worth the travel
Shiro's **724**...............................Local favourite

STEPHEN STRYJEWSKI
Cochon
930 Tchoupitoulas Street, New Orleans
Launched Cochon in partnership with Donald Link in 2006, followed by Cochon Butcher (2009) and Cochon Lafayette (2011).
La Boca **817**.......................................Late nigh
Commander's Palace **819**................Breakfast
The Company Burger **822**...................Regular neighbourhood
The Company Burger **822**...................Bargain
Momofuku Noodle Bar **851**....Wish I'd opened
Parador La Huella **929**..........Worth the travel
Root **817**...Late night
Torrisi Italian Specialties **868**..............Worth the travel

PEDRO SUBIJANA
Akelarre
Paseo Padre Orcoloaga 56, San Sebastián
One of the founding fathers of New Basque cooking. After training in Madrid, he opened Akelarre in his native San Sebastián in 1975.
Arzak **483**..................Regular neighbourhood
Arzak **483**..............................Wish I'd opened
Barkaiztegi **484**......................Local favourite
Bernardo Etxea **485**..............................High end
Calonge Sagardotegia **486**......Local favourite
The Fat Duck **304**..............Worth the travel
Gandarias **487**................................Late night
Kaia Kaipe **481**.....................................High end
Martín Berasategui **482**...................Regular neighbourhood
Martín Berasategui **482**.......Wish I'd opened
Mugaritz **480**.............Regular neighbourhood
Mugaritz **480**.......................Wish I'd opened
Quique Dacosta Restaurante **505**.........Worth the travel
Restaurante Combarro **502**...............High end
Rias de Galicia **517**............................High end
Zuberoa **482**...............Regular neighbourhood
Zuberoa **482**......................Wish I'd opened

ROBERTA SUDBRACK
Roberta Sudbrack
Rua Lineu Paula Machado 916, Rio de Janeiro
Self-taught, she stood behind the stove at Brazil's presidential palace before opening her Rio restaurant in 2005. In 2012, she designed menus for Brazil's Olympic team.
Bras **436**..........................Worth the travel
Braseiro da Gávea **915**...........Local favourite
Garzón **929**.........................Wish I'd opened
Gepetto **915**...Bargain
Jobi **916**..Late night
Olympe **916**..High end
Osteria la Torre **592**.............Worth the travel
L'Ourson qui Boit **444**.........Worth the travel
Padaria Bar Confeitaria Rio Lisboa **916**..........Breakfast
Pousada da Alcobaça **914**...................Regular neighbourhood
Remanso do Bosque **912**......Worth the travel
The River Café **325**..............Worth the travel

MARK SULLIVAN
Spruce
3640 Sacramento Street, San Francisco
Born and raised around San Francisco, Sullivan made his name at 42 Degrees and PlumpJack Squaw Valley. Now chef-partner at Spruce and The Village Pub where the agenda is 'field-to-fork'.
Boulette's Larder **747**.......................Breakfast
Chez Panisse **701**...................Local favourite
Hard Knox Cafe **746**...........................Bargain
Marea **841**.........................Worth the travel
Penrose **705**.......................Wish I'd opened
Quince **747**...High end
Trick Dog **753**...................................Late night
Zuni Café **749**............Regular neighbourhood

BJØRN SVENSSON
Oscarsgate
Inngang Pilestredet 63, Oslo
Started out making pizzas in his Swedish hometown before training at elBulli, Gordon Ramsay and Bagatelle. Has since won plaudits at the pocket-sized Oscarsgate.
Åpent Bakeri **258**...............................Breakfast
Curry & Ketchup **259**...........................Bargain
Grill's Ville **259**..........Regular neighbourhood
Noma **289**........................Worth the travel
Oro **260**...High end
Pjoltergeist **260**................................Late night

AGNAR SVERRISSON
Texture
34 Portman Street, London
Born in Iceland, he worked under Marcus Wareing and Raymond Blanc before launching Texture in 2007.
3 Frakkar **252**.......................Local favourite
Asador Etxebarri **479**...........Worth the travel
Busaba Eathai **347**.............................Bargain
CUT at 45 Park Lane **340**................Breakfast
Hakkasan **342**.............Regular neighbourhood
Hakkasan **342**...................................Late night
Le Manoir aux Quat'Saisons **312**......High end
Zuma **327**.............................Wish I'd opened

JAMES SYHABOUT
Commis
3859 Piedmont Avenue, Oakland
With Manresa, The Fat Duck, Mugaritz and elBulli on his résumé, Thailand-born, California-raised Syhabout became Oakland's only Michelin-starred chef when he launched Commis in 2010.
L'Arpège **458**.........................Worth the travel
Brown Sugar Kitchen **704**........Local favourite
Camino **704**..Breakfast
Penrose **705**.......................Wish I'd opened
Pho Ao Sen **706**...........Regular neighbourhood
Saison **756**...High end

LUIGI TAGLIENTI

Trussardi alla Scala
Piazza della Scala 5, Milan
A defender of Italy's gastronomic culture
and a chef who considers Carlo Cracco his
mentor, Taglienti won his current restaurant
Trussardi alla Scala a Michelin star within
a year.

Antica Trattoria del Gallo **587**.............Regular
neighbourhood
Aromando Bistrot **587**......................Bargain
Café Trussardi **587**.........................Late night
Dal Pescatore **589**..............Worth the travel
Ristorante Cracco **588**.............Local favourite
Ristorante Gastronomico **588**...........High end
Ristorante Giacomo Arengario **588**..Breakfast

TAKUJI TAKAHASHI

Kinobu
416 Iwatoyama-cho, Kyoto
Declared one of Japan's best chefs, Takahashi is the third-generation chef-owner at
Kinobu, a Kyoto kaiseki fixture since 1935.

Chuuka Dining Kyojyuzen **201**..........Late night
Hisata **215**........................Worth the travel
Housen **203**...............................Bargain
Hyotei **203**.........................Local favourite
Inoda Coffee **203**........................Breakfast
Koudaijidoi **202**.................Wish I'd opened
Maison Troisgros **445**............Worth the travel
Shinme **202**...............Regular neighbourhood
Shofukuro **205**..............................High end

SAMI TALLBERG

Following a decade in some of the world's
most renowned kitchens, Tallberg – an
expert on wild food – returned to Helsinki to
consult and sell wild plants to Finland's finest
restaurants.

Babel **649**......................Wish I'd opened
Carelia **298**............Regular neighbourhood
Dishoom Shoreditch **371**....................Regular
neighbourhood
Fafa's **299**................................Late night
Fäviken Magasinet **261**....................High end
Gran Delicato **299**........................Breakfast
Kivukoni Fish Market **646**......Worth the travel
Kosmos **300**........................Local favourite
Relæ **293**..................................Bargain

SAMI TAMIMI

Ottolenghi
287 Upper Street, London
Jerusalem-born Tamimi moved to London in
1997 and ran the kitchen at Baker & Spice
before joining Yotam Ottolenghi in 2002 to set
up their widely acclaimed deli chain.

Abu Zaad **332**...............................Bargain
Ducksoup **348**...........Regular neighbourhood
Honey & Co. **363**..................Wish I'd opened
KaoSarn **357**..............................Late night
NoMad **843**........................Worth the travel
The River Café **325**........................High end
Sushi Bar Makoto **323**.............Local favourite
The Wolseley **345**.........................Breakfast

ARI TAYMOR

Alma Restaurant
952 South Broadway, Los Angeles
Californian-born chef and co-owner of Los
Angeles's Alma Restaurant, which started
life as an ambitious pop-up in 2012. Taymor's
resume includes flour + water and Bar
Tartine.

Le Chateaubriand **466**..........Worth the travel
Intelligentsia Coffee **737**................Breakfast
La Isla Bonita Taco Truck **739**.............Bargain
Lucques **740**.......................Local favourite
Manresa **703**.....................Wish I'd opened
Naturewell **738**..........................Breakfast
Night + Market **740**...Regular neighbourhood
Pizzeria Mozza **741**.......................Late night
Saison **756**................................High end

PETER TEMPELHOFF

The Greenhouse
93 Brommersvlei Road, Cape Town
Launched London diner Automat in 2005,
taking his 'progressive South African' cuisine
back to his native Cape Town in 2006 to
oversee six restaurants within the Relais &
Chateaux hotel group.

Borruso's **646**..............................Bargain
La Colombe **647**....................Local favourite
Overture **651**.....................Worth the travel
Pirates Steakhouse and Pub **648**.....Late night
Superette **648**............................Breakfast
The Tasting Room **651**.......Wish I'd opened
The Test Kitchen **649**.....................High end
Willoughby & Co. **649**.Regular neighbourhood

PEKKA TERÄVÄ

Olo
Pohjoisesplanadi 5, Helsinki
Finn who cooked at Stockholm's Edsbacka
Krog and the Helsinki institution that is
G.W. Sundmans. Champions Modern Nordic
cooking at Olo.

Alain Ducasse au Plaza Athénée **462** High end
L'Atelier de Joël Robuchon Étoile **462**.....Wish
I'd opened
Klaus K Breakfast & Brunch **299**.....Breakfast
Mami **297**.................................Bargain
Michel Bras TOYA Japon **198**.Worth the travel
Trattoria Rivoletto **301**....................Regular
neighbourhood

GIULIO TERRINONI

Acquolina Hostaria
Via Antonio Serra 60, Rome
The traditional food of Lazio is in his blood:
his family ran a restaurant in Fiuggi and even
at the high-end Acquolina the influence of
Roman classics can still be seen.

L'Angolo d'Abruzzo **572**.........Wish I'd opened
Il Convivio Troiani **581**.............Local favourite
All'Oro **580**................................High end
Osteria Francescana **577**......Worth the travel
Ristorante Galleria **582**....................Bargain
Splendor Parthenopes **584**...........Breakfast
Tree Bar **584**..............................Late night
Urbana 47 **584**..........Regular neighbourhood

NAREN THIMMAIAH

Karavalli
66 Residency Road, Bangalore
Hailing from the Coorg district of southwest
India, TV favourite Thimmaiah has been
the face of the iconic Bangalore restaurant
Karavalli for over twenty years.

Café Noir **152**............Regular neighbourhood
Egg Factory **152**..........................Breakfast
Foodhall **153**..............................Bargain
Iggy's **236**.................................High end
Imperial **153**..............................Late night
Le Moulin de Connelles **446**...Worth the travel
MTR – Mavalli Tiffin Rooms **153**..............Local
favourite
Olive Beach **153**.................Wish I'd opened
Toit **154**...............Regular neighbourhood

KEVIN THORNTON
Thornton's Restaurant
The Fitzwilliam Hotel, Dublin
From County Tipperary, described as 'the great philosopher of Irish food', opened Thornton's in 1995, before transferring his eponymous restaurant to Dublin's Fitzwilliam Hotel in 2002.

Avoca Food Market and Salt Café **387**	Regular neighbourhood	
La Bicyclette **702**	Breakfast	
Eataly **862**	Wish I'd opened	
Kai Café + Restaurant **388**	Bargain	
Osteria Mozza **741**	Worth the travel	
The Trocadero **387**	Local favourite	
Vila Joya **524**	High end	
Vintage Cocktail Club **387**	Late night	

JET TILA
Kuma Snow Cream
3735 Spring Mountain Road, Las Vegas
TV personality and founder of The Charleston and Modern Asian Kitchen chain, appointed Culinary Ambassador of Thai Cuisine in 2013. Tila grew up in his family's restaurant kitchens in Los Angeles.

Alinea **827**	Worth the travel
Cooks County **739**	Breakfast
Father's Office **736**	Wish I'd opened
Lawry's The Prime Rib Beverly Hills **729**	Local favourite
Pa Ord Noodle **733**	Bargain
Providence **741**	High end
Ruen Pair **735**	Late night
Yai Restaurant **734**	Regular neighbourhood

BEN TISH
Salt Yard
54 Goodge Street, London
Launched London tapas concern Salt Yard in 2006. In 2008 he became responsible for overseeing the growing Salt Yard Group, whose latest restaurant is London's Ember Yard.

Antepliler **368**	Regular neighbourhood
Berners Tavern **362**	Wish I'd opened
Bistrotheque **355**	Breakfast
Brasserie Zédel **346**	Late night
Delhi Grill **368**	Bargain
J Sheekey **338**	High end
Rules **338**	Local favourite
Il Salviatino **598**	Worth the travel

HIDEKAZU TOJO
Tojo's
1133 Broadway West, Vancouver
Widely credited as the inventor of the California roll, Japanese-born sushi chef Tojo studied in Osaka and moved to Vancouver in 1971, opening his namesake restaurant in 1988.

Bin 941 **668**	Late night
Cioppino's Mediterranean Grill **674**	Regular neighbourhood
Cioppino's Mediterranean Grill **674**	Local favourite
Cioppino's Mediterranean Grill **674**	High end
Marulilu Cafe **673**	Bargain

STEPHEN TOMAN
OX
1 Oxford Street, Belfast
Belfast-born Toman opened OX in 2013 with long-standing friend Alain Kerloc'h, whom he met while working at L'Arpège in Paris.

Amass **286**	Wish I'd opened
L'Arpège **458**	High end
Coppi **381**	Regular neighbourhood
Howard Street **381**	Bargain
Little Italy **381**	Late night
Rayanne House **383**	Breakfast
Relæ **293**	Worth the travel
Tedfords **383**	Local favourite

NEIL ANTHONY TOMES
Alfie's by KEE
10 Chater Road, Central, Hong Kong
Seventeen years cooking across Asia and the Caribbean put Tomes in a great position to oversee Alfie's by KEE.

8½ Otto e Mezzo Bombana **182**	High end
Can-teen **183**	Regular neighbourhood
Fernando's **172**	Worth the travel
Lei Garden **185**	Local favourite
Maranui Café **125**	Worth the travel
Rōnin **186**	Wish I'd opened
Sushi Toku **192**	High end
Yardbird **188**	Wish I'd opened

MITCH TONKS
The Seahorse
5 South Embankment, Dartmouth
Fishmonger turned restaurateur who runs Bristol's RockFish Grill & Seafood Market, The Seahorse and RockFish Seafood in Dartmouth and Plymouth.

Cafe Alf Resco **307**	Breakfast
Crab Shack **307**	Local favourite
Mayflower **305**	Regular neighbourhood
La Petite Maison **343**	Wish I'd opened
La Pineta **599**	Worth the travel
Rasa Sayang **337**	Bargain
Zuma **327**	High end

MICHAEL TOSCANO
Perla
24 Minetta Lane, New York City
Executive chef and co-owner of Perla, Montmartre and Jeffrey's Grocery. Born and raised in Texas, he honed his skills at Mario Batali's Babbo and Manzo.

Le Bernardin **839**	High end
Carnegie Deli **840**	Local favourite
Fifteen **371**	Wish I'd opened
Guido Ristorante **593**	Worth the travel
Per Se **846**	High end
Saigon Shack **853**	Regular neighbourhood
Taqueria Coatzingo **877**	Late night

CHRISTINA TOSI
Momofuku Milk Bar
251 East 13th Street, New York City
Her collaboration with David Chang began in 2009. There are now five New York branches.

Balthazar **868**	Breakfast
The Brooklyn Star **872**	Late night
Caracas Arepa Bar **848**	Bargain
Crif Dogs **848**	Late night
Fōnuts **740**	Wish I'd opened
The Meatball Shop **856**	Late night
Peking Duck House **861**	Bargain
Pies 'n' Thighs **875**	Wish I'd opened
Del Posto **860**	High end
Roberta's **875**	Local favourite
Son of a Gun **742**	Worth the travel
Veselka **852**	Late night

FERNANDO TROCCA
Sucre
Sucre 676, Buenos Aires
Chef-owner at Sucre in northern Buenos Aires, Trocca also overseas the menu for the London-based Argentinean restaurant group, Gaucho Grill.

L'Arpège **458**	High end
Camino **704**	Wish I'd opened
El Cuartito **941**	Late night
La Docena **886**	Bargain
Hong Kong Style **934**	Regular neighbourhood
El Obrero **934**	Local favourite
Tartine Bakery **752**	Breakfast
Varouj **140**	Worth the travel

CLAUDE & THOMAS TROISGROS
Olympe
Rua Curtódio Serrão 62, Rio de Janeiro
Born into a French culinary dynasty, father Claude and his son Thomas settled in Rio, and now run four fine-dining restaurants: flagship Olympe (1978), 66 Bistro, CT Brasserie and CT Boucherie.

Aconchego Carioca **914**	Regular neighbourhood
La Bicyclette **914**	Breakfast
Bira de Guaratiba **915**	Local favourite
Noma **289**	Worth the travel
Quiosque do Português Lagoon **916**	Late night
Roberta Sudbrack **917**	High end

MICHEL TROISGROS
Maison Troisgros
Place Jean Troisgros, Roanne
In 1983 he restored Maison Troisgros, the legendary restaurant made famous by his father and uncle. Has since opened in Paris, Moscow and Tokyo.

Aux Anges 445...........Regular neighbourhood
L'Astrance 469...................Worth the travel
Le Coquillage 433.................Wish I'd opened
Gravelier 430.................................Bargain
La Grenouillère 437.............Local favourite
La Maison de l'Aubrac 463.............Late night
Momofuku Noodle Bar 851....Worth the travel
Zuni Café 749.....................Worth the travel

HADLEIGH TROY
Restaurant Amusé
64 Bronte Street, Perth
Essex-born Troy trained in Perth, Melbourne and London, including stints at London's The Greenhouse and La Noisette, opening Perth's Amusé in 2007.

Ace Pizza 82...............Regular neighbourhood
Bread in Common 82....................Breakfast
Burnt Ends 238....................Worth the travel
Commis 705..........................Worth the travel
Divido 82..Bargain
flour + water 751................Wish I'd opened
Lalla Rookh 83............Regular neighbourhood
Per Se 846......................................High end
Print Hall 83......................Local favourite
Restaurant André 239......................High end
Uncle Billy's 83.............................Late night

ROBERT TRZÓPEK
Previously executive chef at Warsaw's Westin Hotel and Tamka 43, and one-time apprentice at Noma and elBulli, Polish chef Trzópek co-created Harvest (2013).

Bar Mleczny Złota Kurka 613.............Bargain
Butchery & Wine 613.............Local favourite
Concept 13 613.........Regular neighbourhood
Concept 13 613.....................Worth the travel
Meta 614......................................Late night
Metamorfoza 615.................Worth the travel
Nolita 614...........................Worth the travel
Przegryź 614.................................Breakfast

MITSUHARU TSUMURA
Maido
Calle San Martín 399, Lima
Opened celebrated Maido in Lima, serving Japanese-Peruvian fusion cuisine (known as Nikkei), in 2009, having completed culinary studies in Rhode Island and training in Osaka, Japan.

Antigua Taberna Queirolo 906..Local favourite
Azurmendi 482...................Worth the travel
Central 906...................................High end
Fiesta 907.................Regular neighbourhood
La Pava 908...................................Late night
Al Toke Pez 909..............................Bargain

BRAD TURLEY
Goga
1 Yueyang Lu, Shanghai
Californian who in 2010 opened Goga, his compact sixteen-seat Cali-Asian concern, following up with Hai by Goga. Previously worked with Roy Yamaguchi and Floyd Cardoz at New York's Tabla.

100 Century Avenue 170..........Local favourite
Asador Etxebarri 479............Worth the travel
Cha's 168.......................................Late night
Fifty 8° Grill 170........Regular neighbourhood
Grand Brasserie 170...................Breakfast
Roy's 711.........................Wish I'd opened
Tock's 171.................Regular neighbourhood
Ultraviolet 166...............................High end

MICHAEL TUSK
Quince
470 Pacific Avenue, San Francisco
After stints at Chez Panisse and Oliveto, he opened Quince in 2003, with an Italian approach to Northern California's larder, and spin-off Cotogna in 2010.

b. Patisserie 755..........................Breakfast
Chez Panisse 701.................Local favourite
Manresa 703..................................High end
Nopa 754.......................................Late night
Piazza Duomo 591.............Worth the travel
Sightglass 756............................Breakfast
Yank Sing 757...............................Bargain
Zuni Café 749............Regular neighbourhood

GENÇAY ÜÇOK
Meze by Lemon Tree
Meşrutiyet Caddesi 83b, Istanbul
Owns and cooks at Istanbul's Meze by Lemon Tree, a colourful and accomplished modern meyhane, opened in 2010.

Beyti 634.........................Wish I'd opened
Dönerci Şahin Usta 639.....................Bargain
Kale Cafe 639..............................Breakfast
Kanaat Lokantasi 640..............Local favourite
Selçuk Köftecisi 630.............Worth the travel
Seyhmuz Kebab Restaurant 640........Regular
                                       neighbourhood
Sunset Grill & Bar 634...................High end
Tarihi Haliç İşkembecisi 636...........Late night

NAOYA UENO
Gensai
4-16-14 Nakayamate-dori, Kobe
Born in Osaka, he grew up watching his father, Suzo Ueno, cook at Naniwa Kappou Kigawa. Trained further at Kyoto's Kikunoi. Opened Gensai in 2004.

Anonyme 199................Regular neighbourhood
Cafe Bar Kobecco 199.....................Breakfast
Dining Okano 199............................Bargain
Hirasansou 206...................Worth the travel
Ittetsu Ramen 199...........................Bargain
Kikusuizushi Nishimise 199...............High end
NIKU Specialite Macra 200.............Late night
Pizzeria Azzurri 200.........................Bargain
Ca Sento 200.......................Local favourite
Tsukune Ichigo 237...............Worth the travel
Uetsuki 200................Regular neighbourhood

MAURO ULIASSI
Uliassi
Banchina di Levante 6, Senigallia
A former catering-school teacher, Uliassi opened his eponymous restaurant in 1990, whose startling modern Italian food has since seen it win two Michelin stars.

Atlantic Grill 843.................Worth the travel
Lab 590...Late night
Osteria Francescana 577...................High end
Pagaia 591.................Regular neighbourhood
Ristorante Reale 572............Wish I'd opened
Trattoria Cibo e Vino 591...................Regular
                                       neighbourhood

JORGE VALLEJO
Quintonil
Newton 55, Mexico City
Launched his unique and successful take on contemporary Mexican cooking, Quintonil, in 2012, having staged at Noma and worked in Madrid and at Mexico's fine-dining Pujol.

Blanca 872..........................Worth the travel
Corazón de Tierra 880...........Wish I'd opened
eno 883.......................................Breakfast
Nicos 883..Bargain
Noma 289.......................................High end
Pujol 884............................Local favourite
Sud 777 885.............Regular neighbourhood
Taquería El Califa 885.....................Late night

ROGER VAN DAMME
Het Gebaar
Leopoldstraat 24, Antwerp
Dutch cook who opened Het Gebaar in 1994, a luxury tea-room only open during the day that has won particular praise for its desserts.

L'Atelier de Joël Robuchon 459.........Wish I'd
                                         opened
Finjan 410.....................................Late night
't Fornuis 410..............Regular neighbourhood
Hof van Cleve 417.........................High end
Lam en Yin 410...................Worth the travel
Lung Wah 411......................Local favourite
Zuma 188............................Worth the travel

MANOJ VASAIKAR
Indian Zing
236 King Street, London
Owner of Indian Zing, Indian Zilla and Indian Zest, Vasaikar was born in Mumbai and moved to London to work at Chutney Mary and Veeraswamy.

L'Auberge du Pont de Collonges 442	High end
Amaya 326	Wish I'd opened
Aqua Shard 355	Late night
Bukhara 150	Worth the travel
High Road Brasserie 323	Breakfast
HIX 348	Bargain
La Trompette 323	Regular neighbourhood
Sonny's Kitchen 318	Regular neighbourhood

JARI VESIVALO
Olo
Pohjoisesplanadi 5, Helsinki
Ex-Chez Dominique chef brings 'hyper-creative' modern Scandinavian cooking to Helsinki as executive chef at Olo, one of the six restaurants in the city to hold a Michelin star.

Frantzén 270	Wish I'd opened
Gastrobar Emo 299	Regular neighbourhood
Luomo 300	High end
Nokka 300	Local favourite
Restaurant Ask 300	Regular neighbourhood
Street Gastro 301	Late night
Street Gastro 301	Bargain

VIKRAM VIJ
Vij's
1480 West 11th Avenue, Vancouver
Born in India, he trained in Austria before arriving in Canada in 1989. Currently owns Vancouver's Vij's and Rangoli.

Hawksworth Restaurant 668	High end
Maenam 671	Regular neighbourhood
Pidgin 670	Regular neighbourhood
Thomas Haas 672	Local favourite

JORDI VILÀ
Alkimia
Calle Indústria 79, Barcelona
Catalan Vilà learnt his craft in the restaurants of Barcelona, before opening his first, Alkimia, in 2002. A Michelin star, and the management of three further restaurants, have followed.

41 Grados Experience 513	High end
Alinea 827	Worth the travel
Allium 512	Breakfast
Els Casals 496	Worth the travel
Coure 513	Regular neighbourhood
Coure 513	High end
Dos Palillos 518	Wish I'd opened
Gresca 514	Bargain
Hispania 491	Local favourite
Koy Shunka 512	Late night
Koy Shunka 512	High end
Tickets 515	Local favourite

JASON VINCENT
Known affectionately as the 'prince of pork' by industry insiders, the Cleveland-born chef ran Chicago's Nightwood, famed for its farm-to-table philosophy and daily handwritten menu, until 2014.

Acadia 826	High end
Bari 832	Bargain
Fat Rice 826	Regular neighbourhood
Fat Rice 826	Local favourite
Lula 828	Breakfast
Del Posto 860	Worth the travel
Rolf and Daughters 804	Wish I'd opened
State Bird Provisions 750	Wish I'd opened

BENOÎT VIOLIER
Restaurant de l'Hôtel de Ville
Rue d'Yverdon 1, Crissier
Has succeeded in maintaining the three-star excellence at Restaurant de l'Hôtel de Ville after the departure of toque legend Philippe Rochat.

Au Chat Noir 565	Regular neighbourhood
Le Lexique 560	Bargain
Le Pont de Brent 564	High end
Waku Ghin 235	Worth the travel

PAUL VIRANT
Vie
4471 Lawn Avenue, Western Springs
Preservation expert Virant worked at Charlie Trotter's and other Chicago institutions, going on to open Vie just outside Chicago (2004) and, with Boka Restaurant Group, Perennial Virant (2011).

Alinea 827	High end
Avec 832	Wish I'd opened
Big Star 835	Late night
Cuvée World Bistro 709	Worth the travel
Page's Restaurant 773	Regular neighbourhood
Page's Restaurant 773	Breakfast
Pequod's Pizza 827	Local favourite
York Tavern 773	Bargain

CASSY VIRES
Home Wine Kitchen
7322 Manchester Road, St. Louis
Executive chef and owner of St. Louis's Home Wine Kitchen, Vires – also an award-winning food magazine columnist – trained in Houston, Texas.

Cleveland-Heath 772	Worth the travel
Diablitos Cantina 785	Bargain
Niche 787	High end
Sidney Street Cafe 787	Local favourite
Southwest Diner 787	Breakfast
Stone Soup Cottage 783	Wish I'd opened
Taste Bar 788	Late night
Tripel 788	Regular neighbourhood

EBBE VOLLMER
Vollmers
Tegelgårdsgatan 5, Malmö
Returned to his Swedish hometown of Malmö to open Vollmers in 2011. He's worked in Asia and in the UK with Gordon Ramsay.

L'Atelier de Joël Robuchon 337	Regular neighbourhood
Daniel 844	High end
Gaddi's 191	Worth the travel
Le Manoir aux Quat'Saisons 312	Wish I'd opened
Östarps Gästgivaregård 262	Local favourite
Östarps Gästgivaregård 262	Bargain
Radio 296	Worth the travel

MATS VOLLMER
Vollmers
Tegelgårdsgatan 5, Malmö
Mats and brother Ebbe, the fifth generation of a family of restaurateurs, launched their modern Skåne restaurant in Malmö, a hotbed of culinary attractions, in 2011.

L'Astrance 469	High end
L'Astrance 469	Wish I'd opened
Bastard 262	Late night
Donau Bageriet 263	Bargain
Gyoza Robo Bar 263	Regular neighbourhood
Östarps Gästgivaregård 262	Local favourite
Yauatcha 352	Worth the travel

MICHAEL VOLTAGGIO
ink.
8360 Melrose Avenue, Los Angeles
Los Angeles-based chef honed his skills at Naples's Ritz Carlton and Dry Creek Kitchen, earning it a Michelin star, before opening ink., where he serves 'modern Los Angeles cuisine'.

Bouchon 728	Regular neighbourhood
Connie and Ted's 739	Wish I'd opened
Manfreds & Vin 293	Worth the travel
Petrossian Restaurant 741	Breakfast
Red Medicine 729	Late night
Ricky's Fish Tacos 738	Local favourite
Robata Jinya 742	Bargain
Urasawa 730	High end

VICTOR WÅGMAN
Bror
Sankt Peders Stræde 24a, Copenhagen
Swedish graduate of Noma who opened restaurant Bror with fellow New Nordic alumus Samuel Nutter in Copenhagen's Indre By in 2013.

Daniel Berlin Krog 266	Wish I'd opened
La Degustation Bohême Bourgeoise 609	Worth the travel
Geranium 296	High end
La Galette 288	Regular neighbourhood
La Galette 288	Bargain
Noma 289	Local favourite
Slotskøkkenet 282	Wish I'd opened
Søllerød Kro 281	High end
The Bread Station 278	Breakfast

TETSUYA WAKUDA
Tetsuya's
529 Kent Street, Sydney
Arrived in Sydney from Japan in 1982, opening his eponymous restaurant there in 1989, relocating it to larger premises in 2000. Launched in Singapore in 2011.

Bread & Circus **94**............................Breakfast
Café Di Stasio **114**.................Wish I'd opened
Catalina **99**................................Local favourite
deVine **88**......................................Late night
Flower Drum **107**.............................High end
Kahala **205**...........................Worth the travel
Lucio's **96**...................Regular neighbourhood
Pasteur **90**..Bargain

MARCUS WAREING
Marcus
Wilton Place, London
Re-branded the Gordon Ramsay-operated Petrus as Marcus Wareing at The Berkeley (now called Marcus) in 2008. The Gilbert Scott at London's St. Pancras Renaissance followed in 2011.

Alain Ducasse **339**.............................High end
Bar Boulud **326**................................Late night
Chez Bruce **334**........................Local favourite
Colbert **321**.....................................Breakfast
Compartir **491**......................Worth the travel
Medlar **321**................Regular neighbourhood
Pizza Metro Pizza **331**..........................Bargain
Scott's **344**..........................Wish I'd opened

PETER WEEDEN
Newman Street Tavern
48 Neman Street, London
Former Paternoster Chop House head chef, he channeled his obsession with provenance into Newman Street Tavern where – as head chef and partner – he serves elegant, fiercely seasonal British fare.

Bone Daddies Ramen Bar **346**........Late night
Moshi Moshi **358**........Regular neighbourhood
St. John Bar and Restaurant **362**.......Wish I'd opened
St. John Bread & Wine **374**..............Breakfast
The Quality Chop House **360**...............Bargain
The River Café **325**.............................High end
The Sportsman **310**...............Worth the travel
The Wolseley **345**.....................Local favourite

ARJAN WENNEKES
Visaandeschelde
Scheldeplein 4, Amsterdam
Head chef of Visaandeschelde, set in the heart of Amsterdam and reputed to serve the best seafood in town, Wennekes previously worked at Klein Paardenburg, ZIN and Vermeer.

ABaC **520**...High end
Barbecoa **358**......................Wish I'd opened
Gusto di Casto **406**.........................Breakfast
Made's Warung **242**.............Worth the travel
Pata Negra **399**................................Late night
Pure C **395**..............................Local favourite
Ron Gastrobar **404**.....Regular neighbourhood
Sea Palace **399**..................................Bargain

BLAINE WETZEL
The Willows Inn
2579 West Shore Drive, Lummi Island
A Washington State native, he's been cooking at Willows Inn on Lummi Island since 2010. His résumé includes time at L'Auberge in California and Copenhagen's Noma.

Belltown Pizza **720**...........................Late night
La Mar **908**...........................Wish I'd opened
Noma **289**...........................Worth the travel
Saison **756**.......................................High end

ROBIN WICKENS
Royal Mail
98 Parker Street, Melbourne
Worked his way through some of London's finest Michelin-starred kitchens and ran Melbourne's Interlude before stepping into Dan Hunter's shoes as executive chef at Dunkeld's Royal Mail Hotel in 2013.

Bistro Gitan **112**.........Regular neighbourhood
Chez Dré **112**..................................Breakfast
Cumulus Inc. **107**....................Local favourite
Cutler & Co. **110**............................High end
Gekkazan **108**....................................Bargain
Lake House **82**.....................Wish I'd opened
Supper Inn **109**.............................Late night

BAS WIEGEL
De Kas
Kamerlingh Onneslaan 3, Amsterdam
Chef de cuisine at Amsterdam's greenhouse turned restaurant, De Kas. Cultivating the on-site gardens, Wiegel and founder-owner, Gert-Jan Hageman, plate the bounty the day it's picked.

Ciel Bleu Restaurant **400**...................High end
In De Wulf **421**......................Worth the travel
Merkelbach **402**.................................Bargain
Le Pain Quotidien **398**...................Breakfast
Restaurant Jaspers **401**.....................Regular neighbourhood
Restaurant Vermeer **399**.........Local favourite

GERHARD WIESER
Trenkerstube
Keschtngasse 18, Merano
A champion of the produce of South Tyrol, Wieser has run the Trenkerstube restaurant, near the Austrian border, for over a decade, winning it two Michelin stars.

GästeHaus Klaus Erfort **545**..Worth the travel
Geisels Werneckhof **541**......Worth the travel
Geranium **296**......................Worth the travel
Martín Berasategui **482**........Worth the travel
Raffl Kellerlounge **572**.............Local favourite
Il Re della Busa **597**.............Wish I'd opened
Restaurant De Librije **394**....Worth the travel
Rossini Cocktail Bar **573**.................Late night
Sketch **573**...Bargain
Vendôme **544**...................................High end
Vendôme **544**........................Worth the travel

JAMES WILKINS
wilks restaurant
1–3 Chandos Road, Bristol
A glittering career that has taken in stints at Midsummer House, Aubergine and Michel Bras was followed in 2012 by the opening in Bristol of Wilkins's eponymous restaurant, and in 2014 its first Michelin star.

Assk Kahve **638**...............................Breakfast
The Bath Priory Restaurant **312**.............Local favourite
Bras **436**...........................Wish I'd opened
Le Champignon Sauvage **309**.Worth the travel
Domaine de Méjanassère **436**............Bargain
The Felin Fach Griffin **380**...................Regular neighbourhood
Schloss Schauenstein **561**................High end

ALYN WILLIAMS
Alyn Williams at the Westbury
The Westbury Hotel, 37 Conduit Street, London
Londoner Williams spent six years as a ski-instructor before training with Marcus Wareing at the Berkeley. His hotel dining room at the Westbury opened in 2011.

Akash Tandoori **318**...........................Bargain
Brasserie Chavot **340**.............Wish I'd opened
Indian Accent **151**................Worth the travel
Made in Italy **321**.......Regular neighbourhood
Le Manoir aux Quat'Saisons **312**......High end
The Wolseley **345**...........................Breakfast

BRYN WILLIAMS

Odette's
130 Regents Park Road, London
From north Wales, made a name for himself
in 2006 with BBC television's Great British
Menu. He's since revived the long-running
Odette's in London's Primrose Hill.

Benares 339	High end
Bentley's Oyster Bar & Grill 339	Wish I'd opened
Casa Tua 767	Worth the travel
Le Gavroche 341	High end
Polpo 350	Bargain
The Wolseley 345	Local favourite

STEVE WILLIAMS

40 Maltby Street
40 Maltby Street, London
Won The Harwood Arms a Michelin star and
worked at The Ledbury before heading to
Bermondsey to cook up a storm at informal
small-plate wine bar, 40 Maltby Street.

The Anchor & Hope 373	Local favourite
Koya 349	Regular neighbourhood
The Ledbury 331	High end
My Old Place 373	Bargain
Pavilion 365	Breakfast
Ranoush Juice 329	Late night
Le Saint Eutrope 432	Worth the travel

ED WILSON

Terroirs
5 William IV Street, London
Opened Terroirs in London in 2008, serving
small-plate ingredient-led food and natural
wines, followed by Brawn, Soif and The Green
Man & French Horn.

40 Maltby Street 354	Regular neighbourhood
The Clove Club 371	Wish I'd opened
Embassy East 367	Breakfast
Garagistes 80	Worth the travel
Lucky Chip 364	Bargain
The Quality Chop House 360	Local favourite
Umut 2000 361	Late night
The Waterside Inn 304	High end

MICHAEL WILSON

Jing'An
1 Changde Road, Shanghai
Australian who arrived in China in 2012,
fresh from Melbourne's Cutler & Co., to take
charge at Jing'An, the signature restaurant
in the five-star PuLi Hotel.

Attica 113	Worth the travel
Baker & Spice 166	Breakfast
Cumulus Inc. 107	Breakfast
Cutler & Co. 110	High end
Cutler & Co. 110	Wish I'd opened
Dr. Wine 166	Late night
Longrain 101	Regular neighbourhood
Sepia 91	High end

MARTIN WISHART

Restaurant Martin Wishart
54 The Shore, Edinburgh
Trained in starry kitchens in London and
New York, opening his own restaurant in his
native Edinburgh in 1999. A sister restaurant
in Loch Lomond followed, and an Edinburgh
brasserie.

L'Astrance 469	High end
Hakkasan 342	Late night
Les Prés d'Eugénie 430	Worth the travel

JOACHIM WISSLER

Vendôme
Kadettenstrasse, Bergisch Gladbach
Cooking since 1980, his food is provocative,
precise and internationally lauded. His restaurant Vendôme is credited with reinventing
modern German cuisine.

Asador Etxebarri 479	Wish I'd opened
Cölner Hofbräu P. Josef Früh KG 544	Local favourite
Fette Kuh 544	Late night
Le Moissonnier 545	Regular neighbourhood
Restaurant Schwarzwaldstube 540	High end
Steirereck 607	Worth the travel

HARALD WOHLFAHRT

Restaurant Schwarzwaldstube
Tonbachstrasse 237, Baiersbronn
One of Germany's best, Wohlfahrt has trained
countless chefs since arriving at Schwarzwaldstube in 1978. In 2005 he was awarded
a German order of merit.

L'Arnsbourg 428	Regular neighbourhood
Epicure 462	Worth the travel

MICHAEL WOLF

Envy
Prinsengracht 381, Amsterdam
Cooks at Envy, a quirky modern brasserie,
opened in Amsterdam in 2009 by IQ Creative
of Supperclub fame.

Daalder 401	Local favourite
Frantzén 270	High end
Het Houten Huisje 398	Bargain
Jasmijn & Ik 395	Regular neighbourhood
New King 398	Late night
Pure C 395	Wish I'd opened
Steirereck 607	Worth the travel
Vlaamsch Broodhuys 402	Breakfast

PHIL WOOD

Rockpool
11 Bridge Street, Sydney
New Zealand-born head chef of Neil Perry's
legendary Rockpool since 2009, where his
Australian-Asian cooking style, grounded in
French technique, wins multiple plaudits.

Abdul's Restaurant 100	Local favourite
Chairman Mao 98	Local favourite
Ester 89	Regular neighbourhood
Golden Century Seafood 89	Late night
Mikawa Zezankyo 214	Worth the travel
Quay 102	Local favourite
Quay 102	High end
Ramen Ikkyu 93	Bargain
Reuben Hills 101	Breakfast
Sixpenny 95	Wish I'd opened
Spice I Am 101	Local favourite
Sydney Madang 92	Local favourite
Tetsuya's 92	Local favourite
Thanh Binh 95	Local favourite

SIMON WRIGHT

The French Café
210 Symonds Street, Auckland
Made the leap from London to New Zealand
in the 1990s, opening The French Café with
his wife Creghan in 1999, having trained
under Marco Pierre White.

Depot Eatery 128	Wish I'd opened
The Engine Room 128	Regular neighbourhood
Janken 130	Bargain
Ken Yakitori Bar 128	Late night
Kokako Café & Roastery 130	Breakfast
Merediths 131	High end
Restaurant André 239	Worth the travel
The Sugar Club 129	Local favourite

EDUARD XATRUCH

Compartir
Riera Sant Vicenç, Cadaqués
Former head chef at elBulli who, alongside
fellow Adrià disciples Mateu Casañas and
Oriol Castro, opened the more informal
Compartir in Cadaqués in 2012.

Bodega 1900 513	Late night
Dos Palillos 518	Late night
Esportell del Bou 497	Regular neighbourhood
Ca l'Isidre 518	Local favourite
Miramar 494	High end
Petit Comitè 514	Local favourite
El Quim de la Boqueria 519	Breakfast
Restaurante Porvenir 515	Bargain
La Tour d'Argent 455	Wish I'd opened

SEIJI YAMAMOTO
Nihonryori Ryugin
7-17-24 Roppongi, Tokyo
After eleven years of intense study of kaiseki, he opened Nihonryori Ryugin in Tokyo in 2003, where his attention to detail saw him once send an eel for a CT scan.

Amber **182**..............................Worth the travel
Chugoku Hanten Roppongi **214**.......Late night
Au goût du jour Nouvelle Ère **210**.....High end
Mikawa Zezankyo **214**........................Bargain
Sukiyabashi Jiro **212**..............Local favourite
Sushi Takumi Masa **217**......................Regular neighbourhood
Takadahassho **198**...............Worth the travel

JUNYA YAMASAKI
Koya
49 Frith Street, London
Left Tokyo for Paris, where he swapped Fine Art studies for the art of noodle-making at Kunitoraya. Worked at Paris's Rose Bakery, opened its London branch, and launched Koya in 2010.

Attica **113**..............................Worth the travel
Leila's Café **372**...............................Breakfast
One Leicester Street **337**...............Late night
The River Café **325**..........................High end
Silk Road **357**....................................Bargain
St. John Bar and Restaurant **362**.......Wish I'd opened
St. John Bread & Wine **374**................Regular neighbourhood

DANNY YIP
The Chairman
18 Kau U Fong, Hong Kong
Hong Kong based Yip set up The Chairman Group with Josiah Li, which includes Chairman & Yip (1992), Lanterne Rooms (2008) and Malamay (2012) in Canberra and The Chairman in Hong Kong.

Amber **182**.......................................High end
Fook Lam Moon **184**...Regular neighbourhood
Nahm **225**..............................Worth the travel
Le Salon de Thé de Joël Robuchon **186**...........Breakfast
Tsui Wah **189**.......................Local favourite
Tsui Wah **189**................................Bargain

HAJIME YONEDA
Hajime
1-9-11-1f Edobori, Osaka
Osaka-born former electrical engineer whose restaurant Hajime won three Michelin stars just one year after opening.

Brooklyn Roasting Company **210**......Breakfast
Burnt Ends **238**.....................Worth the travel
Mimiu **205**.......................................Bargain
Mizai **202**...................Regular neighbourhood
Sukiyabashi Jiro **212**.......................High end

ALEX YOUNG
Zingerman's Roadhouse
2501 Jackson Avenue, Ann Arbor
Born in London, he moved to California with his family when he was seventeen. Currently serving up his particular style of Southern Comfort food at Zingerman's.

53rd and 6th Halal Cart **839**............Late night
Primo **780**...............................Wish I'd opened

KEN YU
YEN Chinese Restaurant at W Taipei
10 Zhongxiao East Road, Taipei
A twenty-five-year career has seen Yu work in Michelin-starred and hotel kitchens across Asia. He now heads up the YEN Chinese Restaurant on the thirty-first floor of Taipei's W Hotel.

Ā Cái Shūcài Yángròu **173**.............Late night
Ben Teppanyaki **174**.........................High end
Ben Teppanyaki **174**.............Worth the travel
Boon Keng Chicken **174**......................Bargain
Lao Jio **175**..............Regular neighbourhood
Shin Yeh 101 **176**...................Local favourite
Yōnghé Měi Dòujiāng Dàwáng **177**...Breakfast

RICARDO ZARATE
Mo-Chica
514 West 7th Street, Los Angeles
Lima born, he worked in London at Zuma and at Pengelly's before moving to Los Angeles to open the Peruvian-inspired Mo-Chica in 2009, then Picca (2012) and Paichē (2013).

Akasha **731**.....................................Breakfast
Mariscos Ruben **881**..............Worth the travel
El Mercado **908**.....................Worth the travel
Nobu **343**............................Worth the travel
Park's BBQ **734**................................Late night
Providence **741**...............................High end
Ramen Yamadaya **738**.......................Bargain
Sushi Gen **735**............Regular neighbourhood
Urasawa **730**...................................High end
Zuma **327**.............................Wish I'd opened

ROMAN ZAŠTŠERINSKI
Kohvik Moon
Võrgu 3, Tallinn
Ex-chef de cuisine at Tallinn's Restoran Õ, the Russian chef and his wife Jana opened fine-dining destination Kohvik Moon in 2010, with Igor Andrejev sharing kitchen duties.

La Bottega **620**................................Late night
Boulevard Social **297**............Worth the travel
Klaus Kohvik **620**..............................Bargain
Põhjaka Mõis **621**...................Local favourite
Tchaikovsky **621**..............................High end

ANDREW ZIMMERMAN
Sepia
123 North Jefferson Street, Chicago
A musician turned culinary maestro, Zimmerman trained in New York, then headed to Chicago, taking up the reins at Sepia, renowned for its inventive American cuisine in 2009.

Bang Bang Pie Shop **828**..................Breakfast
Au Cheval **832**................................Late night
L2O **827**...High end
The Publican **834**..................Local favourite
Rangoli **835**.............Regular neighbourhood
Schwa **835**..........................Wish I'd opened
SPQR **755**.............................Worth the travel
Udupi Palace **834**.............................Bargain

GERALD ZOGBAUM
Küchenwerkstatt
Hans-Henny-Jahnn-Weg 1, Hamburg
Produce-obsessive who grew up in Lower Saxony and trained in Rhine-Westphalia and Switzerland returned to Hamburg in 2004 to run the kitchen at the Michelin-starred Küchenwerkstatt.

Akari **542**..Bargain
Bullerei **542**.......................Local favourite
Elbgold **543**...................................Breakfast
Erika's Eck **543**................................Bargain
Haerlin **543**....................................High end
Juwelier **543**.............Regular neighbourhood
Mizai **202**..........................Wish I'd opened
Mizai **202**.............................Worth the travel

JOCK ZONFRILLO
Orana
285 Rundle Street, Adelaide
Scottish-born Zonfrillo worked his way up the ranks in London and, seduced by an antipodean sabbatical, settled in Adelaide, launching Orana and Street ADL in 2013, which showcase Australia's indigenous ingredients.

Attica **113**.......................................High end
Dinner by Heston Blumenthal **326**.........Worth the travel
Frank's Pizza Bar & Restaurant **92**.....Bargain
Hey Jupiter **78**...........Regular neighbourhood
Lucia's Pizza & Spaghetti Bar **79**.............Local favourite
Red Door Bakery **79**........................Breakfast
Spice Temple **91**....................Wish I'd opened
Tetsuya's **92**...................................High end
Ying Chow **79**.................................Late night

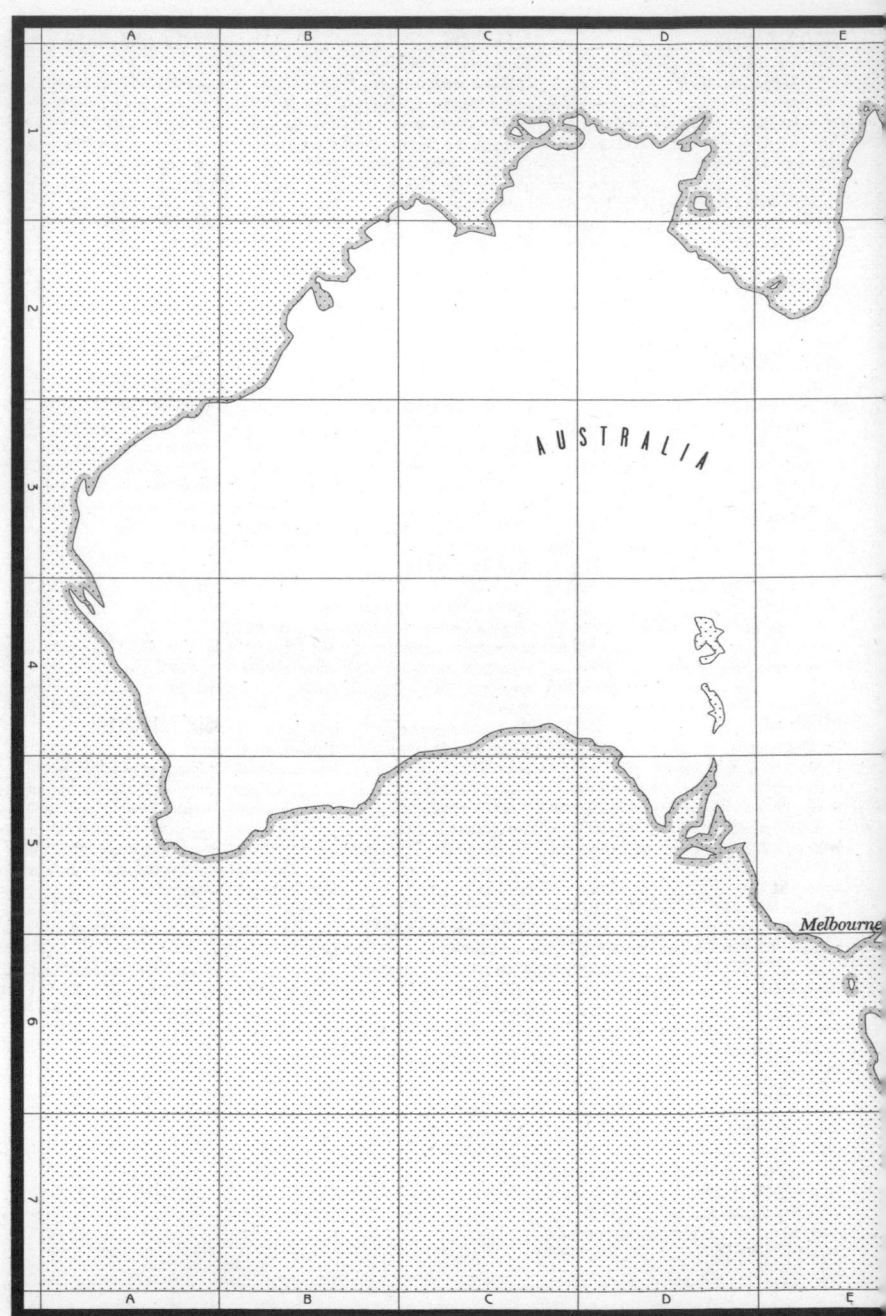

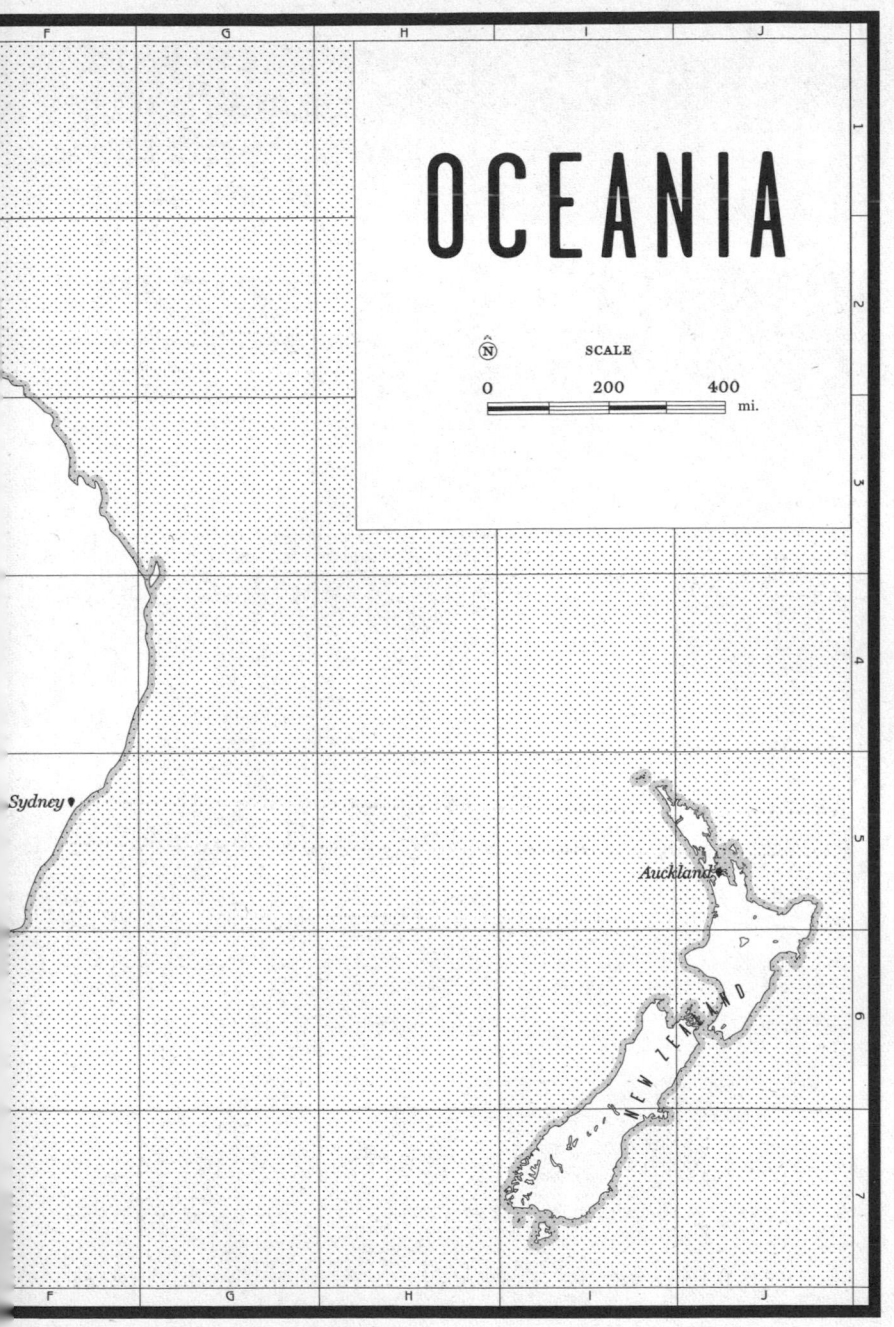

OCEANIA

N

SCALE

0   200   400
                      mi.

Sydney

Auckland

NEW ZEALAND

'GREAT PIZZA, BEER IN CANS AND A PLAYLIST THAT INCLUDES IGGY POP, PATTI SMITH AND AC/DC.'

BEN RUSSELL P74

'Five-star service and a luxurious atmosphere. Pretension and glamour at its best.'

MEYJITTE BOUGHENOUT P78

'It's got plastic tables, fluorescent lights and is open late.'

JOCK ZONFRILLO P79

AUSTRALIA

'INGREDIENTS NOT EVEN HOURS OUT OF THE GROUND, ANIMALS RAISED WITHIN A WHISPER OF THE PLATE AND A TRUE UNDERSTANDING OF TASMANIA AND ITS SURROUNDS.'

LUKE BURGESS P81

AUSTRALIA

SCALE

0   350   700 mi.

AUSTRALIA

• Western Australia pp.82–83

• Queensland pp.74–78

South Australia pp.78–79 •

• New South Wales p.74

• Sydney pp.84–103

• Victoria pp.81–82

Melbourne pp.104–114 •

Tasmania pp.79–81 •

TOWN RESTAURANT AND CAFÉ

Recommended by
Ryan Squires

33 Byron Street
Bangalow
New South Wales 2479
+61 266872555
www.townbangalow.com.au

Opening hours	Open 7 days
Credit cards	Accepted
Price range	Affordable
Style	Smart casual
Cuisine	Modern Australian
Recommended for	Worth the travel

Town would be incongruous enough if it were just the one Byron Bay hinterland restaurant operated by a pair of dangerously overqualified chefs. That it's two restaurants under one roof makes it quite remarkable. Downstairs (or Downtown), it's all about the pastries and the likes of croque monsieur on brioche. Uptown, after dark, it's all dégustation dining. The room isn't brilliant, admittedly, but the prices are small. Katrina and Karl Kanetani left the top end of city dining to 'tree change' here, but the likes of the Gruyère gougères and the rhubarb with rosemary panna cotta and Champagne jelly suggest they certainly haven't gone to seed.

FEDERAL DOMA CAFÉ

Recommended by
Shannon Bennett

3 Albert Street
Federal
New South Wales 2480
+61 266884711

Opening hours	Open 7 days
Reservation policy	No
Credit cards	Not accepted
Price range	Budget
Style	Casual
Cuisine	Japanese
Recommended for	Bargain

'Best Japanese lunch in the country. I'm not sure if it's the setting or what, but it's seriously good Japanese food. Sitting outside in a disused classroom on a Saturday is now my new favourite pastime.'
—Shannon Bennett

HARVEST CAFÉ

Recommended by
Shannon Bennett

18–20 Old Pacific Highway.
Newrybar
New South Wales 2479
+61 266872644
www.harvestcafe.com.au

Opening hours	Open 7 days
Credit cards	Accepted
Price range	Affordable
Style	Smart casual
Cuisine	Modern Australian
Recommended for	Wish I'd opened

'The atmosphere is fantastic and the ingenuity and resourcefulness of maximising all the history in Byron Bay – the old bread oven and the general store vibe – is something I admire. It's a great weekend local. I just love it.'—Shannon Bennett

ALFREDO'S PIZZERIA

Recommended by
Ben Russell

39 Alfred Street
Brisbane
Queensland 4006
+61 732516555
www.alfredos.com.au

Opening hours	Open 7 days
Reservation policy	No
Credit cards	Accepted
Price range	Budget
Style	Casual
Cuisine	Pizza
Recommended for	Regular neighbourhood

'Great pizza, beer in cans and a playlist that includes Iggy Pop, Patti Smith and AC/DC.'—Ben Russell

BECCOFINO

Recommended by
Ryan Squires

10 Vernon Terrace
Brisbane
Queensland 4006
+61 736660207
www.beccofino.com.au

Opening hours	Closed Monday
Reservation policy	No
Credit cards	Accepted
Price range	Affordable
Style	Smart casual
Cuisine	Italian
Recommended for	Local favourite

'They look after you well.'—Ryan Squires

ESQUIRE

Recommended by
Ben Russell

145 Eagle Street
Brisbane
Queensland 4000
+61 732202123
www.esquire.net.au

Opening hours	Closed Monday and Sunday
Credit cards	Accepted
Price range	Expensive
Style	Smart casual
Cuisine	Modern Australian
Recommended for	High end

'Contemporary, classy cooking – a chef's restaurant.'
—Ben Russell

HARAJUKU GYOZA

Recommended by
Ryan Squires

394 Brunswick Street
Brisbane
Queensland 4006
+61 738524624
www.harajukugyoza.com

Opening hours	Open 7 days
Reservation policy	No
Credit cards	Accepted
Price range	Affordable
Style	Casual
Cuisine	Japanese
Recommended for	Late night

'Traditional Japanese dumpling house.'—Ryan Squires

Let's say it straight up: these quite probably won't be the best gyoza you eat in this lifetime. But they are good, and better than that, they're fun. Or at least they're a big part of the fun that is Harajuku Gyoza. Its namesake potsticker dumplings are the name of the game, but compared to the degree of hyper-specialization we see at this level in Japan, the fact that it does duck, chicken and prawn gyoza, let alone offers side dishes (the katsudon is decent) seems positively reckless by Japanese standards. The beers list, though concise, is curated with care. Get ready for some noisy good times.

LEFTY'S OLD TIME MUSIC HALL

Recommended by
Ben Russell

15 Caxton Street
Brisbane
Queensland 4000
www.leftysmusichall.com

Opening hours	Closed Monday and Tuesday
Reservation policy	No
Credit cards	Accepted
Price range	Budget
Style	Casual
Cuisine	Bar Snacks
Recommended for	Wish I'd opened

'Not a restaurant as such, but a music hall with fried foods, a kick-ass country music playlist, cans of beer and whisky.'—Ben Russell

MIEL CONTAINER

Recommended by
Alejandro Cancino,
Ben Russell

96 Albert Street
Brisbane
Queensland 4000
+61 423466503

Opening hours	Closed Sunday
Credit cards	Not accepted
Price range	Budget
Style	Casual
Cuisine	Burgers
Recommended for	Bargain

'A shipping container in the middle of the city serving bulgogi burgers on brioche.'—Ben Russell

MIZU

Recommended by
Ryan Squires

2 Macquarie Street
Brisbane
Queensland 4005
+61 732540488
www.mizurestaurant.com.au

Opening hours	Open 7 days
Reservation policy	No
Credit cards	Accepted
Price range	Affordable
Style	Smart casual
Cuisine	Japanese
Recommended for	Regular neighbourhood

'It's quick, extremely fresh, relaxed and consistent.'
—Ryan Squires

MODA

Recommended by
Alejandro Cancino

12 Edward Street
Brisbane
Queensland 4000
+61 732217655
www.modarestaurant.com.au

Opening hours	Closed Sunday
Credit cards	Accepted
Price range	Affordable
Style	Smart casual
Cuisine	Spanish
Recommended for	Regular neighbourhood

'Simple Spanish food, done properly.'
—Alejandro Cancino

NEW FARM DELI

Recommended by
Alejandro Cancino

900 Brunswick Street
Brisbane
Queensland 4005
+61 733582634
www.newfarmdeli.com.au

Opening hours	Open 7 days
Credit cards	Accepted
Price range	Affordable
Style	Casual
Cuisine	Italian Deli-Café
Recommended for	Breakfast

'Consistently good breakfast. Fresh and well executed.'
—Alejandro Cancino

PEARL CAFÉ

Recommended by
Ben Russell,
Ryan Squires

28 Logan Road
Brisbane
Queensland 4102
+61 733923300

Opening hours	Open 7 days
Credit cards	Accepted
Price range	Affordable
Style	Casual
Cuisine	Café-Bar-Bistro
Recommended for	Breakfast

'This is a place that does everything well.'
—Ben Russell

Sitting, as it does, in the shadow of Brisbane's biggest cricket stadium, Logan Road seems an unlikely bastion of cool, and yet this single block plays host to savvy bars, dealers in fine mid-century furniture and one of the best wine bars in the country. It's also home to Pearl, a café aptly named in the sense that its smallness belies its value. Here the humble slice of toast is elevated by the deployment of three cheeses, braised leek and French mustard; new season pears and poached quince with local yogurt trump fruit salad; and 'chewy rhubarb' and chia seed enliven the porridge. Superior coffee and polished service ice the cake.

PUBLIC

Recommended by
Alejandro Cancino

Upper Level 1
400 George Street
Brisbane
Queensland 4000
+61 732102288
www.lovepublic.com.au

Opening hours	Closed Sunday
Credit cards	Accepted
Price range	Affordable
Style	Smart casual
Cuisine	Small plates
Recommended for	Late night

'I like the ambience and the sharing menu style.'
—Alejandro Cancino

A repository of current trends from 'small plates' and 'dude food' to concrete floors and Scandi furniture, Public manages to wear its New York loft style lightly. Located in Brisbane's central business district, it's made headlines for serving insects – who can resist the sound of wood-roasted scorpions with lobster snow? But the kitchen's strength lies in glammed-up comfort food and fusion with finesse. The sharing concept and late kitchen (until 11.00 p.m.) makes for a lively ambience and suits those splitting 'KFD – Kentucky Fried Duck' and a few beers just as well as it does those hitting the fine wine over wagyu tataki.

RESTAURANT TWO

Recommended by
Alejandro Cancino

2 Edward Street
Brisbane
Queensland 4000
+61 732100600
www.restaurant2.com.au

Opening hours	Closed Monday and Sunday
Credit cards	Accepted
Price range	Expensive
Style	Smart casual
Cuisine	Modern Australian
Recommended for	Local favourite

'One of the longest standing restaurants in Brisbane with a very good reputation.'—Alejandro Cancino

TARO'S RAMEN & CAFÉ

Recommended by
Ryan Squires

363 Adelaide Street
Brisbane
Queensland 4000
+61 738326358
www.taros.com.au

Opening hours	Closed Sunday
Credit cards	Accepted
Price range	Budget
Style	Casual
Cuisine	Ramen Noodles
Recommended for	Bargain

'Authentic.'—Ryan Squires

WARAWARA IZAKAYA

Recommended by
Ben Russell

Level 1 153 Elizabeth Street
Brisbane
Queensland 4000
+61 731083267

Opening hours	Open 7 days
Reservation policy	No
Credit cards	Accepted but not AMEX
Price range	Budget
Style	Casual
Cuisine	Korean-Japanese
Recommended for	Late night

'Open late, Korean pop, kimchi pancakes, chilli fried chicken and always buzzing.'—Ben Russell

OCEAN SEAFOOD

Recommended by
Meyjitte Boughenout

3110 Gold Coast Highway
Gold Coast
Queensland 4217
+61 755703766

Opening hours	Open 7 days
Reservation policy	No
Credit cards	Accepted
Price range	Budget
Style	Casual
Cuisine	Chinese-Malaysian
Recommended for	Late night

'It's definitely the most consistent Chinese restaurant here, I can't get enough of their Shandong chicken.'—Meyjitte Boughenout

PIGS AND PINTS

Recommended by
Meyjitte Boughenout

Chevron Island
54 Thomas Drive
Gold Coast
Queensland 4217
+61 755046404
www.pigsandpints.com.au

Opening hours	Closed Monday and Tuesday
Credit cards	Accepted but not AMEX
Price range	Budget
Style	Casual
Cuisine	Burgers
Recommended for	Regular neighbourhood

'I go at least four nights a week. The decor and the feel of the place remind me of Europe. James Brady is a great chef doing great stuff.'—Meyjitte Boughenout

SUSHI ON JAMES

Recommended by
Meyjitte Boughenout

Shop 3, 2 James Street
Gold Coast
Queensland 4220
+61 755203651

Opening hours	Open 7 days
Reservation policy	No
Credit cards	Accepted but not AMEX
Price range	Budget
Style	Casual
Cuisine	Sushi
Recommended for	Bargain

'Still the best in town.'—Meyjitte Boughenout

VIE BAR & RESTAURANT

Recommended by
Meyjitte Boughenout

Palazzo Versace
94 Seaworld Drive
Gold Coast
Queensland 4217
+61 755098000
www.palazzoversace.com.au

Opening hours	Open 7 days
Credit cards	Accepted
Price range	Affordable
Style	Smart casual
Cuisine	Modern Australian
Recommended for	Local favourite

'The restaurant sits on the waters' edge and provides a beautiful view. Five-star service and a luxurious atmosphere. Pretension and glamour at its best.' —Meyjitte Boughenout

VINTAGE ESPRESSO

Recommended by
Meyjitte Boughenout

1/43 Alfred Street
Gold Coast
Queensland 4218
+61 755277878

Opening hours	Open 7 days
Reservation policy	No
Credit cards	Accepted but not AMEX
Price range	Budget
Style	Casual
Cuisine	Café-Bistro
Recommended for	Breakfast

'It's on my way to the market. The produce is always fresh and the service is great.' —Meyjitte Boughenout

BERARDO'S

Recommended by
Justin North

49 Hastings Street
Noosa
Queensland 4567
+61 754480888
www.berardos.com.au

Opening hours	Open 7 days
Credit cards	Accepted
Price range	Expensive
Style	Smart casual
Cuisine	Modern Australian
Recommended for	Worth the travel

'Any excuse to go to Noosa! I love this place, it's a great restaurant, in a beautiful setting and it showcases the best produce from around the region. Cooked with love and passion.' —Justin North

CAFÉ LE MONDE

Recommended by
Justin North

52 Hastings Street
Noosa
Queensland 4567
+61 754492366
www.cafelemonde.com.au

Opening hours	Open 7 days
Credit cards	Accepted
Price range	Affordable
Style	Casual
Cuisine	International
Recommended for	Breakfast

'Lovely fresh produce, simply prepared, great coffee and located opposite the amazing beach.' —Justin North

HEY JUPITER

Recommended by
Jock Zonfrillo

11 Ebenezer Place
Adelaide
South Australia 5000
+61 416050721

Opening hours	Open 7 days
Reservation policy	No
Credit cards	Accepted but not AMEX
Price range	Budget
Style	Casual
Cuisine	Café
Recommended for	Regular neighbourhood

'It's my first stop on the way in to work each morning. It kinda feels like an extension of our place. French owner Christophe has the best sarcastic, funny personality, he makes it. I enjoy the great food and his great banter. He's old school you know, when he goes on holiday he closes the restaurant. Great coffee, amazing pulled-pork sandwiches with celeriac, mayo, parsley and crackling. A little bit of everything really.' —Jock Zonfrillo

LUCIA'S PIZZA & SPAGHETTI BAR

Recommended by
Jock Zonfrillo

Adelaide Central Market Western Mall
Shop 1, 45 Gouger Street
Adelaide
South Australia 5000
+61 882312303
www.lucias.com.au

Opening hours	Closed Sunday
Reservation policy	No
Credit cards	Not accepted
Price range	Budget
Style	Casual
Cuisine	Italian
Recommended for	Local favourite

'If you come to Adelaide you have to go to the Adelaide markets and when there it's gotta be Lucia's. Growing up in Glasgow as a kid (half Italian) I used to go to an iconic shop beside the River Clyde called Fazzi Bros. Lucia's is real nostalgia for me as it brings back all those wonderful smells. Three generations of women selling fine Italian produce and dishes and all the time that aroma of a great homemade *sugo* simmering away in the background.'—Jock Zonfrillo

RED DOOR BAKERY

Recommended by
Jock Zonfrillo

22 Elizabeth Street
Adelaide
South Australia 5008
+61 883400306
www.reddoorbakery.com.au

Opening hours	Closed Monday
Reservation policy	No
Credit cards	Accepted but not AMEX
Price range	Budget
Style	Casual
Cuisine	Café-Bakery
Recommended for	Breakfast

'Located in a bit of a hipster neighbourhood, this place is a kind of institution. I like the smell of fresh bread and brioche in the morning. Favourites for me are the pork-and-rosemary sausage rolls and fresh sweet morning cakes that change daily.'—Jock Zonfrillo

YING CHOW

Recommended by
Jock Zonfrillo

114 Gouger Street
Adelaide
South Australia 5000
+61 882117998

Opening hours	Open 7 days
Credit cards	Accepted
Price range	Budget
Style	Casual
Cuisine	Chinese
Recommended for	Late night

'It's got plastic tables, fluorescent lights and is open late. Sometimes the crowd are rowdy depending on what's going on in the city, but that's the deal in a late night joint. I go after work some nights for red vinegar ribs. The service is quick and efficient.'—Jock Zonfrillo

BACKDOOR FANNY'S

Recommended by
Rodney Dunn

341 Elizabeth Street
Hobart
Tasmania 7000
+61 362348805
www.sweetenvy.com

Opening hours	Closed Sunday to Friday
Credit cards	Accepted
Price range	Budget
Style	Casual
Cuisine	Barbeque
Recommended for	Bargain

'Gordon Ramsay alumnus Alistair Wise along with wife Teena run a mean patisserie at Sweet Envy. Even more special is Backdoor Fanny's in the alley beside Sweet Envy, where on Saturday evenings in the summer Wise busts out his burger skills on beautiful brioche buns with homemade sauces, pickles and drinks. For afters, sundaes from their restored 1964 Commer Mr Whippy ice-cream van.'—Rodney Dunn

BERTA

Recommended by
Rodney Dunn

323a Elizabeth Street
Hobart
Tasmania 7000
+61 362344844
www.bertahobart.com.au

Opening hours	Closed Monday and Tuesday
Credit cards	Accepted but not AMEX
Price range	Budget
Style	Casual
Cuisine	Café
Recommended for	Regular neighbourhood

'It is light and airy, casual and has the type of food that you could eat every day, from a fried chicken sandwich through to beautiful salads and pasta. There are nice little sweet treats like house-made doughnuts and chocolate-coated honeycomb to have with good coffee.'—Rodney Dunn

GARAGISTES

Recommended by
Rodney Dunn, Ed Wilson

103 Murray Street
Hobart
Tasmania 7000
+61 362310558
www.garagistes.com.au

Opening hours	Closed Sunday to Tuesday
Credit cards	Accepted
Price range	Affordable
Style	Smart casual
Cuisine	Modern Australian
Recommended for	Worth the travel

'Garagistes shows the potential of Tasmania as a food destination by exploring a diverse range of ingredients that have been grown by small local producers, or foraged from the seashores and Tasmanian countryside. Seamlessly married together on local pottery it is always a flavour sensation and a must visit for anybody coming to the state.'—Rodney Dunn

PIGEON HOLE

Recommended by
Luke Burgess, Rodney Dunn

93 Goulburn Street
Hobart
Tasmania 7000
+61 362369306
www.pigeonholecafe.com.au

Opening hours	Closed Monday and Sunday
Reservation policy	No
Credit cards	Accepted
Price range	Budget
Style	Casual
Cuisine	Café
Recommended for	Breakfast

'Like its name it is small and cosy. From its tiny kitchen the chef, Tom Westcott, produces beautiful food using produce from the owner's farm, Weston Farms.'
—Rodney Dunn

SIDECAR

Recommended by
Rodney Dunn

129 Bathurst Street
Hobart
Tasmania 7000
+61 362311338
www.garagistes.com.au/sidecar

Opening hours	Closed Monday and Tuesday
Reservation policy	No
Credit cards	Accepted
Price range	Affordable
Style	Casual
Cuisine	Modern Australian
Recommended for	Late night

'An offshoot of Garagistes and originally designed as a holding pen but shoots far above its weight becoming a destination in its own right. I love to sit down and order the entire menu with everything from excellent house-made charcuterie and artisanally produced natural wines from around the world.'—Rodney Dunn

TRICYCLE CAFE & BAR

Recommended by
Luke Burgess

Salamanca Arts Centre
77 Salamanca Place
Hobart
Tasmania 7000
+61 362237228
www.salarts.org.au

Opening hours	Closed Sunday
Reservation policy	No
Credit cards	Accepted but not AMEX
Price range	Affordable
Style	Casual
Cuisine	Café
Recommended for	Regular neighbourhood

'Working most nights that places are open in Hobart, daytime dining becomes my eating out experience. Inspiration at Tricycle comes from all four corners of the globe with great local products given a twist and plenty of love. Tasty and honest food with vinyl classics.'
—Luke Burgess

THE AGRARIAN KITCHEN

Recommended by
Luke Burgess

650 Lachlan Road
Lachlan
Tasmania 7140
+61 362611099
www.theagrariankitchen.com

Opening hours	Variable
Credit cards	Accepted but not AMEX
Price range	Expensive
Style	Casual
Cuisine	Modern Australian
Recommended for	Local favourite

'This isn't a restaurant (it's actually a cookery school) but it's *the* place that expresses what's possible here. Ingredients not even hours out of the ground, animals raised within a whisper of the plate and a true understanding of Tasmania and its surrounds. Rodney Dunn and Severine Demanet welcome people into their home and cooking school and never fail to deliver a memorable experience and truly delicious food.'
—Luke Burgess

BIRREGURRA GENERAL STORE

Recommended by
Dan Hunter

59 Main Street
Birregurra
Victoria 3242
+61 352362013

Opening hours	Open 7 days
Reservation policy	No
Credit cards	Accepted
Price range	Budget
Style	Casual
Cuisine	Café
Recommended for	Regular neighbourhood

'Good coffee, which is unusual for a small town in country Australia.'—Dan Hunter

BRAE

Recommended by
Luke Burgess, Frank
Camorra, Anthony Lui,
Daniel Puskas

4285 Cape Otway Road
Birregurra
Victoria 3242
+61 352362226
www.braerestaurant.com

Opening hours	Closed Tuesday and Wednesday
Credit cards	Accepted
Price range	Expensive
Style	Smart casual
Cuisine	Modern Australian
Recommended for	High end

'The refined simplicity, focus on the garden and service make this an experience worth going a long way for over and over. You can feel a connection to where they are, nuances abound and inspiration is everywhere. I love this place.'—Luke Burgess

LAKE HOUSE

Recommended by
Robin Wickens

4 King Street
Daylesford
Victoria 3460
+61 353483329
www.lakehouse.com.au

Opening hours	Open 7 days
Credit cards	Accepted
Price range	Expensive
Style	Smart casual
Cuisine	Modern Australian
Recommended for	Wish I'd opened

'This country-house style hotel is somewhere that has always appealed to me, using local produce and working with suppliers.'—Robin Wickens

BREAD IN COMMON

Recommended by
Hadleigh Troy

43 Pakenham Street
Fremantle
Western Australia 6160
+61 893361032
www.breadincommon.com.au

Opening hours	Open 7 days
Reservation policy	No
Credit cards	Accepted
Price range	Budget
Style	Casual
Cuisine	Café-Bakery
Recommended for	Breakfast

'They do brunch rather than breakfast which suits the hours I keep perfectly. Fantastic sourdough and fresh produce in an inspiring setting. It's a great way to start the day.'—Hadleigh Troy

ACE PIZZA

Recommended by
Hadleigh Troy

448 Beaufort Street
Perth
Western Australia 6003
+61 499448000
www.acepizza.com.au

Opening hours	Open 7 days
Credit cards	Accepted
Price range	Affordable
Style	Casual
Cuisine	Italian-American
Recommended for	Regular neighbourhood

'It's relaxed, easygoing and the food is quick and tasty.'
—Hadleigh Troy

DIVIDO

Recommended by
Hadleigh Troy

170 Scarborough Beach Road
Perth
Western Australia 6050
+61 894437373
www.divido.com.au

Opening hours	Closed Sunday
Credit cards	Accepted
Price range	Affordable
Style	Smart casual
Cuisine	Italian
Recommended for	Bargain

'They put together bargain set-menu deals on Mondays and Tuesdays as well as extremely popular Balkan-style banquets every so often, that are not only great value but also cooked with love!'—Hadleigh Troy

LALLA ROOKH

77 Saint Georges Terrace
Perth
Western Australia 6000
+61 893257077
www.lallarookh.com.au

Opening hours	Closed Sunday
Credit cards	Accepted
Price range	Affordable
Style	Casual
Cuisine	Italian
Recommended for	Regular neighbourhood

'Industry professionals who go out of their way to make sure everyone has a great night.'—Hadleigh Troy

PRINT HALL

Brookfield Place
125 Saint Georges Terrace
Perth
Western Australia 6000
+61 862820000
www.printhall.com.au

Opening hours	Closed Sunday
Credit cards	Accepted
Price range	Affordable
Style	Casual
Cuisine	Modern Australian
Recommended for	Local favourite

'A multifaceted venue with a slick fit-out and something for everyone.'—Hadleigh Troy

SILKS

Crown Perth
Great Eastern Highway
Perth
Western Australia 6100
+61 893627551
www.crownperth.com.au

Opening hours	Open 7 days
Credit cards	Accepted
Price range	Expensive
Style	Smart casual
Cuisine	Chinese
Recommended for	Worth the travel

'The best Chinese restaurant I went to last year.'
—Jérôme Lorvellec

THE STABLES BAR

888 Hay Street
Perth
Western Australia 6000
+61 863141300
www.thestablesbar.com.au

Opening hours	Closed Sunday
Credit cards	Accepted
Price range	Affordable
Style	Smart casual
Cuisine	Australian
Recommended for	Late night

'This bar and restaurant in Perth serves very fresh, simple food and also has a large selection of beers.'
—Jérôme Lorvellec

UNCLE BILLY'S

Shop 9, 66 Roe Street
Perth
Western Australia 6003
+61 892289388
www.uncle-billys.com.au

Opening hours	Open 7 days
Credit cards	Not accepted
Price range	Budget
Style	Casual
Cuisine	Chinese
Recommended for	Late night

'It's a late night go-to place that's open until 4.00 a.m. seven nights a week. If we are having Uncle Billy's we will generally order it as takeaway (take out) for the entire team and have it over a beer at the restaurant after a long week.'—Hadleigh Troy

'There aren't many nicer ways to spend a Sunday afternoon than perched on the street overlooking the beach sipping a beer and slurping fresh Sydney rock oysters.'
MIKE EGGERT P86

'NOT FOR THE FAINT HEARTED.'
NEIL PERRY P98

SYDNEY

'It has been a Sydney institution and a restaurant that, over twenty years, has helped define Australian cuisine.'
PETER GILMORE P91

'A must for anyone visiting Sydney.'
MARK BEST P90

'A TRUE AUSTRALIAN ICON.'
REON HOBSON P86

SYDNEY

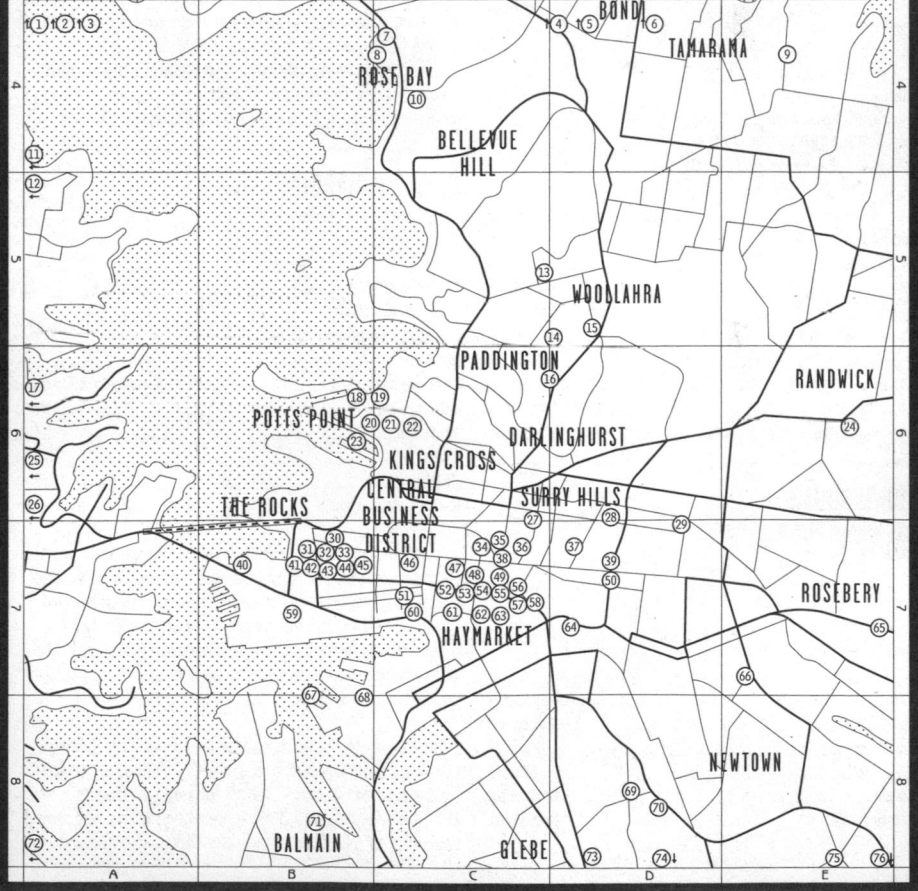

SCALE

0   600   1200   1800 yd.

ROSSO POMODORO PIZZERIA

Recommended by
Martin Benn

Shop 90, 24 Buchanan Street
Balmain
Sydney
New South Wales 2041
+61 295555924
www.rossopomodoro.com.au

Opening hours	Closed Monday
Credit cards	Accepted but not AMEX
Price range	Budget
Style	Casual
Cuisine	Pizza
Recommended for	Late night

'Traditional pizza expertly prepared, utilizing the best produce available. What more could you want late at night?'—Martin Benn

BEROWRA WATERS INN

Recommended by
Reon Hobson

Via East and West Public Wharves
Berowra Waters
Sydney
New South Wales 2082
+61 294561027
www.berowrawatersinn.com

Opening hours	Closed Monday to Thursday
Credit cards	Accepted
Price range	Expensive
Style	Smart casual
Cuisine	Modern European
Recommended for	Wish I'd opened

'Set in dense native bushland and only accessible by seaplane or boat. I can't think of a more idyllic location for a restaurant. A true Australian icon.'—Reon Hobson

BROWN SUGAR

Recommended by
Tomi Björck

106 Curlewis Street
Bondi
Sydney
New South Wales 2026
+61 291301566
www.brownsugarbondi.com.au

Opening hours	Closed Monday
Credit cards	Accepted
Price range	Budget
Style	Casual
Cuisine	Modern Australian
Recommended for	Breakfast

'Amazing breakfast: they've got everything and the flavours are right there. Nice staff and a relaxed atmosphere.'—Tomi Björck

ICEBERGS DINING ROOM AND BAR

Recommended by
Geoff Lindsay

1 Notts Avenue
Bondi
Sydney
New South Wales 2026
+61 293659000
www.idrb.com

Opening hours	Closed Monday
Credit cards	Accepted
Price range	Affordable
Style	Smart casual
Cuisine	Modern Italian
Recommended for	Wish I'd opened

'It's got to be one of the greatest locations in the world. A dreamy pale blue, chartreuse and white room perched above the waves on the cliffs of Bondi. Simple hearty dishes showcasing the best of Australia's ingredients, backed up by fastidious, attentive service. Each time I go, I don't want to leave.'—Geoff Lindsay

SEAN'S PANAROMA

Recommended by
Mike Eggert, Ross Lusted,
Luke Mangan, Bevan Smith

270 Campbell Parade
Bondi
Sydney
New South Wales 2026
+61 293654924
www.seanspanaroma.com.au

Opening hours	Closed Monday and Tuesday
Credit cards	Accepted
Price range	Affordable
Style	Casual
Cuisine	Modern Australian
Recommended for	Local favourite

'Situated on Sydney's most iconic beach, it uses locally farmed organic and biodynamic ingredients. It serves classically rustic fare cooked in a wood-fired oven. There aren't many nicer ways to spend a Sunday afternoon than perched on the street overlooking the beach sipping a beer and slurping fresh Sydney rock oysters.'—Mike Eggert

Sean Moran's restaurant has been serving modern cuisine to local residents, surfers and travellers to Sydney's North Bondi Beach for over a decade. It has a cosy and familial atmosphere with chequered tablecloths and charmingly scribbled chalkboard walls detailing their modern menu and range of boutique Australian wines. The unpretentious atmosphere befits the well-thought-out and eco-conscious menu. Ingredients are seasonal, predominantly grown on Moran's Blue Mountain Farm, thus leaving little by way of a carbon footprint. The prices may sometimes reflect this philosophical approach to cooking but when presented with silk aubergine (eggplant), ocean trout and organic beef of this quality, you tend not to mind.

AZUMA

Recommended by
Neil Perry

Chifley Plaza
1F, 2 Chifley Square
Central Business District
Sydney
New South Wales 2000
+61 292229960
www.azuma.com.au

Opening hours	Closed Sunday
Credit cards	Accepted
Price range	Affordable
Style	Smart casual
Cuisine	Japanese
Recommended for	Regular neighbourhood

'The sashimi is first rate and I love the *sukiyaki* of wagyu beef.'—Neil Perry

BENTLEY RESTAURANT & BAR

Recommended by
Praveen Anand

Radisson Blu Hotel
27 O'Connell Street
Central Business District
Sydney
New South Wales 2000
+61 282140505
www.thebentley.com.au

Opening hours	Closed Sunday
Credit cards	Accepted
Price range	Affordable
Style	Casual
Cuisine	Modern Australian
Recommended for	Worth the travel

'Global cuisine, brilliantly plated and exquisitely combined.'—Praveen Anand

BERTA

Recommended by
Martin Benn

17–19 Alberta Street
Central Business District
Sydney
New South Wales 2000
+61 292646133
www.berta.com.au

Opening hours	Closed Monday and Sunday
Credit cards	Accepted
Price range	Affordable
Style	Smart casual
Cuisine	Italian
Recommended for	Regular neighbourhood

'Contemporary Italian cuisine that evolves so frequently... I never tire of Berta.'—Martin Benn

THE BRIDGE ROOM

Recommended by
Ben Greeno, Neil Perry

GF, 44 Bridge Street
Central Business District
Sydney
New South Wales 2000
+61 292477000
www.thebridgeroom.com.au

Opening hours	Closed Monday and Sunday
Credit cards	Accepted
Price range	Expensive
Style	Smart casual
Cuisine	Modern Australian
Recommended for	Worth the travel

'It feels like home when you walk in there. Ross Lusted's food is thoughtful and exciting.'—Ben Greeno

Ross Lusted's return to the Harbour City after ten years overseas with Aman Resorts has been hailed as his finest hour – The Bridge Room arrived fully formed in 2011 and hasn't looked back. The sleek dining room, in an Art Deco building at the business end of town, is as graceful as the cooking, with parquet floors, banquettes and solid oak tables. Lusted's eclectic style nimbly incorporates elements of farm-to-table, new Nordic and Japanese – with the best dishes (duck with figs and plums, New England spring lamb) slow-smoked robata style over *bincho* charcoal.

CHAT THAI

20 Campbell Street
Central Business District
Sydney
New South Wales 2000
+61 292111808
www.chatthai.com.au

Recommended by
Mark Best, Tomi Björck,
Dan Hong, Kim Öhman

Opening hours	Open 7 days
Credit cards	Accepted
Price range	Budget
Style	Casual
Cuisine	Modern Thai
Recommended for	Late night

'Cheap, fast and delicious regional Thai cuisine. Great produce cooked with care and knowledge.'—Mark Best

CHINATOWN NOODLE KING

1F, 357 Sussex Street
Central Business District
Sydney
New South Wales 2000
+61 292660933

Recommended by
Neil Perry

Opening hours	Open 7 days
Reservation policy	No
Credit cards	Accepted
Price range	Budget
Style	Casual
Cuisine	Chinese
Recommended for	Bargain

'With its spicy hot pots, beer duck laden with chilli and coriander (cilantro), the tea mushroom dish, the cooling and spicy cucumber with chilli oil and the gluten salad, Chinatown Noodle King's not only cheap but delicious. It's hard to beat.'—Neil Perry

DEVINE

32 Market Street
Central Business District
Sydney
New South Wales 2000
+61 292626906
www.devinefoodandwine.com.au

Recommended by
Tetsuya Wakuda

Opening hours	Closed Sunday
Credit cards	Accepted
Price range	Affordable
Style	Casual
Cuisine	Mediterranean
Recommended for	Late night

'Great wine list by the glass, with a wide range of food, from snacks to meals.'—Tetsuya Wakuda

Sydney might be bursting at the seams with newer, cooler wine bars, but deVine has had the turf staked out since before most of the niche operators swirled their first Bornard. The food is a pretty straight-down-the-line mix of contemporary classics (pumpkin and goat's cheese salad dressed with pumpkin-seed oil, say, or fried school prawns with garlic dipping sauce), charcuterie and grills. The unifying theme across the menu is wine-friendliness. A glance down even just the list of drops offered by the glass – Austrian Sauvignon Blanc, sparkling Vouvray, Heathcote Nebbiolo all keeping easy company – confirms that here, at least, the glass comes before the fork.

DIN TAI FUNG

World Square Shopping Centre
1F, 644 George Street
Central Business District
Sydney
New South Wales 2000
+61 292646010
www.dintaifungaustralia.com.au

Recommended by
Dan Hong, Corey Lee

Opening hours	Open 7 days
Credit cards	Accepted
Price range	Budget
Style	Casual
Cuisine	Chinese
Recommended for	Wish I'd opened

'It has to be the most consistent restaurant in the whole world. Their *xiao long bao* (soup dumplings) are legendary and the service is always spot on.' —Dan Hong

EST.

1F, 252 George Street
Central Business District
Sydney
New South Wales 2000
+61 292403000

Recommended by
Luke Mangan

Opening hours	Closed Sunday
Credit cards	Accepted
Price range	Expensive
Style	Smart casual
Cuisine	Modern Australian
Recommended for	High end

'It has one of the most beautiful dining rooms in Sydney and the food is very elegant and refined. It's definitely a restaurant for special occasions.'
—Luke Mangan

ESTER

46–52 Meagher Street
Central Business District
Sydney
New South Wales 2008
+61 280688279
www.ester-restaurant.com.au

Recommended by
James Parry, Daniel
Puskas, Phil Wood

Opening hours	Closed Monday and Sunday
Credit cards	Accepted but not AMEX
Price range	Affordable
Style	Casual
Cuisine	Modern Australian
Recommended for	Regular neighbourhood

'A fantastic space, fun and laid back, with amazing food cooked by a very talented group of chefs headed by Matt Lindsay. There's an awesome blend of Asian and European flavours, a nice little wine list, the whole place is quality and I am always excited to go.'
—Phil Wood

GOLDEN CENTURY SEAFOOD

393–399 Sussex Street
Central Business District
Sydney
New South Wales 2000
+61 292811598
www.goldencentury.com.au

Recommended by
Mark Best, David
Chang, Peter Gilmore,
Ben Greeno, Dan Hong,
Dan Hunter, Ross Lusted,
Isaac McHale, James
Parry, Neil Perry, Daniel
Puskas, Phil Wood

Opening hours	Open 7 days
Credit cards	Accepted
Price range	Affordable
Style	Casual
Cuisine	Cantonese-Seafood
Recommended for	Late night

'It's an enormous restaurant seating upwards of 400 people and it's open till 4.00 a.m.! They serve all the classics, with live seafood from the tanks in the window. You'll pretty much always run into someone you know.'—James Parry

The Cantonese seafood specialist that locals like to call the Golden C, which Sydney's chefs make a habit of calling into late at night after work, is a clear cut above any other Chinese restaurant on Sussex Street – and arguably anywhere else in the city that does small-hours trade. The menu ranges from very affordable noodle dishes to a fantastic selection of live seafood. Insider tips from some of Sydney's finest include: trying the greenlip abalone steamboat with noodles and tofu (the abalone sliced live) and asking for the Charles Leong menu, named after Momofuku Seiōbo's sommelier-at-large.

HAPPY CHEF

Sussex Centre Food Court
401–403 Sussex Street
Central Business District
Sydney
New South Wales 2000
+61 292815832

Recommended by
Luke Mangan

Opening hours	Open 7 days
Reservation policy	No
Credit cards	Not accepted
Price range	Budget
Style	Casual
Cuisine	Chinese
Recommended for	Bargain

'They do the best chicken and spicy beef laksas and it's really cheap!'—Luke Mangan

MALAY-CHINESE TAKEAWAY

Shop 1, 50–58 Hunter Street
Central Business District
Sydney
New South Wales 2000
+61 292316788
www.malaychinese.com.au

Recommended by
Dan Hong

Opening hours	Closed Sunday
Reservation policy	No
Credit cards	Not accepted
Price range	Budget
Style	Casual
Cuisine	Malaysian
Recommended for	Bargain

'I go here for their laksas (best in Sydney) and their special *har mee* (Malaysian prawn[shrimp]noodle soup). It's delicious.'—Dan Hong

MAMAK

Recommended by
Ross Lusted,
Justin North

15 Goulburn Street
Central Business District
Sydney
New South Wales 2000
+61 292111668
www.mamak.com.au

Opening hours	Open 7 days
Reservation policy	No
Credit cards	Accepted
Price range	Budget
Style	Casual
Cuisine	Malaysian
Recommended for	Bargain

'Cheap and quality don't often go together, but Mamak is the exception to the rule. The talent of the chefs spinning the roti in the window is worth the wait in the inevitably long queue.'—Ross Lusted

MR. WONG

Recommended by
Martin Benn, Mark Best,
Peter Doyle, Rodney
Dunn, Luke Mangan

3 Bridge Lane
Central Business District
Sydney
New South Wales 2000
+61 292403000
www.merivale.com.au/mrwong

Opening hours	Open 7 days
Credit cards	Accepted
Price range	Expensive
Style	Smart casual
Cuisine	Cantonese
Recommended for	Late night

'A huge regional Chinese restaurant owned by the Hemmes family. It's in the basement of an old newspaper building and celebrates the warehouse space and Sydney's love of Chinese cuisine. It is a must for anyone visiting Sydney.'—Mark Best

Mr. Wong is a classic big-box Chinatown Canton Palace reimagined with a glam cast of finance-district diners and Wong Kar-wai production values (and prices to boot). That it paid off its hefty fit-out costs in no time flat is local legend, and testament to the brilliance of teaming local chef Dan Hong (a devotee of sneakers, hip-hop culture and Hong Kong dining), import Eric Koh (the *sifu* behind Hakkasan and Yauatcha's dim sum) and master sommelier Franck Moreau (the Burgundy-born genius who oversees a list rich in both Riesling and cool-climate Pinot and Moutai). Come early for dumplings or late for the likes of Sydney's best pepper mud crab — but always prepared to battle with a crowd of like-minded food fans.

PALACE CHINESE RESTAURANT

Recommended by
Dan Hong

Piccadilly Tower
1F, Shop 38, 133–145 Castlereagh Street
Central Business District
Sydney
New South Wales 2000
+61 292836288
www.palacechinese.com.au

Opening hours	Open 7 days
Credit cards	Accepted
Price range	Affordable
Style	Casual
Cuisine	Chinese
Recommended for	Breakfast

'They do the most consistent trolley-style dim sum in Sydney. I'm there at least once every two weeks. They know me now so I get looked after and they are baby friendly! The service is also a cut above most other Chinese restaurants.'—Dan Hong

PASTEUR

Recommended by
Michael Hunter, James Parry,
Tetsuya Wakuda

709 George Street
Central Business District
Sydney
New South Wales 2000
+61 292125622

Opening hours	Open 7 days
Reservation policy	No
Credit cards	Not accepted
Price range	Budget
Style	Casual
Cuisine	Vietnamese
Recommended for	Bargain

'Authentic Vietnamese food with a particularly fantastic pho.'—Tetsuya Wakuda

ROCKPOOL

11 Bridge Street
Central Business District
Sydney
New South Wales 2000
+61 292521888
www.rockpool.com

Opening hours	Closed Sunday
Credit cards	Accepted
Price range	Expensive
Style	Formal
Cuisine	Australian-Asian
Recommended for	High end

'A restaurant that has remained relevant and unique throughout its epic lifespan. Recently relocated and as incredible as ever, it's an industry leader.'—James Parry

ROCKPOOL BAR & GRILL

66 Hunter Street
Central Business District
Sydney
New South Wales 2000
+61 280781900
www.rockpool.com/sydney/bar-and-grill

Opening hours	Closed Sunday
Credit cards	Accepted
Price range	Expensive
Style	Smart casual
Cuisine	Steakhouse
Recommended for	Local favourite

'It has been a Sydney institution and a restaurant that, over twenty years, has helped define Australian cuisine.'
—Peter Gilmore

SEPIA

201 Sussex Street
Central Business District
Sydney
New South Wales 2000
+61 292831990
www.sepiarestaurant.com.au

Opening hours	Closed Monday and Sunday
Credit cards	Accepted
Price range	Expensive
Style	Smart casual
Cuisine	Modern Australian
Recommended for	High end

'Extremely good.'—Michael Wilson

SPICE TEMPLE

10 Bligh Street
Central Business District
Sydney
New South Wales 2000
+61 280781888
www.rockpool.com/sydney/spice-temple/

Opening hours	Closed Sunday
Credit cards	Accepted
Price range	Affordable
Style	Smart casual
Cuisine	Modern Chinese
Recommended for	Local favourite

'Neil Perry has the golden touch – it must be the power in the ponytail! He has helped so many chefs along the way and been at the forefront of Australian gastronomy for years, but he doesn't stop. He's not an institution, he's still very relevant, still very much leading the way.'
—Jock Zonfrillo

Rumour has it that the word 'chilli' appears on the Spice Temple menu 119 times; in truth the number is far smaller. But the words 'hot' and 'numbing' (and, better still, the phrase 'hot and numbing') take up the slack. Neil Perry's tribute to the more fiery cuisines of China is set against a moodily designer backdrop: think Mission Chinese meets Hakkasan, with the soundtrack more the latter than the former. The menu bounces from Szechuan to Yunnan, Hunan to Xinjiang, with the odd excursion to Shaanxi. The constant is clean and vital execution: the seafood in, say, fish drowned in heaven-facing chillies, or the steamed trevalla with salted red and green chilli, sings with freshness, while twice-cooked pork belly is crisp and giving in all the right places under its finely tuned leek and black-bean dressing. Hot stuff.

SUSSEX CENTRE FOOD COURT

Recommended by
Dan Hong

401 Sussex Street
Central Business District
Sydney
New South Wales 2000
+61 292816388

Opening hours	Open 7 days
Reservation policy	No
Credit cards	Not accepted
Price range	Budget
Style	Casual
Cuisine	Street Food
Recommended for	Regular neighbourhood

'Sussex Centre's food court has a range of food stalls, all of which are Asian. Two favourites of mine are Ramen Ikkyu which does amazing *tonkotsu* ramen and Happy Chef which does really good noodle soups and laksa. It's really cheap and there is a lot of variety ranging from Vietnamese, to Thai, Korean and Chinese.'—Dan Hong

SYDNEY MADANG

Recommended by
Neil Perry, Phil Wood

371a Pitt Street
Central Business District
Sydney
New South Wales 2000
+61 292647010

Opening hours	Open 7 days
Credit cards	Accepted
Price range	Budget
Style	Casual
Cuisine	Korean
Recommended for	Regular neighbourhood

'Go for the barbeque, hot pots and loads of kimchi.'
—Neil Perry

TETSUYA'S

Recommended by
Jean Beddington, Alfonso &
Ernesto Iaccarino, Jereme
Leung, Vicky Ratnani, Phil
Wood, Jock Zonfrillo

529 Kent Street
Central Business District
Sydney
New South Wales 2000
+61 292672900
www.tetsuyas.com

Opening hours	Closed Monday and Sunday
Credit cards	Accepted
Price range	Expensive
Style	Smart casual
Cuisine	Modern Japanese
Recommended for	High end

'One of the first restaurants I visited in Australia was Tetsuya's in Sydney. I have a warm place in my heart for Tetsuya's – it is still a beautiful restaurant. It's a classic now like the man himself – a class act indeed.'
—Jock Zonfrillo

PILU AT FRESHWATER

Recommended by
Peter Doyle

Moore Road
Freshwater
Sydney
New South Wales 2096
+61 299383331
www.piluatfreshwater.com.au

Opening hours	Closed Monday
Credit cards	Accepted
Price range	Affordable
Style	Smart casual
Cuisine	Italian
Recommended for	High end

'Friendly staff, in a beautiful location (you can see the surf) and the food is consistently good. The wines are always interesting too.'—Peter Doyle

FRANK'S PIZZA BAR & RESTAURANT

Recommended by
Jock Zonfrillo

137 Parramatta Road
Glebe
Sydney
New South Wales 2050
+61 295193404

Opening hours	Closed Monday
Credit cards	Not accepted
Price range	Budget
Style	Casual
Cuisine	Pizza
Recommended for	Bargain

'Ok, so I have to say you're maybe not going to get the best pizza you've ever eaten in your life. Don't get me wrong, it's delicious, but without getting all cheffy, you *have* to go to Frank's. It's all about the vibe. It's a Sydney institution. It's only 12 bucks (£7; $11) or something, a great pizza and of course there's Frank – the godfather of pizza in Australia. It's all about Frank and it's just cheap.'—Jock Zonfrillo

CHINESE NOODLE HOUSE

Recommended by
Mike Eggert,
Daniel Puskas

8 Quay Street
Haymarket
Sydney
New South Wales 2000
+61 292814508

Opening hours	Open 7 days
Reservation policy	No
Credit cards	Not accepted
Price range	Budget
Style	Casual
Cuisine	Chinese
Recommended for	Bargain

'Handmade noodles and dumplings with great flavours
and at a bargain price. Also the elderly Chinese owner
plays classical music on the violin while you eat.'
—Mike Eggert

KIRORAM SILKWOOD ROAD

Recommended by
Neil Perry

3–6 Harbour Street
Haymarket
Sydney
New South Wales 2000
+61 292830998

Opening hours	Open 7 days
Credit cards	Not accepted
Price range	Budget
Style	Casual
Cuisine	Chinese
Recommended for	Bargain

'Head here for a braise of chicken, tomato, potatoes,
noodles and cumin. This is peasant cooking at it's very
best and crazily cheap.'—Neil Perry

RAMEN IKKYU

Recommended by
Phil Wood

Shop F1A, 401 Sussex Street
Haymarket
Sydney
New South Wales 2000
+61 292810998
www.menikkyu.com.au

Opening hours	Open 7 days
Reservation policy	No
Credit cards	Not accepted
Price range	Budget
Style	Casual
Cuisine	Ramen Noodles
Recommended for	Bargain

'Does a great Tokyo ramen. There aren't many places
where you can go to a food court, order from-a-
counter ramen and have a multi-award winning chef
take your order. Thank you Haru.'—Phil Wood

HUGO'S MANLY

Recommended by
Peter Doyle

Manly Wharf
Shop 1, East Esplanade
Manly
Sydney
New South Wales 2011
+61 281168555
www.hugos.com.au

Opening hours	Open 7 days
Credit cards	Accepted
Price range	Affordable
Style	Smart casual
Cuisine	Italian
Recommended for	Local favourite

'By the water, stylish casual food, and a little hectic but
it's all there for an iconic Sydney casual restaurant.'
—Peter Doyle

BANANA BLOSSOM

Recommended by
Peter Gilmore

Shop 4, 17 Bungan Street
Mona Vale
Sydney
New South Wales 2103
+61 399973889

Opening hours	Closed Sunday
Reservation policy	No
Credit cards	Accepted
Price range	Budget
Style	Casual
Cuisine	Asian
Recommended for	Bargain

'They serve fresh, Asian inspired salads. It's good value
and tasty, healthy food.'—Peter Gilmore

ORMEGGIO AT THE SPIT

Recommended by
Peter Doyle

D'Albora Marinas
The Spit
Mosman
Sydney
New South Wales 2088
+61 299694088
www.ormeggio.com.au

Opening hours	Closed Monday and Tuesday
Credit cards	Accepted
Price range	Affordable
Style	Smart casual
Cuisine	Modern Italian
Recommended for	Regular neighbourhood

'Great location by The Spit water, relaxed, great food, friendly service and very close to home.'—Peter Doyle

Only an Italian in Sydney could create a 'fine-dining' restaurant so impressive yet so utterly approachable. Alessandro Pavoni's Ormeggio at The Spit offers a stunning view of the Middle Harbour sunset, yachts bobbing on the water, an ambitious menu and serious Italian wines. Suitable for a special occasion, but at the same time anybody can swing by for a panino from its kiosk. Lombardy-born Pavoni's contemporary cooking is ardently Italian but always open to wider influences, as in such dishes as wagyu beef with coffee-roasted heirloom carrots and hapuka. The Stressless Sunday menu – a tasting of six courses for A$69 (£37; $62) – offers great value.

PIZZA PESCE BIRRA

Recommended by
Peter Doyle

Shop B, 235 Spit Road
Mosman
Sydney
New South Wales 2088
+61 99684884
www.pizzapescebirra.com.au

Opening hours	Open 7 days
Credit cards	Accepted
Price range	Affordable
Style	Casual
Cuisine	Italian
Recommended for	Bargain

'A good spot for family meals and the menu caters for all ages.'—Peter Doyle

FINE FISH

Recommended by
Reon Hobson

75 Grosvenor Lane
Neutral Bay
Sydney
New South Wales 2089
+61 299084448
www.finefish.com.au

Opening hours	Closed Monday and Sunday
Credit cards	Accepted
Price range	Affordable
Style	Casual
Cuisine	Seafood
Recommended for	Bargain

'As far as hidden gems go, you can't go past Fine Fish. Try the snapper crudo or grilled King George whiting.'
—Reon Hobson

JUGEMU & SHIMBASHI RESTAURANT

Recommended by
Justin North

246 Military Road
Neutral Bay
Sydney
New South Wales 2089
+61 299043011
www.jugemushimbashi.com.au

Opening hours	Closed Monday
Reservation policy	No
Credit cards	Accepted
Price range	Affordable
Style	Casual
Cuisine	Japanese
Recommended for	Regular neighbourhood

'Amazing fresh sushi and sashimi, beautiful soba noodles, good miso and great staff.'—Justin North

BREAD & CIRCUS

Recommended by
Tetsuya Wakuda

21 Fountain Street
Newtown
Sydney
New South Wales 2015
+61 418214425
www.breadandcircus.com.au

Opening hours	Open 7 days
Reservation policy	No
Credit cards	Accepted
Price range	Budget
Style	Casual
Cuisine	Café
Recommended for	Breakfast

'Beautiful salami in an open space with great, fresh juices.'—Tetsuya Wakuda

MARRICKVILLE PORK ROLL
Recommended by
Ben Greeno

36 Illawarra Road
Newtown
Sydney
New South Wales 2204
+61 420966368

Opening hours	Open 7 days
Reservation policy	No
Credit cards	Not accepted
Price range	Budget
Style	Casual
Cuisine	Vietnamese
Recommended for	Bargain

'A hole-in-the-wall place with great banh mi.'
—Ben Greeno

While it's true that Sydney never met a Vietnamese sandwich it didn't like, there is a hierarchy in the banh mi world, and this nano-bakery in the heart of Marrickville's Vietnamese community sits at the top. Is it the bread? No, that's the usual crunchy baguette. The ingredients? The piles of spring onion (scallion), pickled carrot, cucumber, shredded iceberg lettuce and onions are certainly fresh and sliced with care, and the many permutations on the theme of cured and fresh pork are a cut above. But no, it's down to the balance, the particular verve with which Khiem and Emily Du mix everything on a base of pâté and mayo to make for a bite that's crunchy, creamy, spicy and salty all in one hit. That's what brings the queues.

MARY'S
Recommended by
Luke Burgess

6 Mary Street
Newtown
Sydney
New South Wales 2042

Opening hours	Open 7 days
Reservation policy	No
Credit cards	Accepted
Price range	Budget
Style	Casual
Cuisine	Burgers
Recommended for	Late night

'Late-night dining in Hobart is non-existent so my late-night choice involves travel and I love making my way to Mary's just before the burgers get a final call at 11.00 p.m. Throw in a completely smashable natural wine list and lock the doors.'—Luke Burgess

SIXPENNY
Recommended by
Shannon Bennett,
Dan Hunter, Phil Wood

83 Percival Road
Newtown
Sydney
New South Wales 2048
+61 295726666
www.sixpenny.com.au

Opening hours	Closed Monday and Tuesday
Credit cards	Accepted
Price range	Expensive
Style	Smart casual
Cuisine	Modern Australian
Recommended for	Worth the travel

'A couple of friends opened an ambitious fine diner in a suburb of Sydney, with produce coming from their farm in Bowral. I've been multiple times in the couple of years since it opened and love it every time. Dan and Jimmy are really on the way to creating something quite special.'—Phil Wood

THANH BINH
Recommended by
Phil Wood

111 King Street
Newtown
Sydney
New South Wales 2042
+61 295571175
www.thanhbinh.com.au

Opening hours	Closed Monday
Credit cards	Accepted
Price range	Affordable
Style	Casual
Cuisine	Vietnamese
Recommended for	Local favourite

10 WILLIAM ST

Recommended by
Mike Eggert,
Daniel Puskas

10 William Street
Paddington
Sydney
New South Wales 2021
+61 293603310
www.10williamst.com.au

Opening hours	Closed Sunday
Reservation policy	No
Credit cards	Accepted
Price range	Affordable
Style	Casual
Cuisine	Italian
Recommended for	Regular neighbourhood

'The food is fun and always changing and the wine list never disappoints with a fantastic range of natural wines from all over the world.'—Mike Eggert

LUCIO'S

Recommended by
Tetsuya Wakuda

47 Windsor Street
Paddington
Sydney
New South Wales 2021
+61 293805996
www.lucios.com.au

Opening hours	Closed Monday and Sunday
Credit cards	Accepted
Price range	Expensive
Style	Smart casual
Cuisine	Italian
Recommended for	Regular neighbourhood

'Normally I go for lunch. It's a beautiful, art-filled room. I try to choose different dishes each time I go but I keep going back to the crabmeat with green noodles and tomato.'—Tetsuya Wakuda

THE APOLLO

Recommended by
Ross Lusted

44 Macleay Street
Potts Point
Sydney
New South Wales 2011
+61 283540888
www.theapollo.com.au

Opening hours	Open 7 days
Credit cards	Accepted
Price range	Affordable
Style	Smart casual
Cuisine	Australian-Greek
Recommended for	Regular neighbourhood

'They really understand hospitality here and the food is always generous and consistent. It's very relaxing after a busy week in the restaurant.'—Ross Lusted

CHINA DOLL

Recommended by
Luke Mangan

Shop 4, 6 Cowper Wharf Road
Potts Point
Sydney
New South Wales 2011
+61 293806744
www.chinadoll.com.au

Opening hours	Open 7 days
Credit cards	Accepted
Price range	Expensive
Style	Smart casual
Cuisine	Modern Asian
Recommended for	Regular neighbourhood

'Great modern Asian cuisine. Perfect for business lunches.'—Luke Mangan

THE FISH SHOP

Recommended by
Mark Best

22 Challis Avenue
Potts Point
Sydney
New South Wales 2011
+61 293269000
www.merivale.com.au/thefishshop

Opening hours	Open 7 days
Reservation policy	No
Credit cards	Accepted
Price range	Affordable
Style	Casual
Cuisine	Seafood
Recommended for	Regular neighbourhood

'This food is simple, beautifully cooked and delicious. It has a complete lack of pretension and the room and service are efficient and charming.'—Mark Best

FRATELLI PARADISO

Recommended by
Ben Greeno

12–16 Challis Avenue
Potts Point
Sydney New South Wales 2011
+61 293571744
www.fratelliparadiso.com

Opening hours	Open 7 days
Reservation policy	No
Credit cards	Accepted
Price range	Affordable
Style	Casual
Cuisine	Italian
Recommended for	Local favourite

'It's an awesome place to hang out for a long lunch on a sunny weekend.'—Ben Greeno

MONOPOLE

Recommended by
Peter Doyle

71a Macleay Street
Potts Point
Sydney
New South Wales 2011
+61 293604410
www.monopolesydney.com.au

Opening hours	Open 7 days
Credit cards	Accepted
Price range	Affordable
Style	Casual
Cuisine	Modern Australian
Recommended for	Wish I'd opened

'For the simplicity, the unassuming kitchen producing interesting food and the personal approach.'
—Peter Doyle

ROOM 10

Recommended by
Neil Perry

10 Llankelly Place
Potts Point
Sydney
New South Wales 2011
+61 425810174

Opening hours	Open 7 days
Reservation policy	No
Credit cards	Not accepted
Price range	Budget
Style	Casual
Cuisine	Café
Recommended for	Breakfast

'The "two Dans" do fresh juice, great single-origin coffee and I love their toast with avocado and a soft boiled egg on top. Simple produce and well executed, some of the best coffee in town and a wonderful Sydney lane-way experience.'—Neil Perry

This pocket-sized Potts Point café is a short stroll from Kings Cross station and attracts a cool young crowd. Voted the best newcomer in the *Sydney Morning Herald*'s Good Café, shortly after opening in 2011, it's run by a right pair of Dans – Jackson (chef) and Blackman (manager). Freshly squeezed blood orange juice, loose-leaf teas and single-origin coffee courtesy of Mecca, pastries delivered daily by the Black Star patisserie in Newtown, and a short, sharp menu of simple, wholesome dishes. Spread avocado, tomato or ricotta on toast or try their Breakfast Rice made with banana, stewed rhubarb and honey.

JASMIN ONE

Recommended by
Luke Burgess

224 The Boulevard
Punchbowl
Sydney
New South Wales 2196
+61 297407866
www.jasmineonerestaurant.com.au

Opening hours	Open 7 days
Credit cards	Accepted but not AMEX
Price range	Budget
Style	Casual
Cuisine	Lebanese
Recommended for	Bargain

'This is Lebanese food for Lebanese palates and I love the pungency of the spices and pickles. Everything here is delicious. I've tried and I've failed to spend over A$10 (£5.50; $9) each time I visit.'—Luke Burgess

FLYING FISH

Recommended by
Reon Hobson

Jones Bay Wharf
Lower Deck, 19–21 Pirrama Road
Pyrmont
Sydney
New South Wales 2009
+61 295186677
www.flyingfish.com.au

Opening hours	Open 7 days
Credit cards	Accepted
Price range	Expensive
Style	Smart casual
Cuisine	Modern Australian
Recommended for	Late night

'Great way to start the night, breathtaking views and stunning desserts.'—Reon Hobson

MOMOFUKU SEIŌBO

Recommended by
Jason Atherton,
Martin Benn, Mike
Eggert, Dan Hunter,
Andrew McConnell,
Rafael Osterling

The Star
GF, 80 Pyrmont Street
Pyrmont
Sydney
New South Wales 2009
+61 297779000
www.momofuku.com

Opening hours	Closed Sunday
Credit cards	Accepted
Price range	Expensive
Style	Smart casual
Cuisine	Korean
Recommended for	Worth the travel

'Beautiful restaurant design and forward-thinking food that's beautifully presented. They're guaranteed to be playing great music, they have a baller wine list and the front-of-house staff are some of the best.'
—Mike Eggert

That David Chang chose Sydney for his first venture outside New York surprised some. But it makes perfect sense when you consider the city's stellar standard of Asian cooking, against which he knew he'd be judged. Opened in late 2011 in the Star casino, reservations, as at other Momofuku establishments, are secured via their website. It's built around an open kitchen, with an L-shaped dining counter offering the best view of the action. With a black and white picture of AC/DC's Angus Young on the wall, the rock 'n' roll tasting menu of Asian-accented courses is overseen by the very capable Ben Greeno.

CHAIRMAN MAO

Recommended by
Neil Perry, Phil Wood

189 Anzac Parade
Randwick
Sydney
New South Wales 2033
+61 296979189

Opening hours	Closed Tuesday
Credit cards	Accepted
Price range	Affordable
Style	Casual
Cuisine	Chinese
Recommended for	Regular neighbourhood

'The pork dishes are amazing and the spice levels incendiary – I love it. Try the cumin lamb – it's not for the faint hearted.'—Neil Perry

BERNASCONI'S

Recommended by
Luke Mangan

23 Plumer Road
Rose Bay
Sydney
New South Wales 2029
+61 293275717

Opening hours	Open 7 days
Reservation policy	No
Credit cards	Accepted
Price range	Budget
Style	Casual
Cuisine	Café
Recommended for	Breakfast

'They have a great breakfast menu and serve excellent coffee. I love their spring breakfast dish of quinoa, goat's curd, poached eggs and smoked salmon.'
—Luke Mangan

CATALINA

Recommended by
Luke Mangan,
Tetsuya Wakuda

Lyne Park
New South Head Road
Rose Bay
Sydney
New South Wales 2029
+61 293710555
www.catalinarosebay.com.au

Opening hours	Open 7 days
Credit cards	Accepted
Price range	Expensive
Style	Smart casual
Cuisine	Modern Australian
Recommended for	Local favourite

'They have the view, great food and fantastic service.'
—Tetsuya Wakuda

Catalina floats airily above Rose Bay like one of its
namesake seaplanes, and is every inch a pleasure
craft. It's very much 'customer first' here (as it should
be when you're paying prices like these), which goes
some of the way to explaining why the kitchen runs
a separate sushi and sashimi menu in tandem with a
carte stacked with modern European dishes. Thus
a long lunch could wend its way from whiting sliced
paper-thin, *usuzukuri*-style, to roast quail, hazelnuts
and pickled golden beets, and then the signature
roast suckling pig. With a cellar this good, too, there's
no sense in rushing things.

THE SWIMMERS CLUB

Recommended by
Peter Doyle

594 New South Head Road
Rose Bay
Sydney
New South Wales 2029
+61 293276561

Opening hours	Open 7 days
Reservation policy	No
Credit cards	Accepted but not AMEX
Price range	Affordable
Style	Casual
Cuisine	Café-Bistro
Recommended for	Breakfast

'You cannot beat The Swimmers Club for breakfast.'
—Peter Doyle

KITCHEN BY MIKE

Recommended by
Mark Best

85 Dunning Avenue
Rosebery
Sydney
New South Wales 2018
+61 290450910
www.kitchenbymike.com.au

Opening hours	Open 7 days
Reservation policy	No
Credit cards	Accepted but not AMEX
Price range	Budget
Style	Casual
Cuisine	Café
Recommended for	Breakfast

'Owner Mike McEnearney is the "Mike" behind the
food, selecting produce and developing all the menu
items. Formerly an executive chef at Rockpool, he also
spent time in London cooking up a storm at Pharmacy
and with the Conran group. This place is a giant canteen
annex to an design space in a stripped-out warehouse.
Solid, no fuss, home-style food. A central wood oven
produces all sorts of smoky deliciousness. It is gutsy,
earthy and good.'—Mark Best

121BC

Recommended by
Mike Eggert

Shop 4,
50 Holt Street
Surry Hills
Sydney
New South Wales 2010
+61 296991582
www.121bc.com.au

Opening hours	Closed Monday and Sunday
Reservation policy	No
Credit cards	Accepted
Price range	Affordable
Style	Casual
Cuisine	Italian small plates
Recommended for	Wish I'd opened

'Run by the legendary Giorgio De Maria, who has
gathered an exceptional natural Italian wine list and
sells it with gusto. I love the small and simple design
layout that is intimate and comfortable. They also have
some seriously tasty snacks.'—Mike Eggert

ABDUL'S RESTAURANT

Recommended by
Phil Wood

563 Elizabeth Street
Surry Hills
Sydney
New South Wales 2010
+61 296981275
www.abdulsrestaurant.com.au

Opening hours	Open 7 days
Credit cards	Accepted
Price range	Affordable
Style	Casual
Cuisine	Lebanese
Recommended for	Local favourite

CAFE MINT

Recommended by
James Parry

579 Crown Street
Surry Hills
Sydney
New South Wales 2010
+61 293190848
www.cafemint.com.au

Opening hours	Closed Monday
Credit cards	Accepted but not AMEX
Price range	Affordable
Style	Casual
Cuisine	Middle Eastern-European
Recommended for	Breakfast

'A slightly Middle Eastern take on breakfast: spicy lamb mince with hummus or scrambled eggs with spinach, mint and feta. The owner, Hugh Foster, travelled from Bangkok to London by land in the early 1970s. He's full of great stories and always up for a chat.'
—James Parry

FATIMA'S

Recommended by
Mike Eggert, James Parry

294–296 Cleveland Street
Surry Hills
Sydney
New South Wales 2010
+61 296984895
www.fatimas.com.au

Opening hours	Open 7 days
Credit cards	Accepted
Price range	Budget
Style	Casual
Cuisine	Lebanese
Recommended for	Late night

'Late-night Lebanese food. The best falafels and grilled-to-order kebabs, not forgetting the vegetables – grilled okra topped with hummus to chew on while you wait. A visit to Fatima's was almost a daily occurrence once upon a time.'—James Parry

KEPOS STREET KITCHEN

Recommended by
Ross Lusted

96 Kepos Street
Surry Hills
Sydney
New South Wales 2016
+61 293193919
www.keposstreetkitchen.com.au

Opening hours	Closed Monday
Credit cards	Accepted
Price range	Affordable
Style	Casual
Cuisine	Middle Eastern
Recommended for	Breakfast

'It's great to see a different offering for breakfast and Kepos always delivers just that. Great Middle Eastern flavours, home-styled dishes, plus the best fresh orange juice in town.'—Ross Lusted

LONGRAIN

Recommended by
Michael Wilson

85 Commonwealth Street
Surry Hills
Sydney
New South Wales 2010
+61 292802888
www.longrain.com.au

Opening hours	Open 7 days
Credit cards	Accepted
Price range	Affordable
Style	Casual
Cuisine	Modern Asian
Recommended for	Regular neighbourhood

'Good Australian-influenced Thai food and a relaxed atmosphere.'—Michael Wilson

MARQUE

Recommended by
Peter Gilmore, Ross Lusted

4/5 355 Crown Street
Surry Hills
Sydney
New South Wales 2010
+61 293322225
www.marquerestaurant.com.au

Opening hours	Closed Sunday
Credit cards	Accepted
Price range	Expensive
Style	Smart casual
Cuisine	Modern French
Recommended for	High end

'Mark Best is one of Australia's most talented chefs. As a chef it's always an inspiration to dine at Marque, I always learn something after a meal there.'
—Ross Lusted

You sometimes get the impression that Mark Best has ended up at the cutting edge of haute cuisine in Australia simply because he'd be bored anywhere else. His press for innovation and refinement is relentless, across both the food and wine sides of the operation. Barely there swatches of smoked eel complement equally evanescent Parmesan gnocchi, while mustard is the twist in a dessert of mango and coconut. Even the cheese course comes from left field: a soft French goat's cheese paired with the seemingly disparate flavours of pineapple and onion, and played off against a bunch-pressed Tasmanian Riesling. It's edgy dining, but handled with a cool head.

REUBEN HILLS

Recommended by
Neil Perry, Phil Wood

61 Albion Street
Surry Hills
Sydney
New South Wales 2010
+61 292115556
www.reubenhills.com.au

Opening hours	Open 7 days
Reservation policy	No
Credit cards	Accepted
Price range	Budget
Style	Casual
Cuisine	Café
Recommended for	Wish I'd opened

'Breakfast, more often than not, is a piece of toast and a coffee on the way to work, but if I had the time for a long breakfast, Rueben Hills would be the place for it. Great baked eggs, nice produce-driven salads, good espresso and cold infusion coffee.'—Phil Wood

SPICE I AM

Recommended by
Phil Wood

90 Wentworth Avenue
Surry Hills
Sydney
New South Wales 2010
+61 292800928
www.spiceiam.com

Opening hours	Open 7 days
Reservation policy	No
Credit cards	Not accepted
Price range	Budget
Style	Casual
Cuisine	Thai
Recommended for	Local favourite

Opened in 2004, this is the original bistro of four outposts from executive chef Sujet Saenkham, who left a remote village in Central Thailand to work as a Qantas flight attendant before becoming what critics and customers regard as Sydney's most talented Thai chef. Beyond the queues (waiting lines) – no bookings are taken – walls are plastered with reviews, some yellowing, while tables are tightly packed. Service is fast but friendly, and Saenkham's soulful dishes, featuring spice, chillies and locally grown herbs rather than sugar and salt, can – beware – be very hot. These may include an aubergine (eggplant) stir-fry with garlic and shrimp paste, deep-fried mini spring rolls and red duck curry.

THREE BLUE DUCKS

143 Macpherson Street
Tamarama
Sydney
New South Wales 2024
+61 293890010
www.threeblueducks.com

Opening hours	Open 7 days
Credit cards	Accepted
Price range	Affordable
Style	Casual
Cuisine	Australian-Asian
Recommended for	Breakfast

'Relaxed holiday atmosphere, great food, beautiful garden and beautiful people. It's a perfect way to spend a Sydney morning.'—Mike Eggert

The casual look of this breezy café up the hill from Bronte Beach, opened in 2010 by a couple of local surfer dudes, belies an ambitious kitchen. No white linen or creaky service, but the fine dining pedigree shows in the commitment to stellar ingredients. At breakfast, eggs are organic, pastries made on site, sourdough comes from Iggy's Bread down the road and coffee is roasted fifteen minutes away. It's all showcased to dazzling effect in the likes of bacon and organic egg roll with pimento salsa and hollandaise, and pecan and raisin fruit toast with ricotta and home-made berry jam. You can't book for breakfast, so expect to have to wait for a table at weekends.

TASTEBUDS

287 Mona Vale Road
Terry Hills
Sydney
New South Wales 2084
+61 294500873

Opening hours	Open 7 days
Credit cards	Accepted
Price range	Budget
Style	Casual
Cuisine	Café
Recommended for	Breakfast

'It's within a garden centre and has a nice casual atmosphere. I love their corn fritters and bacon.'
—Peter Gilmore

ONE SIX EIGHT

168 Kent Street
The Rocks
Sydney
New South Wales 2000
+61 279004857
www.onesixeightrestaurant.com.au

Opening hours	Closed Monday and Sunday
Credit cards	Accepted
Price range	Affordable
Style	Smart casual
Cuisine	Modern Australian
Recommended for	Regular neighbourhood

'Whether it is a night out or a night in they have you covered from degustation to take away (take out).'
—Reon Hobson

QUAY

Overseas Passenger Terminal
5 Hickson Road
The Rocks
Sydney
New South Wales 2000
+61 292515600
www.quay.com.au

Opening hours	Open 7 days
Credit cards	Accepted
Price range	Expensive
Style	Smart casual
Cuisine	Modern Australian
Recommended for	High end

'Peter Gilmore is a master of flavour and texture. His food is the most delicate and refined in Sydney. I can't go past the mudcrab congee and seasonal "snow egg".'
—Dan Hong

CHISWICK

65 Ocean Street
Woollahra
Sydney
New South Wales 2025
+61 283888688
www.chiswickrestaurant.com.au

Recommended by
Jason Atherton

Opening hours	Open 7 days
Credit cards	Accepted
Price range	Affordable
Style	Casual
Cuisine	Modern Australian
Recommended for	Worth the travel

VINCENT

14 Queen Street
Woollahra
Sydney
New South Wales 2025
+61 280391500
www.vincentfrench.com.au

Recommended by
Ben Greeno

Opening hours	Closed Monday
Credit cards	Accepted
Price range	Affordable
Style	Smart casual
Cuisine	French
Recommended for	Regular neighbourhood

'Light airy room, really well done French food and
French wine list. It reminds me of being in Europe.'
—Ben Greeno

'In my opinion, they roast and serve the best coffee in Australia.'
DAN HUNTER P112

'The best service and maybe the best Chinese food in the world. People come from everywhere to eat here.'
TETSUYA WAKUDA P107

MELBOURNE

'A MELBOURNE INSTITUTION.'
FRANK CAMORRA P 108

'THE PERENNIAL QUEEN OF NIGHT-TIME LIBATION FOR THE HOSPO SET. ONE OF MELBOURNE'S BEST WINE LISTS, KILLER TOASTED SANDWICHES AND A WHO'S WHO OF RESTAURANT COGNOSCENTI.'
GEOFF LINDSAY PP108–9

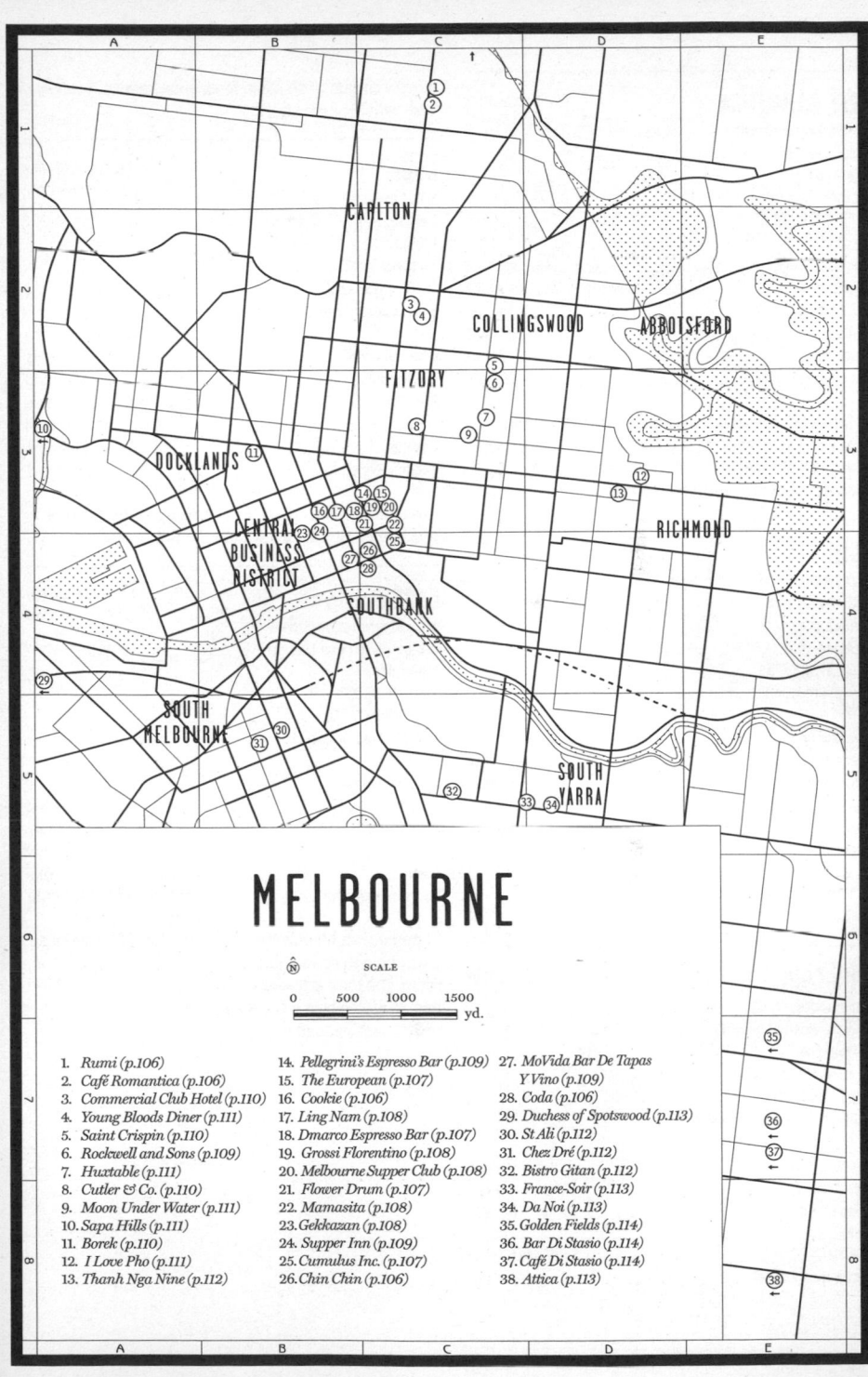

MELBOURNE

Ⓝ SCALE

0   500   1000   1500
yd.

CAFÉ ROMANTICA

Recommended by
Josh Murphy

52–54 Lygon Street
Brunswick East
Melbourne
Victoria 3057
+61 393804437

Opening hours	Open 7 days
Credit cards	Accepted but not AMEX
Price range	Budget
Style	Casual
Cuisine	Italian
Recommended for	Late night

'A late night Brunswick favourite, open twenty-four hours and serving pizza and Peroni. It was the last leg of a night out that went on a little bit longer than it probably should have.'—Josh Murphy

RUMI

Recommended by
Christian F. Puglisi

116 Lygon Street
Brunswick East
Melbourne
Victoria 3057
+61 393888255
www.rumirestaurant.com.au

Opening hours	Open 7 days
Credit cards	Accepted
Price range	Budget
Style	Casual
Cuisine	Lebanese
Recommended for	Worth the travel

'A very inspiring Lebanese restaurant.'
—Christian F. Puglisi

CHIN CHIN

Recommended by
Dan Hunter, Justin North

125 Flinders Lane
Central Business District
Melbourne
Victoria 3000
+61 386632000
www.chinchinrestaurant.com.au

Opening hours	Open 7 days
Credit cards	Not accepted
Price range	Budget
Style	Casual
Cuisine	Southeast Asian
Recommended for	Late night

'Lovely simple fresh Asian food, great service, friendly and swift.'—Justin North

CODA

Recommended by
Bevan Smith

141 Flinders Lane
Central Business District
Melbourne
Victoria 3000
+61 396503155
www.codarestaurant.com.au

Opening hours	Open 7 days
Credit cards	Accepted
Price range	Expensive
Style	Smart casual
Cuisine	Asian-European
Recommended for	Late night

'Great food, vibe, drinks list and pumping busy. Great place to escape for a few hours.'—Bevan Smith

COOKIE

Recommended by
Shannon Bennett

1F, 252 Swanston Street
Central Business District
Melbourne
Victoria 3000
+61 396637660
www.cookie.net.au

Opening hours	Open 7 days
Credit cards	Accepted
Price range	Affordable
Style	Smart casual
Cuisine	Thai
Recommended for	Local favourite

'It epitomizes Melbourne; I love the whole Curtin House concept with its roof-top cinema, book shop and band room. The food is traditional Thai – actually some of the best in Melbourne – cooked by little old ladies.'
—Shannon Bennett

CUMULUS INC.
45 Flinders Lane
Central Business District
Melbourne
Victoria 3000
+61 396501445
www.cumulusinc.com.au

Opening hours	Open 7 days
Credit cards	Accepted but not Diners
Price range	Affordable
Style	Casual
Cuisine	Modern Australian
Recommended for	Local favourite

'For me, this is a restaurant for every occasion when I am in Melbourne – for a coffee or a quick dinner, for a drink or a long lazy lunch. It's hard for a restaurant to achieve all these things but this is one of those restaurants.'—Ross Lusted

Andrew McConnell's all-day restaurant, a stripped-back rag-trade building on arty-fashiony Flinders Lane, has given the already well-established chef a place to let his choice of ingredients speak for themselves. The result is an unimaginably perfect variety of food. Breakfast includes grilled Lyonnaise sausage with smoked hock and braised beans on the one hand and lemon-curd-filled madeleines on the other. À la carte, there are eight varieties of oysters, one starter is a tin of Ortiz anchovies, and there are another eight kinds of charcuterie. This is before even mentioning the cooking… You can never grow tired of Cumulus.

DMARCO ESPRESSO BAR
Shop 11, 103 Little Bourke Street
Central Business District
Melbourne
Victoria 3000
+61 396393676

Opening hours	Closed Saturday and Sunday
Reservation policy	No
Credit cards	Not accepted
Price range	Budget
Style	Casual
Cuisine	Café
Recommended for	Breakfast

'Coffee is consistently excellent, as is the food, which is simple but always makes for a great start to the day.'
—Anthony Lui

THE EUROPEAN
161 Spring Street
Central Business District
Melbourne
Victoria 3000
+61 396504811
www.theeuropean.com.au

Opening hours	Open 7 days
Credit cards	Accepted
Price range	Affordable
Style	Casual
Cuisine	European
Recommended for	Regular neighbourhood

'This is more often than not where I end up. Casual lunches in the wine shop are popular and there's even a grocer and cheesemonger for home supplies. A favourite is their croque monsieur and a glass of Champagne after service on Sunday nights.'
—Josh Murphy

FLOWER DRUM
17 Market Lane
Central Business District
Melbourne
Victoria 3000
+61 396623655
www.flower-drum.com

Opening hours	Open 7 days
Credit cards	Accepted
Price range	Affordable
Style	Smart casual
Cuisine	Chinese
Recommended for	High end

'The best service and maybe the best Chinese food in the world. People come from everywhere, including Hong Kong and Asia, to eat here.'—Tetsuya Wakuda

GEKKAZAN

Recommended by
Robin Wickens

Melbourne's GPO
350 Bourke Street
Central Business District
Melbourne
Victoria 3000
+61 396637767

Opening hours	Open 7 days
Credit cards	Accepted
Price range	Budget
Style	Casual
Cuisine	Japanese
Recommended for	Bargain

'Authentic Japanese classics including brilliant nori rolls.'—Robin Wickens

GROSSI FLORENTINO

Recommended by
Frank Camorra,
Anthony Lui

80 Bourke Street
Central Business District
Melbourne
Victoria 3000
+61 396621811
www.grossiflorentino.com

Opening hours	Closed Sunday
Credit cards	Accepted
Price range	Affordable
Style	Smart casual
Cuisine	Italian
Recommended for	Local favourite

'A Melbourne institution. There has been a hospitality operation on this site since the 1870s making it the oldest restaurant in Melbourne. Grossi Florentino's has something for everyone, from the old-world charm in its upstairs Italian fine-dining room to the more corporate feel of the grill and the relaxed Italian fare in the cellar bar. Generations of Melbournians have loved this restaurant. Since the Grossi family took over in 1999 the old restaurant has been given a new lease of life and energy.'—Frank Camorra

LING NAM

Recommended by
Frank Camorra

204 Little Bourke Street
Central Business District
Melbourne
Victoria 3000
+61 396632347

Opening hours	Open 7 days
Reservation policy	No
Credit cards	Accepted
Price range	Budget
Style	Casual
Cuisine	Chinese
Recommended for	Late night

'A simple Chinese restaurant in Chinatown open until 3.00 a.m. Great place to go with the staff after a busy service. The chilli mud crab gets very messy with a table full of ravenous chefs.'—Frank Camorra

MAMASITA

Recommended by
Shannon Bennett

Level 1, 11 Collins Street
Central Business District
Melbourne
Victoria 3000
+61 396503821
www.mamasita.com.au

Opening hours	Open 7 days
Credit cards	Accepted
Price range	Affordable
Style	Smart casual
Cuisine	Mexican
Recommended for	Late night

'Very simple. I love Mexican food.'—Shannon Bennett

MELBOURNE SUPPER CLUB

Recommended by
Geoff Lindsay

1F, 161 Spring Street
Central Business District
Melbourne
Victoria 3000
+61 396546300

Opening hours	Open 7 days
Credit cards	Accepted
Price range	Affordable
Style	Smart casual
Cuisine	Bar-Small plates
Recommended for	Late night

'The perennial queen of night-time libation for the hospo set. One of Melbourne's best wine lists, killer toasted sandwiches and a who's who of restaurant cognoscenti.'
—Geoff Lindsay

MOVIDA BAR DE TAPAS Y VINO
Recommended by
Bevan Smith

1 Hosier Lane
Central Business District
Melbourne
Victoria 3000
+61 396633038
www.movida.com.au

Opening hours	Open 7 days
Credit cards	Accepted
Price range	Budget
Style	Casual
Cuisine	Small plates
Recommended for	Worth the travel

'The whole package: great food, wine, service and they didn't turn us away when we mentioned our kids would be eating too.'—Bevan Smith

PELLEGRINI'S ESPRESSO BAR
Recommended by
Frank Camorra

66 Bourke Street
Central Business District
Melbourne
Victoria 3000
+61 396621885

Opening hours	Open 7 days
Reservation policy	No
Credit cards	Not accepted
Price range	Affordable
Style	Casual
Cuisine	Italian
Recommended for	Breakfast

'It feels like this classic Italian bar hasn't changed since it opened Melbourne's floodgates to coffee in the 1950s. I have been coming here for a coffee since I first started working in the area. The place exudes charm and nostalgia. It's usually a quick coffee at the counter for me but they also make toasted sandwiches. Just don't expect anything fancy.'—Frank Camorra

SUPPER INN
Recommended by
Robin Wickens

15 Celestial Avenue
Central Business District
Melbourne
Victoria 3000
+61 396634759

Opening hours	Open 7 days
Credit cards	Accepted
Price range	Affordable
Style	Casual
Cuisine	Chinese
Recommended for	Late night

'Cheap Chinese classics. A Melbourne institution and no matter how busy they are, they always manage to find a table for me!'—Robin Wickens

ROCKWELL AND SONS
Recommended by
Anthony Lui

288 Smith Street
Collingwood
Melbourne
Victoria 3066
+61 384150700
www.rockwellandsons.com.au

Opening hours	Closed Tuesday
Credit cards	Accepted
Price range	Affordable
Style	Casual
Cuisine	American
Recommended for	Regular neighbourhood

'This is my son's favourite burger hangout. It's a bit of a departure from what I normally have but it's good to eat and be in an environment that is completely different to where you work and what you deal with every day. Plus the burgers are pretty great as well.'
—Anthony Lui

SAINT CRISPIN

Recommended by
Anthony Lui

300 Smith Street
Collingwood
Melbourne
Victoria 3066
+61 394192202
www.saintcrispin.com.au

Opening hours	Closed Monday and Sunday
Credit cards	Accepted
Price range	Affordable
Style	Smart casual
Cuisine	Modern Australian
Recommended for	Wish I'd opened

'I love the buzz of the dining room, the open kitchen and the interaction between the diners, staff and chefs. I usually leave the menu up to the kitchen and it hasn't failed to impress. It's got that difficult balance between a relaxed and refined fine dining down to a fine art.'
—Anthony Lui

BOREK

Recommended by
Frank Camorra

Queen Victoria Market
Shop 95, Corner of Victoria Street
and Elizabeth Street
Docklands
Melbourne
Victoria 3000
www.qvm.com.au

Opening hours	Closed Monday and Wednesday
Reservation policy	No
Credit cards	Not accepted
Price range	Budget
Style	Casual
Cuisine	Turkish
Recommended for	Bargain

'It's almost unthinkable for me to visit the amazing Queen Victoria food market without purchasing a delicious A$3 (£1.50; $2.80) lamb borek from the ladies at the stall in the deli hall. In fact it's very difficult just to stop at one. There is usually a long queue (waiting line) at the counter but don't be put off – the women handling the demand are super efficient and the wait is well worth it.'—Frank Camorra

COMMERCIAL CLUB HOTEL

Recommended by
Josh Murphy

344 Nicholson Street
Fitzroy
Melbourne
Victoria 3065
+61 394191522

Opening hours	Open 7 days
Credit cards	Accepted
Price range	Budget
Style	Casual
Cuisine	Gastropub
Recommended for	Bargain

'My local pub. A great classic pub menu that is very reasonably priced, and a very comfortable bar where they pour the best glass of Carlton Draft in the city.'
—Josh Murphy

CUTLER & CO.

Recommended by
Robin Wickens,
Michael Wilson

55–57 Gertrude Street
Fitzroy
Melbourne
Victoria 3065
+61 394194888
www.cutlerandco.com.au

Opening hours	Closed Monday
Credit cards	Accepted
Price range	Affordable
Style	Smart casual
Cuisine	Modern Australian
Recommended for	High end

'Exciting food, great wine list and there is always a fantastic, lively atmosphere.'—Robin Wickens

Chef Andrew McConnell has got about a bit. As well as working for Greg Malouf, Australia's guru of Middle Eastern cuisine, he's run restaurants in Hong Kong and Shanghai. No surprise, then, that the menu of intricate and inventive dishes at this former metal workshop in Melbourne's boho Fitzroy suburb is punctuated with global influences. Start with a sashimi of kingfish with fennel and horseradish followed by strip steak with bone marrow and chimichurri. The industrial chic surroundings, featuring whitewashed brick walls and sculpted bar, are as cutting-edge as the food.

HUXTABLE

Recommended by
Shaun Clouston

131 Smith Street
Fitzroy
Melbourne
Victoria 3065
+61 394195101
www.huxtablerestaurant.com.au

Opening hours	Closed Monday
Credit cards	Accepted
Price range	Budget
Style	Casual
Cuisine	Modern Australian
Recommended for	Worth the travel

'Always a favourite when travelling to Melbourne. Tasty and thoughtful food, wine and some great Aussie craft beer.'—Shaun Clouston

MOON UNDER WATER

Recommended by
James Henry

Builders Arms Hotel
211 Gertrude Street   .
Fitzroy
Melbourne
Victoria 3065
+61 394177700
www.buildersarmshotel.com.au

Opening hours	Closed Monday and Sunday
Credit cards	Accepted
Price range	Expensive
Style	Smart casual
Cuisine	Modern International
Recommended for	Worth the travel

'Intelligent and thoughtful cooking as well as being delicious.'—James Henry

YOUNG BLOODS DINER

Recommended by
Josh Murphy

60 Rose Street
Fitzroy
Melbourne
Victoria 3058
+61 394193864
www.theyoungbloods.com.au

Opening hours	Open 7 days
Reservation policy	No
Credit cards	Accepted
Price range	Budget
Style	Casual
Cuisine	Café
Recommended for	Breakfast

'A great restaurant adjacent to a small artists' market. Chef Sascha Randle uses exceptionally fresh local produce and the food is comforting and thoughtful. Great coffee and the open design provides all-natural light – a great start to the morning. There is a rooftop space as well that lends itself to Bloody Marys on slow afternoons in Fitzroy.'—Josh Murphy

SAPA HILLS

Recommended by
Frank Camorra

112 Hopkins Street
Footscray
Melbourne
Victoria 3011
+61 396875729
www.sapahills.com.au

Opening hours	Open 7 days
Credit cards	Accepted
Price range	Budget
Style	Casual
Cuisine	Vietnamese
Recommended for	Regular neighbourhood

'Delicious, simple Vietnamese food that appeals to both my young kids and me. It's the sort of place that is usually packed with families so nobody raises an eyebrow if the kids start to play up. The food is lovely and it's a busy vibrant dining room.'—Frank Camorra

I LOVE PHO

Recommended by
Geoff Lindsay,
Anthony Lui,
Andrew McConnell

264 Victoria Street
Richmond
Melbourne
Victoria 3121
+61 394277749

Opening hours	Open 7 days
Reservation policy	No
Credit cards	Not accepted
Price range	Budget
Style	Casual
Cuisine	Vietnamese
Recommended for	Bargain

'I love to eat pho as the first meal of the day – it's one of the world's greatest restorative tonics. I head to Little Saigon, the Vietnamese community hub of Victoria Street in Richmond and eat at the aptly named I Love Pho. I love the fact that minimal conversation is required both before, during and after the act, that it provides instant gratification to even the most cloudy head, and that the judicious addition of chilli provides enough of an endorphin rush to unfurl the wings of salvation!'
—Geoff Lindsay

THANH NGA NINE

Recommended by
Geoff Lindsay

160 Victoria Street
Richmond
Melbourne
Victoria 3121
+61 394277068

Opening hours	Open 7 days
Credit cards	Accepted
Price range	Budget
Style	Casual
Cuisine	Vietnamese
Recommended for	Bargain

'Again in Little Saigon and clearly showing my bent towards Vietnamese food, Thanh Nga Nine is a great place to sample regional and lesser-known Vietnamese dishes. Don't expect great service or designer fittings, but it is cheap. Try the *banh xeo* (savoury pancakes), the *canh chua ca* (sour fish soup) or the *ca kho to* (braised fish in a claypot).'—Geoff Lindsay

CHEZ DRÉ

Recommended by
Robin Wickens

285–287 Coventry Street
South Melbourne
Melbourne
Victoria 3205
+61 396902688
www.chezdre.com.au

Opening hours	Open 7 days
Reservation policy	No
Credit cards	Accepted
Price range	Affordable
Style	Casual
Cuisine	Café
Recommended for	Breakfast

'Great coffee (always important for breakfast!) and fantastic house-made breads and pastries.'
—Robin Wickens

ST ALI

Recommended by
Dan Hunter

12–18 Yarra Place
South Melbourne
Melbourne
Victoria 3205
+61 396862990
www.stali.com.au

Opening hours	Open 7 days
Reservation policy	No
Credit cards	Accepted
Price range	Affordable
Style	Casual
Cuisine	Café
Recommended for	Breakfast

'In my opinion, they roast and serve the best coffee in Australia.'—Dan Hunter

BISTRO GITAN

Recommended by
Robin Wickens

52 Toorak Road West
South Yarra
Melbourne
Victoria 3141
+61 398675853
www.bistrogitan.com.au

Opening hours	Closed Sunday
Credit cards	Accepted
Price range	Affordable
Style	Smart casual
Cuisine	French Bistro
Recommended for	Regular neighbourhood

'A beautiful little bistro run by a French family with a great wine list.'—Robin Wickens

FRANCE-SOIR

11 Toorak Road
South Yarra
Melbourne
Victoria 3141
+61 398668569
www.france-soir.com.au

Recommended by
Josh Murphy

Opening hours	Open 7 days
Credit cards	Accepted
Price range	Affordable
Style	Smart casual
Cuisine	French Brasserie
Recommended for	Local favourite

'Unbelievably broad and good-value wine list, great simple food. French brasserie in style, it's great for a steak tartare, and they do a wonderful cous cous royale on Monday nights.'—Josh Murphy

DA NOI

95 Toorak Road
South Yarra
Melbourne
Victoria 3141
+61 398665975

Recommended by
Frank Camorra

Opening hours	Closed Sunday
Credit cards	Accepted
Price range	Affordable
Style	Casual
Cuisine	Italian
Recommended for	Wish I'd opened

'Ever since I ate at Da Noi as a young apprentice chef, I have loved this place. A traditional Sicilian daily menu is created by chef-owner Pietro Porcu. The menu changes daily relative to what is in season or what the chef feels like cooking. The idea of throwing away the à la carte menu has always appealed to me from the perspective of a chef but also as a customer.'—Frank Camorra

DUCHESS OF SPOTSWOOD

87 Hudsons Road
Spotswood
Melbourne
Victoria 3015
+61 393916016
www.duchessofspotswood.com.au

Recommended by
Andrew McConnell

Opening hours	Open 7 days
Credit cards	Accepted but not Amex or Diners
Price range	Budget
Style	Casual
Cuisine	Bar-Bistro
Recommended for	Breakfast

ATTICA

74 Glen Eira Road
St Kilda
Melbourne
Victoria 3185
+61 395300111
www.attica.com.au

Recommended by
Junya Yamasaki, Martin Benn,
Alejandro Cancino, Shaun
Clouston, Kobe Desramaults,
Fergus Henderson, Dan Hunter,
Geoff Lindsay, Andrew McConnell,
Michael Meredith, Josh Murphy,
Magnus Nilsson, Christian
Puglisi, Daniel Puskas, René
Redzepi, Michael Wilson,
Jock Zonfrillo

Opening hours	Closed Monday and Sunday
Credit cards	Accepted
Price range	Expensive
Style	Smart casual
Cuisine	Modern Australian
Recommended for	Worth the travel

'Ben Shewry is brilliantly inventive. His restaurant serves some of the most inspiring, thoughtful and delicious food in the world. It's honest, without the trickery that sometimes pervades in modern "cheffy" temples, and is matched by a quietly confident service.'—Geoff Lindsay

Attica's black walls and spotlighting belie the playful nature of head chef Ben Shewry's renowned Melbourne dining room, with dishes much lighter and more vibrant than the decor would have you believe. What the room might lack in personality is made up for by the food, with the famously hands-on chef ploughing his own furrow, often blending Asian and indigenous ingredients for interesting combos. To catch Attica at its best, head down on a Tuesday night when the kitchen is testing and developing new menu ideas – for a snip of what you'd normally pay, experience its five-course menu.

BAR DI STASIO

Recommended by
Shannon Bennett,
Andrew McConnell

31 Fitzroy Street
St Kilda
Melbourne
Victoria 3182
+61 395253999
www.distasio.com.au

Opening hours	Closed Sunday to Thursday
Reservation policy	No
Credit cards	Accepted
Price range	Affordable
Style	Smart casual
Cuisine	Italian
Recommended for	Regular neighbourhood

'I really like it. The bar is great, and Mallory Wall, the maître d', typifies Melbourne. The menu showcases food that is now ingrained as part of our food culture. Many restaurants exist like this, but Di Stasio does it their way and with such great passion.'
—Shannon Bennett

Café Di Stasio is a St Kilda institution, and has been providing the residents of this bohemian neighbourhood with fine Italian food and local wines (the owner also runs a vineyard in the Yarra Valley) for nearly twenty-five years. A recent expansion and refurbishment, however, has allowed the creation of the strikingly minimalist Bar Di Stasio just alongside, where smart staff serve smart customers a range of upscale *aperitivi* to go with their single-vineyard Chardonnay. And being open until late, there's plenty of time to make the most of it all.

CAFÉ DI STASIO

Recommended by
Geoff Lindsay,
Tetsuya Wakuda

31 Fitzroy Street
St Kilda
Melbourne
Victoria 3182
+61 395253999
www.distasio.com.au

Opening hours	Open 7 days
Credit cards	Accepted
Price range	Affordable
Style	Smart casual
Cuisine	Italian
Recommended for	Wish I'd opened

'Simple Italian cuisine with the most attentive and warm service. Every time I go to Melbourne I go there and feel like I've come home.'—Tetsuya Wakuda

GOLDEN FIELDS

Recommended by
Martin Benn

157 Fitzroy Street
St Kilda
Melbourne
Victoria 3182
+61 395254488
www.goldenfields.com.au

Opening hours	Closed Monday
Credit cards	Accepted
Price range	Expensive
Style	Casual
Cuisine	Asian small plates
Recommended for	Local favourite

'Contemporary Asian food at its best.'—Martin Benn

NEW ZEALAND & FIJI

'Exemplary food and service in a stunning rural location.'
AL BROWN P119

What a dream restaurant.'
BENJAMIN BAYLY P118

'It's a hidden jewel of a restaurant. The food is diverse, seasonal, and beautifully cooked and the wine list is exceptional.'
MARTIN BOSLEY P124

FIJI

Ba p.133 ♦

Auckland pp.126–133 ♦

Hawke's Bay p.120 ♦

N E W Z E A L A N D

♦ Wellington pp.123–125

Canterbury pp.118–119 ♦

NEW ZEALAND & FIJI

♦ Otago pp.121–123

SCALE

N̂

0   80   160

mi.

BRACU

Bracu Olive Estate
49 Main Road
Bombay
Auckland 2675
+64 92361030
www.bracu.co.nz

Opening hours	Closed Monday and Tuesday
Credit cards	Accepted
Price range	Affordable
Style	Casual
Cuisine	Modern New Zealand
Recommended for	Wish I'd opened

'I wish I could live in the countryside, cook in a beautiful villa on an olive oil estate and grow my own vegetables like chef Mikey Newlands. What a dream restaurant.'
—Benjamin Bayly

THE OYSTER INN

Recommended by
Miles Kirby

124 Ocean View Road
Oneroa
Waiheke Island
Auckland 1081
+64 93722222
www.theoysterinn.co.nz

Opening hours	Open 7 days
Credit cards	Accepted
Price range	Affordable
Style	Casual
Cuisine	Modern Seafood
Recommended for	Worth the travel

'Great setting, great food, great place.'—Miles Kirby

The Oyster Inn on Waiheke Island, a short ferry trip from Auckland, is what happened when its Kiwi owners left their glamorous fashion and events jobs in London for a new life in New Zealand. Andrew Glenn and Jonathan Rutherfurd-Best created their dream seaside retreat in a stately white building above the ocean, complete with veranda, chichi beach shop, 'fish and chippery' and sunshine yellow vintage camper van. They've lured back another Kiwi, Cristian Hossack (ex-The Providores, London), to helm the kitchen; his 'beachy' bistro menu of fried mussels, oysters, pulled pork sliders and fish pie pleases locals and day trippers.

BURGER AND BEERS INC.

Recommended by
Reon Hobson

355–357 Colombo Street
Christchurch
Canterbury 8023
+64 33543336
www.burgersandbeersinc.co.nz

Opening hours	Open 7 days
Credit cards	Accepted
Price range	Budget
Style	Casual
Cuisine	Burgers
Recommended for	Regular neighbourhood

'Still the best burgers in town – it's where I go to get my Iwi burger fix.'—Reon Hobson

Burger and Beers Inc. does, well, exactly what you might expect. This confessedly 'rock 'n' roller' joint, with its carefully honed menu offering 'grown-up burgers for grown-ups', proves that substance can indeed achieve parity with style. Limited variety does not make the offering dull. One hundred per cent Angus patties are served with unusual accompaniments, such as Béarnaise sauce, roast pumpkin mayo and date chutney. If beef isn't to your liking, scan the right side of the menu for Camembert burgers and other more inventive veggie options. There's an excellent craft beers list.

FIDDLESTICKS RESTAURANT & BAR

Recommended by
Reon Hobson

48 Worcester Boulevard
Christchurch
Canterbury 8013
+64 33650533
www.fiddlesticksbar.co.nz

Opening hours	Open 7 days
Credit cards	Accepted
Price range	Affordable
Style	Smart casual
Cuisine	Modern New Zealand
Recommended for	Breakfast

'For something a little different to start the day try the duck confit hash, malted onion puree and fried egg.'
—Reon Hobson

THE MONDAY ROOM

Recommended by
Reon Hobson

Strategy House
Level 1, 367 Moorhouse Avenue
Christchurch
Canterbury 8011
+64 33775262
www.themondayroom.co.nz

Opening hours	Open 7 days
Credit cards	Accepted
Price range	Affordable
Style	Casual
Cuisine	International
Recommended for	Late night

'After service there is only one place to go and relax.
It's a real hospitality hangout with a great selection
of tapas and yakitori.'—Reon Hobson

The Monday Room's owners had two bars that were
destroyed in the earthquake of 2011. This all-day
venue opened shortly after that disaster and is
now known as one of the best cocktail bars in this
resilient city. It's modern in both aesthetic and menu,
with bare bulbs and exposed brick characterizing
the former, and a geographically rootless tendency
to the latter. Eggy brunch dishes segue to lunchtime
tapas such as garlic prawn sandwich with chilli
mayo; dinner can see great yakitori, sashimi and
other Japanese-influenced dishes. The drinks menu
emphasizes whisky.

SAGGIO DI VINO

Recommended by
Reon Hobson

Carlton Butchery
179 Victoria Street
Christchurch
Canterbury 8013
+64 33794006
www.saggiodivino.co.nz

Opening hours	Open 7 days
Credit cards	Accepted
Price range	Affordable
Style	Smart casual
Cuisine	Modern New Zealand
Recommended for	Local favourite

'Still going strong through two earthquakes and one
relocation. Great cheese trolley (cart).'—Reon Hobson

VENUTI

Recommended by
Reon Hobson

791 Colombo Street
Christchurch
Canterbury 8011
+64 33772454
www.venuti.co.nz

Opening hours	Open 7 days
Credit cards	Accepted but not AMEX
Price range	Affordable
Style	Smart casual
Cuisine	Italian
Recommended for	Bargain

'For a cheap night out without sacrificing on ambience
or service. Try the prosciutto and rocket (arugula)
pizza.'—Reon Hobson

PEGASUS BAY

Recommended by
Reon Hobson, Bevan Smith

Pegasus Bay Winery
263 Stockgrove Road
Waipara
Canterbury 7482
+64 33146869
www.pegasusbay.com

Opening hours	Open 7 days
Credit cards	Accepted
Price range	Expensive
Style	Casual
Cuisine	Modern European
Recommended for	Local favourite

'Exemplary food and service in a stunning rural location.
Everything a restaurant should be.'—Bevan Smith

Food and wine are in harmony at the restaurant at
Pegasus Bay Winery in the Waipara Valley, one of New
Zealand's best winery restaurants. An Italian-inspired
repast of local ingredients in the restaurant or garden
follows on nicely from a morning's tasting, though
Christchurch foodies see it as destination in itself
and regularly drive the half hour here just for lunch.
All dishes come with a recommended wine from the
family winery's 40-hectare (100-acre) vineyard.
Whole Muscovy duck for two with kirsch cherry jus,
fennel, pine nuts and mint sounds like a good excuse
to crack open a bottle of Prima Donna Pinot Noir, the
estate's flagship red.

COMMON ROOM

Recommended by
Terry Lowe

227 Heretaunga Street East
Hastings
Hawke's Bay 4122
+64 276568959
www.commonroombar.com

Opening hours	Closed Sunday to Tuesday
Reservation policy	No
Credit cards	Accepted
Price range	Budget
Style	Casual
Cuisine	Bar Snacks
Recommended for	Late night

'A great meeting place and nice platters.'—Terry Lowe

MAMACITA

Recommended by
Terry Lowe

12 Havelock Road
Hastings
Hawke's Bay 4157
+64 68776200

Opening hours	Closed Monday
Reservation policy	No
Credit cards	Accepted but not AMEX
Price range	Budget
Style	Casual
Cuisine	Mexican
Recommended for	Regular neighbourhood

'It has a vibrant and relaxed atmosphere with simple, fresh and tasty Mexican-style food and very friendly staff.'—Terry Lowe

ROSE AND SHAMROCK VILLAGE INN

Recommended by
Terry Lowe

15 Napier Road
Hastings
Hawke's Bay 4130
+64 68772999
www.roseandshamrock.co.nz

Opening hours	Open 7 days
Reservation policy	No
Credit cards	Accepted
Price range	Affordable
Style	Casual
Cuisine	Gastropub
Recommended for	Bargain

'Reminds me of my mum's cooking with a great selection of beers.'—Terry Lowe

TASTE CORNUCOPIA

Recommended by
Terry Lowe

219 Heretaunga Street East
Hastings
Hawke's Bay 4122
+64 68788730
www.tastecornucopia.co.nz

Opening hours	Closed Saturday and Sunday
Credit cards	Accepted
Price range	Affordable
Style	Casual
Cuisine	Café
Recommended for	Breakfast

'It has a great chef and all the breakfast meals are cooked from scratch.'—Terry Lowe

PACIFICA

Recommended by
Terry Lowe

209 Marine Parade
Napier
Hawke's Bay 4110
+64 68336335
www.pacificarestaurant.co.nz

Opening hours	Closed Sunday
Credit cards	Accepted
Price range	Affordable
Style	Smart casual
Cuisine	Modern New Zealand
Recommended for	Local favourite

'Innovative, cosy and refined.'—Terry Lowe

THE FARM AT CAPE KIDNAPPERS

Recommended by
Terry Lowe

446 Clifton Road
Te Awanga
Hawke's Bay 4157
+64 68751900
www.capekidnappers.com

Opening hours	Open 7 days
Credit cards	Accepted
Price range	Expensive
Style	Formal
Cuisine	Modern New Zealand
Recommended for	High end

'It has got stunning views with a luxurious homely feel and the finest food.'—Terry Lowe

FLEURS PLACE

Recommended by
Ben Batterbury

169 Haven Street
Moeraki
Otago 9482
+64 34394480
www.fleursplace.com

Opening hours	Closed Monday and Tuesday
Credit cards	Accepted
Price range	Affordable
Style	Casual
Cuisine	Seafood
Recommended for	Local favourite

'A restaurant that is renowned in an amazing location with great character and the freshest fish you can eat.' —Ben Batterbury

Moeraki is an old whaling station in Central Otago and its rich seafaring history is preserved in the setting and cooking of Fleurs Place. Sitting right on the jetty, you couldn't get any closer to the sea without being in it, and the local boats deliver their catch right to Fleur Sullivan's door. Blue cod, dory, blue nose, gurnard (sea robin), sole, flounder, groper, crayfish... the menu is dictated by what comes in. One non-fish speciality worth trying is mutton-bird, or titi, which is a local seabird. But it's the fish that has earned Fleurs Place its reputation as a must-stop for locals and passing tourists alike.

RIVERSTONE KITCHEN

Recommended by
Jay Sherwood

1431 State Highway 1, RD 5H
Oamaru
Otago 9493
+64 34313505
www.riverstonekitchen.co.nz

Opening hours	Closed Tuesday and Wednesday
Credit cards	Accepted
Price range	Affordable
Style	Casual
Cuisine	Modern New Zealand
Recommended for	Worth the travel

'The majority of their food is harvested from their own kitchen garden.'—Jay Sherwood

Situated 12 km (7 miles) outside Oamaru in North Otago, Riverstone Kitchen is well placed to base its culinary philosophy on local, seasonal ingredients. They grow in abundance here, as a glimpse in the kitchen garden will testify. With its own jams and ice cream on sale, this light, airy establishment is very much the wholesome country café, but the food is on a different level. Chef Bevan Smith learned his trade in London – at Pont de la Tour and Canteen, via a stint at E'cco Bistro in Brisbane – and it shows. From the Mt Cook salmon to the teashop's cakes, every mouthful makes you feel good.

AMISFIELD BISTRO

Recommended by
Bevan Smith

Amisfield Winery
10 Lake Hayes Road, RD1
Queenstown
Otago 9371
+64 34420556
www.amisfield.co.nz

Opening hours	Open 7 days
Credit cards	Accepted
Price range	Affordable
Style	Casual
Cuisine	Modern New Zealand
Recommended for	Local favourite

ATLAS BEER CAFÉ

Recommended by
Ben Batterbury,
Jay Sherwood

Steamer Wharf
88 Beach Street
Queenstown
Otago 9300
+64 34425995
www.atlasbeercafe.com

Opening hours	Open 7 days
Reservation policy	No
Credit cards	Accepted
Price range	Budget
Style	Casual
Cuisine	Gastropub
Recommended for	Wish I'd opened

'Best beers in town and everything they do they do very well.'—Jay Sherwood

BELLA CUCINA

Recommended by
Jay Sherwood

6 Brecon Street
Queenstown
Otago 9300
+64 34426762
www.bellacucina.co.nz

Opening hours	Open 7 days
Credit cards	Accepted
Price range	Affordable
Style	Casual
Cuisine	Italian
Recommended for	Regular neighbourhood

'I like their wood-fired pizza because the ingredients are always fresh and they constantly change their menu.'—Jay Sherwood

THE BUNKER

Recommended by
Ben Greeno, Jay Sherwood

14 Cow Lane
Queenstown
Otago 9300
+64 34418030
www.thebunker.co.nz

Opening hours	Open 7 days
Credit cards	Accepted
Price range	Affordable
Style	Casual
Cuisine	European
Recommended for	High end

'Their menu is outstanding – their food is perfectly presented and always delicious.'—Jay Sherwood

FERGBURGER

Recommended by
Ben Batterbury

42 Shotover Street
Queenstown
Otago 9300
+64 34411232
www.fergburger.com

Opening hours	Open 7 days
Reservation policy	No
Credit cards	Accepted
Price range	Budget
Style	Casual
Cuisine	Burgers
Recommended for	Late night

'Fergburger is a local legend. If you can be patient enough to survive the permanent queue (waiting line) it's well worth the wait.'—Ben Batterbury

From backstreet, hole-in-the-wall joint to mainstream Main Street success, Queenstown's Fergburger is an Aotearoa burger legend. Open 21/7, the burgers are made with prime New Zealand cuts, chargrilled and served in a soft white roll, that despite its suspect, pillowy consistency heroically holds together long enough to keep its contents – much like the average Kiwi after a night on the town. They burger up everything from beef in the classic quarter-pound Fergburger, to venison in the Sweet Bambi, via making an offer that's hard to refuse with The Codfather, the brutally self-explanatory Little Lamby and the vegetarian-friendly falafel-packed Bun Laden.

KAPPA SUSHI CAFE

Recommended by
Ben Batterbury,
Jay Sherwood

36A The Mall
Queenstown
Otago 9197
+64 34411423

Opening hours	Open 7 days
Reservation policy	No
Credit cards	Accepted
Price range	Budget
Style	Casual
Cuisine	Japanese
Recommended for	Regular neighbourhood

'Delicious bento boxes and the cherry blossoms in the window make me feel like I'm in Japan.'
—Jay Sherwood

NO5 CHURCH LANE

Recommended by
Jay Sherwood

The Spire Hotel
5 Church Lane
Queenstown
Otago 9300
+64 34410004
www.no5churchlane.co.nz

Opening hours	Open 7 days
Credit cards	Accepted
Price range	Affordable
Style	Smart casual
Cuisine	Thai Fusion
Recommended for	Late night

'They have amazing cocktails and tapas.'
—Jay Sherwood

VUDU CAFÉ & LARDER

Recommended by
Ben Batterbury,
Jay Sherwood

16 Rees Street
Queenstown
Otago 9300
+64 34425357
www.vudu.co.nz

Opening hours..Open 7 days
Reservation policy..No
Credit cards..Accepted
Price range..Budget
Style..Casual
Cuisine..Café
Recommended for..Breakfast

'I love the fresh juices and the communal seating.'
—Jay Sherwood

Vudu Café & Larder serves a brilliantly late breakfast (until 5.00 p.m.) in a carefully thought-out room. This collages laser-cut ply with a web of glass jar lights, lab stools and a very large picture of a dramatic mountain landscape (rivalled only by the actual snow-capped ones outside). Sister site to the long-standing Vudu Café, organic plates include free-range poached eggs and grilled halloumi on sourdough with smashed avocado, cherry tomatoes, shaved radish and olive oil, or house-cured Mt. Cook Alpine Salmon with rösti potatoes, poached egg, spinach and beetroot (beet) relish. Small but perfectly formed, Vudu Café & Larder is worth braving the queue (waiting line) for the coffee alone.

YAMA EXPRESS

Recommended by
Ben Batterbury

The Pavilion
1 Beach Street
Queenstown
Otago 9300
+64 34429124

Opening hours..Open 7 days
Credit cards..Accepted
Price range..Budget
Style..Casual
Cuisine..Japanese
Recommended for..Bargain

'Situated in the local shopping mall's food court, this is a real gem in an unusual setting serving consistently great sushi. Beware... it is addictive!'—Ben Batterbury

MIDORI

Recommended by
Bevan Smith

1 Ribble Street
Oamaru
Waitaki
Otago 9400
+64 34349045

Opening hours..Closed Monday
Credit cards..Accepted but not AMEX
Price range..Budget
Style..Casual
Cuisine..Japanese
Recommended for..Regular neighbourhood

'Good sushi and no-fuss cheerful Japanese dishes in an understated setting.'—Bevan Smith

FEDERAL DINER

Recommended by
Bevan Smith

47 Helwick Street
Wanaka
Otago 9305
+64 34435152
www.federaldiner.co.nz

Opening hours..Open 7 days
Credit cards..Accepted
Price range..Budget
Style..Casual
Cuisine..Café
Recommended for..Breakfast

'Great place to refuel, tucked away from the crowds. Busy but it still manages to have a relaxed vibe, good coffee, and a sense of humour.'—Bevan Smith

DRAGONS CHINESE RESTAURANT

Recommended by
Martin Bosley

25 Tory Street
Wellington
Wellington 6011
+64 43843288
www.wellingtondragons.co.nz

Opening hours..Open 7 days
Credit cards..Accepted
Price range..Budget
Style..Casual
Cuisine..Chinese
Recommended for..Bargain

'Yum Cha on a Saturday morning, the best steamed dumplings ever.'—Martin Bosley

FLORIDITAS

Recommended by
Martin Bosley

161 Cuba Street
Wellington
Wellington 6011
+64 43812212
www.floriditas.co.nz

Opening hours	Open 7 days
Credit cards	Accepted
Price range	Affordable
Style	Casual
Cuisine	International
Recommended for	Breakfast

'It has a busy atmosphere, the menu is broad and appealing, the cooking excellent, the service charming and efficient.'—Martin Bosley

A bustling, perennially popular café in Wellington's Cuba Street (though the Havana connection doesn't really stretch any further than the name), Floriditas has built up a loyal following by doing the basics not just very well, but reliably well. The coffee is excellent, the baked goods as impressive as you'll find anywhere (head baker Emily Keshav's wares are now so popular they supply cafés throughout the area) and the service is efficient enough to slice through the queues (waiting lines) before you have time to finish your Bloody Mary. A top New Zealand wine list and signature dishes like smoked mackerel mash further draw the crowds.

HAVANA BAR & RESTAURANT

Recommended by
Martin Bosley

32a–34 Wigan Sreet
Wellington
Wellington 6011
+64 43847039
www.havanabar.co.nz

Opening hours	Closed Sunday
Credit cards	Accepted
Price range	Affordable
Style	Casual
Cuisine	Spanish Tapas
Recommended for	Late night

'It's a hidden jewel of a restaurant. The food is diverse, seasonal, and beautifully cooked and the wine list is exceptional.'—Martin Bosley

Havana unravels within two nineteenth-century cabins on Wigan Street, an area once notorious for its gambling, opium dens and bordellos. Today, classy bar staff mix updated cocktails such as the Cuban Manhattan or roasted apricot Ron Collins, alongside staples like the Negroni or Old Fashioned. Tapas, prepared in the open kitchen, include sautéed prawns in Kashmiri chilli, steamed cockles with home-cured bacon, and halloumi with sweet red pepper relish and rosemary oil. Follow with manuka honey and lime chocolate truffles. Cuban cigars and coffee are also to hand, alongside a vivid soundtrack, making this one of Wellington's best destinations for burning the midnight oil.

LITTLE PENANG

Recommended by
Shaun Clouston

40 Dixon Street
Wellington
Wellington 6011
+64 43829818

Opening hours	Closed Sunday
Credit cards	Accepted but not AMEX
Price range	Budget
Style	Casual
Cuisine	Malaysian
Recommended for	Bargain

'Easily the best Malaysian street food in town. Authentic and well worth the visit.'—Shaun Clouston

MARANUI CAFÉ

Recommended by
Neil Anthony Tomes

Maranui Surf Life Saving Club
The Parade
Wellington
Wellington 6022
+64 43874539
www.maranuicafe.co.nz

Opening hours	Open 7 days
Reservation policy	No
Credit cards	Accepted
Price range	Budget
Style	Casual
Cuisine	Café
Recommended for	Worth the travel

After being nearly destroyed by a fire in 2009 it looked like the end for the 100-year-old Maranui Surf Lifesaving Club. But a spontaneous outpouring of affection (not to mention money) from politicians and concerned locals meant a refurbished clubroom and café opening a little under a year later. Decorated in quirky 1940s surf style, with stunning views over Lyall Bay, it's not hard to see why so many fought for its survival. There's great coffee ('The fire,' reads the menu, 'only made the coffee stronger'), friendly service and crowd-pleasing dishes like Eggs Benedict and the gut-busting, vegetarian Victory Breakfast.

NIKAU CAFÉ

Recommended by
Martin Bosley, Shaun
Clouston

City Art Gallery
101 Wakefield Street
Wellington
Wellington 6011
+64 48014168
www.nikaucafe.co.nz

Opening hours	Closed Sunday
Reservation policy	No
Credit cards	Accepted
Price range	Budget
Style	Casual
Cuisine	Café
Recommended for	Breakfast

'Great coffee, friendly staff, a fantastic sunny courtyard and the best scrambled eggs on the planet.'
—Shaun Clouston

Opened in 1998, the Nikau is Wellington's best-kept secret, serving creative food using good (organic, local, you know the score) ingredients in an improbably attractive corner of the Wellington Gallery. Like many of the town's better coffee shops, they offer excellent coffee and baked goods alongside more substantial dishes like the popular kedgeree or pork saltimbocca, green beans, sage and marsala. The fact that they grow their own vegetables in a courtyard garden, make their own sloe gin and roll their own pasta, perhaps shows the effort and attention to detail that goes into the menu here.

ORTEGA FISH SHACK & BAR

Recommended by
Shaun Clouston

16 Majoribank Street
Wellington
Wellington 6011
+64 43829559
www.ortega.co.nz

Opening hours	Closed Monday and Sunday
Credit cards	Accepted
Price range	Affordable
Style	Smart casual
Cuisine	Seafood
Recommended for	Regular neighbourhood

'A popular venue for local chefs, well-cooked food by one of the country's best chefs. The restaurant has a superb drinks list and great service team in the dining room. If they have it, try a glass of home-made digestif after dinner.'—Shaun Clouston

'IMMACULATE FOOD IN A GLORIOUS SPACE WITH NEAR FAULTLESS SERVICE.'

BEVAN SMITH P130

'AN EXPERIENCE THAT WILL TAKE YOUR BREATH AWAY.'

BENJAMIN BAYLY P131

AUCKLAND

'THIS PLACE DOES MEAN DIRTY DUMPLINGS, WHICH ARE JUST DELICIOUS.'

AL BROWN P131

'It's tapas but with a Kiwiana twist.'

SIMON WRIGHT P128

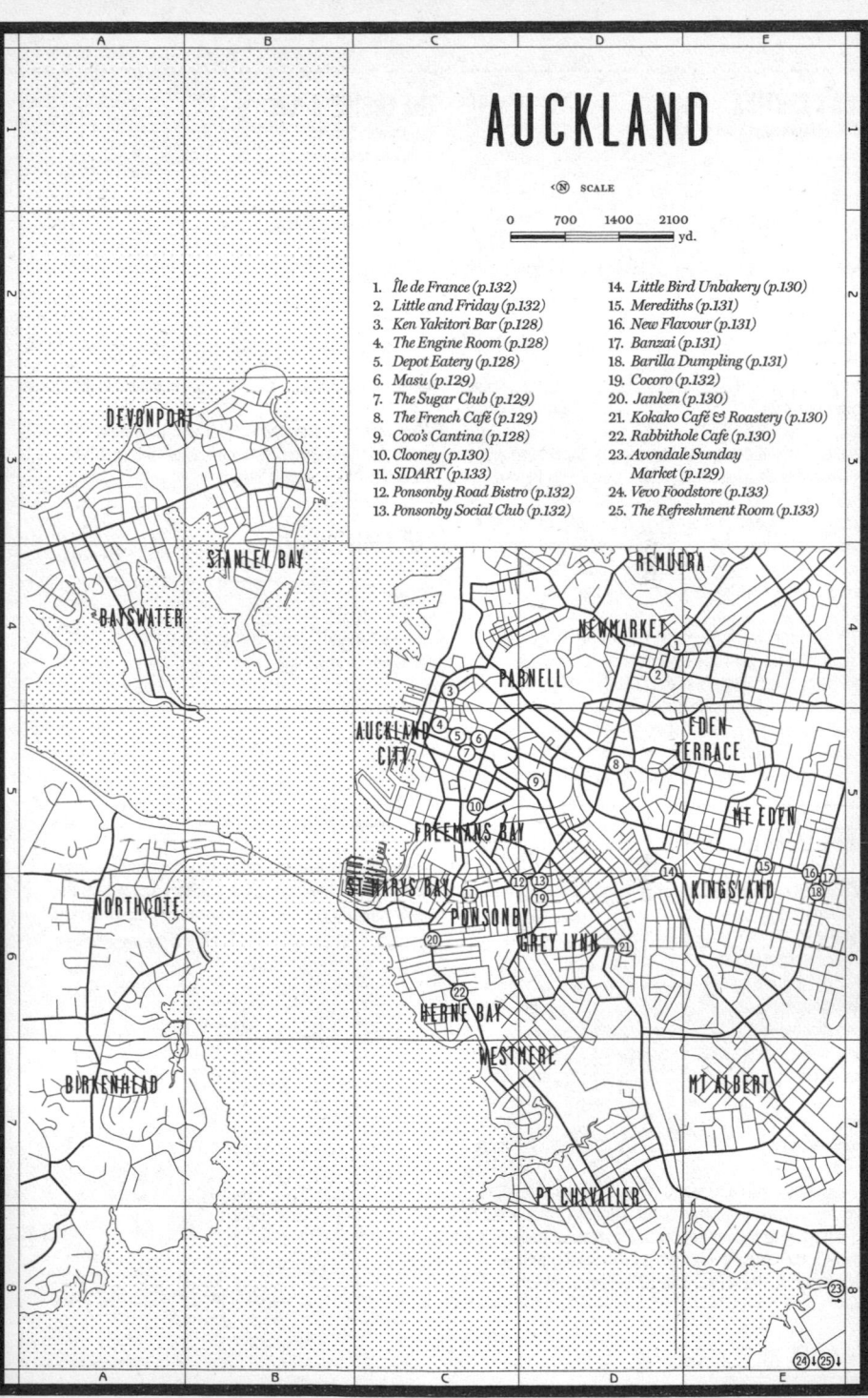

AUCKLAND

◁ N ▷ SCALE

0   700   1400   2100
                                 yd.

COCO'S CANTINA

376 Karangahape Road
Auckland City
Auckland 1010
+64 93007582
www.cocoscantina.co.nz

Recommended by
Al Brown,
Michael Meredith

Opening hours	Closed Monday and Sunday
Reservation policy	No
Credit cards	Accepted
Price range	Budget
Style	Casual
Cuisine	Italian
Recommended for	Wish I'd opened

'Relaxed and super casual. The food is unpretentious but cooked with a lot of heart and soul.'—Al Brown

Karangahape Road is shared by the most undesirable elements of Auckland's seedy underbelly and some of its hippest no-reservations bars and restaurants. Coco's Cantina, a tiny, eccentrically decorated space has been wildly popular since it opened its doors in 2010. Its time-worn air, not to mention its mature selection of Italian food and drink – think bruschetti, meatballs and cocktails for NZ$10 (£5; $8) – is all the more impressive considering this is the first shot at being restaurateurs for its two sister owners. Prepare to enjoy a boisterous night out, and remember – all the cool kids are queuing (waiting in line) these days.

DEPOT EATERY

86 Federal Street
Auckland City
Auckland 1010
+64 93637048
www.eatatdepot.co.nz

Recommended by
Brad Farmerie, Peter
Gordon, Terry Lowe,
Michael Meredith, Bevan
Smith, Simon Wright

Opening hours	Open 7 days
Reservation policy	No
Credit cards	Accepted
Price range	Affordable
Style	Casual
Cuisine	Seafood
Recommended for	Wish I'd opened

'It's tapas but with a Kiwiana twist. It's very simple, but very clever. I think they really fill a hole in the market by managing to appeal to a broad customer base – they're always busy even with a no-booking policy. Turbot sliders. Need I say more?'—Simon Wright

THE ENGINE ROOM

115 Queen Street
Auckland City
Auckland 0627
+64 94809502
www.engineroom.net.nz

Recommended by
Simon Wright

Opening hours	Closed Monday and Sunday
Credit cards	Accepted
Price range	Affordable
Style	Casual
Cuisine	Modern European
Recommended for	Regular neighbourhood

'A great local bistro serving simple food cooked to perfection with great service and an interesting wine list. Brilliant.'—Simon Wright

KEN YAKITORI BAR

55 Anzac Avenue
Auckland City
Auckland 1010
+64 93796500
www.kenyakitori.co.nz

Recommended by
Simon Wright

Opening hours	Open 7 days
Credit cards	Accepted but not AMEX
Price range	Affordable
Style	Casual
Cuisine	Yakitori
Recommended for	Late night

'I love the fact that it's really casual. I can go after work, have a beer, eat great yakitori and watch the chefs cooking right in front of me.'—Simon Wright

MASU

Recommended by
Al Brown

Skycity Grand Hotel
90 Federal Street
Auckland City
Auckland 1010
+64 93636278
www.skycityauckland.co.nz

Opening hours	Open 7 days
Credit cards	Accepted
Price range	Affordable
Style	Smart casual
Cuisine	Modern Japanese
Recommended for	Regular neighbourhood

'Nic Watt's new place is a gorgeous space with pared back, modern Japanese food. The robata grill adds a wonderful charcoal flavour to the dishes. Masu is beautifully executed in every way.'—Al Brown

THE SUGAR CLUB

Recommended by
Simon Wright

Sky Tower
Level 53, 90 Federal Street
Auckland City
Auckland 1010
+64 93636365
www.skycityauckland.co.nz

Opening hours	Open 7 days
Credit cards	Accepted
Price range	Expensive
Style	Smart casual
Cuisine	Fusion
Recommended for	Local favourite

'If you only had one day in Auckland then this place would give you a real taste of what the city is all about. Situated on the top floor of the Sky Tower with views across Auckland, the harbour and outer islands, one of New Zealand's most famous chefs, Peter Gordon, behind the Pacific Rim menu – it's a great package.'
—Simon Wright

AVONDALE SUNDAY MARKET

Recommended by
Peter Gordon

2 Ash Street
Avondale
Auckland 1026
+64 98184931

Opening hours	Closed Monday to Saturday
Reservation policy	No
Credit cards	Not accepted
Price range	Budget
Style	Casual
Cuisine	Street Food
Recommended for	Bargain

'It's a racecourse that becomes a huge farmers' market but one that is full of tatty junk and second-hand goods alongside delicious freshly made Cambodian salads, silken tofu and boil-up (a Maori stew of pork bones, potato and *puha* – a native weed).'—Peter Gordon

THE FRENCH CAFÉ

Recommended by
Martin Bosley, Al
Brown, Peter Gordon,
Michael Meredith,
Bevan Smith

210 Symonds Street
Eden Terrace
Auckland 1010
+64 93771911
www.thefrenchcafe.co.nz

Opening hours	Closed Monday and Sunday
Credit cards	Accepted
Price range	Expensive
Style	Smart casual
Cuisine	French
Recommended for	High end

'A restaurant utterly dedicated to creating the perfect dining experience. It's flawless, from food through to service.'—Martin Bosley

Lauded by critics and showered with awards in the over twenty-five years it's been doing its thing, The French Café is Auckland's own multi-Michelin-starred restaurant, or at least it would be if Michelin operated in the Antipodes. Classic French fine dining with a local twist is the spin, meaning tuna sashimi rubs shoulders with chicken liver parfait for appetizers, and shellfish with enoki mushrooms and smoked dashi sits alongside roast lamb with goat's cheese mash and black olives for mains. Understandably, prices are also starry, but nobody seems to mind—this husband and wife team provides world-class cuisine (him) framed by effortlessly slick service (her).

CLOONEY
Recommended by
Bevan Smith

33 Sale Street
Freemans Bay
Auckland 1010
+64 93581702
www.clooney.co.nz

Opening hours	Closed Monday
Credit cards	Accepted
Price range	Expensive
Style	Smart casual
Cuisine	Modern New Zealand
Recommended for	High end

'Immaculate food in a glorious space with near faultless service.'—Bevan Smith

Close to Skycity, Clooney's chic, polished industrial decor and refined plates helped bring gastronomic gentrification to the once disreputable quarter that is Freemans Bay. Chef Des Harris crafts succinctly described five- and seven-course tasting menus, also available as entirely vegetarian, alongside the à la carte. Starters include glazed eel with oyster, marrow, coriander (cilantro) and pickled tapioca, main course of John Dory with sweet corn, scampi, serrano ham, almonds and pork 'juice', then organic coconut sugar and pineapple cheesecake by pastry chef Justin Lee. General manager/sommelier Gary Olasz fosters a sound connection between dishes and wines, and his list features sought-after producers from home and away. Also worth knowing: BYO on Sundays.

KOKAKO CAFÉ & ROASTERY
Recommended by
Simon Wright

537 Great North Road
Grey Lynn
Auckland 1021
+64 93792868
www.kokako.co.nz

Opening hours	Open 7 days
Reservation policy	No
Credit cards	Accepted but not AMEX
Price range	Budget
Style	Casual
Cuisine	Café
Recommended for	Breakfast

'There's a real buzz about the place, they roast their own coffee on site and the food's completely vegetarian which makes a nice change from the standard bacon and eggs around town.'—Simon Wright

JANKEN
Recommended by
Simon Wright

158 Jervois Road
Herne Bay
Auckland 1011
+64 93600555

Opening hours	Closed Monday
Credit cards	Accepted but not AMEX
Price range	Affordable
Style	Casual
Cuisine	Japanese
Recommended for	Bargain

'It's an organic Japanese restaurant. The food is slightly European but cooked in a Japanese style. At lunch, for NZ$18 (£9; $15) you get a main meal, wholegrain rice, salad, green tea, pickled vegetables and fresh fruit with soy cream. It's all cooked with care and is really tasty.'—Simon Wright

RABBITHOLE CAFE
Recommended by
Peter Gordon

203 Jervois Road
Herne Bay
Auckland 1011
+64 93600755

Opening hours	Open 7 days
Reservation policy	No
Credit cards	Accepted but not AMEX
Price range	Budget
Style	Casual
Cuisine	Café
Recommended for	Breakfast

'The best cheese scones in town, great coffee, and the green scrambled eggs are fabulous, especially when I've just arrived from London after a twenty-five-hour flight and need a tasty pick-me-up.'—Peter Gordon

LITTLE BIRD UNBAKERY
Recommended by
Michael Meredith

385 New North Road
Kingsland
Auckland 1021
+64 95507377
www.littlebirdorganics.co.nz

Opening hours	Closed Monday and Sunday
Reservation policy	No
Credit cards	Accepted but not AMEX
Price range	Budget
Style	Casual
Cuisine	Raw Vegan
Recommended for	Breakfast

The site of the second incarnation of Little Bird at Ponsonby's Summer Street is more romantic than the first (between a marine electronics store and Tent Town). Specializing in raw and organic, positively nutritious cuisine, the business is the brainchild of an architect and his flight-attendant-turned-chef partner who spent too long suffering from several food intolerances. Both locations feature clipboard menus on walls. Dishes include the breakfast Chia Bircher with gluten-free oats, chia, goji berries, apple, almond, lemon, cinnamon and young coconut, or Little Bird's sprouted Grawnola with almond, goji berries and yacon, plus a daily selection of nut 'milks'. Follow on with a 'power bar' and 'teeccino' (herbal coffee).

BANZAI

Recommended by
Michael Meredith

583 Dominion Road
Mount Eden
Auckland 1041
+64 96304489

Opening hours	Closed Monday
Credit cards	Accepted
Price range	Budget
Style	Casual
Cuisine	Japanese
Recommended for	Bargain

BARILLA DUMPLING

Recommended by
Al Brown

571 Dominion Road
Mount Eden
Auckland 1041
+64 96388032

Opening hours	Open 7 days
Credit cards	Not accepted
Price range	Budget
Style	Casual
Cuisine	Asian
Recommended for	Bargain

'This place does mean dirty dumplings, which are just delicious.'—Al Brown

MEREDITHS

Recommended by
Ben Batterbury,
Benjamin Bayly,
Simon Wright

365 Dominion Road
Mount Eden
Auckland 1024
+64 96233140
www.merediths.co.nz

Opening hours	Closed Monday and Sunday
Credit cards	Accepted
Price range	Expensive
Style	Smart casual
Cuisine	International
Recommended for	High end

'Mr Meredith serves up an experience that will take your breath away. A night to remember, a true international chef from New Zealand.'—Benjamin Bayly

Like a microcosm of New Zealand itself, the flavours you'll encounter at Merediths run the gamut from Northern European to Southeast Asian, yet the transition is seamless. It's tasting menus all the way, so prepare to immerse yourself for a good long stint in the intimate surrounds of dark wood and subdued lighting, as course after course of beautifully crafted food is laid before you by the well-trained staff. The wine list is conveniently compact – probably no more than a hundred wines in all – but the country's own offerings are strongly represented and the sommelier will match them to your menu.

NEW FLAVOUR

Recommended by
Benjamin Bayly

541 Dominion Road
Mount Eden
Auckland 1014
+64 96386880

Opening hours	Closed Tuesday
Reservation policy	No
Credit cards	Not accepted
Price range	Budget
Style	Casual
Cuisine	Chinese
Recommended for	Late night

'It's the only place open super-duper late. Good dumplings.'—Benjamin Bayly

ÎLE DE FRANCE

Watercare
2 Nuffield Street
Newmarket
Auckland 1023
+64 95230293
www.iledefrance.co.nz

Opening hours	Closed Sunday
Credit cards	Accepted
Price range	Affordable
Style	Casual
Cuisine	French Brasserie
Recommended for	Bargain

'Amazing classic French food. The chef, Gilles Papst, makes the best terrines I have ever had. Superb French wine list too – such great value.'—Benjamin Bayly

LITTLE AND FRIDAY

12 Melrose Street
Newmarket
Auckland 1023
+64 95248742
www.littleandfriday.com

Opening hours	Open 7 days
Reservation policy	No
Credit cards	Accepted
Price range	Budget
Style	Casual
Cuisine	Café
Recommended for	Breakfast

'Great coffee and extraordinary doughnuts.'—Al Brown

COCORO

56a Brown Street
Ponsonby
Auckland 1021
+64 93600927
www.cocoro.co.nz

Opening hours	Closed Monday and Sunday
Credit cards	Accepted
Price range	Affordable
Style	Casual
Cuisine	Modern Japanese
Recommended for	Wish I'd opened

PONSONBY ROAD BISTRO

165 Ponsonby Road
Ponsonby
Auckland 1011
+64 93601611
www.ponsonbyroadbistro.co.nz

Opening hours	Closed Sunday
Credit cards	Accepted
Price range	Affordable
Style	Casual
Cuisine	Bistro
Recommended for	Regular neighbourhood

'The food is delicious simple fare with a lovely Euro or Asian twist – but very simple twists. Sarah Conway in the kitchen is terrific. One of the owners, Blair Russell or Melissa Morrow, is always on the floor and Melissa is a true gem on the Auckland food scene with her knowledgeable ways and charming service.'—Peter Gordon

PONSONBY SOCIAL CLUB

152 Ponsonby Road
Ponsonby
Auckland 1011
+64 93612320
www.ponsonbysocialclub.co.nz

Opening hours	7 days for dinner
Reservation policy	No
Credit cards	Accepted but not AMEX
Price range	Budget
Style	Casual
Cuisine	Barbeque
Recommended for	Late night

'When I've finished work and am heading home, this is *en route*. Good icy cold beers and martinis, comfort food such as macaroni cheese and great pulled beef burgers.'—Peter Gordon

SIDART

Recommended by
Benjamin Bayly,
Michael Meredith

Three Lamps Plaza
283 Ponsonby Road
Ponsonby
Auckland 1011
+64 93602122
www.sidart.co.nz

Opening hours	Closed Monday and Sunday
Credit cards	Accepted
Price range	Expensive
Style	Smart casual
Cuisine	Modern New Zealand
Recommended for	Local favourite

'The menu changes every week – every time I go there I am blown away by the seasonality of the menu. They offer a unique experience with their "Chefs Table". The service is fantastic and they are constantly evolving.'
—Benjamin Bayly

THE REFRESHMENT ROOM

Recommended by
Benjamin Bayly

233 Scenic Drive
Titirangi
Auckland 0604
+64 98178655
www.therefreshmentroom.co.nz

Opening hours	Closed Monday and Tuesday
Credit cards	Accepted but not AMEX
Price range	Affordable
Style	Casual
Cuisine	Italian
Recommended for	Regular neighbourhood

'A great Sunday night treat. My kids love the home-made pasta and it has amazing views back to the city from the deck.'—Benjamin Bayly

VEVO FOODSTORE

Recommended by
Benjamin Bayly

402c Titirangi Road
Titirangi
Auckland 0604
+64 95551997
www.vevofoodstore.co.nz

Opening hours	Closed Monday
Credit cards	Not accepted
Price range	Budget
Style	Casual
Cuisine	Café-Deli
Recommended for	Breakfast

'Vevo has great staff, Elliot Warne the chef cooks the most amazing eggs. The best coffee in west Auckland.'
—Benjamin Bayly

FLYING FISH

Recommended by
Terry Lowe

Sheraton Fiji Resort
Denarau Island South
Nadi, Ba
Fiji
+679 6750777
www.sheratonfiji.com

Opening hours	Open 7 days
Credit cards	Accepted
Price range	Expensive
Style	Smart casual
Cuisine	Modern Seafood
Recommended for	Worth the travel

'Great use of local produce and a setting to die for.'
—Terry Lowe

Chef Peter Kuruvita has long since moved on from his original Darling Harbour location, but the legacy of his time there is a mini seafood restaurant empire that now stretches all the way to Polynesia. The menu on Denarau Island is a crowd-pleasing mix of local grilled crustaceans and the Indian curries that influence much of the cuisine on these islands. But it would be foolish to ignore the real reason visitors fly all this way – to have dinner by candlelight overlooking the beach, while the hotel's lagoon pool meanders among the tables. A luxury not even Sydney can boast.

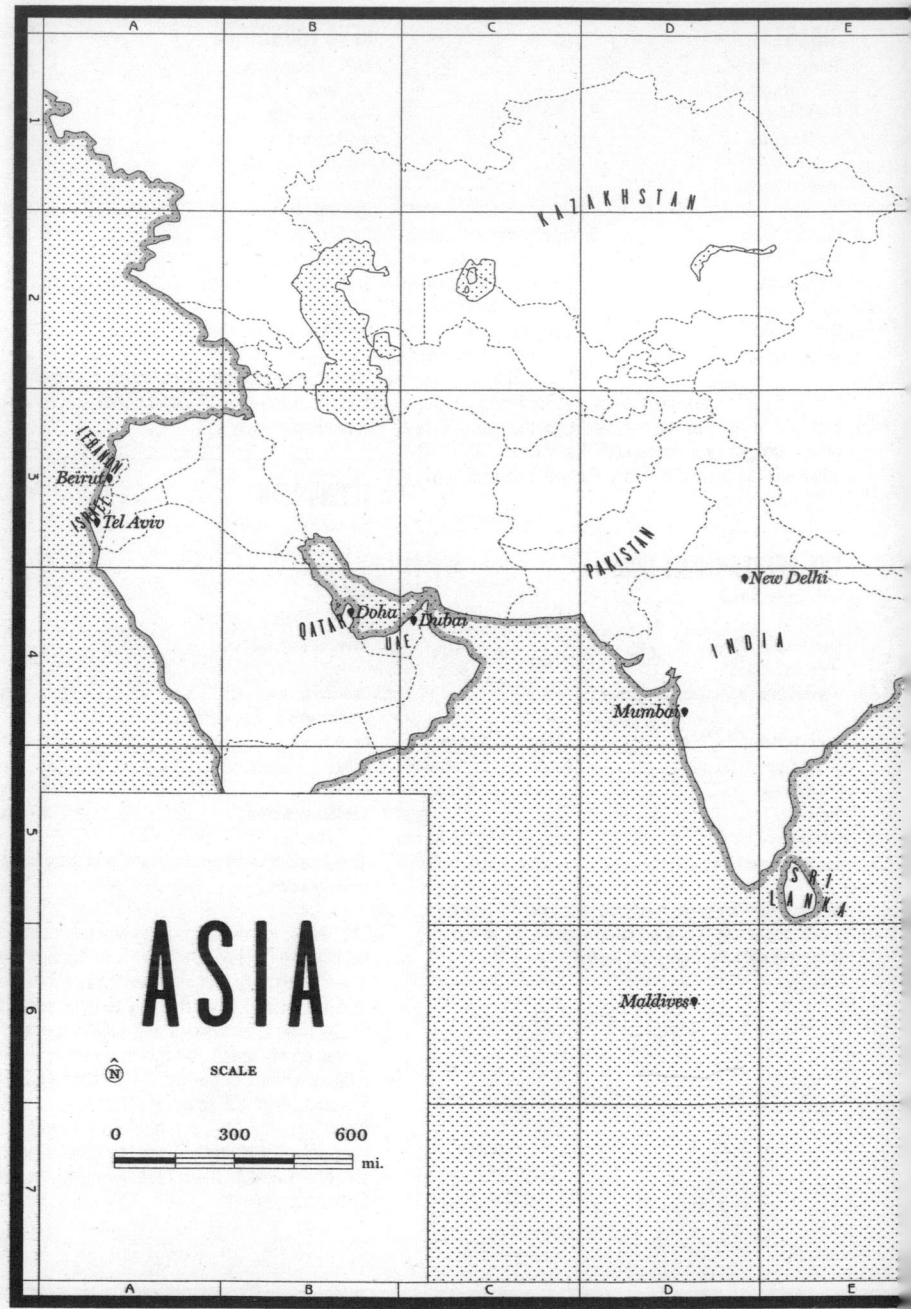

ASIA

SCALE

0   300   600   mi.

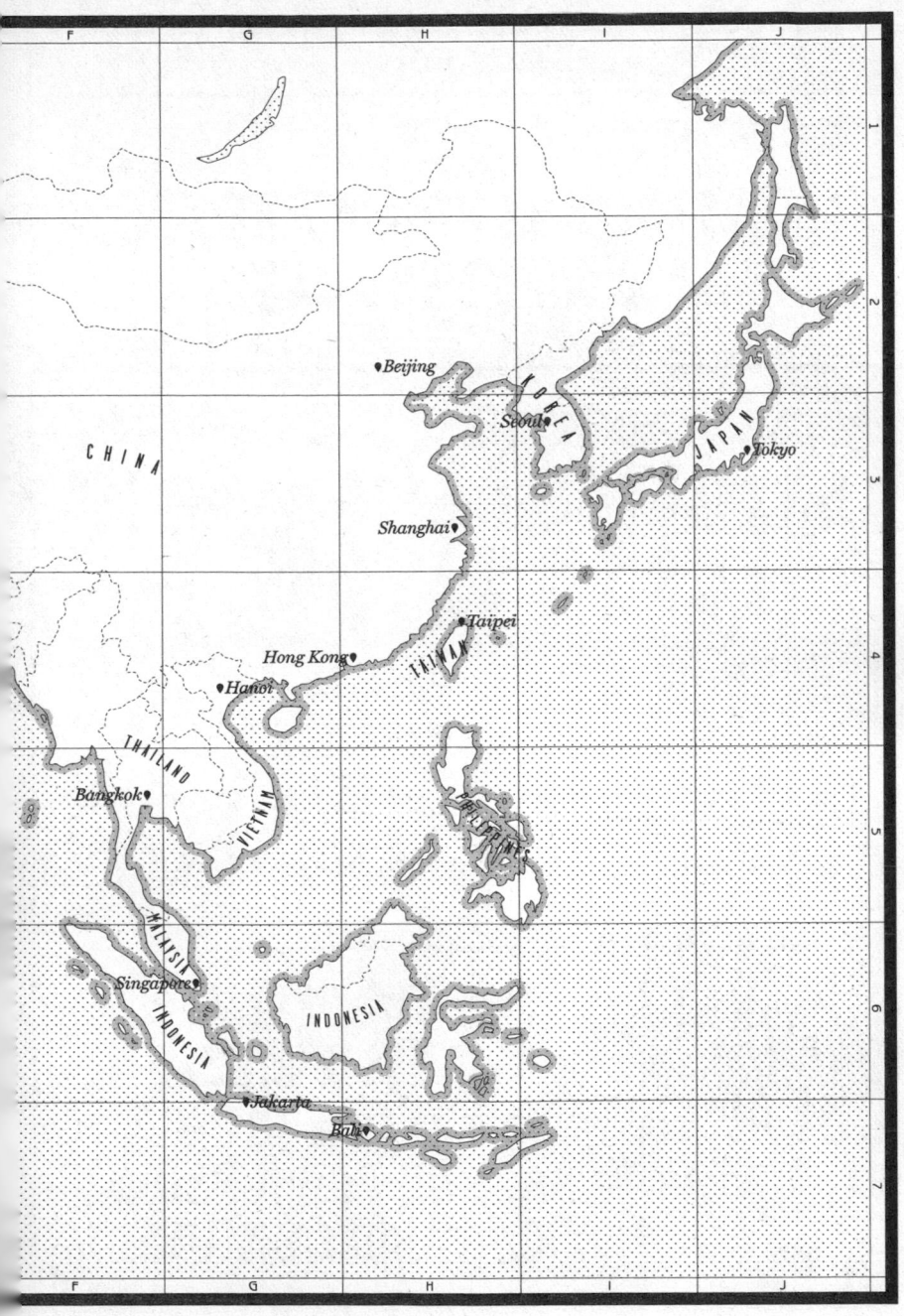

'The best typical Armenian food.'
FERNANDO TROCCA P140

'IT'S SIMPLE AND HONEST. THERE'S NO FAFFING AROUND, WHAT YOU SEE IS WHAT YOU GET.'
IZU ANI P145

SOUTHWEST ASIA

'CASUAL, CHEAP AND EASY TO EAT.'
REIF OTHMAN P147

'THE TRADITION OF A CLASSIC MEZZE IS AT ITS BEST — A SACRED PROCESSION OF TABOULEH AND FATTOUCH'
KAMAL MOUZAWAK P140

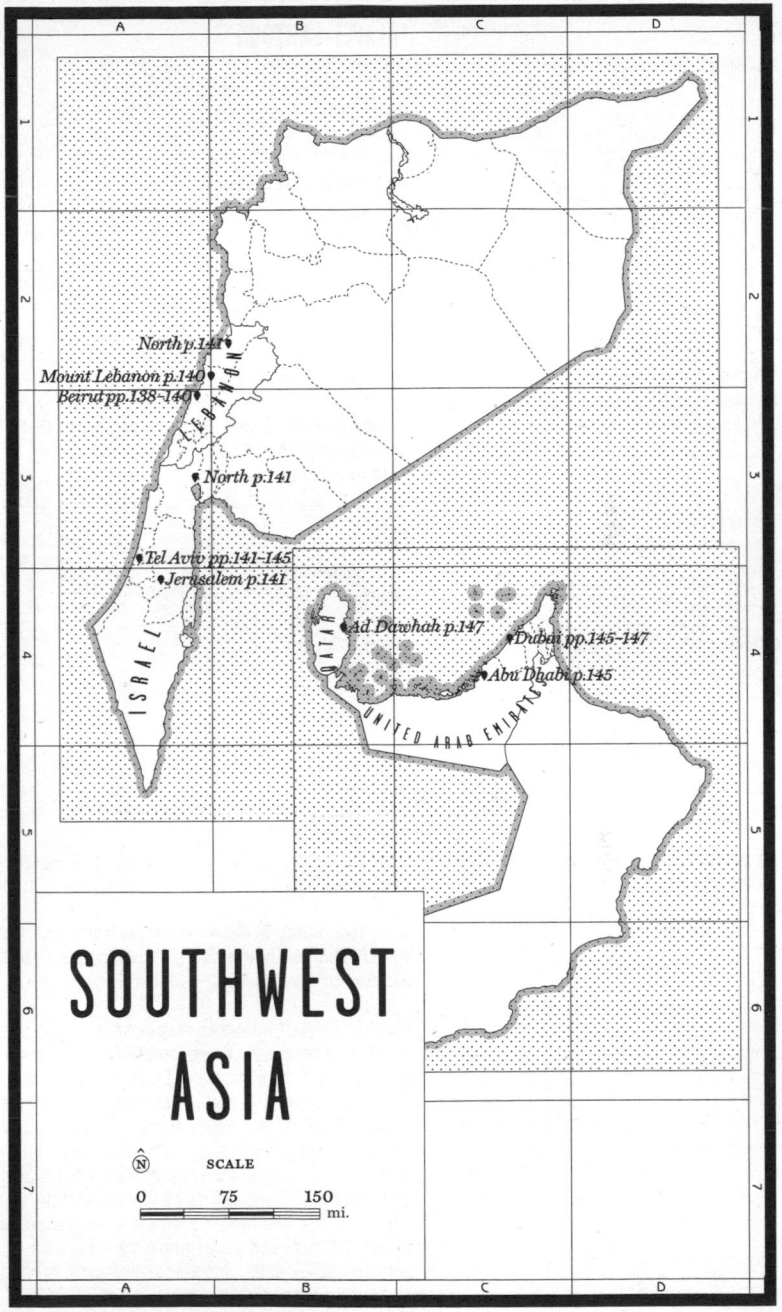

North p.141

Mount Lebanon p.140

Beirut pp.138–140

L E B A N O N

North p.141

Tel Aviv pp.141–145

Jerusalem p.141

I S R A E L

QATAR

Ad Dawhah p.147

Dubai pp.145–147

Abu Dhabi p.145

U N I T E D   A R A B   E M I R A T E S

SOUTHWEST
ASIA

N̂   SCALE

0   75   150
mi.

BOUBOUFFE

Recommended by
Kamal Mouzawak

Avenue Charles Malek
Beirut
Beirut 1100
Lebanon
+961 1334040

Opening hours	Open 7 days
Credit cards	Accepted
Price range	Budget
Style	Casual
Cuisine	Middle Eastern
Recommended for	Late night

'A meat or a chicken shawarma at Boubouffe... best ever! Beautiful meat, perfectly seasoned and cooked on a vertical charcoal burner.'—Kamal Mouzawak

BURGUNDY

Recommended by
Johnny Farah

752 Gouraud Street
Beirut
Beirut 1012
Lebanon
+961 1999820
www.burgundybeirut.com

Opening hours	Closed Sunday
Credit cards	Accepted
Price range	Expensive
Style	Smart casual
Cuisine	Modern French
Recommended for	High end

'High-quality ingredients and very well-executed cooking. An incredible wine list, especially in terms of Burgundy.'—Johnny Farah

FALAFEL SAHYOUN

Recommended by
Johnny Farah

Bechara El Khoury
Beirut
Beirut 1101
Lebanon
+961 1633188
www.falafelsahyoun.com

Opening hours	Closed Sunday
Reservation policy	No
Credit cards	Not accepted
Price range	Budget
Style	Casual
Cuisine	Falafel
Recommended for	Bargain

'Basically, it's excellent falafel for as little as £1.50 ($2) for a sandwich and £2.50 ($4) for a plate.' —Johnny Farah

LIZA

Recommended by
Johnny Farah

Metropolitan Club
Doumani
Beirut
Beirut 1100
Lebanon
+961 1208108
www.lizabeirut.com

Opening hours	Closed Monday
Credit cards	Accepted
Price range	Affordable
Style	Casual
Cuisine	Lebanese
Recommended for	Local favourite

'A perfect mezze of dishes in the perfect surrounding: an old Lebanese house that is incredibly decorated and has comfortable seating.'—Johnny Farah

One of the most beautiful restaurants in Lebanon, Liza Beirut occupies the second floor of a nineteenth-century palace near the Stock Exchange in the upmarket Achrafieh district. It opened in 2013 as an outpost of Liza Asseily's successful Paris original. Interiors, designed by Maria Ousseimi, include delicately patterned wallpapers, polished marble floors and high ceilings – Sunday brunch is the best time to see it in its prime. The food is contemporary Lebanese: tartare of lamb and aubergine (eggplant) with pomegranate seeds, and *kébbé méchwiyé* (grilled meat croquettes with beetroot [beet] dip). The baklava, flavoured with rose hip, is served with a stunning pistachio ice cream.

LE PROFESSEUR

Mar Elias Street
Beirut
Beirut 1105
Lebanon

Opening hours	Closed Sunday
Reservation policy	No
Credit cards	Not accepted
Price range	Budget
Style	Casual
Cuisine	Lebanese
Recommended for	Bargain

'For a morning or daytime *foul* (broad [fava] bean salad), a *balila* (chickpea salad/stew) or a hummus.'
—Kamal Mouzawak

RAFIC AL RASHIDI

Monot Street
Beirut
Beirut 1100
Lebanon
+961 1398800

Opening hours	Open 7 days
Reservation policy	No
Credit cards	Not accepted
Price range	Budget
Style	Casual
Cuisine	Sweets-Pastries
Recommended for	Breakfast

'A *knefeh* (bread filled with melted cheese in a semolina crust, and loads of sugar syrup) at Rashidi – a typical Sunday morning breakfast.'—Kamal Mouzawak

SOUK EL TAYEB

Beirut Souks
Allenby
Beirut
Beirut 1012
Lebanon
+961 1442664
www.soukeltayeb.com

Opening hours	Closed Sunday to Friday
Reservation policy	No
Credit cards	Not accepted
Price range	Budget
Style	Casual
Cuisine	Market-Deli
Recommended for	Breakfast

'Souk El Tayeb is an outdoor farmers' market where I do my week's shopping for the restaurants. It includes small farmers, organic farmers, and also has prepared peasant food, such as *manouche* (a flatbread with various savoury toppings). It even has a seafood stand where you can have oysters with a glass of wine.'
—Johnny Farah

SPORTING CLUB BEACH

Avenue de Paris
Beirut
Beirut 1103
Lebanon
+961 1742481

Opening hours	Open 7 days
Reservation policy	No
Credit cards	Not accepted
Price range	Affordable
Style	Casual
Cuisine	Middle Eastern
Recommended for	Regular neighbourhood

'It's a simple Lebanese mezze and fried fish restaurant, overlooking the blue Mediterranean sea, with the opportunity of having a swim before or after a meal.'
—Johnny Farah

THE TERRACE
Hotel Albergo
137 Rue Abdel Wahab El Inglizi
Beirut
Beirut 1100
Lebanon
+961 1339797
www.albergobeirut.com

Opening hours	Open 7 days
Credit cards	Accepted
Price range	Affordable
Style	Smart casual
Cuisine	International
Recommended for	Breakfast

'A typical Lebanese breakfast at the Albergo Hotel's rooftop restaurant: eggs fried in clay pots, *labneh* (strained yogurt) and small *manaiish* (thyme pizza) – under Beirut's sun and overlooking the city!' —Kamal Mouzawak

AL HALABI
Antelias Square
Antelias
Mount Lebanon 1201
Lebanon
+961 4523555

Opening hours	Open 7 days
Credit cards	Accepted
Price range	Affordable
Style	Smart casual
Cuisine	Lebanese
Recommended for	Local favourite

'Lebanon is synonymous with mezze. At Al Halabi the tradition of a classic mezze is at its best – a sacred procession of tabouleh and fattouch, followed by salads and cold dishes.' —Kamal Mouzawak

FADEL
Naas
Bikfaya
Mount Lebanon 1205
Lebanon
+961 4980979

Opening hours	Open 7 days
Credit cards	Accepted
Price range	Affordable
Style	Smart casual
Cuisine	Lebanese
Recommended for	Local favourite

'A mountain classic. Great food, surrounded by tall pine trees and huge hydrangeas..' —Kamal Mouzawak

VAROUJ
Maracha Royal Street
Bourj Hammoud
Mount Lebanon 1203
Lebanon
+961 3882933

Opening hours	Closed Sunday
Credit cards	Not accepted
Price range	Affordable
Style	Casual
Cuisine	Armenian
Recommended for	Worth the travel

'The best typical Armenian food.' —Fernando Trocca

Rustic, family-run Varouj, lurking in its undistinguished alleyway in Beirut's labyrinthine Armenian neighbourhood Bourj Hammoud is small – four tables small. The owner is the boss here (his son's in the kitchen) and he'll tell you exactly what to order and how much of it. There are no menus and no written bill (the always reasonable final price is seemingly plucked from thin air) but you're in safe hands. Seize the opportunity to sample the frogs' legs, spicy *soujouk* sausage or crunchy bones-in 'small birds' if you're 'allowed'. Be sure to book and enlist a reliable cab driver for directions.

CHEZ MAGUY

Mak'ad el Mir
Batroun
North 1400
Lebanon
+961 3439147

Opening hours	Open 7 days
Credit cards	Not accepted
Price range	Affordable
Style	Casual
Cuisine	Seafood
Recommended for	Regular neighbourhood

'A small shack over the water in Batroun. The freshest fish and seafood prepared in the simplest way.'
—Kamal Mouzawak

MACHNE YUDA

Beit Ya'akov Street 10
Jerusalem
Jerusalem 94323
Israel
+972 25333442
www.machneyuda.co.il

Opening hours	Variable
Credit cards	Accepted
Price range	Expensive
Style	Smart casual
Cuisine	Fusion
Recommended for	Worth the travel

'There's nothing like eating at a colleague's restaurant where you don't have to choose a thing. Yossi's policy is not to create anything, he prefers to take well-known recipes and add his own personal touch.'—Luís Baena

SHRABIC

Main Road
Rameh
North
Israel
+972 49995768

Opening hours	Closed Monday
Reservation policy	No
Credit cards	Not accepted
Price range	Budget
Style	Casual
Cuisine	Middle Eastern
Recommended for	Worth the travel

'Located in the hills of the Galilee, where you can feel the perfect breeze, is Shrabic. Using local ingredients, Yakub makes some of the best Galilean-Palestinian food I have ever tasted. His accurate use of herbs, sours and dough constitute a more than terrific meal.'
—Maoz Alonim

ABU HASSAN

1 Ha' Dolfin Street
Tel Aviv
Tel Aviv 68130
Israel
+972 36820387

Opening hours	Closed Saturday
Reservation policy	No
Credit cards	Accepted
Price range	Budget
Style	Casual
Cuisine	Middle Eastern
Recommended for	Breakfast

'The most-loved hummus on Jaffa. Abu Hassan's hummus, I promise you, is the real deal. The chickpeas are to die for. Abu Hassan's *masabacha* (a speciality hummus) is my favourite way to begin the day, a real breakfast. Your Tel Aviv culinary experience wouldn't be complete if you miss this joint.'—Yair Feinberg

BERTIE

Recommended by
Yair Feinberg

King George Street 88
Tel Aviv
Tel Aviv 64338
Israel
+972 722512950
www.bertie.co.il

Opening hours	Open 7 days
Credit cards	Accepted
Price range	Affordable
Style	Casual
Cuisine	Middle Eastern
Recommended for	Regular neighbourhood

'Relatively new but already packed with eager customers. It's described as a happy "Levant" kitchen – it's a special mix of Tel Avivian bistro and Jerusalemite Mahane Yehuda market joint. Two young talented chefs from the finest restaurants in Tel Aviv (one of them Yishay Malkov, who used to manage Gordon Ramsay's Claridge's in London) set up shop here and are already attracting a following. The place has a chilled-out atmosphere that is both warm and inviting – in short unpretentious. They serve really good food that is made by people who know their stuff.'—Yair Feinberg

THE BUN

Recommended by
Yair Feinberg

Hillel Ha-Zaken Street 18
Tel Aviv
Tel Aviv 63309
Israel
+972 36044725

Opening hours	Closed Saturday
Reservation policy	No
Credit cards	Accepted
Price range	Affordable
Style	Casual
Cuisine	Southeast Asian
Recommended for	Late night

'Two brothers opened this Asian street-food bar near the Carmel market, combining the fresh taste of Asian cuisine with a personal interpretation and a personal touch. The best place to end a tiring day. Good food, good value and personalized and attentive service.'
—Yair Feinberg

CAFE 48

Recommended by
Michael Solomonov

Nahalat Binyamin Street 48
Tel Aviv
Tel Aviv 65163
Israel
+972 35101001
www.cafe48.co.il

Opening hours	Open 7 days
Credit cards	Accepted
Price range	Affordable
Style	Casual
Cuisine	Modern Israeli
Recommended for	Worth the travel

'The food keeps me coming back for more. It's a clean and relevant approach to European-Jewish cuisine.'
—Michael Solomonov

CHANAN MARGILAN

Recommended by
Maoz Alonim

Mesilat Yesharim Street 15
Tel Aviv
Tel Aviv 66534
Israel
+972 36873984

Opening hours	Closed Friday
Credit cards	Accepted
Price range	Budget
Style	Casual
Cuisine	Middle Eastern
Recommended for	Bargain

'One of the best bites in town is Chanan Margilan's dushpara soup. Whenever I seek a good neighbourly lunch I come here, in the south of the city, to eat the best Bukharan food around – meat skewers and traditional, amazingly filled pastries, affordable to all.'
—Maoz Alonim

LUCIFER

Recommended by
Maoz Alonim

Allenby Street 97
Tel Aviv
Tel Aviv 65134
Israel
+972 36851666

Opening hours	Open 7 days
Reservation policy	No
Credit cards	Accepted
Price range	Affordable
Style	Casual
Cuisine	International
Recommended for	Late night

'My ultimate late-night joint is, without a doubt, the Lucifer bar. The name is indicative of its atmosphere – alongside the dark and mystical ambience, the pleasant loudness, the beautiful bartenders and the TV monitors broadcasting the action on the street outside, you can also enjoy some fine beer, delicious pizzas and some of the best hunks of meat in the area.'—Maoz Alonim

THE MINZAR

Recommended by
Maoz Alonim

Allenby Street 60
Tel Aviv
Tel Aviv 6382208
Israel
+972 35173015

Opening hours	Open 7 days
Reservation policy	No
Credit cards	Accepted
Price range	Budget
Style	Casual
Cuisine	Bar Snacks
Recommended for	Local favourite

'The Minzar, or, translated to English, "the Monastery", is one of the city's most important institutions. Despite its ascetic name the Minzar – which is open twenty-four hours a day, seven days a week – hosts some of the city's most intriguing culinary adventures, most infamous drinkers, and provides some of the greatest stories you will ever hear.'—Maoz Alonim

MATI BAR

Recommended by
Maoz Alonim

Matalon Street 41
Tel Aviv
Tel Aviv 66855
Israel

Opening hours	Closed Saturday
Reservation policy	No
Credit cards	Accepted
Price range	Budget
Style	Casual
Cuisine	Bar-Diner
Recommended for	Breakfast

'Named after the infamous Mati, a colourful fellow who drinks for a living and is the owner of this fabulous Eastern European dining establishment, located in the heart of Florentin. Mati's breakfast is comprised of salty fish and pitchers of beer and is no doubt the best breakfast around.'—Maoz Alonim

MIZNON

Recommended by
Ilya Shalev

Ibn Gabirol Street 23
Tel Aviv
Tel Aviv 68178
Israel
+972 37168977

Opening hours	Open 7 days
Reservation policy	No
Credit cards	Accepted
Price range	Budget
Style	Casual
Cuisine	Israeli
Recommended for	Regular neighbourhood

'I tend to visit small places. In particular I prefer the ones where waiters recognize you. One of those that comes to mind is a small corner cafe, called Miznon, in Tel Aviv. Fantastic place, they have no menu, everything goes in a pitta. They just ask you whether you want meat or fish or veggies. Amazing!'—Ilya Shalev

PINAT HASHLOSHA

Recommended by
Yair Feinberg

Panorama GF, Ben-Tzvi Road 84
Tel Aviv
Tel Aviv 68012
Israel
+972 36491777

Opening hours	Closed Saturday
Credit cards	Accepted
Price range	Budget
Style	Casual
Cuisine	Middle Eastern-Asian
Recommended for	Bargain

'Excellent, or perhaps even the best, shawarma in town. Authentic Middle Eastern-Asian steakhouse that serves traditional Bukharan dishes. They also have an open salad bar and freshly baked pittas. The place is usually packed with waiting customers. A treat you should not miss if you want an authentic Israeli dining experience. Kosher.'—Yair Feinberg

RAPHAËL

Recommended by
Yair Feinberg

King David Tower
Ha-Yarkon Street 87
Tel Aviv
Tel Aviv 63432
Israel
+972 35226464
www.raphaeltlv.co.il

Opening hours	Open 7 days
Credit cards	Accepted
Price range	Expensive
Style	Smart casual
Cuisine	Modern International
Recommended for	Local favourite

'Showcases the inspired menu of Chef Rafi Cohen, one of Israel's top chefs. Rafi Cohen creates dishes that are influenced by techniques from different international cuisines, such as North African and French, and top quality raw materials – mostly locally sourced and carefully selected. Dishes served at Raphaël are crammed with Israeli flavours and textures. A highly professional performance.'—Yair Feinberg

SHILA

Recommended by
Yair Feinberg

Ben Yehuda Street 182
Tel Aviv
Tel Aviv 63471
Israel
+972 35221224
www.shila-rest.co.il

Opening hours	Open 7 days
Credit cards	Accepted
Price range	Affordable
Style	Casual
Cuisine	Middle Eastern-Mediterranean
Recommended for	Wish I'd opened

'Definitely my favourite bustling bar/restaurant in Tel Aviv. Sharon Cohen is both chef and owner and it shows. For eight years now, he has consistently managed to give this place his personal touches and with great success. A very modernist cuisine with the best that the Mediterranean has to offer. Sharon uses only the freshest ingredients and marinates them in his pool of creativity until you get a meal that both surprises and delights.'—Yair Feinberg

TAIZU

Recommended by
Yair Feinberg

Levenshtein Tower
Menachem Begin Street 23
Tel Aviv
Tel Aviv 6618356
Israel
+972 35225005
www.taizu.co.il

Opening hours	Open 7 days
Credit cards	Accepted
Price range	Affordable
Style	Smart casual
Cuisine	Asian Fusion
Recommended for	High end

'An Asia-terranean restaurant – a very innovative concept, every meal there is a new and exciting event.' —Yair Feinberg

THAI HOUSE
Recommended by
Maoz Alonim
Bograshov Street 8
Tel Aviv
Tel Aviv 63808
Israel
+972 35178568
www.thai-house.co.il

Opening hours	Open 7 days
Credit cards	Accepted
Price range	Affordable
Style	Casual
Cuisine	Thai
Recommended for	Regular neighbourhood

'Anytime I manage to take some time off from the restaurant you will probably find me in one place and in one place only – Thai House. Being familiar with the traditions of the Thai kitchen in a way that many Thai people are not themselves, Yariv (the owner of the Thai House) created the most authentic, mouth-watering, colourful and spicy menu in town. Going to Thai House is forever a feast.'—Maoz Alonim

YAKIMONO
Recommended by
Maoz Alonim
Sderot Rothschild 19
Tel Aviv
Tel Aviv 63504
Israel
+972 35175171
www.yakimono.co.il

Opening hours	Open 7 days
Credit cards	Accepted
Price range	Affordable
Style	Smart casual
Cuisine	Sushi
Recommended for	High end

'There is no other place in town that serves such high-end Japanese food. Using the freshest, tastiest and exquisite fish and seafood you can find, Yakimono's sushi is something to remember.'—Maoz Alonim

CIPRIANI
Recommended by
Francesco Mazzei
Building 1
Yas Marina
Abu Dhabi
United Arab Emirates
+971 26575400
www.cipriani.com

Opening hours	Open 7 days
Credit cards	Accepted
Price range	Expensive
Style	Smart casual
Cuisine	Italian
Recommended for	Worth the travel

'The best *vitello tonnato* (sliced veal with tuna sauce) and *pollo alla cacciatora* (hunter's chicken stew) of recent times, eaten in front of the marina. It transported me back to Venice.'—Francesco Mazzei

BAKER & SPICE
Recommended by
Izu Ani
Souk Al Bahar
Exit 32 Sheik Zayed
Dubai
United Arab Emirates
+971 44252240
www.bakerandspiceme.com

Opening hours	Open 7 days
Reservation policy	No
Credit cards	Accepted
Price range	Affordable
Style	Casual
Cuisine	Café-Bistro-Deli
Recommended for	Breakfast

'It is simple and honest. There's no faffing around, what you see is what you get.'—Izu Ani

BOULEVARD CAFÉ

Recommended by
Reif Othman

Al Manzil Hotel
Sheikh Mohammed bin Rashid Boulevard
Dubai
United Arab Emirates
+971 44285931
www.almanzilhotel.ae

Opening hours	Open 7 days
Reservation policy	No
Credit cards	Accepted
Price range	Affordable
Style	Smart casual
Cuisine	French
Recommended for	Breakfast

'Good portions of food, nice ambience, friendly staff and good terrace seating for when there's nice weather.'—Reif Othman

Dubai is often at its best when it's pretending to be somewhere else. So it is with this all-day operation attached to the Al Manzil Downtown Dubai hotel, which takes its inspiration from Parisian cafés, views of the towering Burj Khalifa standing in for the Eiffel Tower. It's *petit déjeuner* downtown-Dubai-style with freshly baked croissants, excellent coffee and smart service. The menu extends to tartines, crêpes, waffles, Eggs Benedict and as many ways with the omelette as the emirate has skyscrapers. To make things more authentically Arabesque, there's always the option of a morning shisha on the terrace.

EATALY

Recommended by
Izu Ani

The Dubai Mall
LGF, Financial Centre Road
Dubai
United Arab Emirates
+971 43308899
www.eataly.com

Opening hours	Open 7 days
Credit cards	Accepted
Price range	Affordable
Style	Casual
Cuisine	Italian
Recommended for	Bargain

'They use very few ingredients which I love. Simple Italian food.'—Izu Ani

INDEGO BY VINEET

Recommended by
Alfonso & Ernesto Iaccarino

Grosvenor House
Al Sufouh Road
Dubai
United Arab Emirates
+971 43176000
www.indegobyvineet.com

Opening hours	Open 7 days
Credit cards	Accepted
Price range	Expensive
Style	Smart casual
Cuisine	Modern Indian
Recommended for	Worth the travel

'The way the fish was cooked really impressed us.'
—Alfonso & Ernesto Iaccarino

QBARA

Recommended by
Izu Ani

Wafi Fort Complex
Sheikh Rashid Road
Dubai
United Arab Emirates
+971 47092500
www.qbara.ae

Opening hours	Open 7 days
Credit cards	Accepted
Price range	Affordable
Style	Smart casual
Cuisine	Middle Eastern
Recommended for	Regular neighbourhood

'Their food and approach is different to any other restaurant and it has a really nice atmosphere.'
—Izu Ani

Located in Dubai's buzzing Wafi City complex, this restaurant and bar has serious amounts of 'wow factor'. Set over two storeys in a stand-alone building, the jaw-dropping interior comes on like a contemporary souk, with a riot of carved dark wood, bright silks and Moroccan rugs all topped off with a huge UFO-like chandelier big enough to light a stadium rock band. The mezzanine floor houses various lounge areas or *majlis* that overlook the main dining room, where are served Levantine, Middle Eastern and Moroccan inspired dishes such as duck breast, pomegranate molasses, walnuts and cinnamon.

RAVI

Recommended by
Reif Othman

Satwa (Al Dhiyafa Road)
Dubai
United Arab Emirates
+971 43315353

Opening hours	Open 7 days
Reservation policy	No
Credit cards	Not accepted
Price range	Budget
Style	Casual
Cuisine	Pakistani
Recommended for	Late night

'Casual, cheap and easy to eat.'—Reif Othman

In a city where so much is shiny and new, this Pakistani outpost in Al Satwa, a fixture since 1978, is refreshingly dishevelled by comparison. Open twenty-two hours a day, it's arguably best approached at night when its green and white sign glows. A popular pit stop for cab drivers and moneyed expats alike, its wipe-down outdoor tables are turned at a rate of knots well into the small hours. The lengthy menu of Punjabi classics, from curries and biryanis to chicken tikka, seekh kebabs and lamb chops from the tandoor, might be priced for paupers but the cooking's never impoverished.

REFLETS BY PIERRE GAGNAIRE

Recommended by
Izu Ani

InterContinental Dubai Festival City
Al Rebat Street
Dubai
United Arab Emirates
+971 47011199
www.diningdfc.com

Opening hours	Open 7 days
Credit cards	Accepted
Price range	Expensive
Style	Smart casual
Cuisine	Modern French
Recommended for	High end

'It is refined and their attention to detail is second to none. It's not a quick meal, but a long, leisurely one.'
—Izu Ani

WOK IT

Recommended by
Reif Othman

Zainal Mohebi Plaza
Sheikh Khalifa Bin Zayed Road
Dubai
United Arab Emirates
+971 43885711
www.wokitrestaurant.com

Opening hours	Open 7 days
Credit cards	Accepted
Price range	Budget
Style	Casual
Cuisine	Asian
Recommended for	Regular neighbourhood

'This place serves good Indonesian cuisine that my family loves.'—Reif Othman

WOX

Recommended by
Reif Othman

Grand Hyatt
Sheikh Rashid Rd
Dubai
United Arab Emirates
+971 43172222
www.restaurants.dubai.hyatt.com

Opening hours	Open 7 days
Credit cards	Accepted
Price range	Affordable
Style	Casual
Cuisine	Pan-Asian
Recommended for	Regular neighbourhood

'Wox have a very nice beef pho. Reasonable pricing.'
—Reif Othman

ASTOR GRILL

Recommended by
Alfredo Russo

St Regis Hotel
Doha West Bay
Doha
Ad Dawhah 14435
Qatar
+974 44460105
www.astorgrilldoha.com

Opening hours	Closed Saturday
Credit cards	Accepted
Price range	Expensive
Style	Smart casual
Cuisine	Steakhouse
Recommended for	High end

'For the design.'—Alfredo Russo

CENTRAL & SOUTH ASIA

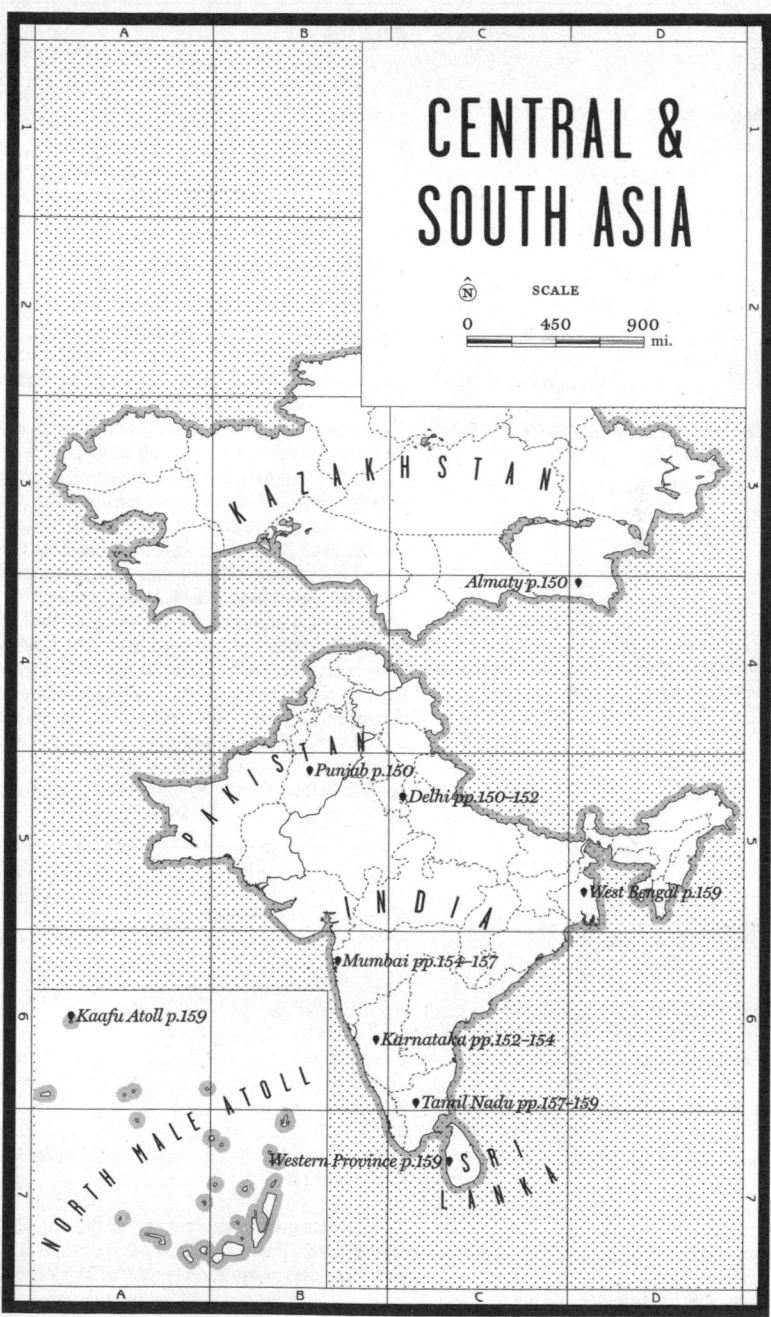

CENTRAL & SOUTH ASIA

$\hat{N}$ SCALE

0   450   900
mi.

KAZAKHSTAN

Almaty p.150

PAKISTAN

Punjab p.150

Delhi pp.150–152

INDIA

West Bengal p.159

Mumbai pp.154–157

Kaafu Atoll p.159

Karnataka pp.152–154

NORTH MALE ATOLL

Tamil Nadu pp.157–159

Western Province p.159

SRI LANKA

LT GRILL

The Ritz-Carlton
Esentai Tower,
77/7 Al-Farabi Avenue
Almaty 050040
Kazakhstan
+7 7273328888
www.ritzcarlton.com

Opening hours	Open 7 days
Credit cards	Accepted
Price range	Expensive
Style	Smart casual
Cuisine	Steakhouse
Recommended for	Worth the travel

'Live music in the restaurant, fashionable diners, clever dishes.'—Thomas Bühner

CUCKOO'S DEN

Roshan Gate
House 2168a Fort Road
Lahore
Punjab 54000
Pakistan
+92 4237662228
Website

Opening hours	Open 7 days
Credit cards	Accepted
Price range	Affordable
Style	Casual
Cuisine	Pakistani
Recommended for	Worth the travel

THE BIG CHILL CAFE

HS-5, Kailash Colony Market
New Delhi
Delhi 110 048
India
+91 1146556828

Opening hours	Open 7 days
Reservation policy	No
Credit cards	Accepted
Price range	Budget
Style	Casual
Cuisine	International
Recommended for	Wish I'd opened

'A small restaurant with brilliant food and great ambience.'—Manoj Goel

BUKHARA

ITC Maurya Hotel
Sardar Patel Marg
New Delhi
Delhi 110 021
India
+91 1126112233
www.itchotels.in

Opening hours	Open 7 days
Credit cards	Accepted
Price range	Expensive
Style	Smart casual
Cuisine	Northwest Indian
Recommended for	Local favourite

'If someone told you that a restaurant hasn't changed their menu in thirty years it would seem crazy or you might think they have a very large menu. Bukhara has a compact menu that's remained unchanged in three decades and it's one of the most successful restaurants in India. I was fortunate to work there just after hotel school. It was then, and continues to be, a mecca for Northwest Indian food. Their kebabs are grilled to perfection and every dish is at its flavourful best. I went back a couple of years ago, after fifteen years, and was pleasantly surprised to see a good number of the staff still there. To me, that always speaks well of a restaurant. They know regulars by name and the service style is incredibly warm and personalized. I love the grandeur of this restaurant, its loyalty to its staff, its belief in its food philosophy and for dishing out a superb experience to its diners.'—Alfred Prasad

CHIMNEY SIZZLERS

Shop 10–16 Yashwant Place
New Delhi
Delhi 110 021
India
+91 1166891090

Opening hours	Open 7 days
Credit cards	Accepted but not AMEX
Price range	Budget
Style	Casual
Cuisine	Indian-Chinese
Recommended for	Bargain

'A cheap and great restaurant to fulfil day-to-day hunger needs. It won't make a hole in your pocket either. The best Indian and Chinese food.'—Manoj Goel

THE CHINA KITCHEN

Recommended by
Manoj Goel

Hyatt Regency Delhi
Bhikaiji Cama Place
New Delhi
Delhi 110 066
India
+91 1166771334
www.delhi.regency.hyatt.com

Opening hours	Open 7 days
Credit cards	Accepted
Price range	Affordable
Style	Casual
Cuisine	Chinese
Recommended for	High end

'The best authentic Chinese food in town.'
—Manoj Goel

GUNPOWDER

Recommended by
Vicky Ratnani

22 Hauz Khas Village
New Delhi
Delhi 110 016
India
+91 1126535700

Opening hours	Closed Monday
Credit cards	Accepted
Price range	Affordable
Style	Casual
Cuisine	South Indian
Recommended for	Worth the travel

INDIAN ACCENT

Recommended by
Alyn Williams

The Manor Hotel
77 Friends Colony West
New Delhi
Delhi 110 065
India
+91 1143235151
www.indianaccent.com

Opening hours	Open 7 days
Credit cards	Accepted
Price range	Expensive
Style	Smart casual
Cuisine	Modern Indian
Recommended for	Worth the travel

'Manish has taken fine dining in India to a new level in his super smart suburban restaurant, serving some of the most exciting and innovative flavour combinations that I have tasted for a long time.'—Alyn Williams

Chef Manish Mehrotra's 'Modern Indian' food at The Manor Hotel's restaurant in southeast New Delhi has an 'Indian Accent' but is fluent in many tongues. The Bihar-born Mehrotra, executive chef of the Old World Hospitality Group, is unafraid of stuffing *galawat* kebab with foie gras, pairing voguish pork belly with exotic bacon, walnut and *munakka* raisin korma or putting homey old *khichdi* (albeit a modern version) on an ambitious fine-dining menu. Mehrotra draws his influences from anything and anywhere, with exciting, never incoherent results. The restaurant itself is plush and glossy with its onyx bar and silver diya tree centrepieces. Excellent wine list.

KARIM'S

Recommended by
Manoj Goel,
Gulam Qureshi

16 Jama Masjid Gali Kababian
New Delhi
Delhi 110 006
India
+91 1123264981
www.karimhoteldelhi.com

Opening hours	Open 7 days
Reservation policy	No
Credit cards	Not accepted
Price range	Affordable
Style	Casual
Cuisine	North Indian
Recommended for	Bargain

'Although the food is a bit spicy and oily, it is always buzzing and has an old world charm.'—Gulam Qureshi

This famous Mughlai venture is almost synonymous with Old Delhi. It was established back in 1911 as a *dhaba* (roadside eatery), catering for travellers from all over the country drawn by King George V's coronation as Emperor of India. The founder's mission was simple: to serve the common man with the same lavish feasts – mutton curry, tandoori meats and biryanis – that his own ancestors had once cooked in the courts of the Mughal emperors. Over a century on, and now in the hands of the fourth generation, it continues to turn out regal meals for *dhaba* prices.

MASALA ART

Recommended by
Manoj Goel

Taj Palace Hotel
Sardar Patel Marg
New Delhi
Delhi 110 021
India
+91 1126110202
www.tajhotels.com

Opening hours	Open 7 days
Credit cards	Accepted
Price range	Affordable
Style	Smart casual
Cuisine	Indian
Recommended for	Regular neighbourhood

'Brilliant execution of food and with great flavours.'
—Manoj Goel

PARANTHE WALI GALI

Recommended by
Manoj Goel

Chandni Chowk
New Delhi
Delhi 110 006
India

Opening hours	Open 7 days
Reservation policy	No
Credit cards	Not accepted
Price range	Budget
Style	Casual
Cuisine	Indian Street Food
Recommended for	Breakfast

'They serve about 100 varieties of *paranthas* (Indian flatbread), and have done for decades, with authentic flavours and tastes.'—Manoj Goel

SWAGATH

Recommended by
Gulam Qureshi

14 Defence Colony Market
New Delhi
Delhi 110 024
India
+91 1124337538
www.swagath.in

Opening hours	Open 7 days
Credit cards	Accepted
Price range	Affordable
Style	Casual
Cuisine	North Indian
Recommended for	Regular neighbourhood

'Their crabs are cooked to perfection in aromatic South Indian spices.'—Gulam Qureshi

WASABI BY MORIMOTO

Recommended by
Rahul Akerkar,
Vicky Ratnani

Taj Mahal Hotel
1 Mansingh Road
New Delhi
Delhi 110 011
India
+91 1166566162
www.tajhotels.com

Opening hours	Open 7 days
Credit cards	Accepted
Price range	Expensive
Style	Formal
Cuisine	Modern Japanese
Recommended for	High End

CAFÉ NOIR

Recommended by
Naren Thimmaiah

U B City Mall
24 Vittal Mallya Road
Bangalore
Karnataka 560 001
India
www.cafenoir.co.in

Opening hours	Open 7 days
Credit cards	Accepted
Price range	Affordable
Style	Casual
Cuisine	Café-Bistro-Deli
Recommended for	Regular neighbourhood

'A typical street-side café known for its burgers, fish and chips and chocolate éclairs.'—Naren Thimmaiah

EGG FACTORY

Recommended by
Naren Thimmaiah

White House
St Marks Road
Bangalore
Karnataka 560 001
India
+91 8042110041
www.theeggfactory.in

Opening hours	Open 7 days
Credit cards	Accepted
Price range	Affordable
Style	Casual
Cuisine	International
Recommended for	Breakfast

'This informal eatery has popularized the breakfast and eggy dishes of Manipal. Try their Manipal Bread Masala.'—Naren Thimmaiah

FOODHALL

Recommended by
Naren Thimmaiah

1MG Road Mall
1/2 Swami Vivekananda Road
Bangalore
Karnataka 560 008
India
+91 8022086533
www.onemgroad.com

Opening hours	Open 7 days
Reservation policy	No
Credit cards	Accepted
Price range	Affordable
Style	Casual
Cuisine	International
Recommended for	Bargain

'Serves tasty international snacks like sandwiches, muffins, cakes, cheeses, and olives.'
—Naren Thimmaiah

IMPERIAL

Recommended by
Naren Thimmaiah

94/95 Residency Road
Bangalore
Karnataka 560 025
India

Opening hours	Open 7 days
Reservation policy	No
Credit cards	Accepted
Price range	Budget
Style	Casual
Cuisine	Indian
Recommended for	Late night

'They're known for their fried chicken kebabs and ghee rice.'—Naren Thimmaiah

KARAVALLI

Recommended by
Manoj Goel

The Gateway Hotel
66 Residency Road
Bangalore
Karnataka 560 025
India
+91 8066604545
www.thegatewayhotels.com

Opening hours	Open 7 days
Credit cards	Accepted
Price range	Affordable
Style	Casual
Cuisine	Indian-Seafood
Recommended for	Worth the travel

'Beautifully designed resturant with great variety of seafood.'—Manoj Goel

MTR – MAVALLI TIFFIN ROOMS

Recommended by
Naren Thimmaiah

14 Lalbagh Road
Bangalore
Karnataka 560 027
India
+91 8022220022
www.mavallitiffinrooms.com

Opening hours	Closed Monday
Credit cards	Not accepted
Price range	Budget
Style	Casual
Cuisine	Indian
Recommended for	Local favourite

'The best restaurant showcasing the local breakfast, snacks and thali (traditional set meal) experience. And more than eighty years old! Try their bisi bele bhath (spicy rice and lentils) and Masala dosa (potato-filled pancake).'—Naren Thimmaiah

OLIVE BEACH

Recommended by
Naren Thimmaiah

16 Wood Street
Bangalore
Karnataka 560 025
India
+91 8041128400
www.olivebarandkitchen.com

Opening hours	Open 7 days
Credit cards	Accepted
Price range	Affordable
Style	Casual
Cuisine	Mediterranean
Recommended for	Wish I'd opened

'I admire Olive Beach the most for the wholesome experience they offer. This is one place which scores on all fronts: great food, fantastic ambience and friendly service. These are the qualities that make a great restaurant!'—Naren Thimmaiah

TOIT

Recommended by
Naren Thimmaiah

298 100 Feet Road
Bangalore
Karnataka 560 038
India
+91 9243406062
www.toit.in

Opening hours	Open 7 days
Credit cards	Accepted
Price range	Affordable
Style	Casual
Cuisine	International
Recommended for	Regular neighbourhood

'This is a trendy and hip place which has good, tasty food. Try their baked nachos, barbeque chicken pizza and lasagne.'—Naren Thimmaiah

ASWAD

Recommended by
Vicky Ratnani

Shivaji Park
Gadkari Chowk
Mumbai
Mumbai Metropolitan Region 400 028
India

Opening hours	Open 7 days
Reservation policy	No
Credit cards	Not accepted
Price range	Budget
Style	Casual
Cuisine	Street Food
Recommended for	Breakfast

'For *kanda poha* (flattened rice with onions and spices).'
—Vicky Ratnani

BADE MIYA

Recommended by
Rahul Akerkar,
Chong Chee Loong,
Vicky Ratnani

Tulloch Road, Apollo Bandar
Colaba
Mumbai
Mumbai Metropolitan Region 400 039
India

Opening hours	Open 7 days
Reservation policy	No
Credit cards	Not accepted
Price range	Budget
Style	Casual
Cuisine	Street Food
Recommended for	Late night

'The velvety rich chicken masala with perfectly baked *roti* (Indian bread) and butter is something you can eat and at a bargain price – other places can be expensive.'—Chong Chee Loong

CANDIES

Recommended by
Chong Chee Loong

5aa Pali Hill
Mumbai
Mumbai Metropolitan Region 400 050
India
+91 26422324
www.candiescafe.com

Opening hours	Closed Monday
Reservation policy	No
Credit cards	Not accepted
Price range	Affordable
Style	Casual
Cuisine	International
Recommended for	Regular neighbourhood

LE CIRQUE SIGNATURE

Recommended by
Chong Chee Loong

The Leela Hotel
Dawood Baug Road
Mumbai
Mumbai Metropolitan Region 400 059
India
+91 2266911344
www.theleela.com

Opening hours	Open 7 days
Credit cards	Accepted
Price range	Expensive
Style	Smart casual
Cuisine	French-Italian
Recommended for	High end

'The food and the service is brilliant. Something you would expect from a five-star place when you dine out for a special occasion or an expensive treat. The menu, the food, the taste of every dish is fabulous.'
—Chong Chee Loong

GAJALEE

Kadamgiri Complex
Hanuman Road
Mumbai
Mumbai Metropolitan Region 400 057
India
+91 2226166470
www.gajalee.com

Opening hours	Open 7 days
Credit cards	Accepted
Price range	Affordable
Style	Casual
Cuisine	Seafood
Recommended for	Regular neighbourhood

'Does a mean Bombil fry.'—Vicky Ratnani

It's named after the Malvani term for an informal gathering, but the flavours at this suburban staple, now with seven outposts from Mangalore to Singapore, are far from casual. This, the original branch, is famous throughout the region for its coastal cuisine: star draws such as the Bombil fry (Bombay duck), tandoori giant crab and clam koshimbir offer a vibrant showcase of Maharashtrian cooking, with its eclectic blend of Konkani and Goan influences. It's not about frills – dishes come 'spicy' or 'very spicy', and dessert is limited to caramel custard or kulfi – but for beautifully fresh seafood it's hard to beat.

IMBISS

Pipewala 4th Pasta Lane
Mumbai
Mumbai Metropolitan Region 400 005
India
+91 2222020455
www.imbissmeatingjoint.com

Opening hours	Open 7 days
Reservation policy	No
Credit cards	Accepted
Price range	Affordable
Style	Casual
Cuisine	German
Recommended for	Regular neighbourhood

'It's got a good vibe. It's an easy going place to visit for good meals.'—Chong Chee Loong

JIMMY BOY

Vikas 11 Bank Street
Mumbai
Mumbai Metropolitan Region 400 023
India
+91 2222700880

Opening hours	Open 7 days
Credit cards	Accepted
Price range	Affordable
Style	Casual
Cuisine	Northwest Indian
Recommended for	Local favourite

'You must try their *akuri* (spicy scrambled eggs) on toast, *salli per idu* (eggs on spiced vegetables), and dhansak.'—Vicky Ratnani

Short of being invited to a local marriage hall like the Albless Baug, this authentic Parsi restaurant, in the historic Fort district, is the only place in town where diners can sample *lagan nu bhonu* – an elaborate multi-course wedding meal served on banana leaves. With its wooden chairs and gentle 1970s soundtrack, it's a nostalgic sort of place, whose kitchen turns out Parsi dishes that have been handed down from generation to generation. Accordingly, classics like dhansak, chicken pilaf and baked custard dominate – all washed down with bottles of raspberry soda, the super-sweet drink seemingly beloved by Parsi wedding-goers.

LEMONGRASS

Palm Spring Link Road
Mumbai
Mumbai Metropolitan Region 400 064
India
+91 28817444
www.lemongrasscafe.in

Opening hours	Open 7 days
Credit cards	Accepted
Price range	Affordable
Style	Casual
Cuisine	Pan-Asian
Recommended for	Regular neighbourhood

'The food is good. It's laid back and I like the atmosphere.'—Chong Chee Loong

LEOPOLD CAFÉ

Recommended by
Chong Chee Loong

Shahid Bhagat Singh Road
Mumbai
Mumbai Metropolitan Region 400 001
India
+91 2222828185
www.leopoldcafe.com

Opening hours	Open 7 days
Credit cards	Accepted
Price range	Affordable
Style	Casual
Cuisine	Café-Bar
Recommended for	Late night

'A very well-known place, with youngsters, locals and tourists. Great place to catch up with friends over some beer.'—Chong Chee Loong

'Getting better with age' is the motto of this classic Colaba hang-out, founded in 1871. From its days as a wholesale oil company, to a horrific 2008 terrorist attack (framed posters now cover the bullet holes), this Irani-run institution has seen it all, and its spirit hasn't been diminished a jot. The menu proudly offers 333 different dishes, running the gamut from cereal to chicken biryani. But it's a joy just to take in the buzzing atmosphere over a late drink – be it cocktail, 'mocktail' or the novelty in-house beer tower: a three-foot-tall cylinder that eliminates the need for refills.

NOOR MOHAMMADI

Recommended by
Vicky Ratnan3

Wazir 179 Abdul Hakim Noor
Mohammadi Chowk
Mumbai Metropolitan Region 400 002
India

Opening hours	Open 7 days
Reservation policy	No
Credit cards	Not accepted
Price range	Budget
Style	Casual
Cuisine	Indian Street Food
Recommended for	Bargain

'Go for biryani and *nalli nihari* (bone marrow stew) – classic meat dishes'—Vicky Ratnani

OLYMPIA COFFEE HOUSE

Recommended by
Vicky Ratnani

Rahim Mansion
1 Shahid Bhagat Singh Road
Mumbai
Mumbai Metropolitan Region 400 039
India

Opening hours	Open 7 days
Reservation policy	No
Credit cards	Not accepted
Price range	Budget
Style	Casual
Cuisine	North West Indian
Recommended for	Breakfast

'For *kheema pao* – minced (ground) meat and soft traditional bread.'—Vicky Ratnani

ROYAL CHINA INDIA

Recommended by
Rahul Akerkar

192 Turner Road
Mumbai
Mumbai Metropolitan Region 400 050
India
+91 2226425533
www.royalchinaindia.com

Opening hours	Open 7 days
Credit cards	Accepted
Price range	Affordable
Style	Smart casual
Cuisine	Cantonese
Recommended for	Regular neighbourhood

'They have great dim sum.'—Rahul Akerkar

SARDAR REFRESHMENT

Recommended by
Vicky Ratnani

166a Tardeo Road Junction
Mumbai
Mumbai Metropolitan Region 400 034
India

Opening hours	Open 7 days
Reservation policy	No
Credit cards	Not accepted
Price range	Budget
Style	Casual
Cuisine	Indian Street Food
Recommended for	Bargain

'Try the *pav bhaji* (vegetable chilli with buns).'
—Vicky Ratnani

SHREE THAKER BHOJANALAY

Recommended by
Rahul Akerkar

31 Dadyseth Agiary Marg
Mumbai
Mumbai Metropolitan Region 400 002
India

Opening hours	Open 7 days
Reservation policy	No
Credit cards	Not accepted
Price range	Budget
Style	Casual
Cuisine	Western Indian
Recommended for	Local favourite

'They serve home-cooked, vegetarian, Gujarati food in a *thali* (set meal) format. It's a different menu at lunch and dinner and changes every day. It's all you can eat for the equivalent of less than £2 ($4)!'—Rahul Akerkar

SUZETTE

Recommended by
Chong Chee Loong

St John Street
Mumbai
Mumbai Metropolitan Region 400 021
India
+91 2226411431
www.suzette.in

Opening hours	Open 7 days
Reservation policy	No
Credit cards	Accepted but not AMEX
Price range	Affordable
Style	Casual
Cuisine	French crêperie
Recommended for	Breakfast

TRISHNA

Recommended by
Chong Chee Loong

7 Sai Baba Marg
Mumbai
Mumbai Metropolitan Region 400 023
India
+91 2222703213
www.trishna.co.in

Opening hours	Open 7 days
Credit cards	Accepted
Price range	Budget
Style	Smart casual
Cuisine	Seafood
Recommended for	Local favourite

'I think this place sums up the city. It's got really good seafood items on its menu. It's in an alley in Kala Godha town. A must visit.'—Chong Chee Loong

Given its present name in 1991, but active for several decades before that, this backstreet restaurant is one of the country's most esteemed destinations for seafood. Frequented by a glittering crowd of Bollywood stars and sportsmen – at lunchtime, when it's easier to snag a table, well-heeled housewives tend to dominate – it's a superior kind of place, although that's not necessarily reflected in the rather routine white interior and old-fashioned banquettes. It is, however, obvious in the superbly cooked seafood, with most patrons making a beeline for the crab in butter pepper garlic sauce, or jumbo prawns tandoor.

MADURAI ARULANANDAM

Recommended by
Praveen Anand

94/1 Usman Road
Chennai
Tamil Nadu 600 017
India
+91 24315223

Opening hours	Open 7 days
Reservation policy	No
Credit cards	Not accepted
Price range	Budget
Style	Casual
Cuisine	Indian
Recommended for	Regular neighbourhood

'Some of the best non-vegetarian dishes prepared in Madurai style. All the dishes made here are consistent in spice levels and taste.'—Praveen Anand

MATHSYA

Recommended by
Praveen Anand

Thanikachalam Road
Chennai
Tamil Nadu 600 008
India
www.mathsyarestaurants.com

Opening hours	Open 7 days
Credit cards	Accepted
Price range	Affordable
Style	Casual
Cuisine	Indian
Recommended for	Late night

'They serve a wide choice of vegetarian dises of both South and North Indian food. Open until 2.00 a.m., they serve the best Udipi cuisine in the city. The owner, Ram Bhatt, always takes great pride in explaining every dish that's served. Try the Karnataka *thali* (traditional set meal), *vella dosai* (sweet pancake) and *rasa vadai* (fritters in broth).'—Praveen Anand

MURUGAN IDLI KADAI

Recommended by
Praveen Anand

46/13 North Usman Road
Chennai
Tamil Nadu 600 017
India

Opening hours	Open 7 days
Reservation policy	No
Credit cards	Not accepted
Price range	Budget
Style	Casual
Cuisine	Indian
Recommended for	Local favourite

'Serves all local breakfast favourites on a banana leaf with unlimited accompaniments. Service is quick and unique.'—Praveen Anand

MYLAI KARPAGAMBAL MESS

Recommended by
Praveen Anand

20 East Mada Street
Chennai
Tamil Nadu 600 017
India

Opening hours	Open 7 days
Reservation policy	No
Credit cards	Not accepted
Price range	Budget
Style	Casual
Cuisine	South Indian
Recommended for	Breakfast

'Exquisitely made *dosai* (pancakes) and *vadai* (fritters) of various types, filter coffee and *badam halwa* (almond dessert).'—Praveen Anand

ROYAL VEGA

Recommended by
Praveen Anand

ITC Hotel Grand Chola
63 Mount Road
Chennai
Tamil Nadu 600 032
India
+91 4422200000
www.itchotels.in

Opening hours	Open 7 days
Credit cards	Accepted
Price range	Affordable
Style	Smart casual
Cuisine	Indian-Vegetarian
Recommended for	Wish I'd opened

'A unique concept serving vegetarian repast of royalty from all over India.'—Praveen Anand

SARAVANAA BHAVAN

Recommended by
Alfred Prasad

101 Dr Radha Krishnan Salai
Chennai
Tamil Nadu 600 004
India
+91 4428115977
www.saravanabhavan.com

Opening hours	Open 7 days
Reservation policy	No
Credit cards	Accepted
Price range	Budget
Style	Casual
Cuisine	Indian-Vegetarian
Recommended for	Late night

'This super success story is the largest vegetarian restaurant chain in the world. There are twenty branches in Chennai, a city I consider home in India. I love this place for its flavours that hit the spot and for its incredible consistency. They open as early as 5.30 a.m. and continue until midnight. I have been caught staring at their kitchen line flow – quite fascinating! It largely has an all-day menu. I am normally there for breakfast every two or three days when I am in India. My favourite dish is *ghee dosa* (pancakes) and *medhu vadai* (black gram flour fritters). To my mind, this place captures the quintessential spirit of the city.'—Alfred Prasad

SHIRAZ ART CAFE

Recommended by
Praveen Anand

Cholamandal Artists' Village
East Coast Road
Chennai
Tamil Nadu 600 041
India
+91 9566031098

Opening hours	Closed Tuesday
Credit cards	Not accepted
Price range	Affordable
Style	Casual
Cuisine	Persian
Recommended for	High end

'Led by Chef Nazrin, this restaurant serves some great homemade Iranian food. Awesome.'—Praveen Anand

THE BANGALA HOTEL

Recommended by
Alfred Prasad

Devakottai Road
Karaikudi
Tamil Nadu 630 001
India
+91 4565220221
www.thebangala.com

Opening hours	Open 7 days
Credit cards	Accepted but not AMEX
Price range	Affordable
Style	Smart casual
Cuisine	Chettinad
Recommended for	Worth the travel

'In the heartland of South India, in the historic Chettinad region, The Bangala makes an incredible effort to preserve the heritage of the Chettiars and their ancient land. In particular, the culinary traditions upheld are a feast for anybody and more so for a chef. I met with the chefs and cooks at the Bangala, who have been cooking for generations, and to gain an understanding of their food calendar and food science was truly inspirational. In London, almost every ingredient is available but in Chettinad, their resourceful approach – from drying ingredients over the summer, sourcing some ingredients from afar and living off the land with their extensive use of game – is truly amazing. The meals here are large and each dish is a feast for the senses. This gastronomic slice of India should be a destination and not a detour.'—Alfred Prasad

KEWPIE'S

Recommended by
Gaggan Anand

2 Elgin Lane
Calcutta
West Bengal 700 020
India
+91 3324861600
www.kewpieskitchen.com

Opening hours	Closed Monday
Credit cards	Accepted but not AMEX
Price range	Affordable
Style	Smart casual
Cuisine	Bengali
Recommended for	Local favourite

'They keep alive traditional Bengali cuisine, which is the most underrated cuisine of India. They cook from recipes that are rarely used now – almost extinct – and their food always inspires me to create.'
—Gaggan Anand

ROYAL INDIAN

Recommended by
Gulam Qureshi

147 Rabindra Sarani
Calcutta
West Bengal 700 001
India
+91 9658570347

Opening hours	Open 7 days
Reservation policy	No
Credit cards	Accepted but not AMEX
Price range	Affordable
Style	Casual
Cuisine	North Indian
Recommended for	Worth the travel

'It's a very small, old restaurant where they do nice mutton chops (Indian lamb chops) and *murgh rizala* (chicken curry in white gravy).'—Gulam Qureshi

GALLE FACE GREEN STREET MARKET

Recommended by
Dharshan Munidasa

Galle Road
Colombo
Western Province 00300
Sri Lanka

Opening hours	Open 7 days
Reservation policy	No
Credit cards	Not accepted
Price range	Budget
Style	Casual
Cuisine	Street Food
Recommended for	Regular neighbourhood

'No fancy infrastructure, just the sunset and Sri Lankan street food at its best.'—Dharshan Munidasa

CELSIUS

Recommended by
Sergio Herman

Huvafen Fushi Resort
North Male Atoll
PO Box 2017
Kaafu Atoll 08390
Maldives
+960 6644222
www.huvafenfushi.peraquum.com

Opening hours	Open 7 days
Credit cards	Accepted
Price range	Expensive
Style	Smart casual
Cuisine	International
Recommended for	High end

'Home-made curries, freshly caught fish, stunning views... and silence, only silence.'—Sergio Herman

'With the Las Vegasification of Macao there are few places to enjoy the old gentle-paced country feel but this is one.'
NEIL ANTHONY TOMES PP172–3

'FRESH BEEF HOT POT AND A FRESHLY SLAUGHTERED COW IS SERVED AT EVERY MEAL.'
JEREME LEUNG P162

'STINKY TOFU IS A SPECIAL FOOD IN ZHEJIANG.'
ALAN SHEN P162

CHINA, MACAO, HONG KONG, TAIWAN & KOREA

'Represents the very essence of Taiwan's food culture.'
LANSHU CHEN P173

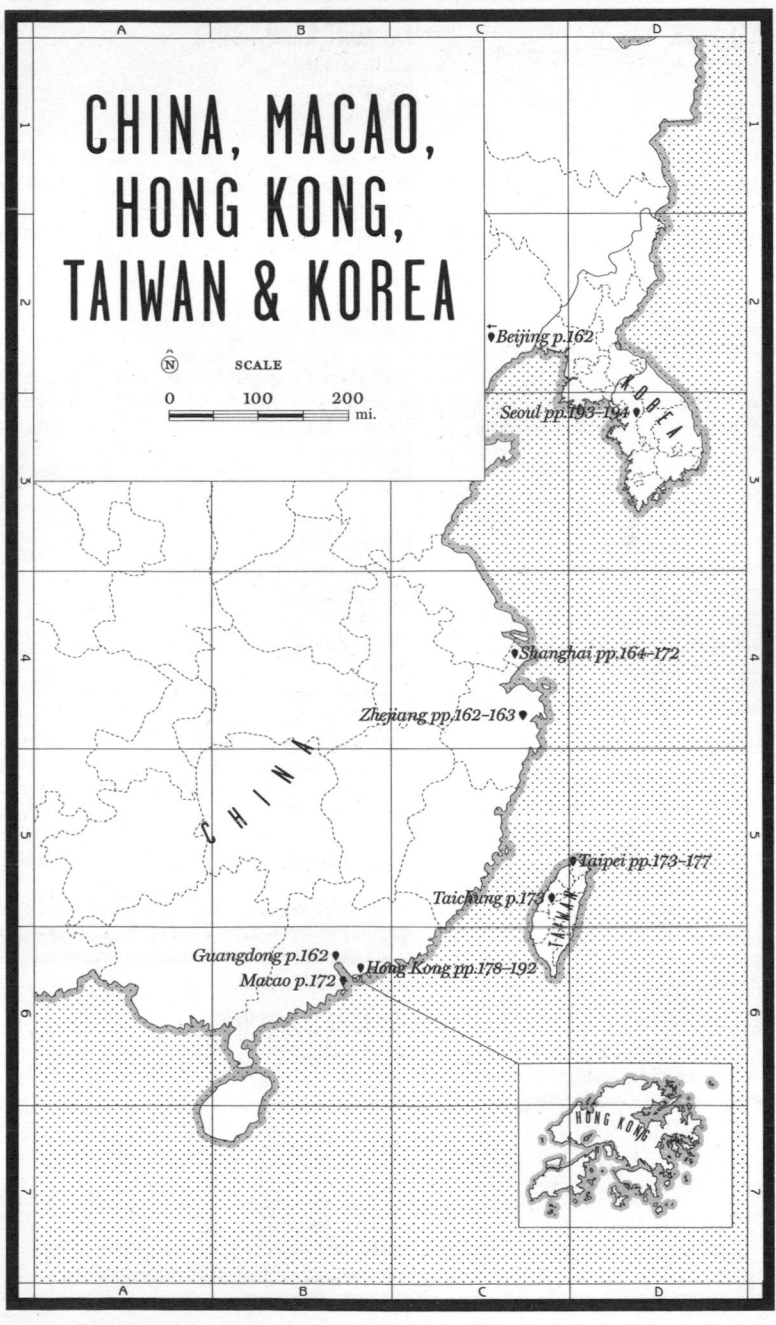

CHINA, MACAO, HONG KONG, TAIWAN & KOREA

(N) SCALE

0   100   200
mi.

Beijing p.162

Seoul pp.193–194

KOREA

Shanghai pp.164–172

Zhejiang pp.162–163

CHINA

Taipei pp.173–177

Taichung p.173

TAIWAN

Guangdong p.162
Macao p.172 *Hong Kong pp.178–192*

HONG KONG

DA DONG ROAST DUCK

Recommended by
Man-Sing Lee

3 Tuanjiehu Lu
Beijing
Beijing 100007
China
+86 1065822892
www.dadongdadong.com

Opening hours	Open 7 days
Credit cards	Accepted
Price range	Affordable
Style	Casual
Cuisine	Modern Chinese
Recommended for	Wish I'd opened

Should you fancy a duck in the city where the Peking variety gained its name – the rebranding as Beijing duck is not sticking, even in China – Da Dong is the place. The Jinbao branch of chef Dong Zhengxiang's eponymous brand follows the success of the Tuanjiehu original and its Dongsishitiao sequel. Locals argue over which produces the best roast duck, made with a lean bird bred for its lower fat content. Moving far beyond fowl, haute European influences are often detectable in the vast modern Chinese menu. If it's only duck you want, call ahead as they're cooked to order.

HAI JI

Recommended by
Jereme Leung

Ping Dong Building 6
GF, 1 Huang Gang Lu
Shantou
Guangdong 515031
China

Opening hours	Open 7 days
Reservation policy	No
Credit cards	Not accepted
Price range	Budget
Style	Casual
Cuisine	Hainanese
Recommended for	Worth the travel

'Serves fresh beef hot pot and a freshly slaughtered cow is served at every meal.'—Jereme Leung

FAT AUNT STINKY TOFU

Recommended by
Alan Shen

118 Dongpo Lu
Hangzhou
Zhejiang 310000
China

Opening hours	Open 7 days
Reservation policy	No
Credit cards	Not accepted
Price range	Budget
Style	Casual
Cuisine	Street Food
Recommended for	Bargain

'Stinky tofu is a special food in Zhejiang. Fat Aunt has been selling this food for more than twenty years. It's only open late at night. "Fat Aunt" is actually my good friend. I enjoy the casual atmosphere, eating cheap but delicious food, and chatting with friends.'—Alan Shen

GOLD CHINO

Recommended by
Alan Shen

Qingchun InTime Department Store
3F, 18 Jingtan Lu
Hangzhou
Zhejiang 310000
China
+86 57186533588

Opening hours	Open 7 days
Credit cards	Not accepted
Price range	Affordable
Style	Smart casual
Cuisine	Asian Fusion
Recommended for	High end

'South Asian food and Cantonese cuisine and a good interior. If I want a change and to try something special or to celebrate, I love to dine here.'—Alan Shen

GRANDMA'S KITCHEN

Recommended by
Alan Shen

2F, 3 Hubin Lu
Hangzhou
Zhejiang 310006
China
+86 57185175778

Opening hours	Open 7 days
Reservation policy	No
Credit cards	Not accepted
Price range	Budget
Style	Casual
Cuisine	Chinese
Recommended for	Wish I'd opened

'A very popular restaurant chain, with ten restaurants in Hangzhou and developing more nearby. It's a perfect place for gathering with friends. Grandma's Kitchen has good-value Zhejiang cuisine dishes and it's a very successful business operation.'—Alan Shen

HAI DI LAO HOTPOT

Recommended by
Alan Shen

Yong Jin Plaza
5F, 135 Yan'an Lu
Hangzhou
Zhejiang 310000
China
+86 57187088050

Opening hours	Open 7 days
Credit cards	Not accepted
Price range	Affordable
Style	Casual
Cuisine	Hot Pot
Recommended for	Late night

'Good service and they're very thoughtful to their guests. There are many choices of hot pot available – the spicy pot is my favourite. Normally it's super busy, but late at night, after finishing work, I can enjoy a nice warm meal there.'—Alan Shen

KRISHNA YUAN HALL

Recommended by
Alan Shen

154 Jie Fang Lu
Hangzhou
Zhejiang 310000
China
+86 57187029012
www.hzkyg.com

Opening hours	Open 7 days
Credit cards	Not accepted
Price range	Budget
Style	Casual
Cuisine	Noodles
Recommended for	Regular neighbourhood

'It has more than 100 years of history and is famous for its noodles.'—Alan Shen

NO.8 DOWNING STREET

Recommended by
Alan Shen

1 Han Lin Jie
Hangzhou
Zhejiang 310000
China
+86 57128880333

Opening hours	Open 7 days
Credit cards	Accepted
Price range	Expensive
Style	Smart casual
Cuisine	Chinese
Recommended for	Local favourite

'A luxury restaurant in town where the top-class guests gather in private rooms. The Chinese style furniture is very tasteful.'—Alan Shen

ZHI WEI GUAN

Recommended by
Alan Shen

156 Jie Fang Lu
Hangzhou
Zhejiang 310000
China
+86 57187922085

Opening hours	Open 7 days
Reservation policy	No
Credit cards	Not accepted
Price range	Budget
Style	Casual
Cuisine	Dim Sum
Recommended for	Breakfast

'Another famous old restaurant in Hangzhou providing local dim sum. It opens early so if I have no time for breakfast at home I'll eat it here.'—Alan Shen

'CLASSIC SHANGHAINESE FOOD THAT YOU WON'T
BE DISAPPOINTED WITH.'
FRANCK-ELIE LALOUM P168

'SIMPLY MAGICAL.'
YANNICK ALLÉNO 166

SHANGHAI

'Great home-style Hunan-
region spicy cuisine.'
WILLY TRULLÁS MORENO P169

'Bird's-eye
views of all
that is classic
Shanghai
and modern
China.'
BRAD TURLEY P170

'I still have
visions of the
lemon tart.
A masterpiece.'
CHRISTOPHE MICHALAK P171

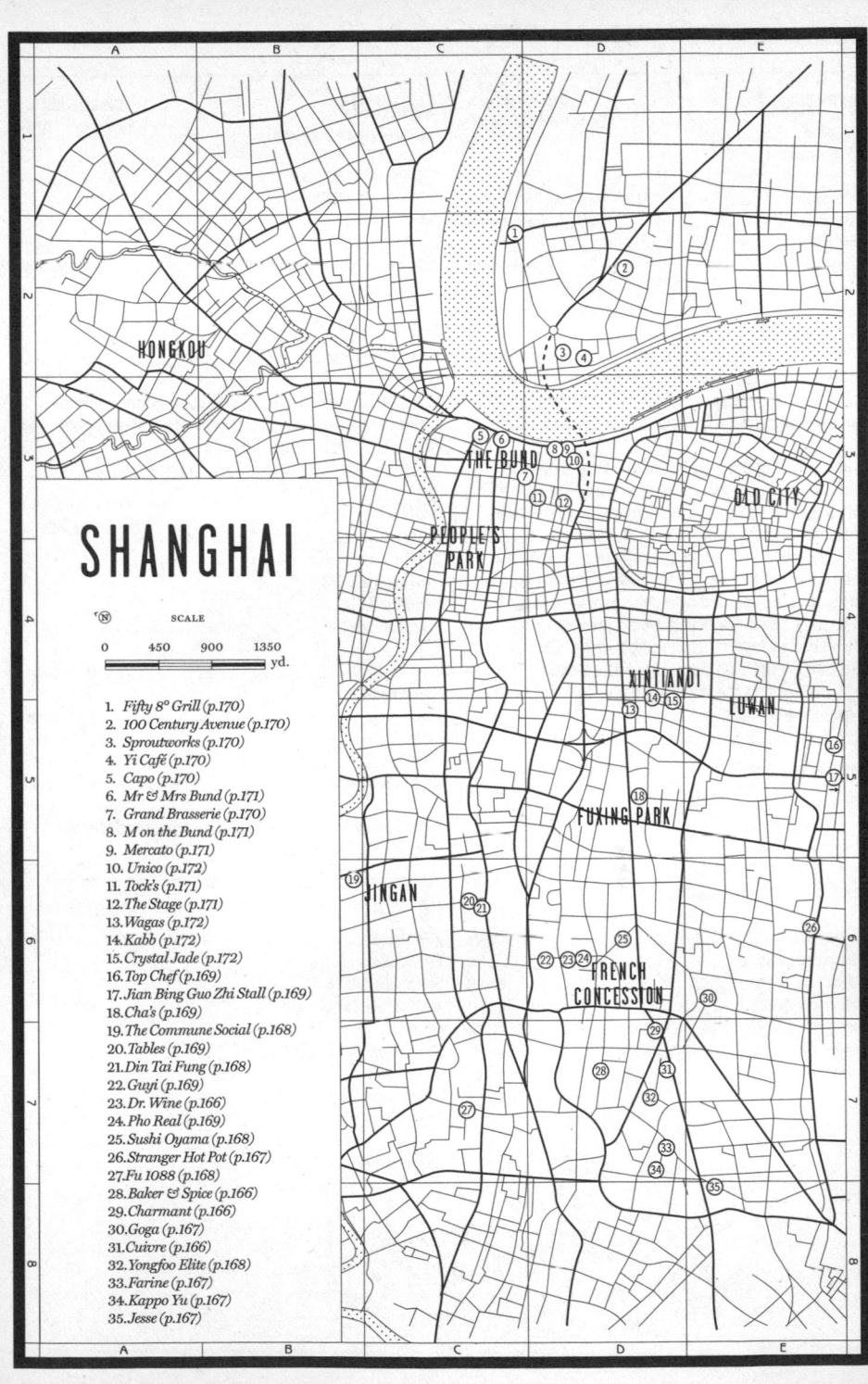

SHANGHAI

N

SCALE

0   450   900   1350
yd.

ULTRAVIOLET
Shanghai
www.uvbypp.cc

Opening hours...............................Closed Monday and Sunday
Credit cards...Accepted
Price range..Expensive
Style...Smart casual
Cuisine...Modern International
Recommended for...Worth the travel

'This restaurant is simply magical. All your senses are awakened and the resulting experience is incredible. This is a truly multidimensional sensory experience that you won't find anywhere else.'—Yannick Alléno

Avant-garde, experimental, immersive: a meal at French chef Paul Pairet's restaurant is like no other. Join nine other guests at a single table in a bare cell-like room with no view for a multisensory experience. The ambience is created by projections on the walls and tabletop that change for each of the twenty-two courses, accompanied by a soundtrack and scents and aromas that are pumped into the room. One minute you're eating 'micro fish no chips with capers and anchovy', in the rain, listening to The Beatles; the next, lobster cocotte to the sight and sound of waves crashing onto rocks.

BAKER & SPICE
195 Anfu Lu
French Concession
Shanghai 200000
+86 2154042733
www.bakerandspice.com.cn

Opening hours...Open 7 days
Reservation policy...No
Credit cards...Accepted
Price range..Budget
Style...Casual
Cuisine..Café-Bakery
Recommended for..Breakfast

CHARMANT
1F, 1414 Huaihai Zhong Lu
French Concession
Shanghai 200000
+86 2164318107

Opening hours...Open 7 days
Credit cards...Accepted
Price range..Budget
Style...Casual
Cuisine...Chinese
Recommended for...Late night

'Simple Taiwanese cuisine with some other general Chinese classics. Open until very late and with good flavours.'—Willy Trullás Moreno

CUIVRE
1502 Huaihai Lu
French Concession
Shanghai 200031
+86 2164374219
www.cuivre.cn

Opening hours...Closed Tuesday
Credit cards...Accepted
Price range..Expensive
Style...Casual
Cuisine..French
Recommended for................................Regular neighbourhood

'This is a very good French bistro – the food is great.'
—Franck-Elie Laloum

DR. WINE
177 Fumin Lu
French Concession
Shanghai 200000
+86 2154035717

Opening hours...Open 7 days
Credit cards...Accepted
Price range..Affordable
Style...Smart casual
Cuisine...Bar-Bistro
Recommended for...Late night

FARINE

Recommended by
Paul Pairet

378 Wukang Lu
French Concession
Shanghai 200031
www.farine-bakery.com

Opening hours	Open 7 days
Reservation policy	No
Credit cards	Accepted
Price range	Affordable
Style	Casual
Cuisine	Café-Bakery
Recommended for	Breakfast

'Better than France.'—Paul Pairet

GOGA

Recommended by
Willy Trullás Moreno

1 Yueyang Lu
French Concession
Shanghai 200030
+86 2164319700
www.goga.gogarestaurants.com

Opening hours	Open 7 days
Credit cards	Not accepted
Price range	Affordable
Style	Casual
Cuisine	American-Asian
Recommended for	Regular neighbourhood

'Love the California-style fusion cuisine from Chef Brad and the Bay Area alternative feeling.'
—Willy Trullás Moreno

JESSE

Recommended by
Jereme Leung

41 Tianping Lu
French Concession
Shanghai 200000
+86 2162829260
www.xinjishi.com

Opening hours	Open 7 days
Credit cards	Accepted
Price range	Affordable
Style	Casual
Cuisine	Shanghaiese
Recommended for	Local favourite

This cornerstone of old-school Shanghainese cuisine – and father of the less well-regarded New Jesse chain – attracts Western dignitaries and local foodies alike. It's a cramped spot with a dozen tables, so reservations are essential, and even then there may be a wait outside on the pavement. Still, what's to follow has earned the spot legendary status: a parade of dishes – *hong shao rou* (braised red pork), drunken shrimp, presented while it's still just about living, or roasted fish head with spring onions (scallions), which must be pre-ordered – that causes diners to crane their necks in admiration as they're ferried through the room.

KAPPO YU

Recommended by
Jereme Leung

33 Wuxing Lu
French Concession
Shanghai 200030
+86 2164667855

Opening hours	Closed Sunday
Credit cards	Accepted
Price range	Expensive
Style	Smart casual
Cuisine	Japanese
Recommended for	High end

'A tiny Japanese restaurant that seats only twenty people per evening. Opens only for dinner and very focused on seasonality. Their Japanese chef makes a special set menu every month and their maki hand rolls are some of the best anywhere.'—Jereme Leung

STRANGER HOT POT

Recommended by
Jereme Leung

268 Zhaojiabang Lu
French Concession
Shanghai 200000
+86 2164316203

Opening hours	Open 7 days
Reservation policy	No
Credit cards	Accepted
Price range	Budget
Style	Casual
Cuisine	Chinese
Recommended for	Late night

'Excellent hot pot stock of chicken and pork stomach with black pepper. Yummy!'—Jereme Leung

SUSHI OYAMA

Recommended by
Willy Trullás Moreno

2F, 20 Donghu Lu
French Concession
Shanghai 200040
+86 2154047705

Opening hours	Closed Sunday
Credit cards	Accepted
Price range	Expensive
Style	Smart casual
Cuisine	Japanese
Recommended for	High end

'Top quality sushi with the best fish bought directly from Nagasaki fish market. It's great to sit at the bar and enjoy observing the craftsmanship of Mr Oyama and taste all the ocean delicacies until you say stop!'
—Willy Trullás Moreno

YONGFOO ELITE

Recommended by
Franck-Elie Laloum

200 Yongfu Lu
French Concession
Shanghai 200031
+86 2154662727
www.yongfooelite.com

Opening hours	Open 7 days
Credit cards	Accepted
Price range	Affordable
Style	Smart casual
Cuisine	Chinese
Recommended for	Local favourite

'Very famous classic Shanghainese food that you won't be disappointed with.'—Franck-Elie Laloum

CHA'S

Recommended by
Brad Turley

30 Sinan Lu
Fuxing Park
Shanghai 200031
+86 2160932062

Opening hours	Open 7 days
Reservation policy	No
Credit cards	Not accepted
Price range	Budget
Style	Casual
Cuisine	Cantonese
Recommended for	Late night

'Cantonese noodle/curry shop open until 2.00 a.m.'
—Brad Turley

THE COMMUNE SOCIAL

Recommended by
Franck-Elie Laloum

511 Jiang Ning Lu
Jingan
Shanghai 200041
+86 2160477638
www.communesocial.com

Opening hours	Closed Monday
Reservation policy	No
Credit cards	Accepted
Price range	Budget
Style	Casual
Cuisine	International
Recommended for	Wish I'd opened

'Really nice modern tapas concept by Jason Atherton.'
—Franck-Elie Laloum

DIN TAI FUNG

Recommended by
Paul Pairet, Franck Pecol

Shanghai Center
GF, 1376 Nanjing Xi Lu
Jingan
Shanghai 200040
+86 2162899182
www.dintaifungusa.com

Opening hours	Open 7 days
Reservation policy	No
Credit cards	Accepted
Price range	Budget
Style	Casual
Cuisine	Taiwanese
Recommended for	Bargain

'Clean and straightforwardly good.'—Paul Pairet

FU 1088

Recommended by
Franck Pecol

375 Zhen Ning Lu
Jingan
Shanghai 200050
+86 2152397878

Opening hours	Open 7 days
Credit cards	Accepted
Price range	Affordable
Style	Smart casual
Cuisine	Modern Chinese
Recommended for	Local favourite

GUYI

Recommended by
Willy Trullás Moreno

1F, 87 Fumin Lu
Jingan
Shanghai 200000
+86 2162495628

Opening hours	Open 7 days
Reservation policy	No
Credit cards	Not accepted
Price range	Budget
Style	Casual
Cuisine	Hunanese
Recommended for	Bargain

'Great home-style Hunan-region spicy cuisine.'
—Willy Trullás Moreno

PHO REAL

Recommended by
Franck Pecol

166 Fumin Lu
Jingan
Shanghai 200000
+86 2154038110
www.phorealgroup.com

Opening hours	Open 7 days
Reservation policy	No
Credit cards	Not accepted
Price range	Budget
Style	Casual
Cuisine	Vietnamese
Recommended for	Bargain

TABLES

Recommended by
Jereme Leung

The Portman Ritz Carlton
1376 Nanjing Xi Lu
Jingan
Shanghai 200040
+86 2162798888
www.ritzcarlton.com/en/Properties/Shanghai

Opening hours	Open 7 days
Credit cards	Accepted
Price range	Expensive
Style	Smart casual
Cuisine	International
Recommended for	Breakfast

'I have champagne brunches on weekends, usually
in one of the top hotels in the city. The Portman Ritz
Carlton is a good choice.'—Jereme Leung

JIAN BING GUO ZHI STALL

Recommended by
Jereme Leung

Behind Luban Lu Xie Tu Lu Bus Stop
Luban Lu
Luwan
Shanghai 200023

Opening hours	Open 7 days
Reservation policy	No
Credit cards	Not accepted
Price range	Budget
Style	Casual
Cuisine	Chinese
Recommended for	Bargain

'It makes excellent Tianjin-style *jian bing guo zi*, which
are essentially pea-flour pancakes with eggs, a crispy
crêpe, sweet-and-chilli sauce and a pickled vegetable
garnish. It doesn't have a name as it literally operates
out of a residential home's kitchen window. It is only
open from 6.00 a.m. to 10.00 a.m. and always has a
long queue (waiting line) of people wanting made-
to-order pancakes. In China, where regulations work a
bit differently, many small establishments like this one
are not officially licensed but are popular with people
anyway. It's cash only, RMB4.5 (40p; 70c) for a pancake
with one egg; RMB1 (10p; 16c) for each additional
egg. The pancake lady puts out a biscuit tin filled with
loose change and guests pay and take their change
themselves – both her hands will be busy making food!'
—Jereme Leung

TOP CHEF

Recommended by
Jereme Leung

169 Mengzi Lu
Luwan
Shanghai 200000
+86 2153028132

Opening hours	Open 7 days
Credit cards	Accepted but not AMEX
Price range	Affordable
Style	Casual
Cuisine	Italian
Recommended for	Regular neighbourhood

'Simple pizzas and very good pastas and seafood with a
reasonable wine list.'—Jereme Leung

CAPO

Recommended by
Paul Pairet

Yifeng Galleria
5F, 99 Beijing Dong Lu
People's Park
Shanghai 200002
+86 2153088332
www.caposhanghai.com

Opening hours	Open 7 days
Credit cards	Accepted
Price range	Affordable
Style	Smart casual
Cuisine	Italian
Recommended for	Regular neighbourhood

'Pizza and glamour.'—Paul Pairet

100 CENTURY AVENUE

Recommended by
Brad Turley

Park Hyatt Shanghai
91–93F, 100 Century Avenue
Pudong
Shanghai 200120
+86 2168881234
www.shanghai.park.hyatt.com

Opening hours	Open 7 days
Credit cards	Accepted
Price range	Expensive
Style	Smart casual
Cuisine	Asian-European
Recommended for	Local favourite

'It has everything you could want, great Asian and Western foods in a buzzing dining room, international crowd and bird's-eye views of all that is classic Shanghai and modern China.'—Brad Turley

FIFTY 8° GRILL

Recommended by
Brad Turley

Mandarin Oriental
111 Pudong Lu
Pudong
Shanghai 200120
+86 2120829938
www.mandarinoriental.com/shanghai

Opening hours	Open 7 days
Credit cards	Accepted
Price range	Expensive
Style	Smart casual
Cuisine	Modern French
Recommended for	Regular neighbourhood

'The best ingredients perfectly executed in a classic European style. Good clean flavours.'—Brad Turley

SPROUTWORKS

Recommended by
Franck-Elie Laloum

Super Brand Mall
B2-06-07, 168 Lujiazui Xi Lu
Pudong
Shanghai 200120
+86 2168905966
www.sproutworks.com.cn

Opening hours	Open 7 days
Credit cards	Accepted
Price range	Budget
Style	Casual
Cuisine	Café
Recommended for	Bargain

'Very good cheap and healthy meals – salad bar, panini, nice main courses for maximum RMB100 (£10; $16).'
—Franck-Elie Laloum

YI CAFÉ

Recommended by
Jereme Leung

Pudong Shangri-La
33 Fu Cheng Lu
Pudong
Shanghai 200120
+86 2158775372
www.shangri-la.com/shanghai/pudongshangrila

Opening hours	Open 7 days
Credit cards	Accepted
Price range	Affordable
Style	Smart casual
Cuisine	International
Recommended for	Breakfast

GRAND BRASSERIE

Recommended by
Franck Pecol,
Brad Turley

Waldorf Astoria Shanghai on the Bund
2 Zhongshan Dong Yi Lu
The Bund
Shanghai 200002
+86 2163229988
www.waldorfastoriashanghai.com

Opening hours	Open 7 days
Credit cards	Accepted
Price range	Expensive
Style	Smart casual
Cuisine	European
Recommended for	Breakfast

'They have it all, plus wine and Champagne, all great quality in beautiful surroundings.'—Brad Turley

M ON THE BUND

Recommended by
Praveen Anand

7F, 20 Guang Dong Lu
The Bund
Shanghai 200002
+86 2163509988
www.m-restaurantgroup.com/mbund

Opening hours	Open / days
Credit cards	Accepted
Price range	Expensive
Style	Formal
Cuisine	International
Recommended for	Worth the travel

'Global cuisine, brilliantly plated and exquisitely combined.'—Praveen Anand

MERCATO

Recommended by
Jason Atherton, John
Jackson, Paul Pairet

6F, 3 Zhongshan Dong Yi Lu
The Bund
Shanghai 200000
+86 2163219922
www.threeonthebund.com

Opening hours	Open 7 days
Credit cards	Accepted
Price range	Affordable
Style	Smart casual
Cuisine	Italian
Recommended for	Regular neighbourhood

'Home away from home which is not even home.'
—Paul Pairet

MR & MRS BUND

Recommended by
Franck-Elie Laloum,
Christophe Michalak,
Alfredo Russo

Bund 18
6F, 18 Zhongshan Dong Yi Lu
The Bund
Shanghai 200002
+86 2163239898
www.mmbund.com

Opening hours	Open 7 days
Credit cards	Accepted
Price range	Affordable
Style	Smart casual
Cuisine	French
Recommended for	Worth the travel

'Paul Pairet is totally off his rocker and his cuisine completely blows your mind! I still have visions of his lemon tart. A masterpiece. His restaurant has a cosy atmosphere in modern surroundings that still make you feel at home... *the* place to go in Shanghai.'
—Christophe Michalak

THE STAGE

Recommended by
Jereme Leung

The Westin Bund Center
88 Henan Zhong Lu
The Bund
Shanghai 200002
+86 2163350577
www.starwoodhotels.com/westin

Opening hours	Open 7 days
Credit cards	Accepted
Price range	Affordable
Style	Casual
Cuisine	International
Recommended for	Breakfast

TOCK'S

Recommended by
Brad Turley

221 Henan Zhong Lu
The Bund
Shanghai 200001
+86 2163463735
www.tocksdeli.com.cn

Opening hours	Open 7 days
Reservation policy	No
Credit cards	Not accepted
Price range	Budget
Style	Casual
Cuisine	Canadian
Recommended for	Regular neighbourhood

'Really good corned beef/smoked beef sandwich shop in town and my first taste of poutine.'—Brad Turley

UNICO

Recommended by
Paul Pairet

2F, 3 Zhongshan Dong Yi Lu
The Bund
Shanghai 200000
+86 2153085399
www.threeonthebund.com

Opening hours	Open 7 days
Credit cards	Accepted
Price range	Affordable
Style	Smart casual
Cuisine	Latin American
Recommended for	Regular neighbourhood

'Pisco and glamour.'—Paul Pairet

CRYSTAL JADE

Recommended by
Paul Pairet

123 Xingye Lu
Xintiandi
Shanghai 200021
+86 2163858752
www.crystaljade.com

Opening hours	Open 7 days
Credit cards	Accepted
Price range	Affordable
Style	Casual
Cuisine	Cantonese
Recommended for	Local favourite

Crystal Jade is one of the most famous dim sum restaurants in Shanghai – there are now two branches in the city. They specialize in great Cantonese and Shanghainese dumplings, but also do brilliant soups: the double-boiled chicken and the *dan dan mien* (spicy peanut) are particularly renowned. Chinese wine can be variable, but bottles of vodka are relatively cheap and a great match for the handmade noodles here. Crystal Jade is popular among affluent Chinese, but since there are pictures on the menu it's great for tourists too. Don't miss the sweet crispy eel.

KABB

Recommended by
Paul Pairet

181 Taicang Lu
Xintiandi
Shanghai 200021
+86 2133070798
www.kabbsh.com

Opening hours	Open 7 days
Credit cards	Accepted
Price range	Budget
Style	Casual
Cuisine	Bar-Bistro
Recommended for	Bargain

'Good value.'—Paul Pairet

WAGAS

Recommended by
Franck-Elie Laloum

1F, 300 Huaihai Zhong Lu
Xintiandi
Shanghai 200021
+86 2154661488

Opening hours	Open 7 days
Reservation policy	No
Credit cards	Accepted
Price range	Affordable
Style	Casual
Cuisine	Café
Recommended for	Breakfast

'A very good coffee shop. Everything is well done, from sandwiches to salads and cakes.'—Franck-Elie Laloum

FERNANDO'S

Recommended by
Neil Anthony Tomes

9 Praia de Hac Sa
Coloane Island South
Macao S.A.R., China
+853 28882264
www.fernando-restaurant.com

Opening hours	Open 7 days
Credit cards	Not accepted
Price range	Affordable
Style	Casual
Cuisine	Portuguese
Recommended for	Worth the travel

'You enter into a reasonably generic frontage and emerge out in the plaza of a small Portuguese hamlet. The food is simple, there's not a massive menu. The last time I went I couldn't decide between the clams or the garlic prawns (shrimp) but fortunately they had allowed for ditherers like myself and I had a prawn

dish with clam sauce! This was lovely when mopped up with a softball-sized puff of bread. They have a stupendous tomato and onion salad, which epitomizes the simplicity here. The salted-codfish balls and succulent suckling pig with crispy skin – a speciality here – are excellent. With the Las Vegasification of Macao there are few places to enjoy the old gentle-paced country feel but this is one of them.'
—Neil Anthony Tomes

TRIPOD KING

Recommended by
Lanshu Chen

14 Jīngchéng Road
Taichung City
Taichung 407
Taiwan
www.tripodking.com.tw

Opening hours	Open 7 days
Credit cards	Accepted but not AMEX
Price range	Affordable
Style	Casual
Cuisine	Hot Pot
Recommended for	Late night

'It's relaxing to have a hot pot with friends late at night after work. A hot pot place always makes you feel warm and convivial. Tripod King (in Mandarin we call it Ding Wang) Spicy Hot Pot serves a very delicious "soup base" with clotted duck blood (it's a super delicacy… don't be scared) and tofu. Their home-made *odens* (Japanese-style hot pots) are nice and there is a lot of quality produce you can choose to add to your hot pot to cook. They'll also adjust the spiciness of the soup base according to the tastes of the guests.'—Lanshu Chen

KEELUNG MIAOKOU NIGHT MARKET

Recommended by
Lanshu Chen

Rénsān Road
Keelung City
Taipei 200
Taiwan

Opening hours	Open 7 days
Reservation policy	No
Credit cards	Not accepted
Price range	Budget
Style	Casual
Cuisine	Street Food
Recommended for	Bargain

'It's a night market in Keelung City, about twenty minutes' drive from Taipei city centre. They have good-quality street food, which represents the very essence of Taiwan's food culture. The famous soup of deep-fried red vinasse eel, the Keelung-style tempura, the thick

soup of pork quenelles are all classic examples of Northern Taiwanese street food.'—Lanshu Chen

Ā CÁI SHŪCÀI YÁNGRÒU

Recommended by
Ken Yu

58, Section 1, Cháng'ān East Road
Taipei City
Taipei 104
Taiwan

Opening hours	Open 7 days
Reservation policy	No
Credit cards	Not accepted
Price range	Budget
Style	Casual
Cuisine	Taiwanese
Recommended for	Late night

'Normally in Taiwan, mutton hot pot is made with a brown sauce. However, the mutton hot pot in this restaurant is a clear soup, and you will not feel greasy after having it – it won't be a burden on your body late at night.'—Ken Yu

BELGIAN BEER CAFÉ LIÈGE

Recommended by
Nicolas De Visch

ATT 4 Fun Mall
6F, 12 Sōngshòu Road
Taipei City
Taipei 110
Taiwan
+886 277378388
www.belgianbeercafe.com.tw

Opening hours	Open 7 days
Credit cards	Accepted
Price range	Affordable
Style	Casual
Cuisine	Belgian
Recommended for	Local favourite

'Very good steak tartare and all my favourite beers.'
—Nicolas De Visch

BEN TEPPANYAKI

Recommended by
Ken Yu

2, Lane 102, Section 1, Ānhé Road
Taipei City
Taipei 106
Taiwan
+886 227032296
www.ben-teppanyaki.com.tw

Opening hours	Open 7 days
Credit cards	Accepted
Price range	Expensive
Style	Smart casual
Cuisine	French-Japanese
Recommended for	High end

'Taiwan has many teppanyaki restaurants, but this is the only place that has surprised me. The average bill is around TWD12,000 (£240; $400). They use the best ingredients, such as wagyu beef and shoulder of lamb – these are the must-eat dishes.'—Ken Yu

BOON KENG CHICKEN

Recommended by
Ken Yu

219, Section 3
Zhōngxiào East Road
Taipei City
Taipei 106
Taiwan
+886 227315522

Opening hours	Open 7 days
Reservation policy	No
Credit cards	Accepted
Price range	Budget
Style	Casual
Cuisine	Singaporean
Recommended for	Bargain

'As my working hours are quite long, I sometimes want to eat a simple meal when I finish work. A bento box to take away (take out) is the easiest and most convenient choice for me. Often I will order Hainanese chicken rice from the restaurant, it costs around TWD160–170 (£3; $5.50) and is convenient and delicious.'—Ken Yu

DA-WAN YAKINIKU

Recommended by
Jereme Leung

22, Lane 177, Section 1
Dūnhuà South Road
Taipei City
Taipei 106
Taiwan
+886 227110179

Opening hours	Open 7 days
Credit cards	Not accepted
Price range	Affordable
Style	Casual
Cuisine	Japanese
Recommended for	Worth the travel

'The best beef grilled on little individual charcoal stoves.'
—Jereme Leung

DIN TAI FUNG

Recommended by
Lanshu Chen

194, Section 2, Xìnyì Road
Taipei City
Taipei 106
Taiwan
+886 223218928
www.dintaifung.com.tw

Opening hours	Closed Sunday
Reservation policy	No
Credit cards	Accepted
Price range	Affordable
Style	Casual
Cuisine	Taiwanese
Recommended for	Regular neighbourhood

'They have the best-quality dim sum, with precise cooking, refined flavours and warm service. I love to go there and have a lovely light meal. I'll have one small cold dish (they call it *hsiao-tsai* – it's one of their signatures) to start, then six pieces of *xiao long bao* (soup dumplings) with a bowl of the famous chicken broth. There are a few Din Tai Fung branches in Taiwan and all of them are good and reliable. You won't be disappointed.'—Lanshu Chen

In their native Taiwan, *xiao long bao* (soup dumplings) generate an almost cult-like obsession, and there are few finer places to indulge than at a branch of Din Tai Fung, now available across Asia and the world, and with nearly twenty outlets in Shanghai alone. What's even more astonishing than their rapid expansion is that standards seem hardly to have suffered – the dumplings themselves are consistently good, made on site behind glass panels; the service is excellent; and the bill won't break the bank.

FIFI

2F, 15, Section 4, Rén'ài Road
Taipei City
Taipei 106
Taiwan
+886 227211970
www.isabelle-wen.com/wenfifi

Recommended by
Nicolas De Visch

Opening hours	Open 7 days
Credit cards	Accepted
Price range	Affordable
Style	Smart casual
Cuisine	Szechuan
Recommended for	Regular neighbourhood

'I love Szechuan food in general and Fifi really maintain a great balance of spicing in all their dishes. It's not a large menu but the spring leek with fermented black beans and fresh chilli is to die for. The steamed sea bass is very fresh and tasty.'—Nicolas De Visch

HACHIBEI

19 Sōnggāo Road
Taipei City
Taipei 110
Taiwan
+886 287865533
www.hachibei.com

Recommended by
Nicolas De Visch

Opening hours	Open 7 days
Credit cards	Accepted
Price range	Affordable
Style	Casual
Cuisine	Yakitori
Recommended for	Wish I'd opened

'I love looking at the open kitchen working; the team is amazing and friendly. I loved the set menu. Amazing all the things you can do with little skewers!'
—Nicolas De Visch

JIANG TAI LANG

6, Section 2, Zhōngshān North Road
Taipei City
Taipei 104
Taiwan
+886 225361101

Recommended by
Nicolas De Visch

Opening hours	Open 7 days
Credit cards	Accepted
Price range	Affordable
Style	Casual
Cuisine	Japanese
Recommended for	Late night

'I love the ambience, it's vibrant and buzzing. With old wooden tables and a great smoky smell, this is the kind of place where you always feel welcome. The quality of the beef was out of this world.'—Nicolas De Visch

JU-DING SHABU SHABU

14, Alley 132, Hu-Lin
Taipei City
Taipei 110
Taiwan

Recommended by
Nicolas De Visch

Opening hours	Open 7 days
Credit cards	Accepted
Price range	Budget
Style	Casual
Cuisine	Hot Pot
Recommended for	Bargain

'Great spot for a nice, calm, family evening. The hot pots are served individually, which is really a plus for me, and the seafood is always fresh with live prawns and abalone. The cuts of pork are great, too, and the lady in charge speaks English. This place is always packed and I am usually the only Westerner!'—Nicolas De Visch

LAO JIO

307 Fùxīng North Road
Taipei City
Taipei 105
Taiwan
+886 227181122

Recommended by
Ken Yu

Opening hours	Open 7 days
Credit cards	Accepted
Price range	Affordable
Style	Casual
Cuisine	Taiwanese
Recommended for	Regular neighbourhood

L'ATELIER DE JOËL ROBUCHON

Recommended by
Nicolas De Visch

28 Sōngrén Road
Taipei City
Taipei 110
Taiwan
+886 287292628
www.robuchon.com.tw

Opening hours	Open 7 days
Credit cards	Accepted
Price range	Expensive
Style	Smart casual
Cuisine	Modern French
Recommended for	High end

'There's no need to talk about the quality of the food, it's always exceptional. I particularly love sitting in front of the kitchen, of course to have a look at the technical aspect, but also because I am amazed how quiet an open kitchen can be.'—Nicolas De Visch

SASA

Recommended by
André Chiang

6, Lane 42, Section 2,
Zhōngshān North Road
Taipei City
Taipei 104
Taiwan
+886 225611246

Opening hours	Closed Monday
Credit cards	Accepted
Price range	Expensive
Style	Smart casual
Cuisine	Japanese
Recommended for	Local favourite

'I keep coming to this small sushi place again and again. Although everyone's tastes are different, I must say that I've never tasted better sushi than that served, surprisingly, by Sasa's Taiwanese chef. It's simple, humble and everything is carefully judged, from the temperature and acidity of the sushi rice to the thickness of the fish – everything seems totally calculated. They don't just use the best and freshest produce, they are also willing to try new flavour combinations and push boundaries. I like it so much that, without exception, every time I visit Taiwan I go to Sasa.'—André Chiang

SHIN YEH 101

Recommended by
Ken Yu

Taipei 101
85F, 7, Section 5, Xìnyì Road
Taipei City
Taipei 110
Taiwan
+886 281010185
www.shinyeh.com.tw

Opening hours	Open 7 days
Credit cards	Accepted
Price range	Expensive
Style	Smart casual
Cuisine	Taiwanese
Recommended for	Local favourite

'I love this restaurant because they serve all the traditional Taiwanese dishes and they have an amazing view of Taipei. I always order their goose meat and mullet roe.'—Ken Yu

Shine Yeh (meaning 'flourishing leaves') offers upmarket Taiwanese cuisine on Floor 85 of skyscraper Taipei 101. It is allegedly the world's largest environmentally friendly building. Quite a contrast to the first Shin Yeh of the late 1970s, which contained only eleven tables. On a clear day it is arguably worth spending a few dollars more on the Connoisseur lunch menu, which secures a window table. Dishes include cold appetizer of baby abalone and jellyfish, then steamed taro nest with fried turnip and shallot, and spring roll filled with cabbage, bean sprouts and peanut (groundnut) powder. Meanwhile, the à la carte offers steamed crab roe with Chinese herbs, and then sweetened almond tofu with peach.

SHORAKU

Recommended by
Lanshu Chen

31, Lane 52, Sìwéi Road
Taipei City
Taipei 106
Taiwan
+886 277091188

Opening hours	Open 7 days
Credit cards	Accepted but not AMEX
Price range	Expensive
Style	Smart casual
Cuisine	Japanese
Recommended for	High end

'They have top-quality produce delivered fresh from Japan, and a nice selection of Japanese wines. The place has been decorated with classic Japanese elegance and tenderness, with about twenty seats and two private rooms. They not only have the best sushi in town, in my opinion, but also cook great warm dishes with amazing balance and layers of flavour, which is relatively rare in Japanese restaurants.'—Lanshu Chen

YŎNGHÉ MĚI DÒUJIĀNG DÀWÁNG

Recommended by
Ken Yu

Lane 120, Guāngfù South Road
Taipei City
Taipei 106
Taiwan
www.soybean.com.tw

Opening hours	Open 7 days
Credit cards	Not accepted
Price range	Budget
Style	Casual
Cuisine	Taiwanese
Recommended for	Breakfast

'This is the most typical Taiwanese breakfast you can find. My favourite dishes are slowly boiled soybean milk, green leek omelette, steamed buns and congee. The soy milk is absolutely delicious and rich in protein – it's my energy resource for the day. The good thing about this place is that they have a lot of branches and they stay open late. Not only for breakfast, it's also good for supper!'—Ken Yu

SHIN YEH

Recommended by
Mak Kwai Pui

34-1, Shuāngchéng Tapei City
Taipei 104
Taiwan
+886 225963255
www.shinyeh.com.tw

Opening hours	Open 7 days
Credit cards	Accepted
Price range	Affordable
Style	Smart casual
Cuisine	Chinese
Recommended for	Worth the travel

'An unforgettable dining experience, a special menu and the food tastes so fresh.'—Mak Kwai Pui

SHI YANG SHAN FANG

Recommended by
Lanshu Chen

7, Lane 350, Section 3, Xīwàn Road
XiZhi City
Taipei 221
Taiwan
+886 226462266
www.shi-yang.com

Opening hours	Closed Monday
Credit cards	Accepted but not AMEX
Price range	Affordable
Style	Casual
Cuisine	Taiwanese
Recommended for	Local favourite

'It's a very special and sophisticated restaurant, serving refined Taiwanese cuisine, which combines a biological concept with Chinese herbal theory. Located in a quiet and secluded mountain area, the restaurant is surrounded by bamboo and numerous native old trees. Driving from the city centre takes about forty minutes but is worthwhile. It is a spiritual tour to dine here; one can feel one's calmness restored and you'll temporarily forget busy city life.'—Lanshu Chen

Memories of the 16 mile (25 km) taxi ride from Nangang Exhibition Center metro station, north of Taipei, fade fast on reaching this secluded haven in sight of the spectacular Wuzhi Mountain. Guests are greeted with tea (no alcohol is served) after being seated in one of three teahouses, simply furnished with low benches, tatamis and flowers. Previously an architect, operator Lin Bin-hui says the idea for Shi Yang Shan Fang – part restaurant, part spiritual retreat – came to him in a dream. Adhering to the mantra of taste and health, a dozen courses (including vegetarian) unfold over three hours. Ingredients, including seafood from Keelung, are presented either raw or boiled, low in oil/salt, and simply adorned.

'Quintessential wonton noodles and soymilk – fast, fresh and delicious.'
MATT ABERGEL P187

HONG KONG

'Great dim sum and snacks.'
MAK KWAI PUI P180

'IT SERVES ONLY ONE THING, BEEF BRISKET NOODLES, AND HAS BEEN DOING IT VERY WELL FOR OVER SIXTY YEARS!'
MAN-SING LEE P184

'IT REALLY SUBMERGES YOU IN HONG KONG LIFE. TONS OF PEOPLE AT BIG ROUND TABLES, NOISE, CONTROLLED CHAOS, A BIG CRAZY FISH TANK FULL OF FRESH FISH, CRABS AND LOBSTERS, NOT TO MENTION ABALONE.'
NEIL ANTHONY TOMES P185

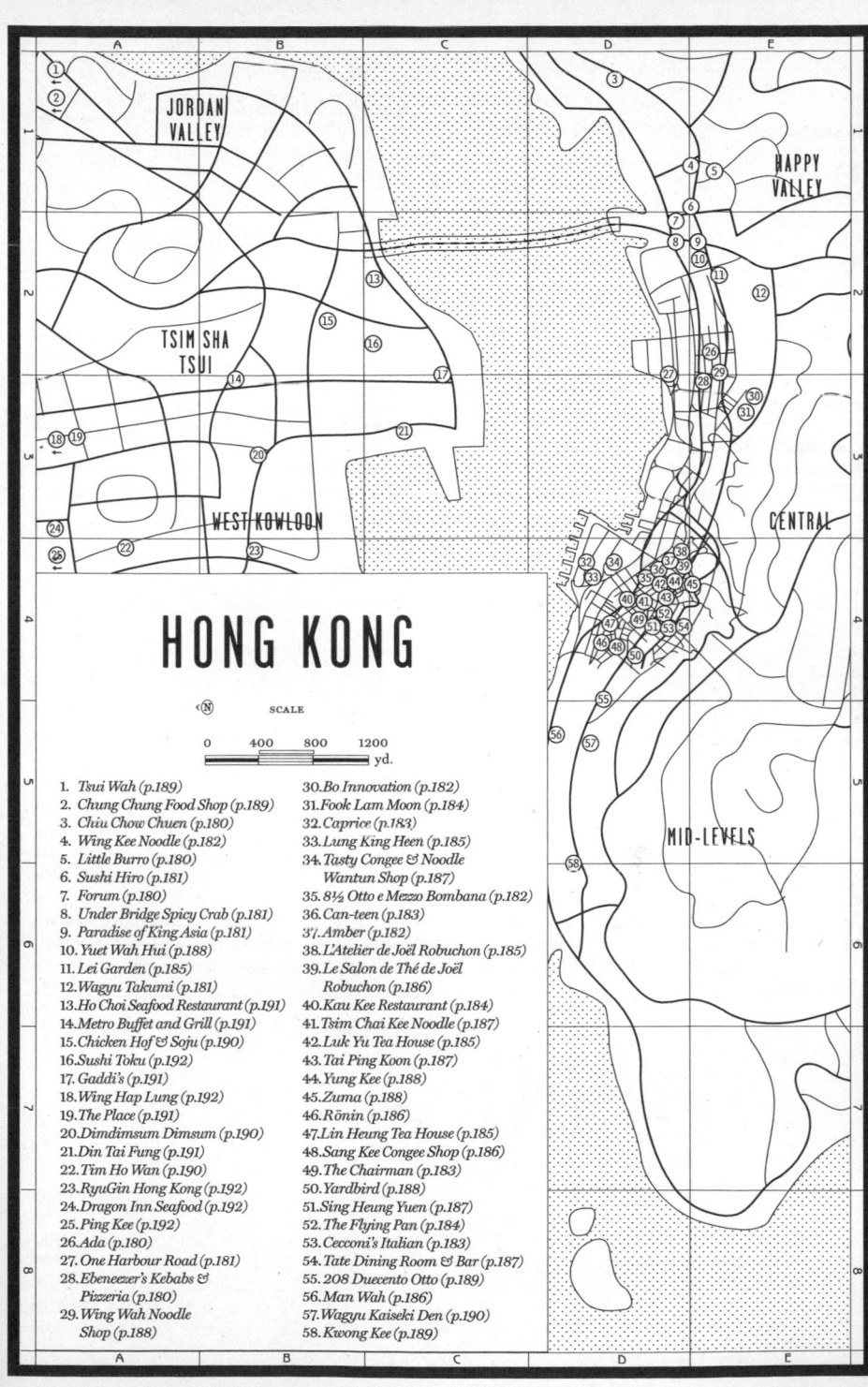

JORDAN VALLEY

HAPPY VALLEY

TSIM SHA TSUI

CENTRAL

WEST KOWLOON

MID-LEVELS

HONG KONG

N

SCALE

0   400   800   1200
yd.

ADA

Recommended by
Esther Sham

Hong Kong Building
GF, 4A–C O'Brien Road
Causeway Bay
Hong Kong
+852 28668338

Opening hours	Open 7 days
Reservation policy	No
Credit cards	Not accepted
Price range	Budget
Style	Casual
Cuisine	Street Food
Recommended for	Bargain

'It's not a restaurant, just a shop selling once-upon-a-time Hong Kong street food like curry fishballs, fake sharkfin soup, steam rice rolls with hoisin and sesame sauce. I can eat like a king for less than HK$50 (£4; $6).'
—Esther Sham

CHIU CHOW CHUEN

Recommended by
Lau Chiu Shing

16 Ngan Mok Street
Causeway Bay
Hong Kong
+852 28871801

Opening hours	Open 7 days
Credit cards	Accepted but not AMEX
Price range	Affordable
Style	Casual
Cuisine	Chinese
Recommended for	Late night

'This restaurant serves traditional Chiu Chow dishes including braised duck meat and duck liver in special sauce, oyster omelette and congee with minced pork. You can get the authentic taste of the Chiu Chow style food here.'—Lau Chiu Shing

EBENEEZER'S KEBABS & PIZZERIA

Recommended by
Uwe Opocensky

G04, Wan Chai Central Building
89 Lockhart Road
Causeway Bay
Hong Kong
+852 25293738
www.ebeneezers.com

Opening hours	Open 7 days
Reservation policy	No
Credit cards	Accepted
Price range	Budget
Style	Casual
Cuisine	Middle Eastern
Recommended for	Late night

'Ebeneezer's reminds me of my youth at home where we had lots of these Turkish stalls. And after a few beers at night nothing is better than a kebab.'
—Uwe Opocensky

FORUM

Recommended by
Mak Kwai Pui

Sino Plaza
1F, 255–257 Gloucester Road
Causeway Bay
Hong Kong
+852 28698282

Opening hours	Open 7 days
Credit cards	Accepted
Price range	Expensive
Style	Smart casual
Cuisine	Chinese
Recommended for	Local favourite

'It is a world famous Chinese restaurant with traditional Cantonese cuisine and an innovative menu. They serve great dim sum and snacks.'—Mak Kwai Pui

LITTLE BURRO

Recommended by
Lori Granito

125 Leighton Road
Causeway Bay
Hong Kong
+852 23363909
www.little-burro.com

Opening hours	Open 7 days
Reservation policy	No
Credit cards	Not accepted
Price range	Budget
Style	Casual
Cuisine	Mexican
Recommended for	Bargain

'Big San Francisco Mission-style burritos at bargain prices. The salsa verde rocks and the guacamole is the best in town. The Kick Ass Carnitas are my favourite. They always have great tunes playing in the background by the DJ-turned-restaurateur owner, Roger de Leon.'
—Lori Granito

ONE HARBOUR ROAD

Recommended by
Matt Abergel

Grand Hyatt Hong Kong Hotel
7F, 1 Harbour Road
Causeway Bay
Hong Kong
+852 25847722
www.hongkong.grand.hyattrestaurants.com/harbourroad

Opening hours	Open 7 days
Credit cards	Accepted
Price range	Affordable
Style	Smart casual
Cuisine	Cantonese
Recommended for	Regular neighbourhood

'Great quality dim sum. It's close to my home and my kids love it.'—Matt Abergel

PARADISE OF KING ASIA

Recommended by
Tim Lai

31–35 Tang Lung Street
Causeway Bay
Hong Kong
+852 25730552

Opening hours	Open 7 days
Credit cards	Accepted but not AMEX or Diners
Price range	Affordable
Style	Casual
Cuisine	Chinese
Recommended for	Regular neighbourhood

SUSHI HIRO

Recommended by
Esther Sham

Henry House
10F, 42 Yun Ping Road
Causeway Bay
Hong Kong
+852 28828752
www.sushihiro.com.hk

Opening hours	Open 7 days
Credit cards	Accepted
Price range	Affordable
Style	Casual
Cuisine	Japanese
Recommended for	Regular neighbourhood

'They actually have three restaurants in the same building. One serves sushi, a second serves tempura and a third serves yakitori. Each of them is focused on their speciality but they do allow diners to cross order from all three. I find I much prefer this than going to a big restaurant serving a huge menu composed of everything but without one speciality.'—Esther Sham

UNDER BRIDGE SPICY CRAB

Recommended by
Richard Ekkebus

Shop 1–2, 414–424 Jaffe Road
Causeway Bay
Hong Kong
+852 28346268
www.underspicycrab.com

Opening hours	Open 7 days
Credit cards	Accepted but not AMEX or Diners
Price range	Affordable
Style	Casual
Cuisine	Cantonese-Seafood
Recommended for	Late night

From a humble stall under the Jaffe Road bypass in the late 1980s, Wong Ching Tuen has grown Under Bridge Spicy Crab into a booming business. This, the original branch on the Jaffe Road, is favoured by those in the know for its after-hours 'ambience' over those nearby on the Lockhart Road. They come, as the name would suggest, for the crab. It's deep-fried and then tossed in a generous helping of a secret chilli mix, with garlic, black beans and spring onion (scallion). To go with your crab, the clams in black bean sauce and the steamed grouper come highly recommended.

WAGYU TAKUMI

Recommended by
Umberto Bombana

The Oakhill
GF, Shop 1, 16 Wood Road
Causeway Bay
Hong Kong
+852 25741299
www.ginsai.com.hk/en/wagyu-takumi

Opening hours	Closed Sunday
Credit cards	Accepted
Price range	Expensive
Style	Smart casual
Cuisine	French-Japanese
Recommended for	Regular neighbourhood

'I like the interpretation of French and Japanese cuisine.'—Umberto Bombana

WING KEE NOODLE

27a Sugar Street
Causeway Bay
Hong Kong
+852 28082877

Opening hours	Open 7 days
Reservation policy	No
Credit cards	Not accepted
Price range	Budget
Style	Casual
Cuisine	Chinese
Recommended for	Late night

'Apart from the list of local delicacies, I also enjoy its lively ambience, which makes it a perfect place for gatherings with friends.'—Man-Sing Lee

8½ OTTO E MEZZO BOMBANA

Landmark Alexandra
Shop 202, 18 Chater Road
Central
Hong Kong
+852 25378859
www.ottoemezzobombana.com

Opening hours	Closed Sunday
Credit cards	Accepted
Price range	Expensive
Style	Smart casual
Cuisine	Modern Italian
Recommended for	High end

'Three-Michelin-star Italian restaurant that's at the top of the Italian dining scene anywhere in the world. It would be at the top in Italy too. Umberto Bombana is a genius and master chef. The food, service, wine and cocktails are heavenly. Go in December for white truffles!'—Donald Berger

AMBER

The Landmark Mandarin Oriental
7F, 15 Queen's Road Central
Central
Hong Kong
+852 21320066
www.amberhongkong.com

Opening hours	Open 7 days
Credit cards	Accepted
Price range	Expensive
Style	Smart casual
Cuisine	Modern European
Recommended for	High end

'Chef Richard Ekkebus has found his home in Asia using pristine Japanese fish in a flawless fine dining setting. Why it doesn't have three Michelin stars still baffles me.'—Matt Abergel

BO INNOVATION

J Residence
2F, Shop 13, 60 Johnston Road
Central
Hong Kong
+852 28508371
www.boinnovation.com

Opening hours	Closed Sunday
Credit cards	Accepted
Price range	Expensive
Style	Smart casual
Cuisine	International
Recommended for	Wish I'd opened

The Wan Chai headquarters of the self-styled proponent of 'X-treme Chinese', with its bare-bones industrial aesthetic, doesn't look like the average Chinese restaurant. But then Alvin Leung isn't your average Chinese chef. With hair dyed to match his purple-tinted glasses and a fondness for tattoos, his image is pure chef as rock star. Self-taught, having worked as an acoustic engineer before taking up cooking late in life as a hobby, at Bo Innovation – and the now recently opened Bo London – he deconstructs the traditional Chinese palate to produce tasting menus via modern techniques borrowed from the cutting edge of Western haute cuisine.

CAN-TEEN

Recommended by
Neil Anthony Tomes

Prince's Building
10 Chater Road
Central
Hong Kong
+852 25246792

Opening hours	Open 7 days
Reservation policy	No
Credit cards	Not accepted
Price range	Budget
Style	Casual
Cuisine	Chinese
Recommended for	Regular neighbourhood

'Great value, very good (most of the time) *char siu* (barbeque pork). *Char siu*, I believe, is one of the most extraordinary contributions to world gastronomy... and I'm not talking about the dried up, purple-ringed bits of packing material you get in the UK, but the luscious, deep-red, sweet and savoury, honey, biscuity lengths of juicy pork cooked in what can only be described as a furnace. Not to be tried at home!'—Neil Anthony Tomes

CAPRICE

Recommended by
Lori Granito

Four Seasons Hotel
8 Finance Street
Central
Hong Kong
+852 31968860
www.fourseasons.com

Opening hours	Open 7 days
Credit cards	Accepted
Price range	Expensive
Style	Smart casual
Cuisine	Modern French
Recommended for	High end

'I go just for a visit to the cheese cellar. A restaurant that's ridiculously expensive, but that thankfully, lives up to the hype.'—Lori Granito

CECCONI'S ITALIAN

Recommended by
Patrick Goubier

43 Elgin Street
Central
Hong Kong
+852 21475500
www.diningconcepts.com.hk/cecconis

Opening hours	Open 7 days
Credit cards	Accepted
Price range	Affordable
Style	Smart casual
Cuisine	Italian
Recommended for	Regular neighbourhood

THE CHAIRMAN

Recommended by
Matt Abergel, Rainer Becker,
Richard Ekkebus

18 Kau U Fong
Central
Hong Kong
+852 25552202
www.thechairmangroup.com

Opening hours	Open 7 days
Credit cards	Accepted
Price range	Affordable
Style	Casual
Cuisine	Modern Cantonese
Recommended for	Worth the travel

'The Chairman serves what I imagine Cantonese food tasted like before people started using pre-made sauces and industrial-quality foods. Honest food, friendly staff.'—Matt Abergel

The Chairman sits in the newly fashionable section of the city that Hong Kong's estate agents (real estate brokers) have decided to christen Noho, as in north of Hollywood Road. Steering away from the traditional and increasingly controversial Cantonese culinary bling that is shark's fin (endangered) and abalone (unsustainable), it has still managed to set out its stall as a destination for quality modern Cantonese cooking. From free-range chicken raised in the New Territories to steamed flower crab with chicken oil and Chinese rice wine, the emphasis here is on the quality of the ingredients, keeping things light and presenting them simply.

THE FLYING PAN

Recommended by
Lori Granito

9 Old Bailey Street
Central
Hong Kong
+852 21406333
www.the-flying-pan.com

Opening hours	Open 7 days
Credit cards	Accepted
Price range	Budget
Style	Casual
Cuisine	American
Recommended for	Late night

'All-night breakfast with just the right combo of carbs to grease. And they serve grits – essential for a Southern gal!'—Lori Granito

Homesick Westerners – perhaps especially those who've had a night on the town – love coming to The Flying Pan, Hong Kong's only twenty-four-hour American-style diner. It's a perfect place to visit after several drinks or a late-finishing service – for bacon and eggs, frittata, a huge burger or a big slab of ham in a toasted bagel with a little omelette folded in. It's also a popular spot for Sunday brunch, where the wide windows, the booths upholstered in blue leather, and the black-and-white tiled floor provide a happy feeling of North American authenticity. With 'bottomless coffee' at only HK\$32 (£2; \$4), there are few better places to linger, any time of day.

FOOK LAM MOON

Recommended by
Corey Lee,
Paul Pairet,
Danny Yip

Newman House
GF, Shop 3
35–45 Johnston Road
Central
Hong Kong
+852 28660663
www.fooklammoon-grp.com

Opening hours	Open 7 days
Credit cards	Accepted
Price range	Expensive
Style	Smart casual
Cuisine	Cantonese
Recommended for	Worth the travel

'A solid and consistent example of why Cantonese food is one of the finest cuisines in the world.'—Corey Lee

The so-called 'cafeteria for the wealthy', Fook Lam Moon, next to the Admiralty and Central business centres, has been serving standout Cantonese seafood dishes for more than forty years. The ambience – varnished wooden floor, starched tablecloths, waiters in smart waistcoats – is appreciated by its upmarket regulars. Three generations of the Chui family have run the four-storey site, which includes private lifts for customers and a valet parking service. The most famous dishes are abalone with oyster sauce or shark's fin and bird's nest soup with bamboo, although more unusual ingredients, such as giant grouper and giant eel are also available, often only by pre-order. Special dim sum are available at weekends.

KAU KEE RESTAURANT

Recommended by
Mango Tsang Chiu Lit,
Man-Sing Lee,
Uwe Opocensky

21 Gough Street
Central
Hong Kong
+852 28505967

Opening hours	Closed Sunday
Reservation policy	No
Credit cards	Not accepted
Price range	Budget
Style	Casual
Cuisine	Cantonese
Recommended for	Bargain

'It serves only one thing, beef brisket noodles, and has been doing it very well for many years! I appreciate its determination to use only fresh ingredients and its food has never disappointed me.'—Man-Sing Lee

Kau Kee is legendary for its beef brisket noodles in curry soup, a classic it has been knocking out for the best part of a century. Little more than a single room, its drinks centre around lemon-flavoured iced tea, and the menu doesn't roam either. Unusually for many Hong Kong noodle joints, Kau Kee doesn't serve fish balls and it limits its noodles to the e-fu egg variety – no flat rice noodles here. Despite occasionally perfunctory service, the long daily queues (waiting lines) testify to the enormous popularity of this Central stalwart, and as a hands-down bargain it's hard to beat.

LEI GARDEN

Recommended by
Umberto Bombana,
Neil Anthony Tomes

CNT Tower
1F, 338 Hennessy Road
Central
Hong Kong
+852 28920333
www.leigarden.hk

Opening hours..Open 7 days
Credit cards...Accepted
Price range..Affordable
Style...Smart casual
Cuisine...Chinese
Recommended for..Local favourite

'It really submerges you in Hong Kong life. There are
tons of people at big round tables, noise, controlled
chaos and a big crazy fish tank full of fresh fish, crabs
and lobsters, not to mention abalone. Great, precise
dim sum.'—Neil Anthony Tomes

LIN HEUNG TEA HOUSE

Recommended by
Tim Lai

160–164 Wellington Street
Central
Hong Kong
+852 25444556

Opening hours..Open 7 days
Reservation policy..No
Credit cards..........................Accepted but not AMEX or Diners
Price range..Budget
Style...Casual
Cuisine...Cantonese
Recommended for..Local favourite

LUK YU TEA HOUSE

Recommended by
Richard Ekkebus

24 Stanley Street
Central
Hong Kong
+852 25235464

Opening hours..Open 7 days
Reservation policy..No
Credit cards...Accepted
Price range..Affordable
Style...Casual
Cuisine...Cantonese
Recommended for..Local favourite

'One of the best tea houses in Hong Kong. Prepare
yourself for tasty and traditionally prepared dim sum.'
—Richard Ekkebus

A true Hong Kong time capsule, the mahogany
booths, gently whirring ceiling fans, stained-glass
windows and Art Deco design make this legendary
teahouse feel like a relic of colonial-era China. It's
also one of the best places to sample proper dim
sum. The English menu changes weekly and might
include duck wrapped in lotus leaves, deep-fried ham
and chicken pie, and large chicken buns. Many of the
staff – white-coated older men, for the most part –
have been here for decades: upstairs is unofficially
reserved for regulars. There was a notorious mafia
hit here in 2002 but things are a lot quieter today.
Try the *sui sin* (narcissus) tea.

LUNG KING HEEN

Recommended by
Paul Pairet

Four Seasons Hotel
8 Finance Street
Central
Hong Kong
+852 31968880
www.fourseasons.com

Opening hours..Open 7 days
Credit cards...Accepted
Price range..Expensive
Style...Smart casual
Cuisine...Chinese
Recommended for..Worth the travel

'High-end dim sum'—Paul Pairet

L'ATELIER DE JOËL ROBUCHON

Recommended by
Patrick Goubier,
Sebastien Lepinoy,
Ben Russell

The Landmark
4F, Shop 401, 15 Queen's Road
Central
Hong Kong
+852 21669000
www.robuchon.hk

Opening hours..Open 7 days
Credit cards...Accepted
Price range..Expensive
Style...Smart casual
Cuisine...French
Recommended for..Regular neighbourhood

'This is one of the best ideas in the past decade – often
imitated but never exceeded. Joël Robuchon's concept
is a revolution to the way people approach fine dining.'
—Sebastien Lepinoy

MAN WAH

Mandarin Oriental Hong Kong Hotel
25F, 5 Connaught Road
Central
Hong Kong
+852 28254003
www.mandarinoriental.com/hongkong

Recommended by
Richard Ekkebus,
Mak Kwai Pui

Opening hours	Open 7 days
Credit cards	Accepted
Price range	Expensive
Style	Smart casual
Cuisine	Modern Cantonese
Recommended for	High end

'This is Hong Kong's signature Cantonese restaurant and it's often referred to as Hong Kong's most beautiful dining space due to its imperial splendor and panoramic views of Victoria Harbour and the cityscape. The menu, by Chef Man-Sing Lee, contains local favourites alongside seasonal specialities with touches of modern flair. No doubt some of the very best Peking duck in town. They also have some excellent steamed seafood dishes and I truly enjoy their great hot-and-sour seafood soup.'—Richard Ekkebus

RŌNIN

8 On Wo Lane
Central
Hong Kong
+852 25475263
www.roninhk.com

Recommended by
Uwe Opocensky, Neil
Anthony Tomes

Opening hours	Closed Sunday
Credit cards	Accepted
Price range	Affordable
Style	Casual
Cuisine	Japanese
Recommended for	Wish I'd opened

'It's small and has a great team. There's a huge selection of sake and whisky, interesting beers and a menu that changes every day.'—Uwe Opocensky

From the founders of boisterous Sheung Wan yakitori bar Yardbird, Rōnin is its smaller, harder-to-find, and equally in-demand (particularly the four seats at the bar) sequel in Central. This time Canadian chef Matt Abergel's menu is mostly seafood focused, from sea bream and squid sashimi, to deep-fried scallop, smoked silver fish tempura, and flower crab with sea urchin roe. Meat gets a look in via marbled Kagoshima beef with maitake mushrooms and egg yolk, and proceedings aren't completely poultry-free with fried quail often making an appearance. Finish the evening with a shochu infused with coffee or chocolate.

LE SALON DE THÉ DE JOËL ROBUCHON

The Landmark
Shop 315, Level 3
16 Des Voeux Road Central
Central
Hong Kong
+852 21669088
www.robuchon.hk

Recommended by
Danny Yip

Opening hours	Open 7 days
Reservation policy	No
Credit cards	Accepted
Price range	Affordable
Style	Smart casual
Cuisine	European
Recommended for	Breakfast

'Great bread and pastries.'—Danny Yip

SANG KEE CONGEE SHOP

7–9 Burd Street
Central
Hong Kong
+852 25411099

Recommended by
Lau Chiu Shing, Richard
Ekkebus, Tim Lai

Opening hours	Closed Sunday
Reservation policy	No
Credit cards	Not accepted
Price range	Budget
Style	Casual
Cuisine	Congee
Recommended for	Breakfast

Run by the same family for over forty years, this specialist in Sheung Wan is worth seeking out for the viscous rice porridge that the locals call breakfast. There's no sign in English, so have the name written down in Chinese, and remember you're here for the congee not the interior design. The choice of ingredients changes according to the seasons, as does the consistency of the congee — the colder the weather, the thicker it gets. You're spoiled for choice if you're after pig — tripe, liver, kidney or meatballs — or fish — head, tail, belly or bones. Other choices include various green vegetables, squid and whole fresh crab.

SING HEUNG YUEN

Recommended by
Tim Lai

2 Mei Lun Street
Central
Hong Kong
+852 25448368

Opening hours	Closed Sunday
Reservation policy	No
Credit cards	Not accepted
Price range	Budget
Style	Casual
Cuisine	Cantonese
Recommended for	Bargain

TAI PING KOON

Recommended by
Esther Sham

60 Stanley Street
Central
Hong Kong
+852 28992780
www.taipingkoon.com

Opening hours	Open 7 days
Credit cards	Accepted
Price range	Budget
Style	Casual
Cuisine	Cantonese-European
Recommended for	Local favourite

'The first "Western" restaurant in the Canton region opened back in the 1860s. It was considered a fancy restaurant back in the old days when the average income was much lower. I have been going to this restaurant ever since I can remember. I always order borscht and my other favorites are Swiss chicken wings, smoked pomfret and roast pigeon. Its exterior and interior decor never changes and some of the staff are so old that you question if they're still legal to work! They're known for their snobbish service, but that's also their signature. It's also interesting to see how people considered them to be a Western restaurant back in the old days when most of their dishes are very Chinese!'—Esther Sham

TASTY CONGEE & NOODLE SHOP

Recommended by
Umberto Bombana

International Finance Centre Mall
3F, 1 Harbour View Street
Central
Hong Kong
+852 22950101
www.tasty.com.hk

Opening hours	Open 7 days
Credit cards	Accepted but not AMEX
Price range	Budget
Style	Casual
Cuisine	Chinese
Recommended for	Bargain

'Very traditional local food.'—Umberto Bombana

TATE DINING ROOM & BAR

Recommended by
Sebastien Lepinoy

59 Elgin Street
Central
Hong Kong
+852 25552172
www.tate.com.hk

Opening hours	Closed Sunday
Credit cards	Accepted
Price range	Expensive
Style	Smart casual
Cuisine	Modern French
Recommended for	Worth the travel

'This restaurant impressed me a lot on my recent trip. There is a mix of strong food knowledge from the chef and innovative food.'—Sebastien Lepinoy

TSIM CHAI KEE NOODLE

Recommended by
Matt Abergel

Jade Centre
Shop B, 98 Wellington Street
Central
Hong Kong
+852 28506471

Opening hours	Open 7 days
Reservation policy	No
Credit cards	Not accepted
Price range	Budget
Style	Casual
Cuisine	Chinese
Recommended for	Bargain

'Quintessential wonton noodles and soy milk – fast, fresh and delicious.'—Matt Abergel

WING WAH NOODLE SHOP

89 Hennessy Road
Central
Hong Kong
+852 25277476

Opening hours	Open 7 days
Reservation policy	No
Credit cards	Not accepted
Price range	Budget
Style	Casual
Cuisine	Chinese
Recommended for	Bargain

'The texture of the noodles is great and always goes well with the broth. I particularly like their congee with meatballs.'—Lau Chiu Shing

YARDBIRD

33–35 Bridges Street
Central
Hong Kong
+852 25479273
www.yardbirdrestaurant.com

Opening hours	Closed Sunday
Reservation policy	No
Credit cards	Accepted but not AMEX or Diners
Price range	Affordable
Style	Casual
Cuisine	Japanese
Recommended for	Wish I'd opened

'Chef Matt Abergel's got the touch, he turns everything to gold... everything but the food! All the staff are passionate and interesting, they're knowledgeable about food. It's a right little hive of social activity that fits in with the chillaxed style of great food and service. The only downside is that when I go there I have to pretend to be cool!'—Neil Anthony Tomes

Smart Soho *izakaya* (bar with restaurant) that's quickly made a name for itself by being an unfussy combination of cocktails and yakitori. The result is the kind of modern casual dining that Hong Kong has never seen before. Opened by Canadian chef Matt Abergel (ex Masa in New York and the Hong Kong branch of Zuma) whose charcoal grill gets the best out of various bits of bird. The skewers menu reads like a chicken autopsy – liver, heart, gizzard, tail, skin and knee – with each part given a different seasoning, whether that's *yuzu kosho* and pepper (neck) or simply sea salt and lemon (oyster).

YUET WAH HUI

Shop B, 405–419 Lockhart Road
Central
Hong Kong
+852 25916803

Opening hours	Open 7 days
Credit cards	Not accepted
Price range	Affordable
Style	Casual
Cuisine	Cantonese-Seafood
Recommended for	Late night

'Excellent seafood.'—Tim Lai

YUNG KEE

32–40 Wellington Street
Central
Hong Kong
+852 25221624
www.yungkee.com.hk

Opening hours	Open 7 days
Credit cards	Accepted
Price range	Affordable
Style	Smart casual
Cuisine	Chinese
Recommended for	Local favourite

'Peking duck hanging in the window, a steady stream of Mercedes, Lexus and Rolls Royces dropping off couture-clad tai tais and high rollers, good food, served by surly waiters – what more could one ask for? That's Hong Kong!'—Lori Granito

ZUMA

5F, The Landmark
15 Queen's Road
Central
Hong Kong
+852 36576388
www.zumarestaurant.com

Opening hours	Open 7 days
Credit cards	Accepted
Price range	Expensive
Style	Smart casual
Cuisine	Modern Japanese
Recommended for	Regular neighbourhood

'On my day off I like to be in a relaxed atmosphere with great, simple and clean food. Zuma offers this with free flowing Champagne, which is a bonus.'
—Uwe Opocensky

CHUNG CHUNG FOOD SHOP

Recommended by
Mak Kwai Pui

Shop 10–12
Shan Mei Street Food Market
Shan Mei Street
Fo Tan East
Hong Kong
+852 26912660

Opening hours	Open 7 days
Reservation policy	No
Credit cards	Not accepted
Price range	Budget
Style	Casual
Cuisine	Chinese
Recommended for	Late night

'A very popular, authentic local restaurant. It's a good price for supper. Pair a glass of beer with a Chinese stir-fry.'—Mak Kwai Pui

TSUI WAH

Recommended by
Man-Sing Lee, Esther
Sham, Danny Yip

81–83 Shung Ling Street
Kowloon
Hong Kong
+852 23246486
www.tsuiwahrestaurant.com

Opening hours	Open 7 days
Reservation policy	No
Credit cards	Not accepted
Price range	Budget
Style	Casual
Cuisine	Cantonese
Recommended for	Local favourite

'The epitome of a *cha chan tang* – a very unique type of tea restaurant in Hong Kong, offering a large variety of food. I like the milk tea and crispy bun with condensed milk.'—Man-Sing Lee

Tsui Wah started life as a simple teahouse back in 1967 but has grown to become a mainstay of Hong Kong's restaurant scene, with eight branches on the island and twenty-six across Hong Kong, Macau and mainland China. The most famous branch is at Wellington, not far from the expat clubbing favourite, Lan Kwai Fong. Several outposts are open twenty-four hours a day, and they're the best ones for breakfast dishes such as crispy toasted bun smeared with condensed milk, served with a silky smooth Hong Kong milk tea. The grouper curry is also excellent; others rave about Kagoshima-style pork cartilage with noodles.

208 DUECENTO OTTO

Recommended by
Lori Granito

208 Hollywood Road
Mid-Levels
Hong Kong
+852 25490208
www.208.com.hk

Opening hours	Open 7 days
Credit cards	Accepted
Price range	Affordable
Style	Smart casual
Cuisine	Italian
Recommended for	Regular neighbourhood

'This place has a fantastic lunch special with very simply cooked but super fresh ingredients. There's a great neighbourhood atmosphere, really good pizzas and a real happy hour vibe. It's upmarket without being too "poncey".'—Lori Granito

KWONG KEE

Recommended by
Lau Chiu Shing

6b Water Street
Mid-Levels
Hong Kong
+852 25486103

Opening hours	Open 7 days
Reservation policy	No
Credit cards	Not accepted
Price range	Budget
Style	Casual
Cuisine	Chinese
Recommended for	Regular neighbourhood

'A very casual family-run eatery that serves home-style dishes. It is nothing fancy, but the food quality is good. My favourite dishes include deep-fried pork cutlet, stir-fried clams in black bean sauce and deep-fried bullet fish.'—Lau Chiu Shing

WAGYU KAISEKI DEN
Recommended by
Lori Granito
Central Park Hotel
263 Hollywood Road
Mid-Levels
Hong Kong
+852 28512820
www.wagyukaisekiden.com.hk

Opening hours	Open 7 days
Credit cards	Accepted
Price range	Expensive
Style	Smart casual
Cuisine	Modern Japanese
Recommended for	Wish I'd opened

'Hands down one of my favourite places. *Always* consistent. Good food and service and great value for money. Good portion sizes too. They serve pancakes with ice cream and even a breakfast pizza! Best of all, it passes my twelve year old "food snob" daughter's test – they don't question why a kid would want both goat's cheese *and* blue cheese on a pizza.'—Lori Granito

TIM HO WAN
Recommended by
Man-Sing Lee, Uwe
Opocensky, Tim Raue
Olympian City Mall
GF, 18 Hoi Ting Road
Tai Kok Tsui
Hong Kong
+852 23322896

Opening hours	Open 7 days
Reservation policy	No
Credit cards	Not accepted
Price range	Budget
Style	Casual
Cuisine	Cantonese
Recommended for	Bargain

'This dim sum restaurant serves the cheapest portion of dim sum for 65 cents (5p; 8c)! The must-have there is the abalone dim sum…'—Tim Raue

CHICKEN HOF & SOJU
Recommended by
Matt Abergel
Kam Kok Mansion
GF, 79 Kimberley Road
Tsim Sha Tsui
Hong Kong
+852 23758080

Opening hours	Open 7 days
Reservation policy	No
Credit cards	Accepted but not AMEX
Price range	Budget
Style	Casual
Cuisine	Korean
Recommended for	Late night

'Serves delicious Korean-style fried chicken, cheesy tamago-style omelettes and draft beer. And they're open until 6.00 a.m.'—Matt Abergel

DIMDIMSUM DIMSUM
Recommended by
Richard Ekkebus
Man Wah Building
21–23 Man Ying Street
Tsim Sha Tsui
Hong Kong
+852 27717766

Opening hours	Open 7 days
Reservation policy	No
Credit cards	Not accepted
Price range	Budget
Style	Casual
Cuisine	Cantonese
Recommended for	Bargain

This unremarkable-looking little dim sum shop in Kowloon has found fame since winning an award for Hong Kong's best dim sum – no mean feat in a city that's drowning in top-drawer dumpling dispensaries. The menu mixes classics with more unusual house specialities. Go beyond Siu Mai and Har Gow for pan-fried tofu skin with chicken and cumin; fried 'nine dishes' and pig's blood with XO sauce; and steamed tripe with black pepper sauce. For those with a sweet tooth a special mention goes to their pineapple buns – made with chunks of fresh fruit – and their sesame seed balls.

DIN TAI FUNG

Recommended by
Uwe Opocensky

Silvercord Shopping Centre
3F, Shop 130, 20 Canton Road
Tsim Sha Tsui
Hong Kong
+852 27306928
www.dintaifung.com.hk

Opening hours	Open 7 days
Reservation policy	No
Credit cards	Accepted
Price range	Budget
Style	Casual
Cuisine	Taiwanese
Recommended for	Bargain

'Simple, tasty and filling. I love dim sum. It is a quick fix
that is amazing value for money.'—Uwe Opocensky

GADDI'S

Recommended by
Ebbe Vollmer

The Peninsula Hong Kong Hotel
1F, 19–21 Salisbury Road
Tsim Sha Tsui
Hong Kong
+852 26966763
www.hongkong.peninsula.com

Opening hours	Open 7 days
Credit cards	Accepted
Price range	Expensive
Style	Formal
Cuisine	French
Recommended for	Worth the travel

HO CHOI SEAFOOD RESTAURANT

Recommended by
Mak Kwai Pui

Empire Centre
68 Mody Road
Tsim Sha Tsui
Hong Kong
+852 23114567
www.hochoi.com

Opening hours	Open 7 days
Reservation policy	No
Credit cards	Accepted
Price range	Budget
Style	Casual
Cuisine	Chinese
Recommended for	Regular neighbourhood

'Consistent standard of food and value for money – you
won't be disappointed!'—Mak Kwai Pui

METRO BUFFET AND GRILL

Recommended by
Mak Kwai Pui

Eaton Hong Kong Hotel
380 Nathan Road
Tsim Sha Tsui
Hong Kong
+852 27101901
www.hongkong.eatonhotels.com

Opening hours	Open 7 days
Credit cards	Accepted
Price range	Affordable
Style	Smart casual
Cuisine	International
Recommended for	Breakfast

'Good location, comfortable environment and a good
place to meet friends for coffee.'—Mak Kwai Pui

THE PLACE

Recommended by
Mango Tsang Chiu Lit

Langham Place Hotel
555 Shanghai Street
Tsim Sha Tsui
Hong Kong
+852 35523028
www.hongkong.langhamplacehotels.com

Opening hours	Open 7 days
Credit cards	Accepted
Price range	Expensive
Style	Smart casual
Cuisine	International
Recommended for	High end

'Offers an array of jet-fresh seafood and international
flavours. It's also family friendly.'
—Mango Tsang Chiu Lit

RYUGIN HONG KONG

Recommended by
Esther Sham

International Commerce Centre
101F, 1 Austin Road West
Tsim Sha Tsui
Hong Kong
+852 23020222
www.ryugin.com.hk

Opening hours	Open 7 days
Credit cards	Accepted
Price range	Expensive
Style	Smart casual
Cuisine	Japanese
Recommended for	High end

'They serve Japanese *kaiseki*, one of my favourite types of cuisine. It's definitely not an everyday type of restaurant.'—Esther Sham

SUSHI TOKU

Recommended by
Neil Anthony Tomes

Cameron Plaza
2F, Shop B, 23–25a Cameron Road
Tsim Sha Tsui
Hong Kong
+852 23013555

Opening hours	Open 7 days
Credit cards	Accepted
Price range	Expensive
Style	Casual
Cuisine	Japanese
Recommended for	High end

'Just great Japanese food!'—Neil Anthony Tomes

WING HAP LUNG

Recommended by
Mak Kwai Pui

392 Portland Street
Tsim Sha Tsui
Hong Kong
+852 23808511

Opening hours	Open 7 days
Reservation policy	No
Credit cards	Not accepted
Price range	Budget
Style	Casual
Cuisine	Chinese
Recommended for	Bargain

'More than eighty years of history, this is a value-for-money restaurant with very good-quality food.'
—Mak Kwai Pui

PING KEE

Recommended by
Esther Sham

102 Chung On Street
Tsuen Wan
Hong Kong
+852 24060488

Opening hours	Open 7 days
Reservation policy	No
Credit cards	Not accepted
Price range	Budget
Style	Casual
Cuisine	Cantonese
Recommended for	Breakfast

'One of a few rare "tea stalls" left on Hong Kong Island. They serve the simplest Hong Kong-style breakfast, such as sausage and egg noodle and toast with condensed milk. They are known for their pork chop but it's still nothing fancy – their seating is just folding tables and plastic stools by the street.'—Esther Sham

DRAGON INN SEAFOOD

Recommended by
Man-Sing Lee

Mile 19.5, Castle Peak Road
Tuen Mun
Hong Kong
+852 24506366

Opening hours	Open 7 days
Credit cards	Accepted
Price range	Affordable
Style	Casual
Cuisine	Seafood
Recommended for	High end

'With a seafood market just next door, guests can select the freshest seafood of a large variety and have the restaurant prepare it for you in your favourite cooking methods. A popular spot for shooting movies back in the 1950s and 1960s, it has retained its favourable ambience.'—Man-Sing Lee

Forty minutes' drive from Central, along the Castle Rock Road into the New Territories, the Dragon Inn has been a Hong Kong fixture since 1939. A popular location during the golden age of Cantonese movies in the 1950s and 1960s, its setting overlooking Castle Peak, plus its distinctive architecture and mini zoo, were a source of cinematic inspiration. Formerly known as the Dragon Inn Villa, but rebuilt and renamed in 1989, its reputation as one of Hong Kong's best seafood destinations remains. Nearby Sam Shing market provides the fish for trademark dishes such as cheese-baked baby lobster, braised whelks, and smoked pomfret.

ANTIBES

2F, Donggwangro 27gil
Seoul
Seoul 137-830
South Korea
+82 25933325

Opening hours	Closed Monday
Credit cards	Accepted
Price range	Affordable
Style	Smart casual
Cuisine	Modern Seafood
Recommended for	Wish I'd opened

'Antibes is a seafood restaurant. The chef-owner has worked in New York and France and he has a high level of technique and respects the ingredients he uses.'
—Jisoo Jang

Antibes is chef Cho Sung-Beom's homage to the Côte d'Azur. It is aptly located in southern Seoul's Seorae Village, an area nicknamed 'Montmartre' by the 550 or so French people who live there. Cho Sung-Beom, whose motto is 'fresh is better than fancy', eschewed fashion design for food, training in Paris then Manhattan before returning to Korea. His notably pretty dishes include caviar blini, sea urchin sushi, clam chowder, yellowtail carpaccio with coriander (cilantro) and lime sauce, then dark chocolate brownies with white chocolate panna cotta. For a memorable experience, indulge in the ten-course tasting menu from the bar beside the open kitchen.

BIM BOM

Seoul 1F,
Hannam dong Dokseodangro 67
Seoul
Seoul 140-884
South Korea
+82 27906245

Opening hours	Closed Monday
Credit cards	Accepted
Price range	Budget
Style	Casual
Cuisine	Café-Bistro-Deli
Recommended for	Breakfast

'The food is humble and the price is reasonable.'
—Jisoo Jang

CONGDU

Deoksugunggil 116-1
Seoul
Seoul 100-120
South Korea
+82 27227002
www.congdu.com

Opening hours	Open 7 days
Credit cards	Accepted
Price range	Expensive
Style	Formal
Cuisine	Modern Korean
Recommended for	Local favourite

'The cuisine is traditional Korean and they use very old, aged soy sauce. The signature dish is fermented Korean crab.'—Jisoo Jang

Fans from far and near have followed Congdu, previously located in Seoul's National History Museum, to this new incarnation. Between the British and US embassies, Congdu is housed within a traditional residence that once had royal connections. Dynamic owner Vivian Han – an ingredient evangelist – has created an eclectic menu of organically inclined dishes that often nod to Korean classics. These may include pine nut soup with soy milk foam, steak tartare with caviar marinated in aged soy, seaweed chicken consommé, and slow-cooked Jeju pork shoulder with kimchi. Sip teas from the varied tea selection alongside. The clean decor is smartly accented with Korean pottery.

JEJU SIC-DANG

Hannam dong 635-3
Seoul
Seoul 140-910
South Korea
+82 27909963

Opening hours	Open 7 days
Credit cards	Accepted
Price range	Affordable
Style	Casual
Cuisine	Korean
Recommended for	Regular neighbourhood

'They do Korean cuisine, specializing in the local food of Jeju. They always use fresh ingredients and every single *ban-chan* (side dish) tastes so good.'
—Jisoo Jang

O'NEUL

Dongbinggo-dong 1-54
Seoul
Seoul 140-230
South Korea
+82 27921054

Opening hours	Open 7 days
Credit cards	Accepted
Price range	Expensive
Style	Smart casual
Cuisine	Modern Korean
Recommended for	High end

'Their cuisine is high-level Korean and they have luxury private rooms so it's quite suitable for anyone who wants to go for a business dinner.'—Jisoo Jang

SANCHEZ

Anguk dong 85
Seoul
Seoul 110-240
South Korea
+82 27350723

Opening hours	Closed Sunday
Credit cards	Accepted
Price range	Budget
Style	Casual
Cuisine	Bar-Bistro
Recommended for	Late night

'A small and cozy bistro. The chef-owner goes to the fish market every morning to find the freshest seafood. He cooks food only once the customer has ordered it so it takes a little bit of time, but it's very tasty.'
—Jisoo Jang

SISILI

Yunnam dong Sungmisanro 198
Seoul
Seoul 121-860
South Korea
+82 23348117

Opening hours	Open 7 days
Credit cards	Accepted
Price range	Affordable
Style	Casual
Cuisine	Korean-Japanese
Recommended for	Bargain

'They are well known for their seafood. The restaurant's interior is quite old fashioned, but there's enough atmosphere for hanging out with old friends.'
—Jisoo Jang

'PROTECTS AND PROMOTES THE CULTURAL HERITAGE OF JAPAN WHILE EXPLORING THE FUTURE OF COOKING.'

MICHAEL ANTHONY P201

'The essence of Kyoto cuisine.'

TAKUJI TAKAHASHI P203

JAPAN

'SET IN A BEAUTIFUL JAPANESE GARDEN WITH A VIEW OF KYOTO FOREST. IT'S FULL OF SURPRISES. YOU WILL HAVE A ONCE-IN-A-LIFETIME EXPERIENCE HERE.'

HIRO SONE P204

'The chef is a god not only in the world of ramen noodles but also in the world of cooking.'

NAOYA UENO P199

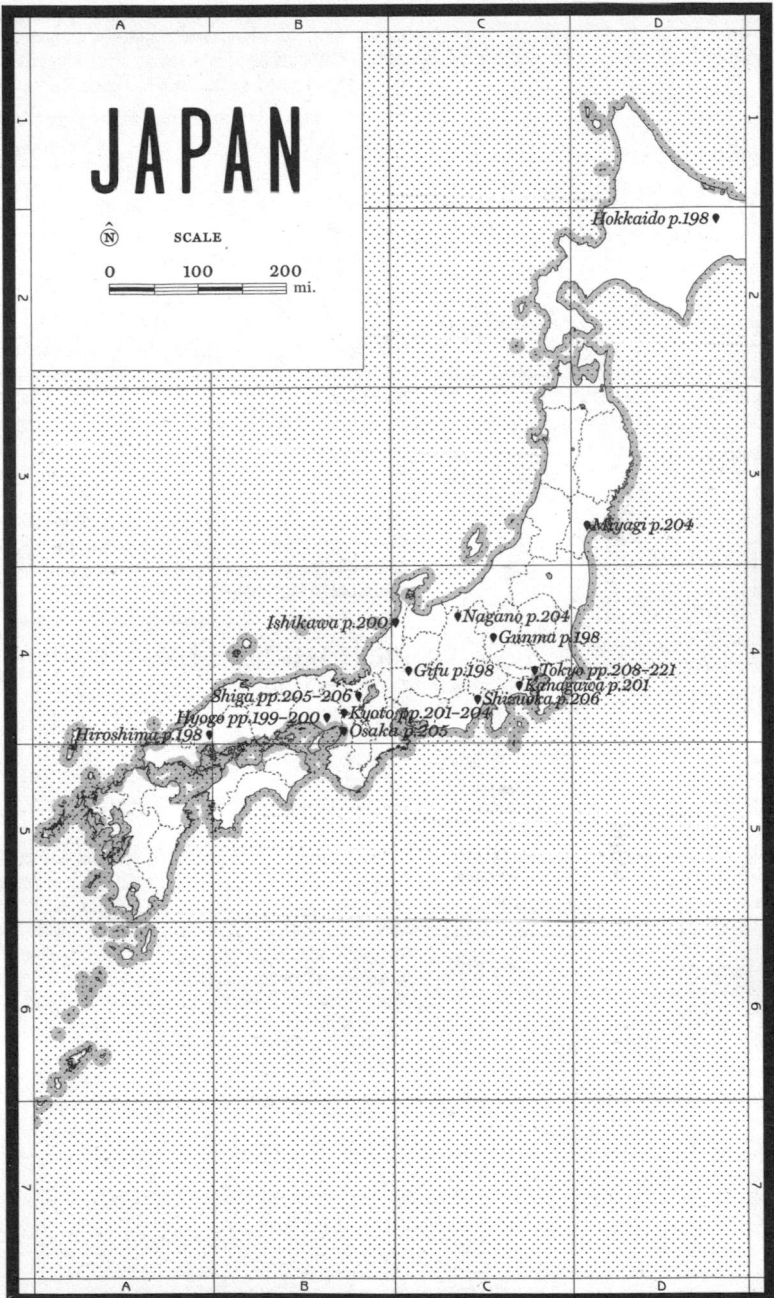

JAPAN

Hokkaido p.198

Miyagi p.204

Ishikawa p.200
Nagano p.204
Gunma p.198
Gifu p.198
Tokyo pp.208–221
Kanagawa p.201
Shiga pp.205–206
Shizuoka p.206
Hyogo pp.199–200
Kyoto pp.201–204
Hiroshima p.198
Osaka p.205

$\widehat{N}$ SCALE

0   100   200
mi.

TAKADAHASSHO
17-2 Sugiyamada-cho
Gifu
Gifu 500-8829
+81 582621750
www.takadahassho.web.fc2.com

Opening hours	Open 7 days
Credit cards	Accepted
Price range	Expensive
Style	Smart casual
Cuisine	Kaiseki
Recommended for	Worth the travel

'This restaurant has the soul of a tea ceremony.'
—Seiji Yamamoto

BETTEI SENJYUAN
6-1-4 Tanigawa
Minakami
Gunma 379-1619
+81 278204141
www.senjyuan.jp

Opening hours	Open 7 days
Credit cards	Accepted
Price range	Expensive
Style	Smart casual
Cuisine	Japanese
Recommended for	Wish I'd opened

'A design mecca of a *ryokan* (Japanese inn), where
the rustic and minimalistic elements of Japanese
design are fused with new and modern elements. In
this beautiful setting is the umeshu bar complete with
hundreds of plum wines!'—Dharshan Munidasa

HASSHO
10-6 Yagenbori
Naka-ku
Hiroshima
Hiroshima 730-0027
+81 822481776
www.hassho.jp

Opening hours	Closed Monday
Reservation policy	No
Credit cards	Not accepted
Price range	Budget
Style	Casual
Cuisine	Japanese
Recommended for	Local favourite

'Hassho is a famous *okonomiyaki* (savoury pancake)
restaurant in Hiroshima, my hometown. Customers
always wait outside to take seats before it opens –
it is really popular.'—Masaharu Morimoto

TAKOTSUBO
4-18 Horikawacho
Naka-ku
Hiroshima
Hiroshima 730-0033
+81 822470101
www.takotubo.com

Opening hours	Closed Wednesday
Credit cards	Accepted but cash only at lunch
Price range	Expensive
Style	Smart casual
Cuisine	Kappo
Recommended for	Wish I'd opened

'Most kappo places are very high-end but Takotsubo
has a more casual atmosphere, so I can enjoy the food
comfortably as though I were at home.'
—Masaharu Morimoto

MICHEL BRAS TOYA JAPON
The Windsor Hotel TOYA
11F, Shimizu
Toyako
Hokkaido 049-5722
+81 142731159
www.windsor-hotels.co.jp

Opening hours	Closed Wednesday
Credit cards	Accepted
Price range	Expensive
Style	Smart casual
Cuisine	Modern French
Recommended for	Worth the travel

KIKUSUIZUSHI NISHIMISE

Recommended by
Naoya Ueno

1-4-15 Matsunouchi
Akashi
Hyogo 673-0016
+81 789287157
www.akashi-sushi.jp/kikusuinishi

Opening hours	Closed Thursday
Credit cards	Accepted
Price range	Expensive
Style	Smart casual
Cuisine	Sushi
Recommended for	High end

'A small sushi restaurant that offers very high-quality sushi in a relaxed environment.'—Naoya Ueno

ITTETSU RAMEN

Recommended by
Naoya Ueno

1-8-11 Kitahirano
Himeji
Hyogo 670-0893
+81 792820208

Opening hours	Closed Monday to Wednesday
Reservation policy	No
Credit cards	Not accepted
Price range	Budget
Style	Casual
Cuisine	Ramen Noodles
Recommended for	Bargain

'The chef is a god not only in the world of ramen noodles but also in the world of cooking. He and his wife do all the work, including growing their own vegetables and they don't add MSG. It takes about an hour-and-a-half along a highway to get here from my house, but since I like the ramen noodles, I come often.'—Naoya Ueno

ANONYME

Recommended by
Naoya Ueno

4-13-3 Shimoyamate-dori
Chuo-ku
Kobe
Hyogo 650-0011
+81 787780956
kobeanony.exblog.jp

Opening hours	Closed Sunday
Credit cards	Accepted
Price range	Affordable
Style	Casual
Cuisine	French-Japanese
Recommended for	Regular neighbourhood

'The chef and his wife manage this eight-seater restaurant. The chef thinks about his food. I respect and trust this restaurant the most.' —Naoya Ueno

CAFE BAR KOBECCO

Recommended by
Naoya Ueno

Yamaura 77 1F, 2-9-2 Kano-cho
Chuo-ku
Kobe
Hyogo 650-0001
+81 782221297

Opening hours	Closed Sunday
Reservation policy	No
Credit cards	Not accepted
Price range	Budget
Style	Casual
Cuisine	Café
Recommended for	Breakfast

'This coffee shop is typical of Kobe, it has a historical air. The room is filled with the aroma of coffee. I feel happy when I'm eating a special sandwich and drinking fresh juice with my family in this cafe, it is a treasure in Kobe.'—Naoya Ueno

DINING OKANO

Recommended by
Naoya Ueno

4-2-8 Shimoyamate-dori
Chuo-ku
Kobe
Hyogo 658-0011
+81 783911161

Opening hours	Closed Saturday and Sunday
Credit cards	Not accepted
Price range	Budget
Style	Casual
Cuisine	Japanese-Indian
Recommended for	Bargain

'The chef has a real understanding of Indian cuisine and cooks Japanese-style curries.'—Naoya Ueno

NIKU SPECIALITE MACRA

Recommended by
Naoya Ueno

2-9-3-1 Kitanagasa-dori
Chuo-ku
Kobe
Hyogo 650-0012
+81 783331002

Opening hours	Closed Monday
Credit cards	Accepted
Price range	Affordable
Style	Casual
Cuisine	Modern Japanese
Recommended for	Late night

'The way they cut meat is innovative in this meat-dish restaurant. I get a sense of the next generation from this place.'—Naoya Ueno

PIZZERIA AZZURRI

Recommended by
Naoya Ueno

Utopia Toa
1F, 3-7-3 Yamamoto-dori
Chuo-ku
Kobe
Hyogo 650-0003
+81 782416036

Opening hours	Closed Thursday
Credit cards	Not accepted
Price range	Budget
Style	Casual
Cuisine	Pizza
Recommended for	Bargain

'They use good-quality ingredients. Although I'm a chef of Japanese cuisine, I understand the wonderful taste of this pizza.'—Naoya Ueno

CA SENTO

Recommended by
Naoya Ueno

4-16-14 Nakayamate-dori
Chuo-ku
Kobe
Hyogo 650-0004
+81 782726882
www.casento.jp

Opening hours	Closed Monday
Credit cards	Accepted
Price range	Expensive
Style	Smart casual
Cuisine	Spanish
Recommended for	Local favourite

'It is a modern Spanish restaurant. I feel the young chef's sharp sense and great possibilities.'
—Naoya Ueno

UETSUKI

Recommended by
Naoya Ueno

3-41-16 Arata-cho
Hyogo-ku
Kobe
Hyogo 658-0032
+81 785115566

Opening hours	Closed Monday
Credit cards	Not accepted
Price range	Affordable
Style	Smart casual
Cuisine	Sushi
Recommended for	Regular neighbourhood

'Although Edo-style sushi is famous, if you go to this sushi restaurant, your view will change. They use the fish from the Tarumi fish port in Kobe. The white fish is the best.'—Naoya Ueno

KINJOHRO

Recommended by
Riki Mizukami

2-23 Funaba-cho
Kanazawa
Ishikawa 920-0911
+81 762218188
www.kinjohro.co.jp

Opening hours	Open 7 days
Credit cards	Accepted
Price range	Expensive
Style	Smart casual
Cuisine	Japanese
Recommended for	Worth the travel

'An example of a restaurant that provides *omotenashi*, which is a culture of hospitality unique to Japan. The dishes and service are the most wonderful in Japan.'
—Riki Mizukami

IROHA SUSHI

Recommended by
Riki Mizukami

Kawashima 1F, 4-48 Oota-machi
Naka-ku
Yokohama
Kanagawa 231-0011
+81 456813366

Opening hours...Closed Sunday
Credit cards..Accepted
Price range...Expensive
Style...Smart casual
Cuisine...Sushi
Recommended for..................................Local favourite

'This chef makes sushi with wild fish. The sushi here is delicious – I like the seaweed roll with seared tuna.'
—Riki Mizukami

CHUUKA DINING KYOJYUZEN

Recommended by
Takuji Takahashi

Gion Ichiban Kan 8-1 Benzaiten-cho
Higashiyama-ku
Kyoto
Kyoto 605-0086
+81 752416288

Opening hours...Closed Monday
Credit cards..Not accepted
Price range...Budget
Style...Casual
Cuisine..Chinese
Recommended for...Late night

'Although it's cheap, it's as delicious as a fine-dining restaurant. A mabo tofu (beancurd, Sichuan-style) is my recommendation. The chef makes anything.'
—Takuji Takahashi

GION MARUYAMA

Recommended by
Masaharu Morimoto

570-171 Minamigawa
Higashiyama-ku
Kyoto
Kyoto 605-0074
+81 755250009
www.gionmaruyama.com

Opening hours...Closed Wednesday
Credit cards..Accepted
Price range...Expensive
Style...Smart casual
Cuisine..Japanese
Recommended for..High end

'This is a traditional Kyoto-style *kaiseki* restaurant located in the centre of Gion, Kyoto. I enjoy multiple courses that are filled with seasonal ingredients, various flavours and remarkable presentation. The decor is also very traditional Japanese.'
—Masaharu Morimoto

KIKUNOI

Recommended by
Michael Anthony

459 Shimokawara-cho
Higashiyama-ku
Kyoto
Kyoto 605-0825
+81 755610015
www.kikunoi.jp

Opening hours...Open 7 days
Credit cards..Accepted
Price range...Expensive
Style...Smart casual
Cuisine..Kaiseki-Kyotonese
Recommended for...Worth the travel

'This restaurant protects and promotes the cultural heritage of Japan while exploring the future of cooking.'—Michael Anthony

To experience exquisite Japanese cuisine in a typical Japanese environment, come to Kikunoi. First the environment: ten private rooms of elegant minimalism where you sit, shoeless, on cushions at low tables. Second the food: a traditional *kaiseki* or flight of courses of artistic brilliance and seasonal harmony from chef Yoshihiro Murata, probably the foremost expert on Kyoto cooking. Pea soup with prawn (shrimp) balls; sea eel and yuba rolls; steamed tilefish with fresh green tea leaves... all served by kimono-clad hostesses. If you don't speak Japanese, don't worry, just let the food lead you to your goal.

KOUDAIJIDOI

Recommended by
Takuji Takahashi

353 Sukiya-mach
Higashiyama-ku
Kyoto
Kyoto 605-0826
+81 755610309

Opening hours	Open 7 days
Credit cards	Accepted
Price range	Expensive
Style	Smart casual
Cuisine	Kaiseki
Recommended for	Wish I'd opened

'This restaurant has a 6,500-square-metre (1.6-acre) garden that makes for wonderful scenery.' —Takuji Takahashi

MIZAI

Recommended by
Hajime Yoneda,
Gerald Zogbaum

Maruyama Park
613 Maruyama-cho
Higashiyama-ku
Kyoto
Kyoto 605-0071
+81 755513310

Opening hours	Closed Wednesday
Credit cards	Not accepted
Price range	Expensive
Style	Formal
Cuisine	Kaiseki
Recommended for	Regular neighbourhood

'It is the best restaurant for Japanese cuisine. The aesthetics are superb on every level.'—Hajime Yoneda

Good timekeeping is essential at this typically diminutive *cha-kaiseki* restaurant on the fringes of Gion. The setting (in Maruyama Park, famous for its cherry blossom) can't be appreciated in a rush, and neither can a meal: everyone is served at the same time, 6.00 p.m., and latecomers cannot be accommodated. Tea is drunk in an anteroom before spaces at the counter fill for rice, wasabi soup and pickled vegetables followed by sashimi, with horse mackerel and scallops being particular highlights. Multiple exquisitely prepared courses of best-quality seasonal produce include, perhaps, grilled wagyu beef with a mild chilli salad. The owner and chef, Hitoshi Ishihara, prepares *matcha* to finish.

SHUHAKU

Recommended by
Hideki Shimoguchi

392 Kinen-cho
Higashiyama-ku
Kyoto
Kyoto 605-0820
+81 755512711
www.kyotoshuhaku.com

Opening hours	Closed Monday
Credit cards	Not accepted
Price range	Expensive
Style	Smart casual
Cuisine	Kaiseki
Recommended for	Regular neighbourhood

'The chef studies cooking and he often creates new dishes. I would recommend this restaurant to a friend or to a specialist of cooking.'—Hideki Shimoguchi

Chef Nobuhisa Yoshida is making quite a name for himself with the French-influenced Japanese food at Shuhaku, a modest restaurant down an alleyway in Kyoto's historic Higashiyama district. Here, you'll be served a set menu of *kaiseki*, a series of bijoux fish and vegetable compilations presented with dazzling precision on an artful array of crockery. Despite the lack of English spoken – this place is off the tourist trail – the atmosphere is less reverent and the prices more forgiving than in more established *kaiseki* restaurants. Book in Japanese, and make sure you eat at the counter so you can watch one of Kyoto's rising stars at work.

SHINME

Recommended by
Takuji Takahashi

38 Nishigawa Tamaya-machi
Kamigyo-ku
Kyoto
Kyoto 602-8286
+81 754613635

Opening hours	Closed Sunday
Credit cards	Not accepted
Price range	Affordable
Style	Casual
Cuisine	Bar
Recommended for	Regular neighbourhood

'It is a Japanese-style bar using very good ingredients. There are lots of different menus and it's a pleasant place.'—Takuji Takahashi

Well-established, homely, family-run, tavern-like eatery close to the Senbon Dori and Nakadachiuri Dori intersection. Beyond a plain white frontage (bar large black characters) the interior is eclectic with stripy stools, an old-school till, an abacus and an innovative approach to a cloakroom (hangers line the walls). Reasonably priced, impeccably fresh plates include fat oysters; tender, almost translucent sashimi; shapely sushi; crisp, fragile tempura; deep bowls of glutinous rice with pickles; and crunchy baby sardines with soy. Incidentally, it's worth knowing a few words of Japanese to get by, Shinme being fairly far from the tourist path.

HOUSEN

Recommended by
Takuji Takahashi

AB 1F, 359 Shimizu-cho
Nakagyo-ku
Kyoto
Kyoto 604-0911
+81 752416288

Opening hours	Closed Monday
Credit cards	Not accepted
Price range	Budget
Style	Casual
Cuisine	Cantonese
Recommended for	Bargain

'It serves Chinese food, which people in Kyoto like. It's a taste of a long-established group of restaurants.'
—Takuji Takahashi

INODA COFFEE

Recommended by
Takuji Takahashi

140 Douyuucho Sanjyo Sagaru
Nakagyou-ku
Kyoto
Kyoto 604-8118
+81 752210507
www.inoda-coffee.co.jp

Opening hours	Open 7 days
Reservation policy	No
Credit cards	Accepted
Price range	Budget
Style	Casual
Cuisine	Café
Recommended for	Breakfast

'The French toast is delicious.'—Takuji Takahashi

GYU HO

Recommended by
Ross Lusted

22-4 Ichijoji Akanomiya-cho
Sakyo-ku
Kyoto
Kyoto 606-8182
+81 757232424
www.gyuho.net

Opening hours	Open 7 days
Reservation policy	No
Credit cards	Not accepted
Price range	Affordable
Style	Casual
Cuisine	Japanese
Recommended for	Worth the travel

'It has ten seats, Kobe beef is cooked on a robata grill and they only serve Bordeaux, which the chef personally selects. It's a real treat if you can get a seat.'
—Ross Lusted

HYOTEI

Recommended by
Matthew Crabbe, Takuji
Takahashi

35 Kusagawa-cho
Sakyo-ku
Kyoto
Kyoto 606-8437
+81 757714116
www.hyotei.co.jp

Opening hours	Closed Thursday
Credit cards	Accepted
Price range	Expensive
Style	Formal
Cuisine	Kaiseki
Recommended for	Local favourite

'The essence of Kyoto cuisine.'—Takuji Takahashi

There are no concessions for the floundering gaijin at the three-Michelin-starred Hyotei, where traditional *kaiseki* – a multi-course menu of Japanese haute cuisine – is served in monastic surroundings. The restaurant is housed in a 400-year-old teahouse, a complex comprising a series of little houses dotted around a manicured garden. Seated on a tatami floor in private rooms, diners are delivered a series of painstakingly beautiful dishes by kimono-clad staff. Sounds expensive? It is: the range of set menus starts at ¥27,000 (around £160/$260). To get a feel for the place without remortgaging your house, the seasonal bento boxes served in the lovely restaurant annex at lunchtime are delicious, and include the famous Hyotei eggs.

BELLOTA

Recommended by
Hisato Nakahigashi

228 Itoya-cho
Shimogyo-ku
Kyoto
Kyoto 600-8424
+81 753515826
www.bellota.jp

Opening hours	Open 7 days
Credit cards	Accepted
Price range	Budget
Style	Casual
Cuisine	Spanish Tapas
Recommended for	Late night

'This restaurant is open until late at night and it's easy to get to after work. It has a good atmosphere, like a bar in a Spanish back street. All of the dishes are delicious, the sauces are tasty and rich in flavour. I can eat without limit and without getting bored.' —Hisato Nakahigashi

KITCHO ARASHIYAMA HONTEN

Recommended by
Hiro Sone

58 Susukinobaba-cho
Ukyo-ku
Kyoto
Kyoto 616-8385
+81 758811101
www.kitcho.com/kyoto

Opening hours	Closed Wednesday
Credit cards	Accepted
Price range	Expensive
Style	Formal
Cuisine	Kaiseki
Recommended for	High end

'This restaurant is in a beautiful Japanese garden with a view of Kyoto Forest. Course after course, every bite is full of surprises. You will have a once-in-a-lifetime experience here.' —Hiro Sone

MIYAGINO

Recommended by
Hiro Sone

Naruko Hotel
36 Naruko Onsen Yumoto
Osaki
Miyagi 989-6823
+81 229832001
www.narukohotel.co.jp

Opening hours	Open 7 days
Credit cards	Accepted
Price range	Expensive
Style	Smart casual
Cuisine	Japanese
Recommended for	Breakfast

'Their breakfast has incredible selections of local classic dishes and ingredients. I always end up eating too much here.' —Hiro Sone

SHOKUNINKAN

Recommended by
Yoshihiro Narisawa

3250-3 Kasuga
Saku
Nagano 384-2205
+81 267522010

Opening hours	Closed Wednesday and Thursday
Credit cards	Not accepted
Price range	Affordable
Style	Casual
Cuisine	Soba Noodles
Recommended for	Worth the travel

'Typical Japanese restaurant that stands alone in its field. It's a hand-made soba restaurant but you can also enjoy various other dishes with local ingredients. The vegetable dishes are especially fantastic. You always enjoy the atmosphere and meal.' —Yoshihiro Narisawa

KIGAWA

Recommended by
David Martin

1-7-7 Dotonbori
Chuo-ku
Osaka
Osaka 542-0071
+81 662113030

Opening hours	Closed Monday
Credit cards	Accepted
Price range	Expensive
Style	Smart casual
Cuisine	Kappo
Recommended for	Worth the travel

'For the purity of grand Japanese cuisine and the kindness of the chef.'—David Martin

MIMIU

Recommended by
Hajime Yoneda

4-6-18 Hirano-cho
Chuo-ku
Osaka
Osaka 541-0046
+81 662315770
www.mimiu.co.jp

Opening hours	Closed Sunday
Credit cards	Accepted
Price range	Affordable
Style	Casual
Cuisine	Udon Noodles
Recommended for	Bargain

'They serve delicious udon noodles every time you walk in.'—Hajime Yoneda

Despite being in the centre of the city (five minutes' walk from Exit 2 of Honmachi station), Mimiu's homely building offers a degree of sanctuary. Udon sukiyaki – a reviving variety of chewy noodles in broth said to have originated here – is the speciality. Ingredients mingled within the steaming hot pot include seafood and duck, as well as vegetables such as crunchy bamboo. However, in addition to the almost addictive, happily affordable, supple noodles, don't forget appetizers, such as tuna sashimi, almost cake-like omelette tamago, and tempura. For dessert, try grape jelly. For parties wishing to slurp noodles out of the gaze of other guests, request the private tatami room.

KAHALA

Recommended by
Tetsuya Wakuda

Kishimoto 1-9-2 Sonezaki-Shinchi
Kita-ku
Osaka
Osaka 530-0002
+81 663456778

Opening hours	Closed Sunday
Credit cards	Accepted
Price range	Expensive
Style	Smart casual
Cuisine	Japanese-European
Recommended for	Worth the travel

'It's always innovative yet simple and flavoursome, in an elegant room. To me, it is one of the best restaurant experiences in the world.'—Tetsuya Wakuda

The best restaurants in Japan are never easy to find, and Kahala, on the third floor of an anonymous residential building near the train station, is no exception. But a reservation here is still as rare as pixie dust, partly due to there being only eight seats, and partly thanks to the exciting, experimental cooking by chef Yoshifumi Mori. What began as a specialist in Kobe beef has developed into a Japanese–European fusion joint, where you are just as likely to be served *jamón ibérico* or Landes duck as the famous 'five-layer millefeuille of Iga beef', cooked in front of guests' very eyes.

SHOFUKURO

Recommended by
Takuji Takahashi

8-11 Yokaichi-honmachi
Higashiomi
Shiga 527-0012
+81 748220003
www.shofukuro.jp

Opening hours	Open 7 days
Credit cards	Accepted
Price range	Expensive
Style	Smart casual
Cuisine	Kaiseki
Recommended for	High end

'This place is very refined and in it Japanese culture is condensed. This restaurant is only interesting if you understand Japanese culture well, otherwise you won't understand it. Before going to the restaurant it would be best to study.'—Takuji Takahashi

HIRASANSOU

Recommended by
Naoya Ueno

94 Katsuragawabomuracho
Otsu
Shiga 520-0475
+81 775992058
www.hirasansou.com

Opening hours..Closed Tuesday
Credit cards...Accepted
Price range...Expensive
Style...Formal
Cuisine...Kaiseki
Recommended for...Worth the travel

'The chef offers Japanese dishes that I love – spring
wild grass, summer sweetfish, autumn matsutake
mushrooms and winter game – all year round.'
—Naoya Ueno

ASABA RYOKAN

Recommended by
Riki Mizukami

3450-1 Syuzenji
Izu
Shizuoka 410-2416
www.ryokancollection.com

Opening hours..Open 7 days
Credit cards...Accepted
Price range...Expensive
Style...Formal
Cuisine...Japanese
Recommended for...Worth the travel

'HAS ITS OWN MAGIC... AND THE SUSHI IS PERFECT.'
ALEX ATALA P213

'An oasis, a timeless restaurant where time has stood still, serving the best unagi in the world.'
DHARSHAN MUNIDASA P215

TOKYO

'IT BLEW ME AWAY WITH ITS STUNNING SIMPLICITY.'
PHIL WOOD P214

THE SHELLFISH DISHES HERE IN SPRING ARE THE MOST DELICIOUS OF ALL THE SUSHI RESTAURANTS IN TOKYO
SEIJI YAMAMOTO P217

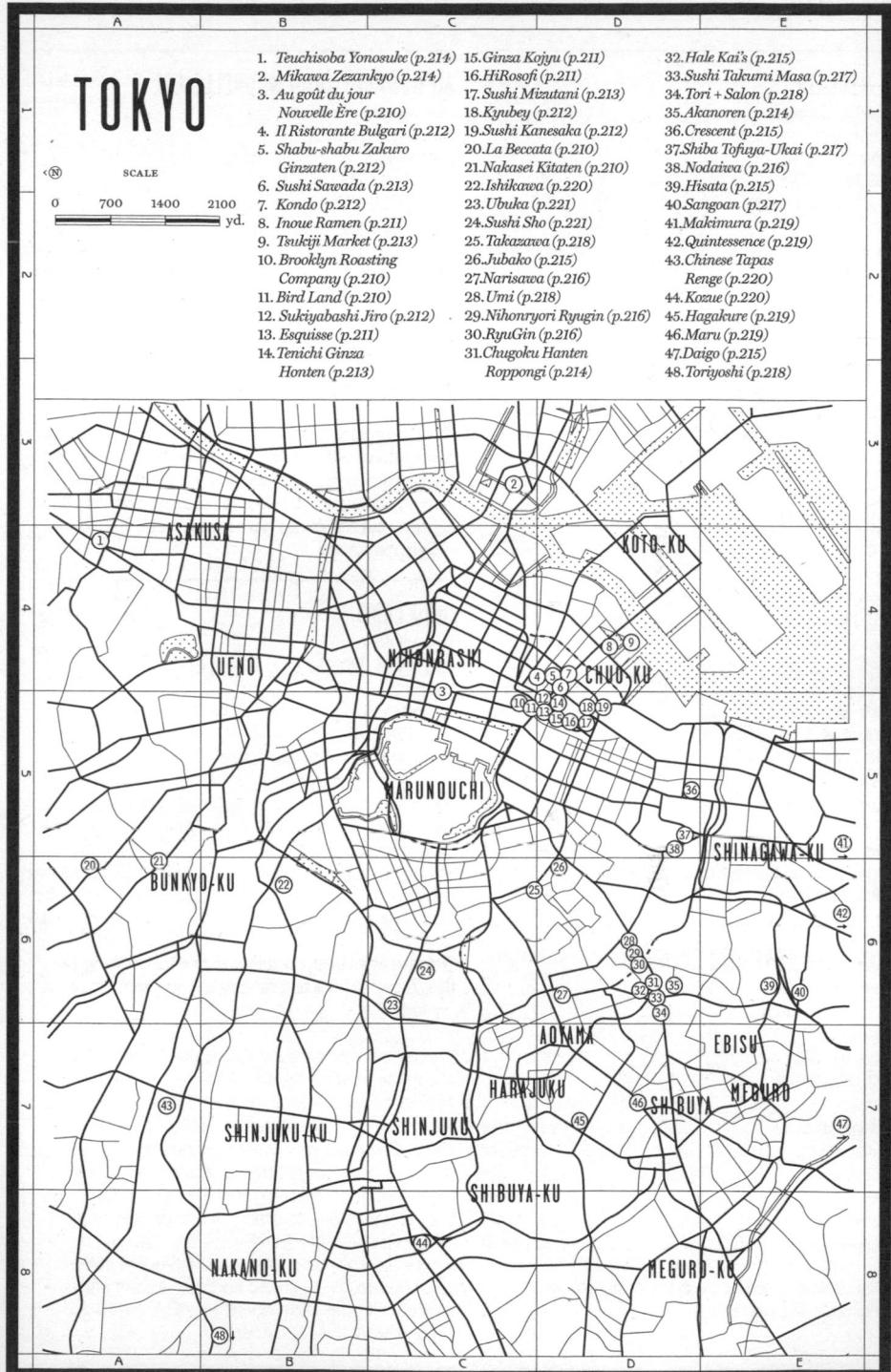

TOKYO

⊙Ⓝ SCALE

0   700   1400   2100
yd.

LA BECCATA

Recommended by
Riki Mizukami

3-34-9-101 Ootsuka
Bunkyo-ku
Tokyo 112-0012
+81 353193459
www.la-beccata.com

Opening hours	Closed Monday
Credit cards	Accepted
Price range	Affordable
Style	Smart casual
Cuisine	Italian
Recommended for	Regular neighbourhood

'This Italian restaurant is comfortable and the food is delicious. The chef adapts the dishes according to the customer's taste. I drop in after work.'—Riki Mizukami

NAKASEI KITATEN

Recommended by
Riki Mizukami

5-10-18 Koishikawa
Bunkyo-ku
Tokyo 112-0002
+81 338300491
www.naka-sei.com

Opening hours	Closed Monday
Credit cards	Not accepted
Price range	Affordable
Style	Casual
Cuisine	Japanese
Recommended for	Local favourite

'This restaurant has a butcher shop and offers delicious dishes that suit the particular cut of meat.'
—Riki Mizukami

BROOKLYN ROASTING COMPANY

Recommended by
Hajime Yoneda

Hankyu Men's Tokyo
6F, 2-5-1 Yuraku-cho
Chiyoda-ku
Tokyo 100-0006
+81 362525402

Opening hours	Open 7 days
Credit cards	Accepted
Price range	Budget
Style	Casual
Cuisine	Café
Recommended for	Breakfast

'They serve very good coffee, their cappuccino is delicious.'—Hajime Yoneda

AU GOÛT DU JOUR NOUVELLE ÈRE

Recommended by
Seiji Yamamoto

Shin-Marunouchi
5F, 1-5-1 Marunouchi
Chiyoda-ku
Tokyo 100-6505
+81 352248070
www.augoutdujour-group.com

Opening hours	Open 7 days
Credit cards	Accepted
Price range	Expensive
Style	Smart casual
Cuisine	French
Recommended for	High end

'This restaurant is my favourite place. The chef has taken into consideration all the elements (how to use an ingredient, the fire, temperature, scent, texture, design, plating up) required for cooking perfectly. It is pricey but the dishes here are perfect.'
—Seiji Yamamoto

BIRD LAND

Recommended by
Gaggan Anand,
Martin Benn

Tsukamoto
B1F, 4-2-15 Ginza
Chuo-ku
Tokyo 104-0061
+81 352501081
www.ginza-birdland.sakura.ne.jp

Opening hours	Closed Monday and Sunday
Credit cards	Accepted
Price range	Affordable
Style	Casual
Cuisine	Yakitori
Recommended for	Wish I'd opened

'Yakitori at its best, I would love to do something like this. They have the tastiest chicken on a skewer... wow.'
—Martin Benn

Western diners weary of taking their chicken 'pink' are in the trustworthy, Michelin-starred hands of Toshihiro Wada at Bird Land. As the name suggests, this smart grill specializes in chicken. But we're in chichi Ginza, not your average neighbourhood, and this is no ordinary yakitori-ya. Wada uses only free-range *shamo* (gamecock) from Oku-kuji, fires his grill with premium *bincho* charcoal, and prefers to pair his poultry with fine Burgundy. The *omakase* (chef's choice menu) typically delivers skewers of salted chicken skin, livers grilled perfectly à point and delicate chicken sashimi with wasabi. There's a second branch in Marunouchi.

ESQUISSE

Recommended by
Marcus Jernmark,
Julien Royer

Royal Crystal Ginza
9F, 5-4-6 Ginza
Chuo-ku
Tokyo 104-0061
+81 355375580
www.esquissetokyo.com

Opening hours...Closed Sunday
Credit cards...Accepted
Price range..Expensive
Style...Smart casual
Cuisine...French-Japanese
Recommended for.............................Worth the travel

'I love how Lionel Beccat creates a very personal cuisine and perfectly pairs Japanese products with French flair.' —Julien Royer

GINZA KOJYU

Recommended by
David Kinch

Carioca
4F, 5-4-8 Ginza
Chuo-ku
Tokyo 104-0061
+81 362159544
www.kojyu.jp

Opening hours...Closed Sunday
Credit cards...Accepted
Price range..Expensive
Style...Formal
Cuisine..Japanese
Recommended for.............................Worth the travel

Located in Ginza, an upmarket area known for its coffeehouses, department stores and boutiques, Ginza Kojyu takes its name from a master potter whose work includes the restaurant's rather alarmingly valuable sake cups. Always drawing inspiration from the most ephemeral, finest market produce, Shizuoka-born chef and sommelier Tooru Okuda presents his Southern heritage via dishes that have earned him three Michelin stars. These may include seasonal wild blue fin toro from Kyushu, *yakimono* broiled fish and meats, and octopus, pumpkin and winter melon. An intimate, comfortable restaurant, panelled in uplifting light wood.

HIROSOFI

Recommended by
Yoshihiro Narisawa

Kojun
4F, 6-8-7 Ginza
Chuo-ku
Tokyo 104-0061
+81 355375855
www.hirosofi.com

Opening hours...Closed Monday
Credit cards...Accepted
Price range..Expensive
Style...Smart casual
Cuisine...Italian
Recommended for...............................Local favourite

'It's the most tasty Italian place in Tokyo. The chef is an influential figure, he's now over sixty but he's a glutton and likes to eat! He's travelled all over the world and reflects what he's eaten in his own dishes which are delicious. And the location is very "Tokyo".' —Yoshihiro Narisawa

INOUE RAMEN

Recommended by
Dharshan Munidasa,
Hiro Sone

4-9-16 Tsukiji
Chuo-ku
Tokyo 104-0045
+81 335420620

Opening hours...Closed Sunday
Reservation policy...No
Credit cards..Not accepted
Price range..Budget
Style...Casual
Cuisine..Ramen Noodles
Recommended for..Bargain

'Iconic in Tsukiji, it only serves one dish and it's simply great.'—Dharshan Munidasa

If you find yourself in Tokyo needing to grab a quick lunch, or you just fancy seeing how the locals do it, Inoue Ramen will satisfy your needs. It's cheap (£5 [$8] should be enough), it's fast (no loitering, they've got jobs to go to and it closes at 1.30 p.m.), it's tasty (tender pork, noodles, bean sprouts and spring onions [scallions] in a bowl of warming broth) and it is all a joyous Japanese jamboree – for the visitor anyway… The locals tuck it away with singular efficiency, but return to their desks sated and energized for the afternoon's shift.

KONDO

Recommended by
Luke Burgess

Sakaguchi
9F, 5-5-13 Ginza
Chuo-ku
Tokyo 104-0061
+81 355680923

Opening hours	Closed Sunday
Credit cards	Accepted
Price range	Expensive
Style	Smart casual
Cuisine	Tempura
Recommended for	High end

'It's not uber-expensive, but it's high-end tempura and it's amazing. The art of frying taken to its height. It's a special occasion to enjoy food prepared and cooked this precisely. The full menu paired with sake leaves you with no doubt this place is serious about frying.'
—Luke Burgess

KYUBEY

Recommended by
Matthew Crabbe,
Masaharu Morimoto

8-7-6 Ginza
Chuo-ku
Tokyo 104-0061
+81 335716523
www.kyubey.jp

Opening hours	Closed Sunday
Credit cards	Accepted
Price range	Expensive
Style	Smart casual
Cuisine	Sushi
Recommended for	High end

'Beautiful sushi in a traditional environment.'
—Matthew Crabbe

IL RISTORANTE BULGARI

Recommended by
Heinz Beck

Ginza Tower
9F, 2-7-12 Ginza
Chuo-ku
Tokyo 104-0061
+81 363620555
www.bulgarihotels.com

Opening hours	Open 7 days
Credit cards	Accepted
Price range	Expensive
Style	Smart casual
Cuisine	Modern Italian
Recommended for	Worth the travel

SHABU-SHABU ZAKURO GINZATEN

Recommended by
Riki Mizukami

Ginza Sanwa
B1F, 4-6-1 Ginza
Chuo-ku
Tokyo 104-0061
+81 335354421

Opening hours	Open 7 days
Credit cards	Accepted
Price range	Expensive
Style	Smart casual
Cuisine	Japanese
Recommended for	Local favourite

SUKIYABASHI JIRO

Recommended by
Josean Alija,
Gaggan Anand,
Seiji Yamamoto,
Hajime Yoneda

Tsukamoto Sogyo
B1F, 4-2-15 Ginza
Chuo-ku
Tokyo 104-0061
+81 335353600
www.sushi-jiro.jp

Opening hours	Closed Sunday
Credit cards	Not accepted
Price range	Expensive
Style	Smart casual
Cuisine	Sushi
Recommended for	High end

'Jiro Ono must be the oldest sushi chef in the world. He has done an outstanding job spreading sushi around the globe. He will go down in history as a great Japanese figure. His whole life was made into a documentary film. Everybody should go to his restaurant once and see his world.'—Seiji Yamamoto

SUSHI KANESAKA

Recommended by
Michael Mina

Misuzu
B1F, 8-10-3 Ginza
Chuo-ku
Tokyo 104-0061
+81 355684411
www.sushi-kanesaka.com

Opening hours	Open 7 days
Credit cards	Accepted
Price range	Expensive
Style	Casual
Cuisine	Sushi
Recommended for	Worth the travel

'Mind blowing! The technique and precision were second to none. Definitely an experience of a lifetime!'—Michael Mina

SUSHI MIZUTANI

Juno
9F, 8-7-7 Ginza
Chuo-ku
Tokyo 104-0061
+81 335735258

Opening hours	Closed Sunday
Credit cards	Not accepted
Price range	Expensive
Style	Casual
Cuisine	Sushi
Recommended for	Worth the travel

SUSHI SAWADA

MC
3F, 5-9-19 Ginza
Chuo-ku
Tokyo 104-0061
+81 335714711

Opening hours	Closed Monday
Credit cards	Accepted
Price range	Expensive
Style	Smart casual
Cuisine	Sushi
Recommended for	Worth the travel

'Has its own magic... and the sushi is perfect.'
—Alex Atala

Sushi master Koji Sawada's seven-seater Tokyo *sushi-ya* is hidden down a quiet Ginza alley where its discreetly marked entrance is obvious only to those in the know. That hasn't stopped Sushi Sawada becoming Tokyo's most-talked-about sushi restaurant, thanks in part to the Michelin Guide anointing it with two stars and the ensuing breathless media coverage. The discreet, panelled room is only for the deepest of pockets but it's arguably the definitive reverential raw fish experience. Expect various types of sea urchin, otoro tuna ever-so-lightly grilled over charcoal, and miniature sushi masterpieces served directly onto the hinoki wood counter.

TENICHI GINZA HONTEN

6-6-5 Ginza
Chuo-ku
Tokyo 104-0061
+81 335711949
www.tenichi.co.jp

Opening hours	Open 7 days
Credit cards	Accepted
Price range	Expensive
Style	Smart casual
Cuisine	Tempura
Recommended for	Local favourite

'Comfortable, cheap, delicious and homely. The employees are also wonderful.'—Riki Mizukami

The original Tenichi unfolds beyond lion sentries in Ginza's heart, below the Sony showroom (fifteen minutes' walk from Exit B4 at Ginza station). Established in the 1930s, the pristine, practically greaseless, fluffy tempura soon attracted an illustrious clientele, including presidents and pop stars. Top-quality morsels, including oyster, scallop, king crab, sea urchin and lotus root, are individually flash-fried at a blistering temperature and served immediately. You can choose to dip them in tentsuyu (dashi broth, soy and mirin) or sprinkle with lemon and salt. Follow with green tea and yuzu sorbet, or perfectly ripened mango.

TSUKIJI MARKET

5-2-1 Tsukiji
Chuo-ku
Tokyo 104-0055
www.tsukiji-market.or.jp

Opening hours	Open 7 days
Reservation policy	No
Credit cards	Not accepted
Price range	Budget
Style	Casual
Cuisine	Seafood
Recommended for	Worth the travel

'After a morning stroll through the back alleys of this gigantic fish heaven, there's nothing like sampling bits and pieces from many shops. *Dashimaki tamago* (rolled omelette) from one and *sencha* (green tea) from another... Keep walking, keep eating and drinking. Sushi can be nice but there are myriad micro genres to enjoy. With so many things to try out, I'm still making new discoveries even after fifteen years!'
—Dharshan Munidasa

TEUCHISOBA YONOSUKE
Recommended by
Riki Mizukami
1-4-4 Motoasakusa
Daito-ku
Tokyo 111-0041
+81 338426400

Opening hours	Closed Sunday
Credit cards	Not accepted
Price range	Budget
Style	Casual
Cuisine	Soba Noodles
Recommended for	Bargain

'The chef carefully selects the Hokkaido buckwheat flour and makes soba. The menu is abundant and delicious.'—Riki Mizukami

MIKAWA ZEZANKYO
Recommended by
Phil Wood, Seiji Yamamoto
1-3-1 Fukuzumi
Eto-ku
Tokyo 135-0032
+81 336438383
www.kayabacho-mikawa.jimdo.com

Opening hours	Closed Wednesday
Credit cards	Accepted
Price range	Expensive
Style	Smart casual
Cuisine	Tempura
Recommended for	Worth the travel

'This place blew me away with its stunning simplicity. A tiny counter restaurant, it completely changed my preconceived ideas of what could be achieved with tempura. There are only eight seats and as you walk in they start making the tempura batter. Dish after dish of the most exquisite tempura served the same way for thirty years... I can't stop thinking about this restaurant and if I'm ever back in Tokyo this will be the first place I re-book.'—Phil Wood

AKANOREN
Recommended by
Matthew Crabbe
Nakaoka
1F, 3-21-24 Nishi-Azabu
Minato-ku
Tokyo 106-0031
+81 334084775

Opening hours	Open 7 days
Reservation policy	No
Credit cards	Not accepted
Price range	Budget
Style	Casual
Cuisine	Ramen Noodles
Recommended for	Late night

'For the fantastic ramen and gyoza.'—Matthew Crabbe

CHUGOKU HANTEN ROPPONGI
Recommended by
Seiji Yamamoto
Oriental
1F, 1-1-5 Nishi-Azabu
Minato-ku
Tokyo 106-0031
+81 334783828
www.chuugokuhanten.com

Opening hours	Open 7 days
Credit cards	Accepted
Price range	Affordable
Style	Smart casual
Cuisine	Chinese
Recommended for	Late night

'They serve à la carte dishes and all of them are very delicious. I think that their Chinese mitten crab is the most delicious in the world. I go to this restaurant once a week.'—Seiji Yamamoto

CRESCENT

Recommended by
Riki Mizukami

1-8-20 Shiba-koen
Minato-ku
Tokyo 105-0011
+81 334363211
www.restaurantcrescent.com

Opening hours	Closed Sunday
Credit cards	Accepted
Price range	Expensive
Style	Formal
Cuisine	French
Recommended for	High end

'The dishes at this restaurant are wonderful, as are the service and interior design. The illuminations of Tokyo Tower are beautiful too.'—Riki Mizukami

Crescent is the aristocrat of Tokyo's haute-cuisine scene. Its appearance is fittingly grand: a Victorian-style English residence worthy of a film set, decorated with heavy drapes, thick carpets, pristine table linen and stained glass. The chef worked under Frédy Girardet in Switzerland and has, since 2009, held two Michelin stars. Expect impeccable bread, exquisite *macarons*, superb beef and shellfish. Choose from a range of menus including the extravagant Confiance, featuring the Crescent hallmark *Compression de Tomate* (a perfect cube of tomato mousse, tartare and jelly), then *Filet de Boeuf Rossini*. Good views of the Tokyo Tower.

DAIGO

Recommended by
Umberto Bombana

Forest Tower
2F, 2-3-1 Atago
Minato-ku
Tokyo 105-0002
+81 334310811
www.atago-daigo.com

Opening hours	Open 7 days
Credit cards	Accepted
Price range	Expensive
Style	Smart casual
Cuisine	Japanese
Recommended for	High end

'It gives a very good expression of Japanese cuisine.'
—Umberto Bombana

HALE KAI'S

Recommended by
Hiro Sone

2-16-4 Nishi-Azabu
Minato-ku
Tokyo 106-0031
+81 334008012

Opening hours	Open 7 days
Credit cards	Accepted
Price range	Affordable
Style	Casual
Cuisine	Japanese-Hawaiian
Recommended for	Late night

'Borderless cuisine, great raw fish dishes and barbeque, and open until 2.30 a.m.'—Hiro Sone

HISATA

Recommended by
Takuji Takahashi

TTC
B1F, 4-2-28 Azabu
Minato-ku
Tokyo 106-0046
+81 334449130

Opening hours	Closed Monday
Credit cards	Accepted
Price range	Expensive
Style	Smart casual
Cuisine	Japanese
Recommended for	Worth the travel

'This restaurant uses locally sourced ingredients and dishes are served on very expensive Bizen ware.'
—Takuji Takahashi

JUBAKO

Recommended by
Dharshan Munidasa

2-17-61 Akasaka
Minato-ku
Tokyo 107-0052
+81 335831319

Opening hours	Closed Sunday
Credit cards	Accepted
Price range	Expensive
Style	Smart casual
Cuisine	Eel
Recommended for	High end

'An oasis, a restaurant where time has stood still, serving the best *unagi* (freshwater eel) in the world.'
—Dharshan Munidasa

NARISAWA

2-6-15 Minami Aoyama
Minato-ku
Tokyo 107-0061
+81 357850799
www.narisawa-yoshihiro.com

Recommended by
Mark Best, André
Chiang, Reif Othman

Opening hours	Closed Sunday
Credit cards	Accepted
Price range	Expensive
Style	Formal
Cuisine	Japanese-French
Recommended for	Worth the travel

'From the moment I stepped inside until the moment I stepped out, everything seemed so flawless. The food has a great balance of flavours with ever-evolving creations. Not only did I taste fabulous, well-executed dishes but I could almost savour the intention and messages expressed through the exquisite cuisine of Chef Narisawa.'—André Chiang

Chef Yoshihiro Narisawa trained in Switzerland at Girardet's, in France at Robuchon's and in Italy at Antica Osteria del Ponte. After nine years in Europe, he returned to Japan, first to Odawara, where he opened La Napuole, then to Minato-ku, Tokyo, where he opened Les Créations de Narisawa, the name of which he later shortened to 'Narisawa'. While his French training, and his molecular gastronomic influences are clear (he has two Michelin stars, after all), the dishes he serves are expressions of the Japanese seasons and the ingredients they provide. This is a fusion worth travelling for.

NIHONRYORI RYUGIN

Side Roppongi
1F, 7-17-24 Roppongi
Minato-ku
Tokyo 106-0032
+81 334238006
www.nihonryori-ryugin.com

Recommended by
Víctor Arguinzóniz,
Alejandro Cancino,
Richard Ekkebus,
Tomoyasu Kamo,
Daniel López

Opening hours	Open 7 days
Credit cards	Accepted
Price range	Expensive
Style	Smart casual
Cuisine	Modern Japanese
Recommended for	Worth the travel

'The setting is amazing. Japanese and avant-garde cuisines are combined to create a perfect and unforgettable experience.'—Daniel López

NODAIWA

1-5-4 Higashiazabu
Minato-ku
Tokyo 106-0044
+81 335837852
www.nodaiwa.co.jp

Recommended by
Gaggan Anand

Opening hours	Closed Sunday
Credit cards	Accepted
Price range	Affordable
Style	Casual
Cuisine	Eel
Recommended for	High end

'Delicious *unagi* (freshwater eel).'—Gaggan Anand

Nodaiwa, Tokyo's most fashionable freshwater eel restaurant, has specialized in *unagi* and nothing but since the mid-nineteenth century. Still family-run – it's now in the hands of the fifth generation – it boasts four addresses in Tokyo, plus one more in Paris. But the one to visit is its flagship, a wonderful beamed *kura* (traditional storehouse) transplanted from the sticks to Nishi-Azabu. Nodaiwa uses only wild eel, traditionally filleted, cooked over embers, steamed, then coated in a secret recipe taré sauce before being grilled one last time. Try it served over rice in a lacquer box or as part of a tasting that includes eel liver soup.

RYUGIN

Side Roppongi
1F, 7-17-24 Roppongi
Minato-ku
Tokyo 106-0032
+81 0334238006
www.nihonryori-ryugin.com

Recommended by
Steffen Hansen,
Hiro Sone

Opening hours	Closed Sunday
Credit cards	Accepted
Price range	Expensive
Style	Smart casual
Cuisine	Modern Japanese
Recommended for	Worth the travel

'Inventive cuisine with extremely fresh Japanese produce.'—Steffen Hansen

SANGOAN

Recommended by
Hiro Sone

510 Shirokane
1F, 5-10-10 Shirokane
Minato-ku
Tokyo 108-0072
+81 334443570

Opening hours	Closed Wednesday
Credit cards	Not accepted
Price range	Affordable
Style	Casual
Cuisine	Japanese
Recommended for	Regular neighbourhood

'Ask for *omakase* (chef's choice menu), which usually contains a few courses of seasonal Japanese vegetable dishes, sashimi, tempura and their homemade soba. It's reasonable and very satisfying.'—Hiro Sone

SHIBA TOFUYA-UKAI

Recommended by
Matthew Crabbe

4-4-13 Shibakoen
Minato-ku
Tokyo 105-0011
+81 334361028
www.ukai.co.jp

Opening hours	Open 7 days
Credit cards	Accepted
Price range	Affordable
Style	Smart casual
Cuisine	Kaiseki
Recommended for	Local favourite

'Beautiful traditional grounds and gardens under Tokyo tower with food and service done the traditional way. All servers are dressed in kimonos.'—Matthew Crabbe

Finding any address in Japan can be a bit of a trial, but there's no excuse for missing Shiba Tofuya-Ukai, set right in the shadow of Tokyo Tower. Encompassing a sprawling – and suitably stunning – Japanese garden, this oasis in the heart of the metropolis serves *kaiseki* cuisine specializing in tofu. As with many such restaurants, exquisite surroundings, immaculate service and world-class food (*kaiseki* is arguably the pinnacle of the Japanese chef's craft) doesn't come cheap, but Shiba Tofuya-Ukai is consistent enough in excellence to draw a regular crowd for both lunch and dinner.

SUSHI TAKUMI MASA

Recommended by
Justin North, Hiro
Sone, Seiji Yamamoto

Seven Nishiazabu
B1F, 4-1-15 Nishiazabu
Minato-ku
Tokyo 106-0031
+81 334999170

Opening hours	Closed Monday
Credit cards	Accepted
Price range	Expensive
Style	Smart casual
Cuisine	Sushi
Recommended for	Regular neighbourhood

'Japanese seafood is of a world-class quality that Japan is proud of. This restaurant offers that seafood with various menus for every season. In spring the shellfish dishes here are the most delicious of all the sushi restaurants in Tokyo.'—Seiji Yamamoto

Amid the international embassies of Nishi-Azabu, a mysterious doorway leads to a seven-seat basement bar, which requires booking at least two weeks in advance. Here, in the cool, laid-back, music-free setting, Masakatsu Oka authors a story of up to forty courses of impeccable sashimi, delicately seasoned sushi and fleetingly grilled fish – particularly lower-fat, white-fleshed fish – with care and friendliness. The result is mesmerizing – an exploration of tastes, textures and lingering aftertastes. Morsels that particularly impress may include smoky pike conger eel, meaty bonito, ultra-rich monkfish liver, and raw and charred baby swordfish.

TAKAZAWA

Sanyo Akasaka
2F, 3-5-2 Akasaka
Minato-ku
Tokyo 107-0052
+81 335055052
www.aroniadetakazawa.com

Opening hours	Open 7 days
Credit cards	Accepted
Price range	Expensive
Style	Smart casual
Cuisine	French-Japanese
Recommended for	Worth the travel

'Contemporary, whimsical, delicious food, with great service.'—Martin Benn

Yoshiaki Takazawa's exclusive Akasaka restaurant has double the number of tables it started out with in 2005, giving global gourmands a princely four tables to fight over. The ex-Park Hyatt chef and sommelier's exquisite French-inflected Japanese multi-course menus are up there with Tokyo's finest, though the restaurant remains, bafflingly, unstarred. While his wife Akiko greets guests warmly (in Japanese or English), Takazawa works alone at his sleekly minimalist open kitchen. Ratatouille, a jewel-bright mosaic of fifteen different vegetables, is his most famous dish and he's known for a playful whimsy grounded in fearsome technique and glorious ingredients. Japanese wines are a focus.

TORI+SALON

Nishi-Azabu FT
2F, 2-25-24 Nishi-Azabu
Minato-ku
Tokyo 106-0031
+81 334866366
www.torisalon.com

Opening hours	Closed Monday
Credit cards	Accepted
Price range	Affordable
Style	Smart casual
Cuisine	Yakitori
Recommended for	Wish I'd opened

'Kazuo Nakayama cuts only twelve amazing free-range chickens and expertly grills them over *bincho* charcoal for something like fifteen customers a day. He seems so relaxed and happy to be doing what he's doing – showcasing what chicken can really taste like.'
—Matt Abergel

UMI

Sannan
1F, 3-2-8 Minami-Aoyama
Minato-ku
Tokyo 107-0062
+81 334013368

Opening hours	Open 7 days
Credit cards	Accepted
Price range	Expensive
Style	Smart casual
Cuisine	Sushi
Recommended for	Worth the travel

'A must-visit restaurant in Tokyo. Absolutely amazing.'
—Alex Atala

A lively ten-seat counter offering immaculate sushi and sashimi in Aoyama (close to Roppongi station). Chef-owner Nagano San sources up to thirty types of fish and crustaceans from Kyushu and Hokkaido. These include tuna, bottarga (which might be cured for up to eight weeks until amber in colour and almost gelatinous), smoked bonito, eel sprinkled with yuzu zest, and sashimi of sardines, whelks and regional clams. Also impressive is the firm shari rice, infused with vinegars and salt, the squid prepared with its entrails, omelette, and densely packed cucumber maki.

TORIYOSHI

Inogashira Park Side
B1, 1-21-1 Kichijyoji-minami-machi
Musashino-ku
Tokyo 180-0003
+81 422484602
www.toriyoshi.jp

Opening hours	Open 7 days
Credit cards	Accepted
Price range	Budget
Style	Casual
Cuisine	Yakitori
Recommended for	Bargain

'My favourite yakitori in Japan, all counter seating.'
—Matthew Crabbe

HAGAKURE

Recommended by
Hiro Sone

2-8-11 Shibuya
Shibuya-ku
Tokyo 150-0033
+81 334003294

Opening hours	Closed Sunday
Credit cards	Not accepted
Price range	Budget
Style	Casual
Cuisine	Japanese
Recommended for	Bargain

'They serve traditional *kushiyaki* (grilled ingredients on skewers) and every imaginable type of innard – even sashimi of innards.'—Hiro Sone

MARU

Recommended by
Matthew Crabbe

Aoyama KT
B1F, 5-50-8 Jingumae
Shibuya-ku
Tokyo 150-0001
+81 364185572
www.maru-mayfont.jp

Opening hours	Open 7 days
Credit cards	Accepted
Price range	Affordable
Style	Casual
Cuisine	Kaiseki
Recommended for	Regular neighbourhood

'Neighbourhood feel, seasonal everything with a simple Japanese flair. The best dish is the corn fritter (when in season).'—Matthew Crabbe

Take a seat at the long wooden counter in this simple but chic room, tucked down a side street in Tokyo's central Aoyama district, and prepare for a feast. Based on Kyoto-style *kaiseki* or multi-course style of dining, owner and chef Keiji Mori offers small sharing dishes made with seasonal ingredients that might include *kamo manjyu* (a traditional bun made with wild duck and lily bulbs); *sakuramasu to hanazansho* (simmered ocean trout and spring vegetables) and *imo tako nankin takiawase* (simmered octopus, taro and pumpkin, served cold). The list of Japanese sake and *shochu* is impressive, but there are also European wines for the less adventurous.

MAKIMURA

Recommended by
Tomoyasu Kamo

3-11-5 Minami-Oi
Shinagawa-ku
Tokyo 140-0013
+81 337686388

Opening hours	Closed Sunday
Credit cards	Accepted
Price range	Expensive
Style	Smart casual
Cuisine	Kaiseki
Recommended for	Worth the travel

QUINTESSENCE

Recommended by
Jason Atherton

Garden City Shinagawa Gotenyama
1F, 6-7-29 Kitashinagawa
Shinagawa-ku
Tokyo 141-0001
+81 362770090
www.quintessence.jp

Opening hours	Closed Sunday
Credit cards	Accepted
Price range	Expensive
Style	Smart casual
Cuisine	Modern French
Recommended for	Worth the travel

Such is the demand for a table at Quintessence, in Tokyo's leafy 'Shinagawa City', that it was recently named in the top ten most difficult restaurants in the world to book. Chef Shuzo Kishida is a fanatic of slow-roasting meat, a technique learned while at Paris's legendary L'Astrance. Kishida's *shonai-sangen* pork with onion-herb sauce, for example, is roasted for one minute, allowed to rest for five more, then roasted for a further minute – a process repeated up to thirty times. There are no written menus for the French-influenced seven-course lunch, or eleven-course dinner, for which only ingredients sourced on the day appear. The predominantly French wine list is considerable.

CHINESE TAPAS RENGE

3-12-1 Shinjyuku
Shinjuku-ku
Tokyo 160-0022
+81 333546776

Opening hours	Closed Monday
Credit cards	Accepted
Price range	Affordable
Style	Casual
Cuisine	Chinese small plates
Recommended for	Bargain

'Fusion-style, elegant Chinese food for both Shanghai aristocrats and any kind of Tokyo taste.'
—Yoshihiro Narisawa

Beloved of cooks who labour in Shinjuku for its late hours and dive-in menu of easy to eat Shanghai-style tapas, Renge has just thirteen seats, most of them at the counter. Served past midnight (early evening is for daters, despite the close quarters), Cantonese favourites including shumai dumplings, roast duck and snacky plates of fried wonton and Shanghai sausage, accessorized with olives and pickled vegetables. Ingredients can tend towards the high end — Kinka ham comes with white asparagus, for example — but there are also half-servings of tantan-men, hairy crab or good, basic ramen in XO sauce.

ISHIKAWA

Takamura
1F, 5-37 Kagurazaka
Shinjuku-ku
Tokyo 162-0825
+81 352250173
www.kagurazaka-ishikawa.co.jp

Opening hours	Closed Sunday
Credit cards	Accepted
Price range	Expensive
Style	Smart casual
Cuisine	Japanese
Recommended for	Worth the travel

'In my limited experience, a real apex in contemporary kaiseki.'—David Kinch

Ishikawa, a temple of gastronomy, is located just behind Kagurazaka's Bishamon temple to Buddha in the geisha district. Beyond an unpretentious black wood exterior unravels an interior of four serene, private dining rooms and a seven-seat counter carved from 400-year-old Japanese cypress trees. Head chef Hideki Ishikawa's dishes, which are more about flavour than presentation, are delivered by polite, often English-speaking, waitresses in kimonos. They might include melted white sesame tofu, tempura turtle with taro, and quail shabu-shabu in sultry broth with five types of mushrooms. The wine list is as extensive as the sake menu.

KOZUE

Park Hyatt Hotel
3-7-1-2 Nishi Shinjuku
Shinjuku-ku
Tokyo 163-1055
+81 353233460
www.tokyo.park.hyatt.com

Opening hours	Open 7 days
Credit cards	Accepted
Price range	Expensive
Style	Smart casual
Cuisine	Modern Japanese
Recommended for	High end

'Very good-quality fresh food, staff wearing traditional kimonos, nice ambience and a view of the city.'
—Reif Othman

SUSHI SHO

Yorindo
1F, 1-11 Yotsuya
Shinjuku-ku
Tokyo 160-0004
+81 333516387

Opening hours	Closed Sunday
Credit cards	Accepted
Price range	Expensive
Style	Casual
Cuisine	Sushi
Recommended for	Worth the travel

'Chef Keiji Nakazawa is the godfather of ageing fish, dispelling the common misconception that fresh fish is best. Visiting his restaurant in Tokyo is a life-changing experience. The restaurant itself is small, with no tables and only ten seats centered around a sushi bar. Even the sushi rice here is special: it's warmer than most with several differently seasoned varieties, paired perfectly with different kinds of fish.'
—Jonathon Sawyer

UBUKA

IS
1F, 2-14 Araki-cho
Shinjuku-ku
Tokyo 160-0007
+81 333567270

Opening hours	Closed Sunday
Credit cards	Accepted
Price range	Expensive
Style	Smart casual
Cuisine	Kaiseki
Recommended for	Regular neighbourhood

'A Japanese restaurant specializing in crab. It's small and casual, managed by a young chef and his wife, but the level is very high. All ingredients are very fresh and fantastic and the price is reasonable.'
—Yoshihiro Narisawa

SOUTHEAST ASIA

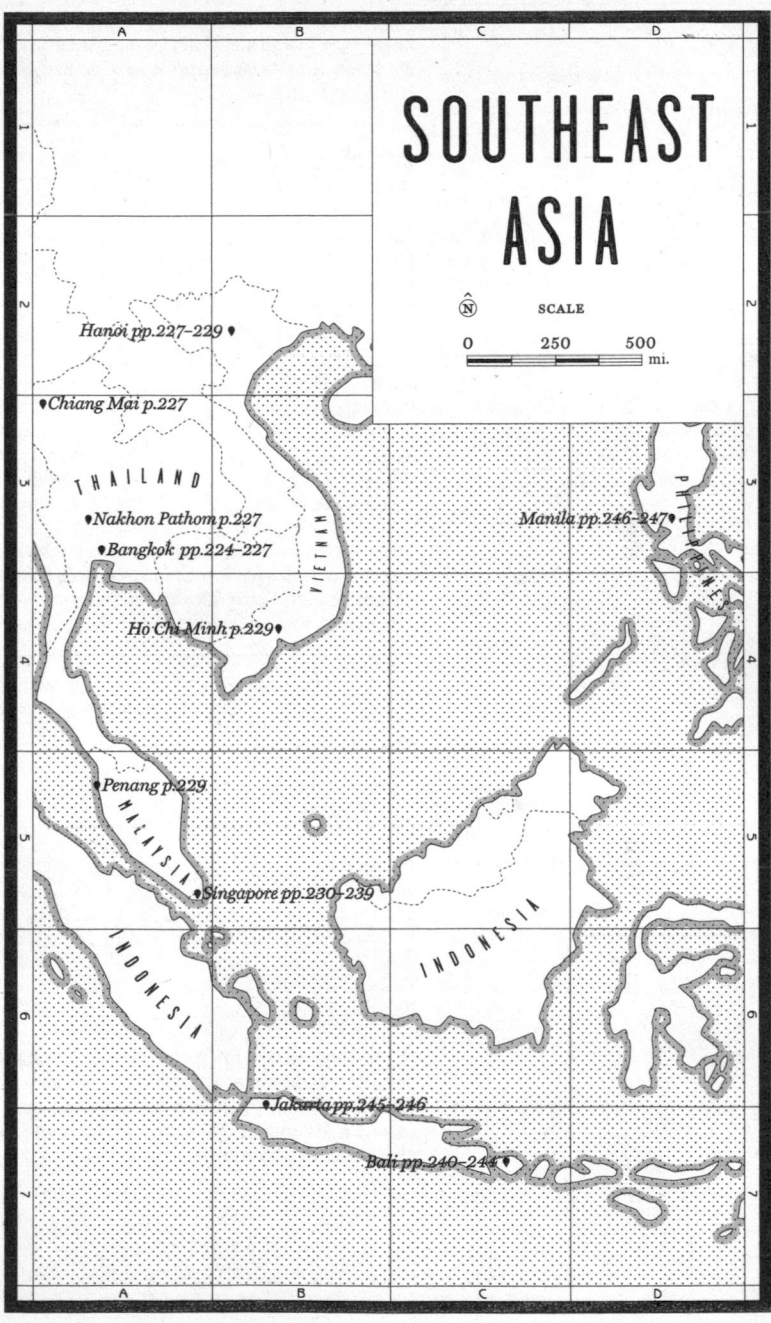

SOUTHEAST
ASIA

SCALE

0   250   500
mi.

Hanoi pp.227–229 ♥

♥Chiang Mai p.227

THAILAND

♥Nakhon Pathom p.227
♥Bangkok pp.224–227

VIETNAM

Manila pp.246–247♥

PHILIPPINES

Ho Chi Minh p.229♥

♥Penang p.229

MALAYSIA

♥Singapore pp.230–239

INDONESIA

INDONESIA

♥Jakarta pp.245–246

Bali pp.240–244 ♥

APPIA

20/4 Sukhumvit 31
Bangkok
Bangkok 10110
Thailand
+66 22612056
www.appia-bangkok.com

Opening hours	Closed Monday
Credit cards	Accepted
Price range	Affordable
Style	Casual
Cuisine	Italian
Recommended for	Regular neighbourhood

'In my opinion it's the best Italian food in the country at the moment. Bold flavours and a warm, friendly atmosphere.'—Dylan Jones & Bo Songvisava

CELADON

The Sukhothai Hotel
13/3 Thanon Sathorn Tai
Bangkok
Bangkok 10120
Thailand
+66 23448888
www.sukhothai.com

Opening hours	Open 7 days
Credit cards	Accepted
Price range	Expensive
Style	Smart casual
Cuisine	Thai
Recommended for	Worth the travel

'The Celadon at the Sukhothai Hotel enables one to experience all the flavours of this magnificent land.' —Italo Bassi

CHAIROJ

467/25 Sri Ayutthaya
Bangkok
Bangkok 10400
Thailand
+66 23544090

Opening hours	Closed Sunday
Credit cards	Not accepted
Price range	Budget
Style	Casual
Cuisine	Thai-Chinese
Recommended for	Regular neighbourhood

'This restaurant has been dishing out delicious home-style Thai-Chinese food for the last forty years. It's simple, easy eating and great value for money.' —Gaggan Anand

COLONNADE

The Sukhothai Hotel
13/3 Thanon Sathorn Tai
Bangkok
Bangkok 10120
Thailand
+66 23448888
www.sukhothai.com

Opening hours	Open 7 days
Credit cards	Accepted
Price range	Expensive
Style	Smart casual
Cuisine	International
Recommended for	Breakfast

'Impeccable service, the design is a feast for the eyes, and after a good night in their fantastic beds there's no place like the Colonnade with its Western-Eastern-cereal-fruit-eggs-et-cetera buffet.'—Julius Jaspers

GAI TAWN PRATUNAM

960–962 Petchburi Soi 30
Bangkok
Bangkok 10400
Thailand
+66 22526325

Opening hours	Open 7 days
Reservation policy	No
Credit cards	Not accepted
Price range	Budget
Style	Casual
Cuisine	Thai
Recommended for	Bargain

'A small hole-in-the-wall spot in Bangkok's Pratunam area, it has been serving the best *khao man gai* (chicken rice Thai-style) in the city for the last forty years. For just over £1 ($2) you get a wholesome meal with water.'—Gaggan Anand

GASTRO 1/6

RMA Institute
22 Sukhumvit Soi Sainamthip 2
Bangkok
Bangkok 10110
Thailand
+66 806036421

Opening hours	Closed Monday
Reservation policy	No
Credit cards	Not accepted
Price range	Budget
Style	Casual
Cuisine	Café
Recommended for	Breakfast

'A hidden oasis in the city, the food's tasty even if
the service is extremely slow.'—Dylan Jones &
Bo Songvisava

Pretty garden café attached to RMA Institute, a quirky
gallery named after the Thai-Chinese word for
'grandmother', ar-ma, as it's where the owner's
own grandmother once lived. Open for breakfast and
brunch, in the case of the latter it offers one of the
few buffet-free experiences in Bangkok. Expect
Spanish-style tortilla, French toast, eggs any style
and a Thai-tinged Full English, where bacon, sausage,
baked beans and sautéed mushrooms sit alongside
garlic-heavy spinach. You fill in a card to place your
order, pay upfront and wait for it to – eventually –
appear at your table. Perfect for a lazy brunch
– but not if you're in a hurry.

NAHM

Metropolitan Hotel
27 Thanon Sathorn Tai
Bangkok
Bangkok 10120
Thailand
+66 26253388
www.metropolitan.bangkok.como.bz

Opening hours	Open 7 days
Credit cards	Accepted
Price range	Expensive
Style	Smart casual
Cuisine	Thai
Recommended for	Worth the travel

'It's thoughtful, intellectual and inspired food showing
how Thai food ought to taste and be eaten.'
—Dylan Jones & Bo Songvisava

Australian Thai-food scholar David Thompson took
Nahm, the modern Thai restaurant he originally
opened in London's Halkin hotel in 1991, to Bangkok
in 2010. Returning to the source of his inspiration, the
restaurant's second iteration, on the ground floor of
the Metropolitan hotel, has arguably eclipsed the food
at the widely championed original, which closed its
doors in late 2012. The reason? The raw materials,
the building blocks for his creative cooking, are now
easily available to him – as opposed to sitting wilting
while they waited to clear UK customs – freshness
being everything in Thai cooking. Skip the à la carte
and take on the tasting menu.

OPPOSITE MESS HALL

27/1 Sukhumvit Soi 51
Bangkok
Bangkok 10110
Thailand
+66 26626330
www.oppositebangkok.com

Opening hours	Closed Monday
Credit cards	Accepted but not AMEX
Price range	Affordable
Style	Casual
Cuisine	Small plates
Recommended for	Regular neighbourhood

'It's real, honest and unpretentious food that's
executed extremely well.'
—Dylan Jones & Bo Songvisava

This lively bar-diner, with long communal tables, open
kitchen and dining counter, arrived in Sukhumvit in the
summer of 2013. It's from the same team behind
WTF, a cultish, tapas-touting bar-cum-gallery on the
other side of the street. Australian chef Jess Barnes,
who first made his name in Bangkok at Quince, rolls
out small plates that look to Asia, Spain, France and
Italy. Alongside the steamed Chinese buns and the
daily-changing line-up of croquettes, crostini, tortilla
and terrines, lies the more creative fusion of dishes
such as smoked bone marrow dumplings in oxtail
broth laced with fermented mooli (daikon) and mustard.

RAAN JAY FAI

Recommended by
Margot Janse

327 Mahachai Road
Bangkok
Bangkok 10200
Thailand
+66 22239384

Opening hours	Closed Saturday
Reservation policy	No
Credit cards	Not accepted
Price range	Affordable
Style	Casual
Cuisine	Thai
Recommended for	Worth the travel

'I was completely bowled over by Jay Fai in Bangkok. A street restaurant run by a sixty-something-year-old woman, who cooks every dish herself on an open fire. Unbelievable flavours and the most amazing crab omelette.'—Margot Janse

SOI 38 NIGHT MARKET

Recommended by
Gaggan Anand

38 Sukhumvit Soi
Bangkok
Bangkok 10110
Thailand

Opening hours	Open 7 days
Reservation policy	No
Credit cards	Not accepted
Price range	Budget
Style	Casual
Cuisine	Thai street food
Recommended for	Late night

'It's a whole street of stalls selling local food and it's perfect for a meal after a night out. Order a beer and enjoy the hot noodles and crab wonton soup.'
—Gaggan Anand

Bangkok is full of night markets, but for optimum hygiene and fresh ingredients the one on Sukhumvit Soi 38, a coconut's throw from the BTS at Thong Lor, is top of the list. Pitch up at a table at any of the stalls from 6.00 p.m. and you could stay there all night, picking from different vendors. Here you'll find one of the city's best renditions of Pad Thai from the old man at Pad Thai Fire Look; sticky rice and mango with one of the biggest smiles in town; duck noodles, crab and pork noodle soup, fruit smoothies, pork satay, just-battered Thai doughnuts with pandan leaf custard and fresh coconut water for all-you-can-eat prices. Later the line-up changes – some stalls close at 8.00 p.m. while others only open at 10.00 p.m.

LA TABLE DE TEE

Recommended by
Alexis Gauthier

69/5 Sala Daeng
Bangkok
Bangkok 10500
Thailand
+66 26363220
www.latabledetee.com

Opening hours	Closed Monday
Credit cards	Accepted
Price range	Affordable
Style	Casual
Cuisine	Thai-French
Recommended for	Worth the travel

'The most exciting place I ate in when I spent two weeks in Bangkok. It's tiny and in a grim dead-end side alley in the centre of town, but it's packed every night with people who've booked three months in advance from all around the world. The eight-course Thai-French tasting menu is about £20 ($33). I don't know who this guy is but he's a genius.'—Alexis Gauthier

Chef Chatree 'Tee' Kachonklin returned to Thailand in 2010, after six years in London kitchens (including Michelin-starred Roussillon), to open his own restaurant when he was a mere twenty-five years old. Still shy of thirty, the precocious talent has made his twenty-cover back-alley gastronomic restaurant the talk of Bangkok's in-crowd. Tee eschews à la carte cooking in favour of a set five-course chef's menu of modern dishes anchored in French and Thai techniques and ingredients. The latest menu is updated weekly on Facebook: hold out hope for pineapple and Kurobuta pork, wild galangal and snapper, and Tee's Siamese Macaroons. Terrific value.

THE VERANDAH

Recommended by
Matthew Harris

Mandarin Oriental Bangkok
48 Oriental Avenue
Bangkok
Bangkok 10500
Thailand
+66 6599000
www.mandarinoriental.com/bangkok

Opening hours	Open 7 days
Credit cards	Accepted
Price range	Expensive
Style	Formal
Cuisine	International
Recommended for	Breakfast

'By the river, great for dim sum.'—Matthew Harris

XIA DUCK NOODLES

Recommended by
Dylan Jones &
Bo (Duangporn) Songvisava

2856 Rama IV Road
Bangkok
Bangkok 10310
Thailand
+66 26713279

Opening hours	Closed Sunday
Reservation policy	No
Credit cards	Not accepted
Price range	Budget
Style	Casual
Cuisine	Chinese
Recommended for	Bargain

'Xia duck noodles is so full of flavour, the blood cakes in the noodle soup with braised duck are so unctuous.'
—Dylan Jones & Bo Songvisava

BAANRAI YARMYEN

Recommended by
Zakary Pelaccio

14 Moo 3 Loi Lanka 3 Jaroenraj
Chiang Mai
Chiang Mai Province 50000
Thailand
+66 53247999

Opening hours	Open 7 days
Credit cards	Accepted
Price range	Affordable
Style	Casual
Cuisine	Northern Thai
Recommended for	Wish I'd opened

TALAT DON WAI

Recommended by
Gaggan Anand

Bang Krathum Don Wai
Nakhon Pathom
Nakhon Pathom Province 73110
Thailand

Opening hours	Open 7 days
Reservation policy	No
Credit cards	Not accepted
Price range	Budget
Style	Casual
Cuisine	Thai street food
Recommended for	Breakfast

'A traditional riverside market behind the Don Wai Temple. It's a non-touristy place. Every Saturday I go there with my wife to eat the freshly made food and return home with a car boot full of fresh produce.'
—Gaggan Anand

LE BEAULIEU

Recommended by
Donald Berger

Hotel Metropole Hanoi
15 Ngô Quyền
Hanoi
Hanoi 110118
Vietnam
+84 438266919
www.sofitel-legend.com/hanoi

Opening hours	Open 7 days
Credit cards	Accepted
Price range	Expensive
Style	Smart casual
Cuisine	French Brasserie
Recommended for	High end

'Located in the Grand Dame of Hanoi, it is like being transported to Paris and pampered like royalty.'
—Donald Berger

BÚN BÒ NAM BỘ

Recommended by
Donald Berger

67 Hàng Điếu
Hanoi
Hanoi 111202
Vietnam
+84 439230701

Opening hours	Open 7 days
Reservation policy	No
Credit cards	Not accepted
Price range	Budget
Style	Casual
Cuisine	Noodles
Recommended for	Bargain

'The best place for the best dish.'—Donald Berger

CHÀ CÁ LÃ VỌNG

Recommended by
Donald Berger

14 Chả Cá
Hanoi
Hanoi 110300
Vietnam
+84 438253929

Opening hours	Open 7 days
Credit cards	Not accepted
Price range	Affordable
Style	Casual
Cuisine	Vietnamese
Recommended for	Bargain

EL GAUCHO

Recommended by
Donald Berger

99 Xuân Diệu
Hanoi
Hanoi 124403
Vietnam
+84 437186991
www.elgaucho.asia

Opening hours	Open 7 days
Credit cards	Accepted
Price range	Expensive
Style	Casual
Cuisine	Argentinian Steakhouse
Recommended for	Wish I'd opened

'Danny the owner opened these restaurants quickly, with incredible attention to detail and staff training. Simply well done.'—Donald Berger

LAKE VIEW FOOD CENTRE

Recommended by
Donald Berger

Hanoi Hotel
D8 Giảng Võ
Hanoi
Hanoi 118402
Vietnam
+84 438452270
www.hanoihotel.com.vn

Opening hours	Open 7 days
Credit cards	Accepted
Price range	Affordable
Style	Smart casual
Cuisine	Chinese
Recommended for	Late night

'It is the busiest late-night restaurant for delicious, fresh, hot Chinese noodles, dumplings, congee and vegetables.'—Donald Berger

MING

Recommended by
Donald Berger

Sofitel Plaza Hotel
1 Thanh Niên
Hanoi
Hanoi 119008
Vietnam
+84 438238888
www.sofitel.com

Opening hours	Open 7 days
Credit cards	Accepted
Price range	Expensive
Style	Smart casual
Cuisine	Dim Sum
Recommended for	Regular neighbourhood

'I have been a dim sum fan since my younger years in Canada, and then, when I was executive chef at the Ritz Carlton in Hong Kong, my appreciation and need for yum cha just continued to develop. The Sofitel Plaza's dim sum is one of the best in Hanoi – properly prepared to Hong Kong standards.'—Donald Berger

PHỞ HỌC GIA TRUYỀN

Recommended by
Donald Berger

40 Xuân Diệu
Hanoi
Hanoi 124403
Vietnam

Opening hours	Open 7 days
Reservation policy	No
Credit cards	Not accepted
Price range	Budget
Style	Casual
Cuisine	Vietnamese
Recommended for	Breakfast

'Pho bo is Vietnam's most classic breakfast dish: hot, savoury, aromatic, full of fresh herbs and flavour, and easy to digest. Streetside sitting, my Vietnamese wife loves it too and it is the best in our neighbourhood. About £1 ($2) a bowl and they don't put in MSG when asked. They have both the par-cooked and well-cooked beef for you to choose from or a combination of the two.'—Donald Berger

QUÁN ĂN NGON

18 Phan Bội Châu
Hanoi
Hanoi 111103
Vietnam
+84 439428162
www.ngonhanoi.com.vn

Opening hours	Open 7 days
Reservation policy	No
Credit cards	Accepted
Price range	Affordable
Style	Casual
Cuisine	Vietnamese
Recommended for	Local favourite

'They serve all the different street dishes in one location. It is chaotic.'—Donald Berger

If you fancy some street food but want the comfort of a restaurant, this buzzing converted French-style villa is for you. Within the restaurant a long list of regional specialities is served from stalls that are manned by former street-food cooks, so you really do get the best of both worlds. They claim to feed thousands of customers every day, many of them locals, who feast on the likes of *bánh canh cua* (crab noodle soup), *gỏi cuốn tôm thịt* (shrimp spring rolls), *nộm chim cút* (quail salad) and *miến xào lươn* (fried eel noodles).

SQUARE ONE

Park Hyatt Hotel
2 Lam Sơn
Ho Chi Minh
Ho Chi Minh 710155
Vietnam
+84 835202359
www.saigon.park.hyattrestaurants.com

Opening hours	Open 7 days
Credit cards	Accepted
Price range	Expensive
Style	Smart casual
Cuisine	Vietnamese-European
Recommended for	Worth the travel

FRUIT N SPICE

202b Jalan Sungai Pinang
Penang Island
Penang 11000
Malaysia
+6012-401 0101
www.fruitnspice.atspace.co.uk

Opening hours	Closed Monday to Friday
Credit cards	Not accepted
Price range	Budget
Style	Casual
Cuisine	Malaysian
Recommended for	Worth the travel

'It's cheap and tasty. A taste of Singapore.'
REIF OTHMAN P232

'STUNNING.'
CLAUS MEYER P233

'FREE-SPIRITED, REFINED AND BEAUTIFUL COOKING.'
TOM KERRIDGE P239

SINGAPORE

'Late at night I like to drop by for some sinful chicken wings.'
SEBASTIEN LEPINOY P236

'A timeless hawker stall'
ANDRÉ CHIANG P233

'Pick anything on the menu, it's sure to be fresh and delicious!'
DAVID ALMANY P233

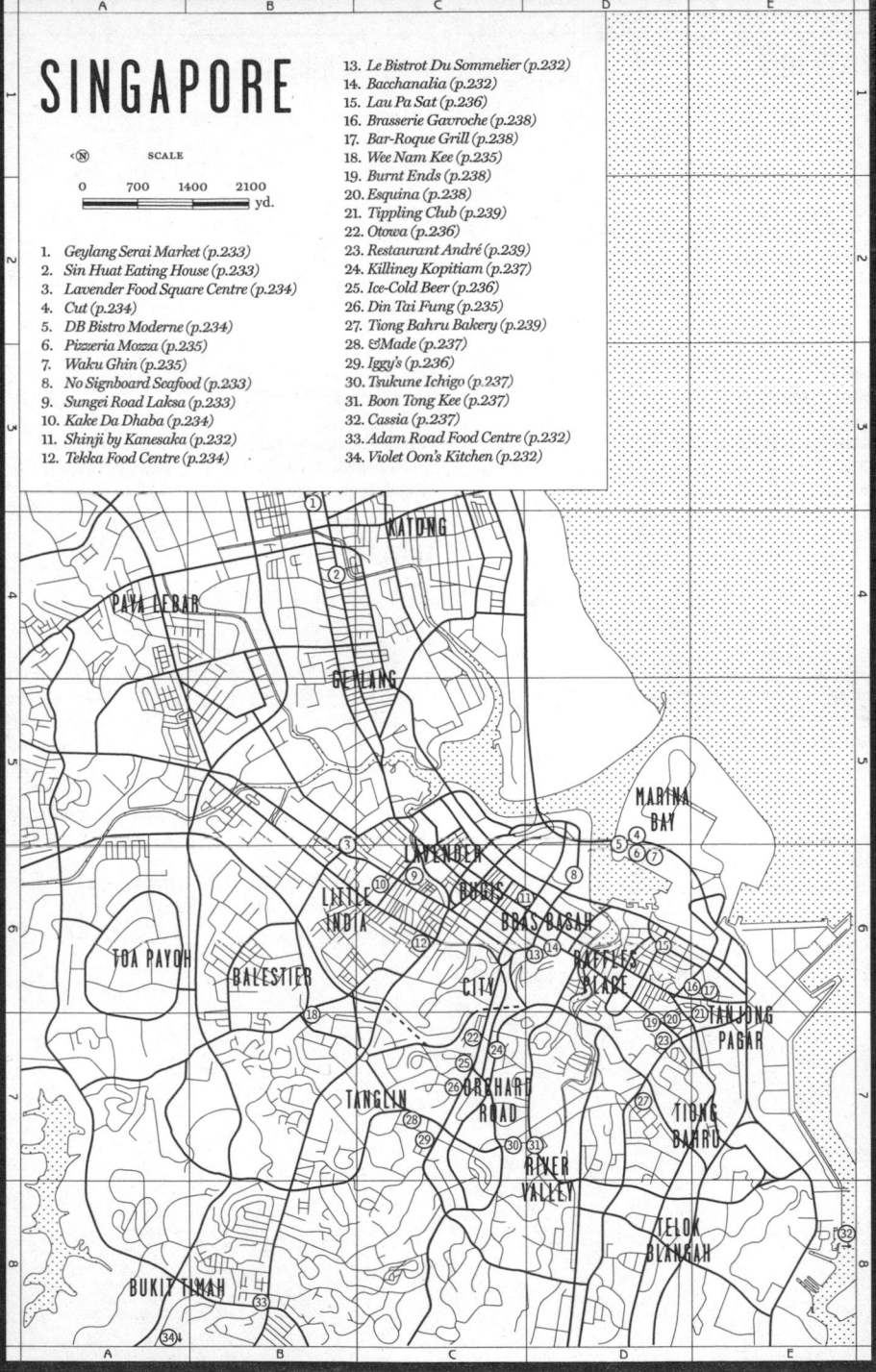

SINGAPORE

SCALE

0   700   1400   2100

yd.

BACCHANALIA

Recommended by
Chong Chee Loong

Masonic Club
23a Coleman Street
Bras Basah
Singapore
179806
+65 65091453
www.bacchanalia.asia

Opening hours	Closed Sunday
Credit cards	Accepted
Price range	Expensive
Style	Smart casual
Cuisine	Modern International
Recommended for	Worth the travel

'I love the ambience and the food. The portion size is perfect and you can share multiple dishes. Executive chef Ivan Brehm has good restaurant experience and is good with what he serves on the table. It's an impressive restaurant to visit.'—Chong Chee Loong

LE BISTROT DU SOMMELIER

Recommended by
Gunther Hubrechsen

53 Armenian Street
Bras Basah
Singapore
179940
+65 63331982
www.lebistrotdusommelier.com

Opening hours	Closed Sunday
Credit cards	Accepted
Price range	Affordable
Style	Smart casual
Cuisine	French
Recommended for	Regular neighbourhood

'This restaurant provides a warm and cosy environment that allows me to brainstorm new ideas for Gunther's.'
—Gunther Hubrechsen

SHINJI BY KANESAKA

Recommended by
Julien Royer

Raffles Hotel
1 Beach Road
Bras Basah
Singapore
189673
+65 63386131
www.shinjibykanesaka.com

Opening hours	Closed Sunday
Credit cards	Accepted
Price range	Expensive
Style	Smart casual
Cuisine	Japanese
Recommended for	High end

'The skills and precision of the Japanese chefs there is just unbelievable. The quality of sushi served and the unique atmosphere are amazing.'—Julien Royer

ADAM ROAD FOOD CENTRE

Recommended by
Reif Othman

2 Adam Road
Bukit Timah
Singapore
289876

Opening hours	Open 7 days
Reservation policy	No
Credit cards	Not accepted
Price range	Budget
Style	Casual
Cuisine	Singaporean Street Food
Recommended for	Bargain

'These places are like food courts that serve all kinds of food. It's cheap and tasty. A taste of Singapore.'
—Reif Othman

VIOLET OON'S KITCHEN
Recommended by
Reif Othman

881 Bukit Timah Road
Bukit Timah
Singapore
279893
+65 64685430
www.violetoonskitchen.com

Opening hours	Closed Monday
Credit cards	Accepted
Price range	Affordable
Style	Casual
Cuisine	Modern Singaporean
Recommended for	Local favourite

'The location is cool, away from the city. The ambience feels like that in New York but they serve very good Singaporean-Peranakan cuisine.'—Reif Othman

NO SIGNBOARD SEAFOOD
Recommended by
David Almany

414 Geylang Road
Geylang
Singapore
389392
+65 68423415
www.nosignboardseafood.com

Opening hours	Open 7 days
Credit cards	Accepted
Price range	Affordable
Style	Casual
Cuisine	Singaporean
Recommended for	Local favourite

'This place sums up Singapore. It is a casual and fun restaurant with unbelievable live seafood. Being here with a couple of good friends and having the chef cook whatever is best that day is a great experience. Pick anything on the menu, it's sure to be fresh and delicious!' —David Almany

SIN HUAT EATING HOUSE
Recommended by
Claus Meyer

659–661 Geylang Road
Geylang
Singapore
389589

Opening hours	Open 7 days
Reservation policy	No
Credit cards	Accepted
Price range	Expensive
Style	Casual
Cuisine	Seafood
Recommended for	Worth the travel

'Informal eatery with stunning food.'—Claus Meyer

GEYLANG SERAI MARKET
Recommended by
Reif Othman

1 Geylang Serai
Katong
Singapore
402001

Opening hours	Open 7 days
Reservation policy	No
Credit cards	Not accepted
Price range	Budget
Style	Casual
Cuisine	Indian-Malaysian Street Food
Recommended for	Bargain

SUNGEI ROAD LAKSA
Recommended by
André Chiang

Jin Shui Kopitiam
27 Jalan Berseh #01–100
Lavender
Singapore
200027

Opening hours	Open 7 days
Reservation policy	No
Credit cards	Not accepted
Price range	Budget
Style	Casual
Cuisine	Singaporean
Recommended for	Breakfast

'A timeless hawker stall. Charcoal-boiled soup, savoury broth with a light coconut fragrance, full-bodied yet light on the palette. At this hidden gem a breakfast laksa is still only SG$2 (£1; $1.50).'—André Chiang

KAKE DA DHABA
Recommended by
David Almany
Hawker Food Centre
Corner of Kitchener and Verdun Road
Little India
Singapore
207278

Opening hours	Open 7 days
Reservation policy	No
Credit cards	Not accepted
Price range	Budget
Style	Casual
Cuisine	Indian
Recommended for	Bargain

'My bargain choice is a small tandoori place called Kake Da Dhaba which is across from my apartment building. Lunch is about SG$10 (£5; $8), for which you will get naan and a large portion of very delicious tandoori chicken. Cheap eats with delicious food!'
—David Almany

LAVENDER FOOD SQUARE CENTRE
Recommended by
David Almany
380 Jalan Besar
Little India
Singapore
209000

Opening hours	Open 7 days
Reservation policy	No
Credit cards	Not accepted
Price range	Budget
Style	Casual
Cuisine	Singaporean Street Food
Recommended for	Late night

'I love going to local food stalls late at night such as the Lavender hawker centre. It has amazing local delicacies such as fried carrot cake and barbeque chicken wings. It's not a restaurant, but it has a lovely outdoor area with great local food and beer.'
—David Almany

TEKKA FOOD CENTRE
Recommended by
Reif Othman
Tekka Centre
665 Buffalo Road #01–201
Little India
Singapore
210665

Opening hours	Open 7 days
Reservation policy	No
Credit cards	Not accepted
Price range	Budget
Style	Casual
Cuisine	Indian Street Food
Recommended for	Bargain

CUT
Recommended by
David Almany
The Shoppes at Marina Bay
2 Bayfront Avenue #B1–71
Marina Bay
Singapore
018972
+65 66888517
www.wolfgangpuck.com

Opening hours	Open 7 days
Credit cards	Accepted
Price range	Expensive
Style	Smart casual
Cuisine	Steakhouse
Recommended for	Regular neighbourhood

DB BISTRO MODERNE
Recommended by
David Almany
The Shoppes at Marina Bay
2 Bayfront Avenue #B1–48
Marina Bay
Singapore
018956
+65 66888525
www.dbbistro.com/singapore

Opening hours	Open 7 days
Credit cards	Accepted
Price range	Expensive
Style	Smart casual
Cuisine	Modern European
Recommended for	Regular neighbourhood

'This is my favourite place for brunch. It's a bright, fun and lively restaurant. They have amazing seafood platters and the executive chef, Jonathan Kinsella, does great truffled scrambled eggs on brioche toast.'
—David Almany

PIZZERIA MOZZA

Recommended by
Massimo Bottura

The Shoppes at Marina Bay
2 Bayfront Avenue #B1–42/46
Marina Bay
Singapore
018972
+65 66888522
www.pizzeriamozza.com

Opening hours	Open 7 days
Credit cards	Accepted
Price range	Affordable
Style	Casual
Cuisine	Italian
Recommended for	Bargain

'Partly as a dare, partly as a joke, I was taken to Mozza in Singapore and it was a huge surprise! Really good pizza.'—Massimo Bottura

WAKU GHIN

Recommended by
David Almany, Anthony Lui,
Benoît Violier

Marina Bay Sands Hotel
10 Bayfront Avenue
Marina Bay
Singapore
018956
+65 66888507
www.marinabaysands.com

Opening hours	Open 7 days
Credit cards	Accepted
Price range	Expensive
Style	Smart casual
Cuisine	Modern Japanese
Recommended for	High end

'Probably one of the best concepts in the world as it is the most refined dining experience I've ever had. The best thing about it is you get to watch all the food being prepared right in front of you.'—David Almany

Marina Bay Sands did a smart thing in getting Tetsuya Wakuda to come and open his first venture outside Australia. This is luxury dining at its most exciting. Having cemented his reputation as one of the world's finest exponents of French-influenced Japanese cooking with Tetsuya's in Sydney, he has now created a whole new experience, where you are taken on a multi-course adventure, moving from room to room as you go. Start with aperitifs in the caviar lounge, move into your private dining room for the ten-course *omakase* menu, and wind up in the main dining room for desserts and digestifs, while enjoying fabulous views of Singapore.

WEE NAM KEE

Recommended by
Claus Meyer, Julien Royer

101 Thomson Road #01–08
Newton
Singapore
307591
+65 62556396

Opening hours	Open 7 days
Credit cards	Accepted
Price range	Affordable
Style	Casual
Cuisine	Hainanese
Recommended for	Bargain

'Fast, tasty and substantial food.'—Julien Royer

Hainanese chicken rice is a beloved staple at food courts and hawker centres across Singapore. The loud, busy, cheap and cheerful Wee Nam Kee is widely considered to offer the city-state's very best. The mini-chain's septuagenarian owner Wee Toon Ouut would put the popularity of his version down to the 'recipe' he has been refining since 1989. Its fans rave not only about the chicken poached in pandan-infused stock but also the fragrant rice and piquant chilli sauce. The original restaurant moved to United Square in 2013. They also run stalls at Gluttons Bay, Marina Square and 112 Katong.

DIN TAI FUNG

Recommended by
Julien Royer

Paragon Shopping Centre
290 Orchard Road
Orchard Road
Singapore
238859
+65 68368336
www.dintaifung.com.sg

Opening hours	Open 7 days
Reservation policy	No
Credit cards	Accepted
Price range	Affordable
Style	Casual
Cuisine	Taiwanese
Recommended for	Local favourite

'Always good, consistent, and their *xiao long bao* (soup dumplings) are delicious.'—Julien Royer

ICE-COLD BEER

9 Emerald Hill Road
Orchard Road
Singapore
229293
+65 67359929
www.ice-cold-beer.com

Opening hours	Open 7 days
Credit cards	Accepted
Price range	Budget
Style	Casual
Cuisine	Bar Snacks
Recommended for	Late night

'Late at night I like to drop by this place for some sinful chicken wings (which might just be the best in town). They also serve outstanding potato chips (fries) that go well with the garlic mayonnaise sauce.'
—Sebastien Lepinoy

IGGY'S

The Hilton Hotel
581 Orchard Road
Orchard Road
Singapore
238883
+65 67322234
www.iggys.com.sg

Opening hours	Closed Sunday
Credit cards	Accepted
Price range	Expensive
Style	Smart casual
Cuisine	International
Recommended for	Worth the travel

'This is a swish restaurant where I've always wanted to have a meal! I went there as part of the group of chefs from India and China on a chef exchange programme through Singapore Tourism. The cuisine is progressive and modern and incorporates ideas and ingredients from Europe, Asia and Australia. We were overwhelmed by the dining experience which was a treat for any chef! The detailing was absolutely brilliant and the whole experience made me proud to belong to this great food industry!'—Naren Thimmaiah

OTOWA

Orchard Plaza
150 Orchard Road 03–16
Orchard Road
Singapore
238841
+65 67335989

Opening hours	Closed Sunday
Credit cards	Accepted
Price range	Affordable
Style	Casual
Cuisine	Japanese
Recommended for	Regular neighbourhood

'It's a small yakitori restaurant in Orchard plaza. I like it because it's a small and intimate restaurant with just twelve seats and one chef preparing the dishes. The experience is very personal.'—David Almany

LAU PA SAT

18 Raffles Quay
Raffles Place
Singapore
048582
+65 62202138
www.laupasat.biz

Opening hours	Open 7 days
Reservation policy	No
Credit cards	Not accepted
Price range	Budget
Style	Casual
Cuisine	Singaporean Street Food
Recommended for	Late night

'I love Cantonese food so my favourite supper is usually a bowl of wonton noodles. Also, after a busy night, I will treat myself to some good dim sum.'
—Gunther Hubrechsen

BOON TONG KEE

Recommended by
Sebastien Lepinoy

425 River Valley Road
River Valley
Singapore
248324
+65 67363213
www.boontongkee.com.sg

Opening hours	Open 7 days
Reservation policy	No
Credit cards	Accepted
Price range	Budget
Style	Casual
Cuisine	Singaporean
Recommended for	Local favourite

'Chicken rice is definitely my favourite local food that I think is iconic to Singapore. The quality and flavour of the rice is key for me and it goes extremely well with a touch of ginger and spicy chilli sauce. It is simply amazing.'—Sebastien Lepinoy

TSUKUNE ICHIGO

Recommended by
Naoya Ueno

399 River Valley Road
River Valley
Singapore
248295
+65 67361340

Opening hours	Closed Sunday
Credit cards	Accepted
Price range	Affordable
Style	Casual
Cuisine	Yakitori
Recommended for	Worth the travel

'The chef offers very delicious yakitori.'—Naoya Ueno

CASSIA

Recommended by
Anatoly Komm

Capella Hotel
1 The Knolls
Sentosa Island
Singapore
098297
+65 65915045
www.capellahotels.com/singapore

Opening hours	Open 7 days
Credit cards	Accepted
Price range	Expensive
Style	Smart casual
Cuisine	Modern Chinese
Recommended for	Worth the travel

KILLINEY KOPITIAM

Recommended by
Gunther Hubrechsen,
Sebastien Lepinoy

67 Killiney Road
Somerset
Singapore
239525
+65 67349648
www.killiney-kopitiam.com

Opening hours	Open 7 days
Reservation policy	No
Credit cards	Not accepted
Price range	Budget
Style	Casual
Cuisine	Café
Recommended for	Breakfast

'Here I like to have kaya toast. It's such a classic Asian breakfast I never get tired of it. I like the mix of soft-boiled eggs with the soy sauce. The highlight is the layer of *kaya* (coconut jam) that is sweet and goes well with the crispy toasted bread.'—Sebastien Lepinoy

&MADE

Recommended by
Sebastien Lepinoy

Pacific Plaza
9 Scotts Road #01–04–06
Tanglin
Singapore
228210
+65 66907566
www.andmade.sg

Opening hours	Open 7 days
Reservation policy	No
Credit cards	Accepted
Price range	Affordable
Style	Casual
Cuisine	Burgers
Recommended for	Regular neighbourhood

'&Made is my favourite burger place in Singapore at the moment. The ambience and vibe of the restaurant is really fun and the burgers are unique as well. There is a French touch that is brought to the table by Chef Bruno Menard that I really like and the sauces go so well on the side. The portion of the burger is also adapted to the local market (it's not too big).'
—Sebastien Lepinoy

BAR-ROQUE GRILL

165 Tanjong Pagar Road #01–00
Tanjong Pagar
Singapore
088539
+65 64449672
www.bar-roque.com.sg

Opening hours	Closed Monday
Credit cards	Accepted
Price range	Affordable
Style	Casual
Cuisine	International
Recommended for	Late night

'The food and drinks are as good and generous as the owners Kori and Stephane. His tarte flambée is fantastic.'—Julien Royer

BRASSERIE GAVROCHE

66 Tras Street
Tanjong Pagar
Singapore
079005
+65 62258266
www.brasseriegavroche.com

Opening hours	Closed Sunday
Credit cards	Accepted
Price range	Affordable
Style	Casual
Cuisine	French Brasserie
Recommended for	Regular neighbourhood

'Really good comfort food, great ambience and good value.'—Julien Royer

BURNT ENDS

20 Teck Lim Road
Tanjong Pagar
Singapore
088391
+65 62243933
www.burntends.com.sg

Opening hours	Closed Monday and Sunday
Credit cards	Accepted
Price range	Affordable
Style	Casual
Cuisine	Australian Barbeque
Recommended for	Worth the travel

'Rustic, down-to-earth yet delicate flavours, friendly and fun atmosphere sitting at the counter talking to Chef Dave. The daily-changing menu keeps me excited every time I visit. It's the only "bistronomy" restaurant in this part of Asia.'—André Chiang

The impressively bearded Australian chef Dave Pynt, who has a pedigree cooking at some of the best restaurants in the world, mans a monster grill in this enormously popular barbecue restaurant, the permanent incarnation of a pop-up he ran in east London. Pynt showcases the extraordinary versatility of this seemingly primitive cooking method, using it to alternately black and char Japanese sea bream previously marinaded in soy and mirin, or to coax the sweetness out of leek hearts. As well as the eighteen-seat wooden counter, for which there are no bookings, there's a private chef's table with a relatively high minimum spend. The smoked quail's eggs are legendary.

ESQUINA

16 Jiak Chuan Road
Tanjong Pagar
Singapore
089267
+65 62221616
www.esquina.com.sg

Opening hours	Closed Monday and Sunday
Reservation policy	No
Credit cards	Accepted
Price range	Affordable
Style	Casual
Cuisine	Spanish Tapas
Recommended for	Worth the travel

Jason Atherton is the chef who set up and launched the all-conquering Maze for Gordon Ramsay, before leaving to open his own acclaimed London restaurant, Pollen Street Social. Esquina, opened in 2011, is his take on a modern Spanish tapas bar, in the unexpected setting that is a post-war colonial building in Singapore's Chinatown. The vibe is casual-chic, a classic L-shaped counter with rather trendy industrial-styled stools, the menu divided simply into five short sections: snacks, including jamon croquetas or crispy baby squid with black ink aïoli; soil; sea; land; desserts. The snappy menu is supplemented by daily specials. Add to that an all-Spanish beer list and servings of sangria.

RESTAURANT ANDRÉ

Recommended by
Pascal Barbot, Tom Kerridge,
Hadleigh Troy, Simon Wright

41 Bukit Pasoh Road
Tanjong Pagar
Singapore
089855
+65 65348880
www.restaurantandre.com

Opening hours	Closed Monday
Credit cards	Accepted
Price range	Expensive
Style	Smart casual
Cuisine	Modern French
Recommended for	Worth the travel

'Free-spirited, refined and beautiful cooking and a chef completely at one with his own style of food.'
—Tom Kerridge

This nineteenth-century terraced house, decked out in antler lampshades, clay figurines and organic crockery, is an atmospheric canvas for Taiwanese-born, French-trained chef André Chiang's artful 'octaphilosophy'. It might sound fishy, but in fact the concept represents the key characteristics of his exploratory eight-course tasting menu: namely, artisan, memory, pure, salt, south, terroir, texture and unique. From warm foie gras jelly with black truffle coulis (memory) to potato gnocchi and caviar (texture), each nouvelle-cuisine-style course comes with a lengthy blurb, but relies on just a few ingredients to work its magic. Natural wines add to the heady mood.

TIPPLING CLUB

Recommended by
Armin Leitgeb

38 Tanjong Pagar Road
Tanjong Pagar
Singapore
088461
+65 64752217
www.tipplingclub.com

Opening hours	Closed Sunday
Credit cards	Accepted
Price range	Expensive
Style	Smart casual
Cuisine	Modern European
Recommended for	Worth the travel

'Ryan Clift is an amazingly creative chef who lives for his job. Experiments are developed until they become a unique new creation.'—Armin Leitgeb

TIONG BAHRU BAKERY

Recommended by
Julien Royer

56 Eng Hoon Street #01–70
Tiong Bahru
Singapore
160056
+65 62203430
www.tiongbahrubakery.com

Opening hours	Open 7 days
Reservation policy	No
Credit cards	Accepted
Price range	Budget
Style	Casual
Cuisine	Café-Bakery
Recommended for	Breakfast

'I like the croissants and the Viennoiseries in general.'
—Julien Royer

BABI GULING CHANDRA

Recommended by
Will Meyrick

Jalan Teuku Umar 140
Denpasar
Bali 80114
Indonesia
+62 361221278

Opening hours	Open 7 days
Reservation policy	No
Credit cards	Not accepted
Price range	Budget
Style	Casual
Cuisine	Balinese
Recommended for	Local favourite

'I'm a big fan of street food and I travel all over Indonesia to search for the best of it. In the city I live in, street food is everywhere but it's not really easy to find the right combination of authenticity and good taste. Babi Guling Chandra has both.'—Will Meyrick

CAFÉ BATU JIMBAR

Recommended by
Chris Salans

Jalan Danau Tamblingan 75a
Denpasar
Bali 80228
Indonesia
+62 361284103
www.cafebatujimbar.com

Opening hours	Open 7 days
Credit cards	Accepted
Price range	Affordable
Style	Casual
Cuisine	Asian Fusion
Recommended for	Breakfast

'I just love this place for the atmosphere and their selection of cakes. But overall they have a great selection of dishes – breakfast and others – and a special food market on Sundays.'—Chris Salans

KURA KURA

Recommended by
Chris Salans

The Oberoi
Seminyak Beach
Denpasar
Bali 80361
Indonesia
+62 361730361
www.oberoihotels.com/oberoi_bali

Opening hours	Open 7 days
Credit cards	Accepted
Price range	Affordable
Style	Smart casual
Cuisine	Asian-European
Recommended for	High end

'Chef Enrico, who has been in Bali for several years now, does a multi-course tasting menu showcasing beautiful ingredients and modern techniques of cooking and presentation. A job very well done.'—Chris Salans

MAMA SAN

Recommended by
Tomi Björck,
Agus Hermawan,
Chris Salans

Jalan Raya Kerobokan 135
Denpasar
Bali 80361
Indonesia
+62 361730436
www.mamasanbali.com

Opening hours	Open 7 days
Credit cards	Accepted
Price range	Affordable
Style	Smart casual
Cuisine	Pan-Asian
Recommended for	Local favourite

'With a wide variety of Thai, Indonesian and Malaysian dishes this is the best place in town for a tasty and refreshing take on Southeast Asian cuisine.'
—Chris Salans

Chesterfields, vintage clocks and atmospheric 1920s prints lend Mama San restaurant, bar and cookery school a colonial feel despite the building's robust, industrial fabric. The menu shows founder Will Meyrick's far-reaching curiosity for Asia. Dishes include roast Peking-style duck with steamed choy sum and red bean sauce, Burmese short rib beef curry with garam masala, and Thai fishcakes with pickled cucumber. Drinks range from Earl Grey tea to 'energizers', and lattes to lassis – and even a Lychee Tiffin Punch. Take note: despite friendly prices, Mama San's management seeks a classy clientele – hence guests wearing 'branded singlets, boardshorts or thongs' are advised to find another haunt.

CUCA

Recommended by
Florian Lamelot

Jalan Yoga Perkanthi
Jimbaran
Bali 80364
Indonesia
+62 361708066
www.cucaflavor.com

Opening hours...Open 7 days
Credit cards...Accepted but not AMEX
Price range...Affordable
Style...Casual
Cuisine...Tapas
Recommended for...............................Local favourite

'I love this place. They opened in 2013 and are already well known in Bali. The seating is great, Chef Kevin creates tasteful tapas/molecular dishes using 100 per cent local ingredients. I recommend the baby octopus or the roasted tiger prawns (jumbo shrimp). I also love their cocktails.'—Florian Lamelot

TEBA MEGA CAFÉ

Recommended by
Florian Lamelot

Jalan Four Seasons Resort
Pantai Muaya
Jimbaran
Bali 80361
Indonesia
+62 361703156
www.indo.com/restaurants/tebacafe

Opening hours...Open 7 days
Credit cards...Not accepted
Price range...Affordable
Style...Casual
Cuisine..Seafood
Recommended for...............................Local favourite

'Teba Mega Café is a very good seafood restaurant in south Jimbaran beach and prices here are still very affordable compared to the north side of Jimbaran. Perfect for sitting on the beach and eating fresh seafood, Balinese style, while enjoying the sunset.' —Florian Lamelot

SARONG

Recommended by
Agus Hermawan

Jalan Petitenget 19
Kerobokan
Bali 80361
Indonesia
+62 3614737809
www.sarongbali.com

Opening hours...Open 7 days
Credit cards..Accepted
Price range...Affordable
Style...Smart casual
Cuisine..Pan-Asian
Recommended for.............................Worth the travel

'The best place for a good meal in Bali. They serve a modern mix of South Asian cuisine.'—Agus Hermawan

WATERCRESS CAFE

Recommended by
Will Meyrick

Jalan Batu Belig 21a
Kerobokan
Bali 80361
Indonesia
+62 3617808030
www.watercressbali.com

Opening hours...Open 7 days
Credit cards...Not accepted
Price range...Affordable
Style...Casual
Cuisine..International
Recommended for..Breakfast

'The food is fresh and the menu has a wide variety, exploring various different flavours. My favourites are the light salads. The crispy sweetcorn cake is a perfect match for the well-made coffee.'—Will Meyrick

CAFÉ ZUCCHINI
Recommended by
Will Meyrick

Jalan Laksamana 49
Kuta
Bali 80361
Indonesia
+62 361736633

Opening hours	Open 7 days
Reservation policy	No
Credit cards	Not accepted
Price range	Budget
Style	Casual
Cuisine	Café
Recommended for	Regular neighbourhood

'Nice vibe with a great range of fresh and clean food options. The menu is simple but it hits the spot every time. After cooking heavily spiced food like I do every night, it is very refreshing.'—Will Meyrick

MADE'S WARUNG
Recommended by
Arjan Wennekes

Jalan Raya Seminyak
Kuta
Bali 80361
Indonesia
+62 361732130
www.madeswarung.com

Opening hours	Open 7 days
Credit cards	Accepted
Price range	Affordable
Style	Casual
Cuisine	Indonesian
Recommended for	Worth the travel

'When I think of this place I want to get on a plane immediately. The food is like a dream and the whole restaurant is in the open air. I've eaten the best gado gado and nasi campur here.'—Arjan Wennekes

Indicative of what's happened to Bali itself, and Seminyak in particular, what was once a sleepy spot serving simple, delicious local dishes has evolved into a slick operation complete with a range of branded merchandise. But much of what made Made's Warung so special when it first opened way back in 1969 – from the reasonably priced menu made up of satays, nasi goreng and gado gado, to the atmosphere in this impressive old wooden pavilion – is all still present and correct. Book in advance to tuck into a whole suckling pig or the Balinese speciality that is *bebek bututu* (twenty-four-hour roast duck).

SARI RATU PADANG
Recommended by
Will Meyrick

Jalan Sunset Road
Jalan Sri Dewi Intersection
Kuta
Bali 80361
Indonesia
+62 3618947482

Opening hours	Open 7 days
Credit cards	Accepted but not AMEX
Price range	Budget
Style	Casual
Cuisine	Indonesian
Recommended for	Late night

'After a big night out I always crave something hot and spicy. Nothing beats *nasi padang* (steamed rice with vegetable and meat dishes). And this restaurant serves a wide range of authentic, heavily spiced dishes to please everyone. A good way to end a night.'
—Will Meyrick

NYOMAN'S BEER GARDEN
Recommended by
Florian Lamelot

Jalan Pantai Mengiat
Nusa Dua
Bali 80361
Indonesia
+62 361775746
www.sendok-bali.com/nyoman-beergarden

Opening hours	Open 7 days
Credit cards	Accepted
Price range	Affordable
Style	Casual
Cuisine	International
Recommended for	Bargain

'A nice little restaurant located in Nusa Dua. The food is simple but delicious, and you can count on Andreas the chef-owner to take good care of you. I always go for one of his German specialities, cheese and ham *spaetzle* (egg noodle or dumpling).'—Florian Lamelot

GOURMET CAFÉ

Jalan Petitenget 77a
Seminyak
Bali 80361
Indonesia
+62 3618095188
www.balicateringcompany.com/cafe

Opening hours	Open 7 days
Reservation policy	No
Credit cards	Accepted but not AMEX
Price range	Budget
Style	Casual
Cuisine	Café
Recommended for	Bargain

'The staff here are great, nothing is ever too much or too little for them. They always deliver appropriate service. The place has nice choices of food. Salad lovers can have do-it-yourself salads at lunch, but for me, the roasted chicken and broccoli is the best dish of all. It's simple yet tasty.'—Will Meyrick

KU DE TA

Jalan Kayu Aya 9
Seminyak
Bali 80361
Indonesia
+62 361736969
www.kudeta.net

Opening hours	Open 7 days
Credit cards	Accepted
Price range	Affordable
Style	Smart casual
Cuisine	Modern International
Recommended for	Late night

'This is one of the places to go to when visiting Bali. The seating is gorgeous and the service efficient. The food is great too! The chef knows how to please every guest. From casual fine dining to international tapas and great cocktails, Ku De Ta is always at the top of its game.'—Florian Lamelot

PETITENGET

Jalan Petitenget 40x
Seminyak
Bali 80361
Indonesia
+62 3614733054
www.petitenget.net

Opening hours	Open 7 days
Credit cards	Accepted
Price range	Affordable
Style	Casual
Cuisine	International
Recommended for	Regular neighbourhood

RYOSHI

Jalan Sunset Road 77x
Seminyak
Bali 80361
Indonesia
+62 3618475950
www.ryoshibali.com

Opening hours	Open 7 days
Credit cards	Accepted
Price range	Budget
Style	Casual
Cuisine	Japanese
Recommended for	Wish I'd opened

'There are many restaurants I admire but mostly because I love their cuisine. One that I admire because I wish I had opened it? Maybe Ryoshi, a Japanese food chain, because the owner has several outlets in Bali, they are all very busy and he seems to always be enjoying himself, travelling and having fun. I wish I knew how to run a restaurant and not be there day in and day out!'—Chris Salans

WARUNG KOLEGA

Jalan Petitenget 98a
Seminyak
Bali 80361
Indonesia
+62 3614732480

Opening hours	Closed Sunday
Reservation policy	No
Credit cards	Not accepted
Price range	Budget
Style	Casual
Cuisine	Indonesian
Recommended for	Bargain

'Along with *kaki limas* (food carts), *warungs* (small local cafés) offer a large selection of dishes from across Indonesia so they are a great way to a) discover new things and b) choose what you want or like to eat.'
—Chris Salans

IBU OKA

Jalan Suweta/Tegal Sari 2
Ubud
Bali 80571
Indonesia
+62 361976345

Opening hours	Open 7 days
Reservation policy	No
Credit cards	Not accepted
Price range	Affordable
Style	Casual
Cuisine	Balinese
Recommended for	Worth the travel

'The restaurant is basically a very simple setup where people sit on the floor in the village meeting hall. The secret is all in the suckling pig, stuffed with Balinese spices and spit-roasted to perfection, served with all the trimmings deep fried in different ways: blood sausage, coconut, mixed green vegetables and the roasting juices of the pig. Simply amazing!'—Chris Salans

LOCAVORE

Jalan Dewi Sita
Ubud
Bali 80571
Indonesia
+62 361977733

Opening hours	Closed Sunday
Credit cards	Accepted
Price range	Affordable
Style	Casual
Cuisine	European-Asian
Recommended for	High end

'As I'm Scottish, I like to get the best value for every penny I spend. Recently, I went to a restaurant called Locavore. It was a nice surprise. I would definitely go there again for a special occasion.'—Will Meyrick

JU-MA-NA

Banjar Kelod
Ungasan
Bali 80364
Indonesia
+62 3613007000
www.banyantree.com/en/bali_ungasan

Opening hours	Closed Monday
Credit cards	Accepted
Price range	Expensive
Style	Smart casual
Cuisine	Modern Seafood
Recommended for	High end

'This stunning sea-view restaurant in the Ungasan area offers an innovative French molecular menu. The food is well executed; the service is efficient and professional with the unique view of the cliff overlooking the ocean. You can go for their set menu or à la carte. My favourite was the wagyu duo with red wine sauce.'
—Florian Lamelot

BANDAR JAKARTA

Recommended by
Florian Lamelot

Pintu Pintu Timur Taman Impian Jaya Ancol
Jakarta
DKI Jakarta 14430
Indonesia
+62 216455472
www.bandar-djakarta.com

Opening hours	Open 7 days
Reservation policy	No
Credit cards	Not accepted
Price range	Affordable
Style	Casual
Cuisine	Seafood
Recommended for	Local favourite

'Located in south Jakarta, this place is one of a kind. Serving up to five thousand covers a day, from live Alaskan king crab, Brittany blue lobster and most of the local live seafood that you can find in Indonesia. I don't go there for the seating or the attentive service but for the freshness of the seafood, grilled the Indonesian way.'—Florian Lamelot

A rumoured capacity of 1,800 at the Ancol branch of this famous seafood restaurant only seems credible when you witness its scale: a colourful, canopied monolith set in a theme park next to a man-made lagoon. Much of the seafood, including the lobsters, is sold live, displayed in bubbling fish tanks from where you can select your dinner. Black pepper crab, grilled octopus and clams with black beans are three of the most famous dishes. Arrive early to watch the sun set over the water. The original has now expanded into three further branches.

BEAUTIKA

Recommended by
Florian Lamelot

Jalan Hang Lekir 1
Jakarta
DKI Jakarta 12120
Indonesia
+62 217226683
www.beautika.net

Opening hours	Open 7 days
Credit cards	Accepted
Price range	Affordable
Style	Casual
Cuisine	Indonesian
Recommended for	Local favourite

'A well-known local restaurant serving a variety of Indonesian food from Manado, North Sulawesi. My favourite dishes are *cakalang* (tuna) and roa fish served with a traditional chilli called *dabu-dabu*. Most of the dishes here are spicy but you can also experience the strong flavour of Indonesian food.'— Florian Lamelot

SKYE

Recommended by
Florian Lamelot

BCA Tower
56F, Jalan M.H. Thamrin Grand Indonesia
Jakarta
DKI Jakarta 10310
Indonesia
+62 2123586996
www.ismaya.com

Opening hours	Open 7 days
Credit cards	Accepted
Price range	Affordable
Style	Smart casual
Cuisine	International
Recommended for	Late night

'This is a stylish, unique restaurant with a 180-degree view of Jakarta. Divided in two, it has an open-air bar serving finger food outside and a Japanese restaurant indoors. The wine and drinks are a good price for Jakarta. The Japanese food on the other side is also quite good but it's the view and the ambience that make the place a stunning spot.' —Florian Lamelot

UNION

Recommended by
Florian Lamelot

Plaza Senayan Courtyard
Jalan Asia Afrika 8
Jakarta
DKI Jakarta 12220
Indonesia
+62 215790586162
www.unionjkt.com

Opening hours	Open 7 days
Credit cards	Accepted
Price range	Affordable
Style	Casual
Cuisine	Brasserie
Recommended for	Local favourite

'Union is one of the busiest places around Senayan that does this New York brasserie style. They serve simple but tasteful dishes with an international touch. The restaurant is busy all day. The ambience is cosmopolitan and refers back to the 1920s. I recommend the whole roasted baby chicken or their pasta.'—Florian Lamelot

VIN+
Jalan Kemang Raya 45b
South Jakarta
DKI Jakarta 12730
Indonesia
+62 2171792577
www.vingroup.biz

Opening hours	Open 7 days
Credit cards	Accepted
Price range	Affordable
Style	Casual
Cuisine	International
Recommended for	Bargain

'Vin+ is a tapas restaurant with a wine cellar. A good
Indonesian chef handles the food, and you can get a
bottle of wine for less than IDR250,000 (£13; $22).
Good food, affordable wine and cosy ambience.'
—Florian Lamelot

GRACE PARK
One Rockwell
GF, Rockwell Drive
Makati City
Metropolitan Manila 1224
Philippines
+63 9399347223

Opening hours	Open 7 days
Credit cards	Accepted
Price range	Affordable
Style	Casual
Cuisine	Italian Bistro
Recommended for	Wish I'd opened

'A farm-to-table menu philosophy. Interiors with a
modern take on shabby chic. Casual but always attentive
service staff. This is a Margarita Fores (the chef and
owner) restaurant at its best.'—Antonio Escalante

TERRY'S
Unit 2 Karrivin Plaza
2316 Pasong Tamo Extension
Makati City
Metropolitan Manila 1223
Philippines
+63 28441816

Opening hours	Open 7 days
Credit cards	Accepted
Price range	Affordable
Style	Casual
Cuisine	Spanish-Basque
Recommended for	Local favourite

'The owner, Juan Carlos de Terry, is a man whose passion
for all things Spanish permeates every aspect of this
iconic Manila restaurant.'—Antonio Escalante

UMU
Dusit Thani Manila Hotel
Ayala Centre
Makati City
Metropolitan Manila 1223
Philippines
+63 22388888
www.dusit.com

Opening hours	Open 7 days
Credit cards	Accepted
Price range	Expensive
Style	Smart casual
Cuisine	Japanese
Recommended for	High end

'Besides the beautiful interiors and attentive service, the
menu is the epitome of elegant simplicity, highlighting
a love for the best ingredients and the importance of
striking visual presentation.'—Antonio Escalante

RAMEN YUSHOKEN

Molito Lifestyle Centre
Madrigal Avenue
Muntinlupa City
Metropolitan Manila 1780
Philippines
+63 28087424

Opening hours...Open 7 days
Reservation policy..No
Credit cards...Accepted
Price range..Budget
Style..Casual
Cuisine...Ramen Noodles
Recommended for...............................Regular neighbourhood

'Why? Because a large, steaming-hot bowl of ramen with a cold Japanese craft beer is a necessity of life.' —Antonio Escalante

NEW HARLEM RESTAURANT

1300 Antonio Arnaiz Avenue
Pasay City
Metropolitan Manila 1300
Philippines
+63 28316128

Opening hours...Open 7 days
Reservation policy..No
Credit cards...Accepted
Price range..Budget
Style..Casual
Cuisine...Filipino-Chinese
Recommended for...Bargain

'Walk too fast and you might miss this hole-in-the-wall establishment. Located in the heart of Pasay City, New Harlem serves Filipino-Chinese classics. The food may be simple but eating here always makes me giddy with excitement.'—Antonio Escalante

JT'S MANUKAN

4 Granada
Quezon City
Metropolitan Manila 1112
Philippines
+63 27219025

Opening hours...Open 7 days
Reservation policy..No
Credit cards...Not accepted
Price range..Budget
Style..Casual
Cuisine...Filipino
Recommended for...Late night

'After a late night of drinking or when I'm missing the tastes of my home province, this open-air sidewalk restaurant hits the spot with the best chicken *inasal* (grilled chicken) I have ever tasted in Manila.' —Antonio Escalante

GLORIA MARIS

Greenhills Shopping Center
Ortigas Avenue
San Juan
Metropolitan Manila 1503
Philippines
+63 25700921

Opening hours...Open 7 days
Credit cards...Accepted
Price range..Affordable
Style..Casual
Cuisine...Cantonese
Recommended for..Breakfast

'Gloria Maris is a Cantonese cuisine institution. Early mornings always start better eating a bowl of congee topped with slices of century eggs and a side of fried bread. All washed down with a glass of soy milk.' —Antonio Escalante

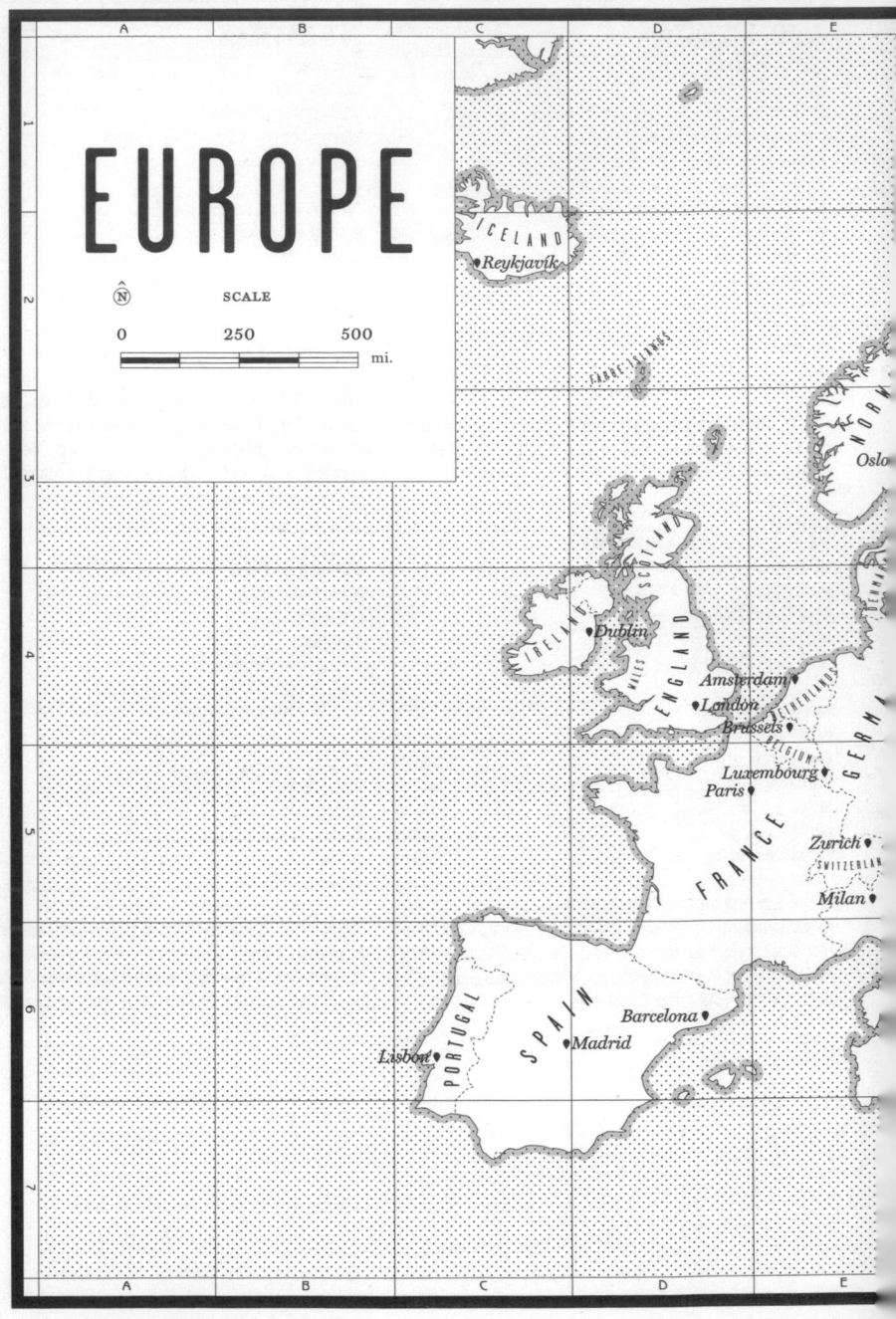

EUROPE

N

SCALE

0   250   500 mi.

ICELAND
Reykjavík

NORW
Oslo

SCOTLAND

IRELAND
Dublin
WALES
ENGLAND
Amsterdam
London
Brussels
NETHERLAND
BELGIUM
Luxembourg
Paris
GERMA

Zurich
SWITZERLAN
Milan

FRANCE

PORTUGAL
Lisbon
SPAIN
Madrid
Barcelona

SWEDEN

FINLAND

RUSSIA

●Helsinki
●Tallinn

●Stockholm

ESTONIA

Moscow ●

●Riga

LATVIA

enhagen

lin

POLAND

●Prague

H REPUBLIC

enna ●

 RIA

LOVENIA

ne

ITALY

GREECE

●Istanbul

TURKEY

●Athens

'IT IS A SCANDINAVIAN RESTAURANT THAT WORKS WITH INGREDIENTS YOU CAN'T FIND ANYWHERE ELSE. YOU'LL FIND A LITTLE BIT OF EVERYTHING IN THEIR KITCHEN.'

FLORA MIKULA P253

ICELAND

'HOME-MADE SOUPS SERVED IN BREAD. GOOD COMFORT FOOD.'

THRAINN FREYR VIGFUSSON P253

'Old-school Icelandic. Whale, puffin, fermented shark... It has been there forever and they aren't going anywhere. As classic as it gets.'

GUNNAR KARL GÍSLASON P252

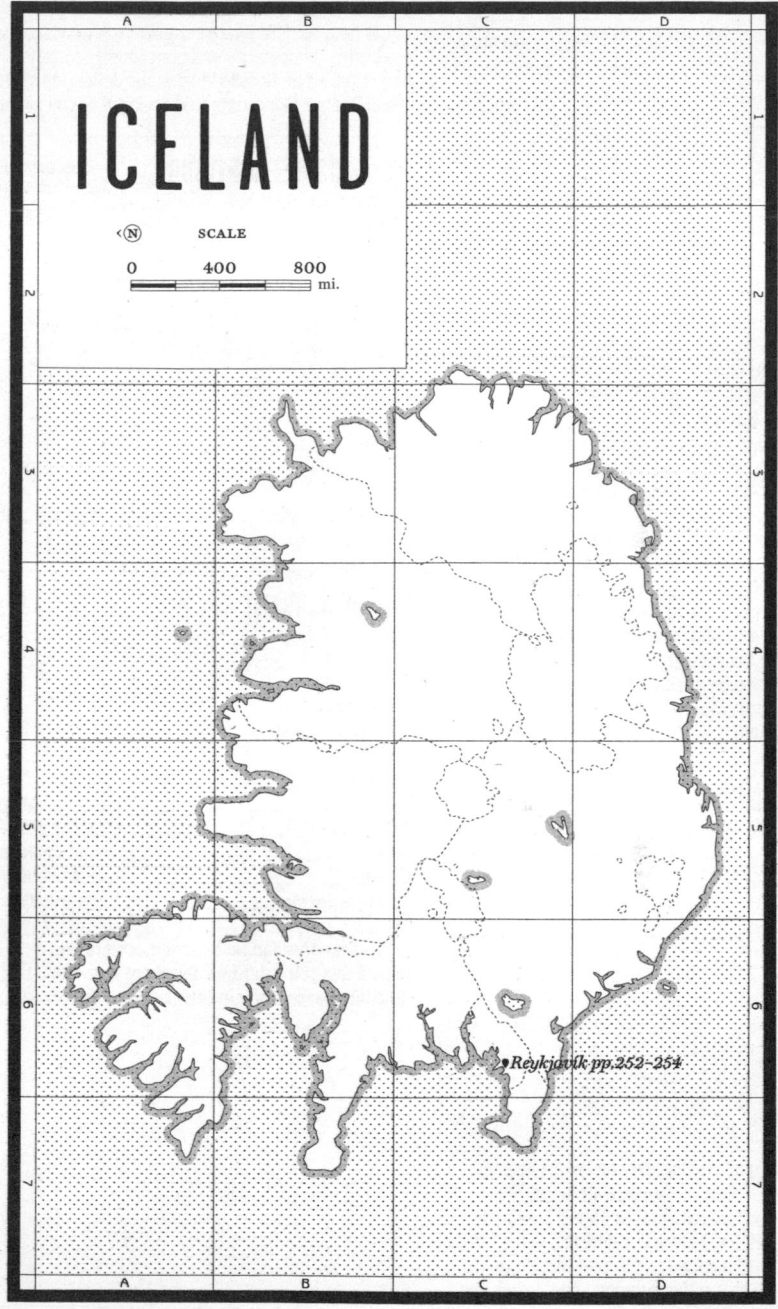

ICELAND

N SCALE

0   400   800 mi.

●Reykjavik pp.252-254

3 FRAKKAR

Baldursgata 14
Reykjavík 101
+354 5523939
www.3frakkar.com

Recommended by
Gunnar Karl Gíslason,
Agnar Sverrisson

Opening hours	Open 7 days
Credit cards	Accepted
Price range	Affordable
Style	Casual
Cuisine	Icelandic
Recommended for	Local favourite

'Old-school Icelandic. Whale, puffin, fermented shark and so on. It has been there forever and they aren't going anywhere. As classic as it gets.'
—Gunnar Karl Gíslason

This family-run Reykjavik institution is a one-stop shop for traditional Icelandic produce, with a loyal local following to prove it. Don't be deterred by the rundown of native specialities such as smoked puffin breast, fried cod chins, guillemot with game sauce and whale sashimi (though only those with Viking blood should tackle the fermented shark). Presentation is far more familiar than the ingredients, with the odd cheffy flourish, and once you're settled into the cosy, old-fashioned dining room, you'll feel right at home. For best value – and almost the same menu – go at lunchtime.

BAKARÍ SANDHOLT

Laugavegur 36
Hverafold 1–3
Reykjavík 101
+354 5513524
www.sandholt.is

Recommended by
Thrainn Freyr Vigfússon

Opening hours	Open 7 days
Reservation policy	No
Credit cards	Accepted but not AMEX or Diners
Price range	Budget
Style	Casual
Cuisine	Café-Bakery
Recommended for	Breakfast

Reykjavik's longest-running artisan bakery opened in 1920 and has been family-run ever since. The award-winning chocolate maker Ásgeir Sandholt, who studied painting before deciding to join the family business, is the fourth generation of the Icelandic baking dynasty to run this shop on Laugavegur, the city's historic central shopping street. Iceland does not have a long history of baking but much of what's on offer at this coffeehouse would not look out of place at the best Parisian patisseries. Macaroons, cakes, croissants, chocolates and generously stuffed baguettes sit alongside indigenous delicacies such as the doughnut-like twists that Icelanders call *kleinur*.

BÆJARINS BEZTU PYLSUR

Tryggvagata 1
Reykjavík 101
+354 8647839
www.bbp.is

Recommended by
Gunnar Karl Gíslason,
Thrainn Freyr Vigfússon

Opening hours	Open 7 days
Reservation policy	No
Credit cards	Accepted
Price range	Budget
Style	Casual
Cuisine	Hot Dogs
Recommended for	Late night

'It's a hot dog stand, there is a line there all day... do I need to say more?'—Gunnar Karl Gíslason

DILL RESTAURANT

The Nordic House
Sturlugötu 5
Reykjavík 101
+354 5521522
www.dillrestaurant.is

Recommended by
Claus Meyer, Flora Mikula

Opening hours	Closed Sunday
Credit cards	Accepted
Price range	Expensive
Style	Smart casual
Cuisine	Modern Nordic
Recommended for	Worth the travel

'It is a Scandinavian restaurant that works with ingredients you can't find anywhere else. You'll find a little bit of everything in their kitchen.'—Flora Mikula

GRÁI KÖTTURINN
Hverfisgata 16a
Reykjavík 101
+354 5511544

Recommended by
Gunnar Karl Gíslason

Opening hours..Open 7 days
Reservation policy...No
Credit cards...Accepted
Price range..Budget
Style..Casual
Cuisine...Icelandic
Recommended for...Breakfast

'It's small and beautiful, super friendly and nice. No better place for a quiet morning coffee and breakfast.' —Gunnar Karl Gíslason

Reykjavik's hipsters – sorry, intellectuals, artists and bohemian types – have their very own breakfast bolt-hole in the form of Grái Kötturinn (Grey Cat). Legendary for its early opening hours as well as its highbrow clientele, the tiny basement room holds just six tables but could fill many more on the strength of its excellent food – think bacon and eggs, American pancakes, bagels and the like – accompanied by a coffee so strong it'll make your heart flutter. Owner Hulda Hakon is, naturally, also an artist, whose works have been displayed in various galleries around the capital.

GRILLID
Hótel Sögu
8F, Við Hagatorg
Reykjavík 107
+354 5259960
www.grillid.is

Recommended by
Thrainn Freyr Vigfússon

Opening hours.....................Closed Monday and Sunday
Credit cards...Accepted
Price range..Expensive
Style..Formal
Cuisine...Modern Icelandic
Recommended for.............................Local favourite

'The most recognized restaurant in Reykjavík, with a history of being the best one here since around 1970. It's a really good Icelandic restaurant.' —Thrainn Freyr Vigfússon

K-BAR
Laugavegur 74
Reykjavík 101
+354 5716666

Recommended by
Gunnar Karl Gíslason

Opening hours..Open 7 days
Reservation policy...No
Credit cards...Accepted
Price range..Budget
Style..Casual
Cuisine...Korean
Recommended for...Late night

'Korean street food and good beers. I love going there after work for a bite and a beer.'—Gunnar Karl Gíslason

SÆMUNDUR Í SPARIFÖTUNUM
KEX Hostel
Skúlagata 28
Reykjavík 101
+354 5616060
www.kexhostel.is/saemundur

Recommended by
Gunnar Karl Gíslason

Opening hours..Open 7 days
Credit cards...Accepted
Price range..Budget
Style..Casual
Cuisine...Gastropub
Recommended for.............................Regular neighbourhood

'Just go there and you will understand why I go there most regularly.'—Gunnar Karl Gíslason

SVARTA KAFFIÐ
Laugavegur 54a
Reykjavík 101
+354 5512999

Recommended by
Thrainn Freyr Vigfússon

Opening hours..Open 7 days
Reservation policy...No
Credit cards...Accepted
Price range..Budget
Style..Casual
Cuisine...Café
Recommended for...Bargain

'Home-made soups served in bread. Good comfort food.'—Thrainn Freyr Vigfússon

VEGAMÓT

Recommended by
Thrainn Freyr Vigfússon

Vegamótastígur 4
Reykjavík 101
+354 5113040
www.vegamot.is

Opening hours	Open 7 days
Credit cards	Accepted
Price range	Affordable
Style	Casual
Cuisine	International
Recommended for	Regular neighbourhood

**'Nice small restaurant in downtown Reykjavík.'
—Thrainn Freyr Vigfússon**

VOX

Recommended by
Thrainn Freyr Vigfússon

Hilton Hotel
Suðurlandsbraut 2
Reykjavík 108
+354 4445050
www.vox.is

Opening hours	Open 7 days
Credit cards	Accepted
Price range	Affordable
Style	Smart casual
Cuisine	Modern Nordic
Recommended for	High end

'Good Nordic food.'—Thrainn Freyr Vigfússon

NORWAY, SWEDEN, DENMARK & FINLAND

NORWAY, SWEDEN, DENMARK & FINLAND

SCALE

0   90   180 mi.

FAROE ISLANDS

Streymoy p.297

NORWAY

SWEDEN

FINLAND

Jämtland pp.261–262

Ulsimaa pp.297–301
Finland Proper p.297

Oslo pp.258–260

Vestfold p.261

Stockholm pp.266, 268–278

Vastra Gotaland pp.266–267

Nordjylland p.282

DENMARK

Midtjylland pp.281–282
Hovedstaden pp.278–281
Copenhagen pp.284–297
Skania pp.262–266
Sjælland pp.282–283
Syddanmark p.283

ÅPENT BAKERI

Recommended by
Jo Bøe Klakegg,
Bjørn Svensson

Inkognito Terrasse 1
Oslo
Oslo 0256
Norway
+47 92046543
www.apentbakeri.no

Opening hours	Closed Sunday
Reservation policy	No
Credit cards	Accepted but not AMEX or Diners
Price range	Budget
Style	Casual
Cuisine	Café-Bakery
Recommended for	Breakfast

'They serve nice, fresh sandwiches, in a pleasant atmosphere.'—Bjørn Svensson

ARAKATAKA

Recommended by
Steffen Hansen,
Esben Holmboe Bang

Mariboes Gate 7
Oslo
Oslo 0183
Norway
+47 23328300
www.arakataka.no

Opening hours	Open 7 days
Credit cards	Accepted
Price range	Affordable
Style	Casual
Cuisine	Modern Nordic
Recommended for	Bargain

'I had a really good meal here. A good atmosphere and tasty food for a very reasonable price.'
—Esben Holmboe Bang

BAGATELLE

Recommended by
Steffen Hansen

Bygdøy Allé 3
Oslo
Oslo 0257
Norway
+47 22444040
www.bagatelle.no

Opening hours	Closed Sunday to Tuesday
Credit cards	Accepted
Price range	Expensive
Style	Smart casual
Cuisine	Modern Nordic
Recommended for	Local favourite

'Made world famous by grand chef Eyvind Hellstrøm. Now Allan Poulsen is head chef and with a fantastic Nordic cuisine Bagatelle is definitely a showcase of the best Norway has to offer. Not to mention the art on the walls – it's like sitting in a gallery.'—Steffen Hansen

LE BENJAMIN

Recommended by
Steffen Hansen

Søndre Gate 6
Oslo
Oslo 0550
Norway
+47 22357944
www.lebenjamin.no

Opening hours	Closed Monday
Credit cards	Accepted but not AMEX or Diners
Price range	Affordable
Style	Casual
Cuisine	French
Recommended for	Regular neighbourhood

'Authentic French bistro with a great wine list and tranching and flambéing in the restaurant.'
—Steffen Hansen

CAFÉ SARA

Recommended by
Jo Bøe Klakegg

Hausmanns Gate 29
Oslo
Oslo 0182
Norway
+47 22034000
www.cafesara.no

Opening hours	Open 7 days
Credit cards	Accepted
Price range	Budget
Style	Casual
Cuisine	International
Recommended for	Late night

'Good Turkish food in slightly dirty premises, but you can sit down and order beer until 3.00 a.m.'
—Jo Bøe Klakegg

CURRY & KETCHUP

Recommended by
Bjørn Svensson

Kirkeveien 51
Oslo
Oslo 0368
Norway
+47 22690522

Opening hours	Open 7 days
Reservation policy	No
Credit cards	Accepted but not Mastercard or AMEX
Price range	Budget
Style	Casual
Cuisine	Indian
Recommended for	Bargain

'Cheap, simple and authentic Indian food.'
—Bjørn Svensson

GRILL'S VILLE

Recommended by
Bjørn Svensson

Frognerveien 9a
Oslo
Oslo 0257
Norway
+47 22437744

Opening hours	Open 7 days
Reservation policy	No
Credit cards	Accepted
Price range	Budget
Style	Casual
Cuisine	American
Recommended for	Regular neighbourhood

'Genuine American hamburger restaurant.'
—Bjørn Svensson

HAI CAFÉ

Recommended by
Jo Bøe Klakegg

Calmeyers Gate 6
Oslo
Oslo 0183
Norway
+47 22203872

Opening hours	Open 7 days
Reservation policy	No
Credit cards	Accepted
Price range	Budget
Style	Casual
Cuisine	Vietnamese
Recommended for	Bargain

'The only good Vietnamese restaurant in Oslo and the cheapest.'—Jo Bøe Klakegg

MAAEMO

Recommended by
Filip Langhoff,
Sasu Laukkonen

Annette Thommessens Plass
Schweigaards Gate 15
Oslo
Oslo 0191
Norway
+47 91994805
www.maaemo.no

Opening hours	Closed Monday and Sunday
Credit cards	Accepted
Price range	Expensive
Style	Smart casual
Cuisine	Modern Nordic
Recommended for	Wish I'd opened

'Such talent, vision and execution are rare to find. These guys and girls are superstars. And the restaurant runs like clockwork.'—Sasu Laukkonen

THE NIGHTHAWK DINER

Recommended by
Steffen Hansen

Seilduksgata 15
Oslo
Oslo 0553
Norway
+47 96627327
www.nighthawkdiner.com

Opening hours	Open 7 days
Credit cards	Accepted
Price range	Affordable
Style	Casual
Cuisine	American
Recommended for	Breakfast

'Authentic diner that is almost always open for limitless coffee and whatever you want for breakfast. Great shakes.'—Steffen Hansen

This retro-styled Oslo diner, with its Edward Hopper-inspired name, might stay open until the small hours but is rarely as sparsely populated as that in Hopper's iconic painting. It's a fine bit of simulacrum, taking in chrome-trimmed booths, apron-wearing waitresses and a jukebox – all of which might look like it's been reclaimed from somewhere stateside were they not so shiny and new. Their burgers, made from organic Norwegian beef, are worthy of investigation but it's the all-day breakfast menu of pancakes, classic egg dishes and the sausage-and-bacon-laden brunch that catch the eye.

OLYMPEN

Grønlandsleiret 15
Oslo
Oslo 0190
Norway
+47 24101999
www.olympen.no

Opening hours...Open 7 days
Credit cards..Accepted
Price range..Affordable
Style..Casual
Cuisine...Norwegian
Recommended for...Local favourite

'It's been in Oslo for as long as I remember. It used to be an institution among the city's serious drinkers. Good traditional food from Norway. Well-made and large portions. Very long list of good beers.' —Jo Bøe Klakegg

ORO

Tordenskioldsgate 6a
Oslo
Oslo 0160
Norway
+47 23010240
www.ororestaurant.no

Opening hours..Closed Sunday
Credit cards..Accepted
Price range...Expensive
Style..Smart casual
Cuisine...Modern International
Recommended for...High end

'Delicate food, great flavours and a splendid wine list.' —Bjørn Svensson

PJOLTERGEIST

Rosteds Gate 15b
Oslo
Oslo 0178
Norway
+47 40237788

Opening hours..............................Closed Monday and Sunday
Credit cards..Accepted
Price range..Affordable
Style..Casual
Cuisine..Icelandic-Asian
Recommended for...Late night

'A very small restaurant with an Icelandic-Asian fusion menu. With their kitchen closing at 12.00 p.m., it's perfect for late-night dining.'—Bjørn Svensson

SAIGON LILLE CAFÉ

Møllergata 32
Oslo
Oslo 0179
Norway
+47 22114813

Opening hours...Open 7 days
Credit cards........................Accepted but not AMEX or Diners
Price range...Budget
Style..Casual
Cuisine..Vietnamese
Recommended for..Bargain

'Authentic Vietnamese cuisine with big portions and good prices.'—Steffen Hanson

While 'bargain' is a relative term in Norway, the Vietnamese food served at Saigon Lille is certainly tasty, and the portions are generous. A no-frills, family-run place tucked down an anonymous alley near Youngstorget, they're never going to win any awards for interior design, but mains priced at around 100kr (£10; $17) is about as reasonable as you're going to find in this town, and the soups (sorry, pho) are also worth your hard-earned money. There's no English or Norwegian menu, so either point at the pictures and hope, or ask a member of staff for his or her favourites.

TACO REPÚBLICA

Torggata 30
Oslo
Oslo 0183
Norway
+47 40057665
www.tacorepublica.no

Opening hours..Closed Monday
Reservation policy...No
Credit cards..Accepted
Price range...Budget
Style..Casual
Cuisine..Mexican
Recommended for...Late night

'Late-night kitchen with real tacos just like you get in Mexico.'—Steffen Hansen

CONRADIS

Nedre Langgate 18
Tønsberg
Vestfold 3126
Norway
+47 33370900
www.conradis.no

Opening hours..Closed Sunday
Credit cards..Accepted
Price range...Affordable
Style..Smart casual
Cuisine...Modern Nordic
Recommended for.............................Regular neighbourhood

'They use local ingredients and are located on the
scenic harbourfront in Tønsberg. Very good chef and
a fine wine list.'—Geir Skeie

ÅRE BAGERI & BREADGARDEN

Årevägen 55
Åre
Jämtland 830 13
Sweden
+46 64752320
www.arebageri.se

Opening hours...Open 7 days
Reservation policy...No
Credit cards..........................Accepted but not AMEX or Diners
Price range..Budget
Style..Casual
Cuisine...Bakery-Café-Deli
Recommended for...Breakfast

ÖLBAREN

Torggränd 2b
Åre
Jämtland 830 13
Sweden
+46 64750023
www.olbaren-are.com

Opening hours.............................Closed Monday and Sunday
Credit cards..Accepted
Price range...Affordable
Style..Casual
Cuisine...Gastropub
Recommended for.............................Regular neighbourhood

FÄVIKEN MAGASINET

Fäviken 216
Järpen
Jämtland 830 05
Sweden
+46 64740177
www.favikenmagasinet.se

Opening hours............................Closed Monday and Sunday
Credit cards............................Accepted but not Diners
Price range...Expensive
Style..Smart casual
Cuisine...Modern Swedish
Recommended for...Worth the travel

'I went for the first time this year and was blown away
by how good the food and the experience of dining
there was. The attention to detail, from the food to
the pacing of the menu to where you sit is amazing.
I thought it was a bit of a trek when I first planned the
trip, but it's more than worth the trouble to get there.'
—James Lowe

To say that Fäviken is worth the journey is high praise
indeed when you consider that your destination is
Järpen in the unspoilt northwest of Sweden, 750 km
(466 miles) north of Stockholm, well on your way
towards the Arctic Circle. It's run by farmer/forager/
hunter/chef Magnus Nilsson, who transforms wild
ingredients into an haute experience for only a handful
of guests. Almost everything served at the strikingly
intimate, twelve-seat, wood-panelled restaurant is
collected, caught, hunted or grown on the vast estate
that surrounds it. Show-stopping dishes include a
charcoal-grilled moose thigh bone, sawn in half on
a block in the dining room, and its marrow served.

NATUR CAFÉ AT KRETSLOPPSHUSET

Recommended by
Magnus Nilsson

Kyrkvägen 5
Mörsil
Jämtland 830 04
Sweden
+46 647665212
www.kretsloppshuset.com

Opening hours	Closed Monday to Wednesday
Credit cards	Accepted
Price range	Affordable
Style	Casual
Cuisine	Swedish
Recommended for	Local favourite

Kretsloppshuset, a name that translates as 'The Circle of Life House', is a sustainable, eco-conscious cooperative run by a forty-strong team of volunteers. From growing organic vegetables to raising free-range chickens in a traditional hen house, Kretsloppshuset's aim, via environmentally sensitive small-scale agriculture, is to provide inspiration for a more sustainable lifestyle. They operate a farm shop and a café where everything served is made from raw ingredients, the majority of which are their own home-grown vegetables. The hippy dream is, it seems, still alive and well in rural northern Sweden.

ÖSTARPS GÄSTGIVAREGÅRD

Recommended by
Ebbe Vollmer,
Mats Vollmer

Gamla Lundavägen 2481–79
Blentarp
Scania 270 35
Sweden
+46 4680229
www.ostarpsgastis.se

Opening hours	Variable
Credit cards	Accepted
Price range	Affordable
Style	Casual
Cuisine	Swedish
Recommended for	Local favourite

'Traditional local Scandinavian cooking at its best! Beautiful setting and as traditional as it gets.'
—Mats Vollmer

The middle-of-nowhere setting in bucolic Skåne is just the place for traditionally prepared Swedish fare. Lennart and Gunilla Vollmer's historic inn, in the family since 1946, comes into its own at Christmas time when its julbord table, groaning with meatballs, salmon and herring every which way, draws visitors from miles around. But that shouldn't detract from

autumn time when local goose with red cabbage and Brussels sprouts makes it annual appearance; nor from its midsummer folk dance; nor its thirty-two-dish holiday smorgasbord. Pretty wooden panels, wall-mounted antlers and miles of lush pastureland paint a picture-perfect scene of Swedish country life.

BASTARD

Recommended by
Daniel Berlin, Robert
Jacobsson, Mats Vollmer

Mäster Johansgatan 11
Malmö
Scania 211 21
Sweden
+46 40121318
www.bastardrestaurant.se

Opening hours	Closed Monday and Sunday
Credit cards	Accepted
Price range	Affordable
Style	Smart casual
Cuisine	Modern European
Recommended for	Late night

'Located in a old Swedish pharmacy with a big back yard for those hot summer nights, it's a pretty special place and you have to visit when here. It might have the greatest atmosphere of any restaurant in the south of Sweden. Come here for a rustic dinner or later in the night for some natural wine and stone-oven-baked pizza in the back yard. They manage to fit in a little piece of a New York brasserie feeling in small-town Malmö.'—Robert Jacobsson

Chef Andreas Dahlberg's illegitimately named Malmö outpost opened in late 2009. A smartly restyled tavern, all dark wood and white butcher's tiles, its doors open each night at 5.00 p.m. and the bar quickly fills up with the city's most fashionable foodies, who drink natural wine and eat charcuterie, sliced by the huge red machine that sits behind the open counter. When the kitchen proper opens at 6.00 p.m., the menu is meat-heavy with a love of offal and game that would please Fergus 'St. John' Henderson. The kitchen is proud of its eco-credentials – a champion of local, organic and high-welfare farming.

CASUAL STREET FOOD

Recommended by
Andreas Dahlberg

Spångatan 32
Malmö
Scania 211 54
Sweden
www.casualstreetfood.se

Opening hours	Closed Sunday
Reservation policy	No
Credit cards	Accepted but not AMEX
Price range	Budget
Style	Casual
Cuisine	Fast Food
Recommended for	Regular neighbourhood

'The most amazing burgers, great place. I like the two guys who run it – they put their heart and soul into what they do.'—Andreas Dahlberg

DONAU BAGERIET

Recommended by
Mats Vollmer

Bergsgatan 27
Malmö
Scania 211 54
Sweden
+46 4079530

Opening hours	Open 7 days
Reservation policy	No
Credit cards	Accepted but not AMEX
Price range	Budget
Style	Casual
Cuisine	Café-Bakery
Recommended for	Bargain

'A bargain? I just buy some freshly baked cheese baguettes at my local baker.'—Mats Vollmer

GYOZA ROBO BAR

Recommended by
Mats Vollmer

Adelgatan 4
Malmö
Scania 211 22
Sweden
+46 40150100
www.gyozarobobar.se

Opening hours	Closed Monday and Sunday
Credit cards	Accepted
Price range	Budget
Style	Casual
Cuisine	Modern Japanese
Recommended for	Regular neighbourhood

'I love Asian food and Gyoza Robo Bar is definitely one of my favourites – nice decor and relaxed service.'
—Mats Vollmer

HAGEN

Recommended by
Robert Jacobsson

Storgatan 41
Malmö
Scania 21145
Sweden
+46 40970970
www.ihagen.se

Opening hours	Closed Saturday and Sunday
Reservation policy	No
Credit cards	Accepted but not AMEX
Price range	Budget
Style	Casual
Cuisine	Café-Bistro
Recommended for	Regular neighbourhood

'This new type of fast-food restaurant serves healthy, tasty food and fast, but in a trendy and honest way, with a laid back interior. It just feels healthier. You can choose from a pulled-pork burger, chilli stews... and if you have room, a lemon crème caramel. All served in five minutes, so no waiting time. I go here as often as possible.'—Robert Jacobsson

JALLA JALLA

Recommended by
Robert Jacobsson

Bergsgatan 16
Malmö
Scania 211 54
Sweden
+46 40303920

Opening hours	Open 7 days
Reservation policy	No
Credit cards	Not accepted
Price range	Budget
Style	Casual
Cuisine	Middle Eastern
Recommended for	Local favourite

'In Malmö we have some fantastic falafel restaurants that everyone's talking about. This is the best one. Comfort food at its best.'—Robert Jacobsson

NORDIC STREET FOOD

Recommended by
Robert Jacobsson

Malmö
Scania
Sweden
+46 706202094
www.nordicstreetfood.com

Opening hours	Variable
Reservation policy	No
Credit cards	Not accepted
Price range	Budget
Style	Casual
Cuisine	Street Food
Recommended for	Bargain

'This is where you go for a quick lunch bite or when out shopping. It serves quality fast food, with locally harvested ingredients. You get pulled pork, cheese burgers and great vegetarian food. These food trucks are common in the UK and the States but they are rare in these parts, so this is a fantastic initiative. I love the cheeseburger...'—Robert Jacobsson

ROSEN BAR & DINING

Recommended by
Robert Jacobsson

Hotel Renaissance
Mäster Johansgatan 15
Malmö
Scania 21121
Sweden
+46 40248524
www.rosenbaranddining.se

Opening hours	Open 7 days
Credit cards	Accepted
Price range	Affordable
Style	Smart casual
Cuisine	Brasserie
Recommended for	Breakfast

'By far the best place for breakfast close by. Malmö is a bit behind on restaurants serving a good breakfast. I think the southern Swedes prefer to eat breakfast at home. Here you will get the stuff that keeps you going through the day. It's a standard hotel breakfast, where you will find all the regular things, but it's the city's best by far.'—Robert Jacobsson

SALTIMPORTEN CANTEEN

Recommended by
Andreas Dahlberg

Grimsbygatan 24
Malmö
Scania 211 20
Sweden
+46 706518426
www.saltimporten.com

Opening hours	Closed Saturday and Sunday
Credit cards	Accepted but not AMEX
Price range	Budget
Style	Casual
Cuisine	Modern Nordic
Recommended for	Bargain

'Best lunch in town.'—Andreas Dahlberg

Having shuttered the acclaimed Trio, rising stars Ola Rudin and Sebastian Persson brought a simpler, more homely version of their New Nordic cooking to this harbourside warehouse in 2013. Open for weekday lunches only, Saltimporten Canteen attracts a hipster crowd, many of whom make the thirty-minute crossing from Copenhagen for the two-dish menu: veal, cucumber, yogurt and mint, perhaps, or beetroot (beet), lingonberry, mustard and spelt. Everything – from the canteen-style tables and benches to the clean-cut compilations on the plate – is carefully pared back. And the bread alone is worth the journey. Check the website first to find out what they're serving before you head over.

SOLDE KAFFEBAR

Recommended by
Andreas Dahlberg

Regementsgatan 2
Malmö
Scania 211 42
Sweden
+46 739357770
www.solde.se

Opening hours	Open 7 days
Reservation policy	No
Credit cards	Accepted
Price range	Budget
Style	Casual
Cuisine	Café
Recommended for	Breakfast

Breakfast at Malmö's Solde Kaffebar (coffee shop) usually means a swift espresso from the La Marzocco and a baguette stuffed with cured wild boar ham or artisan salami. High counters and stools to perch on don't make for lingering, so grab one of the coveted corner seats if you can. Set up in 2006 by a trio of coffee nuts, among them a former pro tennis player and a latte art world champion, the centrally located café is catnip to local hipsters who know their Ethiopian Yirgacheffe from their Sumatra Blue Batak. While you're there, pick up a bag of beans adorned with Solde's signature off-the-wall graphics.

SPOONERY

Recommended by
Daniel Berlin

Östra Stallmästaregatan 2
Malmö
Scania 217 49
Sweden
+46 40265600
www.spoonery.se

Opening hours	Open 7 days
Reservation policy	No
Credit cards	Accepted but not AMEX
Price range	Budget
Style	Casual
Cuisine	Swedish
Recommended for	Bargain

'Easy food cooked with really good produce. Fast and easy to pick up!'—Daniel Berlin

The Spoonery concept is brilliant in its simplicity: slow-cooked food, served at speed. It caters primarily for Slottsstaden's time-poor young professionals with such comforting and hearty dishes as French fish stew with croutons and rouille, prime rib chilli, and creamy venison stew with chanterelles and lingonberries. The bulk of their business is to go, but there are a few seats inside and out for those with the time to linger, with warming bowls of soup or stew served with their freshly baked sourdough on offer for a reasonable 100kr (£9; $15). There's a second branch in the southern Malmö district of Limhamn.

VOLLMERS

Recommended by
Robert Jacobsson

Tegelgårdsgatan 5
Malmö
Scania 211 33
Sweden
+46 40579750
www.vollmers.nu

Opening hours	Closed Sunday
Credit cards	Accepted
Price range	Expensive
Style	Smart casual
Cuisine	Modern Swedish
Recommended for	High end

'Here you have two brothers (the Vollmer brothers) who are really talented chefs and a small restaurant with high-end food. It definitely deserves a star in my book. All the focus is on the experience for us as diners. In the kitchen, great knowledge and raw talent. They serve a Scanian/New Nordic style of food. A cool detail on their menu is that they write the distance from where the main ingredients are farmed, so you know that it's local. Go here when in town.'
—Robert Jacobsson

DANIEL BERLIN KROG

Diligensvägen 21
Tomelilla
Scania 273 92
Sweden
+46 41720300
www.danielberlin.se

Opening hours..................................Closed Sunday to Tuesday
Credit cards...Accepted
Price range...Expensive
Style...Smart casual
Cuisine...Modern Nordic
Recommended for...Worth the travel

'This is as good as it gets. Chef Daniel Berlin is massively talented and does things that few dare to do in a restaurant. It's a place where you can feel that the small things really matter. Simplicity is always the hardest. The food is very delicate, pure and clean. Daniel shoots his wild game himself and digs up the celeriac (celery root) from his back yard. Here the diners know that it's local. This type of restaurant makes you proud to be a chef.'—Robert Jacobsson

Daniel Berlin's parents quit their jobs to work for him in 2009. They're not the only ones to believe in the thirty-two-year-old Swede: René Redzepi himself has tipped him for the top. Berlin draws his inspiration from the landscape and natural larder all around him. Diners come to the Scanian sticks expecting unusual ingredients: Berlin's roasted blackened celeriac (celery root) flesh with Västerbotten cheese, egg yolk with four kinds of cabbage, and quail eggs in the local lardo. An overnight stay at nearby Logi Gamlegård is recommended – the chef or his dad will drive you there after supper.

PALMYRA KEBAB

Årstavägen 57
Årsta
Stockholm 120 54
Sweden
+46 8918012
www.palmyrakebab.se

Opening hours...Open 7 days
Reservation policy...No
Credit cards..Accepted
Price range..Budget
Style..Casual
Cuisine...Sandwiches
Recommended for..Bargain

'Best kebab in town for next to no money at all.'
—Magnus Ek

URBAN DELI

Hesselmans Torg 12
Nacka
Stockholm 131 54
Sweden
+46 859909180
www.urbandeli.org

Opening hours..Open 7 days
Credit cards...Accepted
Price range..Affordable
Style..Casual
Cuisine...International
Recommended for..Breakfast

'It's a new place with a great atmosphere. The food and bread is of a high quality.'—Mathias Dahlgren

BHOGA

Norra Hamngatan 10
Gothenburg
Vastra Gotaland 411 14
Sweden
+46 31138018
www.bhoga.se

Opening hours...............................Closed Monday and Sunday
Credit cards...Accepted
Price range..Affordable
Style...Smart casual
Cuisine...Modern Nordic
Recommended for...Local favourite

'A new restaurant with high ambitions working with a modern cuisine and high-quality wines from small producers.'—Björn Persson

KOKA

Viktoriagatan 12
Gothenburg
Vastra Gotaland 411 25
Sweden
+46 317017979
www.restaurangkoka.se

Opening hours...Closed Sunday
Credit cards...Accepted
Price range...Expensive
Style...Smart casual
Cuisine..Modern Swedish
Recommended for..High end

Having started life as a French bistro in 2000, Björn Persson's Kock & Vin only started taking shape in 2006 when the restaurateur bought the cellar below, upgraded the kitchen and set his sights on creating a world-class restaurant. Eight years later, the restaurant has a new name, a new food philosophy and its modern Swedish cuisine has a Michelin star. However, Koka remains very much a Gothenburg establishment: the menu brims with west-coast produce – salted herring, seaweed, nettles, lovage, langoustine, lingonberry. If you indulge in the seven-course tasting menu, you'll appreciate the comfortable, pared-back dining room; opt for the three-course dinner (£36; €44; $61) and you'll grab yourself a bargain.

MR. P

Recommended by
Björn Persson

Götaplatsen 6
Gothenburg
Vastra Gotaland 412 56
Sweden
+46 31160980
www.mr-p.se

Opening hours...Open 7 days
Reservation policy..No
Credit cards...Accepted
Price range..Affordable
Style..Casual
Cuisine...International
Recommended for...................Regular neighbourhood

The Mr. P in question is one Pontus Fürstenberg, whose substantial art collection helped build the foundations for Gothenburg Art Museum on the floors above. Rather than the stuffy, overpriced tourist trap that's more traditional for art gallery restaurants, this is an informal space populated by friendly staff and serving creative but uncomplicated food such as steak tartare, duck breast with potato cakes, and baked cod with celeriac (celery root) and oyster mushrooms. A particular draw, too, is the bar: obliging bartenders have a huge repertoire of cocktails, making it a very popular date spot despite the inevitable queues (waiting lines).

RESTAURANG 28+

Recommended by
Ben Spalding

Götabergsgatan 28
Gothenburg
Vastra Gotaland 411 34
Sweden
+46 31202161
www.28plus.se

Opening hours..Closed Sunday
Credit cards...Accepted
Price range..Expensive
Style..Smart casual
Cuisine...Modern Swedish
Recommended for...............................Worth the travel

'Just go. Proper timeless Michelin-starred cooking from the charismatic chef Hans Boren and front of house led by the great Ulf Johansson.'—Ben Spalding

SJÖMAGASINET

Recommended by
Björn Persson

Klippans Kulturreservat
Adolf Edelsvärds Gata 5
Gothenburg
Vastra Gotaland 414 51
Sweden
+46 317755920
www.sjomagasinet.se

Opening hours..Closed Sunday
Credit cards...Accepted
Price range..Affordable
Style..Smart casual
Cuisine..Swedish
Recommended for...............................Local favourite

'Classic iconic restaurant.'—Björn Persson

Housed in a harbour-side, timber-clad eighteenth-century warehouse that once belonged to the Swedish East India Company, Sjömagasinet first found fame as a seafood restaurant under legendary Swedish toque, Leif Mannerström. Taken over by Ulf Wagner, who brought Gothenberg its first Michelin star back in 1989, he runs it in partnership with fellow chef Gustav Trägårdh. The menu typically runs from a fennel-laced bouillabaisse, via razor clam and langoustine croquettes, to seafood pot-au-feu or Swedish lamb three ways. Rustic and bedecked with nautical bric-a-brac, dine by the fire in winter and on the pier come summer.

'BEST KEBAB IN SWEDEN. ENOUGH SAID.'

KIM ÖHMAN P277

'A dynamic restaurant that's always striving for perfection.'

MARCUS EAVES P270

'*Herrings and toast skagen.*'

TOMI BJÖRCK P276

STOCKHOLM

'OLD-SCHOOL SWEDISH FOOD IN A REALLY NICE TRADITIONAL SWEDISH ENVIRONMENT.'

NIKLAS EKSTEDT P273

'WHAT ELSE DO YOU NEED WHEN YOU HAVE GREAT SAUSAGES AND BEER?'

ANTON BJUHR P271

STOCKHOLM

N

SCALE

0 500 1000 1500 yd.

1. Chez Betty (p.278)
2. Ramen Ki Mama (p.278)
3. Råkultur (p.275)
4. Esperanto (p.274)
5. Sosta Espresso Bar (p.273)
6. Rolfs Kök (p.273)
7. Volt (p.276)
8. Östermalms Korvspecialist (p.275)
9. Taverna Brillo (p.276)
10. Ekstedt (p.273)
11. Sturehof (p.276)
12. AG (p.271)
13. La Gazelle (p.271)
14. Wienercaféet (p.273)
15. P.A. & Co (p.275)
16. Riche (p.275)
17. Gastrologik (p.274)
18. Speceriet (p.276)
19. Eriks Bakficka (p.274)
20. Max Hamngatan (p.272)
21. Operabaren (p.273)
22. Mathias Dahlgren (p.272)
23. Mathias Dahlgren Matbaren (p.272)
24. Lydmar Hotel (p.272)
25. Rosendals Trädgård (p.270)
26. Petite France (p.271)
27. Pubologi (pp.270–271)
28. 19 Glas (p.270)
29. Frantzén (p.270)
30. Taylors & Jones with the Twist (p.271)
31. Babylon (p.277)
32. Amida Kolgrill (p.277)
33. Pom & Flora (p.278)
34. Nytorget 6 (p.277)
35. Restaurang Gandhi (p.278)
36. Gyrella (p.277)

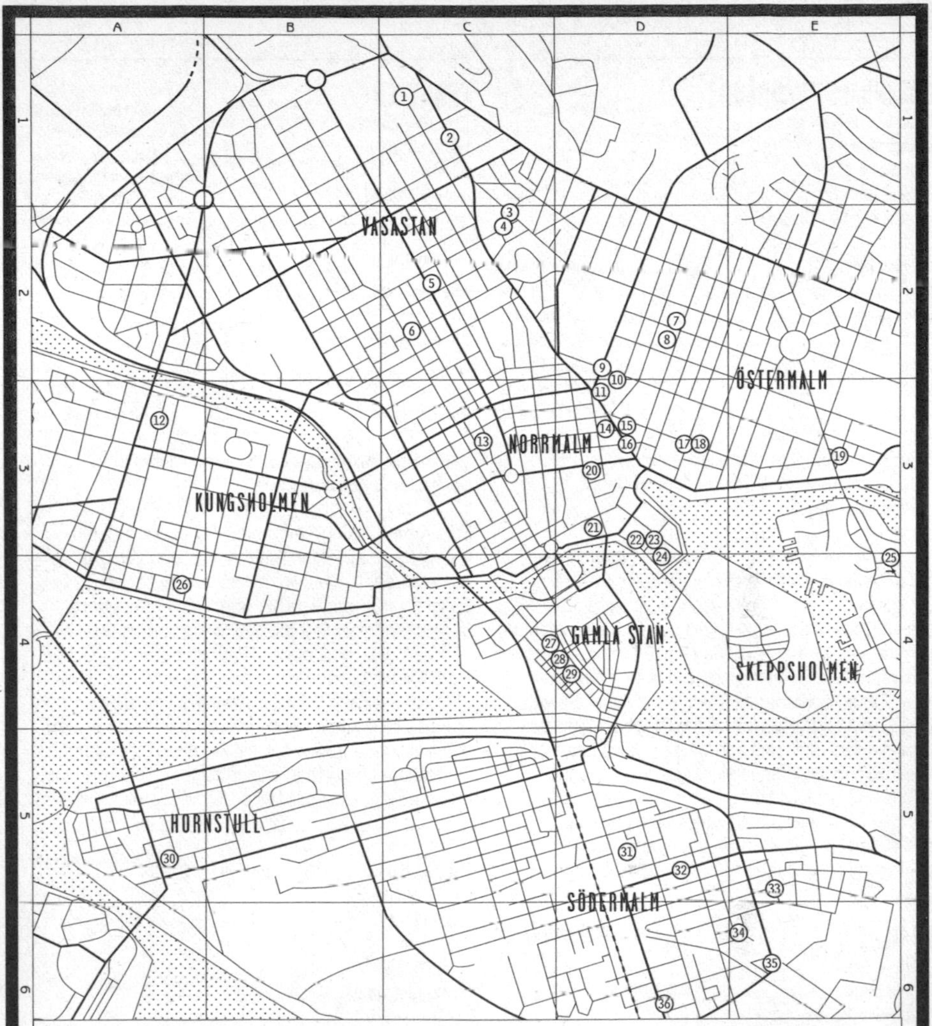

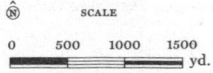

ROSENDALS TRÄDGÅRD

Rosendalsterrassen 12
Djurgården
Stockholm 115 21
+46 854581270
www.rosendalstradgard.se

Recommended by
Mathias Dahlgren

Opening hours	Closed Monday
Reservation policy	No
Credit cards	Accepted
Price range	Budget
Style	Casual
Cuisine	Café-Bakery
Recommended for	Local favourite

'They have more than thirty years experience of gardening and serving organic food in the city.' —Mathias Dahlgren

The 'Rose Valley Garden' café can be found in the old greenhouses of the public garden on the island of Djurgården. Developed under a succession of green-fingered Swedish royals during the nineteenth century, the garden is now a centre for biodynamic cultivation, including a rose garden that features over a hundred varieties. The café is supplied with herbs, fruit and vegetables from the nearby plots and greenhouses and from approved organic and bio-dynamic growers. The menu (sandwiches, soups, salads and glorious home-baking) changes daily to reflect the seasons. Sample dishes include salt-baked root vegetables with sourdough, and cardamom cake with redcurrants. Closed January.

19 GLAS

Stora Nygatan 19
Gamla Stan
Stockholm 111 27
+46 87231919
www.19glas.se

Recommended by
Magnus Ek

Opening hours	Closed Sunday
Credit cards	Accepted
Price range	Affordable
Style	Casual
Cuisine	Bistro
Recommended for	Regular neighbourhood

'A small restaurant with really good food. They work with very good, mostly Swedish products.'—Magnus Ek

FRANTZÉN

Lilla Nygatan 21
Gamla Stan
Stockholm 111 28
+46 8208580
www.restaurantfrantzen.com

Recommended by
Daniel Berlin, Marcus
Eaves, Mikael Einarsson,
Magnus Ek, Stephen
Harris, Nicolai Nørregaard,
Gustav Otterberg, René
Redzepi, Jari Vesivalo,
Michael Wolf

Opening hours	Closed Monday and Sunday
Credit cards	Accepted
Price range	Expensive
Style	Smart casual
Cuisine	Modern Nordic
Recommended for	Worth the travel

'A dynamic restaurant that's always striving for perfection.'—Marcus Eaves

This rapidly rising Stockholm star opened in 2008 in the city's picturesque Old Town. It was established as Frantzén/Lindeberg, a partnership between chef Björn Frantzén and pastry chef Daniel Lindeberg, before the latter left in 2013 to pursue his dream of opening a small bakery. Raw materials are mined from the restaurant's two gardens and from a list of trusted local producers, farmers and growers. Menus are made up of whatever they have in each day and presented in a series of bite-sized courses. Try and book a berth at one of the four front-row counter seats that overlook the action at the kitchen's pass.

PUBOLOGI

Stora Nygatan 20
Gamla Stan
Stockholm 111 27
+46 850640086
www.pubologi.se

Recommended by
Magnus Ek

Opening hours	Closed Sunday
Credit cards	Accepted
Price range	Affordable
Style	Smart casual
Cuisine	Gastropub
Recommended for	Local favourite

'There are interesting dishes using mainly Swedish products and at very affordable prices. It's almost like fine dining but in your local neighbourhood restaurant.' —Magnus Ek

Genre-busting Pubologi in Gamla Stan describes itself as an 'interpretation' of the gastropub and so it is – a very loose interpretation. The twenty-six-cover space with its communal table and craft brews hasn't stopped refining its concept since its 2010 launch, adding a chef's table and upping the gastronomic ante to serve 'fine dining to the people'. The eclectic kitchen mixes ingredients and techniques old and new on the daily-changing 550kr (£51; $85) five-course menu: to wit, raw scallop with browned butter and lemon, and roasted buckwheat ice cream, pickled ume and ginger. The legendary burger is off here but on at sister-bar Tweed.

TAYLORS & JONES WITH THE TWIST

Recommended by
Anton Bjuhr

Långholmsgatan 17–21
Hornstull
Stockholm 117 33
+46 86688078
www.taylorsandjones.com

Opening hours	Open 7 days
Reservation policy	No
Credit cards	Accepted but not AMEX
Price range	Budget
Style	Casual
Cuisine	Hot Dogs
Recommended for	Bargain

'What else do you need when you have great sausages and beer?'—Anton Bjuhr

A British-themed sausage restaurant and bar in Stockholm? Given the craze for all things Scandinavian in the UK at the moment, it seems only natural that influences might work both ways. What started off as a small-scale operation run from the back of a van by two Northern Irish expats has grown into a network of grocers, butchers and now this – a smart, bijou space serving eclectic flavours of gourmet dogs (honey and oregano, pork with rhubarb) at prices that, for Stockholm, are a bargain. A well-chosen craft beer list shows they pay as much attention to drinks as eats.

AG

Recommended by
Björn Frantzén

Kronobergsgatan 37
Kungsholmen
Stockholm 112 33
+46 841068100
www.restaurangag.se

Opening hours	Closed Sunday
Credit cards	Accepted
Price range	Affordable
Style	Casual
Cuisine	Steakhouse
Recommended for	Regular neighbourhood

'I'm a meat lover and they are the best in town.'
—Björn Frantzén

PETITE FRANCE

Recommended by
Anton Bjuhr

John Ericssonsgatan 6
Kungsholmen
Stockholm 112 22
+46 86182800
www.petitefrance.se

Opening hours	Open 7 days
Credit cards	Accepted
Price range	Affordable
Style	Casual
Cuisine	Café-Bistro
Recommended for	Breakfast

'I can practise my French with the bakers while having my petit déjeuner!'—Anton Bjuhr

LA GAZELLE

Recommended by
Niklas Ekstedt

Hötorgshallen Saluhall
Hötorgshallen 42
Norrmalm
Stockholm 111 11
+46 8210212
www.lagazelle.se

Opening hours	Open 7 days
Reservation policy	No
Credit cards	Accepted but not AMEX
Price range	Budget
Style	Casual
Cuisine	Middle Eastern
Recommended for	Bargain

'They have great lamb dishes that are delicious. The staff also know everything about lamb that you need to know.'—Niklas Ekstedt

LYDMAR HOTEL

Recommended by
Magnus Ek

Lydmar Hotel
Södra Blasieholmshamnen 2
Norrmalm
Stockholm 103 24
+46 8223160
www.lydmar.com

Opening hours	Open 7 days
Credit cards	Accepted but not AMEX
Price range	Affordable
Style	Smart casual
Cuisine	Swedish-French
Recommended for	Breakfast

'A relaxed place with large windows facing the park.
They have good coffee and a small breakfast menu
with good-quality food.'—Magnus Ek

MATHIAS DAHLGREN

Recommended by
Steffen Hansen,
Jacob Holmström,
Marcus Samuelsson,
Geir Skeie

Grand Hôtel
Södra Blasieholmshamnen 8
Norrmalm
Stockholm 103 27
+46 86793584
www.mathiasdahlgren.com

Opening hours	Closed Monday and Sunday
Credit cards	Accepted
Price range	Expensive
Style	Smart casual
Cuisine	Modern Swedish
Recommended for	High end

'Always a great experience.'—Jacob Holmström

MATHIAS DAHLGREN MATBAREN

Recommended by
Jacob Holmström,
Kim Öhman

Grand Hôtel
Södra Blasieholmshamnen 8
Norrmalm
Stockholm 103 27
+46 86793584
www.grandhotel.se

Opening hours	Closed Sunday
Credit cards	Accepted
Price range	Affordable
Style	Smart casual
Cuisine	Modern Swedish
Recommended for	High end

'Mathias Dahlgren has a way with food that is simple
yet complex and totally different. Blows you away every
time.'—Kim Öhman

Of the not one but two Mathias Dahlgren restaurants
at Stockholm's Grand Hôtel, Matbaren is the poor
relation with just one Michelin star to its name,
compared with upmarket Matsalen's two. But com-
parisons are otious – both 2007-vintage restaurants
are high achievers, each with their own inimitable
style. Buzzy, popular Matbaren ('food bar'), styled by
Ilse Crawford, presents Dahlgren's unimpeachably
seasonal modern Swedish in good-looking 'medium-
sized' plates, crafted in the impressively fast-paced
open kitchen. Sample dishes include steamed beef
rib buns, salt-baked beetroot (beet) with smoked
goat's cheese, and fallow deer tartare with salted
roe, blood bread, raw onion and smoked butter.

MAX HAMNGATAN

Recommended by
Anton Bjuhr,
Björn Frantzén

Kungsträdgårdsgatan 20
Norrmalm
Stockholm 111 47
+46 86113810
www.max.se

Opening hours	Open 7 days
Reservation policy	No
Credit cards	Accepted
Price range	Budget
Style	Casual
Cuisine	Burgers
Recommended for	Late night

'I tend to go here almost every Friday to grab a burger.'
—Anton Bjuhr

Sweden's own fast-food brand, valiantly expanding
over the past ten years to compete with demonstrably
inferior US interlopers, originated in northern Sweden
in 1968 and is still family-owned. The burgers, made
with Swedish beef, are said to be cooked to order,
and start at 11kr (£1; $2) for a basic patty and bun,
with the much nicer Maxburger at 45kr (£4; $7) and
the Grand de Luxe burgers (Cheese 'n' Bacon, Triple
Cheese, or Chilli 'n' Cheese) at around 65kr (£6; $10).
Don't go in search of a gourmet experience – Max
looks like a chain and tastes like a chain – but do
admire the low-GI, low-carb and low-fat options. The
central branch by Kungsträdgårdsgatan is open until
6.00 a.m.

OPERABAREN

The Royal Opera House
Karl XII:S Torg
Norrmalm
Stockholm 111 86
+46 86765808
www.operakallaren.se

Opening hours..Closed Sunday
Credit cards...Accepted
Price range...Affordable
Style...Smart casual
Cuisine..Swedish
Recommended for...............................Local favourite

'They serve old-school Swedish food in a really nice traditional Swedish environment.'—Niklas Ekstedt

Top-drawer meatballs and herring, framed by a certain degree of formality – this is, after all, Sweden's Royal Opera House – are on the menu at this bourgeois favourite with its handsome turn-of-the-century decor, where the ruling and chattering classes break bread together. Daily specials might include Irish stew, or smoked haddock with spinach, poached egg and hollandaise, both 175kr (£16; $27); among à la carte mains are poached pike perch, 295kr (£27; $45), and steak tartare, 235kr (£21; $36). The same menu is served at the counter in the tiny *Bakficka* ('back pocket') bistro, which has outdoor seating overlooking Kungsträdgårdsgatan, the royal park – a great spot for lunch in summer.

ROLFS KÖK

Tegnérgatan 41
Norrmalm
Stockholm 111 61
+46 8101696
www.rolfskok.se

Opening hours......................................Open 7 days
Credit cards...Accepted
Price range...Affordable
Style...Casual
Cuisine..Swedish-French
Recommended for......................Regular neighbourhood

'Perfect around-the-corner bistro. Amazing rustic food, good wine list. Just a comfort zone.'—Kim Öhman

SOSTA ESPRESSO BAR

Sveavägen 84
Norrmalm
Stockholm 113 59
www.sosta.se

Opening hours..Closed Sunday
Reservation policy...No
Credit cards..Not accepted
Price range...Budget
Style...Casual
Cuisine..Café-Bakery
Recommended for..Breakfast

'Nice espresso and grilled focaccia. Perfect start in the morning.'—Kim Öhman

WIENERCAFÉET

Biblioteksgatan 6–8
Norrmalm
Stockholm 111 46
+46 86112116
www.wienercafeet.com

Opening hours......................................Open 7 days
Credit cards...Accepted
Price range...Affordable
Style..Smart casual
Cuisine..Café-Bakery
Recommended for..Breakfast

'The only place in Stockholm with good Viennoiseries. I come here for croissants and croque monsieurs.' —Jacob Holmström

EKSTEDT

Humlegårdsgatan 17
Östermalm
Stockholm 114 46
+46 86111210
www.ekstedt.nu

Opening hours..........................Closed Monday and Sunday
Credit cards...Accepted
Price range...Expensive
Style..Smart casual
Cuisine...Modern Swedish
Recommended for...High end

'Great food and it's welcoming interior makes you feel special.'—Anton Bjuhr

ERIKS BAKFICKA

Recommended by
Anton Bjuhr

Fredrikshovsgatan 4
Östermalm
Stockholm 115 23
+46 86601599
www.eriks.se

Opening hours	Closed Sunday
Credit cards	Accepted
Price range	Affordable
Style	Casual
Cuisine	Swedish
Recommended for	Regular neighbourhood

'This is a classic!'—Anton Bjuhr

Literally 'back pocket', a *bakficka* is a smaller, more casual offshoot of a grand establishment – in this case, Erik Lallerstedt's Gondolen, a glass-box dining room at the top of a crane overlooking Södermalm. Eriks Bakficka has a classic bistro feel, with parquet floor, wood panelling and marble-topped tables. The menu is deliberately humble, sticking to homely daily specials, such as grilled chicken with fried potatoes, a plate of Baltic herring, and cured salmon with dill mash. Yet even simple Skagen toasts are executed with elan; products are organic, free-range and seasonal; and Erik's signature cheeseburger – not always on the menu but always available to those who ask – is a cult classic.

ESPERANTO

Recommended by
Björn Persson

Kungstensgatan 2
Östermalm
Stockholm 114 25
+46 86962323
www.esperantorestaurant.se

Opening hours	Closed Monday, Tuesday and Sunday
Credit cards	Accepted
Price range	Expensive
Style	Smart casual
Cuisine	International
Recommended for	High end

Swedish chef Sayan Isaksson won gold at the World Culinary Olympics in 2004, but has since shown he can create art on a plate even when there's no podium place at stake. His grand restaurant Esperanto opened in 2005 in what was the foyer of Stockholm's old Jarla Theatre (John Cale and Blondie played there in the 1970s) and was awarded a Michelin star two years later. Isaksson's cuisine is minimal yet flamboyant 'international gastronomy without boundaries' – hence 'Esperanto' – and shows marked French, Japanese and local influences. Choose from a seasonal or dégustation menu of, say, Swedish wagyu, served with fine wines or rare teas.

GASTROLOGIK

Recommended by
Niklas Ekstedt,
Magnus Nilsson

Artillerigatan 14
Östermalm
Stockholm 114 51
+46 86623060
www.gastrologik.se

Opening hours	Closed Monday and Sunday
Credit cards	Accepted
Price range	Expensive
Style	Smart casual
Cuisine	Modern Swedish
Recommended for	Worth the travel

'They have a great wine list, small but very well selected. And it's not too pricey for an upscale restaurant.'
—Niklas Ekstedt

Opened in late 2011 in Östermalm, by chefs Jacob Holmström and Anton Bjuhr, Gastrologik has quickly established a reputation as one of Stockholm's freshest, forward-thinking restaurants. The relaxed modern dining room – a beautifully understated combination of oak floors, white walls, copper lampshades, aquamarine glass and sturdy but stylish Scandinavian furniture – is a suitable setting for daily-changing dishes that are exercises in product-driven simplicity, hence the restaurant's playfully named 'Let Today's Produce Decide' tasting menu. Next door sits Speceriet, their delicatessen, in which the stone oven bakes their sourdough bread.

ÖSTERMALMS KORVSPECIALIST

Recommended by
Jacob Holmström

Nybrogatan 57
Östermalm
Stockholm 114 40
+46 87829579
www.ostermalmskorvspecialist.se

Opening hours	Open 7 days
Reservation policy	No
Credit cards	Not accepted
Price range	Budget
Style	Casual
Cuisine	Hot Dogs
Recommended for	Bargain

'Great sausages for next to no money. Beware the long queues (waiting lines).'—Jacob Holmström

Some Swedes would argue that the world's best hot dog stand is in Stockholm. Known to locals as Bruno's, after its German-born owner Bruno Fortkord, it's near the city's famous Östermalms Saluhall indoor food market. Select your sausage from a list that takes in Argentinian chorizo, Hungarian *kabonos* Tunisian *merguez*, and Slovenian *kransky*, before heading to the heartland of the wurst, with Austria, Switzerland and Germany represented. Vegetarians get grilled halloumi. All are cooked to order and stuffed inside a grilled baguette with sauerkraut and your mustard of choice. Forget ketchup – Bruno has his own home-made spicy tomato sauce.

P.A. & CO

Recommended by
Niklas Ekstedt

Riddargatan 8
Östermalm
Stockholm 114 35
+46 86110845
www.paco.se

Opening hours	Open 7 days
Credit cards	Accepted
Price range	Affordable
Style	Casual
Cuisine	Modern Scandinavian
Recommended for	Regular neighbourhood

'A small bistro in the city centre of Stockholm that always serves a really nice meal for a fair price. The environment is busy but still calm.'—Niklas Ekstedt

For over two decades, this small corner café (on a quiet side street off the busy Stureplan), from the same owner as Bistro Süd, has endeared itself to locals. The decor combines lavish chandeliers with exposed industrial pipes. International dishes include Thai Penang seafood curry or deep-fried halloumi with beetroot (beet), while Swedish fare also features strongly, from meatballs various ways, to an interactive platter of Beef Rydberg. But it is P.A. & Co's signature pudding – Gino, composed of diced strawberries, bananas and kiwi fruits, baked, then topped with grated white chocolate and served with vanilla ice cream – for which guests seem to return with regularity.

RÅKULTUR

Recommended by
Mikael Einarsson, Björn
Frantzén, Gustav Otterberg

Kungstensgatan 2
Östermalm
Stockholm 114 25
+46 86962325
www.rakultur.se

Opening hours	Closed Sunday
Credit cards	Accepted
Price range	Affordable
Style	Smart casual
Cuisine	Japanese
Recommended for	Bargain

'Great value for money, excellent sushi!'
—Björn Frantzén

RICHE

Recommended by
Björn Frantzén

Birger Jarlsgatan 4
Östermalm
Stockholm 114 34
+46 854503560
www.riche.se

Opening hours	Open 7 days
Credit cards	Accepted
Price range	Affordable
Style	Casual
Cuisine	Café-Bar-Bistro
Recommended for	Breakfast

'Great atmosphere and a big menu. Best breakfast in Stockholm.'—Björn Frantzén

SPECERIET

Recommended by
Niklas Ekstedt

Artillerigatan 14
Östermalm
Stockholm 114 51
+46 86623060
www.speceriet.se

Opening hours	Closed Sunday
Reservation policy	No
Credit cards	Accepted
Price range	Affordable
Style	Casual
Cuisine	Modern Swedish
Recommended for	Wish I'd opened

STUREHOF

Recommended by
Tomi Björck, Anton Bjuhr,
Mikael Einarsson, Magnus
Ek, Niklas Ekstedt, Björn
Frantzén, Jacob Holmström,
Kim Öhman

Stureplan 2
Östermalm
Stockholm 114 46
+46 84405730
www.sturehof.com

Opening hours	Open 7 days
Credit cards	Accepted
Price range	Affordable
Style	Smart casual
Cuisine	Seafood
Recommended for	Late night

'You can eat herrings and toast *skagen* from 11.00 a.m. until 1.00 a.m. It feels like you are welcome any time of the day. Nice wine collection and great food.'
—Tomi Björck

A night out with Stockholm's beautiful people should begin and end at Sturehof, the beating heart of Stureplan's social scene. Open 365 days a year, from mid-morning into the early hours, Sturehof is a classic seafood brasserie in a modern metropolitan vein. Opened in 1897 as a German-style beer hall by the name of Malta, it was renamed in 1905, when it became the seafood and fine wine specialist that it is today. Turbot with brown butter, bouillabaisse, lobster soup and fried herring are among the dishes that have stood the test of time. Preening and posing abounds al fresco and in the bars.

TAVERNA BRILLO

Recommended by
Mathias Dahlgren

Sturegatan 6
Östermalm
Stockholm 114 35
+46 851977800
www.tavernabrillo.se

Opening hours	Open 7 days
Credit cards	Accepted
Price range	Affordable
Style	Casual
Cuisine	Italian
Recommended for	Late night

'Stockholm doesn't have many late-night restaurants but this is one of them. I like their pizzas. Still, after 1.00 a.m. you have to look out for a hot-dog stand.'
—Mathias Dahlgren

VOLT

Recommended by
Niklas Ekstedt,
Jacob Holmström

Kommendörsgatan 16
Östermalm
Stockholm 114 48
+46 86623400
www.restaurangvolt.se

Opening hours	Closed Monday and Sunday
Credit cards	Accepted
Price range	Affordable
Style	Smart casual
Cuisine	Modern Swedish
Recommended for	Local favourite

'Great small restaurant with a nice atmosphere and great food with local ingredients.'—Jacob Holmström

The cool young things at Volt in Östermalm have done away with the fuss of the fine dining experience to produce an ambitious restaurant with the buzz of a bistro. The kitchen embraces 'New Nordic', preferring ingredients that are natural and artisanal, and techniques that maximize flavour, texture and excitement. 'Fermented cod roe, onion cream and pickled garlic' or 'lamb cabbage bouillon malt' look and sound modern but there's an appealing note of nostalgia in there too. For the full Volt-age, there's a nine-course menu with a glass of natural wine at every stage.

AMIDA KOLGRILL

Folkungagatan 76
Södermalm
Stockholm 116 22
+46 84420360
www.amida.se

Recommended by
Mathias Dahlgren, Kim
Öhman

Opening hours	Open 7 days
Reservation policy	No
Credit cards	Accepted but not AMEX
Price range	Budget
Style	Casual
Cuisine	Turkish
Recommended for	Bargain

'Best kebab in Sweden. Enough said.'—Kim Öhman

This renowned cheap-eat has been serving grilled meats and charred vegetables to hungry Stockholmares in search of a satisfyingly salty hit for over ten years. Kurdish, Turkish and Persian kebabs and salads dominate the menu in a city not known for its culinary multiculturalism. Think huge plates of mint-specked lamb shish or marinated chicken skewers with mounds of rice, melanges of pickles dusted with sumac. Key to the unique flavour of their meats is the use of a traditional Mesopotamian aromatic charcoal bed. Eat in with a view of the open kitchen or order to take away.

BABYLON

Björns Trädgårdsgränd 4
Södermalm
Stockholm 116 21
+46 86408083

Recommended by
Petter Nilsson

Opening hours	Open 7 days
Reservation policy	No
Credit cards	Accepted
Price range	Budget
Style	Casual
Cuisine	Polish
Recommended for	Regular neighbourhood

'Very close to the subway, yet slightly removed from city stress. Sometimes they have ok *pierogi* (Polish dumplings) for lunch, sometimes cheesecake for dessert.'—Petter Nilsson

GYRELLA

Götgatan 93
Södermalm
Stockholm 116 62
+46 86426570
www.gyrella.se

Recommended by
Kim Öhman

Opening hours	Open 7 days
Reservation policy	No
Credit cards	Accepted but not AMEX
Price range	Budget
Style	Casual
Cuisine	Greek
Recommended for	Late night

'Greek fast food. Does the trick every time.' —Kim Öhman

NYTORGET 6

Nytorget 6
Södermalm
Stockholm 116 40
+46 86409655
www.nytorget6.com

Recommended by
Mikael Einarsson

Opening hours	Open 7 days
Credit cards	Accepted
Price range	Affordable
Style	Casual
Cuisine	Swedish
Recommended for	Breakfast

Taking the address as its name, this large all-day, all-encompassing neighbourhood restaurant has a happy vibe. It gets so popular that customers spill out onto the street, whatever the weather. Fortunately, jaunty canopies, heat lamps and blankets provide defence in cooler months. Inside, eclectic canvases draw the eye, while aromas emanating from the open kitchen stir other senses. An excellent place to start the day, uncomplicated but satisfying dishes include cured and smoked meats, cheeses and pickled cucumbers, and decadent coconut *chokladbollar* (chocolate balls). At weekends brunch runs much of the day. Try *langos* (fried potato bread open sandwich) of shrimp, sour cream, red onion and chives.

POM & FLORA

Bondegatan 64
Södermalm
Stockholm 116 29
+46 841010049
www.pomochflora.se

Opening hours..Open 7 days
Reservation policy...No
Credit cards...............................Accepted but not AMEX
Price range..Budget
Style..Casual
Cuisine..Café
Recommended for..Breakfast

'The chefs used to work in more high-end places.
Now they just give you what you want, without losing
themselves.'—Petter Nilsson

RESTAURANG GANDHI

Katarina Bangata 47
Södermalm
Stockholm 116 39
+46 86439788
www.restauranggandhi.se

Opening hours..Open 7 days
Credit cards.................Accepted but not AMEX or Diners
Price range..Budget
Style..Casual
Cuisine..Indian
Recommended for..Bargain

'They are good at sauces and they are very nice to
children...'—Petter Nilsson

CHEZ BETTY

Roslagsgatan 43
Vasastan
Stockholm 113 54
+46 8292293
www.chezbetty.se

Opening hours...............................Closed Monday and Sunday
Credit cards...Accepted
Price range..Affordable
Style..Casual
Cuisine..French
Recommended for.........................Regular neighbourhood

'A fun restaurant with the simplest food. Its two chefs
both cook and serve. The perfect good food.'
—Gustav Otterberg

RAMEN KI MAMA

Birger Jarlsgatan 93
Vasastan
Stockholm 113 56
+46 8155539
www.kimamma.se

Opening hours..Open 7 days
Credit cards...............................Accepted but not AMEX
Price range..Budget
Style..Casual
Cuisine..Ramen Noodles
Recommended for.........................Regular neighbourhood

'Besides the fact that the restaurant is a one-minute
walk from my home, it's the best place for noodles
in Stockholm.'—Mathias Dahlgren

THE BREAD STATION

Charlottenlund Stationsplads 2
Charlottenlund
Hovedstaden 2920
Denmark
+45 39303736
www.thebreadstation.com

Opening hours..Open 7 days
Reservation policy...No
Credit cards...Accepted
Price range..Budget
Style..Casual
Cuisine...Café-Bakery
Recommended for..Breakfast

'It's located outside the city, about twenty minutes on
the train. Being a chef, it's hard to get up in time for
breakfast but this place is worth it. Set in an old train
station, they have their own mill to grind the flour that
they use for the bread and pastries. It's a good place
to start the day.'—Victor Wågman

GRANOLA

Recommended by
Paul Cunningham,
Jakob Mielcke

Værnedemsvej 5
Frederiksberg
Hovedstaden 1819
Denmark
+45 33250080

Opening hours	Open 7 days
Credit cards	Accepted
Price range	Affordable
Style	Casual
Cuisine	Café
Recommended for	Breakfast

'Go for the eggs!'—Jakob Mielcke

This chic corner café's name is synonymous with 'breakfast' for the foodies on Værnedamsvej. They come in droves daily for their glass tumblers of freshly ground coffee, healthy fruit and vegetable juices with shots of fresh ginger, egg muffins and delicious sandwiches (among the best are vitello tonnato, and chicken and basil). The lovely 1950s-style setting is also a draw. The old grocery counter, coffee mill and vintage signs give the place a French feel but there's no doubt, looking around you, that you're deep in fashionable Copenhagen. The pavement tables are much sought after.

IPSEN & CO.

Recommended by
Rasmus Kofoed

Gammel Kongevej 108
Frederiksberg
Hovedstaden 1850
Denmark
+45 32145527
www.ipsenogco.dk

Opening hours	Open 7 days
Reservation policy	No
Credit cards	Accepted but not AMEX
Price range	Budget
Style	Casual
Cuisine	Café-Bakery
Recommended for	Breakfast

'The owner is always there and there is a friendly atmosphere. Amazing rye bread, yogurt with sea buckthorn jam and great coffee, which is everything I need for a great breakfast.'—Rasmus Kofoed

MIELCKE & HURTIGKARL

Recommended by
Paul Cunningham

Frederiksberg Runddel 1
Frederiksberg
Hovedstaden 2000
Denmark
+45 38348436
www.mhcph.com

Opening hours	Closed Monday and Sunday
Credit cards	Accepted
Price range	Expensive
Style	Smart casual
Cuisine	Modern Danish
Recommended for	High end

'Jakob Mielcke is intelligent, inquisitive and most inventive. He is, in my opinion, the most underrated chef cooking in Copenhagen today. The restaurant is arty and quirky, the service warm and friendly, the food is delicious.'—Paul Cunningham

RESTAURANT MÊLÉE

Recommended by
Brian Mark Hansen,
Claus Meyer

Martensens Allé 16
Frederiksberg
Hovedstaden 1828
Denmark
+45 35131134
www.melee.dk

Opening hours	Closed Monday and Sunday
Credit cards	Accepted
Price range	Affordable
Style	Casual
Cuisine	French
Recommended for	Late night

'A wonderful place serving rustic French food until late.'—Claus Meyer

SÁIGÒN QUÁN

Godthåbsvej 48
Frederiksberg
Hovedstaden 2000
Denmark
+45 38101900
www.saigonquan.dk

Recommended by
Claus Meyer, Thomas
Rode Andersen

Opening hours	Closed Tuesday
Credit cards	Not accepted
Price range	Budget
Style	Casual
Cuisine	Vietnamese
Recommended for	Bargain

'The food is cheap, skillfully prepared and properly seasoned.'—Thomas Rode Andersen

SOKKELUND CAFÉ & BRASSERIE

Smallegade 36e
Frederiksberg
Hovedstaden 2000
Denmark
+45 38106400
www.cafe-sokkelund.dk

Recommended by
Claus Møller
Henriksen

Opening hours	Open 7 days
Credit cards	Accepted
Price range	Affordable
Style	Casual
Cuisine	French Brasserie
Recommended for	Breakfast

'It is a lovely café with good food and good service.'
—Claus Møller Henriksen

VIET-NAM NAM

Godthåbsvej 8
Frederiksberg
Hovedstaden 2000
Denmark
+45 38103764
www.viet-namnam.dk

Recommended by
Rasmus Kofoed

Opening hours	Open 7 days
Credit cards	Accepted
Price range	Affordable
Style	Casual
Cuisine	Vietnamese
Recommended for	Regular neighbourhood

'Casual street food. I really like their flavours, the use of fresh herbs, spices and a tandoori oven, which is very interesting for that kind of food.'—Rasmus Kofoed

TINGGÅRDEN

Frederiksværkvej 182
Frederiksværk
Hovedstaden 3300
Denmark
+45 48712235
www.tinggarden.dk

Recommended by
Claus Meyer

Opening hours	Closed Monday and Tuesday
Credit cards	Accepted but not AMEX
Price range	Affordable
Style	Casual
Cuisine	Danish
Recommended for	Regular neighbourhood

'The food is extremely honest and the ambience is totally down to earth.'—Claus Meyer

In the Zealand town of Frederiksværk (45 minutes' drive northwest of Copenhagen) Tinggården embodies the Danish spirit of *hygge*. A cosy and inviting thatched farmhouse, it offers Danish hospitality in the style of the French country kitchen. This blissful spot – its whitewashed, beamed dining room overlooks an idyllic cobbled courtyard shaded by a walnut tree – has been run as a restaurant since 1987, when Charlotte Vendorf and Jan Friis-Mikkelsen arrived. Sophisticated country cooking – fried sole with potato fricassee, leek and Parmesan/peach tart with raspberry sorbet and soft yogurt cream – meets gently priced French wines.

SØLLERØD KRO

Søllerødvej 35
Holte
Hovedstaden 2840
Denmark
+45 45802505
www.soelleroed-kro.dk

Recommended by
Yves Le Lay, Claus Meyer,
Nicolai Nørregaard,
Christian F. Puglisi,
Victor Wågman

Opening hours	Closed Monday and Tuesday
Credit cards	Accepted
Price range	Expensive
Style	Smart casual
Cuisine	European
Recommended for	High end

'In my opinion the best service in Denmark. Amazing wine list, great food and no risk of leaving hungry!'
—Nicolai Nørregaard

DEN RØDE COTTAGE

Strandvejen 550
Klampenborg
Hovedstaden 2930
Denmark
+45 39904614
www.dengulecottage.dk

Recommended by
Claus Meyer

Opening hours	Open 7 days
Credit cards	Accepted
Price range	Affordable
Style	Smart casual
Cuisine	Modern Nordic
Recommended for	Local favourite

In an idyllic woodland setting in the countryside north of Copenhagen, Den Røde Cottage occupies a nineteenth-century forestry officer's house that, surrounded by ancient beech trees, looks so sweet it could grace a Danish biscuit (cookie) tin. The kitchen is run by Lars Thomsen, formerly of Dragsholm Slot, the monthly changing Nordic menus – three, five, seven or eight courses – devised in partnership with Anita Klemensen, previously of the quirky Copenhagen apartment-based 1.th. Together with Anders Wulff-Sorensen, another ex-city chef who worked at Søllerød Kro, they also run Den Gule Cottage (The Yellow Cottage) in another picture-perfect dwelling, overlooking the coast slightly further south.

RESTAURANT ET

Åboulevarden 7
Aarhus
Midtjylland 8000
Denmark
+45 86138800
www.restaurant-et.dk

Recommended by
Thorsten Schmidt

Opening hours	Closed Sunday
Credit cards	Accepted
Price range	Affordable
Style	Casual
Cuisine	French Bistro
Recommended for	Regular neighbourhood

'Simply fantastic place with honest food that delights all those around the table every time you visit.'
—Thorsten Schmidt

ST. PAULS APOTHEK

Jægergårdsgade 76
Aarhus
Midtjylland 8000
Denmark
+45 86120833
www.stpaulsapothek.dk

Recommended by
Thorsten Schmidt

Opening hours	Closed Monday and Sunday
Credit cards	Accepted
Price range	Affordable
Style	Casual
Cuisine	Modern Nordic
Recommended for	Late night

'They make great beef and cocktails. The place has a buzzing atmosphere even when the clock has passed 2.00 a.m.'—Thorsten Schmidt

MOLSKROEN

Recommended by
Thorsten Schmidt

Hotel Molskroen
Hovedgaden 16
Ebeltoft
Midtjylland 8400
Denmark
+45 86362200
www.molskroen.dk

Opening hours	Open 7 days
Credit cards	Accepted
Price range	Expensive
Style	Smart casual
Cuisine	Modern Nordic
Recommended for	High end

'Located in a naturally beautiful area close to the national park and mountains. Raw ingredients of the highest quality, a skilled chef and a great service team make it one of my favourite places to eat on Sundays.'
—Thorsten Schmidt

EMMERYS

Recommended by
Thorsten Schmidt

Nordre Strandvej 24
Risskov
Midtjylland 8240
Denmark
+45 86255553
www.emmerys.dk

Opening hours	Open 7 days
Reservation policy	No
Credit cards	Accepted
Price range	Budget
Style	Casual
Cuisine	Café-Bakery
Recommended for	Breakfast

'They serve only the very best-quality home-made produce, with a great selection of seasonal specialties. The best service.'—Thorsten Schmidt

SVINKLØV BADEHOTEL RESTAURANT

Recommended by
Mette Hvarre
Gassner

Badehotel
Svinkløvvej 593
Fjerritslev
Nordjylland 9690
Denmark
+45 98218105
www.svinkloev-badehotel.dk

Opening hours	Open 7 days
Credit cards	Accepted but not Mastercard or AMEX
Price range	Affordable
Style	Casual
Cuisine	Modern Danish
Recommended for	Worth the travel

'The atmosphere and setting is priceless and the food is super simple and matches the surroundings perfectly.'—Mette Hvarre Gassner

Svinkløv Badehotel in Northern Jutland harks back to an era of bracing summer breaks on the North Sea. Built in 1925, the thirty-six-room old wooden hotel is all grey – as grey as the skies above on a squally day – but inside, it's cosy and inviting. Lunch looking out over the dunes might take a nostalgic tack with pickled herring, radishes and onions to start, with fried plaice, potatoes and parsley sauce to follow. At dinner, chef Kenneth Hansen shows a modernist bent with plates such as smoked scallops with pickled cucumber and horseradish cream. Open April to October.

SLOTSKØKKENET

Recommended by
Gunnar Karl Gíslason,
Matthew Orlando,
Victor Wågman

Dragsholm Slot
Dragsholm Allé
Hørve
Sjælland 4534
Denmark
+45 59653300
www.dragsholm-slot.dk

Opening hours	Variable
Credit cards	Accepted
Price range	Expensive
Style	Smart casual
Cuisine	Mordern Nordic
Recommended for	High end

'It is a castle from the 1200s, about an hour outside of Copenhagen. It's located in Lammefjord, which is the Garden of Eden for vegetables. The chef, Claus Møller Henrikson, has managed to bring the surrounding area into his kitchen and dining room.

You really feel like you should be eating his food in that dining room and nowhere else. I cannot wait for spring so I can go back to get my fix.'—Matthew Orlando

An hour's drive northwest of Copenhagen, in the Odsherred countryside, lies Dragsholm Slot, one of Denmark's oldest castles – the sort of baroque early thirteenth-century pile that, looking at it from the outside, you can imagine Hamlet sulking around. Now a thirty-six-room hotel, it has two restaurants: the serious Slotskøkkenet – Castle Kitchen – and the casual Spisehus, or Eatery. Claus Møller Henriksen, yet another talented alumnus from Noma's kitchen, where he was sous-chef, oversees both. As at Noma, the focus is very much on vegetable over animal protein, with much of the former grown in the castle's garden and the surrounding island of Zealand.

ELMELY KRO

Holbæk Landevej 63
Ugerløse
Sjælland 4350
Denmark
+45 59188278
www.elmelykro.dk

Recommended by
Claus Møller Henriksen

Opening hours	Closed Monday
Credit cards	Accepted
Price range	Affordable
Style	Casual
Cuisine	Danish
Recommended for	Local favourite

'Genuine Danish food with the taste and identity of an old inn.'—Claus Møller Henriksen

Named after the elm that used to tower over it, this rural, thatched roadside inn showcases the gently updated Danish cuisine of Henrik Nielsen and Poul Bøje Nielsen. Like the duo's fish restaurant, SuRi, half-an-hour's drive north, in Holbæk harbour, expect plenty of 'surf' on the menu, such as lobster with aïoli and green tomato compote, and herring two ways (curried, and marinated with buckthorn), alongside 'turf', including pulled pork from Fjord beasts and pheasant with chestnuts. Despite these smart ingredients and a biodynamic vegetable patch, Elmely Kro remains unpretentious. Indeed, the heated terrace makes a pleasant pit-stop spot for coffee and cake.

RESTAURANT RUDOLF MATHIS

Dosseringen 13
Keterminde
Syddanmark 5300
Denmark
+45 65323233
www.rudolf-mathis.dk

Recommended by
Brian Mark Hansen

Opening hours	Closed Monday and Sunday
Credit cards	Accepted
Price range	Expensive
Style	Smart casual
Cuisine	Seafood
Recommended for	Local favourite

'Local ingredients, respectful cooking.'
—Brian Mark Hansen

KOK & VIN

Store Gråbrødrestræde 19
Odense
Syddanmark 5000
Denmark
+45 31690106
www.kokogvin.dk

Recommended by
Mette Hvarre Gassner

Opening hours	Closed Sunday
Credit cards	Accepted but not AMEX
Price range	Affordable
Style	Casual
Cuisine	French
Recommended for	Bargain

'It is casual, cosy and the food is good.'
—Mette Hvarre Gassner

'It's super cosy and has the most personal touch you'll find in a restaurant in Copenhagen.'
ADAM AAMANN P286

'Serves all the Danish classics.'
NICOLAI NØRREGAARD P290

COPENHAGEN

'COOLEST RESTAURANT IN TOWN.'
RENÉ REDZEPI P286

'You can drink delicious homemade schnapps at noon and not be judged!'
SAMUEL NUTTER P291

'MY FAVOURITE PLACE FOR A HOME-BAKED BUN.'
JAKOB MIELCKE P286

'Luxury.'
BRIAN MARK HANSEN P289

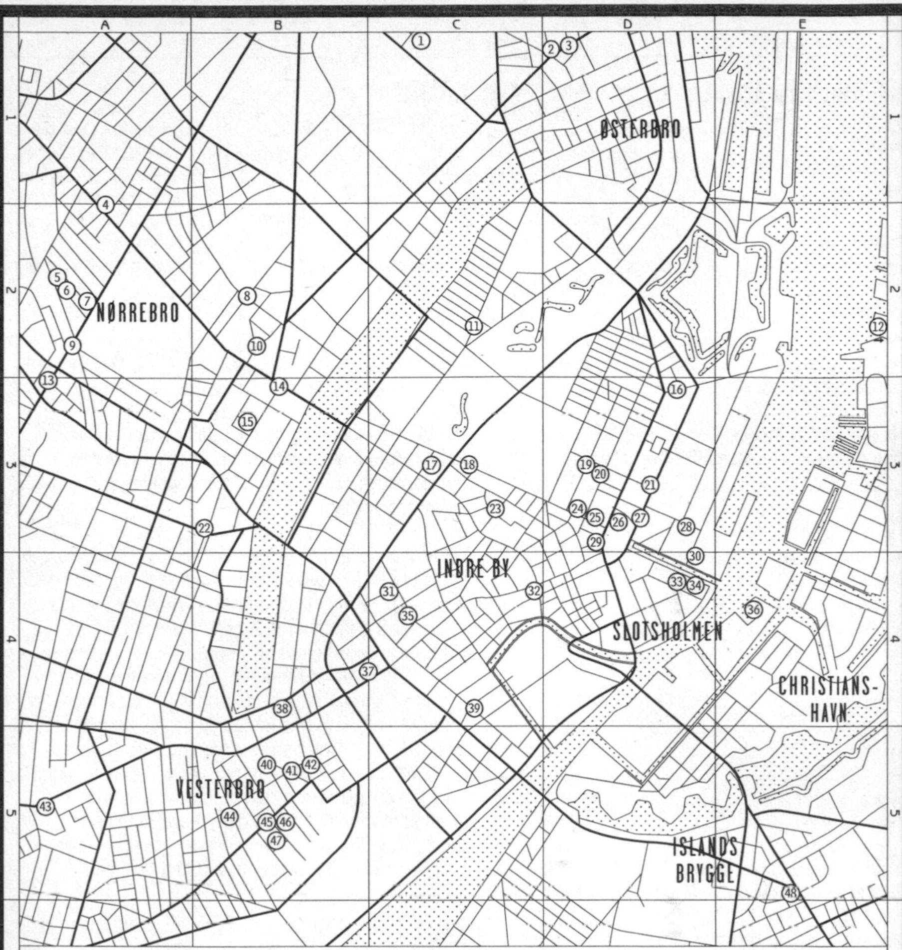

ØSTERBRO
NØRREBRO
INDRE BY
SLOTSHOLMEN
CHRISTIANS-
HAVN
VESTERBRO
ISLANDS
BRYGGE

COPENHAGEN

N
SCALE
0 75 150 225
yd.

1. *Geranium (p.296)*
2. *Hos Fischer (p.296)*
3. *Krummen & Kagen (p.297)*
4. *Kebabistan (p.292)*
5. *Manfreds & Vin (p.293)*
6. *Relæ (p.293)*
7. *The Coffee Collective (p.292)*
8. *Kiin Kiin (p.292)*
9. *Safir Kebab (p.294)*
10. *Selfish (p.294)*
11. *Aamanns Deli & Take Away (p.296)*
12. *Amass (p.286)*
13. *Fu Wa (p.292)*
14. *Beyti (p.291)*
15. *Ranee's (p.293)*
16. *Toldbod Bodega (p.291)*
17. *Torvehallerne (p.291)*
18. *Café Det Vide Hus (p.287)*
19. *Casa D'Antino (p.288)*
20. *Pluto (p.290)*
21. *AOC (pp.286–287)*
22. *Radio (p.296)*
23. *Schønnemann (p.290)*
24. *Atelier September (p.287)*
25. *The Coffee Factory (p.288)*
26. *Geist (pp.288–289)*
27. *Mash (p.289)*
28. *Restaurant Sankt Annæ (p.290)*
29. *Marchal (p.289)*
30. *Told & Snaps (p.291)*
31. *Bror (p.287)*
32. *Cafe Europa 1989 (p.287)*
33. *1.th (p.286)*
34. *Damindra (p.288)*
35. *La Galette (p.288)*
36. *Noma (p.289)*
37. *John's Hotdog Deli (p.295)*
38. *ISSA (p.295)*
39. *Tivolihallen (p.291)*
40. *Cofoco (p.295)*
41. *Noodle House (p.295)*
42. *Bento (p.294)*
43. *Pony (p.296)*
44. *Banzai (p.294)*
45. *Chicky Grill (p.294)*
46. *Paté Paté (p.296)*
47. *Kødbyens Fiskebar (p.295)*
48. *Kaffebaren på Amager (p.286)*

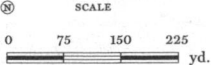

KAFFEBAREN PÅ AMAGER
Æblestien 2
Amager Vest
Copenhagen 2300
+45 26356083

Recommended by
Jakob Mielcke

Opening hours	Open 7 days
Reservation policy	No
Credit cards	Not accepted
Price range	Budget
Style	Casual
Cuisine	Café-Bakery
Recommended for	Breakfast

'This is my favourite place for a home-baked bun, good coffee or yogurt with muesli.'—Jakob Mielcke

1.TH
Herluf Trolles Gade 9
Indre By
Copenhagen 1052
+45 33935770
www.1th.dk

Recommended by
Adam Aamann

Opening hours	Closed Sunday to Tuesday
Credit cards	Accepted
Price range	Expensive
Style	Casual
Cuisine	Modern Danish
Recommended for	High end

'It's super cosy and has the most personal touch you'll find in a restaurant in Copenhagen.'—Adam Aamann

You make a reservation to be invited to the posh Danish dinner party experience that is the 1.th (its name is an abbreviation of 'first floor to the right'). Hosted in a retro-styled apartment in Herluf Trolles Gade behind the Royal Theatre, the ambience is secret society meets old-fashioned Danish hospitality. The creation of Mette Martinussen, who hosted her first dinner party here over a decade ago, you mingle for drinks and canapés in the drawing room, with the twenty or so other diners, before sitting down in an intimate dining room to an innovative ten-course tasting menu.

AMASS
Refshalevej 153
Indre By
Copenhagen 1432
+45 43584330
www.amassrestaurant.com

Recommended by
Andreas Dahlberg,
Mehmet Gürs, Claus Møller
Henriksen, Filip Langhoff,
René Redzepi, Thomas Rode
Andersen, Stephen Toman

Opening hours	Closed Monday and Sunday
Credit cards	Accepted
Price range	Expensive
Style	Smart casual
Cuisine	Modern Nordic
Recommended for	Wish I'd opened

'Coolest restaurant in town, a daily-changing menu with lots of imagination. It has its own vegetable garden and perfect views of the Copenhagen harbour.' —René Redzepi

Shortly before Amass launched in 2013, René Redzepi predicted that it would be that year's hottest European opening. He may well have been right. This venture, from Matt Orlando, the American former head chef of Noma, became not only one of Copenhagen's main destination restaurants but was immediately recognized as a beautiful space: a vast cafeteria with soaring windows and engaging graffiti murals. Housed in a former shipyard in the industrial area of Refshaleøen, its constantly changing menu might include crispy oats with hot-smoked foie gras and walnut marigold, or salted mackerel with grilled skin and spring onion (scallion). Herbs are grown in the garden, where, at night, they light a bonfire.

AOC
Dronningens Tværgade 2
Indre By
Copenhagen 1302
+45 33111145
www.restaurantaoc.dk

Recommended by
Claus Meyer

Opening hours	Closed Monday and Sunday
Credit cards	Accepted
Price range	Expensive
Style	Smart casual
Cuisine	Modern Nordic
Recommended for	Local favourite

The 'Modern/New Nordic Kitchen' trend doesn't begin and end with Noma. Restaurant AOC offers another take on its themes, shifting the focus from obscure Scandinavian ingredients to techniques and combinations designed to thrill all the senses. For an example look no further than ex-Jules Verne chef

Søren Selin's edible pastoral tableau of 'hole in the lake' with celeriac and thyme, or his grilled greens with bleek roe and smoked egg yolk. For the full AOC experience go for the 'sensory evening' of nine-course tasting menu with wines from one of the best collections in town. The surroundings – the white-washed cellar of an old mansion – are beautiful.

ATELIER SEPTEMBER

Gothersgade 30
Indre By
Copenhagen 1123
www.atelierseptember.dk

Recommended by
Bo Bech, Samuel Nutter,
Nicolai Nørregaard,
Matthew Orlando

Opening hours	Closed Sunday
Reservation policy	No
Credit cards	Accepted
Price range	Budget
Style	Casual
Cuisine	Café-Bar-Bistro
Recommended for	Breakfast

'A coffee bar/breakfast spot. I am a coffee geek and always fantasized about having a cool coffee spot with really good bites to eat that are not the same as every other coffee spot. They hit the nail on the head and I am so glad that they opened last year. Plus they serve Koppi coffee, which just happens to be my favourite roastery.'—Matthew Orlando

BROR

Sankt Peders Stræde 24a
Indre By
Copenhagen 1453
+45 32175999
www.restaurantbror.dk

Recommended by
Matthew Orlando,
Björn Persson, Thomas
Rode Andersen

Opening hours	Closed Monday and Tuesday
Credit cards	Accepted
Price range	Affordable
Style	Smart casual
Cuisine	Modern Nordic
Recommended for	Worth the travel

'Run by Samuel Nutter and Victor Wågman, two former sous chefs from Noma, Bror is a no-nonsense place that serves super-delicious food in a chilled-out atmosphere. They are two of the nicest guys I know and that transfers directly into the feeling of eating at their restaurant. A lot of other places call themselves "nose-to-tail", but Bror does it like no other... and they don't even claim it.'—Matthew Orlando

Bror – 'brother' in Danish – is the work of brothers-in-pans and former Noma sous-chefs, English-born Samuel Nutter and Swede Victor Wågman. Opened in wood-panelled, split-level premises near Nørreport station in March 2013, it's a cosy, modern Nordic bistro that pushes a compact seasonal menu. Their short list of constantly changing, tersely described, simple sounding but technically excellent snacks – herring with rye and slow-cooked egg, caramelized shallot with cheese or deep-fried bull balls with tartare sauce – are available à la carte or as a reasonably priced, four-course tasting menu with an accompanying flight of quirky, all-natural wines.

CAFÉ DET VIDE HUS

Gothersgade 113
Indre By
Copenhagen 1123
+45 60612002
www.detvidehus.smartlog.dk

Recommended by
René Redzepi

Opening hours	Open 7 days
Reservation policy	No
Credit cards	Accepted
Price range	Budget
Style	Casual
Cuisine	Café-Patisserie
Recommended for	Breakfast

'Great skyr (Nordic-style yogurt), delicious croissants and killer espressos.'—René Redzepi

CAFE EUROPA 1989

Amagertorv 1
Indre By
Copenhagen 1160
+45 33142889
www.europa1989.dk

Recommended by
Thomas Rode Andersen

Opening hours	Open 7 days
Credit cards	Accepted
Price range	Affordable
Style	Casual
Cuisine	Brasserie
Recommended for	Breakfast

'They have always maintained a high quality in their food, and it is the most Paleo-friendly place to have breakfast by far. You don't have to struggle to avoid the stuff that we don't believe in eating.'
—Thomas Rode Andersen

CASA D'ANTINO

Recommended by
Samuel Nutter

Dronningens Tværgade 43
Indre By
Copenhagen 1302
+45 33151505
www.casadantino.dk

Opening hours.................................Closed Monday and Sunday
Credit cards..Accepted
Price range...Affordable
Style...Casual
Cuisine..Italian
Recommended for...High end

'Not that it is expensive, but this place feels worthy of celebrating a special occasion. It feels luxurious, there is an extensive wine list and best of all you get to sample Mariano Greco's splendid southern Italian food.'—Samuel Nutter

THE COFFEE FACTORY

Recommended by
Paul Cunningham

Gothersgade 21
Indre By
Copenhagen 1123
+45 33141582
www.thecoffeefactory.dk

Opening hours.......................................Open 7 days
Reservation policy...No
Credit cards.............................Accepted but not AMEX
Price range...Budget
Style...Casual
Cuisine...Café
Recommended for.............................Regular neighbourhood

'I drink coffee throughout the day at Bente's Coffee Factory. It's coffee made by people who love coffee, for people who love coffee. Great service, a real *Cheers* sort of place, where I always bump into somebody I know. Cortado-like, "John" is one of Bente's bestsellers. Alongside a quick breakfast of fresh, thickly cut rye bread, there's good salted butter and cheese, and blackcurrant jam. A most pleasant start to my day.'—Paul Cunningham

DAMINDRA

Recommended by
Adam Aamann

Holbergsgade 26
Indre By
Copenhagen 1057
+45 33123375
www.damindra.dk

Opening hours.................................Closed Monday and Sunday
Credit cards.........................Accepted but not AMEX or Diners
Price range...Affordable
Style...Casual
Cuisine..Japanese
Recommended for.............................Regular neighbourhood

'An excellent restaurant, great Japanese-style food at affordable prices. The chef and owner has worked in the Nobu restaurants and I love his cooking style and the flavours.' —Adam Aamann

LA GALETTE

Recommended by
Victor Wågman

Larsbjørnsstræde 9
Indre By
Copenhagen 1454
+45 33323790
www.lagalette.dk

Opening hours...Open 7 days
Credit cards.............................Accepted but not AMEX
Price range...Budget
Style...Casual
Cuisine..Crêpes
Recommended for...Bargain

'It is very relaxed and it offers me time to relax and a good meal. It's been there for more than fifteen years under the same owner and is hidden away, close to our restaurant, actually. You can order these crêpes made with their own wheat and different toppings, savoury or sweet.'—Victor Wågman

GEIST

Recommended by
Mette Hvarre Gassner,
Rebecca Kirhoffer, Rasmus
Kofoed, Jakob Mielcke, Claus
Meyer, Nicolai Nørregaard,
Thomas Rode Andersen

Kongens Nytorv 8
Indre By
Copenhagen 1050
+45 33133713
www.restaurantgeist.dk

Opening hours...Open 7 days
Credit cards..Accepted
Price range...Affordable
Style...Casual
Cuisine...Modern Nordic
Recommended for.............................Regular neighbourhood

'I love the style Bo Bech has been practising ever since he worked for me as a very young chef. He's the daredevil of simplicity. He effortlessly puts very few ingredients together on the plate and makes them interact and become precious in a way that nobody else I know can.'—Thomas Rode Andersen

Danish chef Bo Bech has worked with Europe's finest (including Alain Passard and Alain Senderens); he's had his own TV shows; and he's won a Michelin star (at Paustian). He brings this wealth of experience to Geist, his four-year-old restaurant on Copenhagen's Kongens Nytorv. It's a stylish and very current sort of place, touting ambitious but accessible new Nordic cooking in a multifaceted space that comprises restaurant, 'food bar' and particularly lovely courtyard. Simple-sounding dishes reveal intriguing flavour combinations – salted wasabi cream toffee, baked celeriac (celery root) with condensed buttermilk, avocado with caviar and almond oil – and look gorgeous too.

MARCHAL

Recommended by
Brian Mark Hansen

Hotel d'Angleterre
Kongens Nytorv 34
Indre By
Copenhagen 1050
+45 33120094
www.marchal.dk

Opening hours..............................Open 7 days
Credit cards......................................Accepted
Price range......................................Affordable
Style..Smart casual
Cuisine.....................................Modern Nordic
Recommended for.............................Breakfast

'Luxury.'—Brian Mark Hansen

MASH

Recommended by
Mette Hvarre Gassner

Bredgade 20
Indre By
Copenhagen 1260
+45 33139300
www.mashsteak.dk

Opening hours..............................Open 7 days
Credit cards......................................Accepted
Price range..Expensive
Style..Smart casual
Cuisine..Steakhouse
Recommended for...........................Late night

'There is always time and space for a steak. They serve the best steaks, the best fries and the best sauce Béarnaise. It's a no-brainer and the wine list is super!'
—Mette Hvarre Gassner

NOMA

Strandgade 93
Indre By
Copenhagen 1401
+45 32963297
www.noma.dk

Recommended by
Adam Aamann, Josean Alija, Wojciech Modest Amaro, Pascal Aussignac, Rainer Becker, Daniel Berlin, April Bloomfield, Massimo Bottura, Meyjitte Boughenout, Sean Brock, Jo Bøe Klakegg, André Garrett, Mehmet Gürs, Sam Harris, Claus Møller Henriksen, Diego Hernández Baquedano, Georgianna Hiliadaki, Esben Holmboe Bang, Mark Jordan, Tom Kitchin, Rasmus Kofoed, Normand Laprise, Sasu Laukkonen, Murray McDonald, Michael Meredith, Nenad Mlinarevic, Guillaume Monjuré, Yoshihiro Narisawa, Petter Nilsson, Samuel Nutter, Nicolai Nørregaard, Shuko Oda, Davide Oldani, Enrique Olvera, Neil Perry, Christian F. Puglisi, Mads Refslund, Thomas Rode Andersen, Brian Skinner, Ljubomir Stanisic, Bjørn Svensson, Claude & Thomas Troisgros, Jorge Vallejo, Victor Wågman, Blaine Wetzel

Opening hours.............Closed Monday and Sunday
Credit cards......................................Accepted
Price range..Expensive
Style..Smart casual
Cuisine.....................................Mordern Nordic
Recommended for.......................Wish I'd opened

'René marked a change in the perception of modern restaurateuring. Few restaurants represent, as much as Noma does, the excellence and the will to promote and develop the culture of a land.'—Massimo Bottura

'Probably the best restaurant in the world...' has famously been the opinion of an international jury of chefs, restaurateurs and restaurant critics since Noma first won The World's 50 Best Restaurant Awards in 2010. A 200-year-old harbourside warehouse in Christianshavn, originally built to store goods from Iceland, Greenland and the Faroe Islands, has been the home of René Redzepi's headline-grabbing, agenda-setting dining room since 2003. Not content with pushing boundaries with avant-garde and rediscovered techniques applied to products farmed, fished and foraged from the rich Nordic larder (pantry), in early 2015 the restaurant will move temporarily to Tokyo for a game-changing two-month residency.

PLUTO

Borgergade 16
Indre By
Copenhagen 1300
+45 33160016
www.restaurantpluto.dk

Recommended by
Brian Mark Hansen, Claus
Møller Henriksen, Nicolai
Nørregaard, Thomas
Rode Andersen

Opening hours	Closed Sunday
Credit cards	Accepted
Price range	Affordable
Style	Casual
Cuisine	Nordic-French
Recommended for	Late night

'They don't mind you dropping by any time of day for a few dishes. The problem is that you never seem to be able to keep to just a couple. The place itself, and the first couple of dishes, always give you the munchies. Overall, high-quality products, handled with respect, love, and artisan craftsmanship.'
—Thomas Rode Andersen

RESTAURANT SANKT ANNÆ

Sankt Annæ Plads 12
Indre By
Copenhagen 1250
+45 33125497
www.restaurantsanktannae.dk

Recommended by
Nicolai Nørregaard

Opening hours	Closed Sunday
Credit cards	Accepted
Price range	Affordable
Style	Smart casual
Cuisine	Danish
Recommended for	Local favourite

'Old-school traditional Danish lunch restaurant. Serves all the Danish classics. Great atmosphere and sublime open sandwiches and schnapps.'—Nicolai Nørregaard

SCHØNNEMANN

Hauser Plads 16
Indre By
Copenhagen 1127
+45 33120785
www.restaurantschonnemann.dk

Recommended by
Bo Bech, Claus Møller
Henriksen, Esben Holmboe
Bang, René Redzepi

Opening hours	Closed Sunday
Credit cards	Accepted
Price range	Affordable
Style	Casual
Cuisine	Danish
Recommended for	Local favourite

'I had a stellar meal here, I think it sums up the region really well. The mood, beer, aquavit and heartfelt food.'
—Esben Holmboe Bang

Proudly serving traditional smørrebrød (open sandwiches) since 1877, its dark wooden interior with gingham-draped tables is an essential stop for any right-thinking food tourist on a visit to the Danish capital. The organic meat, poultry and dairy used on the menu might be twenty-first century but the sand on the floor is a reminder of the nineteenth century, when it was warmed by charcoal burners and filled with farmers on their way back from delivering to the market. The sandwiches are huge; the aquavit (a favourite Danish alcoholic drink) list long. If in search of 'New Nordic', go elsewhere – this is a taste of old Copenhagen.

TIVOLIHALLEN

Vester Voldgade 91
Indre By
Copenhagen 1552
+45 33110160
www.tivolihallen.dk

Recommended by
René Redzepi

Opening hours	Closed Sunday
Credit cards	Accepted but not AMEX
Price range	Affordable
Style	Casual
Cuisine	Danish
Recommended for	Local favourite

Locals come to this venerable basement restaurant, which has operated continuously since 1790, for some of the best smørrebrød (open sandwiches) in Denmark. Smoked eel, salmon or herring top rye bread with sprinklings of dill and a smooth lick of butter. The interiors, with warm reds and thick tablecloths, have scarcely been updated since the 1920s, and this place has remained impressively immune to the trans-formations Nordic cuisine has undergone in recent years. A perfect place to stop for cold beers and fresh northern fish after a morning at the nearby National Museum.

TOLD & SNAPS

Recommended by
Samuel Nutter

Toldbodgade 2
Indre By
Copenhagen 1253
+45 33938385
www.toldogsnaps.dk

Opening hours..Open 7 days
Credit cards...Accepted
Price range..Affordable
Style..Casual
Cuisine..Danish
Recommended for..................Regular neighbourhood

'This is a great *smørrebrød* restaurant in Copenhagen. As soon as you walk in, you feel very relaxed and comfortable. They serve great Danish classics and good beers. You can also drink delicious, home-made schnapps at noon and not be judged!'—Samuel Nutter

TOLDBOD BODEGA

Recommended by
René Redzepi

Esplanaden 4
Indre By
Copenhagen 1263
+45 33129331
www.toldbod-bodega.dk

Opening hours...............................Closed Monday
Credit cards...Accepted
Price range..Affordable
Style..Casual
Cuisine..Danish
Recommended for..............................Local favourite

'Vibe and food like how Danes used to eat and live.'
—René Redzepi

TORVEHALLERNE

Recommended by
Adam Aamann

Israels Plads
Frederiksborggade 21
Indre By
Copenhagen 1360
www.torvehallernekbh.dk

Opening hours..Open 7 days
Reservation policy..No
Credit cards...Accepted
Price range..Affordable
Style..Casual
Cuisine..Street Food
Recommended for..Bargain

'There are many inexpensive food treats and a great atmosphere.'—Adam Aamann

BEYTI

Recommended by
Samuel Nutter

Blågårdsgade 1
Nørrebro
Copenhagen 2200
+45 32170003
www.beyti.dk

Opening hours..Open 7 days
Reservation policy..No
Credit cards...Not accepted
Price range..Budget
Style..Casual
Cuisine..Kebab Shop
Recommended for..Late night

'There is not such a late-night scene in Copenhagen, kebabs are about the only option after 10.00 p.m.! This one has an open charcoal grill, does everything to order and serves excellent kebabs.'—Samuel Nutter

THE COFFEE COLLECTIVE

Jægersborggade 10
Nørrebro
Copenhagen 2200
+45 60151525
www.coffeecollective.dk

Opening hours	Open 7 days
Credit cards	Accepted
Price range	Budget
Style	Casual
Cuisine	Café
Recommended for	Breakfast

'For an Italian-style breakfast and a cappuccino.'
—Christian F. Puglisi

The Danes take their coffee very seriously and The Coffee Collective in Nørrebro is widely regarded as probably Copenhagen's very best caffeine dispensary, no small compliment in a city where the competition and the coffee is so strong. A micro-roastery run by a crack team of award-winning Danes – roasters, buyers and baristas – beans are sourced directly from farmers around the world, sustainability and fair trade, as well as quality, at the top of the agenda. If you're a coffee geek you'll be in heaven here: you'll have to try very hard indeed to find a better crema on your cuppa.

FU WA

Jagtvej 7
Nørrebro
Copenhagen 2200
+45 38191740
www.fuwa.dk

Opening hours	Closed Tuesday
Credit cards	Not accepted
Price range	Budget
Style	Casual
Cuisine	Cantonese
Recommended for	Regular neighbourhood

'For affordable and quality dim sum.'
—Christian F. Puglisi

KEBABISTAN

Nørrebrogade 160
Nørrebro
Copenhagen 2200

Opening hours	Open 7 days
Reservation policy	No
Credit cards	Not accepted
Price range	Budget
Style	Casual
Cuisine	Fast Food
Recommended for	Late night

'Definitely the best kebab in town.'—Christian F. Puglisi

KIIN KIIN

Guldbergsgade 21
Nørrebro
Copenhagen 2200
+45 35357555
www.kiin.dk

Opening hours	Closed Sunday
Credit cards	Accepted
Price range	Expensive
Style	Smart casual
Cuisine	Thai
Recommended for	Worth the travel

'I was struck by the creative Thai food at Kiin Kiin, the only Michelin-starred Asian restaurant in the area.'
—Tim Cushman

Eyebrows were raised back in 2006 when Henrik Yde-Andersen opened this modern Thai in then still sketchy Nørrebro. Back then, Kiin Kiin (meaning 'dinner's ready') sold take aways (take outs) from the back door to break even. But by 2008 it had won the Michelin star and stellar reputation that it holds today. The seven-course menu opens with 'street food' snacks in the bar and is followed by inventive reworkings of Thai standards, from 'frozen' red curry to fragrant lobster soup with dim sum. Their own Mikkeller beer, brewed with lemon and lime peel, and the Riesling-championing wine list are both designed for spice.

MANFREDS & VIN

Jægersborggade 40
Nørrebro
Copenhagen 2200
+45 36966593
www.manfreds.dk

Recommended by
Esben Holmboe Bang,
Geoff Hopgood, Sasu
Laukkonen, Claus
Meyer, René Redzepi,
Chad Robertson,
Michael Voltaggio

Opening hours	Closed Monday
Credit cards	Accepted
Price range	Affordable
Style	Casual
Cuisine	Nordic-European small plates
Recommended for	Bargain

'Unpretentious, down-to-earth, vegetable-based food and Johnny Cash on the speakers.'—René Redzepi

Run by the team behind Restaurant Relæ, which sits across the street, Manfreds & Vin began life as more of a take away (take out) before morphing into a wine bar and casual dining room. They have a 200-strong list of natural wines, with the dozen or so selections by the glass available displayed on the blackboard behind the bar. Ingredients are sourced from Relæ's suppliers and dishes are mostly tapas-sized and designed for sharing, whether you order from the short and snappy à la carte or go with one of their set menus. The 'Small Lunch Hunger Menu' is a steal at £20 ($32).

RANEE'S

Blågårds Plads 10
Nørrebro
Copenhagen 2200
+45 35368505
www.ranees.dk

Recommended by
Christian F. Puglisi

Opening hours	Closed Sunday
Credit cards	Accepted
Price range	Budget
Style	Casual
Cuisine	Thai
Recommended for	Bargain

'Great Thai kitchen.'—Christian F. Puglisi

RELÆ

Jægersborggade 41
Nørrebro
Copenhagen 2200
+45 36966609
www.restaurant-relae.dk

Recommended by
Bo Bech, Luke Burgess, André
Chiang, Andreas Dahlberg, Vinny
Dotolo, Thrainn Freyr Vigfússon,
Esben Holmboe Bang, Rasmus
Kofoed, Sasu Laukkonen, Claus
Meyer, Jakob Mielcke, Matthew
Orlando, Peeter Pihel, René
Redzepi, Chad Robertson, Sami
Tallberg, Stephen Toman

Opening hours	Closed Sunday to Tuesday
Credit cards	Accepted
Price range	Expensive
Style	Smart casual
Cuisine	Modern Nordic
Recommended for	Worth the travel

'This is a place that feels liberated, at ease with itself. We share a common wine philosophy, but Relae feels less bound by geography while still respecting its location. I love the feel of the dining room and the casualness glosses over the serious focus this place embodies.'—Luke Burgess

Opened in 2010 by a pair of graduates from Noma, Copenhagen's seminal culinary kingpin: its former head chef, the Sicilian-born, Danish-raised, Christian F. Puglisi, and Dane Kim Rossen, who worked there as a chef and waiter. Relæ sits in Copenhagen's gentrifying but still colourful Nørrebro district, in the northwest of the city. The vibe is informal, the simply styled dining room with open kitchen, an exercise in clever Danish design, form perfectly meeting function in tables built with neat drawers that hold the table settings and menu. The cooking, expressed via a choice of two four-course options – one meat-free – remains seriously ambitious.

SAFIR KEBAB

Recommended by
Rasmus Kofoed

Jagtvej 23
Nørrebro
Copenhagen 2200
+45 35343470
www.safir-kebab.dk

Opening hours	Open 7 day
Reservation policy	No
Credit cards	Accepted
Price range	Budget
Style	Casual
Cuisine	Turkish
Recommended for	Bargain

'Very ethnic. Grilled food, great falafel and really big portions for a small amount of money. Falafel and Turkish pizza are really good here.'—Rasmus Kofoed

SELFISH

Recommended by
Christian F. Puglisi

Elmegade 4
Nørrebro
Copenhagen 2200
+45 35359626
www.selfish.dk

Opening hours	Closed Monday and Sunday
Reservation policy	No
Credit cards	Not accepted
Price range	Budget
Style	Casual
Cuisine	Japanese
Recommended for	Regular neighbourhood

'A great humble sushi place with just four to six seats.'
—Christian F. Puglisi

BANZAI

Recommended by
Jakob Mielcke

Skydebanegade 16
Vesterbro
Copenhagen 1709
+45 36963331
www.restaurantbanzai.dk

Opening hours	Closed Monday and Sunday
Credit cards	Accepted but not AMEX
Price range	Budget
Style	Casual
Cuisine	Japanese
Recommended for	Bargain

'Simple but extremely delicious and true to its Japanese origins.'—Jakob Mielcke

BENTO

Recommended by
Nicolai Nørregaard

Helgolandsgade 16
Vesterbro
Copenhagen 1653
+45 88714646
www.uki.dk

Opening hours	Closed Monday and Sunday
Credit cards	Not accepted
Price range	Affordable
Style	Casual
Cuisine	Sushi
Recommended for	Regular neighbourhood

'The Japanese Uki family serve beautiful Japanese food and some of the best sushi in town. I stop by as often as I can, for dinner or a take away (take out).'
—Nicolai Nørregaard

CHICKY GRILL

Recommended by
Nicolai Nørregaard

Halmtorvet 21
Vesterbro
Copenhagen 1700
+45 33226696

Opening hours	Closed Saturday and Sunday
Reservation policy	No
Credit cards	Not accepted
Price range	Budget
Style	Casual
Cuisine	Diner
Recommended for	Bargain

'This is the exact opposite of the rest of the new and hyped Meat Packing District, which has been undergoing a huge transformation to one of the most hip areas in town. This place offers old-school Danish specialities, comparable with the food my grandparents made for me. The atmosphere is intense and smells of the old days. A hangout for East European hookers, workers and alcoholics – I love it!'—Nicolai Nørregaard

COFOCO

Recommended by
Brian Mark Hansen

Abel Cathrines Gade 7
Vesterbro
Copenhagen 1654
+45 33136060
www.cofoco.dk

Opening hours..Closed Sunday
Credit cards..Accepted
Price range..Affordable
Style..Casual
Cuisine...Modern Danish
Recommended for..Bargain

'They get the best out of everything.'
—Brian Mark Hansen

ISSA

Recommended by
Paul Cunningham

Sankt Jørgens Allé 6
Vesterbro
Copenhagen 1615
+45 31351222
www.issafoods.com

Opening hours..Open 7 days
Credit cards...Not accepted
Price range...Budget
Style..Casual
Cuisine..Japanese
Recommended for..Bargain

'Chef Suzuki is quite simply the best Japanese "cutter" in Copenhagen, in my opinion. Authentic and honest Japanese cooking in simple surroundings. There's no alcohol license, unfortunately.'—Paul Cunningham

JOHN'S HOTDOG DELI

Recommended by
Paul Cunningham

Axeltorv
Vesterbro
Copenhagen 1608
+45 31325848

Opening hours...............................Closed every other Monday
Reservation policy..No
Credit cards...Not accepted
Price range...Budget
Style..Casual
Cuisine...Fast Food
Recommended for..Late night

'John is probably the only classic Danish street *pølsemand* that I know who makes his own sausages

from wonderfully happy pigs, grinds his own mustard and spices his own ketchups.'—Paul Cunningham

KØDBYENS FISKEBAR

Recommended by
Bertrand Grébaut,
Nicolai Nørregaard

Flæsketorvet 100
Vesterbro
Copenhagen 1711
+45 32155656
www.fiskebaren.dk

Opening hours...........................Closed Monday and Sunday
Credit cards..Accepted
Price range..Affordable
Style..Casual
Cuisine..Seafood
Recommended for.....................................Wish I'd opened

'This place has been a huge inspiration to me. It takes a fresh and inventive menu based on seafood and blends it with a relaxed bar atmosphere, natural wines and a contemporary decor that makes you feel right at home.'
—Bertrand Grébaut

NOODLE HOUSE

Recommended by
Claus Meyer,
Samuel Nutter

Abel Cathrines Gade 23
Vesterbro
Copenhagen 1654
+45 38898818
www.wokognudler.dk

Opening hours..Closed Monday
Reservation policy..No
Credit cards...Not accepted
Price range...Budget
Style..Casual
Cuisine..Chinese
Recommended for..Bargain

'Noodle House is a hidden gem down a side street behind Copenhagen's central train station. The food is well cooked and authentic. There always seem to be plenty of chefs from around the city dining here, which is always a good sign.'—Samuel Nutter

PATÉ PATÉ
Slagterboderne 1
Vesterbro
Copenhagen 1716
+45 39695557
www.patepate.dk

Recommended by
Paul Cunningham

Opening hours	Closed Sunday
Credit cards	Accepted
Price range	Affordable
Style	Casual
Cuisine	French Mediterranean
Recommended for	Regular neighbourhood

'Karl the Swede makes honest dishes, rich in flavour. Great salads to wonderful roasts and lots of offal. Housed within an old pâté factory, Karl makes perfect pâtés. The interior is rather industrial, Parisian bohème, resembling an old, battered school classroom.'
—Paul Cunningham

PONY
Vesterbrogade 135
Vesterbro
Copenhagen 1620
+45 33221000
www.ponykbh.dk

Recommended by
Thomas Rode Andersen

Opening hours	Closed Monday
Credit cards	Accepted
Price range	Affordable
Style	Casual
Cuisine	Modern Nordic
Recommended for	High end

RADIO
Julius Thomsens Gade 12
Vesterbro
Copenhagen 1632
+45 25102733
www.restaurantradio.dk

Recommended by
Ebbe Vollmer

Opening hours	Closed Monday and Sunday
Credit cards	Accepted
Price range	Affordable
Style	Casual
Cuisine	Modern Nordic
Recommended for	Worth the travel

AAMANNS DELI & TAKE AWAY
Øster Farimagsgade 10
Østerbro
Copenhagen 2100
+45 35553344
www.aamanns.dk

Recommended by
Paul Cunningham,
Steffen Hansen

Opening hours	Open 7 days
Credit cards	Accepted but not AMEX
Price range	Budget
Style	Casual
Cuisine	Danish
Recommended for	Local favourite

'Adam Aamann's new-wave, Scandinavian open-sandwich movement. Classic combinations with everything made from absolute scratch. Wonderful clean flavours using superb seasonal ingredients.'
—Paul Cunningham

GERANIUM
Per Henrik Lings Allé 4
Østerbro
Copenhagen 2100
+45 69960020
www.geranium.dk

Recommended by
Stefano Baiocco, Brian Mark
Hansen, Mette Hvarre
Gassner, Flora Mikula,
Thorsten Schmidt, Victor
Wågman, Gerhard Wieser

Opening hours	Closed Sunday to Tuesday
Credit cards	Accepted
Price range	Expensive
Style	Smart casual
Cuisine	Modern Nordic
Recommended for	Wish I'd opened

'I was particularly struck by the bold cuisine.'
—Flora Mikula

HOS FISCHER
Victor Borges Plads 12
Østerbro
Copenhagen 2100
+45 35423964
www.hosfischer.dk

Recommended by
Jakob Mielcke

Opening hours	Open 7 days
Credit cards	Accepted
Price range	Affordable
Style	Casual
Cuisine	Italian
Recommended for	Local favourite

'World-class pasta in very cosy surroundings. Inexpensive, but romantic and casual.'—Jakob Mielcke

KRUMMEN & KAGEN
Nordre Frihavnsgade 43
Østerbro
Copenhagen 2100
+45 61270817
www.krummen-kagen.dk

Recommended by
Adam Aamann

Opening hours..Open 7 days
Reservation policy...No
Credit cards................Accepted but not Mastercard or AMEX
Price range...Budget
Style...Casual
Cuisine...Café
Recommended for... Breakfast

KOKS
Hotel Føroyar
45 Oyggjarvegur
Streymoy 100
Faroe Islands
+298 333999
www.koks.fo

Recommended by
Martins Ritins

Opening hours.............................Closed Monday and Sunday
Credit cards...Accepted
Price range..Expensive
Style..Smart casual
Cuisine..Modern Nordic
Recommended for............................Worth the travel

'Incredible chef, with the best lamb and seafood in the
world, especially the langoustine. It's out of the way
but worth the travel.'—Martin Ritins

The waters around the remote eighteen rocky islands
that have been called the 'Nordic Hawaii' are home
to some of the finest seafood on the planet. Noma
has been making use of this environment for years.
Closer to the source, the open kitchen at Koks (which
translates as 'flirt' or 'fusspot'), located in Hotel
Føroyar in the Faroese capital of Tórshavn, offers
creative four, six and eight-course menus inspired by
the exceptional local produce. Cod, crab and langoustine star alongside local lamb and cheese, with only a
few essentials sourced from beyond the islands
finding their way onto the plate.

MAMI
Linnankatu 3
Turku
Finland Proper 20100
Finland
+358 22311111
www.mami.fi

Recommended by
Pekka Terävä

Opening hours..............................Closed Monday and Sunday
Credit cards...Accepted
Price range...Affordable
Style...Casual
Cuisine..Modern Finnish
Recommended for...Bargain

'It's like grandmothers made in the old times.'
—Pekka Terävä

BOULEVARD SOCIAL
Bulevardi 6
Helsinki
Uusimaa 00120
Finland
+358 103229387
www.boulevardsocial.fi

Recommended by
Roman Zaštšerinski

Opening hours......................................Closed Sunday
Credit cards...Accepted
Price range..Expensive
Style...Casual
Cuisine................................Middle Eastern-European
Recommended for............................Worth the travel

'A very interesting approach to food and everything
was so tasty. I can't wait to visit them again.'
—Roman Zaštšerinski

CAFÉ EKBERG

Recommended by
Sasu Laukkonen

Bulevardi 9
Helsinki
Uusimaa 00120
Finland
+358 968118660
www.cafeekberg.fi

Opening hours	Open 7 days
Credit cards	Accepted
Price range	Budget
Style	Casual
Cuisine	Café-Bakery
Recommended for	Breakfast

'Classic café, a rare find in Helsinki.'—Sasu Laukkonen

Café Ekberg, its name emboldened in large, custard-yellow capitals above crimped canopies, stands testament to the energetic orphan who founded it after packing in clockmaking to become apprentice to a master baker. Dating to the 1850s, with ninety seats and its own bakery, specialities include the famed, multilayered, creamy Napoleon cake and canelé-like Champagne Cork. Although also serving lunches from 11.00 a.m., those in the know come for the good-value breakfast buffet, which usually includes porridge, omelettes, cold cuts, marmalades and pastries, alongside some twenty types of fresh breads, from rustic loaves to Basler Brot.

CARELIA

Recommended by
Sami Tallberg

Mannerheimintie 56
Helsinki
Uusimaa 00260
Finland
+358 927090976
www.carelia.info

Opening hours	Open 7 days
Credit cards	Accepted
Price range	Affordable
Style	Casual
Cuisine	French
Recommended for	Regular neighbourhood

'Cool old 1920s pharmacy venue that has an amazing wine list and the food is good traditional French cuisine.'—Sami Tallberg

CHEF & SOMMELIER

Recommended by
Filip Langhoff

Huvilakatu 28
Helsinki
Uusimaa 00150
Finland
+358 400959440
www.chefetsommelier.fi

Opening hours	Closed Monday and Sunday
Credit cards	Accepted
Price range	Affordable
Style	Smart casual
Cuisine	Modern Nordic
Recommended for	Regular neighbourhood

'They work with organic produce. Sasu the chef and Johan the sommelier are extremely talented and they have created a fantastic atmosphere in this small neighbourhood restaurant.'—Filip Langhoff

CHOLO

Recommended by
Tomi Björck

Lönnrotinkatu 9
Helsinki
Uusimaa 00120
Finland
www.cholo.fi

Opening hours	Closed Monday and Sunday
Reservation policy	No
Credit cards	Accepted but not AMEX or Diners
Price range	Budget
Style	Casual
Cuisine	Mexican
Recommended for	Regular neighbourhood

'Amazing burritos with real Mexican flavour and made from scratch. Nice, welcoming and friendly staff.'
—Tomi Björck

The name 'Cholo' derives from the Nahuatl language and means 'Native American': this food, a long way from mushy Tex-Mex, is a brilliant re-creation of Mexican street food, transplanted to the Finnish capital. The tacos are home-made from maize meal, while top beef and pork from local producers make for brilliant, fat burritos. Owner Emanuele 'Manu' Torchio, originally from Mexico, is a serial Helsinki restaurateur: he's in charge of the kitchen, while his Finnish wife, Karina Paakki, does the numbers. This is the place where you unexpectedly learn how well Finnish cider goes with top-notch Mexican food.

FAFA'S

Iso Roobertinkatu 2
Helsinki
Uusimaa 00120
Finland
+358 400183415
www.fafas.fi

Recommended by
Filip Langhoff, Sasu
Laukkonen, Sami Tallberg

Opening hours	Open 7 days
Reservation policy	No
Credit cards	Accepted but not AMEX
Price range	Budget
Style	Casual
Cuisine	Middle Eastern
Recommended for	Late night

'The best falafels in town – perfect after a long day at work.'—Filip Langhoff

GASTROBAR EMO

Kasarmikatu 44
Helsinki
Uusimaa 00130
Finland
+358 105050900
www.emo-ravintola.fi

Recommended by
Jari Vesivalo

Opening hours	Closed Sunday
Credit cards	Accepted
Price range	Affordable
Style	Smart casual
Cuisine	Nordic-European small plates
Recommended for	Regular neighbourhood

'A great place to stop by for a drink and dinner after a hard day in the kitchen.'—Jari Vesivalo

GRAN DELICATO

Kalevankatu 34
Helsinki
Uusimaa 00180
Finland
+358 96940403
www.grandelicato.fi

Recommended by
Filip Langhoff, Sami Tallberg

Opening hours	Closed Sunday
Credit cards	Accepted
Price range	Budget
Style	Casual
Cuisine	Café
Recommended for	Breakfast

'Lively place run by a Greek owner. The sandwich filled with aubergine (eggplant), mortadella, feta and tomato is to die for.'—Sami Tallberg

It's a testament to the popularity of Gran Delicato that since opening as a one-room operation back in 2001 they have expanded into the next-door apartment and opened a new outpost in downtown Helsinki. Its popularity as a breakfast spot is largely thanks to the quality of the Greek coffee, considered to be among the best in town, but freshly squeezed orange juice, fresh salads and sandwiches draw in customers throughout the day. The owner's Greek heritage is reflected in the comfortable, Mediterranean decor and the rather eccentric service – all part of the charm of this quirky neighbourhood deli.

KLAUS K BREAKFAST & BRUNCH

Klaus K Hotel
Bulevardi 2–4
Helsinki
Uusimaa 00120
Finland
+358 207704732
www.klauskhotel.com

Recommended by
Pekka Terävä

Opening hours	Open 7 days
Credit cards	Accepted
Price range	Affordable
Style	Smart casual
Cuisine	European
Recommended for	Breakfast

'It's very simple but the food is very high quality.'
—Pekka Terävä

KOSMOS

Recommended by
Sasu Laukkonen,
Sami Tallberg

Kalevankatu 3
Helsinki
Uusimaa 00100
Finland
+358 9647255
www.kosmos.fi

Opening hours	Closed Sunday
Credit cards	Accepted
Price range	Affordable
Style	Casual
Cuisine	Finnish
Recommended for	Local favourite

'A time-machine trip back to a 1950s to 1980s artist's den. Very traditional Finnish food with French influences. Old-school food but the atmosphere and the venue is the thing.'—Sami Tallberg

LUOMO

Recommended by
Jari Vesivalo

Katariinankatu 1
Helsinki
Uusimaa 00170
Finland
+358 91357287
www.luomo.fi

Opening hours	Closed Monday and Sunday
Credit cards	Accepted
Price range	Expensive
Style	Smart casual
Cuisine	Modern Nordic
Recommended for	High end

'Jouni Toivanen's dishes are always very creative. You never know how he will surprise you.'—Jari Vesivalo

NOKKA

Recommended by
Jari Vesivalo

Kanavaranta 7f
Helsinki
Uusimaa 00160
Finland
+358 961285600
www.ravintolanokka.fi

Opening hours	Closed Sunday
Credit cards	Accepted
Price range	Affordable
Style	Smart casual
Cuisine	Finnish
Recommended for	Local favourite

'Local Finnish cuisine.'—Jari Vesivalo

OLO

Recommended by
Vladislav Djatsuk,
Filip Langhoff

Pohjoisesplanadi 5
Helsinki
Uusimaa 00170
Finland
+358 103206250
www.olo-ravintola.fi

Opening hours	Closed Sunday
Credit cards	Accepted
Price range	Expensive
Style	Smart casual
Cuisine	Modern Nordic
Recommended for	Local favourite

'They are consistently working to improve their product.' —Filip Langhof

Pekka Terävä and Petri Lukkarinen's restaurant Olo is looking good after its 2013 move to the historic surroundings of Lampa House on Helsinki's Market Square. The modernist dining room and stunning glass-roofed courtyard only emphasize the restaurant's entirely justified ambition, in evidence since its 2006 launch. At the pass is ex-Chez Dominique chef Jari Vesivalo, whose tasting menus, inspired by Finland's changing seasons and natural bounty, come in full-length (up to thirty dishes) and abridged form. Look out for scallop and fermented gooseberry; reindeer, lichen and juniper sauce; and caramelized artichokes with chocolate soil. There's an excellent wine cellar too.

RESTAURANT ASK

Recommended by
Jari Vesivalo

Vironkatu 8
Helsinki
Uusimaa 00170
Finland
+358 405818100
www.restaurantask.com

Opening hours	Closed Monday and Sunday
Credit cards	Accepted
Price range	Expensive
Style	Smart casual
Cuisine	Modern Finnish
Recommended for	Regular neighbourhood

SEA HORSE

Recommended by
Sasu Laukkonen

Kapteeninkatu 11
Helsinki
Uusimaa 00140
Finland
+358 9628169
www.seahorse.fi

Opening hours..Open 7 days
Credit cards...Accepted
Price range...Affordable
Style...Casual
Cuisine...Finnish
Recommended for.................................Local favourite

'Good food, big portions, hearty and traditional.
Keep-it-simple cuisine.'—Sasu Laukkonen

Opened in 1934, the Sea Horse, one of Helsinki's
oldest restaurants, has served traditional Finnish
specialities to sailors, artists, piss artists and the
odd jazz legend. Dizzy Gillespie, when he visited,
was supposedly such a fan of their fried herring and
mashed potatoes that he ran into the kitchen, trumpet
in hand, saying 'Please, sir, can I have some more?'
Herrings aside, Finnish favourites on offer include
cabbage rolls and reindeer fillet, served in the sort
of portions that not even a hungry trumpeter could
complain about. Note the restaurant's nickname,
Sikala, which means 'animal house', as late at night
things, and the Finns, can get quite strange.

STREET GASTRO

Recommended by
Jari Vesivalo

Vaasankatu 13
Helsinki
Uusimaa 0500
Finland
+358 447059990
www.streetgastro.fi

Opening hours..Open 7 days
Reservation policy...No
Credit cards...Not accepted
Price range...Budget
Style...Casual
Cuisine..Street Food
Recommended for...Late night

'A good place to have a snack at midnight after a long
day at the office.'—Jari Vesivalo

TEURASTAMON PORTTI

Recommended by
Filip Langhoff

Teurastamo Gate
Työpajankatu 2
Helsinki
Uusimaa 00580
Finland
+358 207559895
www.roolund.fi

Opening hours...Closed Sunday
Reservation policy...No
Credit cards...Accepted
Price range...Budget
Style...Casual
Cuisine..Barbeque
Recommended for..Bargain

'The rosburger and the pulled pork, made on a wood-
fired grill in the old meat-packing district, make for a
perfect lunch.'—Filip Langhoff

TRATTORIA RIVOLETTO

Recommended by
Pekka Terävä

Albertinkatu 38
Helsinki
Uusimaa 00180
Finland
+358 9643455
www.rivolirestaurants.fi

Opening hours..Open 7 days
Credit cards...Accepted
Price range...Affordable
Style...Casual
Cuisine...Italian
Recommended for...............................Regular neighbourhood

'Good pasta dishes.'—Pekka Terävä

'Skye seafood straight off the boats.'
MICHAEL SMITH P377

'THE BEST FISH AND CHIP SHOP EVER.'
ADAM STOKES P377

'STILL THE BEST FINE DINING IN THE UK.'
ISAAC MCHALE P331

UNITED KINGDOM & REPUBLIC OF IRELAND

'WELL WORTH A TRIP INTO THE HIGHLANDS.'
JOCKY PETRIE P377

'CHUNKY CHIPS AND MUSHY PEAS.'
TOM KITCHIN P378

'Beautiful views overlooking the River Lagan.'
STEPHEN TOMAN P383

'WHERE BETTER TO GO LATE AT NIGHT THAN A STREET CALLED "CURRY MILE"?'
ADAM REID P309

UNITED KINGDOM & REPUBLIC OF IRELAND

Ⓝ SCALE

0   50   100
mi.

County of Inverness p.377
Isle of Skye p.377

Perthshire p.379
Argyll p.377
Fife p.378
Edinburgh pp.377–378
Glasgow p.379

SCOTLAND

Ayrshire p.377
Co. Antrim pp.380–383
Durham p.308

Cumbria p.306

ENGLAND

Co. Down p.383
Co. Galway pp.388–389
Co. Westmeath p.390
Lancashire p.311

IRELAND

Co. Dublin pp.385–387
Greater Manchester pp.309–310
Cheshire p.305
Nottinghamshire p.312

Co. Clare p.383
Powys p.380

West Midlands pp.314–315
Co. Waterford pp.389–390
Ceredigion p.379
Suffolk p.314
Co. Cork pp.384–385
Buckinghamshire p.305
Essex p.308
Oxfordshire p.312
Monmouthshire pp.379–380
Gloucestershire p.309

WALES

London pp.316–375
Vale of Glamorgan p.380
Bristol p.305
Berkshire p.304
Wiltshire p.315
Surrey p.314
Kent pp.310–311
Somerset pp.312–313
East Sussex p.308
Devon p.307
Hampshire p.310
Dorset p.308

Cornwall pp.305–306

Jersey p.376

THE CROWN AT BRAY

Recommended by
André Garrett

High Street
Bray
Berkshire
England SL6 2AH
+44 1628621936
www.thecrownatbray.com

Opening hours	Open 7 days
Credit cards	Accepted
Price range	Affordable
Style	Casual
Cuisine	Gastropub
Recommended for	Regular neighbourhood

'Lovely, warm, homely pub, with great food from Heston Blumenthal.'—André Garrett

THE FAT DUCK

Recommended by
Sat Bains, Rainer Becker,
Paul Foster, Nigel Haworth,
Tom Kerridge, Glynn
Purnell, Pedro Subijana

High Street
Bray
Berkshire
England SL6 2AQ
+44 1628580333
www.thefatduck.co.uk

Opening hours	Closed Monday and Sunday
Credit cards	Accepted
Price range	Expensive
Style	Smart casual
Cuisine	Modern British
Recommended for	High end

'Heston has created something so innovative and unique at The Fat Duck. It is a meal of sheer joy.' —Rainer Becker

Imaginative, innovative and creative restaurants are ten a penny these days, but for people who want their levels of crazy turned up to eleven there's still only one place to go — even if it's moving to the other side of the planet. From March 2015 The Fat Duck will temporarily relocate to Melbourne, but far from it becoming a pale imitation of his flagship, Heston Blumenthal is moving his entire kitchen brigade Down Under in an attempt to maintain its levels of creativity and sheer brilliance. After six months the iconic snail porridge and 'Mad Hatter fob watch' — along with the chefs — will return to Berkshire and a fully refurbished Fat Duck, while the venue in Oz will continue as a permanent outpost of Dinner by Heston Blumenthal.

THE HINDS HEAD

Recommended by
Tom Kerridge

High Street
Bray
Berkshire
England SL6 2AB
+44 1628626151
www.hindsheadbray.com

Opening hours	Open 7 days
Credit cards	Accepted
Price range	Affordable
Style	Casual
Cuisine	Gastropub
Recommended for	Regular neighbourhood

'Rock-solid, consistent dishes, thoroughly worthy of its Michelin star.'—Tom Kerridge

THE WATERSIDE INN

Recommended by
Galton Blackiston, Dominic
Chapman, Angela
Hartnett, Ed Wilson

Ferry Road
Bray
Berkshire
England SL6 2AT
+44 1628620691
www.waterside-inn.co.uk

Opening hours	Closed Monday and Tuesday
Credit cards	Accepted
Price range	Expensive
Style	Smart casual
Cuisine	French
Recommended for	High end

'Old-fashioned three-star restaurant that all young chefs and front of house should experience to understand the traditional values of restaurateuring.' —Ed Wilson

MAYFLOWER

Recommended by
Mitch Tonks

3a–5 Haymarket Walk
Bristol
England BS1 3LN
+44 1179250555
www.mayflower-bristol.co.uk

Opening hours...Open 7 days
Credit cards...Accepted but not AMEX
Price range..Affordable
Style...Casual
Cuisine..Chinese
Recommended for.................................Regular neighbourhood

'It's authentic Chinese, only open from 6.00 p.m. to
3.00 a.m. and for dim sum on Sunday. The menu is not
typical, lots of offal, great seafood and a strong Chinese
clientele – the best Chinese outside of London.'
—Mitch Tonks

CASAMIA

Recommended by
Sat Bains

38 High Street
Westbury-on-Trym
Bristol
England BS9 3DZ
+44 1179592884
www.casamiarestaurant.co.uk

Opening hours................................Closed Monday and Sunday
Credit cards...Accepted
Price range..Expensive
Style..Smart casual
Cuisine...Modern British
Recommended for...Worth the travel

THE HAND & FLOWERS

Recommended by
Sat Bains, André Garrett,
Anna Hansen, Tom
Pemberton, Glynn
Purnell, Shaun Searley

126 West Street
Marlow
Buckinghamshire
England SL7 2BP
+44 1628482277
www.thehandandflowers.co.uk

Opening hours...Open 7 days
Credit cards...Accepted
Price range..Affordable
Style...Casual
Cuisine...Gastropub
Recommended for...High end

'Tom has managed to capture the pub, social and
comfortable dining atmosphere with outstanding,
perfectly executed food. Not over-fussy or trying to be
something it's not, just really top food.'—Shaun Searley

STICKY WALNUT

Recommended by
Bruce Poole

11 Charles Street
Chester
Cheshire
England CH2 3AZ
+44 1244400400
www.stickywalnut.com

Opening hours...Open 7 days
Credit cards...Accepted
Price range..Affordable
Style...Casual
Cuisine..British bistro
Recommended for...Worth the travel

'Cracking bistro-type restaurant with bang-on food
and a friendly, fun atmosphere.'—Bruce Poole

THE SEAFOOD RESTAURANT

Recommended by
Dominic Chapman,
Nathan Outlaw

Riverside
Padstow
Cornwall
England PL28 8BY
+44 1841532700
www.rickstein.com

Opening hours...Open 7 days
Credit cards...Accepted
Price range..Expensive
Style..Smart casual
Cuisine..Seafood
Recommended for...Wish I'd opened

'It's the perfect fish restaurant in the perfect
location.'—Dominic Chapman

FRESH FROM THE SEA

Recommended by
Nathan Outlaw

18 New Road
Port Isaac
Cornwall
England PL29 3SB
+44 1208880849
www.freshfromthesea.co.uk

Opening hours	Open 7 days
Reservation policy	No
Credit cards	Accepted
Price range	Budget
Style	Casual
Cuisine	Seafood
Recommended for	Bargain

'Calum's crabs make a fantastic sandwich and they are fished responsibly too.'—Nathan Outlaw

Perfectly formed little fish shop in the picture-perfect fishing village of Port Isaac on the Atlantic coast of North Cornwall. It is run by the husband-and-wife team Calum and Tracey Greenhalgh, who catch their lobster and crab daily from their own boat, the *Mary D*. They specialize in selling and serving sustainable Cornish fish: from hand-line caught mackerel and pollack, to mussels, oysters and clams from the Camel estuary, and smoked fish from the Tregida Smokehouse. They serve lobster salads and rolls, handpicked crab sandwiches and soup, and their own smoked mackerel pâté with toast.

PORTHMINSTER CAFÉ & RESTAURANT

Recommended by
Nathan Outlaw

Porthminster Beach
St Ives
Cornwall
England TR26 2EB
+44 1736795352
www.porthminstercafe.co.uk

Opening hours	Variable
Credit cards	Accepted
Price range	Affordable
Style	Casual
Cuisine	International
Recommended for	Bargain

'Great food, child friendly and literally right on the beach. What more could you ask for?'—Nathan Outlaw

Sat bang on Porthminster Beach, in the popular Cornish seaside town of St Ives, means getting a table here in season takes a bit of forward planning. Nevertheless, with a handsome modern terrace that overlooks the immaculately clean beach, it's invariably packed throughout the summer due to a menu that understands its audience. Lunch offers simple seafood dishes that take in a few Asian influences, alongside a decent- sized vegetarian section and simple bowls of pasta for the kids. Things get a little more elaborate and expensive in the evening – but not prohibitively so – and the kids will still be alright.

L'ENCLUME

Recommended by
Neil Rankin

Cavendish Street
Cartmel
Cumbria
England LA11 6PZ
+44 1539536362
www.lenclume.co.uk

Opening hours	Open 7 days
Credit cards	Accepted
Price range	Expensive
Style	Smart casual
Cuisine	Modern British
Recommended for	Worth the travel

'There is nobody to touch Simon Rogan's cooking. It's perfectly executed, exciting and modern without being naff. The staff balance that formal/informal line perfectly and the service and food is flawless. The whole "we only source local" and "we grow our own veg" thing can get tiresome sometimes for the punter and is usually badly executed but Simon's team do it with as much of an eye for detail as some of the best growers in the country and it shows. They also do a cracking fry-up the next day.'—Neil Rankin

Thanks to L'Enclume the Lake District can offer greater culinary highlights than twee tea rooms and tourist traps churning out 'hearty' quiches for tired ramblers. Operating out of a former blacksmith's forge since 2006, head chef Simon Rogan was in the vanguard of the now ubiquitous approach of using local ingredients and remains one of the most innovative chefs to have graced the UK restaurant scene in the past decade. Rogan's passion for his produce, seeking out a perplexing variety of unusual herbs and vegetables, isn't yawn-inducingly worthy – nor is it PR puff. Rather, it is driven by a desire to serve decent ingredients in an eye-opening manner.

GIDLEIGH PARK

Recommended by
Shaun Hill

Dartmoor National Park
Chagford
Devon
England TQ13 8HH
+44 1647432367
www.gidleigh.com

Opening hours	Open 7 days
Credit cards	Accepted
Price range	Expensive
Style	Smart casual
Cuisine	Modern European
Recommended for	High end

'I used to work there so can't be relied on for dispassionate appraisal but Caines is an exceptional chef and has stood the test of time.'—Shaun Hill

CAFE ALF RESCO

Recommended by
Glynn Purnell,
Mitch Tonks

Lower Street
Dartmouth
Devon
England TQ6 9AN
+44 1803835880
www.cafealfresco.co.uk

Opening hours	Open 7 days
Reservation policy	No
Credit cards	Not accepted
Price range	Budget
Style	Casual
Cuisine	Café-Bar
Recommended for	Breakfast

'The breakfasts are delicious and just what you need after a night out in the fishing town of Brixham. It is lovely to be able to sit outside and see the sea. Also, once breakfast is done – it's Pimm's o'clock!'
—Glynn Purnell

THE SEAHORSE

Recommended by
Nathan Outlaw

5 South Embankment
Dartmouth
Devon
England TQ6 9BH
+44 1803835147
www.seahorserestaurant.co.uk

Opening hours	Closed Monday
Credit cards	Accepted
Price range	Affordable
Style	Smart casual
Cuisine	Seafood
Recommended for	Local favourite

'It showcases the region's finest ingredients. The food is a reflection of the respect and care that is given to those raw materials.'—Nathan Outlaw

The Devon flagship of accountant turned fishmonger turned self taught chef and restaurateur Mitch Tonks is, it shouldn't surprise you to hear, all about fish. While the smart-looking Seahorse on the bank of the River Dart does cater for carnivores with a couple of dishes under the heading 'Today's Meat', the majority, understandably, come here for the kitchen's way with seafood. Tonks's love of Italy comes across in a menu that features *zuppa del pescatore* (an Italian Riviera fisherman's soup), sea bream *al cartoccio* (steamed in a paper bag) and *fritto misto* of monkfish, soft-shell crab, red mullet, whitebait and squid.

CRAB SHACK

Recommended by
Mitch Tonks

3 Queen Street
Teignmouth
Devon
England TQ14 8BY
+44 1626777956
www.crabshackonthebeach.co.uk

Opening hours	Closed Monday and Tuesday
Credit cards	Accepted
Price range	Affordable
Style	Casual
Cuisine	Seafood
Recommended for	Local favourite

'It's run by Rob Simmonds, a crab fisherman and his wife, Amanda, and they serve the area's best shellfish with a big emphasis on crab and lobster. We have the best seafood in the world down here and it's worth travelling for; it never tastes as good in the middle of a city.'—Mitch Tonks

HIX OYSTER & FISH HOUSE

Recommended by
Margot Henderson

Cobb Road
Lyme Regis
Dorset
England DT7 3JP
+44 1297446910
www.hixoysterandfishhouse.co.uk

Opening hours	Variable
Credit cards	Accepted
Price range	Affordable
Style	Smart casual
Cuisine	Seafood
Recommended for	Worth the travel

CRAB HOUSE CAFÉ

Recommended by
Martin Morales

Ferrymans Way
Wyke Regis
Dorset
England DT4 9YU
+44 1305788867
www.crabhousecafe.co.uk

Opening hours	Closed Monday and Tuesday
Credit cards	Accepted
Price range	Affordable
Style	Casual
Cuisine	Seafood
Recommended for	High end

'It's neither high end, nor expensive, but I love to go there on special occasions. Exceptional, freshly caught seafood is on offer, simply cooked and set in a beautiful location.'—Martin Morales

THE RABY HUNT RESTAURANT

Recommended by
Samuel Nutter

The Raby Hunt Inn
Summerhouse
Near Darlington
Durham
England DL2 3UD
+44 1325374237
www.rabyhuntrestaurant.co.uk

Opening hours	Closed Sunday to Tuesday
Credit cards	Accepted
Price range	Expensive
Style	Smart casual
Cuisine	British
Recommended for	Wish I'd opened

'This restaurant is located close to where I grew up in the northeast of England. I had always dreamed of having a restaurant in this very rural area, but always feared that it would not be a success. The head chef and proprietor, James Close, had the guts to do it and has such a fantastic restaurant that has achieved and maintained its first Michelin star.'—Samuel Nutter

THE LANDGATE BISTRO

Recommended by
Timothy Johnson

5–6 Landgate
Rye
East Sussex
England TN31 7LH
+44 1797222829
www.landgatebistro.co.uk

Opening hours	Closed Monday and Tuesday
Credit cards	Accepted
Price range	Affordable
Style	Casual
Cuisine	British
Recommended for	Regular neighbourhood

'Local food cooked simply.'—Timothy Johnson

THE COMPANY SHED

Recommended by
Miles Kirby

129 Coast Road
West Mersea
Essex
England CO5 8PA
+44 1206382700
www.the-company-shed.co.uk

Opening hours	Closed Monday
Reservation policy	No
Credit cards	Not accepted
Price range	Budget
Style	Casual
Cuisine	Seafood
Recommended for	Worth the travel

A weather-beaten hut among the boatyards of West Mersea on the Essex coast, The Company Shed is a quirky fishmonger's with a few tables. Opened in the late 1980s by Heather Haward, originally as a weekend-only concern to sell husband Richard's fish and oysters, it's gained a cult following. The combination of setting, BYOB and the honest pleasures of smoked fish, dressed crab and simply grilled shellfish are irresistible to anyone with a love of seafood and salty air. Make the journey September to April to try the local native oysters that get their distinctive green hue and flavour from the salt marshes.

LE CHAMPIGNON SAUVAGE

Recommended by
James Wilkins

24–26 Suffolk Road
Cheltenham
Gloucestershire
England GL50 2AQ
+44 1242573449
www.lechampignonsauvage.co.uk

Opening hours...............................Closed Monday and Sunday
Credit cards..Accepted
Price range...Affordable
Style..Smart casual
Cuisine...Modern French
Recommended for..Worth the travel

'Great all-round restaurant experience from two very experienced people. Refreshing to be looked after by people who know what they are doing and who are not chasing trends.'—James Wilkins

THE PARLOUR

Recommended by
. Adam Reid

60 Beech Road
Chorlton
Greater Manchester
England M21 9EG
+44 1618814871
www.theparlour.info

Opening hours...Open 7 days
Credit cards..Accepted
Price range...Affordable
Style..Casual
Cuisine...Gastropub
Recommended for............................Regular neighbourhood

'The Parlour shows how Manchester is growing to envelop the suburbs. It does quirky pub food at a good price in a lively and fuss-free style.'—Adam Reid

MUGHLI

Recommended by
Adam Reid

30 Wilmslow Road
Manchester
Greater Manchester
England M14 5TQ
+44 1612480900
www.mughli.com

Opening hours...Open 7 days
Credit cards..Accepted
Price range...Budget
Style..Casual
Cuisine...Indian-Pakistani
Recommended for..Late night

'Where better to go late at night than a street called "Curry Mile"? Mughli provide great food even after I have had a late finish in the kitchen.'—Adam Reid

SUGAR JUNCTION

Recommended by
Adam Reid

60 Tib Street
Manchester
Greater Manchester
England M4 1LG
+44 1618391444
www.sugarjunction.co.uk

Opening hours...Open 7 days
Credit cards..Accepted
Price range...Budget
Style..Casual
Cuisine...Café-Bar-Bistro
Recommended for..Breakfast

'It's in the Northern Quarter and offers simple but hearty breakfasts with good coffee. With its charming 1950s-style theme, it's a great way to start the weekend.'—Adam Reid

THE WHARF

Recommended by
Adam Reid

6 Slate Wharf
Manchester
Greater Manchester
England M15 4SW
+44 1612202960
www.brunningandprice.co.uk/thewharf

Opening hours...Open 7 days
Credit cards..Accepted but not AMEX
Price range...Affordable
Style..Casual
Cuisine...Gastropub
Recommended for..Bargain

'A Brunning and Price pub gives you tasty, affordable food and a good pint as well.'—Adam Reid

YANG SING

Recommended by
Adam Reid

34 Princess Street
Manchester
Greater Manchester
England M1 4JY
+44 1612362200
www.yang-sing.com

Opening hours	Open 7 days
Credit cards	Accepted
Price range	Affordable
Style	Casual
Cuisine	Cantonese
Recommended for	Local favourite

'It might be a big place nowadays but it serves great-quality, tasty food and sums up the ethnic diversity that Manchester offers.'—Adam Reid

THE BLACK RAT RESTAURANT

Recommended by
Tom Adams

88 Chesil Street
Winchester
Hampshire
England SO23 0HX
+44 1962844465
www.theblackrat.co.uk

Opening hours	Open 7 days
Credit cards	Accepted
Price range	Affordable
Style	Smart casual
Cuisine	Modern British
Recommended for	Wish I'd opened

'Beautiful space and beautiful food. They make it feel so effortless, which it is not.'—Tom Adams

THE GOODS SHED RESTAURANT

Recommended by
Stephen Harris

Station Road West
Canterbury
Kent
England CT2 8AN
+44 1227459153
www.thegoodsshed.co.uk

Opening hours	Closed Monday
Credit cards	Accepted
Price range	Affordable
Style	Casual
Cuisine	British bistro
Recommended for	Local favourite

THE SPORTSMAN

Recommended by
Adam Byatt, Kobe
Desramaults, Mike
Eggert, Henry Harris,
Angela Hartnett,
Peter Weeden

Faversham Road
Seasalter
Kent
England CT5 4BP
+44 1227273370
www.thesportsmanseasalter.co.uk

Opening hours	Closed Monday
Credit cards	Accepted
Price range	Affordable
Style	Casual
Cuisine	Gastropub
Recommended for	Worth the travel

'A pub in the middle of nowhere that makes its own butter and you can see the vegetables that they use growing outside and the lambs in the field destined for your plate. The food that is cooked shows a love of craft.'—Henry Harris

What chef-proprietor Stephen Harris likes to describe as a 'grotty rundown pub by the sea' is exactly what The Sportsman was before he took it over in 1999. Today, despite its somewhat desolate location, 3 km (2 miles) outside Whitstable on the Kent coast, it has become a destination, a place of gastronomic pilgrimage based purely on the quality of its cooking. There are two menus – the daily-changing à la carte and a tasting menu that has to be ordered at least forty-eight hours in advance, and for which you'd be advised to put your name down for when you book.

RAJ BARI

Recommended by
Ben Spalding

6–7 Tubs Hill Parade
Sevenoaks
Kent
England TN13 1DH
+44 1732743315
www.rajbari.co.uk

Opening hours	Open 7 days
Credit cards	Accepted but not AMEX
Price range	Budget
Style	Casual
Cuisine	Indian
Recommended for	Regular neighbourhood

'Immaculate Indian food served with style, playfulness and theatre, with well-drilled and equally immaculate waiters. Passion shines through and they just get how to look after the customer.'—Ben Spalding

THE PLEASANT CAFÉ
Recommended by
Timothy Johnson
7 Mount Pleasant Road
Tunbridge Wells
Kent
England TN1 1NT
+44 1892518632

Opening hours..Open 7 days
Reservation policy..No
Credit cards..Not accepted
Price range..Budget
Style...Casual
Cuisine...Café
Recommended for..Breakfast

'For a full English breakfast and a couple of hours of reading.'—Timothy Johnson

DAVID BROWN DELICATESSEN
Recommended by
Stephen Harris
28a Harbour Street
Whitstable
Kent
England CT5 1DB
+44 1227274507

Opening hours..Open 7 days
Credit cards............................Accepted but not AMEX
Price range..Budget
Style...Casual
Cuisine..Mediterranean
Recommended for..............................Regular neighbourhood

ELLIOTT'S COFFEE SHOP
Recommended by
Stephen Harris
1 Harbour Street
Whitstable
Kent
England CT5 1AG
+44 1227276608

Opening hours..Open 7 days
Credit cards...Accepted
Price range..Budget
Style...Casual
Cuisine...Café-Bistro
Recommended for..Breakfast

CLAYTON STREET CHIPPY
Recommended by
Nigel Haworth
9 Clayton Street
Blackburn
Lancashire
England BB6 7AQ

Opening hours..Open 7 days
Reservation policy..No
Credit cards..Not accepted
Price range..Budget
Style...Casual
Cuisine..Fish and Chips
Recommended for...Bargain

THE INN AT WHITEWELL
Recommended by
Nigel Haworth
Whitewell
Forest of Bowland
Lancashire
England BB7 3AT
+44 1200448222
www.innatwhitewell.com

Opening hours..Open 7 days
Credit cards...Accepted
Price range..Affordable
Style...Casual
Cuisine...British
Recommended for.............................Local favourite

RESTAURANT SAT BAINS

Lenton Lane
Nottingham
Nottinghamshire
England NG7 2SA
+44 1159866566
www.restaurantsatbains.com

Opening hours	Closed Monday and Sunday
Credit cards	Accepted
Price range	Expensive
Style	Smart casual
Cuisine	Modern British
Recommended for	Worth the travel

One of the UK's most gastronomically adventurous destination restaurants is unconventionally set on the industrial outskirts of Nottingham. A modern take on the old-fashioned concept of the husband-and-wife-run restaurant with rooms, Sat and Amanda Bains's edgily located, urban oasis is housed in a collection of renovated Victorian farm buildings that predate the panorama of pylons. Book a night in one of the eight rooms plus dinner at either the chef's or the kitchen table – the former overlooking the main kitchen, the latter with your own personal chef – to get closer to the cutting-edge but playful cooking.

LE MANOIR AUX QUAT'SAISONS

Church Road
Great Milton
Oxfordshire
England OX44 7PD
+44 1844278881
www.manoir.com

Opening hours	Open 7 days
Credit cards	Accepted
Price range	Expensive
Style	Smart casual
Cuisine	Modern French
Recommended for	Wish I'd opened

'It's one of Britain's greatest culinary experiences and a truly luxurious place. Any chef would be envious of the extensive kitchen gardens. It's an obvious labour of love for Raymond Blanc and a great success for him.' —Shaun Rankin

SHAUN DICKENS AT THE BOATHOUSE

Station Road
Henley-on-Thames
Oxfordshire
England RG9 1AZ
+44 1491577937
www.shaundickens.co.uk

Opening hours	Closed Monday
Credit cards	Accepted
Price range	Affordable
Style	Smart casual
Cuisine	Modern European
Recommended for	Local favourite

'I love Shaun's food – the dishes are simple, they do not use too many ingredients, yet the ones chosen are perfectly matched so the flavours are incredible. Shaun is hugely passionate about seasonality and using the very best local produce and he spends so much time selecting his suppliers.'—Raymond Blanc

THE BATH PRIORY RESTAURANT

The Bath Priory
Weston Road
Bath
Somerset
England BA1 2XT
+44 1225331922
www.thebathpriory.co.uk

Opening hours	Open 7 days
Credit cards	Accepted
Price range	Expensive
Style	Formal
Cuisine	Modern European
Recommended for	Local favourite

'Stunning gardens in the summer and a good-value lunch menu.'—James Wilkins

THE EASTERN EYE
8a Quiet Street
Bath
Somerset
England BA1 2JS
+44 1225422323
www.easterneye.com

Recommended by
Hywel Jones

Opening hours	Open 7 days
Credit cards	Accepted
Price range	Affordable
Style	Casual
Cuisine	Bengali
Recommended for	Late night

'Brilliant Indian restaurant in the centre of Bath, with a stunning dining room, extremely accommodating staff (even for a late-night table of chefs!) and most importantly, great food. Ask them to create you a bespoke menu and you won't be disappointed.' —Hywel Jones

JIKA JIKA
Princes Buildings
4a George Street
Bath
Somerset
England BA1 2ED
+44 1225429903
www.jikajika.co.uk

Recommended by
Hywel Jones

Opening hours	Open 7 days
Credit cards	Accepted but not AMEX
Price range	Budget
Style	Casual
Cuisine	Café-Bistro
Recommended for	Breakfast

'Fantastic coffee and simple but great-quality food specializing in the West Country's finest produce. A must-visit place if ever I'm in the city centre early in the morning.'—Hywel Jones

THE OLD SPOT
12 Sadler Street
Wells
Somerset
England BA5 2SE
+44 1749689099
www.theoldspot.co.uk

Recommended by
Bruce Poole

Opening hours	Closed Monday
Credit cards	Accepted
Price range	Affordable
Style	Casual
Cuisine	European
Recommended for	Local favourite

'Wonderfully classical and intelligent food with a great wine list, overlooking beautiful Wells Cathedral. What's not to like? I wish I had a place of this quality near where I live!'—Bruce Poole

THE ETHICUREAN
Barley Wood Walled Garden
Long Lane
Wrington
Somerset
England BS40 5SA
+44 1934863713
www.theethicurean.com

Recommended by
Martin Morales

Opening hours	Closed Monday
Credit cards	Accepted
Price range	Affordable
Style	Casual
Cuisine	Modern British
Recommended for	Wish I'd opened

'The Ethicurean team are not just a lovely bunch of guys, they also create some of the most imaginative dishes and drinks from produce gathered no further than one mile from their restaurant. They grow much of what they cook; they forage, hunt, pickle or smoke their produce before artistically displaying it on dishes. The setting is also stunning – set in a walled garden on one side of a valley, it has some of the most spectacular sunsets anywhere in the world.' —Martin Morales

THE BRITISH LARDER SUFFOLK

Orford Road
Bromeswell
Suffolk
England IP12 2PU
+44 1394460310
www.britishlardersuffolk.co.uk

Opening hours..Closed Monday
Credit cards..Accepted but not AMEX
Price range...Affordable
Style..Casual
Cuisine...British
Recommended for...Worth the travel

'I love the way traditional British pubs are evolving into wonderful, upscale restaurants serving no-nonsense, honest food that relies on sourcing good, seasonal ingredients and treating them with respect. This place is a great example of how far pub food has travelled in the last twenty years. Fantastic!'—Marc Fosh

PEA PORRIDGE

28–29 Cannon Street
Bury St Edmunds
Suffolk
England IP33 1JR
+44 1284700200
www.peaporridge.co.uk

Opening hours...............................Closed Monday and Sunday
Credit cards..Accepted but not AMEX
Price range...Affordable
Style..Casual
Cuisine...European
Recommended for...Local favourite

'Solid cooking and full-on flavours. Uncomplicated, tasty food with a maximum of four components per plate.'—Paul Foster

The cosmopolitan cooking comes as quite a surprise at this bijou restaurant, set on a quiet backstreet of a handsome market town. The interior is all English country cottage – stripped wooden floors, pine furniture, an open fire – while the menu gallops gaily from the Middle East, across Spain, France and North Africa, touting the likes of pimentón-infused braised octopus, or Tuscan-style pig's cheeks with polenta. In-the-know locals love the great-value set menus (£16.95/$29 for three courses). Service is as charming as the setting, and the wine list cut from Old World artisan growers. Stop for a pre-dinner drink at The Old Cannon Brewery across the road.

HOO HING SUPERMARKET

Bond Road
Mitcham
Surrey
England CR4 3EB
+44 2086872633
www.hoohing.com

Opening hours...Open 7 days
Reservation policy...No
Credit cards...Accepted
Price range..Budget
Style..Casual
Cuisine...Chinese
Recommended for...Bargain

'The canteen is inside Hoo Hing Chinese supermarket. They do the most delish food at ridiculously cheap prices.'—Ollie Couillaud

THE MALT SHOVEL

Barston Lane
Barston
West Midlands
England B92 0JP
+44 1675443223
www.themaltshovelatbarston.com

Opening hours...Open 7 days
Credit cards...Accepted
Price range...Affordable
Style..Casual
Cuisine...Gastropub
Recommended for................................Regular neighbourhood

'Good-quality, affordable dining and always consistent.'
—Adam Stokes

ADIL

Recommended by
Glynn Purnell

353–355 Ladypool Road
Birmingham
West Midlands
England B12 8LA
+44 1214490335
www.adilbalti.co.uk

Opening hours..Closed Monday
Credit cards..Accepted
Price range..Affordable
Style..Casual
Cuisine..Indian-Pakistani
Recommended for...................................Local favourite

AL FRASH

Recommended by
Glynn Purnell

186 Ladypool Road
Birmingham
West Midlands
England B12 8JS
+44 1217533120
www.alfrash.com

Opening hours.......................................Open 7 days
Credit cards..Accepted
Price range..Budget
Style..Casual
Cuisine..Indian-Pakistani
Recommended for...................................Local favourite

'Birmingham is well known for its curry culture. The
Balti Triangle – the area established in the mid-1970s
by the Pakistani and Kasmiri communities – really
represents the multicultural flavours of my city!'
—Glynn Purnell

IMRANS

Recommended by
Glynn Purnell

262–266 Ladypool Road
Birmingham
West Midlands
England B12 8JU
+44 1214491370
www.imrans.com

Opening hours.......................................Open 7 days
Credit cards..Accepted
Price range..Budget
Style..Casual
Cuisine..Indian-Pakistani
Recommended for...................................Local favourite

SIMPSONS

Recommended by
Adam Stokes

20 Highfield Road
Birmingham
West Midlands
England B15 3DU
+44 1214543434
www.simpsonsrestaurant.co.uk

Opening hours.......................................Open 7 days
Credit cards..Accepted
Price range..Expensive
Style..Smart casual
Cuisine..Modern British
Recommended for...................................Local favourite

'Andreas Antona is the godfather of Birmingham
cooking.'—Adam Stokes

RED LION FREEHOUSE

Recommended by
Bruce Poole

East Chisenbury
Pewsey
Wiltshire
England SN9 6AQ
+44 1980671124
www.redlionfreehouse.com

Opening hours.......................................Open 7 days
Credit cards..................................Accepted but not AMEX
Price range..Affordable
Style..Casual
Cuisine..Gastropub
Recommended for...............................Regular neighbourhood

'Fantastic food and lovely hospitality in a proper pub.
It's a gem.'—Bruce Poole

'THE FOOD IS FILTHY IN ALL THE BEST WAYS.'
NEIL RANKIN P328

'Represents the true side of London'
SAM HARRIS P362

'A FIRST-CLASS FRY UP.'
BEN TISH P355

LONDON

'It's almost as though the fish swims from the counter into your mouth – it's that fresh!'
NUNO MENDES P360

'Dangerously addictive and dangerously messy.'
TOM ADAMS P329

'kedgeree and kippers'
SAMI TAMIMI P344

'in-your-face London'
JACOB KENEDY P359

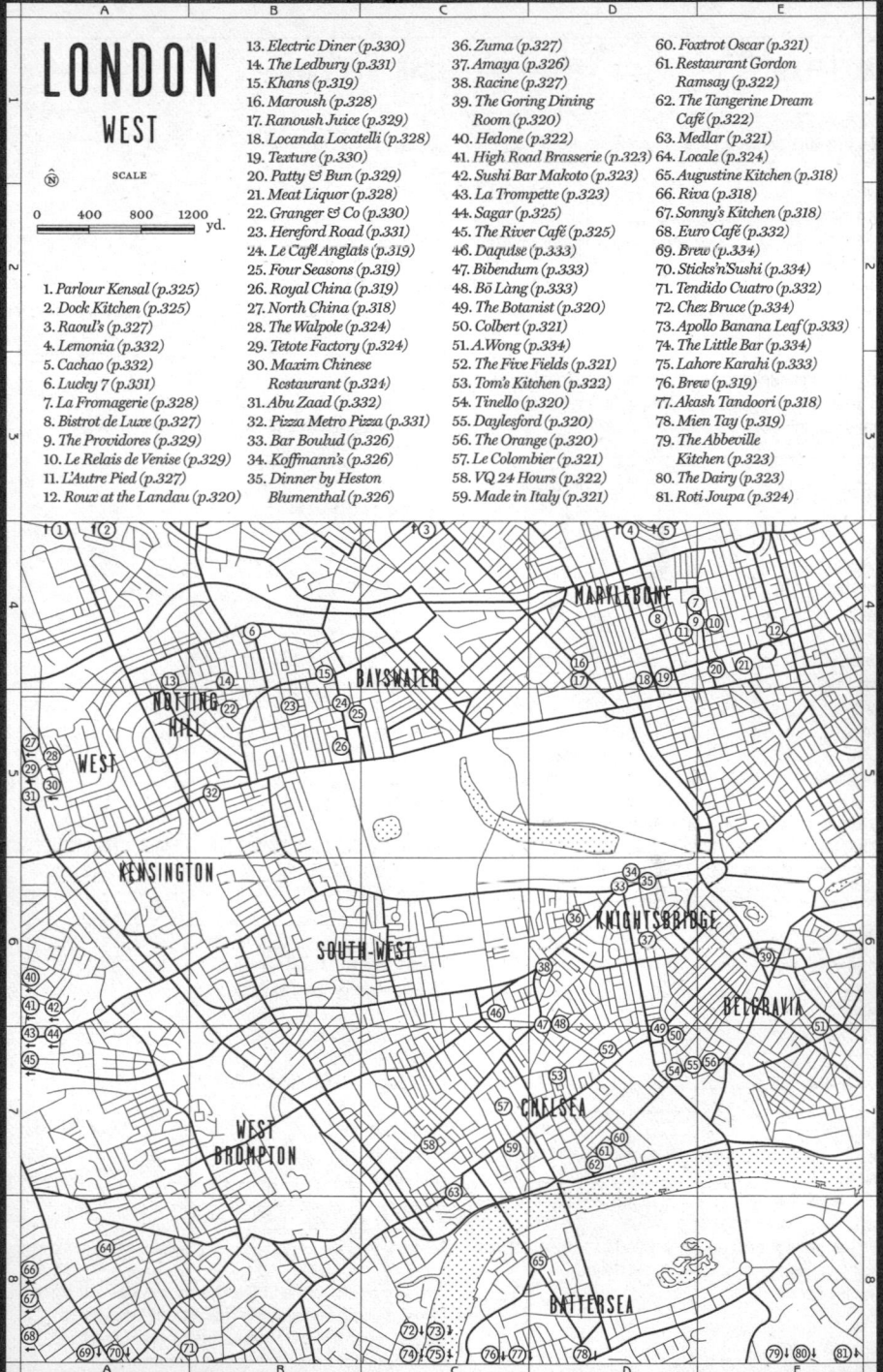

LONDON

WEST

N

SCALE

0   400   800   1200 yd.

STREET FEAST

Recommended by
Ben Spalding

London
+44 7549183866
www.streetfeastlondon.com

Opening hours	Variable
Reservation policy	No
Credit cards	Not accepted
Price range	Budget
Style	Casual
Cuisine	Street Food
Recommended for	Late night

'It's a night market and more people need to wake up and see the revolution happening with Street Feast pioneering it!'—Ben Spalding

NORTH CHINA

Recommended by
Henry Harris

305 Uxbridge Road
Acton
London W3 9QU
+44 2089929183
www.northchina.co.uk

Opening hours	Open 7 days
Credit cards	Accepted
Price range	Affordable
Style	Casual
Cuisine	Chinese
Recommended for	Regular neighbourhood

'My favourite local. Fresh dumplings and a superb Peking duck served as three or four courses. Family run and damn tasty cooking.'—Henry Harris

RIVA

Recommended by
Rainer Becker

169 Church Road
Barnes
London SW13 9HR
+44 2087480434

Opening hours	Open 7 days
Credit cards	Accepted
Price range	Affordable
Style	Smart casual
Cuisine	Italian
Recommended for	Regular neighbourhood

'Riva has great produce. They are so hospitable, but it's low key and the food never lets you down.'
—Rainer Becker

SONNY'S KITCHEN

Recommended by
Rainer Becker,
Manoj Vasaikar

94 Church Road
Barnes
London SW13 0DQ
+44 2087480393
www.sonnyskitchen.com

Opening hours	Open 7 days
Credit cards	Accepted
Price range	Affordable
Style	Smart casual
Cuisine	European
Recommended for	Regular neighbourhood

'I think Sonny's is excellent value for money, with menus designed by Phil Howard, a partner in the restaurant.'—Rainer Becker

AKASH TANDOORI

Recommended by
Alyn Williams

70 Northcote Road
Battersea
London SW11 6QL
+44 8005878129
www.akashtandoori.com

Opening hours	Open 7 days
Credit cards	Accepted
Price range	Budget
Style	Casual
Cuisine	Indian
Recommended for	Bargain

'Akash is a Sunday evening family regular. They cook consistently good Indian food that my kids love too.'
—Alyn Williams

AUGUSTINE KITCHEN

Recommended by
Olivier Limousin

63 Battersea Bridge Road
Battersea
London SW11 3AU
+44 2079787085
www.augustine-kitchen.co.uk

Opening hours	Closed Monday
Credit cards	Accepted
Price range	Affordable
Style	Casual
Cuisine	French
Recommended for	Regular neighbourhood

'It's very traditional and the chef is very good at classic dishes. I like this restaurant because it looks like a small, French *salle à manger* bistro. Good food and good value for money.'—Olivier Limousin

BREW
Recommended by
Adam Byatt

45 Northcote Road
Battersea
London SW11 1NJ
+44 2075852198
www.brew-cafe.com

Opening hours	Open 7 days
Credit cards	Accepted
Price range	Budget
Style	Casual
Cuisine	Café
Recommended for	Breakfast

'Great coffee. They serve freshly cooked, simple brunch offerings, using impeccable ingredients.'—Adam Byatt

MIEN TAY
Recommended by
Robin Gill

180 Lavender Hill
Battersea
London SW11 5TQ
+44 2073500721
www.mientay.co.uk/battersea

Opening hours	Open 7 days
Credit cards	Not accepted
Price range	Budget
Style	Casual
Cuisine	Vietnamese
Recommended for	Bargain

'The food is exceptional traditional Vietnamese and when you step in you automatically imagine you are in a hectic Saigon restaurant.'—Robin Gill

LE CAFÉ ANGLAIS
Recommended by
Thomasina Miers

8 Porchester Gardens
Bayswater
London W2 4DB
+44 2072211415
www.lecafeanglais.co.uk

Opening hours	Open 7 days
Credit cards	Accepted
Price range	Affordable
Style	Casual
Cuisine	French
Recommended for	Regular neighbourhood

FOUR SEASONS
Recommended by
Daniel Boulud

84 Queensway
Bayswater
London W2 3RL
+44 2072294320
www.fs-restaurants.co.uk

Opening hours	Open 7 days
Credit cards	Accepted
Price range	Affordable
Style	Casual
Cuisine	Chinese
Recommended for	Local favourite

KHANS
Recommended by
Omar Allibhoy

13–15 Westbourne Grove
Bayswater
London W2 4UA
+44 2077275420
www.khansrestaurant.com

Opening hours	Open 7 days
Credit cards	Accepted
Price range	Budget
Style	Casual
Cuisine	Indian
Recommended for	Wish I'd opened

'It's a place my Indian grandfather used to visit thirty years ago, and it's still kicking ass with the chillies. There is a reason it's been open for so long.'
—Omar Allibhoy

ROYAL CHINA
Recommended by
Margot Henderson, Jacob Kenedy, Pierre Koffmann, Thomasina Miers

13 Queensway
Bayswater
London W2 4QJ
+44 2072212535
www2.royalchinagroup.biz

Opening hours	Open 7 days
Credit cards	Accepted
Price range	Affordable
Style	Casual
Cuisine	Chinese
Recommended for	Bargain

'I love dim sum for breakfast more than anything.'
—Jacob Kenedy

DAYLESFORD
44b Pimlico Road
Belgravia
London SW1W 8LP
+44 2078818060
www.daylesford.com

Recommended by
Tom Aikens

Opening hours..Open 7 days
Reservation policy..No
Credit cards...Accepted
Price range...Affordable
Style...Casual
Cuisine...British bistro
Recommended for...................................Breakfast

'Fantastic seasonal fare, farm fresh and organic!'
—Tom Aikens

THE GORING DINING ROOM
The Goring
15 Beeston Place
Belgravia
London SW1W 0JW
+44 2073969000
www.thegoring.com

Recommended by
Chris Galvin

Opening hours..Open 7 days
Credit cards...Accepted
Price range...Expensive
Style...Smart casual
Cuisine..British
Recommended for.....................................High end

'When celebrating a special family occasion, we
combine a visit to the restaurant with a stay at this
amazing hotel.'—Chris Galvin

Owned and run by the Goring family for over a century,
this luxury Belgravia hotel was appointed a Royal
Warrant on its 100th anniversary in 2010. From
serving as a plush command centre for the Chief of
Allied Forces during World War I, to being the bride's
family base for the Royal Wedding in 2011, it has
always served the establishment. Its dining room,
revamped in 2005 by Viscount Linley, remains a
bastion of Britishness, where lunch is still called
'luncheon' and the trolley is laden with roast lamb,
steak and kidney pie or roast beef. If class and grace
are boring, then The Goring is a snorefest.

THE ORANGE
37 Pimlico Road
Belgravia
London SW1W 8NE
+44 2078819844
www.theorange.co.uk

Recommended by
Tom Aikens

Opening hours..Open 7 days
Credit cards...Accepted
Price range...Affordable
Style...Casual
Cuisine...British bistro
Recommended for...................................Breakfast

'Has a great kids menu, perfect for my young daughter.'
—Tom Aikens

TINELLO
87 Pimlico Road
Belgravia
London SW1W 8PH
+44 2077303663
www.tinello.co.uk

Recommended by
Giorgio Locatelli

Opening hours...Closed Sunday
Credit cards.............................Accepted but not Diners
Price range...Affordable
Style...Smart casual
Cuisine..Tuscan
Recommended for................Regular neighbourhood

'Friendly and relaxed atmosphere, and Tuscan food in
welcoming surroundings.'—Giorgio Locatelli

THE BOTANIST
7 Sloane Square
Chelsea
London SW1W 8EE
+44 2077300077
www.thebotanistonsloanesquare.com

Recommended by
Heinz Beck

Opening hours..Open 7 days
Credit cards...Accepted
Price range...Affordable
Style...Casual
Cuisine..European
Recommended for...................................Breakfast

'When I am in London, I breakfast at the Botanist as
I prefer to start my day lightly with a glass of their
freshly squeezed orange juice and a plate of fresh fruit,
usually mango and papaya.'—Heinz Beck

COLBERT

Recommended by
Tom Aikens,
Pascal Aussignac,
Marcus Wareing

50–52 Sloane Square
Chelsea
London SW1W 8AX
+44 2077302804
www.colbertchelsea.com

Opening hours	Open 7 days
Credit cards	Accepted
Price range	Affordable
Style	Casual
Cuisine	French Brasserie
Recommended for	Breakfast

'It's great for meetings but equally I can go with my son for a bacon sandwich and cup of tea and fit right in.' —Marcus Wareing

LE COLOMBIER

Recommended by
Pierre Koffmann

145 Dovehouse Street
Chelsea
London SW3 6LB
+44 2073511155
www.le-colombier-restaurant.co.uk

Opening hours	Open 7 days
Credit cards	Accepted
Price range	Affordable
Style	Casual
Cuisine	French
Recommended for	Regular neighbourhood

'Proper classic French food and friendly service. I go for the *plateaux de fruits de mer* (seafood platters) and *chaud froid aux amandes* (ice cream with chocolate sauce and almonds).'—Pierre Koffmann

THE FIVE FIELDS

Recommended by
Pierre Koffmann

8–9 Blacklands Terrace
Chelsea
London SW3 2SP
+44 2078381082
www.fivefieldsrestaurant.com

Opening hours	Closed Monday and Sunday
Credit cards	Accepted
Price range	Expensive
Style	Smart casual
Cuisine	Modern British
Recommended for	High end

'Proper fine dining.'—Pierre Koffmann

FOXTROT OSCAR

Recommended by
Thomasina Miers

79 Royal Hospital Road
Chelsea
London SW3 4HN
+44 2073524448
www.gordonramsay.com/foxtrotoscar

Opening hours	Open 7 days
Credit cards	Accepted
Price range	Affordable
Style	Casual
Cuisine	Modern European
Recommended for	Breakfast

MADE IN ITALY

Recommended by
Alyn Williams

249 Kings Road
Chelsea
London SW3 5EL
+44 2073521880
www.madeinitalygroup.co.uk

Opening hours	Open 7 days
Credit cards	Accepted
Price range	Budget
Style	Casual
Cuisine	Italian
Recommended for	Regular neighbourhood

'They serve simple, delicious, wood-fired pizzas with friendly service.'—Alyn Williams

MEDLAR

Recommended by
Mikael Jonsson, Neil Rankin,
Marcus Wareing

438 Kings Road
Chelsea
London SW10 0LJ
+44 2073491900
www.medlarrestaurant.co.uk

Opening hours	Open 7 days
Credit cards	Accepted
Price range	Affordable
Style	Casual
Cuisine	Modern European
Recommended for	Regular neighbourhood

'It's actually not that pricey, but going there always makes an occasion. Its perfectly pitched service makes you feel special but also puts you at ease. The wine selection and cheese trolley (cart) are worthy of a trip all by themselves but it's the attention to detail in its Frenchified nod to the classics menu that wins me over. There are no foams, jellies or spheres here, it's just a menu you enjoy reading almost as much as eating.'—Neil Rankin

RESTAURANT GORDON RAMSAY

Recommended by
Paul Owens,
Ben Spalding

68 Royal Hospital Road
Chelsea
London SW3 4HP
+44 2073524441
www.gordonramsay.com/royalhospitalroad

Opening hours	Closed Saturday and Sunday
Credit cards	Accepted
Price range	Expensive
Style	Formal
Cuisine	European
Recommended for	High end

'The benchmark in London. A restaurant and kitchen that taught me many disciplines when I trained there.'
—Ben Spalding

THE TANGERINE DREAM CAFÉ

Recommended by
Theo Randall

Chelsea Physic Garden
66 Royal Hospital Road
Chelsea
London SW3 4HS
+44 2073496464
www.tangerinedream.uk.com

Opening hours	Closed Monday and Saturday
Reservation policy	No
Credit cards	Accepted
Price range	Affordable
Style	Casual
Cuisine	Café
Recommended for	Local favourite

'One of my favourite local places. In the summer months, Limpet Barron opens her café in the evenings and cooks delicious food in the oldest and most beautiful garden in Central London.'—Theo Randall

TOM'S KITCHEN

Recommended by
Clare Smyth

27 Cale Street
Chelsea
London SW3 3QP
+44 2073490202
www.tomskitchen.co.uk

Opening hours	Open 7 days
Credit cards	Accepted
Price range	Affordable
Style	Casual
Cuisine	British bistro
Recommended for	Breakfast

VQ 24 HOURS

Recommended by
Steffen Hansen

325 Fulham Road
Chelsea
London SW10 9QL
+44 2073767224
www.vq24hours.com

Opening hours	Open 7 days
Credit cards	Accepted
Price range	Budget
Style	Casual
Cuisine	International
Recommended for	Late night

'The name says it all, open 24/7. Where else can you drink a bottle of Krug in the early-morning hours?'
—Steffen Hansen

HEDONE

Recommended by
Daniel Berlin,
Stephen Harris

301–303 Chiswick High Road
Chiswick
London W4 4HH
+44 2087470377
www.hedonerestaurant.com

Opening hours	Closed Monday and Sunday
Credit cards	Accepted
Price range	Expensive
Style	Smart casual
Cuisine	Modern European
Recommended for	Worth the travel

'It's only about the produce!'—Daniel Berlin

Mikael Jonsson has come a long way: severe food allergies meant he first became a lawyer and then an ingredient-obsessed blogger. When he finally opened this Chiswick restaurant in 2011 it secured a Michelin star in just fourteen months. Its name roughly translates as 'pleasure', and the same earnestness dictates the room's look, with bare bricks and a very open-plan kitchen. There's no fixed menu, but instead a long and elegant procession of dishes celebrating the very best British ingredients such as wild Dorset turbot and Cornish rock oysters. A recent nod from San Pellegrino should see more customers schlepping to the 'burbs.

HIGH ROAD BRASSERIE

Recommended by
Manoj Vasaikar

162–170 Chiswick High Road
Chiswick
London W4 1PR
+44 2087427474
www.brasserie.highroadhouse.co.uk

Opening hours	Open 7 days
Credit cards	Accepted
Price range	Affordable
Style	Casual
Cuisine	European
Recommended for	Breakfast

'Very casual, nice atmosphere. Lean breakfast.'
—Manoj Vasaikar

SUSHI BAR MAKOTO

Recommended by
Sami Tamimi

4 Devonshire Road
Chiswick
London W4 2HD
+44 2089873180
www.sushibarmakato.co.uk

Opening hours	Closed Monday
Credit cards	Accepted
Price range	Affordable
Style	Casual
Cuisine	Sushi
Recommended for	Local favourite

'The thing I love most about London is that you can be transported all over the world through kitchens within a few square miles. Makoto is just one of these: the sushi you are served is second to none. The welcome that customers get from the couple who run the bar is so warm that you feel as though you've been invited to their house.'—Sami Tamimi

LA TROMPETTE

Recommended by
Manoj Vasaikar

3–7 Devonshire Road
Chiswick
London W4 2EU
+44 2087471836
www.latrompette.co.uk

Opening hours	Open 7 days
Credit cards	Accepted
Price range	Affordable
Style	Smart casual
Cuisine	Modern European
Recommended for	Regular neighbourhood

THE ABBEVILLE KITCHEN

Recommended by
Jonathan Jones

47 Abbeville Road
Clapham
London SW4 9JX
+44 2087721110
www.abbevillekitchen.com

Opening hours	Open 7 days
Credit cards	Accepted
Price range	Affordable
Style	Casual
Cuisine	European
Recommended for	Breakfast

'They have the best bacon and sausages from George at Swaledale. Great for lunch and dinner too.'
—Jonathan Jones

THE DAIRY

Recommended by
Tom Aikens

15 The Pavement
Clapham
London SW4 0HY
+44 2076224165
www.the-dairy.co.uk

Opening hours	Closed Monday
Credit cards	Accepted
Price range	Affordable
Style	Casual
Cuisine	British bistro
Recommended for	Bargain

'A lovely local with a good vibe. Good-quality ingredients, partly sourced from their own garden, and a good level of cooking with a British seasonal approach.'—Tom Aikens

ROTI JOUPA

Recommended by
Jonathan Jones

12 Clapham High Street
Clapham
London SW4 7UT
+44 2076278637
www.rotijoupa.com

Opening hours	Closed Sunday
Reservation policy	No
Credit cards	Not accepted
Price range	Budget
Style	Casual
Cuisine	Caribbean
Recommended for	Late night

'Impeccable *roti* (Indian bread) and curried goat. The freshest take away (take out) food I know.' —Jonathan Jones

MAXIM CHINESE RESTAURANT

Recommended by
Alfred Prasad

153–155 Northfield Avenue
Ealing
London W13 9QT
+44 2085671719
www.maxim-ealing.co.uk

Opening hours	Open 7 days
Credit cards	Accepted
Price range	Affordable
Style	Casual
Cuisine	Chinese
Recommended for	Regular neighbourhood

'Everybody should have a neighbourhood gem they feel proud of. Maxim is largely family run and the service is friendly and relaxed, which really hits the right note for a neighbourhood restaurant. It has a lovely, warm and elegant ambience, filled with regular patrons every day of the week. The highlight of Maxim is its freshly made, tasty food. Many times I've seen the big boss herself, Mrs Chow, supervising the kitchen. Her high standards are clearly reflected in the delicious and consistent dishes. My favourites there are prawns (shrimp) in ginger and spring onions (scallions) and the plain noodles. And I highly recommend the salt-and-pepper squid, salt-and-pepper fine beans and the barbeque pork ribs which are delicately spiced and beautifully cooked.' —Alfred Prasad

TETOTE FACTORY

Recommended by
Jocky Petrie

12 South Ealing Road
Ealing
London W5 4QA
+44 2085798391
www.tetotefactory.co.uk

Opening hours	Closed Monday
Reservation policy	No
Credit cards	Accepted but not AMEX
Price range	Budget
Style	Casual
Cuisine	Bakery
Recommended for	Breakfast

'I'm not a big breakfast person, but this tiny bakery is great. Their bread is made with a Japanese twist. The chocolate brioche is very good, as are their baguettes.' —Jocky Petrie

THE WALPOLE

Recommended by
Jocky Petrie

35 St Mary's Road
Ealing
London W5 5RG
+44 2085677918
www.walpole-ealing.co.uk

Opening hours	Closed Monday and Sunday
Credit cards	Accepted but not AMEX
Price range	Affordable
Style	Casual
Cuisine	European Bistro
Recommended for	Bargain

'The portions are huge and the food delicious. There's a great atmosphere too.' —Jocky Petrie

LOCALE

Recommended by
Omar Allibhoy

222 Munster Road
Fulham
London SW6 6AY
+44 2073816137
www.localerestaurants.com

Opening hours	Open 7 days
Credit cards	Accepted
Price range	Affordable
Style	Casual
Cuisine	Italian
Recommended for	Late night

'I always end up at this great Italian restaurant which serves a proper seafood linguine. Whenever I order that dish it never disappoints!' —Omar Allibhoy

THE RIVER CAFÉ

Thames Wharf
Rainville Road
Hammersmith
London W6 9HA
+44 2073864200
www.rivercafe.co.uk

Recommended by
Rainer Becker, Samantha &
Samuel Clark, Andreas Dahlberg
Jeff Galvin, Alexis Gauthier,
Gabrielle Hamilton, Philip
Howard, Jeremy Lee, James
Lowe, Niall McKenna, Thomasina
Miers, Rafael Osterling, Stevie
Parle, Tim Siadatan, Roberta
Sudbrack, Sami Tamimi, Peter
Weeden, Junya Yamasaki

Opening hours	Open 7 days
Credit cards	Accepted
Price range	Expensive
Style	Smart casual
Cuisine	Italian
Recommended for	High end

'A brilliant story of two women opening a restaurant. They were at an age when many are thinking of retiring. It is pioneering stuff. It thrives and has spurred on so many cooks. A lunch on its lovely terrace in the sunshine remains one of life's great pleasures.' —Jeremy Lee

Italian food made by Ruth Rogers and her team with the very best produce money can buy, assembled in neo-rustic style, served in a stylish modern glass-fronted canteen (originally an old oil storage facility before architect Richard Rogers got hold of it), down where the old Thames does flow. That's been the River Café's formula for success since it opened in 1988. Co-founder Rose Gray, who sadly passed away in 2010, would be pleased to see nothing has changed in her absence. Perfect setting meets perfect produce, meets educated service and a wine list, aside from the odd Champagne, that is all-Italian and runs from humble bottles to Super Tuscans.

SAGAR

157 King Street
Hammersmith
London W6 9JT
+44 2087418563
www.sagarveg.co.uk

Recommended by
Martin Morales

Opening hours	Open 7 days
Credit cards	Accepted
Price range	Budget
Style	Casual
Cuisine	Indian-Vegetarian
Recommended for	Bargain

'Freshly made Indian vegetarian food with tasty ingredients, like a masala dosa and a lunch for £6 ($10) which includes some eight items.' —Martin Morales

DOCK KITCHEN

Portobello Docks
342–344 Ladbroke Grove
Kensal Green
London W10 5BU
+44 2089621610
www.dockkitchen.co.uk

Recommended by
Samantha & Samuel Clark,
Thomasina Miers

Opening hours	Open 7 days
Credit cards	Accepted
Price range	Affordable
Style	Smart casual
Cuisine	International
Recommended for	Regular neighbourhood

'Stevie is a very talented chef and as he, like us, trained at the River Café, his approach and food combinations feel very natural to us. The restaurant is also part of Tom Dixon's unique studio near Ladbroke Grove, which in itself is very striking and beautiful.' —Samantha & Samuel Clark

PARLOUR KENSAL

5 Regent Street
Kensal Green
London NW10 5LG
+44 2089692184
www.parlourkensal.com

Recommended by
James Knappett

Opening hours	Open 7 days
Credit cards	Accepted
Price range	Affordable
Style	Casual
Cuisine	Gastropub
Recommended for	Regular neighbourhood

'It's a proper British pub, but the chef really brings the food alive and really makes it interesting, with some great ingredients. There are nice touches, like how you can make your own toast.'—James Knappett

AMAYA

Halkin Arcade
Motcomb Street
Knightsbridge
London SW1X 8JT
+44 2078231166
www.amaya.biz

Recommended by
Manoj Vasaikar

Opening hours	Open 7 days
Credit cards	Accepted
Price range	Expensive
Style	Smart casual
Cuisine	Modern Indian
Recommended for	Wish I'd opened

'Most chic Indian grill in town and a great atmosphere.'
—Manoj Vasaikar

BAR BOULUD

Mandarin Oriental Hyde Park
66 Knightsbridge
Knightsbridge
London SW1X 7LA
+44 2072013899
www.barboulud.com

Recommended by
Paul Foster, Francesco
Mazzei, Glynn Purnell, Clare
Smyth, Marcus Wareing

Opening hours	Open 7 days
Credit cards	Accepted
Price range	Affordable
Style	Smart casual
Cuisine	French
Recommended for	Late night

'The food is simple and approachable, but is of an amazing standard. The service is relaxed and friendly with the attention to detail of a thirty-seat Michelin-starred restaurant.'—Paul Foster

A restaurant in a five-star hotel in the heart of Knightsbridge might seem an unlikely late-night hang-out for anyone other than the supremely wealthy and unimaginative, but then Bar Boulud isn't your typical operation. Firstly, the French bistro-style food, with all manner of charcuterie and tempting titbits, is much more accessible than many hotels offer. Secondly, it does a seriously good burger, including the traditional-style Yankee, the Frenchie (made with confit pork belly and Morbier) and the Piggie (BBQ pulled pork and green chilli mayonnaise). What's more, you can wash it down with one of their uncommonly large selection of draught beers.

DINNER BY HESTON BLUMENTHAL

Mandarin Oriental Hyde Park
66 Knightsbridge
Knightsbridge
London SW1X 7LA
+44 2072013833
www.dinnerbyheston.com

Recommended by
Omar Allibhoy,
Tomi Björck, Christian
Domschitz, Brian Mark
Hansen, Timothy Johnson,
Tony Mantuano, Shuko Oda,
Tom Sellers, Jock Zonfrillo

Opening hours	Open 7 days
Credit cards	Accepted
Price range	Expensive
Style	Smart casual
Cuisine	Modern British
Recommended for	Worth the travel

'As my English husband said as we left Dinner one time, "I'm proud to be English". That's how good the meal was. I did not know pork chops could taste that good. The best ingredients cooked to perfection. I'm not usually one for sweets, but dessert was astonishing.'
—Shuko Oda

Heston Blumenthal's Fat Duck follow-up is a bustling brasserie with a playful menu, much of it surprisingly straightforward despite being inspired by a geeky love of British food history. Overlooking Hyde Park from the handsome rear of Knightsbridge's Mandarin Oriental, its spacious dining room seats 136 at large, luxuriously spaced tables. Inside the vast glass-fronted kitchen, a giant Swiss watch movement turning a series of spits catches the eye. So too the now trademark Meat Fruit — a chicken liver parfait made to resemble a mandarin — and the Tipsy Cake — vanilla-custard-filled brioche served with pineapple roasted on that showcase rotisserie.

KOFFMANN'S

The Berkeley
Wilton Place
Knightsbridge
London SW1X 7RL
+44 2071078844
www.the-berkeley.co.uk/koffmanns

Recommended by
Jacob Kenedy, Tom Kitchin

Opening hours	Open 7 days
Credit cards	Accepted
Price range	Affordable
Style	Smart casual
Cuisine	French
Recommended for	Regular neighbourhood

'I worked with Pierre Koffmann for five years and I always try to go to The Berkeley when I'm in London. Even after all these years he's still my mentor and

I really enjoy spending time with him. For me, Chef is a genius and I love his cooking.'—Tom Kitchin

RACINE

Recommended by
Dominic Chapman

239 Brompton Road
Knightsbridge
London SW3 2EP
+44 2075844477
www.racine-restaurant.com

Opening hours	Open 7 days
Credit cards	Accepted
Price range	Affordable
Style	Smart casual
Cuisine	French
Recommended for	Regular neighbourhood

'The food is always delicious. Great, honest cooking that makes me smile.'—Dominic Chapman

ZUMA

Recommended by
Heinz Beck, Thomas Bühner,
Andreas Caminada, Gert de
Mangeleer, Henry Harris,
Matthew Harris, Alfonso &
Ernesto Iaccarino, Francesco
Mazzei, Theo Randall, Shaun
Rankin, Agnar Sverrisson,
Mitch Tonks, Ricardo Zarate

5 Raphael Street
Knightsbridge
London SW7 1DL
+44 2075841010
www.zumarestaurant.com

Opening hours	Open 7 days
Credit cards	Accepted
Price range	Expensive
Style	Smart casual
Cuisine	Japanese
Recommended for	Wish I'd opened

'Zuma has a fabulous atmosphere coupled with great food and hospitality. They excel on freshness and the quality of their product and you'd be hard pushed to find better Japanese food in London. I can highly recommend the salt-grilled sea bass and the wagyu beef.'—Shaun Rankin

RAOUL'S

Recommended by
Pierre Koffmann

13 Clifton Road
Maida Vale
London W9 1SZ
+44 2072897313
www.raoulsgourmet.com

Opening hours	Open 7 days
Credit cards	Accepted
Price range	Affordable
Style	Casual
Cuisine	European Bistro
Recommended for	Breakfast

L'AUTRE PIED

Recommended by
Ben Spalding

5–7 Blandford Street
Marylebone
London W1U 3DB
+44 2074869696
www.lautrepied.co.uk

Opening hours	Open 7 days
Credit cards	Accepted
Price range	Expensive
Style	Smart casual
Cuisine	Modern French
Recommended for	Local favourite

'An accessible, brilliant, everyday restaurant that is there for the customer, not for ego. Good value and it has a brilliantly talented chef in Andy McFadden. Just a well-rounded restaurant.'—Ben Spalding

BISTROT DE LUXE

Recommended by
Omar Allibhoy, Paul Flynn,
Martin Morales

66 Baker Street
Marylebone
London W1U 7DJ
+44 2079354007
www.galvinrestaurants.com

Opening hours	Open 7 days
Credit cards	Accepted
Price range	Affordable
Style	Smart casual
Cuisine	French
Recommended for	Regular neighbourhood

'A perfectly French, buzzy bistro, with wonderfully rich and perfectly executed food.'—Paul Flynn

LA FROMAGERIE

Recommended by
Omar Allibhoy

2–6 Moxon Street
Marylebone
London W1U 4EW
+44 2079350341
www.lafromagerie.co.uk

Opening hours	Open 7 days
Reservation policy	No
Credit cards	Accepted
Price range	Affordable
Style	Casual
Cuisine	Deli-Café
Recommended for	Breakfast

'This is, in my opinion, the best place to buy cheese in London. You can also purchase quality, fresh produce here. The breakfast is fantastic and the best ingredients are always used. However, be warned, it's not cheap.'
—Omar Allibhoy

LOCANDA LOCATELLI

Recommended by
Yotam Ottolenghi

8 Seymour Street
Marylebone
London W1H 7JZ
+44 2079359088
www.locandalocatelli.com

Opening hours	Open 7 days
Credit cards	Accepted but not Diners
Price range	Expensive
Style	Smart casual
Cuisine	Modern Italian
Recommended for	High end

'It's the most solid of all of London's Italian restaurants. You know exactly what you are going to get, in the best possible sense: delicious, comfortable luxury. For pure comfort, I'd always have the home-made dumplings with cep mushrooms.'—Yotam Ottolenghi

MAROUSH

Recommended by
Sat Bains, Ruth Rogers

21 Edgware Road
Marylebone
London W2 2JE
+44 2077230773
www.maroush.com

Opening hours	Open 7 days
Credit cards	Accepted
Price range	Affordable
Style	Smart casual
Cuisine	Lebanese
Recommended for	Late night

MEAT LIQUOR

Recommended by
Adam Byatt, Michael Deane,
André Garrett, Tom Kerridge,
Neil Rankin, Tom Sellers,
Karam Sethi

74 Welbeck Street
Marylebone
London W1G 0BA
www.meatliquor.com

Opening hours	Open 7 days
Reservation policy	No
Credit cards	Accepted
Price range	Budget
Style	Casual
Cuisine	Burgers
Recommended for	Late night

'Meat Liquor is as far from fine dining as dining out gets. It's dark, loud and busy and the food is filthy in all the best ways. It's the antithesis of almost everything chefs and restaurateurs try to achieve and this is possibly the reason so many of them come here. The food isn't perfect but nothing fills a hole better than a Dead Hippie burger and some chilli cheese fries, especially after a few ales. This is a burger joint that leaves all the others here and in the States for dust and wishing they'd thought of it first.'—Neil Rankin

Meat Liquor – born in late 2011, the child of the rather rock 'n' roll burger van turned pop-up – produces burgers, Philly cheese steaks, chilli dogs, buffalo wings, peanut butter sundaes and so on – all of which, unlike many others, aren't a sad, pale imitation of what you find stateside. The bar does a good selection of microbrews and no-nonsense cocktails served in jars that don't skimp on the liquor. That the queues (waiting lines) of trendy young tattooed things waiting to sink their teeth into a Dead Hippy haven't shortened, even since they opened several additional outposts (Meat Market in Covent Garden; Meat Mission in Shoreditch; another Meat Liquor in Brighton), is testament to their success.

PATTY & BUN

54 James Street
Marylebone
London W1U 1HE
+44 2074873188
www.pattyandbun.co.uk

Recommended by
Tom Adams, Karam Sethi

Opening hours	Closed Monday
Reservation policy	No
Credit cards	Accepted
Price range	Budget
Style	Casual
Cuisine	Burgers
Recommended for	Bargain

'For me, they produce the best burgers in town. Dangerously addictive and dangerously messy. I averaged three a week at one point, which is always a worry.'—Tom Adams

THE PROVIDORES AND TAPA ROOM

109 Marylebone High Street
Marylebone
London W1U 4RX
+44 2079356175
www.theprovidores.co.uk

Recommended by
Brad Farmerie

Opening hours	Open 7 days
Credit cards	Accepted
Price range	Affordable
Style	Casual
Cuisine	Modern International
Recommended for	Breakfast

'Amazing, big punches of flavour, super attentive service, in a relaxed atmosphere – what brunch is all about.'—Brad Farmerie

This Marylebone High Street establishment has been the darling of London brunchers since 2001. Come any time of day and you'll be welcomed by smiling service and knockout blends of flavour, but breakfasts in the Tapa Room will exceed your wildest dreams. Chef Peter Gordon creates true fusion food without forgetting his Kiwi roots, which is reflected in the wine list that includes Bellinis made with New Zealand sparkling wine. Popular favourites include Turkish (poached) eggs with whipped yogurt and hot chilli butter on sourdough, or grilled chorizo with sweet potato and miso mash, garlic labneh and star anise cashew nut praline. A solid Bloody Mary, tamarillo and kiwi fruit smoothies, and excellent coffee provide a memorable morning hit.

RANOUSH JUICE

43 Edgware Road
Marylebone
London W2 2JE
+44 2077235929
www.maroush.com

Recommended by
Henry Harris,
Steve Williams

Opening hours	Open 7 days
Reservation policy	No
Credit cards	Not accepted
Price range	Budget
Style	Casual
Cuisine	Lebanese
Recommended for	Late night

'Open late into the night serving some of the best shawarmas in London. A lamb shawarma kebab and a fresh melon juice will help abate an impending hangover.'—Steve Williams

Even East Enders on a 3.00 a.m. kebab hunt have been known to end up at this Edgware Road staple from the Maroush empire, long overlords of so-called Little Beirut. It's a little rough and ready – there are seats for twenty, but most treat it as a take away (take out), and boozy queues (waiting lines) inevitably gather in the small hours – but benefits from an expert Lebanese production line. The shawarma kebabs are first-rate, whether carved onto the plate or slathered with hummus and pickles in a sandwich, while mezze, baklava and fresh fruit juices offer further fortification for those braving an all-nighter.

LE RELAIS DE VENISE

120 Marylebone Lane
Marylebone
London W1U 2QG
+44 2074860878
www.relaisdevenise.com

Recommended by
Ollie Dabbous

Opening hours	Open 7 days
Reservation policy	No
Credit cards	Accepted
Price range	Affordable
Style	Casual
Cuisine	French
Recommended for	Regular neighbourhood

ROUX AT THE LANDAU

Recommended by
Jacob Kenedy

The Langham
1c Portland Place
Marylebone
London W1B 1JA
+44 2079650165
www.thelandau.com

Opening hours	Open 7 days
Credit cards	Accepted
Price range	Expensive
Style	Smart casual
Cuisine	Modern French
Recommended for	High end

'Chris in the kitchen and Franco on the floor are at the
top of their games. Cocktails in the adjoining artisan
bar are enough to knock anyone for six.'
—Jacob Kenedy

TEXTURE

Recommended by
Raymond Blanc

34 Portman Street
Marylebone
London W1H 7BY
+44 2072240028
www.texture-restaurant.co.uk

Opening hours	Closed Monday and Sunday
Credit cards	Accepted
Price range	Expensive
Style	Smart casual
Cuisine	Modern European
Recommended for	Regular neighbourhood

'My favourite restaurant at the moment is Texture – it's
absolutely wonderful. A wonderful menu and stunning
wine list – what more could you ask for?'
—Raymond Blanc

Agnar Sverrisson and Xavier Rousset absconded
from Raymond Blanc's famed Oxford restaurant Le
Manoir aux Quat'Saisons, where they were head chef
and head sommelier, to open their smart Champagne
bar and restaurant in the capital. The menu is modern
European, but Sverrisson's Icelandic background
brings additional Scandinavian flair to the proceedings,
while Rousset pulls out all the stops with a wine list
of more than 100 different bottles of bubbly alone. To
experience it at its best, ditch the à la carte and opt
for the Scandinavian fish-tasting menu. Order a bottle
of Pol Roger Sir Winston Churchill '99 to wash down
the Icelandic cod.

ELECTRIC DINER

Recommended by
Karam Sethi

191 Portobello Road
Notting Hill
London W11 2ED
+44 2079089696
www.electricdiner.com

Opening hours	Open 7 days
Credit cards	Accepted
Price range	Affordable
Style	Casual
Cuisine	Diner-Café
Recommended for	Wish I'd opened

'I like the menu and brasserie style of the restaurant,
especially since its reopening. It's also a great concept
to have the cinema right next door, especially in a
neighbourhood like Notting Hill. Not only is it packed
for dinner but weekend brunch is always full.'
—Karam Sethi

GRANGER & CO

Recommended by
Tom Aikens

175 Westbourne Grove
Notting Hill
London W11 2SB
+44 2072299111
www.grangerandco.com

Opening hours	Open 7 days
Reservation policy	No
Credit cards	Accepted
Price range	Affordable
Style	Casual
Cuisine	Modern Australian
Recommended for	Breakfast

'Healthy and light breakfast and brunch options in a
nice, relaxing environment.'—Tom Aikens

HEREFORD ROAD

3 Hereford Road
Notting Hill
London W2 4AB
+44 2077271144
www.herefordroad.org

Opening hours..Open 7 days
Credit cards...Accepted
Price range...Affordable
Style..Casual
Cuisine..British
Recommended for.............................Regular neighbourhood

'Hereford Road is my favourite neighbourhood
restaurant. It showcases simple, hearty British cooking.
Hereford Road is simple, honest cooking at its best.'
—Marcus Eaves

The West London chapter of the school of St. John,
Hereford Road first brought its gutsy, no-nonsense
cooking built around British seasonal ingredients to
nearby Notting Hill in 2007. Driven by hardworking
chef-proprietor Tom Pemberton, formerly head chef
of St. John Bread & Wine, it's housed in a Victorian
butcher's shop, open kitchen in the window where
the counter would have been, wrought ironwork on
the ceiling above the red leather upholstered love-
seats. The daily-changing menu delivers perfect
simplicity, from whole fish and helpings of offal to
bowls of rice pudding and jam (jelly). Their set lunch
remains one of London's great bargains.

THE LEDBURY

127 Ledbury Road
Notting Hill
London W11 2AQ
+44 2077929090
www.theledbury.com

Opening hours..Open 7 days
Credit cards...Accepted
Price range..Expensive
Style..Smart casual
Cuisine..Modern European
Recommended for..High end

'Still the best fine dining in the UK.'—Isaac McHale

LUCKY 7

127 Westbourne Park Road
Notting Hill
London W2 5QL
+44 2077276771
www.lucky7london.co.uk

Opening hours..Open 7 days
Reservation policy...No
Credit cards.....................Accepted but not AMEX or Diners
Price range..Budget
Style..Casual
Cuisine..Diner
Recommended for..Bargain

PIZZA METRO PIZZA

147–149 Notting Hill Gate
Notting Hill
London W11 3LF
+44 2077278877
www.pizzametropizza.com

Opening hours..Open 7 days
Credit cards..............................Accepted but not AMEX
Price range..Budget
Style..Casual
Cuisine..Italian
Recommended for..Bargain

'I love a fresh, tasty pizza and it suits my family too. This
one is fairly local and it just gets it right. Even Italians
go there so it can't be bad!'—Marcus Wareing

TENDIDO CUATRO

108–110 New Kings Road
Parsons Green
London SW6 4LY
+44 2073715147
www.cambiodetercio.co.uk

Opening hours	Open 7 days
Credit cards	Accepted
Price range	Affordable
Style	Casual
Cuisine	Spanish
Recommended for	Regular neighbourhood

'I go almost every Sunday with my family. For me, this epitomises what a restaurant should be like: simply somewhere you want to go to, with the people you love, over and over again. The food is good, lots of interesting flavours at a steady pace, which only the Spanish can do. But it is the service and the atmosphere they really get right. You can tell they love their customers.'—Alexis Gauthier

CACHAO

140 Regents Park Road
Primrose Hill
London NW1 8XL
+44 2074834422
www.cachaotoycafe.com

Opening hours	Open 7 days
Credit cards	Accepted
Price range	Budget
Style	Casual
Cuisine	Café
Recommended for	Breakfast

'Grab a table outside in the sunshine on a Sunday morning. Great coffee.'—Theo Randall

LEMONIA

89 Regent's Park Road
Primrose Hill
London NW1 8UY
+44 2075867454
www.lemonia.co.uk

Opening hours	Open 7 days
Credit cards	Accepted but not AMEX
Price range	Affordable
Style	Casual
Cuisine	Greek
Recommended for	Bargain

'Lovely Greek food, very simple and great value. The octopus salad is always good, as are the grilled sardines.'—Theo Randall

EURO CAFÉ

45 Sheen Lane
Sheen
London SW14 8AB
+44 2088783535

Opening hours	Open 7 days
Reservation policy	No
Credit cards	Accepted but not AMEX
Price range	Budget
Style	Casual
Cuisine	British
Recommended for	Breakfast

'This place should win the award for best builder's café. It's a guilty pleasure. Value for money, quick, enormous portions, completely relaxing, it's got the whole collection of rubbish tabloid papers on offer every day and it's my local.'—Martin Morales

ABU ZAAD

29 Uxbridge Road
Shepherd's Bush
London W12 8LH
+44 2087495107
www.abuzaad.co.uk

Opening hours	Open 7 days
Credit cards	Accepted but not AMEX
Price range	Budget
Style	Casual
Cuisine	Middle Eastern
Recommended for	Bargain

'This is a fuss-free, family-friendly restaurant serving the best Syrian food in town. It's where I go when I need a Middle Eastern fix. It's busy, pleasantly chaotic and satisfies all my cravings for home and hummus.'
—Sami Tamimi

BIBENDUM

Recommended by
Jeremy Lee

Michelin House
81 Fulham Road
South Kensington
London SW3 6RD
+44 2075815817
www.bibendum.co.uk

Opening hours	Open 7 days
Credit cards	Accepted
Price range	Affordable
Style	Smart casual
Cuisine	French
Recommended for	High end

'Bibendum remains a peerless dining room of great style and it has the most beautiful light. Ravishing. Oysters, Champagne, snails, a *poulet de bresse* and I love diving deep into the wine cellars. It is an extraordinary use of space in an extraordinary building and remains a testament to the great Terence Conran. Just lovely.'—Jeremy Lee

BO LÀNG

Recommended by
Jacob Kenedy

100 Draycott Avenue
South Kensington
London SW3 3AD
+44 2078237887
www.bolangrestaurant.co.uk

Opening hours	Open 7 days
Credit cards	Accepted but not AMEX
Price range	Affordable
Style	Smart casual
Cuisine	Chinese
Recommended for	Breakfast

'Exemplary dim sum.'—Jacob Kenedy

DAQUISE

Recommended by
Rainer Becker

20 Thurloe Street
South Kensington
London SW7 2LT
+44 2075896117
www.daquise.co.uk

Opening hours	Open 7 days
Credit cards	Accepted
Price range	Affordable
Style	Smart casual
Cuisine	Polish
Recommended for	Late night

'It has a unique atmosphere (retro 1950s and 1960s), very traditional service, and tasty Polish food that actually reminds me of my German heritage, which has some similar dishes. You won't find anything else like it in London.'—Rainer Becker

APOLLO BANANA LEAF

Recommended by
Neil Rankin

190 Tooting High Street
Tooting
London SW17 0SF
+44 2086961423
www.apollobananaleaf.com

Opening hours	Open 7 days
Credit cards	Accepted but not AMEX
Price range	Budget
Style	Casual
Cuisine	Sri Lankan
Recommended for	Bargain

'Tooting is, in my opinion, pound for pound the best area for eating out in the whole of the UK... unless you dislike South Indian or Sri Lankan food that is, because that's pretty much all there is. I have about four or five favourites but I've been to Apollo the most and it's a good place to start. Chicken 65 there is the definitive version for me and the mutton roll and devilled mutton are a staple. There are ups and downs but generally the food is spot on and you could eat like a king for less than £15 ($25). It's also BYO.'—Neil Rankin

LAHORE KARAHI

Recommended by
Jonathan Jones

1 Tooting High Street
Tooting
London SW17 0SN
+44 2087672477
www.lahorekarahirestaurant.co.uk

Opening hours	Open 7 days
Credit cards	Accepted but not AMEX
Price range	Budget
Style	Casual
Cuisine	Pakistani
Recommended for	Bargain

'Fragrant biryani, smoky bread and good mango lassi.'
—Jonathan Jones

THE LITTLE BAR

Recommended by
Ollie Couillaud

145 Mitcham Road
Tooting
London SW17 9PE
+44 2086727317

Opening hours	Open 7 days
Reservation policy	No
Credit cards	Accepted
Price range	Budget
Style	Casual
Cuisine	Bar-Small plates
Recommended for	Wish I'd opened

'Someone's house turned into a wicked little bar. Great drinks and great staff.'—Ollie Couillaud

A.WONG

Recommended by
Jacob Kenedy, Pierre
Koffmann

70 Wilton Road
Victoria
London SW1V 1DE
+44 2078288931
www.awong.co.uk

Opening hours	Closed Sunday
Credit cards	Accepted but not AMEX
Price range	Affordable
Style	Casual
Cuisine	Chinese
Recommended for	Bargain

'Innovative dim sum.'—Pierre Koffmann

CHEZ BRUCE

Recommended by
Jeff Galvin,
Marcus Wareing

2 Bellevue Road
Wandsworth
London SW17 7EG
+44 2086720114
www.chezbruce.co.uk

Opening hours	Open 7 days
Credit cards	Accepted
Price range	Affordable
Style	Smart casual
Cuisine	French
Recommended for	Local favourite

'The food is consistently good, the team are impressive and I have never had a bad meal there. I particularly enjoy the cheese board and talking through the wine list with the sommelier.'—Marcus Wareing

Bruce Poole 'takes it as a compliment' that some find his food old-fashioned. He and Matt Christmas, his kitchen collaborator of ten years, are proud to serve the French-inspired braises, offal dishes, salads and desserts that others eschew. The inspiration is classical, but the style is their own: calf's brains and Puy lentils come with *sauce gribiche* and crisp chicken skin, brandade with mussels and monk's beard, cod with truffle mash and hazelnut dressing. This Wandsworth Common restaurant (twenty-five minutes by cab from town) celebrates two decades in 2015. Its cheese-board and wine list are now legendary.

BREW

Recommended by
Ollie Couillaud

21 High Street
Wimbledon
London SW19 5DX
+44 2089474034
www.brew-cafe.com

Opening hours	Open 7 days
Credit cards	Accepted
Price range	Budget
Style	Casual
Cuisine	Café-Bistro
Recommended for	Breakfast

'The scrambled eggs with chorizo on sourdough is amazing.'—Ollie Couillaud

STICKS'N'SUSHI

Recommended by
Ollie Couillaud

58 Wimbledon Hill Road
Wimbledon
London SW19 7PA
+44 2031418800
www.sticksnsushi.com

Opening hours	Open 7 days
Credit cards	Accepted
Price range	Affordable
Style	Casual
Cuisine	Sushi
Recommended for	Regular neighbourhood

'I take my young son who adores it. We always have a great time and the food is mega!'—Ollie Couillaud

LONDON
CENTRAL

◁Ⓝ SCALE

0   150   300   450
yd.

1. Great Queen Street (p.337)
2. Monmouth Coffee Co. (p.338)
3. The Delaunay (p.337)
4. Rules (p.338)
5. The Ivy (p.338)
6. J Sheekey (p.338)
7. L'Atelier de Joël Robuchon (p.337)
8. Zhengzhong Lanzhou Lamian (p.338)
9. Baozi Inn (p.336)
10. Baiwei (p.336)

11. Beijing Dumpling (p.336)
12. Maison Bertaux (p.349)
13. Café Boheme (p.347)
14. Soho Kitchen & Bar (p.351)
15. Koya Bar (p.349)
16. Koya (p.349)
17. Bar Italia (p.345)
18. Ronnie Scott's (p.351)
19. Rasa Sayang (p.337)
20. One Leicester Street (p.337)
21. Joy King Lau (p.336)
22. Arbutus (p.345)
23. Barrafina (p.346)
24. Ducksoup (p.348)
25. Dean Street Townhouse (p.347)
26. Cay Tre (p.347)
27. Tonkotsu (p.352)
28. New Mayflower (p.336)
29. Wong Kei (p.337)
30. London Jade Garden (p.336)
31. Govinda's Pure Vegetarian (p.348)
32. Quo Vadis (p.350)
33. The Red Fort (p.351)

34. Busaba Eathai (p.347)
35. Bone Daddies Ramen (p.346)
36. Spuntino (p.351)
37. Randall & Aubin (p.350)
38. Bocca di Lupo (p.346)
39. Shoryu Ramen (p.352)
40. The Breakfast Club (p.347)
41. Yauatcha (p.352)
42. Brasserie Zédel (p.346)
43. Andrew Edmunds (p.345)
44. Social Eating House (p.351)
45. Fernandez & Wells (p.348)
46. HIX (p.348)
47. Polpo (p.350)
48. Pitt Cue Co. (p.350)
49. Bentley's Oyster Bar & Grill (p.339)
50. The Fountain (p.340)
51. Wright Brothers (p.352)
52. Aubaine (p.339)
53. Momo (p.343)
54. Cafe Murano (p.352)
55. The Wolseley (p.345)
56. The Gallery (p.341)
57. Gymkhana (p.341)

58. Le Caprice (p.340)
59. Pollen Street Social (p.344)
60. Goodman (p.341)
61. Hibiscus (p.342)
62. Brasserie Chavot (p.340)
63. Hix at The Albemarle (p.342)
64. Umu (p.344)
65. The Square (p.344)
66. Hakkasan (p.342)
67. Benares (p.339)
68. Ikeda (p.343)
69. La Petite Maison (p.343)
70. Murano (p.343)
71. Coya (p.340)
72. The Foyer & Reading Room (pp.340–341)
73. Hélène Darroze (p.342)
74. Nobu (p.343)
75. Scott's (p.344)
76. Alain Ducasse (p.339)
77. Princess Garden of Mayfair (p.344)
78. Le Gavroche (p.341)
79. Cut 45 at Park Lane (p.340)

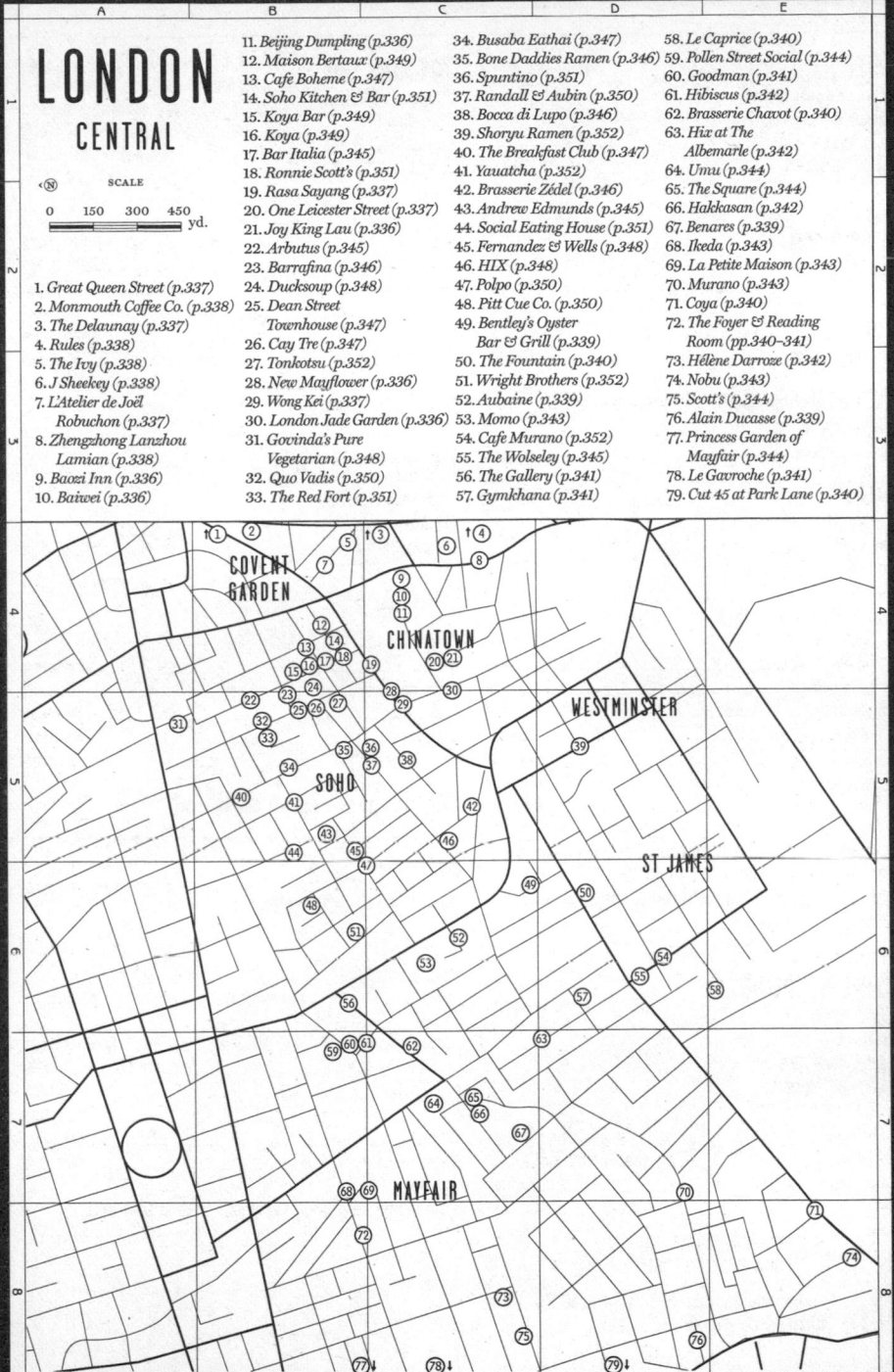

COVENT GARDEN

CHINATOWN

WESTMINSTER

SOHO

ST JAMES

MAYFAIR

BAIWEI
Recommended by
Stevie Parle

8 Little Newport Street
Chinatown
London WC2H 7JJ
+44 2074943605

Opening hours	Open 7 days
Reservation policy	No
Credit cards	Not accepted
Price range	Budget
Style	Casual
Cuisine	Szechuan
Recommended for	Bargain

'It's extremely high quality and not pretentious.'
—Stevie Parle

BAOZI INN
Recommended by
Jason Atherton, Tom Harris

26 Newport Court
Chinatown
London WC2H 7JS
+44 2072876877
www.baoziinnlondon.com

Opening hours	Open 7 days
Reservation policy	No
Credit cards	Not accepted
Price range	Budget
Style	Casual
Cuisine	Chinese
Recommended for	Bargain

'They serve a whole, deeply savoury, porky meatball in a soft, fluffy steamed bun. It's good. This is Chinese street food at its finest transferred to the streets of London.'—Tom Harris

BEIJING DUMPLING
Recommended by
Giorgio Locatelli

23 Lisle Street
Chinatown
London WC2H 7BA
+44 2072876888

Opening hours	Open 7 days
Credit cards	Accepted but not AMEX
Price range	Budget
Style	Casual
Cuisine	Chinese
Recommended for	Late night

'Fantastic hand-made dumplings that must be the tastiest in Chinatown.'—Giorgio Locatelli

JOY KING LAU
Recommended by
Matthew Harris

3 Leicester Street
Chinatown
London WC2H 7BL
+44 2074371132
www.joykinglau.com

Opening hours	Open 7 days
Credit cards	Accepted
Price range	Budget
Style	Casual
Cuisine	Cantonese
Recommended for	Bargain

'Great, cheap dim sum.'—Matthew Harris

LONDON JADE GARDEN
Recommended by
Fergus Henderson

15 Wardour Street
Chinatown
London W1D 6PH
+44 2074375065
www.londonjadegarden.com

Opening hours	Open 7 days
Credit cards	Accepted
Price range	Budget
Style	Casual
Cuisine	Chinese
Recommended for	Bargain

'Dim sum yum!'—Fergus Henderson

NEW MAYFLOWER
Recommended by
Alexis Gauthier

68–70 Shaftesbury Avenue
Chinatown
London W1D 6LY
+44 2077349207
www.newmayflowerlondon.com

Opening hours	Open 7 days
Credit cards	Accepted but not AMEX
Price range	Budget
Style	Casual
Cuisine	Chinese
Recommended for	Late night

'Consistent, and good service.'—Alexis Gauthier

ONE LEICESTER STREET

Recommended by
Junya Yamasaki

1 Leicester Street
Chinatown
London WC2H 7BL
+44 2033018020
www.oneleicesterstreet.com

Opening hours	Variable
Credit cards	Accepted
Price range	Affordable
Style	Smart casual
Cuisine	Modern British
Recommended for	Late night

'Sensitive, quality-guaranteed food.'—Junya Yamasaki

RASA SAYANG

Recommended by
Mitch Tonks

5 Macclesfield Street
Chinatown
London W1D 6AY
+44 2077341382
www.rasasayangfood.com

Opening hours	Open 7 days
Credit cards	Accepted
Price range	Budget
Style	Casual
Cuisine	Malaysian
Recommended for	Bargain

'Really good quality Malaysian curry and you can feast for under £10 ($17) very, very well.'—Mitch Tonks

WONG KEI

Recommended by
Ollie Couillaud

41–43 Wardour Street
Chinatown
London W1D 6PY
+44 2074378408
www.wongkeilondon.com

Opening hours	Open 7 days
Reservation policy	No
Credit cards	Not accepted
Price range	Budget
Style	Casual
Cuisine	Chinese
Recommended for	Late night

'For when you're drunk and hungry at 3.00 or 4.00 a.m.'
—Ollie Couillaud

L'ATELIER DE JOËL ROBUCHON

Recommended by
Bo Bech, Heinz
Beck, Ebbe Vollmer

13–15 West Street
Covent Garden
London WC2H 9NE
+44 2070108600
www.joelrobuchon.co.uk

Opening hours	Open 7 days
Credit cards	Accepted
Price range	Expensive
Style	Smart casual
Cuisine	Modern French
Recommended for	High end

THE DELAUNAY

Recommended by
Angela Hartnett,
Karam Sethi

55 Aldwych
Covent Garden
London WC2B 4BB
+44 2074998558
www.thedelaunay.com

Opening hours	Open 7 days
Credit cards	Accepted
Price range	Affordable
Style	Smart casual
Cuisine	European
Recommended for	Breakfast

'I just love the food. I usually go for a full English or the Viennese breakfast.'—Karam Sethi

GREAT QUEEN STREET

Recommended by
Tom Pemberton

32 Great Queen Street
Covent Garden
London WC2B 5AA
+44 2072420622
www.greatqueenstreetrestaurant.co.uk

Opening hours	Open 7 days
Credit cards	Accepted but not AMEX
Price range	Affordable
Style	Casual
Cuisine	British
Recommended for	Bargain

'Tasty and reasonably priced.'—Tom Pemberton

THE IVY

1–5 West Street
Covent Garden
London WC2H 9NQ
+44 2078364751
www.the-ivy.co.uk

Recommended by
Dominic Chapman, Alexis
Gauthier, Matthew Harris,
Ilya Shalev

Opening hours	Open 7 days
Credit cards	Accepted
Price range	Affordable
Style	Smart casual
Cuisine	Modern European
Recommended for	Local favourite

'Super service and a sense of occasion, even if you just order a shepherd's pie. They serve well-prepared classics. There is a reason why this restaurant is full every night, and has been forever.'—Alexis Gauthier

J SHEEKEY

28–35 St Martin's Court
Covent Garden
London WC2N 4AL
+44 2072402565
www.j-sheekey.co.uk

Recommended by
Pascal Aussignac, Thomasina
Miers, Ben Tish

Opening hours	Open 7 days
Credit cards	Accepted
Price range	Affordable
Style	Smart casual
Cuisine	Seafood
Recommended for	High end

'It's my favourite restaurant in town. Decadent and unpretentious all at once. The food is always consistently amazing and, refreshingly, it never follows trends. The whole turbot for two with a bottle of champagne is as good as it gets for me.'—Ben Tish

MONMOUTH COFFEE COMPANY

27 Monmouth Street
Covent Garden
London WC2H 9EU
+44 2072323010
www.monmouthcoffee.co.uk

Recommended by
Mikael Jonsson

Opening hours	Closed Sunday
Reservation policy	No
Credit cards	Accepted but not AMEX
Price range	Budget
Style	Casual
Cuisine	Coffee Shop
Recommended for	Breakfast

'The coffee is great.'—Mikael Jonsson

RULES

35 Maiden Lane
Covent Garden
London WC2E 7LB
+44 2078365314
www.rules.co.uk

Recommended by
Ben Tish

Opening hours	Open 7 days
Credit cards	Accepted
Price range	Expensive
Style	Smart casual
Cuisine	British
Recommended for	Local favourite

'Sums up our city's food heritage. It's one of London's oldest restaurants and serves expertly cooked braises and old-school pies. It recently had a revamp and the upstairs bar now serves some serious cocktails. A hidden gem.'—Ben Tish

ZHENGZHONG LANZHOU LAMIAN

33 Cranbourn Street
Covent Garden
London WC2H 7AD
+44 2078364399

Recommended by
Martin Morales

Opening hours	Open 7 days
Credit cards	Not accepted
Price range	Budget
Style	Casual
Cuisine	Chinese
Recommended for	Late night

'You can watch the world go by while eating freshly made noodles and great broth.'—Martin Morales

ALAIN DUCASSE

The Dorchester
53 Park Lane
Mayfair
London W1K 1QA
+44 2076298866
www.alainducasse-dorchester.com

Recommended by
Olivier Limousin, Clare
Smyth, Marcus Wareing

Opening hours	Closed Monday and Sunday
Credit cards	Accepted
Price range	Expensive
Style	Smart casual
Cuisine	Modern French
Recommended for	High end

'It got knocked a lot when Chef Jocelyn earned two Michelin stars so soon after opening. However, having recently visited, I thought the service and food were both superb and well worth the three Michelin stars that they now have. The little extras and manager Nicolas really make it a very special experience.'
—Marcus Wareing

AUBAINE

4 Heddon Street
Mayfair
London W1B 4BS
+44 2074402510
www.aubaine.co.uk

Recommended by
Olivier Limousin

Opening hours	Open 7 days
Credit cards	Accepted
Price range	Affordable
Style	Casual
Cuisine	French Bistro
Recommended for	Breakfast

'Every time I have friends visiting me, I always go to Aubaine. The viennoiserie and bread are very nice. I like the decoration too – it looks like you are in the south of France, and there's always good service.'
—Olivier Limousin

BENARES

12a Berkeley Square House
Berkeley Square
Mayfair
London W1J 6BS
+44 2076298886
www.benaresrestaurant.com

Recommended by
Bryn Williams

Opening hours	Closed Sunday
Credit cards	Accepted
Price range	Expensive
Style	Smart casual
Cuisine	Modern Indian
Recommended for	High end

BENTLEY'S OYSTER BAR & GRILL

11–15 Swallow Street
Mayfair
London W1B 4DG
+44 2077344756
www.bentleys.org

Recommended by
Nigel Haworth,
Thomasina Miers,
Bryn Williams

Opening hours	Open 7 days
Credit cards	Accepted
Price range	Expensive
Style	Smart casual
Cuisine	Seafood-Grill
Recommended for	Wish I'd opened

Irish chef Richard Corrigan rebuilt the reputation of this most English of restaurants when he took it over and refurbished it in 2005. First opened in 1916, a classic West End oyster bar and grill, located on a cut-through between Regent's Street and Piccadilly, it now consists of an upper floor grill, where meat sits alongside the fish, and a street level oyster bar. The latter, where marble counter meets red leather upholstery at bar and booth, and seasoned old oyster campaigners in white jackets do their shucking, is a jewel. Outside, a large swathe of Swallow Street does al fresco dining.

BRASSERIE CHAVOT
41 Conduit Street
Mayfair
London W1S 2YF
+44 2071836425
www.brasseriechavot.com

Recommended by
Tom Aikens,
Alyn Williams

Opening hours	Open 7 days
Credit cards	Accepted
Price range	Affordable
Style	Casual
Cuisine	French Brasserie
Recommended for	Wish I'd opened

'Fantastic restaurant. Chef Eric Chavot immediately hit the ground running – considering he was out of the UK for a number of years, he certainly has not lost his touch.'
—Tom Aikens

LE CAPRICE
Arlington House
Arlington Street
Mayfair
London SW1A 1RJ
+44 2076292239
www.le-caprice.co.uk

Recommended by
Thomasina Miers

Opening hours	Open 7 days
Credit cards	Accepted
Price range	Expensive
Style	Smart casual
Cuisine	Modern European
Recommended for	Late night

COYA
118 Piccadilly
Mayfair
London W1J 7NW
+44 2070427118
www.coyarestaurant.com

Recommended by
André Jaeger

Opening hours	Open 7 days
Credit cards	Accepted
Price range	Affordable
Style	Smart casual
Cuisine	Peruvian
Recommended for	Worth the travel

'Peruvian is a cuisine not really known to us. I had a wonderful and most satisfying lunch here. I was impressed by the ease of the service, the taste and quality of the food. I think this is a restaurant concept with great potential.'—André Jaeger

CUT AT 45 PARK LANE
45 Park Lane
Mayfair
London W1K 1PN
+44 2074934554
www.45parklane.com/CUTat45ParkLane

Recommended by
Francesco Mazzei,
Agnar Sverrisson

Opening hours	Open 7 days
Credit cards	Accepted
Price range	Expensive
Style	Smart casual
Cuisine	Steakhouse
Recommended for	High end

'I like to go to CUT at Park Lane for an early brunch.'
—Agnar Sverrisson

THE FOUNTAIN
Fortnum & Mason
181 Piccadilly
Mayfair
London W1A 1ER
+44 8453001707
www.fortnumandmason.com

Recommended by
Shaun Hill

Opening hours	Open 7 days
Credit cards	Accepted
Price range	Affordable
Style	Smart casual
Cuisine	British
Recommended for	Breakfast

'Simple things done well in very snazzy surrounds. Breakfast is not the moment for industrial architecture and cutting-edge grub. Good Eggs Benedict and freshly made coffee served by polite and efficient people is the order of the day.'—Shaun Hill

THE FOYER & READING ROOM
Claridge's
Brook Street
Mayfair
London W1K 4HR
+44 2071078886
www.claridges.co.uk

Recommended by
Adam Byatt,
Jeff Galvin

Opening hours	Open 7 days
Credit cards	Accepted
Price range	Expensive
Style	Smart casual
Cuisine	British
Recommended for	Local favourite

'I go for afternoon tea. It feels incredibly London – sophisticated, generous and so well put together. A real treat and an institution.'—Adam Byatt

THE GALLERY

Sketch
9 Conduit Street
Mayfair
London W1S 2XG
+44 2076594500
www.sketch.uk.com

Recommended by
Pascal Aussignac, Ettore
Botrini, Marcus Eaves, Jeff
Galvin, Sergio Herman

Opening hours..Open 7 days
Credit cards...Accepted
Price range...Expensive
Style...Smart casual
Cuisine..Modern European
Recommended for...Late night

'There is only one restaurant I wished was mine and that is Sketch in London. It has been around for years but every time I'm there it's like I am discovering it all over again! The place bursts with creativity with all of its different concepts and is a total experience for all the senses.'—Sergio Herman

Mourad Mazouz's operation with partner Pierre Gagnaire, opened in 2003, remains the most bizarrely ambitious ever-evolving bar/restaurant/gallery/nightclub that London – perhaps anywhere – has ever seen. For pure fun forget the fine-dining opulence of The Lecture Room and head downstairs to The Gallery instead. Dramatically transformed in mid-2012 to a design courtesy of celebrated Scottish artist Martin Creed, the all-white walls and video projectors retired, replaced with artfully mix-matched furniture, brightly tiled floor and patterned walls. The plan is for a different artist to redesign the room every year or so. Gagnaire's ever-wacky menu continues to mix luxury, comfort and creativity.

LE GAVROCHE

43 Upper Brook Street
Mayfair
London W1K 7QR
+44 2074080881
www.le-gavroche.co.uk

Recommended by
Chris Galvin, Jeff Galvin,
Henry Harris, Fergus
Henderson, Pierre Koffmann,
Paul Owens, Clare Smyth,
Bryn Williams

Opening hours..Closed Sunday
Credit cards...Accepted
Price range...Expensive
Style...Smart casual
Cuisine..French
Recommended for..High end

'You feel stroked inside and out.'—Fergus Henderson

GOODMAN

26 Maddox Street
Mayfair
London W1S 1QH
+44 2074993776
www.goodmanrestaurants.com

Recommended by
Jason Atherton

Opening hours..Closed Sunday
Credit cards...Accepted
Price range...Affordable
Style...Smart casual
Cuisine..Steakhouse
Recommended for...Late night

GYMKHANA

42 Albemarle Street
Mayfair
London W1S 4JH
+44 2030115900
www.gymkhanalondon.com

Recommended by
Stevie Parle, Neil Rankin

Opening hours..Closed Sunday
Credit cards...Accepted
Price range...Affordable
Style...Smart casual
Cuisine...Modern Indian
Recommended for.................................Regular neighbourhood

'There is nothing I dislike about this restaurant. Indian food is hands down my favourite food to eat and here is a place that not only does it with impeccable skill and using the best ingredients, but they also have a great wine and cocktail list. And they have created a space that I would happily move into and never leave. The food menu is such that you never get bored as everything sounds great and almost all of it delivers.'
—Neil Rankin

HAKKASAN

17 Bruton Street
Mayfair
London W1J 6QB
+44 2079071888
www.hakkasan.com

Opening hours	Open 7 days
Credit cards	Accepted
Price range	Expensive
Style	Smart casual
Cuisine	Modern Chinese
Recommended for	Late night

'Glamorous, delicious and there's always a buzz.'
—Philip Howard

HÉLÈNE DARROZE

The Connaught
Carlos Place
Mayfair
London W1K 2AL
+44 2071078880
www.the-connaught.co.uk

Opening hours	Closed Monday and Sunday
Credit cards	Accepted
Price range	Expensive
Style	Formal
Cuisine	Modern French
Recommended for	High end

'A beautiful space which always feels very special.'
—Tom Aikens

The Connaught has seen many fine chefs and France's culinary queen Hélène Darroze is the latest to weave her magic in this historic Mayfair hotel. Her native Landes in southwest France is name-checked several times on the menu: terrine of foie gras from les Landes; corn-fed chicken from les Landes... And she cleverly introduces her native cuisine into her take on the American brunch, served on Saturdays from 11.00 a.m. Charcuterie, terrines and Périgord truffles join smoked salmon, York ham and hot dogs, all in the most stylish and refined of circumstances, of course.

HIBISCUS

29 Maddox Street
Mayfair
London W1S 2PA
+44 2076292999
www.hibiscusrestaurant.co.uk

Opening hours	Closed Sunday
Credit cards	Accepted
Price range	Expensive
Style	Smart casual
Cuisine	Modern French
Recommended for	Worth the travel

It was a brave decision after seven successful years in rural Shropshire to move Hibiscus to metropolitan Mayfair. But since successfully transplanting Hibiscus from Ludlow to London back in 2007, Lyon-born Claude Bosi's reputation as a purveyor of forward-thinking haute cuisine has soared and he's had no reason to look back. The kitchen is discreetly hidden behind a set of swish sliding doors, which open onto an intimate oak-panelled dining room, where the focus is on polished service and Bosi's ever-evolving modern French menus that trawl the British Isles for raw materials and the globe for inspiration.

HIX AT THE ALBEMARLE

Brown's Hotel
Albermarle Street
Mayfair
London W1S 4BP
+44 2075184004
www.hixmayfair.co.uk

Opening hours	Open 7 days
Credit cards	Accepted
Price range	Expensive
Style	Smart casual
Cuisine	British
Recommended for	Late night

'Mark Hix is a great chef for reinventing and reimagining British food.'—Atul Kochar

IKEDA

30 Brook Street
Mayfair
London W1K 5DJ
+44 2076292730
www.ikedarestaurant.com

Recommended by
Margot Henderson

Opening hours	Closed Sunday
Credit cards	Accepted
Price range	Expensive
Style	Smart casual
Cuisine	Japanese
Recommended for	High end

MOMO

25 Heddon Street
Mayfair
London W1B 4BH
+44 2074344040
www.momoresto.com

Recommended by
Theo Randall

Opening hours	Open 7 days
Credit cards	Accepted
Price range	Affordable
Style	Smart casual
Cuisine	Moroccan
Recommended for	Late night

'Great tagine and cous cous, with a dance in the bar afterwards a must.'—Theo Randall

MURANO

20 Queen Street
Mayfair
London W1J 5PP
+44 2074951127
www.muranolondon.com

Recommended by
José Pizarro

Opening hours	Closed Sunday
Credit cards	Accepted
Price range	Expensive
Style	Smart casual
Cuisine	Italian
Recommended for	High end

'I just love Angela's food. Good food handled simply and with great care.'—José Pizarro

NOBU

Metropolitan Hotel
19 Old Park Lane
Mayfair
London W1K 1LB
+44 2074474747
www.noburestaurants.com/london

Recommended by
Ricardo Zarate

Opening hours	Open 7 days
Credit cards	Accepted
Price range	Expensive
Style	Smart casual
Cuisine	Modern Japanese
Recommended for	Worth the travel

LA PETITE MAISON

53–54 Brook's Mews
Mayfair
London W1K 4EG
+44 2074954774
www.lpmlondon.co.uk

Recommended by
Tom Kitchin, Olivier
Limousin, Theo Randall,
Karam Sethi, Mitch Tonks

Opening hours	Open 7 days
Credit cards	Accepted
Price range	Affordable
Style	Smart casual
Cuisine	Niçoise
Recommended for	Wish I'd opened

'I have huge admiration for my dear friend Raphael Duntoye, the chef behind La Petite Maison and the Arts Club in London. He is a fantastically talented chef. La Petite Maison is probably my favourite restaurant in London. I just love the clean cooking and his fantastic ways of mixing flavours.'—Tom Kitchin

This offshoot of the famous Nice hotspot of the same name (Sarkozy is said to be a fan) caters for its similarly starry regulars and the Mayfair set by combining a luxuriously bourgeois French menu with suave but informal service. Dishes are designed for sharing and arrive at the table in their own time, from hors d'oeuvres to rich comforting mains such as truffled macaroni and Mediterranean classics such as salt-baked sea bass. If there's a dish that sums up the whole experience, it's probably the whole Black Leg chicken stuffed with foie gras – roasted to order and well worth the hour's wait.

POLLEN STREET SOCIAL

8–10 Pollen Street
Mayfair
London W1S 1NQ
+44 2072907600
www.pollenstreetsocial.com

Recommended by
Tom Kerridge

Opening hours	Closed Sunday
Credit cards	Accepted
Price range	Expensive
Style	Smart casual
Cuisine	Modern British
Recommended for	Wish I'd opened

'Consistently hits that balance between high-end cuisine, funky fun atmosphere, and a great bar.'
—Tom Kerridge

PRINCESS GARDEN OF MAYFAIR

8–10 North Audley Street
Mayfair
London W1K 6ZD
+44 2074933223
www.princessgardenofmayfair.com

Recommended by
Theo Randall

Opening hours	Open 7 days
Credit cards	Accepted
Price range	Affordable
Style	Smart casual
Cuisine	Chinese
Recommended for	Regular neighbourhood

'Fantastic dim sum, great for a big-table Sunday lunch.'
—Theo Randall

SCOTT'S

20 Mount Street
Mayfair
London W1K 2HE
+44 2074957309
www.scotts-restaurant.com

Recommended by
Philip Howard, Clare Smyth,
Marcus Wareing

Opening hours	Open 7 days
Credit cards	Accepted
Price range	Expensive
Style	Smart casual
Cuisine	Seafood
Recommended for	Wish I'd opened

'I love the decor and the consistent menu – I just wish it was mine!'—Marcus Wareing

THE SQUARE

6–10 Bruton Street
Mayfair
London W1J 6PU
+44 2074957100
www.squarerestaurant.com

Recommended by
Neil Borthwick, Adam Byatt,
Ollie Couillaud, Chris Galvin,
Sam Harris, Angela Hartnett,
Hywel Jones, Bruce Poole

Opening hours	Open 7 days
Credit cards	Accepted
Price range	Expensive
Style	Smart casual
Cuisine	Modern French
Recommended for	High end

'Just total class, and such consistency after so many years. The wine list is one of the best in London, and the over-sized tables for two give an almost regal effect.'—Sam Harris

Now in its third decade, The Square has earned itself a reputation as a perennial source of high-quality fine dining in the heart of Mayfair. Chef patron Philip Howard and head chef Gary Foulkes specialize in taking seasonal and predominantly British ingredients such as Dover sole, prawns (shrimp) and ox cheeks, and applying a twist of French flair that transforms them into sophisticated yet refreshingly unfussy dishes that are simply delicious. A menu like this deserves a stonking good wine list and in this respect The Square doesn't disappoint.

UMU

14–16 Bruton Place
Mayfair
London W1J 6LX
+44 2074998881
www.umurestaurant.com

Recommended by
Ollie Dabbous

Opening hours	Closed Sunday
Credit cards	Accepted
Price range	Expensive
Style	Smart casual
Cuisine	Japanese
Recommended for	High end

THE WOLSELEY
160 Piccadilly
Mayfair
London W1J 9EB
+44 2074996996
www.thewolseley.com

Recommended by
Tom Aikens, Jason Atherton,
Dominic Chapman, Marcus
Eaves, Chris Galvin, André
Garrett, Steffen Hansen,
Matthew Harris, Nigel
Haworth, Philip Howard, Atul
Kochhar, Francesco Mazzei,
Tom Oldroyd, José Pizarro,
Bruce Poole, Ruth Rogers,
Karam Sethi, Ilya Shalev, Sami
Tamimi, Peter Weeden, Alyn
Williams, Bryn Williams

Opening hours...Open 7 days
Credit cards...Accepted
Price range...Expensive
Style...Smart casual
Cuisine..European
Recommended for..Breakfast

'The space is great – the combination of London
heritage with Viennese café grandeur transports you to
the 1920s and feels a long way from the streets of
Piccadilly outside. The food is classic, comforting and
reliable: always a good way to start the day. The breakfast
menu has something for everyone – oysters, scrambled
eggs, apple strudel, a simple croissant. I always have
the kedgeree and kippers with mustard butter.'
—Sami Tamimi

Such is its overwhelmingly popularity as a breakfast
venue, many of its loyal regulars never go to The
Wolseley for either lunch or dinner, although it's
typically full for both. The lengthy morning menu is
packed with comfort: crumpets, kedgeree, crispy
bacon rolls, Eggs Benedict, fried haggis with duck
eggs, Omelette Arnold Bennett and a fine selection of
Viennese pastries – to name but a fraction of what's
on offer. But it's also about the setting and the
sumptuous space. Once the Piccadilly showroom for
the old marque it's named after, it's now a sweeping
grand café in the European style.

ANDREW EDMUNDS
46 Lexington Street
Soho
London W1F 0LP
+44 2074375708
www.andrewedmunds.com

Recommended by
James Knappett

Opening hours...Open 7 days
Credit cards..Accepted but not AMEX
Price range...Affordable
Style...Smart casual
Cuisine..Bistro
Recommended for..Bargain

ARBUTUS
63–64 Frith Street
Soho
London W1D 3JW
+44 2077344545
www.arbutusrestaurant.co.uk

Recommended by
André Garrett

Opening hours...Open 7 days
Credit cards...Accepted
Price range...Affordable
Style...Casual
Cuisine..Bistro
Recommended for..Bargain

'Great price and a tasty lunch menu.'—André Garrett

BAR ITALIA
22 Frith Street
Soho
London W1D 4RF
+44 2074374520
www.baritaliasoho.co.uk

Recommended by
Chris Galvin, Margot
Henderson, Tom Oldroyd,
Alfred Prasad

Opening hours...Open 7 days
Reservation policy..No
Credit cards..Accepted but not AMEX
Price range...Affordable
Style...Casual
Cuisine..Coffee Shop
Recommended for...Late night

'I love its classic Italian café look, its bustling energy
and the sense of community. You see all sorts of
characters there, which just adds to the charm of this
legendary café. I love their tiramisù, coffee and
friendliness. Great place to wrap up a night out.'
—Alfred Prasad

BARRAFINA

54 Frith Street
Soho
London W1D 4SL
www.barrafina.co.uk

Recommended by
Jason Atherton, Robin Gill,
Angela Hartnett, Margot
Henderson, Adam Stokes

Opening hours	Open 7 days
Reservation policy	No
Credit cards	Accepted
Price range	Affordable
Style	Casual
Cuisine	Tapas
Recommended for	Regular neighbourhood

'Nieves and head chef Jose rule Spanish food in London. I love the sardines a la plancha and gambas aioli.'—Angela Hartnett

The Hart brothers' tribute to Barcelona's legendary Cal Pep consists of only twenty-three stools around a marble counter. The crammed open kitchen behind it produces top-class tapas, from grilled meat and game, to seafood cooked a la plancha. Throw in an excellent all-Iberian wine list and good-natured service that deals efficiently and politely with the inevitable waiting throng come peak times. Relax, grab a draught of cold Cruzcampo or two and a plate of *jamón* while you wait, and watch Soho go by.

BOCCA DI LUPO

12 Archer Street
Soho
London W1D 7BB
+44 2077342223
www.boccadilupo.com

Recommended by
Thomasina Miers

Opening hours	Open 7 days
Credit cards	Accepted
Price range	Affordable
Style	Casual
Cuisine	Italian
Recommended for	Regular neighbourhood

BONE DADDIES RAMEN BAR

31 Peter Street
Soho
London W1F 0AR
+44 2072878581
www.bonedaddiesramen.com

Recommended by
Adam Byatt, Miles Kirby,
Peter Weeden

Opening hours	Open 7 days
Reservation policy	No
Credit cards	Accepted
Price range	Budget
Style	Casual
Cuisine	Ramen Noodles
Recommended for	Late night

'Ramen heaven.'—Miles Kirby

Despite the unmarked facade, this NYC-style ramen bar isn't high on subtlety: diners are barraged with rock music and images of Japanese rockabillies, while menu options such as Cock Scratchings and swift service mean it's probably not a place to take a parent or a date. The cooking, helmed by ex-Zuma and ex-Nobu head chef Ross Shonhan, is just as punchy, with rich takes on classics like *tonkotsu* ramen – with its twenty-hour simmered pork bones – packing a serious amount of flavour for the price. A good list of sake, shochu and whisky keeps the young Soho crowd happy.

BRASSERIE ZÉDEL

20 Sherwood Street
Soho
London W1F 7ED
+44 2077344888
www.brasseriezedel.com

Recommended by
Ben Tish

Opening hours	Open 7 days
Credit cards	Accepted
Price range	Affordable
Style	Smart casual
Cuisine	French Brasserie
Recommended for	Late night

'It's a very central location so it's a great place to go after drinks in Soho. Always tasty and delicious – the steak tartare and chips (fries) is good – and it's no nonsense, the service is quick and it's unbelievable value for money. There's also a great bar next door if you fancy another.'—Ben Tish

THE BREAKFAST CLUB

Recommended by
Adam Stokes

33 D'Arblay Street
Soho
London W1F 8EU
+44 2074342571
www.thebreakfastclubcafes.com

Opening hours...Open 7 days
Credit cards.................................Accepted but not AMEX
Price range...Budget
Style..Casual
Cuisine..Café-Bistro
Recommended for...Breakfast

'Cool and quirky. Great sausages and duck eggs.'
—Adam Stokes

BUSABA EATHAI

Recommended by
Omar Allibhoy, Pascal
Aussignac, Atul Kochhar,
Francesco Mazzei,
Agnar Sverrisson

106–110 Wardour Street
Soho
London W1F 0TR
+44 2072558686
www.busaba.com

Opening hours...Open 7 days
Reservation policy...No
Credit cards...Accepted
Price range...Budget
Style..Casual
Cuisine..Thai
Recommended for...Bargain

'Lovely Thai flavours, great value for money and very
quick and efficient service.'—Agnar Sverrisson

CAFE BOHEME

Recommended by
Olivier Limousin

13 Old Compton Street
Soho
London W1D 5JQ
+44 2077340623
www.cafeboheme.co.uk

Opening hours...Open 7 days
Credit cards...Accepted
Price range..Affordable
Style..Casual
Cuisine...French Bistro
Recommended for...Late night

'Always busy with a fun vibe and good food.'
—Olivier Limousin

CAY TRE

Recommended by
Alexis Gauthier,
Stevie Parle

42–43 Dean Street
Soho
London W1D 4PZ
+44 2073179118
www.caytresoho.co.uk

Opening hours...Open 7 days
Credit cards...Accepted
Price range...Budget
Style..Casual
Cuisine...Vietnamese
Recommended for...Bargain

'For Vietnamese food this place is hard to beat. Very
fresh ingredients, varied menu and extremely good
value. I go a lot.'—Alexis Gauthier

DEAN STREET TOWNHOUSE

Recommended by
Alexis Gauthier,
Tom Oldroyd

69–71 Dean Street
Soho
London W1D 3SE
+44 2074341775
www.deanstreettownhouse.com

Opening hours...Open 7 days
Credit cards...Accepted
Price range..Affordable
Style...Smart casual
Cuisine..British
Recommended for...Breakfast

'Great buzzy atmosphere, not too stuffy and always
good food.'—Alexis Gauthier

This handsome Georgian townhouse in the heart of
Soho has seen some action over the years, notably
as the Gargoyle club, a louche drinking den frequented
by arty souls such as Francis Bacon and Lucian Freud.
Since then its various parts have been a snooker club
and a sauna, and most recently it was a branch of
a grim pub chain. It suits its latest role as a stylish
Soho House-operated boutique hotel with an all-day
dining room doing simple British food. It's a luxuriously
relaxed place to start the day, the menu offering
everything from baskets of pastries to Manx kippers.

DUCKSOUP

Recommended by
Margot Henderson, Miles
Kirby, Sami Tamimi

41 Dean Street
Soho
London W1D 4PY
+44 2072874599
www.ducksoupsoho.co.uk

Opening hours	Open 7 days
Reservation policy	No
Credit cards	Accepted
Price range	Affordable
Style	Casual
Cuisine	European small plates
Recommended for	Regular neighbourhood

'It's a small place with a long bar. The decor is pared down – white tiles, bare lights – with the focus, instead, on great food. The plates are for sharing and they have the confidence to let the ingredients do the talking. No frills or foams! The wines are really interesting too: there's a focus on natural wines, which you can have by the glass.'—Sami Tamimi

FERNANDEZ & WELLS

Recommended by
Yotam Ottolenghi

73 Beak Street
Soho
London W1F 9SR
+44 2072878124
www.fernandezandwells.com

Opening hours	Open 7 days
Reservation policy	No
Credit cards	Accepted
Price range	Budget
Style	Casual
Cuisine	Café-Bar-Bistro
Recommended for	Breakfast

'The coffee is exceptionally good. It's also a place where I can justify eating an *jamón ibérico* and tomato sandwich before midday.'—Yotam Ottolenghi

GOVINDA'S PURE VEGETARIAN

Recommended by
Tom Oldroyd

Radha-Krishna Temple
10 Soho Street
Soho
London W1D 3DL
+44 2074405229
www.iskcon-london.org/visiting/govinda-s-restaurant

Opening hours	Open 7 days
Credit cards	Accepted
Price range	Budget
Style	Casual
Cuisine	Vegetarian
Recommended for	Bargain

'Although I will probably live to regret letting you in on this, the Hare Krishna temple just off Soho Square offers up some of the tastiest cheap eats in Central London.'—Tom Oldroyd

HIX

Recommended by
Angela Hartnett, Thomasina
Miers, Manoj Vasaikar

66–70 Brewer Street
Soho
London W1F 9UP
+44 2072923518
www.hixsoho.co.uk

Opening hours	Open 7 days
Credit cards	Accepted
Price range	Affordable
Style	Smart casual
Cuisine	British
Recommended for	Late night

'Very casual food with substance and good wine. Lots of seasonal produce used.'—Manoj Vasaikar

Mark Hix's Soho flagship, like the man himself, is often at its best late at night. The buzz of the street-level dining room tends to crescendo until it closes, by which time there is the basement bar and its cocktail menu in which to take refuge. The simple British seasonal approach of the kitchen is applied to everything from shellfish to steaks. The informal ambience is arguably a double-edged sword – while you'll feel comfortable enough to eat a late-night dinner here after a few too many, so does everyone else. But then who comes here for a quiet dinner?

KOYA
49 Frith Street
Soho
London W1D 4SG
www.koya.co.uk

Recommended by
Izu Ani, Samantha & Samuel Clark, Anna Hansen, Sasu Laukkonen, Jeremy Lee, Jocky Petrie, Steve Williams

Opening hours..Open 7 days
Reservation policy..No
Credit cards.............................Accepted but not AMEX
Price range..Budget
Style...Casual
Cuisine...Japanese
Recommended for...............Regular neighbourhood

'An exemplary renaissance of Alastair Little's eponymous restaurant with sublime cooking of Junya Yamasaki's wonderful dishes.'—Jeremy Lee

It would be damning Koya with faint praise to say it's the best udon noodle shop in London, because in truth there's not really a lot of competition at the moment (if you don't count Koya Bar, its sister restaurant next door). Radiating a low-key authenticity, Koya's udon noodles — made on site in the traditional way, served with umami-rich stocks and a range of toppings — would hold their own back in Japan. Similarly, the site that first found fame in the 1980s as Alastair Little's Soho home now feels authentically Japanese, its understated interior a mix of utilitarian tables and chairs, white walls hung with wooden menu boards and a mosaic-tiled floor.

KOYA BAR
50 Frith Street
Soho
London W1D 4SQ
www.koyabar.co.uk

Recommended by
James Lowe

Opening hours..Open 7 days
Reservation policy..No
Credit cards.............................Accepted but not AMEX
Price range..Budget
Style...Casual
Cuisine...Japanese
Recommended for..Breakfast

'The newest addition to one of the best restaurants in London is this bar-restaurant next door to the original Koya. It features the udon and fabulous stocks that have made Koya such a favourite, as well as things like kedgeree porridge and bacon and egg udon at breakfast time.'—James Lowe

MAISON BERTAUX
28 Greek Street
Soho
London W1D 5DQ
+44 2074376007
www.maisonbertaux.com

Recommended by
Jeremy Lee

Opening hours..Open 7 days
Reservation policy..No
Credit cards..Accepted
Price range..Budget
Style...Casual
Cuisine...French Patisserie
Recommended for..Breakfast

'I have been eating here since a dim and distant youth. They are the best in London.'—Jeremy Lee

This old Soho spot boasts of being London's oldest patisserie, originally opened by Communards who, having fled Paris following the failure of the Fourth French Revolution, took refuge in cake. While it's true that the service can be hit and miss, it never fails to be entertainingly theatrical. The French fancies and cream cakes, still baked daily on the premises, are a reliable source of calories and le café au lait 'c'est bon'. Whether it's from a window table at street level or out on the pavement (sidewalk), there are few better vantage points from which to watch Soho go by.

PITT CUE CO.

1 Newburgh Street
Soho
London W1F 7RB
www.pittcue.co.uk

Opening hours	Open 7 days
Reservation policy	No
Credit cards	Accepted
Price range	Affordable
Style	Casual
Cuisine	Barbeque
Recommended for	Bargain

'Not a cheap restaurant exactly but it's definitely the number-one bargain in town. It has an unrivalled commitment to serving the best barbeque, beer and bourbon around.'—Marcus Eaves

Following a successful summer residency operating out of a van on the South Bank, the Pitt Cue Co. made these bijou premises off Carnaby Street their permanent home. Head here for a late lunch early in the week to avoid the queues (waiting lines) for a stool in the pint-sized bar or to grab a table in their basement bunker of a dining room. Chef Tom Adams's skill with a smoker, combined with the sourcing of the perfect cuts of pork and beef, make for a carnivores' Shangri-La. A short list of craft beers, ciders and bourbon-based cocktails provide the liquid refreshment.

POLPO

41 Beak Street
Soho
London W1F 9SB
+44 2077344479
www.polpo.co.uk

Opening hours	Open 7 days
Reservation policy	No
Credit cards	Accepted
Price range	Affordable
Style	Casual
Cuisine	Italian small plates
Recommended for	Wish I'd opened

'I'm a massive fan of this place and its emphasis on simply great food in a chilled-out, stripped-back environment. Polpo opened in 2009 and it's still one of the hottest tables in London.'—Marcus Eaves

QUO VADIS

26–29 Dean Street
Soho
London W1D 3LL
+44 2074379585
www.quovadissoho.co.uk

Opening hours	Closed Sunday
Credit cards	Accepted
Price range	Affordable
Style	Smart casual
Cuisine	British
Recommended for	Regular neighbourhood

'From menu to mouth, this restaurant never fails to deliver. I am yet to have a bad experience there. The slick, friendly and attentive service sets the scene in which Jeremy Lee's timeless cooking is readily received.'—Tom Oldroyd

The arrival in 2011 of Jeremy Lee at Quo Vadis, after years at the Blueprint Café, breathed new life into the old Soho landmark that's been running as a restaurant since 1929. He has a smart, seasonal way with British produce and remains one of the best cooks of game in London, if not the country. Trademark dishes include baked salsify wrapped in phyllo pastry and topped with grated Parmesan, a smoked eel and horseradish sandwich and the classic Elizabeth David dessert – although Lee prefers to talk about 'puddings' – St Emilion au chocolat. The 'Theatre Set' menu is a steal.

RANDALL & AUBIN

14–16 Brewer Street
Soho
London W1F 0SG
+44 2072874447
www.randallandaubin.com

Opening hours	Open 7 days
Credit cards	Accepted
Price range	Affordable
Style	Casual
Cuisine	French Seafood
Recommended for	Regular neighbourhood

'There is a great, buzzy Soho vibe; day or night it's always vibrant there. And the oysters are divine.'
—Yotam Ottolenghi

THE RED FORT
Recommended by
Dominic Chapman

77 Dean Street
Soho
London W1D 3SH
+44 2074372525
www.redfort.co.uk

Opening hours	Open 7 days
Credit cards	Accepted
Price range	Affordable
Style	Smart casual
Cuisine	Indian
Recommended for	Late night

'Probably the best curry in London. Brilliant chef and restaurant.'—Dominic Chapman

RONNIE SCOTT'S
Recommended by
Chris Galvin

47 Frith Street
Soho
London W1D 4HT
+44 2074390747
www.ronniescotts.co.uk

Opening hours	Open 7 days
Credit cards	Accepted
Price range	Affordable
Style	Smart casual
Cuisine	International
Recommended for	Late night

'I love jazz and this place makes for a great night out.'
—Chris Galvin

SOCIAL EATING HOUSE
Recommended by
Marcus Eaves

58 Poland Street
Soho
London W1F 7NR
+44 2079933251
www.socialeatinghouse.com

Opening hours	Closed Sunday
Credit cards	Accepted
Price range	Affordable
Style	Casual
Cuisine	Modern British
Recommended for	Local favourite

'New-wave "bistronomy". It's a slick operation with a chilled-out, funky vibe and stunning food.'
—Marcus Eaves

SOHO KITCHEN & BAR
Recommended by
Tom Aikens

19–21 Old Compton Street
Soho
London W1D 5JJ
+44 2077345656
www.sohokitchenandbar.co.uk

Opening hours	Open 7 days
Credit cards	Accepted
Price range	Affordable
Style	Casual
Cuisine	Bar-Diner
Recommended for	Late night

'Great location in Soho and they serve an all-day menu into the early hours with comfort-food favourites, plus a good selection of cocktails.'—Tom Aikens

SPUNTINO
Recommended by
Adam Byatt, Shaun
Hill, Karam Sethi

61 Rupert Street
Soho
London W1D 7PW
www.spuntino.co.uk

Opening hours	Open 7 days
Reservation policy	No
Credit cards	Accepted
Price range	Affordable
Style	Casual
Cuisine	Italian-American
Recommended for	Bargain

'I particularly like their core dishes – truffled egg and fontina on toast, the best sliders in London – and they have very reasonable house wines.'—Shaun Hill

Russell Norman's follow-up to Polpo channels the aesthetic of a hip Brooklyn diner meets a fashion-forward Lower Eastside speakeasy. It's darkly lit with artfully aged white tiles on the walls, rusty tin on the ceiling, alt-rock soundtrack and a U-shaped zinc-topped counter around which sit twenty-six fixed stools. No telephone, no reservations, and a long wait at peak times for the menu of Italian-American small plates that take in various sliders, meatballs and pizzette. The popcorn machine churns out complimentary cups of the salty snack laced with chilli to make you thirsty for the predominantly Italian and reasonably priced wine list.

TONKOTSU

Recommended by
Tom Oldroyd

63 Dean Street
Soho
London W1D 4QG
+44 2074370071
www.tonkotsu.co.uk

Opening hours	Open 7 days
Reservation policy	No
Credit cards	Accepted
Price range	Budget
Style	Casual
Cuisine	Ramen Noodles
Recommended for	Late night

'If I'm in need of something a little more substantial, then you'll find me at Tonkotsu's bar, my head simmering in a steaming bowl of slippery ramen broth.'
—Tom Oldroyd

WRIGHT BROTHERS

Recommended by
Rainer Becker

13 Kingly Street
Soho
London W1B 5PW
+44 2074343611
www.thewrightbrothers.co.uk

Opening hours	Open 7 days
Credit cards	Accepted
Price range	Affordable
Style	Smart casual
Cuisine	Seafood
Recommended for	Regular neighbourhood

'Simple, good, honest food in a vibrant location – and great oysters!'—Rainer Becker

YAUATCHA

Recommended by
Matthew Harris,
Mats Vollmer

15–17 Broadwick Street
Soho
London W1F 0DL
+44 2074948888
www.yauatcha.com

Opening hours	Open 7 days
Credit cards	Accepted
Price range	Affordable
Style	Smart casual
Cuisine	Chinese
Recommended for	Worth the travel

'I had the big menu and the Peking duck I got as the last dish was perfect. Impressed!'—Mats Vollmer

CAFE MURANO

Recommended by
Neil Borthwick

33 St James's Street
St James's
London SW1A 1HD
+44 2033715559
www.cafemurano.co.uk

Opening hours	Closed Sunday
Credit cards	Accepted
Price range	Affordable
Style	Casual
Cuisine	Italian Bistro
Recommended for	Late night

'It's rare in London to find a place where you can get a stunning bowl of pasta and a glass of wine in an informal, buzzy room. Their post-theatre menu is fantastic value. Of course I love the grown-up big sister Murano too when I have more time to indulge.'
—Neil Borthwick

SHORYU RAMEN

Recommended by
Atul Kochhar,
Yotam Ottolenghi

9 Regent Street
St James's
London SW1Y 4LR
www.shoryuramen.com

Opening hours	Open 7 days
Reservation policy	No
Credit cards	Accepted
Price range	Budget
Style	Casual
Cuisine	Ramen Noodles
Recommended for	Late night

'I love places which do one thing very well – you know you are in good hands. Noodles late at night hit the spot for me: comforting, easy, sustaining and quick.'
—Yotam Ottolenghi

LONDON

EAST

(N) SCALE

0   400   800   1200
━━━━━━━━━━━━━━━━ yd.

40 MALTBY STREET

Recommended by
James Lowe, Ed Wilson

40 Maltby Street
Bermondsey
London SE1 3PA
+44 2072379247
www.40maltbystreet.com

Opening hours	Closed Sunday to Tuesday
Reservation policy	No
Credit cards	Accepted but not AMEX
Price range	Affordable
Style	Casual
Cuisine	British
Recommended for	Regular neighbourhood

'The best daily-changing menu of simple seasonal food and a great wine list. You always leave happy and content with life.'—Ed Wilson

Locals weren't too pleased when this idiosyncratic venture in a rattling railway arch hit the headlines, but with its serious food and no-fuss presentation, it wasn't going to stay secret for long. Maltby Street was dubbed the 'next Borough Market', and while that hasn't really happened, it has spawned good ad-hoc eateries – not least this wine bar and shop with a handful of tables and limited service hours. There are unusual natural wines from France, Italy and Slovenia at goodish mark-ups, but it's the (mismatched) small plates – deep fried duck eggs, say, or glazed Yorkshire ham – which really take centre stage.

CAFE EAST

Recommended by
Sam Harris

100 Redriff Road
Bermondsey
London SE16 7LH
www.cafeeastpho.co.uk

Opening hours	Closed Tuesday
Reservation policy	No
Credit cards	Not accepted
Price range	Budget
Style	Casual
Cuisine	Vietnamese
Recommended for	Bargain

'The best pho soup in London, so authentic.'
—Sam Harris

CASSE-CROÛTE

Recommended by
Olivier Limousin

109 Bermondsey Street
Bermondsey
London SE1 3XB
+44 2074072140
www.cassecroute.co.uk

Opening hours	Open 7 days
Credit cards	Accepted
Price range	Affordable
Style	Casual
Cuisine	French Bistro
Recommended for	Local favourite

'Typical French bistro with everything reminding me of my country – the music, the food, the aperitifs...'
—Olivier Limousin

THE GARRISON

Recommended by
Tom Sellers

99–101 Bermondsey Street
Bermondsey
London SE1 3XB
+44 2070899355
www.thegarrison.co.uk

Opening hours	Open 7 days
Credit cards	Accepted
Price range	Affordable
Style	Casual
Cuisine	Gastro pub
Recommended for	Breakfast

'Nice variety on the menu so I can get whatever I am in the mood for.'—Tom Sellers

JOSÉ

Recommended by
Tom Sellers

104 Bermondsey Street
Bermondsey
London SE1 3UB
www.josepizarro.com/restaurants/jose

Opening hours	Open 7 days
Reservation policy	No
Credit cards	Accepted
Price range	Budget
Style	Casual
Cuisine	Tapas
Recommended for	Regular neighbourhood

'The food is great, the venue is small and intimate and the atmosphere is really friendly.'—Tom Sellers

ZUCCA

184 Bermondsey Street
Bermondsey
London SE1 3TQ
+44 2073786809
www.zuccalondon.com

Recommended by
Adam Byatt, Angela
Hartnett, Philip Howard,
José Pizarro, Clare Smyth

Opening hours	Closed Monday
Credit cards	Accepted but not AMEX
Price range	Affordable
Style	Casual
Cuisine	Italian
Recommended for	Regular neighbourhood

'A great local restaurant serving the kind of food I like to eat regularly.'—Philip Howard

Since opening in 2010 in fashionable Bermondsey Street, not far from the foodie hub of Borough Market, Zucca has become a fixture on the London food scene. Part of the new wave of affordable, rustic Italians in London, plain, excellently executed dishes such as grilled octopus, sprouting (baby) broccoli, rosemary and anchovy, and home-made pasta with lentils, walnuts and basil are served up in this plain but cheerful canteen-like space. The simple stylishness keeps prices down – all the better to enjoy the extensive, all-Italian wine list that saw Zucca win *Decanter* magazine's 'Restaurant of the Year' title in 2011.

BISTROTHEQUE

23–27 Wadeson Street
Bethnal Green
London E2 9DR
+44 2089837900
www.bistrotheque.com

Recommended by
Ben Tish

Opening hours	Open 7 days
Credit cards	Accepted
Price range	Affordable
Style	Casual
Cuisine	Bistro
Recommended for	Breakfast

'Apart from a first-class fry up when you need it most (on a hangover), there's always amazing entertainment in the form of a transvestite playing renditions of pop and club classics.'—Ben Tish

CIAO BELLA

86–90 Lamb's Conduit Street
Bloomsbury
London WC1N 3LZ
+44 2072424119
www.ciaobellarestaurant.co.uk

Recommended by
Fergus Henderson

Opening hours	Open 7 days
Credit cards	Accepted
Price range	Affordable
Style	Casual
Cuisine	Italian
Recommended for	Regular neighbourhood

'They tolerate kids, the best people-watching in Lamb's Conduit Street, you can sit outside comfortably to smoke, which suits some of us, and they leave the grappa on the table.'—Fergus Henderson

AQUA SHARD

The Shard
31F, 31 St Thomas Street
Borough
London SE1 9RY
+44 2030111256
www.aquashard.co.uk

Recommended by
Manoj Vasaikar

Opening hours	Open 7 days
Credit cards	Accepted
Price range	Expensive
Style	Smart casual
Cuisine	British
Recommended for	Late night

'Great atmosphere. London looks beautiful from up there. Great cocktails.'—Manoj Vasaikar

BRINDISA CHORIZO GRILL

Recommended by
Alfred Prasad

Borough Market
The Floral Hall
Stoney Street
Borough
London SE1 9AF
+44 2074071036
www.brindisa.com

Opening hours	Closed Sunday
Reservation policy	No
Credit cards	Accepted
Price range	Budget
Style	Casual
Cuisine	Spanish
Recommended for	Bargain

'Love their double chorizo sandwich – under £5 ($8)
– with high-quality chorizo, just taken off a sizzling
grill, sandwiched in a ciabatta with crisp rocket
(arugula) and juicy piquillo peppers. Just across the
street is Monmouth Café for a perfect filter coffee.
Meal done for under £7 ($12).'—Alfred Prasad

HUTONG

Recommended by
José Pizarro

The Shard
33F, 31 St Thomas Street
Borough
London SE1 9RY
+44 2030111257
www.aquahutong.co.uk

Opening hours	Open 7 days
Credit cards	Accepted
Price range	Expensive
Style	Smart casual
Cuisine	Chinese
Recommended for	Regular neighbourhood

'The food and the view are both amazing!'
—José Pizarro

MAGDALEN

Recommended by
Sam Harris

152 Tooley Street
Borough
London SE1 2TU
+44 2074031342
www.magdalenrestaurant.co.uk

Opening hours	Closed Sunday
Credit cards	Accepted
Price range	Affordable
Style	Smart casual
Cuisine	British
Recommended for	Regular neighbourhood

'This place seems to have been missed by Londoners
– such is the shame, as the quality of cooking is some
of the best in town. My meal is perfect every time, and
I'm very fussy!'—Sam Harris

OBLIX

Recommended by
Giorgio Locatelli

The Shard
32F, 31 St Thomas Street
Borough
London SE1 9RY
+44 2072686700
www.oblixrestaurant.com

Opening hours	Open 7 days
Credit cards	Accepted
Price range	Expensive
Style	Smart casual
Cuisine	International
Recommended for	Local favourite

'The food is great and the view is breathtaking.'
—Giorgio Locatelli

FRANCO MANCA

Recommended by
Jonathan Jones, Mikael
Jonsson, Isaac McHale,
Shuko Oda

Unit 4, Market Row
Brixton
London SW9 8LD
+44 2077383021
www.francomanca.co.uk

Opening hours	Open 7 days
Reservation policy	No
Credit cards	Accepted but not AMEX
Price range	Budget
Style	Casual
Cuisine	Pizza
Recommended for	Bargain

'Every time I am stunned by how good it is, and how
cheap the bill is at the end.'—Isaac McHale

HONEST BURGERS

Recommended by
Robin Gill

Unit 12, Brixton Village
Brixton
London SW9 8PR
+44 2077337963
www.honestburgers.co.uk

Opening hours..Open 7 days
Reservation policy...No
Credit cards..Accepted
Price range..Budget
Style..Casual
Cuisine..Burgers
Recommended for..Bargain

'Honest Burgers has simply the best burger in town.
Always an interesting beer list too.'—Robin Gill

KAOSARN

Recommended by
Sami Tamimi

Unit 96, Brixton Village
Brixton
London SW9 8PR
+44 2070958922

Opening hours..Closed Monday
Credit cards..Not accepted
Price range..Budget
Style..Casual
Cuisine..Thai
Recommended for..Late night

'The atmosphere in Brixton market is great – you can
eat in the market cheaply so there's always a really
mixed and happy crowd there, tucking into lots of
different things. Drinks in one place, burgers in
another, coffee and cake right next door. There is
something for everyone. And you can get the best
marinated chicken with sticky rice and a green papaya
salad south of the river if you're happy to join the
queue (waiting line) outside KaoSarn.'—Sami Tamimi

SILK ROAD

Recommended by
Shuko Oda,
Junya Yamasaki

49 Camberwell Church Street
Camberwell
London SE5 8TR
+44 2077034832

Opening hours..Open 7 days
Credit cards..Not accepted
Price range..Budget
Style..Casual
Cuisine..Chinese
Recommended for..Bargain

'At least twice a month I get a craving for their spicy
stir-fried cabbage and chewy belt noodles. Cheap and
cheerful.'—Shuko Oda

Camberwell's no frills Silk Road specializes in the
food of Xinjiang, China's northwest frontier province.
The basic set-up of communal tables and punishingly
hard benches isn't what brings London's gluttons
back again and again: that would be the fascinating
regional cuisine with its central Asian and Chinese
influences and the great value it represents. Few
leave without trying the fried pork dumplings, chilli
and cumin lamb skewers and 'big plate' chicken in
fiery broth, with its side of hand-pulled noodles for
optimal slurping. A feast and a few Tsingtao beers
still leave change from £20 ($33).

TASTE OF SIAM

Recommended by
Giorgio Locatelli

45 Camden High Street
Camden
London NW1 7JH
+44 2073800665
www.taste-of-siam.co.uk

Opening hours..Open 7 days
Credit cards..Accepted
Price range..Budget
Style..Casual
Cuisine..Thai
Recommended for..Bargain

'It's cheap and cheerful.'—Giorgio Locatelli

BARBECOA

Recommended by
Arjan Wennekes

20 New Change Passage
City of London
London EC4M 9AG
+44 2030058555
www.barbecoa.com

Opening hours	Open 7 days
Credit cards	Accepted
Price range	Affordable
Style	Casual
Cuisine	Barbeque
Recommended for	Wish I'd opened

'A very good concept, with its own butchery. The whole atmosphere is screaming "We have the best meat in town". Also, the design of the kitchen, with the big Argentinian grill in front of the window, is amazing.' —Arjan Wennekes

DUCK & WAFFLE

Recommended by
Paul Foster, Atul Kochhar,
Neil Rankin, Shaun
Searley, Adam Stokes

Heron Tower
110 Bishopsgate
City of London
London EC2N 4AY
+44 2036407310
www.duckandwaffle.com

Opening hours	Open 7 days
Credit cards	Accepted
Price range	Affordable
Style	Smart casual
Cuisine	European
Recommended for	Breakfast

'Even if the food was half as good as it actually is, I'd still enjoy eating there purely because of the views. To get food that actually delivers in a restaurant that high up is a huge gain for London. Dan has a filthy mind when it comes to food and that is never better utilised than during breakfast/brunch, which for me is all about layering on the carbs, fats and sugars. I don't eat breakfast that often, but if I want healthy I'll buy some porridge and stay at home. If I'm going out then there is no better place.'—Neil Rankin

HAWKSMOOR

Recommended by
Robin Gill

10 Basinghall Street
City of London
London EC2V 5BQ
+44 2073978120
www.thehawksmoor.com

Opening hours	Closed Saturday and Sunday
Credit cards	Accepted
Price range	Expensive
Style	Smart casual
Cuisine	Steakhouse
Recommended for	Breakfast

'The Hawksmoor breakfast is a beast of a feast and they have great cocktails too. Perfect cure after a heavy night.'—Robin Gill

The weekday breakfast menu offered only at this branch of Hawksmoor is worth a special trip to the City. Not least for the that's-what-I-call-a-power-breakfast excess of their eye-opening platter for two, which includes a smoked bacon chop; their own-recipe sausages made with pork, beef and mutton; black pudding (blood sausage); short-rib bubble and squeak (cabbage and mashed potatoes); grilled bone marrow; 'Trotter baked beans'; fried eggs; grilled mushrooms; and roast tomatoes. Combine that with several Bloody Marys – you can pimp your own from a buffet of condiments should you wish – and you'll be set up for the day. Or possibly for a lie-down.

MOSHI MOSHI

Recommended by
Peter Weeden

Liverpool Street Station
Unit 24
City of London
London EC2M 7QH
+44 2072473227
www.moshimoshi.co.uk

Opening hours	Closed Saturday and Sunday
Credit cards	Accepted
Price range	Affordable
Style	Casual
0Cuisine	Sushi
Recommended for	Regular neighbourhood

'Caroline Bennett's team serve excellent, fresh, sustainably caught Cornish fish. I like to be able to trust restaurants, and here I can.'—Peter Weeden

SWEETINGS

39 Queen Victoria Street
City of London
London EC4N 4SF
+44 2072483062
www.sweetingsrestaurant.com

Recommended by
Fergus Henderson,
Jacob Kenedy

Opening hours.............................Closed Saturday and Sunday
Reservation policy..No
Credit cards...Accepted
Price range...Affordable
Style...Casual
Cuisine..Seafood
Recommended for...Local favourite

'It's been around for about 200 years and is perfectly unfussy, unspoilt, in-your-face London with friendly service and brilliant seafood.'—Jacob Kenedy

Serving simply prepared fish in the City of London since 1889, without being pompous Sweetings revels in being fantastically old fashioned, a right earned by having survived two world wars and more financial crashes than you can a shake a skate wing at. It's the like of crab bisque, smoked eel, potted shrimps, fried whitebait and scallops and bacon to start, with main courses running from extravagant, simply prepared catches such as turbot and Dover sole, to their infinitely more affordable fish pie and salmon cake. Puddings are hefty boarding-school classics such as baked jam roll and spotted dick.

CARAVAN

11–13 Exmouth Market
Clerkenwell
London EC1R 4QD
+44 2078338115
www.caravanonexmouth.co.uk

Recommended by
Brad Farmerie

Opening hours...Open 7 days
Credit cards...Accepted
Price range...Affordable
Style...Casual
Cuisine...Modern International
Recommended for..Breakfast

'Maybe the best coffee you have ever had, with delicious food and casual, cool service.'
—Brad Farmerie

Caravan sits at the mouth of Exmouth Market, where creatives and crusties rub shoulders with Post Office workers. The all-day menu, a well-travelled selection of snacks, small plates and grown-up main courses,

is no slouch. But it's perhaps for breakfast or a relaxed weekend brunch, sat over their take on the classic fry-up (fry breakfast) or a plate of baked eggs with chorizo, that its charms are best appreciated. They roast their own coffee beans in the basement: the combination of aroma, choice – from Flat Whites to proper filter – and quality are more than enough to satisfy even the most discerning of coffee geeks.

THE MODERN PANTRY

47–48 St John's Square
Clerkenwell
London EC1V 4JJ
+44 2075539210
www.themodernpantry.co.uk

Recommended by
Pascal Aussignac, Ollie
Dabbous, Angela Hartnett

Opening hours...Open 7 days
Credit cards...Accepted
Price range...Affordable
Style...Casual
Cuisine...Modern International
Recommended for..Breakfast

'I love Anna Hansen's cuisine and her approach to British ingredients with a fusion twist.'
—Pascal Aussignac

The Modern Pantry's bright ground-floor café, with its all-white tables and chairs that amplify the light through its large front windows across St John's Square, is the perfect morning venue. Raised in New Zealand, chef-proprietor Anna Hansen puts as much care into breakfast as she does lunch and dinner. Expect the likes of ricotta pancakes, soft-boiled eggs with Vegemite soldiers (strips of toast) and grilled chorizo with plantain fritters. Star of the show is a, rightly celebrated, Sri Lankan-inspired omelette filled with sugar-cured prawns (shrimp), green chilli, spring onions (scallions) and coriander (cilantro), topped with a smoked chilli sambal. The smoothies also demand your attention.

MORITO
Recommended by
Yotam Ottolenghi

32 Exmouth Market
Clerkenwell
London EC1R 4QE
+44 2072787007
www.morito.co.uk

Opening hours	Open 7 days
Credit cards	Accepted
Price range	Affordable
Style	Casual
Cuisine	Tapas
Recommended for	Regular neighbourhood

'The atmosphere is great, the crowd is mixed, the tapas is first class. Stopping by for a snack and a drink on Exmouth Market always reminds me why I love living and working in London. And I could eat a bucket of the beetroot (beet) borani with feta, dill, walnuts and nigella seeds.'—Yotam Ottolenghi

MORO
Recommended by
Angela Hartnett, Jacob Kenedy, Miles Kirby, Tom Pemberton, Tim Siadatan, Michael Smith

34–36 Exmouth Market
Clerkenwell
London EC1R 4QE
+44 2078338336
www.moro.co.uk

Opening hours	Open 7 days
Credit cards	Accepted
Price range	Affordable
Style	Casual
Cuisine	North African-Spanish
Recommended for	Regular neighbourhood

'Diverse, cosmopolitan, interesting, busy, fun, exciting and unique – just like London.'—Tom Siadatan

OTTO'S
Recommended by
Jonathan Jones

182 Gray's Inn Road
Clerkenwell
London WC1X 8EW
+44 2077130107
www.ottos-restaurant.com

Opening hours	Closed Sunday
Credit cards	Accepted
Price range	Expensive
Style	Casual
Cuisine	French
Recommended for	High end

'Pressed duck over two courses and very well-priced Burgundy. It is a labour of love for the incredibly hospitable Otto.'—Jonathan Jones

THE QUALITY CHOP HOUSE
Recommended by
Isaac McHale, Neil Rankin, Peter Weeden, Ed Wilson

88–94 Farringdon Road
Clerkenwell
London EC1R 3EA
+44 2072781452
www.thequalitychophouse.com

Opening hours	Open 7 days
Credit cards	Accepted
Price range	Affordable
Style	Casual
Cuisine	British
Recommended for	Local favourite

'Like the rest of London, The Quality Chop House has a rich past, but has been reinvented and reinvigorated by some clever people to make it what it is today. Go.' —Isaac McHale

SUSHI TETSU
Recommended by
James Knappett, Nuno Mendes

12 Jerusalem Passage
Clerkenwell
London EC1V 4JP
+44 2032170090
www.sushitetsu.co.uk

Opening hours	Closed Monday and Sunday
Credit cards	Accepted
Price range	Expensive
Style	Smart casual
Cuisine	Sushi
Recommended for	High end

'A wonderful sushi experience that is very personal and very special. It's almost as if the fish swims from the counter into your mouth – it's that fresh! The chef and his wife are the perfect hosts and make you feel totally at home sitting at the small eight-seat counter.' —Nuno Mendes

MANGAL OCAKBASI

Recommended by
Nuno Mendes,
Yotam Ottolenghi

10 Arcola Street
Dalston
London E8 2DJ
+44 2072758981
www.mangal1.com

Opening hours	Open 7 days
Reservation policy	No
Credit cards	Not accepted
Price range	Budget
Style	Casual
Cuisine	Turkish
Recommended for	Bargain

'The no-frills focus on the kebabs, the kebabs! I always have the adana kofte with yogurt, tomato and butter sauce.'—Yotam Ottolenghi

SÖMINE

Recommended by
Samantha & Samuel Clark

131 Kingsland High Street
Dalston
London E8 2PB
+44 2072547384

Opening hours	Open 7 days
Reservation policy	No
Credit cards	Accepted
Price range	Budget
Style	Casual
Cuisine	Turkish
Recommended for	Late night

'A twenty-four-hour Turkish restaurant on the corner of Kingsland Road and Crossway. We go there for Turkish mezze, yogurt soups and delicious slow-cooked dishes. The Turkish restaurants around Dalston and Stoke Newington were a great influence on Moro, before and when we first opened. There are many and it is hard to have a bad meal if you stick to the basics: marinated lamb kofte or shish kebab, quail or chicken, grilled over charcoal with the freshest of chopped salads, yogurt and bread. The perfect late-night sustenance and Sömine happens to be open late; in fact it never closes!'—Samantha & Samuel Clark

TAVA RESTAURANT

Recommended by
Isaac McHale

17 Stoke Newington Road
Dalston
London N16 8BH
+44 2072493666

Opening hours	Open 7 days
Credit cards	Accepted
Price range	Budget
Style	Casual
Cuisine	Turkish
Recommended for	Late night

'London doesn't really do much late-night stuff, considering its size. This is always my pick of late-night eats after work, great *lahmacun*.'—Isaac McHale

UMUT 2000

Recommended by
Tom Harris, Ed Wilson

6 Crossway
Dalston
London N16 8HX
+44 2072490903
www.umut2000.com

Opening hours	Open 7 days
Credit cards	Not accepted
Price range	Budget
Style	Casual
Cuisine	Turkish
Recommended for	Late night

'Smoky grilled lamb, the best sumac and onions, great breads and endless ice-cold bottles of Efes beer. There are lots of great Turkish restaurants in East London but Umut 2000 is always where I head to after a night out.'—Tom Harris

THE SIRLOIN

Recommended by
Fergus Henderson

94 Cowcross Street
Farringdon
London EC1M 6BH
+44 2072501442

Opening hours	Open 7 days
Credit cards	Accepted but not AMEX
Price range	Affordable
Style	Casual
Cuisine	Gastropub
Recommended for	Breakfast

'Offers a steadying fry up and pint of Guinness early in the morning. Strangely, every time I've been it's just me in the dining room, adding calmness to the start of the day.'—Fergus Henderson

This dining room can be found above the Farringdon boozer, The Hope, giving the whole the nickname The Hope & Sir Loin. On the doorstep of Smithfield meat market, it used to open stupidly early to serve meaty breakfasts to traders – those that humped carcasses for a living and drank pints, and those of the financial variety that guzzled Champagne. These days The Hope doesn't open its doors until a civilized 7.00 a.m. and only serves breakfast upstairs to large parties that book ahead. But their Full English – egg, sausage, bacon, liver, kidney and a sirloin steak – is still served in the ground-floor bar.

ST. JOHN BAR AND RESTAURANT

Recommended by
Andreas Dahlberg,
Semsa Denizsel, Sam
Harris, Tom Harris, Margot
Henderson, Jonathan Jones,
Miles Kirby, Jeremy Lee,
Jp McMahon, Carlo Mirarchi,
Tom Oldroyd, Tom Pemberton,
Ruth Rogers, Shaun Searley,
Tom Sellers, Peter Weeden,
Junya Yamasaki

26 St John Street
Farringdon
London EC1M 4AY
+44 2072510848
www.stjohnrestaurant.com

Opening hours	Open 7 days
Credit cards	Accepted
Price range	Affordable
Style	Casual
Cuisine	British
Recommended for	Local favourite

'This place represents the true side of London, not the over-hyped glamour of some of the Mayfair establishments. It marries the balance of an old working-class establishment with a cutting-edge, up-to-date one. It's one of a kind, and only a city like London could have a restaurant like this.'—Sam Harris

Arguably the most seminal London restaurant of the last twenty years, the original branch of St. John has barely changed since it opened back in 1994. The birthplace of Fergus Henderson's famed 'nose-to-tail' philosophy, the twice-daily-changing menu is still tersely written, strictly seasonal and still likes to make use of bits of beast that Anglo-Saxon chefs used to throw away, until he made them fashionable. The other star is the Georgian building, an old smokehouse, its high ceilings, whitewashed walls and surfeit of natural light somehow managing to make it feel like nowhere else in London, and somewhere that couldn't exist anywhere else.

BERNERS TAVERN

Recommended by
Ben Tish

10 Berners Street
Fitzrovia
London W1T 3NP
+44 2079087979
www.bernerstavern.com

Opening hours	Open 7 days
Credit cards	Accepted
Price range	Affordable
Style	Smart casual
Cuisine	British
Recommended for	Wish I'd opened

'It has to be the most beautiful dining room I've been in – anywhere – and Ian Schrager designed it. The food is fantastic too. It's rammed to the rafters for breakfast, lunch, afternoon tea and dinner seven days a week.'—Ben Tish

Jason Atherton's glamorous new all-day dining venture capped a remarkable 2013 for the chef, who also found time to launch Soho's Little Social and the Social Eating House. Naturally enough, given its setting in Ian Schrager's £33m ($55m) Edition Hotel, it's a jaw-dropping space, with Grand Central Station-style chandeliers, walls packed with paintings, and an impressive backlit bar. With Atherton's long-time lieutenant Phil Carmichael heading up the kitchen, the inventive modern British cooking is just as stellar, balancing witty modernist touches reminiscent of his first venture, Pollen Street Social, with barbecued pulled pork sandwiches and crowd-pleasing roasts.

BUBBLEDOGS

70 Charlotte Street
Fitzrovia
London W1T 4QG
+44 2076377770
www.bubbledogs.co.uk

Recommended by
Paul Foster, Matthew
Gaudet, Mette Hvarre
Gassner, Nuno Mendes,
Josh Murphy

Opening hours	Closed Monday and Sunday
Credit cards	Accepted
Price range	Affordable
Style	Casual
Cuisine	Hot Dogs
Recommended for	Wish I'd opened

'Fast food and grower Champagne. It seems like a no-brainer now that I think about it.'—Josh Murphy

Run by an ex-Noma duo, this Champagne-and-hot-dog joint opened in 2012, and immediately won over both the hip and the jaded. Its concept is clever: single-estate Champagnes served not with caviar, as you'd expect, but gourmet dogs – from the Naked (a dog in a bun), to gussied-up versions like the Date Dog (heavy on the garlic). Sides include potato Tots and fresh coleslaw. The space itself is handsome, with exposed brick, reclaimed oak floorboards and a copper-clad bar – although the unisex toilets aren't for everyone. The owners' small-plate venture, Kitchen Table, is also on the premises.

DABBOUS

39 Whitfield Street
Fitzrovia
London W1T 2SF
+44 2073231544
www.dabbous.co.uk

Recommended by
Tom Pemberton, Thrainn
Freyr Vigfússon

Opening hours	Closed Monday and Sunday
Credit cards	Accepted
Price range	Affordable
Style	Casual
Cuisine	Modern European
Recommended for	Wish I'd opened

'Simple but beautiful presentation. Quality food in a trendy atmosphere.'—Tom Pemberton

Critics' darling on opening in 2012 meant Dabbous's compact thirty-six-cover dining room found itself booked until kingdom come. Believe the hype – the universal praise for the playful French-meets-Nordic-in-London cooking of its well-travelled young chef Ollie Dabbous (ex of Texture and Le Manoir) is more than justified. The gritty, no-frills, industrial aesthetic of the dining room – artfully distressed concrete, meshed metal, exposed ducting – has its detractors. But perhaps it's partially why everything – particularly the set lunch and the tasting menus – seems so reasonably priced and so much fun. The basement bar does classy cocktails and a short menu of bar snacks.

HONEY & CO.

25a Warren Street
Fitzrovia
London W1T 5LZ
+44 2073886175
www.honeyandco.co.uk

Recommended by
Yotam Ottolenghi
Sami Tamimi

Opening hours	Closed Sunday
Credit cards	Accepted
Price range	Affordable
Style	Casual
Cuisine	Middle Eastern
Recommended for	Wish I'd opened

'It's hard to get a restaurant up and running and consistently in demand in London. Honey & Co. is a small, exceptionally good restaurant which has done just this. I don't wish I'd opened it – it's in the best hands – but I do wish I'd created their deconstructed cheesecake with a *kadaifi* pastry base. And they won't disclose the recipe!'—Yotam Ottolenghi

KITCHEN TABLE

70 Charlotte Street
Fitzrovia
London W1T 4QG
+44 2076377770
www.kitchentablelondon.co.uk

Recommended by
Paul Foster, Adam Reid,
Shaun Searley

Opening hours	Closed Monday and Sunday
Credit cards	Accepted
Price range	Expensive
Style	Smart casual
Cuisine	Modern European
Recommended for	Wish I'd opened

'The interaction the chefs have with the customers is great. There is a rawness and complete transparency to the restaurant as you literally sit around James Knappett's kitchen and watch him prepare your food. The best dining experience topped off with some of the best food being cooked right now.'—Shaun Searley

PIED À TERRE

Recommended by
Tom Pemberton

34 Charlotte Street
Fitzrovia
London W1T 2NH
+44 2076361178
www.pied-a-terre.co.uk

Opening hours	Closed Sunday
Credit cards	Accepted
Price range	Expensive
Style	Smart casual
Cuisine	Modern French
Recommended for	High end

'Consistent, excellent, with a lightness of touch.'
—Tom Pemberton

RIDING HOUSE CAFÉ

Recommended by
Rainer Becker

43–51 Great Titchfield Street
Fitzrovia
London W1W 7PQ
+44 2079270840
www.ridinghousecafe.co.uk

Opening hours	Open 7 days
Credit cards	Accepted
Price range	Affordable
Style	Casual
Cuisine	British bistro
Recommended for	Breakfast

'Not many places get breakfast right. They do.'
—Rainer Becker

ROKA

Recommended by
Miles Kirby, Glynn Purnell,
Karam Sethi

37 Charlotte Street
Fitzrovia
London W1T 1RR
+44 2075806464
www.rokarestaurant.com

Opening hours	Open 7 days
Credit cards	Accepted
Price range	Expensive
Style	Smart casual
Cuisine	Modern Japanese
Recommended for	High end

'I usually go for anything on the robata menu,
especially the lamb cutlets with Korean spices.'
—Karam Sethi

LARDO

Recommended by
Tom Harris

197–205 Richmond Road
Hackney
London E8 3NJ
+44 2089852683
www.lardo.co.uk

Opening hours	Open 7 days
Credit cards	Accepted but not AMEX
Price range	Affordable
Style	Casual
Cuisine	Italian
Recommended for	Regular neighbourhood

'My kids go crazy for the pizzas, and they're amazing,
Damien is a great cook. But for me, it's date night,
sitting with my wife at the pass, drinking a Negroni
Sbagliato and sharing fennel-pollen salami and a bit
of lardy loin.'—Tom Harris

LUCKY CHIP

Recommended by
Ed Wilson

Netil Market Trailer
11–25 Westgate Street
Hackney
London E2 9AG
www.luckychipuk.com

Opening hours	Closed Sunday to Friday
Reservation policy	No
Credit cards	Accepted
Price range	Budget
Style	Casual
Cuisine	Burgers
Recommended for	Bargain

'The Kevin Bacon eaten outdoors is the best burger in
London.'—Ed Wilson

PALM2

Recommended by
Miles Kirby

152–156 Lower Clapton Road
Hackney
London E5 0QJ
+44 2085331787
www.palm2.co.uk

Opening hours	Open 7 days
Credit cards	Accepted
Price range	Budget
Style	Casual
Cuisine	International
Recommended for	Local favourite

'This place represents all walks of life in the borough of Hackney. Interesting produce and great *gözleme* (savoury Turkish pastry) to go. The pop-up space upstairs hosts some great nights too.'—Miles Kirby

In the fashionable East London frontier that Clapton has become, this hip grocers-cum-event space is a community hub in rapidly gentrifying E5. The shop punts everything from E5 Bakehouse bread to interesting wines and craft beers; it has a deli counter that does cheese, meat and fish, and a good selection of quality fruit and veg. Their upstairs event space hosts everything from the acquired taste that is Ukulele Wednesdays, to more obviously delicious residencies that are pizza pop-ups, sushi master classes, sake tastings, Ghanaian and Nepalese evenings, dim sum lunches and weekend brunches. Every food- and drink-geek's dream local.

PAVILION

Recommended by
Stevie Parle, Shaun Searley,
Steve Williams

Victoria Park
Crown Gate West
Hackney
London E9 7DE
+44 2089800030
www.the-pavilion-cafe.com

Opening hours	Open 7 days
Reservation policy	No
Credit cards	Accepted
Price range	Budget
Style	Casual
Cuisine	Café
Recommended for	Breakfast

'Situated in Victoria Park next to a lake, they focus on quality, locally sourced produce. No frills, simply food perfectly executed – just what you want for breakfast. And the coffee is always spot on.'—Shaun Searley

RAW DUCK

Recommended by
Nuno Mendes

197 Richmond Road
Hackney
London E8 3NJ
+44 2089866534
www.rawduckhackney.co.uk

Opening hours	Open 7 days
Credit cards	Accepted but not AMEX
Price range	Budget
Style	Casual
Cuisine	Café-Bistro
Recommended for	Regular neighbourhood

'It's a little place in Hackney that is open all day. They have a great natural wine list and a really interesting small menu that changes throughout the day.'
—Nuno Mendes

VIOLET

Recommended by
Henry Harris

47 Wilton Way
Hackney
London E8 3ED
+44 2072758360
www.violetcakes.com

Opening hours	Closed Monday
Reservation policy	No
Credit cards	Accepted
Price range	Budget
Style	Casual
Cuisine	Bakery
Recommended for	Breakfast

'Superlative baking and properly made coffee.'
—Henry Harris

THE WINDSOR CASTLE

Recommended by
Miles Kirby

135 Lower Clapton Road
Hackney
London E5 8EQ
+44 2089856096
www.thewindsorcastleclapton.com

Opening hours	Open 7 days
Credit cards	Accepted
Price range	Affordable
Style	Casual
Cuisine	British bistro
Recommended for	Regular neighbourhood

'Great pub with excellent food.'—Miles Kirby

BEAGLE

Recommended by
Nuno Mendes

397–400 Geffrye Street
Hoxton
London E2 8HZ
+44 2076132967
www.beaglelondon.co.uk

Opening hours	Open 7 days
Credit cards	Accepted
Price range	Affordable
Style	Casual
Cuisine	British bistro
Recommended for	Breakfast

'The brunch menu here is amazing. The whole breakfast menu is super decadent and super tasty. Last time I was there I had the portobello mushrooms, toasted brioche, poached eggs and hollandaise. They also do a great blood cake and hash browns.'
—Nuno Mendes

BRAWN

Recommended by
Angela Hartnett,
Margot Henderson

49 Columbia Road
Hoxton
London E2 7RG
+44 2077295692
www.brawn.co

Opening hours	Open 7 days
Credit cards	Accepted but not AMEX
Price range	Affordable
Style	Casual
Cuisine	Bar-Bistro
Recommended for	Regular neighbourhood

'Brilliant food.'—Angela Hartnett

The likeable follow-up to Terroirs, Brawn sits on Columbia Road, in the hip heart of the East End. Utilitarian furniture meets whitewashed walls, Pop art, amusingly random bric-a-brac and a soundtrack that's big on reggae. It's staffed by a mixture of pretty young things and arty bearded blokes. The gutsy, daily-changing menu, made for sharing, is divided into five fairly self-explanatory sections: 'Taste Ticklers', 'Pig', 'Larder', 'Stove' and 'Pudding'. All of which is designed to go with a wine list that's big on natural wines – or 'cloudy reds and murky whites' as they like to describe them.

THE BREAKFAST CLUB

Recommended by
Pascal Aussignac

2–4 Rufus Street
Hoxton
London N1 6PE
+44 2077295252
www.thebreakfastclubcafes.com

Opening hours	Open 7 days
Credit cards	Accepted
Price range	Budget
Style	Casual
Cuisine	Diner-Café
Recommended for	Breakfast

'Great diversity of food, atmosphere, smiley service, cool 1980s music.'—Pascal Aussignac

EMBASSY EAST

Recommended by
Ed Wilson

285 Hoxton Street
Hoxton
London N1 5JX
+44 2077398340
www.embassyeast.co.uk

Opening hours	Open 7 days
Credit cards	Accepted but not AMEX
Price range	Budget
Style	Casual
Cuisine	Café
Recommended for	Breakfast

'The best grilled cheese sandwiches and coffee, by a great bunch of New Zealanders.'—Ed Wilson

SÔNG QUÊ CAFÉ

Recommended by
Greg Marchand

134 Kingsland Road
Hoxton
London E2 8DY
+44 2076133222
www.songque.co.uk

Opening hours	Open 7 days
Credit cards	Accepted but not AMEX or Diners
Price range	Budget
Style	Casual
Cuisine	Vietnamese
Recommended for	Bargain

'A great Vietnamese place full of Vietnamese and locals. They serve a killer quail.'—Greg Marchand

THE TOWPATH CAFÉ

Recommended by
Samantha & Samuel
Clark, Miles Kirby

42 De Beauvoir Crescent
Hoxton
London N1 5SB

Opening hours	Closed Monday
Reservation policy	No
Credit cards	Accepted
Price range	Budget
Style	Casual
Cuisine	Café
Recommended for	Local favourite

'An idyllic spot beside Regent's Canal in East London. The Towpath is a pretty hard location to beat, especially as it is combined with some of the most delicious food. Not surprisingly it is very popular.'
—Samantha & Samuel Clark

TRIP KITCHEN

Recommended by
Miles Kirby

TripSpace Projects
Arch 339–340, Acton Mews
Hoxton
London E8 4EA
+44 2079239417
www.tripspace.co.uk

Opening hours	Closed Monday and Tuesday
Credit cards	Accepted
Price range	Affordable
Style	Casual
Cuisine	Modern Turkish
Recommended for	Breakfast

'Great take on modern Turkish food and excellent coffee.'—Miles Kirby

AFGHAN KITCHEN

Recommended by
Miles Kirby

35 Islington Green
Islington
London N1 8DU
+44 2073598019

Opening hours	Closed Monday and Sunday
Credit cards	Not accepted
Price range	Budget
Style	Casual
Cuisine	Afghan
Recommended for	Bargain

'The chicken and yogurt at the Afghan Kitchen is a bargain.'—Miles Kirby

ANTEPLILER

Recommended by
Jacob Kenedy, Ben Tish

139 Upper Street
Islington
London N1 1QP
+44 2072265441
www.anteplilerislington.co.uk

Opening hours	Open 7 days
Credit cards	Accepted but not AMEX or Diners
Price range	Budget
Style	Casual
Cuisine	Turkish
Recommended for	Bargain

'London is blessed with any number of Turkish restaurants – this is by far the best, and at bargain prices. They make brilliant baklava, too, for after the pide, mezze and grills.'—Jacob Kenedy

This welcoming Turkish restaurant is a rather different beast to its Green Lanes sister – all neon mosaics and Ottoman chic, in lieu of a functional canteen and patisserie – but has thankfully remained immune to the prices of its gentrified Islington neighbours. The food remains just as honest as before, too, with superior standards such as hummus, borek and kebabs, alongside Antep kitchen specials, originating from the Gaziantep province, near the Syrian border. Of particular wallet-friendly note are the wood-fired-oven *lahmacun*: thin Turkish pizzas topped with lamb, herbs and salad, and rolled up to create the most extraordinary comfort food.

LE COQ

Recommended by
Tim Siadatan

292–294 St Paul's Road
Islington
London N1 2LH
+44 2073595055
www.le-coq.co.uk

Opening hours	Closed Monday
Credit cards	Accepted
Price range	Affordable
Style	Casual
Cuisine	Rotisserie
Recommended for	Late night

'You can go at 10:30 p.m. and get the best rotisserie chicken in London, in under five minutes.'
—Tim Siadatan

DELHI GRILL

Recommended by
Ben Tish

21 Chapel Market
Islington
London N1 9EZ
+44 2072788100
www.delhigrill.com

Opening hours	Open 7 days
Credit cards	Accepted
Price range	Budget
Style	Casual
Cuisine	Indian
Recommended for	Bargain

'Delhi Grill serves delicious, fresh and interesting Indian tandoor grills, home-made breads and chutneys, and healthy, spicy salads. Always under £20 ($33) per head – even with a beer.'—Ben Tish

THE DUKE OF CAMBRIDGE

Recommended by
Francesco Mazzei

30 St Peter's Street
Islington
London N1 8JT
+44 2073593066
www.dukeorganic.co.uk

Opening hours	Open 7 days
Credit cards	Accepted
Price range	Affordable
Style	Casual
Cuisine	Gastropub
Recommended for	Local favourite

MAISON D'ÊTRE

Recommended by
Tim Siadatan

154 Canonbury Road
Islington
London N1 2UP
www.maisondetrecafe.co.uk

Opening hours	Open 7 days
Reservation policy	No
Credit cards	Accepted
Price range	Budget
Style	Casual
Cuisine	Café-Bistro
Recommended for	Breakfast

'Nice staff, great coffee and superb granola.'
—Tim Siadatan

OTTOLENGHI

Recommended by
Fisun Ercan,
Anna Hansen

287 Upper Street
Islington
London N1 2TZ
+44 2072881454
www.ottolenghi.co.uk

Opening hours	Open 7 days
Credit cards	Accepted
Price range	Affordable
Style	Casual
Cuisine	Modern International
Recommended for	Local favourite

'Eclectic menus. Fresh, vibrant food served all day, every day. Their use of global ingredients reflects modern living in London.'—Anna Hansen

PALMERA OASIS

Recommended by
Miles Kirby

332 Essex Road
Islington
London N1 3PB
+44 2077046149
www.palmeraoasis.co.uk

Opening hours	Open 7 days
Credit cards	Accepted but not AMEX or Diners
Price range	Budget
Style	Casual
Cuisine	Lebanese
Recommended for	Late night

'Extra tahini sauce.'—Miles Kirby

SMOKEHOUSE

Recommended by
Paul Day, Shaun Searley

63–69 Canonbury Road
Islington
London N1 2DG
+44 2073541144
www.smokehouseislington.co.uk

Opening hours	Open 7 days
Credit cards	Accepted
Price range	Affordable
Style	Casual
Cuisine	Gastropub
Recommended for	Regular neighbourhood

'I love their use of the Big Green Egg ceramic barbeque as I use it myself and I enjoy sampling all the creative ways it can be used. The food at Smokehouse is great and is accompanied by an extensive beer list.'
—Shaun Searley

SUNDAY

Recommended by
Anna Hansen

169 Hemingford Road
Islington
London N1 1DA
+44 2076073868

Opening hours	Open 7 days
Credit cards	Accepted
Price range	Affordable
Style	Casual
Cuisine	Café
Recommended for	Breakfast

'Fantastic brunches in a cute, friendly neighbourhood restaurant. It has a lovely garden out the back with a huge old fig tree, which is perfect in the summer. The food is generous, consistent and tasty.'—Anna Hansen

TRULLO

Recommended by
Miles Kirby

300–302 St Paul's Road
Islington
London N1 2LH
+44 2072262733
www.trullorestaurant.com

Opening hours	Open 7 days
Credit cards	Accepted but not AMEX or Diners
Price range	Affordable
Style	Casual
Cuisine	Italian
Recommended for	Regular neighbourhood

CARAVAN

Recommended by
Giorgio Locatelli

Granary Building
1 Granary Square
King's Cross
London N1C 4AA
+44 2071017661
www.caravankingscross.co.uk

Opening hours	Open 7 days
Credit cards	Accepted
Price range	Affordable
Style	Casual
Cuisine	Modern International
Recommended for	Wish I'd opened

'It does pizza, small eats and it's a fun but relaxing environment.'—Giorgio Locatelli

THE BEGGING BOWL

Recommended by
Matthew Harris

168 Bellenden Road
Peckham
London SE15 4BW
+44 2076352627
www.thebeggingbowl.co.uk

Opening hours	Open 7 days
Reservation policy	No
Credit cards	Accepted
Price range	Affordable
Style	Casual
Cuisine	Thai small plates
Recommended for	Worth the travel

'Fantastic, fresh, authentic.'—Matthew Harris

It's tempting to describe The Begging Bowl as an instant success, but this is merely the latest stop on chef Andy Oliver's personal Thai-food odyssey, which has involved six months in Bangkok restaurant Bo. Lan, a sous position at Alan Yau's Naamyaa, and... oh, the slight distraction of being a MasterChef finalist in 2009. All this experience and relentless enthusiasm is on display in this bright and informal Peckham restaurant, where colourful regional Thai dishes are made with the best British ingredients – think vermicelli noodles with Dorset crab, or Woodvale venison with chilli jam. Customers are treated like old friends, and prices are never unreasonable.

ALBION CAFE

Recommended by
Sam Harris

2–4 Boundary Street
Shoreditch
London E2 7DD
+44 2077291051
www.albioncaff.co.uk

Opening hours	Open 7 days
Reservation policy	No
Credit cards	Accepted
Price range	Affordable
Style	Casual
Cuisine	British
Recommended for	Breakfast

'The home-made breads are worth the trip alone, as are their pastries.'—Sam Harris

BEIGEL BAKE

Recommended by
Robin Gill, Tom Harris

159 Brick Lane
Shoreditch
London E1 6SB
+44 2077290616

Opening hours	Open 7 days
Reservation policy	No
Credit cards	Not accepted
Price range	Budget
Style	Casual
Cuisine	Bakery
Recommended for	Local favourite

'Bagels are part of my DNA. I've been going there since I was a kid and the first night I could legally drive, I drove all the way from Shepherd's Bush to Brick Lane to buy a salt beef and mustard bagel to celebrate. It was 3.00 a.m. and well worth the trip. I used to take girls there on dates and when I got married, the bagels at my wedding weren't going to come from anywhere else.'—Tom Harris

BURRO E SALVIA

Recommended by
Martin Morales

52 Redchurch Street
Shoreditch
London E2 7DP
+44 2077394429
www.burroesalvia.co.uk

Opening hours	Open 7 days
Credit cards	Accepted but not AMEX
Price range	Affordable
Style	Casual
Cuisine	Italian Deli-Café
Recommended for	Regular neighbourhood

'There is an incredibly high level of human craftsmanship in what they offer. It's a small pasta specialist where the focus is on real, artisanal Italian food similar in ethos to our very own values.'—Martin Morales

THE CLOVE CLUB

Shoreditch Town Hall
380 Old Street
Shoreditch
London EC1V 9LT
+44 2077296496
www.thecloveclub.com

Opening hours	Closed Sunday
Credit cards	Accepted
Price range	Expensive
Style	Smart casual
Cuisine	Modern British
Recommended for	Wish I'd opened

'What a great cuisine guys! At a more than reasonable price in the centre of London, you find an authentically British menu with a contemporary touch. The restaurant is well maintained and elegant in the rooms of the old town hall. At the bar, quality drinks with character are prepared and the competence and courtesy of the staff is really top class.'—Massimo Bottura

Cult Dalston pop-up, The Clove Club found a permanent home in a section of Shoreditch Town Hall, opening in March 2013. The space is split between bar and dinner-only dining room. The latter, a handsome combination of lofty ceiling and open kitchen with show pass, serves a take-it-or-leave-it five-course menu with a few snacks thrown in for fun. The cooking combines carefully sourced British produce, a Nordic sensibility and more far-flung influences – notably a fondness for Korean condiments. Lunch, served in the bar, offers a more pared-back menu but the full tasting can be booked ahead of time.

DISHOOM SHOREDITCH

7 Boundary Street
Shoreditch
London E2 7JE
+44 2074209324
www.dishoom.com

Opening hours	Open 7 days
Credit cards	Accepted
Price range	Affordable
Style	Casual
Cuisine	Indian
Recommended for	Late night

'Great atmosphere and a really fun restaurant.'
—Stevie Parle

FIFTEEN

15 Westland Place
Shoreditch
London N1 7LP
+44 2033751515
www.fifteen.net

Opening hours	Open 7 days
Credit cards	Accepted
Price range	Affordable
Style	Casual
Cuisine	European
Recommended for	Wish I'd opened

'At Fifteen, Jamie Oliver has set up an apprenticeship programme to give unemployed young people a job and a chance to have a better life through learning how to cook. I admire Jamie Oliver for all of his philanthropic efforts.'—Michael Toscano

HOI POLLOI

Ace Hotel
100 Shoreditch High Street
Shoreditch
London E1 6JQ
+44 2088806100
www.hoi-polloi.co.uk

Opening hours	Open 7 days
Credit cards	Accepted
Price range	Affordable
Style	Smart casual
Cuisine	Modern British
Recommended for	Breakfast

'I love the glamorous room and buzzy atmosphere.'
—Isaac McHale

KÊU BÁNH MÌ DELI

332 Old Street
Shoreditch
London EC1V 9DR
+44 2077391164
www.keudeli.co.uk

Recommended by
Isaac McHale

Opening hours	Closed Sunday
Reservation policy	No
Credit cards	Accepted
Price range	Budget
Style	Casual
Cuisine	Vietnamese
Recommended for	Regular neighbourhood

'Local Vietnamese baguette place. Head and shoulders above all others I have ever tried, they have just the right bread, layers of flavour and everything's done really well.'—Isaac McHale

This Vietnamese deli in Shoreditch specializes in Bánh mì, the filled baguettes that are the delicious bastard child of Indochina's French colonial era. Kêu, from the team behind the nearby Vietnamese stalwarts Viet Grill and Cây Tre, have their baguettes baked for them by the Sally Clarke bakery. They're softer than a traditional French stick, as they should be, despite not being made with rice flower as they are back in Vietnam. Fillings include lemongrass-infused mackerel with mooli (daikon) and coriander (cilantro); spiced pork belly, ham terrine and chicken liver pâté; and pork meatballs in a spicy gravy.

LEILA'S CAFÉ

17 Calvert Avenue
Shoreditch
London E2 7JP
+44 2077299789

Recommended by
Tom Adams, Neil
Borthwick, Tom Harris,
Junya Yamasaki

Opening hours	Closed Monday and Tuesday
Reservation policy	No
Credit cards	Accepted
Price range	Budget
Style	Casual
Cuisine	Café-Bistro-Deli
Recommended for	Breakfast

'Polish breakfast for me, ham and eggs for my wife, toast and jam for the kids. It doesn't get any better than this. And before we go, we'll visit Leila's shop next door which is full of all the most delicious things.'
—Tom Harris

An annexe of Lelia's Shop, which sits next door, styled like an old-fashioned grocers by virtue of the fact that that's exactly what it was until the mid-1960s, its shelves today stocked like that of a lovably eclectic delicatessen. The café has a truly open kitchen, with nothing between those cooking and the communal tables. Depending on your tolerance level, the eccentric service could at times be described as borderline surly. But that doesn't deter its loyal and fashionable following, who come for the atmosphere, the simple home-cooked dishes and the excellent coffee.

ROCHELLE CANTEEN

Rochelle School
Arnold Circus
Shoreditch
London E2 7ES
+44 2077295677
www.arnoldandhenderson.com

Recommended by
Neil Borthwick, Gabrielle
Hamilton, Miles Kirby

Opening hours	Closed Saturday and Sunday
Credit cards	Accepted
Price range	Budget
Style	Casual
Cuisine	British
Recommended for	Regular neighbourhood

'I was actually moved to eat with my fingers, suck the bones clean, and then lift the plate to my lips and drain every last drop of broth. It was unapologetically straightforward cooking.'—Gabrielle Hamilton

Occupying the converted bike sheds of a Victorian school, what began as a canteen for the local arty souls has become a Shoreditch institution. Open weekdays only, it's run by Melanie Arnold and Margot Henderson (other half of Fergus of St. John fame) and doubles up as the headquarters for their in-demand catering company. Come summertime, they set up tables outside, overlooking the school's grassy playground. The menu changes daily and is very much of the school of St. John – short, British, seasonal, tersely descriptive and delicious.

TAS FIRIN
Recommended by
Tom Adams
160 Bethnal Green Road
Shoreditch
London E2 6DG
+44 2077296446

Opening hours	Open 7 days
Reservation policy	No
Credit cards	Not accepted
Price range	Budget
Style	Casual
Cuisine	Turkish
Recommended for	Late night

'Brilliant *ocakbasi*. Great *lahmacun* (meat-topped flatbread) and *pide* (Turkish pizza) – amazing booze sponges.'—Tom Adams

TRAMSHED
Recommended by
Angela Hartnett
32 Rivington Street
Shoreditch
London EC2A 3LX
+44 2077490478
www.chickenandsteak.co.uk

Opening hours	Open 7 days
Credit cards	Accepted
Price range	Affordable
Style	Casual
Cuisine	Steakhouse
Recommended for	Regular neighbourhood

THE ANCHOR & HOPE
Recommended by
Jeremy Lee, Tom Pemberton,
Steve Williams
36 The Cut
Southwark
London SE1 8LP
+44 2079289898
www.charleswells.co.uk

Opening hours	Closed Sunday
Reservation policy	No
Credit cards	Accepted but not AMEX
Price range	Affordable
Style	Casual
Cuisine	Gastropub
Recommended for	Bargain

'Jonathan Jones writes a beautiful menu at most reasonable prices. It's brilliant, I love it and I am always happy there.'—Jeremy Lee

With its robust, well-priced cooking and decent ales, this decade-plus institution near the Old and Young Vic theatres embodies the gastropub's original (and oft-abused) virtues. Accordingly, it's more pubby than pretentious, with a plain, curtained-off dining room whose no-bookings policy usually means a longish wait in the bar for dinner. But, as you'd expect from a venture created by St. John graduates – by way of The Eagle – the cooking makes excellent use of head-to-tail ingredients in appealing dishes such as chopped rabbit and deep-fried pig's head, and non-carnivores are also well served by the daily-changing menu. Good – suitably traditional – desserts too.

MY OLD PLACE
Recommended by
Steve Williams
88–90 Middlesex Street
Spitalfields
London E1 7EZ
+44 2072472200
www.oldplace.co.uk

Opening hours	Open 7 days
Credit cards	Not accepted
Price range	Budget
Style	Casual
Cuisine	Szechuan
Recommended for	Bargain

'Fantastic Szechuan food near Liverpool Street.'
—Steve Williams

ST. JOHN BREAD & WINE

94–96 Commercial Street
Spitalfields
London E1 6LZ
+44 2072510848
www.stjohngroup.uk.com

Recommended by
Tom Adams, Neil Borthwick,
Samantha & Samuel Clark,
Paul Foster, Angela Hartnett,
James Knappett, James Lowe,
Brad McDonald, Nuno Mendes,
Carlo Mirarchi, Shuko Oda,
Tom Pemberton, Andy Ricker,
Tim Siadatan, Peter Weeden,
Junya Yamasaki

Opening hours	Open 7 days
Credit cards	Accepted
Price range	Affordable
Style	Casual
Cuisine	British
Recommended for	Local favourite

'A purely London institution. One afternoon, many years ago, I walked in and sat by myself and watched the kitchen at work. I had a dish of braised and smoked pork belly with carrots and a little bit of the braising liquid, accompanied with mustard. It was one of the most satisfying meals I have had in London.'
—Nuno Mendes

St. John's second outpost lies across from Spital-fields Market and runs a staggered, just shy of all-day, menu from breakfast – via elevenses, lunch and early afternoon nibbles – through to supper. Built around its bakery and wine shop, the cooking naturally reflects the British seasonal nose-to-tail approach that is St. John's trademark but tailors it more to tapas-style sharing. The open kitchen and bakery overlook a no-nonsense dining room, brightly lit with whitewashed walls, tightly packed with simple wooden tables and chairs. If there's one complaint, it's that the latter don't favour bony behinds.

UPSTAIRS AT THE TEN BELLS

84 Commercial Street
Spitalfields
London E1 6LY
+44 7530492986
www.tenbells.com

Recommended by
Robin Gill

Opening hours	Closed Monday
Credit cards	Accepted but not AMEX
Price range	Affordable
Style	Casual
Cuisine	Modern British
Recommended for	Local favourite

'I love that the setting is a 300-year-old public house bathed in history, but the food is as the city: modern, with mixed cultural influences and full of inspiring combinations. Most of all, I love that you feel like you are at a friend's house and totally relaxed.'—Robin Gill

HERMAN ZE GERMAN

19 Villiers Street
Strand
London WC2N 6NE
www.herman-ze-german.co.uk

Recommended by
Tim Siadatan

Opening hours	Open 7 days
Reservation policy	No
Credit cards	Accepted
Price range	Budget
Style	Casual
Cuisine	German
Recommended for	Wish I'd opened

'Great bratwurst, sauerkraut and chips (fries). Makes me smile every time I think about it – I think it will go far.'—Tim Siadatan

THE INDIA CLUB

Hotel Strand Continental
143 Strand
Strand
London WC2R 1JA
+44 2078364880
www.strand-continental.co.uk

Recommended by
José Pizarro

Opening hours	Open 7 days
Credit cards	Accepted
Price range	Budget
Style	Casual
Cuisine	Indian
Recommended for	Bargain

'I like the food. The staff are great. Makes me feel like I'm in India in another era. And it's BYO!'—José Pizarro

Established by India's first High Commissioner to the UK in 1946 as a meeting place for civil servants, The India Club, found up a flight of stairs off The Strand, appears to have changed little since. Portraits of Gandhi line the walls of the almost old-school class-room-like colonial canteen. A loyal clientele that ranges from students to barristers comes here for bargain dishes, from the £5 ($8) kebabs to a whole chicken for £10 ($17). Bring your own drinks (no corkage), or sip masala tea (£1.60/$2.70 per cup). South Indian dishes include masala dosa, dahi vada, bhuna lamb and Mughlay chicken – with optional accompaniments of pickles and chutneys (60p/$1).

TERROIRS

Recommended by
Tom Kerridge

5 William IV Street
Strand
London WC2N 4DW
+44 2070360660
www.terroirswinebar.com

Opening hours	Closed Sunday
Credit cards	Accepted
Price range	Affordable
Style	Casual
Cuisine	French
Recommended for	Bargain

'Brilliant, rustic French cooking, simple terrines and great pork products.'—Tom Kerridge

BRAVI RAGAZZI

Recommended by
Matthew Harris

2a Sunnyhill Road
Streatham
London SW16 2UH
+44 2087694966
www.braviragazzipizzeria.co.uk

Opening hours	Open 7 days
Reservation policy	No
Credit cards	Accepted but not AMEX
Price range	Budget
Style	Casual
Cuisine	Pizza
Recommended for	Late night

'Great sourdough pizza.'—Matthew Harris

LAHORE KEBAB HOUSE

Recommended by
Atul Kochhar

2–10 Umberston Street
Whitechapel
London E1 1PY
+44 2074819737
www.lahore-kebabhouse.com

Opening hours	Open 7 days
Credit cards	Accepted
Price range	Budget
Style	Casual
Cuisine	Pakistani
Recommended for	Bargain

'Serves the best traditional Indian food in London without a doubt. The lamb chops – they're famous for a reason!'—Atul Kochar

TAYYABS

Recommended by
Ollie Dabbous, Henry Harris

83–89 Fieldgate Street
Whitechapel
London E1 1JU
+44 2072479543
www.tayyabs.co.uk

Opening hours	Open 7 days
Credit cards	Accepted
Price range	Budget
Style	Casual
Cuisine	Indian-Pakistani
Recommended for	Bargain

'Grilled lamb chops, dry meat curry and naan. Great buzz, always a queue (waiting line) and it's BYO.'
—Henry Harris

No one comes to Tayyabs for the ambience. Forty years after opening, E1's worst-kept secret is more cut and thrust than ever, from the location round the back of Whitechapel High Street to the hour-plus queues (waiting lines) – and that's with a reservation – and the ferocious noise levels. However, the Punjabi food – specifically the sizzling lamb chops and groaning mixed grill plate, as well as fresh-from-the-tandoor naan – makes it all worthwhile, especially with change from £20 ($33). Don't get caught out by the BYO policy – bring an extra beer or two so you can enjoy a pre-dinner drink while you wait for a table.

GREEN ISLAND RESTAURANT

Recommended by
Shaun Rankin

Green Island
St Clement
Jersey
Channel Islands JE2 6LS
+44 1534857787
www.greenisland.je

Opening hours	Closed Monday
Credit cards	Accepted
Price range	Affordable
Style	Casual
Cuisine	Mediterranean
Recommended for	Local favourite

'They do a fantastic seafood plate that has to be enjoyed leisurely on the terrace with a chilled bottle of Sancerre.'—Shaun Rankin

SIAM GARDEN

Recommended by
Mark Jordan

6 Parade Arcade
St Helier
Jersey
Channel Islands JE2 3QP
+44 1534766776
www.siamgardenjersey.com

Opening hours	Open 7 days
Credit cards	Accepted
Price range	Budget
Style	Casual
Cuisine	Thai
Recommended for	Regular neighbourhood

'This fantastic little Thai restaurant is run by some Thai women and they do the best Thai food that I have ever tasted. Everything is made fresh to order and to original recipes.'—Mark Jordan

THE BASS & LOBSTER

Recommended by
Shaun Rankin

Gorey Coast Road
St Martin
Jersey
Channel Islands JE3 6EU
+44 1534859590
www.bassandlobster.com

Opening hours	Closed Monday
Credit cards	Accepted
Price range	Affordable
Style	Casual
Cuisine	Seafood
Recommended for	Regular neighbourhood

'I have two small children, which can be a handful at times, so it's important to feel comfortable when out dining as a family and know that nothing is a problem. The service coupled with great, honest food ticks all of the boxes for our family.'—Shaun Rankin

BIG VERN'S

Recommended by
Mark Jordan

La Grande Route des Mielles
St Ouen
Jersey
Channel Islands JE3 7FN
+44 1534481705

Opening hours	Open 7 days
Reservation policy	No
Credit cards	Accepted but not AMEX
Price range	Affordable
Style	Casual
Cuisine	Diner-Café
Recommended for	Breakfast

'My favourite place to go for breakfast has to be Big Vern's down alongside the five-mile beach on St Ouen's Bay. It's a café right on the beach and they make an awesome breakfast. I love the feel of the restaurant, it's very rustic with surf pictures on the walls and has a really relaxed, surfy style about it. My kids love it there.'—Mark Jordan

EL TICO BEACH CANTINA

Recommended by
Shaun Rankin

La Grande Route des Mielles
St Ouen
Jersey
Channel Islands JE3 7FN
+44 1534482009
www.elticojersey.com

Opening hours	Open 7 days
Credit cards	Accepted
Price range	Affordable
Style	Casual
Cuisine	International
Recommended for	Breakfast

'I can tuck into a smoky bacon roll while the kids enjoy stacks of Yankee Pancakes with mascarpone cream and maple syrup. The standout feature of this cantina is the breathtaking view over the long stretch of St Ouen's Bay – the perfect spot for a bracing sea walk after all that breakfast.'—Shaun Rankin

THE HAWTHORN RESTAURANT

Recommended by
Jocky Petrie

5 Keil Crofts
Benderloch
Argyll
Scotland PA37 1QS
+44 1631720777

Opening hours	Closed Monday
Credit cards	Accepted but not AMEX
Price range	Affordable
Style	Casual
Cuisine	British
Recommended for	Worth the travel

'This small husband-and-wife-run restaurant is well
worth a trip into the Highlands.'—Jocky Petrie

WEE HURRIE

Recommended by
Adam Stokes

Troon Harbour
Troon
Ayrshire
Scotland KA10 6DH

Opening hours	Closed Monday
Reservation policy	No
Credit cards	Not accepted
Price range	Budget
Style	Casual
Cuisine	Fish and Chips
Recommended for	Bargain

'The best fish-and-chip shop ever and it's next to a
wholesale fish market in a harbour.'—Adam Stokes

ROCPOOL

Recommended by
Michael Smith

1 Ness Walk
Inverness
County of Inverness
Scotland IV3 5NE
+44 1463717274
www.rocpoolrestaurant.com

Opening hours	Closed Sunday
Credit cards	Accepted
Price range	Affordable
Style	Casual
Cuisine	Brasserie
Recommended for	Regular neighbourhood

'Consistently delivers delicious food. Steven, the owner,
is always there, leading from the front and welcoming
regulars, families and tourists alike with typical
Highland charm.'—Michael Smith

LOCH BAY

Recommended by
Michael Smith

Stein
Isle of Skye
County of Inverness
Scotland IV55 8GA
+44 1470592235
www.lochbay-seafood-restaurant.co.uk

Opening hours	Closed Sunday to Tuesday
Credit cards	Accepted
Price range	Affordable
Style	Casual
Cuisine	Seafood
Recommended for	Local favourite

'Skye seafood straight off the boats, cooked simply.'
—Michael Smith

THE KITCHIN

Recommended by
Neil Borthwick

78 Commercial Quay
Edinburgh
Scotland EH6 6LX
+44 1315551755
www.thekitchin.com

Opening hours	Closed Monday and Sunday
Credit cards	Accepted
Price range	Expensive
Style	Smart casual
Cuisine	Modern Scottish
Recommended for	Worth the travel

'I admire the from-nature-to-plate philosophy. Tom has
a real passion for Scottish ingredients and it shows.'
—Neil Borthwick

ONDINE RESTAURANT

Recommended by
Tom Kitchin

2 George IV Bridge
Edinburgh
Scotland EH1 1AD
+44 1312261888
www.ondinerestaurant.co.uk

Opening hours	Closed Sunday
Credit cards	Accepted
Price range	Affordable
Style	Casual
Cuisine	Seafood
Recommended for	Local favourite

'Edinburgh's food scene is brilliant at the moment. It's amazing to see chefs making the most of the high-quality produce available right on our doorstep. Roy Brett's restaurant Ondine, off the Royal Mile, is one of my favourites in Edinburgh. The shellfish is of fantastic quality and I especially like Roy's commitment to sustainable Scottish fish and shellfish.'—Tom Kitchin

URBAN ANGEL

Recommended by
Tom Kitchin

121 Hanover Street
Edinburgh
Scotland EH2 1DJ
+44 1312256215
www.urban-angel.co.uk

Opening hours	Open 7 days
Credit cards	Accepted but not AMEX
Price range	Budget
Style	Casual
Cuisine	Café-Bistro
Recommended for	Breakfast

'It's a little gem for breakfast! They do delicious scrambled eggs and freshly made artisan bread.'
—Tom Kitchin

ANSTRUTHER FISH BAR

Recommended by
Tom Kitchin

42–44 Shore Anstruther
Fife
Scotland KY10 3AQ
+44 1333310518
www.anstrutherfishbar.co.uk

Opening hours	Open 7 days
Reservation policy	No
Credit cards	Accepted but not AMEX
Price range	Budget
Style	Casual
Cuisine	Fish and Chips
Recommended for	Bargain

'The family-run Anstruther Fish Bar is situated in a small fishing village in Fife. Their fish is caught fresh every day from the local quayside and they serve it traditionally with chunky chips (fries) and mushy peas. Something I love to do when I can is get together with family and friends and head outside of Edinburgh city centre. Whenever I do, I always make a stop at Anstruther – there's nothing better than enjoying the views over the bay with a delicious fish supper.'
—Tom Kitchin

THE PEAT INN

Recommended by
Tom Kitchin

On the B940
near St Andrews
Fife
Scotland KY15 5LH
+44 1334840206
www.thepeatinn.co.uk

Opening hours	Closed Monday and Sunday
Credit cards	Accepted
Price range	Affordable
Style	Smart casual
Cuisine	Scottish
Recommended for	High end

'I love The Peat Inn. Geoffrey Smeddle and his wife, Katherine, do a fantastic job up there and the food is always first class.'—Tom Kitchin

CITATION TAVERNE & RESTAURANT

40 Wilson Glasgow
Glasgow
Scotland G1 1HD
+44 1415596799
www.citation-glasgow.com

Opening hours	Open 7 days
Credit cards	Accepted
Price range	Affordable
Style	Casual
Cuisine	British bistro
Recommended for	Breakfast

'Order their Full Écosse and you won't need to eat again for the entire day!'—Michael Smith

ANDREW FAIRLIE

Gleneagles Hotel
Auchterarder
Perthshire
Scotland PH3 1NF
+44 1764694267
www.andrewfairlie.co.uk

Opening hours	Closed Sunday
Credit cards	Accepted
Price range	Expensive
Style	Smart casual
Cuisine	Modern French
Recommended for	High end

'Luxury in a relaxed atmosphere.'—Michael Smith

BALLINLUIG MOTOR GRILL

Ballinluig Services, A9
Ballinluig
Perthshire
Scotland PH9 0LG
+44 1796482212
www.ballinluigservices.co.uk

Opening hours	Open 7 days
Reservation policy	No
Credit cards	Accepted but not AMEX
Price range	Budget
Style	Casual
Cuisine	British
Recommended for	Bargain

'When travelling to Edinburgh or Glasgow I always stop at this authentic "truckers" diner for sausage, egg and chips served by local ladies in tabards.'—Michael Smith

THE HARBOURMASTER

Harbourmaster Hotel
Pen Cei
Aberaeron
Ceredigion
Wales SA46 0BT
+44 1545570755
www.harbour-master.com

Opening hours	Open 7 days
Credit cards	Accepted
Price range	Affordable
Style	Casual
Cuisine	British
Recommended for	Wish I'd opened

'A truly stunning location on the harbour's edge in Aberaeron. Over the past decade it's developed into a national icon. A thriving business built on great Welsh food and true Welsh hospitality.'—Hywel Jones

THE HARDWICK

Old Raglan Road
Abergavenny
Monmouthshire
Wales NP7 9AA
+44 1873854220
www.thehardwick.co.uk

Opening hours	Open 7 days
Credit cards	Accepted
Price range	Affordable
Style	Casual
Cuisine	British
Recommended for	Local favourite

'Wales is fortunate to have a chef of Stephen Terry's calibre plying his trade there and flying the flag for Welsh produce with such clear passion. A restaurant that suits all occasions and an extremely family friendly one too.'—Hywel Jones

A London-restaurant-scene legend, chef Stephen Terry returned to his native Wales to take ownership of a pub called the Horse & Jockey on the outskirts of Abergavenny, the Monmouthshire market town famous for the Walnut Tree and the annual food festival it hosts each September. Reopened as The Hardwick four weeks after he first took it over in 2005, it has since grown into an award-winning restaurant with rooms. Terry's unfussy menu makes the most of the best local ingredients, combining them with the good taste and technical ability with which he originally made his name.

THE WALNUT TREE

Recommended by
Jacob Kenedy,
Bruce Poole

Llanddewi Skirrid
Abergavenny
Monmouthshire
Wales NP7 8AW
+44 1873852797
www.thewalnuttreeinn.com

Opening hours	Closed Monday and Sunday
Credit cards	Accepted but not AMEX
Price range	Affordable
Style	Casual
Cuisine	Modern British
Recommended for	Worth the travel

'Shaun Hill has more nous than most in my game and a philosophy we can all aspire to.'—Jacob Kenedy

One of the Britain's great cooking heroes, Shaun Hill 'retired' to Abergavenny to take over The Walnut Tree in 2007. He formerly ran the fine and tiny Merchant House in Ludlow, where he always cooked alone. He has more help in the kitchen here, a famous dining destination on and off since the 1960s. The cooking, wonderfully straightforward but with the sort of seasoned skill that only years at the stove can bring, makes use of local produce sourced from Monmouth-shire's rich larder (pantry). Make a proper meal of it and book a room in one of their two nearby cottages.

THE FELIN FACH GRIFFIN

Recommended by
James Wilkins

Felin Fach
Brecon
Powys
Wales LD3 0UB
+44 1874620111
www.felinfachgriffin.co.uk

Opening hours	Open 7 days
Credit cards	Accepted but not AMEX
Price range	Affordable
Style	Casual
Cuisine	Gastropub
Recommended for	Regular neighbourhood

'I love to go walking on the Brecon Beacons and this place is the perfect welcoming country pub with a log fire, good beers and good food.'—James Wilkins

THE FIG TREE

Recommended by
Hywel Jones

The Esplanade
Penarth
Vale of Glamorgan
Wales CF64 3AU
+44 2920702512
www.thefigtreepenarth.co.uk

Opening hours	Closed Monday
Credit cards	Accepted but not AMEX
Price range	Affordable
Style	Casual
Cuisine	British
Recommended for	Regular neighbourhood

'A great neighbourhood restaurant run by Mike Caplain and Sandy Guppy. Fantastic seaside location, great food, service and value with a refreshingly large vegetarian offering on the menu. '—Hywel Jones

CANTEEN AT THE MAC

Recommended by
Niall McKenna

Metropolitan Arts Centre
10 Exchange Street West
Belfast
County Antrim
Northern Ireland BT1 2NJ
+44 2890235053
www.themaclive.com

Opening hours	Open 7 days
Credit cards	Accepted but not AMEX
Price range	Affordable
Style	Casual
Cuisine	Café-Bistro
Recommended for	Breakfast

'Great on a Sunday morning with the papers and the kids can have a wander around. I love the ambience of the place – it is open, cleverly designed with gallery spaces and there is always a relaxed vibe.'
—Niall McKenna

COPPI

Recommended by
Stephen Toman

St Anne's Square
Belfast
County Antrim
Northern Ireland BT1 2LR
+44 2890311959
www.coppi.co.uk

Opening hours	Open 7 days
Credit cards	Accepted
Price range	Affordable
Style	Casual
Cuisine	Italian Bistro
Recommended for	Regular neighbourhood

'Chilled-out vibe in beautiful surroundings, great for a Sunday evening.'—Stephen Toman

THE GREAT ROOM RESTAURANT

Recommended by
Niall McKenna

The Merchant Hotel
16 Skipper Street
Belfast
County Antrim
Northern Ireland BT1 2DZ
+44 2890234888
www.themerchanthotel.com

Opening hours	Open 7 days
Credit cards	Accepted
Price range	Affordable
Style	Smart casual
Cuisine	Brasserie
Recommended for	High end

'To be honest it is hard to beat the Champagne high tea at The Merchant Hotel. The building and dining room are truly breathtaking and the afternoon tea is classic. The drinks, service and atmosphere at their award-winning cocktail bar are second to none.'
—Niall McKenna

HOWARD STREET

Recommended by
Stephen Toman

56 Howard Street
Belfast
County Antrim
Northern Ireland BT1 6PG
+44 2890248362
www.howardstbelfast.com

Opening hours	Closed Monday and Sunday
Credit cards	Accepted
Price range	Affordable
Style	Casual
Cuisine	Mediterranean
Recommended for	Bargain

'Great for pre-theatre.'—Stephen Toman

LITTLE ITALY

Recommended by
Stephen Toman

13 Amelia Street
Belfast
County Antrim
Northern Ireland BT2 7GS
+44 2890314914

Opening hours	Open 7 days
Reservation policy	No
Credit cards	Accepted
Price range	Budget
Style	Casual
Cuisine	Pizza - Takeaway
Recommended for	Late night

'Best pizzas in town.'—Stephen Toman

MOURNE SEAFOOD BAR
34–36 Bank Street
Belfast
County Antrim
Northern Ireland BT1 1HL
+44 2890248544
www.mourneseafood.com

Recommended by
Niall McKenna

Opening hours	Open 7 days
Credit cards	Accepted
Price range	Budget
Style	Casual
Cuisine	Seafood
Recommended for	Bargain

'I tend to pop in here for a pint of prawns (shrimp) or a bowl of mussels. It is a traditional fish restaurant and you get exactly what you ask for.'—Niall McKenna

The flagship branch of Mourne Seafood (there is a another at Dundrum, on the County Down coast) is as pleasantly unpretentious as a seafood restaurant gets. Located in the very heart of the city, down a side alley along from the legendary Belfast pub that is Kelly's Cellars, Mourne's menu always includes hugely generously portions of classic beer-battered fish and chips; a whole grilled catch with boiled buttered potatoes; and oysters and mussels sourced from Mourne's own beds. If you're after something more elaborate – say a seafood risotto or a ceviche – the daily specials have you covered.

THE RAJ
461 Lisburn Road
Belfast
County Antrim
Northern Ireland BT9 7EQ
+44 2890662168
www.therajbelfast.com

Recommended by
Michael Deane

Opening hours	Open 7 days
Credit cards	Accepted
Price range	Affordable
Style	Casual
Cuisine	Indian-Pakistani
Recommended for	Regular neighbourhood

'Great cooking and great friends.'—Michael Deane

SHU
253 Lisburn Road
Belfast
County Antrim
Northern Ireland BT9 7EN
+44 2890381655
www.shu-restaurant.com

Recommended by
Niall McKenna

Opening hours	Closed Sunday
Credit cards	Accepted
Price range	Affordable
Style	Smart casual
Cuisine	British bistro
Recommended for	Regular neighbourhood

'It has classically cooked food and the service and atmosphere are great. It's always a good night out and the chef, Brian McCann, always has something funny to tell you.'—Niall McKenna

THE SPHINX
74 Stranmillis Road
Belfast
County Antrim
Northern Ireland BT9 5AD
+44 2890681881
www.sphinxkebabs.com

Recommended by
Michael Deane

Opening hours	Open 7 days
Reservation policy	No
Credit cards	Not accepted
Price range	Budget
Style	Casual
Cuisine	Kebab Shop
Recommended for	Late night

'Local, fresh and tasty. Owned by famous butcher Earl Jenkins.'—Michael Deane

Laying claim to Belfast's best kebab since 1980, The Sphinx sits in a student-friendly stretch of Stranmillis, in the south of the city. Its doner kebabs have been shortlisted for a national award, the no-nonsense Irish Kebab – just lamb-stuffed pitta without any of that pesky salad – a bestseller. Not that The Sphinx's versatile menu keeps to kebabs, extending to fish 'n' chips, burgers and fried chicken. The exact recipe for their supposedly Egyptian-inspired Sphinx special sauce remains a secret. But it's there on the Sphinx Kebab, Sphinx Burger, Sphinx Fish, Sphinx Chicken Salad and smothered on the Sphinx Chips (fries).

TEDFORDS

Recommended by
Stephen Toman

5 Donegall Quay
Belfast
County Antrim
Northern Ireland BT1 3EA
+44 2890434000
www.tedfordsrestaurant.com

Opening hours	Closed Monday and Sunday
Credit cards	Accepted
Price range	Affordable
Style	Smart casual
Cuisine	Modern French
Recommended for	Local favourite

'One of the longest-serving restaurants in Belfast, showcasing our amazing seafood. Beautiful views overlooking the River Lagan.'—Stephen Toman

RAYANNE HOUSE

Recommended by
Stephen Toman

60 Demense Road
Belfast
County Down
Northern Ireland BT18 9EX
+44 2890425859
www.rayannehouse.com

Opening hours	Open 7 days
Credit cards	Accepted
Price range	Affordable
Style	Casual
Cuisine	British
Recommended for	Breakfast

'Local porridge and yogurt, a great selection for breakfast and child friendly.'—Stephen Toman

BISTRO AT BALLOO HOUSE

Recommended by
Niall McKenna

1 Comber Road
Killinchy
County Down
Northern Ireland BT23 6PA
+44 2897541210
www.ballooinns.com

Opening hours	Open 7 days
Credit cards	Accepted
Price range	Affordable
Style	Casual
Cuisine	British bistro
Recommended for	Local favourite

'I like the fact that the bar always has a turf fire going, no matter what the time of year. The smell always evokes a great sense of familiarity in the big, bustling room. This place is great for Sunday lunch as it is outside of Belfast and supports local producers really well. The menu always has a great selection of fish and meat.'—Niall McKenna

DINING ROOM

Recommended by
Cathal Armstrong

Gregans Castle Hotel
Corkscrew Hill
Ballyvaughan
County Clare
Republic of Ireland
+353 657077005
www.gregans.ie/dining

Opening hours	Closed Wednesday and Sunday
Credit cards	Accepted
Price range	Expensive
Style	Smart casual
Cuisine	Modern Irish
Recommended for	Worth the travel

'It was hands down the best meal I've ever had in Ireland.'—Cathal Armstrong

WILD HONEY INN

Recommended by
Ultan Cooke

Kincora Road
Lisdoonvarna
County Clare
Republic of Ireland
+353 657074300
www.wildhoneyinn.com

Opening hours	Closed Tuesday
Reservation policy	No
Credit cards	Accepted but not AMEX
Price range	Affordable
Style	Casual
Cuisine	Gastropub
Recommended for	Wish I'd opened

'Aidan McGrath is a first-class chef who has a quaint restaurant with a bar and rooms on the west coast. The food is the mature offerings of a chef who has been there, done that and knows what's important.'
—Ultan Cooke

FARMGATE CAFÉ

Recommended by
Ross Lewis

The English Market
Cork
County Cork
Republic of Ireland
+353 214278134
www.farmgate.ie

Opening hours	Closed Sunday
Credit cards	Accepted
Price range	Budget
Style	Casual
Cuisine	Irish
Recommended for	Local favourite

'I think it sums up what is good about Irish food.'
—Ross Lewis

The Cork English Market is even more impressive when viewed from a height, which is just one of the reasons to sit down and tuck into lunch at Kay Harte's daytime Farmgate Café. With an enviably short supply chain, oysters are shucked to order, one of the staff popping downstairs to the fishmonger Pat O'Connell as the need arises. Food is local and the cooking is skilfully simple. Traditional dishes – such as tripe and onions with drisheen (black pudding/blood sausage) and lamb's liver and bacon with champ – can be washed down with craft beer.

HOUSE CAFÉ

Recommended by
Jocky Petrie

Cork Opera House
Emmet Place
Cork
County Cork
Republic of Ireland
+353 214905277

Opening hours	Closed Sunday
Credit cards	Accepted
Price range	Affordable
Style	Casual
Cuisine	Café-Bistro
Recommended for	Bargain

'Best fish I've ever eaten. I've never had a meal here I didn't thoroughly enjoy. Superb desserts too.'
—Jocky Petrie

JACKIE LENNOX CHIP SHOP

Recommended by
Jocky Petrie

137 Bandon Road
Cork
County Cork
Republic of Ireland
+353 214316118

Opening hours	Open 7 days
Reservation policy	No
Credit cards	Not accepted
Price range	Budget
Style	Casual
Cuisine	Fish and Chips
Recommended for	Late night

'There is something unbeatable about their chips (fries). It's the only place I can finish the whole bag every time.'—Jocky Petrie

People in Cork don't go for fish and chips, they go for 'a Lennox's'. Ireland's first purpose-built chippy, opened in 1951 by Jackie and Eileen Lennox on Bandon Road, is still doing its founder proud. From midday until after midnight, the second and third generation Lennoxes turn out the city's best battered cod, haddock and proper chips from the old-fashioned counter. Despite the demand – queues regularly stretch out along the pavement – real attention is paid to produce, so potato, cheese and onion pies are made each morning, chicken and beef are 100 per cent Irish, and cod and haddock fished from sustainable stocks. Even the battered sausage is local.

FISHY FISHY CAFÉ

Recommended by
Paul Flynn,
Ross Lewis

Crowley's Quay
Kinsale
County Cork
Republic of Ireland
+353 214700415
www.fishyfishy.ie

Opening hours	Open 7 days
Credit cards	Accepted but not AMEX
Price range	Affordable
Style	Casual
Cuisine	Seafood
Recommended for	Wish I'd opened

'Always busy because they serve the freshest fish, cooked simply and it is in a beautiful part of Ireland.'
—Paul Flynn

Having evolved from a small fish shop that serves a limited number of fish dishes at lunchtime, Martin

Shanahan's second, larger Fishy Fishy restaurant has an enviable position at the end of the pier in Kinsale, a fashionable fishing village in Cork. On a sunny day there are few better places to be than the courtyard, in the shade of mature trees, with a bottle of crisp white wine and simply cooked fish from local boats. But it's no secret, so at lunchtime you may have to wait at the bar for a table; they do, however, take bookings for dinner.

BALLYMALOE RESTAURANT

Recommended by
Paul Flynn,
Ross Lewis

Ballymaloe House
Shanagarry
County Cork
Republic of Ireland
+353 214652531
www.ballymaloe.ie

Opening hours..Open 7 days
Credit cards...Accepted
Price range...Expensive
Style...Smart casual
Cuisine...Irish
Recommended for..Breakfast

'They take breakfast very seriously here. Organic porridge and hot breakfasts with free-range bacon and sausages and eggs from the farm.'—Ross Lewis

Not many people know this: you don't need to be staying at Ballymaloe, the renowned country house of the Allen family, to go for breakfast there – a reservation will do. Most of the produce is from their 160-hectare (400-acre) organic farm and just about everything is home-made. Breakfast includes soda bread and scones, and home-made muesli and yogurt, which can be piled up with seasonal fruit such as rhubarb, gooseberries, pears and apples. Eggs are from their own hens, the sausages are from Woodside, the black and white puddings (blood sausage) are from Rosscarbery, and there's always fresh fish from nearby Ballycotton.

CHAPTER ONE

Recommended by
Paul Flynn,
Niall McKenna

Basement of Writers Museum
18–19 Parnell Square
Dublin 1
County Dublin
Republic of Ireland
+353 18732266
www.chapteronerestaurant.com

Opening hours................................Closed Monday and Sunday
Credit cards...Accepted
Price range...Expensive
Style...Smart casual
Cuisine...Irish
Recommended for..Worth the travel

'True Irish hospitality at its best. You are greeted with a smile and you always feel the welcome. The food is seasonal and local and the service is impeccable.'
—Niall McKenna

Ross Lewis's restaurant beneath the Dublin Writer's Museum is a warm bastion of Irish hospitality at its very best. Housed in the basement of a handsome eighteenth-century townhouse, once the family home of John Jameson of the distilling dynasty, the dining room is a welcoming combination of exposed brickwork and sage-green carpet, its walls hung with work by emerging Irish artists. Lewis's menus champion the very best of Ireland's larder (pantry), with a penchant for pork, game and seafood in cooking that's both refined and generous. As befits the building's history, there's a lengthy list of Irish whiskeys for after dinner.

M & L CHINESE RESTAURANT

Recommended by
Ross Lewis

13 Cathedral Street
Dublin 1
County Dublin
Republic of Ireland
+353 18748038
www.mlchineserestaurant.com

Opening hours	Open 7 days
Credit cards	Not accepted
Price range	Affordable
Style	Casual
Cuisine	Szechuan
Recommended for	Late night

'Unexpected' is probably one of the better words to describe this inexpensive Szechuan restaurant, situated down one of Dublin's side streets, which is frequented by the Chinese community and more adventurous diners. For an authentic experience and the full Szechuan heat, either visit with a Chinese friend and order from the Chinese menu, or refuse vehemently to order from the English menu. Pointing to the more interesting dishes being demolished at other tables is one way of doing this, but if there's resistance, insist on 'original' Chinese food, so that the staff choose the dishes and you enjoy the pay-off of your perseverance.

L'ECRIVAIN

Recommended by
Ross Lewis

109a Lower Baggot Street
Dublin 2
County Dublin
Republic of Ireland
+353 16611919
www.lecrivain.com

Opening hours	Closed Sunday
Credit cards	Accepted
Price range	Expensive
Style	Smart casual
Cuisine	French
Recommended for	High end

'It's run by chef Derry Clarke and his wife, Sally Anne, who are building on over twenty-five years of tradition yet still serving first-class food in a warm and friendly environment.'—Ross Lewis

Derry Clarke's established canteen to the Dublin establishment occupies a pair of Georgian coach houses in a courtyard mews off Lower Baggot Street. His sensible response to Ireland's economic ructions was to introduce a three-course lunch menu for a

rather reasonable €35 (£29; $48). However, you can still indulge yourself like the Celtic Tiger is ever roaring, as opposed to purring apologetically, with a multi-course tasting menu and a wine list that continues to list magnums of vintage Grands Crus. As always, the cooking showcases the kitchen's fine French technique let loose on the best Irish produce.

THE GREENHOUSE DUBLIN

Recommended by
Ultan Cooke, Paul
Flynn, Jp McMahon

Dawson Street
Dublin 2
County Dublin
Republic of Ireland
+353 16767015
www.thegreenhouserestaurant.ie

Opening hours	Closed Monday and Sunday
Credit cards	Accepted
Price range	Expensive
Style	Smart casual
Cuisine	Modern Irish
Recommended for	High end

'I don't get to Dublin much but The Greenhouse is first class and well worth the trip. It's one to watch – a few more accolades are definitely due.'—Ultan Cooke

RESTAURANT PATRICK GUILBAUD

Recommended by
Paul Flynn

21 Upper Merrion Street
Dublin 2
County Dublin
Republic of Ireland
+353 16764192
www.restaurantpatrickguilbaud.ie

Opening hours	Closed Monday and Sunday
Credit cards	Accepted
Price range	Expensive
Style	Smart casual
Cuisine	Modern French
Recommended for	High end

THE TROCADERO

Recommended by
Kevin Thornton

4 Saint Andrew Street
Dublin 2
County Dublin
Republic of Ireland
+353 16775545
www.trocadero.ie

Opening hours	Open 7 days
Credit cards	Accepted
Price range	Affordable
Style	Smart casual
Cuisine	European
Recommended for	Local favourite

'Late night, great food and staff.'—Kevin Thornton

Long a haunt of Dublin's literati and thespians, the 'Troc' is probably the most nostalgic restaurant in town, filled with old-time showbiz glamour. Liberty-style lampshades, gilt mirrors, bordello-red upholstery and photo-lined walls create a decadent feel, and with the legendary Robert Doggett running the show front of house, the atmosphere is more clubby than restaurant. As the Olympia Theatre is nearby, the pre-theatre menu is popular, but the real action starts later in the evening with people, who all seem to know each other, dropping into the bar or tucking into unpretentious food such as grilled steak and sole on the bone.

VINTAGE COCKTAIL CLUB

Recommended by
Kevin Thornton

15 Crown Alley
Dublin 2
County Dublin
Republic of Ireland
+353 167553547
www.vintagecocktailclub.com

Opening hours	Open 7 days
Credit cards	Accepted
Price range	Affordable
Style	Casual
Cuisine	Irish
Recommended for	Late night

'It's a cool place.'—Kevin Thornton

AVOCA FOOD MARKET & SALT CAFÉ

Recommended by
Kevin Thornton

11a The Crescent
Monkstown
County Dublin
Republic of Ireland
+353 12020230
www.avoca.ie

Opening hours	Open 7 days
Credit cards	Accepted
Price range	Affordable
Style	Casual
Cuisine	Café-Bistro-Deli
Recommended for	Regular neighbourhood

'Family-run restaurant.'—Kevin Thornton

THAT'S AMORE

Recommended by
Ross Lewis

107 Monkstown Road
Monkstown
County Dublin
Republic of Ireland
+353 12845400
www.thatsamoremonkstown.ie

Opening hours	Open 7 days
Credit cards	Accepted
Price range	Affordable
Style	Casual
Cuisine	Italian Bistro
Recommended for	Regular neighbourhood

'Small neighbourhood Italian restaurant run by Marco Valeri and Silvia Leo. Homely atmosphere and they serve good, fresh pasta and pizza.'—Ross Lewis

OWENMORE RESTAURANT

Recommended by
Ultan Cooke

Ballynahinch Castle Hotel
Recess
Connemara
County Galway
Republic of Ireland
+353 9531006
www.ballynahinch-castle.com

Opening hours	Open 7 days
Credit cards	Accepted
Price range	Expensive
Style	Smart casual
Cuisine	Modern Irish
Recommended for	High end

'Set in the unique location of Ballynahinch Castle, it has the whole package with a first-class restaurant. Whenever I can sneak off, this is where I go.'
—Ultan Cooke

ARD BIA AT NIMMOS

Recommended by
Jp McMahon

Spanish Arch
Long Walk
Galway
County Galway
Republic of Ireland
+353 91561114
www.ardbia.com

Opening hours	Open 7 days
Credit cards	Accepted but not AMEX
Price range	Affordable
Style	Casual
Cuisine	Café-Bistro
Recommended for	Breakfast

'Producer-focused menu, wonderful ambience, great location.'—Jp McMahon

ASIAN TEA HOUSE

Recommended by
Ultan Cooke

15 Mary Street
Galway
County Galway
Republic of Ireland
+353 91563749
www.asianteahouse.ie

Opening hours	Closed Tuesday in winter months
Credit cards	Accepted
Price range	Affordable
Style	Casual
Cuisine	Pan-Asian
Recommended for	Late night

'An award-winning Asian restaurant with some real classics that always hit the spot.'—Ultan Cooke

GALWAY FARMERS MARKET

Recommended by
Jp McMahon

Beside St Nicholas's Church
Shop Street
Galway
County Galway
Republic of Ireland
www.galwaymarket.com

Opening hours	Closed Monday to Friday
Reservation policy	No
Credit cards	Not accepted
Price range	Budget
Style	Casual
Cuisine	Street Food
Recommended for	Bargain

'I really enjoy the street food from this market by St Nicholas's Church. There's loads of great food, from falafels to sushi.'—Jp McMahon

KAI CAFÉ & RESTAURANT

Recommended by
Ultan Cooke, Jp McMahon,
Kevin Thornton

20 Sea Road
Galway
County Galway
Republic of Ireland
+353 91526003
www.kaicaferestaurant.com

Opening hours	Open 7 days
Credit cards	Accepted
Price range	Affordable
Style	Casual
Cuisine	Modern Irish
Recommended for	Regular neighbourhood

'Run by Kiwi chef Jess Murphy, Kai is a charming restaurant focusing on local produce and it never fails to wow with real passionate cooking.'—Ultan Cooke

KAPPA-YA

Recommended by
Ultan Cooke

4 Middle Street
Galway
County Galway
Republic of Ireland
+353 91865930
www.kappa-ya.com

Opening hours	Closed Sunday
Credit cards	Accepted but not AMEX
Price range	Affordable
Style	Casual
Cuisine	Japanese
Recommended for	Bargain

'A small Japanese place with some amazing dishes. It's real value for money and, although often quiet, it's where you will find chefs from other restaurants eating lunch on their day off.'—Ultan Cooke

SHERIDANS CHEESEMONGERS

Recommended by
Jp McMahon

14 Church Yard Street
Galway
County Galway
Republic of Ireland
+353 91564832
www.sheridanscheesemongers.com

Opening hours	Closed Monday and Sunday
Reservation policy	No
Credit cards	Accepted but not AMEX
Price range	Affordable
Style	Casual
Cuisine	Bar-Small plates
Recommended for	Late night

'Great wines, fantastic cured Irish meat and artisan raw-milk cheeses from Ireland.'—Jp McMahon

UPSTAIRS@MCCAMBRIDGE'S

Recommended by
Ultan Cooke

McCambridge's of Galway
38–39 Shop Street
Galway
County Galway
Republic of Ireland
+353 91562259
www.mccambridges.com

Opening hours	Open 7 days
Credit cards	Accepted
Price range	Budget
Style	Casual
Cuisine	Café-Bistro-Deli
Recommended for	Breakfast

'An old general store and deli that recently opened a restaurant upstairs, which specalizes in simple hearty fare and seems to get it right on all the little things that count. Their brunch offerings are fantastic.' —Ultan Cooke

THE HOUSE RESTAURANT

Recommended by
Paul Flynn

Cliff House Hotel
Middle Road
Ardmore
County Waterford
Republic of Ireland
+353 2487800
www.thecliffhousehotel.com

Opening hours	Closed Monday and Sunday
Credit cards	Accepted
Price range	Expensive
Style	Smart casual
Cuisine	Modern Irish
Recommended for	Regular neighbourhood

'One of Ireland's greatest hotel experiences. The food and the view are both spectacular.'—Paul Flynn

GENOA'S TAKEAWAY

Recommended by
Paul Flynn

30 Gratten Square
Dungarvan
County Waterford
Republic of Ireland
+353 5843539

Opening hours	Open 7 days
Reservation policy	No
Credit cards	Not accepted
Price range	Budget
Style	Casual
Cuisine	Fast Food
Recommended for	Late night

'I love their battered sausages.'—Paul Flynn

THE SHAMROCK RESTAURANT

Recommended by
Paul Flynn

4 O'Connell Street
Dungarvan
County Waterford
Republic of Ireland
+353 5842242

Opening hours	Closed Sunday
Credit cards	Accepted but not AMEX
Price range	Budget
Style	Casual
Cuisine	Irish
Recommended for	Breakfast

'Proper, no-nonsense food and always a genuine welcome.'—Paul Flynn

L'ATMOSPHERE

Recommended by
Paul Flynn

19 Henrietta Street
Waterford
County Waterford
Republic of Ireland
+353 51858426
www.restaurant-latmosphere.com

Opening hours	Open 7 days
Credit cards	Accepted but not AMEX
Price range	Affordable
Style	Casual
Cuisine	French Bistro
Recommended for	Bargain

'The best French bistro classics in Ireland.'—Paul Flynn

THE FATTED CALF

Recommended by
Jp McMahon

Glasson
Athlone
County Westmeath
Republic of Ireland
+353 906485208
www.thefattedcalf.ie

Opening hours	Closed Monday and Tuesday
Credit cards	Accepted
Price range	Affordable
Style	Casual
Cuisine	Bar-Bistro
Recommended for	Local favourite

'It's a great place to stop off at when travelling between Galway and Dublin. It has a farmer-focused menu, there's attention to seasonal and local produce, and a gastropub ambience.'—Jp McMahon

The midlands is not renowned as the culinary centre of Ireland, but since taking over the Village Inn pub in 2010, Feargal O'Donnell has given the cross-country driver a reason to stop. With roaring fires and bare wooden tables, The Fatted Calf exudes an authentic, old-world charm, and the hearty food, which has a strong Irish focus, follows in the same vein. Their home-raised Tamworth pigs feature strongly on the menu with traditional dishes like crispy crubeens made from pigs' trotters (feet), pulled pork, pork belly, home-cured ham and McGeogh's black puddings (blood sausages). Plus there's an impressive selection of Irish craft beers.

'Zeeland mussels, lobster and oysters, all prepared in a pure and beautiful manner.'

SERGIO HERMAN P395

NETHERLANDS

'THE BAR IS A BIG PARTY WITH THE BEST COCKTAILS YOU'VE EVER HAD. THE FOOD IS REALLY CREATIVE AND LIGHT. IT IS A PLEASURE TO EAT THE SEXY FOOD.'

ARJAN WENNEKES P395

'Calf's liver and fried eel'

JONNIE BOER P394

'ALWAYS VIBRATING WITH ACTION.'

JULIUS JASPERS P404

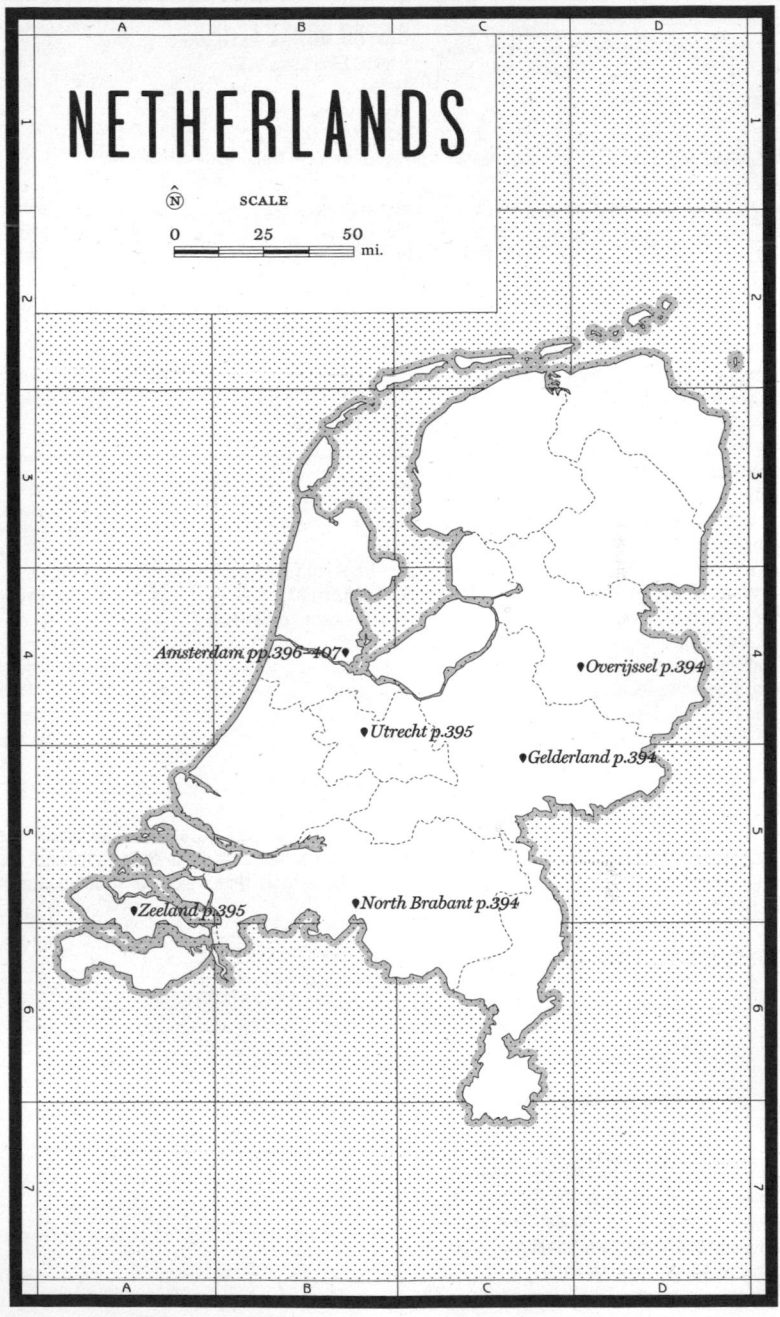

NETHERLANDS

N

SCALE

0   25   50
mi.

●Amsterdam pp.396–407

●Overijssel p.394

●Utrecht p.395

●Gelderland p.394

●Zeeland p.395

●North Brabant p.394

DE LEEST

Kerkweg 1
Vaassen
Gelderland 8171 VT
+31 578571382
www.restaurantdeleest.nl

Opening hours	Closed Monday and Sunday
Credit cards	Accepted
Price range	Expensive
Style	Smart casual
Cuisine	Modern European
Recommended for	Worth the travel

'It's just one hour away from Amsterdam. Jakob is a great chef. It's worth the trip!'—Andreas Caminada

Husband and wife team Jacob Jan Boerma and Kim Veldman have transformed an old shoemaker's shop in the sleepy Dutch town of Vaassen into a hive of gastronomic creativity. Still a best-kept secret outside the Netherlands – in spite of its three Michelin stars – their restaurant De Leest (est. 2002) is relaxed, modern and understated: all the better to enjoy Boerma's visually arresting cooking. The well-travelled chef has classical roots and relishes luxury ingredients, but his style is light, adventurous and global. Locally foraged sea vegetables, innovative techniques and honest hospitality define the experience. The lunch menu is famously good value.

AVANT-GARDE VAN GROENINGE

Philips Stadion
Frederiklaan 10d
Eindhoven
North Brabant 5616 NH
+31 402505640
www.restaurantavantgarde.nl

Opening hours	Closed Monday and Sunday
Credit cards	Accepted
Price range	Expensive
Style	Smart casual
Cuisine	Contemporary French
Recommended for	Worth the travel

'I was initially intrigued because this Michelin-starred restaurant is located in PSV Eindhoven's Philips football stadium with views of the pitch. Technically the food was really strong and the flavours were spot on. A very impressive restaurant.'—Marc Fosh

BISTRO BONNE FEMME

Samuel Hirschstraat 5
Zwolle
Overijssel 8011 PT
+31 384222780
www.bistrobonnefemme.nl

Opening hours	Open 7 days
Credit cards	Accepted but not AMEX
Price range	Affordable
Style	Casual
Cuisine	French Bistro
Recommended for	Regular neighbourhood

'It's a classic French bistro where they serve quick and easy dishes. I regularly eat calf's liver and fried eel.'—Jonnie Boer

RESTAURANT DE LIBRIJE

Broerenkerkplein 13–15
Zwolle
Overijssel 8011 TW
+31 384212083
www.restaurantdelibrije.nl

Opening hours	Closed Monday and Sunday
Credit cards	Accepted
Price range	Expensive
Style	Smart casual
Cuisine	Modern European
Recommended for	High end

'There's no better food and service than here. Fantastic wine list, great menus and à la carte and always the feeling you're more than welcome. '—Julius Jaspers

JASMIJN & IK

Recommended by
Michael Wolf

Kanaalstraat 219
Utrecht
Utrecht 3531 CH
+31 302938907
www.jasmijnenik.nl

Opening hours..............................Closed Monday and Tuesday
Credit cards...Accepted
Price range...Affordable
Style...Smart casual
Cuisine...Asian
Recommended for..............................Regular neighbourhood

'It's an Asian restaurant with small dishes and fresh ingredients. I really like the sweet-and-sour taste of their dishes. They do about forty covers, which makes it really cosy and relaxed.'—Michael Wolf

PURE C

Recommended by
Peter Goossens,
Cyril Molard, Markus
Mraz, Arjan Wennekes,
Michael Wolf

Strand Hotel
Boulevard de Wielingen 49
Cadzand
Zeeland 4506 JK
+31 117396036
www.sergioherman.com

Opening hours..............................Closed Monday and Tuesday
Credit cards...Accepted
Price range...Expensive
Style...Smart casual
Cuisine..Modern European
Recommended for...Worth the travel

'The bar is a big party with the best cocktails you've ever had. The food is really creative and light. It is a pleasure to eat the sexy food.'—Arjan Wennekes

The beach at wind-whipped Cadzand in Zeeland is the setting for Pure C, Sergio Herman's style-conscious 'resto bar'. 'A little like Ibiza on the North Sea,' muses Herman, Holland's top chef and winner of three Michelin stars at Oud Sluis, which closed in 2013. Herman and his protégé Syrco Bakker have created a sexily futuristic destination restaurant at the Strandhotel, with food that won its own star within a year of the restaurant's 2010 launch. Pure C is hip and youthful – the chefs' 'whites' are by G-Star – but Bakker's audacious Zeeland-meets-Asia style, rich in sea vegetables and North Sea seafood, is serious, grown-up stuff.

AUBERGE DES MOULES

Recommended by
Sergio Herman

Visserslaan 3
Philippine
Zeeland 4553 BE
+31 115491265
www.aubergedesmoules.com

Opening hours...Closed Monday
Credit cards...Accepted
Price range...Affordable
Style...Smart casual
Cuisine..Seafood
Recommended for...Local favourite

'This restaurant works with regional specialities from the sea, such as Zeeland mussels, lobster and oysters, all prepared in a pure and beautiful manner.' —Sergio Herman

Zeelanders take their mussels very seriously: in Philippine, as elsewhere throughout the province, a statue immortalizing the mollusc holds pride of place in the village square. Accordingly, although small, the town boasts about as many mussel restaurants as inhabitants – the first among them being this relaxed but upmarket venture, of forty years' standing, which is steeped in the local fishermen's culture. Photos of the town during its days as a thriving port adorn the walls, and although that's no longer the case, juicy mussels are still brought in fresh twice a day. Locals rub elbows with visitors from nearby Belgium.

'Sitting by the window for dinner looking at the boats on the Amstel River is a real moment of happiness for me.'
ARJAN WENNEKES P404

NICOLAS DE VISCH P402

AMSTERDAM

'DESSERTS WITH BACON OR CHICKEN. IT'S WEIRD BUT VERY COOL.'
ARJAN WENNEKES P404

'The food is botanically inspired and the concept is fantastic.'
STEFANO BAIOCCO P401

'New Amsterdam cuisine with a local vegetable garden.'
ROBERT KRANENBORG P406

'IT'S THE PLACE TO BE IN AMSTERDAM FOR A WAKE-UP BREAKFAST.'
ONNO KOKMEIJER P406

AMSTERDAM

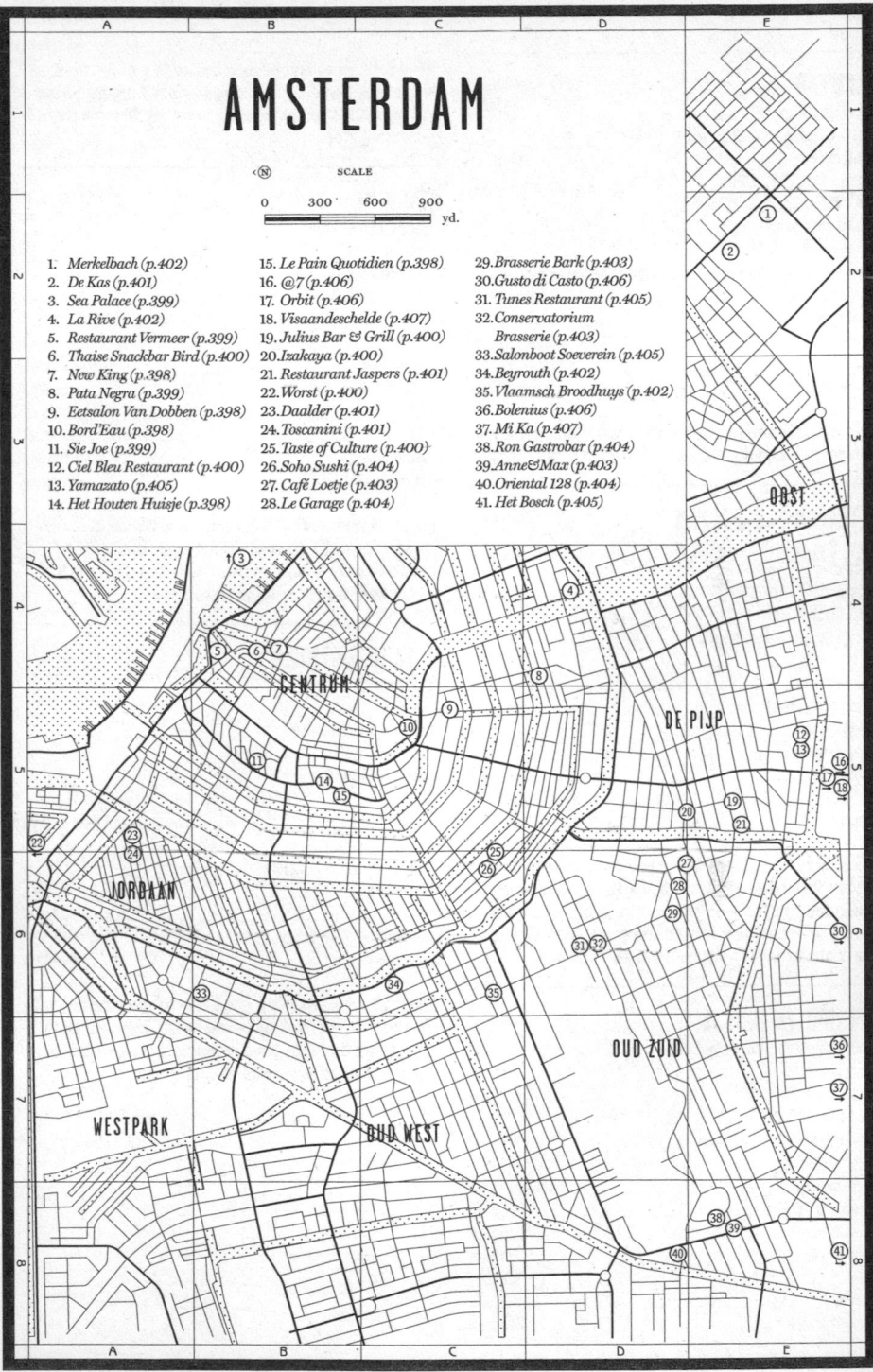

N

SCALE

0   300   600   900
yd.

OOST

CENTRUM

DE PIJP

JORDAAN

OUD ZUID

WESTPARK

OUD WEST

BORD'EAU

Recommended by
Robert Kranenborg

Hotel de L'Europe
Nieuwe Doelenstraat 2–14
Centrum
Amsterdam 1012 CP
+31 205311777
www.bordeau.nl

Opening hours	Closed Monday and Sunday
Credit cards	Accepted
Price range	Expensive
Style	Smart casual
Cuisine	Modern French
Recommended for	High end

'Two Michelin stars in two-and-a-half years, great style of food, service and ambience.'—Robert Kranenborg

EETSALON VAN DOBBEN

Recommended by
Jean Beddington,
Onno Kokmeijer

Korte Reguliersdwardsstraat 5–7–9
Centrum
Amsterdam 1017 BH
+31 206244200
www.eetsalonvandobben.nl

Opening hours	Open 7 days
Reservation policy	No
Credit cards	Not accepted
Price range	Budget
Style	Casual
Cuisine	Dutch
Recommended for	Local favourite

'There are many places where you can get good sandwiches, however, this is by far the most famous one in the city. The food's always fresh and of a high quality. Add the quick service and you'll know why it is so popular with locals.'—Onno Kokmeijer

HET HOUTEN HUISJE

Recommended by
Michael Wolf

Nieuwezijds Voorburgwal 289
Centrum
Amsterdam 1012 RL
+31 206256542
www.hethoutenhuisje.com

Opening hours	Open 7 days
Reservation policy	No
Credit cards	Accepted
Price range	Budget
Style	Casual
Cuisine	Café
Recommended for	Bargain

'It's a little wooden house in the middle of Amsterdam where they serve organic chips (fries), burgers, wraps and juices. It's run by a family and they all work there.' —Michael Wolf

NEW KING

Recommended by
Julius Jaspers,
Michael Wolf

Zeedijk 115–117
Centrum
Amsterdam 1012 AV
+31 206252180
www.newking.nl

Opening hours	Open 7 days
Credit cards	Accepted
Price range	Budget
Style	Casual
Cuisine	Chinese
Recommended for	Bargain

'Steamed buns with Peking duck and hoisin, steamed *har kau* (prawn [shrimp] dumplings), fried *sui kau* (pork and prawn dumplings)... delicious dim sum for a couple of euros.'—Julius Jaspers

LE PAIN QUOTIDIEN

Recommended by
Bas Wiegel

Spuistraat 266
Centrum
Amsterdam 1012 VW
+31 206222555
www.lepainquotidien.nl

Opening hours	Open 7 days
Reservation policy	No
Credit cards	Accepted
Price range	Budget
Style	Casual
Cuisine	Café-Bakery
Recommended for	Breakfast

'Opens at 7.00 a.m. It's a good way to start the day with a fresh breakfast: freshly baked bread, fresh fruits... I like the fact that they keep it simple. It's also nice to visit with the family.'—Bas Wiegel

PATA NEGRA

Recommended by
Arjan Wennekes

Utrechtsestraat 124
Centrum
Amsterdam 1017 VT
+31 204226250
www.pata-negra.nl

Opening hours	Open 7 days
Credit cards	Accepted
Price range	Affordable
Style	Casual
Cuisine	Spanish Tapas
Recommended for	Late night

'For me, this is the best tapas bar in town. Always busy and a joyful place to be. Sit down at the bar and let the cooks surprise you.'—Arjan Wennekes

SEA PALACE

Recommended by
Arjan Wennekes

Oosterdokskade 8
Centrum
Amsterdam 1011 AE
+31 206264777
www.seapalace.nl

Opening hours	Open 7 days
Credit cards	Accepted
Price range	Affordable
Style	Casual
Cuisine	Chinese
Recommended for	Bargain

'The dim sum lunch is nice. Go there with your friends and order the whole dim sum and steamed bun menu.'
—Arjan Wennekes

RESTAURANT VERMEER

Recommended by
Bas Wiegel

Prins Hendrikkade 59–72
Centrum
Amsterdam 1012 AD
+31 205564885
www.restaurantvermeer.nl

Opening hours	Closed Sunday
Credit cards	Accepted
Price range	Expensive
Style	Smart casual
Cuisine	Modern European
Recommended for	Local favourite

'I really like and appreciate their way of using local products like fish, meat and of course the vegetables.'
—Bas Wiegel

Named after Johannes Vermeer, the Dutch painter of middle-class life, this spacious restaurant unravels beyond the facades of the tall old houses of five-star hotel NH Barbizon Palace (opposite Centraal station). Michelin-starred Christopher Naylor, who trained with Albert Roux, cares for vegetables, particularly evident in his seasonal vegetable casserole. Dishes on the seven-course From the Land menu include oysters with manzanilla, avocado, yogurt and cucumber purée, then braised/glazed veal cheek with apricot, cabbage and ponzu. Coffee soufflé with lemongrass/lemon sorbet is a standout dessert from the à la carte. Competitive pricing of both food and wine list, helpfully packaged by sommelier Simon Veldman, makes Vermeer a favourite with Amsterdammers.

SIE JOE

Recommended by
Agus Hermawan

Gravenstraat 24a
Centrum
Amsterdam 1012 NM
+31 206241830
www.siejoe.com

Opening hours	Closed Sunday
Reservation policy	No
Credit cards	Not accepted
Price range	Budget
Style	Casual
Cuisine	Indonesian
Recommended for	Bargain

'Indonesian restaurants have become a real Dutch phenomenon and Sie Joe reminds us why.'
—Agus Hermawan

Run by the same Chinese-Indonesian family for over twenty years, the tiny, unassuming Sie Joe is a commendably authentic little slice of Jakarta and a welcome change from the myriad *rijsttafel* joints that are more common round these parts. The short menu of Indonesian classics (think satays and nasi goreng) contains nothing over €10 (£8; $14), is all generously proportioned and served with a familiar family touch. With only fifteen covers, and no reservations taken, finding a spot at popular times can be a struggle, but for the price you can barely do better in Amsterdam.

TASTE OF CULTURE

Recommended by
Julius Jaspers

Korte Leidsedwarsstraat 139–141
Centrum
Amsterdam 1017 PZ
+31 204271136
www.tasteofculture.net

Opening hours	Open 7 days
Credit cards	Accepted but not AMEX
Price range	Affordable
Style	Casual
Cuisine	Chinese
Recommended for	Late night

'The best Chinese food in the city after 9.00 p.m., and open until very late.'—Julius Jaspers

THAISE SNACKBAR BIRD

Recommended by
Jonnie Boer

Zeedijk 77
Centrum
Amsterdam 1012 AS
+31 204206289
www.thai-bird.nl

Opening hours	Open 7 days
Reservation policy	No
Credit cards	Not accepted
Price range	Budget
Style	Casual
Cuisine	Thai
Recommended for	Bargain

'A cafeteria that serves delicious Thai food.'
—Jonnie Boer

WORST

Recommended by
Robert Kranenborg

Barentszstraat 171
Centrum
Amsterdam 1013 NM
+31 206256167
www.deworst.nl

Opening hours	Closed Monday
Credit cards	Accepted but not AMEX
Price range	Affordable
Style	Casual
Cuisine	Bar-Bistro
Recommended for	Breakfast

'Wine bar with the best charcuterie.'
—Robert Kranenborg

CIEL BLEU RESTAURANT

Recommended by
Bas Wiegel

Hotel Okura
Ferdinand Bolstraat 333
De Pijp
Amsterdam 1072 LH
+31 206787450
www.cielbleu.nl

Opening hours	Closed Sunday
Credit cards	Accepted
Price range	Expensive
Style	Smart casual
Cuisine	Modern French
Recommended for	High end

'A really special place. Amazing flavours and creations. I think it's one of the best in Amsterdam.'—Bas Wiegel

IZAKAYA

Recommended by
Robert Kranenborg

Sir Albert Hotel
Albert Cuypstraat 2–6
De Pijp
Amsterdam 1072 CT
+31 203053090
www.izakaya-amsterdam.com

Opening hours	Open 7 days
Credit cards	Accepted
Price range	Affordable
Style	Casual
Cuisine	Modern Japanese
Recommended for	Wish I'd opened

'Asian dishes but not traditional.'—Robert Kranenborg

JULIUS BAR & GRILL

Recommended by
Robert Kranenborg

Ceintuurbaan 256–260
De Pijp
Amsterdam 1072 GH
+31 203446406
www.juliusbargrill.nl

Opening hours	Open 7 days
Credit cards	Accepted
Price range	Affordable
Style	Casual
Cuisine	Barbeque
Recommended for	Late night

'A barbeque specialist.'—Robert Kranenborg

RESTAURANT JASPERS
Ceintuurbaan 196
De Pijp
Amsterdam 1072 GC
+31 204715233
www.restaurantjaspers.com

Opening hours	Closed Monday and Sunday
Credit cards	Accepted
Price range	Affordable
Style	Smart casual
Cuisine	Modern European
Recommended for	Regular neighbourhood

'This place is not too big and the food served is fresh and flavoursome. I like it because the service has a personal touch, it's friendly and the food is good. It's a perfect evening out.'—Bas Wiegel

DAALDER
Lindengracht 90
Jordaan
Amsterdam 1015 KK
+31 206248864
www.daalderamsterdam.nl

Recommended by
Michael Wolf

Opening hours	Open 7 days
Credit cards	Accepted
Price range	Affordable
Style	Casual
Cuisine	Modern European
Recommended for	Local favourite

'It's the coolest place in Amsterdam. The food is really modern – you wouldn't expect it to be because the restaurant looks like an old café but it is.'
—Michael Wolf

TOSCANINI
Lindengracht 75
Jordaan
Amsterdam 1015 KD
+31 206232813
www.restauranttoscanini.nl

Recommended by
Agus Hermawan,
Robert Kranenborg

Opening hours	Closed Sunday
Credit cards	Accepted
Price range	Affordable
Style	Casual
Cuisine	Italian
Recommended for	Local favourite

'Classic Italian kitchen and ambience.'
—Robert Kranenborg

DE KAS
Kamerlingh Onneslaan 3
Oost
Amsterdam 1097 DE
+31 204624562
www.restaurantdekas.nl

Recommended by
Stefano Baiocco

Opening hours	Closed Sunday
Credit cards	Accepted
Price range	Affordable
Style	Smart casual
Cuisine	Mediterranean
Recommended for	Wish I'd opened

'The restaurant is situated inside an early-twentieth-century conservatory. The food is botanically inspired and the concept is fantastic.'—Stefano Baiocco

Saved from the wrecking ball and soulless redevelopment by chef Gert Jan Hageman, this municipal nursery on the southern edge of Amsterdam opened as his restaurant in 2001. The restored 1926 hothouse, its brick chimney preserved, is now a spacious modern dining room showered with natural light. Given the setting, Hagemen decided the best way forward was to become a grower, with vegetables and herbs for the seriously seasonal, Mediterranean-inspired menu either grown on site or on their own land about 10 km (6 miles) away. Book the chef's table for a tasting menu that makes the most of all those fresh vegetables and herbs.

MERKELBACH

Recommended by
Bas Wiegel

Middenweg 72
Oost
Amsterdam 1097 BS
+31 206650880
www.huizefrankendael.nl

Opening hours	Open 7 days
Credit cards	Accepted but not cash
Price range	Affordable
Style	Casual
Cuisine	Modern European
Recommended for	Bargain

'A really nice building located in a park. A tasty meal with good ingredients.'—Bas Wiegel

Chef Geert Burema, an advocate of the Slow Food movement, offers very reasonably priced all-day menus at Merkelbach, which is situated in the restored coach house of a historic summer palace turned art gallery and events space. Dishes range from a simple breakfast croissant or sweetly flavoured *suikerbrood* bread with butter (€2.50; £2; $3), to steak tartare with piquillo and Espelette peppers for lunch, and a three-course set dinner for under €30 (£25; $41) featuring Burema's market fish with saffron, lemon confit, capers, *cime di rapa*, anchovies and potato. Overlooking the grandeur of Frankendael Park's formal gardens, a table on the terrace is particularly sought after.

LA RIVE

Recommended by
Jean Beddington,
Nicolas De Visch

Intercontinental Hotel
Professor Tulpplein 1
Oost
Amsterdam 1018 GX
+31 205203264
www.restaurantlarive.nl

Opening hours	Open 7 days
Credit cards	Accepted
Price range	Expensive
Style	Smart casual
Cuisine	Fusion
Recommended for	Worth the travel

'Sitting by the window for dinner looking at the boats on the Amstel River is a real moment of happiness for me. Having the Dover sole fillet with local grey prawns (shrimp), simple but so good.'—Nicolas De Visch

BEYROUTH

Recommended by
Jean Beddington

Kinkerstraat 18
Oud West
Amsterdam 1053 DV
+31 206160635
www.restaurant-beyrouth.nl

Opening hours	Open 7 days
Credit cards	Accepted but not AMEX
Price range	Affordable
Style	Casual
Cuisine	Lebanese
Recommended for	Regular neighbourhood

'Really good mezzes.'—Jean Beddington

VLAAMSCH BROODHUYS

Recommended by
Michael Wolf

Eerste Constantijn Huygensstraat 64
Oud West
Amsterdam 1054 BR
+31 206899131
www.vlaamschbroodhuys.nl

Opening hours	Open 7 days
Reservation policy	No
Credit cards	Accepted but not cash
Price range	Budget
Style	Casual
Cuisine	Café-Bakery
Recommended for	Breakfast

'It's a bakery with different sandwiches but also a lot of sweet things. Their bread is really good and fresh. Sometimes I take it home but I'll often enjoy it there. Usually I eat their bread with a sweet topping; their jam is amazing and of course it's home-made.'
—Michael Wolf

ANNE&MAX

Amstelveenseweg 196
Oud Zuid
Amsterdam 1075 XS
+31 207549436
www.annemax.nl

Opening hours	Open 7 days
Reservation policy	No
Credit cards	Not accepted
Price range	Affordable
Style	Casual
Cuisine	Café
Recommended for	Breakfast

'Great coffee and healthy food – their daily-changing salads are low on calories. Also, the service is friendly.'
—Agus Hermawan

BRASSERIE BARK

Van Baerlestraat 120
Oud Zuid
Amsterdam 1071 BD
+31 206750210
www.bark.nl

Opening hours	Open 7 days
Credit cards	Accepted
Price range	Affordable
Style	Casual
Cuisine	Brasserie
Recommended for	Late night

'This is a famous restaurant in the museum quarter of Amsterdam. The kitchen is open until midnight for fresh seafood dishes.'—Onno Kokmeijer

Chef-owner Peter Janssen's busy Parisian-style brasserie is very popular with concertgoers before and after the main event (his kitchen stays open until half-past midnight). The dark banquettes at this corner site flank big windows. Janssen concentrates on crustaceans, such as North Sea crab, lobster (decadently served with Canadian scallops), native and rock oysters on ice and Dutch shrimp cocktail. Just add Muscadet. Fleshier fish includes salmon (smoked with wasabi mayonnaise), Dover sole meunière, swordfish steaks and tuna sashimi. From the land, there are veal kidneys with mustard sauce, braised rabbit and lamb roulade. Finish with parfait of prunes with Armagnac.

CAFÉ LOETJE

Johannes Vermeerstraat 52
Oud Zuid
Amsterdam 1071 DT
+31 206628173
amsterdam.loetje.com

Opening hours	Open 7 days
Credit cards	Accepted but not AMEX
Price range	Affordable
Style	Casual
Cuisine	European
Recommended for	Wish I'd opened

'They only serve steaks of the highest quality and at moderate prices. The steaks are served in three shifts in the evening, a concept that is increasingly popular in the Netherlands.'—Onno Kokmeijer

CONSERVATORIUM BRASSERIE

Conservatorium Hotel
Van Baerlestraat 27
Oud Zuid
Amsterdam 1071 AN
+31 205700000
www.conservatoriumhotel.com

Opening hours	Open 7 days
Credit cards	Accepted
Price range	Affordable
Style	Casual
Cuisine	French Brasserie
Recommended for	Breakfast

'Wonderful location.'—Jean Beddington

LE GARAGE

Ruysdaelstraat 54–56
Oud Zuid
Amsterdam 1071 XE
+31 206797176
www.restaurantlegarage.nl

Opening hours	Open 7 days
Credit cards	Accepted
Price range	Affordable
Style	Casual
Cuisine	International
Recommended for	Local favourite

'Great food for almost twenty-five years, international à la carte with a French touch. Former patron Joop Braakhekke is a national symbol of hospitality, his successor, Erwin Walthaus, no less so. Always vibrating with action, great people-watching, see and be seen. Try the tuna pizza and the ribeye. Best crème brûlée in town.'—Julius Jaspers

ORIENTAL 128

Amstelveenseweg 128
Oud Zuid
Amsterdam 1075 XL
+31 206392090
www.oriental128.nl

Opening hours	Closed Monday
Credit cards	Accepted
Price range	Affordable
Style	Casual
Cuisine	Chinese
Recommended for	Regular neighbourhood

'The best Chinese restaurant in the neighbourhood. Serves great wine and has a classy atmosphere.'
—Agus Hermawan

RON GASTROBAR

Sophialaan 55
Oud Zuid
Amsterdam 1075 BP
+31 204961943
www.rongastrobar.nl

Opening hours	Open 7 days
Credit cards	Accepted
Price range	Affordable
Style	Casual
Cuisine	Small plates
Recommended for	Regular neighbourhood

'The food is very creative, the staff are young and dynamic and they always surprise me. They also serve desserts with bacon or chicken. It's weird but very cool.'—Arjan Wennekes

Sensing that guests craved a less formal atmosphere, in 2010 the then two-Michelin-starred chef Ron Blaauw dispensed with the linen tablecloths and sought to simplify his dishes. The re-launched Ron Gastrobar (now holding one Michelin star) is a friendly neighbourhood restaurant with almost all plates priced at €15 (£12; $21). After freshly baked bread humbly served in a paper bag, dishes include the wittily titled McFlurry of Foie Gras with tangerine, wagyu burger with grilled onions and tarragon sorrel cream, Ron's Cauliflower (an update of the traditional Dutch dish of meatballs and cauliflower) and pudding of barbecued banana with dulce de leche.

SOHO SUSHI

Lange Leidsedwarsstraat 33
Oud Zuid
Amsterdam 1017 NG
+31 204285858
www.sohosushi.nl

Opening hours	Open 7 days
Credit cards	Accepted
Price range	Affordable
Style	Casual
Cuisine	Sushi
Recommended for	Late night

'Serves a decent choice of fresh, home-made sushi for a light dinner or late-night snack in the city centre.'
—Agus Hermawan

TUNES RESTAURANT

Recommended by
Jean Beddington

Conservatorium Hotel
Van Baerlestraat 27
Oud Zuid
Amsterdam 1071 AN
+31 205700000
www.conservatoriumhotel.com

Opening hours	Closed Sunday
Credit cards	Accepted
Price range	Expensive
Style	Smart casual
Cuisine	Modern European
Recommended for	High end

'This place is going from strength to strength. The chef, Schilo van Coevorden, is a master of innovation and balance.'—Jean Beddington

YAMAZATO

Recommended by
Jean Beddington,
Onno Kokmeijer,
Iñigo Peña

Hotel Okura Amsterdam
Ferdinand Bolstraat 333
Oud Zuid
Amsterdam 1072 LH
+31 206787450
www.yamazato.nl

Opening hours	Open 7 days
Credit cards	Accepted
Price range	Expensive
Style	Smart casual
Cuisine	Japanese
Recommended for	High end

'This was the first traditional Japanese restaurant in Europe to be awarded a Michelin star, which is quite an achievement considering the down-to-earth eating culture for which the Netherlands is known. Yamazato is the best no-nonsense restaurant and a unique culinary experience.'—Onno Kokmeijer

Outside it's all canals and bicycles, but inside Yamazato you're transported to a very different world. With its modern take on *sukiya* (teahouse) decor, kimono-wearing serving staff and ornamental carp pond, you could be in Kyoto. This upmarket hotel restaurant was one of the first to introduce *kaiseki ryori*, or Japanese haute cuisine, to Western palates over thirty years ago. The traditional nine-course *hana kaiseki* set menu is the way to go here, but there's also an à la carte selection of sushi, sashimi and specialities such as grilled eel with *kabayaki* (sweet soy and mirin) sauce.

SALONBOOT SOEVEREIN

Recommended by
Onno Kokmeijer

Rederij Cruise with Us
Frederik Hendrikstraat 23 Hs
Westerpark
Amsterdam 1052 HJ
+31 207742764
www.cruisewithus.nl

Opening hours	By private arrangement
Credit cards	Accepted
Price range	Expensive
Style	Smart casual
Cuisine	European
Recommended for	High end

'Combining a tour in one of the old classic boats on the canals of Amsterdam with a private dinner is a unique and unforgettable experience.'—Onno Kokmeijer

HET BOSCH

Recommended by
Agus Hermawan

Jollenpad 10
Zuid
Amsterdam 1081 KC
+31 206445800
www.hetbosch.com

Opening hours	Closed Sunday
Credit cards	Accepted
Price range	Affordable
Style	Smart casual
Cuisine	Modern French
Recommended for	Wish I'd opened

'Nice location at the edge of the city, close to the Amsterdamse Bos, with a terrace at the waterside. The chef is my favourite in town.'—Agus Hermawan

ORBIT

Recommended by
Onno Kokmeijer

Scheldestraat 95
Zuid
Amsterdam 1078 GJ
+31 206722922
www.restaurantorbit.nl

Opening hours	Closed Monday
Credit cards	Accepted
Price range	Affordable
Style	Casual
Cuisine	Asian
Recommended for	Regular neighbourhood

'Orbit offers new Asian-style cuisine in a pleasant atmosphere with a nice balance between local and international guests.'—Onno Kokmeijer

@7

Recommended by
Onno Kokmeijer

Scheldestraat 92
Zuideramstel
Amsterdam 1078 GN
+31 0206709295
www.at7online.nl

Opening hours	Open 7 days
Credit cards	Accepted
Price range	Budget
Style	Casual
Cuisine	Café
Recommended for	Breakfast

'It's the place to be in Amsterdam for a wake-up breakfast. They serve a lovely espresso and very nice energising smoothies. Restaurant @7 is not only the perfect place for breakfast but also for lunch or a high tea.'—Onno Kokmeijer

@7 is so named because it serves food seven days a week and opens at 7.00 a.m. Monday to Friday. (The doors don't open until 8.00 a.m. and 9.00 a.m. on Saturday and Sunday mornings respectively.) It's a bright café serving fresh coffee, home-made apple pie and muffins, wild smoked fish and excellent brunch. But perhaps it's most famous for its Brazilian health shakes at around €5 (£4; $6) apiece. @7 is hugely dog- and child-friendly: they'll provide water and treats for pets and there's a special play area, with toys, for youngsters. Round the corner is Amstelpark, which has a kid's playground and a city farm.

BOLENIUS

Recommended by
Robert Kranenborg

George Gershwinlaan 30
Zuideramstel
Amsterdam 1082 MT
+31 204044411
www.bolenius-restaurant.nl

Opening hours	Closed Sunday
Credit cards	Accepted
Price range	Affordable
Style	Smart casual
Cuisine	Modern European
Recommended for	Local favourite

'New Amsterdam cuisine with a local vegetable garden.' —Robert Kranenborg

GUSTO DI CASTO

Recommended by
Arjan Wennekes

Van Leijenberghlaan 216
Zuideramstel
Amsterdam 1082 DC
+31 206448903
www.gustodicasto.nl

Opening hours	Open 7 days
Reservation policy	No
Credit cards	Accepted
Price range	Affordable
Style	Casual
Cuisine	Italian Deli-Café
Recommended for	Breakfast

'Every day they have the best Italian sandwiches. When you're there it feels like you're in Italy. Order the Capitalista or Quattro.'—Arjan Wennekes

MI KA

Buitenveldertselaan 158a
Zuideramstel
Amsterdam 1081 AB
+31 206614077

Opening hours	Closed Sunday
Reservation policy	No
Credit cards	Not accepted
Price range	Budget
Style	Casual
Cuisine	Asian
Recommended for	Bargain

'A nice mixture of traditional home-style dishes from Korea and Japan.'—Jean Beddington

VISAANDESCHELDE

Scheldeplein 4
Zuideramstel
Amsterdam 1078 GR
+31 206751583
www.visaandeschelde.nl

Opening hours	Open 7 days
Credit cards	Accepted
Price range	Affordable
Style	Smart casual
Cuisine	Seafood
Recommended for	High end

'Serves a wide variety of fresh, seasonal fish. A favourite for fish fans.'—Agus Hermawan

Chef Michiel Deenik's popular fish restaurant is easily reached, being opposite the RAI exhibition centre. Dinner features intricate three, four, five or eight-course menus (light lunches are also available). Dishes show Asian influences, such as the starter of shellfish salad with quinoa, which comes with *tom kha kai* and green curry marshmallow, and the surf and turf main of fried pike perch with braised pork belly, black pudding and fish gravy seasoned with Chinese five-spice. Also worth mentioning is the lavish oriental-style lobster with rice noodles, oriental vegetables and Malaysian sambal paste. Desserts, by contrast, are more straightforward—such as the pretty fusion of blood orange, fennel and almond sorbets.

'TRADITIONAL FLEMISH CUISINE IN A MODERN CLASSIC INTERIOR.'

SERGIO HERMAN P422

BELGIUM & LUXEMBOURG

'Art on a plate.'

FILIP CLAEYS P410

'It blew my mind. I had the most amazing sea bass ever, baked in a crust of broken oyster shells and seaweed.'

KOBE DESRAMAULTS P412

'FOR BREAKFAST, YOU CAN'T BEAT THEIR PISTOLET BELGE.'

SANG-HOON DEGEIMBRE P414

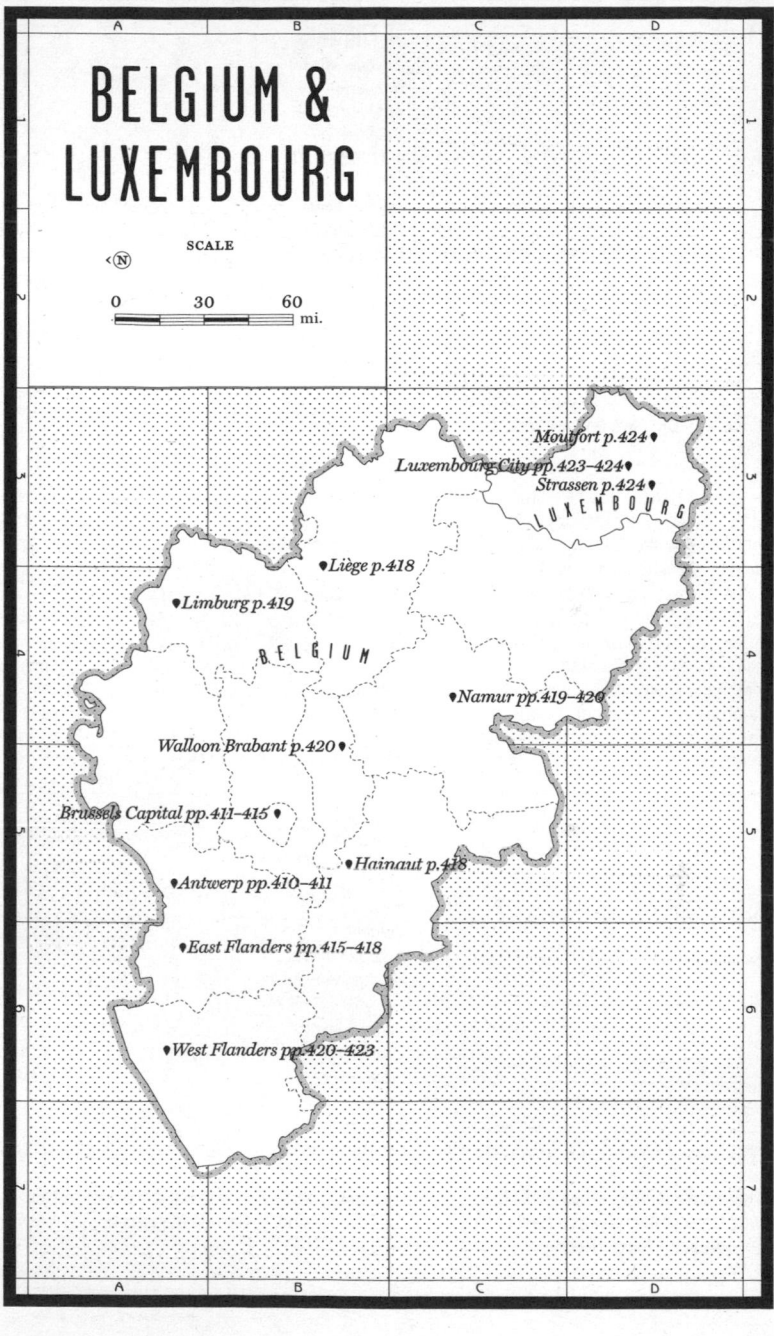

BELGIUM & LUXEMBOURG

SCALE

〈Ⓝ〉

0   30   60

mi.

Moutfort p.424 ♥

Luxembourg City pp.423–424 ♥

Strassen p.424 ♥

LUXEMBOURG

♥ *Liège p.418*

♥ *Limburg p.419*

BELGIUM

♥ *Namur pp.419–420*

Walloon Brabant p.420 ♥

Brussels Capital pp.411–415 ♥

♥ *Hainaut p.418*

♥ *Antwerp pp.410–411*

♥ *East Flanders pp.415–418*

♥ *West Flanders pp.420–423*

CAFÉ STANNY
Recommended by
Sergio Herman

Stanleystraat 1
Antwerp
Antwerp 2018
Belgium
+32 32895467

Opening hours	Closed Sunday
Reservation policy	No
Credit cards	Not accepted
Price range	Affordable
Style	Casual
Cuisine	Gastropub
Recommended for	Bargain

'Daily specials for a fair price, mostly organic and the alternative ambience is laid back and relaxed.'
—Sergio Herman

Located on Stanleystraat, near Berchem station, Café Stanny's bright red frontage accented by neat neon sign marks it out as something of a local landmark. Perennially popular, the neighbourhood pub has a laid-back, friendly vibe. Expect a good selection of beers from the young staff at Stanny's blue counter. These include Gagel, Seef and Tripel Karmeliet. The small but regularly changing menu of home-made dishes offers great value sustenance. Expect spaghetti Bolognese, home-made meatballs and meatloaf, as well as steaming soups and large omelettes. At weekends Stanny stays open until the wee hours.

FINJAN

Graaf van Hoornestraat 1
Antwerp
Antwerp 2000
Belgium
+32 32487714
www.finjan.be

Opening hours	Open 7 days
Credit cards	Accepted
Price range	Budget
Style	Casual
Cuisine	Middle Eastern
Recommended for	Late night

'Excellent Lebanese cuisine. The restaurant is open until early in the morning, they give you lovely food and service with a smile.'—Sergio Herman

'T FORNUIS
Recommended by
Peter Goossens,
Roger van Damme

Reyndersstraat 24
Antwerp
Antwerp 2000
Belgium
+32 32336270

Opening hours	Closed Saturday and Sunday
Credit cards	Accepted
Price range	Expensive
Style	Smart casual
Cuisine	French
Recommended for	Regular neighbourhood

HET GEBAAR
Recommended by
Filip Claeys,
Peter Goossens

Leopoldstraat 24
Antwerp
Antwerp 2000
Belgium
+32 32323710
www.hetgebaar.be

Opening hours	Closed Monday and Sunday
Credit cards	Accepted
Price range	Affordable
Style	Smart casual
Cuisine	Modern Belgian
Recommended for	Worth the travel

'Art on a plate.'—Filip Claeys

LAM EN YIN
Recommended by
Gert de Mangeleer,
Roger van Damme

Reyndersstraat 17
Antwerp
Antwerp 2000
Belgium
+32 32328838
www.lam-en-yin.be

Opening hours	Closed Monday and Tuesday
Credit cards	Accepted
Price range	Affordable
Style	Casual
Cuisine	Chinese
Recommended for	Worth the travel

'Authentic, serene, simple but extremely tasteful Chinese cuisine.'—Gert de Mangeleer

LUNG WAH
Van Wesenbekestraat 38
Antwerp
Antwerp 2060
Belgium
+32 32978258

Recommended by
Roger van Damme

Opening hours..Closed Thursday
Credit cards...Not accepted
Price range...Budget
Style...Casual
Cuisine..Chinese
Recommended for..Local favourite

'T ZILTE
Hanzestedenplaats 5
Antwerp
Antwerp 2000
Belgium
+32 32834040
www.tzilte.be

Recommended by
Peter Goossens

Opening hours..........................Closed Saturday and Sunday
Credit cards...Accepted
Price range...Expensive
Style...Smart casual
Cuisine...Modern European
Recommended for..High end

DE SCHONE VAN BOSKOOP
Appelkantstraat 10
Boechout
Antwerp 2530
Belgium
+32 34541931
www.deschonevanboskoop.be

Recommended by
Peter Goossens

Opening hours.............................Closed Monday and Sunday
Credit cards...Accepted
Price range...Expensive
Style...Smart casual
Cuisine...Modern European
Recommended for...Worth the travel

NUANCE
Kiliaanstraat 6
Duffel
Antwerp 2570
Belgium
+32 15634265
www.resto-nuance.be

Recommended by
Peter Goossens

Opening hours......................Closed Tuesday and Wednesday
Credit cards...Accepted
Price range...Expensive
Style...Smart casual
Cuisine...Modern European
Recommended for...High end

FRITURE RENÉ
Place de la Résistance 14
Anderlecht
Brussels-Capital 1070
Belgium
+32 25232876

Recommended by
Peter Goossens,
David Martin

Opening hours.............................Closed Monday and Tuesday
Reservation policy..No
Credit cards...Accepted
Price range..Affordable
Style...Casual
Cuisine..Belgian
Recommended for..Local favourite

'For the tavern atmosphere, the traditional Belgian dishes and the exceptional choice of teas.'
—David Martin

Friendly, family-run, reasonably priced bistro that stays open until late, seven days a week. Established in 1932 in the busy Anderlecht district (about twenty minutes by metro from the city centre), Friture René delivers fuss-free classics. These include prawn (shrimp) croquettes, steak cut to order, rugged meatballs in tomato sauce and garlic-scented mussels (baked or steamed). Be sure to order a side of twice-cooked frites – best dipped in Béarnaise – alongside a pick from the good beer, wine or even tea lists. Soak in the night-time atmosphere at the little bar or grab one of the small tables covered in checked plastic.

LA PAIX

Rue Ropsy-Chaudron 49
Anderlecht
Brussels-Capital 1070
Belgium
+32 25230958
www.lapaix.eu

Recommended by
Sang-Hoon Degeimbre,
Peter Goossens

Opening hours	Closed Saturday and Sunday
Credit cards	Accepted
Price range	Affordable
Style	Smart casual
Cuisine	French Brasserie
Recommended for	Regular neighbourhood

'This is a brasserie in the purest tradition, although the chef adds a nice, modern touch while maintaining what's important: the taste and comfort of typical dishes.'—Sang-Hoon Degeimbre

Opposite the grand old abattoir, La Paix, with roots dating back to 1892, is appropriately known for its pure-strain Simmental beef. In addition to fillet, côte de boeuf or even veal brains, other dishes by TV chef David Martin show finesse and often incorporate Asian touches – such as the amuse-bouche of goat's cheese with green tea, and starter of carpaccio of langoustines in miso. Desserts on the other hand are unapologetically rich: Dame Blanche, a home-made ice cream accompanied by a jug of chocolate sauce, for instance. Despite holding a Michelin star, the tone of the dining room, with its huge windows, dark wood and high ceilings, is quite relaxed.

BON BON

Avenue de Tervueren 453
Brussels
Brussels-Capital 1150
Belgium
+32 23466615
www.bon-bon.be

Recommended by
Kobe Desramaults,
Peter Goossens,
Tomoyasu Kamo

Opening hours	Closed Saturday and Sunday
Credit cards	Accepted
Price range	Expensive
Style	Smart casual
Cuisine	Modern Mediterranean
Recommended for	High end

'It blew my mind. I had the most amazing sea bass ever, baked in a crust of broken oyster shells and seaweed.'—Kobe Desramaults

Christophe Hardiquest is among the most celebrated younger chefs in Belgium; at Bon Bon, his wife Stéphanie manages front of house. There's no menu: diners choose from a blackboard whose dishes change daily according to what looked best in the market that morning. The wood-floored dining room, with its chandeliers, red curtains and grey chairs, evokes a kind of utilitarian luxury. Diners enjoy dishes such as roasted langoustines with confit of bacon and Sarazen sauce; or sesame-coated Anjou pigeon in spiced consommé. The seven-course tasting menu isn't cheap, but there's a reasonably priced lunch deal.

LA BUVETTE

Chaussée d'Alsemberg 108
Brussels
Brussels-Capital 1060
Belgium
+32 25341303
www.la-buvette.be

Recommended by
David Martin

Opening hours	Closed Monday and Sunday
Credit cards	Accepted
Price range	Affordable
Style	Smart casual
Cuisine	Modern European
Recommended for	Bargain

'A former butchers, go for the atmosphere, an intelligent chef and contemporary cuisine. The €35 (£30; $50) menu is unbeatable value for money!' —David Martin

LE CABESTAN

Place Saint-Job 16
Brussels
Brussels-Capital 1180
Belgium
+32 23754437

Recommended by
Sang-Hoon Degeimbre

Opening hours	Open 7 days
Reservation policy	No
Credit cards	Not accepted
Price range	Budget
Style	Casual
Cuisine	Bistro
Recommended for	Late night

'For when I'm feeling peckish at the end of the evening or after a night out. It's rare to find a restaurant that's open late at night. Le Cabestan has simple cuisine with a great atmosphere.'—Sang-Hoon Degeimbre

LE CHAT NOIR

Rue Jules Van Praetstraat 8
Brussels
Brussels-Capital 1000
Belgium
+32 25121077
www.restolechatnoir.be

Opening hours..Open 7 days
Credit cards...Accepted
Price range...Affordable
Style..Casual
Cuisine...Belgian
Recommended for.......................................Late night

COMME CHEZ SOI

Place Rouppe 23
Brussels
Brussels-Capital 1000
Belgium
+32 25122921
www.commechezsoi.be

Opening hours...........................Closed Monday and Sunday
Credit cards...Accepted
Price range...Expensive
Style..Smart casual
Cuisine...Belgian
Recommended for.......................................High end

HET KRIEKSKE

Kapittel 10
Brussels
Brussels-Capital 1500
Belgium
+32 23801421

Opening hours...............................Closed Monday and Tuesday
Credit cards...Accepted
Price range...Affordable
Style..Casual
Cuisine...Belgian
Recommended for...................Regular neighbourhood

LE PAIN QUOTIDIEN

Rue Antoine Dansaert 16a
Brussels
Brussels-Capital 1000
Belgium
+32 25022361
www.lepainquotidien.be

Opening hours..Open 7 days
Reservation policy..No
Credit cards...Accepted
Price range..Budget
Style..Casual
Cuisine..Café-Bakery
Recommended for.......................................Breakfast

'One big breakfast table, organic produce, cosy atmosphere.'—Gert de Mangeleer

PÂTISSERIE LE SAINT-AULAYE

Rue Vanderkindere 377
Brussels
Brussels-Capital 1180
Belgium
+32 23457785
www.saintaulaye.be

Opening hours...Closed Monday
Reservation policy..No
Credit cards...Accepted
Price range..Budget
Style..Casual
Cuisine..Patisserie
Recommended for.......................................Breakfast

'The welcome, the smell of the croissants, the cakes, the quiches, the extraordinary bread...'—David Martin

AL PICCOLO MONDO

Recommended by
Lionel Rigolet

Rue Jourdan 19
Brussels
Brussels-Capital 1060
Belgium
+32 25388794
www.alpiccolomondo.com

Opening hours	Open 7 days
Credit cards	Accepted
Price range	Affordable
Style	Casual
Cuisine	French-Italian
Recommended for	Late night

'An Italian restaurant that's open every day and late into the night.'—Lionel Rigole

PISTOLET ORIGINAL

Recommended by
Lionel Rigolet

Rue Joseph Stevens 24
Brussels
Brussels-Capital 1000
Belgium
+32 28808098
www.pistolet-original.be

Opening hours	Open 7 days
Reservation policy	No
Credit cards	Accepted
Price range	Budget
Style	Casual
Cuisine	Café-Bakery
Recommended for	Breakfast

'For breakfast, you can't beat their *pistolet Belge* (traditional Belgian bread).'—Lionel Rigolet

LE POECHENELLEKELDER

Recommended by
Lionel Rigolet

Rue du Chêne 5
Brussels
Brussels-Capital 1000
Belgium
+32 25119262
www.poechenellekelder.be

Opening hours	Open 7 days
Reservation policy	No
Credit cards	Not accepted
Price range	Budget
Style	Casual
Cuisine	Bar Snacks
Recommended for	Local favourite

'A typical Brussels-style establishment opposite the Manneken Pis statue. A pleasant place to go for a glass of wine in the evening after service, or after lunch on Sunday.'—Lionel Rigolet

PREGO!

Recommended by
Lionel Rigolet

Place Jourdan 58–61
Brussels
Brussels-Capital 1040
Belgium
+32 22307935
www.pregoprego.be

Opening hours	Open 7 days
Credit cards	Accepted but not AMEX
Price range	Affordable
Style	Casual
Cuisine	Italian
Recommended for	Regular neighbourhood

'It's easy and pleasant.'—Lionel Rigolet

TOUCAN SUR MER

Recommended by
Lionel Rigolet

Avenue Louis Lepoutre 17
Brussels
Brussels-Capital 1050
Belgium
+32 23400740
www.toucanbrasserie.com

Opening hours	Open 7 days
Credit cards	Accepted
Price range	Affordable
Style	Casual
Cuisine	Seafood
Recommended for	Bargain

'Go for the seafood platter.'—Lionel Rigolet

ORIENTALIA

Recommended by
Tomoyasu Kamo

Chaussée de Charleroi 277
Saint-Gilles
Brussels-Capital 1060
Belgium
+32 25207575

Opening hours	Closed Monday and Sunday
Credit cards	Not accepted
Price range	Affordable
Style	Casual
Cuisine	Lebanese
Recommended for	Regular neighbourhood

LE CHALET DE LA FORÊT

Recommended by
Peter Goossens,
Tomoyasu Kamo

Drève de Lorraine 43
Uccle
Brussels-Capital 1180
Belgium
+32 23745416
www.lechaletdelaforet.be

Opening hours...............................Closed Saturday and Sunday
Credit cards...Accepted
Price range...Expensive
Style..Smart casual
Cuisine...Modern French
Recommended for.....................................Worth the travel

DE HERMELIJN

Recommended by
Peter Goossens

Wannegemdorp 7
Wannegem-Lede
Brussels-Capital 9772
Belgium
+32 93836411
www.dehermelijn.be

Opening hours.......................Closed Wednesday and Thursday
Credit cards...Accepted
Price range...Affordable
Style...Casual
Cuisine...Belgian
Recommended for................................Regular neighbourhood

'T HUIS VAN LEDE

Recommended by
Peter Goossens

Lededorp 7
Wannegem-Lede
Brussels-Capital 9772
Belgium
+32 93835096
www.thuisvanlede.be

Opening hours..............................Closed Monday and Sunday
Credit cards...Accepted
Price range...Affordable
Style...Casual
Cuisine...Modern Belgian
Recommended for................................Regular neighbourhood

PLEIN 25

Recommended by
Peter Goossens

Elsegemplein 25
Elsegem
East Flanders 9790
Belgium
+32 56602525
www.plein25.be

Opening hours.........................Closed Wednesday and Sunday
Credit cards...Accepted
Price range...Affordable
Style...Casual
Cuisine...Bistro
Recommended for................................Regular neighbourhood

J.E.F.

Recommended by
Kobe Desramaults

Lange Streenstraat 10
Gent
East Flanders 9000
Belgium
+32 93368058
www.j-e-f.be

Opening hours..............................Closed Monday and Sunday
Credit cards...Accepted
Price range...Affordable
Style...Casual
Cuisine...Belgian
Recommended for................................Regular neighbourhood

'Down to earth but creative cooking in a cool setting.'
—Kobe Desramaults

J.E.F. is named after Jason Blanckaert and his girlfriend Femke Dequidt, who set up the restaurant in the middle of Ghent's old town. The off-white walls and aged, bare tables give the place a clean and sturdy look – it's not fancy, but the food is innovative, on-trend and very reasonably priced. Snails come with bone marrow and smoked bread croutons, assorted shellfish with oyster tartare, samphire and seafood broth, and they have a dessert of pear with sorrel, coffee and basil and lime sorbet. The set lunch has two choices for each course and there's a cracking selection of Belgian beers.

DE LIEVE

Recommended by
Kobe Desramaults

Sint-Margrietstraat 1
Gent
East Flanders 9000
Belgium
+32 92232947
www.eetkaffee-delieve.be

Opening hours	Closed Saturday and Sunday
Credit cards	Accepted
Price range	Budget
Style	Casual
Cuisine	Belgian
Recommended for	Bargain

'It's been an institution for years. Go in for a quick lunch: traditional food, lots of it and it's cheap too.' —Kobe Desramaults

Eetkaffee De Lieve, on the corner of Lievestraat and Sint-Margrietstraat, is an old favourite among Ghent natives. The large café has been going since the mid-1980s, serving good food at excellent prices. It's always been popular with students, artists and tourists. The genial owners command proceedings effectively, and the kitchen claims to take its inspiration from no less a figure than Escoffier. On the menu are a great prawn (shrimp) cocktail, some stews, meatballs, and haddock in mustard sauce, and a fabulous Dame Noire for dessert. Potatoes are a notable highlight, either as chips (fries), mash or croquettes.

MARTINO

Recommended by
Kobe Desramaults, Peter
Goossens

Vlaanderenstraat 125
Gent
East Flanders 9000
Belgium
+32 92250104

Opening hours	Closed Monday and Tuesday
Credit cards	Accepted
Price range	Affordable
Style	Casual
Cuisine	International
Recommended for	Late night

'It's been in the family for generations. It opens at 6.00 p.m. and closes at 1.30 a.m. Order cheese and eggs – amazing (definitely after some beers).' —Kobe Desramaults

Martino was recently refurbished, and the old neon signs were stripped away. It's now a brightly lit and functional late-night café, serving great pasta carbonara, spaghetti bolognese, cheeseburgers (often with egg), sandwiches, steak tartare and so on, typically with copious quantities of chips (fries). The place is rather an institution among Ghent's students and clubbers – who, let's face it, often overlap – lingering over a final drink and a burger at the end of a night out. Perhaps the most famous dish is the steak martino, which sees the beef smothered in a rich, spicy sauce.

'T NIEUW STADION

Recommended by
Peter Goossens

Brusselsesteenweg 664
Gent
East Flanders 9050
Belgium
+32 92308833
www.nieuwstadion.be

Opening hours	Closed Tuesday
Credit cards	Accepted
Price range	Affordable
Style	Smart casual
Cuisine	Belgian
Recommended for	Bargain

SIMON SAYS

Recommended by
Kobe Desramaults

Sluizeken 8
Gent
East Flanders 9000
Belgium
+32 92330343
www.simon-says.be

Opening hours	Closed Monday
Credit cards	Accepted
Price range	Budget
Style	Casual
Cuisine	Café
Recommended for	Breakfast

'A great place for breakfast. Watch out, this place is always packed with a cool crowd but has a warm environment.'—Kobe Desramaults

Simon Says is a new and stylish bed and breakfast in the middle of Ghent's Patershol district, where many of the city's best restaurants are clustered. The dining room is painted in turquoise, while handsome gold objects from Antwerp artist Panamarenko hang from the walls. For breakfast: freshly baked croissants and other pastries from the local baker, cereals and good marmalade. They do organic brunches with Fairtrade Belgian chocolate as well. The café is closed to non-residents on Monday, allowing bed-and-breakfast guests to enjoy breakfast whenever they like.

VOLTA

Recommended by
Kobe Desramaults,
Peter Goossens

Nieuwe Wandeling 2b
Gent
East Flanders 9000
Belgium
+32 93240500
www.volta-gent.be

Opening hours............................Closed Monday and Sunday
Credit cards...Accepted
Price range..Affordable
Style...Casual
Cuisine..Modern European
Recommended for...............................Regular neighbourhood

'Down-to-earth but creative cooking in a cool setting.'
—Kobe Desramaults

One of the most exciting restaurants in Belgium, Volta is a huge former turbine hall a few minutes' walk from the centre of Ghent. It serves a seven-course tasting menu in the evenings, while the €25 (£21; $34) set lunch menu is great value. Expect crunchy white cabbage with smoked eel and parsley root, or a rib-eye of veal with onion and pickles. When the weather is fine they open the sixty-cover terrace, and there's a wood-beamed private dining room upstairs. Surprisingly for such original cooking, Volta is very popular with families.

VRIJMOED

Recommended by
Peter Goossens

Vlaanderenstraat 22
Gent
East Flanders 9000
Belgium
+32 92799977
www.vrijmoed.be

Opening hours............................Closed Monday and Sunday
Credit cards..................................Accepted but not AMEX
Price range...Expensive
Style..Smart casual
Cuisine..Modern European
Recommended for...Local favourite

BISTRO DE KRUIDEN MOLEN

Recommended by
Gert de Mangeleer,
Peter Goossens

Dorpsstraat 1
Klemskerke
East Flanders 8420
Belgium
+32 59235178
www.kruidenmolen.be

Opening hours...................Closed Wednesday and Thursday
Credit cards..Not accepted
Price range..Affordable
Style...Casual
Cuisine..Belgian
Recommended for...Local favourite

'Authenticity in both the recipes and the drinks.'
—Gert de Mangeleer

HOF VAN CLEVE

Recommended by
Filip Claeys,
Roger van Damme

Riemegemstraat 1
Kruishoutem
East Flanders 9770
Belgium
+32 93835848
www.hofvancleve.com

Opening hours............................Closed Monday and Sunday
Credit cards...Accepted
Price range...Expensive
Style..Smart casual
Cuisine...Modern Belgian
Recommended for...High end

'The best restaurant in Belgium. A top three-star place.'
—Filip Claeys

BRASSERIE BOULEVARD

Recommended by
Peter Goossens

Kortijksesteenweg 175
Sint-Martens-Latem
East Flanders 9830
Belgium
+32 92791200
www.blvd.be

Opening hours...Closed Sunday
Credit cards..................................Accepted but not AMEX
Price range..Affordable
Style...Casual
Cuisine..Belgian Brasserie
Recommended for...Local favourite

BRASSERIE LATEM

Kortrijksesteenweg 9
Sint-Martens-Latem
East Flanders 9830
Belgium
+32 92823617
www.brasserielatem.be

Opening hours	Closed Sunday
Credit cards	Accepted
Price range	Expensive
Style	Smart casual
Cuisine	Belgian Brasserie
Recommended for	Local favourite

B&B SOFIE LACHAERT

Sint-Jozefstraat 30
Tielrode
East Flanders 9140
Belgium
+32 37111963
www.lachaert.com

Opening hours	Open 7 days
Credit cards	Accepted
Price range	Affordable
Style	Casual
Cuisine	Breakfast
Recommended for	Breakfast

'This is the most inspiring place of all places. It's poetry, it's translucent, it's anything but just a B&B with a breakfast.'—Sergio Herman

BENOIT & BERNARD DEWITTE

Beertegemstraat 52
Zingem
East Flanders 9750
Belgium
+32 93845652
www.benoitdewitte.be

Opening hours	Closed Monday and Sunday
Credit cards	Accepted
Price range	Expensive
Style	Smart casual
Cuisine	Modern European
Recommended for	Local favourite

LA TABLE DU BOUCHER

Rue d'Havré 49
Mons
Hainaut 7000
Belgium
+32 65316838
www.latableduboucher.be

Opening hours	Open 7 days
Credit cards	Accepted
Price range	Expensive
Style	Smart casual
Cuisine	French
Recommended for	Regular neighbourhood

'For their welcome, the best meat in Belgium, and for the generosity of the chef that comes through in the food.'—David Martin

ENOTECA

Rue de la Casquette 5
Liège
Liège 4000
Belgium
+32 42222464
www.enoteca.be

Opening hours	Closed Sunday
Credit cards	Accepted
Price range	Affordable
Style	Casual
Cuisine	Italian
Recommended for	Bargain

'Tasty food, very well served, quick and excellent value for money.'—Arabelle Meirlaen

ARABELLE MEIRLAEN

Chemin de Bertrandfontaine 7
Marchin
Liège 4570
Belgium
+32 85255555
www.arabelle.be

Opening hours	Closed Monday and Sunday
Credit cards	Accepted
Price range	Expensive
Style	Smart casual
Cuisine	Modern European
Recommended for	High end

SLAGMOLEN

Recommended by
Peter Goossens

Molenweg 177
Opglabbeek
Limburg 3660
Belgium
+32 89854888
www.slagmolen.be

Opening hours	Closed Tuesday and Wednesday
Credit cards	Accepted
Price range	Expensive
Style	Smart casual
Cuisine	French
Recommended for	High end

L'AIR DU TEMPS

Recommended by
Peter Goossens

Rue de la Croix Monet 2
Eghezee
Namur 5310
Belgium
+32 81813048
www.airdutemps.be

Opening hours	Closed Monday and Tuesday
Credit cards	Accepted
Price range	Expensive
Style	Smart casual
Cuisine	Modern French
Recommended for	High end

True to its name, L'Air du Temps is an avant-garde restaurant with a sensory mission. Having been a butcher before becoming a sommelier, Korean-born chef Sang-Hoon Degeimbre moved to modernist cookery methods. Fastidious research and a menu that has been perfected over time earned the chef first one Michelin star, then two. Unlike that of many gastronomic innovators, the chef's menu is accessible, where the likes of kimchi is cleverly paired with more conventional European ingredients. The menu dégustation comes as a series of artfully garnished and technicolored creations. Provenance is central to this developmental venture.

LE PAIN QUOTIDIEN

Recommended by
Sang-Hoon
Degeimbre

Avenue du Bourgmestre Jean Materne 54
Jambes
Namur 5100
Belgium
+32 81308888
www.lepainquotidien.be

Opening hours	Open 7 days
Reservation policy	No
Credit cards	Accepted
Price range	Budget
Style	Casual
Cuisine	Café-Bakery
Recommended for	Breakfast

'Their sourdough bread, the smell of freshly baked croissants, a decor blending rustic wood with a perfect range of products... all with that distinctive conviviality found at a *table d'hôte* (multi-course set meal).'—Sang-Hoon Degeimbre

BRASSERIE FRANÇOIS

Recommended by
Sang-Hoon Degeimbre

Place Saint-Aubain 3
Namur
Namur 5000
Belgium
+32 81221123
www.brasseriefrancois.be

Opening hours	Open 7 days
Credit cards	Accepted
Price range	Affordable
Style	Casual
Cuisine	French
Recommended for	Bargain

'The cod mousseline is just perfect – the ingredients, baking and quality of the mousseline are impeccable. Plus their meatballs in tomato sauce are exactly how I like them.'—Sang-Hoon Degeimbre

Brasserie François is a beautiful early nineteenth-century building, designed in Napoleon III style, next to Namur's celebrated baroque cathedral. The restaurant has two floors: a brasserie downstairs with a wood and brass bar and a seafood counter, and a huge panelled room upstairs with seven-metre (23-feet) high walls. The food is classic Parisian bistro: duck foie gras terrine with muscat jelly and brioche; veal kidneys *à la moutarde*; or veal brains in a caper butter for the more adventurous. If the weather is fine the covered terrace outside is lovely – with a cold Belgian beer.

L'EAU VIVE

Route de Floreffe 37
Profondeville
Namur 5170
Belgium
+32 81411151
www.eau-vive.be

Recommended by
Peter Goossens

Opening hours	Closed Tuesday and Wednesday
Credit cards	Accepted
Price range	Expensive
Style	Smart casual
Cuisine	Modern European
Recommended for	High end

AUX PETITS OIGNONS

Chaussée de Tirlemont 260
Jodoigne
Walloon Brabant 1370
Belgium
+32 10760078
www.auxpetitsoignons.be

Recommended by
Sang-Hoon Degeimbre

Opening hours	Closed Tuesday and Wednesday
Credit cards	Accepted but not AMEX
Price range	Affordable
Style	Smart casual
Cuisine	French
Recommended for	Local favourite

'The cuisine here uses fine products with technical prowess, yet is constantly seeking to hit the right note. The homely dishes are popular with the hordes of diners who flock to this charming address.' —Sang-Hoon Degeimbre

BISTRO CHRISTOPHE

Garenmarkt 34
Bruges
West Flanders 8000
Belgium
+32 50344892
www.christophe-brugge.be

Recommended by
Filip Claeys,
Gert de Mangeleer

Opening hours	Closed Tuesday and Wednesday
Credit cards	Accepted
Price range	Affordable
Style	Casual
Cuisine	French Bistro
Recommended for	Late night

'Good steak tartare, nice atmosphere and open until 1.00 a.m.' —Filip Claeys

FRITUUR BOSRAND

Koning Albert L Laan 108
Bruges
West Flanders 8200
Belgium
+32 494527552

Recommended by
Gert de Mangeleer

Opening hours	Open 7 days
Reservation policy	No
Credit cards	Not accepted
Price range	Budget
Style	Casual
Cuisine	Fast Food
Recommended for	Bargain

'Real top-quality Belgian frites.' —Gert de Mangeleer

HERTOG JAN

Torhoutse Steenweg 479
Bruges
West Flanders 8200
Belgium
+32 50673446
www.hertog-jan.com

Recommended by
Peter Goossens,
David Martin

Opening hours	Closed Monday and Sunday
Credit cards	Accepted
Price range	Expensive
Style	Formal
Cuisine	Modern European
Recommended for	High end

'It's a magical place where you eat in the kitchen gardens. There's a purity to the cuisine – it's to the point. Creativity and the best vegetables you'll ever taste with over 500 herbs and vegetables that come straight from the farm. Some of the best service in Belgium. A place you must go once in your lifetime.' —David Martin

DE JONKMAN

Maalsesteenweg 438
Bruges
West Flanders 8310
Belgium
+32 50360767
www.dejonkman.be

Recommended by
Peter Goossens

Opening hours	Closed Monday and Sunday
Credit cards	Accepted
Price range	Expensive
Style	Smart casual
Cuisine	Modern Belgian
Recommended for	High end

ROCK FORT

Langestraat 15
Bruges
West Flanders 8000
Belgium
+32 50334113
www.rock-fort.be

Opening hours............................Closed Saturday and Sunday
Credit cards...Accepted
Price range..Affordable
Style..Casual
Cuisine...Belgian
Recommended for...............................Regular neighbourhood

'Great vibe, good wines, and quality food for its price.'
—Gert de Mangeleer

LE SIPHON

Damse Vaart-Oost 1
Damme
West Flanders 8340
Belgium
+32 50620202
www.siphon.be

Opening hours............................Closed Saturday and Sunday
Credit cards..Not accepted
Price range..Affordable
Style..Casual
Cuisine...Traditional Belgian
Recommended for...............................Regular neighbourhood

'Traditional Belgian food with nice childhood memories.'
—Filip Claeys

L'AUBERGE IN DE ZON

Dikkebusstraat 80
De Klijte
West Flanders 8950
Belgium
+32 57212626
www.indezon.be

Opening hours............................Closed Monday and Tuesday
Credit cards..Accepted
Price range..Affordable
Style..Casual
Cuisine...Belgian
Recommended for...Local favourite

'Serves traditional Flemish and French food in an authentic setting. Start the meal with some pâté, rillettes, pork fat, bread and pickles. It has some very good draft beers!'—Kobe Desramaults

L'Auberge In De Zon is a handsome tavern a mile or so from the French border. Brown-bricked, with a red-tiled roof it overlooks a lush garden. A bright and soulful place with stained-glass windows and bare brick, there's often a band playing with an accordion and a double bass. The food is infinitely better than you might expect for a venue like this: starters of young snails de Bourgogne and mains of roasted horse steak, crown of lamb with parsley and garlic butter, or eel with a prawn (shrimp) cream and chives. The set menu even includes half a bottle of wine per person.

IN DE WULF

Wulvestraat 1
Dranouter
West Flanders 8950
Belgium
+32 57445567
www.indewulf.be

Opening hours............................Closed Monday and Tuesday
Credit cards..Accepted
Price range...Expensive
Style..Smart casual
Cuisine..Modern Belgian
Recommended for..Worth the travel

'A timeless cuisine that takes you to the very roots of the ingredients on your plate. And it has a magnificent wine list.'—Guillaume Monjuré

Kobe Desramaults's hideaway isn't the most accessible of places, tucked away 160 km (100 miles) north of the French–Belgian border, but you'll be glad you tracked down this former farm turned restaurant with rooms. Its wild location is a suitable backdrop for what's on offer: a procession of small dishes often made with unpronounceable ingredients (kerremelkstampers or Keiemtaler, anyone?) plucked from the farm's environs. Hardened gastronomes will know the score — Ostend oysters in a whey sauce, seabuckthorn and foraged herbs aplenty, all impeccably presented on a baffling array of dinnerware. Could this be Belgium's answer to Noma? In a word, (whisper it) yes.

LA DURÉE

Recommended by
Peter Goossens

Leenstraat 28
Izegem
West Flanders 8870
Belgium
+32 51310031
www.laduree.be

Opening hours	Closed Monday and Sunday
Credit cards	Accepted
Price range	Expensive
Style	Smart casual
Cuisine	Modern European
Recommended for	High end

BARTHOLOMEUS

Recommended by
Peter Goossens

Zeedijk-Heist 267
Knokke-Heist
West Flanders 8301
Belgium
+32 50517576
www.restaurantbartholomeus.be

Opening hours	Closed Tuesday to Thursday
Credit cards	Accepted
Price range	Expensive
Style	Smart casual
Cuisine	Modern European
Recommended for	High end

BRASSERIE BRISTOL

Recommended by
Sergio Herman

Zeedijk 291
Knokke-Heist
West Flanders 8301
Belgium
+32 50512112
www.brasseriebristol.be

Opening hours	Closed Wednesday and Thursday
Credit cards	Accepted
Price range	Affordable
Style	Smart casual
Cuisine	Belgian Brasserie
Recommended for	Regular neighbourhood

'Traditional Flemish cuisine in a modern classic interior. The welcome is always warm and the food always tastes good.'—Sergio Herman

DEMARÉ

Recommended by
Peter Goossens

Kustlaan 119
Knokke-Heist
West Flanders 8300
Belgium
+32 50611314

Opening hours	Closed Monday and Tuesday
Reservation policy	No
Credit cards	Accepted
Price range	Budget
Style	Casual
Cuisine	Bakery
Recommended for	Breakfast

LE NOUVEAU BLÉ D'OR

Recommended by
Peter Goossens

Emile Verhaerenlaan 16
Knokke-Heist
West Flanders 8300
Belgium
+32 50339981

Opening hours	Closed Wednesday
Reservation policy	No
Credit cards	Accepted but not Amex
Price range	Budget
Style	Casual
Cuisine	Bakery
Recommended for	Breakfast

SEL GRIS

Recommended by
Peter Goossens

Zeedijk 314
Knokke-Heist
West Flanders 8301
Belgium
+32 50514937
www.restaurantselgris.be

Opening hours	Closed Wednesday and Thursday
Credit cards	Accepted but not AMEX
Price range	Expensive
Style	Smart casual
Cuisine	Modern European
Recommended for	High end

BOURY

Recommended by
Peter Goossens

Diksmuidsesteenweg 53
Roeselare
West Flanders 8800
Belgium
+32 51626462
www.restaurantboury.be

Opening hours........................Closed Tuesday and Wednesday
Credit cards..Accepted
Price range..Expensive
Style..Smart casual
Cuisine..Modern European
Recommended for...High end

BERTO

Recommended by
Peter Goossens

Holstraat 32
Waregem
West Flanders 8790
Belgium
+32 56443015
www.berto-waregem.be

Opening hours................................Closed Monday and Sunday
Credit cards....................................Accepted but not AMEX
Price range..Expensive
Style..Smart casual
Cuisine..Modern French
Recommended for...Local favourite

ESCABECHE

Recommended by
Peter Goossens

Stationsstraat 166
Waregem
West Flanders 8790
Belgium
+32 56328697
www.escabechedeluxe.be

Opening hours................................Closed Monday and Sunday
Credit cards....................................Accepted but not AMEX
Price range..Affordable
Style..Casual
Cuisine..Spanish Tapas
Recommended for...Local favourite

RESTAURANT CLAIREFONTAINE

Recommended by
Cyril Molard

9 Place de Clairefontaine
Luxembourg City
Luxembourg 1341
+352 462211
www.restaurantclairefontaine.lu

Opening hours..............................Closed Saturday and Sunday
Credit cards..Accepted
Price range..Expensive
Style..Formal
Cuisine..French
Recommended for...Local favourite

'The best restaurant in Luxembourg. It's a famous and gourmet table.'—Cyril Molard

With no fewer than eleven starred restaurants, Luxembourg has more Michelin stars per capita than any other country. Restaurant Clairefontaine, moments from the Place Guillaume II and the Grand Ducal Palace, is arguably one of the best to have garnered an award. Run by tennis fanatic turned chef Arnaud Magnier (who trained with Bernard Loiseau) and his wife Edwige, dishes often feel playful despite the formality of the dining rooms. These include the hamburger 'Kobe-style' with foie gras, Breton lobster with iced black truffle, wood pigeon from Vosges, and thoroughly truffled Bresse chicken cooked within a pig's bladder. Follow on with Grand Marnier soufflé.

RESTAURANT L'ADRESSE

Recommended by
Thierry Duhr

32 Rue Notre Dame
Luxembourg City
Luxembourg 2240
+352 27858468

Opening hours..Closed Sunday
Credit cards..Accepted
Price range..Affordable
Style..Casual
Cuisine..French Bistro
Recommended for...Late night

'Good atmosphere, good food.'—Thierry Duhr

LA TABLE DU PAIN

Recommended by
Cyril Molard

19 Avenue Monterey
Luxembourg City
Luxembourg 2163
+352 241608
www.tabledupain.lu

Opening hours	Open 7 days
Credit cards	Accepted
Price range	Affordable
Style	Smart casual
Cuisine	French
Recommended for	Breakfast

'Delicious and indulgent products.'—Cyril Molard

WASABI

Recommended by
Cyril Molard

104 Rue de Remich
Moutfort
Luxembourg 5330
+352 357281
www.wasabi.lu

Opening hours	Closed Monday and Sunday
Credit cards	Accepted
Price range	Affordable
Style	Casual
Cuisine	Japanese
Recommended for	Bargain

'Authentic Asian flavours.'—Cyril Molard

BISTRONOME

Recommended by
Cyril Molard

373 Route d'Arlon
Strassen
Luxembourg 8011
+352 26313190
www.bistronome.lu

Opening hours	Closed Monday and Sunday
Credit cards	Accepted
Price range	Expensive
Style	Smart casual
Cuisine	French Bistro
Recommended for	Regular neighbourhood

'Quality ingredients, consistency and flavour.'
—Cyril Molard

'A fisherman's hut right in the middle of the salt marshes that serves great food.'
OLLIE COUILLAUD P438

'SIMPLE, TRADITIONAL REGIONAL CUISINE, SET IN THE MIDDLE OF THE MEADOWS WITH A VIEW OVERLOOKING MONT BLANC.'
EMMANUEL RENAUT P443

'THIS PLACE JUST OOZES FRENCHNESS.'
YVES CAMDEBORDE P433

FRANCE & MONACO

'DREAMY.'
RENEE ERICKSON P436

'AN ASTOUNDING GASTRONOMIC EXPERIENCE THAT VARIES ACCORDING TO THE SEASON. THIS IS PROVENCE IN ALL ITS GLORY.'
YANNICK ALLÉNO P438

'You can buy and eat oysters on the dock with the fishermen; I like them with a dash of shallot and Cabernet Sauvignon vinegar.'
SHAUN RANKIN P432

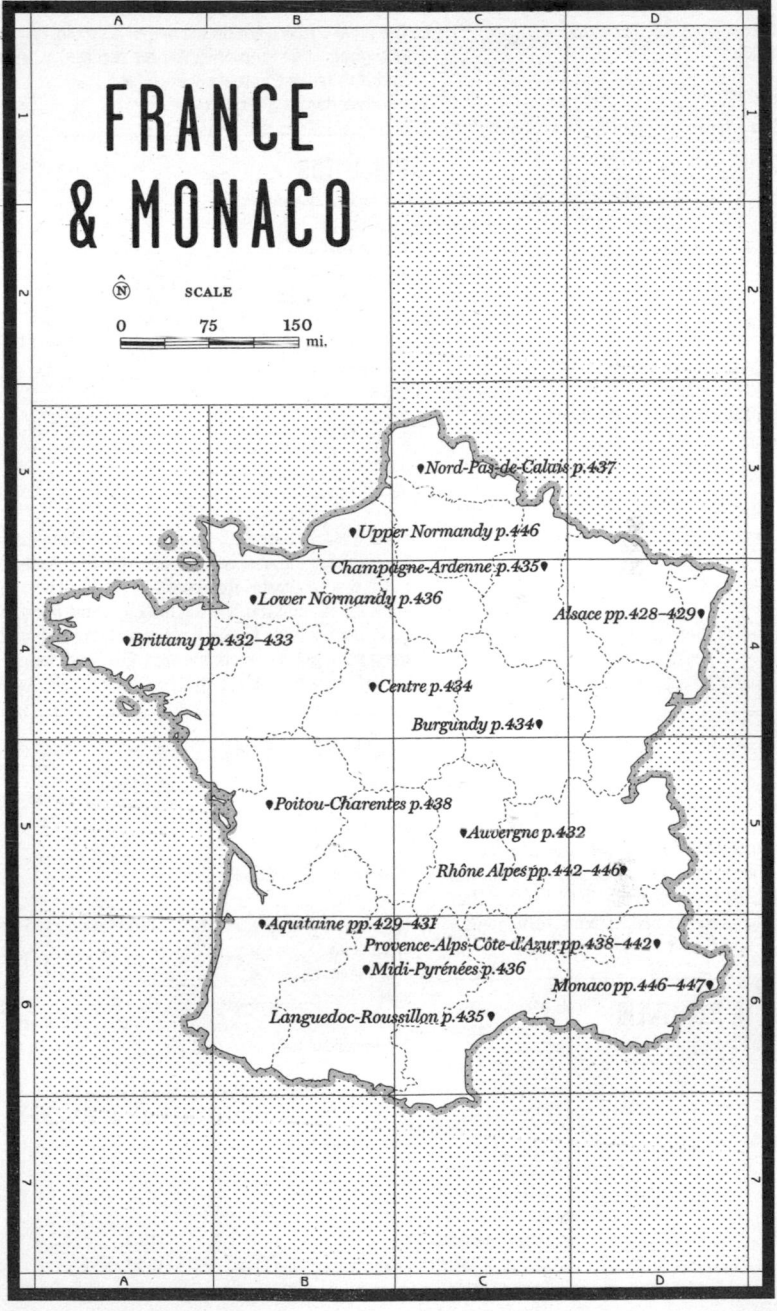

FRANCE
& MONACO

N

SCALE

0   75   150 mi.

♦Nord-Pas-de-Calais p.437

♦Upper Normandy p.446

Champagne-Ardenne p.435♦

♦Lower Normandy p.436

Alsace pp.428–429♦

♦Brittany pp.432–433

♦Centre p.434

Burgundy p.434♦

♦Poitou-Charentes p.438

♦Auvergne p.432

Rhône Alpes pp.442–446♦

♦Aquitaine pp.429–431

Provence-Alpes-Côte-d'Azur pp.438–442♦

♦Midi-Pyrénées p.436

Monaco pp.446–447♦

Languedoc-Roussillon p.435♦

L'ARNSBOURG

Recommended by
Alexandre Gauthier,
Harald Wohlfahrt

18 Untermuhlthal
Baerenthal
Alsace 57230
+33 387065085
www.arnsbourg.com

Opening hours	Closed Tuesday and Wednesday
Credit cards	Accepted
Price range	Expensive
Style	Formal
Cuisine	Modern French
Recommended for	High end

'This is a very good restaurant. It has an intimate atmosphere and the standard is high. Plus, it's not far from the area of Baiersbronn and you get fantastic value for money.'—Harald Wohlfahrt

L'AUBERGE DE L'ILL

Recommended by
Izu Ani,
Lori Granito,
Jean Joho

2 Rue de Collonges au Mont d'Or
Illhaeusern
Alsace 68970
+33 389718900
www.auberge-de-l-ill.com

Opening hours	Closed Monday and Tuesday
Credit cards	Accepted
Price range	Expensive
Style	Smart casual
Cuisine	Alsatian
Recommended for	Worth the travel

'Um, everything. Seriously, they even have a resident stork! The Haeberlin family continues to impress. Food, decor, service... it's no surpise that they're one of the longest-running three-Michelin-starred restaurants in the world.'—Lori Granito

AUBERGE DE LA NACHTWEID

Recommended by
Oliver James Sheridan

Chemin de la Nachtweid
Ostwald
Alsace 67540
+33 388665888
www.auberge-nachtweid.fr

Opening hours	Open 7 days
Credit cards	Accepted but not AMEX
Price range	Budget
Style	Casual
Cuisine	Eastern French
Recommended for	Local favourite

'You won't find a more typical Alsace restaurant. All the local classics are on the menu. It's fresh, tasty and good value for money. You are received as friends and they make you feel comfortable.'
—Oliver James Sheridan

BINCHSTUB

Recommended by
Oliver James Sheridan

6 Rue du Tonnelet Rouge
Strasbourg
Alsace 67000
+33 388134773
www.binchstub.fr

Opening hours	Open 7 days
Reservation policy	No
Credit cards	Accepted
Price range	Budget
Style	Casual
Cuisine	Alsatian
Recommended for	Late night

'A nice place to go with your mates late at night. Simplicity is the best word to describe this place. They make the best tartes flambées and the local beer and wine list is good too. You eat directly at the bar and you can't book a table so you have to be lucky enough to get a seat, but it's worth the wait. Easy and cheap – a sort of tapas bar Alsace style.'—Oliver James Sheridan

BRASSERIE LES HARAS

Recommended by
Armin Leitgeb

23 Rue des Glacières
Strasbourg
Alsace 67000
+33 388240000
www.les-haras-brasserie.com

Opening hours	Closed Monday and Sunday
Credit cards	Accepted
Price range	Affordable
Style	Casual
Cuisine	French Brasserie
Recommended for	Wish I'd opened

'Probably the most beautiful brasserie in France at the moment. Beautiful architecture and amazing food.'
—Armin Leitgeb

LA CASSEROLE

Recommended by
Oliver James Sheridan

24 Rue des Juifs
Strasbourg
Alsace 67000
+33 388364968
www.restaurantlacasserole.fr

Opening hours	Closed Monday and Sunday
Credit cards	Accepted
Price range	Expensive
Style	Smart casual
Cuisine	Modern French
Recommended for	High end

'A Michelin-starred restaurant, very exclusive and cosy with only about twenty seats. Local classics but with a "gastronomique" touch. The team members are young and enthusiastic. I will say this: classic transformed into *fantastique*!'—Oliver James Sheridan

LA CUILLER À POT

Recommended by
Oliver James Sheridan

18b Rue Finkwiller
Strasbourg
Alsace 67000
+33 388355630
www.lacuillerapot.com

Opening hours	Closed Monday and Sunday
Credit cards	Accepted
Price range	Affordable
Style	Casual
Cuisine	French
Recommended for	Wish I'd opened

'It feels like you have been invited to eat at a friend's house, with the husband in the kitchen and the wife in the dining room. It's a small and very cosy restaurant and the food is simple and so well executed – faultless from beginning to end.'—Oliver James Sheridan

MOUSTIQUE ET FRELON

Recommended by
Oliver James Sheridan

7 Place Clément
Strasbourg
Alsace 67000
+33 388229775

Opening hours	Closed Sunday
Credit cards	Accepted but not AMEX
Price range	Budget
Style	Casual
Cuisine	Italian
Recommended for	Bargain

'A very small Italian restaurant that serves great pizzas and pasta. I love Italian food so it's always a pleasure to eat here.'—Oliver James Sheridan

LE PENJAB

Recommended by
Oliver James Sheridan

12 Rue des Tonneliers
Strasbourg
Alsace 67000
+33 388323637
www.lepenjab.fr

Opening hours	Open 7 days
Credit cards	Accepted
Price range	Budget
Style	Casual
Cuisine	Indian
Recommended for	Regular neighbourhood

'Of course you can guess that it is an Indian restaurant. I often go here because I'm a Brit living in France and it's very rare to eat a top-quality curry over here, but at last I've found it. There's a nice ambience, it's clean, the decor is very sober and the food is fresh and full of flavour. It takes me back to London!'
—Oliver James Sheridan

CHÂTEAU DE BRINDOS

Recommended by
Xabier Diez Esteibar

Château de Brindos
1 Allée du Château
Anglet
Aquitaine 64600
+33 559238980
www.chateaudebrindos.com

Opening hours	Open 7 days
Credit cards	Accepted
Price range	Affordable
Style	Smart casual
Cuisine	French
Recommended for	Worth the travel

'It's worth the travel for its amazing surroundings and the great regional French cuisine.'
—Xabier Diez Esteibar

GRAVELIER

114 Cours de Verdun
Bordeaux
Aquitaine 33000
+33 556481715
www.gravelier.fr

Opening hours	Closed Saturday and Sunday
Credit cards	Accepted
Price range	Affordable
Style	Casual
Cuisine	Modern French
Recommended for	Bargain

LA TUPINA

6 Rue Porte de la Monnaie
Bordeaux
Aquitaine 33800
+33 556915637
www.latupina.com

Opening hours	Open 7 days
Credit cards	Accepted
Price range	Affordable
Style	Casual
Cuisine	Southwest French
Recommended for	Worth the travel

'All the spirit of Southwest French cuisine is at La Tupina. Simple food, great produce and superb atmosphere.'—Pascal Aussignac

In a grand old fireplace, centrepiece of the dining room, sits the titular *tupiña* (Basque for 'cast-iron kettle'). It's still used, as it has been ever since the place opened in 1968, in the summer to make chips (fries) and in winter to warm soup, the smell of which infuses every corner of the handsome nineteenth-century building. Service is sparkling, the food comforting and robust, and, of course (this being Bordeaux), the wine is world-class. It's a restaurant so utterly French it could have been created as a set for a Disney movie, but La Tupina is no artifice – it's a Bordeaux institution.

LES PRÉS D'EUGÉNIE

234 Rue René Vielle
Eugénie les Bains
Aquitaine 40320
+33 558050607
www.michelguerard.com

Opening hours	Open 7 days
Credit cards	Accepted
Price range	Expensive
Style	Smart casual
Cuisine	Modern French
Recommended for	High end

'Here you will experience timeless, understated excellence.'—Marcus Eaves

Despite being 500 miles from Paris, this family-run Relais & Châteaux-registered restaurant (three Michelin stars for thirty-seven years) and spa have long managed to court an upmarket clientele. Inspired by his wife Christine, daughter of the founder of Biotherm skincare products, Michel Guérard coined the term '*cuisine minceur*' (slimming cuisine) in the mid-1970s. Light but flavoursome dishes adhering to this philosophy include Champvallon lamb with thyme, and sea bass ceviche with mango, while dishes from the diet-free carte include Chinese-inspired 'soft pillows' of morels and wild mushrooms in truffle sauce, and soufflé of lemon verbena (from the garden) with raspberry coulis.

LE RELAIS DE LA POSTE

24 Avenue de Maremne
Magescq
Aquitaine 40140
+33 558477025
www.relaisposte.com

Opening hours	Closed Monday and Tuesday
Credit cards	Accepted
Price range	Expensive
Style	Smart casual
Cuisine	Southwest French
Recommended for	High end

CAP E TOT

Recommended by
Yves Camdeborde

10 Carrère du Château
Morlanne
Aquitaine 64370
+33 559816268

Opening hours	Open 7 days
Credit cards	Accepted but not AMEX
Price range	Affordable
Style	Casual
Cuisine	French Bistro
Recommended for	Wish I'd opened

'David Ducassou and I worked together in Paris but he went back to his home village to try to breathe new life into it. He has managed to bring the people of this village together and give new life to the place, notably by giving local farmers the chance to return to growing excellent produce, which he then showcases at this exquisite restaurant.'—Yves Camdeborde

LA FERME D'ORTHE

Recommended by
Julien Duboué

9 Rue de la Fontaine
Orthevielle
Aquitaine 40300
+33 558730103
www.lafermedorthe.fr

Opening hours	Closed Monday
Credit cards	Accepted
Price range	Budget
Style	Casual
Cuisine	French Bistro
Recommended for	Bargain

'Here you'll get a very good, well made, simple meal.'
—Julien Duboué

AU BON COIN LES PIEDS DE COCHON

Recommended by
Julien Duboué

223 Rue de Château
Peyrehorade
Aquitaine 40300
+33 558730045
www.auboncoin40.fr

Opening hours	Open 7 days
Credit cards	Not accepted
Price range	Affordable
Style	Casual
Cuisine	French
Recommended for	Breakfast

'One of the things I treasure most is the experience of eating pig's trotters (feet) at this restaurant in my hometown. This experience is best on Wednesday mornings because of the street market that goes on. All the farmers from the nearby towns come here to eat.'—Julien Duboué

L'AUBERGE DU PAS DE VENT

Recommended by
Julien Duboué

281 Avenue Pas de Vent
Pouillon
Aquitaine 40350
+33 558983465
www.auberge-dupasdevent.com

Opening hours	Closed Wednesday
Credit cards	Accepted but not AMEX
Price range	Affordable
Style	Casual
Cuisine	Southwest French
Recommended for	Local favourite

'Fresh, traditional cuisine from Les Landes.'
—Julien Duboué

MICHEL TRAMA

Recommended by
Ollie Couillaud

52 Rue Royale
Puymirol
Aquitaine 47270
+33 553953146
www.aubergade.com

Opening hours	Open 7 days
Credit cards	Accepted
Price range	Expensive
Style	Smart casual
Cuisine	Modern French
Recommended for	Worth the travel

'One of the best meals I've ever had.'—Ollie Couillaud

Michel Trama, champion diver turned two-Michelin-starred chef and cigar aficionado, runs this former monastery with wife, Maryse. The thirteenth-century building's theatrical interiors, where sofas rest on lion-like feet, may not be to everyone's taste. However, Trama's witty dishes are worth the flight to Toulouse, or the train journey to Agen. These include signature foie-gras hamburger, lobster lasagne, and truffled potatoes en papillote. From mid-December until mid-March take Trama's Tout Truffle menu — a eulogy to the black fungus. Desserts include *cristalline* of green apple or Double Corona Trama, crafted with chocolate and tobacco leaf.

LE SAINT EUTROPE

Recommended by
Jonathan Jones,
Steve Williams

4 Rue Saint Eutrope
Clermont-Ferrand
Auvergne 63000
+33 473343041
www.sainteutrope.com

Opening hours	Closed Saturday to Monday
Credit cards	Accepted but not AMEX
Price range	Affordable
Style	Casual
Cuisine	French Bistro
Recommended for	Worth the travel

'A fantastic, tiny, beautiful bistro with an old-fashioned charm and brilliant cooking.'—Jonathan Jones

RÉGIS ET JACQUES MARCON

Recommended by
Philip Howard

Larsiallas
St Bonnet-le-Froid
Auvergne 43290
+33 471599372
www.regismarcon.fr

Opening hours	Closed Tuesday and Wednesday
Credit cards	Accepted
Price range	Expensive
Style	Smart casual
Cuisine	Modern French
Recommended for	Worth the travel

'World-class cooking in a spectacular rural environment.'—Philip Howard

In the wilds of the remote Haute-Loire, master of the mushroom Régis Marcon and his son Jacques create dishes that garner three Michelin stars, using the rich natural pantry in their midst. Dishes – such as lobster cassoulet with green lentils from nearby Le Puy, then mushroom tea scented with tansy served between fish and meat courses, and lamb with cep granita – are served in a sleekly modern dining room. By day this clever redux of the original auberge has interrupted views over the Ardèche River and Monts du Velay (bedrooms are sympathetically sunk into the grounds), while at night its ceiling lights sparkle. Follow on with local cheeses and rum-free, raspberry-rich baba.

MAISON DECORET

Recommended by
Pascal Barbot

15 Rue du Parc
Vichy
Auvergne 03200
+33 470976506
www.maisondecoret.com

Opening hours	Closed Tuesday and Wednesday
Credit cards	Accepted
Price range	Expensive
Style	Smart casual
Cuisine	Modern French
Recommended for	Worth the travel

It might seem a little out of the way in the slow-paced, chintzy town of Vichy, but there's nothing provincial about rising star Jacques Decoret's cooking. The former winner of the coveted Ouvrier de France award set up this one-star venture with the help of his wife Martine, who was behind the restaurant's chic white interiors. (The Napoleon III-era chalet also boasts five tasteful guest rooms.) The *menu confiance* allows Decoret carte blanche to explore his sophisticated flavour combinations, but he's not immune to fun: foie gras with the 'sweetness and acidities' of green pumpkin and orange, say, or a certain penchant for plastic TV trays.

CANCALE OYSTER STANDS

Recommended by
Shaun Rankin

Rue des Parcs
Cancale
Brittany 35260

Opening hours	Open 7 days
Reservation policy	No
Credit cards	Not accepted
Price range	Budget
Style	Casual
Cuisine	Seafood
Recommended for	Bargain

'One of my favourite things to do is head to Cancale where you can buy and eat oysters on the dock with the fishermen. I like them with a sprinkling of shallot and a dash of Cabernet Sauvignon vinegar.'
—Shaun Rankin

RESTAURANT PATRICK JEFFROY

Recommended by
Jean-Marie Baudic

Hôtel de Carantec
20 Rue du Kelenn
Carantec
Brittany 29660
+33 298670047
www.hoteldecarantec.com

Opening hours	Closed Monday and Tuesday
Credit cards	Accepted
Price range	Expensive
Style	Casual
Cuisine	Modern French
Recommended for	Local favourite

'An honest, genuine chef, a very beautiful restaurant and a gorgeous view. The products and food are always delicious. A real pleasure.'—Jean-Marie Baudic

LE BON SENS

Recommended by
Jean-Marie Baudic

5 Rue Saint-Nicolas
Guingamp
Brittany 22200
+33 296387216

Opening hours	Closed Sunday
Credit cards	Accepted but not AMEX
Price range	Budget
Style	Casual
Cuisine	French Bistro
Recommended for	Bargain

'Serves really cheap and good food with an excellent wine selection. A very nice place.'—Jean-Marie Baudic

AUBERGE DU PONT D'ACIGNÉ

Recommended by
Flora Mikula

Le Pont d'Acigné
Noyal-sur-Vilaine
Brittany 35530
+33 299625255
www.auberge-du-pont-dacigne.com

Opening hours	Closed Monday and Tuesday
Credit cards	Accepted
Price range	Expensive
Style	Casual
Cuisine	French
Recommended for	High end

'When I need to recharge my batteries I go to this place in Brittany. I love going there. I particularly like the way Chef Sylvain Guillemot's cuisine has developed over time.'—Flora Mikula

CHAR À BANCS

Recommended by
Jean-Marie Baudic

Ferme-Auberge de la famille Lamour
Moulin de la Ville Geffroy
Plélo
Brittany 22170
+33 296741363
www.ferme-auberge-charabancs-bretagne.com

Opening hours	Closed Tuesday
Credit cards	Accepted but not AMEX
Price range	Affordable
Style	Casual
Cuisine	French
Recommended for	Regular neighbourhood

'A safe bet. A family atmosphere and a place in symbiosis with nature.'—Jean-Marie Baudic

L'AUBERGE DES GLAZICKS

Recommended by
Yves Camdeborde

7 Rue de la Plage
Plomodiern
Brittany 29550
+33 298815232
www.aubergedesglazick.com

Opening hours	Closed Monday and Tuesday
Credit cards	Accepted but not AMEX
Price range	Expensive
Style	Smart casual
Cuisine	French
Recommended for	High end

'This place just oozes Frenchness and a sense of well being. It is set in a little village in Brittany and the cuisine is to die for. Time stands still here – it's a pure joy. The chef is passionate about cooking.'
—Yves Camdeborde

LE COQUILLAGE

Recommended by
Michel Troisgros

Château Richeux
St-Méloir des Ondes
Brittany 35350
+33 299896476
www.maisons-de-bricourt.com

Opening hours	Open 7 days
Credit cards	Accepted
Price range	Expensive
Style	Smart casual
Cuisine	French Seafood
Recommended for	Wish I'd opened

BISSOH

Recommended by
Tomoyasu Kamo

1a Rue du Faubourg St Jacques
Beaune
Burgundy 21200
+33 380249950
www.bissoh.com

Opening hours	Closed Monday and Tuesday
Credit cards	Accepted but not AMEX
Price range	Affordable
Style	Smart casual
Cuisine	Japanese-French
Recommended for	Wish I'd opened

CAVES MADELEINE

Recommended by
Josep Roca, Gabriel Rucker

8 Rue Faubourg Madeleine
Beaune
Burgundy 21200
+33 380229330

Opening hours	Closed Thursday and Sunday
Credit cards	Accepted
Price range	Affordable
Style	Smart casual
Cuisine	Burgundian
Recommended for	Worth the travel

'One of most memorable bottles of wine there and the food was simple but perfect.'—Gabriel Rucker

Very much off the track beaten by those devoted to the Red Guide, this rural French bistro has been popularized via word of mouth and because of an ability to pair excellent wines with brilliantly cooked classic French dishes. The usual suspects are all done very well. From confit duck to andouille and boeuf bourguignon to snail cassolette, the regional authenticity always feels nourishing. Net curtains drape in the windows of a fairly unsuspecting facade behind which diners sit cheek by jowl on communal wooden tables. Wines are available to take away; a mere €6 (£5; $8) corkage is charged for consumption in house.

LA COLLINE DU COLOMBIER

Recommended by
Alexandre Gauthier

La Colline du Colombier
Iguerande
Burgundy 71340
+33 385840724
www.troisgros.fr

Opening hours	Closed Tuesday and Wednesday
Credit cards	Accepted
Price range	Expensive
Style	Casual
Cuisine	French
Recommended for	Wish I'd opened

RELAIS BERNARD LOISEAU

Recommended by
Guy Savoy

2 Rue d'Argentine
Saulieu
Burgundy 21210
+33 380905353
www.bernard-loiseau.com

Opening hours	Closed Tuesday and Wednesday
Credit cards	Accepted
Price range	Expensive
Style	Smart casual
Cuisine	Modern French
Recommended for	Regular neighbourhood

LES HAUTES ROCHES

Recommended by
Ljubomir Stanisic

86 Quai de la Loire
Rochecorbon
Centre 37210
+33 247528888
www.leshautesroches.com

Opening hours	Open 7 days
Credit cards	Accepted
Price range	Expensive
Style	Smart casual
Cuisine	French
Recommended for	Worth the travel

'A beautiful location overlooking one of the largest wild rivers in Europe. The head chef, Didier Edon, is one of the most fascinating people I have ever met and they serve an unbeatable artichoke dish.'
—Ljubomir Stanisic

LE PARC

Recommended by
Patrick O'Connell

Domaine les Crayères
64 Boulevard Henry Vasnier
Reims
Champagne-Ardenne 51100
+33 326249000
www.lescrayeres.com

Opening hours	Closed Monday and Tuesday
Credit cards	Accepted
Price range	Expensive
Style	Smart casual
Cuisine	Modern French
Recommended for	Worth the travel

L'ASSIETTE CHAMPENOISE

Recommended by
Emilio Garip

40 Avenue Paul Vaillant-Couturie
Tinqueux
Champagne-Ardenne 51430
+33 326846464
www.assiettechampenoise.com

Opening hours	Closed Tuesday
Credit cards	Accepted
Price range	Expensive
Style	Smart casual
Cuisine	Modern French
Recommended for	Worth the travel

'It's a perfect restaurant, one that you enjoy from the moment you step foot in the place. Their tableware and silverware are second to none and cater to all courses. It must be one of the few places that serves Krug by the glass. Chef Arnaud Lallement is always on hand and his cooking is superb. The cheese selection is incredible and you can always round off the evening with a cigar and an XO Cognac. It's in a hotel so there's no need to worry about the time or having to drive home afterwards and you can enjoy one of the best breakfasts in the world the following morning.'
—Emilio Garip

AUBERGE DU VIEUX PUITS

Recommended by
Paul Pairet

5 Avenue Saint-Victor
Fontjoncouse
Languedoc-Roussillon 11360
+33 468440737
www.aubergeduvieuxpuits.fr

Opening hours	Closed Monday and Tuesday
Credit cards	Accepted
Price range	Expensive
Style	Smart casual
Cuisine	Modern French
Recommended for	Worth the travel

'Delicate, powerful flavours.'—Paul Pairet

The cuisine of Gilles Goujon, son of a fighter pilot, is rated three stars by Michelin and therefore 'worth a special journey'. A GPS is essential when making this pilgrimage. The sleepy Languedoc hamlet of Fontjoncouse is populated by fewer than a hundred – including some of the restaurant's sixteen chefs. Dishes are beautiful tableaux: from lightly poached oyster with a smoky 'pearl' that must be broken with a miniature hammer, to vol-au-vent of rabbit's kidney, and an assiette of five types of tomato. Considering the location, it is advisable to book one of the pretty rooms by the pool. The freshly baked breakfast arrives in a basket.

LA RÉSERVE RIMBAUD

Recommended by
Julien Duboué

820 Avenue St Maur
Montpellier
Languedoc-Roussillon 34000
+33 467725253
www.reserve-rimbaud.com

Opening hours	Closed Monday
Credit cards	Accepted
Price range	Affordable
Style	Smart casual
Cuisine	Southern French
Recommended for	Worth the travel

'A very pleasant waterfront restaurant with great food by the chef Charles Fontes.'—Julien Duboué

LA CALE

The Beachfront
Blainville-sur-Mer
Lower Normandy 50560
+33 233472272

Opening hours	Variable
Reservation policy	No
Credit cards	Accepted
Price range	Affordable
Style	Casual
Cuisine	French
Recommended for	Worth the travel

'Basic simple food: wood-roasted leg of lamb, snails, mussels in cider and cream... and it's serve-yourself wine and bread. All the while you are perched above acres of oyster beds. Dreamy.'—Renee Erickson

LE BACARETTO

44 Rue de la Chaussée
Honfleur
Lower Normandy 14600
+33 231148311

Opening hours	Closed Wednesday and Thursday
Credit cards	Accepted
Price range	Budget
Style	Casual
Cuisine	French Bistro
Recommended for	Wish I'd opened

'A bistro in all its splendour. Everything is home-made, from the pastry to the bread and desserts. Excellent charcuterie and cheese. They don't use packaged salad here, for sure. The wine is, like everything else, exceptional. This bistro has a soul – its own soul, its own identity. It's lively. The owner has got it all. Well done.'—Jean-Marie Baudic

SAQUANA

22 Place Hamelin
Honfleur
Lower Normandy 14600
+33 231894080
www.alexandre-bourdas.com

Opening hours	Closed Monday to Wednesday
Credit cards	Accepted
Price range	Expensive
Style	Casual
Cuisine	Modern French
Recommended for	Regular neighbourhood

DOMAINE DE MÉJANASSÈRE

Méjanassère
Entraygues-sur-Truyère
Midi-Pyrénées 12140
+33 565445476
www.domaine-de-mejanassere.fr

Opening hours	Variable
Credit cards	Accepted
Price range	Affordable
Style	Casual
Cuisine	French
Recommended for	Bargain

'Beautiful old country house totally lost in the Aveyron countryside. The owner grows all his own vegetables, fruits, leaves and herbs in the garden. He has his own vines and makes wine, bakes his own bread and pâtés in the log fire and roasts a pig each night on the spit. It's the perfect place to relax, is not expensive and the view from the little terrace at the back of the restaurant is spectacular.'—James Wilkins

BRAS

Route de l'Aubrac
Laguiole
Midi-Pyrénées 12210
+33 565511820
www.bras.fr

Opening hours	Closed Monday
Credit cards	Accepted
Price range	Expensive
Style	Smart casual
Cuisine	Modern French
Recommended for	Worth the travel

'Michel Bras was a complete visionary when he opened this restaurant and it is still utterly magical. Sébastien, his son, has taken over the kitchen and has managed to honour the legacy of his father's work, while also adding his own personal touch and talent.'
—Pierre Gagnaire

LA COUR DE RÉMI

Recommended by
Alexandre Gauthier

1 Rue Baillet
Bermicourt
Nord-Pas-de-Calais 62130
+33 321033333
www.lacourderemi.com

Opening hours	Open 7 days
Credit cards	Accepted
Price range	Affordable
Style	Smart casual
Cuisine	Northern French
Recommended for	Regular neighbourhood

'High-end bistronomy in a nice setting.'
—Alexandre Gauthier

LE CHATILLON

Recommended by
Alexandre Gauthier

6 Rue Charles Tellier
Boulogne-sur-Mer
Nord-Pas-de-Calais 62200
+33 321314395
www.le-chatillon.com

Opening hours	Closed Sunday
Credit cards	Accepted but not AMEX
Price range	Affordable
Style	Casual
Cuisine	Seafood
Recommended for	Breakfast

'The atmosphere is reminiscent of a fishing port. Good for eating a savoury sailor's breakfast, washed down with a coffee and a strong glass of brandy.'
—Alexandre Gauthier

LA GRENOUILLÈRE

Recommended by
Yves Camdeborde, Kobe
Desramaults, Carlo
Mirarchi, Cyril Molard,
Michel Troisgros

19 Rue de la Grenouillère
La Madeleine-sous-Montreuil
Nord-Pas-de-Calais 62170
+33 321060722
www.lagrenouillere.fr

Opening hours	Variable
Credit cards	Accepted
Price range	Expensive
Style	Formal
Cuisine	Modern French
Recommended for	Worth the travel

'Alexandre Gauthier has created a world of his own, a place totally unique to him. When you go there, you get sucked into his universe. The table setting, the decor in the bedrooms, the crockery, the general attitude… If you spend two days there it infuses your whole being. He creates a convincingly authentic atmosphere devoid of commercialism. He achieves this because he loves it and you really sense that.'—Yves Camdeborde

The Auberge de la Grenouillère opened as early as 1920 in the pretty village of Montreuil-sur-Mer, a few miles from Le Touquet. It once specialized in dishes involving frogs but, at least since 2003 – when chef Alexandre Gauthier (then aged just twenty-three) took over the kitchen from his father – the cuisine has ranged far wider. Gauthier's cooking is bold and vigorous: Norway lobster comes to the table on a bed of still-smoking juniper twigs; morel mushrooms are stuffed with sweetbreads and then covered in tiny cones of raw turnip; a white chocolate and potato shell, once broken into, reveals a sticky centre of strawberry compote. One of the best restaurants in this part of France.

LE CAVEAU

Recommended by
Alexandre Gauthier

40 Place du Général de Gaulle
Montreuil-sur-Mer
Nord-Pas-de-Calais 62170
+33 321060521
www.lecaveau.fr

Opening hours	Closed Monday
Credit cards	Accepted but not AMEX
Price range	Budget
Style	Casual
Cuisine	Brasserie
Recommended for	Bargain

'Traditional cuisine in a welcoming setting. I go for the Welsh rarebit.'—Alexandre Gauthier

LE RELAIS DES SALINES

Recommended by
Ollie Couillaud

Port des Salines
Le Grand-Village-Plage
Poitou-Charentes 17370
+33 546758242
www.lerelaisdessalines.com

Opening hours	Open 7 days
Credit cards	Accepted but not AMEX
Price range	Affordable
Style	Casual
Cuisine	French Seafood
Recommended for	Local favourite

'A fisherman's hut right in the middle of the salt marshes that serves great food.'—Ollie Couillaud

This part of the world is famous for its seafood, and where better to enjoy it than this colourful little shed right on the waterfront. Although the decor is best described as 'no frills', the menu is anything but. There are the famous Oléron oysters, of course, collected from the local salt marshes, but also meaty Atlantic cod with vanilla, hake fillet with chorizo sauce – the best ingredients served in surprisingly experimental ways. It's understandably popular, not just with the tourists that flock here in summer but also with a grateful local crowd, so you'd be well advised to book.

RESTAURANT EDOUARD LOUBET

Recommended by
Yannick Alléno

Domaine de Capelongue
Les Claparèdes
Bonnieux
Provence-Alpes-Côte d'Azur 84480
+33 490758978
www.capelongue.com

Opening hours	Closed Tuesday and Wednesday
Credit cards	Accepted
Price range	Expensive
Style	Smart casual
Cuisine	Provençal
Recommended for	High end

'Édouard Loubet lets his creative talent shine through an astounding gastronomic experience that varies according to the season. This is Provence in all its glory.'—Yannick Alléno

High up in a lavender-sniffer's paradise, Édouard Loubet adds the hot, herbal flavours of Provence to food that, for all its refinement, remains pleasingly simple to eat. It's served in an airy dining room in a restored stone farmhouse, with distressed wood and pale linens that are also sported in the seventeen bedrooms. There's fern-infused milk in a '100 per cent Lubéron' asparagus carbonara, and nostalgia in specialities like a rack of lamb in a nest of wild thyme, served with Loubet's grandmother's wildly luxurious potato gratin. For dessert, cedar from the local forest makes it into the soufflé. On summer afternoons head outside for a more relaxed menu.

LA CHÈVRE D'OR

Recommended by
Yoann Conte

Rue du Barri
Èze
Provence-Alpes-Côte d'Azur 06360
+33 492106661
www.chevredor.com

Opening hours	Open 7 days
Credit cards	Accepted
Price range	Expensive
Style	Smart casual
Cuisine	French
Recommended for	Wish I'd opened

'I like the view, the setting, the lush greenery, the surrounding mountains and sea and the historic village.'—Yoann Conte

BRASSERIE OM

Recommended by
Michel Portos

25 Quai des Belges
Marseille
Provence-Alpes-Côte d'Azur 13001
+33 491338033

Opening hours	Open 7 days
Credit cards	Accepted
Price range	Affordable
Style	Casual
Cuisine	French Brasserie
Recommended for	Breakfast

'Chic, popular, reliable and friendly. With a view overlooking the old port, this joint is a killer, not forgetting of course the OM (Olympique de Marseille – Marseille football team) logo!'—Michel Portos

CHEZ MICHEL

Recommended by
Michel Portos

6 Rue des Catalans
Marseille
Provence-Alpes-Côte d'Azur 13007
+33 491523063
www.restaurant-michel-13.fr

Opening hours	Open 7 days
Credit cards	Accepted
Price range	Expensive
Style	Smart casual
Cuisine	French Seafood
Recommended for	Local favourite

'Another historic address – even my grandfather used to come here. They serve the best bouillabaisse in Marseille. It's bang opposite the Plage des Catalans, the beach I used to go to as a child.'—Michel Portos

If you want to sample the definitive bouillabaisse, the classic Provençal fish stew that originated in Marseille, then look no further than this smart bistro adjacent to the old port. Check out the display of fresh fish in the boat-shaped counter, then take your seat for the main event. First comes the soup: saffron-rich poaching liquor made from whole rockfish, blitzed and sieved to remove the bones. Meanwhile, white-jacketed waiters fillet prime fish tableside and present them as a platter with saffron potatoes. Other local specialities include *bourride* (fish stew thickened with garlic mayonnaise) or grilled fresh fish of your choice.

CHEZ SAUVEUR

Recommended by
Michel Portos

10 Rue d'Aubagne
Marseille
Provence-Alpes-Côte d'Azur 13001
+33 491543396
www.chezsauveur.fr

Opening hours	Closed Monday and Sunday.
Credit cards	Accepted
Price range	Budget
Style	Casual
Cuisine	Pizza
Recommended for	Bargain

'One of the best pizzas in Marseille, served in surroundings that haven't changed at all in the last fifty years!'—Michel Portos

Nothing much has changed at Chez Sauveur, one of Marseille's oldest pizzerias, since it opened back in 1943. The wood-fired pizzas still come out of the original oven, and are prepared to exactly the same recipe –

the only difference being that these days the ads lining the walls have become fashionably 'vintage'. Although the young owner has attracted a hipper clientele of late, this remains a family-friendly neighbourhood favourite, with punters of all ages enjoying Sicilian specialities like calzoni. If too packed to find a place, you can also get your Marguerite or Meridionale to go.

AU FALAFEL

Recommended by
Michel Portos

5 Rue Lulli
Marseille
Provence-Alpes-Côte d'Azur 13001
+33 491540855
www.aufalafel.com

Opening hours	Closed Saturday
Credit cards	Accepted but not AMEX
Price range	Budget
Style	Casual
Cuisine	Israeli
Recommended for	Regular neighbourhood

'A little local restaurant. There is a pavement terrace for relaxing outside on sunny days. Simple, good food that hits the spot! And the ingredients are fresh.' —Michel Portos

LE MAS DE LULLI

Recommended by
Michel Portos

4 Rue Lulli
Marseille
Provence-Alpes-Côte d'Azur 13001
+33 491332590

Opening hours	Open 7 days
Credit cards	Accepted
Price range	Budget
Style	Casual
Cuisine	French-Italian
Recommended for	Late night

'A small, historic restaurant nestled in the old town centre and crawling with its night owls and artists. The kitchen turns out decent cuisine if you want to grab dinner after a show without necessarily resorting to a hamburger.'—Michel Portos

PERON

Recommended by
Michel Portos

56 Corniche du Président John Kennedy
Marseille
Provence-Alpes-Côte d'Azur 13007
+33 491521522
www.restaurant-peron.com

Opening hours	Open 7 days
Credit cards	Accepted
Price range	Expensive
Style	Casual
Cuisine	French Seafood
Recommended for	Wish I'd opened

'Set in an historic address, with a stunning view over the Mediterranean sea and tastefully updated decor.'
—Michel Portos

LE PETIT NICE

Recommended by
Michel Portos

17 Rue des Braves
Marseille
Provence-Alpes-Côte d'Azur 13007
+33 491592592
www.passedat.fr

Opening hours	Closed Monday and Sunday
Credit cards	Accepted
Price range	Expensive
Style	Smart casual
Cuisine	Seafood
Recommended for	High end

'I come here for the setting, for the view, and above all for the creativity of the chef, Gérald Passédat! The only three-Michelin-starred restaurant for miles around.'
—Michel Portos

Gérald Passédat was born in this neo-Greek villa, purchased by his grandfather, and continues to draw inspiration from its spectacular views of the Mediterranean. Apt to go into a paean about the personality of the little-known fish (the 'solitary' comber, the 'flirtatious' wrasse) that form the basis of his three-star cooking, Passédat reserves his greatest passion for his cult take on southern favourite bouillabaisse. The corner table has impressive panoramic views – as does the terrace where you can swim and sip pastis, should you opt for a night in one of the hotel's restful suites.

BOULANGERIE ERIC KAYSER

Recommended by
Jérôme Lorvellec

Route de Sospel
Menton
Provence-Alpes-Côte d'Azur 06500
+33 493965977

Opening hours	Open 7 days
Reservation policy	No
Credit cards	Accepted
Price range	Budget
Style	Casual
Cuisine	Bakery
Recommended for	Breakfast

'It is a typical French boulangerie and patisserie with very nice croissants and a nice atmosphere.'
—Jérôme Lorvellec

FLEUR DE SEL

Recommended by
Jérôme Lorvellec

2 Rue du Vieux Collège
Menton
Provence-Alpes-Côte d'Azur 06500
+33 493448734

Opening hours	Closed Monday and Sunday
Credit cards	Accepted but not AMEX
Price range	Budget
Style	Casual
Cuisine	French crêperie
Recommended for	Bargain

'If you want to eat a traditional salted or sweet crêpe you must go there.'—Jérôme Lorvellec

LE MIRAZUR

Recommended by
Steffen Hansen,
Stephen Harris, Mikael
Jonsson, Sasu Laukkonen,
Jérôme Lorvellec

30 Avenue Aristide Briand
Menton
Provence-Alpes-Côte d'Azur 06500
+33 492418686
www.mirazur.fr

Opening hours	Closed Monday and Tuesday
Credit cards	Accepted
Price range	Expensive
Style	Smart casual
Cuisine	Modern Provençal
Recommended for	Worth the travel

'I've been there five times now and the chef, Mauro, keeps surprising me every time. Incredibly pure tastes and real cooking from the heart.'—Sasu Laukkonen

Le Mirazur overlooks the gleaming Côte d'Azur, metres (yards) from Italy's border. 'Food's aromas awaken the oldest memories' believes Argentinian head chef Mauro Colagreco, who left home for France to learn the 'building blocks of cuisine' with Alain Ducasse, Alain Passard and the late Bernard Loiseau. He breathed life back into a shell that had been closed for years, sowing an edible garden in the process. Colagreco's South American heritage is evident in ingredients such as quinoa, mate (for macaroons) and dulce de leche, although dishes such as the deconstructed Vietnamese spring roll show Colagreco's increasing interest in Asia.

L'O À LA BOUCHE

Recommended by
Mauro Colagreco

59 Porte de France
Menton
Provence-Alpes-Côte d'Azur 06500
+33 493353925

Opening hours	Closed Wednesday
Credit cards	Accepted
Price range	Affordable
Style	Casual
Cuisine	French Bistro
Recommended for	Regular neighbourhood

'A small, family-run restaurant serving good, down-to-earth food. Home-made pasta, fresh fish harpoon-caught by the owner's son, vegetables from the market... It's like eating at home.'
—Mauro Colagreco

LA MERENDA

Recommended by
Mauro Colagreco

4 Rue Raoul Bosio
Nice
Provence-Alpes-Côte d'Azur 06000
www.lamerenda.net

Opening hours	Closed Saturday and Sunday
Credit cards	Not accepted
Price range	Affordable
Style	Casual
Cuisine	Niçoise
Recommended for	Local favourite

'Local family food cooked by a great friend and chef.'
—Mauro Colagreco

Cash only, no phone, closed every weekend, tiny and quirky, La Merenda in Nice's Old Town is one of a kind. Dominique Le Stanc, who previously ran the star-studded Le Chantecler, took it over in the mid-1990s as a going concern that had been serving simple

Niçoise cuisine for some twenty years. He changed very little. All the cooking is done solo from the simple, open kitchen at the back. The menu, scrawled on a blackboard, is a short selection of local classics that, depending on the time of year, might include *pâtes au pistou*, *tripes à la Niçoise* and *tarte aux blettes*.

LE RELAIS DES MAURES

Recommended by
Tom Oldroyd

1 Avenue Koeklin
Rayol-Canadel-sur-Mer
Provence-Alpes-Côte d'Azur 83820
+33 494056127
www.lerelaisdesmaures.fr

Opening hours	Open 7 days
Credit cards	Accepted but not AMEX
Price range	Affordable
Style	Casual
Cuisine	French Mediterranean
Recommended for	Worth the travel

'A Michelin-rated restaurant attached to a handful of gorgeous bedrooms with balconies overlooking the sea. The place was empty when I went and I had the chef all to myself. What a lesson in ingredient-led cooking. Incredible food and wine.'—Tom Oldroyd

AU GRAND INQUISITEUR

Recommended by
Jérôme Lorvellec

15 Rue du Château
Roquebrune-Cap-Martin
Provence-Alpes-Côte d'Azur 06190
+33 493350537
www.augrandinquisiteur.com

Opening hours	Closed Monday
Credit cards	Accepted
Price range	Affordable
Style	Casual
Cuisine	French
Recommended for	Local favourite

'French classic but always on top.'—Jérôme Lorvellec

HOSTELLERIE JÉRÔME

Recommended by
Mauro Colagreco

20 Rue du Comté de Cessole
La Turbie
Provence-Alpes-Côte d'Azur 06320
+33 492415151
www.hostelleriejerome.com

Opening hours	Closed Monday and Tuesday
Credit cards	Accepted
Price range	Expensive
Style	Formal
Cuisine	French
Recommended for	High end

'I like the work of Bruno and his wife Marion: gourmet food, fresh produce, skilled work and exceptional wines.' —Mauro Colagreco

CAFÉ BRUNET

Recommended by
Yoann Conte

18 Place Gabriel Fauré
Annecy-le-Vieux
Rhone-Alpes 74940
+33 450276565
www.cafebrunet.com

Opening hours	Closed Monday and Sunday
Credit cards	Accepted
Price range	Affordable
Style	Casual
Cuisine	Café-Bistro
Recommended for	Regular neighbourhood

'The chef produces snappy cuisine. The place is very relaxed, with a nice terrace outside.' —Yoann Conte

CHEZ LUIGI

Recommended by
Yoann Conte

87 Rue Charlet Straton
Chamonix-Mont-Blanc
Rhone-Alpes 74400
+33 450540660

Opening hours	Closed in winter
Credit cards	Accepted
Price range	Budget
Style	Casual
Cuisine	Italian
Recommended for	Bargain

'You can enjoy a plate of tagliatelle carbonara at an altitude of 1,200 meters (3,937 feet) here, in the village of Chamonix, a place steeped in history and my own personal memories.' —Yoann Conte

LA SCIERIE

Recommended by
Yoann Conte

321–331 Route du Col des Aravis
La Clusaz
Rhone-Alpes 74220
+33 450633468
www.la-scierie.com

Opening hours	Open 7 days
Credit cards	Accepted but not AMEX
Price range	Affordable
Style	Smart casual
Cuisine	French
Recommended for	Local favourite

'The decor is heavy on wood, there is a fireplace, and the menu is full of fresh, local produce and specialities from the Savoie region.' —Yoann Conte

L'AUBERGE DU PONT DE COLLONGES

Recommended by
Pierre Koffmann,
Dietmar Priewe,
César Santos,
Manoj Vasaikar

40 Quai de la Plage
Collonges-au-Mont-d'Or
Rhone-Alpes 69660
+33 472429090
www.bocuse.fr

Opening hours	Open 7 days
Credit cards	Accepted
Price range	Expensive
Style	Smart casual
Cuisine	French
Recommended for	Worth the travel

'Paul is a great chef, I've always admired him and he inspired me to become a chef and to introduce my country's cuisine to the world. His restaurant is incredible and serves excellent food.' —César Santos

LE KINTESSENCE

Recommended by
Yoann Conte

Le K2 Hôtel
Route des Clarines
Courchevel 1850
Rhone-Alpes 73120
+33 479400880
www.hotellek2.com

Opening hours	Open 7 days
Credit cards	Accepted
Price range	Expensive
Style	Smart casual
Cuisine	French-Japanese Fusion
Recommended for	Worth the travel

'This is high-end luxury. It's in a fantastic location with magnificent views and total comfort.'—Yoann Conte

LE SCIOZIER

Recommended by
Emmanuel Renaut

Route du Gateau
Flumet
Rhone-Alpes 73590
+33 479317519
www.termedusciozier.com

Opening hours	Variable
Credit cards	Not accepted
Price range	Affordable
Style	Casual
Cuisine	French
Recommended for	Local favourite

'Simple, traditional regional cuisine, set in the middle of the meadows with a view overlooking Mont Blanc.'
—Emmanuel Renaut

HOSTELLERIE DU PORT DE GROSLÉE

Recommended by
Guy Savoy

Le Port
Groslée
Rhone-Alpes 01680
+33 474397101
www.hostellerieduportdegroslee.fr

Opening hours	Closed Monday
Credit cards	Accepted but not AMEX
Price range	Affordable
Style	Casual
Cuisine	Eastern French
Recommended for	Bargain

LA BOÎTE À CAFÉ

Recommended by
Guillaume Monjuré

3 Rue de l'Abbé Rozier
Lyon
Rhone-Alpes 69001
+33 427014871
www.cafemokxa.com

Opening hours	Open 7 days
Reservation policy	No
Credit cards	Accepted but not AMEX
Price range	Budget
Style	Casual
Cuisine	Café-Bakery
Recommended for	Breakfast

'A wide array of finely brewed coffees, prepared using both syphon vacuum and Chemex coffee makers. A laid-back atmosphere.'—Guillaume Monjuré

LA BRASSERIE GEORGES

Recommended by
Matthew Kirkley

30 Cours de Verdun
Lyon
Rhone-Alpes 69002
+33 472565454
www.brasseriegeorges.com

Opening hours	Open 7 days
Credit cards	Accepted
Price range	Affordable
Style	Casual
Cuisine	Classic French
Recommended for	Wish I'd opened

'I am jealous that this restaurant exists and also resentful that it wouldn't work in any other city but Lyon. It's a monstrously large banquet-hall-style space specializing in foods near and dear to my heart: *choucroute garni* (sauerkraut with meats), seafood platters and ice-cream sundaes. The sheer size of the place combined with its very high-quality food is a spectacle to behold.'—Matthew Kirkley

This shrine to Lyonnaise gastronomy, the oldest brasserie in the city, does everything on a large scale – be it the 650-odd covers, or the fact that it once served the biggest sauerkraut in the world. Beneath the lustrous frescoes of this Art Deco brasserie, Ernest Hemingway, Paul Verlaine and Jacques Brel spent many a night nursing the Brasserie's home brew – a tradition since its inception, when Lyon water was considered of impeccable quality. These days the luminaries may be gone, but Brasserie Georges remains a buzzing place to while away an evening over regional specialities like tripe with pommes Lyonnais and Lyon sausage with pistachio.

BRASSERIE LÉON DE LYON

Recommended by
Jocky Petrie

1 Rue Pleney
Lyon
Rhone-Alpes 69001
+33 472101112
www.bistrotsdecuisiniers.com

Opening hours	Open 7 days
Credit cards	Accepted
Price range	Affordable
Style	Casual
Cuisine	French Brasserie
Recommended for	Wish I'd opened

'The place is steeped in history and serves some great classic dishes. It reminds me of my favourite movie, *Ratatouille*.'—Jocky Petrie

LA CAVE DE CÉCILE

12 Rue Longue
Lyon
Rhone-Alpes 69001
+33 478273099

Opening hours	Closed Sunday
Credit cards	Accepted
Price range	Budget
Style	Casual
Cuisine	French
Recommended for	Bargain

'This is a great place to hang out with friends. I go for their roast chicken and sautéed potatoes. There is also a nice line-up of wines.'—Guillaume Monjuré

On a backstreet in the heart of Lyon's Presqu'île (between the Rhône and Saône rivers) is chef and wine-enthusiast Cécile Ducroux's charming bistro. There's room for about two dozen diners, at simple wooden tables and chairs, who pack in to delight in the daily-changing, market-driven menu of traditional, homely French and Lyonnaise dishes. There might be creamed courgette (zucchini) soup, pot-au-feu, roast guinea fowl and then apricot clafoutis to finish. The list of about eighty wines is drawn mainly from small organic and natural producers from across France but specializing in Côtes du Rhône and Burgundy.

CHEZ TERRA

81 Rue Duguesclin
Lyon
Rhone-Alpes 69006
+33 478890504

Opening hours	Closed Monday and Sunday
Credit cards	Accepted
Price range	Affordable
Style	Casual
Cuisine	Japanese
Recommended for	Regular neighbourhood

'Fresh, high-quality ingredients, cooked to perfection. A fine selection of saké.'—Guillaume Monjuré

L'OURSON QUI BOIT

23 Rue Royale
Lyon
Rhone-Alpes 69001
+33 478272337

Opening hours	Closed Wednesday and Sunday
Credit cards	Accepted but not AMEX
Price range	Affordable
Style	Casual
Cuisine	Japanese-French
Recommended for	Worth the travel

'An amazing chef. There's an enormous amount of technique and great ingredients. Minimalist and full of personality.'—Roberta Sudbrack

RESTAURANT DANIEL ET DENISE

156 Rue de Créqui
Lyon
Rhone-Alpes 69003
+33 478606653
www.daniel-et-denise.fr

Opening hours	Closed Saturday and Sunday
Credit cards	Accepted
Price range	Affordable
Style	Casual
Cuisine	Lyonnaise
Recommended for	Local favourite

'Authentic cuisine from Lyon based on local products.' —Guillaume Monjuré

Offering offal in abundance, the first of the two Daniel et Denise is close to Part-Dieu station. Lyonnaise dishes devised and often cooked by German-born chef Joseph Viola – Meilleur Ouvrier de France 2004 – include frisée salad with roasted pig's ears, calf's brain pan-fried in butter, deep-fried breaded tripe, and beef bourguignon. If you still feel like continuing after such hearty fare, desserts include roasted pineapple with vanilla ice cream or crème brûlée. As well as Viola's cooking, the interior adheres to the traditional bouchon semiotics: from red chequered tablecloths protected by crackly paper, to the frying pans festooned in the part-tiled dining room.

FLOCONS DE SEL

1775 Route du Leutaz
Megève
Rhone-Alpes 74120
+33 450214999
www.floconsdesel.com

Recommended by
Guillaume Cantin, Matthew
Kirkley, Reto Lampart,
Guillaume Monjuré

Opening hours	Closed Tuesday and Wednesday
Credit cards	Accepted
Price range	Expensive
Style	Smart casual
Cuisine	Modern French
Recommended for	Worth the travel

'This is a gourmet address not too far from Lyon.'
—Guillaume Monjuré

Having manned the kitchens at Paris's uber-luxury Hotel Crillon and London's Claridge's, Emmanuel Renaut sought a more tranquil canvas for his talents. His choice — an alpine chalet with a handful of high-end design rooms and a spa offering treatments based on the chef's favourite plants — paid off, and in 2012 he scooped a third Michelin star. Today, skiers and gourmets from Geneva can get a workout with the two-and-a-quarter hour, nine-course 'hike' menu, typically immersed in the locale, with Lake Geneva fish, Savoie biscuit (cracker) and mountain cheese. Up here the air is rarefied, but then again, so is Renaut's cuisine.

LA SAUVAGEONNE

Hameau du Leutaz
Megève
Rhone-Alpes 74120
+33 450919081
www.restaurant-sauvageonne.com

Recommended by
Emmanuel Renaut

Opening hours	Open 7 days
Credit cards	Accepted
Price range	Affordable
Style	Smart casual
Cuisine	French-Asian
Recommended for	Late night

'Good food served in a magical setting tucked down the road leading to the little hamlet of Leutaz. The atmosphere suits all ages and it's open late.'
—Emmanuel Renaut

AUX ANGES

6 Place Georges Clemenceau
Roanne
Rhone-Alpes 42300
+33 477781985
www.aux-anges.com

Recommended by
Michel Troisgros

Opening hours	Closed Sunday
Credit cards	Accepted
Price range	Affordable
Style	Smart casual
Cuisine	Modern French
Recommended for	Regular neighbourhood

MAISON TROISGROS

Place Jean Troisgros
Roanne
Rhone-Alpes 42300
+33 477716697
www.troisgros.fr

Recommended by
Massimiliano Alajmo,
Alexandre Gauthier,
Claus Meyer, Patrick
O'Connell, Josep Roca,
Takuji Takahashi

Opening hours	Closed Tuesday and Wednesday
Credit cards	Accepted
Price range	Expensive
Style	Formal
Cuisine	French
Recommended for	High end

'Quality, atmosphere and flavour.'—Alexandre Gauthier

Maison Troisgros represents the epitome of the finest and most traditional haute cuisine. The Troisgros family is one of France's best-known culinary dynasties, with a cooking heritage spanning more than eighty years, of which their flagship restaurant has held three Michelin stars for an impressive forty-five. With Michel behind the stove the cooking has become less fussy but no less produce focused. Many restaurants today make great boasts of creating menus 'according to what is available in the market' but MT was doing it when they were still in their infancy and is still the master of ad hoc hospitality.

MAISON PIC

Recommended by
Normand Laprise,
Clasu Meyer,
Michel Portos

285 Avenue Victor Hugo
Valence
Rhone-Alpes 26000
+33 475441532
www.pic-valence.fr

Opening hours	Closed Monday and Sunday
Credit cards	Accepted
Price range	Expensive
Style	Smart casual
Cuisine	Modern French
Recommended for	Worth the travel

'I had a great meal here that I found impressively accomplished and also striking for its flavours and service. Overall, a fantastic culinary experience.'
—Michel Portos

Located on the Route Nationale 7 (the road provides the name of the trendy on-site bistro), the century-old Maison Pic has always been on gastro-tourists' radar. Home to one of France's oldest kitchen dynasties, these days it's run by Anne-Sophie Pic – the only woman in France with three Michelin stars (although her ancestors had already won and lost that many twice). Such pedigree is worked into the boutique hotel's design, which features the Pic family's photo archive. In the restaurant, the 'Menu Essentiel' exemplifies Anne-Sophie's perfectionist streak, with dishes like langoustines with aniseed and cinnamon leaf striving to outdo the over-achieving Pics of the past.

GEORGES BLANC

Recommended by
Patrick Goubier

Place du Marché
Vonnas
Rhone-Alpes 01540
+33 474509090
www.georgesblanc.com

Opening hours	Closed Monday and Tuesday
Credit cards	Accepted
Price range	Expensive
Style	Smart casual
Cuisine	French
Recommended for	Worth the travel

LE MOULIN DE CONNELLES

Recommended by
Naren Thimmaiah

40 route d'Amfreville sous les Monts
Connelles
Upper Normandy 27430
+33 232595333
www.moulin-de-connelles.fr

Opening hours	Open 7 days
Credit cards	Accepted but not AMEX
Price range	Expensive
Style	Smart casual
Cuisine	French
Recommended for	Worth the travel

'This charming riverside restaurant in the Rouen countryside is housed in an old-world mansion. The set menus are evenly balanced and, with select wines, make a great dinner proposition. I'm a firm believer in a wholesome meal experience: great food, crisp service and lovely ambience. This place was just that.'
—Naren Thimmaiah

BEEFBAR

Recommended by
Rolf Fliegauf

42 Quai Jean-Charles Rey
Monte Carlo 98000
Monaco
+377 97770929
www.beefbar.com

Opening hours	Open 7 days
Credit cards	Accepted but not Diners
Price range	Expensive
Style	Smart casual
Cuisine	Steakhouse
Recommended for	Wish I'd opened

'The restaurant is on the port in Monte Carlo. You sit next to the sea and inside it's very beautiful. The concept is great. They have a special oven – like a grill – and they serve different parts of different meats. You can also choose from a variety of outstanding mashed potatoes. They have a shuttle service and every five minutes you'll see a Ferrari, Bentley, Maserati or Rolls Royce arrive. It's spectacular.'—Rolf Fliegauf

LE LOUIS XV

Hôtel de Paris
Place du Casino
Monte Carlo 98000
Monaco
+377 98068864
www.alain-ducasse.com

Recommended by
Stefano Baiocco, Italo
Bassi, Oriol Castro, Richard
Ekkebus, Davide Oldani,
Nathan Outlaw, Paul Pairet,
Jordi Roca

Opening hours	Closed Tuesday and Wednesday
Credit cards	Accepted
Price range	Expensive
Style	Formal
Cuisine	Mediterranean
Recommended for	High end

'It is a luxury venue par excellence. I like it because
one is truly aware of the highest standards of
professionalism in everything.'—Stefano Baiocco

The ultimate expression of Monégasque glamour, Le
Louis XV, an opulent Versailles grand-siècle-inspired
palace of pleasure, opened in 1987, is perhaps the
greatest achievement and defining project of Alain
Ducasse's star-studded career. Leaving aside the
swan-like service, a dining room in which Marie-
Antoinette would have felt at home, the gilded hand-
bag stools, the bespoke crockery and silverware, the
400,000-bottle cellar and a mineral water list longer
then the average bistro's carte du vin – it's the quality
of Riviera-led cooking, which takes the very best
from sea, garden and farm, that remains at its
luxurious heart.

'IT'S GOT THAT VERY FRENCH KIND OF PARISIAN ATMOSPHERE THAT I ADORE.'

YVES CAMDEBORDE P456

'Raw scallops over a perfect Jerusalem artichoke puree all held in a savoury, shortbread-style pastry crust. A touch of salt and cracked black pepper. Excellent.'

MATT DILLON P470

PARIS

'It still has the most beautiful view in Paris!'

PIERRE GAGNAIRE P455

'It's a very romantic atmosphere, it's like a hunting lodge in the middle of Paris.'

GIORGIO LOCATELLI P463

'REPRESENTS EVERYTHING THE CAPITAL HAS TO OFFER IN TERMS OF CULINARY DELIGHTS.'

AKRAME BENALLAL P455

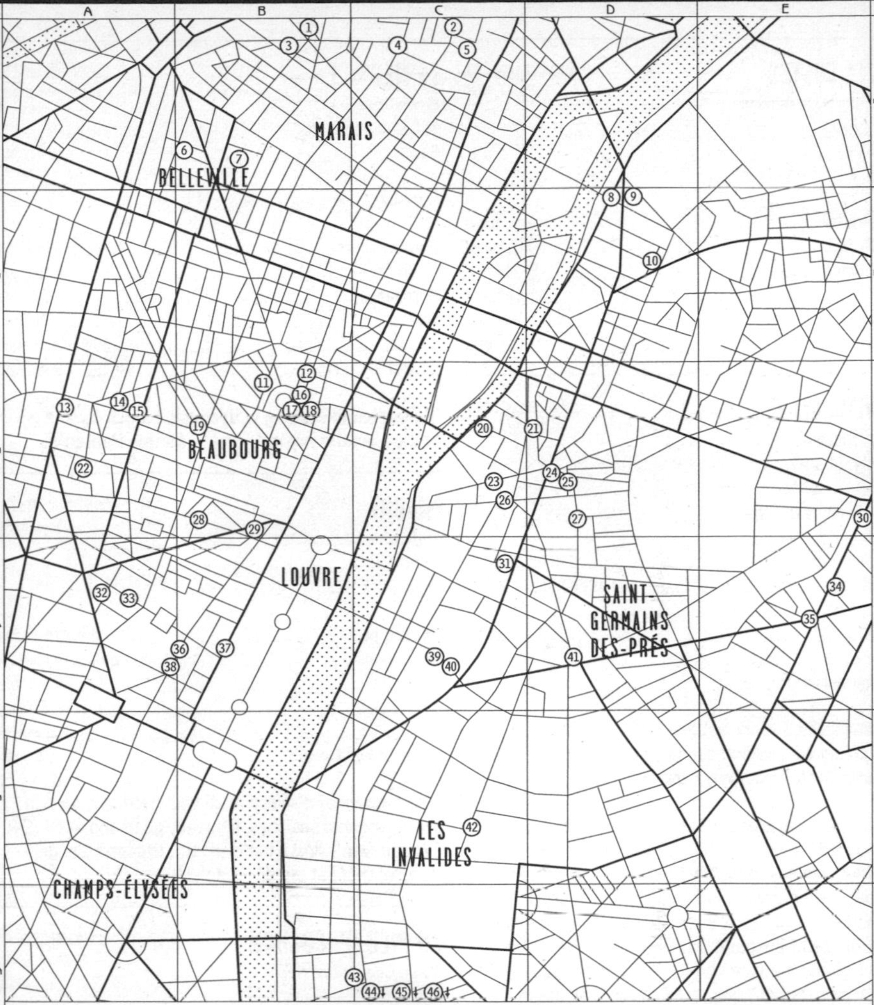

MARAIS
BELLEVILLE
BEAUBOURG
LOUVRE
SAINT-GERMAINS DES-PRÉS
LES INVALIDES
CHAMPS-ÉLYSÉES

PARIS

1er–7e

SCALE

0 300 600 900 yd.

1. *Le Mary Celeste (p.454)*
2. *Le Pavillon de la Reine (p.454)*
3. *Candelaria (p.454)*
4. *Café des Musées (p.454)*
5. *L'Ambroisie (pp.454–455)*
6. *L'Ami Louis (p.453)*
7. *Taing Song-Heng (p.454)*
8. *La Tour d'Argent (p.455)*
9. *L'AOC (p.455)*
10. *Terroir Parisien (p.455)*
11. *Au Pied de Cochon (p.450)*
12. *La Tour de Montlhéry (p.451)*
13. *Passage 53 (p.453)*
14. *Silencio (p.453)*
15. *Saturne (p.453)*
16. *La Poule au Pot (p.451)*
17. *Yam'Tcha (p.451)*
18. *Midory (p.450)*
19. *Chez Georges (p.452)*
20. *Ze Kitchen Galerie (p.458)*
21. *Allard (p.455)*
22. *Aux Lyonnais (p.452)*
23. *Agapé Substance (p.455)*
24. *Le Comptoir du Relais (p.457)*
25. *L'Avant Comptoir (p.456)*
26. *Semilla (p.457)*
27. *Pouic Pouic (p.457)*
28. *Kunitoraya (p.450)*
29. *Zen (p.452)*
30. *La Closerie des Lilas (p.456)*
31. *Café de Flore (p.456)*
32. *Pascade (p.452)*
33. *Les Orchidées (p.452)*
34. *Art Macaron (p.456)*
35. *La Rotonde (p.457)*
36. *Hôtel Costes (p.450)*
37. *Le Meurice (p.450)*
38. *Sur Mesure par Thierry Marx (p.451)*
39. *L'Atelier de Joël Robuchon Saint-Germain (p.459)*
40. *Gaya (p.460)*
41. *Brasserie Lutetia (p.456)*
42. *L'Arpège (p.458)*
43. *Brasserie Thoumieux (p.459)*
44. *L'Ami Jean (p.458)*
45. *Les Fables de la Fontaine (p.459)*
46. *Le Jules Verne (p.460)*

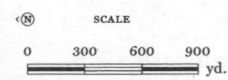

HÔTEL COSTES

239 Rue Saint-Honoré
Paris 75001
+33 142445000
www.hotelcostes.com

Recommended by
Paul Pairet

Opening hours	Open 7 days
Credit cards	Accepted
Price range	Expensive
Style	Smart casual
Cuisine	French
Recommended for	High end

KUNITORAYA II

5 Rue Villedo
Paris 75001
+33 147030774
www.kunitoraya.com

Recommended by
Johnny Farah

Opening hours	Closed Monday
Credit cards	Accepted but not AMEX
Price range	Affordable
Style	Casual
Cuisine	Japanese
Recommended for	Worth the travel

'An unexpected specialist of Japanese food, using French ingredients and culinary methods, resulting in a perfect taste.'—Johnny Farah

Twenty years ago Japanese chef Masafumi Nomoto introduced Parisians to the delights of slurping cheap, fat udon noodles in his packed out, no-reservations canteen, Kunitoraya. Now that there's another branch – Nomoto took over Chez Pauline, the famous ex haut lieu of Burgundy cuisine across the street – the original's been re-christened Kunitoraya 1. The noodle, hot or cold, remains the star, but in this unlikely decor of imposing 1900s brasserie mirrors, wall clocks and dark wood panelling you can now book a table for excellent tempura or *onigiri*. In the evenings the chef sends out his small-plate feast of sashimis, whelks and leeks in miso sauce or grated radish with broad (fava) beans.

LE MEURICE

Le Meurice
228 Rue de Rivoli
Paris 75001
+33 144581055
www.lemeurice.com

Recommended by
Steffen Hansen

Opening hours	Open 7 days
Credit cards	Accepted
Price range	Expensive
Style	Formal
Cuisine	Classic French
Recommended for	High end

'Be treated like a king with classic French cuisine at the absolute highest level.'—Steffen Hansen

MIDORY

49 Rue de l'Arbre Sec
Paris 75001
+33 142974730

Recommended by
Daniel Rose

Opening hours	Closed Sunday
Credit cards	Accepted but not AMEX
Price range	Affordable
Style	Casual
Cuisine	Japanese
Recommended for	Bargain

'The sushi chef makes a maki with fried salmon skin and fermented radishes. It's really good and at €5 (£4; $7) you won't find a better deal... except if you get three of them at once.'—Daniel Rose

AU PIED DE COCHON

6 Rue Coquillière
Paris 75001
+33 140137700
www.pieddecochon.com

Recommended by
Michael Smith

Opening hours	Open 7 days until late
Credit cards	Accepted
Price range	Affordable
Style	Casual
Cuisine	Classic French
Recommended for	Late night

'It serves pig's trotters (feet) and chips (fries) twenty-four hours a day. What more is there to say?'—Michael Smith

LA POULE AU POT

Recommended by
Greg Marchand

9 Rue Vauvilliers
Paris 75001
+33 142363296
www.lapouleaupot.com

Opening hours	Closed Monday
Credit cards	Accepted but not AMEX
Price range	Affordable
Style	Casual
Cuisine	Classic French
Recommended for	Late night

'Open late for classic French fare like steak frites and bone marrow.'—Greg Marchand

SUR MESURE PAR THIERRY MARX

Recommended by
Tomaž Kavčič

Mandarin Oriental Hotel
251 Rue Saint-Honoré
Paris 75001
+33 170987300
www.mandarinoriental.com

Opening hours	Closed Monday and Sunday
Credit cards	Accepted
Price range	Expensive
Style	Smart casual
Cuisine	Modern French
Recommended for	Worth the travel

'A unique, warm and well-designed restaurant with splendid service and brilliant food. Definitely the best restaurant I have ever visited in Paris. The ambience is a mix of authenticity and luxury, the table setting is great for privacy, the chef combines pure tastes with amazing ways of serving them, the service is impeccable and dinner is not a meal but a wonderful dining experience. Attentive waiters are all experts in their field. Exciting aromas, theatrical demonstrations, precise combinations of flavours and attention to detail make it worth the extravagant cost!'—Tomaž Kavčič

LA TOUR DE MONTLHÉRY

Recommended by
Jean-Marie Baudic, Greg
Marchand, Daniel Rose

5 Rue des Prouvaires
Paris 75001
+33 142362182

Opening hours	Closed Saturday and Sunday
Credit cards	Accepted but not AMEX
Price range	Budget
Style	Casual
Cuisine	Classic French
Recommended for	Late night

'A must-go place. A rare, old-fashioned bistro with traditional dishes and service. An old French tradition.'
—Jean-Marie Baudic

One of those bastions of French cuisine that's so old it's got more than one name, Chez Denise/La Tour de Montlhéry is a relic of all-night market action at Les Halles, serving rillettes, *pâté de campagne*, leeks vinaigrette, tripe and *onglet* through the night. Charming in red and white checks, the tables are set close together, ready to receive dozens of hungry night owls who devour mounds of frites along with their earthy offal or game choices, and chilled Brouilly by the litre. Beloved of students, insomniacs, clubbers, workmen and tourists, and definitely more fun after midnight.

YAM'TCHA

Recommended by
Bertrand Grébaut

4 Rue Sauval
Paris 75001
+33 140260807
www.yamtcha.com

Opening hours	Closed Monday and Sunday
Credit cards	Accepted but not AMEX
Price range	Expensive
Style	Smart casual
Cuisine	French-Chinese
Recommended for	High end

'I'm always particularly struck by the intense, bold nature of the cuisine here, which shakes me up every time I visit. The dishes are diverse, intelligent and unfailingly progressive.'—Bertrand Grébaut

Adeline Grattard spent three years with Pascal Barbot at L'Astrance, and three in restaurants in China. In 2009 she pitched her twenty-cover, verging-on-austere restaurant perfectly as Paris moved on from traditional French high-end formality and woke up to post-sushi Asian diversity and refinement. With her husband Chi Wan, cooking from a minuscule open kitchen – 'we want to stay in touch with our clients as if we were all at home' – she offers just one service an evening. Like a sommelier, Chi Wan matches his teas (there's a wine list too) to Grattard's breathtakingly sensual cooking – Challans duck, cockles sautéed with black soya, and aubergines (eggplant) *à la sichuanaise*.

ZEN

8 Rue de l'Échelle
Paris 75001
+33 142619399

Opening hours	Open 7 days
Credit cards	Accepted but not AMEX
Price range	Budget
Style	Casual
Cuisine	Japanese
Recommended for	Bargain

'This little Japanese-style restaurant serves fabulous sushi at extremely reasonable prices.'—Yannick Alléno

CHEZ GEORGES

1 Rue du Mail
Paris 75002
+33 142600711

Opening hours	Closed Saturday and Sunday
Credit cards	Accepted but not AMEX
Price range	Affordable
Style	Casual
Cuisine	French Bistro
Recommended for	Wish I'd opened

'It's almost everything I want from a restaurant.'
—Fergus Henderson

Paris is coming down with establishments that go by the name of Chez Georges. While the Latin Quarter's Chez Georges old-school caves bar is certainly worth stopping by for *un verre* or *deux*, the chances are that if anyone recommends a Chez Georges they're most likely talking about this Bourse bistro. Opened by Georges Brouillet back in 1964, you get the impression that very little has changed since – from the menu crammed with comforting bourgeois classics to its well-heeled regulars. Although, admittedly, the latter now have to grudgingly share the invariably packed, long narrow room with camera-happy tourists.

AUX LYONNAIS

32 Rue Saint Marc
Paris 75002
+33 158002206
www.auxlyonnais.com

Opening hours	Closed Monday and Sunday
Credit cards	Accepted
Price range	Affordable
Style	Smart casual
Cuisine	French Bistro
Recommended for	Worth the travel

LES ORCHIDÉES

Hôtel Park Hyatt Paris-Vendôme
5 Rue de la Paix
Paris 75002
+33 158711060
www.paris.vendome.hyatt.com

Opening hours	Open 7 days
Credit cards	Accepted
Price range	Expensive
Style	Casual
Cuisine	Modern International
Recommended for	Breakfast

'This is a Paris spot that I just adore, especially for its breakfast. The hotel is quite understated, chic and low-key, but it still always manages to be lively and friendly.'—Yannick Alléno

PASCADE

14 Rue Daunou
Paris 75002
+33 142601100
www.pascade-alexandre-bourdas.com

Opening hours	Open 7 days
Credit cards	Accepted
Price range	Affordable
Style	Casual
Cuisine	French
Recommended for	Bargain

'They serve a speciality from the Aveyron region, a *Pascade*, which is a type of sweet or savoury caramelised crêpe-cum-soufflé. You haven't lived unless you've tried it at least once.'
—Christophe Michalak

PASSAGE 53

Recommended by
Mikael Jonsson,
Arabelle Meirlaen

53 Passage des Panoramas
Paris 75002
+33 142330435
www.passage53.com

Opening hours	Closed Monday and Sunday
Credit cards	Accepted but not AMEX
Price range	Expensive
Style	Smart casual
Cuisine	French-Japanese
Recommended for	Worth the travel

'A tiny restaurant in an old passage in the heart of Paris serving modern, pure and original food.'
—Mikael Jonsson

Ex Astrance and Mugaritz, chef Shinichi Sato heads an all-Japanese brigade in the kitchen of this discreet dining room, hidden in one of Paris's nineteenth-century *passages*. Expect a daily-changing, highly produce-led Menu Surprise of up to a dozen courses: calamari comes with shaved raw cauliflower and a cauliflower foam; turbot is garlanded with cabbage, turnip and enoki mushrooms; Dordogne pork arrives pink with bergamot jam and parsnip. Passage 53 has white art on white walls, linen tablecloths and is tiny, with only seventeen comfortable seats, so book ahead. Expect steep prices, attentive service and a Burgundy-leaning wine list.

SATURNE

Recommended by
Sang-Hoon Degeimbre,
James Henry,
Gwendal Le Ruyet

17 Rue Notre-Dame des Victoires
Paris 75002
+33 142603190
www.saturne-paris.fr

Opening hours	Closed Saturday and Sunday
Credit cards	Accepted but not AMEX
Price range	Expensive
Style	Smart casual
Cuisine	Modern French
Recommended for	High end

'Not expensive for what it is. Excellent wine and somehow the food seems to get better with every visit.'
—James Henry

Located across from the Paris Bourse, Sven Chartier and Ewen Lemoigne's minimalist *cave à manger* is refined enough to please a pinstriped clientele by day, then offers the cool crowd a suave alternative to bad-boy bistronomy at dinner. The chef/sommelier pair previously worked together at *terroir*-driven Racines, and Chartier's reverence for pristine produce plus Lemoigne's elite library of biodynamic and 'natural' wines now represent the high end of the hip dining scene. The six-course Carte Blanche menu might feature smoked eel with beetroot (beet) and horse-radish or raw diver-caught scallop with sea urchin, then suckling pig with roast corn, squash and pickled onion, matched with wines from the Loire, Jura, Slovenia or Sardinia.

SILENCIO

Recommended by
Alexandre Gauthier

142 Rue Montmartre
Paris 75002
+33 140131232
www.silencio-club.com

Opening hours	Closed Monday and Sunday
Reservation policy	No
Credit cards	Accepted
Price range	Affordable
Style	Smart casual
Cuisine	Bar-Diner
Recommended for	Late night

L'AMI LOUIS

Recommended by
Ruth Rogers,
Guy Savoy

32 Rue du Vertbois
Paris 75003
+33 148877748

Opening hours	Closed Monday and Tuesday
Credit cards	Accepted
Price range	Expensive
Style	Casual
Cuisine	French Bistro
Recommended for	Local favourite

CAFÉ DES MUSÉES

Recommended by
Bertrand Grébaut

49 Rue de Turenne
Paris 75003
+33 142729617
www.cafedesmusees.fr

Opening hours	Open 7 days
Credit cards	Accepted
Price range	Affordable
Style	Casual
Cuisine	French Bistro
Recommended for	Local favourite

'This is a rare, typically Parisian brasserie. It offers generous helpings of good, traditional cuisine, such as steak tartare with chips (fries), *entrecôte* with Béarnaise sauce, chicken liver terrine and stuffed mushrooms.'—Bertrand Grébaut

CANDELARIA

Recommended by
Greg Marchand,
Flora Mikula

52 Rue de Saintonge
Paris 75003
+33 142744128
www.candelariaparis.com

Opening hours	Open 7 days
Reservation policy	No
Credit cards	Accepted but not AMEX
Price range	Budget
Style	Casual
Cuisine	Mexican
Recommended for	Late night

'To grab a bite to eat and a glass of wine with friends I go to Candelaria. I love the way it feels like a speakeasy, where you can sample real nachos and drink a to-die-for Margarita.'—Flora Mikula

LE MARY CELESTE

Recommended by
Flora Mikula

1 Rue Commines
Paris 75003
www.lemaryceleste.com

Opening hours	Open 7 days
Credit cards	Accepted
Price range	Budget
Style	Casual
Cuisine	French
Recommended for	Wish I'd opened

'What I like here is the concept of a cocktail-bar-cum-oyster bar and a menu based around vegetables.'
—Flora Mikula

LE PAVILLON DE LA REINE

Recommended by
Bertrand Grébaut

Hôtel Pavillon de la Reine
28 Place des Vosges
Paris 75003
+33 140291919
www.pavillon-de-la-reine.com

Opening hours	Open 7 days
Credit cards	Accepted
Price range	Expensive
Style	Smart casual
Cuisine	French
Recommended for	Breakfast

'They serve the perfect French breakfast here. Everything is impeccable: the bread, the jam, the pastries… the bonus being that it has a sun-filled, paved courtyard right in the middle of the Marais.'
—Bertrand Grébaut

TAING SONG-HENG

Recommended by
Bertrand Grébaut

3 Rue Volta
Paris 75003
+33 142783170

Opening hours	Closed Sunday
Reservation policy	No
Credit cards	Not accepted
Price range	Budget
Style	Casual
Cuisine	Vietnamese-Thai
Recommended for	Bargain

'This is a tiny Vietnamese canteen in the oldest building in Paris. You can have one of the city's best beef pho here for only €8 (£6.50; $11).'—Bertrand Grébaut

L'AMBROISIE

Recommended by
Konstantin Filippou, Matthew
Kirkley, Greg Marchand

9 Place des Vosges
Paris 75004
+33 142785145
www.ambroisie-paris.com

Opening hours	Closed Monday and Sunday
Credit cards	Accepted
Price range	Expensive
Style	Formal
Cuisine	French
Recommended for	Local favourite

'I still believe this to be the greatest kitchen cooking today. Breathtakingly pristine produce and perfectly executed classical cooking define the restaurant. It's a high wire act, and they charge accordingly. Simply brilliant.'—Matthew Kirkley

L'AOC

Recommended by
Flora Mikula

14 Rue des Fossés Saint-Bernard
Paris 75005
+33 143542252
www.restoaoc.com

Opening hours	Closed Monday and Sunday
Credit cards	Accepted but not AMEX
Price range	Affordable
Style	Casual
Cuisine	French
Recommended for	Local favourite

'I love going there. They serve up homemade terrines and pork products as well as roasted joints of meat.'
—Flora Mikula

TERROIR PARISIEN

Recommended by
Akrame Benallal

20 Rue Saint-Victor
Paris 75005
+33 144315454
www.yannick-alleno.com

Opening hours	Open 7 days
Credit cards	Accepted
Price range	Affordable
Style	Smart casual
Cuisine	French Bistro
Recommended for	Local favourite

LA TOUR D'ARGENT

Recommended by
Pierre Gagnaire,
Eduard Xatruch

15 Quai de la Tournelle
Paris 75005
+33 143542331
www.latourdargent.com

Opening hours	Closed Monday and Sunday
Credit cards	Accepted
Price range	Expensive
Style	Formal
Cuisine	Classic French
Recommended for	High end

'It still has the most beautiful view in Paris!'
—Pierre Gagnaire

AGAPÉ SUBSTANCE

Recommended by
Konstantin Filippou

66 Rue Mazarine
Paris 75006
+33 143293383
www.agapesubstance.com

Opening hours	Closed Monday and Sunday
Credit cards	Accepted
Price range	Expensive
Style	Smart casual
Cuisine	Modern French
Recommended for	Wish I'd opened

'Michelin-star cooking doesn't always have to take up a lot of space. It's the vision that counts – the kitchen and the cellar – and you can see it being realized wonderfully here.'—Konstantin Filippou

The concept of the open kitchen takes a leap forward at Agapé Substance, where, in a rather narrow Saint-Germain dining room, you effectively sit in the kitchen, perched either side of a long twenty-four-seat bench. Set up by David Toutain and Laurent Lapaire, formerly chef and head waiter, respectively, of L'Arpège, the kitchen is now run by the experimental twenty-nine-year-old Gaëtan Gentil. While its name – what's the best translation? Love Stuff? Material Love? – sounds like it's trying way too hard (it doesn't trip off the tongue any easier in French), the creative, market-driven menus that trawl the globe for inspiration don't come across as forced – rather, inspired.

ALLARD

Recommended by
Akrame Benallal

41 Rue Saint-André des Arts
Paris 75006
+33 158002342
www.restaurant-allard.fr

Opening hours	Open 7 days
Credit cards	Accepted
Price range	Expensive
Style	Smart casual
Cuisine	French
Recommended for	Local favourite

'This place offers typically Parisian cuisine that represents everything the capital has to offer in terms of culinary delights.'—Akrame Benallal

ART MACARON

Recommended by
Julien Duboué

129 Boulevard du Montparnasse
Paris 75006
+33 143213249
www.artmacaron.com

Opening hours	Closed Monday
Reservation policy	No
Credit cards	Accepted
Price range	Affordable
Style	Casual
Cuisine	Café-Patisserie
Recommended for	Breakfast

'A special place that is still part of the undiscovered Paris. The excellent French toast and hot chocolate are highlights. The macarons, the house speciality, are delicious.'—Julien Duboué

L'AVANT COMPTOIR

Recommended by
Julien Duboué,
Alexandre Gauthier

Hôtel Relais Saint-Germain
9 Carrefour de l'Odéon
Paris 75006
+33 144270797
www.hotel-paris-relais-saint-germain.com

Opening hours	Open 7 days
Reservation policy	No
Credit cards	Accepted but not AMEX
Price range	Budget
Style	Casual
Cuisine	Small plates
Recommended for	Regular neighbourhood

'A place I go to regularly with friends for its tapas by the star chef Yves Camdeborde. They have great natural wines on their menu.'—Julien Duboué

BRASSERIE LUTETIA

Recommended by
Emilio Garip

Hotel Lutetia
45 Boulevard Raspail
Paris 75006
+33 149544676
www.lutetia-paris.com

Opening hours	Open 7 days
Credit cards	Accepted
Price range	Affordable
Style	Casual
Cuisine	French Brasserie
Recommended for	Breakfast

'The service is excellent, the fruit selection is varied, the eggs are cooked just the way you like them and the ham, bread, croissants and coffee are all very good too.'—Emilio Garip

CAFÉ DE FLORE

Recommended by
Yves Camdeborde

172 Boulevard Saint-Germain
Paris 75006
+33 145485526
www.cafedeflore.fr

Opening hours	Open 7 days
Reservation policy	No
Credit cards	Accepted
Price range	Affordable
Style	Smart casual
Cuisine	Classic French
Recommended for	Breakfast

'When I go there in the morning, I feel like I'm in the 1930s. It has been around since that era and the clientele is pretty caricatural. It's got that very French kind of Parisian atmosphere that I adore.'
—Yves Camdeborde

The one to choose – rather than rival Les Deux Magots on the same stretch (Sartre and de Beauvoir preferred the Flore) – this Saint-Germain giant among literary cafés is somewhat pricy, but what price an existentialist espresso and forty-five minutes watching the Left Bank go by in style? Be sure to carry a copy of *Libé*, wear a leather flying jacket, and order Mariage Frères Earl Grey and some toast and jam, or an *omelette aux fines herbes* and a bottle of Gevrey-Chambertin.

LA CLOSERIE DES LILAS

Recommended by
Jean-François Piège

171 Boulevard du Montparnasse
Paris 75006
+33 140513450
www.closeriedeslilas.fr

Opening hours	Open 7 days
Credit cards	Accepted
Price range	Expensive
Style	Smart casual
Cuisine	French
Recommended for	Late night

'The ambience here is quintessential old-style Paris, exuding that unmistakable atmosphere of Paris at night that never fails to delight.'—Jean-François Piège

LE COMPTOIR DU RELAIS

Hôtel Relais Saint-Germain
9 Carrefour de l'Odéon
Paris 75006
+33 144270797
www.hotel-paris-relais-saint-germain.com

Recommended by
Andreas Dahlberg,
Alexandre Gauthier,
Carlo Mirarchi

Opening hours	Open 7 days
Credit cards	Accepted
Price range	Expensive
Style	Smart casual
Cuisine	French Bistro
Recommended for	Breakfast

'French breakfast: an egg, good ham, a croissant and an espresso.'—Alexandre Gauthier

Yves Camdeborde is one of the founding fathers of *la bistronomie*, the movement that dismissed starry codes in favour of simple bistro cuisine made gastronomic. Camdeborde's Comptoir has been a Basque trailblazer of all things pig and has not emptied since the day it opened. Such is Camdeborde's fame and reputation, you'll be hard pushed to get a table. But he has thoughtfully opened a hotel on one side – where you can stay and wait a day or two to pounce – and the great L'Avant Comptoir, a small-plate and tapas stand-up counter, on the other, when shoulder to shoulder's what you're after.

POUIC POUIC

9 Rue Lobineau
Paris 75006
+33 143267195
www.pouicpouicstgermain.fr

Recommended by
Guy Savoy

Opening hours	Closed Monday and Sunday
Credit cards	Accepted but not AMEX
Price range	Affordable
Style	Casual
Cuisine	French Bistro
Recommended for	Late night

'I don't go out at night anymore, but I keep Pouic Pouic as my bolthole.'—Guy Savoy

LA ROTONDE

105 Boulevard du Montparnasse
Paris 75006
+33 143266884
www.rotondemontparnasse.com

Recommended by
Flora Mikula

Opening hours	Open 7 days
Credit cards	Accepted
Price range	Affordable
Style	Casual
Cuisine	French Brasserie
Recommended for	Late night

'Open until 2.00 a.m., this is a Parisian brasserie in the truest sense of the word. I come here for some quiet time and to enjoy a good sole meunière, or an *entrecôte* steak with chips (fries) and Béarnaise sauce.'
—Flora Mikula

SEMILLA

54 Rue de Seine
Paris 75006
+33 143543450

Recommended by
Peter Doyle

Opening hours	Open 7 days
Credit cards	Accepted but not AMEX
Price range	Affordable
Style	Smart casual
Cuisine	Modern French
Recommended for	Worth the travel

'A perfect example of the new-wave Parisian restaurants, but with a bigger menu choice and a Meilleurs Ouvriers de France (best craftsman of France) chef in the kitchen producing well-crafted food at very affordable prices with friendly service. Just brilliant.'
—Peter Doyle

ZE KITCHEN GALERIE

Recommended by
Christophe Michalak

4 Rue des Grands Augustins
Paris 75006
+33 144320032
www.zekitchengalerie.fr

Opening hours	Closed Sunday
Credit cards	Accepted
Price range	Expensive
Style	Smart casual
Cuisine	French-Asian
Recommended for	Wish I'd opened

'I'm nuts about William Ledeuil's food. I love his Asian-inspired blend of lemongrass, coconut and ginger. Undoubtedly one of the best restaurants in Paris. I'm blown away every time.'—Christophe Michalak

William Ledeuil was one of the first French chefs to cook some sense into the existing chilli, cumin and lemongrass Asian fusion cacophony. When he opened Ze Kitchen Galerie in 2001 he had never been to the countries whose food was the foundation of his menu, learning everything from cookbooks and whatever he could glean from suppliers in Paris's 13th arrondissement. After years of researching, refining and spending time in the Far East, he won his Michelin star in 2008 and Gault et Millau Chef of the Year in 2010 for his cuisine, largely built around light, fragrant broths and emulsions. His restaurant filled with contemporary art brings flashes of ballsy colour to the hallowed greyness of Saint Germain des Prés.

L'AMI JEAN

Recommended by
Julien Duboué,
Björn Persson

27 Rue Malar
Paris 75007
+33 147058689
www.lamijean.fr

Opening hours	Closed Monday and Sunday
Credit cards	Accepted
Price range	Affordable
Style	Casual
Cuisine	French Bistro
Recommended for	Wish I'd opened

'The best bistro in Paris. You can find the best produce from all over France in the amazing cuisine of chef Stéphane Jégo. The cool, laid-back atmosphere and the well-served dishes make it my favourite place to have lunch.'—Julien Duboué

Stéphane Jégo's pedigree (Christian Constant at the Crillon and Cambdeborde at La Régalade) and talent make it tough to get a place at L'Ami Jean's famous farm table. Renowned for his roasts and braises, some of his meat dishes – like the Kobe *côte de boeuf* or half-raw quail with head and beak intact – border on downright filthy. The decor is a bistro-punk layering of weird brown junk, in a room lit like a dentist's surgery (office). But clients' eyes are on their plates and, although prices are soaring, you get the feeling they'd gladly pay twice as much for another shot at Jégo's mythical rice pudding.

L'ARPÈGE

Recommended by
Rahul Akerkar, Andrew Carmellini,
Paul Cunningham, Stephen
Harris, Linton Hopkins, Gunther
Hubrechsen, Dan Hunter, Mikael
Jonsson, Jakob Mielcke, Flora
Mikula, Daniel Puskas, James
Syhabout, Stephen Toman,
Fernando Trocca

84 Rue de Varenne
Paris 75007
+33 147050906
www.alain-passard.com

Opening hours	Closed Saturday and Sunday
Credit cards	Accepted
Price range	Expensive
Style	Smart casual
Cuisine	Modern French
Recommended for	High end

'So delicious and thoughtful at the same time. Vegetables shine and ingredients are paramount.' —James Syhabout

In 2001, Alain Passard raised an eyebrow or two among his countrymen when he took red meat off the menu at L'Arpège, pledging instead to explore the virtues of veg. Michelin didn't seem to mind. Chef Passard kept his trio of stars, bought a kitchen garden 230 km (140 miles) outside Paris and now ferries his organic harvest to the city early each morning to grace plates in the hushed dining room the same afternoon. There's flesh too – the duck is particularly fine – and the much-imitated 'hot-cold egg'. It all comes at a three-star price, so it's worth noting that the lunch *dégustation*, at less than half the price of the evening menu, is a more affordable way in.

L'ATELIER DE JOËL ROBUCHON

Recommended by
Ivo Adam, Pascal
Barbot, Akrame Benallal,
Michael Deane, Johnny
Farah, Emilio Garip, Peter
Goossens, Jérôme Lorvellec,
Reto Mathis, Vicky Ratnani,
Emmanuel Renaut, Jordi
Roca, Fabio Rossi, David
Sasek, Roger van Damme

5 Rue de Montalembert
Paris 75007
+33 142225656
www.joel-robuchon.com

Opening hours..Open 7 days
Credit cards...Accepted
Price range..Expensive
Style...Smart casual
Cuisine...French
Recommended for.......................................Wish I'd opened

'Every chef fantasizes about having opened this place themselves. Joël Robuchon had the cunning to come up with the idea of creating a pioneering notion of space, where you have your meal sitting around the kitchen, and where normal dining codes go out of the window. It's a unique concept that has opened us up to a new way of eating at top restaurants, with very good value for money.'—Akrame Benallal

The concept may be dated now but the Asian feel, small-plate, chef-gawking counter that Robuchon created in 2003 conquered a sceptical Paris clientele. L'Atelier's door opens from the inside out, meaning staff control entry, and its booking system is a pain, but once inside its black lacquer cocoon with the sleek brigade busy making gorgeous five-bite morsels, all's well. No wonder the Ateliers took off – the menu allows clients a bit of luxurious everything. About twenty tasting plates on one side; on the other, larger mains and desserts. Stick to the small ones! After the foie gras-stuffed quail with truffled mashed potato, sweetbreads with bay and rosemary, and a couple of other taste poppers, the *chocolat tendance* – an Araguani chocolate ganache, cocoa-nib ice cream and Oreo cookies – is a no-brainer.

BRASSERIE THOUMIEUX

Recommended by
Greg Marchand,
Christophe Michalak

79 Rue Saint-Dominique
Paris 75007
+33 147054975
www.thoumieux.fr

Opening hours...............................Closed Saturday and Sunday
Credit cards...Accepted
Price range..Expensive
Style...Smart casual
Cuisine...French Bistro
Recommended for.......................................Wish I'd opened

'It feels like you're in a friend's house (well, a very rich friend's house). A low ceiling, great furniture, laid-back service, great wine list and excellent food make it one of my favourite dining spots in Paris.'—Greg Marchand

When wunderkind Thierry Costes (Café Etienne Marcel, Café Marly, Georges) teamed up with brazen ex-Crillon chef Jean-François Piège to transform this classic brasserie in the 7th arrondissement, the locals grumbled and the critics sneered but everybody else flocked. When they subsequently opened the excellent chef's table above the restaurant – instantly gaining two Michelin stars – revamped the rooms and Piège became a judge on French TV's Top Chef, things got serious. Now that the place is deliciously dark, noisy and louche, no one really cares whether they can see their (comfort) food. *Calamars à la carbonara*, eggiest crème caramel with dainty *langues de chat* and stellar tartes are picked at by *le beau monde*.

LES FABLES DE LA FONTAINE

Recommended by
Julien Duboué

131 Rue Saint-Dominique
Paris 75007
+33 144183755
www.lesfablesdelafontaine.net

Opening hours..Open 7 days
Credit cards...Accepted
Price range..Expensive
Style...Smart casual
Cuisine...Seafood
Recommended for................................Regular neighbourhood

'A small cosy Michelin-starred restaurant where I go to eat when I'm looking for great seafood cuisine.'
—Julien Duboué

GAYA

Recommended by
Tim Lai

44 Rue du Bac
Paris 75007
+33 145447373
www.pierre-gagnaire.com

Opening hours	Closed Sunday
Credit cards	Accepted
Price range	Expensive
Style	Smart casual
Cuisine	Seafood
Recommended for	Wish I'd opened

'The young team, led by Nicolas Fontaine, is full of passion and energy. This is a dream team for every chef and restaurant owner. Lucky Pierre Gagnaire.'—Tim Lai

LE JULES VERNE

Recommended by
Pavel Mencl, Shaun Rankin,
Alfredo Russo

Eiffel Tower
Avenue Gustave Eiffel
Paris 75007
+33 145556144
www.lejulesverne-paris.com

Opening hours	Open 7 days
Credit cards	Accepted
Price range	Expensive
Style	Formal
Cuisine	Modern French
Recommended for	High end

'What an amazing location for dining! At an altitude of 125 m (410 ft) it has to be one of the best restaurant views in the world. With such a renowned reputation for food and service you can't beat it for a romantic treat.'—Shaun Rankin

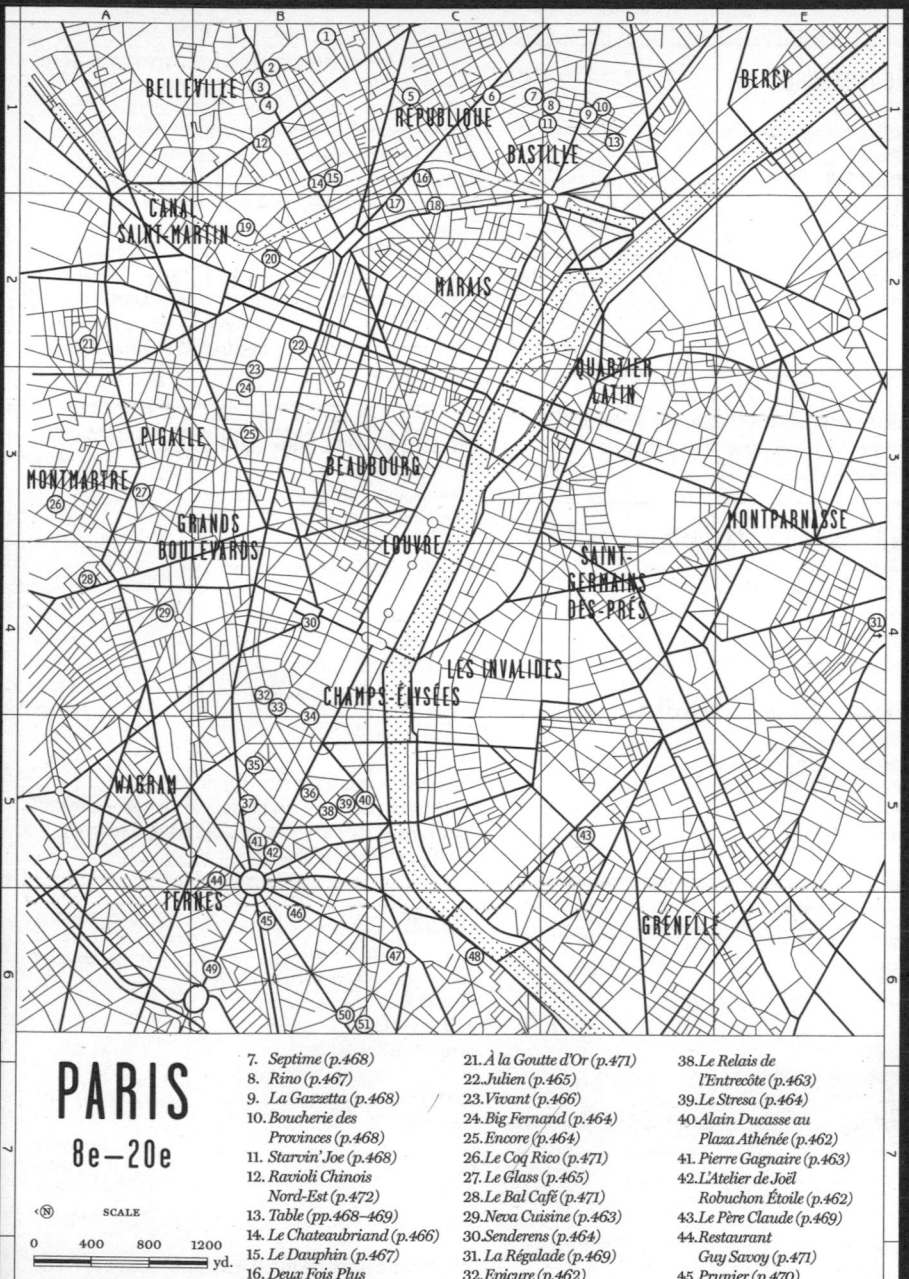

PARIS
8e–20e

<N> SCALE

0   400   800   1200
yd.

1. *Roseval (p.472)*
2. *Le Baratin (p.472)*
3. *Lao Siam (p.471)*
4. *Le Pacifique (p.472)*
5. *La Buvette (p.466)*
6. *Bones (p.466)*
7. *Septime (p.468)*
8. *Rino (p.467)*
9. *La Gazzetta (p.468)*
10. *Boucherie des Provinces (p.468)*
11. *Starvin' Joe (p.468)*
12. *Ravioli Chinois Nord-Est (p.472)*
13. *Table (pp.468–469)*
14. *Le Chateaubriand (p.466)*
15. *Le Dauphin (p.467)*
16. *Deux Fois Plus de Piment (p.467)*
17. *L'Entrée des Artistes (p.467)*
18. *Le Repaire de Cartouche (p.467)*
19. *Ten Belles (p.465)*
20. *Le Verre Volé (p.465)*
21. *À la Goutte d'Or (p.471)*
22. *Julien (p.465)*
23. *Vivant (p.466)*
24. *Big Fernand (p.464)*
25. *Encore (p.464)*
26. *Le Coq Rico (p.471)*
27. *Le Glass (p.465)*
28. *Le Bal Café (p.471)*
29. *Neva Cuisine (p.463)*
30. *Senderens (p.464)*
31. *La Régalade (p.469)*
32. *Epicure (p.462)*
33. *Le 114 Faubourg (p.462)*
34. *Le Laurent (p.463)*
35. *Apicius (p.462)*
36. *La Maison de l'Aubrac (p.463)*
37. *Le Taillevent (p.464)*
38. *Le Relais de l'Entrecôte (p.463)*
39. *Le Stresa (p.464)*
40. *Alain Ducasse au Plaza Athénée (p.462)*
41. *Pierre Gagnaire (p.463)*
42. *L'Atelier de Joël Robuchon Étoile (p.462)*
43. *Le Père Claude (p.469)*
44. *Restaurant Guy Savoy (p.471)*
45. *Prunier (p.470)*
46. *Restaurant Akrame (p.470)*
47. *Carette (p.470)*
48. *L'Astrance (p.469)*
49. *Kifuné (p.470)*
50. *Le Stella (p.470)*
51. *La Pâtisserie des Rêves (p.470)*

LE 114 FAUBOURG

Recommended by
Julien Duboué,
Chris Galvin

Hôtel Le Bristol
114 Rue du Faubourg Saint-Honoré
Paris 75008
+33 153434444
www.lebristolparis.com

Opening hours	Open 7 days
Credit cards	Accepted
Price range	Expensive
Style	Smart casual
Cuisine	Modern French
Recommended for	Worth the travel

'One of the most beautiful restaurant rooms in the world – you get a real sense of arrival here.'
—Chris Galvin

ALAIN DUCASSE AU PLAZA ATHÉNÉE

Recommended by
Andreas Caminada,
Julien Duboué, Peter
Goossens, Pekka Terävä

Plaza Athénée Hotel
25 Avenue Montaigne
Paris 75008
+33 153676500
www.alain-ducasse.com

Opening hours	Closed Saturday and Sunday
Credit cards	Accepted
Price range	Expensive
Style	Formal
Cuisine	French
Recommended for	High end

'For me, it is always a great restaurant experience.'
—Andreas Caminada

APICIUS

Recommended by
Olivier Limousin

20 Rue d'Artois
Paris 75008
+33 143801966
www.restaurant-apicius.com

Opening hours	Closed Saturday and Sunday
Credit cards	Accepted
Price range	Expensive
Style	Formal
Cuisine	French
Recommended for	Worth the travel

'Although this restaurant is in the middle of Paris, it's like a castle. The food is amazing – I had a really nice time there.'—Olivier Limousin

Chef Jean-Pierre Vigato's Michelin-starred destination restaurant is beautifully housed in a nineteenth-century mansion close to the Champs-Élysées. Gently refined, bourgeois dishes are crafted from carefully sourced ingredients such as oysters from Jersey, langoustines and blue lobsters from Brittany, spider crabs from Normandy, veal from Corrèze and black Périgord truffles. Highlights from the, alas, appropriately priced menu include tea-smoked langoustines, wild Brittany turbot on the bone for two, a whole lobe of sweetbread, plus tangy bergamot and grapefruit sorbet. The gardens surrounding the house certainly help confer a sense of escape from the clamour of the city's streets.

L'ATELIER DE JOËL ROBUCHON ÉTOILE

Recommended by
Italo Bassi,
Niko Romito,
Pekka Terävä

Drugstore Publicis
133 Avenue des Champs Elysées
Paris 75008
+33 147237575
www.atelier-robuchon-etoile.com

Opening hours	Open 7 days
Credit cards	Accepted
Price range	Expensive
Style	Smart casual
Cuisine	French
Recommended for	Wish I'd opened

'I love this restaurant! From a professional and commercial point of view, the format chosen – elegant but casual at the same time – is definitely a winning combination.'—Niko Romito

EPICURE

Recommended by
Yoann Conte, Yves Le Lay,
Harald Wohlfahrt

Hôtel Le Bristol
112 Rue du Faubourg Saint-Honoré
Paris 75008
+33 153434340
www.lebristolparis.com

Opening hours	Open 7 days
Credit cards	Accepted
Price range	Expensive
Style	Formal
Cuisine	French
Recommended for	Worth the travel

'It's always a pleasure to eat here when I come to Paris.'
—Yoann Conte

The grand restaurant at L'Hôtel Le Bristol, relaunched as Epicure in 2011 in the dramatically but classically refurbished garden room of the five-star luxury hotel, is the quintessential Parisian multi-Michelin-starred haute cuisine experience. Headed up by Chevalier de la Légion d'Honneur Eric Frechon, a friend of former French President Nicolas Sarkozy, it's the place to go for the seriously luxurious ingredients synonymous with posh French nosh: think foie gras, caviar, lobster, frog's legs and grand cru chocolate. For sheer impact, however, try the Bresse chicken *en vessie* (stuffed with truffles and cooked inside a pig's bladder).

LE LAURENT

Recommended by
Giorgio Locatelli

41 Avenue Gabriel
Paris 75008
+33 142250039
www.le-laurent.com

Opening hours	Closed Sunday
Credit cards	Accepted
Price range	Expensive
Style	Smart casual
Cuisine	Modern French
Recommended for	High end

'It has a very romantic atmosphere – it's like a hunting lodge in the middle of Paris.'—Giorgio Locatelli

LA MAISON DE L'AUBRAC

Recommended by
Michel Troisgros

37 Rue Marbeuf
Paris 75008
+33 143590514
www.maison-aubrac.com

Opening hours	Open 7 days
Credit cards	Accepted but not AMEX
Price range	Affordable
Style	Casual
Cuisine	Steakhouse
Recommended for	Late night

'The meat is absolutely delicious.'—Michel Troisgros

NEVA CUISINE

Recommended by
Akrame Benallal

2 Rue de Berne
Paris 75008
+33 145221891

Opening hours	Closed Saturday and Sunday
Credit cards	Accepted but not AMEX
Price range	Expensive
Style	Casual
Cuisine	French Bistro
Recommended for	Bargain

'I come here especially for its sweetbread. You eat extremely well here and not only is it very good value for money but the desserts are outstanding.'
—Akrame Benallal

PIERRE GAGNAIRE

Recommended by
Akrame Benallal,
Umberto Bombana, Carlo
Crisci, Ramón Freixa,
Matthew Gaudet, Joan
Roca, Daniel Rose

6 Rue Balzac
Paris 75008
+33 158361250
www.pierre-gagnaire.com

Opening hours	Closed Saturday and Sunday
Credit cards	Accepted
Price range	Expensive
Style	Formal
Cuisine	Modern French
Recommended for	High end

'Pierre Gagnaire is in a league of his own. If you ask me, he doesn't have three stars to his name but four. He has his own trademark cuisine that is like nothing you have ever experienced before. He is writing a whole new chapter of culinary history, all on his own.'
—Akrame Benallal

LE RELAIS DE L'ENTRECÔTE

Recommended by
Daniel Rose

15 Rue Marbeuf
Paris 75008
+33 149520717
www.relaisentrecote.fr

Opening hours	Open 7 days
Reservation policy	No
Credit cards	Accepted but not AMEX
Price range	Affordable
Style	Casual
Cuisine	Steakhouse
Recommended for	Wish I'd opened

'One of the best restaurants in Paris. You never come away disappointed.'—Daniel Rose

SENDERENS

9 Place de la Madeleine
Paris 75008
+33 142652290
www.senderens.fr

Opening hours	Closed Monday and Sunday
Credit cards	Accepted
Price range	Expensive
Style	Formal
Cuisine	French
Recommended for	Worth the travel

'Always good food.'—Paul Owens

LE STRESA

7 Rue Chambiges
Paris 75008
+33 147235162
www.lestresa.com

Opening hours	Closed Saturday and Sunday
Credit cards	Accepted
Price range	Expensive
Style	Formal
Cuisine	Italian
Recommended for	Regular neighbourhood

'A little Italian restaurant that is cosy and welcoming.'
—Yannick Alléno

LE TAILLEVENT

15 Rue Lamennais
Paris 75008
+33 144951501
www.taillevent.com

Opening hours	Closed Saturday and Sunday
Credit cards	Accepted
Price range	Expensive
Style	Formal
Cuisine	French
Recommended for	Worth the travel

BIG FERNAND

55 Rue du Faubourg Poissonnière
Paris 75009
+33 173705152
www.bigfernand.com

Opening hours	Closed Sunday
Reservation policy	No
Credit cards	Accepted but not AMEX
Price range	Budget
Style	Casual
Cuisine	Burgers
Recommended for	Regular neighbourhood

'They serve the best burger in Paris. You get the most amazing welcome here and the atmosphere is crazy!'
—Christophe Michalak

Among a dozen bouncy newcomers to a seedyish furriers' quarter between the 9th and 10th arrondissements, Big Fernand is a shoo-in for best Paris burger bar. This is fast food very much à la Française: beef (identifiably Charolais, Blonde d'Aquitaine, Normande or Salers) squidged into doughy buns (baked daily next door in their own bakery) with Fourme d'Ambert or Tomme de Savoie cheese. The staff are humorous, the burgers have names like Alphonse (milk-fed lamb with grilled aubergine, €13; £11; $20) and Bartholomé (beef with raclette cheese, bacon and confit onion, €12; £10; $17), and a long queue at lunchtime is inevitable.

ENCORE

43 Rue Richer
Paris 75009
+33 172609772
www.encore-restaurant.fr

Opening hours	Closed Saturday and Sunday
Credit cards	Accepted but not AMEX
Price range	Affordable
Style	Casual
Cuisine	Asian-European
Recommended for	Regular neighbourhood

'I often pop in for a quick lunch or long dinner. The Japanese chef Yoshie Morie cooks some amazing food.'
—Greg Marchand

LE GLASS

7 Rue Frochot
Paris 75009
+33 980729883
www.glassparis.com

Recommended by
Greg Marchand

Opening hours	Open 7 days
Credit cards	Accepted
Price range	Budget
Style	Casual
Cuisine	Hot Dogs
Recommended for	Late night

'Great cocktail bar and hot dogs.'—Greg Marchand

JULIEN

16 Rue du Faubourg Saint-Denis
Paris 75010
+33 147701206
www.julienparis.com

Recommended by
Yannick Alléno

Opening hours	Open 7 days
Credit cards	Accepted
Price range	Affordable
Style	Smart casual
Cuisine	French Brasserie
Recommended for	Late night

'This brasserie is listed as a historical monument. It's an institution, serving refined cuisine.'—Yannick Alléno

The bowl-you-over beauty and sheer age of this landmark on trendified Faubourg St-Denis are so extraordinary it ought to be an ossified monument, but arty Parisians still choose to dine here, beneath the art nouveau mouldings and Charles Buffet's towering mirrors. The food is a far cry in every way from the tripe or veal kidneys young bohemians would save up for in the 1960s. Nowadays the menu features Caesar salad with Landes chicken, Norwegian salmon with a sesame crust, and roasted duck breast with Parmesan crumble – well, it is owned by the Flo Group. Order the profiteroles with warm Valrhona chocolate sauce, sit back, and think of Piaf.

TEN BELLES

10 Rue de la Grange aux Belles
Paris 75010
+33 142409078
www.tenbelles.com

Recommended by
James Henry

Opening hours	Open 7 days
Reservation policy	No
Credit cards	Accepted but not AMEX
Price range	Budget
Style	Casual
Cuisine	Café-Bakery
Recommended for	Breakfast

'They roast their own coffee and serve sausage rolls. It was opened by the team behind Le Bal Café.'—James Henry

LE VERRE VOLÉ

67 Rue de Lancry
Paris 75010
+33 148031734
www.leverrevole.fr

Recommended by
Nicolai Nørregaard,
Louis-Philippe Riel

Opening hours	Open 7 days
Credit cards	Accepted but not AMEX
Price range	Affordable
Style	Casual
Cuisine	French
Recommended for	Regular neighbourhood

'I think it is the perfect restaurant for a city because the food changes radically every day while the place retains the same atmosphere – so if you feel comfortable there, you can go back every day without ever getting bored. I believe it is the liveliest restaurant ever. It is always changing, with customers coming back again and again. It is a restaurant that is always there when you need it while being different every time – for some this is a negative point but, to my mind, it is the exact opposite.'—Louis-Philippe Riel

VIVANT

43 Rue des Petites Écuries
Paris 75010
+33 142464355
www.vivantparis.com

Opening hours	Closed Saturday and Sunday
Credit cards	Accepted
Price range	Affordable
Style	Smart casual
Cuisine	French
Recommended for	Worth the travel

'It was super laid back and incredibly creative. Their wine list was absolutely over the top!'—Mindy Segal

BONES

43 Rue Godefroy Cavaignac
Paris 75011
+33 980753208
www.bonesparis.com

Opening hours	Closed Monday and Sunday
Credit cards	Accepted but not AMEX
Price range	Affordable
Style	Casual
Cuisine	Modern French
Recommended for	Wish I'd opened

'Probably the most fun I've had dining. Aside from the incredible food, that it's fun might be what makes Bones so successful. James makes his own bread, butter and charcuterie, processes all of his own seafood and uses fruit and vegetables direct from growers. Offal is often the star, and there is usually a whole suckling pig on the bar being stuffed into rolls with cabbage salad. A single duck heart with horseradish was startlingly satisfying.'—Josh Murphy

Aussie chef James Henry hadn't been in Paris long before a reputation-making year at Au Passage won him a cult following that has tailed him to Bones. Bones opened in the 'très Brooklyn' 11th arrondissement in January 2013, in an old Irish pub that was stripped to the 'bones'. The lighting is low and the music is loud. The bar is a destination in its own right for suckling pig sandwiches, small plates and natural wines, while the twenty-five-cover restaurant does a €40 (£33; $56) four-course *prix fixe*. Expect the likes of veal carpaccio with home-made bottarga and marinated mackerel with Meyer lemon.

LA BUVETTE

67 Rue Saint-Maur
Paris 75011
+33 983569411

Opening hours	Closed Monday and Tuesday
Reservation policy	No
Credit cards	Accepted but not AMEX
Price range	Budget
Style	Casual
Cuisine	Small plates
Recommended for	Regular neighbourhood

'I like the informal atmosphere here, where you can just pop in for a quick bite or an aperitif.'
—Flora Mikula

LE CHATEAUBRIAND

129 Avenue Parmentier
Paris 75011
+33 143574595
www.lechateaubriand.net

Opening hours	Closed Monday and Sunday
Credit cards	Accepted
Price range	Affordable
Style	Casual
Cuisine	French Brasserie
Recommended for	Wish I'd opened

'A restaurant of the future before anyone could see it.'
—René Redzepi

Sat on a sycamore-shaded avenue in Belleville, Le Chateaubriand occupies a handsome old bistro, its 1930s facade and interior largely unchanged. With its lack of airs and graces, championing of pungent natural wines and a take-it-or-leave-it five-course fixed price menu at dinner – there are those who don't get why it's created such a stir since opening in 2006. But that's their loss, because the cooking, which keeps things as raw and unadulterated as possible while mixing French staples with less familiar foreign flavours, makes it clear why chef-owner Inaki Aizpitarte has become the poster boy for the 'bistronomique' movement.

LE DAUPHIN

Recommended by
Flora Mikula

131 Avenue Parmentier
Paris 75011
+33 155287888
www.restaurantledauphin.net

Opening hours................................Closed Monday and Sunday
Credit cards..Accepted but not AMEX
Price range...Affordable
Style..Casual
Cuisine...French
Recommended for.....................................Local favourite

'I like this place, the atmosphere is a bit bobo
(bourgeois bohemian).'—Flora Mikula

DEUX FOIS PLUS DE PIMENT

Recommended by
James Henry

33 Rue Saint-Sébastien
Paris 75011
+33 158309935

Opening hours...Open 7 days
Reservation policy..No
Credit cards...Accepted
Price range..Budget
Style...Casual
Cuisine...Chinese
Recommended for..Bargain

'The only place in Paris for a dose of serious spice.'
—James Henry

L'ENTRÉE DES ARTISTES

Recommended by
Sven Chartier

8 Rue de Crussol
Paris 75011
+33 950996711

Opening hours...Closed Sunday
Credit cards...Accepted
Price range..Budget
Style...Casual
Cuisine..Small plates
Recommended for......................................Late night

'You come here to eat well and drink delicious cocktails.'
—Sven Chartier

LE REPAIRE DE CARTOUCHE

Recommended by
Yves Camdeborde

8 Boulevard des Filles du Calvaire
Paris 75011
+33 147002586

Opening hours................................Closed Monday and Sunday
Credit cards..Accepted but not AMEX
Price range...Budget
Style..Casual
Cuisine...French
Recommended for.....................................Bargain

'The €14 (£11.50; $19) menu is quite traditional, but
full of flavour and based on fresh ingredients which are
exceptional.'—Yves Camdeborde

RINO

Recommended by
Jean-François Piège,
Louis-Philippe Riel

46 Rue Trousseau
Paris 75011
+33 148069585

Opening hours................................Closed Monday and Sunday
Credit cards..Accepted
Price range...Affordable
Style..Smart casual
Cuisine..Italian
Recommended for.....................................High end

'The food here is very authentic and it is a place where
I can easily feel alone with my girlfriend even though it
is small and always packed. It is also where you can eat
the best pasta in Paris.'—Louis-Philippe Riel

If you're in Paris looking for first-class modern
European cuisine in unpretentious surroundings,
head over to the arty Sainte-Marguerite quartier in
the 11th arrondissement, where Rome's Giovanni
'Rino' Passerini is cooking up a storm. In a small,
well-managed dining room with light-coloured walls,
some bare brick and simple wooden furniture, you
can choose from a daily-changing menu that combines
influences and ingredients from all over Europe in a
highly imaginative and often surprising way. Rino has
a genuine talent for marrying textures and flavours in
dishes befitting fine dining, without the fine-dining price.

SEPTIME

80 Rue de Charonne
Paris 75011
+33 143673829
www.septime-charonne.fr

Recommended by
Mike Lata, Ken Oringer,
Kevin Pemoulie

Opening hours	Closed Saturday and Sunday
Credit cards	Accepted but not AMEX
Price range	Affordable
Style	Casual
Cuisine	Modern French
Recommended for	Worth the travel

'A killer new modern French restaurant in an edgy neighbourhood (11th arrondissement). Chef Grébaut's got a real playful yet elegant cooking style and the service is straight-forward and friendly.'—Ken Oringer

Rarely has a restaurant in Paris condensed and combined so many world trends. The room is an industrial-style loft, the waiters kindly attentive, carefully unshaven and if they don't have tattoos yet they're just about to. Bernard Grébaut is eminently celeb-able, good-looking, speaks his mind, loves poetry, was trained by Passard and pocketed a Michelin star aged only twenty-seven. His gentle, sensitive cuisine enfolds the new Nordic codes in solid French technique – veal with foie gras bouillion, white asparagus, sauce gribiche, oysters, plus flowers everywhere. Although despairingly hip and hard to book, it's exhilarating to witness the emergence of a blazing new talent.

STARVIN' JOE

42 Rue de Charonne
Paris 75011

Recommended by
Sven Chartier

Opening hours	Open 7 days
Reservation policy	No
Credit cards	Accepted
Price range	Budget
Style	Casual
Cuisine	Burgers
Recommended for	Bargain

'Just a simple burger, in a homemade bun made with good quality meat. At €10 (£8; $14) all in, it's the best value for money around.'—Sven Chartier

BOUCHERIE DES PROVINCES

20 Rue d'Aligre
Paris 75012
+33 143439164

Recommended by
Flora Mikula

Opening hours	Closed Monday
Credit cards	Accepted but not AMEX
Price range	Affordable
Style	Casual
Cuisine	Steakhouse
Recommended for	Bargain

'I go there for the hanger steak.'—Flora Mikula

LA GAZZETTA

29 Rue de Cotte
Paris 75012
+33 143474705
www.lagazzetta.fr

Recommended by
Andreas Dahlberg

Opening hours	Closed Monday and Sunday
Credit cards	Accepted
Price range	Affordable
Style	Smart casual
Cuisine	Modern French
Recommended for	Worth the Travel

This elegant 1930s bistro was given a new lease of life in 2006 with the arrival of former chef and now part-owner Petter Nilsson and the team from Le Fumoir. Close to the marché d'Aligre, Paris's hippest market, the lunch is magically priced: three small plates from a choice of four to team with salad or charcuterie and le dessert du jour, all for less than €20 (£16; $27). In the evening a more sparkly but still tight, and fantastically good value, evening menu – asparagus and bonito with verbina butter; duck foie gras with new potatoes, saffron and mustard; hay and chicory ice cream – has made La Gazzetta a serious gastronomic destination.

TABLE

3 Rue de Prague
Paris 75012
+33 143431226
www.tablerestaurant.fr

Recommended by
Matthew Crabbe

Opening hours	Closed Saturday and Sunday
Credit cards	Accepted
Price range	Expensive
Style	Smart casual
Cuisine	Modern French
Recommended for	Worth the travel

'Honest food and ambience, Bruno is a terrific host.'
—Matthew Crabbe

A cook and critic prepared to put his money where his mouth is, in spring 2013 Bruno Verjus donned his whites in earnest. A radically produce-driven destination dining room, in a neighbourhood dense with popular bistros, Table attracts gourmet pilgrims and restaurant world insiders who are undaunted by its high prices and limited choice. Verjus and his two chefs work reverently with artisan charcuterie (Blonde d'Aquitaine 'ham', black pork from Saint-Géry), vegetables grown by Joël Thiébault (who also supplies Alain Passard at L'Arpège), and exceptional cuts of meat or whole fish destined for the La Cornue rotisserie. Verjus himself designed the dining space and open kitchen, and personally selects the bio wines, including rare examples of more mature *vins natures*.

LA RÉGALADE

49 Avenue Jean Moulin
Paris 75014
+33 145456858

Recommended by
Julien Duboué,
Christophe Michalak,
Emmanuel Renaut

Opening hours	Closed Saturday and Sunday
Credit cards	Accepted but not AMEX
Price range	Affordable
Style	Smart casual
Cuisine	French Bistro
Recommended for	Bargain

'Generous, gourmet cuisine, including pig's trotters (feet) and tartare. Good food that is halfway between gastro and bistro, in a fun, convivial atmosphere.' —Emmanuel Renaut

Ferocious talent Yves Camdeborde sent shock waves through Paris kitchens when he left behind the starry Hôtel de Crillon in 1992 to open a tiny bistro in the 14th arrondissement. Credited as the forerunner of the *la bistronomique* movement, his quaint tiled bistro touted haute skills and ingredients at bistro prices. Camdeborde has sinced moved on (to Le Comptoir) but new owner Bruno Doucet keeps the generous spirit alive, inviting guests to dig in to foie gras with macerated figs ahead of an unashamedly Gallic feast of sea bass with a fricassée of potatoes and artichokes, saddle of rabbit with pan-fried courgettes (zucchini) and pine nuts and a pain perdu with red berries and ice cream. A second Régalade opened on the Rue Saint-Honoré in 2010.

LE PÈRE CLAUDE

51 Avenue de la Motte-Picquet
Paris 75015
+33 147340305
www.lepereclaude.com

Recommended by
Christophe Michalak

Opening hours	Open 7 days
Credit cards	Accepted
Price range	Affordable
Style	Casual
Cuisine	French Bistro
Recommended for	Late night

'This surely has to be one of the few restaurants that take you hostage, serving you late into the night. Try Christian Parra's black pudding (blood sausage)... an absolute must.'—Christophe Michalak

L'ASTRANCE

4 Rue Beethoven
Paris 75016
+33 140508440
www.astrancerestaurant.com

Recommended by
Yves Camdeborde, Anatoly
Komm, Franck-Elie Laloum,
Corey Lee, Greg Marchand,
Jocky Petrie, Daniel Puskas,
Jack Riebel, Michel
Troisgros, Mats Vollmer,
Martin Wishart

Opening hours	Closed Saturday to Monday
Credit cards	Accepted
Price range	Expensive
Style	Smart casual
Cuisine	Modern French
Recommended for	Worth the travel

'Fabulous Paris restaurant, Chef Pascal Barbot cooked me the meal of my life!'—Jack Riebel

This small (but tall!), out of the way, airy, three-Michelin-starred restaurant is soaked in relaxed confidence, as is Pascal Barbot's concise cooking. Root vegetables, flowers and herbs are very much the stars, sitting together raw, fermented and poached, or spiked with notes of smoke, citrus and pickle. Barbot rightly prides himself on the very careful pairing of wine with the tasting menu (for instance, Challans duck and raspberries, with a Gevrey Chambertin 'Vieilles Vignes' 2005) and, unlike many lazier *grandes tables*, here it would be a shame not to let yourself be guided from start to finish. You're in good hands.

CARETTE

Recommended by
Akrame Benallal,
Pierre Gagnaire

4 Place du Trocadéro
Paris 75016
+33 147279885

Opening hours	Open 7 days
Credit cards	Accepted
Price range	Affordable
Style	Casual
Cuisine	Café-Patisserie
Recommended for	Breakfast

'I like this place because it hasn't changed since it opened in 1927. Utterly timeless, it has managed to stay exactly the same all these years.'—Akrame Benallal

LA PÂTISSERIE DES RÊVES

Recommended by
Pascal Barbot

111 Rue de Longchamp
Paris 75016
+33 147040024
www.lapatisseriedesreves.com

Opening hours	Closed Monday
Reservation policy	No
Credit cards	Accepted
Price range	Affordable
Style	Casual
Cuisine	Patisserie
Recommended for	Local favourite

PRUNIER

Recommended by
Matt Dillon

16 Avenue Victor Hugo
Paris 75016
+33 144173585
www.prunier.com

Opening hours	Closed Sunday
Credit cards	Accepted
Price range	Expensive
Style	Smart casual
Cuisine	French Seafood
Recommended for	High end

'The service is so unreal. Classic but not pretentious. Beautiful, comfortable seats. The caviar was mind-blowing. I just celebrated my fortieth birthday here and had one of the best dishes I've eaten in my life. Raw scallops over a perfect Jerusalem artichoke puree all held in a savoury, shortbread-style pastry crust. A touch of salt and cracked black pepper. Excellent.'
—Matt Dillon

RESTAURANT AKRAME

Recommended by
Pierre Gagnaire

19 Rue Lauriston
Paris 75016
+33 140671116
www.akrame.com

Opening hours	Closed Saturday and Sunday
Credit cards	Accepted
Price range	Expensive
Style	Casual
Cuisine	Modern French
Recommended for	Regular neighbourhood

'I really enjoy having dinner at Akrame. I like the chef's culinary creations.'—Pierre Gagnaire

LE STELLA

Recommended by
Pierre Gagnaire

133 Avenue Victor Hugo
Paris 75016
+33 156905600

Opening hours	Open 7 days
Credit cards	Accepted
Price range	Affordable
Style	Smart casual
Cuisine	French Brasserie
Recommended for	Late night

'After the theatre or a football match, I often go and eat a plate of oysters at Le Stella. The staff are very welcoming, the atmosphere is calm and you can have quite a relaxed time here.'—Pierre Gagnaire

KIFUNÉ

Recommended by
Pierre Gagnaire

44 Rue Saint-Ferdinand
Paris 75017
+33 145721119

Opening hours	Closed Sunday
Credit cards	Accepted but not AMEX
Price range	Affordable
Style	Casual
Cuisine	Japanese
Recommended for	Local favourite

'You would think it was a restaurant in Tokyo and it's a hot spot for the Japanese crowd. Their beef tataki is excellent.'—Pierre Gagnaire

RESTAURANT GUY SAVOY
Recommended by
Saipin Chutima

18 Rue Troyon
Paris 75017
+33 143804061
www.guysavoy.com

Opening hours	Closed Monday and Sunday
Credit cards	Accepted
Price range	Expensive
Style	Formal
Cuisine	French
Recommended for	High end

'An interior design that leaves the diner in awe of its beauty. The food is carefully prepared and the flavours in each dish leave the mind mesmerized.'
—Saipin Chutima

Just like Pierre Gagnaire and Joël Robuchon, Guy Savoy has grown a global empire, opening in Las Vegas and Singapore, from this intimate three-Michelin-starred restaurant where the service is ultra-personalized from the minute the client opens the door. Elsewhere in Paris, three modern bistro/brasseries – Le Chiberta, Les Bouquinistes and L'Atelier Maître Albert – serve simpler versions of Savoy's classicism but his artichoke soup with black truffles, parmesan and mushroom brioche with black truffle butter remains one of France's most celebrated dishes. Chefs return again and again to soak up the Savoy magic and inspiration.

À LA GOUTTE D'OR
Recommended by
Akrame Benallal

41 Rue de la Goutte d'Or
Paris 75018
+33 142649916
www.lagouttedor.net

Opening hours	Closed Sunday
Credit cards	Accepted
Price range	Budget
Style	Casual
Cuisine	North African-French
Recommended for	Regular neighbourhood

'You get a good, honest meal here. The place is down to earth, just like me.'—Akrame Benallal

LE BAL CAFÉ
Recommended by
Greg Marchand,
Daniel Rose

Le Bal
6 Impasse de la Défense
Paris 75018
+33 144707551
www.le-bal.fr

Opening hours	Closed Monday and Tuesday
Credit cards	Accepted but not AMEX
Price range	Affordable
Style	Casual
Cuisine	British
Recommended for	Breakfast

'I love going there on Sunday mornings for a fry-up brunch. They make a slick coffee and their English-breakfast-style menu transports me to London for an hour or two. The little park opposite is perfect for kids to run around in and there's often enough space to park a pushchair – no small detail!'—Daniel Rose

LE COQ RICO
Recommended by
Greg Marchand

98 Rue Lepic
Paris 75018
+33 142598289
www.lecoqrico.com

Opening hours	Open 7 days
Credit cards	Accepted
Price range	Affordable
Style	Casual
Cuisine	French
Recommended for	Regular neighbourhood

'Great neo-rotisserie to go to for Sunday lunch with the kids. They have amazing roast chicken. And afterwards I love going for a digestive walk near the Sacré Cœur.'
—Greg Marchand

LAO SIAM
Recommended by
Flora Mikula

49 Rue de Belleville
Paris 75019
+33 140400968

Opening hours	Open 7 days
Credit cards	Accepted but not AMEX
Price range	Budget
Style	Casual
Cuisine	Thai
Recommended for	Regular neighbourhood

LE PACIFIQUE

35 Rue de Belleville
Paris 75019
+33 142496680

Recommended by
Bertrand Grébaut

Opening hours	Open 7 days
Credit cards	Accepted
Price range	Budget
Style	Casual
Cuisine	Chinese
Recommended for	Late night

'This is a traditional Chinese restaurant open until 2.00 a.m., where you'll find a fantastic mápó tòfu (tofu in spicy sauce) and a very good crispy fried pork belly.'
—Bertrand Grébaut

LE BARATIN

3 Rue Jouye-Rouve
Paris 75020
+33 143493970

Recommended by
Sven Chartier, Andreas Dahlberg, Bertrand Grébaut, James Henry, Paul Pairet, Josep Roca

Opening hours	Closed Monday and Sunday
Credit cards	Accepted but not AMEX
Price range	Affordable
Style	Casual
Cuisine	French Bistro
Recommended for	Regular neighbourhood

'It's good, simple and fuss-free. Plus, in my opinion, they have the best wine cellar in Paris.'
—Bertrand Grébaut

Raquel Carena and Philippe 'Pinuche' Pinoteau have admirably ridden the wave of global fame and *New York Times* profiles to keep Le Baratin the way it has always been – a crammed, no-nonsense, local bistro with a splash of charm, plus slavish, personal devotion to the highest-quality wine and ingredients. Chefs love revitalizing their tired palates with Raquel's motherly, delicate handling of fish and vegetables from Breton superstar Annie Bertin. She holds their awe and respect as much as the Passards and Ducasses for the dozens of remarkably inventive dishes that spring from her heart and tiny kitchen every day.

RAVIOLI CHINOIS NORD-EST

11 Rue Civiale
Paris 75020
+33 175508803

Recommended by
Greg Marchand

Opening hours	Closed Wednesday
Reservation policy	No
Credit cards	Not accepted
Price range	Budget
Style	Casual
Cuisine	Chinese
Recommended for	Bargain

'A great little hole-in-the-wall place serving steamed or grilled *jiaozi*, a kind of Chinese gyoza traditionally served at Chinese new year in the northeast of China. A bargain at €5 (£4; $7) for ten pieces.'—Greg Marchand

ROSEVAL

1 Rue d'Eupatoria
Paris 75020
+33 953562414
www.roseval.fr

Recommended by
Petter Nilsson

Opening hours	Closed Saturday and Sunday
Credit cards	Accepted but not AMEX
Price range	Expensive
Style	Casual
Cuisine	Modern French
Recommended for	Late night

SPAIN

'THE BEST PLACE TO CELEBRATE THE UNLIMITED HORIZONS OF PLEASURE.'
GASTÓN ACURIO P493

'I eat the sea bass in a salt crust, sea cucumbers and Balearic prawns with my feet in the sand.'
SERGIO HERMAN P478

'CLASSIC VALENCIAN RABBIT-AND MOUNTAIN-SNAIL PAELLA AND PACO TORREBLANCA CHOCOLATES. IT WILL BLOW YOU AWAY.'
JOCKY PETRIE P506

'One of those magical sensations that makes life worth living.'
ANDONI LUIS ADURIZ P480

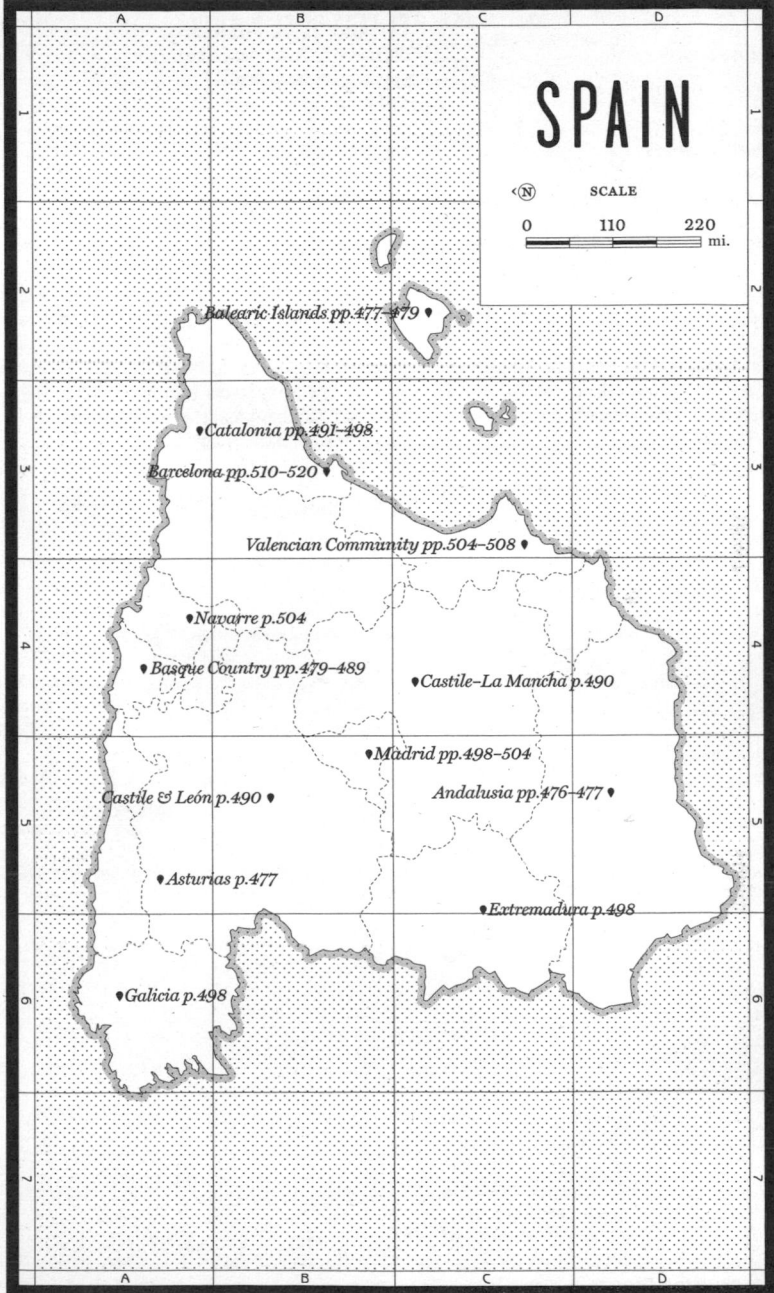

SPAIN

SCALE

0   110   220
mi.

Balearic Islands pp.477–479 ♥

♥ Catalonia pp.491–498

Barcelona pp.510–520 ♥

Valencian Community pp.504–508 ♥

♥ Navarre p.504

♥ Basque Country pp.479–489   ♥ Castile–La Mancha p.490

♥ Madrid pp.498–504

Castile & León p.490 ♥   Andalusia pp.476–477 ♥

♥ Asturias p.477

♥ Extremadura p.498

♥ Galicia p.498

EL CAMPERO

Avenida Constitución Local 5c
Barbate
Andalusia 11160
+34 956432300
www.restauranteelcampero.es

Opening hours	Closed Monday
Credit cards	Accepted
Price range	Affordable
Style	Smart casual
Cuisine	Seafood
Recommended for	Worth the travel

'El Campero is in the heart of the traditional tuna fishing region of Jerez and during tuna fishing season it serves a mouth-watering tuna tasting menu.'
—Samantha & Samuel Clark

LAS REJAS

Estrada El Lentiscal
Bolonia
Andalusia 11391
+34 956688546

Opening hours	Variable
Credit cards	Accepted but not AMEX
Price range	Affordable
Style	Casual
Cuisine	Seafood
Recommended for	Bargain

'The place is unique, near one of the most beautiful, untouched beaches in Cádiz. They serve the best fresh fish that I've ever eaten.'—Ángel León

APONIENTE

Calle Puerto Escondido 6
El Puerto de Santa María
Andalusia 11500
+34 956851870
www.aponiente.com

Opening hours	Closed Monday and Sunday
Credit cards	Accepted
Price range	Expensive
Style	Smart casual
Cuisine	Modern Seafood
Recommended for	Worth the travel

'Ángel León is as much fisherman as he is chef. He coaxes flavours from the sea to create dishes that are worthy of envy.'—Dan Barber

EL FARO DE EL PUERTO

Carretera de Fuentebravía Km. 0.5
El Puerto de Santa María
Andalusia 11500
+34 956870952
www.elfarodelpuerto.com

Opening hours	Open 7 days
Credit cards	Accepted
Price range	Affordable
Style	Smart casual
Cuisine	Andalusian
Recommended for	Local favourite

'They use the best products and produce some great cooking. One of my favourite dishes is the anchovy toast. The restaurant has great staff, especially the chef, Fernándo Córdoba.'—Ángel León

RESTAURANTE EL ARRIATE

Calle Los Moros 4
El Puerto de Santa María
Andalusia 11500
+34 630746946
www.restauranteelarriate.com

Opening hours	Closed Monday
Credit cards	Accepted but not AMEX
Price range	Affordable
Style	Casual
Cuisine	Andalusian
Recommended for	Regular neighbourhood

'They're fantastic at cooking vegetables and the staff make me feel like I'm at home.'—Ángel León

RESTAURANTE VENTA PINTO

Recommended by
Ángel León

Carretera Barbate-Vejer s/n
Vejer de la Frontera
Andalusia 11150
+34 956450069
www.ventapinto.com

Opening hours	Open 7 days
Credit cards	Accepted
Price range	Affordable
Style	Casual
Cuisine	Andalusian
Recommended for	Breakfast

'I like their artisan bread with *la manteca colorá* (lard seasoned with paprika).'—Ángel León

EL HÓRREO

Recommended by
Alberto Chicote

Calle Antromero AS-239
Antromero
Asturias 33449
+34 985871470

Opening hours	Open 7 days
Credit cards	Accepted
Price range	Affordable
Style	Casual
Cuisine	Seafood
Recommended for	Wish I'd opened

'The restaurant is absolutely remote, the way of cooking is not like mine, but they have the best seafood I have ever tasted.'—Alberto Chicote

CASA MARCIAL

Recommended by
Quique Dacosta

La Salgar s/n
Parres
Asturias 33549
+34 985840991
www.casamarcial.com

Opening hours	Closed Monday
Credit cards	Accepted
Price range	Affordable
Style	Smart casual
Cuisine	Modern Spanish
Recommended for	Worth the travel

CASA GERARDO

Recommended by
Quique Dacosta

Antigua Carretera AS-19 Km. 9
Prendes
Asturias 33438
+34 985887797
www.restaurantecasagerardo.com

Opening hours	Closed Monday
Credit cards	Accepted
Price range	Affordable
Style	Smart casual
Cuisine	Northern Spanish
Recommended for	Worth the travel

ES XARCU

Recommended by
Joan Roca

Cala Es Xarco
Sant Josep
Ibiza
Balearic Islands 07830
+34 971187867
www.esxarcu.com

Opening hours	Variable
Credit cards	Accepted
Price range	Affordable
Style	Casual
Cuisine	Spanish Grill
Recommended for	Local favourite

Few restaurants can boast a terrace with a view as picturesque as Es Xarcu's, which is located directly on the sandy shores of a Sant Josep cove. Locals don't come for the view alone, however, but for the traditional food that is cooked simply over a flame for maximum flavour. The menu is comfortingly basic, with starters such as handcarved *jamón* (ham), *boquerones* and fresh prawns (shrimp) *a la plancha* making way for simple mains of freshly caught fish that are merely thrown on the grill. There are no delusions of grandeur here, with the cheap plastic chairs and the daily lunchtime scramble only adding to the experience.

RESTAURANT ES TORRENT

Platja d'es Torrent
Sant Josep
Ibiza
Balearic Islands 07839
+34 971802160
www.estorrent.net

Recommended by
Filip Claeys,
Sergio Herman

Opening hours	Open 7 days
Credit cards	Accepted but not AMEX
Price range	Expensive
Style	Casual
Cuisine	Seafood
Recommended for	Wish I'd opened

'My heart lies here. With my friends I eat the sea bass in a salt crust, the sea cucumbers and the Balearic prawns (shrimp) with my feet in the sand.'
—Sergio Herman

Depending on whether you are a 'have not' or a 'have yacht', you can drop anchor close to Es Torrent before taking shade under a straw umbrella and dining with your feet in the sand. What started as a stall a decade ago has become Ibiza's most des res (desirable restaurant). Open April to October, specialities of the long, fish-focused, market menu include whole sea bass baked in salt crust, spiny lobster stew for two, and the – hard to define in terms of taste and texture – sea cucumber. The wine list is full of excellent reds and the best national whites, which wonderfully suit the seaside location.

ES MOLÍ D'EN BOU

Protur Sa Coma Playa Hotel and Spa
Calle Lilles s/n
Sa Coma
Majorca
Balearic Islands 07560
+34 971569663
www.esmolidenbou.es

Recommended by
Marc Fosh

Opening hours	Closed Monday
Credit cards	Accepted but not AMEX
Price range	Expensive
Style	Smart casual
Cuisine	Majorcan
Recommended for	High end

'Local celebrity chef, Tomeu Caldentey, creates innovative, stunning food based on traditional Mallorcan flavours at this modern restaurant. Try and book the chef's table – superb experience!'—Marc Fosh

FIBONACCI

Vicario Joaquin Fuster 95
Palma
Majorca
Balearic Islands 07006
+34 971264258
www.fibonacci-bakery.com

Recommended by
Marc Fosh

Opening hours	Open 7 days
Reservation policy	No
Credit cards	Accepted
Price range	Budget
Style	Casual
Cuisine	Café-Bakery
Recommended for	Breakfast

'It's in the old fishing quarter of Palma known as Portixol. Great coffee and home-made pastries and breads that are to die for. Being right next to the Mediterranean sea completes the experience.'
—Marc Fosh

JOAN MARC RESTAURANT

Plaça del Blanquer 10
Inca
Majorca
Balearic Islands 07300
+34 971500804
www.joanmarcrestaurant.com

Recommended by
Marc Fosh

Opening hours	Closed Monday
Credit cards	Accepted
Price range	Affordable
Style	Casual
Cuisine	Majorcan
Recommended for	Regular neighbourhood

'Joan Marc is a very talented Spanish chef and his restaurant is an absolute jewel in the quiet old town of Inca. The food is uncomplicated but really well executed and the well-chosen ingredients speak for themselves. Also the price for the quality is a major draw.'—Marc Fosh

SA CUINA DE N'AINA

Recommended by
Marc Fosh

Carrer Rafal 31
Sencelles
Majorca
Balearic Islands 07140
+34 971872992
www.sacuinadenaina.com

Opening hours	Closed Monday and Tuesday
Credit cards	Accepted
Price range	Affordable
Style	Casual
Cuisine	Majorcan
Recommended for	Local favourite

'A little gem, hidden away in a small village. Chef Aina Carbonell, cooks classic Majorcan food to perfection. Try her *arroz brut*, a rustic dish of rice, game and vegetables in a hearty stock, or the local suckling pig which is slow-roasted until crisp and tender. Both are delicious.'—Marc Fosh

ASADOR ETXEBARRI

Recommended by
Andoni Luis Aduriz, Josean Alija, Juan Mari & Elena Arzak, Pascal Barbot, Alberto Chicote, Ashley Christensen, Greg & Gabrielle Quiñónez Denton, Matt Dillon, Robin Gill, James Henry, Julius Jaspers, Pierre Koffmann, Donald Link, David Martin, Willy Trullás Moreno, Paul Pairet, Franck Pecol, Neil Perry, Louis-Philippe Riel, Didem Şenol Tiryakioğlu, Hiro Sone, Agnar Sverrisson, Brad Turley, Joachim Wissler

Plaza de San Juan 1
Atxondo
Basque Country 48291
+34 946583042
www.asadoretxebarri.com

Opening hours	Closed Monday
Credit cards	Accepted
Price range	Expensive
Style	Smart casual
Cuisine	Basque Grill
Recommended for	Worth the travel

'Represents the essence of Basque gastronomy. In my eyes, Víctor Arguinzóniz is the best grill-house chef in the world.'—Josean Alija

There's no food without fire at Víctor Arguinzóniz's homage to the Iberian-born tradition of the *asador* (grill restaurant). It sits in the bucolic Basque Country village of Axpe, nestled at the foot of mount Alluitz, halfway between San Sebastián and Bilbao. Every dish that makes it onto Arguinzóniz's strictly seasonal tasting menu is flavoured with a smoky kiss from his charcoal-fired grill: seafood, marbled beef, vegetables, eggs, cheese, butter – even the desserts – smoked milk often making an appearance. Ingredients are predominantly sourced from the surrounding unfairly fertile Atxondo valley – even the charcoal for the grill, is made from local oak.

ASADOR INDUSI

Recommended by
Josean Alija

Calle Maestro García Rivero 7
Bilbao
Basque Country 48011
+34 944417176
www.asador-bilbao.com

Opening hours	Open 7 days
Credit cards	Accepted
Price range	Affordable
Style	Casual
Cuisine	Basque Grill
Recommended for	Regular neighbourhood

'A grill-house specializing in charcoal-grilled meats.'
—Josean Alija

BAITA GAMINIZ

Recommended by
Josean Alija

Calle Alameda de Mazarredo 20
Bilbao
Basque Country 48001
+34 944242267
www.baitagaminiz.com

Opening hours	Closed Monday
Credit cards	Accepted
Price range	Affordable
Style	Casual
Cuisine	Modern Basque
Recommended for	Regular neighbourhood

'A restaurant that serves modern local cuisine and that specializes in fish.'—Josean Alija

It might lie within sight of the Guggenheim, but this Bilbao favourite has won fans far closer to home than hungry tourists looking for a lunch spot. Legions of loyal locals testify to the keen pricing – €50 (£42; $69) for the tasting menu – as well as the comfortable, calm ambience and the excellence of the cooking. Chef Guillermo Fernández uses traditional Basque cuisine as a springboard to original creations. *Bacalao* (salt cod) is the reason to come. If you've enjoyed it in the restaurant, you can buy twenty varieties of it in the Baita Gaminiz shop next door. Book in advance, particularly if you're aiming to score a table on the pretty riverside terrace.

NERUA

Guggenheim Bilbao Museum
Avenida Abandoibarra 2
Bilbao
Basque Country 48001
+34 944000430
www.nerua.com

Recommended by
Andoni Luis Aduriz, Víctor
Arguinzóniz, Juan Mari &
Elena Arzak, Quique Dacosta,
Alberto Landgraf

Opening hours	Closed Monday
Credit cards	Accepted
Price range	Expensive
Style	Smart casual
Cuisine	Modern Basque
Recommended for	Worth the travel

'Watching how the colour of the walls of the Guggenheim Museum in Bilbao changes while you are having an aperitif on Nerua's top-floor terrace is one of those magical sensations that makes life worth living.'
—Andoni Luis Aduriz

TXAKOLI SIMÓN

Camino San Roque 89
Bilbao
Basque Country 48015
+34 944457499
www.txakolisimon.com

Recommended by
Josean Alija

Opening hours	Open 7 days
Credit cards	Accepted
Price range	Affordable
Style	Casual
Cuisine	Basque Grill
Recommended for	Regular neighbourhood

'Excellent pork chop.'—Josean Alija

MUGARITZ

Otazulueta Baserria
Aldura Aldea 20
Errenteria
Basque Country 20100
+34 943522455
www.mugaritz.com

Recommended by
Víctor Arguinzóniz, Juan Mari &
Elena Arzak, José Avillez, Massimo
Bottura, Alejandro Cancino, Quique
Dacosta, Wylie Dufresne, Paul
Foster, Matthew Gaudet, Hernán
Gipponi, Rodolfo Guzmán, Anna
Hansen, Dan Hunter, Anatoly
Komm, William Mahi, Michael
Meredith, David Muñoz, Petter
Nilsson, Paul Pairet, James Parry,
Neil Perry, Pedro Subijana

Opening hours	Closed Monday
Credit cards	Accepted
Price range	Expensive
Style	Smart casual
Cuisine	Modern Spanish
Recommended for	Worth the travel

'Andoni's is a truly global cuisine. It's cooking that begins, first and foremost, with a concept before moving on to the raw materials. Consistently flawless technique. A unique experience.'—Massimo Bottura

The smell of barbecue greets visitors to this cutting-edge restaurant tucked away in the hills outside San Sebastián, where head chef Andoni Luis Aduriz believes it's a universal childhood aroma. It's academic, really, as everything you're served once seated in the bright and spacious dining room is unrecognizable – designed to startle, amaze and even challenge your ideas about food. The techno-emotional cooking approach means a succession of wildly creative dishes such as 'edible stones'. There are no Basque favourites such as hake and salsa verde on the menu. In fact, there isn't even a menu – you simply put yourself at the kitchen's mercy.

ELKANO

Calle de Herrerieta 2
Getaria
Basque Country 20808
+34 943140024
www.restauranteelkano.com

Recommended by
Andoni Luis Aduriz, Josean
Alija, Juan Mari & Elena
Arzak, Daniel López, Iñigo
Peña, José Pizarro

Opening hours	Variable
Credit cards	Accepted but not AMEX
Price range	Expensive
Style	Smart casual
Cuisine	Seafood
Recommended for	Regular neighbourhood

'A family-run restaurant in a coastal village near San Sebastián. It is named after the first man who sailed around the world, who was also from Getaria. It serves the best Basque fish and seafood.'—Andoni Luis Aduriz

The philosophy at Elkano, which sits on the seafront at Getaria, an hour west of San Sebastián, is quite simple: fresh fish, chargrilled. Except some strange alchemy seems to occur when the piscine produce of the Guipuzcoan coast meets Pedro Arregui's coals in the open air. Superlative turbot and hake are delivered unadorned to clothed tables in the unselfconsciously old-fashioned dining room – terracotta tiles, dark wooden beams. Lobster, clams, baby squid and coral-pink prawns (shrimp) all receive the same treatment, partnered by a compact selection of Spanish wines, including the region's own dry sparkling Chacolí. Round off with another local speciality – the indulgent custard-filled *Panchineta*.

KAIA KAIPE

General Arnao 4
Getaria
Basque Country 20808
+34 943140500
www.kaia-kaipe.com

Recommended by
Martín Berasategui,
Iñigo Peña,
Pedro Subijana

Opening hours	Open 7 days
Credit cards	Accepted
Price range	Affordable
Style	Smart casual
Cuisine	Seafood
Recommended for	Regular neighbourhood

'One of a lot of really good restaurants in and around San Sebastián.'—Martín Berasategui

Situated about 25 km (15 miles) along the coast from San Sebastián, Getaria catches the eye for the rocky outcrop that juts out into the sea, attached by a spit of land. On this spit, overlooking the little harbour, stands Kaia Kaipe. You can imagine how fresh the fish is. If you get a table outside, you can watch it coming in. Turbot, hake, langoustines, lobster... cooked as well as any fish you will ever have the pleasure of eating. This speciality brings in the local regulars, as well as fish fanciers from far and wide, which all makes for a very rewarding experience.

ALAMEDA

Minasoroeta Kalea 1
Hondarribia
Basque Country 20280
+34 943642789
www.restaurantealameda.net

Recommended by
Juan Mari & Elena Arzak

Opening hours	Closed Monday
Credit cards	Accepted
Price range	Affordable
Style	Casual
Cuisine	Modern Spanish
Recommended for	Worth the travel

This third-generation restaurant, run by the three Txapartegi brothers, lies in a tiny seaside hamlet, just a seven-minute ferry ride from France, that's starting to steal some of nearby San Sebastián's limelight. Chef Gorka, who trained under Martín Berasategui, is a rising star in the region thanks to his contemporary Basque cuisine – tuna in citrus paired with liquefied tomato and sprouts, scallop ravioli with wild mushrooms and asparagus – which is more about respecting the local produce than indulging in experimental high jinks. The spacious dining room feels a long way from Donostia's madding crowds, and the food is more affordable too.

AZURMENDI

Corredor del Txorierri, exit 25
Larrabetzu
Basque Country 48195
+34 944558866
www.azurmendi.biz

Recommended by
Bruno Oteiza & Mikel
Alonso, Pascal Barbot,
Quique Dacosta,
Mitsuharu Tsumura

Opening hours	Closed Monday
Credit cards	Accepted
Price range	Expensive
Style	Casual
Cuisine	Modern Basque
Recommended for	Worth the travel

'The best gastronomic experience of my life. Eneko Atxa has achieved the perfect balance of home-made flavours and avant-garde cuisine. The service, work ethic, creativity and location make this restaurant unique in the world. I would come all the way from Peru just to eat at Azurmendi.'—Mitsuharu Tsumura

Eneko Atxa is Azurmendi's young, passionate and impressively earringed chef. The restaurant opened in 2005 in a warehouse-style building ten minutes outside Bilbao. The dining room is brightly lit, with tall windows, and the decor is stylish and modern — sensible lighting and an open, airy space. Atxa's food is bold and experimental, his dishes bearing names such as 'the garden' (edible soil with young vegetables) or 'heart of the countryside', but there are nods to a more rustic Basque heritage in a dish of Iberian pork with wild garlic flowers and broad beans. They serve an excellent txakoli wine produced by their own winery.

MARTÍN BERASATEGUI

Loidi Kalea 4
Lasarte-Oria
Basque Country 20160
+34 943366471
www.martinberasategui.com

Recommended by
Ettore Botrini, José
Cordeiro, Quique Dacosta,
Xabier Diez Esteibar,
Peter Knogl, William Mahi,
Aizpea Oihaneder Perez,
Pedro Subijana,
Gerhard Wieser

Opening hours	Closed Monday and Tuesday
Credit cards	Accepted
Price range	Expensive
Style	Smart casual
Cuisine	Modern Spanish
Recommended for	Wish I'd opened

'It has a good philosophy, a clear line, but is still constantly innovative.'—Peter Knogl

As if you need another reason for going to San Sebastián, a visit to Martín Berasategui is the cherry on the icing on the cake. And a warm toasted almond cake at that. Located a short drive outside the Basque capital, the restaurant is a haven of calm simplicity, while in the kitchen an orchestra of sous-chefs plays tirelessly to Berasategui's score. Not one for gilding the lily, he has become a master at extracting the maximum from his pure ingredients. Expect not a lavish feast, but delicate portions of intense flavour that melt in the mouth and leave a long-lasting impression.

ZUBEROA

Araneder Bidea
Oiartzun
Basque Country 20180
+34 943491228
www.zuberoa.com

Recommended by
Víctor Arguinzóniz, Juan
Mari & Elena Arzak,
Martín Berasategui,
Aizpea Oihaneder Perez,
Iñigo Peña, Pedro Subijana

Opening hours	Variable
Credit cards	Accepted
Price range	Expensive
Style	Smart casual
Cuisine	Modern Basque
Recommended for	Wish I'd opened

'It represents elegance, superb flavour and real cooking. It's a fantastic place.'—Martín Berasategui

The setting — a convivial old stone building in a 600-year-old village outside San Sebastián — may be quaint, but there is nothing quaint about the cooking. This is traditional Basque food brought bang up to date by chef Hilario Arbelaitz, who stakes his reputation on the quality of his ingredients and his ability to arrange them enticingly on the plate. Seafood plays the lead role, as you would expect in this part of the world, and the flavours are rich and warming, but Arbelaitz is not afraid to throw in the odd exotic ingredient, such as coconut or pineapple, or even both.

MUGURUZA

Recommended by
Martín Berasategui

Calle Torre-Atze 8-bajo
Pasai San Pedro
Basque Country 20110
+34 943394944

Opening hours	Closed Sunday
Reservation policy	No
Credit cards	Not accepted
Price range	Budget
Style	Casual
Cuisine	Basque
Recommended for	Breakfast

'Generally known as "Falcon Crest". I love going for a good walk and ending up here for breakfast. And there is no coffee, juice, toast or pastry in sight: here you eat breakfast like the old, wise sailors used to do: meatballs, meat stew, *ajoarriero* (cod with oil, garlic and peppers), fried fish, liver and onions, etc. Delicious.'
—Martín Berasategui

AGORREGI

Recommended by
Xabier Diez Esteibar

Portuetxe Kalea 15
San Sebastián
Basque Country 20018
www.agorregi.com

Opening hours	Closed Sunday
Credit cards	Accepted but not AMEX
Price range	Affordable
Style	Casual
Cuisine	Modern Basque
Recommended for	Bargain

'Friendly service and the food is simple and affordable.'
—Xabier Diez Esteibar

AKELARRE

Recommended by
Andoni Luis Aduriz, Víctor
Arguinzóniz, Juan Mari & Elena
Arzak, Martín Berasategui,
Quique Dacosta,
Rob Evans, Florian Lamelot,
Aizpea Oihaneder Perez,
Martín Rebaudino

Paseo Padre Orcoloaga 56
San Sebastián
Basque Country 20008
+34 943311209
www.akelarre.net

Opening hours	Closed Monday
Credit cards	Accepted
Price range	Expensive
Style	Smart casual
Cuisine	Modern Basque
Recommended for	Worth the travel

'A real institution. A major benchmark in haute cuisine and the cutting-edge Basque cuisine we produce here.'
—Martín Berasategui

Should you tire of San Sebastián's abundant *pintxos* (Basque tapas) bars, venture a little out of town for an altogether more ethereal and quirky demonstration of Basque hospitality. Admired by professional chefs the world over, Pedro Subijana of the three-Michelin-starred Akelarre is one of the founding fathers of New Basque cuisine. Injecting much-needed humour into high-concept cooking, his restaurant – perched above the Bay of Biscay – has pursued culinary innovation and technical perfection with tongue firmly in cheek for over thirty years. Two tasting menus, one based on *Aranori* (fish) and one on *Bekarki* (meat), are beautifully conceived and pleasingly playful.

ARZAK

Recommended by
Andoni Luis Aduriz, Bruno
Oteiza & Mikel Alonso,
Víctor Arguinzóniz, Martín
Berasategui, José Cordeiro,
Ollie Couillaud, Quique
Dacosta, Xabier Diez
Esteibar, Dylan Jones & Bo
(Duangporn) Songvisava,
José Pizarro, Glynn Purnell,
Pedro Subijana

Avenida Alcalde José Elósegui 273
San Sebastián
Basque Country 20015
+34 943278465
www.arzak.es

Opening hours	Closed Monday and Sunday
Credit cards	Accepted
Price range	Expensive
Style	Smart casual
Cuisine	Modern Basque
Recommended for	Worth the travel

'When I first ate there it was so cutting edge it blew my mind. It's the first time I have seen a chef using burnt vegetables: burnt leek vinaigrette, wow!'
—Glynn Purnell

Despite its three Michelin stars, there are no Arzak franchises – Juan Mari and his daughter Elena stay behind the stove, where the Arzak family has been for over 100 years. The cooking has come some distance since the building's former incarnation as a wine tavern, built by Juan Mari's grandparents. The monochrome dining room provides an urbane backdrop for the 'New Basque' cuisine, which works classic local ingredients into avant-garde compilations: sardines and strawberries; peach curd with seaweed; 'chorizo and tonic' on an upside-down Schweppes can. Fish – particularly hake – is exquisite. Book the chef's table to observe the father-daughter team at work.

ASADOR EKAITZ
Recommended by
Daniel López
Paseo Padre Orkolaga 131
San Sebastián
Basque Country 20008
+34 943212024
www.asadorekaitz.com

Opening hours	Closed Monday and Tuesday
Credit cards	Accepted
Price range	Affordable
Style	Casual
Cuisine	Spanish Grill
Recommended for	Regular neighbourhood

'It's a grill-house that serves simple, traditional food prepared with great care and very few rules. I like to order the Spanish tomato salad, the steak, and the cheese tart.'—Daniel López

ASADOR PORTUETXE
Recommended by
Wylie Dufresne
Portuetxe Kalea 43
San Sebastián
Basque Country 20018
+34 943215018
www.asadorportuetxe.com

Opening hours	Open 7 days
Credit cards	Accepted
Price range	Affordable
Style	Casual
Cuisine	Basque
Recommended for	Worth the travel

'They serve simple Spanish fare. I wouldn't miss the cuttlefish and caramelized onions.'—Wylie Dufresne

In the heart of the spirited Basque region of northern Spain, this traditional restaurant, replete with huge decorative wine barrels and ancient wooden beams, specializes in fresh fish and large hunks of meat cooked over charcoal grills. Portuetxe is in the style of a Basque farmhouse (the building is four hundred years old) and is diligent in the preparation of seasonal vegetables and offers an impressive wine list with over 350 bins. This is classic but casual – resistant to the modernism that has characterized some of San Sebastián's more famed restaurants. To accompany the meat and fish try the artichokes for which it is well known.

BAR NESTOR
Recommended by
Aizpea Oihaneder Perez
Pescaderia Kalea 11
San Sebastián
Basque Country 20003
+34 943424873
www.barnestor.com

Opening hours	Closed Monday
Credit cards	Accepted but not AMEX
Price range	Affordable
Style	Casual
Cuisine	Basque
Recommended for	Late night

'The speciality is an amazing potato tortilla and tomato salad (when in season). They serve excellent steak too.'
—Aizpea Oihaneder Perez

BAR TXEPETXA
Recommended by
Andoni Luis Aduriz
Calle Pescadería 5
San Sebastián
Basque Country 20003
+34 943422227
www.bartxepetxa.com

Opening hours	Closed Monday
Reservation policy	No
Credit cards	Accepted but not AMEX
Price range	Budget
Style	Casual
Cuisine	Pintxos
Recommended for	Bargain

'Good for having an informal meal without breaking the bank.'—Andoni Luis Aduriz

BARKAIZTEGI
Recommended by
Pedro Subijana
Paseo de Barkaiztegi 42
San Sebastián
Basque Country 20014
+34 943451304
www.barkaiztegi.com

Opening hours	Closed Sunday
Credit cards	Accepted
Price range	Affordable
Style	Casual
Cuisine	Basque
Recommended for	Local favourite

BERNARDINA VINOTECA

Recommended by
Juan Mari & Elena Arzak

Calle de Vitoria-Gasteiz 6
San Sebastián
Basque Country 20018
+34 943314899
www.vinotecabernardina.com

Opening hours	Closed Wednesday
Credit cards	Accepted
Price range	Budget
Style	Casual
Cuisine	Pintxos
Recommended for	Regular neighbourhood

In the labyrinthine streets of the Parte Vieja, this stylish wine and *pintxo* bar, with its bare brick walls and plate-glass windows, attracts a convivial local crowd. The main attraction, hanging above the bar, is the *jamón* (from Joselito, one of Spain's top producers), which is served in a panoply of ways, from bite-sized dishes of bacon and roasted peppers to ham tortillas and croquettes. The short, sweet and wallet-friendly *pintxo* list also takes in tuna tacos and mini-hamburgers. Plenty of superior national and international wines by the glass offer an added reason to linger long after brunch.

BERNARDO ETXEA

Recommended by
Pedro Subijana

Calle del Puerto 7
San Sebastián
Basque Country 20003
+34 943422055
www.bernardoetxea.com

Opening hours	Closed Thursday
Credit cards	Accepted
Price range	Affordable
Style	Smart casual
Cuisine	Basque
Recommended for	High end

'There aren't many expensive places in the area, you only pay a lot if you eat seafood and drink expensive wines, which you can do at Bernardo Etxea.'
—Pedro Subijana

LA BODEGA DONOSTIARRA

Recommended by
Andoni Luis Aduriz

Calle Peña y Goñi 13
San Sebastián
Basque Country 20002
+34 943011380
www.bodegadonostiarra.com

Opening hours	Closed Sunday
Credit cards	Accepted
Price range	Budget
Style	Casual
Cuisine	Pintxos
Recommended for	Local favourite

'You can eat *pintxos* here for a reasonable price.'
—Andoni Luis Aduriz

Enjoy a traditional San Sebastián bar experience, while avoiding the heaving streets of the old town, at old-timer Bodega Donostiarra, established in 1928 in the district of Gros. Behind the undistinguished blue frontage and frosted glass windows is a real locals' local, though it receives a huge influx of non-Donostiarras during the International Film Festival at the nearby Kursaal. A mouth-watering menu of *pintxos* (Basque tapas) and meaty grills, including the 800 g (28 oz) chuleta steak, goes down well with a *txikito* of wine or two. Don't miss the tuna, anchovy and *guindilla* (pepper) *pintxo*, a celebration of the region's traditional canned seafood.

BODEGÓN ALEJANDRO

Recommended by
Andoni Luis Aduriz,
Ettore Botrini

Fermín Calbetón 4
San Sebastián
Basque Country 20003
+34 943427158
www.bodegonalejandro.com

Opening hours	Closed Monday
Credit cards	Accepted
Price range	Affordable
Style	Casual
Cuisine	Basque
Recommended for	Regular neighbourhood

'Bodegón Alejandro serves food from the local market. You can go with the family and order according to how much time you have at your disposal and your mood.'
—Andoni Luis Aduriz

BORDA BERRI

Fermín Calbetón 12
San Sebastián
Basque Country 20003
+34 943430342

Opening hours	Closed Monday
Reservation policy	No
Credit cards	Accepted
Price range	Budget
Style	Casual
Cuisine	Pintxos
Recommended for	Bargain

In a city overwhelmed with good *pintxo* bars, Iñaki Gulín and Marc Clua's follow-up to *nueva cocina* hotspot La Cuchara, located just a few streets away, manages to stand out from the competition thanks to its earthy Basque flavours and spirited vibe. Opened six years ago, the homely spot features yellow walls, vintage photographs and black-and-white chequered floors, attracting a youthful, rock 'n' roll crowd. *Pintxos* are made to order, and many come hot, with mushroom risotto and braised veal cheeks in wine particularly oversubscribed. A blackboard (chalkboard) behind the bar also advertises *bocatas* (sandwiches) for lunch on the cheap.

CALONGE SAGARDOTEGIA

Paseo Orkolaga 8
San Sebastián
Basque Country 20008
+34 943213251
www.calongesagardotegia.es

Opening hours	Closed Monday
Credit cards	Accepted
Price range	Affordable
Style	Casual
Cuisine	Basque
Recommended for	Local favourite

'This *sidrería* (cider bar) is very typical when the season starts, after Christmas.'—Pedro Subijana

CASA UROLA

Fermín Calbetón 20
San Sebastián
Basque Country 20003
+34 943441371
www.casaurolajatetxea.es

Opening hours	Open 7 days
Credit cards	Accepted
Price range	Affordable
Style	Casual
Cuisine	Modern Basque
Recommended for	Local favourite

'A traditional restaurant in San Sebastián's old town, where fresh ingredients play the leading role.' —Daniel López

ELOSTA

Paseo Colón 41
San Sebastián
Basque Country 20002
+34 843630325
www.elostarestaurante.com

Opening hours	Closed Monday
Credit cards	Accepted
Price range	Affordable
Style	Casual
Cuisine	Spanish-Asian
Recommended for	Late night

'It's a casual place that blends Basque and Japanese cuisine. They serve a variety of high-quality sushi rolls and *tiraditos* (Peruvian raw fish dishes). You can also enjoy meat and fish dishes that showcase the chef's Basque roots.'—Daniel López

A FUEGO NEGRO

Calle 31 de Agosto 31
San Sebastián
Basque Country 20003
+34 650135373
www.afuegonegro.com

Opening hours	Closed Monday
Credit cards	Accepted
Price range	Budget
Style	Casual
Cuisine	Pintxos
Recommended for	Worth the travel

'It has a contemporary style and they serve the most modern, fun and unexpected *pintxos* in San Sebastián's old town. The music is also amazing.'
—Xabier Diez Esteibar

GANBARA JATETXEA

Calle de San Jeronimo 21
San Sebastián
Basque Country 20003
+34 943422575
www.ganbarajatetxea.com

Opening hours	Closed Monday
Credit cards	Accepted
Price range	Budget
Style	Casual
Cuisine	Pintxos
Recommended for	Regular neighbourhood

GANDARIAS

Calle 31 de Agosto 23
San Sebastián
Basque Country 20003
+34 943426362
www.restaurantegandarias.com

Opening hours	Open 7 days
Credit cards	Accepted but not AMEX
Price range	Affordable
Style	Casual
Cuisine	Pintxos
Recommended for	Late night

'I don't usually do late night, but Gandarias in Donosti is a good place to do so.'—Pedro Subijana

San Sebastián's old town is awash with atmospheric bars, their counters loaded with *pintxos* (Basque tapas) and hams hanging from their ceilings. Gandarias is one such establishment and is as essential a stop on a serious gourmet tour of the city as it is on a late-night bar crawl. Its restaurant is known for its bloody, marbled steaks and excellent wine cellar (strong on Riojas), while the always lively bar is recommended for its classic *pintxos* and blackboard specials. Specialities include the *brocheta di chipirón* (squid), *ensaladilla rusa* (Russian salad) and, of course, the celebrated acorn-fed Joselito ham.

GELTOKI

Calle Easo 61
San Sebastián
Basque Country 20006
+34 943450902

Opening hours	Open 7 days
Reservation policy	No
Credit cards	Accepted
Price range	Budget
Style	Casual
Cuisine	Bakery
Recommended for	Breakfast

LA GUINDA

Zabaleta 55
San Sebastián
Basque Country 20002
+34 843981715

Opening hours	Open 7 days
Credit cards	Accepted but not AMEX
Price range	Budget
Style	Casual
Cuisine	Bakery-Café-Deli
Recommended for	Breakfast

'It's the perfect place to start the day as it's very cosy and the people are as delightful as everything they cook. They serve great coffee, freshly squeezed juices, a wide variety of breads and pastries and, my favourite, whole-meal (whole wheat) bread with grated tomato and olive oil. It's also a favourite when I fancy eating something different: I love their salads, toasted sandwiches and original dishes.'—Daniel López

HAIZEA BAR

Calle de Aldamar 8
San Sebastián
Basque Country 20003
+34 943425710

Opening hours	Open 7 days
Reservation policy	No
Credit cards	Not accepted
Price range	Budget
Style	Casual
Cuisine	Pintxos
Recommended for	Worth the travel

IBAI

Calle de Getaria 15
San Sebastián
Basque Country 20005
+34 943428764

Opening hours	Closed Saturday and Sunday
Credit cards	Not accepted
Price range	Expensive
Style	Casual
Cuisine	Basque
Recommended for	Local favourite

'The menu is very limited because they only work with seasonal ingredients. You enjoy what nature has to offer, depending on the season.'—Íñigo Peña

If Ibai had silver service, it would be regarded as one of the finest restaurants in the world. Instead, tucked away beneath a Donostia tapas bar, it's a secret, unpretentious gem, a rustic dining room with five cloth-clad and heavily subscribed tables. In fact, you need to persevere if you want to get a table because the locals snap them up fast. This is down to the food and the high quality of the ingredients. Ibai serves the freshest of fresh fish (either fried or slow-cooked in the oven), shellfish and vegetables, embellished with local truffles, local wine and good old local hospitality.

KOKOTXA

Campanario 11
San Sebastián
Basque Country 20003
+34 943421904
www.restaurantekokotxa.com

Opening hours	Variable
Credit cards	Accepted but not AMEX
Price range	Affordable
Style	Casual
Cuisine	Modern Basque
Recommended for	Regular neighbourhood

'I like their creativity, the ingredients they use and the location.'—Aizpea Oihaneder Perez

MIRADOR DE ULÍA

Paseo de Ulía 193
San Sebastián
Basque Country 20013
+34 943272707
www.miradordeulia.es

Opening hours	Closed Monday and Tuesday
Credit cards	Accepted
Price range	Expensive
Style	Smart casual
Cuisine	Modern Basque
Recommended for	Regular neighbourhood

'I go here because of their enthusiasm for innovation and the spectacular views of the bay of San Sebastián.'—Xabier Diez Esteibar

PASTELERIA GAZTELO

Zarautz Kalea 76
San Sebastián
Basque Country 20018
+34 943226584

Opening hours	Open 7 days
Reservation policy	No
Credit cards	Not accepted
Price range	Budget
Style	Casual
Cuisine	Bakery
Recommended for	Breakfast

'Traditional artisan bakery with great pastries.'—Xabier Diez Esteibar

LA RAMPA

Del Muelle Ibilbidea 26–27
San Sebastián
Basque Country 20003
+34 943421652
www.restaurantelarampa.com

Opening hours	Closed Wednesday
Credit cards	Accepted
Price range	Affordable
Style	Casual
Cuisine	Spanish-Basque
Recommended for	Wish I'd opened

'I like its location in the port of San Sebastián and their amazing ingredients: from the sea straight to your plate.'—Xabier Diez Esteibar

RESTAURANTE NI NEU

Recommended by
Andoni Luis Aduriz

Avenida de la Zurriola 1
San Sebastián
Basque Country 20002
+34 943003162
www.restaurantenineu.com

Opening hours	Closed Monday
Credit cards	Accepted
Price range	Budget
Style	Casual
Cuisine	Modern Spanish
Recommended for	Bargain

TAMBORIL

Recommended by
Juan Mari & Elena Arzak

Calle Pescaderia 2
San Sebastián
Basque Country 20003
www.bartamboril.com

Opening hours	Open 7 days
Reservation policy	No
Credit cards	Accepted
Price range	Budget
Style	Casual
Cuisine	Pintxos
Recommended for	Bargain

VA BENE DISCO BURGER

Recommended by
Martín Berasategui,
Iñigo Peña

Calle de Blas de Lezo 4
San Sebastián
Basque Country 20007

Opening hours	Open 7 days
Reservation policy	No
Credit cards	Accepted
Price range	Budget
Style	Casual
Cuisine	Burgers
Recommended for	Late night

'In San Sebastián restaurants close early so if you ever get really hungry at midnight, for example, there is nothing better than going to the Va Bene hamburger joint. They serve first-rate sandwiches and hamburgers, made from good products and with a lot of care. They enjoy widespread success.'—Martín Berasategui

XARMA JATETXEA

Recommended by
Martín Berasategui

Avenida de Tolosa 123
San Sebastián
Basque Country 20018
+34 943317162
www.xarmajatetxea.com

Opening hours	Closed Monday
Credit cards	Accepted
Price range	Affordable
Style	Casual
Cuisine	Modern Basque
Recommended for	Bargain

'They serve cutting-edge cuisine at reasonable prices. It is always an appetising and stimulating place to go.' —Martín Berasategui

IRIARTE JATETXEA

Recommended by
Aizpea Oihaneder Perez

Plaza Pedro María Otaño 1
Zizurkil
Basque Country 20150
+34 943692537
www.iriartejatetxea.net

Opening hours	Open 7 days
Credit cards	Accepted
Price range	Budget
Style	Casual
Cuisine	Pintxos
Recommended for	Bargain

'I go here for their home-made dishes, prepared with love and joy.'—Aizpea Oihaneder Perez

CASA FITO

Recommended by
Filip Claeys

Carretera General del Sur 4
Granadilla
Tenerife
Canary Islands 38594
+34 922777179
www.casafitochimiche.com

Opening hours	Open 7 days
Credit cards	Accepted but not AMEX
Price range	Budget
Style	Casual
Cuisine	Tenerife-Spanish
Recommended for	Bargain

'Top food and a six-course menu for €20 (£17; $28).' —Filip Claeys

KABUKI

Abama Golf & Spa Resort
Carretera General TF-47
Guia de Isora
Tenerife
Canary Islands 38687
+34 902105600
www.abamahotelresort.com

Opening hours	Closed Tuesday
Credit cards	Accepted
Price range	Expensive
Style	Formal
Cuisine	Modern Japanese
Recommended for	Worth the travel

EL CAPRICHO

Paraje de la Vega
León
Castile and León 24767
+34 987664224
www.bodega-capricho.com

Opening hours	Closed Monday
Credit cards	Accepted
Price range	Affordable
Style	Casual
Cuisine	Steakhouse
Recommended for	Worth the travel

'Truly, this is one of the most unique restaurants in the world. The owner, José Gordon, is a 'beef whisperer', because he understands beef like no one else. In the United States, the animal is usually slaughtered at about three years old, but José allows his animals to grow up to fifteen years, and the result is a meat that has an astonishingly bold and silky texture. No other beef comes close to it!'—José Andrés

COCINANDOS

Calle las Campanillas 1
León
Castile and León 24008
+34 987071378
www.cocinandos.com

Opening hours	Closed Monday and Sunday
Credit cards	Accepted but not AMEX
Price range	Affordable
Style	Smart casual
Cuisine	Modern Spanish
Recommended for	Worth the travel

'I admire their tasting menu, which changes weekly, their open kitchen and their innovative dishes.'
—Aizpea Oihaneder Perez

RESTAURANTE LAS REJAS

Calle del General Borrero 49
Las Pedroñeras
Castile-La Mancha 16660
+34 967161089
www.manueldelaosa.com

Opening hours	Closed Monday and Sunday
Credit cards	Accepted
Price range	Expensive
Style	Smart casual
Cuisine	Modern Spanish
Recommended for	Worth the travel

RESTAURANTE TIERRA

Hotel Valdepalacios
Carretera de Oropesa a Puente del Arzobispo Km. 9
Oropesa
Castile-La Mancha 45572
+34 925457534
www.valdepalacios.es

Opening hours	Open 7 days
Credit cards	Accepted
Price range	Expensive
Style	Smart casual
Cuisine	Modern Spanish
Recommended for	Worth the travel

'I was blown away by the cuisine there.'—José Mendin

HISPANIA

Recommended by
Jordi Vilà

Carretera Real 54
Arenys de Mar
Catalonia 08350
+34 937910457
www.restauranthispania.com

Opening hours	Closed Monday
Credit cards	Accepted but not AMEX
Price range	Affordable
Style	Smart casual
Cuisine	Catalan
Recommended for	Local favourite

'Situated on the outskirts of Barcelona, this restaurant serves well-prepared, typical Catalan cuisine. You can enjoy dishes such as the *sang i fetge* (a Catalan liver dish), *mongetes del ganxet* (a Catalan bean dish) or *pelota con garbanzos* (chickpeas with dough balls), prepared on request.'—Jordi Vilà

HOTEL VAL DE RUDA

Recommended by
Iñigo Peña

Hotel Val de Ruda
Baqueira Beret 1500
Baqueira
Catalonia 25598
+34 973645258
www.hotelvalderudabaqueira.com

Opening hours	Open 7 days
Credit cards	Accepted but not AMEX
Price range	Affordable
Style	Casual
Cuisine	Mediterranean
Recommended for	Breakfast

'Having breakfast here means that I'll have a good day of snow ahead.'—Iñigo Peña

TOC AL MAR

Recommended by
Joan Roca

Carrer de Platja d'Aiguablava 6
Begur
Catalonia 17255
+34 972113232
www.tocalmar.cat

Opening hours	Variable
Credit cards	Accepted but not AMEX
Price range	Affordable
Style	Casual
Cuisine	Seafood
Recommended for	Late night

COMPARTIR

Recommended by
Julius Jaspers, Albert
Raurich, Jordi Roca,
Marcus Wareing

Riera Sant Vicenç
Cadaqués
Catalonia 17488
+34 972258482
www.compartircadaques.com

Opening hours	Variable
Credit cards	Accepted
Price range	Affordable
Style	Casual
Cuisine	Modern Spanish
Recommended for	Worth the travel

'In a beautiful part of Spain, this restaurant is owned by three chefs, who all previously worked with Ferran Adrià. The theme of the restaurant is sharing dishes, the food is fabulous with local influences, but of course, there are touches of genius. I visited twice in a week and loved the outside tables, the service and the feel of the place. Worth a visit.'—Marcus Wareing

The picture-book whitewashed fishing village of Cadaqués is a dream location, and Compartir (Catalan for 'share') could be many people's idea of a dream restaurant. Hidden in a beautifully restored 300-year-old house, complete with terrace walled with local slate for when the weather is good (unusually for Costa Brava restaurants, Compartir is open year-round), guests enjoy innovative sharing plates such as water-melon and tomatoes with blood orange foam, bacallà with 'honey air' or mussels with Béarnaise sauce — combinations worthy of the three founding chefs' pedigree (they previously worked with Ferran Adrià at elBulli).

CAN JUBANY

Recommended by
Carles Abellan

Carreterra de Sant Hilari
Calldetenes
Catalonia 08506
+34 938891023
www.canjubany.com

Opening hours	Closed Monday and Tuesday
Credit cards	Accepted
Price range	Expensive
Style	Smart casual
Cuisine	Modern Catalan
Recommended for	Worth the travel

'This is a high-end restaurant that has been very tastefully redecorated. You feel at ease here and the service is very attentive. A cuisine with both a creative and traditional feel to it, which is very well prepared. It is a great restaurant that deserves its three Michelin stars.'—Carles Abellan

A disciple of the modernist Catalonian school of gastronomy, Nandu Jubany has created a picturesque retreat that masterfully showcases the produce of his own farm and gardens. Like many of his contemporaries, his dishes often start at a traditional base before being reinterpreted by modern molecular innovations. This includes the likes of stewed peas with confit pork collar or lightly pickled oysters with seaweed and beetroot foam. Precise craft and immaculate service wow and please equally throughout. Outside is rural Catalonia; inside is serenity, with minimalist design resting tastefully within the building's historical character. Jubany has mastered the marriage of old and new in all aspects of his restaurant.

RESTAURANT CAN XIFRA

Recommended by
Jordi Roca

Mas Artigas
Cartellà
Catalonia 17199
+34 972428546
www.canxifra.com

Opening hours	Closed Wednesday
Credit cards	Accepted
Price range	Affordable
Style	Casual
Cuisine	Catalan
Recommended for	Regular neighbourhood

Styled in the inviting farmhouse aesthetic of rural Catalonia, Can Xifra has rustic terracotta-tiled flooring, open brick walls and wooden-beamed ceilings. It is a simple affair situated within view of the outstanding Rocacorba Mountain, about 7 km (4 miles) outside Girona. Bold food, such as roasted shoulder of lamb, braised wild boar and stewed rabbit, is served in positively unpretentious surroundings. An obvious aim to provide robust sustenance with unfussy house wines is a welcome reminder that, despite innovations from Ferran Adrià loyalists all over Spain, there remains a place for the hearty traditionalists.

EMPORIUM RESTAURANT

Recommended by
Mateu Casañas

Emporium Hotel
Calle Santa Clara 31
Castelló d'Empúries
Catalonia 17486
+34 972250593
www.emporiumhotel.com

Opening hours	Closed Monday
Credit cards	Accepted but not AMEX
Price range	Affordable
Style	Casual
Cuisine	Modern Spanish
Recommended for	High end

'Emporium is a place where two generations, one that knows how to adapt (the parents) and another that knows how to innovate (the children), do some amazing work.' —Mateu Casañas

EL MOTEL

Recommended by
Josep Roca

Hotel Empordà
Avenida Salvador Dalí i Domènech 170
Figueres
Catalonia 17600
+34 972500562
www.elmotel.cat

Opening hours	Open 7 days
Credit cards	Accepted
Price range	Affordable
Style	Smart casual
Cuisine	Modern Catalan
Recommended for	Local favourite

CAN MARQUÈS

Recommended by
Joan Roca,
Josep Roca

Plaça Calvet i Rubalcaba 3
Girona
Catalonia 17001
+34 972201001
www.canmarques.com

Opening hours	Closed Sunday
Credit cards	Accepted
Price range	Affordable
Style	Casual
Cuisine	Catalan
Recommended for	Breakfast

It describes itself as 'one of the most traditional restaurants in Girona'. Currently overseen by the fourth generation of the founding family, Can Marquès's interior subtly pays tribute to the innovations of restaurant design. It strikes a careful balance between old and new, modern furniture sitting comfortably among traditional wooden dressers and cabinets stacked with wine bottles and glassware. Exceptional value can be found in the *menú del día* – three courses with a drink for €14.50 (£12; $20). It is in part defined by its proximity to the city market, which lies opposite and which elicits a wealth of exciting produce. For breakfast try the scrambled eggs with prawns (shrimp) and garlic.

CAN ROCA

Recommended by
Joan Roca, Jordi Roca,
Josep Roca

Carretera de Taialà 42
Girona
Catalonia 17007

Opening hours	Closed Monday and Sunday
Credit cards	Accepted
Price range	Affordable
Style	Casual
Cuisine	Catalan
Recommended for	Regular neighbourhood

EL CELLER DE CAN ROCA

Recommended by
Gastón Acurio, Albert Adrià,
Andoni Luis Aduriz, Josean
Alija, Wojciech Modest Amaro,
Juan Mari & Elena Arzak, José
Avillez, Jordi Butrón Melero,
Mateu Casañas, Oriol Castro,
Alberto Chicote, Jordi Cruz,
Quique Dacosta, Ramón
Freixa, Brad Holmes, Thomas
McNaughton, Arabelle
Meirlaen, David Muñoz, Fabio
Rossi, Nikos Roussos, Shaun
Searley, Clare Smyth,
Adam Stokes

Can Sunyer 48
Girona
Catalonia 17007
+34 972222157
www.cellercanroca.com

Opening hours	Closed Monday and Sunday
Credit cards	Accepted
Price range	Expensive
Style	Smart casual
Cuisine	Modern Catalan
Recommended for	Worth the travel

'The best place to celebrate the unlimited horizons of pleasure.'—Gastón Acurio

While molecular gastronomy fans flocked to elBulli and The Fat Duck, the pioneering trio of brothers at El Celler de Can Roca in Girona remained Spain's little secret. Eating in the clean-cut Scandi-style dining room is an experience that plays with mood and memory. Traditional Catalonian ingredients are given innovative treatment to create playful dishes such as caramelized olives hanging from a bonsai tree or the famous Journey to Havana – a tobacco-flavoured 'cigar' sitting on an 'ashtray' – or desserts that replicate Calvin Klein or Lancôme scents. Having achieved a third star in 2009, the €130 (£109; $181) seven-course menu looks like very good value.

UMAI

Plaça Josep Pla 18
Girona
Catalonia 17001
+34 972417872
www.umaigirona.com

Opening hours	Closed Sunday
Credit cards	Accepted but not AMEX
Price range	Affordable
Style	Casual
Cuisine	Sushi
Recommended for	Late night

CAL TET

Cal Tet Hotel
Carrer Santa Anna 38
L'Estartit
Catalonia 17258
+34 972751179
www.caltet.com

Opening hours	Open 7 days
Credit cards	Accepted
Price range	Affordable
Style	Casual
Cuisine	Seafood
Recommended for	Regular neighbourhood

Eating out on Spain's Costa Brava is not a simple toss-up between eye-popping molecular gastronomy à la Ferran Adrià and greasy calamares in a beachfront bar. The *marisqueria* (seafood restaurant) Cal Tet, in the fishing village-turned-resort of L'Estartit, is where local families go to enjoy their region's traditional dishes. Since 1971 the Giménez family have staked their reputation on dazzling shellfish from local and Galician waters, serving Catalan classics such as *mariscada* (seafood stew of sea snails, winkles and mussels) and *fideuada* (pasta 'paella'), for parties of two or more, accompanied by the local Empordà wine.

MIRAMAR

Passeig Marítim 7
Llançà
Catalonia 17490
+34 972380132
www.restaurantmiramar.com

Opening hours	Closed Monday
Credit cards	Accepted
Price range	Expensive
Style	Smart casual
Cuisine	Modern Spanish
Recommended for	High end

'Located in Empordà, a beautiful place to spend the weekend, Miramar is currently one of the best restaurants around. Its tasting menu is nothing short of spectacular. The service, coordinated by chef Paco Peréz's wife, Montse, makes you feel as if you were in your own home. The combination of fine cuisine and a personal touch make this the place to enjoy a world-class dining experience.'—Eduard Xatruch

LES COLS

Mas les Cols
Carretera de la Canya
Olot
Catalonia 17800
+34 972269209
www.lescols.com

Opening hours	Closed Monday
Credit cards	Accepted
Price range	Expensive
Style	Smart casual
Cuisine	Modern Spanish
Recommended for	Worth the travel

'Perhaps less well-known internationally, this is one of a few restaurants in Spain that are benchmarks for innovation, creativity and cooking with local products.'
—Quique Dacosta

ALMADRABA RESTAURANT

Recommended by
Mateu Casañas

Almadraba Park Hotel
Avinguda Díaz Pacheco 70
Roses
Catalonia 17480
+34 972256550
www.almadrabapark.com

Opening hours	Open 7 days
Credit cards	Accepted but not AMEX
Price range	Affordable
Style	Smart casual
Cuisine	Seafood
Recommended for	Local favourite

'The place is run by Jaume Subirós and is a favourite when it comes to relaxation and enjoyment. You can try any of their perfectly cooked seafood specialties in a beautiful garden that is as close to the sea as it gets in this area.'—Mateu Casañas

CAL CAMPANER

Recommended by
Mateu Casañas

Carrer del Mossèn Carles Feliu 23
Roses
Catalonia 17480
+34 972256954

Opening hours	Closed Monday
Credit cards	Accepted but not AMEX
Price range	Affordable
Style	Casual
Cuisine	Seafood
Recommended for	Regular neighbourhood

'It's a family restaurant that only serves fresh fish from Roses. So much so that when the fish runs out they close for the day. They also have a long history of family members dedicated to running the place. Today, Joan Romero is in charge of the kitchen.'—Mateu Casañas

LA COSA NOSTRA

Recommended by
Mateu Casañas

23 Avinguda Jaume I
Roses
Catalonia 17480
+34 972256445

Opening hours	Closed Tuesday
Credit cards	Accepted but not AMEX
Price range	Budget
Style	Casual
Cuisine	Italian
Recommended for	Bargain

'My family and I regularly visit Fabri at La Cosa Nostra restaurant. He is from Sicily and his pasta dishes are spectacular. He runs the kitchen himself and serves the guests with only a couple of helpers to assist him.'
—Mateu Casañas

ELS BRANCS

Recommended by
Mateu Casañas

Hotel Vistabella
Avinguda de José Díaz Pacheco 26
Roses
Catalonia 17480
+34 972256008
www.elsbrancs.com

Opening hours	Closed Monday
Credit cards	Accepted
Price range	Expensive
Style	Smart casual
Cuisine	Modern Spanish
Recommended for	Late night

'An unbeatable location with some of the best views of the bay of Roses. Their constant hard work undoubtedly pays off.'—Mateu Casañas

RAFA'S

Recommended by
Albert Adrià

Calle Sant Sebastià 56
Roses
Catalonia 17480
+34 972254003

Opening hours	Variable
Credit cards	Accepted
Price range	Affordable
Style	Casual
Cuisine	Seafood
Recommended for	Wish I'd opened

'A tiny place in Roses that unfailingly serves only the best grilled fish.'—Albert Adrià

The second most-famous restaurant to open in the vicinity of Roses on the Costa Brava has long been celebrated as a favourite of the brothers Adrià of elBulli fame. When Ferran Adrià let slip that it was his favourite place to eat when he wasn't in his kitchen, a meal at Rafa's quickly became part of the pilgrimage for those en route to the erstwhile home of molecular gastronomy. There's no menu, the fantastically fresh plancha-kissed seafood on offer being whatever has come in that morning. Call ahead as it opens and closes according to the quality of the catch available each day.

RASPA & WINE

Recommended by
Mateu Casañas

Almadraba Park Hotel
Avinguda Diaz Pacheco 71
Roses
Catalonia 17480
+34 972256554
www.raspawine.com

Opening hours	Open 7 days
Credit cards	Accepted but not AMEX
Price range	Affordable
Style	Casual
Cuisine	Tapas
Recommended for	Local favourite

'Experience the casual vibe of the tapas bar.'
—Mateu Casañas

SI US PLAU

Recommended by
Mateu Casañas

Avinguda de Rhode 58
Roses
Catalonia 17480
+34 972254264

Opening hours	Closed Tuesday
Reservation policy	No
Credit cards	Not accepted
Price range	Budget
Style	Casual
Cuisine	Bar-Bistro
Recommended for	Breakfast

'This is a restaurant and bar located right on the seafront. Breakfast with the view of the bay of Roses and with people you care about... There's no competition!'—Mateu Casañas

ELS CASALS

Recommended by
Josep Roca, Jordi Vilà

Els Casals Hotel
Camí de la Guàrdia
Sagàs
Catalonia 08517
+34 938251200
www.elscasals.cat

Opening hours	Variable
Credit cards	Accepted
Price range	Expensive
Style	Smart casual
Cuisine	Modern Spanish
Recommended for	High end

'A mountain cooking project that uses large quantities of home-grown produce. Here, both the restaurant and the cuisine represent a very Catalan way of life.'
—Jordi Vilà

Head about 90 km (55 miles) north of Barcelona and you'll find the small town of Sagàs in the Pre-Pyrenees and this rural ten-bedroom hotel surrounded by its own farmland, which has its restaurant in a converted stable block. Dozens of varieties of vegetables and herbs, including Sant Pau beans, Blanca de Bufet potatoes and Montserrat tomatoes, grow in the garden, and the fields are home to free-range cattle and other livestock. All of which is used well – along with other local, seasonable produce – by chef Oriol Rovira, who serves dishes such as braised Galician oxtail with garlic and onions.

RESTAURANT VILLA MÁS

Recommended by
Josep Roca

Passeig San Pol 95
San Feliu de Guixols
Catalonia 17220
+34 972822526
www.restaurantvillamas.com

Opening hours	Variable
Credit cards	Accepted
Price range	Affordable
Style	Casual
Cuisine	Seafood
Recommended for	Worth the travel

In the summer, you dine in the courtyard of this early twentieth-century modernist villa set in the bay of Sant Feliu de Guíxols, an hour north of Barcelona. Former DJ and now chef Carlos Orta serves the freshest seafood, such as red prawns (shrimp) from Palamos, scorpion fish, grilled grouper and marinated sardines on potato confit. There are regional specialities, including *salmorejo* (a type of gazpacho), and inventive pairings such as pig's trotter with sea cucumber. For wine lovers there's an internationally noted selection of Burgundy vintages pegged at close-to-retail prices, although you'll still need deep pockets to enjoy them.

HOTEL TORRE MARTÍ

Carrer de Ramon Llull 11
Sant Julià de Vilatorta
Catalonia 08504
+34 938888372
www.hoteltorremarti.com

Recommended by
Jean-Marie Baudic

Opening hours	Open 7 days
Credit cards	Accepted but not AMEX
Price range	Affordable
Style	Smart casual
Cuisine	Modern Catalan
Recommended for	Worth the travel

'I like the simplicity and the warm welcome you get in this idyllic, quiet hotel. Such a calm and peaceful place. You can tell the Catalan food they serve is made with heart and the pleasure of sharing.'—Jean-Marie Baudic

SANT PAU

Carrer Nou 10
Sant Pol de Mar
Catalonia 08395
+34 937600662
www.ruscalleda.com

Recommended by
Quique Dacosta,
Riki Mizukami

Opening hours	Closed Monday and Sunday
Credit cards	Accepted
Price range	Expensive
Style	Smart casual
Cuisine	Modern Spanish
Recommended for	Worth the travel

'Among the best restaurants in Spain and one of the best showcases of my country to the world. Pure magic.' —Quique Dacosta

LA NANSA

Carrer de la Carreta 24
Sitges
Catalonia 08870
+34 938941927
www.restaurantlanansa.com

Recommended by
Oriol Castro

Opening hours	Closed Wednesday
Credit cards	Accepted but not AMEX
Price range	Affordable
Style	Casual
Cuisine	Catalan
Recommended for	Regular neighbourhood

'One of Sitges's most traditional restaurants, located in an old townhouse.'—Oriol Castro

PIC NIC

Passeig de la Ribera
Sitges
Catalonia 08870
+34 938110040
www.restaurantpicnic.com

Recommended by
Oriol Castro

Opening hours	Open 7 days
Credit cards	Accepted
Price range	Affordable
Style	Casual
Cuisine	Tapas
Recommended for	Regular neighbourhood

'They serve some really good rice dishes prepared with coastal ingredients.'—Oriol Castro

ESPORTELL DEL BOU

Carrer Diputat Orga 3–5
Tarragona
Catalonia 43491
+34 977604868
www.esportelldelbou.com

Recommended by
Eduard Xatruch

Opening hours	Closed Tuesday
Credit cards	Accepted
Price range	Affordable
Style	Casual
Cuisine	Catalan
Recommended for	Regular neighbourhood

'It has a welcoming atmosphere and the service is very friendly. There are several inner courtyards and my daughter has a lot of fun playing there. Their *calçotadas* – traditional gastronomic feasts that take place from December to April when the *calçots* (green onions) are in season – are amazing.'—Eduard Xatruch

BAR SPORT

Recommended by
Oriol Castro

Barri Marítim de la Indústria
Torredembarra
Catalonia 43830
+34 977645629

Opening hours	Open 7 days
Credit cards	Not accepted
Price range	Budget
Style	Casual
Cuisine	Spanish Tapas
Recommended for	Bargain

'A small, family-owned town bar that mainly serves tapas, but their octopus is heavenly. The father often cooks some really good seafood dishes.'—Oriol Castro

CA L'ENRIC

Recommended by
Jordi Roca

Carretera Camprodon s/n
La Vall De Bianya
Catalonia 17813
+34 972290015
www.calenric.net

Opening hours	Closed Monday
Credit cards	Accepted but not AMEX
Price range	Affordable
Style	Smart casual
Cuisine	Modern Spanish
Recommended for	Local favourite

ATRIO

Recommended by
Dario Barrio, Quique Dacosta

Atrio Hotel
Plaza de San Mateo 1
Cáceres
Extremadura 10003
+34 927242928

Opening hours	Open 7 days
Credit cards	Accepted
Price range	Expensive
Style	Smart casual
Cuisine	Modern Spanish
Recommended for	Worth the travel

'Cooking that is a sensory delight. Well worth the trip.'
—Dario Barrio

The new incarnation of chef Toño Pérez and José Polo's Atrio in Cáceres, Extremadura, designed by renowned architects Luis M. Mansilla and Emilio Tuñón Alvarez, opened in 2011. Situated on a small square beside the convent of San Pablo and the church of San Mateo in the beautiful, historic part of the city, black granite floors and white oak walls adorned with contemporary art are the setting for Pérez's famous creations – such as roast scallops with creamy boletus and truffle, and *jamón ibérico* with lobster, pimentón and garlic – and Polo's celebrated wine selection, kept in an incredible, purpose-built cellar.

CULLER DE PAU

Recommended by
Ricard Camarena

Reboredo 73
O Grove
Galicia 36980
+34 986732275
www.cullerdepau.com

Opening hours	Closed Tuesday
Credit cards	Accepted
Price range	Affordable
Style	Smart casual
Cuisine	Modern Spanish
Recommended for	Worth the travel

'I like Javier Olleros's cooking style. The way he handles local ingredients is inspiring.'—Ricard Camarena

CASA LUCIO

Recommended by
María Marte

Calle Cava Baja 35
Madrid
Madrid 28005
+34 913658217
www.casalucio.es

Opening hours	Closed Monday
Credit cards	Accepted
Price range	Affordable
Style	Smart casual
Cuisine	Spanish
Recommended for	Local favourite

'Casa Lucio is one of Madrid's most iconic restaurants. I like that its signature dish, the scrambled eggs, has crossed borders. I especially recommend the onion soup and any of their meats, which are exquisite. The service is excellent and you really feel the weight of history when you enter. Many historical figures have been there before you and their names are engraved on some of the chairs.'—María Marte

EL CHAFLÁN

Recommended by
Dario Barrio

Avenida de Pio XII 34
Madrid
Madrid 28016
+34 913506193
www.elchaflan.com

Opening hours	Closed Sunday
Credit cards	Accepted
Price range	Affordable
Style	Smart casual
Cuisine	Modern Spanish
Recommended for	Regular neighbourhood

'It's my favourite restaurant. Juan Pablo Felipe, at the heart of the business, is one of the best cooks I know.'
—Dario Barrio

CISNE AZUL

Recommended by
Michael Caballo

Calle de Gravina 19
Madrid
Madrid 28004
+34 915213799

Opening hours	Closed Sunday
Credit cards	Not accepted
Price range	Affordable
Style	Casual
Cuisine	Spanish
Recommended for	Wish I'd opened

'The best and maybe the only completely wild-mushroom-driven restaurant. One person cooking, crazy busy insane place, I just love what they do.'
—Michael Caballo

In Chueca, an area that's bursting with inviting restaurants, you could be forgiven for passing Cisne Azul by. Don't. Especially if you're a fungophile. The aggressively lit dining room may be well past its best, but the crowd of well-heeled Madrileños don't care – they just want to get stuck into the mushrooms. Porcini, morels, chanterelles, whatever's in season, you'll find it here, grilled, fried, paired with foie gras, lobster tail, goat's cheese or topped with an egg. You'll be shoulder to shoulder with your fellow diners throughout the week, especially on Friday and Saturday, though gracious waiting staff won't rush you along. It's a local place, so take your phrase book or, better still, a local.

CORRAL DE LA MORERIA

Recommended by
Dario Barrio

Calle de la Morería 17
Madrid
Madrid 28005
+34 913658446
www.corraldelamoreria.com

Opening hours	Open 7 days
Credit cards	Accepted
Price range	Affordable
Style	Casual
Cuisine	Spanish
Recommended for	Wish I'd opened

'Considered the best flamenco venue in the world, its gastronomic offering has been reinvigorated under José Luis Estevan, who has converted it into a gastronomic temple.'—Dario Barrio

DIVERXO

Recommended by
Quique Dacosta, Michael
Ferraro, Jorge Rausch

NH Eurobuilding
Calle Padre Damián 23
Madrid
Madrid 28036
www.diverxo.com

Opening hours	Closed Monday and Sunday
Credit cards	Accepted
Price range	Expensive
Style	Smart casual
Cuisine	Spanish-Asian
Recommended for	Worth the travel

'Simply the most impressive gastronomic experience I have ever had. It can't be explained, it can only be wondered at!'—Jorge Rausch

DON LAY

Recommended by
David Muñoz

Paseo de Extremadura 30
Madrid
Madrid 28011
+34 914634546

Opening hours	Closed Tuesday
Credit cards	Accepted
Price range	Affordable
Style	Casual
Cuisine	Cantonese
Recommended for	Late night

'Best Chinese in town. Perhaps the best in Spain.'
—David Muñoz

ESTADO PURO

Recommended by
Dario Barrio

Hotel NH Paseo del Prado
Plaza Cánovas del Castillo 4
Madrid
Madrid 28014
+34 913302400
www.tapasenestadopuro.com

Opening hours	Open 7 days
Credit cards	Accepted
Price range	Affordable
Style	Casual
Cuisine	Tapas
Recommended for	Local favourite

'A tapas restaurant headed up by the famous chef Paco Roncero.'—Dario Barrio

LA GABINOTECA

Recommended by
Ramón Freixa,
María Marte

Calle Fernández de la Hoz 53
Madrid
Madrid 28003
+34 913991500
www.lagabinoteca.com

Opening hours	Closed Sunday
Credit cards	Accepted
Price range	Affordable
Style	Casual
Cuisine	Spanish
Recommended for	Late night

'It's a place with a cool vibe and good-looking people, where you can enjoy traditional cooking with a few fun twists. The decor is modern, the wine list is fun, the croquettes are to die for and their veal escalopes come extra large. If you're going there for the first time with a food-loving friend, make sure you order the "Juan Palomo" dessert.'—Ramón Freixa

ISAAC SALIDO

Recommended by
Dario Barrio

Calle Villalar 11
Madrid
Madrid 28001
+34 915762175
www.isaacsalido.es

Opening hours	Closed Sunday
Reservation policy	No
Credit cards	Accepted
Price range	Budget
Style	Casual
Cuisine	Café
Recommended for	Breakfast

'They serve really delicious home-made cakes for breakfast and I like their chocolate brownies. It's a multi-purpose space and turns into a hair salon at 11.00 a.m.'—Dario Barrio

KABUKI WELLINGTON

Recommended by
Andoni Luis Aduriz,
María Marte

Hotel Wellington
Calle de Velázquez 6
Madrid
Madrid 28001
+34 915777877
www.restaurantekabuki.com

Opening hours	Closed Sunday
Credit cards	Accepted
Price range	Expensive
Style	Smart casual
Cuisine	Japanese Fusion
Recommended for	High end

'Ricardo Sanz is in charge of the food in this restaurant which combines traditional Japanese recipes and local products, producing dishes like the quail egg sushi with white truffle. And on top of that, Kabuki offers desserts by Oriol Balaguer, one of the best pastry chefs in the world.'—María Marte

MAMÁ FRAMBOISE

Calle de Fernando VI 23
Madrid
Madrid 28004
+34 913914364
www.mamaframboise.com

Opening hours	Open 7 days
Reservation policy	No
Credit cards	Accepted
Price range	Budget
Style	Casual
Cuisine	Café-Patisserie
Recommended for	Breakfast

'They have the best pastries and I like to have a pain au chocolat, a freshly squeezed carrot and apple juice and, of course, a cappuccino.'—Ramón Freixa

MATILDA CAFÉ CANTINA

Calle de Almadén 15
Madrid
Madrid 28014
+34 914298029

Opening hours	Closed Sunday
Credit cards	Accepted
Price range	Budget
Style	Casual
Cuisine	Spanish
Recommended for	Breakfast

'It is a small place with personality; the owners always serve you with a smile. They have home-made menus for breakfast, exquisite coffee and serve tasty tomato on toast with olive oil. You go there for the decor, the messages on the walls and the family atmosphere.'
—María Marte

MERCADO DE SAN MIGUEL

Plaza de San Miguel
Madrid
Madrid 28005
+34 915424936
www.mercadodesanmiguel.es

Opening hours	Open 7 days
Reservation policy	No
Credit cards	Not accepted
Price range	Budget
Style	Casual
Cuisine	Street Food
Recommended for	Wish I'd opened

'The market's essence and the tapas blend perfectly to create a concept that I would like to have been part of myself.'—Mateu Casañas

MERCADO SAN ANTÓN

Calle Augusto Figueroa 24
Madrid
Madrid 28004
+34 913300730
www.mercadosananton.com

Opening hours	Open 7 days
Reservation policy	No
Credit cards	Not accepted
Price range	Budget
Style	Casual
Cuisine	Spanish
Recommended for	Regular neighbourhood

'Not only is it a trendy wholesale food market in the Chueca district, it is also a place where you can get tapas and snacks. I enjoy looking at the merchandise, the cheeses, the seafood, talking to the staff and taking the time to enjoy a variety of high-quality products – in short, learning the fun way!'—María Marte

LA PANAMERICANA

Calle de Hortaleza 72
Madrid
Madrid 28004
+34 915241397
www.lapanamericana.es

Opening hours	Open 7 days
Credit cards	Accepted
Price range	Affordable
Style	Casual
Cuisine	Latin American
Recommended for	Late night

'The dishes are all about the fusion cuisine of South America. The ceviche, the seafood *sopa de mariscos en cafetera* (seafood soup in a coffee machine) and the *parrilla criolla* (Creole grill), cooked by Emiliano Reyes, a connoisseur of fusion cuisine, make me feel close to the land where I was born.'—María Marte

RAMÓN FREIXA MADRID

Calle Claudio Coello 67
Madrid
Madrid 28001
+34 917818262
www.ramonfreixamadrid.com

Recommended by
Dario Barrio,
Quique Dacosta

Opening hours	Closed Monday and Sunday
Credit cards	Accepted
Price range	Expensive
Style	Smart casual
Cuisine	Modern Spanish
Recommended for	High end

'A really sophisticated restaurant where no detail is overlooked.'—Dario Barrio

Nothing says 'special occasion' quite like dinner at Ramon Freixa's ravishing Madrid restaurant. Jaws hit the floor at the first sight of the chandeliers, mosaic floor and magnificent mirrored ceiling. Classically trained Catalan chef Freixa backs up style with substance: his highly evolved cuisine was awarded two Michelin stars within two years of the restaurant opening in 2009. Both 'traditional' and 'modern' dishes are served – it's not often one finds a stew of salt cod tripe and broad beans with prawns (shrimp) and 'exploding' tangerine segments on the same menu. Cooking is in Freixa's blood – his father was a top chef and it's his excellent bread that's served here.

RESTAURANTE COMBARRO

Calle Reina Mercedes 12
Madrid
Madrid 28020
+34 915547784
www.combarro.com

Recommended by
Pedro Subijana

Opening hours	Open 7 days
Credit cards	Accepted
Price range	Affordable
Style	Smart casual
Cuisine	Galician-Seafood
Recommended for	High end

This elegant and refined dining room close to Madrid's city centre specializes in the cuisine of Galicia and especially its seafood. If you've never tried the scary looking but oh-so-delicious *percebes* (gooseneck barnacles) that are death-defyingly harvested by hand from Galician cliff sides, this is the place to eat them. There are other *outré* species such as the eel-like lamprey, but the more familiar dishes such as octopus and a range of grilled or baked fish are equally attractive propositions. You don't have to indulge in full-on fine-dining though – there's tapas in the handsome wood-panelled bar with its impressive display of hanging hams.

RESTAURANTE EL PESCADOR

Calle José Ortega y Gasset 75
Madrid
Madrid 28006
+34 914021290
www.marisqueriaelpescador.net

Recommended by
Ramón Freixa

Opening hours	Closed Sunday
Credit cards	Accepted but not AMEX
Price range	Affordable
Style	Casual
Cuisine	Seafood
Recommended for	Regular neighbourhood

'This is one of those restaurants that you never tire of. It's like having the sea at your table. I always order something to share: oysters, prawns (shrimp) and ham are all good choices, as is the Evaristo-style sole for two as a main course. If you have a sweet tooth, the *filloas* (crêpes) are a must for dessert.'—Ramón Freixa

RESTAURANTE MEATING

Calle de Valenzuela 7
Madrid
Madrid 28014
+34 914316997
www.restaurantemeating.com

Recommended by
Dario Barrio

Opening hours	Closed Sunday
Credit cards	Accepted
Price range	Affordable
Style	Casual
Cuisine	Spanish
Recommended for	Bargain

'They serve first-rate meat and vegetables. Honest cooking.'—Dario Barrio

SACHA

Calle Juan Hurtado de Mendoza 11
Madrid
Madrid 28036
+34 913455952

Recommended by
Alberto Chicote,
Bertrand Grébaut,
David Muñoz

Opening hours	Closed Sunday
Credit cards	Accepted
Price range	Affordable
Style	Casual
Cuisine	Spanish
Recommended for	Worth the travel

'A very typical bistro turning out powerful, classic dishes. This place reminds us that simplicity is always best.'—Bertrand Grébaut

SANTCELONI

Hotel Hesperia Madrid
Paseo de la Castellana 57
Madrid
Madrid 28010
+34 912108840
www.restaurantesantceloni.com

Recommended by
Quique Dacosta,
Ramón Freixa

Opening hours	Closed Sunday
Credit cards	Accepted
Price range	Expensive
Style	Smart casual
Cuisine	Madrileno
Recommended for	Local favourite

'It's both traditional and contemporary. The service is great, the food is delicate and subtle, the cheeseboard is heavenly and the winery is unique. Fresh ingredients cooked to perfection.'—Ramón Freixa

SERGI AROLA GASTRO

Calle de Zurbano 31
Madrid
Madrid 28010
+34 913102169
www.sergiarola.es

Recommended by
Quique Dacosta,
Vicky Ratnani

Opening hours	Closed Sunday
Credit cards	Accepted
Price range	Expensive
Style	Formal
Cuisine	Modern Spanish
Recommended for	Worth the travel

SUDESTADA

Calle Ponzano 85
Madrid
Madrid 28003
+34 915334154
www.sudestada.es

Recommended by
David Muñoz

Opening hours	Closed Monday and Sunday
Credit cards	Accepted
Price range	Affordable
Style	Smart casual
Cuisine	Modern Asian
Recommended for	High end

'One of the two best Thai restaurants in the world (the other being Nahm in Bangkok). For me, they are on the same level. A creative and personal understanding of Thai food and the experience in the restaurant is amazing.'—David Muñoz

TABERNA DE LA DANIELA

General Pardiñas 21
Madrid
Madrid 28001
+34 915752329
www.tabernaladaniela.com

Recommended by
Omar Allibhoy

Opening hours	Open 7 days
Credit cards	Accepted
Price range	Budget
Style	Casual
Cuisine	Madrileno
Recommended for	Local favourite

'This restaurant serves the best Cocido Madrileño – a rich soup with thin angel hair pasta, chickpeas and stewed beef in tomato sauce and seasonal greens. It's a must try if you're in Madrid.'—Omar Allibhoy

LA TERRAZA

Casino de Madrid
Calle de Alcalá 15
Madrid
Madrid 28014
+34 915321275
www.casinodemadrid.es

Recommended by
Alberto Chicote, Quique
Dacosta, Ramón Freixa

Opening hours	Closed Sunday
Credit cards	Accepted
Price range	Expensive
Style	Formal
Cuisine	Modern Spanish
Recommended for	High end

'The place is great, both in winter to enjoy the inside of the restaurant and in summer to gaze at the stars. The wonderful balcony boasts one of the best views of Madrid. The avant-garde style is well thought out and the cooking is sensible and creative. You are surprised again and again – Paco's workshop is a must-see.'
—Ramón Freixa

TRICICLO

Calle Santa María 28
Madrid
Madrid 28014
+34 910244798
www.eltriciclo.es

Recommended by
David Muñoz

Opening hours	Closed Sunday
Credit cards	Accepted
Price range	Affordable
Style	Smart casual
Cuisine	Tapas
Recommended for	Regular neighbourhood

VIRIDIANA

Calle de Juan de Mena 14
Madrid
Madrid 28014
+34 915311039
www.restauranteviridiana.com

Recommended by
María Marte, David Muñoz

Opening hours	Open 7 days
Credit cards	Accepted
Price range	Affordable
Style	Casual
Cuisine	Modern International
Recommended for	Wish I'd opened

'A gastronomic restaurant with over twenty years of experience using products of the highest quality in a

warm atmosphere and with excellent service. Abraham Garcia was the first to dare to create imaginative combinations and to play with various textures. The Iberian sirloin steak stuffed with Torta del Casar cheese with Grenache reduction and roasted figs is delightful.'
—María Marte

EL CRUCERO

Calle Mayor 1
Corella
Navarre 31591
+34 948781683
www.elcrucerocorella.com

Recommended by
Susan Spicer

Opening hours	Open 7 days
Credit cards	Not accepted
Price range	Budget
Style	Casual
Cuisine	Café-Bistro
Recommended for	Worth the travel

LA TABERNA DEL GOURMET

Calle San Fernando 10
Alicante
Valencian Community 03002
+34 965204233
www.latabernadelgourmet.com

Recommended by
Quique Dacosta

Opening hours	Open 7 days
Credit cards	Accepted
Price range	Affordable
Style	Smart casual
Cuisine	Tapas
Recommended for	Local favourite

'A restaurant at the top of its creative game.'
—Quique Dacosta

L'ESCALETA

Pujada Estació Nord 205
Cocentaina
Valencian Community 03820
+34 965592100
www.lescaleta.com

Recommended by
Quique Dacosta

Opening hours	Closed Monday
Credit cards	Accepted
Price range	Affordable
Style	Smart casual
Cuisine	Modern Spanish
Recommended for	Local favourite

'Here you'll find all that you could hope for in a creative restaurant.'—Quique Dacosta

CASA FEDERICO

Recommended by
Quique Dacosta

Carrer Ausiàs March 22
Dénia
Valencian Community 03700
+34 965783041
www.casafederico.es

Opening hours..Open 7 days
Credit cards..Accepted
Price range..Affordable
Style...Casual
Cuisine..Seafood
Recommended for.............................Regular neighbourhood

'Local Dénia seafood cuisine.'—Quique Dacosta

EL FARALLÓ

Recommended by
Quique Dacosta

Carrer del Fénix 10
Dénia
Valencian Community 03700
+34 966430652
www.elfarallo.com

Opening hours..Closed Monday
Credit cards..Accepted
Price range..Affordable
Style...Casual
Cuisine..Seafood
Recommended for.............................Regular neighbourhood

EL MARINO

Recommended by
Quique Dacosta

Plaza del Oculista Buigues 4
Dénia
Valencian Community 03700
+34 965783566
www.elmarinodenia.com

Opening hours..Closed Monday
Credit cards..Accepted
Price range..Affordable
Style...Casual
Cuisine..Seafood
Recommended for.............................Regular neighbourhood

PEIX & BRASES

Recommended by
Quique Dacosta

Plaza Benidorm 16
Dénia
Valencian Community 03700

Opening hours..Open 7 days
Credit cards..Accepted
Price range..Affordable
Style...Casual
Cuisine...Seafood-Grill
Recommended for.............................Regular neighbourhood

'They focus on the quality of the fish, brought directly from the fish market in Dénia.'—Quique Dacosta

QUIQUE DACOSTA RESTAURANTE

Recommended by
Andoni Luis Aduriz,
Josean Alija, Ricard
Camarena, Sang-Hoon
Degeimbre, Hernán
Gipponi, Ángel León,
Pedro Subijana

Carretera Las Marinas
Dénia
Valencian Community 03700
+34 965784179
www.quiquedacosta.es

Opening hours.............................Closed Monday and Tuesday
Credit cards..Accepted
Price range..Expensive
Style...Formal
Cuisine..Modern Spanish
Recommended for...Worth the travel

'One of the most important gastronomic experiences that you can have in the world today.'
—Andoni Luis Aduriz

Chef Quique Dacosta takes his place among the Spanish avant-garde giants such as Ferran Adrià due to his desire to create truly original dishes. Following elBulli's closure, his Costa Blanca restaurant has become the new place of pilgrimage for globetrotting gastronomes. Inside the glass and concrete building, which resembles both a modern art gallery and a rustic Spanish retreat, Dacosta experiments with underutilised plants, such as cacti, as well as more traditional Spanish ingredients, in an attempt to create an 'edible landscape'. As you might imagine, dishes are colourful, often surprising and occasionally slightly bonkers – but always memorable.

RESTAURANTE LA CUINA

Carreterra de les Marines 2
Dénia
Valencian Community 03700
+34 965787080

Opening hours	Closed Tuesday
Credit cards	Accepted
Price range	Budget
Style	Casual
Cuisine	Tapas
Recommended for	Regular neighbourhood

'Very honest in their work.'—Quique Dacosta

LA FINCA

Partida de Perleta 7
Elche
Valencian Community 03295
+34 965456007
www.lafinca.es

Opening hours	Closed Monday
Credit cards	Accepted
Price range	Expensive
Style	Smart casual
Cuisine	Modern Spanish
Recommended for	Local favourite

'A first-class gastronomic restaurant.'
—Quique Dacosta

RESTAURANTE PARPALLÓ

Avenida Luís Pericot 57
La Drova
Valencian Community 46758
+34 962807229

Opening hours	Closed Wednesday
Credit cards	Not accepted
Price range	Budget
Style	Casual
Cuisine	Valencian
Recommended for	Bargain

'They make the best *empanadillas* (a Spanish pasty) in the world!'—Ricard Camarena

RESTAURANTE CASA PEPA

Partida de Pamís 7–30
Ondara
Valencian Community 03760
+34 965766606
www.restaurantecasapepa.com

Opening hours	Closed Monday
Credit cards	Accepted
Price range	Affordable
Style	Smart casual
Cuisine	Spanish
Recommended for	Regular neighbourhood

'Incredibly good value for money.'—Quique Dacosta

LA SIRENA RESTAURANTE

Avenida de Madrid 14
Petrer
Valencian Community 03610
+34 965371718
www.lasirena.net

Opening hours	Closed Monday
Credit cards	Accepted
Price range	Affordable
Style	Casual
Cuisine	Spanish
Recommended for	Local favourite

'A restaurant recognized at the highest level worldwide.'
—Quique Dacosta

PACO GANDÍA

Calle San Francisco 10
Pinoso
Valencian Community 03650
+34 965478023
www.pacogandia.com

Opening hours	Closed Monday
Credit cards	Accepted
Price range	Affordable
Style	Casual
Cuisine	Valencian
Recommended for	Worth the travel

'This lunch-only restaurant serves classic Valencian rabbit-and-mountain-snail paella and Paco Torreblanca chocolates. It will blow you away.'—Jocky Petrie

ASKUA

Recommended by
Ricard Camarena,
Quique Dacosta

Carrer de Felip Maria Garín 4
Valencia
Valencian Community 46021
+34 963375536
www.askuarestaurante.com

Opening hours	Closed Sunday
Credit cards	Accepted but not AMEX
Price range	Affordable
Style	Casual
Cuisine	Spanish Grill
Recommended for	Regular neighbourhood

'Very special, ingredient-based cuisine in a place
where I always feel at home thanks to the amazing
warmth of its owners.'—Ricard Camarena

CASA CARMELA

Recommended by
Ricard Camarena

Carrer d'Isabel de Villena 155
Valencia
Valencian Community 46011
+34 963710073
www.casa-carmela.com

Opening hours	Closed Monday
Credit cards	Accepted
Price range	Affordable
Style	Casual
Cuisine	Valencian
Recommended for	Local favourite

'A truly genuine menu.'—Ricard Camarena

GARNACHA TINTA

Recommended by
Quique Dacosta

Calle Doctor Romagosa 3
Valencia
Valencian Community 46002
+34 963813840
www.garnachatinta.es

Opening hours	Open 7 days
Credit cards	Accepted but not AMEX
Price range	Affordable
Style	Casual
Cuisine	Spanish
Recommended for	Breakfast

'I don't usually have breakfast but Garnacha Tinta is
perhaps the ideal place for breakfast or lunch. The
service, the quality of the pastries and cakes, as well
as the typical Valencian lunches, are all prepared with
great gusto.'—Quique Dacosta

MOLTTO

Recommended by
Ricard Camarena

Plaza de la Reina 9
Valencia
Valencian Community 46001
+34 960114155
www.moltto.es

Opening hours	Open 7 days
Credit cards	Accepted
Price range	Budget
Style	Casual
Cuisine	Valencian
Recommended for	Breakfast

'I love its location and the fantastic range of pastries
and savoury treats on offer.'—Ricard Camarena

EL POBLET

Recommended by
Daniel Achilles

Calle de Correos 8
Valencia
Valencian Community 46002
+34 961111106
www.elpobletrestaurante.com

Opening hours	Closed Sunday
Credit cards	Accepted
Price range	Affordable
Style	Casual
Cuisine	Modern Spanish
Recommended for	Worth the travel

'It impressed me from the start: the interior, the
incredible hospitality, a seldom-seen feeling for forms
and colours, and of course – I can safely say – the
spectacular cuisine. Quique Dacosta has his very own
independent style which is based on the variety of
regional produce. And all this happens on what
I would call an artistic level.'—Daniel Achilles

RAUSELL

Recommended by
Ricard Camarena

Calle Ángel Guimerá 61
Valencia
Valencian Community 46008
+34 963843193
www.rausell.es

Opening hours	Closed Monday and Tuesday
Credit cards	Accepted
Price range	Affordable
Style	Casual
Cuisine	Valencian
Recommended for	Wish I'd opened

'It has an amazing bar and take away (take out) area, as well as a cosy dining room run by the Rausell brothers. Their business model is unbeatable.'
—Ricard Camarena

RESTAURANTE RIFF

Recommended by
Quique Dacosta

Calle Conde Altea 18
Valencia
Valencian Community 46005
+34 963335353
www.restaurante-riff.com

Opening hours	Closed Monday and Sunday
Credit cards	Accepted
Price range	Expensive
Style	Smart casual
Cuisine	Modern Spanish
Recommended for	Local favourite

RICARD CAMARENA

Recommended by
Quique Dacosta

Calle Doctor Sumsi 4
Valencia
Valencian Community 46005
+34 963355418
www.ricardcamarena.com

Opening hours	Closed Monday and Sunday
Credit cards	Accepted
Price range	Expensive
Style	Smart casual
Cuisine	Modern Spanish
Recommended for	Local favourite

'A unique representation of one of the most dynamic gastronomic and creative regions in Spain.'
—Quique Dacosta

LA SALITA

Recommended by
Quique Dacosta

Calle de Séneca 12
Valencia
Valencian Community 46021
+34 963817516
www.lasalitarestaurante.com

Opening hours	Closed Sunday
Credit cards	Accepted
Price range	Affordable
Style	Casual
Cuisine	Modern Spanish
Recommended for	Local favourite

TASTEM

Recommended by
Quique Dacosta

Calle Ernesto Ferrer 14
Valencia
Valencian Community 46021
+34 963696851
www.tastem.com

Opening hours	Closed Monday
Credit cards	Accepted
Price range	Affordable
Style	Casual
Cuisine	Japanese
Recommended for	Late night

'A very interesting Japanese restaurant where native chefs serve Japanese cuisine that is very true to the original.'—Quique Dacosta

TORREBLANCA

Recommended by
Quique Dacosta

Calle Conde Salvatierra 35
Valencia
Valencian Community 46004
+34 963941249
www.torreblanca.net

Opening hours	Open 7 days
Reservation policy	No
Credit cards	Accepted
Price range	Affordable
Style	Casual
Cuisine	Café-Patisserie
Recommended for	Breakfast

'It's owned by Paco Torreblanca. It's a treat to have breakfast in one of his pastry shops – he is, after all, one of the best pastry chefs in the world.'
—Quique Dacosta

'REPRESENTS THE HISTORY OF A CITY.'

ALBERT ADRIÀ P518

'Some of the most innovative pastries in town.'

ALBERT RAURICH P519

BARCELONA

'A FANTASTIC BEACH BAR BY THE SEA WITH INCREDIBLE PAELLAS.'

ALBERT RAURICH P516

'A RESTAURANT THAT MAKES LIFE WORTH LIVING.'

OMAR ALLIBHOY P515

'WHEN A CHEF DISCOVERS NEW FLAVOURS, HE STEPS INTO ANOTHER AROMATIC WORLD WITH HIS CURIOSITY AWAKENED.'

CARMELO CHIARAMONTE P516

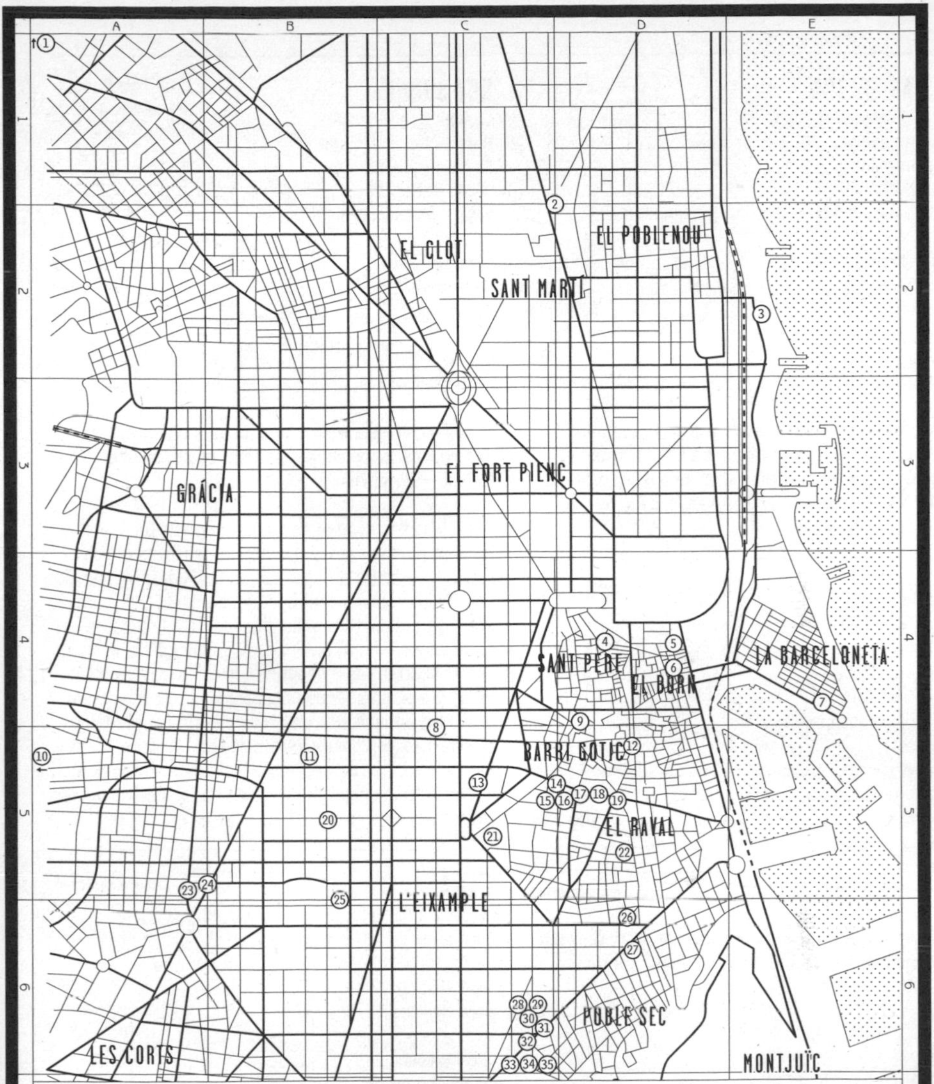

EL CLOT

EL POBLENOU

SANT MARTÍ

GRÀCIA

EL FORT PIENC

SANT PERE

LA BARCELONETA

EL BORN

BARRI GÒTIC

EL RAVAL

L'EIXAMPLE

PUBLE SEC

LES CORTS

MONTJUÏC

BARCELONA

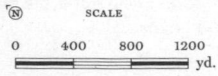

SCALE

0   400   800   1200   yd.

LA MAR SALADA

Recommended by
Jordi Butrón Melero

Passeig de Joan de Borbó 58
La Barceloneta
Barcelona 08003
+34 932212127
www.lamarsalada.cat

Opening hours	Closed Tuesday
Credit cards	Accepted
Price range	Affordable
Style	Casual
Cuisine	Seafood
Recommended for	Wish I'd opened

'Marc Singla prepares serious and honest seafood cuisine with full flavours and for a large number of diners. Cooking at a certain level for a few people is really simple. Doing it for 200 people is not as easy.' —Jordi Butrón Melero

ALLIUM

Recommended by
Jordi Vilà

Carrer del Call 17
Barri Gòtic
Barcelona 08002
+34 933023003
www.alliumrestaurant.es

Opening hours	Closed Sunday
Credit cards	Accepted
Price range	Affordable
Style	Casual
Cuisine	Catalan
Recommended for	Breakfast

'A charming place serving home-made food. They put a lot of emphasis on the simpler things.' —Jordi Vilà

KOY SHUNKA

Recommended by
Joan Roca, Jordi Vilà

Copons 7
Barri Gòtic
Barcelona 08002
+34 934127939
www.koyshunka.com

Opening hours	Closed Monday
Credit cards	Accepted
Price range	Expensive
Style	Smart casual
Cuisine	Japanese
Recommended for	Late night

'A Japanese restaurant where food is prepared, by hand, and cooked at the counter in front of you by Chef Hideki.' —Jordi Vilà

Barcelona has acquired a healthy appetite for Japanese food in recent years. Following the success of their original restaurant Shunka, owners Hideki Matsuhisa and Xu Zhangchao opened Koy Shunka in 2008, which itself garnered a Michelin star in 2013. Behind an anonymous door in an anonymous back alley in the gothic quarter lies a beautiful grey slate room dominated by a polished wood counter, where a maximum of twenty-four diners watch as a series of stunning MediterrAsian dishes are meticulously prepared before their eyes. It's not cheap, and a tasting menu can stretch well on into the night, but you won't hear any complaints from anyone lucky enough to score a reservation.

VIENA

Recommended by
Albert Adrià

La Rambla del Estudis 115
Barri Gòtic
Barcelona 08002
+34 933171492
www.viena.es

Opening hours	Open 7 days
Reservation policy	No
Credit cards	Accepted
Price range	Budget
Style	Casual
Cuisine	Bakery-Café-Deli
Recommended for	Bargain

'It's a fast-food restaurant that focuses on quality. They have one the best sandwiches in the world, the *jamón ibérico* sandwich.' —Albert Adrià

CAL PEP

Recommended by
Oriol Castro, Jason Fox,
Kim Öhman, Cal Peternell

Plaça de les Olles 8
El Born
Barcelona 08003
+34 933107961
www.calpep.com

Opening hours	Closed Sunday
Credit cards	Accepted
Price range	Affordable
Style	Casual
Cuisine	Tapas
Recommended for	Late night

'They serve tasty Spanish food over a bar and people love it.'—Kim Öhman

TLAXCAL

Recommended by
Carles Abellan

Carrer del Comerç 27
El Born
Barcelona 08003
+34 932684134
www.tlaxcal.com

Opening hours	Closed Tuesday
Credit cards	Accepted but not AMEX
Price range	Budget
Style	Casual
Cuisine	Mexican
Recommended for	Late night

'They serve very well-prepared traditional Mexican dishes using very authentic products and it is excellent value for money.'—Carles Abellan

BODEGA 1900

Recommended by
Wojciech Modest Amaro,
Quique Dacosta,
Eduard Xatruch

Carrer de Tamarit 91
L'Eixample
Barcelona 08015
+34 933252659
www.ca.bodega1900.com

Opening hours	Closed Monday and Sunday
Credit cards	Accepted
Price range	Affordable
Style	Casual
Cuisine	Catalan
Recommended for	Wish I'd opened

'Simple concept based on fantastic ingredients.'
—Wojciech Modest Amaro

41 GRADOS EXPERIENCE

Recommended by
Pier Bussetti, Quique
Dacosta, Robin Gill,
Rasmus Kofoed, Willy
Trullás Moreno, Albert
Raurich, Jordi Vilà

Avinguda Paral-lel 164
L'Eixample
Barcelona 08015
+34 696592571
www.41grados.es

Opening hours	Closed Monday and Sunday
Credit cards	Accepted but not Diners
Price range	Expensive
Style	Smart casual
Cuisine	Modern International
Recommended for	Worth the travel

'Without doubt one of the best restaurants in the world. Albert Adrià has gone back to giving life to elBulli snacks and has also created a new type of fantastic gastronomic concept.'—Albert Raurich

COURE

Recommended by
Jordi Butrón Melero,
Jordi Vilà

Passatge de Marimon 20
L'Eixample
Barcelona 08021
+34 932007532
www.restaurantcoure.es

Opening hours	Closed Monday and Sunday
Credit cards	Accepted
Price range	Affordable
Style	Casual
Cuisine	Modern Catalan
Recommended for	Regular neighbourhood

'On entering this fine-dining restaurant, you are met with a friendly and cosy bar for only ten diners. You sit down, you follow the advice of the chef, Albert Ventura, and without realizing it, time passes pleasantly amid the delicious tapas and agreeable conversation. It's a must.'—Jordi Butrón Melero

Barcelona's bistronomics movement is about ambitious chefs serving exciting food while keeping costs to a minimum. The modern Catalan dishes chef Albert Ventura produces in his basement restaurant are aimed at the heights of Michelin-starred gastronomy, but at just €35 (£29; $49) for a seasonal menu, this classy cooking doesn't have to be a rare treat. On the ground floor are squeezed ten stools at a small tapas bar, where you can enjoy a taste of the theatrics from below – without the white tablecloths and for an even more reasonable chunk of cash.

GRESCA

Carrer de Provença 230
L'Eixample
Barcelona 08036
+34 934516193
www.gresca.net

Recommended by
Albert Raurich,
Jordi Vilà

Opening hours	Closed Sunday
Credit cards	Accepted
Price range	Affordable
Style	Casual
Cuisine	Modern Catalan
Recommended for	Bargain

'Rafa's originality and courage is reflected in his dishes. His rebelliousness, informality and passion for cooking and all that goes with gastronomy is a real reflection of what is going on in Catalonia.'
—Albert Raurich

With just twenty-six covers, the narrow, minimalist dining room with its white linen and white walls focuses the diner's full attention on the plate. Which is no bad thing as the dinnerware here is the canvas for talented and creative chef Rafael Peña. A graduate of the school of Spanish modernism sustained by both Ferran Adrià and Martín Berasategui, Peña's style of 'bistronomia' fuses traditional bistro food with the haute-cuisine ideals of gastronomy to produce dishes — a flower-shaped egg-white soufflé with soft yolk centre, for instance — that are as affordable as they are delicious.

HISOP

Passatge de Marimón 9
L'Eixample
Barcelona 08021
+34 932413233
www.hisop.net

Recommended by
Jason Fox

Opening hours	Closed Sunday
Credit cards	Accepted
Price range	Affordable
Style	Smart casual
Cuisine	Modern Catalan
Recommended for	Worth the travel

'Casual but sophisticated, and not at outrageous prices.'
—Jason Fox

LOLITA TAPERÍA

Tamarit 104
L'Eixample
Barcelona 08015
+34 934245231
www.lolitataperia.com

Recommended by
Albert Raurich

Opening hours	Closed Monday and Sunday
Reservation policy	No
Credit cards	Accepted
Price range	Budget
Style	Casual
Cuisine	Tapas
Recommended for	Bargain

'Lolita Tapería is what used to be the Inopia Bar owned by Albert Adrià and Joan Martinez. Albert went on to open Tickets and Juanito continues to serve great tapas for €30–40 (£25–33; $42–55) per person.'
—Albert Raurich

The wildly popular Inopia, opened by Albert Adrià and Joan Martínez, quickly graduated from neighbourhood tapas bar to become one of Barcelona's most sought-after hang-outs when it opened in 2006. Now that Adrià has moved on and the restaurant has been renamed Lolita Tapería, the neighbourhood feel has returned – that's not to say that Martínez is letting standards slip. The familiar faces behind the counter are still as welcoming as ever, the laidback decor as effortlessly cool and the food as appealing as it is unshowy. Long-term fans might recognize the potato-and-beef-filled *Bomba d'Eixample*. Other highlights include hake roe in spicy oil and the *Gos d'Atura* hot dog, all at down-to-earth prices.

PETIT COMITÈ

Passatge de la Concepció 13
L'Eixample
Barcelona 08008
+34 935500620
www.petitcomite.cat

Recommended by
Eduard Xatruch

Opening hours	Open 7 days
Credit cards	Accepted
Price range	Affordable
Style	Casual
Cuisine	Modern Catalan
Recommended for	Local favourite

'Nandu Jubany offers an impressive repertoire of perfectly cooked Catalan dishes.'—Eduard Xatruch

RESTAURANTE PORVENIR

Recommended by
Eduard Xatruch

Carrer de Villarroel 157
L'Eixample
Barcelona 08036
+34 934531046

Opening hours	Closed Monday
Credit cards	Not accepted
Price range	Budget
Style	Casual
Cuisine	Galician
Recommended for	Bargain

'I found this place by chance. It offers traditional Galician dishes at a very reasonable price. The main specialities are *lacón* (dried pork shoulder), grilled pig's ear and Galician-style octopus. The staff are very kind and you feel at home here.'—Eduard Xatruch

TAPAS 24

Recommended by
Albert Raurich,
Joan Roca

Calle Diputación 269
L'Eixample
Barcelona 08007
+34 934880977
www.carlesabellan.es

Opening hours	Closed Sunday
Reservation policy	No
Credit cards	Accepted
Price range	Affordable
Style	Casual
Cuisine	Tapas
Recommended for	Wish I'd opened

'More than admiring it, I wouldn't mind it being mine! The rock 'n' roll spirit of Carles Abellan in its purest form. I can assure you that you'll eat fantastically well here.'—Albert Raurich

The Eixample tapas bar from chef Carles Abellan, who did sixteen years under you-know-who of elBulli fame, and also runs the long-running and rather more experimental Commerc24, and Bravo24 in the W hotel. In a small, brightly lit basement, the short menu of crowd-pleasing snacks is designed as a cutlery wrapper and scrawled across mirrors and blackboards. These include classic salt cod croquettas, Catalan favourites such as tripe stew, and the posh fast-food hits that are the Bikini – a ham and cheese toasted sandwich flecked with black truffle – and the McFoie Burger – a beef and foie gras pâté in a crispy bun.

TICKETS

Recommended by
Omar Allibhoy, Gaggan
Anand, Felipe Bronze, Pier
Bussetti, Quique Dacosta,
Ramón Freixa, William
Mahi, Jp McMahon, Paul
Pairet, Jordi Roca, José
Santaella, Jordi Vilà

Avinguda Paral-lel 164
L'Eixample
Barcelona 08015
www.ticketsbar.es

Opening hours	Closed Monday and Sunday
Credit cards	Accepted
Price range	Affordable
Style	Casual
Cuisine	Tapas
Recommended for	Worth the travel

'The best meal I have ever had in my life! A restaurant that makes life worth living.'—Omar Allibhoy

This is what the elBulli brothers did next. Their next trick, after running the most famously oversubscribed restaurant the world has ever seen, was to open a tapas bar. Or, to be more precise, a tapas bar and a casual restaurant that does tapas, the way elBulli was a formal restaurant that did tapas. Sitting next to Tickets, 41 Grados Experience, closer to a traditional tapas bar in terms of the space, serves creative cocktails and snacks. Tickets itself is arranged with counters, colourful furniture and a series of stations that prepare everything from local seafood delicacies to wacky desserts.

DOS CIELOS

Recommended by
Quique Dacosta,
Albert Raurich

ME Hotel
Calle Pere IV 272–286
El Poblenou
Barcelona 08005
+34 933672070
www.doscielos.com

Opening hours	Closed Monday and Sunday
Credit cards	Accepted
Price range	Expensive
Style	Smart casual
Cuisine	Modern Spanish
Recommended for	High end

'I think that the Torres brothers' cooking is some of the most interesting and stylish in Barcelona.'
—Albert Raurich

XIRINGUITO ESCRIBÀ

Recommended by
Albert Raurich

Avenida del Litoral 42
El Poblenou
Barcelona 08005
+34 932210729
www.xiringuitoescriba.com

Opening hours	Open 7 days
Credit cards	Accepted
Price range	Affordable
Style	Casual
Cuisine	Seafood
Recommended for	Regular neighbourhood

'A fantastic beach bar by the sea with incredible paellas made by maestro and friend Joan Escribà.'
—Albert Raurich

If the tourist throng on Las Ramblas gets too much, just remember you're only ten minutes away from paella on a sandy white beach at this casual seaside joint in Barcelona's smart Olympic port neighbourhood. There's cuttlefish, langoustines and Galician mussels in the classic seafood version; mushrooms and asparagus paella for vegetarians; and the Valencian take on the dish called *Fideuà* that's made with noodles instead of rice. But this isn't just any beach restaurant – with talented chef Joan Escribà in charge of the menu there's an imaginative range of dishes, including 'sea and mountain': guinea fowl and prawn (shrimp).

CASA DE TAPAS CAÑOTA

Recommended by
Oriol Castro

Carrer Lleida 7
Poble Sec
Barcelona 08004
+34 933259171
ww.casadetapas.com

Opening hours	Closed Monday
Credit cards	Accepted
Price range	Affordable
Style	Casual
Cuisine	Tapas
Recommended for	Late night

ESPAI KRU

Recommended by
Jordi Butrón Melero

Carrer Lleida 7
Poble Sec
Barcelona 08004
+34 934248152
www.espaikru.com

Opening hours	Closed Monday
Credit cards	Accepted
Price range	Affordable
Style	Casual
Cuisine	Modern Seafood
Recommended for	High end

'Fish and seafood in all their splendour. If you want to impress or celebrate an event, this is the place for you. Excellent ingredients handled with the utmost respect. The cuts and the presentation in both the traditional and creative recipes are enviably accurate.'
—Jordi Butrón Melero

PAKTA

Recommended by
Carmelo Chiaramonte,
Quique Dacosta

Carrer Lleida 5
Poble Sec
Barcelona 08004
+34 936240177
www.ca.pakta.es

Opening hours	Closed Monday and Sunday
Credit cards	Accepted
Price range	Expensive
Style	Smart casual
Cuisine	Japanese-Peruvian
Recommended for	Worth the travel

'An indescribable experience. Peruvian food is not that well known and when a chef discovers new flavours, he steps into another aromatic world with his curiosity awakened. The staff's hospitality, the simple and beautiful furnishings and Japanese cooking blend magically with Peruvian cooking.'
—Carmelo Chiaramonte

QUIMET I QUIMET

Poeta Cabanyes 25
Poble Sec
Barcelona 08004
+34 934423142

Recommended by
Oriol Castro,
Willy Trullás Moreno

Opening hours	Closed Sunday
Reservation policy	No
Credit cards	Accepted
Price range	Affordable
Style	Casual
Cuisine	Tapas
Recommended for	Late night

'A wine cellar filled with bottles and amazing canned goods. A magical place.'—Oriol Castro

A prince among Barcelona tapas joints, Quimet i Quimet has been in the Quim family for four generations, since it was built at the start of the twentieth century. There are no chairs and just a couple of tables, and the walls are hung with bottles of wine and spirits from all over the world, and some of the best canned foods in Spain. The specialities here are the *montaditos*, little open sandwiches of which Señor Quim improvises perhaps dozens every night – they might feature salmon with truffled honey or tuna with caviar and balsamic syrup. There's a vast selection of wines and house beer on tap.

RIAS DE GALICIA

Carrer Lleida 7
Poble Sec
Barcelona 08004
+34 934248152
www.riasdegalicia.com

Recommended by
Ferran Adrià,
Pedro Subijana

Opening hours	Open 7 days
Credit cards	Accepted
Price range	Expensive
Style	Smart casual
Cuisine	Galician-Seafood
Recommended for	High end

'A formidable seafood restaurant.'—Ferran Adrià

The late 1980s/early 1990s time warp of a dining room aside, it's hard to fault anything else bar the steepness of the bill at this Galician seafood specialist. Although, these days that's the price of fish this rare. Aside from the vintage Joselito ham with which you can start your meal and the large range of cheeses with which you can finish, the only land food on offer is simply prepared suckling pig, kid and veal. Indulge in the lengthiest list of wacky and wonderful shellfish delicacies you're ever likely to see this side of a high-end Tokyo sushi bar.

BACOA

Ronda de la Universitat 31
El Raval
Barcelona 08007
+34 932507290
www.bacoa.es

Recommended by
Jordi Butrón Melero

Opening hours	Open 7 days
Reservation policy	No
Credit cards	Accepted but not AMEX
Price range	Budget
Style	Casual
Cuisine	Burgers
Recommended for	Bargain

'They serve the best hamburgers in Barcelona. It has a young and relaxed atmosphere. The mix of local ingredients and excellent value for money, plus some original and tasty combinations make Bacoa an easy and appetising option when you are in the centre of Barcelona.'—Jordi Butrón Melero

BAR PINOTXO

Mercat de La Boqueria 466–470
La Rambla 89
El Raval
Barcelona 08002
+34 933171731
www.pinotxobar.com

Recommended by
Ferran Adrià, José
Andrés, Oriol Castro,
Ramón Freixa, Willy
Trullás Moreno,
Cal Peternell

Opening hours	Open 7 days
Reservation policy	No
Credit cards	Not accepted
Price range	Budget
Style	Casual
Cuisine	Tapas
Recommended for	Breakfast

'When I worked at elBulli, before we started work we used to go shopping at La Boqueria market and we would always meet at Pinotxo. I would have coffee and a crunchy cream-filled pastry there every morning. Juanito, the owner, is an amazing person: he enchants all of his clients with his happiness and friendliness. No one goes to La Boqueria in Barcelona without stopping by Pinotxo.'—Oriol Castro

DOS PALILLOS

Carrer d'Elisabets 9
El Raval
Barcelona 08001
+34 933040513
www.dospalillos.com

Recommended by
Carles Abellan, Albert Adrià,
Ferran Adrià, Jordi Vilà,
Eduard Xatruch

Opening hours	Closed Monday and Sunday
Credit cards	Accepted
Price range	Expensive
Style	Smart casual
Cuisine	Asian small plates
Recommended for	Regular neighbourhood

'In my opinion, one of the best restaurants in the city, serving Asian cuisine that is full of little gems. Its owner, Albert Raurich, was head chef at elBulli for seven years.'—Albert Adrià

You've been executive chef at the most renowned restaurant on the planet for the best part of a decade – what do you do next? The answer for Albert Raurich, who ran the kitchen at elBulli from 1999 until 2007, is to open an Asian-inspired tapas bar. Located beside the Casa Camper hotel (with a second branch at their Berlin hotel), Dos Palillos serves small plates in its no-nonsense front bar, where you perch perilously on plastic crates. Behind the bead curtain at the back lies a more formal, low-lit dining room with counter seating that offers a multi-coursed menu of Asian-Iberian dishes.

FORN MISTRAL

Ronda Sant Antoni 96
El Raval
Barcelona 08001
+34 933018037
www.fornmistral.com

Recommended by
Jordi Butrón Melero

Opening hours	Closed Sunday
Reservation policy	No
Credit cards	Not accepted
Price range	Budget
Style	Casual
Cuisine	Café-Bakery
Recommended for	Breakfast

'An unpretentious neighbourhood café/bakery. It's very homely and accessible. The number of options, both sweet and savoury, is endless. I go there for breakfast every Monday and I always face the same dilemma: deciding what I most fancy from the variety of options. If you pick the famous *ensaimada* (a pastry from Mallorca), you've chosen wisely.'—Jordi Butrón Melero

GRANJA VIADER

Xuclà 6
El Raval
Barcelona 08001
+34 933183486
www.granjaviader.cat.mialias.net

Recommended by
Albert Adrià

Opening hours	Closed Sunday
Credit cards	Accepted but not AMEX
Price range	Budget
Style	Casual
Cuisine	Café-Bakery
Recommended for	Breakfast

'A classic place where a very famous Catalan chocolate drink called *el Cacaolat* was invented. This place represents the history of a city.'—Albert Adrià

CA L'ISIDRE

Carrer de les Flors 12
El Raval
Barcelona 08001
+34 934411139
www.calisidre.com

Recommended by
Eduard Xatruch

Opening hours	Closed Sunday
Credit cards	Accepted
Price range	Expensive
Style	Smart casual
Cuisine	Spanish
Recommended for	Local favourite

'Isidre Gironés and his whole family represent the revival of Barcelona quality over the decades – they use exceptional ingredients that are handled with the utmost respect.'—Eduard Xatruch

PASTELERIA ESCRIBÀ

Recommended by
Albert Raurich

Gran Vía de les Corts Catalanes 546
El Raval
Barcelona 08011
+34 934547535
www.escriba.es

Opening hours	Open 7 days
Reservation policy	No
Credit cards	Accepted
Price range	Affordable
Style	Casual
Cuisine	Café-Patisserie
Recommended for	Breakfast

'A Barcelona classic. Christian makes fantastic baked goods and some of the most innovative pastries in town.'—Albert Raurich

The name Escribà is known in sweet-toothed Barcelona circles both as a traditional family-run bakery dating back to 1906 and as the producer of avant-garde chocolate sculptures almost worthy of a Turner Prize. The Gran Vía flagship is a showcase for fourth-generation pastry chef Christian Escribà's fashion-fabulous creations (including very wearable sugar rings and not-quite-so-practical chocolate shoes) as well as a great spot for coffee and a pastry. The flavoured croissants are famous: try *sobra-sada* (cured sausage) and honey, vanilla and rose or chocolate and banana. The gorgeous La Rambla shop, an Art Nouveau gem, is another must-see.

EL QUIM DE LA BOQUERIA

Recommended by
Carles Abellan, Antonio
Escalante, Jason Fox,
Eduard Xatruch

Mercat de La Boqueria
La Rambla 91
El Raval
Barcelona 08001
www.elquimdelaboqueria.cat

Opening hours	Closed Monday and Sunday
Reservation policy	No
Credit cards	Accepted
Price range	Affordable
Style	Casual
Cuisine	Tapas
Recommended for	Breakfast

'I love it because the breakfasts are incredible, the ingredients are amazing (it's in La Boqueria market) and Quim is a real character.'—Eduard Xatruch

Cava hangover be damned, the time to get to Barcelona's legendary food market, La Boqueria, is at 7.00 a.m., when its top bar, El Quim De La Boqueria (established 1987), fries its first egg. This is when the Catalan capital's top chefs gather for a breakfast beer and Quim Márquez Durán's famous eggs, practically deep-fried in olive oil and served with *chipirones* (baby squid) or foie gras and wild mushrooms. Quim's exceptional ingredients are the pick of the market. The eighteen stools at its modest counter are among the city's most sought after – it's strictly first come, first served.

SUCULENT

Recommended by
Albert Adrià, Jordi
Butrón Melero

Rambla del Raval 43
El Raval
Barcelona 08001
+34 934436579
www.suculent.com

Opening hours	Closed Monday and Tuesday
Credit cards	Accepted
Price range	Affordable
Style	Casual
Cuisine	Spanish
Recommended for	Regular neighbourhood

'I go to places that prepare a menu or food that I can't make at home. I like sharing dishes in the middle of the table, tapas, rice dishes and so on. Suculent is a small, welcoming place with an excellent culinary range that combines quality products with excellent techniques.' —Albert Adrià

The best seats in this former wine house, tucked away in the old city, are at the wooden bar, where you can watch your drinks being poured. The young chef, Antonio Romero, cooks classic dishes updated for modern palates, including *butifarra* sausage with cuttlefish meatballs or slow-cooked oxtail; the cheesecake might include Brie. Although many locals know about this nicely designed place – with its white walls, split levels and design features, including forks and spoons painted on the walls – it's on few tourists' radars. Things really get going at the weekend, when the fish comes off the boats, and there's live flamenco on Sunday evenings.

MOSQUITO

Recommended by
Carles Abellan

Carders 46
Sant Pere
Barcelona 08003
+34 932687569
www.mosquitotapas.com

Opening hours	Open 7 days
Credit cards	Accepted but not AMEX
Price range	Budget
Style	Casual
Cuisine	Asian small plates
Recommended for	Bargain

'It offers healthy, tasty and very cheap Vietnamese food that is good for a quick and easy meal.'
—Carles Abellan

ABAC

Recommended by
Quique Dacosta,
Arjan Wennekes

ABaC Hotel
Avinguda del Tibidabo 1
Sarrià-Sant Gervasi
Barcelona 08022
+34 933196600
www.abacbarcelona.com

Opening hours	Closed Monday and Sunday
Credit cards	Accepted
Price range	Expensive
Style	Smart casual
Cuisine	Modern Catalan
Recommended for	High end

'A very high-class restaurant with a kitchen full of surprises. There are also influences of elBulli, but in their own way.'—Arjan Wennekes

There is something of the Great Gatsby in the serene interior and Michelin-starred Catalonian cuisine of ABaC. It could be that chef Jordi Cruz is a youthful devotee to style and quality. Proof is in the fact that he received his first star at the age of twenty-five. Or it might be that the food is a successful meeting of tradition and innovation. The restaurant's elBulli-style cooking has given birth to an annual seasonal portfolio of tartares that should be on your to-order list. If you have a minute between indulging in the pioneering molecular gastronomy, try to wander by the formidably modern, stainless-steel kitchen to watch the action.

EL BOQUERÓN DE PLATA

Recommended by
Oriol Castro

Carrer Mare de Déu de Lorda 24
Trinitat Vella
Barcelona 08033
+34 932742327

Opening hours	Closed Monday
Reservation policy	No
Credit cards	Not accepted
Price range	Budget
Style	Casual
Cuisine	Spanish
Recommended for	Late night

'My lifelong favourite bar. It's known for three things: fried fish of the day, *butifarra* sausage with anchovies and tomato, and Arbequina olives.'—Oriol Castro

'In a place like this, simple, immediate, expressive cooking is very easy. The Atlantic wind tenderly kissing your face.'

CARMELO CHIARAMONTE P526

PORTUGAL

'The most creative chef working in Portugal today. He tells stories, of sea and land, and does so without losing sight of the flavours.'

LJUBOMIR STANISIC P524

'TYPICAL, PROUDLY PORTUGUESE CUISINE.'

LUÍS BAENA P534

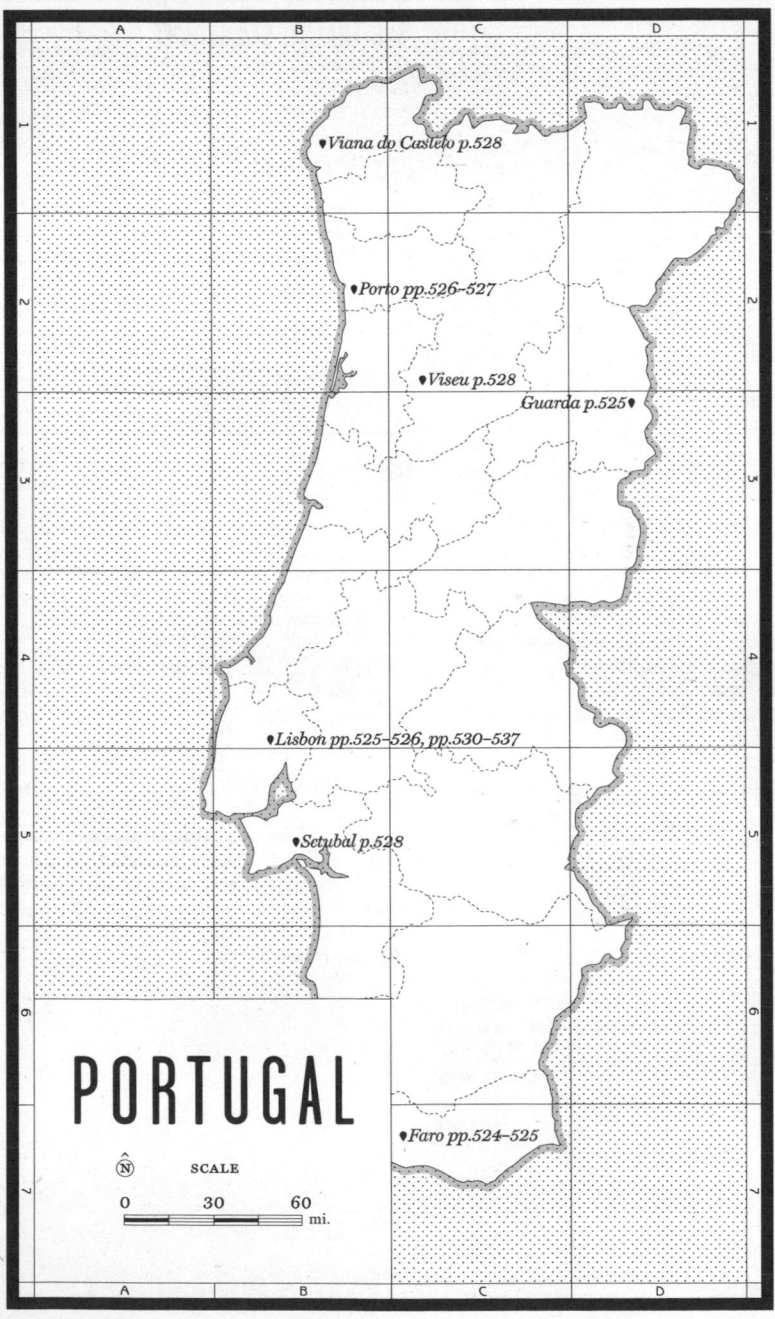

♦Viana do Castelo p.528

♦Porto pp.526–527

♦Viseu p.528

Guarda p.525♦

♦Lisbon pp.525–526, pp.530–537

♦Setúbal p.528

PORTUGAL

N

SCALE

0   30   60
mi.

♦Faro pp.524–525

VILA JOYA

Vila Joya & Joy Jung Spa
Estrada da Galé
Albufeira
Faro 8200-416
+351 289591795
www.vilajoya.com

Opening hours..Closed Wednesday
Credit cards...Accepted
Price range...Expensive
Style...Smart casual
Cuisine..Modern European
Recommended for...Local favourite

'Good food by the sea with great sunsets.'
—Kevin Thornton

Some say that Vila Joya houses Portugal's very best
restaurant. Those who have made the trip to this
idyllic stretch of the Algarve, and this seafront
dining room in particular, would have little cause
to disagree. Chef Dieter Koschina makes the most
of stunning local Albufeiran seafood and market
produce to construct a menu that is recognizably
Portuguese yet utterly luxurious by any international
standards. Signature dishes, including lobster with
cauliflower and imperial caviar, and fillet and head of
veal with Madeira jus, have won them two Michelin
stars, and a spot in the San Pellegrino World's 50
Best Restaurants.

RESTAURANTE HENRIQUE LEIS

Vale Formoso
Almancil
Faro 8135-035
+351 289393438
www.henriqueleis.com

Opening hours................................Closed Monday and Sunday
Credit cards...................................Accepted but not Diners
Price range...Expensive
Style...Smart casual
Cuisine..Gourmet
Recommended for...High end

RESTAURANTE SÃO GABRIEL

Estrada Vale do Lobo
Almancil
Faro 8135-106
+351 289394521
www.sao-gabriel.com

Opening hours...Closed Monday
Credit cards...Accepted
Price range...Expensive
Style...Smart casual
Cuisine..Modern European
Recommended for...Worth the travel

'Delicate Portuguese-inspired cuisine.'
—Miguel Castro e Silva

OCEAN

Vila Vita Parc Hotel
Rua Anneliese Pohl
Porches
Faro 8400-450
+351 282310100
www.vilavitaparc.com

Opening hours.........................Closed Tuesday and Wednesday
Credit cards...Accepted
Price range...Expensive
Style...Formal
Cuisine..Modern Portuguese
Recommended for...High end

'Austrian chef Hans Neuner is, in my opinion, the most
creative chef working in Portugal today. He goes far
beyond simply preparing food, he creates a backdrop
on which to serve it. He tells stories, of sea and land,
and does so without losing sight of the flavours.'
—Ljubomir Stanisic

EMO GOURMET RESTAURANT

Recommended by
Luís Baena

Avenida dos Descobrimentos
Vilamoura
Faro 8125-309
+351 289317000
www.tivolihotels.com

Opening hours	Open 7 days
Credit cards	Accepted
Price range	Expensive
Style	Formal
Cuisine	Modern Portuguese
Recommended for	High end

'Chef Bruno Costa has a technical mastery that enables him to enhance regional products, which results in astounding contemporary cuisine.'—Luís Baena

ROBALO

Recommended by
Miguel Castro e Silva

Largo do Cinema 4
Sabugal
Guarda 6320-455
+351 271753566

Opening hours	Closed Sunday
Credit cards	Accepted but only Visa
Price range	Affordable
Style	Casual
Cuisine	Portuguese
Recommended for	Worth the travel

'Whenever I go and spend a few days in Beira Alta, I start with a meal at Robalo. I greet João and don't even look at the menu. Charcoal-grilled lamb and a few spicy sausages to start make for a simple but satisfying meal.'—Miguel Castro e Silva

CASA DA GUIA

Recommended by
José Cordeiro

Avenida Nossa Senhora do Cabo 101
Cascais
Lisbon 2750-374
+351 214843215
www.casadaguia.com

Opening hours	Open 7 days
Credit cards	Accepted
Price range	Affordable
Style	Casual
Cuisine	European
Recommended for	Breakfast

FORTALEZA DO GUINCHO

Recommended by
José Cordeiro

Fortaleza do Guincho Hotel
Estrada do Guincho
Cascais
Lisbon 2750-642
+351 214870491
www.fortalezadoguincho.pt

Opening hours	Open 7 days
Credit cards	Accepted
Price range	Expensive
Style	Smart casual
Cuisine	French-Portuguese
Recommended for	High end

A seventeenth-century fortress keeping watch over the vast Atlantic from Cascais, due west of Lisbon, Fortaleza do Guincho is now a five-star hotel and Michelin-starred restaurant, under the creative hand of celebrated Alsatian chef Antoine Westermann. The style is essentially French but the ingredients are largely Portuguese, and seventeen years at this post has added a battery of local culinary knowledge to Westermann's armoury. Whether you choose the seasonal, à la carte or tasting menu – the latter comprising six courses including *amuse-bouches* and *mignardises* – expect a barrage of flavour and exquisite texture, complemented by a suitably excellent selection of wine.

PORTO SANTA MARIA

Recommended by
José Cordeiro

Estrada do Guincho
Cascais
Lisbon 2750-640
+351 214879450
www.portosantamaria.com

Opening hours	Open 7 days
Credit cards	Accepted
Price range	Affordable
Style	Smart casual
Cuisine	Portuguese-Seafood
Recommended for	Wish I'd opened

RESTAURANTE RIO'S

Recommended by
José Cordeiro

Complexo Turistico da Piscina Oceânica de Oeiras
Avenida Marginal
Oeiras
Lisbon 2780-267
+351 214411324
www.bholding.com.pt

Opening hours..Closed Monday
Credit cards..Accepted
Price range...Affordable
Style..Casual
Cuisine..Mediterranean
Recommended for................................Regular neighbourhood

RESTAURANTE DA ADRAGA

Recommended by
Carmelo Chiaramonte

Rua da Praia da Adraga 63
Sintra
Lisbon 2703-063
+351 219280028
www.restaurantedaadraga.com

Opening hours..Open 7 days
Credit cards........................Accepted but only VISA
Price range...Affordable
Style..Casual
Cuisine.....................................Portuguese-Seafood
Recommended for..Wish I'd opened

'Next to the sea, the best fish, freshly caught by local
fishermen. A magical corner, it would be wonderful
to cook here. In a place like this, simple, immediate,
expressive cooking is very easy. The Atlantic wind
tenderly kissing your face.'—Carmelo Chiaramonte

IL GALLO D'ORO

Recommended by
José Cordeiro

The Cliff Bay Hotel
Estrada Monumental 147
Funchal
Madeira Island 9004-532
+351 291707700
www.portobay.com

Opening hours..Open 7 days
Credit cards..Accepted
Price range..Expensive
Style..Formal
Cuisine..International
Recommended for................................Worth the travel

RESTAURANTE SAO VALENTIM

Recommended by
José Cordeiro

Rua Herois de Franca 335
Matosinhos
Porto 4450-158
+351 229379204

Opening hours..Closed Tuesday
Credit cards..Accepted
Price range...Affordable
Style..Casual
Cuisine.....................................Portuguese-Seafood
Recommended for................................Regular neighbourhood

RESTAURANTE O SAPO

Recommended by
José Cordeiro

Rua da Estrada 25
Penafiel
Porto 4560-173
+351 255752326

Opening hours..Closed Monday
Credit cards..Accepted
Price range...Affordable
Style..Casual
Cuisine..Portuguese
Recommended for..Bargain

CONFEITARIA TAVI

Recommended by
José Cordeiro

Rua Senhora da Luz 363
Porto
Porto 4150-698
+351 226180152
www.tavi.pt

Opening hours..Open 7 days
Reservation policy...No
Credit cards..Accepted
Price range...Affordable
Style..Casual
Cuisine...European
Recommended for..Breakfast

ODE PORTO WINE HOUSE

Recommended by
José Cordeiro

Largo do Terreiro 7
Porto
Porto 4050-301
+351 913200010

Opening hours	Closed Monday
Credit cards	Not accepted
Price range	Affordable
Style	Smart casual
Cuisine	Portuguese
Recommended for	Local favourite

Housed in a tall, crooked building overlooking Porto's Estiva Quay on the Douro, ODE exudes backstreet charm with its barrel-laden dining room and slate tabletops. As its name suggests, it's a place to savour the region's best wine – they have a carefully selected cellar of over 100 bins – but the food deserves great credit too, with an emphasis on farm-to-table, organic produce. This really is Slow Food: the northern Portuguese bread *broa de Avintes* is made in house, a process that takes six hours. It's this care and love for the region's traditions and ingredients that makes ODE an ode to the *terroir* of Grande Porto.

RESTAURANTE DOP

Recommended by
José Cordeiro

Palácio das Artes
Largo de São Domingos 18
Porto
Porto 4050-545
+351 222014313
www.ruipaula.com

Opening hours	Closed Sunday
Credit cards	Accepted
Price range	Affordable
Style	Smart casual
Cuisine	Modern Portuguese
Recommended for	Local favourite

Chef Rui Paula opened DOP in 2010, in a glorious neo-classical palace that was once the home of the Lisbon Bank – the local district is a world heritage site. His sixty-five-cover restaurant represents a stylish, modern take on classic Portuguese cuisine: tasting menus of differing lengths include dishes such as lobster with squid-ink spaghetti, mussels, razor clams and lobster bouillon. Tripe and salt cod also make regular appearances. There is a mezzanine area for smokers, while guests downstairs can sit at communal tables. Paula, who has recently opened a venue in Brazil, is strengthening his position as a leading Portuguese chef.

RESTAURANTE PAJÚ

Recommended by
José Cordeiro

Rua Faria Guimarães 309
Porto
Porto 4000-206
+351 225021555

Opening hours	Closed Sunday
Credit cards	Accepted
Price range	Affordable
Style	Casual
Cuisine	European
Recommended for	Late night

SHIS

Recommended by
José Cordeiro

Esplanada do Castelo
Porto
Porto 4150-623
+351 226189593
www.shisrestaurante.com

Opening hours	Open 7 days
Credit cards	Accepted
Price range	Affordable
Style	Smart casual
Cuisine	International
Recommended for	Wish I'd opened

THE YEATMAN

Recommended by
José Cordeiro

The Yeatman Hotel
Rua do Choupelo
Porto
Porto 4400-088
+351 220133100
www.the-yeatman-hotel.com

Opening hours	Open 7 days
Credit cards	Accepted
Price range	Expensive
Style	Smart casual
Cuisine	Modern Portuguese
Recommended for	High end

VALE DO GAIO

Recommended by
Miguel Castro e Silva

Vale do Gaio Hotel
Barragem Trigo de Morais
Alcácer do Sal
Setubal 7595-034
+351 265669610
www.valedogaio.com

Opening hours	Open 7 days
Credit cards	Accepted
Price range	Affordable
Style	Smart casual
Cuisine	Portuguese
Recommended for	Local favourite

'Excellent if you want to get away for a couple of days
and relax.'—Miguel Castro e Silva

RESTAURANTE O GAIO

Recommended by
José Cordeiro

Rua Agostinho José Taveira 6
Ponte de Lima
Viana do Castelo 4990-072
+351 258941251
www.restaurantegaio.pai.pt

Opening hours	Open 7 days
Credit cards	Accepted
Price range	Budget
Style	Casual
Cuisine	Portuguese
Recommended for	Bargain

RESTAURANTE DOC

Recommended by
Henrique Sá Pessoa

Estrada Nacional 222
Armamar
Viseu 5110-204
+351 254858123
www.ruipaula.com

Opening hours	Open 7 days
Credit cards	Accepted
Price range	Expensive
Style	Smart casual
Cuisine	Modern Portuguese
Recommended for	Worth the travel

'Excellent service, creative cuisine, good produce,
great view and location, fantastic wine list.'
—Henrique Sá Pessoa

'GOOD ATMOSPHERE, EXQUISITE SERVICE AND I LIKE THE IMAGINATIVE DETAIL OF THEIR CREATIONS.'

HENRIQUE SÁ PESSOA P535

LISBON

'It's a tavern that serves authentic food and a fabulous plate of salt cod.'

CHAKALL P533

'THE SEAFOOD DELIGHTS THAT YOU FIND HERE ARE 100 PER CENT FRESH, AS THOUGH THE OCEAN WAS TAKING OVER THE CITY. SIMPLE, WELL PREPARED AND SATISFYING.'

LUÍS BAENA P532

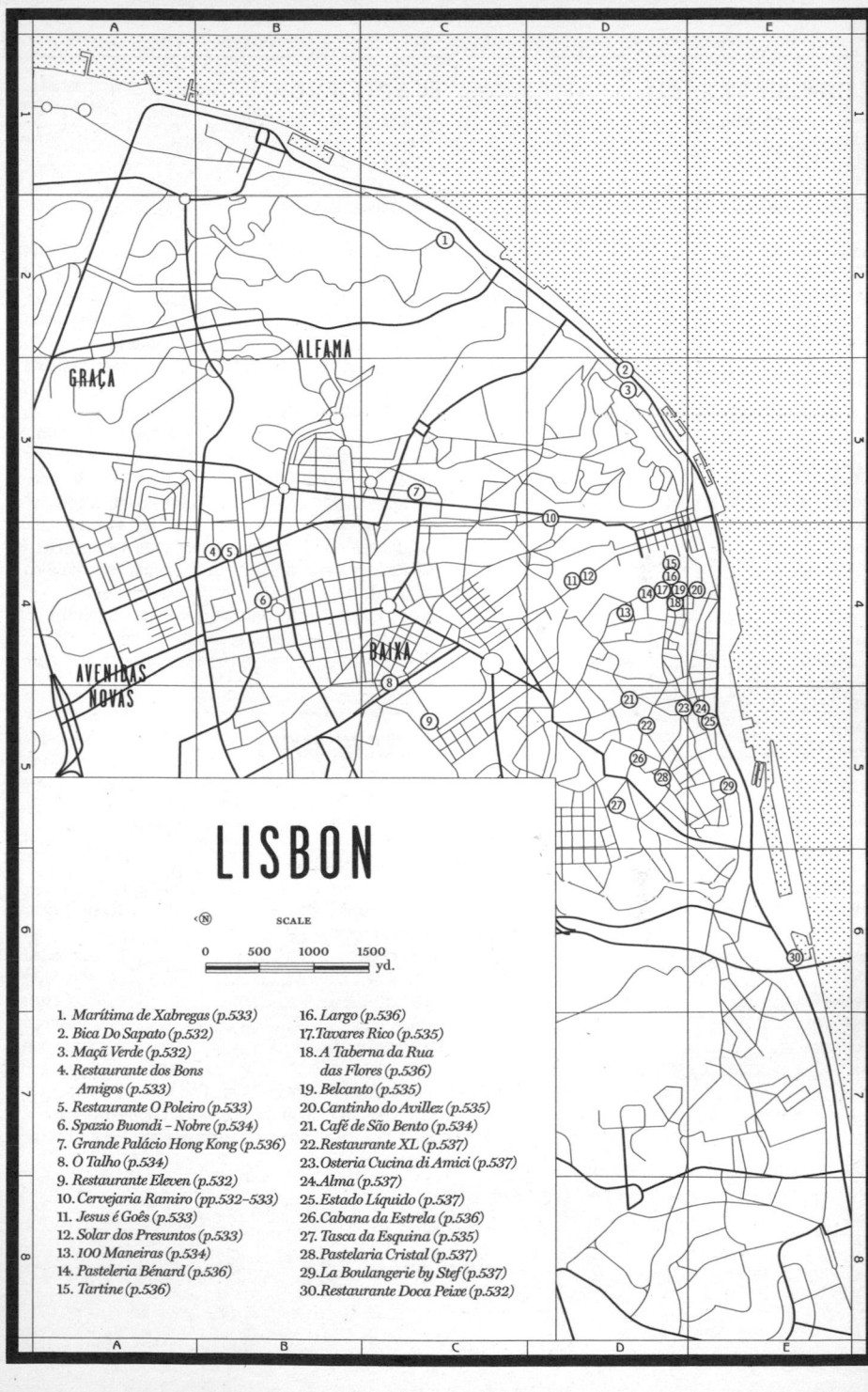

LISBON

⊙N SCALE

0   500   1000   1500
                    yd.

RESTAURANTE DOCA PEIXE

Recommended by
Miguel Castro e Silva

Doca de Santo Amaro
Alcântara
Lisbon 1350-353
+351 213973565
www.docapeixe.com

Opening hours	Open 7 days
Credit cards	Accepted
Price range	Affordable
Style	Casual
Cuisine	Seafood
Recommended for	Regular neighbourhood

'A good choice if you like fish.'—Miguel Castro e Silva

MAÇÃ VERDE

Recommended by
José Cordeiro

Rua dos Caminhos de Ferro 84
Alfama
Lisbon 1100-108
+351 218868780

Opening hours	Closed Sunday
Reservation policy	No
Credit cards	Accepted but not AMEX
Price range	Budget
Style	Casual
Cuisine	Portuguese
Recommended for	Bargain

RESTAURANTE ELEVEN

Recommended by
José Cordeiro

Amália Rodrigues Garden
Rua Marquês de Fronteira
Amoreiras
Lisbon 1070-051
+351 213862211
www.restauranteleven.com

Opening hours	Closed Sunday
Credit cards	Accepted
Price range	Expensive
Style	Smart casual
Cuisine	European
Recommended for	Regular neighbourhood

BICA DO SAPATO

Recommended by
José Cordeiro

Avenida Infante Dom Henrique
Avenidas Novas
Lisbon 1900-436
+351 218810320
www.bicadosapato.com

Opening hours	Open 7 days
Credit cards	Accepted
Price range	Affordable
Style	Smart casual
Cuisine	Modern Portuguese
Recommended for	Local favourite

On an old cobbled street in Lisbon's old town – alongside a tramway leading to the sea – is Bica Do Sapato, a warehouse-space restaurant, sushi bar and adjacent club co-owned by actor John Malkovich. The lofty, minimalist space and Euro-vogue decor is mirrored in the restaurant's libertarian take on Portuguese classics. The coast location means that the sushi is fresh and fish, rigntly, dominates the Bica Do Sapato menu. Conveniently located across the street, for post-dinner shape-throwing, is Club Lux where skilfully prepared cocktails and generously iced beverages are served to a young and undeniably hip crowd.

CERVEJARIA RAMIRO

Recommended by
José Avillez, Luís Baena,
Henrique Sá Pessoa,
Ljubomir Stanisic

Avenida Almirante Reis 1h
Avenidas Novas
Lisbon 1150-007
+351 218851024
www.cervejariaramiro.pt

Opening hours	Closed Monday
Reservation policy	No
Credit cards	Accepted
Price range	Affordable
Style	Casual
Cuisine	Seafood
Recommended for	Regular neighbourhood

'The seafood delights that you find here are 100 per cent fresh, as though the ocean was taking over the city. Simple, well prepared and satisfying.'—Luís Baena

Cervejaria (meaning 'beerhouse') downplays the charms of this downtown seafood specialist. Sure, the scruffy neighbourhood and the 1970s decor are not pulls, but beer certainly isn't the main reason that, for over fifty years, Lisboetas have been waiting in line here. That accolade goes to the superb seafood. Start with the house *pata negra* (cured ham), before getting stuck into some super-size Portuguese *carabineiros* (prawns/shrimp), *santola* (crab) and sea-salty *percebes* (gooseneck barnacles). Leave room for the famous *prego* steak sandwich. Wash it all down with local beer or a bottle of ice-cold Vinho Verde. Seasoned staff are quick – the queue (waiting line) moves fast – but always cheery.

JESUS É GOÊS

Recommended by
Ljubomir Stanisic

Rua de São José 23
Avenidas Novas
Lisbon 1150-321
+351 211545812

Opening hours	Closed Sunday
Credit cards	Not accepted
Price range	Affordable
Style	Casual
Cuisine	Indian-Pakistani
Recommended for	Bargain

'The chef of Jesus é Goês (the restaurant's name translates as "Jesus is Goan") learnt from his mother and from many years in the kitchens of Tentações de Goa, another restaurant that I really like.'
—Ljubomir Stanisic

MARÍTIMA DE XABREGAS

Recommended by
Miguel Castro e Silva,
Chakall

Rua da Manutenção 40
Avenidas Novas
Lisbon 1900-360
+351 218682235
restaurantemaritimadexabregas.com.pt

Opening hours	Closed Saturday
Credit cards	Accepted
Price range	Affordable
Style	Casual
Cuisine	Portuguese
Recommended for	Regular neighbourhood

'I regularly eat at this restaurant near my home. It's a tavern that serves authentic food and a fabulous plate of salt cod.'—Chakall

RESTAURANTE DOS BONS AMIGOS

Recommended by
Chakall

Rua Doutor Gama Barros 12
Avenidas Novas
Lisbon 1700-145
+351 218452680
www.restaurantebonsamigos.pt

Opening hours	Open 7 days
Credit cards	Accepted
Price range	Affordable
Style	Casual
Cuisine	Portuguese
Recommended for	Late night

'It's quiet and you can eat late there.'—Chakall

RESTAURANTE O POLEIRO

Recommended by
Chakall

Rua de Entrecampos 30a
Avenidas Novas
Lisbon 1700-158
+351 217976265
www.opoleiro.com

Opening hours	Closed Sunday
Credit cards	Accepted
Price range	Affordable
Style	Casual
Cuisine	Portuguese
Recommended for	Local favourite

'They serve typical Portuguese food, lovingly prepared, and it has a very welcoming atmosphere.'—Chakall

SOLAR DOS PRESUNTOS

Recommended by
Chakall, Vítor Sobral,
Ljubomir Stanisic

Rua das Portas de Santo Antão 150
Avenidas Novas
Lisbon 1150-269
+351 213424253
www.solardospresuntos.com

Opening hours	Closed Sunday
Credit cards	Accepted
Price range	Affordable
Style	Casual
Cuisine	Modern Portuguese
Recommended for	Local favourite

'Traditional Portuguese hospitality and gastronomy are taken to the highest level here. *Pataniscas* (cod fritters), *pastéis de bacalhau* (salt cod croquettes), *rissóis* (meat/fish croquettes) and roast goat are all on offer.'—Vítor Sobral

SPAZIO BUONDI – NOBRE

Recommended by
José Cordeiro

Avenida Sacadura Cabral 53b
Avenidas Novas
Lisbon 1000-273
+351 217970760
www.justanobre.pt

Opening hours	Open 7 days
Credit cards	Accepted
Price range	Affordable
Style	Casual
Cuisine	Portuguese
Recommended for	Local favourite

'They serve typical, proudly Portuguese cuisine. They really make the most of seasonal ingredients and, when in season, the lamprey eel and the goat are not to be missed.'—Luís Baena

O TALHO

Recommended by
Luís Baena,
José Cordeiro

Rua Carlos Testa 1b
Avenidas Novas
Lisbon 1050-046
+351 213154105
www.otalho.pt

Opening hours	Closed Sunday
Credit cards	Accepted
Price range	Affordable
Style	Casual
Cuisine	Steakhouse
Recommended for	Wish I'd opened

'Following his international training, young Chef Kiko decided to work primarily with the local Mirandesa beef and his recipes are masterful and creative.'
—Luís Baena

100 MANEIRAS

Recommended by
Henrique Sá Pessoa,
Vítor Sobral

Rua do Teixeira 35
Bairro Alto
Lisbon 1200-459
+351 910307575
www.restaurante100maneiras.com

Opening hours	Open 7 days
Credit cards	Accepted
Price range	Expensive
Style	Smart casual
Cuisine	Fusion
Recommended for	Wish I'd opened

'I like the surroundings, the excellent location, the bar menu and the concept.'—Henrique Sá Pessoa

CAFÉ DE SÃO BENTO

Recommended by
José Cordeiro,
Ljubomir Stanisic

Rua de São Bento 212
Bairro Alto
Lisbon 1200-821
+351 213952911
www.cafesaobento.com

Opening hours	Open 7 days
Credit cards	Accepted
Price range	Affordable
Style	Smart casual
Cuisine	Steakhouse
Recommended for	Late night

'A great Azorean steak will always sort you out after you've had a night out. It has an old-style English feel to it that is rather alien to me but which also makes me feel as though I'm abroad.'—Ljubomir Stanisic

With its typically Portuguese blue-and-white ceramic tiles, you might walk straight past this very modest-looking joint. But that would be a mistake, because they've been serving some of the best steak in the city here for over thirty years. A re-creation of a traditional Lisbon café, the low ceiling, wood-panelled bar and red leather bucket seats create a clubby feel, ideal for a late-night feast. They've improved on the nineteenth-century classic *Bife á Marrare* (steak in pepper sauce) by replacing rump with fillet (tenderloin) and tweaking and refining the sauce to piquant, creamy perfection.

TAVARES RICO
Rua da Misericórdia 37
Bairro Alto
Lisbon 1200-270
+351 213421112
www.restaurantetavares.net

Recommended by
José Cordeiro

Opening hours..Closed Sunday
Credit cards..Accepted
Price range...Expensive
Style...Formal
Cuisine...Modern European
Recommended for...High end

TASCA DA ESQUINA
Rua Domingos Sequeira 41c
Campo de Ourique
Lisbon 1350-119
+351 210993939
www.tascadaesquina.com

Recommended by
Luís Baena,
José Cordeiro,
Henrique Sá Pessoa,
Ljubomir Stanisic

Opening hours..Closed Sunday
Credit cards..Accepted
Price range...Affordable
Style..Smart casual
Cuisine..Portuguese
Recommended for.......................................Local favourite

'Chef Vítor Sobral manages to give classic Portuguese dishes a personal touch, remaining faithful to tradition but with a modern twist. He also incorporates new elements from his many travels, as the Portuguese have always done over centuries of their adventurous cuisine.'—Luís Baena

Chef Vítor Sobral masterminded Tasca da Esquina, a minimalistic corner restaurant that has raised the bar of tapas joints in the capital since its inception in 2007. Sobral is largely recognized as one of the pioneers of national *petiscos* – the Portuguese sibling of Spanish tapas – of which there are plenty to nibble on as you watch the world go by through the restaurant's vast glass frontage. Opt either for the *Hoje Há* (on the menu today) of daily-changing dishes or, if you want something more traditional, pick from the *Há Lá Carta*, a fixed menu of classics that seldom changes.

BELCANTO
Largo de São Carlos 10
Chiado
Lisbon 1200-410
+351 213420607
www.belcanto.pt

Recommended by
Miguel Castro e Silva, José
Cordeiro, Henrique Sá
Pessoa, Vítor Sobral

Opening hours...............................Closed Monday and Sunday
Credit cards..Accepted
Price range...Expensive
Style..Smart casual
Cuisine...Modern Portuguese
Recommended for...High end

'Good atmosphere, exquisite service and I like the imaginative detail of their creations.'
—Henrique Sá Pessoa

Chef José Avillez has taken over the space that formerly played host, in the form of a gentleman's club, to opera patrons and artists from the nearby Teatro Nacional de São Carlos. It has been designed to act as an arena in which this promising chef – who has worked under both Ferran Adrià and Alain Ducasse – can flourish. A formal and sophisticated makeover has retained some signs of the past, such as bookshelves, wood-panelling and grand lighting. Modern Portuguese cuisine, however, has replaced the pole dancers of old. The likes of twice-cooked leg of lamb, a 'dip into the sea' comprising sea bass and seaweed, and red mullet with 'Lisbon's sidewalk stones' come from a menu that aims – ambitiously – to tell stories and stir emotions.

CANTINHO DO AVILLEZ
Rua dos Duques de Bragança 7
Chiado
Lisbon 1200-162
+351 211992369
www.cantinhodoavillez.pt

Recommended by
José Cordeiro

Opening hours..Closed Sunday
Credit cards..Accepted
Price range...Affordable
Style..Smart casual
Cuisine...Modern Portuguese
Recommended for...............................Regular neighbourhood

LARGO

Recommended by
José Cordeiro

Rua Serpa Pinto 10a
Chiado
Lisbon 1200-445
+351 213477225
www.largo.pt

Opening hours	Open 7 days
Credit cards	Accepted
Price range	Affordable
Style	Casual
Cuisine	Modern Portuguese
Recommended for	Regular neighbourhood

PASTELARIA BÉNARD

Recommended by
José Avillez

Rua Garrett 104
Chiado
Lisbon 1200-205
+351 213473133

Opening hours	Closed Sunday
Reservation policy	No
Credit cards	Accepted
Price range	Budget
Style	Casual
Cuisine	Café-Bakery
Recommended for	Breakfast

'This pastry shop is in the Chiado neighbourhood, next door to my restaurants. It has a good terrace and is one of Lisbon's most renowned spots.'—José Avillez

A TABERNA DA RUA DAS FLORES

Recommended by
José Avillez

Rua das Flores 103
Chiado
Lisbon 1200-194
+351 213479418

Opening hours	Closed Sunday
Reservation policy	No
Credit cards	Not accepted
Price range	Affordable
Style	Casual
Cuisine	Portuguese
Recommended for	Local favourite

'It's a cosy, unique place that offers traditional cuisine.'
—José Avillez

TARTINE

Recommended by
Henrique Sá Pessoa

Rua Serpa Pinto 15a
Chiado
Lisbon 1200-443
+351 213429108
www.tartine.pt

Opening hours	Closed Sunday
Reservation policy	No
Credit cards	Accepted but not AMEX
Price range	Affordable
Style	Casual
Cuisine	Café-Bakery
Recommended for	Breakfast

'I like their freshly baked bread and the atmosphere.'
—Henrique Sá Pessoa

GRANDE PALÁCIO HONG KONG

Recommended by
José Avillez

Rua Pascoal de Melo 8a
Graça
Lisbon 1170-294
+351 213123349
www.restaurante-chines.com

Opening hours	Open 7 days
Credit cards	Accepted
Price range	Budget
Style	Casual
Cuisine	Chinese
Recommended for	Bargain

'It's my favourite Chinese restaurant in Lisbon.'
—José Avillez

CABANA DA ESTRELA

Recommended by
Miguel Castro e Silva

Rua Bela Vista à Lapa 18
Lapa
Lisbon 1200-612
+351 213971934

Opening hours	Closed Sunday
Credit cards	Not accepted
Price range	Affordable
Style	Casual
Cuisine	Portuguese
Recommended for	Bargain

'A little tavern that serves excellent traditional food.'
—Miguel Castro e Silva

PASTELARIA CRISTAL

Recommended by
Miguel Castro e Silva

Rua Buenos Aires 25a
Lapa
Lisbon 1200-622
+351 213961557
www.pastelariacristal.pt

Opening hours	Open 7 days
Credit cards	Not accepted
Price range	Budget
Style	Casual
Cuisine	Café-Bakery
Recommended for	Breakfast

'They sell high-quality products.'—Miguel Castro e Silva

RESTAURANTE XL

Recommended by
Miguel Castro e Silva

Calçada da Estrela 57–63
Lapa
Lisbon 1200-661
+351 213956118
www.xl.besttables.com

Opening hours	Closed Sunday
Credit cards	Accepted
Price range	Affordable
Style	Casual
Cuisine	Portuguese
Recommended for	Late night

'A restaurant with a very diverse clientele that serves lots of different dishes, not just the usual steaks.' —Miguel Castro e Silva

ALMA

Recommended by
José Cordeiro

Calçada Marquês de Abrantes 92
Santos
Lisbon 1200-720
+351 213963527
www.alma.co.pt

Opening hours	Closed Monday and Sunday
Credit cards	Accepted but not Diners
Price range	Affordable
Style	Smart casual
Cuisine	Modern Portuguese
Recommended for	Regular neighbourhood

LA BOULANGERIE BY STEF

Recommended by
Ljubomir Stanisic

Rua do Olival 46
Santos
Lisbon 1100-318
+351 936155742

Opening hours	Closed Monday
Credit cards	Not accepted
Price range	Affordable
Style	Casual
Cuisine	Breakfast-Brunch
Recommended for	Breakfast

'They make the best French croissants in Lisbon and the foie gras brunch is always an incentive to go. It's a good place to take children and read the papers.' —Ljubomir Stanisic

ESTADO LÍQUIDO

Recommended by
Henrique Sá Pessoa

Largo de Santos 5a
Santos
Lisbon 1200-808
+351 213972022
www.estadoliquido.com

Opening hours	Open 7 days
Credit cards	Accepted
Price range	Affordable
Style	Casual
Cuisine	Japanese
Recommended for	Late night

'Good sushi and friendly service!'—Henrique Sá Pessoa

OSTERIA CUCINA DI AMICI

Recommended by
Henrique Sá Pessoa

Rua das Madres 52–54
Santos
Lisbon 1200-710
+351 213960584
www.osteria.pt

Opening hours	Open 7 days
	Closed Tuesday
Credit cards	Not accepted
Price range	Affordable
Style	Casual
Cuisine	Italian
Recommended for	Bargain

'Very good food and good value for money.' —Henrique Sá Pessoa

'MY FAVOURITE PLACE TO DRINK KÖLSCH AND EAT A GREAT STEAK TARTARE IS THE BRAUHAUS AT THE FRÜH BREWERY.'
JOACHIM WISSLER P544

GERMANY

'The atmosphere's great. You all sit at the same long tables. The local beer flowing, the Bavarians singing. It's iconic of Munich. Just what I imagined before going there.'
OLIVER JAMES SHERIDAN P541

'CHEEKY AND ALWAYS OPEN FOR ANYTHING NEW.'
DIETMAR PRIEWE P542

'SOME OF THE BEST BAKERS IN TOWN.'
GERALD ZOGBAUM P543

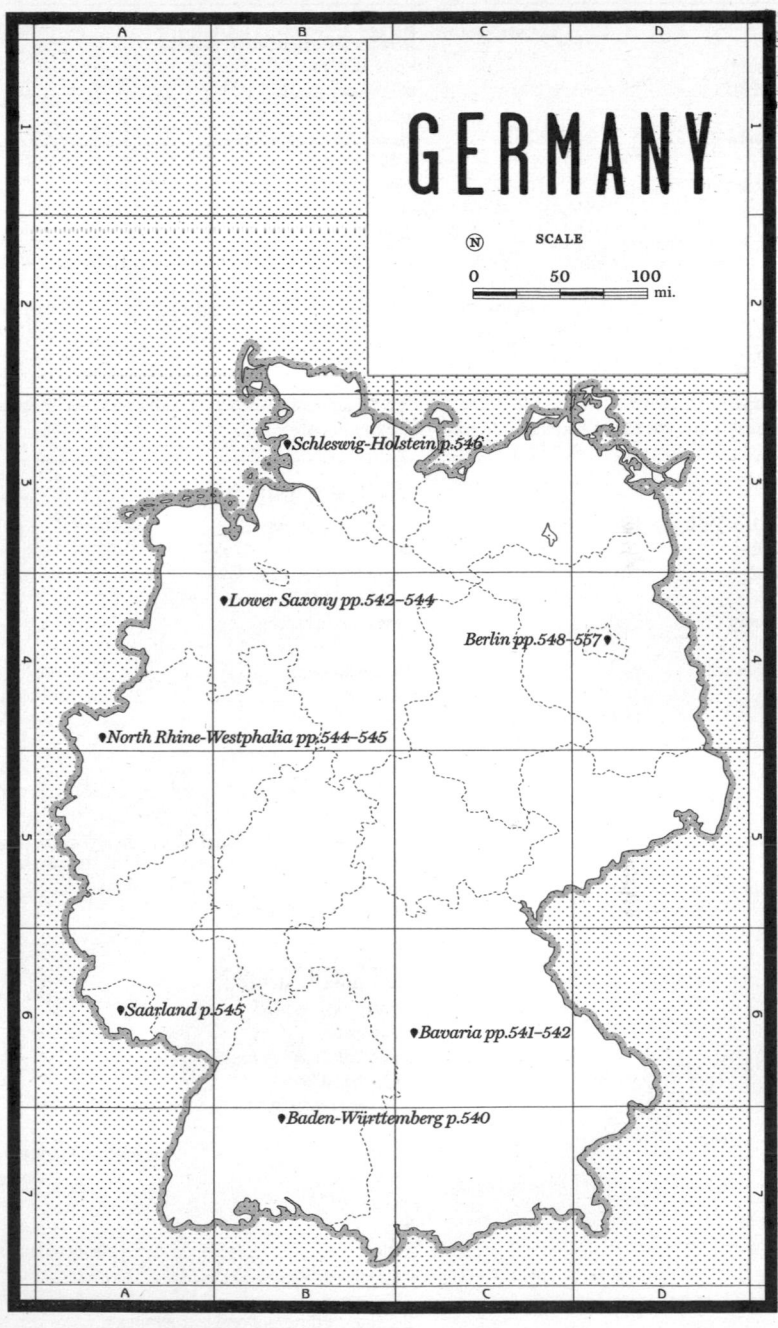

GERMANY

N

SCALE

0   50   100

mi.

♦ Schleswig-Holstein p.546

♦ Lower Saxony pp.542–544

Berlin pp.548–557 ♦

♦ North Rhine-Westphalia pp.544–545

♦ Saarland p.545

♦ Bavaria pp.541–542

♦ Baden-Württemberg p.540

SILBERBURG

Recommended by
Rolf Fliegauf

Hotel Traube Tonbach
Tonbachstrasse 237
Baiersbronn
Baden-Württemberg 72270
+49 74424920
www.traube-tonbach.de

Opening hours	Open 7 days
Credit cards	Accepted
Price range	Expensive
Style	Smart casual
Cuisine	German
Recommended for	Breakfast

'A really traditional hotel. Mostly I love the Silberburg breakfast. The quality and the choice is amazing so you can have an outstanding breakfast.'—Rolf Fliegauf

SCHWARZWALDSTUBE

Recommended by
Joachim Wissler

Hotel Traube Tonbach
Tonbachstrasse 237
Baiersbronn
Baden-Württemberg 72270
+49 7442492622
www.traube-tonbach.de

Opening hours	Closed Monday and Tuesday
Credit cards	Accepted
Price range	Expensive
Style	Smart casual
Cuisine	French
Recommended for	High End

'Celebrating a special occasion is not hard in Germany. Harald Wohlfahrt's Schwarzwaldstube is perfect.'
—Joachim Wissler

HOTEL RESTAURANT MÜHLE

Recommended by
Peter Knogl

Hotel Mühle
Mühlenstrasse 26
Binzen
Baden-Württemberg 79589
+49 76216072
www.muehle-binzen.de

Opening hours	Open 7 days
Credit cards	Accepted
Price range	Affordable
Style	Smart casual
Cuisine	German
Recommended for	Local favourite

'It is an authentic restaurant with good-quality food.'
—Peter Knogl

LA VILLA SCHMIDT

Recommended by
Oliver James Sheridan

Ludwig-Trick-Strasse 12
Kehl
Baden-Württemberg 77694
+49 7851886677
www.lavillakehl.com

Opening hours	Closed Monday
Credit cards	Accepted
Price range	Affordable
Style	Casual
Cuisine	German
Recommended for	Breakfast

'Great place for a brunch. I love to go there and chill out on my day off. The food is good and the Sunday roast is spot on. It's good value for money too.'
—Oliver James Sheridan

RESTAURANT AMADOR

Recommended by
Dietmar Priewe

Flosswörthstrasse 38
Mannheim
Baden-Württemberg 68199
+49 6218547496
www.restaurant-amador.de

Opening hours	Closed Monday and Sunday
Credit cards	Accepted
Price range	Expensive
Style	Formal
Cuisine	Modern European
Recommended for	High end

'Something different and extraordinary.'
—Dietmar Priewe

RESIDENZ HEINZ WINKLER

Recommended by
Heinz Beck

Kirchplatz 1
Aschau im Chiemgau
Bavaria 83229
+49 805217990
www.residenz-heinz-winkler.de

Opening hours	Open 7 days
Credit cards	Accepted
Price range	Expensive
Style	Formal
Cuisine	Modern German
Recommended for	Local favourite

'Unfortunately it's not possible for me to go there regularly but I love this place.'—Heinz Beck

FISCH POSEIDON

Recommended by
Armin Leitgeb

Westenriederstrasse 13
Munich
Bavaria 80331
+49 89299296
www.fisch-poseidon.de

Opening hours	Closed Sunday
Reservation policy	No
Credit cards	Accepted
Price range	Affordable
Style	Casual
Cuisine	Seafood
Recommended for	Breakfast

'It's a beautiful fish shop that serves some amazing specialities for breakfast like bouillabaisse, seafood, oysters...'—Armin Leitgeb

GEISEL'S VINOTHEK

Recommended by
Armin Leitgeb

Hotel Excelsior
Schützenstrasse 11
Munich
Bavaria 80335
+49 89551370
www.excelsior-hotel.de

Opening hours	Open 7 days
Credit cards	Accepted
Price range	Affordable
Style	Smart casual
Cuisine	Italian-Bavarian
Recommended for	Late night

'Later at night I want some ambience even for food. It's a hotspot for meeting people and has good food.' —Armin Leitgeb

GEISELS WERNECKHOF

Recommended by
Gerhard Wieser

Werneckstrasse 11
Munich
Bavaria 80802
+49 8938879568
www.geisels-werneckhof.de

Opening hours	Closed Monday and Sunday
Credit cards	Accepted
Price range	Expensive
Style	Smart casual
Cuisine	Asian-German
Recommended for	Worth the travel

HOFBRÄUHAUS

Recommended by
Oliver James Sheridan

Platzl 9
Munich
Bavaria 80331
+49 892901360
www.hofbraeuhaus.de

Opening hours	Open 7 days
Reservation policy	No
Credit cards	Accepted
Price range	Budget
Style	Casual
Cuisine	German
Recommended for	Worth the travel

'The atmosphere's great. You all sit at the same long tables. The local beer flowing, the Bavarians singing. It's just iconic of Munich. Just what I imagined before going there.'—Oliver James Sheridan

TANTRIS

Recommended by
Armin Leitgeb, Thomas
Rode Andersen

Johann-Fichte Strasse 7
Munich
Bavaria 80805
+49 893619590
www.tantris.de

Opening hours	Closed Monday and Sunday
Credit cards	Accepted
Price range	Expensive
Style	Smart casual
Cuisine	Modern European
Recommended for	High end

'The experience was mind-blowing. Not in terms of new thinking but in terms of consistency. Hans Haas cooks as he's been doing since the beginning of the 1990s and still does it brilliantly. And we're not talking twenty covers a night here. Cooking that precisely and with so much passion for more than 100 guests every night for so long is an amazing task. Warm, tasty food, seasoned with a watchmaker's precision and accompanied with perfect wine service by American sommelier Justin Leone who prepared an unforgettable experience for us.'—Thomas Rode Andersen

Property magnate Fritz Eichbauer could have bought a castle for what he invested in Tantris, his impossibly extravagant temple of fine dining and Pop art — 'but then where would I have gone to eat?' Back in 1971, Eichbauer's accountant doubtless balked at the expenditure lavished on stone carvings, orange carpet for the floor and walls, and avant-garde exposed concrete and steel for the exterior, but Tantris has become a fiercely protected icon of 1970s design. Chef Hans Haas's elegant modern European cuisine, honoured with two Michelin stars, is positively understated by comparison. Go for broke with the eight-course gourmet menu.

AKARI

Recommended by
Gerald Zogbaum

Papenhuder Strasse 67
Hamburg
Lower Saxony 22087
+49 402200803
www.restaurant-akari.de

Opening hours	Closed Tuesday
Credit cards	Not accepted
Price range	Affordable
Style	Casual
Cuisine	Japanese
Recommended for	Bargain

'A small, Japanese family-run restaurant in my neighbourhood. There are authentic Japanese dishes (agedashi tofu, soba noodles, udon, tempura) and the family is really nice. Unpretentious, simple Japanese.' —Gerald Zogbaum

BULLEREI

Recommended by
Dietmar Priewe,
Gerald Zogbaum

Lagerstrasse 34b
Hamburg
Lower Saxony 20357
+49 4033442110
www.bullerei.com

Opening hours	Open 7 days
Credit cards	Accepted
Price range	Affordable
Style	Casual
Cuisine	German
Recommended for	Wish I'd opened

'Cheeky and always open for anything new. Actually there's something for everybody.'—Dietmar Priewe

CARLS AN DER ELBPHILHARMONIE

Recommended by
Dietmar Priewe

Elbphilharmonie Hamburg
Am Kaiserkai 69
Hamburg
Lower Saxony 20457
+49 40300322400
www.carls-brasserie.de

Opening hours	Open 7 days
Credit cards	Accepted
Price range	Affordable
Style	Casual
Cuisine	French
Recommended for	Late night

'Great view of the harbour with a kind of French mood.' —Dietmar Priewe

ELBGOLD

Recommended by
Gerald Zogbaum

Mühlenkamp 6a
Hamburg
Lower Saxony 22303
+49 2027882223
www.elbgold.com

Opening hours	Open 7 days
Reservation policy	No
Credit cards	Not accepted
Price range	Budget
Style	Casual
Cuisine	Café
Recommended for	Breakfast

'This is actually a coffee roasters. You'll find the best croissants, bagels, wholemeal (whole-wheat) and sourdough breads from some of the best bakers in town, topped with fresh ingredients. The tea is also good.'—Gerald Zogbaum

ERIKA'S ECK

Recommended by
Gerald Zogbaum

Sternstrasse 98
Hamburg
Lower Saxony 20357
+49 40433545
www.erikas-eck.de

Opening hours	Closed Sunday
Credit cards	Not accepted
Price range	Budget
Style	Casual
Cuisine	German
Recommended for	Bargain

HAERLIN

Recommended by
Gerald Zogbaum

Fairmont Hotel Vier Jahreszeiten
Neuer Jungfernstieg 9
Hamburg
Lower Saxony 20354
+49 2034943310
www.restaurant-haerlin.de

Opening hours	Closed Monday and Sunday
Credit cards	Accepted
Price range	Expensive
Style	Smart casual
Cuisine	Modern Mediterranean
Recommended for	High end

'Chef Rüffer cooks modern food very well. Creative, light, high-quality, great aromatic cuisine. The restaurant is very enjoyable.'—Gerald Zogbaum

JIM BLOCK

Recommended by
Dietmar Priewe

Dammtorstrasse 29–32
Hamburg
Lower Saxony 20354
+49 04032088360
www.jim-block.de

Opening hours	Open 7 days
Reservation policy	No
Credit cards	Accepted
Price range	Budget
Style	Casual
Cuisine	Burgers
Recommended for	Bargain

'Just fresh and delicious.'—Dietmar Priewe

JUWELIER

Recommended by
Gerald Zogbaum

Weidenallee 27
Hamburg
Lower Saxony 20357
+49 4025481678
www.juwelier-restaurant.de

Opening hours	Open 7 days
Credit cards	Not accepted
Price range	Affordable
Style	Casual
Cuisine	German
Recommended for	Regular neighbourhood

'Simple, tasty dishes and a reasonably priced menu. It is charming, pleasant and delicious. There are a few tables outside the restaurant where you can sit and enjoy some people-watching in the summer.'
—Gerald Zogbaum

11A KÜCHE MIT GARTEN

Recommended by
Thomas Bühner

Am Küchengarten 11a
Hannover
Lower Saxony 30449
+49 5115901111
www.11a-restaurant.de

Opening hours	Open 7 days
Credit cards	Accepted
Price range	Budget
Style	Casual
Cuisine	Modern European
Recommended for	Bargain

'Located in a former public restroom in a park, it's down to earth and the food's really tasty – just fabulous.'—Thomas Bühner

SEESTEG

Recommended by
Thomas Bühner

Hotel Seesteg
Damenpfad 36a
Norderney
Lower Saxony 26548
+49 4932893635
www.seesteg-norderney.de

Opening hours	Open 7 days
Credit cards	Accepted
Price range	Affordable
Style	Smart casual
Cuisine	Modern European
Recommended for	Breakfast

'The sea view, the lounge music from the "Milch Bar" opposite and the friendly and efficient service make for a relaxing day ahead.'—Thomas Bühner

AQUA

Recommended by
Peter Goossens

The Ritz-Carlton Hotel
Parkstrasse 1
Wolfsburg
Lower Saxony 38440
+49 5361606056
www.restaurant-aqua.com

Opening hours	Closed Monday and Sunday
Reservation policy	No
Credit cards	Accepted
Price range	Expensive
Style	Formal
Cuisine	Modern European
Recommended for	Worth the travel

VENDÔME

Recommended by
Daniel Achilles,
Gerhard Wieser

Schloss Bensberg Hotel
Kadettenstrasse
Bergisch Gladbach
North Rhine-Westphalia 51429
+49 2204421941
www.schlossbensberg.com

Opening hours	Closed Monday and Tuesday
Credit cards	Accepted
Price range	Expensive
Style	Formal
Cuisine	Modern German
Recommended for	High end

'Joachim Wissler's cuisine is truly unique and the long journey to the restaurant is definitely worth it.'
—Daniel Achilles

Although the name might have originated from Paris's Place Vendôme, any French connection ends there. In fact, chef Joachim Wissler is, unlike many of his countrymen, more concerned with the 'treasures of our own neglected cuisine', so diners might well come across workaday German ingredients such as sauerkraut and *knäckebrot* (crispbread) in his 'New German' cooking. However, this being the three-star restaurant of a luxury hotel set in a baroque castle, regional culinary traditions are elevated by molecular cooking techniques and vibrant presentation, delivered, perhaps, in a twenty-one-course menu. Set in the hills above Cologne, the dining room, refurbished in 2007, is light-filled and more approachable than you'd imagine.

CÖLNER HOFBRÄU P. JOSEF FRÜH KG

Recommended by
Joachim Wissler

Am Hof 12–18
Cologne
North Rhine-Westphalia 50667
+49 2212613215
www.frueh.de

Opening hours	Open 7 days
Credit cards	Not accepted
Price range	Budget
Style	Casual
Cuisine	Bar-Bistro
Recommended for	Local favourite

'Our region is dominated by Kölsch beer breweries. Each brewery has its own brewery bar. My favourite place to drink Kölsch and eat a great steak tartare is the brauhaus at the Früh brewery.'—Joachim Wissler

FETTE KUH

Recommended by
Joachim Wissler

Bonner Strasse 43
Cologne
North Rhine-Westphalia 50677
+49 22137627775

Opening hours	Closed Tuesday
Reservation policy	No
Credit cards	Not accepted
Price range	Budget
Style	Casual
Cuisine	Burgers
Recommended for	Late night

'It's a burger bar where everything is freshly prepared with organic products sourced from the local area. They serve a good glass of wine too.'—Joachim Wissler

LE MOISSONNIER

Recommended by
Joachim Wissler

Krefelder Strasse 25
Cologne
North Rhine-Westphalia 50670
+49 221729479
www.lemoissonnier.de

Opening hours	Closed Monday and Sunday
Credit cards	Accepted
Price range	Expensive
Style	Smart casual
Cuisine	French
Recommended for	Regular neighbourhood

'The Moissonnier family have a restaurant with the charm of a Parisian bistro and the creativity and cuisine of a high-end restaurant. I feel at home there.'
—Joachim Wissler

POPPENBORG

Recommended by
Thomas Bühner

Brockhäger Strasse 9
Harsewinkel
North Rhine-Westphalia 33428
+49 52472241

Opening hours	Closed Wednesday
Credit cards	Accepted
Price range	Affordable
Style	Smart casual
Cuisine	Classic French
Recommended for	Local favourite

'The hosts are incredibly friendly and the chef is still young at heart, despite his sixty-five years. He's a master of classical cooking but always looks to the younger chefs for inspiration.'—Thomas Bühner

Heinz and Anne Poppenborg, husband-and-wife team behind this elegant, if outwardly unassuming, hotel-restaurant in Harsewinkel, have been running this assured operation since the early 1980s. Today the atmosphere is one of practised hospitality. Guests can choose between the haute cuisine French-inflected tasting menu served in the main restaurant (turbot with black truffle, curried Norway lobster), amid cut-glass mirrors and Art Deco touches, or — more popular with the locals — the more traditional comfort food served in the *Stübchen* (little room), where a plate of Wiener Schnitzel or wild garlic ravioli (in season) won't break the bank.

VICTOR'S

Recommended by
Cyril Molard

Victor's Residenz Hotel Schloss Berg
Schlossstrasse 27–29
Perl-Nenning
Saarland 66706
+49 686679118
www.victors-gourmet.de

Opening hours	Closed Monday and Tuesday
Credit cards	Accepted
Price range	Expensive
Style	Formal
Cuisine	Modern European
Recommended for	High end

'This three-Michelin-starred restaurant is exceptional, wonderful and beautiful.'—Cyril Molard

GÄSTEHAUS KLAUS ERFORT

Recommended by
Tim Raue,
Gerhard Wieser

Mainzer Strasse 95
Saarbrücken
Saarland 66121
+49 6819582682
www.gaestehaus-erfort.de

Opening hours	Closed Monday and Sunday
Credit cards	Accepted but not AMEX
Price range	Expensive
Style	Smart casual
Cuisine	French
Recommended for	Worth the travel

The rise of Klaus Erfort's haute dining venue has a pleasingly Germanic sense of precision: first star achieved not long after opening in 2002, second in 2004, and third in 2007. Never one to court publicity, he's usually to be spied in the glass-fronted kitchen of this white mansion — a rare beauty spot in an otherwise unlovely industrial town — toiling away on perfectly executed plates of classic French cuisine. Rather than bamboozling diners' senses, Erfort's cooking conjures intense flavours from just a handful of ingredients, offering a pure, elevated experience that's matched by endless park views from the terrace.

DORINT SÖL'RING HOF

Hotel Dorint Söl'ring Hof
Am Sandwall 1
Rantum
Schleswig-Holstein 25980
+49 4651836200
www.soelring-hof.de

Opening hours	Closed Monday
Credit cards	Accepted
Price range	Expensive
Style	Formal
Cuisine	Modern German
Recommended for	Local favourite

'Johannes King is an incredibly friendly and decent person. He pampers his guests in the open, country-style kitchen with a superb menu and perfect wines.' —Christian Lohse

CAFÉ WIEN

Strandstrasse 13
Westerland
Schleswig-Holstein 25980
+49 46515335
www.cafe-wien-sylt.de

Opening hours	Open 7 days
Credit cards	Accepted but not AMEX
Price range	Budget
Style	Casual
Cuisine	Café-Bakery
Recommended for	Breakfast

'Traditional and fun. A good mixture of old and new school.' —Dietmar Priewe

STRANDHAUS

Lornsenweg 13
Westerland
Schleswig-Holstein 25980
+49 46512998874
www.strandhaus-sylt.de

Opening hours	Open 7 days
Credit cards	Accepted
Price range	Budget
Style	Casual
Cuisine	European
Recommended for	Regular neighbourhood

'Simple, delicious, uncomplicated... just chilling in the middle of the dunes.' —Dietmar Priewe

'THE BEST CURRYWURST IN TOWN.'

THOMAS KURT P551

BERLIN

'A typical Berlin restaurant with a rustic atmosphere and good, traditional home cooking.'

DANIEL ACHILLES P554

'IT'S JUST A FEW STEPS AWAY FROM THE BUSY KÜRSTENDAMM. THEY SERVE GREAT FRESHLY BAKED BREAD AND AN AWESOME FLAMMKUCHEN.'

TIM RAUE P551

'Captures the atmosphere of fine dining in Berlin.'

GAL BEN MOSHE P551

BERLIN

<N>   SCALE

0   650   1300   1950
                              yd.

AROMA

Recommended by
Gal Ben Moshe

Kantstrasse 35
Charlottenburg
Berlin 10625
+49 3037591628

Opening hours	Open 7 days
Credit cards	Accepted
Price range	Budget
Style	Casual
Cuisine	Chinese
Recommended for	Late night

'Aroma is a very authentic Chinese restaurant that specializes in dim sum. They are open until 3.00 a.m. (which is quite rare in Berlin) and they seem to always be busy with a mostly Chinese clientele. I like their pork bao (steamed bun) and after a long, hard day of work I like to eat a few of these on my way home from the restaurant.'—Gal Ben Moshe

EL BORRIQUITO

Recommended by
Thomas Kurt

Wielandstrasse 6
Charlottenburg
Berlin 10625
+49 303129929
www.el-borriquito.de

Opening hours	Open 7 days
Credit cards	Accepted but not AMEX
Price range	Budget
Style	Casual
Cuisine	Spanish
Recommended for	Late night

'A restaurant where chefs and night owls meet after midnight. The wine list is good and the high-quality Spanish dishes are authentic. Plus, the atmosphere is great.'—Thomas Kurt

LA CRÉMERIE

Recommended by
Gal Ben Moshe

Windscheidstrasse 22
Charlottenburg
Berlin 10627
+49 3031809288

Opening hours	Closed Sunday
Reservation policy	No
Credit cards	Accepted but not AMEX
Price range	Affordable
Style	Casual
Cuisine	Café-Deli
Recommended for	Regular neighbourhood

'The owner personally imports cheese and wines from the top affineur in Paris. I like to go there for a cheese plate and a glass of wine and talk with the owner about cheese, wine and food in general. I'll also go there for private and business meetings because it has a charming intimate atmosphere, almost romantic, and the quality of the things he has is unbelievable.' —Gal Ben Moshe

PARIS BAR

Recommended by
Christian Lohse

Kantstrasse 152
Charlottenburg
Berlin 10623
+49 303138052
www.parisbar.net

Opening hours	Open 7 days
Credit cards	Accepted
Price range	Affordable
Style	Casual
Cuisine	Café-Bar
Recommended for	Wish I'd opened

'Paris Bar is an old West Berlin institution, an iconic bar with a terrific art collection and down-to-earth French cuisine.'—Christian Lohse

SETS

Recommended by
Tim Raue

Schlüterstrasse 36
Charlottenburg
Berlin 10629
+49 3056738797
www.setsberlin.de

Opening hours	Open 7 days
Credit cards	Accepted but only debit cards
Price range	Budget
Style	Casual
Cuisine	Café
Recommended for	Breakfast

'Just a few steps away from the busy Kurfürstendamm, they serve great freshly baked bread and an awesome *flammkuchen* (tarte flambée).'—Tim Raue

The name's an abbreviation: it stands for *sitzen, essen, trinken, schlafen* (sit, eat, drink, sleep), all things you can do at this brasserie, bed and breakfast. You could add 'w' for 'wait' – as you might well have to do if you pitch up on a Sunday, the busiest day of the week for this chic Charlottenburg breakfast destination off the Kurfürstendamm. Breakfast options vary from robust *Bauernfrühstück* (farmer's breakfast) to *Eier im Glas* (eggs in a glass) and muesli. The beautiful people that frequent SETs also rate it for cocktails, salads, cakes and creatively topped *Flammkuchen*.

CURRY 36

Recommended by
Thomas Kurt

Mehringdamm 36
Kreuzberg
Berlin 10961
+49 302517368
www.curry36.de

Opening hours	Open 7 days
Reservation policy	No
Credit cards	Not accepted
Price range	Budget
Style	Casual
Cuisine	Fast Food
Recommended for	Bargain

'The best currywurst in town.'—Thomas Kurt

In a city with countless stalls and even a museum dedicated to the Berlin-born cult of the currywurst – sliced pork sausage coated with spicy ketchup – this Imbiss (German street-food stall), opened back in 1980, has somehow managed to gain favour over much of the competition. Perhaps it's the convenient

location near Mehringdamm U-Bahn station or the long hours they keep – the late-night queues (waiting lines) include a diverse mix of tourists, taxi drivers and loyal locals. You'll always be asked *mit oder ohne*, with or without, referring to your sausage and its skin. Undecided? Order a mixed double to get one of each.

HARTMANNS

Recommended by
Gal Ben Moshe

Fichtestrasse 31
Kreuzberg
Berlin 10967
+49 3061201003
www.hartmanns-restaurant.de

Opening hours	Closed Sunday
Credit cards	Accepted
Price range	Expensive
Style	Smart casual
Cuisine	Modern German
Recommended for	High end

'I really like Stefan Hartmann's food – it's effortlessly tasty, elegant and smart. He really manages to combine German flavours with classical techniques and good flavour combinations. He captures the atmosphere of fine dining in Berlin.'—Gal Ben Moshe

HENNE

Recommended by
Daniel Achilles

Leuschnerdamm 25
Kreuzberg
Berlin 10999
+49 0306147730
www.henne-berlin.de

Opening hours	Closed Monday
Credit cards	Not accepted
Price range	Budget
Style	Casual
Cuisine	German
Recommended for	Local favourite

HORVÁTH

Recommended by
Christian Lohse

Paul-Lincke-Ufer 44a
Kreuzberg
Berlin 10999
+49 03061289992
www.restaurant-horvath.de

Opening hours	Closed Monday
Credit cards	Accepted
Price range	Expensive
Style	Smart casual
Cuisine	International
Recommended for	High end

'Sebastian Frank's food is closely connected to nature. Well-prepared produce and attentive and friendly service.'—Christian Lohse

RIO GRANDE

Recommended by
Thomas Kurt

May-Ayim-Ufer 9
Kreuzberg
Berlin 10997
+49 3061074981
www.riogrande-berlin.de

Opening hours	Open 7 days
Credit cards	Accepted
Price range	Affordable
Style	Casual
Cuisine	German
Recommended for	Wish I'd opened

'At Rio Grande guests are treated to local and seasonal produce – the foundation for the restaurant's modern, urban cuisine. The dishes are alpine (the owners are Austrian) and you can taste their culinary origin. Situated directly on the waterfront of the Spree, it's a very special place.'—Thomas Kurt

Rio Grande is as close as it gets to eating on the water without getting your feet wet. This contemporary Austrian all-day brasserie looks out over the River Spree and the Oberbaum Bridge through magnificent arched windows. Such a view makes an occasion of a casual breakfast, a bargain set lunch (three courses for under €10 [£8; $14]) or even a slice of apple strudel. The Rio Grande day begins with platters of Tyrolean ham, mountain cheese, salami, pickles and horseradish, before the lunch crowd arrives for schnitzel, goulash or Caesar salad. Three- and four-course menus with matching wines are available at dinnertime.

TIM RAUE

Recommended by
Konstantin Filippou

Rudi-Dutschke Strasse 26
Kreuzberg
Berlin 10969
+49 3025937930
www.tim-raue.com

Opening hours	Closed Monday and Sunday
Credit cards	Accepted
Price range	Expensive
Style	Smart casual
Cuisine	Modern Asian
Recommended for	Regular neighbourhood

'Urban, contemporary and unpretentious Michelin-starred cooking.'—Konstantin Filippou

VAN LOON RESTAURANTSCHIFFE

Recommended by
Thomas Kurt

Carl-Herz-Ufer 5
Kreuzberg
Berlin 10961
+49 306926293
www.vanloon.de

Opening hours	Open 7 days
Credit cards	Accepted but only debit cards
Price range	Budget
Style	Casual
Cuisine	German
Recommended for	Breakfast

'Van Loon is an old Dutch sailing barge that has been converted into a restaurant. Guests dine on the top deck while enjoying the vista across the Landwehr Canal. The menu includes fresh crab, home-pickled salmon and home-made jam. The breakfast is great and the service is attentive and friendly.'—Thomas Kurt

3 MINUTES SUR MER

Recommended by
Marco Müller

Torstrasse 167
Mitte
Berlin 10115
+49 3067302052
www.3minutessurmer.de

Opening hours	Open 7 days
Credit cards	Not accepted
Price range	Affordable
Style	Smart casual
Cuisine	French Bistro
Recommended for	Regular neighbourhood

BANDOL SUR MER

Torstrasse 167
Mitte
Berlin 10115
+49 3076302051

Opening hours	Open 7 days
Credit cards	Not accepted
Price range	Affordable
Style	Smart casual
Cuisine	French Bistro
Recommended for	Local favourite

CHICAGO WILLIAMS BBQ

Hannoversche Strasse 2
Mitte
Berlin 10115
+49 3028042422
www.chicagowilliamsbbq.de

Opening hours	Open 7 days
Credit cards	Not accepted
Price range	Budget
Style	Casual
Cuisine	Barbeque
Recommended for	Bargain

COCOLO RAMEN

Gipsstrasse 3
Mitte
Berlin 10119
+49 1723047584
www.oliverprestele.de

Opening hours	Open 7 days
Reservation policy	No
Credit cards	Not accepted
Price range	Budget
Style	Casual
Cuisine	Ramen Noodles
Recommended for	Regular neighbourhood

'When I take a stroll in the area around Hackescher Markt on my days off, I usually go to Cocolo Ramen to enjoy one of the best Japanese ramen-noodle soups in town. Everything is perfect about this place: the design is great, with simple wooden furniture and lovely lighting; you can watch the chefs at work; the food is always fresh and extremely tasty... What I like best about this restaurant is that it has a personal touch – something you don't often see in Berlin's Mitte.' —Daniel Achilles

COOKIES CREAM

Behrenstrasse 55
Mitte
Berlin 10117
+49 3027492940
www.cookiescream.com

Opening hours	Closed Monday and Sunday
Credit cards	Accepted
Price range	Affordable
Style	Casual
Cuisine	Vegetarian
Recommended for	Wish I'd opened

THE GRAND

Hirtenstrasse 4
Mitte
Berlin 10178
+49 302789099555
www.the-grand-berlin.com

Opening hours	Open 7 days
Credit cards	Accepted
Price range	Affordable
Style	Smart casual
Cuisine	Modern European
Recommended for	Local favourite

'A typical big-city restaurant and with Rainer Möckl as manager you are guaranteed an entertaining evening. The venue is impressively situated inside a school dating back to 1842. The Berlin Mitte crowd represents the new Berlin.'—Thomas Kurt

MONSIEUR VUONG

Recommended by
Daniel Achilles

Alte Schönhauser Strasse 46
Mitte
Berlin 10119
+49 3099296924
www.monsieurvuong.de

Opening hours	Closed Sunday
Reservation policy	No
Credit cards	Accepted but not AMEX
Price range	Budget
Style	Casual
Cuisine	Vietnamese
Recommended for	Wish I'd opened

'Considering the quality of the food, the atmosphere, and the location, the spring rolls here are a bargain. The restaurant is always busy and there's a delightful, relaxed atmosphere. From time to time you'll spot someone famous, but even if there aren't any stars around, there'll always be someone to look at. There are an incredible number of beautiful people here. I haven't found out yet how they manage to do that…'
—Daniel Achilles

A decade on, Mitte's bright young things still carry a torch for Monsieur Vuong. This cool Vietnamese canteen – no reservations taken – is never without a queue (waiting line), though the charming staff will soon have you seated. Credit to the concept: the compact menu with just a handful of regular dishes (exemplary pho, summer rolls, etc.) and a couple of daily specials makes for swift decision-making. Join one of the communal tables inside or out and discover freshly made *bo xao la lot* (beef with betel leaves) or *ga xoai* (chicken in mango and coconut sauce), accompanied by cold Saigon beer.

ROSENBURGER

Recommended by
Marco Müller

Brunnenstrasse 196
Mitte
Berlin 10119
+49 3024083037

Opening hours	Open 7 days
Reservation policy	No
Credit cards	Not accepted
Price range	Budget
Style	Casual
Cuisine	Burgers
Recommended for	Late night

YUMCHA HEROES

Recommended by
Daniel Achilles

Weinbergsweg 8
Mitte
Berlin 10119
+49 3076213035
www.yumchaheroes.de

Opening hours	Open 7 days
Credit cards	Accepted but not AMEX
Price range	Budget
Style	Casual
Cuisine	Chinese
Recommended for	Late night

'After a tiring day in the kitchen Yumcha Heroes is the perfect place to wind down. They serve small fried or steamed dumplings stuffed with meat, vegetables or seafood. I can watch the chefs skilfully filling the tiny dumplings, chat with the really lovely owner, or just enjoy the food and the relaxed atmosphere.'
—Daniel Achilles

ZUR LETZTEN INSTANZ

Recommended by
Daniel Achilles

Waisenstrasse 14–16
Mitte
Berlin 10179
+49 302425528
www.zurletzteninstanz.com

Opening hours	Open 7 days
Credit cards	Accepted
Price range	Affordable
Style	Casual
Cuisine	German
Recommended for	Local favourite

'A typical Berlin restaurant with a rustic atmosphere and good, traditional home cooking.'—Daniel Achilles

Since 1621, Berlin's oldest restaurant, Zur Letzten Instanz, has fed everyone from celebrities and visiting dignitaries to hungry tourists, apprehensive about their first Eisbein experience. This traditional hostelry, its medieval home restored after World War Two, is the place to come for all the hearty classics of the Berlin kitchen. Besides the mammoth pork knuckles, there are daily dishes such as *Königsberger Klopse* (veal and caper meatballs) and pike quenelles; while on the evening menu, there's also a roast of the day and smaller plates such as currywurst and pork belly with *mostarda*. Local beers are by the likes of Schultheiss and Berliner.

THE BIRD

Recommended by
Gal Ben Moshe

Am Falkplatz 5
Prenzlauer Berg
Berlin 10437
+49 3051053283
www.thebirdinberlin.com

Opening hours	Open 7 days
Credit cards	Not accepted
Price range	Budget
Style	Casual
Cuisine	Burgers
Recommended for	Local favourite

'I find it hard to think about someone I know who came to visit Berlin and didn't stop to have a burger at The Bird. OK, Berlin is probably not famed for its burgers, but to say that this is one of the top burger joints in Berlin would not be an exaggeration. Inside an English muffin sits 250 g (9 oz) of meaty joy made of German premium brisket. It is just a top burger, with top condiments and top hand-cut chips (fries). The atmosphere is priceless and sitting on the edge of the famous Mauerpark, it is the perfect place for a Sunday lunch after the *flohmarkt* (flea market). It is a real joy.'
—Gal Ben Moshe

Berliners have no beef with The Bird, a New York-style hangout touting burgers and USDA steak in the land of pork. Established in Prenzlauer Berg in 2006, The Bird nails the hip Brooklyn look with its exposed brick walls, scrawled blackboard menu, craft beers and squeezy bottles of ketchup. It bristles with New York 'tude' too: forget happy hour, here they do 'angry hour'. And as for paying by card? 'Fuhgeddaboutit'. Everything is made from scratch, from the pickles in your Ghetto Deluxe burger with American cheese, to the Coffee Chipotle Sauce with your BBQ Brisket Sandwich. Branches in Hamburg and Kreuzberg.

SAUVAGE

Recommended by
Thomas Rode Andersen

Winsstrasse 30
Prenzlauer Berg
Berlin 10405
+49 38100025
www.sauvageberlin.com

Opening hours	Closed Monday and Tuesday
Credit cards	Accepted but not AMEX
Price range	Affordable
Style	Casual
Cuisine	Paleo Cuisine
Recommended for	Wish I'd opened

'They're trying to do the full paleo monty.'
—Thomas Rode Andersen

The Leite-Poço brothers opened Sauvage, the world's first 'Paleo' restaurant, in Berlin in 2011. While the original branch, now renamed Paleothek, functions as a café and centre for all things Paleo, the newer Prenzlauer Berg branch advances the cause of caveman cooking with a gastronomic touch. Taking a cue from our prehistoric ancestors' diet, Sauvage eschews grains, gluten, refined sugar and dairy in favour of wild meat and fish, seasonal vegetables, nuts and seeds. This is no mere gimmick: beef ragout tart with goji berries and walnuts, and duck breast and confit leg with quince are produced with considerable flair.

DOLORES

Recommended by
Gal Ben Moshe

Bayreuther Strasse 36
Schöneberg
Berlin 10789
+49 54821590
www.dolores-online.de

Opening hours	Open 7 days
Reservation policy	No
Credit cards	Not accepted
Price range	Budget
Style	Casual
Cuisine	Mexican
Recommended for	Bargain

'A Mexican taqueria that can only be described as delicious. Really, really delicious. It is the fast food equivalent of fine dining, with the quality of ingredients and the attention to detail in preparations. You really can't go wrong there. The burrito costs €4.50 (£3.70; $6), which is pricy for Berlin fast food, but it is still a bargain for the amazing quality you get, and together with the tortilla chips (€2.50 [£2; $3.40], but worth every cent) they are worth a meal and half.'
—Gal Ben Moshe

HERMANNS EINKEHR

Recommended by
Christian Lohse

Emser Strasse 24
Schöneberg
Berlin 10719
+49 3088717475
www.hermannseinkehr.de

Opening hours	Closed Sunday
Credit cards	Not accepted
Price range	Affordable
Style	Casual
Cuisine	German
Recommended for	Local favourite

'Chef de cuisine Bernd Schwarz serves Swabian classics, which go well with the excellent draft beers on offer. The atmosphere is rustic and very peaceful!'
—Christian Lohse

Somewhat off the beaten track on a quiet and leafy strasse in Wilmersdorf is the cosy and welcoming Hermanns Einkehr. Specialists in the *Schwäbisch* cuisine of Baden-Württemberg, you'd expect to see *Spätzle* on the menu (in this case with Allgäu cheese), *Maultaschen* (large meat ravioli) and punchy Black Forest beers, but more of a surprise is the appearance of *ibérico* pork fillet and a wide-ranging wine list to complement the accomplished, albeit commendably inexpensive, comfort food. Traditional regional German cuisine with the occasional gourmet nod, served with a smile — it's no wonder local Berliners flock here every night.

HOT SPOT

Recommended by
Christian Lohse

Eisenzahnstrasse 66
Schöneberg
Berlin 10709
+49 03089006878
www.restaurant-hotspot.de

Opening hours	Open 7 days
Credit cards	Accepted but not AMEX
Price range	Affordable
Style	Casual
Cuisine	Chinese
Recommended for	Regular neighbourhood

'I would say it's one of the best Chinese restaurants in Berlin. The cuisine is very spicy Szechuan, the hosts are wonderful and the wine list is sensational.'
—Christian Lohse

5-CINCO

Recommended by
Alfredo Russo

Das Stue Hotel
Drakestrasse 1
Tiergarten
Berlin 10787
+49 303117220
www.5-cinco.com

Opening hours	Closed Monday and Sunday
Credit cards	Accepted
Price range	Expensive
Style	Smart casual
Cuisine	Modern Spanish
Recommended for	High end

'For the design.'—Alfredo Russo

CAFÉ EINSTEIN

Recommended by
Christian Lohse,
Marco Müller

Kurfürstenstrasse 58
Tiergarten
Berlin 10785
+49 3026391918
www.cafeeinstein.com

Opening hours	Open 7 days
Credit cards	Accepted
Price range	Affordable
Style	Casual
Cuisine	Café
Recommended for	Breakfast

'The ancestral home of the Einstein café chain is furnished in the style of a Viennese coffee house. The atmosphere is wonderful and the cakes, styles of bread and *Kaiserschmarrn* (Austrian pancake dessert) are a delight.'—Christian Lohse

Wild rumours still fly about regarding the old villa on the Kurfürstenstrasse that houses Café Einstein. True or false, the grand nineteenth-century property has certainly seen its fair share of history, having been a secret gambling club under Jewish ownership before the Nazis moved in. It re-emerged from its past in 1978 as the Berlin home of Austrian coffeehouse culture, complete with newspapers on sticks, schnitzel, strudel and creamy 'melange' coffee. Weekly-changing menus offer international breakfasts and elegant dishes such as whole artichoke, rack of lamb with herby gnocchi, and Wiener Tafelspitz. Its wood-panelled Lebensstern bar is upstairs.

FACIL

Recommended by
Hywel Jones,
Marco Müller

The Mandala Hotel
5F, Potsdamer Strasse 3
Tiergarten
Berlin 10785
+49 30590051234
www.facil.de

Opening hours	Closed Saturday and Sunday
Credit cards	Accepted
Price range	Expensive
Style	Formal
Cuisine	Modern European
Recommended for	Worth the travel

'A favourite of ours over the years during our visits to my wife's home town. Amazing terrace in the summer. Recently promoted to two stars.'—Hywel Jones

HUGOS

Recommended by
Thomas Kurt

InterContinental Berlin Hotel
Budapester Strasse 2
Tiergarten
Berlin 10787
+49 30260201263
www.hugos-restaurant.de

Opening hours	Closed Sunday
Credit cards	Accepted
Price range	Expensive
Style	Smart casual
Cuisine	Modern European
Recommended for	High end

'Michelin-starred chef Thomas Kammeier celebrates international haute cuisine that delights with local ingredients and authentic flavours. The maître d' Olaf Rode and his team provide a friendly yet discreet service. And the panoramic views across Berlin from the fourteenth floor are something very special indeed.' —Thomas Kurt

RESTAURANTSCHIFF PATIO

Recommended by
André Jaeger

Helgoländer Ufer
Kirchstrasse 13a
Tiergarten
Berlin 10557
+49 3040301700
www.patio-berlin.de

Opening hours	Closed Sunday
Credit cards	Accepted
Price range	Affordable
Style	Smart casual
Cuisine	European
Recommended for	Local favourite

'Located by the River Spree, this is a family-owned and operated restaurant which specializes in serving seasonal, local produce: spring chicken and fish fresh out of the lakes.'—André Jaeger

AUSTERIA BRASSERIE

Recommended by
Thomas Kurt

Hundekehlestrasse 33
Wilmersdorf
Berlin 14199
+49 308818461
www.austeria-brasserie.de

Opening hours	Open 7 days
Credit cards	Accepted
Price range	Affordable
Style	Smart casual
Cuisine	French Brasserie
Recommended for	Regular neighbourhood

'A classic restaurant that offers a fine selection of fresh seafood and high-quality meat. All the dishes are presented in an unpretentious way. In the summer months, guests can sit outside on the wonderful patio, which has a marvellous atmosphere. The wine list is extensive, they have an assorted range of cigars, and the service is very personal.'—Thomas Kurt

'An open
kitchen with an
open mind.'
IVO ADAM PP560–561

'A REAL
INSTITUTION
IN ZURICH.'
NENAD MLINAREVIC P567

SWITZERLAND

'Great cheese
fondue.'
HEIKO NIEDER P566

'In the middle of the
evening, the lights cut
out and somebody
has to put a coin in a
box for the electricity
to come back on. It's
totally funny and
everybody loves it.'
ROLF FLIEGAUF P563

'TRADITIONAL AND
LOCAL DISHES SUCH
AS CAPUNS, MALUNS
AND PIZOKEL. THIS
IS MY FAVOURITE
PLACE TO GO FOR
LOCAL FOOD.'
ANDREAS CAMINADA P561

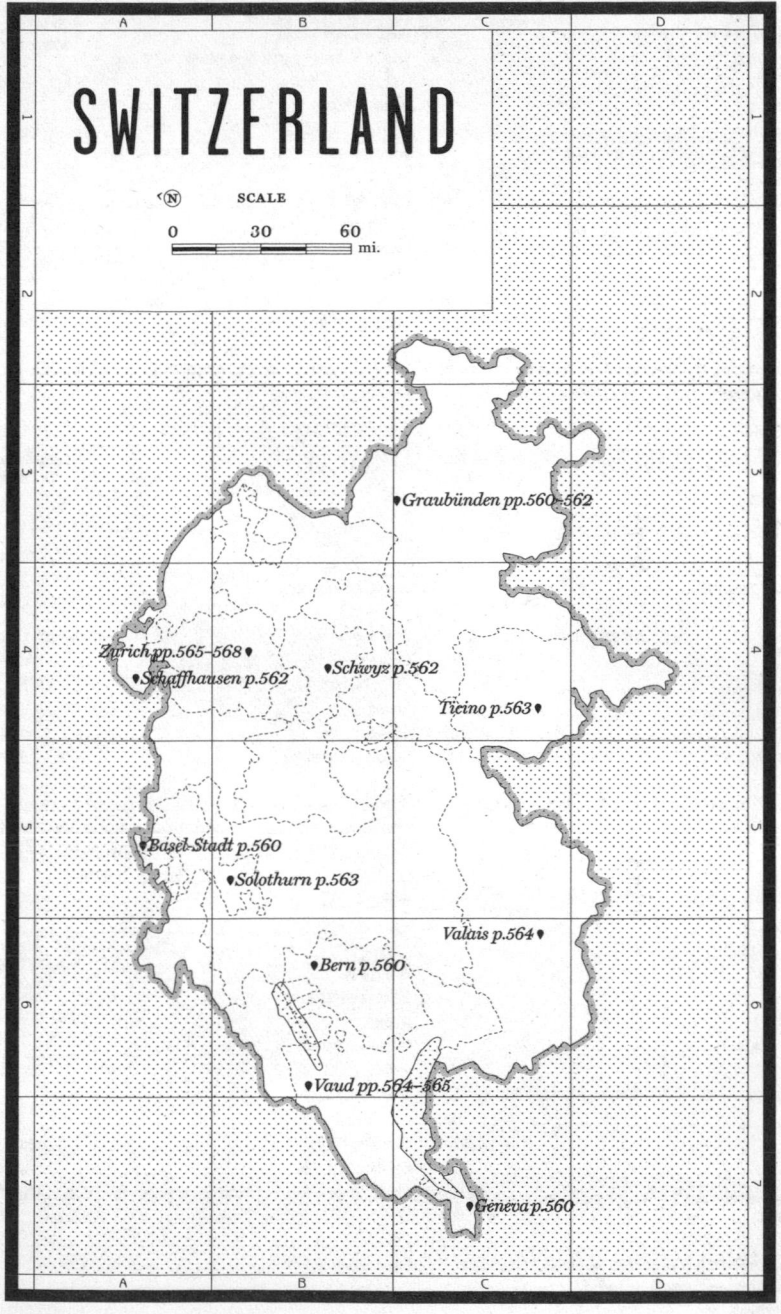

SWITZERLAND

N

SCALE

0   30   60 mi.

Graubünden pp.560–562

Zurich pp.565–568

Schaffhausen p.562

Schwyz p.562

Ticino p.563

Basel-Stadt p.560

Solothurn p.563

Valais p.564

Bern p.560

Vaud pp.564–565

Geneva p.560

MERCEDES SPOT

Recommended by
Peter Knogl

Schneidergasse 28
Basel
Basel-Stadt 4051
+41 612622000

Opening hours	Open 7 days
Reservation policy	No
Credit cards	Accepted
Price range	Budget
Style	Smart casual
Cuisine	Café-Bar
Recommended for	Breakfast

'I never have breakfast, but when I go for a coffee, I like the elegant atmosphere of this bar.'—Peter Knogl

RESTAURANT WIESENGARTEN

Recommended by
Peter Knogl

Weilstrasse 51
Riehen
Basel-Stadt 4125
+41 616412642
www.wiesengartenmusetti.ch

Opening hours	Closed Monday and Tuesday
Credit cards	Accepted
Price range	Expensive
Style	Smart casual
Cuisine	Italian
Recommended for	Regular neighbourhood

'A pleasant atmosphere and authentic Italian fare.'
—Peter Knogl

BASTA

Recommended by
Marcus Lindner

Bernerhof Gstaad
Promenade
Gstaad
Bern 3780
+41 337488844
www.bernerhof-gstaad.ch

Opening hours	Closed Monday and Sunday
Credit cards	Accepted
Price range	Affordable
Style	Casual
Cuisine	Italian
Recommended for	Bargain

'Fresh pasta, fresh fish and plates of appetizers. I like the choice of portions, small or large.'
—Marcus Lindner

WASSERNGRAT

Recommended by
Marcus Lindner

Top of Wasserngrat Mountain
Gstaad
Bern 3780
+41 337449622
www.wasserngrat.ch

Opening hours	Open 7 days
Credit cards	Accepted
Price range	Expensive
Style	Casual
Cuisine	Swiss
Recommended for	Worth the travel

'An impressive view to share with your friends.'
—Marcus Lindner

LE LEXIQUE

Recommended by
Benoît Violier

Rue de la Faucille 14
Geneva
Geneva 1201
+41 227333131
www.lelexique.ch

Opening hours	Closed Monday and Sunday
Credit cards	Accepted
Price range	Affordable
Style	Casual
Cuisine	French Bistro
Recommended for	Bargain

'Cyrille Montanier offers a cuisine based on simple cooking methods, appropriate seasoning and beautiful flavours. The place has a bistro atmosphere that I particularly appreciate for a lunch in town.'
—Benoît Violier

AIFACH

Recommended by
Ivo Adam

Unterseestrasse
Arosa
Graubünden 7050
+41 815330851
www.aifach.ch

Opening hours	Open 7 days
Credit cards	Accepted
Price range	Affordable
Style	Casual
Cuisine	Swiss
Recommended for	Worth the travel

'Located on the Mediterranean side of Switzerland, Aifach means "simple" in the dialect of the beautiful canton of Graubünden. An open kitchen with an open mind, just one menu, very easy going.'—Ivo Adam

B12

Recommended by
Andreas Caminada

Brandisstrasse 12
Chur
Graubünden 7000
+41 812505440
www.brandis12.ch

Opening hours	Closed Monday and Sunday
Credit cards	Accepted
Price range	Affordable
Style	Casual
Cuisine	Swiss
Recommended for	Breakfast

'Very nice bircher muesli and very good brioche, cakes and marmalades.'—Andreas Caminada

SCHLOSS SCHAUENSTEIN

Recommended by
Nenad Mlinarevic,
James Wilkins

Schlossgasse 1
Fürstenau
Graubünden 7414
+41 816321080
www.schauenstein.ch

Opening hours	Closed Monday and Tuesday
Credit cards	Accepted
Price range	Expensive
Style	Smart casual
Cuisine	Modern European
Recommended for	High end

'One of the best, if not *the* best meal I have ever had. The attention to detail on the plate was phenomenal.'
—James Wilkins

WALDHEIM

Recommended by
Andreas Caminada

Via Runs 1
Laax
Graubünden 7031
+41 819214151
www.restaurant-waldheim.ch

Opening hours	Closed Monday and Sunday
Credit cards	Accepted
Price range	Affordable
Style	Casual
Cuisine	Swiss
Recommended for	Regular neighbourhood

'Traditional and local dishes such as *capuns* (Spätzle dough, meat and cheese rolled in chard leaves), *maluns* (a buttery potato dish) and *pizokel* (Swiss pasta). This is my favourite place to go for local food.'
—Andreas Caminada

LA PADELLA

Recommended by
Reto Mathis

Hotel Donatz
Plazzet 15
Samedan
Graubünden 7503
+41 818524666
www.hoteldonatz.ch

Opening hours	Closed Monday
Credit cards	Accepted
Price range	Affordable
Style	Smart casual
Cuisine	Swiss
Recommended for	Regular neighbourhood

'The menu is seasonal and the food always very well cooked.'—Reto Mathis

THE PIZ

Recommended by
Reto Mathis

Hotel Piz St Moritz
Via dal Bagn 6
St Moritz
Graubünden 7500
+41 818321111
www.piz-stmoritz.ch

Opening hours	Open 7 days
Credit cards	Accepted
Price range	Affordable
Style	Casual
Cuisine	Pizza
Recommended for	Bargain

'They make a fierce Pizza Crudo with rocket (arugula).'
—Reto Mathis

PIZZERIA CARUSO

Recommended by
Rolf Fliegauf

Hotel Laudinella
Via Tegiatscha 17
St Moritz
Graubünden 7500
+41 818360000
www.laudinella.ch

Opening hours	Open 7 days
Credit cards	Accepted
Price range	Affordable
Style	Casual
Cuisine	Pizza
Recommended for	Late night

'You can get pizza until 1.00 a.m. and it's really good. It's a fun place to eat late at night.'—Rolf Fliegauf

RESTAURANT LES SAISONS

Recommended by
Marcus Lindner,
Reto Mathis

Kempinski Grand Hotel des Bains
Via Mezdi 27
St Moritz
Graubünden 7500
+41 818383081
www.kempinski.com

Opening hours	Open 7 days
Credit cards	Accepted
Price range	Expensive
Style	Smart casual
Cuisine	Modern European
Recommended for	Breakfast

'The offer is hands down the most versatile and best value in town.'—Reto Mathis

DA VITTORIO – ST MORITZ

Recommended by
Reto Mathis

Carlton Hotel
Via Johannes Badrutt 11
St Moritz
Graubünden 7500
+41 818367030
www.carlton-stmoritz.ch

Opening hours	Closed Monday and Sunday
Credit cards	Accepted
Price range	Expensive
Style	Smart casual
Cuisine	Italian
Recommended for	High end

'An offshoot of the Italian restaurant whose original property is in Bergamo, Italy, which has three Michelin stars. Run by three charismatic brothers, they make fantastic Italian food, especially tasty seafood and to-die-for *paccheri*.'—Reto Mathis

RESTAURANT GEMEINDEHAUS

Recommended by
André Jaeger

Hauptstrasse 78
Merishausen
Schaffhausen 8232
+41 526531131
www.gmeindhuus.ch

Opening hours	Open 7 days
Credit cards	Accepted
Price range	Affordable
Style	Casual
Cuisine	Swiss
Recommended for	Bargain

'It is the town hall of a small country village. Lovely old restaurant, nicely renovated. The tenant is a young chef who aims to offer the best cordon bleu cuisine and indeed he does. There is a selection of meats and cheeses for you to order. You can also choose from several Swiss specialities, all at incredibly attractive prices.'—André Jaeger

RESTAURANT ADELBODEN

Recommended by
André Jaeger

Schlagstrasse
Steinen
Schwyz 6422
+41 8321242
www.wiget-adelboden.ch

Opening hours	Closed Monday and Sunday
Credit cards	Accepted
Price range	Expensive
Style	Smart casual
Cuisine	Classic French
Recommended for	High end

'Run by couple Ruth and Franz Wiget, it is a true gem of a place, located on a mountain with a stunning view. The cuisine is modern, personalized and the service is superb. Franz Wiget was the Swiss Gault Millau Chef of the Year in 2012. His cuisine is very refined and based on the very best produce available in his region. He is very inventive and never fails to amaze his patrons with new and surprising flavours.'—André Jaeger

RATHSKELLER OLTEN

Recommended by
Reto Lampart

Klosterplatz 5
Olten
Solothurn 4600
+41 622122160
www.rathskeller-olten.ch

Opening hours	Closed Sunday
Credit cards	Accepted
Price range	Budget
Style	Casual
Cuisine	Swiss
Recommended for	Local favourite

'Rathskeller Olten is popularly known as *Chübel*, that is to say a place where people from all walks of life meet: old, young, poor and rich. It's a traditional pub and renowned for its home-made hamburgers.'
—Reto Lampart

RESTAURANT FELSENBURG

Recommended by
Reto Lampart

Aarauerstrasse 157
Olten
Solothurn 4600
+41 622962277

Opening hours	Open 7 days
Credit cards	Accepted
Price range	Affordable
Style	Casual
Cuisine	Italian
Recommended for	Regular neighbourhood

'Felsenburg is a long-established Italian restaurant with a good wine list. You can enjoy great pasta or a fine piece of meat from the grill. Fuss free and very good.'—Reto Lampart

EDEN ROC

Recommended by
Ivo Adam

Hotel Eden Roc
Via Albarelle 16
Ascona
Ticino 6612
+41 917857171
www.edenroc.ch

Opening hours	Open 7 days
Credit cards	Accepted
Price range	Expensive
Style	Formal
Cuisine	Modern European
Recommended for	Breakfast

'My standard breakfast consists of an espresso and a fresh orange juice, but the brunch at Eden Roc on Sunday morning is my once-in-a-while indulgence. No wishes unfulfilled.'—Ivo Adam

GROTTO BALDORIA

Recommended by
Ivo Adam,
Rolf Fliegauf

Via Sant'Omobono 9
Ascona
Ticino 6612
+41 917913298
www.grottobaldoria.ch

Opening hours	Open 7 days
Credit cards	Not accepted
Price range	Budget
Style	Casual
Cuisine	Italian
Recommended for	Local favourite

'It's a traditional Italian trattoria. You don't get a table on your own when you come in but sit between other people instead – I always have nice conversations with the other guests. There's also no menu, so you have to eat what you're given. In the middle of the evening, the lights cut out and somebody has to put a coin in a box for the electricity to come back on. It's totally funny and everybody loves it.'—Rolf Fliegauf

TENTAZIONI

Recommended by
Ivo Adam

Via Cantonale
Cavigliano
Ticino 6654
+41 917807071
www.ristorante-tentazioni.ch

Opening hours	Closed Monday
Credit cards	Accepted
Price range	Expensive
Style	Smart casual
Cuisine	Swiss
Recommended for	Regular neighbourhood

'It's small, it's cosy and Andreas Schwab serves dishes you will adore. Don't ask for the menu, ask Andreas to make what he thinks will suit you.'—Ivo Adam

CHEZ VRONY

Recommended by
Ivo Adam

Findeln
Zermatt
Valais 3920
+41 279672552
www.chezvrony.ch

Opening hours	Open 7 days
Credit cards	Accepted
Price range	Affordable
Style	Casual
Cuisine	Swiss
Recommended for	Breakfast

'Take a bit-more-than-one-hour walk up the hill from Zermatt centre and visit Vrony and her partner in an Alpine-chic environment. It's perfect for lunch, too.'
—Ivo Adam

LE PONT DE BRENT

Recommended by
Benoît Violier

Route de Blonay 4
Brent
Vaud 1817
+41 219645230
www.lepontdebrent.ch

Opening hours	Closed Monday and Sunday
Credit cards	Accepted but not Diners
Price range	Expensive
Style	Smart casual
Cuisine	Contemporary French
Recommended for	High end

'Stéphane Décotterd took over Le Pont de Brent four years ago, succeeding Gérard Rabaey with brio. This elegant establishment is particularly appropriate for special occasions and family outings. I appreciate the subtle and delicate cuisine of the chef.'—Benoît Violier

RESTAURANT DE L'HÔTEL DE VILLE

Recommended by
Reto Lampart,
Sebastien Lepinoy,
Heiko Nieder

Rue d'Yverdon 1
Crissier
Vaud 1023
+41 216340505
www.restaurantcrissier.com

Opening hours	Closed Monday and Sunday
Credit cards	Accepted
Price range	Expensive
Style	Formal
Cuisine	French
Recommended for	High end

'This three-Michelin-starred restaurant offers classic French food for serious foodies and gourmet-food lovers.'—Sebastien Lepinoy

Once the domain of legendary chef Frédy Girardet, Benoît Violier and wife Brigitte had a tough act to follow when they took over the reins in 2012. They've got off to an impeccable start, winning three Michelin stars within a year. Set on a hill outside Lausanne, this former town hall looks more like a picture-perfect wine château than a municipal building. Inside are the white-linen-covered, well-spaced tables and tasteful muted decor you might expect from a pillar of haute cuisine. Created by a team of twenty-two chefs, the dishes – such as purple Valais asparagus served cold with foie gras and truffles – are precise, detailed and exquisite.

RÔTISSERIE AU GAULOIS

Recommended by
Carlo Crisci

Route du Dîme 3
Croy
Vaud 1322
+41 244531489
www.au-gaulois.com

Opening hours	Closed Monday and Tuesday
Credit cards	Accepted
Price range	Expensive
Style	Smart casual
Cuisine	Rotisserie
Recommended for	Regular neighbourhood

'Quality food, nice setting and atmosphere.'
—Carlo Crisci

L'ÉCU VAUDOIS

Recommended by
Carlo Crisci

Place de la Dîme 1
Gollion
Vaud 1124
+41 218611241

Opening hours	Closed Saturday and Sunday
Credit cards	Accepted but not AMEX
Price range	Budget
Style	Casual
Cuisine	Swiss
Recommended for	Bargain

'For its simplicity, warm welcome and proximity.'
—Carlo Crisci

ANNE-SOPHIE PIC

Recommended by
Ivo Adam

Beau-Rivage Palace
Place du Port 17-19
Lausanne
Vaud 1000
+41 216133339
www.brp.ch

Opening hours	Closed Monday and Sunday
Credit cards	Accepted
Price range	Expensive
Style	Formal
Cuisine	French
Recommended for	High end

'Feminine cooking at its best. Great signature, very extroverted flavours, very perfectionist. A great chef!'
—Ivo Adam

LA BRASSERIE DU GRAND CHÊNE

Recommended by
Carlo Crisci

Lausanne Palace & Spa
Grand Chêne 7–9
Lausanne
Vaud 1002
+41 213313131
www.lausanne-palace.com

Opening hours	Open 7 days
Credit cards	Accepted
Price range	Expensive
Style	Smart casual
Cuisine	French Brasserie
Recommended for	Late night

'The hospitality is exceptional and the restaurant serves quality food.'—Carlo Crisci

AU CHAT NOIR

Recommended by
Benoît Violier

Rue Beau-Séjour 27
Lausanne
Vaud 1003
+41 213129585

Opening hours	Closed Saturday and Sunday
Credit cards	Accepted
Price range	Expensive
Style	Casual
Cuisine	French
Recommended for	Regular neighbourhood

'In the centre of Lausanne, this restaurant offers a cuisine based on local and fresh produce in a warm atmosphere. The walls are decorated with pictures of the many and illustrious artists who frequented it, reflecting the establishment's reputation. I particularly appreciate the chef's seasonal cuisine; it's generous and full of flavour.'—Benoît Violier

RESTAURANT DU JORAT

Recommended by
Carlo Crisci

Grand'Rue 16
Mézières
Vaud 1083
+41 219031128
www.restaurantdujorat.ch

Opening hours	Closed Monday and Sunday
Credit cards	Accepted
Price range	Expensive
Style	Smart casual
Cuisine	Eastern French
Recommended for	Regular neighbourhood

'Nice setting and good-quality food.'—Carlo Crisci

AUBERGE DE LA VEVEYSE

Recommended by
Carlo Crisci

Route de Châtel-Saint-Denis 212
St-Légier-La Chiésaz
Vaud 1806
+41 219436760
www.auberge-de-la-veveyse.ch

Opening hours	Closed Monday and Sunday
Credit cards	Accepted
Price range	Expensive
Style	Smart casual
Cuisine	French
Recommended for	Regular neighbourhood

'Nice atmosphere and family feel.'—Carlo Crisci

DÜBI IMBISS

Recommended by
Heiko Nieder

Dübendorf Bahnhof
Bettlistrasse 1
Dübendorf
Zurich 8600
+41 765064526

Opening hours	Open 7 days
Credit cards	Accepted
Price range	Budget
Style	Casual
Cuisine	Turkish
Recommended for	Bargain

'Huge, delicious kebabs at a sensational price compared with other kebab shops in Switzerland.'—Heiko Nieder

AH-HUA

Recommended by
Heiko Nieder

Ankerstrasse 110
Zurich 8004
+41 442403888
www.ah-hua.ch

Opening hours	Closed Monday
Credit cards	Accepted
Price range	Affordable
Style	Casual
Cuisine	Thai
Recommended for	Regular neighbourhood

'Very good, authentic Asian food in a relaxed atmosphere.'—Heiko Nieder

CHÄSALP

Recommended by
Heiko Nieder

Tobelhofstrasse 236
Zurich 8044
+41 442607575
www.chaesalp.ch

Opening hours	Open 7 days
Credit cards	Accepted
Price range	Affordable
Style	Casual
Cuisine	Swiss
Recommended for	Local favourite

'Great cheese fondue, real local flavours and a cosy atmosphere. A good place to spend time with friends and family.'—Heiko Nieder

In a semi-rural setting on the outskirts of the city, this converted barn with its stone walls, wooden beams and simple wooden tables and chairs is the place to try the great Swiss tradition of fondue. They're not saying what's in the house fondue, made from a generations-old recipe, but it's bound to contain the local Gruyère cheese. But why stop there when there are versions made with Champagne, truffles or Calvados? The long menu also includes more than a dozen macaroni dishes, including veal, morels and cream. In the summer grab a table outside overlooking the neighbouring fields and woods.

CONFISERIE SPRÜNGLI

Recommended by
Nenad Mlinarevic

1F, Bahnhofstrasse 21
Zurich 8022
+41 442244616
www.spruengli.ch

Opening hours	Open 7 days
Credit cards	Accepted
Price range	Affordable
Style	Smart casual
Cuisine	Swiss
Recommended for	Breakfast

'The best traditional Swiss food and an interesting mixture of guests. It has been owned by the same family for many years.'—Nenad Mlinarevic

GLOBUS

Recommended by
Marcus Lindner

Globus Zurich Bellevue
Theaterstrasse 12
Zurich 8001
+41 585786767
www.globus.ch

Opening hours	Open 7 days
Reservation policy	No
Credit cards	Accepted
Price range	Affordable
Style	Casual
Cuisine	International
Recommended for	Wish I'd opened

'There's always a lot of people; it is a place to meet for fine dining at any time of the day.'—Marcus Lindner

HUMMER- & AUSTERNBAR

Recommended by
André Jaeger

Bahnhofstrasse 87
Zurich
Zurich 8001
+41 442277621
www.hummerbar.ch

Opening hours	Open 7 days
Credit cards	Accepted
Price range	Expensive
Style	Smart casual
Cuisine	French Seafood
Recommended for	Late night

'A classic restaurant with a young French chef, Filipe Alloin. I can have a wonderful meal, light and enhancing, even late in the evening.'—André Jaeger

KAFISCHNAPS

Recommended by
Heiko Nieder

Kornhausstrasse 57
Zurich 8037
+41 435388116
www.kafischnaps.ch

Opening hours	Open 7 days
Credit cards	Accepted
Price range	Affordable
Style	Casual
Cuisine	Café-Bar
Recommended for	Breakfast

'Great breakfast, trendy location, tasty coffee!'
—Heiko Nieder

KRONENHALLE

Recommended by
Andreas Caminada,
Nenad Mlinarevic

Rämistrasse 4
Zurich 8001
+41 442629900
www.kronenhalle.ch

Opening hours	Open 7 days
Credit cards	Accepted
Price range	Expensive
Style	Formal
Cuisine	Swiss
Recommended for	Local favourite

'It's a real institution in Zurich and has a renowned, very stylish bar with an arty atmosphere. Cosmopolitan guests go there for specific dishes that have been on the menu forever.'—Nenad Mlinarevic

Housed in a stunning Biedermeier-style building, Kronenhalle is one of Zurich's most famous restaurants. The interior's dark wood-panelled walls display an art collection that includes works by Klee, Chagall and Matisse. Choose between the brasserie, Swiss Gallery or the Chagall Room. Chef Peter Schärer's market-driven menus cover everything from classics such as herring with cream and sliced calf's liver with onions and rösti, to seasonal specialities such as veal filet mignons with fresh morels and white asparagus. Visit the cosy bar with its green leather sofas, mahogany wall panelling and polished parquet floor for a Ladykiller: gin, Cointreau, apricot brandy, pineapple juice and passion fruit juice.

MIRACLE

Recommended by
Nenad Mlinarevic

Fröhlichstrasse 37
Zurich 8008
+41 443822005
www.miracle-seefeld.ch

Opening hours	Open 7 days
Credit cards	Accepted
Price range	Affordable
Style	Casual
Cuisine	Italian
Recommended for	Bargain

'The best pizza in town and great value for money!'
—Nenad Mlinarevic

NAGASUI

Recommended by
Nenad Mlinarevic

Selnaustrasse 16
Zurich 8001
+41 442883888
www.nagasui.ch

Opening hours	Closed Sunday
Credit cards	Accepted
Price range	Affordable
Style	Smart casual
Cuisine	Asian
Recommended for	Regular neighbourhood

'Authentic, very tasty Asian cuisine.'—Nenad Mlinarevic

OLD CROW

Recommended by
Marcus Lindner

Schwanengasse 4
Zurich 8001
+41 432335335
www.oldcrow.ch

Opening hours	Closed Sunday
Reservation policy	No
Credit cards	Accepted
Price range	Budget
Style	Casual
Cuisine	Bar Snacks
Recommended for	Late night

'They serve nearly 100 whisky varieties and the atmosphere is lively.'—Marcus Lindner

THE RESTAURANT

Recommended by
Marcus Lindner

The Dolder Grand
Kurhausstrasse 65
Zurich 8032
+41 444566000
www.thedoldergrand.com

Opening hours	Closed Monday and Sunday
Credit cards	Accepted
Price range	Expensive
Style	Formal
Cuisine	Modern European
Recommended for	High end

'Fanciful and fantastic food in a great restaurant.'
—Marcus Lindner

RESTAURANT CAMINO

Recommended by
Reto Lampart

Freischützgasse 4
Zurich 8004
+41 442402121
www.restaurant-camino.ch

Opening hours	Closed Sunday
Credit cards	Accepted
Price range	Affordable
Style	Casual
Cuisine	Mediterranean
Recommended for	Regular neighbourhood

'Restaurant Camino is a young establishment that uses fresh, market-sourced ingredients. It has a very good wine list and two charming hosts, a mother and her daughter.'—Reto Lampart

SALA OF TOKYO

Recommended by
André Jaeger

Limmatstrasse 29
Zurich 8005
+41 442715290
www.sala-of-tokyo.ch

Opening hours	Closed Monday and Sunday
Credit cards	Accepted
Price range	Expensive
Style	Smart casual
Cuisine	Japanese
Recommended for	Regular neighbourhood

'For many years it's been the most authentic Japanese restaurant in the area. It has very high standards and the service is superb and friendly.'—André Jaeger

TIBITS

Recommended by
Andreas Caminada

Seefeldstrasse 2
Zurich 8008
+41 442603222
www.tibits.ch

Opening hours	Open 7 days
Reservation policy	No
Credit cards	Accepted
Price range	Affordable
Style	Casual
Cuisine	Vegetarian
Recommended for	Late night

'A vegetarian restaurant open until midnight with great salads and vegetables.'—Andreas Caminada

WIRTSCHAFT NEUMARKT

Recommended by
Marcus Lindner

Neumarkt 5
Zurich 8001
+41 442527939
www.wirtschaft-neumarkt.ch

Opening hours	Closed Sunday
Credit cards	Accepted
Price range	Affordable
Style	Casual
Cuisine	Swiss
Recommended for	Local favourite

'Friendly service and local food at its best.'
—Marcus Lindner

'A shack on the beach in Liguria serving only fish and lasagnette al pesto.'

RUTH ROGERS P585

'THE BEST PIZZA I HAVE EVER TASTED.'

CHRISTIAN F. PUGLISI P573

ITALY

'RAZOR-SHARP CUISINE WITH THE WHOLE REGION LAID OUT ON A PLATE.'

EMMANUEL RENAUT P591

'TRUE COUNTRY DINING IN SICILY.'

CARMELO CHIARAMONTE P597

'IF IT WAS THE LAST MEAL OF YOUR LIFE, YOU WOULD DIE HAPPY.'

ROBIN GILL P574

'THE BEST SEAFOOD IN THE WHOLE OF ITALY, LIGHT AND FULL OF FLAVOUR.'

IGLES CORELLI P576

Alto Adige pp.572–573 ♥

♥ Trentino p.597

Friuli-Venezia Giulia pp.579–580 ♥

Lombardy pp.585–589 ♥

♥ Veneto pp.599–601

♥ Piedmont pp.591–594

♥ Emilia Romagna pp.575–579

♥ Liguria p.585

Tuscany pp.598–599 ♥

♥ Marche pp.590–591 ♥

♥ Abruzzo p.572

Lazio pp.580–585 ♥

♥ Puglia p.595

Campania pp.573–575 ♥

Calabria p.573 ♥

Sicily pp.595–597 ♥

ITALY

$\hat{N}$ SCALE

0   80   160
mi.

L'ANGOLO D'ABRUZZO
Recommended by
Giulio Terrinoni
Piazza Aldo Moro 8–9
Carsoli
L'Aquila
Abruzzo 67061
+39 0863997429
www.langolodiabruzzo.it

Opening hours	Closed Monday
Credit cards	Accepted
Price range	Affordable
Style	Smart casual
Cuisine	Abruzzese
Recommended for	Wish I'd opened

'A classic restaurant, excellent raw materials, great wine cellar and being a barbeque enthusiast, I love the open barbeque in the middle of the room.'
—Giulio Terrinoni

RISTORANTE REALE
Recommended by
Mauro Uliassi
Contrada Santa Liberata
Castel di Sangro
L'Aquila
Abruzzo 67031
+39 086469382
www.ristorantereale.com

Opening hours	Closed Monday and Tuesday
Credit cards	Accepted
Price range	Expensive
Style	Smart casual
Cuisine	Modern Italian
Recommended for	Wish I'd opened

'Niko Romito is an example of entrepreneurship and business in the restaurant industry.'—Mauro Uliassi

TAVERNA DE LI CALDORA
Recommended by
Niko Romito
Piazza Umberto I 13
Pacentro
L'Aquila
Abruzzo 67030
+39 086441139
www.tavernacaldora.it

Opening hours	Closed Tuesday
Credit cards	Accepted
Price range	Affordable
Style	Casual
Cuisine	Abruzzese
Recommended for	Local favourite

'This place represents my region because it has always chosen, worked with and offered the great raw materials of Abruzzo.'—Niko Romito

RISTORANTE AL METRÒ
Recommended by
Niko Romito
Via Ferdinando Magellano 35
San Salvo Marina
Chieti
Abruzzo 66050
+39 0873803428
www.ristorantealmetro.it

Opening hours	Closed Monday
Credit cards	Accepted
Price range	Affordable
Style	Casual
Cuisine	Italian seafood
Recommended for	Regular neighbourhood

TAVERNA 58
Recommended by
Niko Romito
Corso Gabriele Manthonè 46
Pescara
Abruzzo 65127
+39 085690724
www.taverna58.it

Opening hours	Closed Sunday
Credit cards	Accepted
Price range	Budget
Style	Casual
Cuisine	Italian
Recommended for	Bargain

'In twenty years of activity, this place has always been synonymous with high quality. A menu of three dishes does not exceed €20 (£16.50; $28).'—Niko Romito

RAFFL KELLERLOUNGE
Recommended by
Gerhard Wieser
Piazza Duomo 32
Merano
Bolzano
Alto Adige 39012
+39 0473232825
www.rafflkeller.it

Opening hours	Closed Monday and Sunday
Reservation policy	No
Credit cards	Accepted
Price range	Affordable
Style	Casual
Cuisine	Bar-Small plates
Recommended for	Local favourite

ROSSINI COCKTAIL BAR

Recommended by
Gerhard Wieser

Freiheitsstrasse 19
Merano
Bolzano
Alto Adige 39012
+39 0473491085
www.rossini-bar.it

Opening hours	Open 7 days
Reservation policy	No
Credit cards	Accepted
Price range	Affordable
Style	Casual
Cuisine	Bar Snacks
Recommended for	Late night

SKETCH

Recommended by
Gerhard Wieser

Passerpromenade 40
Merano
Bolzano
Alto Adige 39012
+39 0473211800
www.sketch.bz

Opening hours	Closed Monday
Credit cards	Accepted
Price range	Budget
Style	Casual
Cuisine	Café-Bar
Recommended for	Bargain

LIMONAIA

Recommended by
Davide Oldani

Hotel Rosa Alpina
Strada Micurà de Ru 20
San Cassiano
Bolzano
Alto Adige 39030
+39 0471849500
www.rosalpina.it

Opening hours	Open 7 days
Credit cards	Accepted
Price range	Affordable
Style	Smart casual
Cuisine	Breakfast
Recommended for	Breakfast

'My benchmark for breakfast in the Dolomites is the
restaurant in the Hotel Rosa Alpina because of the
purity of the products and above all the importance
given to local produce.'—Davide Oldani

LAPPRODO

Recommended by
Francesco Mazzei

Hotel Cala del Porto
Via Roma 22
Vibo Marina
Vibo Valentia
Calabria 89900
+39 0963577763
www.lapprodo.com

Opening hours	Open 7 days
Credit cards	Accepted
Price range	Expensive
Style	Smart casual
Cuisine	Seafood
Recommended for	Worth the travel

PEPE IN GRANI

Recommended by
Christian F. Puglisi

Vicolo San Giovanni Battista 3
Caiazzo
Caserta
Campania 81013
+39 0823862718
www.pepeingrani.it

Opening hours	Closed Monday
Credit cards	Accepted but not AMEX
Price range	Budget
Style	Casual
Cuisine	Pizza
Recommended for	Worth the travel

'The best pizza I have ever tasted.'—Christian F. Puglisi

L'OLIVO

Recommended by
Alexandre Gauthier

Capri Palace
Via Capodimonte 14
Anacapri
Naples
Campania 80071
+39 0819780111
www.capripalace.com

Opening hours	Open 7 days
Credit cards	Accepted
Price range	Expensive
Style	Smart casual
Cuisine	Modern Italian
Recommended for	Worth the travel

LA CONCA DEL SOGNO

Via San Marciano 9
Massa Lubrense
Naples
Campania 80061
+39 0818081036
www.concadelsogno.it

Opening hours	Open 7 days
Credit cards	Accepted
Price range	Affordable
Style	Casual
Cuisine	Seafood
Recommended for	Wish I'd opened

'Perched on a cliff and only accessible by boat, it has a cave with natural sea water keeping all the shellfish alive. The food is simple southern Italian cooking but the restaurant makes you feel that if it was the last meal of your life, you would die happy.'—Robin Gill

LO SCOGLIO DA TOMMASO

Lo Scoglio Hotel
Piazze delle Sirene 15
Massa Lubrense
Naples
Campania 80061
+39 0818081026
www.hotelloscoglio.com

Opening hours	Open 7 days
Credit cards	Accepted
Price range	Affordable
Style	Casual
Cuisine	Campanian
Recommended for	Regular neighbourhood

PIZZARIA LA NOTIZIA

Via Michelangelo da Caravaggio 53
Naples
Naples
Campania 80126
+39 0817142155
www.pizzarialanotizia.com

Opening hours	Closed Monday
Reservation policy	No
Credit cards	Accepted but not AMEX
Price range	Budget
Style	Casual
Cuisine	Pizza
Recommended for	Late night

'Because the pizza epitomizes Naples and because it's a single and complete dish.'
—Alfonso & Ernesto Iaccarino

DON ALFONSO

Don Alfonso 1890
Corso Sant'Agata 11–13
Sant'Agata sui Due Golfi
Naples
Campania 80064
+39 0818780026
www.donalfonso.com

Opening hours	Closed Monday and Tuesday
Credit cards	Accepted
Price range	Expensive
Style	Formal
Cuisine	Campanian
Recommended for	Worth the travel

'An unforgettable restaurant that grows its own produce. The food and the hosts are extraordinary.'
—Giorgio Locatelli

RISTORANTE TASSO

Via Correale 11
Sorrento
Naples
Campania 80067
+39 0818785809
www.ristorantetasso.com

Opening hours	Open 7 days
Credit cards	Accepted
Price range	Affordable
Style	Casual
Cuisine	Campanian
Recommended for	Bargain

'We love their antipasti.'—Alfonso & Ernesto Iaccarino

TORRE DEL SARACINO

Recommended by
Carmelo Chiaramonte

Via Torretta 9
Vico Equense
Naples
Campania 80069
+39 0818028555
www.torredelsaracino.it

Opening hours	Closed Monday
Credit cards	Accepted
Price range	Expensive
Style	Smart casual
Cuisine	Modern Italian
Recommended for	High end

'It was here that I first understood what a perfect dish is: when you are not sure whether to savour every mouthful or to wolf it all down. This fantastic dish is a citrus and redfish risotto. The sea air that you breathe in here does the rest. This chef's cooking is authentic, you never experience the taste of "dead" food cooked inside a vacuum-sealed bag. The combination of ingredients is delightful and there is no attempt to always include five colours in every dish. Ungarnished cooking, nakedly authentic.'—Carmelo Chiaramonte

AL CONVENTO

Recommended by
Moreno Cedroni

Piazza San Francesco 16
Cetara
Salerno
Campania 84010
+39 089261039
www.alconvento.net

Opening hours	Closed Wednesday
Credit cards	Accepted
Price range	Affordable
Style	Casual
Cuisine	Campanian
Recommended for	Worth the travel

'Home cooking with high-quality raw materials in a disarmingly beautiful town.'—Moreno Cedroni

RISTORANTE ZASS

Recommended by
Moreno Cedroni

Il San Pietro di Positano
Via Laurito 2
Positano
Salerno
Campania 84017
+39 089875455
www.ilsanpietro.it

Opening hours	Open 7 days
Credit cards	Accepted
Price range	Expensive
Style	Smart casual
Cuisine	Campanian
Recommended for	High end

'Unique location, excellent food.'—Moreno Cedroni

CAMINETTO D'ORO

Recommended by
Theo Randall

Via dè Falegnami 4
Bologna
Bologna
Emilia-Romagna 40121
+39 051263494
www.caminettodoro.it

Opening hours	Closed Sunday
Credit cards	Accepted
Price range	Affordable
Style	Smart casual
Cuisine	Bolognese
Recommended for	Worth the travel

'The restaurant is family run and the chef is a wonderful lady called Maria whose food is original and utterly delicious.'—Theo Randall

SAN DOMENICO

Recommended by
Igles Corelli

Via Gaspare Sacchi 1
Imola
Bologna
Emilia-Romagna 40026
+39 054229000
www.sandomenico.it

Opening hours	Closed Monday
Credit cards	Accepted
Price range	Expensive
Style	Smart casual
Cuisine	Modern Italian
Recommended for	High end

'The food and ambience are magical, almost *belle époque*.'—Igles Corelli

MAGNOLIA RISTORANTE

Recommended by
Jean Beddington

Viale Trento 31
Cesenatico
Forlì-Cesena
Emilia-Romagna 47042
+39 054781598
www.magnoliaristorante.it

Opening hours	Closed Wednesday
Credit cards	Accepted
Price range	Expensive
Style	Smart casual
Cuisine	Modern Italian
Recommended for	Worth the travel

'A superb mix of modern techniques and traditional ingredients.'—Jean Beddington

Dishes such as grilled wild turbot with artichokes, grilled pigeon with black truffle, *frutti di mare* with ripe, sweet tomatoes, and home-made honeyed tarte Tatin make Magnolia a worthwhile destination. Located on a quiet crossroads near the canal in the outskirts of popular tourist town Cesenatico, the curvaceous villa, which also serves as a cookery school, has a minimalist interior. Leading the young team is Michelin-starred chef Alberto Faccani, a member of Jeunes Restaurateurs d'Europe. Alongside Faccani's dishes, the 500-label-strong wine list by sommelier Tomas Buda shows inquisitiveness, with a number of organic and biodynamic bins.

LA CAPANNA DI ERACLIO

Recommended by
Igles Corelli

Via Per Le Venezie 30
Codigoro
Ferrara
Emilia-Romagna 44021
+39 0533712154

Opening hours	Closed Wednesday and Thursday
Credit cards	Accepted
Price range	Expensive
Style	Smart casual
Cuisine	Seafood
Recommended for	Local favourite

'Grazia Soncini serves the best seafood in the whole of Italy, light and full of flavour. The fish could not be fresher. The ambience and surrounding area give it a 1950s feel.'—Igles Corelli

HOSTARIA DEL RIO

Recommended by
Jenn Louis

Via Guglielmo Marconi 23
Castelvetro
Modena
Emilia-Romagna 41014
+39 059790278
www.hostariadelrio.it

Opening hours	Closed Tuesday and Wednesday
Credit cards	Accepted
Price range	Affordable
Style	Casual
Cuisine	Modenese
Recommended for	Worth the travel

'Three sisters own this restaurant: one waits tables, two cook. The food was so simple – as excellent Italian food should be – and the service was so thoughtful and kind. When I asked how they made their gnocchi, they offered me a thirty-minute lesson the following morning, what hospitality!'—Jenn Louis

L'ERBA DEL RE

Recommended by
Massimo Bottura

Via Castel Maraldo 45
Modena
Modena
Emilia-Romagna 41121
+39 059218188
www.lerbadelre.it

Opening hours	Closed Sunday
Credit cards	Accepted
Price range	Expensive
Style	Smart casual
Cuisine	Modern Italian
Recommended for	Regular neighbourhood

'It's my favourite restaurant in Modena. You can have great traditional cuisine as well as some modern Italian dishes.'—Massimo Bottura

Although served in a stark, beige dining room, a love of colour characterizes the precise dishes of Arezzo-born accountancy graduate turned head chef Luca Marchini. While well-heeled food pilgrims come from miles to splash their Euros on the ten-course tasting menu, the locals more often than not stick to the traditional menu which at €45 (£37; $62) is half the price. Dishes include home-made tortellini in capon stock, Parmesan risotto with aged balsamic vinegar, rabbit with raspberries and crudités, and even an English trifle layered with walnut liqueur. Particularly praised by Michelin, the entirely European wine list runs to almost thirty pages.

MON CAFÉ

Recommended by
Massimo Bottura

Corso Canalchiaro 128
Modena
Modena
Emilia-Romagna 41121
+39 059223257
www.mon-cafe.it

Opening hours	Closed Monday
Credit cards	Accepted but not AMEX
Price range	Affordable
Style	Casual
Cuisine	Café-Bar-Bistro
Recommended for	Breakfast

'A very elegant café. The best coffee in Modena, the best pastries, great cocktails and wines of exceptional quality.'—Massimo Bottura

OSTERIA FRANCESCANA

Recommended by
Gaggan Anand, Luke Dale-
Roberts, Margot Janse,
Anatoly Komm, Ross Lewis,
Gal Ben Moshe, Davide
Oldani, Fabio Rossi, Giulio
Terrinoni, Mauro Uliassi

Via Stella 22
Modena
Modena
Emilia-Romagna 41121
+39 059210118
www.osteriafrancescana.it

Opening hours	Closed Sunday
Credit cards	Accepted
Price range	Expensive
Style	Smart casual
Cuisine	Modern Italian
Recommended for	Worth the travel

'There was so much inspiration everywhere and some of the dishes made me emotional, showing me the bridge between traditional and avante-garde cooking.'
—Gaggan Anand

Deconstruction, reinterpretation and concentration are recurring themes at Massimo Bottura's Modena restaurant, where even the most traditional of dishes from the Emilia-Romagna region is given the modern treatment. The jazz-loving chef, like his beloved music, mixes things up in unconventional ways – his take on mortadella sees its key ingredients stripped out and served separately – yet he also adheres strictly to tradition when it counts, particularly in his peerless pasta dishes. Bottura's effervescent personality pervades Osteria Francescana: seldom is he seen without his trademark trainers (sneakers), which enable him to bound around the kitchen with an energy that would put an athlete to shame.

PASTICCERIA BAR DONDI

Recommended by
Massimo Bottura

Strada Vignolese 578
Modena
Modena
Emilia-Romagna 41125
+39 059362248

Opening hours	Open 7 days
Reservation policy	No
Credit cards	Accepted
Price range	Budget
Style	Casual
Cuisine	Café-Bar
Recommended for	Breakfast

'Luca makes extraordinary pastry cream! When I leave on a trip, or return on a morning international flight, I stop in there to get my fill of *cannoli*.'
—Massimo Bottura

RISTORANTE CORALE VERDI

Recommended by
Gualtiero Marchesi

Vicolo Asdente 9
Parma
Parma
Emilia-Romagna 43100
+39 0521208291

Opening hours	Closed Monday
Credit cards	Accepted but not AMEX
Price range	Affordable
Style	Casual
Cuisine	Parmese
Recommended for	Regular neighbourhood

'It is a stone's throw from the Maria Luigia park and where Chef Sante cooks. I always order the tortelli stuffed with pumpkin, beetroot (beet) greens or meat. I like the atmosphere, the summer garden area and the live music.'—Gualtiero Marchesi

TRATTORIA DA SAVINO

Recommended by
Fabio Rossi

Via Cavallino 32
Coriano
Rimini
Emilia-Romagna 47853
+39 0541656206
www.trattoriadasavino.com

Opening hours	Closed Monday
Credit cards	Accepted
Price range	Budget
Style	Casual
Cuisine	Italian Bistro
Recommended for	Bargain

'A trattoria where you eat well, it's quick and doesn't cost much.'—Fabio Rossi

SCACCIANOIA CAFFÈ

Recommended by
Fabio Rossi

Via Scacciano 106
Misano Adriatico
Rimini
Emilia-Romagna 47843
+39 0541694854

Opening hours	Open 7 days
Reservation policy	No
Credit cards	Accepted
Price range	Budget
Style	Casual
Cuisine	Café-Bar
Recommended for	Breakfast

'I go for breakfast here almost every morning. It's a family-run café with regular daily customers, a morning meeting place for neighbours where you know everyone. It's quite a big place, so you can sit down and read the paper or chat with other people.'
—Fabio Rossi

IL PIASTRINO

Recommended by
Fabio Rossi

Via Parco Begni 5
Pennabili
Rimini
Emilia-Romagna 47864
+39 0541928106
www.piastrino.it

Opening hours	Closed Tuesday and Wednesday
Credit cards	Accepted
Price range	Affordable
Style	Smart casual
Cuisine	Italian
Recommended for	Local favourite

'The location and the decor make this place unique, very welcoming and warm. The cooking is superior.'
—Fabio Rossi

BARRUMBA

Recommended by
Fabio Rossi

Lungomare Augusto Murri 79
Rimini
Rimini
Emilia-Romagna 47900
+39 0541307541
www.barrumba.it

Opening hours	Open 7 days
Credit cards	Accepted
Price range	Budget
Style	Casual
Cuisine	Bar Snacks
Recommended for	Late night

'Only open in summer, there are always lots of people here every evening until late at night. It is very informal, with loud music and you can snack on a good pizza.'
—Fabio Rossi

ROSE & CROWN

Recommended by
Fabio Rossi

Viale Regina Elena 2
Rimini
Rimini
Emilia-Romagna 47900
+39 0541391398
www.roseandcrown.it

Opening hours	Open 7 days
Credit cards	Accepted but not AMEX or Diners
Price range	Budget
Style	Casual
Cuisine	Bar Snacks
Recommended for	Late night

'Rose & Crown is an English-style pub with a good beer selection, excellent hamburgers and live music. You can also play darts.'—Fabio Rossi

POVERO DIAVOLO

Via Roma 30
Torriana
Rimini
Emilia-Romagna 47825
+39 0541675060
www.ristorantepoverodiavolo.com

Opening hours................................Closed Wednesday
Credit cards.....................Accepted but not AMEX or Diners
Price range..Expensive
Style...Casual
Cuisine...Modern Italian
Recommended for...............................Wish I'd opened

'I love the aggressive yet balanced flavours, the *cotto-non-cotto* style of cooking and the herbs and spices.'—Igles Corelli

AL CACCIATORE

La Subida
Via Subida 52
Cormons
Gorizia
Friuli-Venezia Giulia 34071
+39 048160531
www.lasubida.it

Opening hours..................Closed Tuesday and Wednesday
Credit cards..Accepted
Price range..Affordable
Style...Casual
Cuisine..Northern Italian
Recommended for..................................Local favourite

'The atmosphere is fabulous in the house of the Sirk family. In the heart of the Collio, this restaurant has great wines and unforgettable landscapes. They serve northern Italian cuisine and you have the opportunity to taste ham and cheeses personally selected by the owners, Joško and Loredana Sirk.'—Emanuele Scarello

TRATTORIA AI CIODI

Isola di Anfora
Grado
Gorizia
Friuli-Venezia Giulia 34073
+39 3357522209
www.portobusoaiciodi.it

Opening hours...Open 7 days
Credit cards...Not accepted
Price range..Affordable
Style...Casual
Cuisine..Seafood
Recommended for...............................Wish I'd opened

'A welcome retreat. The nature that surrounds this place is wild, almost untouched! It's on the Laguna di Grado, an island currently only inhabited by its owners and a few fishermen. You eat wonderful, expertly prepared fish here. At sunset you can take your boat and go back to where you came from or you can stay in one of the cottages they rent out and enjoy a unique, magical silence.'—Emanuele Scarello

TRATTORIA SANDRA

Piazza Duca D'Aosta 27
Grado
Gorizia
Friuli-Venezia Giulia 34073
+39 043180529
www.trattoriasandra.it

Opening hours...Closed Thursday
Credit cards............................Accepted but not AMEX
Price range..Affordable
Style..Smart casual
Cuisine..Seafood
Recommended for..........................Regular neighbourhood

'As you enter the restaurant you are greeted warmly and you instantly feel welcome and at ease. It offers the best in traditional seafood dishes (made only from freshly caught seafood) in a warm and friendly atmosphere, all very hospitable; the service is great.' —Tomaž Kavčič

CAFFETTERIA TORINESE
Recommended by
Emanuele Scarello
Piazza Grande 9
Palmanova
Udine
Friuli-Venezia Giulia 33057
+39 0432920732
www.caffetteriatorinese.com

Opening hours	Open 7 days
Reservation policy	No
Credit cards	Accepted
Price range	Budget
Style	Casual
Cuisine	Italian Bar-Deli
Recommended for	Breakfast

'The brioche and the pastries in general are simply incredible. This place is perfect for a quick lunch or supper too, and the gastronomic offerings are absolutely outstanding.'—Emanuele Scarello

BIRRERIA GAMBRINUS
Recommended by
Emanuele Scarello
Via Paolo Sarpi 18
Udine
Udine
Friuli-Venezia Giulia 33100
+39 3468211801

Opening hours	Open 7 days
Reservation policy	No
Credit cards	Accepted
Price range	Budget
Style	Casual
Cuisine	Bar Snacks
Recommended for	Late night

'They offer an extensive selection of beers to accompany good cheeses and excellent sandwiches.'
—Emanuele Scarello

CONCORDIA
Recommended by
Emanuele Scarello
Piazza I Maggio 21
Udine
Udine
Friuli-Venezia Giulia 33100
+39 0432505813
www.ristoranteconcordia.com

Opening hours	Closed Monday
Credit cards	Accepted
Price range	Affordable
Style	Casual
Cuisine	Italian
Recommended for	Bargain

'Their pizzas are always light and crispy, perfect for when you feel like something good without giving it too much thought.'—Emanuele Scarello

ALL'ORO
Recommended by
Giulio Terrinoni
The First Hotel
Via del Vantaggio 14
Rome
Rome
Lazio 00186
+39 0697996907
www.ristorantealloro.it

Opening hours	Closed Sunday
Credit cards	Accepted
Price range	Expensive
Style	Formal
Cuisine	Modern Italian
Recommended for	High end

'I have enormous respect for Chef Riccardo Di Giacinto and his wife, Ramona. They serve authentic and flavoursome food.'—Giulio Terrinoni

ANTICO FORNO ROSCIOLI

Recommended by
Heinz Beck

Via dei Chiavari 34
Rome
Rome
Lazio 00186
+39 066864045
www.salumeriaroscioli.com

Opening hours	Closed Sunday
Reservation policy	No
Credit cards	Accepted
Price range	Budget
Style	Casual
Cuisine	Bakery-Pizza
Recommended for	Breakfast

'One of the oldest bakeries in Rome, located in the heart of the city.'—Heinz Beck

L'ARCANGELO

Recommended by
Şemsa Denizsel

Via Giuseppe Gioacchino Belli 59
Rome
Rome
Lazio 00193
+39 063210992
www.ristorantelarcangelo.com

Opening hours	Closed Sunday
Credit cards	Accepted
Price range	Affordable
Style	Smart casual
Cuisine	Roman
Recommended for	Worth the travel

'For its perfect pillows of gnocchi.'—Şemsa Denizsel

IL CONVIVIO TROIANI

Recommended by
Giulio Terrinoni

Vicolo dei Soldati 31
Rome
Rome
Lazio 00186
+39 066869432
www.ilconviviotroiani.com

Opening hours	Closed Sunday
Credit cards	Accepted
Price range	Expensive
Style	Smart casual
Cuisine	Roman
Recommended for	Local favourite

'A high-quality, historic restaurant that has been around for twenty-five years. It is constantly able to reinvent itself, proven by the fact that today it is an organic restaurant. I recommend the Amatriciana.' —Giulio Terrinoni

IMÀGO

Recommended by
Rahul Akerkar

Hassler Hotel
Piazza Trinità dei Monti 6
Rome
Rome
Lazio 00187
+39 0669934726
www.imagorestaurant.com

Opening hours	Open 7 days
Credit cards	Accepted
Price range	Expensive
Style	Formal
Cuisine	Modern Italian
Recommended for	Worth the travel

Located on the top floor of the Hotel Hassler, at the summit of the Spanish Steps, Imàgo offers stunning views of spectacular Rome. In fact, it takes something very special to divert one's attention from what's outside the window to what's being served within, but Neapolitan chef Francesco Apreda comes up with the goods. His cooking reflects a versatility and fine eye for detail garnered in London and Tokyo and an affinity with his native cuisine that keeps the locals coming back for more. Save room for dessert – Apreda's first love.

THE JERRY THOMAS PROJECT

Recommended by
Heinz Beck

Vicolo Cellini 30
Rome
Rome
Lazio 00186
+39 0696845937
www.thejerrythomasproject.it

Opening hours	Closed Monday and Sunday
Credit cards	Not accepted
Price range	Affordable
Style	Casual
Cuisine	Bar Snacks
Recommended for	Worth the travel

'A bar recently opened in the historical centre of Rome.' —Heinz Beck

IL PAGLIACCIO

Via dei Banchi Vecchi 129a
Rome
Rome
Lazio 00186
+39 0668809595
www.ristoranteilpagliaccio.com

Opening hours	Closed Monday and Sunday
Credit cards	Accepted
Price range	Expensive
Style	Formal
Cuisine	Modern Italian
Recommended for	High end

'Anthony Genovese is one of the most professional and knowledgeable chefs I have ever met. He juggles spices like no other. Eating in his restaurant is a unique experience.'—Pier Bussetti

The distinctive cuisine of Calabrian Anthony Genovese unravels behind titillating frosted windows off medieval Rome's Via dei Banchi Vecchi. Drawing on his extensive travels from France, his birthplace, to England, Japan, Malaysia, Thailand, then back to Italy, Genovese crafts dishes worthy of two Michelin stars. To match a wine from his 600-strong list, sommelier Matteo Zappile must decode Genovese's unusual sounding combinations of ingredients. These range from crab, salsify ice cream, apple and mint, to pigeon, carrot cream, endive and vinegar with a waft of cocoa. Meanwhile, pastry chef Marion Lichtle conceives sweet temptations to finish, including pear bonbon, ricotta ice cream and honeyed walnuts.

LA PERGOLA

Rome Cavalieri Hotel
Via Alberto Cadlolo 101
Rome
Rome
Lazlo 00136
+39 635092152
www.romecavalieri.com

Opening hours	Closed Monday and Sunday
Credit cards	Accepted
Price range	Expensive
Style	Formal
Cuisine	European
Recommended for	High end

PIZZARIUM

Via della Meloria 43
Rome
Rome
Lazio 00136
+39 0639745416

Opening hours	Closed Sunday
Reservation policy	No
Credit cards	Accepted
Price range	Budget
Style	Casual
Cuisine	Pizza
Recommended for	Wish I'd opened

'What a great concept! Pizza by the slice, but so many different variations – it's amazing what Gabriele Bonci is topping his pizzas with that we're not used to seeing in the US. You can try a few and pair them with local beers and organic wines.'—Tony Mantuano

RISTORANTE GALLERIA

Galleria Alberto Sordi 53
Via dei Sabini 15
Rome
Rome
Lazio 00187
+39 0685355431
www.galleria-restaurant.it

Opening hours	Open 7 days
Credit cards	Accepted
Price range	Affordable
Style	Casual
Cuisine	Italian Bistro
Recommended for	Bargain

'Excellent for a quick but high-quality lunch.'
—Giulio Terrinoni

RISTORANTE LAGANÀ

Recommended by
Ethan Stowell

Via dell'Orso 44
Rome
Rome
Lazio 00186
+39 0668301161
www.ristorantelagana.it

Opening hours	Open 7 days
Credit cards	Accepted
Price range	Affordable
Style	Casual
Cuisine	Italian
Recommended for	Worth the travel

'I first stumbled across Laganà around midnight after a very unsuccessful experience at another restaurant around the corner. Still hungry and drawn in by the crowd of people outside I decided to check it out. Little did I know that the crowd of people outside were not people leaving, they were people waiting to get in. I couldn't believe it! An hour-and-a-half wait at midnight? It blew my mind. I almost didn't bother but I'm very glad I did. It was one of the most beautiful and romantic meals I've ever had. Every time I have been back, the food has been just as good as I remember and that's hard to do.'—Ethan Stowell

Run by Calabrian Mimmo and his family, Laganà, with its bricky interior, red-and-white tablecloths and fairy lights fringing the entrance, could all too easily be written off as a tourist haunt. But that would belittle both its enduring charm and the kitchen's consistency. In fact, dishes satisfy the diner's blessed trinity: they are simple, copious and flavoursome. These include carpaccio of bream, roast lamb from Lazio with porcini, grilled lobster, the gamut of pasta, and — on demand — tripe. Follow with home-made Sicilian cassata or tiny wild strawberries with creamy vanilla ice cream. The candlelit tables on the cobbles of the narrow Via dell'Orso are romantic in summertime.

ROMEO

Recommended by
Heinz Beck

Via Silla 26a
Rome
Rome
Lazio 00192
+39 0632110120
www.romeo.roma.it

Opening hours	Open 7 days
Credit cards	Accepted
Price range	Affordable
Style	Casual
Cuisine	Italian Bistro
Recommended for	Bargain

Romeo, subtitled 'Chef and Baker', is a collaboration between Cristina Bowerman, of Glass Hostaria, and Pierluigi and Alessandro Roscioli of the famous Roman bakery and deli dynasty. The result, in a former Alfa Romeo showroom near the Vatican, is a gourmet food store, café and restaurant for the twenty-first century. The playfully futuristic design contrasts with the centuries of artisan tradition that have gone into many of the excellent wines, cheeses, salumi and baked goods in stock. On the other hand, more on-trend creations such as foie gras panino with chips (fries) and mango ketchup have found an appreciative audience.

ROSCIOLI

Recommended by
Daniel Costa, Şemsa
Denizsel, René Redzepi,
Daniel Rose

Via dei Giubbonari 21
Rome
Rome
Lazio 00186
+39 066875287
www.salumeriaroscioli.com

Opening hours	Closed Sunday
Credit cards	Accepted
Price range	Affordable
Style	Smart casual
Cuisine	Bar-Bistro-Deli
Recommended for	Worth the travel

'Great pasta and perfect charcuterie.'—René Redzepi

The Roscioli name is Roman shorthand for fine food, wine and pizza. The third generation of the family is now dispensing sought-after slices of pizza bianca and sourdough loaves at the Via dei Chiavari bakery, while the family's old grocery store nearby has been operating as a wine bar, restaurant and deluxe deli since 2002. On entering, it's temptation from all sides: perfectly kept cheeses and cured meats at the deli counter, world-class wines (from a cellar of thousands) on every shelf, and a menu based around the produce they punt. A contender for Rome's best carbonara, say some.

IL SAN LORENZO

Recommended by
Heinz Beck

Via dei Chiavari 4–5
Rome
Rome
Lazio 00186
+39 066865097
www.ilsanlorenzo.it

Opening hours	Open 7 days
Credit cards	Accepted
Price range	Expensive
Style	Smart casual
Cuisine	Seafood
Recommended for	Regular neighbourhood

'A very good fish restaurant in the centre of the city.'
—Heinz Beck

SPLENDOR PARTHENOPES

Recommended by
Giulio Terrinoni

Via Vittoria Colonna 32c
Rome
Rome
Lazio 00193
+39 066833710
www.splendorparthenopes.com

Opening hours	Open 7 days
Credit cards	Accepted but not Diners
Price range	Affordable
Style	Smart casual
Cuisine	Café-Bar-Bistro
Recommended for	Breakfast

'It's a restaurant that could be found in any capital in the world. Only natural products are used for a very light breakfast. The pastry chef is Fabio Trinti and the croissants are an absolute must.'—Giulio Terrinoni

TREE BAR

Recommended by
Giulio Terrinoni

Via Flaminia 226
Rome
Rome
Lazio 00196
+39 0632652754
www.treebar.info

Opening hours	Open 7 days
Credit cards	Accepted but not AMEX or Diners
Price range	Affordable
Style	Casual
Cuisine	Italian Bar-Bistro-Deli
Recommended for	Late night

'Modern and eco-friendly, the name is indicative of its mission. Only first-class products are used and the meat is excellent.'—Giulio Terrinoni

URBANA 47

Recommended by
Giulio Terrinoni

Via Urbana 47
Rome
Rome
Lazio 00184
+39 0647884006
www.urbana47.it

Opening hours	Open 7 days
Credit cards	Accepted
Price range	Affordable
Style	Casual
Cuisine	Italian Bistro
Recommended for	Regular neighbourhood

'Nestled in one of Rome's oldest neighbourhoods, it serves dishes based on local products. It is the first real "green", sustainable restaurant in Rome. Extremely elegant setting and, in my opinion, the most beautiful bistro in Rome. Marco Proietti is the chef there.'
—Giulio Terrinoni

TRATTORIA DA LAURA

Recommended by
Ruth Rogers

Near San Fruttuoso Abbey
Via San Fruttuoso
Camogli
Genoa
Liguria 16032
+39 0185772589

Opening hours	Open 7 days
Credit cards	Not accepted
Price range	Affordable
Style	Casual
Cuisine	Ligurian
Recommended for	Wish I'd opened

'A shack on the beach in Liguria serving only fish and *lasagnette al pesto*.'—Ruth Rogers

NAPUL'È

Recommended by
Jérôme Lorvellec

Corso Nazario Sauro 5
Sanremo
Imperia
Liguria 18038

Opening hours	Open 7 days
Credit cards	Accepted
Price range	Budget
Style	Casual
Cuisine	Pizza
Recommended for	Regular neighbourhood

'I like pizza very much and the pizzas here are like the great ones I ate in Naples.'—Jérôme Lorvellec

LA SPIAGGETTA

Recommended by
Mauro Colagreco

Via Romana Antica s/n
Ventimiglia
Imperia
Liguria 18039
+39 0184227020
www.balzirossi.it

Opening hours	Open 7 days
Credit cards	Accepted
Price range	Affordable
Style	Casual
Cuisine	Ligurian
Recommended for	Breakfast

'Located on a little private beach in Italy, just over the French border, this is a wonderful, peaceful place serving fresh products and – most importantly – Italian-style "ristretto" coffee!'—Mauro Colagreco

TRATTORIA GIANNI FRANZI

Recommended by
Ruth Rogers

Piazza Marconi 5
Vernazza
Spezia
Liguria 19018
+39 0187821003
www.giannifranzi.it

Opening hours	Closed Wednesday
Credit cards	Accepted
Price range	Affordable
Style	Casual
Cuisine	Ligurian
Recommended for	Worth the travel

DA VITTORIO

Recommended by
Emanuele Scarello

Via Cantalupa 17
Brusaporto
Bergamo
Lombardy 24060
+39 035681024
www.davittorio.com

Opening hours	Open 7 days
Credit cards	Accepted
Price range	Expensive
Style	Smart casual
Cuisine	Lombardian
Recommended for	High end

'Everything here is generous, magnificent and perfect. But the most intriguing thing is that these magnificent dishes are created by such a precise and happy hand.'
—Emanuele Scarello

PASTICCERIA VENETO

Recommended by
Stefano Baiocco

Via Salvo D'Acquisto 8
Brescia
Brescia
Lombardy 25128
+39 030392586

Opening hours	Open 7 days
Reservation policy	No
Credit cards	Accepted
Price range	Budget
Style	Casual
Cuisine	Patisserie
Recommended for	Breakfast

'When I have time, I like to head to Brescia and have breakfast in Iginio Massari's pastry shop. He's an international master. Everything is of the highest quality but I like the leavened products most of all.'
—Stefano Baiocco

RISTORANTE PIZZERIA NABLUS

Recommended by
Stefano Baiocco

Via Supiane 1
Gardone Riviera
Brescia
Lombardy 25083
+39 036543671
www.ristorantenablus.com

Opening hours	Closed Tuesday
Credit cards	Accepted but not Mastercard or AMEX
Price range	Affordable
Style	Casual
Cuisine	Pizza
Recommended for	Late night

'This restaurant is in a beautiful location with panoramic views. The service is friendly and informal, the food is simple but well prepared and uses good-quality ingredients. Try the sourdough pizza, topped with fresh artichokes, Parmesan and mortadella... it's to die for!'—Stefano Baiocco

LA TORTUGA

Recommended by
Stefano Baiocco

Via XXIV Maggio 5
Gargnano
Brescia
Lombardy 25084
+39 036571251
www.ristorantelatortuga.it

Opening hours	Closed Tuesday
Credit cards	Accepted
Price range	Expensive
Style	Smart casual
Cuisine	Lombardian
Recommended for	Regular neighbourhood

'It is a family-run restaurant and a very comfortable venue. Danilo and Orietta are exceptional in the dining room, and in the kitchen Maria prepares one of the best lake fish dishes around.'—Stefano Baiocco

VILLA FELTRINELLI

Recommended by
Igles Corelli,
Pierre Gagnaire

Via Rimembranza 38–40
Gargnano
Brescia
Lombardy 25084
+39 0365798000
www.villafeltrinelli.com

Opening hours	Open 7 days
Credit cards	Accepted
Price range	Expensive
Style	Formal
Cuisine	Modern Italian
Recommended for	Worth the travel

'The setting is romantic, pure luxury: comfort, calm, space... The cuisine alone is worth the trip!'
—Pierre Gagnaire

LA SOSTA

Recommended by
Stefano Baiocco

Via Cecina 82
Toscolano-Maderno
Brescia
Lombardy 25088
+39 0365644295

Opening hours	Closed Wednesday
Credit cards	Not accepted
Price range	Budget
Style	Casual
Cuisine	Lombardian
Recommended for	Bargain

'It is a restaurant that has been preparing the same dishes for years: cured meats, two pasta dishes and grilled meat. The quality is always consistent and the value for money is almost embarrassing. Another strength of this place is the friendliness of the people who work there. Your typical crazy gang!'
—Stefano Baiocco

RISTORANTE20

Recommended by
Davide Oldani

Via Vittorio Veneto 14
Cornaredo
Milan
Lombardy 20010
+39 3285885980
www.ristorante20.it

Opening hours	Closed Monday
Reservation policy	No
Credit cards	Accepted but not AMEX
Price range	Budget
Style	Casual
Cuisine	Lombardian
Recommended for	Bargain

'It's my local trattoria.'—Davide Oldani

ANTICA TRATTORIA DEL GALLO

Recommended by
Luigi Taglienti

Via Privata Gerli 3
Gaggiano
Milan
Lombardy 20083
+39 029085276
www.trattoriadelgallo.com

Opening hours	Closed Monday and Tuesday
Credit cards	Accepted but not AMEX
Price range	Affordable
Style	Casual
Cuisine	Italian Bistro
Recommended for	Regular neighbourhood

'Excellent for rediscovering the excellence and real flavours of our country.'—Luigi Taglienti

AROMANDO BISTROT

Recommended by
Luigi Taglienti

Via Pietro Moscati 13
Milan
Milan
Lombardy 20154
+39 0236744172

Opening hours	Closed Monday
Credit cards	Accepted but not AMEX
Price range	Affordable
Style	Casual
Cuisine	Italian Bar-Bistro-Deli
Recommended for	Bargain

'Sunday lunch in the homes of Milan's wealthy reinterpreted with meticulous food preparation and an excellent wine list.'—Luigi Taglienti

CAFÉ TRUSSARDI

Recommended by
Luigi Taglienti

Piazza della Scala 5
Milan
Milan
Lombardy 20121
+39 0280688295
www.cafetrussardi.com

Opening hours	Closed Sunday
Credit cards	Accepted
Price range	Affordable
Style	Smart casual
Cuisine	Café-Bar-Bistro
Recommended for	Late night

'Located in front of the La Scala theatre, it's the place for post-theatre excellence in Milan.'—Luigi Taglienti

DRY

Recommended by
Davide Oldani

Via Solferino 33
Milan
Milan
Lombardy 20121
+39 0263793414
www.drymilano.it

Opening hours	Open 7 days
Credit cards	Accepted
Price range	Budget
Style	Smart casual
Cuisine	Pizza
Recommended for	Late night

'I have complete respect for the small Neapolitan pizza with its distinctive outer edge and perfect natural fermentation – top quality.'—Davide Oldani

IL LUOGO DI AIMO E NADIA

Via Raimondo Montecuccoli 6
Milan
Milan
Lombardy 20147
+39 02416886
www.aimoenadia.com

Opening hours	Closed Sunday
Credit cards	Accepted
Price range	Expensive
Style	Smart casual
Cuisine	Modern Italian
Recommended for	Worth the travel

'The meal of my life.'—Rodrigo Oliveira

RISTORANTE BERTON

Viale della Liberazione 13
Milan
Milan
Lombardy 20124
+39 0267075801
www.ristoranteberton.com

Opening hours	Closed Sunday
Credit cards	Accepted
Price range	Expensive
Style	Smart casual
Cuisine	Modern Italian
Recommended for	Local favourite

'For its quality, service and the chef's impeccable professionalism.'—Davide Oldani

RISTORANTE CRACCO

Via Victor Hugo 4
Milan
Milan
Lombardy 20123
+39 02876774
www.ristorantecracco.it

Opening hours	Closed Sunday
Credit cards	Accepted
Price range	Expensive
Style	Formal
Cuisine	Modern Italian
Recommended for	Local favourite

'A world-renowned icon of Italian high cuisine, this restaurant knows how to marry a contemporary experience with the promotion of high-quality local products.'—Luigi Taglienti

Carlo Cracco's elegant vault of a dining room opened in 2001 as Cracco-Peck, a partnership with the famous Milanese food store that plies its reassuringly expensive wares just around the corner. In a city where tradition tends to triumph over creativity in terms of restaurants, Cracco, who parted with Peck in 2007, has carved out a niche and courted controversy, as an innovator and risk taker, by embracing avantgarde techniques and – appropriately, in that this is Milan – fashion. Leave aside the à la carte and the 'traditional' tasting menu and, instead, go 'creative' to experience his latest collection of dishes.

RISTORANTE GASTRONOMICO

Palazzo Parigi Hotel
Corso di Porta Nuova 1
Milan
Milan
Lombardy 20121
+39 0262562555
www.palazzoparigi.com

Opening hours	Open 7 days
Credit cards	Accepted
Price range	Expensive
Style	Formal
Cuisine	Modern Italian
Recommended for	High end

'Pure luxury in Milan. The dishes are Chef Carlo Cracco's creations.'—Luigi Taglienti

RISTORANTE GIACOMO ARENGARIO

Via Guglielmo Marconi 1
Milan
Milan
Lombardy 20123
+39 0272093814
www.giacomoarengario.com

Opening hours	Open 7 days
Credit cards	Accepted
Price range	Affordable
Style	Casual
Cuisine	Bar-Bistro
Recommended for	Breakfast

'Inside the Museo del Novecento (Milan's contemporary art museum), you get a breathtaking view of the Piazza del Duomo (cathedral square). It is excellent for coffee and reading the newspapers.'—Luigi Taglienti

TRATTORIA DEL NUOVO MACELLO
Recommended by Gualtiero Marchesi

Via Cesare Lombroso 20
Milan
Milan
Lombardy 20137
+39 0259902122
www.trattoriadelnuovomacello.it

Opening hours	Closed Sunday
Credit cards	Not accepted
Price range	Affordable
Style	Casual
Cuisine	Lombardian
Recommended for	Local favourite

'This is a charming old Milanese trattoria where the hospitality is gracious and the food traditional and prepared the way it should be. The *cotoletta alla Milanese* (veal cutlet), for example, is perfect.' —Gualtiero Marchesi

Milan's old meat district is not the slickest part of town, but it's the logical destination for those who seek the old-school version of Milan's famous *cotoletta* dish. This family-run restaurant, honest but not without style, has been here since 1928. They cleave to the original take on the breaded veal cutlet: thick-cut, cooked on the bone and served medium, and none of your big flappy elephant ears. Tripe, *pasta e fagioli* (pasta with beans) and osso bucco are cooked with equal care, but there are plenty of more outward-looking options, including pork fillet with salted hazelnut sauce, nigella salt and apples. Afterwards, hail the cheese trolley.

ZAZÀ RAMEN
Recommended by Gualtiero Marchesi

Via Solferino 48
Milan
Milan
Lombardy 20121
+39 0236799000
www.zazaramen.it

Opening hours	Closed Tuesday
Credit cards	Accepted
Price range	Budget
Style	Casual
Cuisine	Japanese
Recommended for	Bargain

'They serve many different bowls of ramen, it is decorated in pale wood and there are no tablecloths. The atmosphere is contemporary, pleasant, fast-paced and interesting.'—Gualtiero Marchesi

ZERO
Recommended by Davide Oldani

Corso Magenta 87
Milan
Milan
Lombardy 20123
+39 0245474733
www.zeromagenta.it

Opening hours	Open 7 days
Credit cards	Accepted
Price range	Expensive
Style	Smart casual
Cuisine	Modern Japanese
Recommended for	Regular neighbourhood

'Fresh products and unusual combinations make for a modern Japanese cuisine.'—Davide Oldani

DAL PESCATORE
Recommended by Massimo Bottura, Jennifer Jasinski, Luigi Taglienti

Località Runate 15
Canneto sull'Oglio
Mantua
Lombardy 46013
+39 0376723001
www.dalpescatore.com

Opening hours	Closed Monday and Tuesday
Credit cards	Accepted
Price range	Expensive
Style	Smart casual
Cuisine	Mantuan
Recommended for	Local favourite

'The Santini family's restaurant is not actually in the Emilia-Romagna region (it's a stone's throw from the border), but their cooking is representative of the best flavours and aromas of the Emilia-Romagna/Mantua area. An example to all restaurateurs of my generation.' —Massimo Bottura

Sit back and stay awhile – you'll be reluctant to leave! The Santini family are renowned for treating customers like old friends at their world-class restaurant, set in isolated splendour an hour's drive from Milan. Dal Pescatore, originally a humble osteria, has been in the same hands for three generations. Serving refined Mantuan cuisine, the three-Michelin-starred kitchen is run by Nadia Santini, considered one of Italy's finest chefs, along with her son Giovanni and mother-in-law Bruna. Produce takes pride of place, and rigorously indigenous dishes such as *tortelli di zucca*, snails with porcini and *agnolini in brodo* often feature on the two tasting menus: the *Primavera* and *Campagna*.

AL MANDRACCHIO

Recommended by
Stefano Baiocco

Largo Fiera della Pesca 11
Ancona
Ancona
Marche 60125
+39 071202990

Opening hours	Closed Monday
Credit cards	Accepted
Price range	Affordable
Style	Casual
Cuisine	Seafood
Recommended for	Local favourite

'I work in the Lake Garda area but I'm originally from Ancona. This restaurant is situated in a characteristic part of my city: the port. In the kitchen, Mariano prepares dishes with exclusively Adriatic fish. In fact, during the fishing protection period, the restaurant closes. I come here primarily for the creativity of the chef.'—Stefano Baiocco

OSTERIA TEATRO STRABACCO

Recommended by
Stefano Baiocco

Via Guglielmo Oberdan 2
Ancona
Ancona
Marche 60122
+39 07156748
www.strabacco.it

Opening hours	Closed Monday
Credit cards	Accepted
Price range	Affordable
Style	Casual
Cuisine	Marchese
Recommended for	Late night

'It is a late-night venue, an ideal place to taste traditional fare from the Le Marche region.'
—Stefano Baiocco

IL LAGHETTO

Recommended by
Moreno Cedroni

Contrada Portonovo
Portonovo
Ancona
Marche 60020
+39 071801183
www.illaghetto.com

Opening hours	Open 7 days
Credit cards	Accepted
Price range	Affordable
Style	Casual
Cuisine	Italian seafood
Recommended for	Regular neighbourhood

'This charming place is rich in traditional flavours and fragrances.'—Moreno Cedroni

LE BOUDOIR

Recommended by
Moreno Cedroni

Via Armellini 13
Senigallia
Ancona
Marche 60019
+39 07165853
www.leboudoir.it

Opening hours	Open 7 days
Credit cards	Accepted but not AMEX or Diners
Price range	Affordable
Style	Casual
Cuisine	Café-Bar-Bistro
Recommended for	Breakfast

'A fascinating place that reminds you of a Parisian bistro in the middle of Senigallia's historic centre, where you go to see and be seen.'—Moreno Cedroni

LAB

Recommended by
Mauro Uliassi

Via Ottorino Manni 25
Senigallia
Ancona
Marche 60019
+39 0717926659
www.lab-bar.it

Opening hours	Closed Wednesday
Credit cards	Accepted
Price range	Budget
Style	Casual
Cuisine	Bar Snacks
Recommended for	Late night

'Late in the evening, I like going here. It's a bar on the beach in Senigallia.'—Mauro Uliassi

LUNA ROSSA

Via Leonardo da Vinci 35bis
Senigallia
Ancona
Marche 60019
+39 0717920800

Opening hours	Open 7 days
Credit cards	Accepted
Price range	Affordable
Style	Casual
Cuisine	Marchese
Recommended for	Late night

'A family-run place, full of friends, with a varied menu and very good pizza.'—Moreno Cedroni

PAGAIA

Recommended by
Mauro Uliassi

Via Bovio 1bis
Senigallia
Ancona
Marche 60019
+39 0717922557
www.ristorantepagaia.it

Opening hours	Closed Tuesday
Credit cards	Accepted
Price range	Affordable
Style	Casual
Cuisine	Italian seafood
Recommended for	Regular neighbourhood

'I like this place because it serves good and simple food. The professionals in the kitchen love their work.'
—Mauro Uliassi

TRATTORIA CIBO E VINO

Recommended by
Moreno Cedroni,
Mauro Uliassi

Via Fagnani 16–18
Senigallia
Ancona
Marche 60019
+39 07163206

Opening hours	Closed Monday
Credit cards	Accepted but not AMEX or Diners
Price range	Affordable
Style	Casual
Cuisine	Italian seafood
Recommended for	Bargain

'The freshest fish, a real respect for raw materials in an informal atmosphere.'—Moreno Cedroni

ULIASSI

Recommended by
Jean Beddington, Moreno
Cedroni

Banchina di Levante 6
Senigallia
Ancona
Marche 60019
+39 07165463
www.uliassi.it

Opening hours	Closed Monday
Credit cards	Accepted
Price range	Expensive
Style	Smart casual
Cuisine	Modern Italian
Recommended for	Local favourite

'For quality and know-how.'—Moreno Cedroni

PIAZZA DUOMO

Recommended by
Massimo Bottura,
Davide Oldani, Emmanuel
Renaut, Michael Tusk

Piazza Risorgimento 4
Alba
Cuneo
Piedmont 12051
+39 0173366167
www.piazzaduomoalba.it

Opening hours	Closed Monday and Sunday
Credit cards	Accepted
Price range	Expensive
Style	Formal
Cuisine	Modern Italian
Recommended for	High end

'I love Enrico Crippa's restaurant for razor-sharp cuisine, with the whole region laid out on a plate: white Alba truffles, local veal and hazelnuts from the Piedmont region and Barbaresco wine – pure joy only three hours from Megève.'—Emmanuel Renaut

Piazza Duomo, the ambitious restaurant in the heart of Alba, brings together the culinary daring of Enrico Crippa and the vision of influential wine producers, the Ceretto family. Crippa's style is extraordinarily visual, a style reflected in the bold pink restaurant interiors with their magnificent fresco by Francesco Clemente. Seasonal produce from the restaurant's kitchen garden is given due prominence: consider Crippa's Salad 21…31…41 with scores of rare flowers and leaves, his egg yolk and caviar Uova e Uova Salad or his panna cotta Matisse with its 'cut-outs' of pea, raspberry and so on. Tasting menus mix new dishes and Crippa signatures.

ANTICA TORRE

Recommended by
Jeremy Lee

Via Torino 71
Barbaresco
Cuneo
Piedmont 12050
+39 0173635170
www.anticatorrebarbaresco.com

Opening hours	Closed Thursday
Credit cards	Accepted but not AMEX
Price range	Affordable
Style	Casual
Cuisine	Piedmontese
Recommended for	Worth the travel

'It is a beautiful restaurant. It was a beautiful day. The *vendemmia* (grape harvest) was moments away. The grapes lined the roads. The wine was ace. The food was ace. The company was ace. The table a joy. Lovely.'
—Jeremy Lee

You'd expect to eat well in the heart of Piedmont, but this friendly and authentic little trattoria is impressive even by the standards of this most food-friendly part of the world. Local speciality *tajarin* ribbon pasta, vitello tonnato and veal ravioli make Antica Torre popular with locals and tourists alike, all year round. But it's truffle season when the real magic happens: choose your desired size and colour of *fungo* (budget allowing) and they will shave it delicately over almost every dish on the menu. A pretty outdoor terrace and second-floor restaurant with stunning views of the town add to the charm.

OSTERIA LA TORRE

Recommended by
Roberta Sudbrack

Via dell'Ospedale 22
Cherasco
Cuneo
Piedmont 12062
+39 0172488458

Opening hours	Closed Monday
Credit cards	Accepted but not AMEX or Diners
Price range	Affordable
Style	Casual
Cuisine	Piedmontese
Recommended for	Worth the travel

'Amazing food, some of the best I've ever tried. Chef Marco runs the place with his family. The food is full of emotion. The ingredients all come from local suppliers and are very fresh and alive. Exquisite and unforgettable…'—Roberta Sudbrack

TRATTORIA DELLA POSTA

Recommended by
Chris McDonald

Località Sant'Anna 87
Monforte d'Alba
Cuneo
Piedmont 12065
+39 017378120
www.trattoriadellaposta.it

Opening hours	Closed Thursday
Credit cards	Accepted
Price range	Affordable
Style	Smart casual
Cuisine	Piedmontese
Recommended for	Wish I'd opened

'Romantic with professional service, great Piedmontese cuisine, an extensive local wine list and some very rare grappa. The cheese board is exceptional.'
—Chris McDonald

RISTORANTE GARDEN

Recommended by
Giorgio Rapicavoli

Albergo dell'Agenzia
Via Fossano 21
Pollenzo
Cuneo
Piedmont 12042
+39 0172458600
www.albergoagenzia.com

Opening hours	Open 7 days
Credit cards	Accepted
Price range	Affordable
Style	Smart casual
Cuisine	Piedmontese
Recommended for	Worth the travel

'The Albergo dell'Agenzia is a beautiful hotel and culinary school. The location is stunning and the food at the restaurant is even better. The *tajarin* pasta with a ragu of sausage from Bra is probably the best thing I have ever eaten.'—Giorgio Rapicavoli

OSTERIA DA GEMMA

Via Marconi 6
Roddino
Cuneo
Piedmont 12050
+39 0173794252
www.leradicieleali.it

Opening hours	Closed Monday and Tuesday
Credit cards	Accepted
Price range	Affordable
Style	Casual
Cuisine	Piedmontese
Recommended for	Wish I'd opened

'This osteria in the sleepy hill town of Roddino is a culinary gem. There's no menu, they just send out what's good that day. They've got the best *tajarin* pasta and the best set-meal deal in Piedmont. I'd definitely like to come back to this place. Homely atmosphere, lots of locals hanging out. Here is the food we had: two kinds of home-made whole *salami di Langa*, *carne cruda* (chopped raw beef), *insalata russa* (Russian salad), *vitello tonnato* (cold sliced veal with a tuna sauce), *tajarin al ragù* – the best *tajarin* pasta on our trip – *ravioli al ragù*, *coniglio* (rabbit), *brasato* (braised beef), green beans, strudel, *bunet* (chocolate terrine), *meringata* (meringue cake) and one-and-a-half bottles of house wine, all for €58 (£49; $80).'—Hiro Sone

GUIDO RISTORANTE

Tenuta di Fontanafredda
Via Alba 15
Serralunga d'Alba
Cuneo
Piedmont 12050
+39 0173626162
www.guidoristorante.it

Opening hours	Closed Monday
Credit cards	Accepted
Price range	Expensive
Style	Smart casual
Cuisine	Piedmontese
Recommended for	Worth the travel

'I had one of the most elegant, flavourful and exciting meals of my life there. Expertly executed Piedmontese cuisine from start to finish.'—Michael Toscano

COMBAL.ZERO

Piazzale Mafalda di Savoia
Rivoli
Turin
Piedmont 10098
+39 0119565225
www.combal.org

Opening hours	Closed Monday and Sunday
Credit cards	Accepted
Price range	Expensive
Style	Smart casual
Cuisine	Modern Italian
Recommended for	High end

LA CREDENZA

Via Cavour 22
San Maurizio Canavese
Turin
Piedmont 10077
+39 0119278014
www.ristorantelacredenza.it

Opening hours	Closed Tuesday and Wednesday
Credit cards	Accepted
Price range	Expensive
Style	Smart casual
Cuisine	Modern Italian
Recommended for	Local favourite

LA BARRIQUE

Corso Dante Alighieri 53
Turin
Turin
Piedmont 10126
+39 011657900
www.labarriqueristorante.it

Opening hours	Closed Sunday
Credit cards	Accepted
Price range	Affordable
Style	Smart casual
Cuisine	Modern Italian
Recommended for	Local favourite

CAFFÈ AL BICERIN

Recommended by
Kamal Mouzawak

Piazza della Consolata 5
Turin
Turin
Piedmont 10122
+39 0114369325
www.bicerin.it

Opening hours	Closed Wednesday
Reservation policy	No
Credit cards	Accepted but not AMEX
Price range	Budget
Style	Casual
Cuisine	Café-Patisserie
Recommended for	Worth the travel

'My favourite café in the world. It's a tiny place with two red velvet benches and white marble tables. Unchanged for the last 250 years.'—Kamal Mouzawak

LIBERY

Recommended by
Pier Bussetti

Via Legnano 14
Turin
Turin
Piedmont 10128
+39 0114546040

Opening hours	Closed Monday
Credit cards	Accepted
Price range	Budget
Style	Casual
Cuisine	Pizza
Recommended for	Regular neighbourhood

'The only pizzeria I know that does not skimp on ingredients. I recommend the *Bufala* pizza, which is topped with an exceptional buffalo mozzarella after the pizza has come out of the oven.'—Pier Bussetti

Cavernous, whitewashed, full of wrought-iron furniture and always bustling (evening bookings are essential), this gourmet pizzeria really flies the flag for northern Italian pizza. We're talking thin sourdough base with blackened chunky crusts, gilded with, for instance, burrata, sausage and artichoke. Given the ingredients are cherry-picked from local suppliers – such as eggs from Parisi and flour from Gragano – this is good value for a standout meal. That and the much-loved Baladin, the local beer that arrives in carafes from the taps.

VINTAGE 1997

Recommended by
Alfredo Russo

Piazza Solferino 16
Turin
Turin
Piedmont 10121
+39 0115136722
www.vintage1997.com

Opening hours	Closed Sunday
Credit cards	Accepted
Price range	Affordable
Style	Smart casual
Cuisine	Piedmontese
Recommended for	Local favourite

DOLCE STIL NOVO

Recommended by
Yair Feinberg

Piazza della Repubblica 4
Venaria Reale
Turin
Turin
Piedmont 10078
+39 0114992343
www.dolcestilnovo.com

Opening hours	Closed Monday
Credit cards	Accepted
Price range	Expensive
Style	Smart casual
Cuisine	Modern Italian
Recommended for	Worth the travel

'Chef Alfredo Russo actually created a "new Italian style" in cooking. His cuisine is founded on the combination of an absolute respect for Italian tradition and a constant search and wish for innovation. Every dish leaves you overwhelmed. The absolute purity of flavour always stands out. I had one of the best meals of my life there.'—Yair Feinberg

RISTORANTE DA TUCCINO

Recommended by
Corrado Assenza

Via Santa Caterina 69
Polignano a Mare
Bari
Puglia 70044
+39 0804241560
www.tuccino.it

Opening hours	Closed Monday
Credit cards	Accepted
Price range	Expensive
Style	Smart casual
Cuisine	Seafood
Recommended for	Worth the travel

'It has the sea on its doorstep. Absolutely nothing is left to chance in offering customers the freshest fish Puglia has to offer. The customer's joy and pleasure is never compromised. With ample room for growth, given the imminent generational change-over (brutally dictated by life), enormous credit goes to the older generation, while the strength of young Vito leaves us with hope for a bright future.'—Corrado Assenza

LA MADIA

Recommended by
Corrado Assenza

Corso Filippo Re Capriata 22
Licata
Agrigento
Sicily 92027
+39 0922771443
www.ristorantelamadia.it

Opening hours	Closed Tuesday
Credit cards	Accepted but not Diners
Price range	Expensive
Style	Smart casual
Cuisine	Modern Sicilian
Recommended for	Local favourite

Licata, a nondescript town in southern Sicily barely mentioned in travel guides, is an odd place to find a high-end (nay, trailblazing) kitchen. It is, however, the birthplace of Michelin-starred chef Pino Cuttaia, who opened La Madia in 2000 and quickly gained a reputation as one of the best chefs on the island. Be warned – few navigation systems can find the place and there's no obvious signage, so seek help from a local when you reach the town. A simple, modern take on traditional Sicilian cuisine is the hallmark of Cuttaia: his tasting menus offer clever and dazzlingly presented riffs on classics such as arancini and cannoli, plus more adventurous fare such as red prawns (shrimp) with bottarga mayonnaise and mandarin oil.

A PUTIA DO CALABRISI

Recommended by
Carmelo Chiaramonte

Via Concordia 185
Catania
Catania
Sicily 95121

Opening hours	Closed Sunday
Reservation policy	No
Credit cards	Accepted but not AMEX
Price range	Budget
Style	Casual
Cuisine	Sicilian
Recommended for	Breakfast

'It's a very popular place, the last really original one, almost suspended in time. There are lots of wine barrels at the entrance, communal tables with paper tablecloths, and you spend about €10 (£8; $14) per person. The chef only cooks lunch – a different speciality every day. My favourite dish is the stewed pork lips. It's rare to find a place where you can meet new people and make notes on the tablecloth. It's also one of the few places in the city where you can taste authentic "mamma's" food, prepared by the women of the family.'—Carmelo Chiaramonte

RISTORANTE MM

Recommended by
Carmelo Chiaramonte

Piazza Pardo 34
Catania
Catania
Sicily 95121
+39 095348897

Opening hours	Closed Sunday
Credit cards	Accepted but not AMEX
Price range	Affordable
Style	Casual
Cuisine	Seafood
Recommended for	Breakfast

'It has tables facing my trusted fishmonger, Lombardo Orazio e Fratelli. I don't eat sweet pastries for breakfast, just raw fish, some bread and coffee. It's a special place to me, as I can clear my mind amid the bustle of the market. A two- to three-hour visit awakens the nose to endless aromatic experiences, from the fragrances of fruit to those of the salty sea. A true breadbasket of inspiration.'
—Carmelo Chiaramonte

CHARLESTON

Recommended by
Heinz Beck

Via Generale Vincenzo Magliocco 15
Palermo
Palermo
Sicily 90141
+39 091450171
www.ristorantecharleston.com

Opening hours	Open 7 days
Credit cards	Accepted
Price range	Affordable
Style	Smart casual
Cuisine	Modern Sicilian
Recommended for	Wish I'd opened

'I love this restaurant for its architectural beauty and its position – it's so close to the sea... beautiful.'
—Heinz Beck

MAJORE

Recommended by
Tim Raue

Via Martiri Ungheresi 12
Chiaramonte Gulfi
Ragusa
Sicily 97012
+39 0932928019
www.majore.net

Opening hours	Closed Monday
Credit cards	Accepted
Price range	Budget
Style	Casual
Cuisine	Sicilian
Recommended for	Regular neighbourhood

'At my hideway in Sicily there is Majore. It serves only pork dishes from pigs they farm themselves. In a four-course menu for just €20 (£16.50; $28) you'll get a selection of cold cuts, a ravioli dish and a sausage you will never forget. There is also a wine list with more than 400 labels, priced like they were in the 1990s...'
—Tim Raue

RISTORANTE DUOMO

Recommended by
Massimiliano Alajmo,
Corrado Assenza

Via Capitano Bocchieri 31
Ragusa
Ragusa
Sicily 97100
+39 0932651265
www.cicciosultano.it

Opening hours	Closed Sunday
Credit cards	Accepted
Price range	Expensive
Style	Smart casual
Cuisine	Modern Sicilian
Recommended for	Local favourite

'The chef makes Sicilian food culture contemporary and avant-garde.'—Corrado Assenza

I SAPORI DEL VAL DI NOTO

Recommended by
Corrado Assenza

Ronco Bernardo Leanti 9
Noto
Syracuse
Sicily 96017
+39 0931839322
www.isaporidelvaldinoto.it

Opening hours	Closed Monday
Credit cards	Accepted but not AMEX or Diners
Price range	Budget
Style	Casual
Cuisine	Sicilian
Recommended for	Local favourite

'A place where you can enjoy a pizza of a quality far above the mediocrity all too often found in this type of restaurant.'—Corrado Assenza

RISTORANTE CROCIFISSO

Recommended by
Corrado Assenza

Via Principe Umberto 48
Noto
Syracuse
Sicily 96017
+39 0931571151
www.ristorantecrocifisso.it

Opening hours	Closed Wednesday
Credit cards	Accepted
Price range	Affordable
Style	Casual
Cuisine	Sicilian
Recommended for	Local favourite

RISTORANTE DAMMUSO

Recommended by
Corrado Assenza

Via Rocco Pirri 10–12
Noto
Syracuse
Sicily 96017
+39 0931835786
www.ristorantedammuso.it

Opening hours	Closed Tuesday
Credit cards	Accepted
Price range	Affordable
Style	Casual
Cuisine	Sicilian
Recommended for	Local favourite

'A familiar atmosphere.'—Corrado Assenza

TRATTORIA DEL GALLO

Recommended by
Carmelo Chiaramonte

Via Roma 228
Palazzolo Acreide
Syracuse
Sicily 96010
+39 0931881334

Opening hours	Closed Wednesday
Credit cards	Accepted but not AMEX
Price range	Budget
Style	Casual
Cuisine	Sicilian
Recommended for	Local favourite

'You can eat at the counter and enjoy unbeatable fried potato croquettes and fried meatballs. The atmosphere is always friendly and interesting. There are black Sicilian truffles in this region and sometimes you can eat them here with pasta or a pork dish. True Sicilian country dining.'—Carmelo Chiaramonte

IL RE DELLA BUSA

Recommended by
Gerhard Wieser

Hotel Lido Palace
Viale Carducci 10
Riva del Garda
Trento
Trentino 38066
+39 0464021899
www.lido-palace.it

Opening hours	Open 7 days
Credit cards	Accepted
Price range	Expensive
Style	Formal
Cuisine	Italian
Recommended for	Wish I'd opened

LOCANDA MARGON

Recommended by
Jonathon Sawyer

Via Margone di Ravina 15
Trento
Trento
Trentino 38123
+39 0461349401
www.locandamargon.it

Opening hours	Closed Tuesday
Credit cards	Accepted
Price range	Expensive
Style	Smart casual
Cuisine	Modern Italian
Recommended for	High end

'Located three kilometres from Trento, this is Ferrari's signature restaurant. In my opinion it's the best Italy has to offer. Chef Alfio Ghezzi has such an eye for detail. His attention and hand are seen in everything, right down to the custom-designed plate. Not only does he support his restaurant, but he also proudly trumpets the farms, vineyards and lardo of Trento.'
—Jonathon Sawyer

For an oenologist with a love of food, this fine-dining hilltop salotto overlooking Trento has to be a utopian prospect. Many Italian wine producers convert farmhouses into informal restaurants but the Lunelli family, owners of the Ferrari winery, has been rather more ambitious. Since Alfio Ghezzi took over the kitchen and won them a Michelin star, Locanda Margon has thronged with gastro tourists and wine lovers. Imaginative wine pairings are suggested throughout and seasonally-changing menus might include ziti with razor clams or roe deer loin with coffee polenta. For a truly immersive experience fit in a cellar tour and wine tasting beforehand.

IL SALVIATINO

Recommended by
Ben Tish

Hotel Il Salviatino
Via del Salviatino 21
Fiesole
Florence
Tuscany 50137
+39 0559041111
www.salviatinoagenda.com

Opening hours	Open 7 days
Credit cards	Accepted
Price range	Expensive
Style	Smart casual
Cuisine	Tuscan
Recommended for	Worth the travel

'A simply stunning hotel and restaurant just outside Florence. The food is served on the terrace overlooking the Tuscan countryside. Beautiful ingredients and local produce are prepared with deftness. Chianina beef, local tomatoes and fragrant herbs from their own garden.'—Ben Tish

ENOTECA PINCHIORRI

Recommended by
Luca Gozzani

Via Ghibellina 87
Florence
Florence
Tuscany 50122
+39 055242757
www.enotecapinchiorri.it

Opening hours	Closed Monday and Sunday
Credit cards	Accepted
Price range	Expensive
Style	Formal
Cuisine	Modern Italian
Recommended for	Worth the travel

'Because it's in the most beautiful city in the world and the dishes are unforgettable.'—Luca Gozzani

TRATTORIA CAMMILLO

Recommended by
Ollie Dabbous

Borgo San Jacopo 57r
Florence
Florence
Tuscany 50125
+39 055212427

Opening hours	Closed Tuesday and Wednesday
Credit cards	Accepted
Price range	Affordable
Style	Smart casual
Cuisine	Tuscan
Recommended for	Worth the travel

TRATTORIA FRATELLI BRIGANTI

Recommended by
Italo Bassi

Piazza Giovanbattista Giorgini 12r
Florence
Florence
Tuscany 50134
+39 055475255

Opening hours	Closed Thursday
Credit cards	Not accepted
Price range	Budget
Style	Casual
Cuisine	Italian Bistro
Recommended for	Bargain

'Humble trattoria with excellent products, which they produce themselves.'—Italo Bassi

DARIO DOC

Recommended by
Massimiliano Alajmo

Via XX Luglio 11
Panzano in Chianti
Florence
Tuscany 50022
+39 055852020
www.dariocecchini.com

Opening hours	Closed Sunday
Reservation policy	No
Credit cards	Accepted
Price range	Budget
Style	Casual
Cuisine	Burgers
Recommended for	Bargain

'It's a place that represents Italy perfectly, with quality ingredients and low prices.'—Massimiliano Alajmo

LA PINETA

Recommended by
Mitch Tonks

Via dei Cavalleggeri Nord 27
Bibbona
Livorno
Tuscany 57020
+39 0586600016
www.lapinetadizazzeri.it

Opening hours	Closed Monday
Credit cards	Accepted
Price range	Expensive
Style	Smart casual
Cuisine	Seafood
Recommended for	Worth the travel

'A beach restaurant serving some of the best seafood I've ever eaten. It's been there for many years and has a Michelin star but is very unpretentious. They have stuck to cooking the best fish very simply but with excellent execution. Guests come here knowing that the owner sources better seafood than anyone else and for me that's the reason you go out to eat fish.' —Mitch Tonks

IL CAFFÈ SOTTO I PORTICI

Recommended by
Igles Corelli

Piazza del Mercato 18
Pescia
Pistoia
Tuscany 51017
+39 057247016

Opening hours	Closed Monday
Reservation policy	No
Credit cards	Accepted
Price range	Budget
Style	Casual
Cuisine	Café-Bar-Bistro
Recommended for	Regular neighbourhood

'Wonderful. The decor is very pleasant and it overlooks the little piazza. I sometimes go there and eat a large salad or a plate of pasta. It's also a good way to start the day with a cappuccino and to hear what's new in town.' —Igles Corelli

RISTORANTE DA GIOVANNI

Recommended by
Massimiliano Alajmo

Via Pietro Maroncelli 22
Padua
Padua
Veneto 35129
+39 049772620
www.ristorantedagiovannipd.it

Opening hours	Closed Sunday
Credit cards	Accepted
Price range	Affordable
Style	Casual
Cuisine	Venetian
Recommended for	Local favourite

'It is a historic restaurant that serves old-style boiled meats.'—Massimiliano Alajmo

LE CALANDRE

Recommended by
Fabio Rossi

Via Liguria 1
Sarmeola di Rubano
Padua
Veneto 35030
+39 049630303
www.calandre.com

Opening hours	Closed Monday and Sunday
Credit cards	Accepted
Price range	Expensive
Style	Smart casual
Cuisine	Modern Italian
Recommended for	High end

'A great, impeccably managed restaurant. I have never been able to fault a thing and everything I have tasted there has been first class. Ingenious cooking, and flawless service in the dining room.'—Fabio Rossi

Helmed by Massimiliano Alajmo, the youngest ever chef to receive three Michelin stars, Le Calandre has 'foodie pilgrimage' written all over it. Ignore the unlovely location in the Paduan suburbs and you'll find regional classics given a molecular spin, such as Veneto staple risotto with a sprinkling of powdered liquorice. For more experimental fare, there's the In. gredienti menu: this is also the name of the restaurant's gourmet grocery, which stocks pure essences produced in collaboration with a master perfumer. Alajmo's mother Rita taught him everything he knows: head next door to casual sibling venue Il Calandrino for her famous *zuccotto*.

ANTICA OSTERIA CERA

Recommended by
Corrado Assenza

Via Marghera 24
Campagna Lupia
Venice
Veneto 30010
+39 0415185009
www.osteriacera.it

Opening hours	Closed Monday
Credit cards	Accepted
Price range	Expensive
Style	Smart casual
Cuisine	Seafood
Recommended for	Wish I'd opened

'Nestled in the countryside, far from the city bustle, it's a sanctuary devoted to fish. Every detail of a dish's preparation is attended to with the utmost devotion and knowledge of the raw ingredients. Fish and clients pampered by great professionals makes for an unforgettable lunch. The service is discreet, polite and relaxed.'—Corrado Assenza

ALLE TESTIERE

Recommended by
Tom Oldroyd

Calle del Mondo Novo 5801
Venice
Venice
Veneto 30122
+39 0415227220
www.osterialletestiere.it

Opening hours	Closed Monday and Sunday
Credit cards	Accepted but not AMEX or Diners
Price range	Affordable
Style	Casual
Cuisine	Venetian
Recommended for	High end

'I would take a day trip to Venice and end the evening with dinner at one of the city's beautiful and hidden bacari, such as Alle Testiere.'—Tom Oldroyd

There are only twenty-four seats spread over nine tables at this tiny *osteria* and most of them are usually filled with Venetians. One of the notable exceptions to the generally accepted wisdom that Venice is one of the hardest places in Italy to find a decent meal, Alle Testiere specializes in serving local seafood. Typically taxing to track down, despite its proximity to St Mark's and the Rialto, it's housed in a beautiful old bacaro, its tables covered with brown paper instead of white cloth. Despite this informality there's sophistication from the kitchen and a serious wine list that focuses on quirky local producers.

CORTE SCONTA

Recommended by
Tom Oldroyd

Calle del Pestrin 3886
Venice
Venice
Veneto 30122
+39 0415227024
www.cortescontavenezia.it

Opening hours	Closed Monday and Sunday
Credit cards	Accepted but not AMEX or Diners
Price range	Affordable
Style	Casual
Cuisine	Venetian
Recommended for	High end

ENOITECA MASCARETA

Recommended by
Massimiliano Alajmo

Calle Lunga Santa Maria Formosa 5183
Venice
Venice
Veneto 30122
+39 0415230744
www.ostemaurolorenzon.it

Opening hours	Open 7 days
Credit cards	Accepted
Price range	Budget
Style	Casual
Cuisine	Venetian
Recommended for	Late night

'Mauro Lorenzon is the ideal late-night host.'
—Massimiliano Alajmo

The offspring of established Venetian osteria Al Mascaron, this intimate *enoteca* (wine bar) has over time proved more popular than its forebear. Owner Mauro Lorenzon, famously charismatic and always wearing a bow tie, will match your choice of *cicchetti* (Venetian tapas) with the perfect wine. Many rave about the prosciutto here, not to mention the cheeseboard, crostini, traditional bean soups, cuttlefish pasta and *baccalà* served in antipasti-sized portions. Whether it's a late-night bite and *ombra* (literally 'shadow', a white wine to follow food) or anything else from a hefty wine list, menu and ambience conspire for fun well into the early hours.

HARRY'S BAR
Calle Vallaresso 1323
Venice
Venice
Veneto 30124
+39 0415285777
www.cipriani.com

Recommended by
Massimiliano Alajmo

Opening hours..Open 7 days
Credit cards..Accepted
Price range..Expensive
Style...Smart casual
Cuisine..Bar-Bistro
Recommended for...Wish I'd opened

RISTORANTE QUADRI
Piazza San Marco 121
Venice
Venice
Veneto 30124
+39 0415222105
www.alajmo.it

Recommended by
Massimiliano Alajmo,
Tony Mantuano

Opening hours...Closed Monday
Credit cards..Accepted
Price range..Expensive
Style...Smart casual
Cuisine...Modern Italian
Recommended for..High end

'A restaurant in a spectacular, romantic setting. The
food is delicious and the hospitality is even better.'
—Tony Mantuano

TAPASOTTO
Galleria Pellicciai 12
Verona
Verona
Veneto 37121
+39 045591477
www.tapasotto.it

Recommended by
Italo Bassi

Opening hours...Closed Monday
Credit cards.................................Accepted but not AMEX
Price range..Budget
Style..Casual
Cuisine..Tapas
Recommended for...Late night

'Unpretentious and informal.'—Italo Bassi

'PRAGUE GOLDEN–ERA STYLE ARCHITECTURE AND FOOD THAT'S VERY POPULAR WITH THE LOCALS.'

PAUL DAY P609

AUSTRIA, CZECH REPUBLIC, POLAND & SLOVENIA

'The only restaurant in Vienna on a boat on the Danube Canal. The food is excellent, but you can also jump into the Danube for a swim.'

CHRISTIAN DOMSCHITZ P606

Pomerania p.615♥

Masovia pp.613–615♥

P O L A N D

Prague pp.608–613♥   Moravia-Silesia p.608♥

Central Bohemia p.607♥

C Z E C H   R E P U B L I C

Lower Austria p.604♥
Vienna pp.605–607♥

Salzburg p.604♥

Tirol pp.603–605♥

A U S T R I A

Goriška pp.615–616♥

S L O V E N I A

AUSTRIA, CZECH REPUBLIC, POLAND & SLOVENIA

Ⓝ   SCALE

0   90   180
▬▬▬▬▬▬▬ mi.

DER FLOH

Recommended by
Markus Mraz

Tullnerstrasse 1
Langenlebarn
Lower Austria 3425
Austria
+43 227262809
www.derfloh.at

Opening hours	Closed Tuesday and Wednesday
Credit cards	Accepted
Price range	Affordable
Style	Smart casual
Cuisine	Austrian
Recommended for	Bargain

'Austrian restaurant culture is still being treasured in this restaurant and the chef never runs out of ideas. A family-run establishment which is comfortable, fuss-free and simply great.'—Markus Mraz

IKARUS

Recommended by
Stefano Baiocco

Salzburg Airport
Wilhelm-Spazier-Strasse 7a
Salzburg
Salzburg 5020
Austria
+43 66221970
www.hangar-7.com

Opening hours	Open 7 days
Credit cards	Accepted
Price range	Expensive
Style	Smart casual
Cuisine	International
Recommended for	Wish I'd opened

'The restaurant, owned by the Red Bull group, offers a unique concept found nowhere else in the world. Each month it invites a chef from another country to work there, ensuring an incredible and different experience every time.'—Stefano Baiocco

OBAUER

Recommended by
Thomas Rode Andersen

Hotel Obauer
Markt 46
Werfen
Salzburg 5450
Austria
+43 646852120
www.obauer.com

Opening hours	Closed Monday and Tuesday
Credit cards	Accepted
Price range	Affordable
Style	Smart casual
Cuisine	Modern Austrian
Recommended for	Worth the travel

'Both Rudi and Karl Obauer are legends in the Alp region, having reigned for decades, and both have amazed me ever since I started in the industry. They changed my gastronomic perspective. For two decades they've been doing what they do best and maintaining it.'—Thomas Rode Andersen

In the shadow of majestic Schloss Hohenwerfen in Austria's Salzach Valley lies the pretty market town of Werfen, home to Restaurant-Hotel Obauer. Brothers Karl and Rudi Obauer began the ongoing modernization of their family's restaurant in 1979, gaining exposure to other chefs and cuisines as they went along, via internships at Troisgros, Alain Chapel and Au Crocodile. The Obauers give local ingredients a starring role: trout strudel and *Werfen* lamb are Obauer classics; while chilli tripe with cockscombs, and wild mushroom soup with goose breast, dates and sauerkraut reveal their bolder side. The hotel's breakfasts are magnificent too.

ROSENGARTEN SIMON TAXACHER

Recommended by
Armin Leitgeb

Hotel Rosengarten
Aschauerstrasse 46
Kirchberg
Tirol 6365
Austria
+43 53574201
www.restaurant.rosengarten-taxacher.com

Opening hours	Closed Tuesday and Wednesday
Credit cards	Accepted
Price range	Expensive
Style	Smart casual
Cuisine	Modern European
Recommended for	Local favourite

'This family establishment is now run by the son, Simon Taxacher who earned his nineteenth point in the Gault Millau in 2014. It's great to see young chefs achieve their dreams and contribute to the culinary growth of the region.'—Armin Leitgeb

SCHWEDENKAPELLE

Recommended by
Armin Leitgeb

Klausenbach 67
Kitzbühel
Tirol 6370
Austria
+43 535665870
www.schwedenkapelle.com

Opening hours	Closed Monday and Tuesday
Credit cards	Accepted
Price range	Affordable
Style	Casual
Cuisine	Modern Austrian
Recommended for	Regular neighbourhood

'The job these brothers are doing is probably the most honest in casual local food in Tirol.'—Armin Leitgeb

DER METZGERWIRT

Recommended by
Armin Leitgeb

Dorfstrasse 16
Uderns
Tirol 6271
Austria
+43 528862559
www.dermetzgerwirt.at

Opening hours	Variable
Credit cards	Accepted
Price range	Affordable
Style	Casual
Cuisine	Austrian
Recommended for	Bargain

'The quality and the philosophy behind the food is worth a little detour.'—Armin Leitgeb

CAFÉ ANZENGRUBER

Recommended by
Christian Domschitz,
Konstantin Filippou

Schleifmuhlgasse 19
Vienna
Vienna 1040
Austria
+43 15878297

Opening hours	Closed Sunday
Reservation policy	No
Credit cards	Not accepted
Price range	Affordable
Style	Casual
Cuisine	Austrian
Recommended for	Late night

'A cross between a traditional coffee house and a gastropub in Vienna's new Soho – at least that's what the locals say. Here you get the best of the best: legendary goulash, stuffed peppers and Viennese schnitzels – even at midnight. The restaurant is also a hub for artists.'—Christian Domschitz

DO & CO RESTAURANT

Recommended by
Konstantin Filippou

Do & Co Hotel
Stephansplatz 12
Vienna
Vienna 1010
Austria
+43 15353969
www.docohotel.com

Opening hours	Open 7 days
Credit cards	Accepted
Price range	Expensive
Style	Smart casual
Cuisine	International
Recommended for	Breakfast

'This restaurant is affiliated with the Albertina Museum. It surprises time and again with a truly great breakfast and sensible, tasteful combinations. The atmosphere is great and there's an open-air terrace in the summer months.'—Konstantin Filippou

HOLY MOLY!
Badeschiff
Donaukanal
Vienna
Vienna 1010
Austria
+43 69915130750
www.badeschiff.at

Recommended by
Christian Domschitz

Opening hours	Closed Sunday
Credit cards	Accepted
Price range	Affordable
Style	Casual
Cuisine	Modern Austrian
Recommended for	Local favourite

'This is the only restaurant in Vienna on a boat on the Danube Canal. The food is excellent, but you can also jump into the Danube for a swim during the summer months. The view across Vienna is spectacular.'
—Christian Domschitz

MEIXNER'S GASTWIRTSCHAFT
Buchengasse 64
Vienna
Vienna 1100
Austria
+43 16042710
www.meixners-gastwirtschaft.at

Recommended by
Christian Domschitz

Opening hours	Closed Monday
Credit cards	Accepted
Price range	Affordable
Style	Casual
Cuisine	Austrian
Recommended for	Regular neighbourhood

'This restaurant takes me back to my roots as it's in the neighbourhood where I grew up. Karl Meixner shares my gastronomic taste for "no frills".'
—Christian Domschitz

MOCHI
Praterstrasse 15
Vienna
Vienna 1020
Austria
+43 19251380
www.mochi.at

Recommended by
Markus Mraz

Opening hours	Closed Sunday
Credit cards	Not accepted
Price range	Affordable
Style	Casual
Cuisine	Japanese Fusion
Recommended for	Regular neighbourhood

'A small restaurant with great Asian cuisine, a lovely and comforting atmosphere and winning service.'
—Markus Mraz

MRAZ & SOHN
Wallensteinstrasse 59
Vienna
Vienna 1200
Austria
+43 13304594
www.mrazundsohn.at

Recommended by
Christian Domschitz

Opening hours	Closed Saturday and Sunday
Credit cards	Accepted
Price range	Expensive
Style	Smart casual
Cuisine	Modern Austrian
Recommended for	Worth the travel

'A crazy chef and a friend of mine, who once served me one of the longest menus: white wine dishes for lunch, red wine dishes for dinner and desserts shortly before midnight.'—Christian Domschitz

SERVITENWIRT
Servitengasse 7
Vienna
Vienna 1090
Austria
+43 13152387
www.servitenwirt.at

Recommended by
Markus Mraz

Opening hours	Open 7 days
Credit cards	Accepted
Price range	Affordable
Style	Casual
Cuisine	European
Recommended for	Local favourite

'Superb regional cuisine.'—Markus Mraz

It doesn't get much more atmospheric than the Servitenwirt in Servitenviertel – Dr Freud's old neighbourhood, which oozes fin-de-siècle charm. A traditional inn with wooden benches and antique glass pendant lights, its terrace leads on to the church square. To the sound of the bells of the Servitenkirche, Matthias Eichblatt (recently arrived from the well-regarded Hill) has evolved Servitenwirt's menu. He continues to cook the *gutbürgerlich* classics you'd expect – schnitzel, goulash and pancakes – but alongside them has introduced lighter, modern dishes such as Arctic char dressed with tomato and cucumber jelly. Good local beer and Austrian wines.

SKOPIK & LOHN

Recommended by
Konstantin Filippou

Leopoldsgasse 17
Vienna
Vienna 1020
Austria
+43 12198977
www.skopikundlohn.at

Opening hours	Closed Monday and Sunday
Credit cards	Accepted
Price range	Affordable
Style	Casual
Cuisine	European
Recommended for	Local favourite

'Every city needs a restaurant like this, where the intellectual elite meets the foodies. It features a fantastic urban atmosphere with a reasonably priced but fun menu, where I always find something that's just right for me. And the owner takes good care of all his guests.'—Konstantin Filippou

STEIRERECK

Recommended by
Christian Domschitz, Thomas
Kurt, Markus Mraz, Joachim
Wissler, Michael Wolf

Am Heumarkt 2a
Vienna
Vienna 1030
Austria +43 17133168
www.steirereck.at

Opening hours	Closed Saturday and Sunday
Credit cards	Accepted
Price range	Expensive
Style	Smart casual
Cuisine	Modern Austrian
Recommended for	Worth the travel

'The perfect restaurant. The service is world-class, attentive, friendly, professional – you can't do better…

Excellent cuisine that's creative, imaginative and down-to-earth all at the same time. Beautifully located in Vienna's Stadtpark.'—Thomas Kurt

STOMACH

Recommended by
Christian Domschitz

Seegasse 26
Vienna
Vienna 1090
Austria
+43 13102099
www.stomach.at

Opening hours	Closed Monday and Tuesday
Credit cards	Not accepted
Price range	Affordable
Style	Casual
Cuisine	Austrian
Recommended for	Regular neighbourhood

'I think the area of Servitenviertel has a unique French flair. Stomach is a small, traditional Viennese restaurant offering some great specialities: appetizers that feature pumpkin seed oil (home-made by the chef's sister), an oven-baked Austrian sirloin dish, and an incredible home-made flourless chocolate cake, served with whipped cream.'—Christian Domschitz

U SAPÍKŮ

Recommended by
Pavel Mencl

Klokočná 8
Klokočná
Central Bohemia 25164
Czech Republic
+420 323641186
www.klokocna.cz

Opening hours	Closed Monday and Tuesday
Credit cards	Accepted but not AMEX
Price range	Affordable
Style	Casual
Cuisine	Czech
Recommended for	Local favourite

MIURA RESTAURANT

Recommended by
Gwendal Le Ruyet

Hotel Miura
Čeladná 887
Čeladná
Moravia-Silesia 73912
Czech Republic
+420 558761100
www.miura.cz

Opening hours	Open 7 days
Credit cards	Accepted
Price range	Affordable
Style	Smart casual
Cuisine	Czech
Recommended for	High end

'This hotel is a masterpiece. The chef, Michael Göth, knows his suppliers perfectly. His cooking is borderless.'—Gwendal Le Ruyet

BAKESHOP PRAHA

Recommended by
David Sasek

Kozí 918/1
Prague
Prague 11000
Czech Republic
+420 222316823
www.bakeshop.cz

Opening hours	Open 7 days
Reservation policy	No
Credit cards	Accepted
Price range	Budget
Style	Casual
Cuisine	Bakery-Café-Deli
Recommended for	Breakfast

'Absolutely the top place for breakfast. They do all kinds of products: home-made sourdough, cakes, sandwiches, granola and croissants. They prepare nice coffee for you, all the staff are very friendly and you can sit and eat your breakfast on the bench in front of the bakery. It has been open for seventeen years and it's always overcrowded.'
—David Sasek

BISTRO SANTINKA

Recommended by
David Sasek

Náměstí Na Santince
Prague
Prague 16000
Czech Republic
+420 725975365
www.santinka.cz

Opening hours	Open 7 days
Credit cards	Accepted
Price range	Budget
Style	Casual
Cuisine	Bistro
Recommended for	Bargain

'A pleasant place with usually one three-course menu offer for the day.'—David Sasek

CAFÉ DE PARIS

Recommended by
Gwendal Le Ruyet

Maltézské Náměstí 537/4
Prague
Prague 11800
Czech Republic
+420 603160718
www.cafedeparis.cz

Opening hours	Open 7 days
Credit cards	Not accepted
Price range	Budget
Style	Casual
Cuisine	French
Recommended for	Late night

'A cosy little restaurant that's been here for many years and that's open until midnight. *Entrecôte* and chips (fries) is a classic here.'—Gwendal Le Ruyet

CAFÉ IMPERIAL

Recommended by
Pavel Mencl

Na Poříčí 15
Prague
Prague 11000
Czech Republic
+420 246011440
www.cafeimperial.cz

Opening hours	Open 7 days
Credit cards	Accepted
Price range	Affordable
Style	Smart casual
Cuisine	Brasserie
Recommended for	Breakfast

'Historical interior, perfect food, good service, central location.'—Pavel Mencl

CAFÉ SAVOY
Vítězná 124/5
Prague
Prague 15000
Czech Republic
+420 257311562
cafesavoy.ambi.cz

Opening hours	Open 7 days
Credit cards	Accepted
Price range	Affordable
Style	Smart casual
Cuisine	Czech
Recommended for	Local favourite

'Prague golden-era (late 1930s) style architecture and food. Very popular with the locals.'—Paul Day

ČERSTVĚ PRAŽENÁ KÁVA
Truhlářská 33
Prague
Prague 11000
Czech Republic
+420 602644499
www.cerstve-prazena-kava.cz

Opening hours	Closed Sunday
Reservation policy	No
Credit cards	Not accepted
Price range	Budget
Style	Casual
Cuisine	Café
Recommended for	Breakfast

'Coffee is my breakfast. In the morning you will find me behind the counter of the best coffee place in Prague. The beans are ground just for your cup right before your eyes.'—Gwendal Le Ruyet

CUKRKÁVALIMONÁDA
Lázeňská 290/7
Prague
Prague 11800
Czech Republic
+420 257225396
www.cukrkavalimonada.com

Opening hours	Open 7 days
Credit cards	Not accepted
Price range	Budget
Style	Casual
Cuisine	Café-Bistro
Recommended for	Bargain

'The best place to stop, have an omelette, a piece of cake and a coffee before you head for the castle.'
—Gwendal Le Ruyet

LA DEGUSTATION BOHÊME BOURGEOISE
Haštalská 18
Prague
Prague 11000
Czech Republic
+420 222311234
www.ladegustation.cz

Opening hours	Open 7 days
Credit cards	Accepted
Price range	Affordable
Style	Smart casual
Cuisine	Czech
Recommended for	High end

'I was blown away. The level of service, passion and vision was amazing. They knew exactly what they were about and delivered a great dining experience from the moment I arrived.'—Adam Reid

La Degustation Bohême Bourgeoise showcases chef Oldřich Sahajdák's intelligent take on Czech cuisine. His six-course menu is inspired by the work of nineteenth-century Czech cookery writer, Marie B. Svobodová, while the eleven-course menu embraces more modern techniques and influences. Both feature small plates partnered with wines, beers and fruit juices chosen by the team of three sommeliers. Typical dishes include langoustine, oyster and amaranth matched with home-made lemonade, catfish with cabbage and almonds with South Moravian Sauvignon Blanc, and mature *olomoucké tvarůžky* – a cheese that claims fame in having its own museum – with traditional wheat beer.

DIVINIS

Recommended by
David Sasek

Týnská 21
Prague
Prague 11000
Czech Republic
+420 222325440
www.divinis.cz

Opening hours	Closed Sunday
Credit cards	Accepted
Price range	Affordable
Style	Smart casual
Cuisine	Italian
Recommended for	Regular neighbourhood

'A very nicely designed, romantic restaurant with great Italian food and fresh products. Cosy and bright with an attractive interior and a great ambience.'—David Sasek

KALINA

Recommended by
David Sasek

Dlouhá 616/12
Prague
Prague 11000
Czech Republic
+420 222317715
www.kalinarestaurant.cz

Opening hours	Closed Sunday
Credit cards	Accepted
Price range	Affordable
Style	Casual
Cuisine	French
Recommended for	Regular neighbourhood

'Perfect French cuisine with a perfect wine selection and pairing.'—David Sasek

KASTROL

Recommended by
Paul Day

Ohradské Náměstí 1625/2
Prague
Prague 15500
Czech Republic
+420 607048992
www.restauracekastrol.cz

Opening hours	Open 7 days
Credit cards	Not accepted
Price range	Affordable
Style	Casual
Cuisine	Czech
Recommended for	Regular neighbourhood

'Czech cuisine and locally sourced produce.'—Paul Day

KATSURA

Recommended by
Paul Day

Evropská 370/15
Prague
Prague 16000
Czech Republic
+420 296559298
www.katsura.cz

Opening hours	Closed Tuesday
Credit cards	Accepted
Price range	Affordable
Style	Casual
Cuisine	Japanese
Recommended for	Regular neighbourhood

'Located in an old staff canteen of the Communist-era Diplomat Hotel, they serve perfect sushi and sashimi.' —Paul Day

KRYSTAL MOZAIKA BISTRO

Recommended by
Oldřich Sahajdák

Sokolovská 101/99
Prague
Prague 18600
Czech Republic
+420 222318152
www.krystal-bistro.cz

Opening hours	Open 7 days
Credit cards	Accepted
Price range	Budget
Style	Casual
Cuisine	Bistro
Recommended for	Regular neighbourhood

'It's a very lively place, warm staff and fresh, easy but tasty food. Czech cuisine, with the touch of a Parisian bistro.'—Oldřich Sahajdák

LAS ADELITAS

Recommended by
Paul Day

Americká 684/8
Prague
Prague 12000
Czech Republic
+420 222542031
www.lasadelitas.cz

Opening hours	Open 7 days
Credit cards	Accepted
Price range	Affordable
Style	Casual
Cuisine	Mexican
Recommended for	Late night

'Loud music, great tacos and mescal.'—Paul Day

LOKÁL

Dlouhá 33
Prague
Prague 11000
Czech Republic
+420 222316265
lokal-dlouha.ambi.cz

Recommended by
Paul Day, Pavel Mencl,
Oldřich Sahajdák

Opening hours	Open 7 days
Credit cards	Accepted
Price range	Budget
Style	Casual
Cuisine	Czech
Recommended for	Local favourite

'Czech folklore is to drink beer so it has to be this
place. Great beer, great location, crowded, and nice
food like our mothers used to cook.'—Oldřich Sahajdák

MALÝ BUDDHA

Úvoz 46
Prague
Prague 11000
Czech Republic
+420 220513894
www.malybuddha.cz

Recommended by
David Sasek

Opening hours	Closed Monday
Credit cards	Not accepted
Price range	Budget
Style	Casual
Cuisine	Asian Fusion
Recommended for	Bargain

'Fresh food in a Nepalese/Asian style.'—David Sasek

MŮJ ŠÁLEK KÁVY

Křižíkova 386/105
Prague
Prague 18600
Czech Republic
+420 222981874
www.mujsalekkavy.cz

Recommended by
Paul Day

Opening hours	Open 7 days
Credit cards	Accepted but not AMEX
Price range	Budget
Style	Casual
Cuisine	Café-Bistro
Recommended for	Breakfast

'Perfect for coffee heads.'—Paul Day

Můj šálek kávy fits the zeitgeist of edgy but emerging
Karlín, an area off the tourist trail. The inside mixes
black-and-white photographs by the co-owner with a
huge mural grafted on otherwise bare bricks, oversized
industrial lights and blackboards. Baristas carefully
brew organic, fair-trade coffees from beans sourced
from producers in Central and South America and
Africa. These include honeyed Panama Los Lajones
or lighter El Salvador Finca El Carmen Natural
Panamera. Pancakes with large dollops of sour
cream are great for breakfast, as are poached eggs
with hollandaise, or Bradan Rost salmon. The terrace
is a nice spot to catch the summer's fleeting rays.

NOODLES

Hotel Yasmin
Politických Vězňů 913/12
Prague
Prague 11000
Czech Republic
+420 234100110
www.noodles.cz

Recommended by
Pavel Mencl

Opening hours	Open 7 days
Credit cards	Accepted
Price range	Budget
Style	Casual
Cuisine	International
Recommended for	Bargain

'Perfect all-around-the-world noodles and pasta.'
—Pavel Mencl

POLÉVKÁRNA

Sokolovská 97
Prague
Prague 18600
Czech Republic
+420 775114050
www.polevkarna.cz

Recommended by
Oldřich Sahajdák

Opening hours	Closed Saturday and Sunday
Reservation policy	No
Credit cards	Not accepted
Price range	Budget
Style	Casual
Cuisine	Czech
Recommended for	Bargain

'They have great soups that you can take away (take
out). It's focused mostly on seasonal vegetables. The
food is simple, cheap and very nice. You can sit by the
large window and look out onto the street while you're
eating.'—Oldřich Sahajdák

RESTAURACE NA KOPCI

Recommended by
Gwendal Le Ruyet

K Závěrce 2774/20
Prague
Prague 15000
Czech Republic
+420 251553102
www.nakopci.com

Opening hours	Open 7 days
Credit cards	Accepted
Price range	Affordable
Style	Smart casual
Cuisine	Czech
Recommended for	Regular neighbourhood

'The foie gras rolled in pistachio nuts is superb.'
—Gwendal Le Ruyet

SANSHO

Recommended by
Oldřich Sahajdák,
David Sasek

Petrská 1170/25
Prague
Prague 11000
Czech Republic
+420 222317425
www.sansho.cz

Opening hours	Closed Monday and Sunday
Credit cards	Accepted
Price range	Affordable
Style	Casual
Cuisine	Asian Fusion
Recommended for	Wish I'd opened

'I think this is the best "funky Asian" restaurant in town. They buy most of their ingredients from local farmers and suppliers and they know how to cook. They cook nose-to-tail style. I always enjoy my time there.'
—Oldřich Sahajdák

SAPA MARKET

Recommended by
Paul Day

Libušská 319/126
Prague
Prague 14200
Czech Republic
www.sapa-praha.cz

Opening hours	Open 7 days
Reservation policy	No
Credit cards	Not accepted
Price range	Budget
Style	Casual
Cuisine	Vietnamese Street Food
Recommended for	Bargain

'Vietnam out of Vietnam. Everything is a bargain. Real authentic Vietnamese food.'—Paul Day

SASAZU

Recommended by
Pavel Mencl

Bubenské Nábřeží 306
Prague
Prague 17004
Czech Republic
+420 284097455
www.sasazu.com

Opening hours	Open 7 days
Credit cards	Accepted
Price range	Affordable
Style	Smart casual
Cuisine	Asian Fusion
Recommended for	Regular neighbourhood

'Perfect food, a professional approach and service, and a great interior.'—Pavel Mencl

THE TAVERN

Recommended by
Paul Day

Chopinova 1521/26
Prague
Prague 12000
Czech Republic
www.thetavern.cz

Opening hours	Closed Monday
Credit cards	Not accepted
Price range	Budget
Style	Casual
Cuisine	Burgers
Recommended for	Regular neighbourhood

'Fantastic In-N-Out-style burger. Friendly and very cosy.'—Paul Day

LE TERROIR

Recommended by
Oldřich Sahajdák

Vejvodova 1
Prague
Prague 11000
Czech Republic
+420 222220260
www.leterroir.cz

Opening hours	Closed Monday and Sunday
Credit cards	Accepted
Price range	Expensive
Style	Smart casual
Cuisine	Modern European
Recommended for	High end

'One of the best restaurants in the Czech Republic. It's focused on seafood and local farmers' meat, such as rabbit or duck, and it has great wines.'
—Oldřich Sahajdák

YAMATO

Recommended by
David Sasek

U Kanálky 14
Prague
Prague 12000
Czech Republic
+420 222212617
www.yamato.cz

Opening hours	Closed Sunday
Credit cards	Accepted
Price range	Affordable
Style	Casual
Cuisine	Sushi
Recommended for	Late night

'Yamato is a tiny family-run Japanese restaurant with a nice atmosphere.'—David Sasek

BAR MLECZNY ZŁOTA KURKA

Recommended by
Robert Trzópek

Ulica Marszałkowska 55/73
Warsaw
Masovia 00-676
Poland
+48 226213280
www.barzlotakurka.pl

Opening hours	Open 7 days
Reservation policy	No
Credit cards	Accepted but not AMEX or Diners
Price range	Budget
Style	Casual
Cuisine	Polish
Recommended for	Bargain

'A *bary mleczny* (milk bar) is one item on the list of things worth trying in Poland. They are part of our history. Classic dishes made by our parents and grandparents at home.'—Robert Trzópek

BUTCHERY & WINE

Recommended by
Robert Trzópek

Ulica Żurawia 22
Warsaw
Masovia 00-515
Poland
+48 22502 3118
www.butcheryandwine.pl

Opening hours	Closed Sunday
Credit cards	Accepted
Price range	Affordable
Style	Casual
Cuisine	Steakhouse
Recommended for	Local favourite

'The first and best steakhouse in town. People in Poland love this kind of food.'—Robert Trzópek

CONCEPT 13

Recommended by
Robert Trzópek

Vitkac Department Store
Ulica Bracka 9
Warsaw
Masovia 00-501
Poland
+48 223107373
www.likusrestauracje.pl

Opening hours	Open 7 days
Credit cards	Accepted
Price range	Affordable
Style	Smart casual
Cuisine	Modern European
Recommended for	Regular neighbourhood

'Head chef Dariusz Barański is, for me, one of the future best chefs in Poland. He's a most creative and talented chef. The restaurant has a good-value lunch. It's well-designed and in a good location.'
—Robert Trzópek

MAKA I WODA

Recommended by
Wojciech Modest Amaro

Ulica Chmielna 13a
Warsaw
Masovia 00-021
Poland
+48 225059187

Opening hours	Open 7 days
Credit cards	Accepted but not AMEX
Price range	Budget
Style	Casual
Cuisine	Italian
Recommended for	Bargain

'Great original pizza and pasta. I enjoy eating there with my family.'—Wojciech Modest Amaro

The 'flour and water' of the restaurant's name focus immediate attention on the quality of raw materials that go into the Neapolitan pizza served here. Happily, for Warsaw's pizza purists, it all stands up to scrutiny: the flour is Caputo, direct from Naples, the tomatoes are thin-skinned San Marzano and the cheese is delicate, creamy *mozzarella di bufala*. In addition to the pizze *bianche* and *rosse*, you'll find seasonal dishes such as octopus, farro and preserved orange salad, and home-made *garganelli* with speck. The interior is modern urban, the spectacular tiled wood-fired oven burning proudly at centre stage.

META

Recommended by
Robert Trzópek

Ulica Mazowiecka 11
Warsaw
Masovia 00-052
Poland
+48 226924288
www.metanamazowieckiej.pl

Opening hours	Open 7 days
Credit cards	Accepted
Price range	Budget
Style	Casual
Cuisine	Polish
Recommended for	Late night

'The design is late 1980s, the food is simple and made especially for eating with vodka: herring, beef tartare and cold legs of pork.'—Robert Trzópek

NOLITA

Recommended by
Robert Trzópek

Ulica Wilcza 46
Warsaw
Masovia 00-999
Poland
+48 222920424
www.nolita.pl

Opening hours	Closed Sunday
Credit cards	Accepted
Price range	Affordable
Style	Smart casual
Cuisine	Modern European
Recommended for	Worth the travel

PRZEGRYŹ

Recommended by
Robert Trzópek

Ulica Mokotowska 52
Warsaw
Masovia 00-001
Poland
+48 22621 7177

Opening hours	Open 7 days
Credit cards	Accepted
Price range	Budget
Style	Casual
Cuisine	Polish
Recommended for	Breakfast

'All the ingredients are organic and from good suppliers. Double chicken broth made by the owner is the best cure for a hangover.'—Robert Trzópek

STARY DOM

Recommended by
Wojciech Modest Amaro

Ulica Puławska 104/106
Warsaw
Masovia 02-620
Poland
+48 226464208
www.restauracjastarydom.pl

Opening hours	Open 7 days
Credit cards	Accepted
Price range	Affordable
Style	Smart casual
Cuisine	Polish
Recommended for	Local favourite

'Traditional Polish food and liqueurs. Good for family brunch, lunch or dinner.'—Wojciech Modest Amaro

Expect hearty, home-made, traditional dishes and an abundance of vodka from the thirty-strong list at Stary Dom, a cosy slice of old Warsaw on Puławska, one of the capital's main streets. These include tripe soup or borscht, veal-stuffed pierogi dumplings (with an optional shot of vodka), steak tartare prepared at your table (also offered with vodka), and a house special of roast wild boar with juniper berry and Śliwowica (plum brandy) reduction. A favourite of jockeys and horse-racing fans in the 1950s, the spacious, wooden-vaulted, neighbourhood staple attracts the occasional star, being co-owned by Polish actor Piotr Adamczyk.

METAMORFOZA

Recommended by
Robert Trzópek

Ulica Szeroka 22/23
Gdansk
Pomerania 80-835
Poland
+48 583203030
www.restauracjametamorfoza.pl

Opening hours	Closed Monday
Credit cards	Accepted
Price range	Expensive
Style	Smart casual
Cuisine	Modern Polish
Recommended for	Worth the travel

Firmly planted on the Tri-City's culinary map, this laudable fine-dining venture, run by Justyna Zdunek, offers a modern take on the tastes and traditions of historic Pomerania, situated on the south shore of the Baltic Sea. Given her mission to promote the culinary culture of her homeland – a television programme has followed the restaurant's efforts to establish a poultry farm and restock nearby lakes with Polish fish – there's plenty of prime local produce on the menu. It's not all down to earth, though: the seven-course tasting menu – beef cheek with beetroot (beet), pike-perch with pickled cabbage – features impressive molecular flourishes.

HIŠA FRANKO

Recommended by
Shaun Hill

Staro Selo 1
Kobarid
Goriška 5222
Slovenia
+386 53894120
www.hisafranko.com

Opening hours	Open 7 days
Credit cards	Accepted
Price range	Expensive
Style	Smart casual
Cuisine	Modern Slovenian
Recommended for	Worth the travel

'It's the contrast between expectation and delivery. Quiet, rustic and set in a wood in northern Slovenia, this place delivers two- to three-star food and an enlightening selection of boutique Slovenian wines.' —Shaun Hill

Much admired by those who make the journey, the secluded, light-pink-walled restaurant (with rooms) slumbers on the valley floor near the Italian border. Chef Ana Ros exploits a bountiful local larder of game, mountain lamb, trout and up to 200 types of cheese. The latter, along with the cellar of biodynamic Slovenian wines, is the preserve of Ros's partner, Valter Kramar, whose father was the first owner of Hiša Franko. Ros's dishes include beetroot (beet) ravioli with cottage cheese, foie gras and fennel; a 'sea garden' of tomato water, sea bass, sea herbs and oyster ice cream; and dry porcini and 'blonde' chocolate ice cream with plum, kefir (fermented milk) and elder blossom jelly.

GOSTILNICA MANDRIJA

Recommended by
Tomaž Kavčič

Ajševica 81
Nova Gorica
Goriška 5000
Slovenia
+386 41752584
www.mandrija.si

Opening hours	Closed Tuesday and Wednesday
Credit cards	Accepted but not AMEX
Price range	Affordable
Style	Casual
Cuisine	Slovenian
Recommended for	Bargain

'A very nice place, especially for nature and horse lovers. Prices are good and they have made great progress in their cuisine. The menu is short and simple but well selected. The service is very good, there's a nice presentation of the dishes, and the ingredients are of high quality. The meat is excellent – very tender and tasty.'—Tomaž Kavčič

ABRAM TOURIST FARM

Recommended by
Tomaž Kavčič

Nanos 6
Vipava
Goriška 5271
Slovenia
+386 51662002
www.abram-si.com

Opening hours	Variable
Credit cards	Not accepted
Price range	Affordable
Style	Casual
Cuisine	Slovenian
Recommended for	Local favourite

'This family farm is more than 500 years old and is situated on a karst tableland called Nanos, 920 metres (3018 feet) above sea level with a great view of the sea. There's a nice atmosphere and it's child-friendly. You feel like you're at home. The waiters are young and committed. The food – ecologically produced in keeping with the local tradition – is original and genuine, with very generous portions, and you can taste different local dishes, such as Istrian stew, roast veal and dumplings.'—Tomaž Kavčič

GOSTILNA PRI LOJZETU

Recommended by
Emanuele Scarello

Dvorec Zemono
Vipava
Goriška 5271
Slovenia
+386 53687007
www.prilojzetu.si

Opening hours	Closed Monday and Tuesday
Credit cards	Accepted
Price range	Affordable
Style	Casual
Cuisine	Slovenian
Recommended for	Regular neighbourhood

'Here, the best regional produce of both land and sea is prepared with great *legerdemain*. Real musts are the sea bass cooked on a Piran salt slab and, in summer, an aperitif in the garden with its splendid view over the Vipava vineyards. The hospitality is exemplary thanks to Tomaž and Flavia, who make anyone who comes up to the Castello di Zemono feel like a king or queen.'
—Emanuele Scarello

'THEY GROW EVERYTHING THEMSELVES AND THE FOOD IS VERY HONEST AND PURE. BIG RESPECT.'

ROMAN ZAŠTŠERINSKI P621

ESTONIA, LATVIA & RUSSIA

'DELICIOUS FOOD FROM THE NORDIC ISLANDS, INSPIRED BY THE COOKING TRADITIONS OF MUHU AND THE SURROUNDING ISLANDS.'

VLADISLAV DJATSUK P622

'PERFECTLY PREPARED RUSSIAN HOME-STYLE FOOD.'

MATT ABERGEL P623

'You'd think you were in Paris not Riga.'

MARTINS RITINS P622

ESTONIA

LATVIA

RUSSIA

ESTONIA, LATVIA & RUSSIA

N̂

SCALE

0   140   280 mi.

LA BOTTEGA

Recommended by
Roman Zaštšerinski

Vene 4
Tallinn
Harjumaa 10123
Estonia
+372 6277733
www.labottega.ee

Opening hours	Open 7 days
Credit cards	Accepted
Price range	Affordable
Style	Smart casual
Cuisine	Italian
Recommended for	Late night

'This trattoria offers fantastic Sardinian food.'
—Roman Zaštšerinski

CHEDI

Recommended by
Vladislav Djatsuk

Sulevimägi 1
Tallinn
Harjumaa 10123
Estonia
+372 6461676
www.chedi.ee

Opening hours	Open 7 days
Credit cards	Accepted
Price range	Affordable
Style	Smart casual
Cuisine	Modern Asian
Recommended for	Late night

'I like to sit in Chedi on late evenings because it's an Asian restaurant that brings some magic through its food.'—Vladislav Djatsuk

KLAUS KOHVIK

Recommended by
Roman Zaštšerinski

Kalasadama 8
Tallinn
Harjumaa 10415
Estonia
+372 56919010
www.klauskohvik.ee

Opening hours	Open 7 days
Credit cards	Accepted but not AMEX
Price range	Budget
Style	Casual
Cuisine	Café-Bistro
Recommended for	Bargain

'It has a very good price and quality level. You get what you pay for.'—Roman Zaštšerinski

KOHVIK MOON

Recommended by
Vladislav Djatsuk,
Yves Le Lay

Võrgu 3
Tallinn
Harjumaa 10415
Estonia
+372 6314575
www.kohvikmoon.ee

Opening hours	Open 7 days
Credit cards	Accepted
Price range	Affordable
Style	Casual
Cuisine	Baltic Fusion
Recommended for	Regular neighbourhood

'It's good value, and very tasty Russian-Estonian food.'
—Yves Le Lay

Since 2009, Tallinn's arty waterfront neighbourhood of Kalamaja has been home to Kohvik Moon, a friendly local headed by a pair of chefs, Roman Zaštšerinski (ex Restoran Ö) and his cousin Igor Andrejeviga, along with Roman's wife Jana. Moon (Estonian for 'poppy') offers quirky good looks, vintage details and a new approach to modern Estonian cuisine without haute-cuisine trappings but with a tight focus on strong local ingredients and recipes. Follow fried herring, pickled potatoes, grapefruit and keta roe with duck breast, sauerkraut pie and smoked plum sauce, then finish with aronia berry schnapps. Closed July.

KOLM SIBULAT

Recommended by
Vladislav Djatsuk

Telliskivi 2
Tallinn
Harjumaa 10611
Estonia
+372 6644055
www.kolmsibulat.eu

Opening hours	Open 7 days
Credit cards	Accepted
Price range	Budget
Style	Casual
Cuisine	Baltic Fusion
Recommended for	Bargain

'A simple and relaxed restaurant.'—Vladislav Djatsuk

LEIB RESTO JA AED

Recommended by
Vladislav Djatsuk,
Peeter Pihel

Uus 31
Tallinn
Harjumaa 10111
Estonia
+372 6119026
www.leibresto.ee

Opening hours	Closed Sunday
Credit cards	Accepted
Price range	Affordable
Style	Casual
Cuisine	European
Recommended for	Local favourite

Dominated by its grill, the grassy terrace with comfy, fleece-wrapped seats makes Leib Resto ja Aed mighty popular with locals. 'Leib', meaning bread (traditionally black in Estonia), is a great accompaniment to hearty dishes such as creamy trout soup with tarragon, pike perch with organic buckwheat and mousseline, or hearty grass-fed rib-eye with celeriac (celery root), roasted garlic cream and red cabbage. Follow on with crème brûlée or sea buckthorn tart with strawberry ice cream. Expect a carefully stocked cellar too, seeing as Kristjan Peäske (co-owner with Janno Lepik, ex Rhodes W1) is a multi-award-winning sommelier.

TCHAIKOVSKY

Recommended by
Roman Zaštšerinski

Telegraaf Hotel
Vene 9
Tallinn
Harjumaa 10123
Estonia
+372 6000610
www.telegraafhotel.com

Opening hours	Open 7 days
Credit cards	Accepted
Price range	Affordable
Style	Smart casual
Cuisine	French-Russian
Recommended for	High end

'I think it's the best restaurant in Tallinn at the moment, and it serves gourmet Russian food which is very dear to me.'—Roman Zaštšerinski

PÕHJAKA MÕIS

Recommended by
Vladislav Djatsuk, Peeter
Pihel, Roman Zaštšerinski

Põhjaka Manor
Mäeküla
Paide
Järvamaa 72604
Estonia
+372 5267795
www.pohjaka.ee

Opening hours	Variable
Credit cards	Accepted
Price range	Affordable
Style	Casual
Cuisine	Modern Baltic
Recommended for	Local favourite

'They grow everything themselves and the food is very honest and pure. Big respect.'—Roman Zaštšerinski

In 2007 a trio of chefs began to breathe life back into a derelict nineteenth-century manor house between Tallinn and Tartu. The majority of typically Estonian dishes cost less than €10 (£8; $14) and are served to a 1980s soundtrack (from vinyl LPs). The dishes include marinated lamprey eels, home-cured and smoked charcuterie with black bread, rabbit stew, fillet of wild boar with mushroom sauce and roast onion, and Pavlova with sea buckthorn sauce. The millefeuille (here known as Napoleon Cake) is a staple. Ingredients are mostly sourced from the manor's garden (for their jams and compotes, for example) and also their farm, roamed by hens and pigs.

ALEXANDER

Recommended by
Vladislav Djatsuk

Pädaste Manor
Muhu Island
Saaremaa 94716
Estonia
+372 4548800
www.padaste.ee

Opening hours	Open 7 days
Credit cards	Accepted
Price range	Expensive
Style	Smart casual
Cuisine	Modern Baltic
Recommended for	High end

'Located at Pädaste Manor, its high ceilings open up views of the sunny conservatory and the ancient trees in the manor park. The team at Alexander offers delicious food from the Nordic islands, inspired by the cooking traditions of Muhu and the surrounding islands and valuing local traditions and the diverse tastes of different seasons.'—Vladislav Djatsuk

The impressive Pädaste Manor hotel, on Muhu Island, was largely built in the sixteenth century. But there is nothing old-fashioned about the food at Alexander, its flagship restaurant. A new chef, the Dane Yves Le Lay, has maintained Peeter Pihel's new Nordic cookery in extravagant nine-course tasting menus. Dishes include duck gizzards with apple, leek and whitefish roe, and local cheeses served with the island's own honey. The dining room, much of which is in a sunny conservatory, overlooks the winter garden; beyond is the property's private beach. Alexander has been named Estonia's Best Restaurant four years in a row.

KUKŠU MUIŽA

Recommended by
Martins Ritins

Kukšas
Jaunsātu Pagasts
Kurzeme 3128
Latvia
+371 63181545
www.kuksumuiza.lv

Opening hours	By appointment
Credit cards	Accepted
Price range	Expensive
Style	Casual
Cuisine	Latvian
Recommended for	Wish I'd opened

'Filled with authentic antiques and has its own kitchen garden.'—Martins Ritins

ART CAFÉ SIENNA

Recommended by
Martins Ritins

Strēlnieku Iela 3
Riga 1010
Latvia
+371 26142286
www.sienna.lv

Opening hours	Open 7 days
Credit cards	Accepted
Price range	Affordable
Style	Smart casual
Cuisine	Café-Patisserie
Recommended for	Breakfast

'You'd think you were in Paris not Riga (Riga before the war was called little Paris). The quiche is so rich and pure. Croque Monsieur, crêpes and rich, decadent cakes are all served... Escoffier would be proud.'
—Martins Ritins

The pavement tables at Riga's bohemian Art Café Sienna offer glorious views of the Art Nouveau buildings on Strēlnieku Street. There are further distractions inside, where *Vogue* magazines pile up on vintage tables, paintings by local artists line the walls, and books and antiques fill every corner. Part grandma's house, part Les Deux Magots, this eccentric café is known for excellent coffee, fine teas, and cakes from the acclaimed pastry kitchen at top Riga restaurant Vincents. Enjoy a quick croissant in the morning or while away an afternoon over eclairs, fresh berry tarts and a bottle of Champagne.

FOODBOX

Recommended by
Martins Ritins

Antonijas Iela 6a
Riga 1010
Latvia
+371 28205998
www.foodbox.lv

Opening hours	Closed Sunday
Reservation policy	No
Credit cards	Not accepted
Price range	Budget
Style	Casual
Cuisine	Turkish
Recommended for	Bargain

'It's a Turkish kebab establishment, but the difference here is that the owner bakes his own pittas and makes his own giros.'—Martins Ritins

KOYA

Recommended by
Martins Ritins

Andrejostas Iela 4
Riga 1045
Latvia
+371 27757255
www.koyarestaurant.com

Opening hours	Closed Monday
Credit cards	Accepted
Price range	Affordable
Style	Smart casual
Cuisine	Modern Latvian
Recommended for	Regular neighbourhood

'There's a great view of the harbour and a talented young chef, Jolanta Vaļēviča. It's great for a lazy Sunday brunch.'—Martins Ritins

Koya went from being an abandoned warehouse to destination restaurant in time for Riga's year in the spotlight as European Capital of Culture. Overlooking the Daugava River and harbour, diners can sit on the large terrace or beneath the recovered timber roof, while bands and DJs pump out atmosphere. Although Koya could all too easily be written off as too cool for school, dishes don't disappoint. They range from generous ostrich tartare with quail's egg and truffle toast, to veal broth with grilled peppers and bean sprouts, and catfish fillet with blue mussels, white asparagus and artichokes. Follow on with rowan parfait with almond crisps, alongside a cocktail of Persimmon Tea with kumquats, cinnamon sugar and Earl Grey soda.

VĪNA STUDIJA

Recommended by
Martins Ritins

Elizabetes Iela 10
Riga 1010
Latvia
+371 67283205
www.vinastudija.lv

Opening hours	Open 7 days
Credit cards	Accepted but not AMEX
Price range	Affordable
Style	Casual
Cuisine	Bar-Small plates
Recommended for	Late night

'Have a light antipasti and a glass of Riesling. Chef Elmāru is not just a chef, he's a comedian.'
—Martins Ritins

CAFE PUSHKIN

Recommended by
Matt Abergel,
Brad Farmerie

Tverskoy Bulvar 26a
Moscow
Moscow Oblast 125009
Russia
+7 4957390033
www.cafe-pushkin.ru

Opening hours	Open 7 days
Credit cards	Accepted
Price range	Expensive
Style	Formal
Cuisine	Russian
Recommended for	Worth the travel

'Cafe Pushkin was recommended to me on a quick trip to Moscow. I honestly expected it to be a tourist trap, but I was pleasantly surprised by the perfectly prepared Russian home-style food that was served. It reminded me of a refined version of my great-grandmother's cooking.'—Matt Abergel

DELICATESSEN

Recommended by
Ilya Shalev

Building 2
Sadovaya-Karetnaya Ulitsa 20
Moscow
Moscow Oblast 127051
Russia
+7 4956993952
www.newdeli.ru

Opening hours	Closed Monday and Sunday
Reservation policy	No
Credit cards	Accepted
Price range	Budget
Style	Casual
Cuisine	Deli
Recommended for	Local favourite

'A small restaurant run by the self-taught genius Ivan Shishkin. The food is very tasty.'—Ilya Shalev

PAUL

Recommended by
Pier Bussetti

Tverskaya Ulitsa 23/12
Moscow
Moscow Oblast 125009
Russia
+7 4955604948
Website

Opening hours	Open 7 days
Reservation policy	No
Credit cards	Accepted
Price range	Budget
Style	Casual
Cuisine	Bakery-Café
Recommended for	Breakfast

'Originally a French bakery, it's now owned by a Russian company. Despite the franchise, the quality is good.'
—Pier Bussetti

RAGOUT

Recommended by
Pier Bussetti

Bolshaya Gruzinskaya Ulitsa 69
Moscow
Moscow Oblast 123056
Russia
+7 4956626458
www.ragout.ru

Opening hours	Open 7 days
Credit cards	Accepted
Price range	Affordable
Style	Casual
Cuisine	Café-Bar-Bistro
Recommended for	Bargain

'A cross between a bistro and pseudo-gourmet restaurant with high-quality products and reasonable prices – especially at lunchtime.'—Pier Bussetti

The brainchild of Alexei Zimin, a leading food writer, magazine editor and TV presenter. Although also featuring a café and atelier, it is Ragout's sleek bar and grill that attracts the fashionably dressed locals, particularly at weekends when it stays open until late. In this otherwise low-lit room, two illuminated counters meet. One features imaginative libations by mixologist Natalia Davydova, including a Bloody Mary crafted with bacon-infused vodka. The other dispenses Zimin's European-accented dishes, such as duck breast with mango ceviche, halloumi salad with pears and kimchi, curried pumpkin and apple soup with toasted sunflower seeds and brioche, and mini churros with strawberry sauce.

UILLIAM'S

Recommended by
Brad Farmerie

Malaya Bronnaya Ulitsa 20a
Moscow
Moscow Oblast 123104
Russia
+7 4956506462
www.uilliams.ru

Opening hours	Open 7 days
Credit cards	Accepted
Price range	Affordable
Style	Smart casual
Cuisine	European
Recommended for	Worth the travel

'The best hidden gem in the city, serving super-tasty European cuisine in a beautiful room with beautiful people and a beautiful Molteni stove in the middle of an open kitchen.'—Brad Farmerie

'Uses daily fresh fish from the South Aegean Sea, which is in front of the restaurant.'
MUSTAFA CIHAN KIPÇAK P630

'IT IS REALLY NICE TO SEE HOW YOU CAN PORTRAY AN ENTIRE NATION WITH FOOD. ERGON EXEMPLIFIES GREECE'S VERSATILITY.'
KONSTANTIN FILIPPOU P629

'BEST KEBAB IN THE COUNTRY.'
ÜRYAN DOĞMUŞ P630

GREECE, TURKEY & CYPRUS

'WITH THE VIEW OF THE ACROPOLIS, IT IS THE PERFECT SPOT FOR ME, BECAUSE I AM VERY SLEEPY IN THE MORNING AND I LIKE MY BREAKFAST WITH A LITTLE SOFTNESS.'
WILLIAM MAHI PP628–629

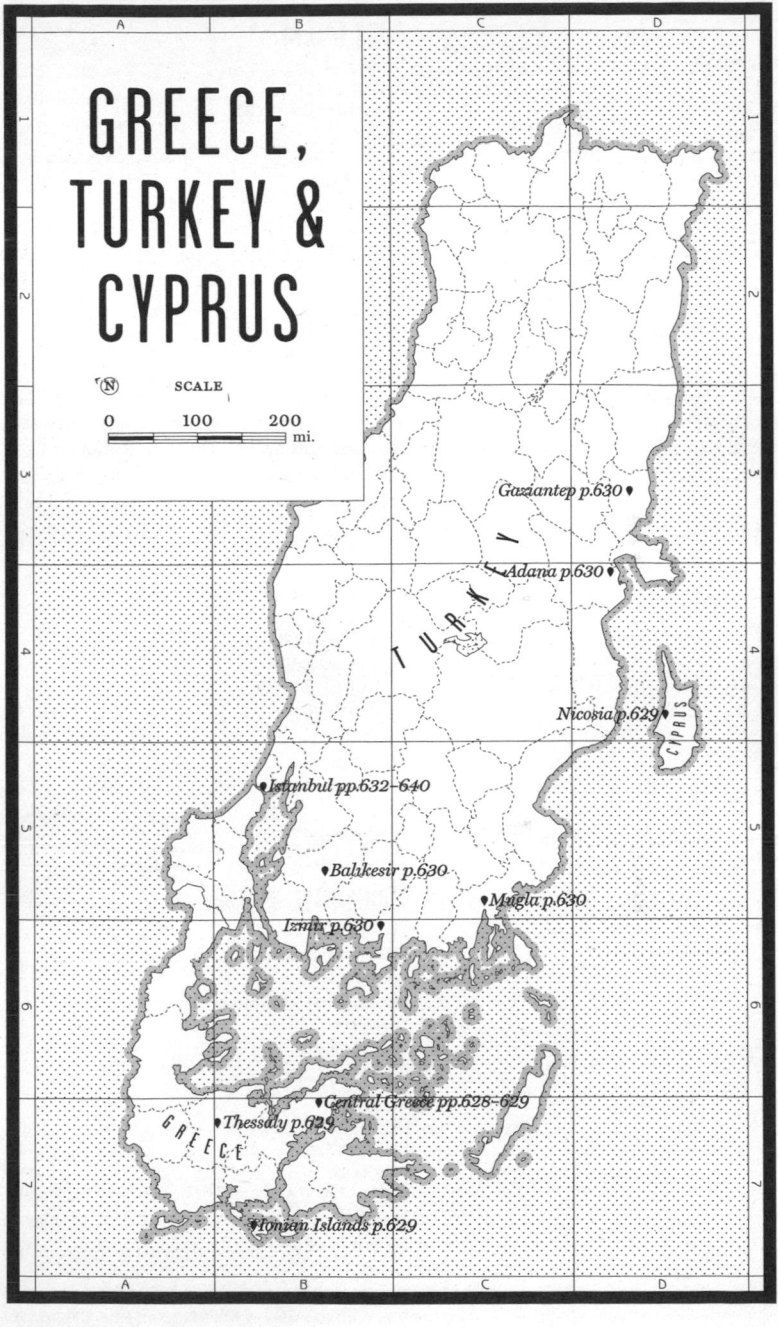

GREECE, TURKEY & CYPRUS

N   SCALE

0   100   200
                        mi.

A   B   C   D

TURKEY

Gaziantep p.630 ♦

♦ Adana p.630 ♦

Nicosia p.629 ♦   CYPRUS

♦ Istanbul pp.632–640

♦ Balıkesir p.630

Muğla p.630 ♦

Izmir p.630 ♦

♦ Central Greece pp.628–629

♦ Thessaly p.629

GREECE

♦ Ionian Islands p.629

ALERIA

Megalou Alexandrou 57
Athens
Central Greece 104 35
Greece
+30 2105222633
www.aleria.gr

Recommended by
Georgianna Hiliadaki,
Nikos Roussos

Opening hours	Closed Sunday
Credit cards	Accepted
Price range	Affordable
Style	Casual
Cuisine	Mediterranean
Recommended for	Regular neighbourhood

'Chef Gikas Xenakis cooks deliciously modern Greek cuisine. Most favourable in the summer when you can sit in the beautiful yard.'—Georgianna Hiliadaki

NEW TASTE

New Hotel
Filellinon 16
Athens
Central Greece 105 57
Greece
+30 2103273000
www.yeshotels.gr

Recommended by
Georgianna Hiliadaki,
Nikos Roussos

Opening hours	Open 7 days
Credit cards	Accepted
Price range	Affordable
Style	Casual
Cuisine	Mediterranean
Recommended for	Breakfast

'Beautiful space, very nice pastries, best place in Athens for a Sunday brunch in the heart of the city.'
—Georgianna Hiliadaki

PBOX EATERY

Levidou 11
Athens
Central Greece 145 62
Greece
+30 2108088818
www.p-box.gr

Recommended by
Georgianna Hiliadaki

Opening hours	Open 7 days
Credit cards	Accepted
Price range	Affordable
Style	Casual
Cuisine	Greek-Asian
Recommended for	Bargain

'Nice atmosphere, an all-day chic and casual place, where there is a very interesting combination of Greek and Asian cuisine.'—Georgianna Hiliadaki

PSOMI & ALATI

Eleftheroton Square 8
Athens
Central Greece 152 32
Greece
+30 2106848178
www.psomialati.gr

Recommended by
Nikos Roussos

Opening hours	Closed Monday
Credit cards	Accepted but not AMEX
Price range	Affordable
Style	Casual
Cuisine	Modern Greek
Recommended for	Bargain

TUDOR HALL RESTAURANT

King George Hotel
Vasileos Georgiou A Street 3
Athens
Central Greece 105 64
Greece
+30 2103330265
www.tudorhall.gr

Recommended by
William Mahi

Opening hours	Open 7 days
Credit cards	Accepted
Price range	Affordable
Style	Smart casual
Cuisine	Mediterranean
Recommended for	Breakfast

'The service is very attentive, without being over the top. With the view of the Acropolis, it is the perfect spot for me, because I'm very sleepy in the morning

and I like my breakfast with a little softness.'
—William Mahi

KLIMATARIA
Benitses
Corfu
Ionian Islands 490 84
Greece
+30 2661071201
www.klimataria-restaurant.gr

Recommended by
Ettore Botrini

Opening hours	Open 7 days
Credit cards	Not accepted
Price range	Affordable
Style	Casual
Cuisine	Corfiot
Recommended for	Local favourite

AGNADIO
By the Monastery of Evangelistria
Skiathos
Thessaly 370 02
Greece
+30 2427022016

Recommended by
Dominic Chapman

Opening hours	Open 7 days
Credit cards	Accepted
Price range	Affordable
Style	Casual
Cuisine	Greek
Recommended for	Worth the travel

'Agnadio serves really delicious traditional Greek food. The service is friendly and very professional. The view is probably the best view from any restaurant in Europe. It's a very good restaurant that I look forward to visiting when I am in Greece.'—Dominic Chapman

ERGON
Kouskoura 5
Thessaloniki
Thessaly 546 22
Greece
+30 2310284224
www.ergonproducts.gr

Recommended by
Konstantin Filippou

Opening hours	Open 7 days
Reservation policy	No
Credit cards	Accepted but not AMEX
Price range	Affordable
Style	Casual
Cuisine	Greek
Recommended for	Bargain

'It's really nice to see how you can portray an entire nation with food. Ergon exemplifies Greece's versatility and offers more than 1,200 traditional Greek products in its stores and adjoining restaurants.'
—Konstantin Filippou

ZANETTOS
Trikoupi 65
Nicosia
Nicosia 1015
Cyprus
+357 22765501
www.zanettos.com

Recommended by
Ettore Botrini

Opening hours	Closed Sunday
Credit cards	Accepted
Price range	Budget
Style	Casual
Cuisine	Cypriot
Recommended for	Worth the travel

This old-town taverna provides visiting tourists, local politicians and passing celebrities (check out the walls' hall of fame) with a masterclass in mezze. Zanettos doesn't muck around with menus – expect a stream of Cypriot dishes prepared from fresh produce gathered from Nicosia's farmers' market. Dinner might kick off with garlicky tahini, perky green salads and crisp fried courgette (zucchini) strips, but save space for the signature halloumi, smoked Cypriot sausage, pitta and piping hot souvlaki, fresh from the coals. And all for €20 (£16; $28) a head. Like it or not, your visit will undoubtedly include a hello from the ebullient owner. Book for after 9.00 p.m. if you want to dine with the locals.

YÜZEVLER KEBAP

Recommended by
Üryan Doğmuş

Ziya Paşa Bulvari 25/a
Adana
Adana 64018
Turkey
+90 3224547513
www.yuzevler.com.tr

Opening hours..Open 7 days
Credit cards..Accepted but not AMEX
Price range...Budget
Style..Casual
Cuisine..Turkish
Recommended for............................Worth the travel

'Best kebab in the country. There's nothing too
interesting about the service or design but the food is
a once in a lifetime experience. As a chef, I have eaten
very tasty food a number of times but nothing
compares to the kebab at Yüzevler.'—Üryan Doğmuş

BAY NIHAT LALE

Recommended by
Şemsa Denizsel

Sahil Yolu 21
Cunda Island
Balıkesir 10405
Turkey
+90 2663271063
www.baynihat.com.tr

Opening hours..Open 7 days
Credit cards..Accepted but not AMEX
Price range..Affordable
Style...Smart casual
Cuisine..Mezze
Recommended for............................Worth the travel

'For the most wonderful seafood mezzes and foraged
greens.'—Şemsa Denizsel

METANET LOKANTASI

Recommended by
Şemsa Denizsel

Kozluca Caddesi 11
Şahinbey
Gaziantep 27240
Turkey
+90 3422314666

Opening hours..Open 7 days
Reservation policy...No
Credit cards..Not accepted
Price range...Budget
Style..Casual
Cuisine..Turkish
Recommended for............................Worth the travel

'They make the most wonderful *beyran*, a local breakfast
staple, which is a spicy rice and lamb soup with loads
of garlic.'—Şemsa Denizsel

SELÇUK KÖFTECISI

Recommended by
Gençay Üçok

Şahabettin Dede Caddesi 10
Selçuk
Izmir 35920
Turkey
+90 2328926696

Opening hours..Open 7 days
Credit cards............................Accepted but not AMEX or Diners
Price range...Budget
Style..Casual
Cuisine..Turkish
Recommended for............................Worth the travel

'Honest cooking, specializing in the local cuisine of the
region. All very fresh and high-quality produce. Very
hospitable staff. Simple but very tasty home-made
dishes like grilled meatballs and sautéed exotic wild
greens and vegetables.'—Gençay Üçok

SARDUNYA

Recommended by
Mustafa Cihan Kipçak

Selimiye Köyü
Marmaris
Mugla 48700
Turkey
+90 2524464003
www.sardunya.info

Opening hours..Open 7 days
Credit cards..Accepted
Price range..Affordable
Style...Smart casual
Cuisine..Turkish
Recommended for............................Worth the travel

'There is no doubt that Sardunya is the best fish
restaurant for me. They use daily fresh fish from the
South Aegean Sea, which is in front of the restaurant,
and they get all their other ingredients fresh from
Selimiye village. Because of this all their products are
ecological and organic. You'll always see the owner of
the restaurant there and you can feel the warm homey
approach.'—Mustafa Cihan Kipçak

ISTANBUL

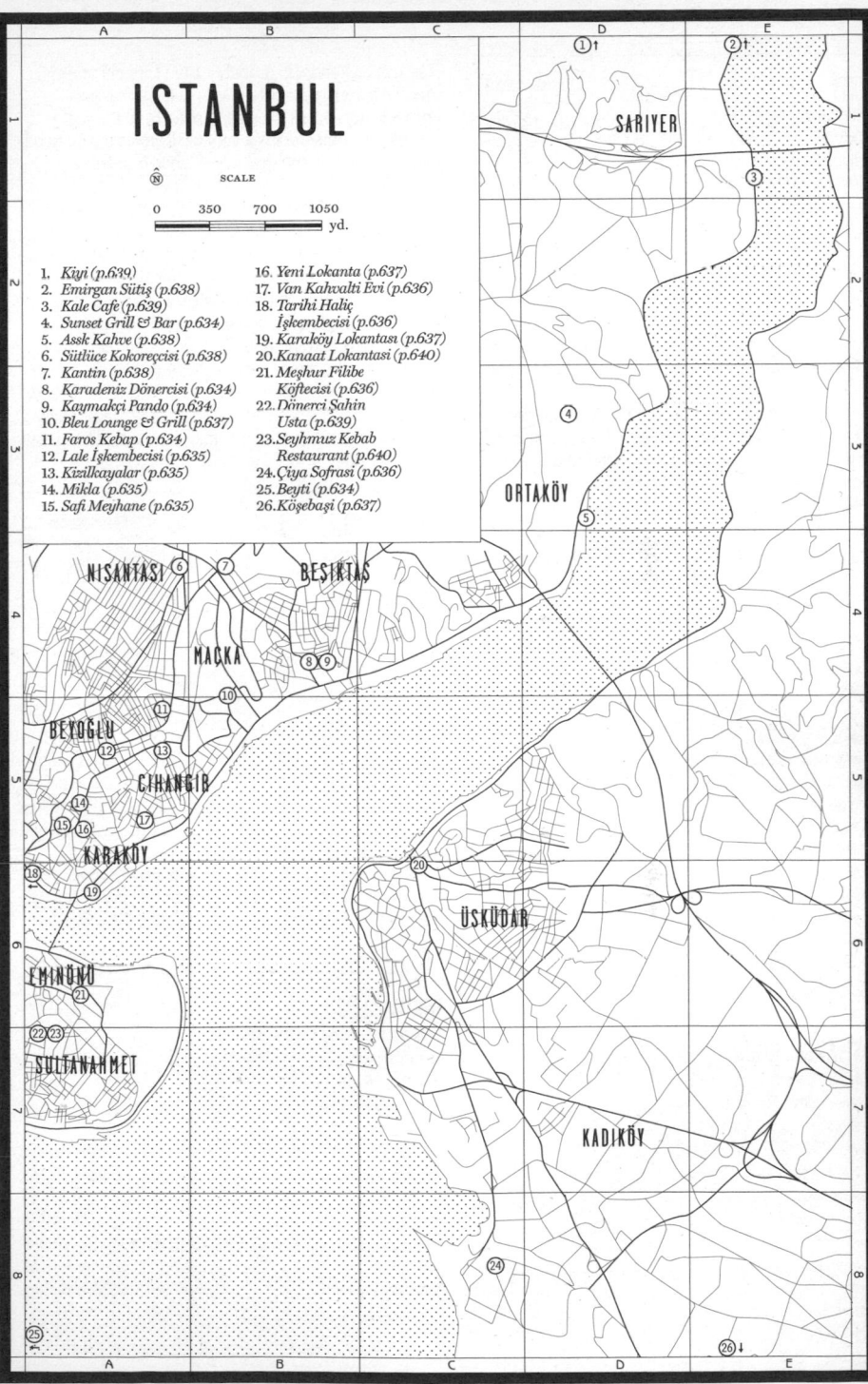

BEYTI

Orman Sokak 8
Bakirkoy
Istanbul 34153
+90 2126632990
www.beyti.com

Opening hours	Closed Monday
Credit cards	Accepted
Price range	Affordable
Style	Smart casual
Cuisine	Turkish
Recommended for	Local favourite

'Beyti is a symbol of Istanbul. You can find still find Mr
Beyti (who is ninety years old) here. He continues to
control the quality and guest satisfaction. As a meat
restaurant there is no other like Beyti.'
—Mustafa Cihan Kipçak

KARADENIZ DÖNERCISI

Balıkçılar Çarşısı
Mumcu Bakkal Sokak 6
Beşiktaş
Istanbul 34353
+90 2122617693

Opening hours	Open 7 days
Reservation policy	No
Credit cards	Not accepted
Price range	Budget
Style	Casual
Cuisine	Turkish
Recommended for	Bargain

'It is cheap, but also good. Asım Usta makes a good
döner kebab and the value for money is excellent. By
the way, you can find Asım by following the long line
in Beşiktaş Çarşı.'—Mustafa Cihan Kipçak

KAYMAKÇI PANDO

Balıkçılar Çarşısı
Mumcu Bakkal Sokak 6
Beşiktaş
Istanbul 34353

Opening hours	Open 7 days
Reservation policy	No
Credit cards	Not accepted
Price range	Budget
Style	Casual
Cuisine	Café
Recommended for	Breakfast

'The owner, Pando, is probably 100 years old and still
there. It's the tiniest eatery with only buffalo-milk
kaymak, eggs, fresh bread and milk. Even the tea
comes from outside. It's a very basic place but so good
you barely notice the grime.'—Şemsa Denizsel

How much this *kaymak* specialist in Beşiktaş market
has changed since it opened back in 1895, it's hard to
say. A clotted cream made from skimming simmered
buffalo milk, *kaymak* is a Turkish breakfast delight,
and Kaymakçi Pando does the very best in Istanbul.
Run by eighty-nine-year-old Pando, it's an unapologetically scruffy place but its four inside tables and
– assuming it's not raining – those on the pavement
outside are never empty. Freshly baked white bread,
dipped in *kaymak* with honey, and a side of fried eggs,
drowning in butter, with hot milk or a cup of black tea
– way to go.

SUNSET GRILL & BAR

Ulus Parkı
Yol Sokak 2
Beşiktaş
Istanbul 34353
+90 2122870357
www.sunsetgrillbar.com

Opening hours	Open 7 days
Credit cards	Accepted
Price range	Expensive
Style	Smart casual
Cuisine	International
Recommended for	High end

'Nice view over the Bosphorus, consistently good
service, an impressive wine cellar and a "posh" feel to
the place, which is handy for special-occasion dinners.'
—Gençay Üçok

FAROS KEBAP

Şehit Muhtar Bey Caddesi 28
Beyoğlu
Istanbul 34437
+90 2122503356
www.faroskebab.com

Opening hours	Open 7 days
Credit cards	Accepted
Price range	Affordable
Style	Casual
Cuisine	Turkish
Recommended for	Regular neighbourhood

'It is a new kebab restaurant, but it's different from the others because of the atmosphere. It looks like a modern bistro or coffee shop but it is a kebab house, which is very interesting for us. As for food, they are using their own sources for ingredients such as pistachios from Siirt and almonds from Datça. And their baker, who I call "Fırın Ustası", is quite possibly the best in town.'
—Mustafa Cihan Kipçak

LALE İŞKEMBECISI

Recommended by
Şemsa Denizsel

Tarlabaşı Bulvarı 13
Beyoğlu
Istanbul 34437
+90 2122526969
www.laleiskembecisi.com.tr

Opening hours	Open 7 days
Reservation policy	No
Credit cards	Accepted but not Amex
Price range	Budget
Style	Casual
Cuisine	Tripe
Recommended for	Late night

'Serves very garlicky tripe soup.'—Şemsa Denizsel

MIKLA

Recommended by
Şemsa Denizsel,
Üryan Doğmuş, Niklas
Ekstedt, Fisun Ercan,
Mustafa Cihan Kipçak,
Didem Şenol Tiryakioğlu

The Marmara Pera Hotel
Meşrutiyet Caddesi 15
Beyoğlu
Istanbul 34430
+90 2122935656
www.miklarestaurant.com

Opening hours	Closed Sunday
Credit cards	Accepted
Price range	Expensive
Style	Smart casual
Cuisine	Modern Turkish
Recommended for	High end

'As a chef in Istanbul, Mikla was my first stop. The food is always well presented and delicious. They have a great research team for local ingredients, so you can taste products from every region of Turkey, and the servers know what they are doing.'—Üryan Doğmuş

SAFI MEYHANE

Recommended by
Üryan Doğmuş

Meşrutiyet Caddesi 84
Beyoğlu
Istanbul 34437
+90 5302404908
www.safimeyhane.com

Opening hours	Open 7 days
Credit cards	Accepted
Price range	Budget
Style	Casual
Cuisine	Mezze
Recommended for	Wish I'd opened

'It is a mezze and rakı restaurant in Istanbul. For me, to have a restaurant like Safi is a retirement plan. Very simple and good food with a friendly environment. No stress for the owner.'—Üryan Doğmuş

KIZILKAYALAR

Recommended by
Şemsa Denizsel

Siraselviler Caddesi 6
Cihangir
Istanbul 34433
+90 2164111177
www.kizilkayalar.com.tr

Opening hours	Open 7 days
Reservation policy	No
Credit cards	Not accepted
Price range	Budget
Style	Casual
Cuisine	Fast Food
Recommended for	Late night

'Wet burgers that are very garlicky.'—Şemsa Denizsel

Kizilkayalar first managed to distinguish itself from Istanbul's vast sea of fast-food stands in the late 1970s, when some bright spark, noting that the döner market was somewhat flooded, came up with the concept of the Islak Burger (wet burger). Their sweetly pungent smell first hits you in the long queue (waiting line) outside. The burgers are doused in an oily, tomato sauce, containing relationship-ending quantities of garlic, then steamed for several hours inside their sticky bun to produce the world's slipperiest slider. Order two right from the start, as putting your hand back into your pocket after your first is a very messy business.

VAN KAHVALTI EVI

Recommended by
Üryan Doğmuş

Defterdar Yokuşu 52
Cihangir
Istanbul 34433
+90 2122936437

Opening hours	Open 7 days
Reservation policy	No
Credit cards	Accepted but not AMEX
Price range	Affordable
Style	Casual
Cuisine	Turkish breakfast
Recommended for	Breakfast

'The quality is really good for the price. The way that they serve breakfast, family-style, and the atmosphere really makes me feel like I'm at home and that's a very good feeling for breakfast.'—Üryan Doğmuş

MEŞHUR FILIBE KÖFTECISI

Recommended by
Şemsa Denizsel

Ankara Caddesi 112
Eminönü
Istanbul 34110
+90 2125193976

Opening hours	Closed Sunday
Reservation policy	No
Credit cards	Not accepted
Price range	Budget
Style	Casual
Cuisine	Turkish
Recommended for	Bargain

'Delicious, cheap and satisfying. It serves simply grilled meatballs with a bean salad.'—Şemsa Denizsel

TARIHI HALIÇ İŞKEMBECISI

Recommended by
Gençay Üçok

Abdulezelpaşa Caddesi 315
Eminönü
Istanbul 34083
+90 2125349414
www.haliciskembecisi.com

Opening hours	Open 7 days
Reservation policy	No
Credit cards	Accepted
Price range	Budget
Style	Casual
Cuisine	Turkish
Recommended for	Late night

'It is a strong Turkish tradition to eat tripe soup late at night or early morning, especially if you have had a night out drinking. This particular tripe soup shop has been operating since 1938 and apparently has reached perfection in preparation of this "love it or hate it" kind of soup. For those who aren't brave enough to try it, the shop does also serve "sheep's head and foot soup" and for those who want to be just boring, there's lentil soup!'—Gençay Üçok

ÇIYA SOFRASI

Recommended by
Carrie Nahabedian,
Stevie Parle

Güneslibahce Sokak 44
Kadiköy
Istanbul 34710
+90 2163303190
www.ciya.com.tr

Opening hours	Open 7 days
Credit cards	Accepted but not AMEX
Price range	Budget
Style	Smart casual
Cuisine	Turkish
Recommended for	Worth the travel

'The chef there is extremely talented and travelled around Turkey collecting recipes and changing them in a wonderful way. You won't eat like this anywhere else in the world.'—Stevie Parle

EUROPE / GREECE, TURKEY & CYPRUS / ISTANBUL

KÖŞEBAŞI

Bağdat Caddesi 235/1
Kadiköy
Istanbul 34730
+90 2164675353
www.kosebasi.com

Recommended by
Carrie Nahabedian

Opening hours	Open 7 days
Credit cards	Accepted
Price range	Affordable
Style	Smart casual
Cuisine	Turkish
Recommended for	Worth the travel

'Great food and kebabs and mezze of the highest order.
The food is so flavourful and juicy, just bursting with
Turkish spices and rich marinades. The warm grilled
breads of the Caucasus Mountain regions, whole
grilled fish wrapped in grape leaves – it may sound
common, but it is far from it.'—Carrie Nahabedian

KARAKÖY LOKANTASI

Kemankes Caddesi 37a
Karaköy
Istanbul 34425
+90 2122924455
www.karakoylokantasi.com

Recommended by
Üryan Doğmuş

Opening hours	Open 7 days
Credit cards	Accepted but not AMEX
Price range	Budget
Style	Casual
Cuisine	Turkish
Recommended for	Regular neighbourhood

'As a chef I can feel the difference between fresh and
dated food and every time I go to Karaköy Lokantasi I
eat fresh food. The service is not fancy but I've never
had a problem.'—Üryan Doğmuş

YENI LOKANTA

Kumbaracı Yokuşu 66
Karaköy
Istanbul 34435
+90 2122922550
www.lokantayeni.com

Recommended by
Didem Şenol Tiryakioğlu

Opening hours	Closed Sunday
Credit cards	Accepted
Price range	Affordable
Style	Smart casual
Cuisine	Modern Turkish
Recommended for	Local favourite

'The smoked butter is to die for.'
—Didem Şenol Tiryakioğlu

Yeni Lokanta is a paradigm of so-called 'new Turkish
cuisine': classic regional ingredients handled in
dexterous, modern ways. The name means 'new
canteen' or 'new eatery' and is a nod to this innovative
genre. A wide marble-clad entrance leads to a bar
covered in beautiful Iznik tiles, while delicate green
lamps dangle above the tables. The standout dishes
are the *mantı* (Turkish dumplings), which are usually
filled with meat but here come stuffed with dried
aubergine and served in a spicy red pepper sauce
flavoured with pomegranate molasses. For dessert,
try the mastic pudding with mastic ice cream.

BLEU LOUNGE & GRILL

The Ritz-Carlton Hotel
Askerocagi Caddesi 6
Maçka
Istanbul 34367
+90 2123344444
www.ritzcarlton.com

Recommended by
Üryan Doğmuş

Opening hours	Open 7 days
Credit cards	Accepted
Price range	Affordable
Style	Smart casual
Cuisine	International
Recommended for	Late night

'I want to be sure of what I eat at night – it must be clean,
fresh and tasty. Bleu satisfies all my needs in terms of
those three. Since it is an outlet of Ritz-Carlton, the
service is perfect.'—Üryan Doğmuş

KANTIN

Akkavak Sokağı 30
Nişantaşı
Istanbul 34365
+90 2122193114
www.kantin.biz

Opening hours	Closed Sunday
Reservation policy	No
Credit cards	Accepted
Price range	Affordable
Style	Smart casual
Cuisine	Modern Turkish
Recommended for	Local favourite

'Şemsa Denizsel is the lady kickin' ass in the kitchen. Refined, contemporary and casual local cooking at its best. In my opinion it is a perfect role model for what a contemporary "Istanbullu" eatery should be.' —Mehmet Gürs

Şemsa Denizsel is often referred to as the 'Turkish Alice Waters', her ingredient-led, farm-to-table food philosophy bearing much in common with the famous Californian's. Kantin, as its name suggests, is an upmarket local canteen for professionals in the smart Nişantaşı district. Downstairs is a deli with a handsome garden; upstairs is a dining room with crisp linen and cut flowers on the tables. Dishes, chalked on the blackboard, might include tabbouleh with modern accents such as candied almonds and oat-crusted chicken schnitzel or perhaps a bonito shish kebab.

SÜTLÜCE KOKOREÇCISI

Corner of Halaskargazi Caddesi
and Çarsı Sokak
Nişantaşı
Istanbul 34360
+90 2122308036

Opening hours	Open 7 days
Reservation policy	No
Credit cards	Accepted but not AMEX
Price range	Budget
Style	Casual
Cuisine	Fast Food
Recommended for	Bargain

'Whenever I pass by Sütlüce, I can't resist the smell of *kokoreç* (lamb-intestine dish). The *kokoreç* they cook here is the real stuff, they cook it on a coal fire and serve it with great spices. It is nothing fancy, just street food. There is always a traffic jam around, there's no air conditioning or roof and you have to eat on the pavement (sidewalk), but it's worth it.' —Üryan Doğmuş

ASSK KAHVE

Muallim Naci Caddesi 64
Ortaköy
Istanbul 34345
+90 2122654734
www.asskkahve.com

Opening hours	Open 7 days
Reservation policy	No
Credit cards	Accepted
Price range	Budget
Style	Casual
Cuisine	Café
Recommended for	Breakfast

'They have a few sites in Istanbul but the one down on the Bosphorus is just the most amazing location. A perfect view of all the boats coming and going down the Bosphorus, beautiful sunshine and a good Turkish breakfast make it a great start to a day off in Istanbul.' —James Wilkins

EMIRGAN SÜTIŞ

Emirgan Mektebi Sk 3
Sarıyer
Istanbul 34450
+90 2125737724
www.sutis.com.tr

Opening hours	Open 7 days
Reservation policy	No
Credit cards	Accepted
Price range	Affordable
Style	Smart casual
Cuisine	Turkish
Recommended for	Breakfast

'The most important thing is that they use high-quality products. It may not be a boutique place, but the food is delicious and the quality of the service is impressive. The location is superb as it's so close to the Bosphorus. You can have a breakfast at Emirgan, the old Ottoman territory, and watch the ships go by while sitting below the giant trees.' —Mustafa Cihan Kipçak

KALE CAFE

Recommended by
Gençay Üçok

Yahya Kemal Caddesi 16
Sarıyer
Istanbul 34470
+90 2122650097
www.kalecafe.com

Opening hours	Open 7 days
Credit cards	Accepted
Price range	Affordable
Style	Casual
Cuisine	Turkish
Recommended for	Breakfast

'This is where one should be in Istanbul on a sunny weekend morning: Rumeli Hisarı, by the magnificent views of the Bosphorus, to enjoy a slow and lasting "Ceremonial Turkish Breakfast". Scrambled eggs with pastrami, a good selection of local cheeses and olives, fresh clotted cream to go along with honey and jams... Try to get there before 10.00 a.m., otherwise it can be hard to find a table.'—Gençay Üçok

KIYI

Recommended by
Mehmet Gürs

Kefeliköy Caddesi 126
Sariyer
Istanbul 34470
+90 2122620002
www.kiyi.com.tr

Opening hours	Open 7 days
Credit cards	Accepted
Price range	Budget
Style	Casual
Cuisine	Mezze-Seafood
Recommended for	Regular neighbourhood

'It's a great fish restaurant. Few but great mezze, always fresh fish, grilled to perfection. The place is refined but has a nice casual feel.'—Mehmet Gürs

A mezze and seafood restaurant on the European side of the Bosphorus, ramshackle Kiyi eclipses its better-groomed competitors by 'maximizing the full potential of seasonal fish'. This is fresh, traditional Turkish cuisine, with mezze of squid, prawns (shrimp) and mussels, and vine leaves, sea beans and cheesy cigarette pastries. Take your pick from a long fish menu that changes seasonally, including grilled gurnard (sea robin), scorpion fish or lightly floured red mullet. Open since 1964, Kiyi's history of local custom, a sea view and decor of wood panels and creeping vines gives eating seafood here a dash of shabby chic.

DÖNERCI ŞAHIN USTA

Recommended by
Didem Şenol Tiryakioğlu,
Gençay Üçok

Kılıççılar Sokak 7
Sultanahmet
Istanbul 34110
+90 2125265297
www.donercisahinusta.com

Opening hours	Open 7 days
Reservation policy	No
Credit cards	Not accepted
Price range	Budget
Style	Casual
Cuisine	Turkish
Recommended for	Bargain

'Slices of very juicy döner kebab cooked on a coal fire, spread out onto a fresh puffy loaf of *pide* (flatbread) and wrapped together with some greens and red onions. You could order a "double meat" portion to enjoy it better and it will still cost you no more than twenty liras (£5; $9). You might have to line up in front of this small hole in the wall to taste "probably the last proper example of döner kebab available in town". Be sure to get there before 2.00 p.m. and remember that they have no seating.'—Gençay Üçok

This tiny hole in the wall, flanked by jewellers, represents an unsurpassable pit stop after shopping in the nearby Grand Bazaar. The enterprise, with its garish orange awning, has been going since the late 1960s, and there's always a queue (waiting line) for the very short menu. The choice is döner kebab with onions and tomatoes, served in a wrap or stuffed into pitta bread. The meat is so succulent, a sauce is hardly necessary. Be warned: it's only open for lunch and the kebab is usually finished by about 2.00 p.m. — so don't leave it too late.

SEYHMUZ KEBAB RESTAURANT

Recommended by
Gençay Üçok

Medrese Sokak 2
Sultanahmet
Istanbul 34110
+90 2125261613
www.seyhmuzkebab.com

Opening hours..Closed Sunday
Reservation policy..No
Credit cards...Not accepted
Price range...Budget
Style..Casual
Cuisine..Turkish
Recommended for.............................Regular neighbourhood

'Delicacies of Mardin Province prepared with great skill and labour. Always a genuine welcome, but if you haven't finished the food on your plate, you might end up being grilled by one of the chefs or waiters, so a real "feel-at-home" mood is also standard. Go for the house special, charcoal-grilled Şeyhmuz meatball, and roll it into a piping hot flatbread with fresh greens, you'll remember it for years.'—Gençay Üçok

KANAAT LOKANTASI

Recommended by
Gençay Üçok

Selmanipak Cadessi 9
Üsküdar
Istanbul 34672
+90 2165533791
www.kanaatlokantasi.com.tr

Opening hours...Open 7 days
Reservation policy..No
Credit cards...Not accepted
Price range...Budget
Style..Casual
Cuisine..Turkish
Recommended for.....................................Local favourite

'Traditional local delicacies varying from casseroles to cold stews and desserts, all executed with experience and respect to the traditions of Turkish home cooking. Probably the best example of Istanbul's typical lunch restaurants, where there is something for everyone. It is also very vegetarian friendly.'—Gençay Üçok

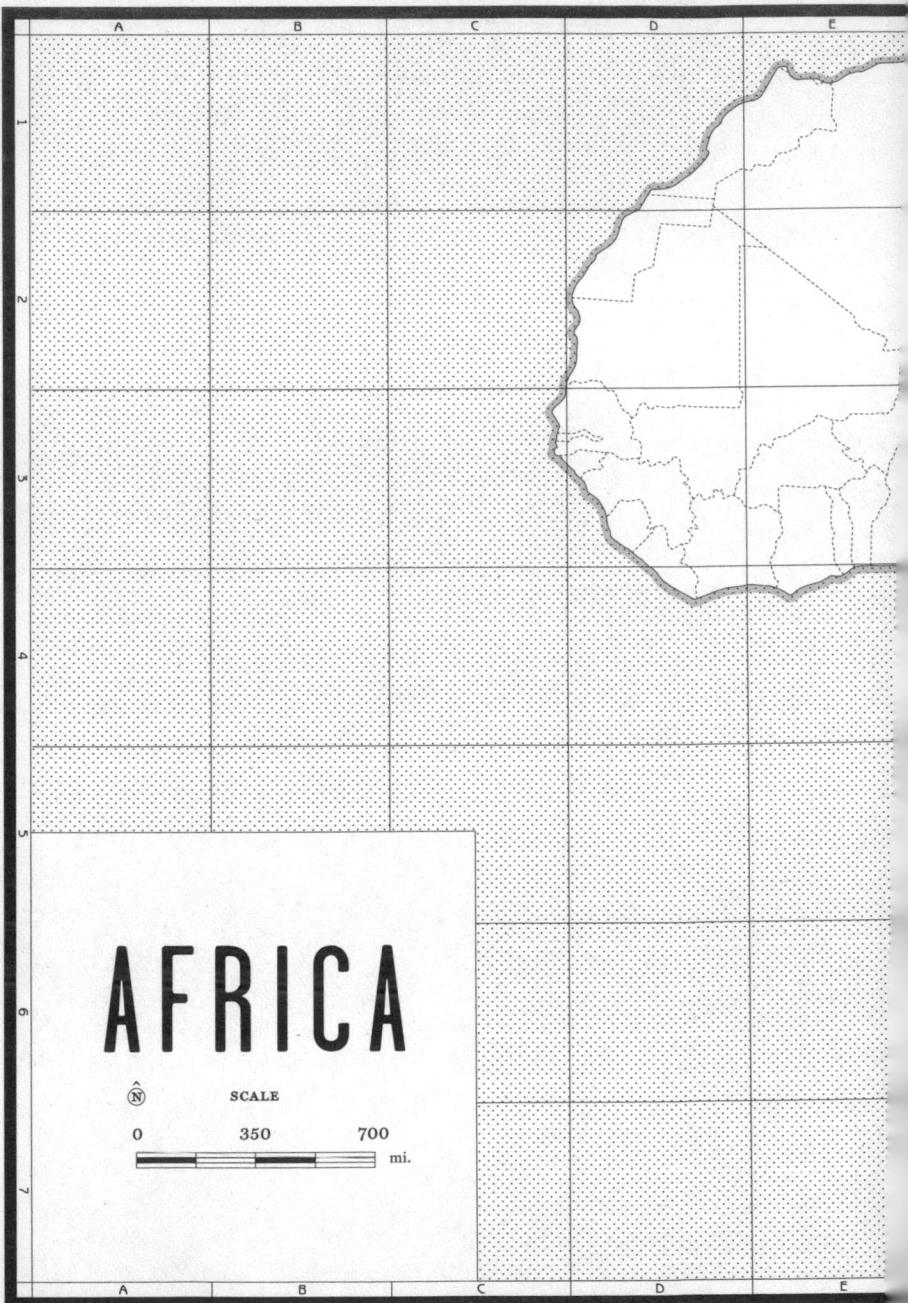

AFRICA

N̂

SCALE

0   350   700
                    mi.

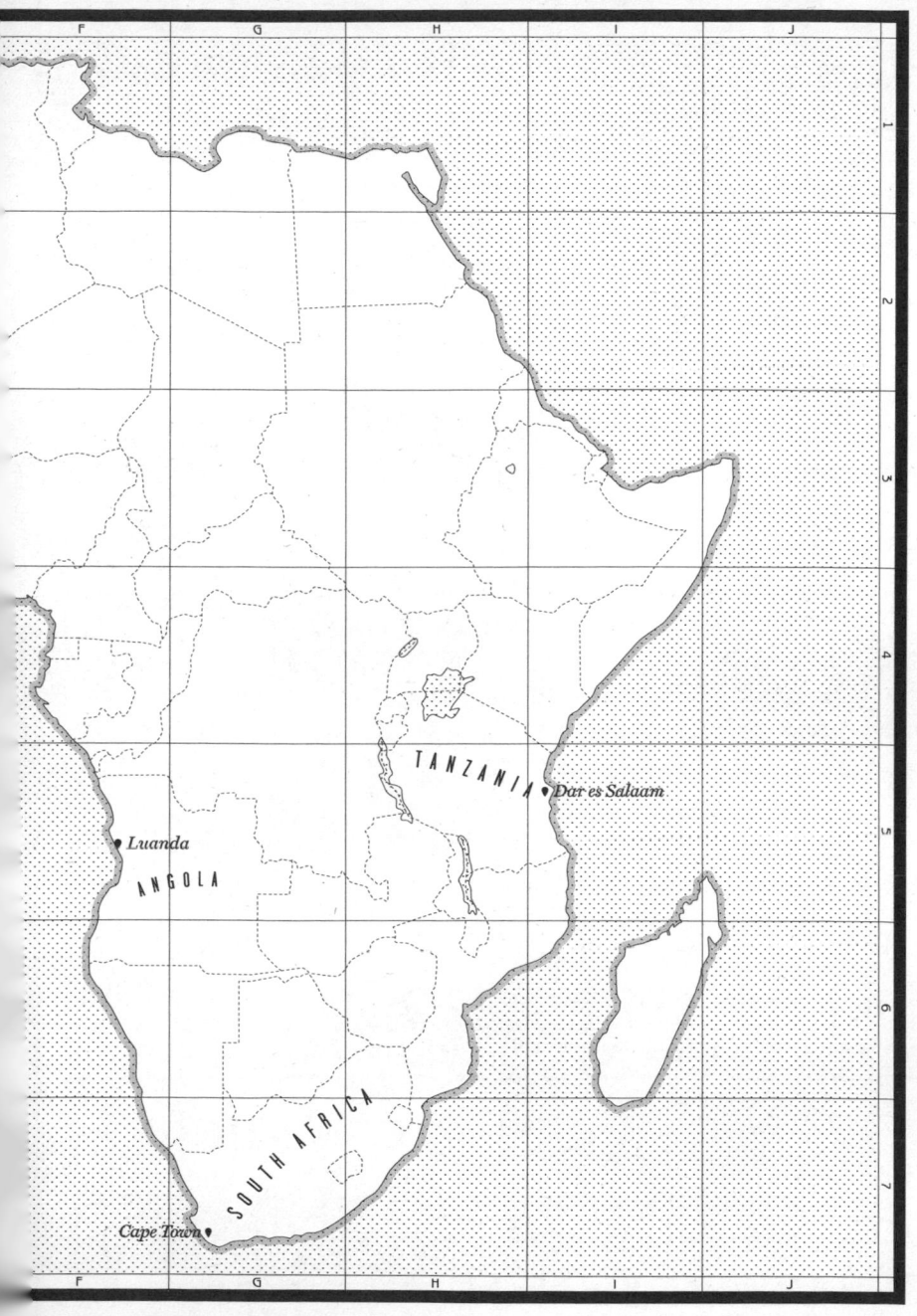

F G H I J

TANZANIA ●Dar es Salaam

●Luanda

ANGOLA

SOUTH AFRICA

Cape Town●

'The girls do a killer breakfast full of love.'
LUKE DALE-ROBERTS P647

'A traditional braai in the township with the locals.'
SCOT KIRTON P647

'FOR ITS INNOVATIVE CELEBRATION OF THE HERITAGE OF CAPE DUTCH CUISINE.'
MARGOT JANSE P650

ANGOLA, TANZANIA & SOUTH AFRICA

'CONSTANTLY PUSHING THE CULINARY BOUNDARIES. WELL WORTH A VISIT.'
PETER TEMPELHOFF P647

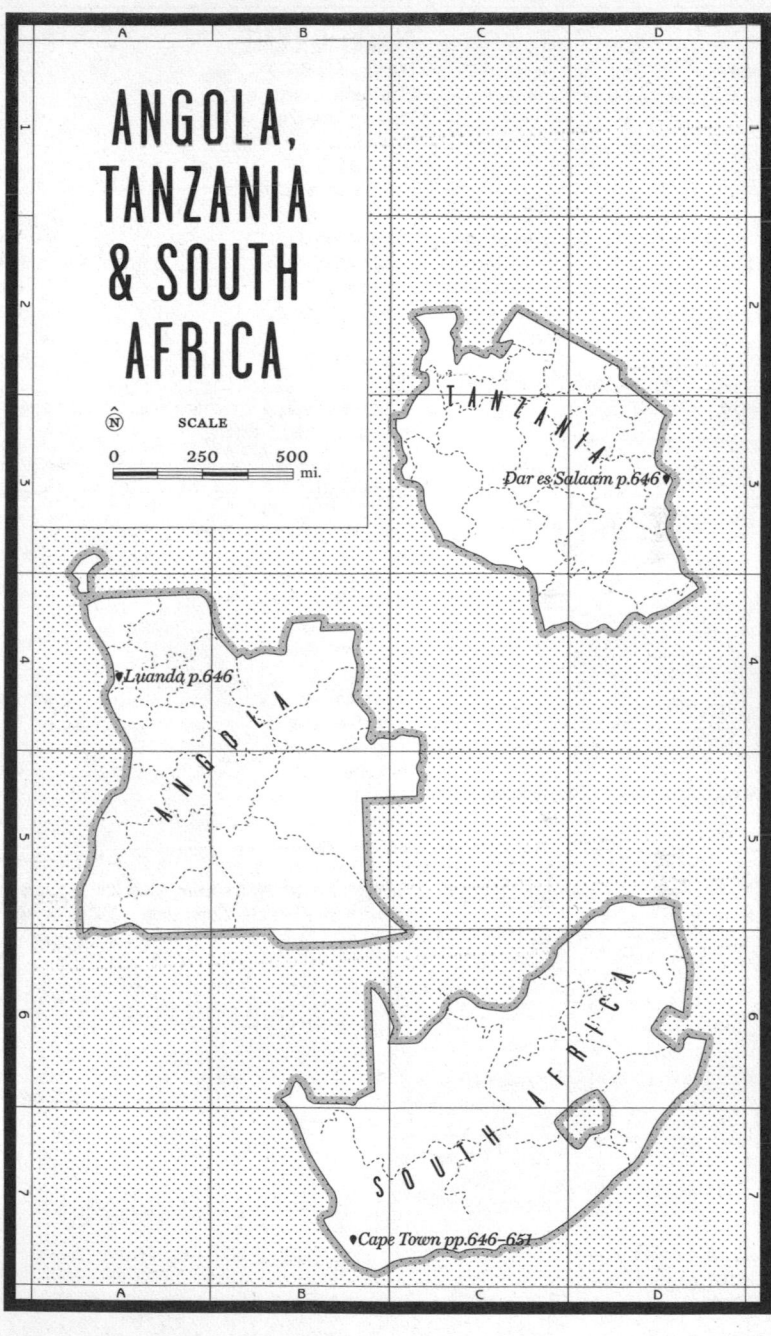

ANGOLA, TANZANIA & SOUTH AFRICA

$\hat{N}$ SCALE

0   250   500 mi.

TANZANIA

Dar es Salaam p.646 ♥

Luanda p.646

ANGOLA

SOUTH AFRICA

♥ Cape Town pp.646–651

KYMBU

Recommended by
Chakall

Vila Espa Condominium
Avenida Pedro de Castro Van-Duném Loy
Luanda
Angola
+244 954540888

Opening hours	Open 7 days
Credit cards	Not accepted
Price range	Expensive
Style	Smart casual
Cuisine	Portuguese-Angolan
Recommended for	Worth the travel

'It's a wonderful place, fitted out entirely in wood, and the food is excellent.'—Chakall

KIVUKONI FISH MARKET

Recommended by
Sami Tallberg

Ocean Road
Dar es Salaam
Tanzania

Opening hours	Open 7 days
Reservation policy	No
Credit cards	Not accepted
Price range	Budget
Style	Casual
Cuisine	Street Food
Recommended for	Worth the travel

'Seafood at its best, cooked simply with piri piri sauce.'
—Sami Tallberg

95 KEEROM

Recommended by
Luke Dale-Roberts

95 Keerom Street
Cape Town
Western Cape 8000
South Africa
+27 0214220765
www.95keerom.com

Opening hours	Closed Sunday
Credit cards	Accepted
Price range	Affordable
Style	Casual
Cuisine	Italian
Recommended for	Local favourite

'Great classic Italian in a stylish setting.'
—Luke Dale-Roberts

BANANA JAM CAFÉ

Recommended by
Scot Kirton

157 Second Avenue
Cape Town
Western Cape 7708
South Africa
+27 0216740186
www.bananajamcafe.co.za

Opening hours	Open 7 days
Credit cards	Accepted but not AMEX
Price range	Budget
Style	Casual
Cuisine	Caribbean
Recommended for	Bargain

'Simple food with a Caribbean influence, and easy on the pocket.'—Scot Kirton

BORRUSO'S

Recommended by
Peter Tempelhoff

Corner of Main Road and Mains Avenue
Cape Town
Western Cape 7708
South Africa
+27 0217615822
www.borrusos.net

Opening hours	Open 7 days
Reservation policy	No
Credit cards	Accepted
Price range	Budget
Style	Casual
Cuisine	Pizza
Recommended for	Bargain

'Really casual trattoria serving great Italian pizzas and decent pastas.'—Peter Tempelhoff

BURRATA

Recommended by
Luke Dale-Roberts

The Old Biscuit Mill
373–375 Albert Road
Cape Town
Western Cape 7925
South Africa
+27 0214476505
www.burrata.co.za

Opening hours	Closed Sunday
Credit cards	Accepted
Price range	Budget
Style	Casual
Cuisine	Italian
Recommended for	Bargain

'They do a great authentic pizza which is affordable and delicious along with some lovely other options.'
—Luke Dale-Roberts

CARNE SA

Recommended by
Scot Kirton

70 Keerom Street
Cape Town
Western Cape 8000
South Africa
+27 214243460
www.carne-sa.com

Opening hours	Closed Sunday
Credit cards	Accepted
Price range	Affordable
Style	Smart casual
Cuisine	Italian Steakhouse
Recommended for	Wish I'd opened

'Great meat done simply, but properly.'—Scot Kirton

LA COLOMBE

Recommended by
Peter Tempelhoff

Constantia Uitsig Wine Estate
Spaanschemat River Road
Cape Town
Western Cape 7806
South Africa
+27 0217942390
www.constantia-uitsig.com

Opening hours	Open 7 days
Credit cards	Accepted
Price range	Affordable
Style	Smart casual
Cuisine	Modern South African
Recommended for	Local favourite

'It has been serving consistently excellent food for over a decade now, has been as high as twelfth in the world and is constantly pushing the culinary boundaries. Well worth a visit.'—Peter Tempelhoff

FOUR & TWENTY

Recommended by
Luke Dale-Roberts

23 Wolfe Street
Cape Town
Western Cape 7800
South Africa
+27 0217620975
www.fourandtwentycafe.co.za

Opening hours	Closed Monday
Credit cards	Accepted but not AMEX
Price range	Budget
Style	Casual
Cuisine	Café-Bakery
Recommended for	Breakfast

'The girls do a killer breakfast full of love.'
—Luke Dale-Roberts

MZOLI'S PLACE

Recommended by
Scot Kirton

NY155, Shop 3
Gugulethu
Cape Town
Western Cape 7750
South Africa

Opening hours	Open 7 days
Reservation policy	No
Credit cards	Not accepted
Price range	Budget
Style	Casual
Cuisine	Barbeque
Recommended for	Local favourite

'A traditional *braai* (barbeque) in the township with the locals, a great atmosphere and a buzz of music and laughter.'—Scot Kirton

OLYMPIA CAFÉ

Recommended by
Scot Kirton

134 Main Road
Cape Town
Western Cape 7975
South Africa
+27 0217886396

Opening hours	Open 7 days
Reservation policy	No
Credit cards	Accepted
Price range	Budget
Style	Casual
Cuisine	Café
Recommended for	Breakfast

'Good, wholesome breakfast with an unpretentious atmosphere located on the seaside.'—Scot Kirton

PIRATES STEAKHOUSE AND PUB

Recommended by
Peter Tempelhoff

160 Main Road
Cape Town
Western Cape 7801
South Africa
+27 0217975659
www.piratessteakhouse.co.za

Opening hours	Open 7 days
Credit cards	Accepted
Price range	Budget
Style	Casual
Cuisine	Steakhouse
Recommended for	Late night

'You can have a great meal at 2.00 a.m. The steak is always good and there's a fun bar for afterwards.'
—Peter Tempelhoff

RAFIKI'S

Recommended by
Scot Kirton

13 Kloof Nek Road
Cape Town
Western Cape 8001
South Africa
+27 0214264731
www.rafikis.co.za

Opening hours	Open 7 days
Credit cards	Accepted
Price range	Budget
Style	Casual
Cuisine	Bar-Small plates
Recommended for	Late night

'Late-night chilli poppers and a cold beer after a long day.'—Scot Kirton

ROYALE EATERY

Recommended by
Luke Dale-Roberts

273 Long Street
Cape Town
Western Cape 8000
South Africa
+27 0214224536
www.royaleeatery.com

Opening hours	Closed Sunday
Credit cards	Accepted but not AMEX
Price range	Budget
Style	Casual
Cuisine	Burgers
Recommended for	Late night

'Good burgers!'—Luke Dale-Roberts

SUPERETTE

Recommended by
Peter Tempelhoff

66 Albert Road
Cape Town
Western Cape 7915
South Africa
+27 0218025525
www.superette.co.za

Opening hours	Closed Sunday
Reservation policy	No
Credit cards	Accepted
Price range	Budget
Style	Casual
Cuisine	Café
Recommended for	Breakfast

'Open, airy, great coffee, fast service, hearty dishes.'
—Peter Tempelhoff

Superette is the favoured daytime hangout of rapidly gentrifying Woodstock's ever-growing bevy of designers, creatives and beautiful people. It enjoys a plum spot on the ground floor of retail and design hub Woodstock Exchange, where its sunshine-yellow Tolix stools, bright white tiles and covetable pendant lights spell easy urban cool. Take your pick from not one but two local coffee roasters (Deluxe Coffeeworks and Rosetta Roastery) and a daily-changing breakfast, brunch and lunch menu of oversized sandwiches, colourful salads and fine baking. Behind Superette are Cameron Munro and Justin Rhodes, the entrepreneurial spirits from Whatiftheworld Gallery and the Neighbourgoods Market.

TASHAS

Recommended by
Scot Kirton

Constantia Village
Constantia Main Road
Cape Town
Western Cape 7806
South Africa
+27 0217945449
www.tashas.co.za

Opening hours	Open 7 days
Reservation policy	No
Credit cards	Accepted
Price range	Budget
Style	Casual
Cuisine	Café-Bistro
Recommended for	Regular neighbourhood

'Modern, fresh and vibey lunches with a generous selection of food items.'—Scot Kirton

THE TEST KITCHEN

Recommended by
Scot Kirton,
Peter Tempelhoff

The Old Biscuit Mill
375 Albert Road
Cape Town
Western Cape 7915
South Africa
+27 0214472337
www.thetestkitchen.co.za

Opening hours	Closed Monday and Sunday
Credit cards	Accepted
Price range	Affordable
Style	Smart casual
Cuisine	Modern South African
Recommended for	High end

'Phenomenal attention to detail, vibrant service, always busy, great food.'—Peter Tempelhoff

WILLOUGHBY & CO.

Recommended by
Peter Tempelhoff

Victoria Wharf
Shop 6132, V & A Waterfront
Cape Town
Western Cape 8001
South Africa
+27 0214186116
www.willoughbyandco.co.za

Opening hours	Open 7 days
Reservation policy	No
Credit cards	Accepted
Price range	Affordable
Style	Casual
Cuisine	Japanese
Recommended for	Regular neighbourhood

'It has simple and delicious sushi and is always packed with locals.'—Peter Tempelhoff

BABEL

Recommended by
Margot Janse,
Sami Tallberg

Babylonstoren
Klapmuts Simondium Road
Franschhoek
Western Cape 7670
South Africa
+27 0218633852
www.babylonstoren.com

Opening hours	Open 7 days
Credit cards	Accepted
Price range	Affordable
Style	Casual
Cuisine	Modern South African
Recommended for	Wish I'd opened

'Babel is situated on the incredible Babylonstoren farm which dates back to 1690. It is a very beautiful 250-hectare working fruit and vegetable farm. The restaurant has everything at its fingertips and cooks with the seasons.'—Margot Janse

BREAD & WINE

Recommended by
Margot Janse

Môreson Farm
Happy Valley Road
Franschhoek
Western Cape 7690
South Africa
+27 0218763692
www.moreson.co.za

Opening hours	Open 7 days
Credit cards	Accepted
Price range	Affordable
Style	Casual
Cuisine	Bistro
Recommended for	Regular neighbourhood

'Neil Jewell is the amazing chef at Bread & Wine and the top charcutier in South Africa. His charcuterie is of incredible quality and his à la carte menu is honest yet innovative. I know I will have a great afternoon when I go there, eating and drinking fabulous fare, amid vineyards and lemon orchards.'—Margot Janse

CAFÉ DES ARTS

Recommended by
Margot Janse

7 Reservoir West Street
Franschhoek
Western Cape 7690
South Africa
+27 0218762952
www.cafedesarts.co.za

Opening hours	Closed Sunday
Credit cards	Accepted but not AMEX
Price range	Budget
Style	Casual
Cuisine	Café-Bakery
Recommended for	Breakfast

'It is a small, very relaxed, unpretentious restaurant run by passionate owners Chris and Louise. Delicious pastries and the best scrambled eggs in town. Great value for money.'—Margot Janse

PIERNEEF À LA MOTTE

Recommended by
Margot Janse

La Motte Wine Estate
R45 Main Road
Franschhoek
Western Cape 7690
South Africa
+27 0218768800
www.la-motte.com

Opening hours	Closed Monday
Credit cards	Accepted
Price range	Affordable
Style	Smart casual
Cuisine	Modern South African
Recommended for	High end

'For its innovative celebration of the heritage of Cape Dutch cuisine.'—Margot Janse

Amid the drama of the Franschhoek Valley, the neatly trimmed La Motte wine estate is calm and its restaurant grown-up. Named after the South African landscape artist collected by the owning Rupert family, Pierneef à La Motte shows off Cape Winelands cuisine from seventeenth-century settlement onwards. Chef Chris Erasmus (a Shane Osborn protégé) uses produce from the kitchen garden in dishes such as citrus-cured Franschhoek salmon trout with grilled cucumber and horseradish, radish terrine and apple puffs, and smoked and pickled lamb *soutribbetjie* (a SA barbeque classic) with creamed corn and summer peas. As you'd expect, staff know their wine inside out, and there's opportunity to splurge.

THE TASTING ROOM

Le Quartier Français Hotel
9 Wilhelmina Street
Franschhoek
Western Cape 7690
South Africa
+27 0218762151
www.lqf.co.za

Opening hours	Closed Sunday
Credit cards	Accepted
Price range	Expensive
Style	Smart casual
Cuisine	Modern South African
Recommended for	Wish I'd opened

'It is one of the best restaurants in the world and always delivers on quality and ingenuity.'
—Peter Tempelhoff

JORDAN RESTAURANT

Jordan Wine Estate
Stellenbosch Kloof Road
Stellenbosch
Western Cape 7604
South Africa
+27 0218813612
www.jordanwines.com

Opening hours	Open 7 days
Credit cards	Accepted
Price range	Affordable
Style	Casual
Cuisine	Modern South African
Recommended for	Regular neighbourhood

'Relaxed. You can sense the character of the chef, George Jardine, in the food.'—Luke Dale-Roberts

OVERTURE

Hidden Valley Estate
Annandale Road
Stellenbosch
Western Cape 7600
South Africa
+27 0218802721
www.dineatoverture.co.za

Opening hours	Closed Monday
Credit cards	Accepted
Price range	Affordable
Style	Smart casual
Cuisine	Modern South African
Recommended for	Worth the travel

'A well-run establishment which serves perfectly prepared plates and has great service.'
—Peter Tempelhoff

Opened in 2007 by chef-patron Bertus Basson and business partner Craig Cormack, Overture, on the Hidden Valley estate in Stellenbosch, has become one of South Africa's most illustrious wineland addresses. The setting helps: the bold glass and stone building opens out onto an expansive deck with glorious views of the valley's vineyards. As does Basson's food: prettily plated but generous, his seasonal menus (from two to ten courses) take in local flavours in the form of steak tartare with *slaphakskeentjies* (a South African onion salad) and jacopever fish with sweet corn. Local wines from boutique producers feature alongside Hidden Valley's own.

RUST EN VREDE

Rust en Vrede Wine Estate
Annandale Road
Stellenbosch
Western Cape 7600
South Africa
+27 0218813757
www.rustenvrede.com

Opening hours	Closed Monday and Sunday
Credit cards	Accepted
Price range	Expensive
Style	Formal
Cuisine	Modern French
Recommended for	High end

'It's beautiful, original and comfortable without feeling stuffy.'—Luke Dale-Roberts

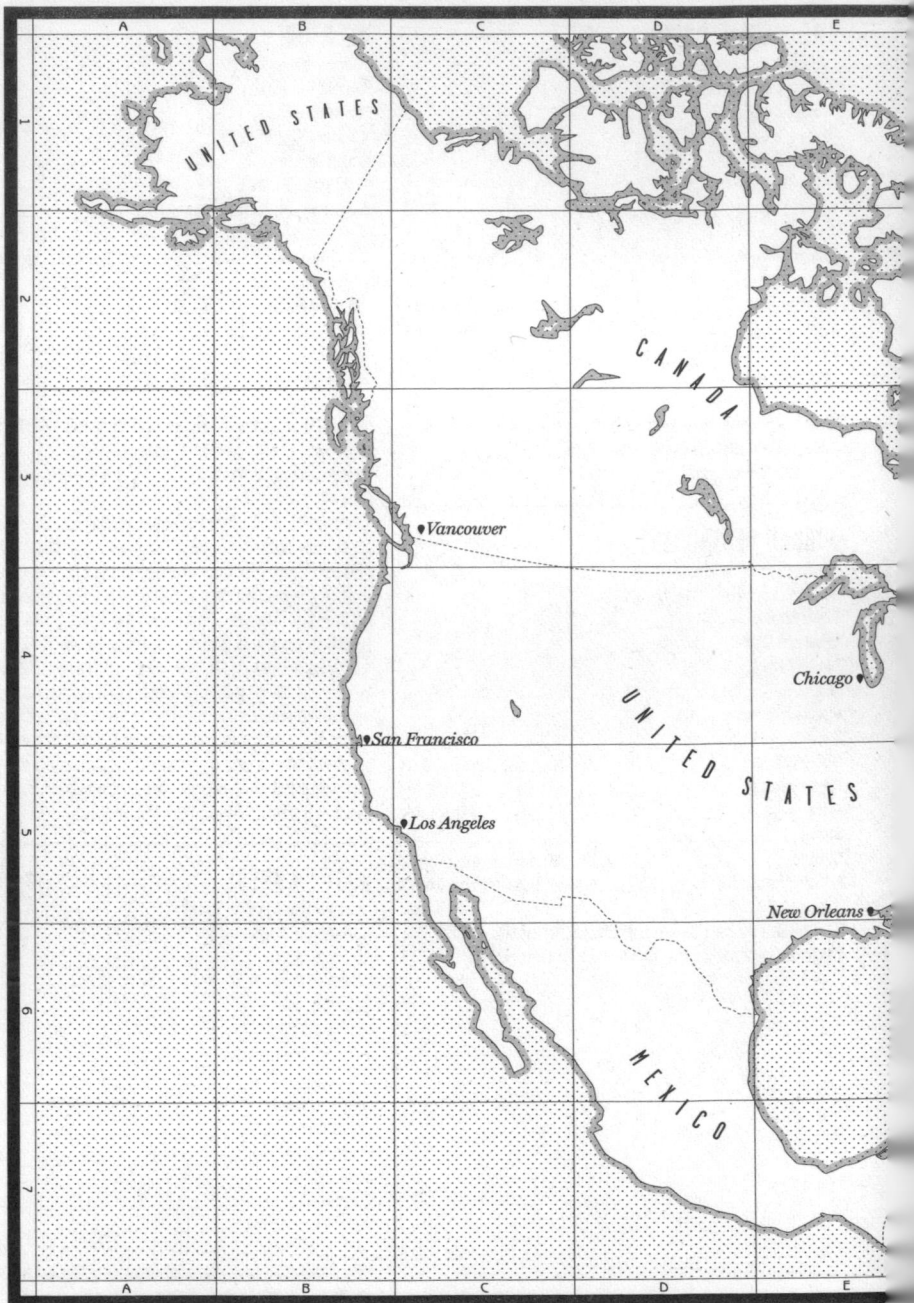

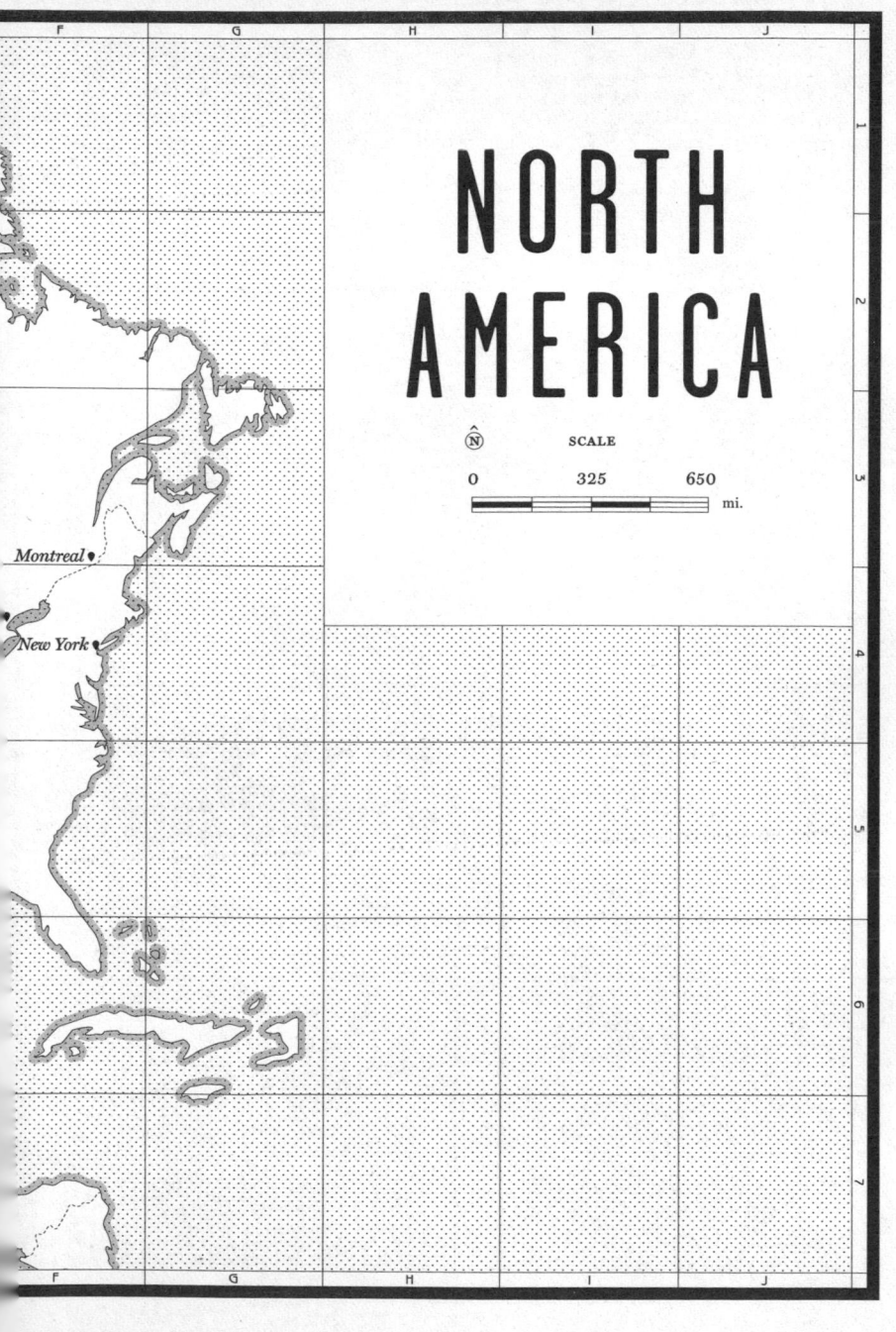

NORTH AMERICA

N

SCALE

0   325   650
mi.

Montreal •

• New York •

'TRADITIONAL QUÉBÉCOIS COMFORT FOOD THAT DOES YOU A WORLD OF GOOD.'
LOUIS BOUCHARD TRUDEAU P664

'TWO TURKEY FLIPS AND A CHOCOLATE MILK.'
JEREMY CHARLES P662

CANADA

'A Calgary pioneer of local regionalized cuisine.'
JOHN JACKSON & CONNIE DESOUSA P658

'Always a great place to go for Jiggs dinner.'
MURRAY MCDONALD P660

'FORAGING FOR MUSHROOMS, SEAWEED AND OTHER INDIGENOUS EDIBLES IS THE CORNERSTONE OF THEIR CUISINE.'
BRAD HOLMES P660

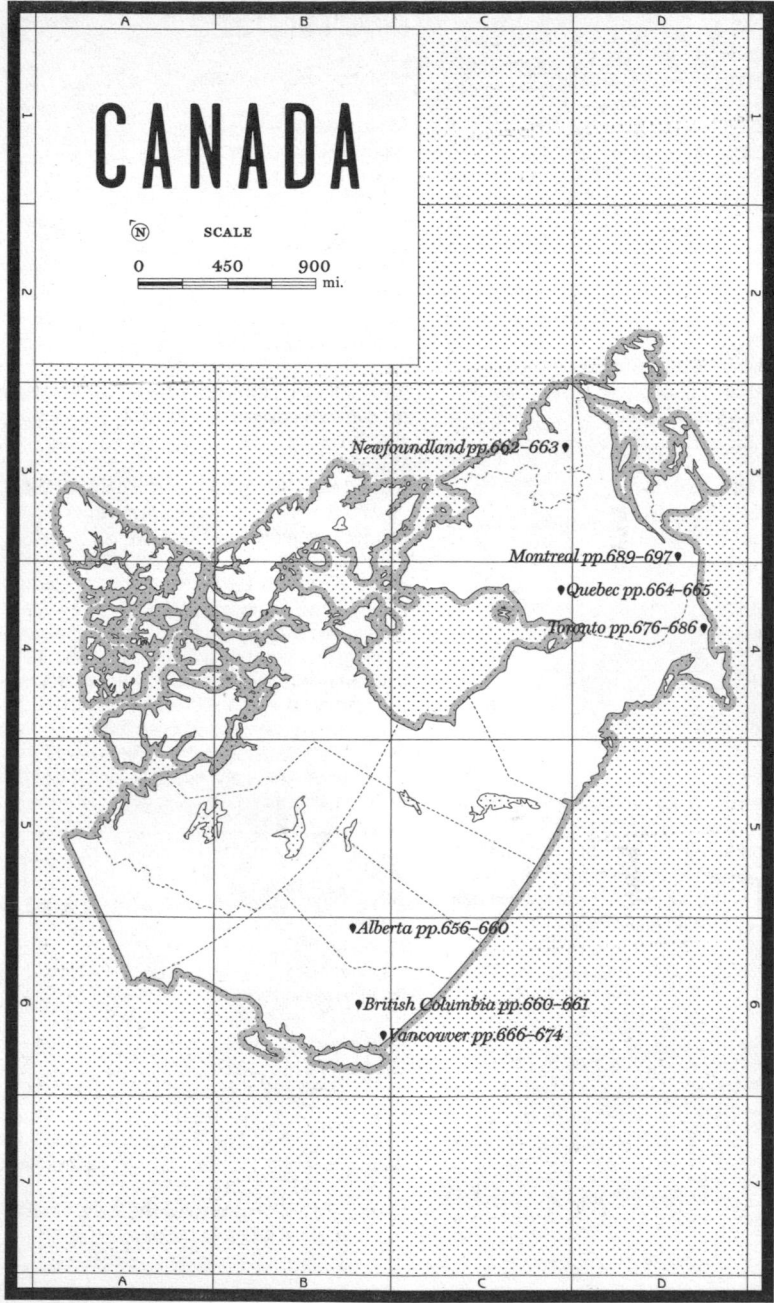

CANADA

SCALE

0   450   900 mi.

Newfoundland pp.662–663 ♥

Montreal pp.689–697 ♥

♥Quebec pp.664–665

Toronto pp.676–686 ♥

♥Alberta pp.656–660

♥British Columbia pp.660–661

♥Vancouver pp.666–674

CANDELA
Recommended by
John Jackson &
Connie DeSousa
1919 4 Street Southwest
Calgary
Alberta T2S 0G8
+1 4037190049
www.candelalounge.com

Opening hours...Open 7 days
Credit cards...Accepted
Price range..Affordable
Style..Casual
Cuisine..Small plates
Recommended for...............................Regular neighbourhood

'They are changing the culinary landscape of Calgary
and Alberta through innovation and collaboration.'
—John Jackson & Connie DeSousa

CASSIS BISTRO
Recommended by
John Jackson & Connie
DeSousa, Justin Leboe
Suite 105
2505 17th Avenue Southwest
Calgary
Alberta T3E 7V3
+1 4032620036
www.thecassisbistro.ca

Opening hours...Closed Monday
Credit cards...Accepted
Price range..Affordable
Style..Smart casual
Cuisine..French
Recommended for...Breakfast

'At Cassis the menu is straightforward yet creative
and delicious. Through its simplicity it truly lets the
ingredients shine. This is a go-to neighbourhood spot
for us.'—John Jackson & Connie DeSousa

CHARCUT ROAST HOUSE
Recommended by
Justin Leboe
Suite 101
899 Centre Street Southwest
Calgary
Alberta T2G 1B8
+1 4039842180
www.charcut.com

Opening hours...Open 7 days
Credit cards...Accepted
Price range..Affordable
Style..Smart casual
Cuisine..Steakhouse
Recommended for......................................Local favourite

'One of the four or five restaurants that helped ignite
the current movement of restaurants in Calgary.'
—Justin Leboe

Calgary chefs John Jackson and Connie DeSousa's
downtown restaurant gets its name from its in-
house charcuterie bar and custom-built chargrill
(charbroiler). As you might expect, the 'urban-rustic'
menu primarily caters for carnivores. At lunchtime,
the signature grilled and pressed rotisserie meat
sandwiches and express lunches beckon. Come the
evening, the menu opens with French- and Italian-
inspired small plates and charcuterie boards – the
pig head mortadella and brassica mustard with
warm raclette cheese is a house favourite – the main
events along the lines of chargrilled whole fish and T-
bones. Great drinks and late hours put the emphasis
on fun over formality.

CIBO
Recommended by
John Jackson &
Connie DeSousa
1012 17th Avenue Southwest
Calgary
Alberta T2T 0A5
+1 4039844755
www.cibocalgary.com

Opening hours...Open 7 days
Credit cards...Accepted
Price range..Affordable
Style..Casual
Cuisine..Italian
Recommended for...............................Regular neighbourhood

'Owned and operated by chefs and likeminded people.'
—John Jackson & Connie DeSousa

DINER DELUXE

Recommended by
Justin Leboe

804 Edmonton Trail Northeast
Calgary
Alberta T2E 3J6
+1 4032765499
www.dinerdeluxe.com

Opening hours	Open 7 days
Reservation policy	No
Credit cards	Accepted
Price range	Affordable
Style	Casual
Cuisine	Diner
Recommended for	Breakfast

'Great vibe and no run-of-the-mill breakfast items
here.'—Justin Leboe

DOWNTOWNFOOD

Recommended by
John Jackson &
Connie DeSousa

628 8th Avenue Southwest
Calgary
Alberta T2P 1G4
+1 5873533474
www.downtownfood.ca

Opening hours	Closed Sunday
Credit cards	Accepted
Price range	Expensive
Style	Smart casual
Cuisine	Asian-American
Recommended for	Regular neighbourhood

'We visit regularly.'—John Jackson & Connie DeSousa

MODEL MILK

Recommended by
John Jackson &
Connie DeSousa

308 17th Avenue Southwest
Calgary
Alberta T2G 1P3
+1 4032657343
www.modelmilk.ca

Opening hours	Open 7 days
Credit cards	Accepted
Price range	Affordable
Style	Smart casual
Cuisine	Modern Canadian
Recommended for	Late night

'We love them and what they contribute to our city's
dining scene!'—John Jackson & Connie DeSousa

Justin Leboe is a chef with an established haute
pedigree, his CV including The French Laundry, Daniel

and, closer to home, Accolade in Toronto. But in 2011
when he opened Model Milk, housed in a converted Art
Deco dairy in Uptown Calgary, he served up Southern
fried chicken, waffles and gravy, and 'Sunday suppers'
of BBQ ribs. On his menu, which does sharing plates
and traditional mains, easy comforts sit alongside the
more grown-up likes of foie gras parfait, hand-made
cavatelli, and beetroot (beets) with burrata. A fine
modern wine list and an extensive list of bourbons
encourage lingering into the early hours.

NOTABLE

Recommended by
John Jackson &
Connie DeSousa

4611 Bowness Road Northwest
Calgary
Alberta T3B 0B2
+1 4032884372
www.notabletherestaurant.ca

Opening hours	Closed Monday
Credit cards	Accepted but not AMEX
Price range	Affordable
Style	Smart casual
Cuisine	Modern Canadian
Recommended for	Regular neighbourhood

PHO HOAI

Recommended by
Justin Leboe

132 3rd Avenue Southeast
Calgary
Alberta T2G 4Z4
+1 4032648174

Opening hours	Open 7 days
Reservation policy	No
Credit cards	Accepted but not AMEX
Price range	Budget
Style	Casual
Cuisine	Vietnamese
Recommended for	Bargain

'Some of the best Vietnamese soup I have ever
tasted.'—Justin Leboe

RIVER CAFÉ

25 Prince's Island Park
Calgary
Alberta T2P 0R1
Canada
+1 4032617670
www.river-cafe.com

Recommended by
John Jackson &
Connie DeSousa

Opening hours	Open 7 days
Credit cards	Accepted
Price range	Expensive
Style	Smart casual
Cuisine	Modern Canadian
Recommended for	Breakfast

'River Café is a Calgary pioneer of local regionalized cuisine. Their brunch is not to be missed for both locals and people visiting our city. We love to bring out-of-town guests for the spectacular showcase of local dishes and the one-of-a-kind scenic view.'
—John Jackson & Connie DeSousa

ROUGE

1240 8th Avenue Southeast
Calgary
Alberta T2G 0M7
+1 4035312767
www.rougecalgary.com

Recommended by
John Jackson &
Connie DeSousa

Opening hours	Closed Sunday
Credit cards	Accepted
Price range	Expensive
Style	Smart casual
Cuisine	French
Recommended for	Local favourite

'Paul Rogalski, the culinary director-owner of Rouge, opened the doors to this Calgary institution in 2003. His massive backyard garden and historic dining room truly create a stage to showcase his localized fine dining cuisine. Paul has helped put our city on the map, most recently being recognized by San Pellegrino in its World's Best Restaurants list.'—John Jackson & Connie DeSousa

SHIKIJI

1608 Centre Street Northeast
Calgary
Alberta T2E 2R9
+1 4035200093
www.shikiji.ca

Recommended by
John Jackson &
Connie DeSousa

Opening hours	Open 7 days
Credit cards	Accepted
Price range	Affordable
Style	Casual
Cuisine	Japanese
Recommended for	Regular neighbourhood

TEATRO

200 8th Avenue Southeast
Calgary
Alberta T2G 0K7
+1 4032901012
www.teatro.ca

Recommended by
Justin Leboe

Opening hours	Open 7 days
Credit cards	Accepted
Price range	Expensive
Style	Smart casual
Cuisine	Italian
Recommended for	High end

'The chef John Michael MacNeil is uber-talented.'
—Justin Leboe

UNA PIZZA + WINE

618 17th Avenue Southwest
Calgary
Alberta T2S 0B4
+1 4034531183
www.unapizzeria.com

Recommended by
John Jackson & Connie
DeSousa, Justin Leboe

Opening hours	Open 7 days
Reservation policy	No
Credit cards	Accepted
Price range	Affordable
Style	Casual
Cuisine	Pizza
Recommended for	Late night

'One of our go-to late-night spots. We love the energy of the space and have become great friends with the owners and staff over the years.'—John Jackson & Connie DeSousa

VINTAGE CHOPHOUSE

Recommended by
John Jackson &
Connie DeSousa

320 11th Avenue Southwest
Calgary
Alberta T2R 0C5
+1 4032627262
www.vintagechophouse.com

Opening hours	Open 7 days
Credit cards	Accepted
Price range	Expensive
Style	Smart casual
Cuisine	Steakhouse
Recommended for	High end

'Stellar wine list and some of the best steaks in town.'
—John Jackson & Connie DeSousa

DUCHESS BAKE SHOP

Recommended by
Daniel Costa

10720 124th Street Northwest
Edmonton
Alberta T5M 0H1
+1 7804884999
www.duchessbakeshop.com

Opening hours	Closed Monday
Reservation policy	No
Credit cards	Accepted
Price range	Budget
Style	Casual
Cuisine	Café-Bakery
Recommended for	Breakfast

'All of the pastries are made properly and the room is beautiful. I love a simple croissant and they make them perfectly.'—Daniel Costa

IZAKAYA TOMO

Recommended by
Daniel Costa

3739 99th Street
Edmonton
Alberta T6E 6J7
+1 7804409152
www.izakayatomo.net

Opening hours	Closed Monday
Credit cards	Accepted but not AMEX
Price range	Affordable
Style	Casual
Cuisine	Japanese
Recommended for	Late night

'This is a fun place where you can get many *izakaya* dishes like raw octopus marinated in wasabi and great sake.'—Daniel Costa

LEVA

Recommended by
Daniel Costa

11053 86th Avenue Northwest
Edmonton
Alberta T6G 0X1
+1 7804795382
www.levabar.com

Opening hours	Open 7 days
Reservation policy	No
Credit cards	Accepted but not AMEX
Price range	Affordable
Style	Casual
Cuisine	Café-Bar
Recommended for	Regular neighbourhood

'Leva is an Italian café that has a simple, flavourful menu. I like the fact that you can stand up at the bar and have a proper espresso or sit down and enjoy a glass of wine and great simple pizza followed by fresh gelato.'—Daniel Costa

RED OX INN

Recommended by
Daniel Costa

9420 91st Street Northwest
Edmonton
Alberta T6C 1Z5
+1 7804655727
www.theredoxinn.com

Opening hours	Closed Monday
Credit cards	Accepted
Price range	Affordable
Style	Smart casual
Cuisine	Modern Canadian
Recommended for	High end

'Great food, great service and great owners. A cosy restaurant that has great food and wine.'—Daniel Costa

THANH-THANH
Recommended by
Daniel Costa

10718 101st Street Northwest
Edmonton
Alberta T5H 2S3
+1 7804265068
www.thanhthanh.ca

Opening hours................................Closed Monday and Sunday
Reservation policy...No
Credit cards..Accepted
Price range..Budget
Style..Casual
Cuisine...Vietnamese
Recommended for..Bargain

'It is fast and fresh. Living in Edmonton can be quite
cold so warming up with a bowl of soup is perfect.'
—Daniel Costa

TRES CARNALES TAQUERÍA
Recommended by
Daniel Costa

10119 100a Street
Edmonton
Alberta T5J 0R5
+1 7804290911
www.trescarnales.com

Opening hours...Closed Sunday
Reservation policy...No
Credit cards...Accepted but not AMEX
Price range..Budget
Style..Casual
Cuisine...Mexican
Recommended for...............................Regular neighbourhood

'Tres Carnales is a Mexican taquería that offers great
tacos like al pastor (with pineapple and pork) and
pollo asado (grilled chicken). The three owners are
passionate and energetic about all things Mexican.'
—Daniel Costa

WATERFRONT RESTAURANT
Recommended by
Lee Cooper

104 1180 Sunset Drive
Kelowna
British Columbia V1Y 9W6
+1 2509791222
www.waterfrontrestaurant.ca

Opening hours...Closed Sunday
Credit cards..Accepted
Price range...Affordable
Style..Smart casual
Cuisine...International
Recommended for...Local favourite

'Delicious food. Committed to showcasing British
Columbia's best produce, fish and meats.'—Lee Cooper

POINT-NO-POINT RESORT
Recommended by
Brad Holmes

10829 West Coast Road
Shirley
British Columbia V9Z 1G9
+1 2506462020
www.pointnopointresort.com

Opening hours..Open 7 days
Credit cards...Accepted but not AMEX
Price range...Affordable
Style..Casual
Cuisine...International
Recommended for..High end

'Rent one of their rustic cabins with a fireplace and an
outdoor hot tub. Eat a delicious dinner with local wine
watching the sun set over the ocean from the original
dining room (sixty years in operation).'—Brad Holmes

SOOKE HARBOUR HOUSE
Recommended by
Brad Holmes

1528 Whiffin Spit Road
Sooke
British Columbia V9Z 0T4
+1 2506423421
www.sookeharbourhouse.com

Opening hours..........................Closed Tuesday and Wednesday
Credit cards..Accepted
Price range...Affordable
Style..Casual
Cuisine..Seafood
Recommended for...Local favourite

'Hyper-local long before the term "100-mile diet"
was coined. Foraging for mushrooms, seaweed and
other indigenous edibles is the cornerstone of their
cuisine.'—Brad Holmes

BRASSERIE L'ECOLE
Brad Holmes
1715 Government Street
Victoria
British Columbia V8W 1Z4
+1 2504756260
www.lecole.ca

Opening hours	Closed Monday and Sunday
Reservation policy	No
Credit cards	Accepted
Price range	Affordable
Style	Casual
Cuisine	French
Recommended for	Late night

'Well-executed French brasserie food with a touch of West Coast and open later than most places in Victoria. A definite go-to place.'—Brad Holmes

FOL EPI
Recommended by
Brad Holmes
398 Harbour Road
Victoria
British Columbia V9A 0B7
+1 2504778882
www.folepi.ca

Opening hours	Open 7 days
Reservation policy	No
Credit cards	Not accepted
Price range	Budget
Style	Casual
Cuisine	Café-Bakery
Recommended for	Breakfast

'The bread we serve at Ulla comes from here. Cliff Leir mills his flour on site and bakes delicious stuff in his wood-fired oven. A pastry and a coffee here makes a great breakfast.'—Brad Holmes

RELISH FOOD AND COFFEE
Recommended by
Brad Holmes
920 Pandora Avenue
Victoria
British Columbia V8V 3P3
+1 2505908464
www.relishfoodcoffee.com

Opening hours	Closed Monday and Sunday
Reservation policy	No
Credit cards	Accepted but not AMEX
Price range	Budget
Style	Casual
Cuisine	Café
Recommended for	Bargain

'Delicious breakfast and lunch from a daily-changing menu. Everything is made in-house and with care.'
—Brad Holmes

TIBETAN KITCHEN
Recommended by
Brad Holmes
680 Broughton Street
Victoria
British Columbia V8W 1C9
Canada
+1 2503835664
www.tibetankitchen.com

Opening hours	Closed Sunday
Credit cards	Accepted
Price range	Affordable
Style	Casual
Cuisine	Himalayan-Nepalese
Recommended for	Regular neighbourhood

'Serves delicious Tibetan food. A great place to have a warming, rich curry or to try Tibetan specialities. They use meat from local, humanely raised animals.'
—Brad Holmes

UCHIDA EATERY/SHOKUDO
Recommended by
Brad Holmes
A22–633 Courtney Street
Victoria
British Columbia V8W 1B9
+1 2503887383

Opening hours	Closed Saturday and Sunday
Reservation policy	No
Credit cards	Accepted but not AMEX
Price range	Budget
Style	Casual
Cuisine	Japanese
Recommended for	Regular neighbourhood

'Small, lunch-only spot. Great Japanese fare using fresh, local products. Small menu with daily-changing specials.'—Brad Holmes

FOGO ISLAND INN

Recommended by
Jeremy Charles,
Chris McDonald

210 Main Road
Fogo Island
Newfoundland A0G 2X0
+1 7096583444
www.fogoislandinn.ca

Opening hours	Open 7 days
Credit cards	Accepted
Price range	Expensive
Style	Smart casual
Cuisine	Modern Canadian
Recommended for	Worth the travel

'Chef Murray McDonald is developing his own style of Newfoundland cooking. Lots of cod, which I love, seaweed and lichens and this is one of the few places in North America where it is legal to serve true game in a restaurant. The staff are mostly local and completely charming.'—Chris McDonald

There's a distinctly end-of-the-earth feel to Fogo Island, the remote and rugged setting for this luxury ecolodge, opened in spring 2013. Minimalist, Scandi-inspired design allows guests to be drawn in by the wildness of the surroundings: passing icebergs or migrating humpbacks in the gunmetal waters of the North Atlantic. Menus in the whitewashed, glass-walled dining room — the best table sits in the 'bow' — make the most of the island's abundant fish and crustacea as well as foraged plants and berries. The juniper-smoked turbot alone is worth the forty-five-minute ferry ride from Newfoundland. Breakfast, lunch and dinner are served all week, all year, but sunsets, which bathe the space in a rich amber glow, are not to be missed.

NICOLE'S CAFÉ

Recommended by
Murray McDonald

159 Main Road
Fogo Island
Newfoundland A0G 2X0
+1 7096583663
www.nicolescafe.ca

Opening hours	Closed Monday and Sunday
Credit cards	Accepted but not AMEX
Price range	Affordable
Style	Casual
Cuisine	Newfoundland Regional
Recommended for	Regular neighbourhood

'It was the only full-service restaurant on Fogo Island until we opened, with a focus on local food and traditions. Always a great place to go for Jiggs dinner.'
—Murray McDonald

CHINCHED BISTRO

Recommended by
Murray McDonald

7 Queen Street
St. John's
Newfoundland A1C 4K2
+1 7097223100
www.chinchedbistro.com

Opening hours	Closed Monday and Sunday
Credit cards	Accepted
Price range	Affordable
Style	Casual
Cuisine	Bistro
Recommended for	Bargain

'I wouldn't call it cheap but it's great value for what you get. Shaun and Michelle cook great high-end comfort food. The food's made from scratch and locally sourced – the only way to go.'—Murray McDonald

DUKE OF DUCKWORTH

Recommended by
Jeremy Charles

325 Duckworth Street
St. John's
Newfoundland A1C 1H5
+1 7097396344
www.dukeofduckworth.com

Opening hours	Open 7 days
Reservation policy	No
Credit cards	Accepted
Price range	Budget
Style	Casual
Cuisine	Bar-Bistro
Recommended for	Local favourite

'Local watering hole, amazing fish and chips (fries), truly a landmark.'—Jeremy Charles

FABULOUS FOODS LIMITED

Recommended by
Jeremy Charles

166 Merrymeeting Road
St. John's
Newfoundland A1C 2W4
+1 7095797666

Opening hours	Closed Sunday
Reservation policy	No
Credit cards	Accepted but not AMEX
Price range	Budget
Style	Casual
Cuisine	Canadian
Recommended for	Bargain

'Two turkey flips and a chocolate milk. It's a small take away (take out) in Rabbit Town that's been around forever.'—Jeremy Charles

FIXED COFFEE & BAKING
183 Duckworth Street
St. John's
Newfoundland A1C 1G3
+1 7095767797
www.fixedcoffee.com

Opening hours	Open 7 days
Reservation policy	No
Credit cards	Accepted
Price range	Budget
Style	Casual
Cuisine	Café-Bakery
Recommended for	Breakfast

'Funky new café with amazing bagels and coffee. My son is a huge fan of the muffins.'—Jeremy Charles

MALLARD COTTAGE
8 Barrows Road
St. John's
Newfoundland A1A 1G8
+1 7092377314
www.mallardcottage.ca

Opening hours	Variable
Credit cards	Accepted
Price range	Affordable
Style	Casual
Cuisine	Modern Canadian
Recommended for	Regular neighbourhood

'Cosy, amazing space with great food.'—Jeremy Charles

An eighteenth-century Irish cottage in the quaint St. John's fishing village of Quidi Vidi – chef Todd Perrin, his wife Kim Doyle and business partner Stephen Lee spent years painstakingly restoring this handsome heritage property. It opened as Mallard Cottage in late 2013 on a winning ticket of sparkling local produce, craft beer and fun. Expect live music sessions, crackling fires, hearty weekend brunches and scrawled daily menus that take pride in their no-nonsense gutsiness. Typical dishes include coldwater shrimp; kraut with flounder roe; duck leg curry, potato, cauliflower and chickpea; and pig face sandwich with chips (fries).

RAYMONDS
95 Water Street
St. John's
Newfoundland A1C 1A4
+1 7095795800
www.raymondsrestaurant.com

Opening hours	Closed Monday and Sunday
Credit cards	Accepted
Price range	Expensive
Style	Smart casual
Cuisine	Modern French-Canadian
Recommended for	High end

'One of the best restaurants in Canada. The Jeremys (chef Jeremy Charles and sommelier Jeremy Bonia) have got it down. Great service and great locally sourced food. And chef Jeremy is a really nice guy, always looking to help other chefs out.'
—Murray McDonald

THE UNDERBELLY
YellowBelly Brewery
288 Water Street
St. John's
Newfoundland A1C 5J9
+1 7097573784
www.yellowbellybrewery.com

Opening hours	Open 7 days
Credit cards	Accepted but not AMEX
Price range	Affordable
Style	Casual
Cuisine	Canadian
Recommended for	Late night

'Located in the basement of the YellowBelly Brewery, The UnderBelly is a great late-night wind down for us.'
—Jeremy Charles

L'AFFAIRE EST KETCHUP

Recommended by
Louis Bouchard Trudeau

46 Rue Saint-Joseph Est
Quebec City
Quebec G1K 3A6
+1 4185299020

Opening hours	Closed Monday and Sunday
Credit cards	Accepted
Price range	Affordable
Style	Casual
Cuisine	Modern French-Canadian
Recommended for	Local favourite

'This was one of the first restaurants in Quebec to open a small, intimate space, seating only fifteen to twenty people. When you look around this place, it's like walking into a guy's apartment. You're basically eating out in a restaurant that feels like home.'
—Louis Bouchard Trudeau

LE BUFFET DE L'ANTIQUAIRE

Recommended by
Louis Bouchard Trudeau

95 Rue Saint-Paul
Quebec City
Quebec G1K 3V8
+1 4186922661

Opening hours	Open 7 days
Reservation policy	No
Credit cards	Accepted but not AMEX
Price range	Budget
Style	Casual
Cuisine	Diner-Café
Recommended for	Bargain

'It's like going to eat at your grandmother's house. Traditional Québécois comfort food that does you a world of good.'—Louis Bouchard Trudeau

CHEZ GASTON

Recommended by
Louis Bouchard Trudeau

332 Dorchester
Quebec City
Quebec G1K 6A2
+1 4185230677
www.chezgaston.ca

Opening hours	Open 7 days
Reservation policy	No
Credit cards	Accepted
Price range	Budget
Style	Casual
Cuisine	Canadian
Recommended for	Late night

'This is where you come for the ultimate snack. Perfect *poutines* (French fries with fresh cheese curds, topped with brown gravy). The service is professional, even late at night. A great group of people to end the evening with.'—Louis Bouchard Trudeau

LE CLOCHER PENCHÉ

Recommended by
Louis Bouchard Trudeau

203 Rue Saint-Joseph Est
Quebec City
Quebec G1K 3B1
+1 4186400597
www.clocherpenche.ca

Opening hours	Closed Monday
Credit cards	Accepted but not AMEX
Price range	Affordable
Style	Casual
Cuisine	French-Canadian Bistro
Recommended for	Breakfast

'One of the first new restaurants to open up in the Saint-Roch district. Quality always comes first at this establishment, which serves refined, spot-on cuisine. Their brunches are unique and highly imaginative.'
—Louis Bouchard Trudeau

MANOIR MONTMORENCY

Recommended by
Jean-Marie Baudic

2490 Avenue Royale
Quebec City
Quebec G1C 1S1
+1 4186633330

Opening hours	Open 7 days
Credit cards	Accepted
Price range	Affordable
Style	Smart casual
Cuisine	Canadian
Recommended for	Breakfast

'The buffet is rich and exceptionally diverse, and I like the quality of the products they use. The service is good too.'—Jean-Marie Baudic

LE MOINE ÉCHANSON

Recommended by
Louis Bouchard Trudeau

585 Rue Saint-Jean
Quebec City
Quebec G1R 1P5
+1 4185247832
www.lemoineechanson.com

Opening hours	Open 7 days
Credit cards	Accepted
Price range	Affordable
Style	Casual
Cuisine	French-Canadian Bistro
Recommended for	Wish I'd opened

'I like the friendly atmosphere here, the selection of natural wines and the dishes piled high with generous helpings of rustic food. This is proper grub.'
—Louis Bouchard Trudeau

PATENTE ET MACHIN

Recommended by
Louis Bouchard Trudeau

82 Rue St-Joseph Ouest
Quebec City
Quebec G1K 1W9
+1 5819813999

Opening hours	Open 7 days
Credit cards	Accepted
Price range	Affordable
Style	Casual
Cuisine	Modern Canadian
Recommended for	Regular neighbourhood

'A simple place with a great party atmosphere that is good for hanging out with the boys. There is a long bar where you can see the chefs at work, producing rustic, no-frills cooking. The dishes on the blackboard (chalk board) menu change constantly... even throughout the evening. Your plate will always contain three staples: vegetables, starchy food and protein.'—Louis Bouchard Trudeau

LA TANIÈRE

Recommended by
Louis Bouchard Trudeau

2115 Rang Saint-Ange
Quebec City
Quebec G2G 0E8
+1 4188724386
www.restaurantlataniere.com

Opening hours	Closed Monday, Tuesday and Sunday
Credit cards	Accepted
Price range	Expensive
Style	Smart casual
Cuisine	Modern French-Canadian
Recommended for	High end

'Game features strongly on the menu here. The cuisine surprises you at every turn, using groundbreaking techniques that deliver sleek dishes tinged with emotion.'—Louis Bouchard Trudeau

'Chef Vikram Vij's Canadian-
and Indian-influenced cuisine
best sums up our multicultural
and diverse city.'

DAVID HAWKSWORTH P669

'A GAME CHANGER
FOR THE WEST
COAST.'

BRAD HOLMES P668

VANCOUVER

'They sling
the snappiest
fresh-pressed
juices out of
the snappiest
little truck.'

BRIAN SKINNER P670

'AN OLD-SCHOOL
ICONIC FAVOURITE
FOR THE CITY. IT IS
EXCEPTIONALLY
EXPENSIVE AND
OLD SCHOOL BUT I
HAD A BLAST.

ANDREA CARLSON P668

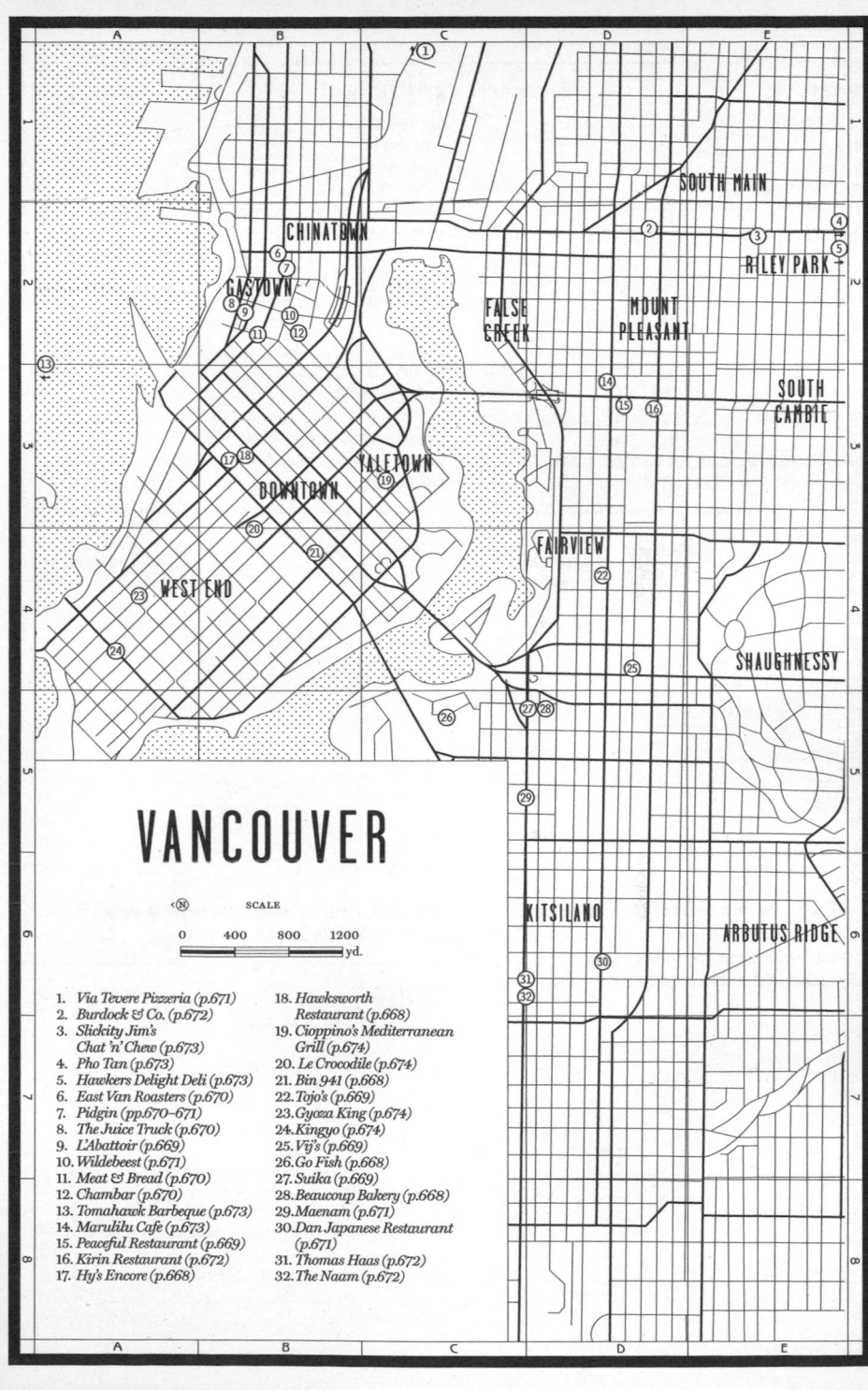

BIN 941
941 Davie Street
Downtown
Vancouver
British Columbia V6Z 1B9
+1 6046831246
www.bin941.com

Opening hours	Open 7 days
Reservation policy	No
Credit cards	Accepted but not AMEX
Price range	Affordable
Style	Smart casual
Cuisine	Tapas
Recommended for	Late night

'A small tapas restaurant but the food and presentation are very stylish.'—Hidekazu Tojo

HAWKSWORTH RESTAURANT
Rosewood Hotel Georgia
801 West Georgia Street
Downtown
Vancouver
British Columbia V6C 1P7
+1 6046737000
www.hawksworthrestaurant.com

Recommended by
Andrea Carlson, Brad
Holmes, Edward Lee,
Vikram Vij

Opening hours	Open 7 days
Credit cards	Accepted
Price range	Affordable
Style	Smart casual
Cuisine	Modern Canadian
Recommended for	Worth the travel

'Chef David's flagship restaurant impresses on so many levels and is a game changer for the West Coast. Taking some well-worn ideas and turning them on their side is really making the restaurant stand out.'—Brad Holmes

HY'S ENCORE
637 Hornby Street
Downtown
Vancouver
British Columbia V6C 2G3
+1 6046837671
www.hyssteakhouse.com

Recommended by
Andrea Carlson

Opening hours	Open 7 days
Credit cards	Accepted
Price range	Expensive
Style	Smart casual
Cuisine	Steakhouse
Recommended for	Local favourite

'An old-school iconic favourite for the city. I went there for the first time recently. It is exceptionally expensive and old school but I had a blast.'—Andrea Carlson

BEAUCOUP BAKERY
2150 Fir Street
Fairview
Vancouver
British Columbia V6J 3B5
+1 6047324222
www.beaucoupbakery.com

Recommended by
Andrea Carlson

Opening hours	Open 7 days
Reservation policy	No
Credit cards	Accepted but not AMEX
Price range	Affordable
Style	Casual
Cuisine	Café-Bakery
Recommended for	Breakfast

'New pastry shop in town doing some really beautiful baking.'—Andrea Carlson

GO FISH
1505 West 1st Avenue
Fairview
Vancouver
British Columbia V6J 1E8
+1 6047305040
www.bin941.com

Recommended by
David Hawksworth

Opening hours	Closed Monday
Reservation policy	No
Credit cards	Accepted
Price range	Budget
Style	Casual
Cuisine	Seafood
Recommended for	Wish I'd opened

'This fish-and-chip shack close to Granville Island is always busy and diners have an unforgettable view of the marina and mountains, plus the rent is cheap!'
—David Hawksworth

PEACEFUL RESTAURANT
Recommended by
Lee Cooper,
Brian Skinner

532 West Broadway
Fairview
Vancouver
British Columbia V5Z 1E9
+1 6048799878
www.peacefulrestaurant.com

Opening hours	Open 7 days
Reservation policy	No
Credit cards	Not accepted
Price range	Budget
Style	Casual
Cuisine	Chinese
Recommended for	Bargain

'Family run, Szechuan cuisine, inexpensive and always good.'—Lee Cooper

SUIKA
Recommended by
Andrea Carlson

1626 West Broadway
Fairview
Vancouver
British Columbia V6J 1X6
+1 6047301678
www.suika-snackbar.com

Opening hours	Open 7 days
Credit cards	Accepted
Price range	Budget
Style	Casual
Cuisine	Japanese
Recommended for	Late night

'Suika is open late so it's super convenient for post-service snacks and it's delicious. Their staff win for team spirit! I once saw someone in a full chicken suit at Halloween – where else in Vancouver would you see that?! The udon with kimchi and cured roe is one of my favourites.'—Andrea Carlson

TOJO'S
Recommended by
Andrea Carlson

1133 Broadway West
Fairview
Vancouver BC V6H 1G1
+1 6048728050
www.tojos.com

Opening hours	Closed Sunday
Credit cards	Accepted
Price range	Expensive
Style	Smart casual
Cuisine	Japanese
Recommended for	Local favourite

'The most iconic Japanese chef in Vancouver.'
—Andrea Carlson

VIJ'S
Recommended by
Andrea Carlson,
David Hawksworth

1480 West 11th Avenue
Fairview
Vancouver BC V6H 1L1
+1 6047366664
www.vijsrestaurant.ca

Opening hours	Open 7 days
Reservation policy	No
Credit cards	Accepted
Price range	Affordable
Style	Smart casual
Cuisine	Indian
Recommended for	Local favourite

'Chef Vikram Vij's Canadian- and Indian-influenced cuisine best sums up our multicultural and diverse city.'—David Hawksworth

L'ABATTOIR
Recommended by
David Hawksworth

217 Carrall Street
Gastown
Vancouver
British Columbia V6B 2J2
+1 6045681701
www.labattoir.ca

Opening hours	Open 7 days
Credit cards	Accepted
Price range	Affordable
Style	Casual
Cuisine	Modern French-Canadian
Recommended for	High end

'It has a space with great energy, warm staff and the menu features truly innovative food.'
—David Hawksworth

CHAMBAR
Recommended by
Lee Cooper

562 Beatty Street
Gastown
Vancouver
British Columbia V6B 2L3
+1 6048797119
www.chambar.com

Opening hours	Open 7 days
Credit cards	Accepted
Price range	Affordable
Style	Casual
Cuisine	Modern European
Recommended for	Wish I'd opened

'Always busy, fun and lively. Great before and after the hockey game.'—Lee Cooper

EAST VAN ROASTERS
Recommended by
Andrea Carlson

Rainier Hotel
319 Carrall Street
Gastown
Vancouver
British Columbia V6B 2J4
+1 6046297562
www.eastvanroasters.com

Opening hours	Closed Monday and Sunday
Reservation policy	No
Credit cards	Accepted but not AMEX
Price range	Budget
Style	Casual
Cuisine	Café
Recommended for	Wish I'd opened

'I am super happy with what I've got on the go with Burdock but I do admire the new Portland Hotel Society's operation, East Van Roasters – Vancouver's only bean-to-bar roaster making chocolate and roasting coffee in the Downtown Eastside (DTES). They employ women from the neighbourhood and work with affiliated projects like Hives for Humanity to create remarkable honey and cocoa-nib caramels.'
—Andrea Carlson

THE JUICE TRUCK
Recommended by
Brian Skinner

Corner of Abbott Street and Water Street
Gastown
Vancouver
British Columbia V6B 1B2
+1 6047198861
www.thejuicetruck.ca

Opening hours	Closed Sunday
Reservation policy	No
Credit cards	Accepted but not AMEX
Price range	Budget
Style	Casual
Cuisine	Juices and Smoothies
Recommended for	Wish I'd opened

'They sling the snappiest fresh-pressed juices out of the snappiest little truck. Killer business, killer dudes!'—Brian Skinner

MEAT & BREAD
Recommended by
Brad Holmes

370 Cambie Street
Gastown
Vancouver
British Columbia V6B 1H7
www.meatandbread.ca

Opening hours	Closed Sunday
Reservation policy	No
Credit cards	Accepted
Price range	Budget
Style	Casual
Cuisine	Sandwiches
Recommended for	Wish I'd opened

'Delicious. Genius.'—Brad Holmes

PIDGIN
Recommended by
Andrea Carlson,
Vikram Vij

350 Carrall Street
Gastown
Vancouver
British Columbia V6B 2J3
+1 6046209400
www.pidginvancouver.com

Opening hours	Open 7 days
Credit cards	Accepted
Price range	Affordable
Style	Casual
Cuisine	Asian Fusion
Recommended for	Regular neighbourhood

'Casual but very tasty food; great neighbourhood place done really well. The execution of their food is very interesting as they use the whole animal. The room is small but there's a real attention to detail.'—Vikram Vij

WILDEBEEST

Recommended by
Andrea Carlson

120 West Hastings Street
Gastown
Vancouver
British Columbia V6B 1G8
+1 6046876880
www.wildebeest.ca

Opening hours	Open 7 days
Credit cards	Accepted
Price range	Affordable
Style	Casual
Cuisine	Modern Canadian
Recommended for	Local favourite

'An excellent example of forward-thinking young chefs collaborating to create meat-centric modern dishes.'
—Andrea Carlson

VIA TEVERE PIZZERIA

Recommended by
Daniel Puskas

1190 Victoria Drive
Grandview-Woodland
Vancouver
British Columbia V5L 4G5
+1 6043361803
www.viateverepizzeria.com

Opening hours	Closed Monday
Reservation policy	No
Credit cards	Accepted
Price range	Budget
Style	Casual
Cuisine	Pizza
Recommended for	Worth the travel

'Because the pizzas are so damn good.'—Daniel Puskas

DAN JAPANESE RESTAURANT

Recommended by
David Hawksworth

2511 West Broadway
Kitsilano
Vancouver
British Columbia V6K 2E9
+1 6046776930
www.danrestaurant.com

Opening hours	Closed Tuesday
Credit cards	Accepted
Price range	Affordable
Style	Smart casual
Cuisine	Japanese
Recommended for	Regular neighbourhood

'This friendly sushi restaurant is owned and operated by chef Ken Oda and his wife Tomoko. The food is always consistent and everything is perfect.'
—David Hawksworth

MAENAM

Recommended by
Andrea Carlson,
Vikram Vij

1938 West 4th Avenue
Kitsilano
Vancouver
British Columbia V6J 1M5
+1 6047305579
www.maenam.ca

Opening hours	Open 7 days
Credit cards	Accepted
Price range	Budget
Style	Casual
Cuisine	Thai
Recommended for	Regular neighbourhood

'Some of the best Thai food that I have ever had the pleasure of tasting.'—Andrea Carlson

THE NAAM
2724 West 4th Avenue
Kitsilano
Vancouver
British Columbia V6K 1R1
+1 6047387151
www.thenaam.com

Recommended by
Brian Skinner

Opening hours..Open 7 days
Reservation policy..No
Credit cards...Accepted
Price range..Budget
Style..Casual
Cuisine..Fusion
Recommended for...............................Local favourite

'Not for the food, but for the twenty-four-hour service
and the history – Greenpeace was started here man!
Perhaps not the same as it once was but it will always
be an institution.'—Brian Skinner

THOMAS HAAS
2539 West Broadway Avenue
Kitsilano
Vancouver
British Columbia V6K 2E9
+1 6047361848
www.thomashaas.com

Recommended by
Andrea Carlson,
David Hawksworth,
Vikram Vij

Opening hours................................Closed Monday and Sunday
Reservation policy..No
Credit cards...Accepted
Price range..Budget
Style..Casual
Cuisine...Café-Bakery
Recommended for......................................Breakfast

'Thomas Haas is a fourth-generation pastry chef – he
grew up making pastries in his family's pastry shop
in the Black Forest in Germany – and his are by far
the best pastries in town. And it's next to Bel Café of
course!'—David Hawksworth

BURDOCK & CO.
2702 Main Street
Mount Pleasant
Vancouver
British Columbia V5T 3E8
+1 6048790077
www.burdockandco.com

Recommended by
Brian Skinner

Opening hours..Open 7 days
Credit cards...Accepted
Price range..Affordable
Style...Smart casual
Cuisine...Modern Canadian
Recommended for..High end

'Chef Andrea Carlson's food is the most honest and
humbling of the Vancouver high-end dining scene.
Seemingly effortless, always inspiring.'—Brian Skinner

KIRIN RESTAURANT
201 City Square
555 West 12th Avenue
Mount Pleasant
Vancouver
British Columbia V5Z 3X7
+1 6048798038
www.kirinrestaurants.com

Recommended by
David Hawksworth

Opening hours..Open 7 days
Credit cards...Accepted
Price range..Affordable
Style..Casual
Cuisine..Chinese
Recommended for...Bargain

'It serves great seafood and the food is always fresh
and consistent.'—David Hawksworth

MARULILU CAFE

Recommended by
Hidekazu Tojo

451 West Broadway Street
Mount Pleasant
Vancouver
British Columbia V5Y 1R4
+1 6045684211

Opening hours	Open 7 days
Reservation policy	No
Credit cards	Accepted but not AMEX
Price range	Budget
Style	Casual
Cuisine	Japanese
Recommended for	Bargain

'Friendly and they serve classic Japanese home-style dishes.'—Hidekazu Tojo

TOMAHAWK BARBEQUE

Recommended by
Lee Cooper

1550 Philip Avenue
North Vancouver
Vancouver
British Columbia V7P 2V8
+1 6049882612
www.tomahawkrestaurant.com

Opening hours	Open 7 days
Reservation policy	No
Credit cards	Accepted
Price range	Budget
Style	Casual
Cuisine	Diner-Café
Recommended for	Breakfast

'Quirky family restaurant. It's been in business for more than eighty years. Great bacon.'—Lee Cooper

HAWKERS DELIGHT DELI

Recommended by
Brian Skinner

4127 Main Street
Riley Park
Vancouver
British Columbia V5V 3P6
+1 6047098188

Opening hours	Closed Sunday
Reservation policy	No
Credit cards	Not accepted
Price range	Budget
Style	Casual
Cuisine	Malaysian-Indonesian
Recommended for	Regular neighbourhood

'Cheap, legit, Malaysian-Indonesian street food. Four bucks (£2) gets you a *roti canai* (flatbread) that rivals the best off the streets of Borneo. Six bucks (£3), a sizzling hot plate of *nasi goreng* (Indonesian stir-fried rice).'—Brian Skinner

PHO TAN

Recommended by
Andrea Carlson

4598 Main Street
Riley Park
Vancouver
British Columbia V5V 3R5
+1 6048733345

Opening hours	Open 7 days
Reservation policy	No
Credit cards	Not accepted
Price range	Budget
Style	Casual
Cuisine	Vietnamese
Recommended for	Bargain

'It opens early (10.30 a.m.; good breakfast place), it's fast and always delicious. #38 is my go-to choice. At New Year's the owner gave me some very curious Vietnamese fruit... *vu sua* a.k.a. star apple or "breast-milk fruit".'—Andrea Carlson

SLICKITY JIM'S CHAT 'N' CHEW

Recommended by
Brian Skinner

3475 Main Street
Riley Park
Vancouver
British Columbia V5V 3M9
+1 6048736760
www.slickityjims.com

Opening hours	Open 7 days
Reservation policy	No
Credit cards	Accepted
Price range	Budget
Style	Casual
Cuisine	Diner
Recommended for	Breakfast

'The room is lively, packed and never boring. Good place for a hangover brunch with endless pots of coffee.'—Brian Skinner

LE CROCODILE
Recommended by
Lee Cooper
909 Burrard Street
West End
Vancouver
British Columbia V6Z 2N2
+1 6046694298
www.lecrocodilerestaurant.com

Opening hours	Closed Sunday
Credit cards	Accepted
Price range	Affordable
Style	Smart casual
Cuisine	French
Recommended for	High end

'Classy old-school French dining. Outstanding service.'
—Lee Cooper

Now into its fourth decade, Le Crocodile makes earning and keeping its A-list clientele of movie stars, gourmets and CEOs look effortless. Chef-patron Michel Jacob named the downtown restaurant in homage to the three-Michelin-starred Au Crocodile in his native Strasbourg. His take on the classic French restaurant couples haute cuisine with the cosseting warmth of a luxury bistro. There's a traditional bent to the place – all frog's legs, lobster bisque, fine Bordeaux and black-clad waiters – but it's so charming and so assured, it's hard not to be seduced time and time again. The five-course dégustation comes recommended.

GYOZA KING
Recommended by
David Hawksworth
1508 Robson Street
West End
Vancouver
British Columbia V6G 1C2
+1 6046698278
www.gyokingroup.com

Opening hours	Open 7 days
Credit cards	Accepted but not AMEX
Price range	Budget
Style	Casual
Cuisine	Japanese
Recommended for	Late night

'It's great quality but, more importantly, it's also near work and open late.'—David Hawksworth

KINGYO
Recommended by
Lee Cooper
871 Denman Street
West End
Vancouver
British Columbia V6G 2L9
+1 6046081677
www.kingyo-izakaya.ca

Opening hours	Open 7 days
Credit cards	Accepted
Price range	Affordable
Style	Casual
Cuisine	Japanese
Recommended for	Late night

'Tasty Japanese *izakaya*. Cold beer.'—Lee Cooper

CIOPPINO'S MEDITERRANEAN GRILL
Recommended by
Hidekazu Tojo
1133 Hamilton Street
Yaletown
Vancouver
British Columbia V6B 5P6
+1 6046887466
www.cioppinos.wordpress.com

Opening hours	Closed Sunday
Credit cards	Accepted
Price range	Affordable
Style	Smart casual
Cuisine	Italian
Recommended for	Regular neighbourhood

'Best Italian in Vancouver.'—Hidekazu Tojo

'TRUCKERS, GANGSTERS AND VEAL SANDWICHES, 24 HOURS, 365 DAYS A YEAR.'
ANTHONY ROSE P685

'THEY HAVE VERY ROUGH, BIG FLAVOURS WITH LOTS OF CHILLIES.'
CHRIS MCDONALD P678

'*It's sexy.*'
MICHAEL HUNTER P680

TORONTO

'POETRY. ASTONISHING TECHNIQUE, INGREDIENTS ... JUST, WOW. THE ULTIMATE HUMBLING EXPERIENCE FOR A CHEF. SO STUDIED, SO PRECISE — SINGULAR MASTERY OF A STYLE. NOTHING ELSE LIKE IT IN MOST PLACES IN THE WORLD, CERTAINLY NOT IN TORONTO.'
MICHAEL CABALLO P679

TORONTO

(N) SCALE

0   300   600   900
yd.

1. *Kaiseki Yu-zen Hashimoto (p.679)*
2. *Mt. Everest Restaurant (p.682)*
3. *Pantheon (p.679)*
4. *Allen's (p.679)*
5. *Sukhothai (p.678)*
6. *Starfish Oyster Bed & Grill (p.681)*
7. *George Restaurant (p.681)*

8. *The Senator (p.681)*
9. *Barberian's Steakhouse (p.681)*
10. *Cava (p.682)*
11. *Café Boulud (p.686)*
12. *Sassafraz (p.686)*
13. *Japango (p.683)*
14. *Nota Bene (p.683)*
15. *360 Restaurant (p.683)*
16. *Forestview Chinese Restaurant (p.678)*
17. *SiChuan House Cuisine (p.678)*
18. *Taste of China (p.678)*
19. *King's Noodle Restaurant (p.678)*
20. *Jacob's & Co. Steakhouse (p.680)*
21. *Le Sélect Bistro (pp.680–681)*
22. *Bar Buca (p.680)*
23. *Buca (p.680)*

24. *Vesta Lunch (p.678)*
25. *House of Chan (p.685)*
26. *Rhum Corner (p.685)*
27. *Bar Isabel (p.682)*
28. *Boom Breakfast & Co (p.683)*
29. *Pizzeria Libretto (p.685)*
30. *Pho Tien Thanh (p.684)*
31. *Commisso Bros. & Racco (p.685)*
32. *Sky Ranch (p.686)*
33. *Bairrada Churrasqueira (p.679)*
34. *Farmhouse Tavern (p.682)*
35. *Phoenix Restaurant (p.682)*
36. *Favourites Dining Room (p.684)*
37. *Grand Electric (p.684)*
38. *Electric Mud BBQ (p.683)*
39. *Food & Liquor (p.684)*
40. *Cheese Boutique (p.680)*

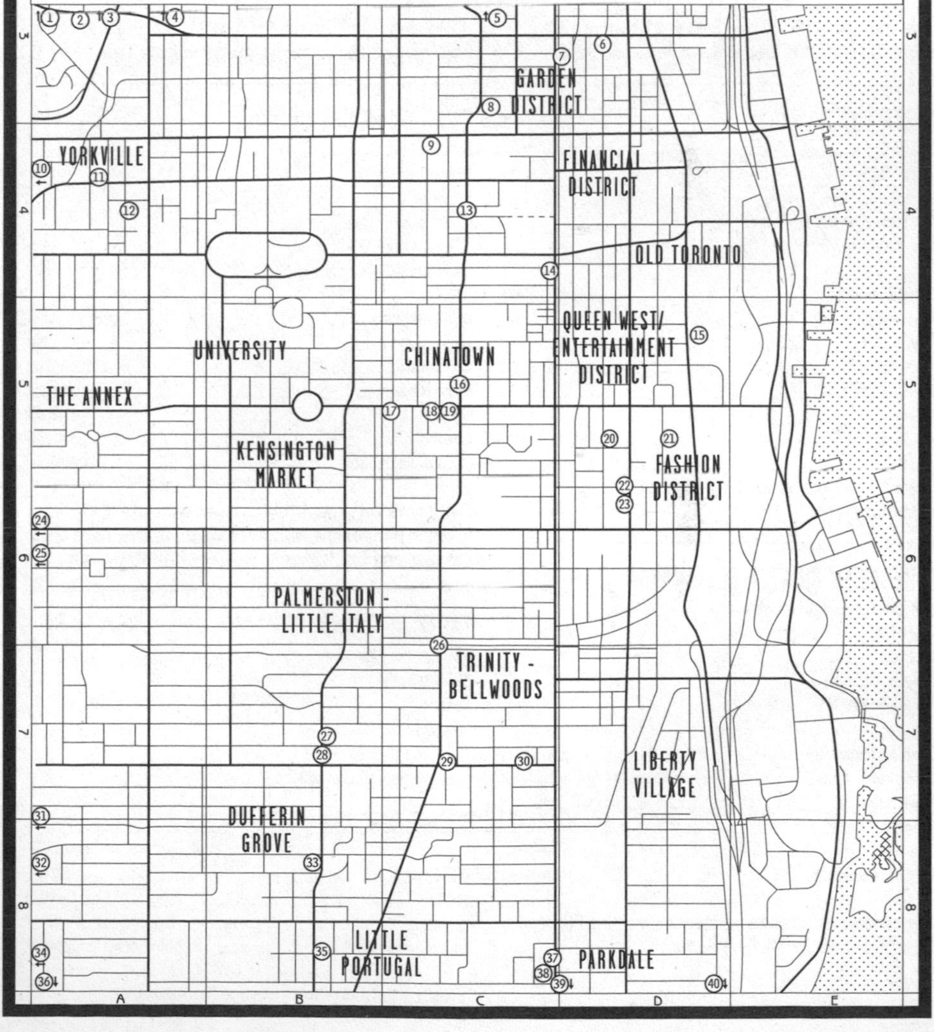

GARDEN DISTRICT

YORKVILLE

FINANCIAL DISTRICT

OLD TORONTO

UNIVERSITY

CHINATOWN

QUEEN WEST/ ENTERTAINMENT DISTRICT

THE ANNEX

KENSINGTON MARKET

FASHION DISTRICT

PALMERSTON - LITTLE ITALY

TRINITY - BELLWOODS

LIBERTY VILLAGE

DUFFERIN GROVE

LITTLE PORTUGAL

PARKDALE

SUKHOTHAI
Recommended by
Basilio Pesce

274 Parliament Street
Cabbagetown South
Toronto
Ontario M5A 3A4
+1 4169138846
www.sukhothaifood.ca

Opening hours	Closed Sunday
Credit cards	Accepted
Price range	Budget
Style	Casual
Cuisine	Thai
Recommended for	Local favourite

'The *khao soi* (curried noodles) and fresh rolls are addictive! Best Thai food in town.'—Basilio Pesce

VESTA LUNCH
Recommended by
Anthony Rose

474 Dupont Street
Casa Loma
Toronto
Ontario M5R 1W5
+1 4165374318

Opening hours	Open 7 days
Reservation policy	No
Credit cards	Not accepted
Price range	Budget
Style	Casual
Cuisine	Diner
Recommended for	Wish I'd opened

'I want that lunch counter so very bad, please.'
—Anthony Rose

FORESTVIEW CHINESE RESTAURANT
Recommended by
Michael Hunter

468 Dundas Street West
Chinatown
Toronto
Ontario M5T 1G9
+1 4165970319

Opening hours	Open 7 days
Credit cards	Accepted but not AMEX
Price range	Budget
Style	Casual
Cuisine	Dim Sum
Recommended for	Breakfast

'I enjoy everything about authentic dim sum. For me it's a huge treat.'—Michael Hunter

KING'S NOODLE RESTAURANT
Recommended by
Susur Lee

296 Spadina Avenue
Chinatown
Toronto
Ontario M5T 2E7
+1 4165981817
www.kingsnoodle.ca

Opening hours	Closed Wednesday
Credit cards	Not accepted
Price range	Budget
Style	Casual
Cuisine	Chinese
Recommended for	Late night

'Chinese at night is comfort food for me, the barbeque pork on rice, the soups, all great!'—Susur Lee

SICHUAN HOUSE CUISINE
Recommended by
Chris McDonald

394 Spadina Avenue
Chinatown
Toronto
Ontario M5T 2G5
+1 4165979333
www.sichuanhouse.ca

Opening hours	Open 7 days
Reservation policy	No
Credit cards	Not accepted
Price range	Budget
Style	Casual
Cuisine	Chinese
Recommended for	Late night

'They have very rough, big flavours with lots of chillies. I love the pork elbow with five spices but they have duck tongues and frog's legs as well.'—Chris McDonald

TASTE OF CHINA
Recommended by
Susur Lee

338 Spadina Avenue
Chinatown
Toronto
Ontario M5T 2G2
+1 4163488828
www.tasteofchinarestaurant.ca

Opening hours	Open 7 days
Credit cards	Accepted but not AMEX
Price range	Budget
Style	Casual
Cuisine	Cantonese-Seafood
Recommended for	Regular neighbourhood

'Fresh, great Cantonese cuisine.'—Susur Lee

PANTHEON

Recommended by
Michael Caballo

407 Danforth Avenue
The Danforth
Toronto
Ontario M4K 1P1
+1 4167781929
www.pantheonrestaurant.ca

Opening hours	Open 7 days
Credit cards	Accepted
Price range	Affordable
Style	Casual
Cuisine	Greek
Recommended for	Bargain

'Some of the best Greek food for pure enjoyability –
whole fried whitings with some marinated hot
peppers... heaven.'—Michael Caballo

Surrounded by impressive competition in Toronto's
Greektown, Pantheon is consistently described as
the best Hellenic restaurant in the city. The menu is
straightforward but well-put-together, with octopus
salad – marinated, seared on the charcoal grill and
served with a minty dressing – dandelion greens
and large plates of sausages, dolmades and grilled
calamari. You'll frequently hear the chatter of Greek
voices bouncing off the hand-painted frescoes, which
evoke sunny days in Ancient Greece; the outside
seating works well for summer people-watching.
Honey cake often emerges for dessert, sometimes
at no extra charge.

KAISEKI YU-ZEN HASHIMOTO

Recommended by
Michael Caballo

Japanese Canadian Cultural Centre
6 Garamond Court
Don Mills
Toronto
Ontario M3C 1Z5
+1 4164447100
www.kaiseki.ca

Opening hours	Open 7 days
Credit cards	Accepted
Price range	Expensive
Style	Smart casual
Cuisine	Japanese
Recommended for	High end

'Poetry. Astonishing technique, ingredients... just,
wow. The ultimate humbling experience for a chef.
So studied, so precise – singular mastery of a style.
Nothing else like it in most places in the world, certainly
not in Toronto.'—Michael Caballo

BAIRRADA CHURRASQUEIRA

Recommended by
Chris McDonald

1000 College Street
Dufferin Grove
Toronto
Ontario M6H 1A7
+1 4165398239
www.bairrada.ca

Opening hours	Closed Monday
Credit cards	Accepted
Price range	Affordable
Style	Casual
Cuisine	Portuguese
Recommended for	Regular neighbourhood

'A very reasonable Portuguese restaurant with a lovely
large backyard and a Euro feel with families dining
together.'—Chris McDonald

ALLEN'S

Recommended by
Anthony Rose

143 Danforth Avenue
East York
Toronto
Ontario M4K 1N2
+1 4164633086
www.allens.to

Opening hours	Open 7 days
Credit cards	Accepted
Price range	Budget
Style	Casual
Cuisine	Irish Pub
Recommended for	Regular neighbourhood

'It makes me feel right at home. Good, simple, and love
in all the food.'—Anthony Rose

CHEESE BOUTIQUE

Recommended by
Anthony Rose

45 Ripley Avenue
Etobicoke
Toronto
Ontario M6S 3P2
+1 4167626292
www.cheeseboutique.com

Opening hours	Open 7 days
Reservation policy	No
Credit cards	Accepted
Price range	Affordable
Style	Casual
Cuisine	Deli
Recommended for	Bargain

'It's not that it's cheap but they give me an espresso as soon as I walk in to the shop. Then I just have Afrim Pristine sample me on a ton of cheese, meats and things until I'm stuffed.'—Anthony Rose

BAR BUCA

Recommended by
Basilio Pesce

75 Portland Street
Fashion District
Toronto
Ontario M5V 2M9
+1 4165992822
www.barbuca.com

Opening hours	Open 7 days
Reservation policy	No
Credit cards	Accepted
Price range	Budget
Style	Casual
Cuisine	Italian
Recommended for	Wish I'd opened

'Great food in a great room. The concept is small bites and they have the best coffee in the city. The true osteria experience.'—Basilio Pesce

BUCA

Recommended by
Michael Hunter, Susur
Lee, Basilio Pesce

604 King Street West
Fashion District
Toronto
Ontario M5V 1M6
+1 4168651600
www.buca.ca

Opening hours	Open 7 days
Credit cards	Accepted
Price range	Affordable
Style	Smart casual
Cuisine	Italian
Recommended for	High end

'It's sexy. It serves hardy, rustic Italian food with a contemporary spin. I love making charcuterie and salumi and they have a huge ageing room behind glass to show off their talents.'—Michael Hunter

JACOB'S & CO. STEAKHOUSE

Recommended by
Susur Lee

12 Brant Street
Fashion District
Toronto
Ontario M5V 2M1
+1 4163660200
www.jacobssteakhouse.com

Opening hours	Open 7 days
Credit cards	Accepted
Price range	Expensive
Style	Smart casual
Cuisine	Steakhouse
Recommended for	High end

LE SÉLECT BISTRO

Recommended by
Michael Caballo

432 Wellington Street West
Fashion District
Toronto
Ontario M5V 1E3
+1 4165966405
www.leselect.com

Opening hours	Open 7 days
Credit cards	Accepted
Price range	Affordable
Style	Smart casual
Cuisine	French Bistro
Recommended for	Regular neighbourhood

'The room is one of the most beautiful, romantic, warm, elegant and comfortable dining rooms in the city. Perfect bistro atmosphere. The food is all of those

adjectives as well! Technical and delicious. I'm always impressed by the finesse and sheer deliciousness. The most precise foie gras terrine in the city.'
—Michael Caballo

BARBERIAN'S STEAKHOUSE

Recommended by
Geoff Hopgood,
Chris McDonald

7 Elm Street
Garden District
Toronto
Ontario M5G 1H1
+1 4165970335
www.barberians.com

Opening hours	Open 7 days
Credit cards	Accepted
Price range	Expensive
Style	Smart casual
Cuisine	Steakhouse
Recommended for	Local favourite

'It has been here for more than fifty years and in the same family. It's a classic Canadian steak house. I like the porterhouse and the salad with blue cheese dressing.'—Chris McDonald

The maple-leaf flag waves proudly outside Barberian's, which has stood in the same spot, and been owned by the same family, since Harry Barberian opened a teetotal steak house here in 1959. Since then the owners have obtained an alcohol licence – just as well, since the 800-bin wine list now needs to be housed in a two-storey cellar. The rather masculine menu recalls an earlier era of dining out, with oysters, snails and Caesar salad as starters and house chocolate mousse, baked Alaska and frozen chocolate eclair for dessert. As well as abroad range of different cuts and sizes of steak, specials such as grilled capon and salmon complete the picture.

GEORGE RESTAURANT

Recommended by
Paul Newman

111c Queen Street East
Garden District
Toronto
Ontario M5C 1S2
+1 4168636006
www.georgeonqueen.com

Opening hours	Closed Sunday
Credit cards	Accepted
Price range	Expensive
Style	Smart casual
Cuisine	International
Recommended for	Worth the travel

'They have interesting menu compilations.'
—Paul Newman

THE SENATOR

Recommended by
Geoff Hopgood

249 Victoria Street
Garden District
Toronto
Ontario M5B 1V8
+1 4163647517
www.thesenator.com

Opening hours	Open 7 days
Credit cards	Accepted
Price range	Affordable
Style	Casual
Cuisine	Diner
Recommended for	Breakfast

'They serve classic grub from beef dips to meatloaf. But I really like their breakfast: eggs, bacon, fried potatoes (home fries), baked beans and challah toast.'
—Geoff Hopgood

STARFISH OYSTER BED & GRILL

Recommended by
Paul Newman

100 Adelaide Street East
Garden District
Toronto
Ontario M5C 1K9
+1 4163667827
www.starfishoysterbed.com

Opening hours	Open 7 days
Credit cards	Accepted
Price range	Affordable
Style	Smart casual
Cuisine	Seafood
Recommended for	Worth the travel

'Amazing fresh oysters and mussels.'—Paul Newman

FARMHOUSE TAVERN

Recommended by
Geoff Hopgood

1627 Dupont Street
Junction Triangle
Toronto
Ontario M6P 3S7
+1 4165619114
www.farmhousetavern.tumblr.com

Opening hours	Closed Monday to Wednesday
Credit cards	Accepted
Price range	Affordable
Style	Casual
Cuisine	Modern Canadian
Recommended for	Local favourite

'Local, farm-focused, great food and service.'
—Geoff Hopgood

MT. EVEREST RESTAURANT

Recommended by
Chris McDonald

804 Eglinton Avenue East
Leaside
Toronto
Ontario M4G 2L1
+1 6477488849
www.mteverestrestaurant.ca

Opening hours	Closed Monday
Credit cards	Accepted
Price range	Budget
Style	Casual
Cuisine	Himalayan-Nepalese-Indian
Recommended for	Bargain

'The restaurant is spotless and the staff are gracious.
Their Indian food is very fresh.'—Chris McDonald

BAR ISABEL

Recommended by
Louis Bouchard Trudeau,
Suzanne Goin, Geoff
Hopgood, Michael Hunter

797 College Street
Little Italy
Toronto
Ontario M6G 1C6
+1 4165322222
www.barisabel.com

Opening hours	Open 7 days
Credit cards	Accepted
Price range	Affordable
Style	Smart casual
Cuisine	Spanish
Recommended for	Worth the travel

'The space is really beautiful. I had the most amazing
grilled octopus!'—Suzanne Goin

PHOENIX RESTAURANT

Recommended by
Basilio Pesce

1151 College Street
Little Portugal
Toronto
Ontario M6H 1B5
+1 4165386891
www.phoenixrestaurant.ca

Opening hours	Open 7 days
Credit cards	Accepted
Price range	Budget
Style	Casual
Cuisine	Vietnamese
Recommended for	Bargain

'Great Vietnamese food. The pho is a standout, with
a nice clean broth. They also have a good selection of
other traditional dishes under the "chef's specials".'
—Basilio Pesce

CAVA

Recommended by
Murray McDonald

1560 Yonge Street
Midtown
Toronto
Ontario M4T 2S9
+1 4169799918
www.cavarestaurant.ca

Opening hours	Open 7 days
Credit cards	Accepted
Price range	Affordable
Style	Smart casual
Cuisine	Spanish
Recommended for	Worth the travel

'Chef Chris McDonald's execution and passion for
cuisine from the Iberian peninsula really shows
through. Great food, great people and a fantastic
spot to relax. Small plates and wine – count me in.'
—Murray McDonald

360 RESTAURANT

CN Tower
301 Front Street West
Old Toronto
Toronto
Ontario M5V 2T6
+1 4163625411
www.cntower.ca

Opening hours	Open 7 days
Credit cards	Accepted
Price range	Expensive
Style	Smart casual
Cuisine	Modern Canadian
Recommended for	Local favourite

'I had a pretty amazing experience there for my twenty-first birthday. Not to mention it's a great place for a date to watch the sun set over a bottle of wine and a cheese board.'—Michael Hunter

JAPANGO

122 Elizabeth Street
Old Toronto
Toronto
Ontario M5G 1P5
+1 4165995557
www.japango.net

Opening hours	Open 7 days
Credit cards	Accepted
Price range	Affordable
Style	Casual
Cuisine	Sushi
Recommended for	Regular neighbourhood

'Best sushi in town. It's a super-small joint – try the signature roll.'—Geoff Hopgood

NOTA BENE

180 Queen Street West
Old Toronto
Toronto
Ontario M5V 3X3
+1 4169776400
www.notabenerestaurant.com

Opening hours	Closed Sunday
Credit cards	Accepted
Price range	Affordable
Style	Smart casual
Cuisine	Modern Canadian
Recommended for	High end

BOOM BREAKFAST & CO

808 College Street
Palmerston
Toronto
Ontario M6G 1C8
+1 4165343447
www.boombreakfast.com

Opening hours	Open 7 days
Reservation policy	No
Credit cards	Accepted but not AMEX
Price range	Budget
Style	Casual
Cuisine	Diner
Recommended for	Breakfast

'My son loves it, I enjoy taking him for breakfast there.'
—Susur Lee

ELECTRIC MUD BBQ

5 Brock Avenue
Parkdale
Toronto
Ontario M6K 2K3
+1 4165168286
www.electricmudbbq.com

Opening hours	Closed Tuesday
Reservation policy	No
Credit cards	Not accepted
Price range	Budget
Style	Casual
Cuisine	Barbeque
Recommended for	Wish I'd opened

'I love barbeque and they do it well. I really like the roadhouse feel of this place. It almost transports you to a Southern side-of-the-road-type barbeque shack.'
—Geoff Hopgood

FOOD & LIQUOR

Recommended by
Basilio Pesce

1610 Queen Street West
Parkdale
Toronto
Ontario M6R 1A8
+1 6477487113
www.foodandliquor.ca

Opening hours	Closed Tuesday and Wednesday
Reservation policy	No
Credit cards	Accepted but not AMEX
Price range	Budget
Style	Casual
Cuisine	Asian Fusion
Recommended for	Late night

'Casual bar with great bar bites and dumplings. Open until 2.00 a.m., it's a great spot to grab a drink and a nibble after work.'—Basilio Pesce

GRAND ELECTRIC

Recommended by
Geoff Hopgood

1330 Queen Street West
Parkdale
Toronto
Ontario M6K 1L4
+1 4166273459
www.grandelectricbar.com

Opening hours	Open 7 days
Reservation policy	No
Credit cards	Not accepted
Price range	Budget
Style	Casual
Cuisine	Mexican
Recommended for	Bargain

'Tacos are C$3.50 (£2; $3) each. They are all delicious but definitely try the scrapple taco.'—Geoff Hopgood

FAVOURITES DINING ROOM

Recommended by
Anthony Rose

Woodbine Racetrack
555 Rexdale Boulevard
Rexdale
Toronto
Ontario M9W 5L2
+1 4166757223
www.woodbineentertainment.com

Opening hours	Variable
Credit cards	Accepted but not AMEX
Price range	Affordable
Style	Casual
Cuisine	International
Recommended for	High end

'If I have some dough to spend I love me a dinner and a show.'—Anthony Rose

PHO TIEN THANH

Recommended by
Susur Lee

57 Ossington Avenue
Trinity-Bellwoods
Toronto
Ontario M6J 2Y9
+1 4165886997

Opening hours	Open 7 days
Reservation policy	No
Credit cards	Not accepted
Price range	Budget
Style	Casual
Cuisine	Vietnamese
Recommended for	Bargain

'The best pho in town! I always get the rare beef noodle soup and spring rolls.'—Susur Lee

PIZZERIA LIBRETTO
221 Ossington Avenue
Trinity-Bellwoods
Toronto
Ontario M6J 2Z8
+1 4165328000
www.ossington.pizzerialibretto.com

Recommended by
Basilio Pesce

Opening hours	Open 7 days
Reservation policy	No
Credit cards	Accepted
Price range	Budget
Style	Casual
Cuisine	Pizza
Recommended for	Regular neighbourhood

'The best pizza in town. Classic Neapolitan pizza at a good price, done right. I usually skip over between lunch and dinner for a quick bite. The wine list is small but smart.'—Basilio Pesce

RHUM CORNER
926 Dundas Street West
Trinity-Bellwoods
Toronto
Ontario M6J 1W3
+1 6473469356
www.rhumcorner.com

Recommended by
Michael Caballo

Opening hours	Closed Tuesday and Wednesday
Reservation policy	No
Credit cards	Not accepted
Price range	Budget
Style	Casual
Cuisine	Haitian
Recommended for	Late night

'Creative, fun, delicious, unique – hundreds of rums and Piña Colada slushies on tap. This is a Haitian-influenced place – unique flavours that are great to experience.'—Michael Caballo

Jen Agg owns three of Toronto's coolest restaurants – though she is reluctant to countenance that adjective – all within a block or two of each other. Rhum Corner, a Haitian-themed rum bar, is her most recent. Bare bricks and white tiles provide modern touches, while a huge painting of a naked Haitian sunbather decorates one wall. Over forty kinds of rum provide a deliciously smoky and varied counterpoint to the food. This sees legumes with goat meat, fried pork shoulder with fried plantain and malanga fritters with *picklese* (a spicy Haitian condiment made from shredded cabbage). Best Piña Colada in town, too.

COMMISSO BROS. & RACCO
8 Kincourt Street
York
Toronto
Ontario M6M 3E1
+1 4166517671
www.commissobakery.com

Recommended by
Anthony Rose

Opening hours	Open 7 days
Reservation policy	No
Credit cards	Not accepted
Price range	Budget
Style	Casual
Cuisine	Bakery-Deli
Recommended for	Late night

'Truckers, gangsters and veal sandwiches, twenty-four hours, 365 days a year.'—Anthony Rose

Commisso Bros. began serving Italian-Canadians the tastes of the old country back in 1957 – and now continues to do so round the clock, seven days a week, 365 days a year. Persistent rumours of mob links (one former owner was shot dead outside the store in 2002) do little to dissuade customers from trooping through the door night after night for veal Parmigiana, porchetta, big greasy pizzas and the store's own artisan breads. A large parking lot means there's always space, and you'll even find an olive bar and, in the summer, fresh gelato. A proud nugget of blue-collar Canadiana.

HOUSE OF CHAN
876 Eglinton Avenue West
York
Toronto
Ontario M6C 2B6
+1 4167815575
www.houseofchan.ca

Recommended by
Anthony Rose

Opening hours	Open 7 days
Reservation policy	No
Credit cards	Accepted
Price range	Expensive
Style	Smart casual
Cuisine	Steakhouse-Chinese
Recommended for	Local favourite

'As old school as it gets, really clubby with the best lobster and steaks in town. American-Chinese food is a dying luxury.'—Anthony Rose

SKY RANCH

Recommended by
Anthony Rose

2473 Dufferin Street
York
Toronto
Ontario M6B 3P9
+1 4167870491
www.skyranch.sites.toronto.com

Opening hours	Closed Monday
Credit cards	Accepted
Price range	Affordable
Style	Casual
Cuisine	Argentinian
Recommended for	Breakfast

'Who doesn't want Argentinian steak for breakfast? Plus, if you're still hungry afterwards, California Sandwiches is across the street, kinda.'—Anthony Rose

CAFÉ BOULUD

Recommended by
Chris McDonald,
Paul Newman

Four Seasons Hotel
60 Yorkville Avenue
Yorkville
Toronto
Ontario M4W 0A4
+1 4169636000
www.cafeboulud.com/toronto

Opening hours	Open 7 days
Credit cards	Accepted
Price range	Affordable
Style	Smart casual
Cuisine	French
Recommended for	High end

'I love Daniel's food and I have had many great meals at Café Boulud in New York and am delighted that he has opened here. His sommeliers are excellent.'
—Chris McDonald

SASSAFRAZ

Recommended by
Michael Hunter

100 Cumberland Street
Yorkville
Toronto
Ontario M5R 1A6
+1 4169642222
www.sassafraz.ca

Opening hours	Open 7 days
Credit cards	Accepted
Price range	Affordable
Style	Smart casual
Cuisine	Modern Canadian
Recommended for	High end

'They have one of the most beautiful restaurant dining rooms in the city. Huge skylights lighting up a massive living wall and a waterfall. It's a special spot.'
—Michael Hunter

'IT EMBODIES THE SPIRIT OF MONTREAL
– LIVELY, STEEPED IN TRADITION,
BUT A BIT UNTAMED.'

COREY LEE P695

MONTREAL

'*Currently
the cream of
Montreal's
top-end
restaurants.*'

SÉGUÉ LEPAGE P696

'STEAMING
PILES OF
CANADIAN
SNOW CRAB.'

JUSTIN DEVILLIER P690

'ONE OF THE BEST
VALUE RESTAURANTS IN
MONTREAL. MONUMENTAL
WINE LIST.'

DAVID MCMILLAN & FRÉDÉRIC MORIN P692

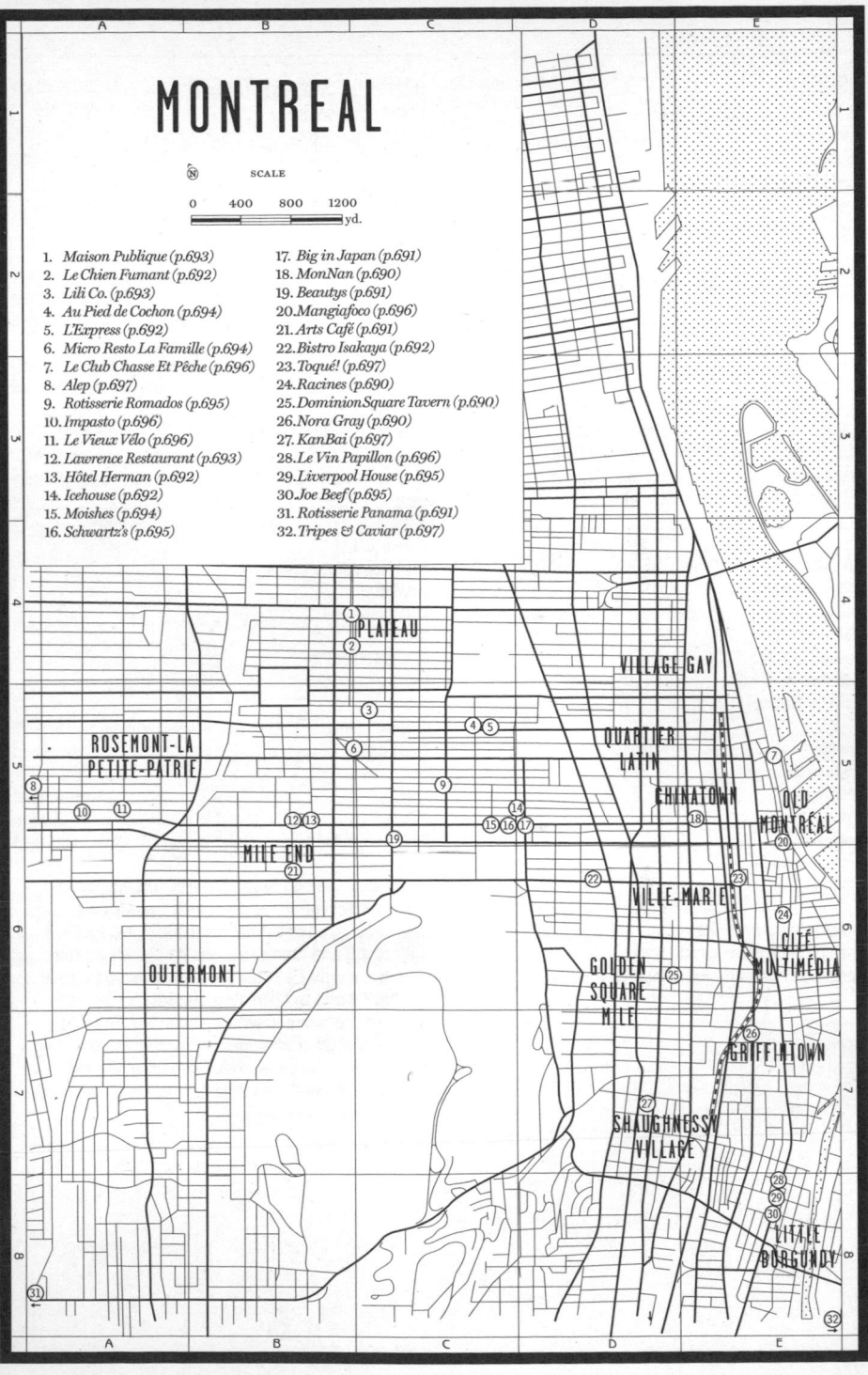

MONNAN

Recommended by
David McMillan &
Frédéric Morin

43 Rue de la Gauchetière Est
Chinatown
Montreal
Quebec H2Z 1K3
+1 5148667123
www.restaurantmonnan.com

Opening hours	Open 7 days
Credit cards	Accepted
Price range	Affordable
Style	Casual
Cuisine	Chinese
Recommended for	Late night

'Skilled at seafood. It might sound crazy but they're also skilled at deep-frying things in a light way. You don't feel like you're drinking the deep-fat frier.'
—David McMillan & Frédéric Morin

RACINES

Recommended by
Guillaume Cantin

444 Rue McGill
Cité Multimedia
Montreal
Quebec H2Y 2G1
+1 5145440444
www.racines.ca

Opening hours	Closed Monday and Sunday
Credit cards	Accepted
Price range	Affordable
Style	Casual
Cuisine	European small plates
Recommended for	Local favourite

'This restaurant exemplifies the creativity found in Montreal today with its young chef, Simon Mathys. The cuisine is spot-on and unpretentious, bringing out pure, clean flavours.'—Guillaume Cantin

DOMINION SQUARE TAVERN

Recommended by
Guillaume Cantin

1243 Rue Metcalfe
Golden Square Mile
Montreal
Quebec H3B 2V5
+1 5145645056
www.dominiontavern.com

Opening hours	Open 7 days
Credit cards	Accepted
Price range	Affordable
Style	Casual
Cuisine	French-Canadian Bistro
Recommended for	Regular neighbourhood

'The overall concept works well at this restaurant that neatly combines decor, atmosphere and food. The cuisine has a homely, British touch.'—Guillaume Cantin

NORA GRAY

Recommended by
Justin Devillier

1391 Rue Saint-Jacques
Griffintown
Montreal
Quebec H3C 1H2
+1 5144196672
www.noragray.com

Opening hours	Closed Monday and Sunday
Credit cards	Accepted
Price range	Affordable
Style	Smart casual
Cuisine	Italian
Recommended for	Wish I'd opened

'You walk in and go through velvet curtains, which reveal the restaurant and tiny little bar. It's on a dark street in a residential neighbourhood. I walked right past it and didn't even see it – there's no sign. Funnily enough, I was thinking this would be a great neighbourhood to open a restaurant. It's the chef's version of Italian food with an urban feel. The fried calf's brains were amazing and so were the steaming piles of Canadian snow crab. I also loved the ambience and staff – by the time I left I felt like I was part of the crew.'—Justin Devillier

ROTISSERIE PANAMA

Recommended by
David McMillan &
Frédéric Morin

1150 Boulevard Curé-Labelle
Laval
Montreal
Quebec H7V 2V5
+1 4509348009
www.rotisseriepanama.com

Opening hours	Open 7 days
Credit cards	Accepted
Price range	Affordable
Style	Casual
Cuisine	Greek
Recommended for	Bargain

'They do grilled chicken, Greek salad, greens. Dirt cheap. On Fridays and Saturdays, they have big plates of braised lamb.'—David McMillan & Frédéric Morin

ARTS CAFÉ

Recommended by
Fisun Ercan

201 Avenue Fairmount Ouest
Le Plateau-Mont-Royal
Montreal
Quebec H2T 2M8
+1 5142740919
www.artscafemontreal.com

Opening hours	Open 7 days
Reservation policy	No
Credit cards	Accepted but not AMEX
Price range	Budget
Style	Casual
Cuisine	Café
Recommended for	Breakfast

'On weekdays I like to stop by here before going to work. Their coffee is good, which is very important for me along with the food for breakfast. Very good scones, breakfast sandwiches and fresh salads. Hip ambience without being hectic.'—Fisun Ercan

BEAUTYS

Recommended by
Louis-Philippe Riel

93 Avenue du Mont-Royal Ouest
Le Plateau-Mont-Royal
Montreal
Quebec H2T 2S5
+1 5148498883
www.beautys.ca

Opening hours	Open 7 days
Reservation policy	No
Credit cards	Accepted
Price range	Budget
Style	Casual
Cuisine	Diner-Café
Recommended for	Breakfast

'The decor of this Jewish diner hasn't changed since the 1950s, the food is always comforting and the service is by far the best I have ever seen in this kind of restaurant.'—Louis-Philippe Riel

BIG IN JAPAN

Recommended by
Fisun Ercan,
Normand Laprise

3723 Boulevard Saint-Laurent
Le Plateau-Mont-Royal
Montreal
Quebec H2X 2V7
+1 5148472222
www.biginjapan.ca

Opening hours	Open 7 days
Credit cards	Accepted but not AMEX
Price range	Affordable
Style	Casual
Cuisine	Japanese
Recommended for	Bargain

'When I'm in the mood for a big bowl of ramen soup or some funky sandwiches, I go to Big in Japan.'
—Fisun Ercan

BISTRO ISAKAYA

Recommended by
Normand Laprise

3469 Avenue du Parc
Le Plateau-Mont-Royal
Montreal
Quebec H2X 2H6
+1 5148458226
www.bistroisakaya.com

Opening hours	Closed Monday
Credit cards	Accepted
Price range	Budget
Style	Casual
Cuisine	Japanese
Recommended for	Bargain

LE CHIEN FUMANT

Recommended by
Fisun Ercan,
Martin Juneau

4710 Rue de Lanaudière
Le Plateau-Mont-Royal
Montreal
Quebec H2J 3Z2
+1 5145242444
www.lechienfumant.com

Opening hours	Closed Monday
Credit cards	Accepted but not AMEX
Price range	Affordable
Style	Casual
Cuisine	Modern Canadian
Recommended for	Late night

'Because they close late here, the wine list is short but first-rate and their cured meats are just perfect.'
—Martin Juneau

L'EXPRESS

Recommended by
David McMillan &
Frédéric Morin

3927 Rue Saint-Denis
Le Plateau-Mont-Royal
Montreal
Quebec H2W 2M4
+1 5148455333
www.restaurantlexpress.ca

Opening hours	Open 7 days
Credit cards	Accepted but not AMEX
Price range	Affordable
Style	Casual
Cuisine	French Bistro
Recommended for	Regular neighbourhood

'Classic French bistro. I've been eating there for more than twenty years. Nothing has changed. One of the best-value restaurants in Montreal. Monumental wine list. Possibly the cheapest place to drink wine. Don't

forget to ask for the wine inventory. They'll bring out a secret list with everything they have in the basement.'
—David McMillan & Frédéric Morin

HÔTEL HERMAN

Recommended by
Martin Juneau,
Ségué Lepage

5171 Boulevard Saint-Laurent
Le Plateau-Mont-Royal
Montreal
Quebec H2T 1R9
+1 5142787000
www.hotelherman.com

Opening hours	Closed Tuesday
Credit cards	Accepted
Price range	Affordable
Style	Smart casual
Cuisine	Modern Canadian
Recommended for	Local favourite

'A fabulous address, serving genuine and intelligent cuisine… my favourite restaurant.'—Ségué Lepage

ICEHOUSE

Recommended by
Ségué Lepage

51 Rue Roy Est
Le Plateau-Mont-Royal
Montreal
Quebec H2W 1L8
+1 5144396691

Opening hours	Closed Monday
Reservation policy	No
Credit cards	Accepted
Price range	Budget
Style	Casual
Cuisine	Tex-Mex
Recommended for	Late night

'This is an unpretentious Tex-Mex restaurant. Warm and friendly, serving simple dishes with sharp flavours and superb cocktails.'—Ségué Lepage

LAWRENCE RESTAURANT

Recommended by
Guillaume Cantin,
Martin Juneau

5201 Boulevard Saint-Laurent
Le Plateau-Mont-Royal
Montreal
Quebec H2T 2L9
+1 5145031070
www.lawrencerestaurant.com

Opening hours...Closed Monday
Credit cards..Accepted
Price range...Affordable
Style...Casual
Cuisine..Bistro
Recommended for...Breakfast

'This restaurant focuses mainly on lunches and in my opinion it's the best value for money in town… My favourite lunch spot in Montreal.'—Martin Juneau

Shabby chic meets industrial cool at this popular forty-seat neighbourhood bistro. Exposed pipework and yards of gunmetal grey paintwork are the setting for bare wood tables, simple bistro chairs and the odd wooden bench. Weekend brunch is hugely popular, with everything from scones to baked eggs, celeriac (celery root) and oyster mushrooms on offer – but meat lovers will save their appetite for dinner. British-born chef Marc Cohen has his own butchery in the restaurant's basement, meaning there's plenty of nose-to-tail action on the menu, including lamb offal with beetroots (beets) and mint, and braised oxtail with oysters, stout and mash.

LILI CO.

Recommended by
Fisun Ercan

4650 Rue Mentana
Le Plateau-Mont-Royal
Montreal
Quebec H2J 3B9
+1 5145077278
www.restolilico.com

Opening hours...Open 7 days
Credit cards..Accepted
Price range...Affordable
Style...Casual
Cuisine..Modern Canadian
Recommended for...Breakfast

'For Sunday brunch it's difficult to choose just one place since a lot of restaurants are doing very creative brunch menus but Lili Co.'s grilled octopus, baked eggs, Vietnamese-style crêpes, grilled blood sausages, and nut pancakes are popular – although the menu changes regularly. Very friendly service, open kitchen

(even when I'm not working I like to feel the dynamism of the kitchen so small, open-kitchen restaurants attract me the most), and the nicely presented, flavourful food pleases me.'—Fisun Ercan

MAISON PUBLIQUE

Recommended by
Lee Cooper,
Chris Cosentino,
David McMillan &
Frédéric Morin

4720 Rue Marquette
Le Plateau-Mont-Royal
Montreal
Quebec H2J 3Y6
+1 5145070555
www.maisonpublique.com

Opening hours...Closed Monday and Tuesday
Credit cards..Accepted but not AMEX
Price range...Affordable
Style...Casual
Cuisine..British
Recommended for...Worth the travel

'Outstanding food in a comfortable room. The food is cooked by Derek Dammann who is one of the chefs I admire most.'—Lee Cooper

This neighbourhood pub-restaurant's British connections stretch beyond its slicked-up boozer aesthetic: it's backed by Jamie Oliver. But the gutsy menu is very much the work of local chef-owner Derek Dammann (an Oliver alumnus), whose love of seasonal gastropub cooking is evident in the likes of smoked mackerel, Welsh rarebit, Charlevoix pork with salsa verde and pig's ear salad. There's an all-Canadian wine list, a line-up of ciders and a popular weekend brunch featuring an English breakfast loaded with blood pudding, bone marrow and pork chops – offal is a speciality here. Maison Publique (geddit?) doesn't take reservations for brunch, so pitch up and grab a seat at the long counter where you can watch the chefs at work.

MICRO RESTO LA FAMILLE

Recommended by
Ségué Lepage

418 Rue Gilford
Le Plateau-Mont-Royal
Montreal
Quebec H2J 1N2
+1 5145088700

Opening hours	Closed Monday and Sunday
Reservation policy	No
Credit cards	Not accepted
Price range	Budget
Style	Casual
Cuisine	Modern Canadian
Recommended for	Breakfast

'There's only room for nine in this micro restaurant set up by the two Daniel-Six brothers (chef and pastry chef). This is raw talent in its purest form!'
—Ségué Lepage

Micro it may be – there are just nine stools to perch on – but this new Plateau hotspot has made waves with its very macro, market-driven flavours. There are a handful of chalked-up mains, and great organic wines (courtesy of the wine importer co-owner), but it's the brunch that excels. From the sweet (brownies, fruit-studded muffins and Ricard-drenched *canelés*) to the savoury (duck brioche, bacon slab squash soup), it hits all the right notes, with excellent coffee to boot. Original member and pastry chef Jérémy Daniel-Six recently moved on – but reports so far suggest that the family is still going strong.

MOISHES

Recommended by
David McMillan &
Frédéric Morin

3961 Boulevard Saint-Laurent
Le Plateau-Mont-Royal
Montreal
Quebec H2W 1Y4
+1 5148453509
www.moishes.ca

Opening hours	Open 7 days
Credit cards	Accepted
Price range	Expensive
Style	Smart casual
Cuisine	Steakhouse
Recommended for	Local favourite

'An often-forgotten Montreal classic. This steakhouse has been here for almost eighty years. It's right near Schwartz's. The father started it and his son still runs the place with his brother. Steak, chicken, chopped liver, pickles, cabbage... It represents a slice of what Montreal is about. There'll be all types of people – a great cross-section. It's a real power room, lots of politicians.'—David McMillan & Frédéric Morin

AU PIED DE COCHON

Recommended by
Yves Le Lay, Hernán Gipponi,
Michael Hunter, Normand
Laprise, David McMillan &
Frédéric Morin

536 Avenue Duluth Est
Le Plateau-Mont-Royal
Montreal
Quebec H2L 1A9
+1 5142811114
www.restaurantaupieddecochon.ca

Opening hours	Closed Monday and Tuesday
Credit cards	Accepted
Price range	Affordable
Style	Smart casual
Cuisine	Modern French
Recommended for	Worth the travel

'I travelled with other local chefs to cook at the Montreal Lumière Festival. The night my friend Juan Pedro Rastellino and I had dinner in that restaurant was unforgettable. We ate a record number of dishes because we chefs like to try everything. The restaurant pays great homage to pork and foie gras. Delicious!'
—Hernán Gipponi

Martin Picard's cult Québécois outpost has carved out a decadent reputation for itself since opening in 2001. Picard made his name here with his pork and foie gras-fixated menu, which incorporates these ingredients into everything – including the local delicacy that is poutine (chips [fries] topped with cheese curd and gravy), burgers, more typically French applications such as terrines and boudin noir tarts – and stuffing it generously inside the restaurant's namesake. Meanwhile, Picard's famous duck-in-a-can is magret and more foie gras, cooked and brought to the table in said can and dumped on toast topped with celeriac purée.

ROTISSERIE ROMADOS
Recommended by
Louis-Philippe Riel
115 Rue Rachel Est
Le Plateau-Mont-Royal
Montreal
Quebec H2W 1C8
+1 5148491803
www.romados.ca

Opening hours	Open 7 days
Reservation policy	No
Credit cards	Not accepted
Price range	Budget
Style	Casual
Cuisine	Portuguese
Recommended for	Bargain

'This Portuguese rotisserie makes the juiciest roast chicken ever at all hours. Getting a C$9 (£5; $8) half-chicken and going to eat it in the park nearby is always a good time. Most importantly, nothing has ever changed in the restaurant, which is a perfect example of its kind.'—Louis-Philippe Riel

SCHWARTZ'S
Recommended by
David McMillan & Frédéric
Morin, Louis-Philippe Riel
3895 Boulevard Saint-Laurent
Le Plateau-Mont-Royal
Montreal
Quebec H2W 1X9
+1 5148424813
www.schwartzsdeli.com

Opening hours	Open 7 days
Reservation policy	No
Credit cards	Not accepted
Price range	Budget
Style	Casual
Cuisine	Deli-Café
Recommended for	Late night

'There's nothing more satisfying than a smoked meat sandwich with a cherry coke.'—Louis-Philippe Riel

JOE BEEF
Recommended by
Fisun Ercan, Martin
Juneau, Normand Laprise,
Corey Lee, Ségué Lepage
2491 Rue Notre-Dame Ouest
Little Burgundy
Montreal
Quebec H3J 1N6
+1 5149356504
www.joebeef.ca

Opening hours	Closed Monday and Sunday
Credit cards	Accepted but not AMEX
Price range	Affordable
Style	Casual
Cuisine	Steakhouse-Seafood
Recommended for	Local favourite

'Simply delicious cooking happening here and it embodies the spirit of Montreal: lively, steeped in tradition, but a bit untamed.'—Corey Lee

Despite its hard-to-come-by tables, Joe Beef has its feet firmly on the ground. There's a whiff of rebellion in the air in the noisy little dining room, where the menu is chalked up on a blackboard and diners are seated elbow to elbow at well-worn wooden tables. Emphasis is on the food: impeccably sourced, simply prepared and delivered in supersize portions. Dinner (there's no lunch service) might start with a trip to the oyster bar for half a dozen New Brunswicks, before New York strip with beef-fat fries or the ever-popular lobster spaghetti. Ask knowledgeable staff for wine recommendations. Call long in advance to secure a table, particularly for the ones in the lovely kitchen garden.

LIVERPOOL HOUSE
Recommended by
Ségué Lepage
2501 Notre-Dame West
Little Burgundy
Montreal
Quebec H3J 1N6
+1 5143136049
www.joebeef.ca

Opening hours	Closed Monday and Sunday
Credit cards	Accepted
Price range	Affordable
Style	Casual
Cuisine	Modern European
Recommended for	Wish I'd opened

'I have great respect for David McMillan and Frédéric Morin. They have a vision when it comes to cuisine and they stick to it. It's a major success story.'
—Ségué Lepage

LE VIN PAPILLON

2519 Rue Notre-Dame Ouest
Little Burgundy
Montreal
Quebec H3J 1N4
www.vinpapillon.com

Recommended by
Guillaume Cantin,
Martin Juneau,
Ségué Lepage

Opening hours...................Closed Monday and Sunday
Reservation policy...No
Credit cards............................Accepted but not AMEX
Price range...Affordable
Style..Casual
Cuisine...Small plates
Recommended for............................Wish I'd opened

'The vegetables here are prepared in an extremely original way and the wine list is magnificent.'
—Guillaume Cantin

LE CLUB CHASSE ET PÊCHE

423 Rue Saint-Claude
Old Montreal
Montreal
Quebec H2Y 3B6
+1 5148611112
www.leclubchasseetpeche.com

Recommended by
Ségué Lepage

Opening hours...................Closed Monday and Sunday
Credit cards..Accepted
Price range...Affordable
Style..Smart casual
Cuisine...........................Modern French-Canadian
Recommended for...................................High end

'This place is currently the cream of Montreal's high-end restaurants.'—Ségué Lepage

Since it opened in late 2004, Le Club Chasse et Pêche has become known as one of the best restaurants in Montreal. Set back from a cobbled street in the city's old quarter, with a crest of antlers and fish hanging by the door, it serves fresh and modern Canadian cuisine with a special emphasis – as the name suggests – on game and fish. The menu comprises venison, guinea fowl, lobster and Arctic char as well as their take on a 'surf and turf': calf's sweetbreads with crab, trompette mushrooms and horseradish. It's a loud and boisterous place popular with young Montrealers.

MANGIAFOCO

105 Rue Saint-Paul Ouest
Old Montreal
Montreal
Quebec H2Y 1Z5
+1 5144198380
www.mangiafoco.ca

Recommended by
Guillaume Cantin

Opening hours...................................Open 7 days
Credit cards..Accepted
Price range...Affordable
Style..Casual
Cuisine..Italian
Recommended for...................................Late night

'This is the place to go for a good, honest pizza and a glass of wine.'—Guillaume Cantin

IMPASTO

48 Rue Dante
Rosemont-La Petite-Patrie
Montreal
Quebec H2S 1J5
+1 5145086508
www.impastomtl.com

Recommended by
Basilio Pesce

Opening hours...................Closed Monday and Sunday
Credit cards..Accepted
Price range...Affordable
Style..Casual
Cuisine..Italian
Recommended for...........................Worth the travel

'Very traditional Italian food. Simple, honest cooking done right in a modern, stylish room.'—Basilio Pesce

LE VIEUX VÉLO

59 Rue Beaubien Est
Rosemont-La Petite-Patrie
Montreal
Quebec H2S 1R1
+1 5144395595

Recommended by
Martin Juneau

Opening hours...................................Open 7 days
Reservation policy...No
Credit cards............................Accepted but not AMEX
Price range...Budget
Style..Casual
Cuisine..Café
Recommended for.................................Breakfast

'This neighbourhood restaurant offers very good breakfast dishes, as well as exceptional coffee and particularly interesting burgers...'—Martin Juneau

KANBAI

Recommended by
Fisun Ercan

1813 Rue Sainte-Catherine Ouest
Shaughnessy Village
Montreal
Quebec II3II 1M2
+1 5149336699

Opening hours	Open 7 days
Credit cards	Not accepted
Price range	Budget
Style	Casual
Cuisine	Chinese
Recommended for	Bargain

'It's an atypical Chinese restaurant for Montreal: they mostly specialize in Szechuan and Hunan cuisine. It has a huge menu but poached fish fillet in hot chilli oil is one of the favourites. Dry-fried green beans, sizzling aubergine (eggplant) and sizzling duck are popular too. Szechuan pepper is quite abundant in the dishes. For those who like spicy Asian food this restaurant is a delicious option. For C\$50 (£30; \$50) there is enough food on the table for six to eight people.'—Fisun Ercan

TRIPES & CAVIAR

Recommended by
Fisun Ercan

3725 Wellington Street
Verdun
Montreal
Quebec H4G 1V1
+1 5148191791
www.tripesandcaviar.com

Opening hours	Closed Monday and Tuesday
Credit cards	Not accepted
Price range	Affordable
Style	Casual
Cuisine	Modern Canadian
Recommended for	Regular neighbourhood

'A young, very energetic and audacious chef-owner whose bold menus change regularly. Offal, seafood and meat dishes feature, along with some vegetable dishes. I also admire him because he uses every piece of the animal, which many people throw out. You can find whole-roasted salmon head, cod rillettes, wagyu beef and ratte potato parfait, pig's tail, and it goes on.'—Fisun Ercan

TOQUÉ!

Recommended by
Guillaume Cantin,
Louis-Philippe Riel

900 Place Jean-Paul-Riopelle
Ville-Marie
Montreal
Quebec H2Z 2B2
+1 5144992084
www.restaurant-toque.com

Opening hours	Closed Monday and Sunday
Credit cards	Accepted
Price range	Expensive
Style	Smart casual
Cuisine	Modern French-Canadian
Recommended for	High end

'I believe it was the first and, more importantly, currently is one of the only restaurants which understands and uses the resources of Quebec to offer a real gastronomic experience to its customers.'—Louis-Philippe Riel

ALEP

Recommended by
Martin Juneau

199 Rue Jean-Talon Est
Villeray-Saint-Michel-Parc-Extension
Montreal
Quebec H2R 1S8
+1 5142706396
www.restaurantalep.com

Opening hours	Closed Monday and Sunday
Credit cards	Accepted
Price range	Affordable
Style	Smart casual
Cuisine	Syrian-Armenian
Recommended for	Regular neighbourhood

'This is a terrific Middle Eastern restaurant, where the wine list is fantastic and almost entirely made up of natural wines. Plus, it's family friendly.'
—Martin Juneau

'Delicious, home-style Cal-Mex cooking in the heart of the agricultural Central Coast of California. It's a true taste of this place that we call home.'
DAVID KINCH P708

'It's loved by locals and travellers for the beautiful bounties of Hawaii.'
BRAD TURLEY P711

'The perfect after-surf meal to get your day going.'
MATTHEW ORLANDO P706

USA WEST

'Some of the best and most exciting food in the Pacific Northwest.'
ANDY RICKER P719

'The most eye-boggling selection of booze in the world.'
MATT DILLON P721

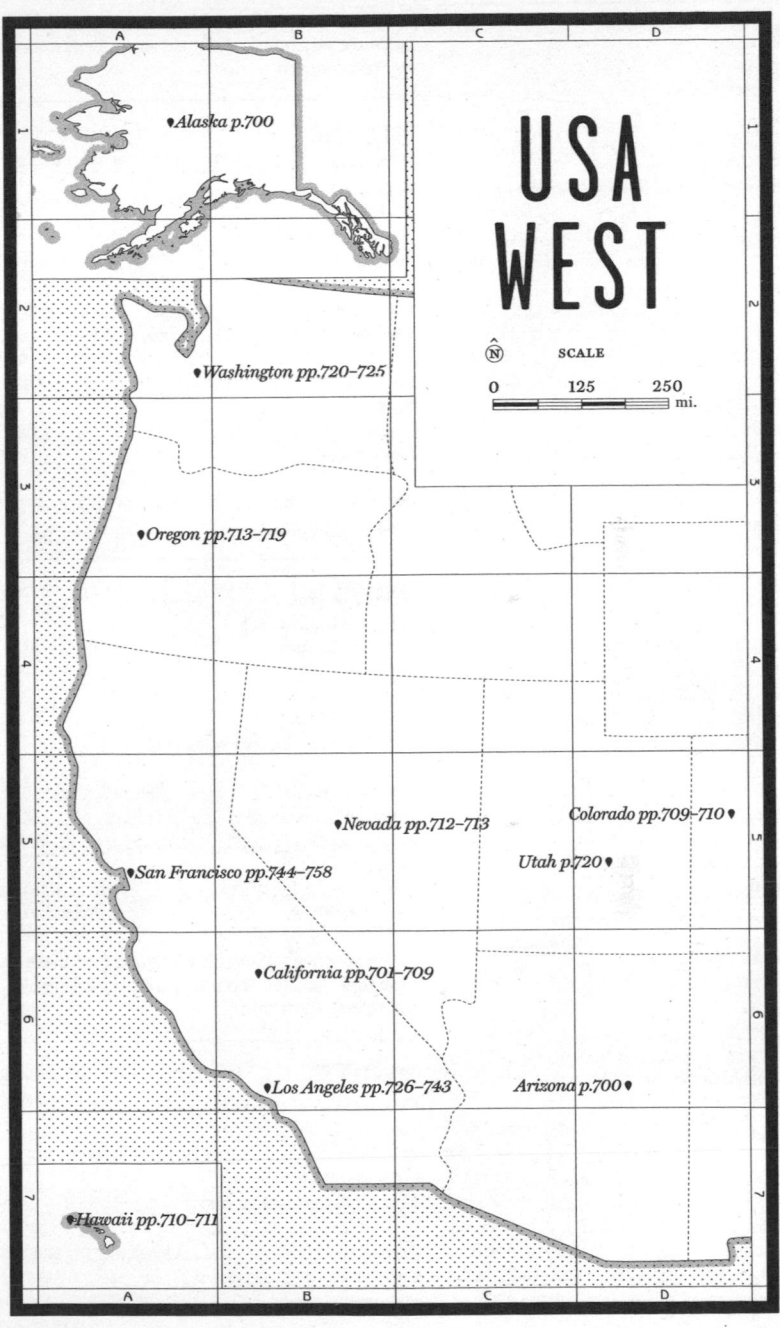

USA
WEST

N̂ SCALE

0   125   250
━━━━━━━━━━━ mi.

●Alaska p.700

●Washington pp.720–725

●Oregon pp.713–719

●Nevada pp.712–713   Colorado pp.709–710 ●

●San Francisco pp.744–758   Utah p.720 ●

●California pp.701–709

●Los Angeles pp.726–743   Arizona p.700 ●

●Hawaii pp.710–711

CITY DINER
3000 Minnesota Drive
Anchorage
Alaska 99503
+1 9072772489
www.citydineranchorage.com

Opening hours	Open 7 days
Reservation policy	No
Credit cards	Accepted
Price range	Budget
Style	Casual
Cuisine	American
Recommended for	Breakfast

'Excellent eggs and a simple, comfort food menu.'
—Drew Johnson

CROW'S NEST
The Hotel Captain Cook
939 West 5th Avenue
Anchorage
Alaska 99501
+1 9072766000
www.captaincook.com/dining/crows-nest

Opening hours	Closed Sunday
Credit cards	Accepted
Price range	Expensive
Style	Smart casual
Cuisine	International
Recommended for	High end

'Good food preparation with creative ideas.'
—Drew Johnson

SPENARD ROADHOUSE
1049 West Northern Lights Boulevard
Anchorage
Alaska 99503
+1 9077707623
www.spenardroadhouse.com

Opening hours	Open 7 days
Reservation policy	No
Credit cards	Accepted
Price range	Budget
Style	Casual
Cuisine	American
Recommended for	Local favourite

'Great use of local ingredients when available. The food is simple yet creative and great value. Great cocktails!'
—Drew Johnson

TACO KING
3003 Tanglewood Drive
Anchorage
Alaska 99517
+1 9077716059
www.tacokingak.com

Opening hours	Open 7 days
Reservation policy	No
Credit cards	Accepted
Price range	Budget
Style	Casual
Cuisine	Mexican
Recommended for	Bargain

'Somewhat authentic Mexican cuisine at a great price.'
—Drew Johnson

WHALE'S TAIL
The Hotel Captain Cook
939 West 5th Avenue
Anchorage
Alaska 99501
+1 9072766000
www.captaincook.com/whales-tail

Opening hours	Closed Sunday to Tuesday
Credit cards	Accepted
Price range	Affordable
Style	Casual
Cuisine	American small plates
Recommended for	Wish I'd opened

'One of the few restaurants with good food that's open past 10.00 p.m. Hip and trendy with a great simple menu.'—Drew Johnson

BINKLEY'S
6920 East Cave Creek Road
Cave Creek
Arizona 85331
+1 4804371072
www.binkleysrestaurant.com

Opening hours	Closed Monday and Sunday
Credit cards	Accepted
Price range	Expensive
Style	Smart casual
Cuisine	Modern American
Recommended for	Worth the travel

CHEZ PANISSE

1517 Shattuck Avenue
Berkeley
California 94709
+1 5105485525
www.chezpanisse.com

Recommended by
Andreas Dahlberg, James
Henry, Thomas McNaughton,
Craig Stoll, Mark Sullivan,
Michael Tusk

Opening hours	Closed Sunday
Credit cards	Accepted
Price range	Expensive
Style	Smart casual
Cuisine	Modern American
Recommended for	Wish I'd opened

'An iconic, excellent restaurant. It has a sense of community and longevity, with the best products and a great philosophy.'—James Henry

IPPUKU

2130 Center Street
Berkeley
California 94704
+1 5106651969
www.ippukuberkeley.com

Recommended by
Russell Moore

Opening hours	Open 7 days
Credit cards	Accepted
Price range	Affordable
Style	Casual
Cuisine	Japanese
Recommended for	Regular neighbourhood

'A super-delicious lunchtime combination of soba and tempura (dinner is great too but you can only get soba for lunch). Koichi makes the soba by hand and Ryogi makes the tempura perfect and delicate.'
—Russell Moore

IYASARE

1830 4th Street
Berkeley
California 94710
+1 5108458100
www.iyasare-berkeley.com

Recommended by
Hiro Sone

Opening hours	Closed Tuesday
Credit cards	Accepted
Price range	Affordable
Style	Casual
Cuisine	Japanese
Recommended for	Worth the travel

'A kappo-style restaurant, specializing in charcoal-grill cooking with fresh Californian produce and many types of miso from Japan. Good sake and Japanese craft beer selections'—Hiro Sone

LITTLE SAIGON

1717 University Avenue
Berkeley
California 94703
+1 5105499594

Recommended by
Cal Peternell

Opening hours	Open 7 days
Reservation policy	No
Credit cards	Accepted
Price range	Budget
Style	Casual
Cuisine	Vietnamese
Recommended for	Bargain

SPOON

933 Ashby Avenue
Berkeley
California 94710
+1 5107049555
www.spoonashby.com

Recommended by
Russell Moore

Opening hours	Open 7 days
Reservation policy	No
Credit cards	Accepted
Price range	Budget
Style	Casual
Cuisine	Korean
Recommended for	Breakfast

'A funny little Korean place that opens at 9.00 a.m. and serves Korean breakfast, like mixed-grain porridge with black sesame. That, and the *banchan* that comes with it, makes for a perfect breakfast.'—Russell Moore

Though spoilt for choice in Los Angeles when it comes to Korean food, the Bay area proves more of a challenge when trying to get your fix of bibimbap and kimchi. Fortunately the team behind popular Bowl'd in Albany (billed as a 'Korean Rice Bar') have opened Spoon in nearby Berkeley, which they're calling a 'Korean Bistro'. Spoon is open from 9.00 a.m. for Korean breakfast and brunch. Expect sunny-side-egg-topped kimchi fried rice, tofu pancakes, porridge with abalone, and steamed egg soufflé. Friendly service and generous portions that deliver plenty of 'bibim-bang' for your buck.

VIK'S CHAAT CORNER
Recommended by
Cal Peternell
2390 4th Street
Berkeley
California 94710
+1 5106444432
www.vikschaatcorner.com

Opening hours..Open 7 days
Reservation policy...No
Credit cards...Accepted
Price range..Budget
Style..Casual
Cuisine...Indian
Recommended for.....................Regular neighbourhood

BIG SUR BAKERY
Recommended by
Justin Cogley
47540 Highway 1
Big Sur
California 93920
+1 8316670520
www.bigsurbakery.com

Opening hours..Open 7 days
Credit cards...Accepted
Price range...Affordable
Style..Casual
Cuisine...Modern American
Recommended for..................................Local favourite

'Built in 1936 to feed hungry travellers. Iconic location, wood-fired oven, and when they are out of food, they are out.'—Justin Cogley

LA BICYCLETTE
Recommended by
Kevin Thornton
29 Dolores Street
Carmel-by-the-Sea
California 93923
+1 8316229899
www.labicycletterestaurant.com

Opening hours..Open 7 days
Credit cards...Accepted
Price range...Affordable
Style..Casual
Cuisine..French Bistro
Recommended for..................................Breakfast

'Good food, fresh bread and good choice for breakfast.'
—Kevin Thornton

CARMEL BELLE
Recommended by
Justin Cogley
Doud Craft Studios
Ocean Avenue and San Carlos Street
Carmel-by-the-Sea
California 93921
+1 8316241600
www.carmelbelle.com

Opening hours..Open 7 days
Reservation policy...No
Credit cards...Accepted
Price range..Budget
Style..Casual
Cuisine...Modern American
Recommended for...Breakfast

'Straightforward – the owners buy everything at local markets and it's all made in house.'—Justin Cogley

KOI PALACE
Recommended by
René Redzepi,
Evan Rich
Serramonte Plaza
365 Gellert Boulevard
Daly City
California 94015
+1 6509929000
www.koipalace.com

Opening hours..Open 7 days
Credit cards...Accepted
Price range...Affordable
Style..Casual
Cuisine..Chinese
Recommended for..High end

'Ideal for Sunday dim sum near San Francisco.'
—René Redzepi

DONOSTIA

Recommended by
David Kinch

424 North Santa Cruz Avenue
Los Gatos
California 95030
+1 4087978688
www.donostiapintxos.com

Opening hours	Closed Sunday
Reservation policy	No
Credit cards	Accepted
Price range	Affordable
Style	Casual
Cuisine	Basque
Recommended for	Late night

'Fun, friendly and open late. The chef is from San Sebastián and I like what comes off his plancha.'
—David Kinch

MANRESA

Recommended by
Matthew Accarrino, Justin Cogley, Alexandre Gauthier, Mehmet Gürs, Stuart Brioza & Nicole Krasinski, Hiro Sone, Ari Taymor, Michael Tusk

320 Village Lane
Los Gatos
California 95030
+1 4083544330
www.manresarestaurant.com

Opening hours	Closed Monday and Tuesday
Credit cards	Accepted
Price range	Expensive
Style	Smart casual
Cuisine	Modern American
Recommended for	High end

'To start with you can't beat the location. Between Santa Cruz and San Francisco, up high but close to the sea... what else do you want? Then there is their amazing relationship with Love Apple Farms. As a bonus throw in a cool guy like David and you have a winner...'—Mehmet Gürs

Nestled in a well-heeled San Francisco Bay suburb, Manresa might be easily missed by the unobservant but it is no culinary wallflower. Enigmatic and humble, chef-proprietor David Kinch has been thrilling diners with his unfussy yet inventive presentations of California's bounty for over ten years. A 'chef's chef', his two-Michelin-star food defies categorization, though a tip o' the hat to Alice Waters at Chez Panisse might give you an idea of what to expect. The ingredient-led tasting menu, which champions produce supplied by local biodynamic growers at Love Apple Farm, and shuns sous vide, siphons and molecular experimentation, has won Manresa widespread acclaim.

COMPAGNO'S MARKET AND DELI

Recommended by
Justin Cogley

2000 Prescott Avenue
Monterey
California 93940
+1 8313755987
www.compagnos.com

Opening hours	Open 7 days
Reservation policy	No
Credit cards	Accepted
Price range	Budget
Style	Casual
Cuisine	Deli-Café
Recommended for	Regular neighbourhood

'Tons of history, right near the naval base in Monterey, and they make *huge* sandwiches. Inexpensive, neighbourhood sandwich shop.'—Justin Cogley

RED'S DONUTS

Recommended by
Justin Cogley

433 Alvarado Street
Monterey
California 93940
+1 8313729761
www.redsdonuts.com

Opening hours	Open 7 days
Reservation policy	No
Credit cards	Accepted
Price range	Budget
Style	Casual
Cuisine	Bakery
Recommended for	Bargain

'Best deal around. Huge apple fritters. Monday and Tuesday "Specials" are $5 (£3) for a dozen. Made fresh daily since 1950.'—Justin Cogley

GOTT'S ROADSIDE

The Oxbow Public Market
644 1st Street
Napa
California 94559
+1 7072246900
www.gotts.com

Recommended by
Mathias Dahlgren

Opening hours	Open 7 days
Reservation policy	No
Credit cards	Accepted
Price range	Budget
Style	Casual
Cuisine	American
Recommended for	Wish I'd opened

'Great location, affordable and tasty food from people of our time.'—Mathias Dahlgren

Gott's Roadside is a gourmet burger joint, Northern California-style. The four-strong mini chain started life when winemaker Joel Gott and his brother Duncan took over Taylor's Refresher, a rundown St. Helena drive-in, back in 1999. Renamed Gott's Roadside in 2010, the hero product is their high-welfare Niman Ranch burgers, charred medium-well but always served with a pink centre, always best consumed with a side of their unimpeachable chips (fries). Their fish tacos and house-made chilli, made with Anchor Steam Beer, have a loyal following too. They proudly champion local producers, craft breweries and winemakers.

BOOT AND SHOE SERVICE

3308 Grand Avenue
Oakland
California 94610
+1 5107632668
www.bootandshoeservice.com

Recommended by
Daniel Patterson

Opening hours	Closed Monday
Reservation policy	No
Credit cards	Accepted
Price range	Affordable
Style	Casual
Cuisine	Italian
Recommended for	Regular neighbourhood

'I have kids. Kids like pizza. The pizza is great, as are the salads and vegetable offerings, as well as terrific cocktails. Great vibe.'—Daniel Patterson

The sequel to Pizzaiolo does the same thing with quality wood-fired Neapolitan-style pizzas for the Oakland neighbourhood of Grand Lake that its older sibling does up in Temescal. Unlike Pizzaiolo, they don't take reservations here, but their bar is a rather pleasant holding pen when waiting for a table. The name has been recycled from the business that previously occupied the premises, the old shoe repair shop's sign and much of the building's original character – exposed bricks, beamed ceiling and scuffed floor – retained. A breakfast and brunch café in adjoining premises was added to the mix in 2011.

BROWN SUGAR KITCHEN

2534 Mandela Parkway
Oakland
California 94607
+1 5108397685
www.brownsugarkitchen.com

Recommended by
James Syhabout

Opening hours	Closed Monday
Reservation policy	No
Credit cards	Accepted
Price range	Affordable
Style	Casual
Cuisine	Southern American
Recommended for	Local favourite

CAMINO

3917 Grand Avenue
Oakland
California 94610
+1 5105475035
www.caminorestaurant.com

Recommended by
Suzanne Goin, Alejandro
Morales, Cal Peternell,
James Syhabout, Fernando
Trocca

Opening hours	Closed Tuesday
Credit cards	Accepted
Price range	Affordable
Style	Casual
Cuisine	Modern American
Recommended for	Worth the travel

'I crave their food.'—Suzanne Goin

COMMIS

3859 Piedmont Avenue
Oakland
California 94611
+1 5106533902
www.commisrestaurant.com

Recommended by
André Chiang,
Chris Cosentino, Jason Fox,
Hadleigh Troy

Opening hours	Closed Monday and Tuesday
Credit cards	Accepted
Price range	Expensive
Style	Smart casual
Cuisine	Modern American
Recommended for	Wish I'd opened

'Simply beautiful. Minimalist decoration, delicate flavours, elegant cuisine. It's a place where you can simply focus on the food and nothing else. Small restaurant, grand cuisine!'—André Chiang

Understated and gastronomically ambitious, James Syhabout's Commis immediately demanded attention when it opened in 2009. Not least for Syhabout's CV, which includes stretches at The Fat Duck and elBulli before he returned to California to help open Daniel Patterson's Coi in San Francisco and work under David Kinch at Manresa in Los Gatos. Raised in Oakland, the son of a Thai mother and a Chinese father, his menus take a cerebral approach to Northern California's ample larder (pantry), combining modern European flair with the occasional Asian technique. Try and claim a sought-after berth at the six-seat counter overlooking the open kitchen.

HAWKER FARE

2300 Webster Street
Oakland
California 94612
+1 5108328896
www.hawkerfare.com

Recommended by
Daniel Patterson

Opening hours	Closed Sunday
Reservation policy	No
Credit cards	Accepted
Price range	Budget
Style	Casual
Cuisine	Southeast Asian
Recommended for	Bargain

'Delicious Thai food made with care.'
—Daniel Patterson

Expect rice bowls but never noodles at this busy, loud, graffiti-strewn Southeast Asian eatery and take away (take out). Street-food-style dishes, many of which are under $10 (£6), include scrambled mung bean crêpes to share, skewered chicken hearts and rice bowls of grilled satay beef short ribs marinated in coconut milk and turmeric. Either bring your own wine and pay the corkage, or order a Linden Street Tap (brewed exclusively for Hawker Fare) or the arrestingly titled Dying Bastard cocktail (ginger beer, bitters, gin, brandy, whiskey and lime). End with a pineapple and rum Jell-O shot and an Ovaltine sundae with fudge.

EL PAISA

2900 International Boulevard
Oakland
California 94601
+1 5103845465

Recommended by
Russell Moore

Opening hours	Open 7 days
Reservation policy	No
Credit cards	Not accepted
Price range	Budget
Style	Casual
Cuisine	Mexican
Recommended for	Bargain

'A little taquería that makes its own chorizo and makes delicious *suadero* (thinly cut beef) along with perfect little onions and a different violently hot salsa every day. Not the usual chicken, steak and *carnitas* (pulled pork).'—Russell Moore

PENROSE

3311 Grand Avenue
Oakland
California 94610
+1 5104441649
www.penroseoakland.com

Recommended by
Mark Sullivan,
James Syhabout

Opening hours	Closed Sunday
Reservation policy	No
Credit cards	Accepted
Price range	Affordable
Style	Casual
Cuisine	Modern American
Recommended for	Wish I'd opened

'This place is sexy: from the bar design and the space to cooking everything over a fire. Fantastic drinks and loud acoustics. A great place to gather and let loose.'
—James Syhabout

PHO AO SEN

1139 East 12th Street
Oakland
California 94606
+1 5108355588
www.phoaosen.com

Opening hours	Open 7 days
Reservation policy	No
Credit cards	Accepted
Price range	Budget
Style	Casual
Cuisine	Vietnamese
Recommended for	Bargain

'I love my noodles. The *bun bo hue* (beef noodle soup) is also great served with shaved banana leaves and pig's blood.'—James Syhabout

PIZZAIOLO

5008 Telegraph Avenue
Oakland
California 94609
+1 5106524888
www.pizzaiolooakland.com

Opening hours	Closed Sunday
Credit cards	Accepted
Price range	Affordable
Style	Casual
Cuisine	Italian
Recommended for	Regular neighbourhood

Charlie Hallowell, 'child of Chez Panisse' inspired by his eight years in the kitchen at Alice Water's seminal Berkeley restaurant, opened Pizzaiolo in Oakland in 2005. Located on Telegraph Avenue, in the maple-lined heart of the Temescal district of the city, it has developed a cult following for its simple menu built around a line-up of antipasti, a handful of pasta dishes, the occasional large plate and – the main event – a selection of wood-fired Neapolitan-style pizzas, made with organic flour and almost exclusively topped with seasonal sustainably farmed produce sourced directly from local farmers. Alice must be very proud.

HANA

101 Golf Course Drive
Rohnert Park
California 94928
+1 7075860270
www.hanajapanese.com

Opening hours	Open 7 days
Credit cards	Accepted
Price range	Affordable
Style	Casual
Cuisine	Japanese
Recommended for	Regular neighbourhood

'I've been a fan of Ken Tominaga's for more than ten years. I love the brightness, fresh flavours and his approach to Japanese cuisine. It is my family's go-to spot.'—Michael Mina

POTATO SHACK CAFE

120 West I Street
San Diego
California 92024
+1 7604361282
www.potatoshackcafe.com

Opening hours	Open 7 days
Reservation policy	No
Credit cards	Not accepted
Price range	Budget
Style	Casual
Cuisine	Diner-Café
Recommended for	Breakfast

'They serve the best pan-roasted potatoes I have ever had. Throw a couple of fried eggs into the mix and have it with a Bloody Mary and it becomes the perfect after-surf meal to get your day going.'
—Matthew Orlando

CAFE DELMARETTE
1126 Pacific Avenue
Santa Cruz
California 95060
+1 8314201025
www.cafedelmarette.com

Opening hours	Closed Tuesday
Reservation policy	No
Credit cards	Accepted
Price range	Budget
Style	Casual
Cuisine	Café-Bakery
Recommended for	Bargain

'Great sandwiches and coffee. The sandwiches are limited but constantly change and are respectfully made with products from the local farmers' market. I go back as often as I can.'—David Kinch

SOIF
105 Walnut Avenue
Santa Cruz
California 95060
+1 8314232020
www.soifwine.com

Opening hours	Open 7 days
Credit cards	Accepted
Price range	Affordable
Style	Casual
Cuisine	Modern American
Recommended for	Regular neighbourhood

'A little wine bar that I frequent for a glass of wine and a simple plate of food.'—David Kinch

VERVE COFFEE ROASTERS
1540 Pacific Avenue
Santa Cruz
California 95062
+1 8316007784
www.vervecoffeeroasters.com

Opening hours	Open 7 days
Reservation policy	No
Credit cards	Accepted
Price range	Affordable
Style	Casual
Cuisine	Coffee Shop
Recommended for	Breakfast

'Fantastic coffee.'—David Kinch

THE FREMONT DINER
2698 Fremont Drive
Sonoma
California 95476
+1 707938/370
www.thefremontdiner.com

Opening hours	Open 7 days
Reservation policy	No
Credit cards	Accepted
Price range	Budget
Style	Casual
Cuisine	Diner
Recommended for	Wish I'd opened

'Honest, good food cooked with ingredients from their farm at the back of the diner. I absolutely love this place.'—Gunnar Karl Gíslason

EL MOLINO CENTRAL
11 Central Avenue
Sonoma
California 95476
+1 7079391010
www.elmolinocentral.com

Opening hours	Open 7 days
Reservation policy	No
Credit cards	Accepted
Price range	Budget
Style	Casual
Cuisine	Mexican
Recommended for	Wish I'd opened

'It is a complete thought. It has a simple, beautiful and understated feel and delicious food. Everything fits together.'—Russell Moore

THE RESTAURANT AT MEADOWOOD

Meadowood
900 Meadowood Lane
St. Helena
California 94574
+1 7079671205
www.therestaurantatmeadowood.com

Recommended by
Matthew Accarrino,
Brad Farmerie, Jason
Fox, Linton Hopkins,
Thomas McNaughton,
Russell Moore, Paul
Qui, Evan Rich

Opening hours...................................Closed Sunday
Credit cards..Accepted
Price range..Expensive
Style...Smart casual
Cuisine....................................Modern American
Recommended for.......................................High end

'It dives so deeply into the region we are cooking in. It is a great expression of what a blow-out meal should be. It has a sense of time and place.'
—Thomas McNaughton

The 'other' three-Michelin-starred Napa restaurant (often compared to The French Laundry), Meadowood is off the scenic Silverado Trail, past redwood trees. Illinois-born head chef Chris Kostow claims to 'curate' bespoke dishes for his guests in the polished concrete and wood dining room rather than hand out menus – albeit at a price. The tasting menu costs $225 (£135), plus the same again for wine matches. Nevertheless, dishes that gentrify locally foraged and sustainable ingredients have included slithers of razor clams with smoked avocado and cannellini beans, and wagyu with wild mushrooms. Incidentally, the bar/lounge serves a more accessibly priced menu.

CARNITAS TREJO

370 East Lake Avenue
Watsonville
California 95076
+1 8317688863

Recommended by
David Kinch

Opening hours...................................Closed Tuesday
Reservation policy...No
Credit cards......................................Not accepted
Price range...Budget
Style...Casual
Cuisine..Mexican
Recommended for..................Regular neighbourhood

'I love it because it's delicious, home-style Cal-Mex cooking in the heart of the agricultural Central Coast of California. It's a true taste of this place that we call home.'—David Kinch

BOUCHON

6534 Washington Street
Yountville
California 94599
+1 7079448037
www.bouchonbistro.com

Recommended by
André Jaeger,
Timothy Johnson

Opening hours.................................Open 7 days
Credit cards..Accepted
Price range..Affordable
Style..Casual
Cuisine..French
Recommended for........................Wish I'd opened

'Why? It assembles the finest traditional French cuisine in a very easy manner. With all the modern trends that unfortunately resemble each other in many ways, eating at a restaurant like Bouchon is highly satisfying without being boring or common. Wholesome food, prepared with the best ingredients, will never lose its value. Many have tried to do French brasserie cuisine, but few have succeeded like Thomas Keller. I take a bow in front of him. Not only does he educate, he gives true pleasure.'—André Jaeger

CICCIO

6770 Washington Street
Yountville
California 94599
+1 7079451000
www.ciccionapavalley.com

Recommended by
Matthew Accarrino

Opening hours.......................Closed Monday and Tuesday
Reservation policy...No
Credit cards..Accepted
Price range..Affordable
Style..Casual
Cuisine..Italian
Recommended for...Bargain

'The food is simple, the prices are inexpensive and everything tastes good.'—Matthew Accarrino

Napa natives Frank and Karen Altamura, founders of the Altamura Winery, took over this one-time Italian general store with their sons in 2012. Their breezily attractive, no-reservations hangout has a reputation for first-class pizza and a seven-strong Negroni menu. Just as alluring are wines from the Altamuras' own vineyards, their own-grown herbs and vegetables, and a regularly changing menu of Italian 'stuff that isn't pizza'. Squash blossom and garlic scape pizza isn't the only thing to emerge from the colourfully tiled wood-fired oven, which is also used to produce the likes of whole roasted fish with Calabrian chillies, and wood-fired artichokes with walnut *bagna càuda*.

THE FRENCH LAUNDRY
6640 Washington Street
Yountville
California 94599
+1 7079442380
www.frenchlaundry.com

Recommended by
Matthew Accarrino, Jason Atherton, Rodney Dunn, André Garrett, Brian Mark Hansen, Yves Le Lay, Corey Lee, Alfred Prasad, Geir Skeie

Opening hours	Open 7 days
Credit cards	Accepted
Price range	Expensive
Style	Formal
Cuisine	Modern French
Recommended for	Wish I'd opened

'It is every chef's dream. Need I say more?'
—Alfred Prasad

REDD
6480 Washington Street
Yountville
California 94599
+1 7079442222
www.reddnapavalley.com

Recommended by
Christopher Hodgson

Opening hours	Open 7 days
Credit cards	Accepted
Price range	Affordable
Style	Smart casual
Cuisine	Modern American
Recommended for	Worth the travel

'I returned recently and it was just as outstanding as the first time I went years ago when I was first entering the culinary world. Bravo chef Reddington, bravo.'
—Christoper Hodgson

CUVÉE WORLD BISTRO
305 Gold Rivers Court
Basalt
Colorado 81621
+1 9709274000
www.cuveebistro.com

Recommended by
Paul Virant

Opening hours	Closed Sunday
Credit cards	Accepted
Price range	Affordable
Style	Casual
Cuisine	International
Recommended for	Worth the travel

'They have something for everyone: solid pizza, great nachos and excellent soups.'—Paul Virant

FRASCA FOOD AND WINE
1738 Pearl Street
Boulder
Colorado 80302
+1 3034426966
www.frascafoodandwine.com

Recommended by
Jennifer Jasinski

Opening hours	Closed Sunday
Credit cards	Accepted
Price range	Expensive
Style	Casual
Cuisine	Frulian
Recommended for	High end

'They have an incredible wine list, off-the-chart service and perfectly made Fruilian cuisine.'—Jennifer Jasinski

A member of the Slow Food organization, Frasca, in Colorado, takes inspiration from Friuli, northeast Italy. Leading sommelier Bobby Stuckey has cultivated a wine list that saw Frasca win Outstanding Wine Program from the James Beard Foundation. His selections partner well with chef Lachlan Mackinnon-Patterson's dishes, which often nod to local producers. These include Colorado wagyu hanger steak, and Broken Arrow Ranch quail with farro. From further afield, try finely sliced Quebec veal loin salad. Although ideal for a special occasion blowout, Frasca also offers a popular $50 (£30) Monday night tasting menu.

COLT & GRAY
1553 Platte Street
Denver
Colorado 80202
+1 3034771447
www.coltandgray.com

Recommended by
Jennifer Jasinski

Opening hours	Closed Monday
Credit cards	Accepted
Price range	Affordable
Style	Smart casual
Cuisine	Modern American
Recommended for	Regular neighbourhood

'Ask the chef to make you a tasting menu.'
—Jennifer Jasinski

NEW SAIGON

Recommended by
Jennifer Jasinski

630 South Federal Boulevard
Denver
Colorado 80219
+1 3039364954
www.newsaigon.com

Opening hours	Closed Monday
Credit cards	Accepted
Price range	Affordable
Style	Casual
Cuisine	Vietnamese
Recommended for	Bargain

'New Saigon is killer, real Vietnamese food. Have the duck curry or green papaya salad.'—Jennifer Jasinski

PATZCUARO'S

Recommended by
Jennifer Jasinski

2616 West 32nd Avenue
Denver
Colorado 80211
+1 3034554389
www.patzcuaros.com

Opening hours	Open 7 days
Reservation policy	No
Credit cards	Accepted
Price range	Budget
Style	Casual
Cuisine	Mexican
Recommended for	Regular neighbourhood

'Go for the *carnitas* (pulled pork) or *tacos de cabeza* (beef head tacos).'—Jennifer Jasinski

PHO DUY

Recommended by
Jennifer Jasinski

945 South Federal Boulevard
Denver
Colorado 80219
+1 3039371609

Opening hours	Open 7 days
Reservation policy	No
Credit cards	Accepted
Price range	Budget
Style	Casual
Cuisine	Pho
Recommended for	Bargain

'The tendon, brisket and rare beef pho are great.'
—Jennifer Jasinski

SUSHI SASA

Recommended by
Jennifer Jasinski

Suite 80 2401 15th Street
Denver
Colorado 80202
+1 3034337272
www.sushisasa.com

Opening hours	Open 7 days
Credit cards	Accepted
Price range	Affordable
Style	Casual
Cuisine	Sushi
Recommended for	Regular neighbourhood

'I love the squid in Korean sauce and anything on their special menu is gonna be great.'—Jennifer Jasinski

EGGS 'N THINGS

Recommended by
Masaharu Morimoto

343 Saratoga Road
Honolulu
Hawaii 96815
+1 8089233447
www.eggsnthings.com

Opening hours	Open 7 days
Reservation policy	No
Credit cards	Accepted but not AMEX
Price range	Budget
Style	Casual
Cuisine	Diner
Recommended for	Breakfast

'I like their pancakes and they always welcome me with a warm smile.'—Masaharu Morimoto

Cranking out omelettes, pancakes and crêpes since 1974, this much-loved diner is rammed with locals and tourists who like to breakfast all day long. Seats under the green-painted balcony are always in demand, but you'll get the same (obscene) amount of whipped cream on your waffles wherever you sit, and however long you have to queue (wait in line). Obligingly, staff are clad in aloha wear and rarely neglect a coffee cup, fostering a sense of good-natured retro indulgence bolstered by the liberal consumption of ham, or Spam, and eggs. Later, the pancakes come with *ahi* (tuna) or chicken, and the waffles with ice cream. Branches in Ala Moana and Waikiki Beach.

ROY'S

Recommended by
Brad Turley

6600 Kalanianaole Highway
Honolulu
Hawaii 96825
+1 8083967697
www.royshawaii.com

Opening hours	Open 7 days
Credit cards	Accepted
Price range	Affordable
Style	Casual
Cuisine	Hawaiian-Asian
Recommended for	Wish I'd opened

'After more then twenty years it's still at the top. It's loved by locals and travellers for the beautiful bounties of Hawaii on the beachfront doorstep, the most amazing view while preparing for dinner, the best sunsets and Roy's trademark aloha spirit.'—Brad Turley

SHIROKIYA

Recommended by
Masaharu Morimoto

Suite 2250
1450 Ala Moana Boulevard
Honolulu
Hawaii 96814
www.shirokiya.com

Opening hours	Open 7 days
Reservation policy	No
Credit cards	Accepted
Price range	Budget
Style	Casual
Cuisine	International
Recommended for	Bargain

'Shirokiya is a Japanese department store. They have many Japanese goods including electronics, Sanrio toys, accessories, homewares and so on. They also have a cafeteria and food court. When I go there, I feel like I'm in Japan. After shopping, I eat a bento box – there are so many choices. The price is very reasonable.'
—Masaharu Morimoto

TOWN

Recommended by
Russell Moore

3435 Waialae Avenue
Honolulu
Hawaii 96816
+1 8087355900
www.townkaimuki.com

Opening hours	Closed Sunday
Credit cards	Accepted
Price range	Affordable
Style	Casual
Cuisine	Modern American
Recommended for	Worth the travel

'It's a fun restaurant that is trying to do something different. It was great a few years ago but it's even better now. They use really interesting, local Hawaiian ingredients from cool farms like Ma'o in Waianae. It reminds me of a Bay Area restaurant but they aren't held back with Mediterranean ingredients, they use what grows in Hawaii.'—Russell Moore

O'O FARM

Recommended by
Brendan McGill

651 Waipoli Road
Kula
Hawaii 96790
+1 8086674341
www.oofarm.com

Opening hours	Closed Friday to Sunday
Credit cards	Accepted
Price range	Affordable
Style	Casual
Cuisine	Modern International
Recommended for	Worth the travel

'Upcountry Maui has a very unique micro-climate. At the base of the mountain you see the sugar cane and pineapple fields that you'd expect, but as you climb Haleakala (in your car) you pass through eucalyptus forest and enter a truly temperate climate where beetroot (beets), chard and turnips grow year-round. The local hardwoods supply the fuel at this little farm-to-table luncheonette, where Chef JJ pulls from the bounty of the farm and the incredible Pacific seafood. I defy anyone to visit, eat, go to the farmers' markets and stay for a day or two and not want to drop everything and move there.'—Brendan McGill

L'ATELIER DE JOËL ROBUCHON

MGM Grand Hotel Casino
3799 Las Vegas Boulevard South
Las Vegas
Nevada 89109
+1 7028917358
www.mgmgrand.com

Opening hours	Open 7 days
Credit cards	Accepted
Price range	Expensive
Style	Smart casual
Cuisine	Modern French
Recommended for	High end

'An extravagant restaurant in an amazing city with everything you desire, if you can afford it.'
—Steffen Hansen

BOUCHON

The Venetian Resort and Casino
3355 Las Vegas Boulevard South
Las Vegas
Nevada 89109
+1 7024146200
www.bouchonbistro.com

Opening hours	Open 7 days
Credit cards	Accepted
Price range	Affordable
Style	Smart casual
Cuisine	French
Recommended for	Worth the travel

'Wow, I love the brunch. The quiche is sublime and the boudin blanc is out of this world. A must after-party place if you're in Vegas.'—Raúl Correa

BLUEBERRY HILL

3790 East Flamingo Road
Las Vegas
Nevada 89121
+1 7024339999
www.blueberryhillrestaurants.com

Opening hours	Open 7 days
Reservation policy	No
Credit cards	Accepted
Price range	Budget
Style	Casual
Cuisine	Diner
Recommended for	Breakfast

'One of my favourite breakfast and late-night breakfast joints in Las Vegas. It's family owned with 1950s-diner appeal. Their pancakes are spectacular and their waffles are amazing.'—Saipin Chutima

CASA DI AMORE

2850 East Tropicana Avenue
Las Vegas
Nevada 89121
+1 7024334967
www.casadiamore.com

Opening hours	Closed Tuesday
Credit cards	Accepted
Price range	Affordable
Style	Casual
Cuisine	Italian-American
Recommended for	Late night

'I love this place for late-night dining. It's open until 5.00 a.m. but if you go before 10.00 p.m. you get to enjoy their show of two gentlemen singing tunes from the old days. Their food is amazing and the interior recalls the Frank Sinatra days. The staff are wonderful and they all have a history with the restaurant. My favourite dishes are the Pomodoro Fresco and the Gypsy Pasta.'—Saipin Chutima

LE CIRQUE

Recommended by
Saipin Chutima

Bellagio Hotel & Casino
3600 Las Vegas Boulevard South
Las Vegas
Nevada 89109
+1 8662597111
www.bellagio.com/lecirque

Opening hours	Closed Monday
Credit cards	Accepted
Price range	Expensive
Style	Smart casual
Cuisine	Modern French
Recommended for	High end

'Besides the flavours of the food, the artistic design on the plating gives each dish a characteristic that brings the food alive.'—Saipin Chutima

EAT

Recommended by
Saipin Chutima

707 Carson Street
Las Vegas
Nevada 89101
+1 7025341515
www.eatdtlv.com

Opening hours	Open 7 days
Reservation policy	No
Credit cards	Accepted
Price range	Budget
Style	Casual
Cuisine	American
Recommended for	Breakfast

'The food is very fresh and each meal has been carefully made to perfection. You can never go wrong with their Down Town Eggs Benedict.'—Saipin Chutima

JOYFUL HOUSE

Recommended by
Saipin Chutima

4601 Spring Mountain Road
Las Vegas
Nevada 89102
+1 7028898881
www.joyfulhouselv.com

Opening hours	Open 7 days
Credit cards	Accepted
Price range	Affordable
Style	Casual
Cuisine	Cantonese
Recommended for	Regular neighbourhood

'Joyful House has my favourite goby cod dish. I normally order the steamed whole fish and the chef cooks it in his sauce. Besides the fish, I always order the house soup, which consists of beef broth with lotus barks and roots – a very healthy dish with a homey feeling to each bite.'—Saipin Chutima

SAGE

Recommended by
Bruce Bromberg

Aria Resort & Casino
3730 Las Vegas Boulevard South
Las Vegas
Nevada 89149
+1 8772302742
www.aria.com/dining/restaurants/sage

Opening hours	Open 7 days
Credit cards	Accepted
Price range	Expensive
Style	Smart casual
Cuisine	Modern American
Recommended for	Worth the travel

There's a surprisingly homespun feel about the menu at this swanky hotel restaurant in one of the Strip's typically small and unassuming luxury resorts. By Vegas standards the glossy executive-lounge dining room is a masterclass in restraint, and though you'll find all the staples – wagyu, foie gras and truffle – the kitchen follows suit, with ingredient-led dishes such as organic chicken with buckwheat Spätzle, artichoke and stinging nettles, heirloom baby beetroot (beets), and celeriac (celery root) and hazelnut soup. You won't escape with your trousers on – the mains hover around the $40 (£24) mark – but this is Vegas, so the $89 (£53) pre-theatre menu is a (relative) steal.

AVA GENE'S

Recommended by
Andy Ricker

3377 Southeast Division Street
Portland
Oregon 97202
+1 9712290571
www.avagenes.com

Opening hours	Open 7 days
Credit cards	Accepted
Price range	Affordable
Style	Smart casual
Cuisine	Italian
Recommended for	Regular neighbourhood

'Ava Gene's nails it on all levels: food, ambience, design and service. Beautiful Italian/Pacific Northwest cuisine.'—Andy Ricker

BARWARES

Recommended by
Greg & Gabrielle
Quiñónez Denton

4605 Northeast Fremont Street
Portland
Oregon 97213
+1 9712290995
www.smallwarespdx.com

Opening hours	Open 7 days
Credit cards	Accepted
Price range	Budget
Style	Casual
Cuisine	American-Asian
Recommended for	Late night

'We love chef Johanna Ware and her boldly flavoured,
Asian-inspired dishes.'
—Greg & Gabrielle Quiñónez Denton

BEAST

Recommended by
Brendan McGill

5425 Northeast 30th Avenue
Portland
Oregon 97211
+1 5038416968
www.beastpdx.com

Opening hours	Closed Monday and Tuesday
Credit cards	Accepted
Price range	Expensive
Style	Casual
Cuisine	Modern French
Recommended for	Wish I'd opened

'Chef Naomi Pomeroy purpose-built the place to serve
forty and turns it twice a night. The only food option is
the tasting menu and the only drink option is a wine
flight paired with the dinner. Don't want all the wine?
Fine, drink water. It takes tremendous confidence to
do this – she nailed it and brought home a James
Beard Award. Not to mention the economics of eighty
guests at $100 (£60) a pop in a small forty-seat
restaurant.'—Brendan McGill

BINH MINH BAKERY AND DELI

Recommended by
Andy Ricker

6812 Northeast Broadway Street
Portland
Oregon 97213
+1 5032573868

Opening hours	Closed Monday
Reservation policy	No
Credit cards	Accepted
Price range	Budget
Style	Casual
Cuisine	Vietnamese
Recommended for	Bargain

'Best banh mi in Portland, which is saying something
considering how many places are dedicated to the
Vietnamese torpedo of awesomeness. They make their
own baguette that's perfect for banh mi: light, crispy
crust, soft crumb and narrow profile. The sandwich
itself has a small amount of everything: meat, *cu cai*
(radish), raw chilli, coriander (cilantro), cucumber, a
smear of sketchy pâté and a squirt of soy sauce in
perfect ratio to the bread. This makes it the closest to
the banh mi I have eaten in Vietnam.'—Andy Ricker

BOXER RAMEN

Recommended by
Sarah Pilner & Jasper Shen

1025 Southwest Stark Street
Portland
Oregon 97205
+1 5038948260
www.boxerramen.com

Opening hours	Open 7 days
Reservation policy	No
Credit cards	Not accepted
Price range	Budget
Style	Casual
Cuisine	Ramen Noodles
Recommended for	Wish I'd opened

'It's a brilliant concept and it works.'
—Sarah Pilner & Jasper Shen

BUNK SANDWICHES

211 Southwest 6th Avenue
Portland
Oregon 97204
+1 5033282865
www.bunksandwiches.com

Opening hours	Open 7 days
Reservation policy	No
Credit cards	Accepted
Price range	Budget
Style	Casual
Cuisine	Sandwiches
Recommended for	Bargain

'Grab a quick sandwich with Italian cured meats and cheeses.'—Gabriel Rucker

CASTAGNA

1752 Southeast Hawthorne Boulevard
Portland
Oregon 97214
+1 5032317373
www.castagnarestaurant.com

Opening hours	Closed Sunday to Tuesday
Credit cards	Accepted
Price range	Expensive
Style	Smart casual
Cuisine	Modern American
Recommended for	Worth the travel

'Everything was perfectly executed and the experience was completely unexpected.'—Jason Franey

CHEN'S GOOD TASTE

18 Northwest 4th Avenue
Portland
Oregon 97209
+1 5032233838

Opening hours	Open 7 days
Reservation policy	No
Credit cards	Accepted
Price range	Budget
Style	Casual
Cuisine	Chinese
Recommended for	Bargain

'Chen's is simple: roast pork and smoked duck hanging in the window, tables lined up in rows and quick, efficient service. Lunch for two totals about $15 (£9), is traditionally crafted and so, so soulful.'—Jenn Louis

CLUB 21

2035 Northeast Glisan Street
Portland
Oregon 97232
+1 5032355690

Opening hours	Open 7 days
Reservation policy	No
Credit cards	Accepted
Price range	Budget
Style	Casual
Cuisine	Fast Food
Recommended for	Late night

'Dive bars never have good food but this one does. Their burger is made from naturally raised cows, the Cheddar is made in Oregon and the buns are soft and never stale.'—Jenn Louis

GRAIN & GRISTLE

1473 Northeast Prescott Street
Portland
Oregon 97211
+1 5032985007
www.grainandgristle.com

Opening hours	Open 7 days
Reservation policy	No
Credit cards	Accepted
Price range	Budget
Style	Casual
Cuisine	Gastropub
Recommended for	Late night

'Their burgers are good.'—Sarah Pilner & Jasper Shen

JAKE'S FAMOUS CRAWFISH

401 Southwest 12th Avenue
Portland
Oregon 97205
+1 5032261419

Opening hours	Open 7 days
Credit cards	Accepted
Price range	Affordable
Style	Smart casual
Cuisine	Seafood
Recommended for	Local favourite

'This Downtown restaurant has been here forever. The classic, old, wooden bar is the best place to sit and drink. Somehow, over the years, it has hardly changed.'—Jenn Louis

LINCOLN RESTAURANT
Recommended by
Anita Lo
3808 North Williams Avenue
Portland
Oregon 97227
+1 5032886200
www.lincolnpdx.com

Opening hours	Closed Monday and Sunday
Credit cards	Accepted
Price range	Affordable
Style	Casual
Cuisine	American-Italian
Recommended for	Worth the travel

'Jenn Louis makes smart, delicious food with impeccable ingredients.'—Anita Lo

Jenn Louis and David Welch – the husband and wife team behind Lincoln, which opened in 2008 (plus 2011's Sunshine Tavern) – have helped transform the once-gritty North Williams Avenue scene. Lincoln is now a Portland fixture with its Northwest-centric food, craft beer and wine offering, with Louis at the stove and Welch at the bar. Louis's simple, seasonal food speaks to modern Portland tastes: thyme flatbread with salmon tartare and sea urchin, and carrot risotto with fennel pollen and duck egg are the very definition of 'ingredient-driven', while polenta (cornmeal) onion rings and Burgundy snails with garlic and bruschetta offer clever comfort.

LITTLE BIRD BISTRO
Recommended by
Greg & Gabrielle
Quiñónez Denton
219 Southwest 6th Avenue
Portland
Oregon 97204
+1 5036885952
www.littlebirdbistro.com

Opening hours	Open 7 days
Credit cards	Accepted
Price range	Affordable
Style	Casual
Cuisine	French Bistro
Recommended for	Wish I'd opened

'A great Downtown Portland bistro that serves really tasty French bistro classics alongside other, more creative dishes – the best of both worlds.'
—Greg & Gabrielle Quiñónez Denton

LOVELY'S FIFTY FIFTY
Recommended by
Greg & Gabrielle
Quiñónez Denton
4039 North Mississippi Avenue
Portland
Oregon 97227
+1 5032814060
www.lovelysfiftyfifty.com

Opening hours	Closed Monday
Reservation policy	No
Credit cards	Accepted
Price range	Budget
Style	Casual
Cuisine	Pizza
Recommended for	Regular neighbourhood

'This wood-fired pizza joint serves one of our favourite pies in town. Besides the great sourdough crust, we are huge fans of everything else that is also not pizza: oven-roasted vegetables, perfectly dressed salads, and awesome, house-made ice cream.'
—Greg & Gabrielle Quiñónez Denton

LUCE
Recommended by
Renee Erickson
2140 East Burnside Street
Portland
Oregon 97214
+1 5032367195
www.luceportland.com

Opening hours	Open 7 days
Reservation policy	No
Credit cards	Accepted
Price range	Affordable
Style	Casual
Cuisine	Italian
Recommended for	Wish I'd opened

'It feels like a special spot in Italy that you stumble upon and go back four times before your trip is over. Simple food, great wines, bright decor.'
—Renee Erickson

MAURICE PASTRY LUNCHEONETTE
Recommended by
Mindy Segal
921 Southwest Oak Street
Portland
Oregon 97205
+1 5032249921
www.mauricepdx.com

Opening hours	Closed Sunday
Reservation policy	No
Credit cards	Accepted
Price range	Affordable
Style	Casual
Cuisine	Café-Bakery
Recommended for	Wish I'd opened

'I love the premise and it seems like a restaurant I would love to open!'—Mindy Segal

NED LUDD
Recommended by
Greg & Gabrielle
Quiñónez Denton
3925 Northeast Martin
Luther King Jr Boulevard
Portland
Oregon 97212
+1 5032886900
www.nedluddpdx.com

Opening hours	Closed Tuesday
Credit cards	Accepted
Price range	Affordable
Style	Casual
Cuisine	Modern American
Recommended for	Local favourite

'Hyper-local, rustic, delicious food.'
—Greg & Gabrielle Quiñónez Denton

NOISETTE
Recommended by
Gabriel Rucker
1937 Northwest 23rd Place
Portland
Oregon 97210
+1 5037194599
www.noisetterestaurant.com

Opening hours	Closed Sunday to Wednesday
Credit cards	Accepted
Price range	Expensive
Style	Smart casual
Cuisine	Modern French
Recommended for	High end

'Très classique.'—Gabriel Rucker

NONG'S KHAO MAN GAI
Recommended by
Brad Farmerie,
Jenn Louis
Southwest 10th and Alder Street
Portland
Oregon 97205
+1 9712553480
www.khaomangai.com

Opening hours	Closed Saturday and Sunday
Reservation policy	No
Credit cards	Accepted
Price range	Budget
Style	Casual
Cuisine	Thai
Recommended for	Bargain

'Nong only sells one thing, chicken and rice, but she does it well. I like it so much that I have eaten it twice in the same day.'—Brad Farmerie

NOSTRANA
Recommended by
Jenn Louis
1401 Southeast Morrison Street
Portland
Oregon 97214
+1 5032342427
www.nostrana.com

Opening hours	Open 7 days
Credit cards	Accepted
Price range	Affordable
Style	Casual
Cuisine	Italian
Recommended for	High end

'Portland isn't really known for high-end dining, but for our style, I would say Nostrana is a great place for a celebration. On special occasions I love to order the kilo porterhouse, grilled somewhere between medium-rare and medium. Grilled over a wood fire, it is a great, great steak.'—Jenn Louis

EL NUTRI TACO

Recommended by
Sarah Pilner & Jasper Shen

2124 Northeast Alberta
Portland
Oregon 97211
+1 5034738447
www.elnutritacopdx.com

Opening hours	Open 7 days
Reservation policy	No
Credit cards	Accepted
Price range	Budget
Style	Casual
Cuisine	Mexican
Recommended for	Bargain

'They use fresh vegetables and cook and season their meat nicely. Also it's cheap.'
—Sarah Pilner & Jasper Shen

OLYMPIC PROVISIONS SOUTHEAST

Recommended by
Greg & Gabrielle
Quiñónez Denton

107 Southeast Washington Street
Portland
Oregon 97214
+1 5039543663
www.olympicprovisions.com

Opening hours	Open 7 days
Credit cards	Accepted
Price range	Affordable
Style	Casual
Cuisine	Modern European
Recommended for	Breakfast

'The best Eggs Benedict anywhere, ever. Thinly shaved sweetheart ham, a generous dollop of zesty hollandaise and, in the summer, they'll even griddle up a fat slice of heirloom tomato to add to the mix.'
—Greg & Gabrielle Quiñónez Denton

OVERLOOK FAMILY RESTAURANT

Recommended by
Sarah Pilner &
Jasper Shen

1332 North Skidmore Street
Portland
Oregon 97217
+1 5032880880

Opening hours	Open 7 days
Reservation policy	No
Credit cards	Accepted
Price range	Budget
Style	Casual
Cuisine	Diner-Café
Recommended for	Breakfast

'It's like going out to brunch without having to wait in line.'—Sarah Pilner & Jasper Shen

PAADEE

Recommended by
Greg & Gabrielle
Quiñónez Denton

6 Southeast 28th Avenue
Portland
Oregon 97214
+1 5033601453
www.paadeepdx.com

Opening hours	Open 7 days
Credit cards	Accepted
Price range	Budget
Style	Casual
Cuisine	Thai
Recommended for	Bargain

'Wonderful Thai food, great ambience and amazing drinks.'—Greg & Gabrielle Quiñónez Denton

PALEY'S PLACE

Recommended by
Gabriel Rucker

1204 Northwest 21st Avenue
Portland
Oregon 97209
+1 5032432403
www.paleysplace.net

Opening hours	Open 7 days
Credit cards	Accepted
Price range	Affordable
Style	Casual
Cuisine	French
Recommended for	Local favourite

'Where I got my chops and it is nice to go home.'
—Gabriel Rucker

PHO HUNG

Recommended by
Sarah Pilner &
Jasper Shen

4717 Southeast Powell Boulevard
Portland
Oregon 97206
+1 5037753170
www.pho-hung.com

Opening hours	Open 7 days
Reservation policy	No
Credit cards	Accepted
Price range	Budget
Style	Casual
Cuisine	Vietnamese
Recommended for	Regular neighbourhood

'The pho is consistently good. It's cheap and non-pretentious.'—Sarah Pilner & Jasper Shen

LE PIGEON

Recommended by
Andy Ricker, Sarah Pilner &
Jasper Shen

738 East Burnside Street
Portland
Oregon 97214
+1 5035468796
www.lepigeon.com

Opening hours	Open 7 days
Credit cards	Accepted
Price range	Expensive
Style	Casual
Cuisine	Modern French
Recommended for	Local favourite

'Total creative freedom, obsessive dedication to the foodstuffs and wines of the area, a DIY design aesthetic and informal service cranking out some of the best and most exciting food in the Pacific Northwest for years now, and getting stronger and more focused every passing year.'—Andy Ricker

Gabriel Rucker's East Burnside flagship (a sister bistro, Little Bird, continues the avian theme) is a warm and cosy spot where young Portlanders take refuge from the inclement local climate. With a slew of communal tables, chandeliers and a chef's counter, the theatrical space pivots around an open kitchen, where the jovial staff go about creating some of the most inventive dishes in the region. Chef candy like beef cheeks, sweetbreads and marrow dominate the short but ever-rotating menu, and are even worked into desserts such as foie gras profiteroles. The tasting menu, paired with exciting, lesser-known wines, is just as well publicized.

PODNAH'S PIT

Recommended by
Jenn Louis

1625 Northeast Killingsworth Street
Portland
Oregon 97211
+1 5032813700
www.podnahspit.com

Opening hours	Open 7 days
Reservation policy	No
Credit cards	Accepted
Price range	Budget
Style	Casual
Cuisine	Barbeque
Recommended for	Breakfast

'I am a sucker for a savoury Mexican breakfast, so a Texan barbeque joint serving lardy biscuits and chilli verde sopa (green chilli soup) with fried eggs is totally my jam.'—Jenn Louis

ROE

Recommended by
Greg & Gabrielle
Quiñónez Denton

Block + Tackle
3113 Southeast Division Street
Portland
Oregon 97202
+1 5032321566
www.roe-pdx.com

Opening hours	Closed Sunday to Tuesday
Credit cards	Accepted
Price range	Expensive
Style	Smart casual
Cuisine	Seafood
Recommended for	High end

'Roe serves a beautiful and refined tasting menu that focuses on seafood and modern technique.'—Greg & Gabrielle Quiñónez Denton

ZILLA SAKÉ

Recommended by
Jenn Louis

1806 Northeast Alberta Street
Portland
Oregon 97211
+1 5032888372
www.zillasakehouse.com

Opening hours	Open 7 days
Credit cards	Accepted
Price range	Budget
Style	Casual
Cuisine	Sushi
Recommended for	Regular neighbourhood

'This slightly hipster sushi joint is small and quirky. Kate has been running the kitchen for years, serving simple, seasonal and straightforward sashimi, sushi and nigiri. The fish is just what it should be: absolute quality.'—Jenn Louis

FORAGE

Recommended by
Matthew Orlando

370 East 900 South
Salt Lake City
Utah 84111
+1 8017087834
www.foragerestaurant.com

Opening hours	Closed Monday and Sunday
Credit cards	Accepted
Price range	Expensive
Style	Smart casual
Cuisine	Modern American
Recommended for	Worth the travel

'It was an amazing meal and such a great surprise. Chef Bowman Brown is killing it in a landscape that is quite foreign to most of us. Completely landlocked, he is cooking from the mountains and rivers around him. I highly recommend it if you are in Salt Lake City.' —Matthew Orlando

THE WILLOWS INN

Recommended by
Andrew Carmellini,
— Jason Fox,
Jason Franey

The Willows Inn
2579 West Shore Drive
Lummi Island
Washington 98262
+1 3607582620
www.willows-inn.com

Opening hours	Closed Monday to Wednesday
Credit cards	Accepted
Price range	Expensive
Style	Smart casual
Cuisine	Modern American
Recommended for	Worth the travel

'Delicious foraged food and fantastic technique.' —Jason Franey

BA BAR

Recommended by
Ethan Stowell

550 12th Avenue
Seattle
Washington 98122
+1 2063282030
www.babarseattle.com

Opening hours	Open 7 days
Reservation policy	No
Credit cards	Accepted
Price range	Budget
Style	Casual
Cuisine	Vietnamese
Recommended for	Late night

'Ba Bar is a super-cool, all-day/all-night Vietnamese spot that serves great food and cocktails. And, if you go late at night on a Wednesday, you can partake in Kung Fu Karaoke! Always a bunch of restaurant folks there as well.' —Ethan Stowell

BELLTOWN PIZZA

Recommended by
Blaine Wetzel

2422 1st Avenue
Seattle
Washington 98121
+1 2064412653
www.belltownpizza.net

Opening hours	Open 7 days
Reservation policy	No
Credit cards	Accepted
Price range	Budget
Style	Casual
Cuisine	Pizza
Recommended for	Late night

'Fun atmosphere, even on weekdays.' —Blaine Wetzel

CAFÉ BESALU

Recommended by
Ethan Stowell

5909 24th Avenue Northwest
Seattle
Washington 98107
+1 2067891463
www.cafebesalu.com

Opening hours	Closed Monday and Tuesday
Reservation policy	No
Credit cards	Accepted but not AMEX
Price range	Budget
Style	Casual
Cuisine	Café-Bakery
Recommended for	Breakfast

'Besalu is a small pastry shop in Ballard, which is a great neighbourhood in Seattle, and they serve the best croissant I have ever had. I've tried many times to find a better croissant and it just hasn't happened. I honestly feel very fortunate that this place is ten minutes away from my house.' —Ethan Stowell

CAFÉ PRESSE
1117 12th Avenue
Seattle
Washington 98122
+1 2067097674
www.cafepresseseattle.com

Opening hours	Open 7 days
Credit cards	Accepted but not AMEX
Price range	Budget
Style	Casual
Cuisine	French
Recommended for	Breakfast

'French-bistro classics – pain au chocolat, Croque Monsieur, omelette aux fines herbes, pommes frites – and a cappuccino. Sometimes if I really need to fuel up I order the cold chicken with a side salad and a bucket of mayo. If it's a day off, steak tartare with frites and a pichet of red wine.'—Brendan McGill

CANLIS
2576 Aurora Avenue North
Seattle
Washington 98109
+1 2062833313
www.canlis.com

Opening hours	Closed Sunday
Credit cards	Accepted
Price range	Expensive
Style	Formal
Cuisine	Modern American
Recommended for	High end

'Canlis is Seattle's one true fine-dining restaurant. The food is fantastic, the service is great, the wine list is stellar and the view can't be beat.'—Ethan Stowell

CANON
928 12th Avenue
Seattle
Washington 98122
+1 2065529755
www.canonseattle.com

Opening hours	Open 7 days
Reservation policy	No
Credit cards	Accepted
Price range	Affordable
Style	Casual
Cuisine	Modern American
Recommended for	Late night

'The best cocktails in the city matched with great food. The best cocktail bar service in the city. The most eye-boggling selection of booze in the world. Did I say the best service ever? They never let it get too crowded. Awesome.'—Matt Dillon

Best build up your thirst for Canon, which claims the Western Hemisphere's largest library of spirits. The walls are a larder of aged spirits and premium whiskeys, shelves only breaking where they meet the windows, although natural light is anathema to late-night barflies. 'Lavish Libations' include the heady Truffled Old Fashioned and the bold Canon with bitters, rye and triple sec foam. The menu is wry: 'Alcohol, eggs, sex, undercooked foods and most enjoyable things in life can and will kill you if you give them enough time. Live life to the fullest until then...' Particularly strong is 'ration' of bone marrow with smoked garlic gremolata.

IL CORVO
217 James Street
Seattle
Washington 98104
+1 2065380999
www.ilcorvopasta.com

Opening hours	Closed Saturday and Sunday
Reservation policy	No
Credit cards	Accepted
Price range	Budget
Style	Casual
Cuisine	Italian
Recommended for	Bargain

'Bustling spot with delicious pasta.'—Renee Erickson

DELANCEY

Recommended by
Renee Erickson

1415 Northwest 70th Street
Seattle
Washington 98117
+1 2068381960
www.delanceyseattle.com

Opening hours	Closed Monday and Tuesday
Credit cards	Accepted
Price range	Affordable
Style	Casual
Cuisine	Pizza
Recommended for	Regular neighbourhood

'Perfect pizza and delicious, wood-oven-roasted vegetable dishes.'—Renee Erickson

DICK'S DRIVE-IN

Recommended by
Ethan Stowell

115 Broadway East
Seattle
Washington 98102
+1 2063231300
www.ddir.com

Opening hours	Open 7 days
Reservation policy	No
Credit cards	Not accepted
Price range	Budget
Style	Casual
Cuisine	Burgers
Recommended for	Bargain

'You only get this answer if you're from Seattle. It's a great burger, but it's less about the burger and more about the history of Dick's in Seattle.'—Ethan Stowell

GREEN LEAF

Recommended by
Ethan Stowell

418 8th Avenue South
Seattle
Washington 98104
+1 2063401388
www.greenleaftaste.com

Opening hours	Open 7 days
Reservation policy	No
Credit cards	Accepted
Price range	Budget
Style	Casual
Cuisine	Vietnamese
Recommended for	Regular neighbourhood

'The lunch spot I eat at most regularly is Green Leaf in the International District. I love Vietnamese cuisine and culture. Having spent some time there (best vacation spot ever) I have a huge amount of respect for how regional, seasonal and traditional the cuisine is. Green Leaf lives up to that sense of fresh, modest and delicious food that I found throughout my travels.'
—Ethan Stowell

LITTLE UNCLE

Recommended by
Brendan McGill

88 Yesler Way
Seattle
Washington 98104
+1 2062238529
www.littleuncleseattle.com

Opening hours	Closed Monday and Sunday
Reservation policy	No
Credit cards	Accepted
Price range	Affordable
Style	Casual
Cuisine	Thai
Recommended for	Regular neighbourhood

'It's in the Pioneer Square neighbourhood next to Altstadt and I always find myself down there around lunchtime. Wylie Frank and Poncharee Kounpungchart (PK) are the perfect example of the chef-owner couple. Wylie was the sous chef at Lark, he married PK, they went and travelled all over Thailand and came back cooking this unbelievable Thai food. They started as a pop-up at La Bête, opened a window on Capitol Hill and now a full-service restaurant down in the Square. The food is ballsy, full-flavoured "chef food."'
—Brendan McGill

MAEKAWA BAR

Recommended by
Brendan McGill

601 South King Street
Seattle
Washington 98104
+1 2066220634
www.maekawabar.com

Opening hours	Closed Monday
Credit cards	Accepted but not AMEX
Price range	Budget
Style	Casual
Cuisine	Japanese
Recommended for	Late night

'Legit *izakaya*. I like it because it's in a thoroughly un-gentrified corner of Chinatown, in a plaza of other Japanese businesses (travel agency, video game store, karaoke spot, "American-style" bar) so it gives a sense of immersion. I go for *geso kimchi*, *takoyaki*, *shishamo* and *bonito tataki*. I'm bummed because the menu seems to be getting a little more gaijin friendly. I vote for more hardcore classics.'—Brendan McGill

A single unit on the second floor of a modest mall in Seattle's Chinatown International District is the unlikely home of one of Seattle's best-loved Japanese outposts. This is a tiny *izakaya* with a big reputation for unpretentious grub that goes well with beer. Takoyaki octopus balls, squid legs with kimchi, and baked oysters with 'special mayo sauce' are established 'house favourites', and the likes of fried chicken wings and ramen the works represent post-stadium eating at its beer-friendly best. Kirin and Sapporo are served in pints and jugs (pitchers), with last orders after midnight at the weekend.

MANEKI
Recommended by
Matt Dillon

304 6th Avenue South
Seattle
Washington 98104
+1 2066222631
www.manekirestaurant.com

Opening hours	Closed Monday
Credit cards	Accepted
Price range	Budget
Style	Casual
Cuisine	Japanese
Recommended for	Bargain

'A real Japanese *izakaya* experience. Wheel of fortune, ancient bartenders and takoyaki. Perfect.'—Matt Dillon

MONSOON
Recommended by
Jason Franey

615 19th Avenue East
Seattle
Washington 98112
+1 2063252111
www.monsoonseattle.com

Opening hours	Open 7 days
Credit cards	Accepted
Price range	Affordable
Style	Casual
Cuisine	Vietnamese
Recommended for	Breakfast

'The dumplings are amazing.'—Jason Franey

PALACE KITCHEN
Recommended by
Drew Johnson

2030 5th Avenue
Seattle
Washington 98121
+1 2064482001
www.tomdouglas.com

Opening hours	Open 7 days
Credit cards	Accepted
Price range	Affordable
Style	Casual
Cuisine	Modern American
Recommended for	Worth the travel

'Creative menu with excellent local ingredients and proper execution.'—Drew Johnson

PHO VIET ANH
Recommended by
Jason Franey

372 Roy Street
Seattle
Washington 98109
+1 2063521881
www.phovietanh.com

Opening hours	Open 7 days
Reservation policy	No
Credit cards	Accepted
Price range	Budget
Style	Casual
Cuisine	Vietnamese
Recommended for	Bargain

'Classic pho done really well with no frills.'
—Jason Franey

LE PICHET
Recommended by
Renee Erickson

1933 1st Avenue
Seattle
Washington 98101
+1 2062561499
www.lepichetseattle.com

Opening hours	Open 7 days
Credit cards	Accepted but not AMEX
Price range	Affordable
Style	Casual
Cuisine	French
Recommended for	Late night

'Classic French food that is satisfying with delicious, inexpensive French wines by the glass.'
—Renee Erickson

POPPY

Recommended by
Matt Dillon

622 Broadway East
Seattle
Washington 98102
+1 2063241108
www.poppyseattle.com

Opening hours	Open 7 days
Credit cards	Accepted
Price range	Affordable
Style	Casual
Cuisine	Modern American
Recommended for	Regular neighbourhood

'I really love Jerry Traunfeld's restaurant Poppy on Capitol Hill. No one has a better feel for spices and herbs than he does. His Indian-inspired way of dining with a focus on Northwest foods is unbelievable. The service is always wonderful and it's a truly unique restaurant in Seattle.'—Matt Dillon

SHIRO'S

Recommended by
Ethan Stowell

2401 2nd Avenue
Seattle
Washington 98121
+1 2064439844
www.shiros.com

Opening hours	Open 7 days
Credit cards	Accepted
Price range	Affordable
Style	Casual
Cuisine	Japanese
Recommended for	Local favourite

'Shiro has been making sushi in Seattle for at least thirty years. He has worked at, influenced, or started all of the best sushi restaurants in Seattle. He's our most iconic, and in my opinion, best chef working in Seattle today. When you go in make sure you get there a half-hour before opening so that you can get a spot at the counter with Shiro.'—Ethan Stowell

STAPLE & FANCY

Recommended by
Jason Franey

4739 Ballard Avenue Northwest
Seattle
Washington 98107
+1 2067891200
www.ethanstowellrestaurants.com

Opening hours	Open 7 days
Credit cards	Accepted
Price range	Affordable
Style	Casual
Cuisine	Italian
Recommended for	Regular neighbourhood

'It's a fun, reliable, seasonal and delicious spot. Ethan Stowell does great things with his menu.'
—Jason Franey

SUSHI KAPPO TAMURA

Recommended by
Brendan McGill

2968 Eastlake Avenue East
Seattle
Washington 98102
+1 2065470937
www.sushikappotamura.com

Opening hours	Open 7 days
Credit cards	Accepted
Price range	Expensive
Style	Smart casual
Cuisine	Japanese
Recommended for	High end

'The best *omakase* (chef's choice menu) sushi experience in Seattle right now. I ate the freshest, locally sourced seafood, one course after another, for hours.'—Brendan McGill

VIF WINE AND COFFEE

Recommended by
Renee Erickson

4401 Fremont Avenue North
Seattle
Washington 98103
+1 2065577357
www.vifseattle.com

Opening hours	Closed Monday
Reservation policy	No
Credit cards	Accepted
Price range	Budget
Style	Casual
Cuisine	Café-Bar
Recommended for	Breakfast

'Charred toast with ricotta and honey. Perfectly made
coffee. Yum.'—Renee Erickson

THE WALRUS AND THE CARPENTER

Recommended by
Craig Stoll

4743 Ballard Avenue Northwest
Seattle
Washington 98107
+1 2063959227
www.thewalrusbar.com

Opening hours	Open 7 days
Reservation policy	No
Credit cards	Accepted
Price range	Affordable
Style	Casual
Cuisine	Seafood
Recommended for	Worth the travel

An oyster bar on Rain City's Ballard Avenue, The
Walrus and the Carpenter oozes utilitarian elegance
with its stripped floorboards, whitewashed walls and
baskets of fruit, oysters and liquor decorating the
steel bar. The daily-changing menu promises a choice
of around six varieties of fresh oyster and even more
of them on the fish menu (fried and gratinéed), which
also includes more creative dishes such as scallop
tartare with lemon crème and black truffle. Salads and
puddings are equally bright and original – imagine
roasted Medjool dates with olive oil and sea salt. The
wine list is a mixture of French, Italian and West Coast
American options designed to complement seafood.

'IT'S LIKE A TARANTINO FILM IN YOUR MOUTH.'

ZACH POLLACK P740

LOS ANGELES

'The epitome of southern Californian cooking.'

JOSEPH CENTENO P737

'OPEN UNTIL 4.00 A.M. AND A FAVOURITE FOR ANGELINOS IN THE KNOW.'

JET TILA P735

'Wolfgang Puck is still the king of LA.'

JON SHOOK P730

'IT SERVES ONE OF MY FAVOURITE BURGERS IN THE CITY.'

VINNY DOTOLO P729

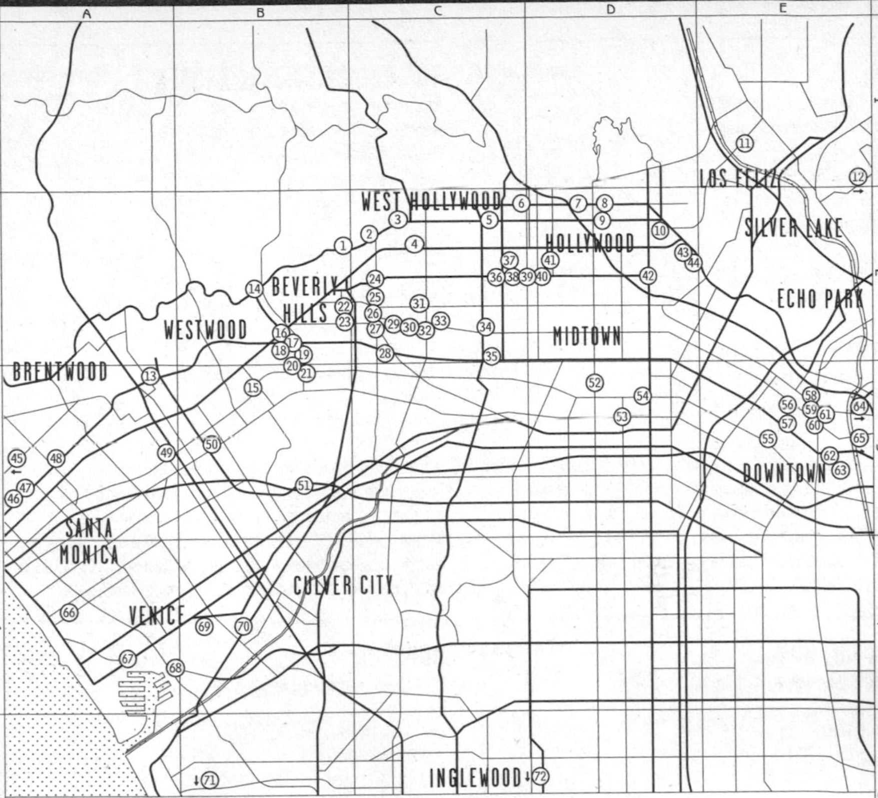

LOS ANGELES

SCALE

0   1500   3000   4500
yd.

1. *Night + Market (p.740)*
2. *Sushi Park (p.742)*
3. *The Restaurant (p.741)*
4. *Connie and Ted's (p.739)*
5. *In-N-Out Burger (p.733)*
6. *Loteria Grill (p.734)*
7. *Yai Restaurant (p.734)*
8. *Ruen Pair (p.735)*
9. *Pa Ord Noodle (p.733)*
10. *Ricky's Fish Tacos (p.738)*
11. *Canelé (p.728)*
12. *Hui Tou Xiang (p.736)*
13. *800 Degrees (p.743)*
14. *Fountain Coffee Room (p.729)*

15. *Hinoki & The Bird (p.731)*
16. *Bouchon (p.728)*
17. *SUGARFISH by Sushi Nozawa (p.730)*
18. *Urasawa (p.730)*
19. *Spago (p.730)*
20. *Honor Bar (p.729)*
21. *South Beverly Grill (p.730)*
22. *Ed's Coffee Shop (p.740)*
23. *Petrossian Restaurant & Boutique (p.741)*
24. *Lucques (p.740)*
25. *Lawry's The Prime Rib (p.729)*
26. *Matsuhisa Restaurant (p.729)*
27. *The Bazaar by José Andrés (p.728)*
28. *Red Medicine (p.729)*
29. *Son of a Gun (p.742)*
30. *Fōnuts (p.740)*
31. *Cooks County (p.739)*
32. *Robata Jinya (p.742)*
33. *Short Cake (p.742)*
34. *Graffiti Sublime Coffee (p.733)*
35. *Genwa Korean BBQ (p.733)*
36. *Pizzeria Mozza (p.741)*
37. *Trois Mec (p.743)*
38. *Osteria Mozza (p.741)*
39. *chi SPACCA (p.739)*
40. *Providence (p.741)*
41. *Cactus Tacos (p.733)*
42. *Sqirl (p.733)*
43. *Intelligentsia Coffee (p.737)*

44. *Naturewell (p.738)*
45. *Father's Office (p.736)*
46. *Mélisse (p.737)*
47. *Rustic Canyon (p.737)*
48. *Milo and Olive (p.737)*
49. *Tsujita Annex (p.737)*
50. *The Apple Pan (p.743)*
51. *Sushi Zo (p.731)*
52. *Pollo a la Brasa (p.734)*
53. *Papa Cristo's (p.734)*
54. *Park's BBQ (p.734)*
55. *Terroni Downtown LA (p.732)*
56. *Bäco Mercat (p.731)*
57. *Cole's (p.732)*
58. *Daikokuya (p.735)*
59. *KaGaYa (p.735)*
60. *Kokekokko (p.735)*
61. *Sushi Gen (p.735)*
62. *Daily Dose Café (p.732)*
63. *Bestia (p.732)*
64. *In-N-Out Burger (p.728)*
65. *Guisados (p.730)*
66. *La Isla Bonita Taco Truck (p.739)*
67. *Gjelina (p.738)*
68. *Paichē (p.736)*
69. *A-Frame (p.731)*
70. *Akasha (p.731)*
71. *Manhattan Beach Post (p.736)*
72. *Ramen Yamadaya (p.738)*

CANELÉ

Recommended by
Suzanne Goin, Christian
Page, Zach Pollack

3219 Glendale Boulevard
Atwater Village
Los Angeles
California 90039
+1 3236667133
www.canele-la.com

Opening hours	Closed Monday
Reservation policy	No
Credit cards	Accepted
Price range	Affordable
Style	Casual
Cuisine	Modern European
Recommended for	Breakfast

'An outstanding fried chicken sandwich, superb shrimp and grits, but what takes the cake is their French toast. It's epic. The Kobe Bryant of French toast, both in its towering stature and in its jaw-dropping perfection. That's about as far as the metaphor goes...'
—Zach Pollack

THE BAZAAR BY JOSÉ ANDRÉS

Recommended by
Carles Abellan

SLS Hotel Beverly Hills
465 South La Cienega Boulevard
Beverly Hills
Los Angeles
California 90048
+1 3102465555
www.thebazaar.com

Opening hours	Open 7 days
Credit cards	Accepted
Price range	Expensive
Style	Smart casual
Cuisine	Tapas
Recommended for	Worth the travel

'I like food that is prepared in miniature using different styles and always with a nod to Spanish cooking, where tradition and creativity go hand in hand. Designed by Philippe Starck, with different rooms for each occasion within the same restaurant, it's a really cool, current and modern place.'—Carles Abellan

IN-N-OUT BURGER

Recommended by
Saipin Chutima

13850 Francisquito Avenue
Baldwin Park
Los Angeles
California 91706
+1 8007861000
www.in-n-out.com

Opening hours	Open 7 days
Reservation policy	No
Credit cards	Accepted
Price range	Budget
Style	Casual
Cuisine	Burgers
Recommended for	Bargain

'Being from California, In-N-Out will always be a part of me. It was always the comfort food when we were exhausted from work. I always get the number two with both kinds of onions, chopped peppers and extra tomato.'—Saipin Chutima

BOUCHON

Recommended by
Michael Voltaggio

235 North Canon Drive
Beverly Hills
Los Angeles
California 90210
+1 3102719910
www.bouchonbistro.com

Opening hours	Open 7 days
Credit cards	Accepted
Price range	Affordable
Style	Smart casual
Cuisine	French
Recommended for	Regular neighbourhood

'I love eating oysters, cheese, etc. The execution of Thomas Keller's French-bistro-inspired cuisine is never short of perfection. Service is always as precise as the food, in an inviting yet refined way, that makes you leave feeling taken care of.'—Michael Voltaggio

FOUNTAIN COFFEE ROOM

The Beverly Hills Hotel
9641 Sunset Boulevard
Beverly Hills
Los Angeles
California 90210
+1 3102762251
www.beverlyhillshotel.com

Opening hours	Open 7 days
Reservation policy	No
Credit cards	Accepted
Price range	Budget
Style	Casual
Cuisine	Diner-Café
Recommended for	Breakfast

'I go with my daughter. It's our spot. When you walk in, it smells like sugar cooking.'—Jon Shook

HONOR BAR

Recommended by
Vinny Dotolo

122 South Beverly Drive
Beverly Hills
Los Angeles
California 90212
+1 3105500292
www.hillstone.com

Opening hours	Open 7 days
Reservation policy	No
Credit cards	Accepted
Price range	Budget
Style	Casual
Cuisine	American
Recommended for	Regular neighbourhood

'It serves one of my favourite burgers in the city.'
—Vinny Dotolo

LAWRY'S THE PRIME RIB

Recommended by
Jet Tila

100 North La Cienega Boulevard
Beverly Hills
Los Angeles
California 90211
+1 3106522827
www.lawrysonline.com

Opening hours	Open 7 days
Credit cards	Accepted
Price range	Affordable
Style	Smart casual
Cuisine	Steakhouse
Recommended for	Local favourite

'I've been eating there all my life, I remember eating there with my grandparents. You'd be hard pressed to find someone from LA that hasn't been there. Still the best prime rib, creamed spinach, and Yorkshire pudding in America. You feel the history of LA when dining there.'—Jet Tila

MATSUHISA RESTAURANT

Recommended by
Matt Molina,
Jon Shook

129 North La Cienega Boulevard
Beverly Hills
Los Angeles
California 90211
+1 3106599639
www.nobumatsuhisa.com

Opening hours	Open 7 days
Credit cards	Accepted
Price range	Expensive
Style	Smart casual
Cuisine	Japanese
Recommended for	Regular neighbourhood

'It's my favourite sushi restaurant. They remember me, there is a great staff, and the quality of sushi is among the best in the country.'—Jon Shook

RED MEDICINE

Recommended by
Vinny Dotolo, Claus
Meyer, Steve Samson,
Michael Voltaggio

8400 Wilshire Boulevard
Beverly Hills
Los Angeles
California 90211
+1 3236515500
www.redmedicinela.com

Opening hours	Open 7 days
Credit cards	Accepted
Price range	Affordable
Style	Casual
Cuisine	Asian-American
Recommended for	Late night

'I think Jordan Kahn is one of the most talented young chefs in the city. It's the one place you can't leave without having dessert.'—Vinny Dotolo

SOUTH BEVERLY GRILL

Recommended by
Jon Shook

122 South Beverly Drive
Beverly Hills
Los Angeles
California 90212
+1 3105500242
www.hillstone.com

Opening hours	Open 7 days
Credit cards	Accepted
Price range	Affordable
Style	Smart casual
Cuisine	American
Recommended for	Wish I'd opened

'Consistency, consistency, consistency.'—Jon Shook

SPAGO

Recommended by
Suzanne Goin,
Jon Shook

176 North Canon Drive
Beverly Hills
Los Angeles
California 90210
+1 3103850880
www.wolfgangpuck.com

Opening hours	Open 7 days
Credit cards	Accepted
Price range	Expensive
Style	Smart casual
Cuisine	Modern American
Recommended for	Local favourite

'Wolfgang Puck is still the king of LA. I'm not quite sure I like the new design of the restaurant, but the iconic dishes at Spago still make me feel nostalgic for old LA.' —Jon Shook

SUGARFISH BY SUSHI NOZAWA

Recommended by
Matt Molina

212 North Canon Drive
Beverly Hills
Los Angeles
California 90210
+1 3102766900
www.sugarfishsushi.com

Opening hours	Open 7 days
Reservation policy	No
Credit cards	Accepted
Price range	Affordable
Style	Casual
Cuisine	Sushi
Recommended for	Regular neighbourhood

URASAWA

Recommended by
Steve Samson, Michael
Voltaggio, Ricardo Zarate

218 North Rodeo Drive
Beverly Hills
Los Angeles
California 90210
+1 3102478939

Opening hours	Closed Monday and Sunday
Credit cards	Accepted
Price range	Expensive
Style	Smart casual
Cuisine	Japanese
Recommended for	High end

'Each piece of food is treated with so much care and respect for the ingredient. Chef Hiro is a true craftsman and it's inspiring to watch him work. The sushi is perfect but the goma tofu and shabu shabu are so surprising.'—Michael Voltaggio

GUISADOS

Recommended by
Josef Centeno

2100 East Cesar E Chavez Avenue
Boyle Heights
Los Angeles
California 90033
+1 3232647201
www.guisados.co

Opening hours	Open 7 days
Reservation policy	No
Credit cards	Accepted
Price range	Budget
Style	Casual
Cuisine	Mexican
Recommended for	Bargain

'All the tacos are awesome!'—Josef Centeno

HINOKI & THE BIRD

Recommended by
Luke Mangan

10 Century Drive
Century City
Los Angeles
California 90067
+1 3105521200
www.hinokiandthebird.com

Opening hours..............................Closed Monday and Sunday
Credit cards..Accepted
Price range..Affordable
Style..Smart casual
Cuisine..Asian-American
Recommended for..Wish I'd opened

'Fabulous fit-out and a great Asian-inspired menu. It's a restaurant I wish I'd opened in Sydney as I think Sydney-siders would really embrace it.'—Luke Mangan

SUSHI ZO

Recommended by
Vinny Dotolo,
Tom Sellers

9824 National Boulevard
Cheviot Hills
Los Angeles
California 90064
+1 3108423977

Opening hours..Closed Sunday
Credit cards..Accepted
Price range..Expensive
Style..Casual
Cuisine..Sushi
Recommended for..Worth the travel

'The best sushi I have eaten in my life. The quality of the fish was amazing, and I loved the setting.'
—Tom Sellers

A-FRAME

Recommended by
Massimo Bottura

12565 Washington Boulevard
Culver City
Los Angeles
California 90066
+1 3103987700
www.aframela.com

Opening hours..Open 7 days
Reservation policy..No
Credit cards..Accepted
Price range..Affordable
Style..Casual
Cuisine..Modern American
Recommended for..Bargain

'Organic ingredients for a fast, healthy and different snack in Los Angeles. A quick country outing in the city. Among wooden walls and camping seats, it is an easy and unusual way to treat yourself to some down time.'
—Massimo Bottura

AKASHA

Recommended by
Ricardo Zarate

9543 Culver Boulevard
Culver City
Los Angeles
California 90232
+1 3108451700
www.akasharestaurant.com

Opening hours..Open 7 days
Credit cards..Accepted
Price range..Affordable
Style..Casual
Cuisine..Modern American
Recommended for..Breakfast

BÄCO MERCAT

Recommended by
Neal Fraser

408 South Main Street
Downtown
Los Angeles
California 90013
+1 2136878808
www.bacomercat.com

Opening hours..Open 7 days
Credit cards..Accepted
Price range..Affordable
Style..Casual
Cuisine..Modern Spanish
Recommended for..Local favourite

'It is a great expression of tasty food served in a modern way. Josef does a great job with all the dishes on the menu. "Caesar" Brussels sprouts – enough said.'
—Neal Fraser

BESTIA

Recommended by
Michael Schwartz

2121 East 7th Place
Downtown
Los Angeles
California 90021
+1 2135145724
www.bestiala.com

Opening hours	Open 7 days
Credit cards	Accepted
Price range	Affordable
Style	Casual
Cuisine	Italian
Recommended for	Worth the travel

'There is passion, hard work and the talent of chef Ori Menashe and pastry chef Genevieve Gergis, the husband-and-wife team behind this multi-regional Italian restaurant in the Arts District of Downtown Los Angeles. As you can guess – Bestia means "Beast" in Italian – they have an impressive house-cured meats programme, as well as sourdough from Ori's own yeast culture, to match. From fresh pizza dough fired in the wood-burning oven to freshly made fusilli, *agnolotti*, *casarecce* and more, Bestia is an honest mom-and-pop restaurant that's going to be around a long time.' —Michael Schwartz

COLE'S

Recommended by
Josef Centeno

118 East 6th Street
Downtown
Los Angeles
California 90014
+1 2136224090
www.colesfrenchdip.com

Opening hours	Open 7 days
Credit cards	Accepted
Price range	Budget
Style	Casual
Cuisine	American
Recommended for	Late night

'I go for their grilled-cheese sandwiches, tomato soup and an Old-Fashioned from Cole's Red Car Bar.' —Josef Centeno

DAILY DOSE CAFÉ

Recommended by
Steve Samson

Suite 104 1820 Industrial Street
Downtown
Los Angeles
California 90021
+1 2132819300
www.dailydoseinc.com

Opening hours	Open 7 days
Reservation policy	No
Credit cards	Accepted
Price range	Budget
Style	Casual
Cuisine	Café
Recommended for	Breakfast

'I am trying to be really healthy and eat at least one vegan meal a day. They make a great vegan breakfast salad.' —Steve Samson

Downtown Los Angeles doesn't get much more atmospheric than Daily Dose, tucked down an alleyway off Industrial Street. This verdant Arts District spot, brick-paved and tumbling with greenery, serves 'honest food' done right seven days a week. Breakfast could be anything from fruit with raw honey or baguette, butter and jam, to a mighty three-egg omelette with rocket (arugula) salad and root veggies, accompanied by perfectly pulled shots of Intelligentsia Coffee. Sandwiches are generously proportioned: the Cheeky Bastard pairs beef cheeks, green onions and *pico de gallo*; Mike The Mechanic has mortadella and caramelized onions atop toasted rye.

TERRONI DOWNTOWN LA

Recommended by
Josef Centeno

802 South Spring Street
Downtown
Los Angeles
California 90014
+1 3239540300
www.terroni.com

Opening hours	Open 7 days
Credit cards	Accepted
Price range	Affordable
Style	Casual
Cuisine	Italian
Recommended for	Breakfast

'I like their poached eggs with porchetta, crispy aubergine (eggplant), tomato and smoked mozzarella.' —Josef Centeno

PA ORD NOODLE
Recommended by
Jet Tila
5301 Sunset Boulevard
East Hollywood
Los Angeles
California 90027
+1 3234613945

Opening hours..Open 7 days
Reservation policy..No
Credit cards...Not accepted
Price range...Budget
Style...Casual
Cuisine...Thai
Recommended for...Bargain

'Tom yum noodle soup, pork belly with broccoli over rice, both for about $12 (£7)... no joke!'—Jet Tila

SQIRL
Recommended by
Vinny Dotolo
Suite 4, 720 North Virgil Avenue
East Hollywood
Los Angeles
California 90029
+1 3232848147
www.sqirlla.com

Opening hours..Open 7 days
Reservation policy..No
Credit cards...Accepted
Price range...Budget
Style...Casual
Cuisine...Modern American
Recommended for...Breakfast

'It's like a continuous brunch. There's great savoury food and great sweet food. And I can bring the kid there.'—Vinny Dotolo

GENWA KOREAN BBQ
Recommended by
Neal Fraser
5115 Wilshire Boulevard
Hancock Park
Los Angeles
California 90036
+1 3235490760
www.genwakoreanbbq.com

Opening hours..Open 7 days
Reservation policy..No
Credit cards...Accepted
Price range...Affordable
Style...Casual
Cuisine...Korean
Recommended for...Late night

'Beef *bibimbap* and grilled prime *kalbi*. Both great, and great *banchan* to boot.'—Neal Fraser

GRAFFITI SUBLIME COFFEE
Recommended by
Matt Molina
180 South La Brea Avenue
Hancock Park
Los Angeles
California 90036

Opening hours..Open 7 days
Reservation policy..No
Credit cards...Accepted
Price range...Affordable
Style...Casual
Cuisine...Coffee Shop
Recommended for...Breakfast

CACTUS TACOS
Recommended by
Matt Molina
950 Vine Street
Hollywood
Los Angeles
California 90038
+1 3234645865

Opening hours..Open 7 days
Reservation policy..No
Credit cards...Accepted
Price range...Budget
Style...Casual
Cuisine...Mexican
Recommended for...Bargain

IN-N-OUT BURGER
Recommended by
Vinny Dotolo
7009 Sunset Boulevard
Hollywood
Los Angeles
California 90028
+1 8007861000
www.in-n-out.com

Opening hours..Open 7 days
Reservation policy..No
Credit cards...Accepted
Price range...Budget
Style...Casual
Cuisine...Burgers
Recommended for...Local favourite

'Los Angeles is very car-culture driven. Fast food was sort of pioneered here, even though we assume that LA is one of the healthier-eating cities. In-N-Out is iconic Southern California.'—Vinny Dotolo

LOTERIA GRILL
Recommended by
Neal Fraser
6627 Hollywood Boulevard
Hollywood
Los Angeles
California 90028
+1 3234652500
www.loteriagrill.com

Opening hours	Open 7 days
Credit cards	Accepted
Price range	Budget
Style	Casual
Cuisine	Mexican
Recommended for	Breakfast

'Chorizo and eggs, or *chilaquiles* with *carnitas* and mole. Both are amazing. I eat the chorizo and eggs more often, but when you need to fill the belly and the soul, go for the *chilaquiles*. They are spectacular.'
—Neal Fraser

YAI RESTAURANT
Recommended by
Jet Tila
5757 Hollywood Boulevard
Hollywood
Los Angeles
California 90028
+1 3234620292
www.yai.menutoeat.com

Opening hours	Open 7 days
Reservation policy	No
Credit cards	Not accepted
Price range	Budget
Style	Casual
Cuisine	Thai
Recommended for	Regular neighbourhood

'I eat here a few times a month, at least. It's always a solid meal, in a comfortable, unpretentious environment. Most Thai restaurants have one or two dishes that are great; Yai has an entire portfolio that is great. Best wok-cooked noodles in town and they cook their own pork belly. It's boiled until tender, air dried, and then deep fried. So perfect!'—Jet Tila

PAPA CRISTO'S
Recommended by
Vinny Dotolo
2771 West Pico Boulevard
Koreatown
Los Angeles
California 90006
+1 3237372970
www.papacristos.com

Opening hours	Closed Monday and Tuesday
Credit cards	Accepted
Price range	Budget
Style	Casual
Cuisine	Greek
Recommended for	Bargain

'I like *souvlaki* (skewered meat) sandwiches – I grew up eating them. It's cheap and filling – it's the perfect lunch.'—Vinny Dotolo

PARK'S BBQ
Recommended by
Matt Molina,
Ricardo Zarate
955 South Vermont Avenue
Koreatown
Los Angeles
California 90006
+1 2133801717
www.parksbbq.com

Opening hours	Open 7 days
Credit cards	Accepted
Price range	Affordable
Style	Casual
Cuisine	Korean
Recommended for	Local favourite

POLLO A LA BRASA
Recommended by
Steve Samson
764 South Western Avenue
Koreatown
Los Angeles
California 90005
+1 2133871531

Opening hours	Closed Tuesday
Reservation policy	No
Credit cards	Accepted
Price range	Budget
Style	Casual
Cuisine	Peruvian
Recommended for	Bargain

'A Peruvian, rotisserie-chicken place in Koreatown. Look for it by the stack of wood lining the side wall. Really great, smoky, roasted chicken.'—Steve Samson

DAIKOKUYA

327 East 1st Street
Little Tokyo
Los Angeles
California 90012
+1 2136261680
www.dkramen.com

Recommended by
Josef Centeno,
Neal Fraser,
Christian Page

Opening hours	Open 7 days
Reservation policy	No
Credit cards	Not accepted
Price range	Budget
Style	Casual
Cuisine	Ramen Noodles
Recommended for	Bargain

'10 bucks (£6) and you get an amazing bowl of ramen. Good, fast, cheap and full of flavour.'—Neal Fraser

KAGAYA

418 East 2nd Street
Little Tokyo
Los Angeles
California 90012
+1 2136171016
www.kagaya.dla.menuclub.com

Recommended by
Josef Centeno

Opening hours	Closed Monday
Credit cards	Accepted
Price range	Expensive
Style	Casual
Cuisine	Japanese
Recommended for	High end

'I go for pristine shabu shabu.'—Josef Centeno

KOKEKOKKO

203 South Central Avenue
Little Tokyo
Los Angeles
California 90012
+1 2136870690

Recommended by
Steve Samson

Opening hours	Closed Sunday
Credit cards	Accepted
Price range	Affordable
Style	Casual
Cuisine	Japanese
Recommended for	Regular neighbourhood

'I live in Downtown Los Angeles, so I often go to this place. I love Japanese food. I've gone there for years and years. A lot of the other Japanese places will do different things, but here they always do perfect chicken. The chef is this crazy guy. He uses really high-quality chicken. He cooks the chicken rare. If you use a good ingredient, you can do it. He just kisses them on the grill. They're blackened and rare.'—Steve Samson

SUSHI GEN

422 East 2nd Street
Little Tokyo
Los Angeles
California 90012
+1 2136170552
www.sushigen.org

Recommended by
Neal Fraser,
Ricardo Zarate

Opening hours	Closed Sunday
Credit cards	Accepted
Price range	Affordable
Style	Casual
Cuisine	Japanese
Recommended for	Regular neighbourhood

'The fish here is amazing. As good as, and sometimes better than, sushi bars at twice the cost. Always amazing. I have lunch there as often as possible.'—Neal Fraser

RUEN PAIR

5257 Hollywood Boulevard
Los Feliz
Los Angeles
California 90027
+1 3234660153

Recommended by
Jet Tila

Opening hours	Open 7 days
Reservation policy	No
Credit cards	Not accepted
Price range	Budget
Style	Casual
Cuisine	Thai
Recommended for	Late night

'Open until 4.00 a.m., it's a favourite for Angelinos in the know. From papaya salad and pork jerky, to roast duck curry, it's the place to pre or post party for me.'—Jet Tila

MANHATTAN BEACH POST

1142 Manhattan Avenue
Manhattan Beach
Los Angeles
California 90266
+1 3105455405
www.eatmbpost.com

Opening hours..Open 7 days
Credit cards...Accepted
Price range..Affordable
Style...Casual
Cuisine..Modern American
Recommended for................................Local favourite

'*Great*, unique food, laid-back and friendly atmosphere,
by the beach. When you think of Los Angeles, you think
of the beach.'—Steve Samson

PAICHĒ

13488 Maxella Avenue
Marina del Rey
Los Angeles
California 90292
+1 3108936100
www.paichela.com

Opening hours..Open 7 days
Credit cards...Accepted
Price range..Affordable
Style...Casual
Cuisine..Peruvian-Japanese
Recommended for................................Worth the travel

'Every restaurant Ricardo Zarate opens is amazing. The
menu is a mix of Peruvian and Japanese. Must tries are
his tuna tartar, Amazonian fish and his selection of
sashimi.'—Luke Mangan

HUI TOU XIANG

704 West Las Tunas Drive
San Gabriel
Los Angeles
California 91776
+1 6262819888
www.huitouxiang.com

Opening hours..Open 7 days
Reservation policy..No
Credit cards...Not accepted
Price range..Budget
Style...Casual
Cuisine..Chinese
Recommended for..Breakfast

'I go for the pan-fried *hui tou* dumplings.'
—Josef Centeno

FATHER'S OFFICE

1018 Montana Avenue
Santa Monica
Los Angeles
California 90403
+1 3107362224
www.fathersoffice.com

Opening hours..Open 7 days
Reservation policy..No
Credit cards...Accepted
Price range..Budget
Style...Casual
Cuisine..Gastropub
Recommended for................................Wish I'd opened

'Such a brilliant concept. The food and drinks are
all perfect. The best burger in the US by far, and an
amazing collection of libations curated by chef Sang
Yoon.'—Jet Tila

MÉLISSE

Recommended by
Jon Shook

1104 Wilshire Boulevard
Santa Monica
Los Angeles
California 90401
+1 3103950881
www.melisse.com

Opening hours.............................Closed Monday and Sunday
Credit cards...Accepted
Price range..Expensive
Style...Smart casual
Cuisine...Modern French
Recommended for..High end

'Josiah is awesome. I love him.'—Jon Shook

MILO AND OLIVE

Recommended by
Christian Page

2723 Wilshire Boulevard
Santa Monica
Los Angeles
California 90403
+1 3104536776
www.miloandolive.com

Opening hours..Open 7 days
Reservation policy..No
Credit cards...Accepted
Price range...Budget
Style...Casual
Cuisine...Bakery-Pizza
Recommended for...............................Regular neighbourhood

RUSTIC CANYON

Recommended by
Josef Centeno

1119 Wilshire Boulevard
Santa Monica
Los Angeles
California 90401
+1 3103937050
www.rusticcanyonwinebar.com

Opening hours..Open 7 days
Credit cards...Accepted
Price range...Affordable
Style...Casual
Cuisine...Modern American
Recommended for..Local favourite

'Jeremy Fox's food is the epitome of Southern
Californian cooking.'—Josef Centeno

TSUJITA ANNEX

Recommended by
Vinny Dotolo

2050 Sawtelle Boulevard
Sawtelle
Los Angeles
California 90025
+1 3102310222
www.tsujita-la.com/annex.html

Opening hours..Open 7 days
Reservation policy..No
Credit cards...Not accepted
Price range...Budget
Style...Casual
Cuisine...Ramen Noodles
Recommended for...Wish I'd opened

'It's delicious, simple and affordable. And the *tsukemen*
(dipping noodles) they serve is not typical.'
—Vinny Dotolo

INTELLIGENTSIA COFFEE

Recommended by
Ari Taymor

3922 West Sunset Boulevard
Silver Lake
Los Angeles
California 90029
+1 3236636173
www.intelligentsiacoffee.com

Opening hours..Open 7 days
Reservation policy..No
Credit cards...Accepted
Price range...Affordable
Style...Casual
Cuisine...Coffee Shop
Recommended for...Breakfast

NATUREWELL

Recommended by
Ari Taymor

3824 West Sunset Boulevard
Silver Lake
Los Angeles
California 90026
+1 3236645894
www.naturewell.me

Opening hours	Open 7 days
Reservation policy	No
Credit cards	Accepted
Price range	Affordable
Style	Casual
Cuisine	Vegetarian
Recommended for	Breakfast

'I don't like to feel bogged down during the day, so I find the power of raw green vegetable smoothies incredibly energizing.'—Ari Taymor

RICKY'S FISH TACOS

Recommended by
Michael Voltaggio

1400 North Virgil Avenue
Silver Lake
Los Angeles
California 90027
+1 3239067290

Opening hours	Open 7 days
Reservation policy	No
Credit cards	Not accepted
Price range	Budget
Style	Casual
Cuisine	Mexican
Recommended for	Local favourite

'Ricky's is more of a food stand or truck, which Los Angeles is known for. It's a great example of a family recipe that has found its way from Ensenada to Los Angeles and has not gotten lost in translation.'
—Michael Voltaggio

RAMEN YAMADAYA

Recommended by
Ricardo Zarate

3118 West 182nd Street
Torrance
Los Angeles
California 90504
+1 3103805555
www.ramen-yamadaya.com

Opening hours	Open 7 days
Reservation policy	No
Credit cards	Not accepted
Price range	Budget
Style	Casual
Cuisine	Ramen Noodles
Recommended for	Bargain

GJELINA

Recommended by
Josef Centeno

1429 Abbot Kinney Boulevard
Venice
Los Angeles
California 90291
+1 3104501429
www.gjelina.com

Opening hours	Open 7 days
Credit cards	Accepted
Price range	Affordable
Style	Smart casual
Cuisine	Modern American
Recommended for	Local favourite

Gjelina's the hip Venice hangout that caused a stir by turning down a pregnant Victoria Beckham's special request. Gjelina's Cali-Med salads, sexy brunches and wood-oven pizzas are just right as they are, thank you very much. When it opened in 2008 it was the dream neighbourhood joint. Now that word's got out about its guanciale and green olive pizza, charred romanesco with Fresno chilli and anchovy, and butterscotch pot de crème, there are almost more out-of-towners here than there are local artists and surfers. Tables in the backyard have the edge — just — over the industrial chic interior. Reservations are like gold dust but there's always GTA (Gjelina Take Away) next door.

LA ISLA BONITA TACO TRUCK
4th Street and Rose Avenue
Venice
Los Angeles
California 90291
+1 3106636603

Recommended by
Ari Taymor

Opening hours	Closed Thursday
Reservation policy	No
Credit cards	Not accepted
Price range	Budget
Style	Casual
Cuisine	Mexican
Recommended for	Bargain

'Best prawn (shrimp) burrito, period.'—Ari Taymor

CHI SPACCA
6610 Melrose Avenue
West Hollywood
Los Angeles
California 90036
+1 3232971133
www.chispacca.com

Recommended by
David Almany

Opening hours	Open 7 days
Credit cards	Accepted
Price range	Affordable
Style	Casual
Cuisine	Italian
Recommended for	Worth the travel

'Nancy Silverton just opened this amazing restaurant
– it is worth a journey for sure. The chef makes all of
his own salami, charcuterie, and butchers whole pigs,
which makes up a fair bit of the menu. There's an open
kitchen and you are literally right in front of all the
action. The open kitchen comes with a huge wood-
burning grill and wood-burning pizza oven, which
make absolutely delicious food. Plus it is very small,
with seating for only thirty people, so it is very
intimate.'—David Almany

CONNIE AND TED'S
8171 Santa Monica Boulevard
West Hollywood
Los Angeles
California 90046
+1 3238482722
www.connieandteds.com

Recommended by
Michael Voltaggio

Opening hours	Open 7 days
Credit cards	Accepted
Price range	Affordable
Style	Casual
Cuisine	Seafood
Recommended for	Wish I'd opened

'I'm from the East Coast and I always miss the lobster/
shellfish shack restaurants where the food is so
comforting and delicious. They nail it here with the
steamer clams, lobster rolls, shellfish platters, fritters...'
—Michael Voltaggio

COOKS COUNTY
8009 Beverly Boulevard
West Hollywood
Los Angeles
California 90048
+1 3236538009
www.cookscountyrestaurant.com

Recommended by
Jet Tila

Opening hours	Open 7 days
Credit cards	Accepted
Price range	Affordable
Style	Casual
Cuisine	Modern American
Recommended for	Breakfast

'I love this restaurant. The combination of farm
ingredients, thoughtful cooking and Roxana Jullapat's
pastry make this the perfect place. You can indulge or
keep it light, but you always leave satisfied. I love that
the chefs, Daniel and Roxana, are always procuring
direct from the farmers. They incorporate only the
season's best offerings into their ever-changing menu.
They are always delicately teaching us how to eat with
the seasons.'—Jet Tila

ED'S COFFEE SHOP

460 North Robertson Boulevard
West Hollywood
Los Angeles
California 90048
+1 3106598625

Recommended by
Jon Shook

Opening hours	Open 7 days
Reservation policy	No
Credit cards	Accepted
Price range	Budget
Style	Casual
Cuisine	Diner-Café
Recommended for	Bargain

'Ed's wife still works there, and the prices have barely gone up since the day it opened.'—Jon Shook

FŌNUTS

8104 West 3rd Street
West Hollywood
Los Angeles
California 90048
+1 3235923075
www.fonuts.com

Recommended by
Christina Tosi

Opening hours	Open 7 days
Reservation policy	No
Credit cards	Accepted
Price range	Budget
Style	Casual
Cuisine	Café-Bakery
Recommended for	Wish I'd opened

LUCQUES

8474 Melrose Avenue
West Hollywood
Los Angeles
California 90069
+1 3236556277
www.lucques.com

Recommended by
Ari Taymor

Opening hours	Open 7 days
Credit cards	Accepted
Price range	Affordable
Style	Smart casual
Cuisine	Modern American
Recommended for	Local favourite

'This, for me, is the iconic LA restaurant. Beautiful, thoughtful food, an elegant room, excellent service and classic cooking make it an amazing special occasion restaurant.'—Ari Taymor

Los Angeles restaurateurs Suzanne Goin and Caroline Styne (A.O.C., Tavern) began their immensely successful partnership in 1998 with the opening of West Hollywood's Lucques. The stellar site (it was once Harold Lloyd's carriage house) strikes that balance between dreamy date destination and neighbourhood hangout: it's all in the walled patio, close tables and flattering, 'barely there' lighting. Oh, and the seasonally spot-on Californian cooking of Goin, a chef even Alice Waters describes as 'a standout'. Try *kampachi crudo*, green harissa and pomegranate salsa, and braised rabbit with hand-cut noodles. Fixed-price Sunday Suppers have spawned a cookbook and many loyal fans.

NIGHT + MARKET

9043 Sunset Boulevard
West Hollywood
Los Angeles
California 90069
+1 3102759724
www.nightmarketla.com

Recommended by
Josef Centeno,
Zach Pollack,
Ari Taymor

Opening hours	Closed Monday
Credit cards	Accepted
Price range	Budget
Style	Casual
Cuisine	Modern Thai
Recommended for	Regular neighbourhood

'Tantalizingly delicious, rough around the edges, loud, in-your-face yet impeccably balanced. It's like a Tarantino film in your mouth.'—Zach Pollack

'We make food for drunkards' goes the claim on the Night + Market website. Kris Yenbamroong set up his cult West Hollywood Thai, adjacent to his parents' more mainstream Talésai, in 2010. His express purpose: serving *aharn klam lao* (food to facilitate drinking). With a love of pork to the fore, the menu is about Thai bar snacks that aren't afraid to turn up the heat. Staples such as spiced pork larb with fresh herbs, and home-made fermented pork sausage with raw cabbage, chilli and peanuts (groundnuts), fit the brief. Be prepared for it to get loud at the communal tables.

OSTERIA MOZZA

Recommended by
Christian Page,
Kevin Thornton

6602 Melrose Avenue
West Hollywood
Los Angeles
California 90038
+1 3232970100
www.osteriamozza.com

Opening hours	Open 7 days
Credit cards	Accepted
Price range	Expensive
Style	Smart casual
Cuisine	Italian
Recommended for	High end

'They were able to accommodate us at midnight for eight people for a ten-course menu!'—Kevin Thornton

PETROSSIAN RESTAURANT

Recommended by
Michael Voltaggio

321 North Robertson Boulevard
West Hollywood
Los Angeles
California 90048
+1 3102716300
www.petrossian.com

Opening hours	Open 7 days
Credit cards	Accepted
Price range	Expensive
Style	Smart casual
Cuisine	French
Recommended for	Breakfast

'They put caviar in every dish: caviar scrambled eggs, caviar flatbread, caviar everything!'—Michael Voltaggio

PIZZERIA MOZZA

Recommended by
Suzanne Goin,
Ari Taymor

641 North Highland Avenue
West Hollywood
Los Angeles
California 90036
+1 3232970101
www.pizzeriamozza.com

Opening hours	Open 7 days
Credit cards	Accepted
Price range	Affordable
Style	Casual
Cuisine	Pizza
Recommended for	Regular neighbourhood

'My kids are obsessed with it. The first time they went, the chef, Matt Molina, took them to the kitchen and let

them taste all the *gelati* (ice cream). Now they tell all their friends to go get the *gelato* tasting.'
—Suzanne Goin

PROVIDENCE

Recommended by
Jet Tila,
Ricardo Zarate

5955 Melrose Avenue
West Hollywood
Los Angeles
California 90038
+1 3234604170
www.providencela.com

Opening hours	Open 7 days
Credit cards	Accepted
Price range	Expensive
Style	Smart casual
Cuisine	Seafood
Recommended for	High end

'There are very few high-end places in Los Angeles proper but when it's time to splurge, I like Providence. Chef Michael Cimarusti is one of the best seafood specialists in America and his tasting menu is phenomenal.'—Jet Tila

THE RESTAURANT

Recommended by
Jean-François Piège

Chateau Marmont
8221 Sunset Boulevard
West Hollywood
Los Angeles
California 90046
+1 3238485908
www.chateaumarmont.com

Opening hours	Open 7 days
Credit cards	Accepted
Price range	Expensive
Style	Smart casual
Cuisine	American
Recommended for	Breakfast

There's not an official dress code at Chateau Marmont, but best bring your sunglasses, otherwise you might feel left out. Built on Sunset Boulevard in 1927, modelled loosely on a Loire Valley château, breakfast in its restaurant provides an accessible hit of Hollywood hotel glamour for those who can't afford to cough up for a room — and somewhere to start the day for those who can. The menu takes in the usual American classics: buttermilk pancakes, two types of French toast (one plain brioche, the other almond crunchy) and a soft-boiled egg that they describe as coming with 'accoutrements' rather than toast.

ROBATA JINYA
8050 West 3rd Street
West Hollywood
Los Angeles
California 90048
+1 3236538877
www.jinya-la.com

Opening hours	Open 7 days
Credit cards	Accepted
Price range	Affordable
Style	Casual
Cuisine	Japanese
Recommended for	Bargain

'It's a chain-type ramen place but they also serve fresh vegetables and meats grilled on the robata. There is a variety of food and then the comforting bowl of ramen always ties it all together.'—Michael Voltaggio

SHORT CAKE
The Original Farmers Market
Stall 316 6333 West 3rd Street
West Hollywood
Los Angeles
California 90036
+1 3237617976
www.shortcakela.com

Opening hours	Open 7 days
Reservation policy	No
Credit cards	Accepted
Price range	Budget
Style	Casual
Cuisine	Café-Bakery
Recommended for	Breakfast

SON OF A GUN
8370 West 3rd Street
West Hollywood
Los Angeles
California 90048
+1 3237829033
www.sonofagunrestaurant.com

Opening hours	Open 7 days
Credit cards	Accepted
Price range	Affordable
Style	Casual
Cuisine	Modern American
Recommended for	Worth the travel

'It's worth the trip all the way to Los Angeles just to taste the local, highly modern cuisine here. This is not really the kind of restaurant you'd ever find in France. I have a particular soft spot for the lobster roll, which has the traditional basics, but with a staunchly modernized twist.'—Jean-François Piège

Jon Shook and Vinny Dotolo's fish-focused follow-up to their carnivorous Animal is a masterpiece of *mise-en-scène*. Shiny varnished wainscoting, wall-mounted fish, vintage lifebuoys and bottles of rum evoke an old-fashioned American seafood shack, albeit one where bearded hipsters replace bearded sea dogs. Greasy hands work happily, the length of Son of a Gun's communal table, tucking into 'peel and eat' prawns (shrimp), prawn toast with Sriracha mayo and fried chicken sandwiches. On a more elegant note, there are dainty lobster rolls with celery and lemon aioli and prettily plated scallops with *yuzu kosho* and pickled shitake. All that's missing is a sea view.

SUSHI PARK
8539 Sunset Boulevard
West Hollywood
Los Angeles
California 90069
+1 3106520523

Opening hours	Closed Sunday
Credit cards	Accepted
Price range	Expensive
Style	Casual
Cuisine	Sushi
Recommended for	Worth the travel

'Sushi Park is great. I had such a good time there and it really makes you realize why people talk so highly of West Coast sushi.'—Marcus Samuelsson

TROIS MEC
716 North Highland Avenue
West Hollywood
Los Angeles
California 90038
www.troismec.com

Opening hours............................Closed Saturday and Sunday
Credit cards...Accepted
Price range..Expensive
Style..Casual
Cuisine..Modern American
Recommended for................................Wish I'd opened

'It's a really interesting place. The whole concept is really cool. It incorporates a lot of ideas. The cooks run the food and explain the dishes. The wine is great. It's in a nondescript part of a strip mall – very LA. I had an awesome, unique meal there.'—Steve Samson

THE APPLE PAN
10801 West Pico Boulevard
West Los Angeles
Los Angeles
California 90064
+1 3104753585

Opening hours..Closed Monday
Reservation policy...No
Credit cards..Not accepted
Price range..Budget
Style..Casual
Cuisine..Burgers
Recommended for.....................................Late night

'It's got everything you want late at night: a little greasy, a little healthy and, of course, pie.'—Jon Shook

800 DEGREES
10889 Lindbrook Drive
Westwood
Los Angeles
California 90024
+1 3104431911
www.800degreespizza.com

Opening hours...Open 7 days
Reservation policy...No
Credit cards..Accepted
Price range..Budget
Style..Casual
Cuisine..Pizza
Recommended for.....................................Wish I'd opened

'800 degrees is another fast, casual business that I think is doing an amazing job, and I see a lot of potential for them in the years to come. Their business model of bringing high-quality food to mainstream America is brilliant and, at the same time, employing so many people.'—José Andrés

'The crab is quickly becoming an iconic San Francisco dish.'
COREY LEE P746

'IT HAS DEFINED SAN FRANCISCO FOOD FOR THE LAST TWENTY YEARS.'
DANIEL PATTERSON P749

'I often order a second plate of the same dish here – it's that good.'
CHAD ROBERTSON P747

SAN FRANCISCO

'Tartine is enough of a reason, by itself, to move to San Francisco.'
CHRISTIAN F. PUGLISI P752

'QUIRKY, CHARACTERFUL, NONCONFORMIST AND BRILLIANTLY ROCK 'N' ROLL...'
SANG-HOON DEGEIMBRE P751

'IT'S THE BEST RESTAURANT IN THE UNITED STATES.'
DAVID CHANG P756

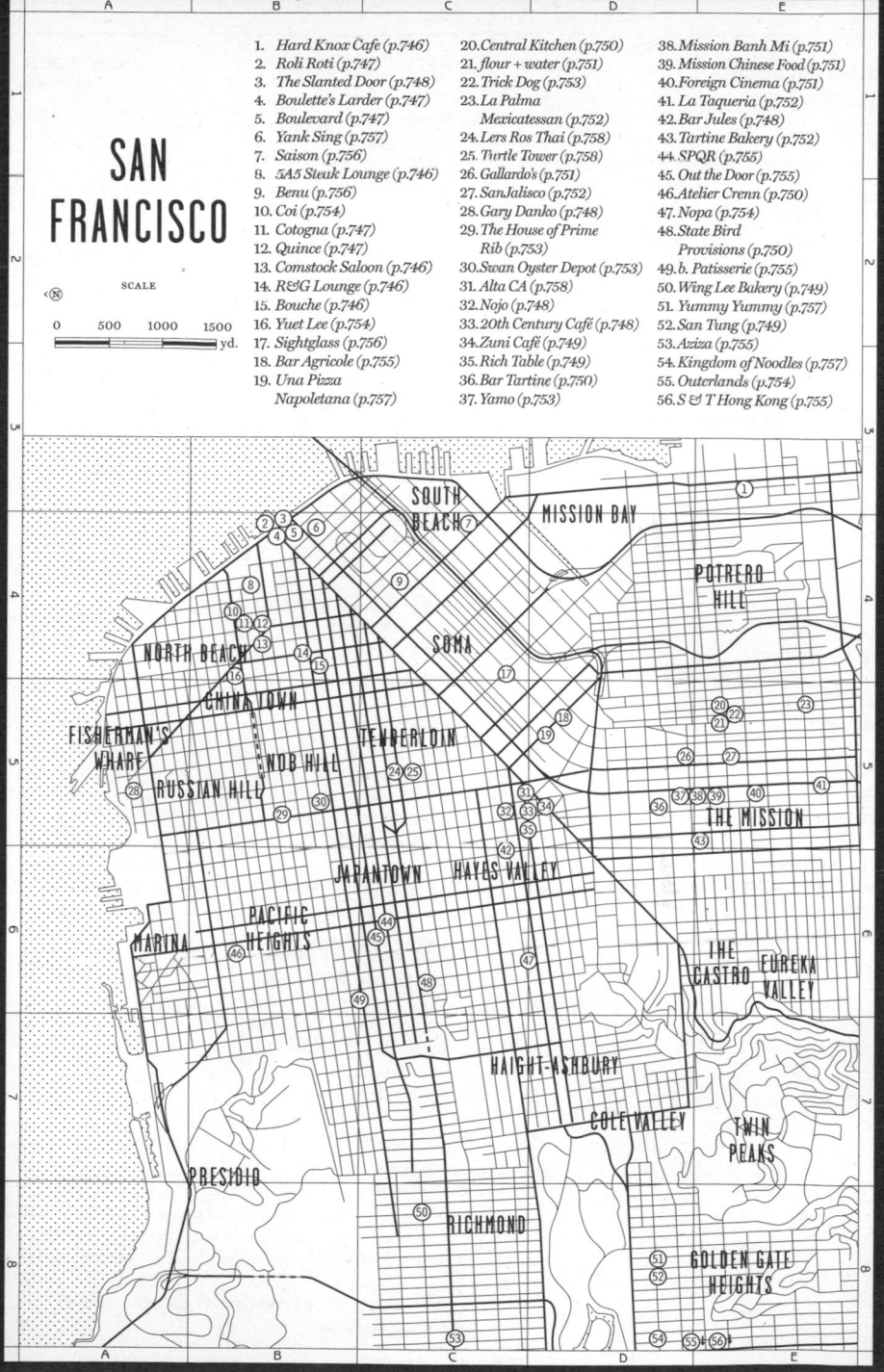

COMSTOCK SALOON
Recommended by
Jason Fox
155 Columbus Avenue
Chinatown
San Francisco
California 94133
+1 4156170071
www.comstocksaloon.com

Opening hours	Open 7 days
Credit cards	Accepted
Price range	Budget
Style	Casual
Cuisine	American
Recommended for	Late night

'Order the pot pie or rabbit, if it's on the menu.'
—James Fox

R&G LOUNGE
Recommended by
Corey Lee, Michael Mina
631 Kearny Street
Chinatown
San Francisco
California 94108
+1 4159827877
www.rnglounge.com

Opening hours	Open 7 days
Credit cards	Accepted
Price range	Affordable
Style	Casual
Cuisine	Cantonese
Recommended for	Regular neighbourhood

'Best Cantonese restaurant in San Francisco. The crab is quickly becoming an iconic San Francisco dish.'
—Corey Lee

HARD KNOX CAFE
Recommended by
Mark Sullivan
2526 3rd Street
Dogpatch
San Francisco
California 94107
+1 4156483770
www.hardknoxcafe.com

Opening hours	Open 7 days
Reservation policy	No
Credit cards	Accepted
Price range	Budget
Style	Casual
Cuisine	Southern American-Creole
Recommended for	Bargain

'It has a great neighbourhood feel, with great beers on tap and Southern fried chicken.'—Mark Sullivan

BOUCHE
Recommended by
Jason Fox
603 Bush Street
Downtown
San Francisco
California 94108
+1 4159560396
www.bouchesf.com

Opening hours	Open 7 days
Credit cards	Accepted
Price range	Affordable
Style	Casual
Cuisine	Modern French
Recommended for	Late night

'I like just about anything at Bouche.'—James Fox

5A5 STEAK LOUNGE
Recommended by
Paul Newman
244 Jackson Street
Embarcadero
San Francisco
California 94111
+1 4159892539
www.5a5stk.com

Opening hours	Open 7 days
Credit cards	Accepted
Price range	Expensive
Style	Smart casual
Cuisine	Steakhouse
Recommended for	Worth the travel

'Very contemporary and fun with fantastic steaks!'
—Paul Newman

BOULETTE'S LARDER

1 Ferry Building Marketplace
Embarcadero
San Francisco
California 94111
+1 4153991155
www.bouletteslarder.com

Opening hours	Closed Monday and Saturday
Credit cards	Accepted
Price range	Affordable
Style	Casual
Cuisine	Modern American
Recommended for	Breakfast

'Amaryll cooks what I want to eat, every day. She takes the finest ingredients and makes incredibly delicious, produce-driven, healthy, decadent food. I often order a second plate of the same dish here. It's that good.'
—Chad Robertson

BOULEVARD

1 Mission Embarcadero
San Francisco California 94105
+1 4155436084
www.boulevardrestaurant.com

Opening hours	Open 7 days
Credit cards	Accepted
Price range	Expensive
Style	Smart casual
Cuisine	Modern American
Recommended for	Local favourite

COTOGNA

490 Pacific Avenue
Embarcadero
San Francisco
California 94133
+1 4157758508
www.cotognasf.com

Opening hours	Open 7 days
Credit cards	Accepted
Price range	Affordable
Style	Casual
Cuisine	Italian
Recommended for	Worth the travel

'When I ate at Cotogna in San Francisco I had a very serious case of restaurant envy!'—Gabrielle Hamilton

QUINCE

470 Pacific Avenue
Embarcadero
San Francisco
California 94133
+1 4157758500
www.quincerestaurant.com

Opening hours	Closed Sunday
Credit cards	Accepted
Price range	Expensive
Style	Formal
Cuisine	Modern European
Recommended for	High end

'The pastas are to die for, and there is an elegant bar where you can order à la carte from the *prix fixe* menu. Plus, I don't like to be pinned down to a reservation, so it's nice knowing you can have a special meal on the fly when dining at the bar at Quince.'—Mark Sullivan

ROLI ROTI

Ferry Plaza Farmers Market
1 Ferry Building
Embarcadero
San Francisco
California 94111
+1 5107800300
www.roliroti.com

Opening hours	Closed Sunday to Wednesday, and Friday
Reservation policy	No
Credit cards	Not accepted
Price range	Budget
Style	Casual
Cuisine	Rotisserie
Recommended for	Bargain

'Thomas's porchetta is always perfectly cooked and who can resist it when he sops up the pork juices with the ciabatta? The best!'—Michael Mina

THE SLANTED DOOR

Recommended by
Miles Kirby

1 Ferry Building
Embarcadero
San Francisco
California 94111
+1 4158618032
www.slanteddoor.com

Opening hours	Open 7 days
Credit cards	Accepted
Price range	Affordable
Style	Smart casual
Cuisine	Vietnamese
Recommended for	Worth the travel

GARY DANKO

Recommended by
Timothy Johnson

800 North Point Street
Fisherman's Wharf
San Francisco
California 94109
+1 4157492060
www.garydanko.com

Opening hours	Open 7 days
Credit cards	Accepted
Price range	Expensive
Style	Formal
Cuisine	Modern American
Recommended for	Wish I'd opened

Gary Danko's eponymous San Francisco restaurant has become a go-to for traditional cooking that makes the most of America's high-quality produce without any fuss. First impressions reveal little to make it stand out from other middle-class destinations of its type: crisp white linen, hushed tones and a laden cheese trolley which is ceremoniously pushed around the room. But that's the point. The reassuringly familiar package leaves you under no illusion of what you're going to get, which is a polished haute cuisine meal, the kind of which you'd happily eat every day if only your arteries could stand it.

20TH CENTURY CAFÉ

Recommended by
Stuart Brioza & Nicole
Krasinski

198 Gough Street
Hayes Valley
San Francisco
California 94102
+1 4156212380
www.20thcenturycafe.com

Opening hours	Closed Monday
Reservation policy	No
Credit cards	Accepted
Price range	Budget
Style	Casual
Cuisine	Café-Bakery
Recommended for	Breakfast

'Eastern European, hand-made, savoury and sweet pastries, and hand-pulled espresso.'
—Stuart Brioza & Nicole Krasinski

BAR JULES

Recommended by
Miles Kirby

609 Hayes Street
Hayes Valley
San Francisco
California 94102
+1 4156215482
www.barjules.com

Opening hours	Closed Monday
Credit cards	Accepted
Price range	Affordable
Style	Casual
Cuisine	Modern American
Recommended for	Worth the travel

NOJO

Recommended by
Jason Fox

231 Franklin Street
Hayes Valley
San Francisco
California 94102
+1 4158964587
www.nojosf.com

Opening hours	Closed Tuesday
Credit cards	Accepted
Price range	Budget
Style	Casual
Cuisine	Japanese
Recommended for	Breakfast

'I go to Nojo for brunch. They offer a unique spin on Japanese *izakaya* plus brunch.'—Jason Fox

RICH TABLE

199 Gough Steet
Hayes Valley
San Francisco
California 94102
+1 4153559085
www.richtablesf.com

Opening hours..Open 7 days
Credit cards...Accepted
Price range..Affordable
Style..Casual
Cuisine..Modern American
Recommended for..Wish I'd opened

'Great concept, atmosphere and sensational food.'
—Martin Bosley

This restaurant's decor is of stripped-back simplicity:
heavy wooden tables and white-painted wooden walls
are drenched in light from the huge windows at the
front of the room. In contrast, the food, as the name
suggests, is generous, decorative and very carefully
sourced. Dishes include New York steak with Sungold
tomatoes and black-eyed beans (peas); and king salmon
with buckwheat, pak choi (bok choy) and ginger. The
pairings are intelligent, the plating sensitive. Chef
patrons Evan and Sarah Rich, who have worked in
some of San Francisco's best restaurants, bring
high-end techniques to the farm-to-table movement,
with brilliant results.

ZUNI CAFÉ

1658 Market Street
Hayes Valley
San Francisco
California 94102
+1 4155522522
www.zunicafe.com

Opening hours..Closed Monday
Credit cards...Accepted
Price range..Affordable
Style..Casual
Cuisine..International
Recommended for....................................Local favourite

'My first great meal in San Francisco was at Zuni in
1990. It has defined San Francisco food for the last
twenty years. The respect for ingredients, the simple
but well-executed preparations, the casual style of
service and open, airy design have been incredibly
influential. And it's still a great restaurant!'
—Daniel Patterson

Judy Rodgers, who passed away in 2013, was
synonymous with Zuni Café, still an icon of San
Francisco dining. Her legacy lives on not only in the
staunchly seasonal daily-changing menu, where her
famous brick oven roast chicken with Tuscan bread
salad, the house-cured anchovies with celery and
Parmesan or the Zuni Caesar salad can still always
be found, but also in the casual yet perfectionist
streak of the whole operation. Opened in 1979 –
Rodgers joined in 1987 – Zuni deals in rustic French
and Italian flavours, married with excellent Bay Area
ingredients. Oysters and artisan cheeses are taken
seriously here.

WING LEE BAKERY

503 Clement Street
Inner Richmond
San Francisco
California 94118
+1 4156689481

Opening hours..Open 7 days
Reservation policy..No
Credit cards..Not accepted
Price range..Budget
Style..Casual
Cuisine..Chinese
Recommended for...Bargain

SAN TUNG

1031 Irving Street
Inner Sunset
San Francisco
California 94122
+1 4152420828
www.santungrestaurant.com

Opening hours......................................Closed Wednesday
Credit cards...Accepted
Price range..Budget
Style..Casual
Cuisine...Chinese-Korean
Recommended for...Bargain

'One of the few Chinese-Korean restaurants I've found
in the US. The best fried chicken.'—Corey Lee

STATE BIRD PROVISIONS

1529 Fillmore Street
Japantown
San Francisco
California 94115
+1 4157951272
www.statebirdsf.com

Opening hours	Open 7 days
Credit cards	Accepted
Price range	Affordable
Style	Casual
Cuisine	American small plates
Recommended for	Wish I'd opened

'State Bird Provisions serves fresh, clever and slightly eccentric food served in a yum cha style. It's amazing food.'—Al Brown

Its name cheekily conjures up California's state bird, the quail, a crunchy deep-fried version of which, served with wafer-thin slices of onion stewed in lemon and rosemary, is a trademark dish. Opened in 2012 by husband and wife, Stuart Brioza and Nicole Krasinski – formerly chefs at the now defunct Rubicon – the open kitchen of this bijou, darkly lit and basically decorated forty-five seater (exposed concrete, pinboard (tackboard) covered walls, simple wooden chairs and tables) overlooks Fillmore from a large plate-glass window. The shtick? A reasonably priced, short selection of creative dishes punted around the room by waiters pushing dim sum-style trolleys.

ATELIER CRENN

3127 Fillmore Street
Marina
San Francisco
California 94123
+1 4154400460
www.ateliercrenn.com

Opening hours	Closed Monday and Sunday
Credit cards	Accepted
Price range	Expensive
Style	Smart casual
Cuisine	French
Recommended for	High end

BAR TARTINE

561 Valencia Street
Mission
San Francisco
California 94110
+1 4154871600
www.bartartine.com

Opening hours	Open 7 days
Credit cards	Accepted
Price range	Affordable
Style	Casual
Cuisine	Modern International
Recommended for	Regular neighbourhood

'They make interesting products in house, such as their own vinegars. It is refreshing to see a different style of food from a Californian perspective. It is like Eastern European meets Japanese meets Northern Californian.' —Thomas McNaughton

CENTRAL KITCHEN

3000 20th Street
Mission
San Francisco
California 94110
+1 4158267004
www.centralkitchensf.com

Opening hours	Open 7 days
Credit cards	Accepted
Price range	Affordable
Style	Smart casual
Cuisine	Modern American
Recommended for	Worth the travel

'Clearly dedicated to using only quality ingredients, which are sustainable and locally sourced. The menu defines a style of cuisine.'—Martin Bosley

FLOUR + WATER

Recommended by
Jason Fox,
Hadleigh Troy

2401 Harrison Street
Mission
San Francisco
California 94110
+1 4158267000
www.flourandwater.com

Opening hours	Open 7 days
Credit cards	Accepted
Price range	Affordable
Style	Casual
Cuisine	Modern Italian
Recommended for	Wish I'd opened

'They serve the sort of food I love to cook, the way
I would like to serve it!'—Hadleigh Troy

FOREIGN CINEMA

Recommended by
Chad Robertson,
Craig Stoll

2534 Mission Street
Mission
San Francisco
California 94110
+1 4156487600
www.foreigncinema.com

Opening hours	Open 7 days
Credit cards	Accepted
Price range	Affordable
Style	Casual
Cuisine	Modern American
Recommended for	Local favourite

GALLARDO'S

Recommended by
Chad Robertson

3248 18th Street
Mission
San Francisco
California 94110
+1 4154369387

Opening hours	Open 7 days
Credit cards	Not accepted
Price range	Budget
Style	Casual
Cuisine	Mexican
Recommended for	Bargain

'I go to Gallardo's for *birria* (lamb stew with chickpeas)
and *pozole* (pork and hominy stew) with fresh, house-
made tortillas on the weekends. It is super busy all the
time and everything is made in small batches, fresh
every day.'—Chad Robertson

MISSION BANH MI

Recommended by
Jason Fox

Duc Loi Market
2200 Mission Street
Mission
San Francisco
California 94110
+1 4155511773
www.missionbanhmi.com

Opening hours	Open 7 days
Reservation policy	No
Credit cards	Accepted
Price range	Budget
Style	Casual
Cuisine	Vietnamese
Recommended for	Bargain

MISSION CHINESE FOOD

Recommended by
Sang Hoon Degeimbre

2234 Mission Street
Mission
San Francisco
California 94110
+1 4158632800
www.missionchinesefood.com

Opening hours	Closed Wednesday
Reservation policy	No
Credit cards	Accepted
Price range	Budget
Style	Casual
Cuisine	Chinese
Recommended for	Wish I'd opened

'Quirky, characterful, nonconformist and brilliantly rock
'n' roll. Totally uninhibited, enjoyable cuisine designed
for everyone.'—Sang-Hoon Degeimbre

LA PALMA MEXICATESSAN

2884 24th Street
Mission
San Francisco
California 94110
+1 4156471500
www.lapalmasf.com

Opening hours..Open 7 days
Reservation policy..No
Credit cards..Accepted
Price range..Budget
Style..Casual
Cuisine..Mexican
Recommended for...Bargain

'Love the *huarache* (flatbread topped with meat, salsa, cheese) and the Mexican market.'—Stuart Brioza & Nicole Krasinski

Sixty years old, this family-run take away (take out) and 'Mexicatessen' (Mexican delicatessen) has become an institution. Come lunchtime the queue (waiting line) snakes far from the door here in San Francisco's Mission District. They come for hand-made tortillas and sopes, and fried plantain chips. Powerful, almost industrial, fans do their best to cool the heat emanating from the substantial plancha – source of the action. The few tables outside, nudging a wall with a technicolour mural, are highly sought after. Try chicken pupusa (a thick handmade, griddled corn flatbread) or chile verde taco with re-fried beans and well- spiced pork. The only problem with La Palma is that they close early (6.00 p.m.).

SANJALISCO

901 South Van Ness Avenue
Mission
San Francisco
California 94110
+1 4156488383
www.sanjalisco.com

Opening hours..Open 7 days
Reservation policy..No
Credit cards..Accepted
Price range..Budget
Style..Casual
Cuisine..Mexican
Recommended for......................................Breakfast

'The *chorizo con huevos* is like a light pillowy cloud, an almost soufflé-like texture. It is the perfect combination with a cold Modelo and the stone-ground guacamole.' —Thomas McNaughton

LA TAQUERIA

2889 Mission Street
Mission
San Francisco
California 94110
+1 4152857117

Opening hours..Open 7 days
Reservation policy..No
Credit cards..Not accepted
Price range..Budget
Style..Casual
Cuisine..Mexican
Recommended for...Bargain

'Any day of the week for the *cabeza* (beef head) tacos with salsa fresca, crema, and lots of fresh coriander (cilantro).'—Chad Robertson

TARTINE BAKERY

600 Guerrero Street
Mission
San Francisco
California 94110
+1 4154872600
www.tartinebakery.com

Opening hours..Open 7 days
Reservation policy..No
Credit cards..Accepted
Price range..Budget
Style..Casual
Cuisine..Café-Bakery
Recommended for......................................Breakfast

'Undoubtedly the best bread I have had, and their croissant with ham and cheese is the best way a human being can start the day... As if you needed more, Tartine is enough of a reason, by itself, to move to San Francisco.'—Christian F. Puglisi

TRICK DOG

Recommended by
Mark Sullivan

3010 20th Street
Mission
San Francisco
California 94114
+1 4154712999
www.trickdogbar.com

Opening hours	Open 7 days
Reservation policy	No
Credit cards	Accepted
Price range	Budget
Style	Casual
Cuisine	Bar Snacks
Recommended for	Late night

'They craft their drinks like scientists in a lab, are always spot on, and offer great bar snacks.'
—Mark Sullivan

YAMO

Recommended by
Jason Fox

3406 18th Street
Mission
San Francisco
California 94110
+1 4155538911

Opening hours	Closed Sunday
Reservation policy	No
Credit cards	Not accepted
Price range	Budget
Style	Casual
Cuisine	Burmese
Recommended for	Bargain

THE HOUSE OF PRIME RIB

Recommended by
Evan Rich

1906 Van Ness Avenue
Nob Hill
San Francisco
California 94109
+1 4158854605
www.houseofprimerib.net

Opening hours	Open 7 days
Credit cards	Accepted
Price range	Affordable
Style	Smart casual
Cuisine	Steakhouse
Recommended for	Local favourite

'It is old school and straight to the point and they cook a great prime rib.'—Evan Rich

SWAN OYSTER DEPOT

Recommended by
Chris Cosentino, Rodney
Dunn, Stuart Brioza & Nicole
Krasinski, Steven Satterfield,
Sarah Pilner & Jasper
Shen, Craig Stoll

1517 Polk Street
Nob Hill
San Francisco
California 94109
+1 4156732757

Opening hours	Closed Sunday
Reservation policy	No
Credit cards	Not accepted
Price range	Affordable
Style	Casual
Cuisine	Seafood
Recommended for	Wish I'd opened

'The restaurant is as straightforward as can be. It's been open since 1912. It's a small, intimate spot, with classic counter seating and a family staff that is only concerned about keeping the quality at its best. You'll find great seafood treated so simply. It's a true city gem with great goodwill. They serve classic San Francisco dishes, local oysters, sea urchin, Dungeness crab, great chowder... the list just goes on.'—Chris Cosentino

Not many restaurants get to celebrate a century in business. The Depot didn't take credit cards or reservations when they opened in 1912 – and they don't now. Open from breakfast through to late afternoon, the lunchtime queue (waiting line) for the twenty stools at the marble counter moves quickly. Many regulars just pop in for a plate of oysters, a cup of chowder or the Swan Special – a prawn (shrimp) cocktail and a beer – and are gone. Beyond that it's simply prepared seafood, from dressed crab to various salads and cocktails. There's no wine list but they have Anchor Steam Beer, a fine foil for anything on the menu.

COI

373 Broadway Street
North Beach
San Francisco
California 94133
+1 4153939000
www.coirestaurant.com

Opening hours..............................Closed Monday and Sunday
Credit cards..Accepted
Price range...Expensive
Style...Smart casual
Cuisine...Modern American
Recommended for..Worth the travel

'Daniel Patterson gets better and better and his food tells a real story.'—David Kinch

Daniel Patterson's imaginative Californian cuisine has secured nods from the Michelin men and a place in the World's 50 Best Restaurants list. With its decorous exterior and bold positioning in North Beach, Coi *is* San Francisco. Its eleven-course ever-changing tasting menu combines modern techniques with local wild and foraged ingredients and meticulous presentation to create plates that surprise and always encourage discussion. The restaurant's unusual name (pronounced 'kwa') is an archaic French word meaning 'tranquil': an apt reflection of Patterson and his unique culinary vision.

YUET LEE

1300 Stockton Street
North Beach
San Francisco
California 94133
+1 4159826020

Opening hours...Closed Tuesday
Reservation policy..No
Credit cards..Accepted
Price range...Budget
Style..Casual
Cuisine..Chinese
Recommended for...Late night

Yuet Lee, in the North Beach area of San Francisco, is often described as one of the city's 'best-kept secrets' but it's actually a no-frills food joint that has been blogged about so frequently that it's actually better known than most other places. Yet it's easy to believe that this Chinatown favourite remains undiscovered, such is the modest interior and no-reservations policy that doesn't go down well with

tourists. But not so for the late-night revellers who can regularly be seen winding down in the small hours to a steaming bowl of frog rice pudding, braised duck feet or the legendary salt and pepper squid.

NOPA

560 Divisadero Street
North Panhandle
San Francisco
California 94117
+1 4158648643
www.nopasf.com

Opening hours..Open 7 days
Credit cards..Accepted
Price range...Affordable
Style..Casual
Cuisine...Modern American
Recommended for...Late night

'Great food, warm service and terrific drinks and wine.'—Daniel Patterson

This bustling neighbourhood joint north of the Panhandle – hence the name – is popular with restaurant workers after a little post-shift sustenance. Located in an old bank, well served by a series of 3.6-m (12-foot) tall windows, it's an evening-only operation, except on weekends when it opens for brunch. The menu, which focuses on delivering comfort from seasonal farm-sourced organic produce and a wood-fired grill, is what chef Laurence Jossel bills as 'urban rustic'. The balcony level is best for watching the scene unfold in the dining room below; the large communal table or the bar for being a part of it.

OUTERLANDS

4001 Judah Street
Outer Sunset
San Francisco
California 94122
+1 4156616140
www.outerlandssf.com

Opening hours...Closed Monday
Credit cards..Accepted
Price range...Affordable
Style..Casual
Cuisine...Modern American
Recommended for....................................Regular neighbourhood

'The chef and owners take a lot of pride in what they do, and the food is always fresh and new.'—Evan Rich

S & T HONG KONG

Recommended by
Jason Fox

2578 Noriega Street
Outer Sunset
San Francisco
California 94122
+1 4156658338

Opening hours	Open 7 days
Credit cards	Accepted
Price range	Budget
Style	Casual
Cuisine	Chinese
Recommended for	Bargain

B. PATISSERIE

Recommended by
Michael Tusk

2821 California Street
Pacific Heights
San Francisco
California 94115
+1 4154401700
www.bpatisserie.com

Opening hours	Closed Monday
Reservation policy	No
Credit cards	Accepted
Price range	Affordable
Style	Casual
Cuisine	Café-Patisserie
Recommended for	Breakfast

'I like a good pastry and a cup of coffee. The kouign
amann here is a favourite of mine.' —Michael Tusk

OUT THE DOOR

Recommended by
Matthew Accarrino

2232 Bush Street
Pacific Heights
San Francisco
California 94115
+1 4159239575
www.outthedoors.com

Opening hours	Open 7 days
Credit cards	Accepted
Price range	Affordable
Style	Casual
Cuisine	Vietnamese
Recommended for	Regular neighbourhood

'Chef Charles Phan uses local ingredients to create a
Vietnamese-inspired menu. It's a great lunch spot and
occasional breakfast location – they have great seasonal omelettes. The menu is inexpensive, varied and
changes frequently.' —Matthew Accarrino

SPQR

Recommended by
Benjamin Bayly, Jason Fox,
Andrew Zimmerman

1911 Fillmore Street
Pacific Heights
San Francisco
California 94115
+1 4157717779
www.spqrsf.com

Opening hours	Open 7 days
Credit cards	Accepted
Price range	Affordable
Style	Casual
Cuisine	Modern Italian
Recommended for	Worth the travel

'The most inspiring Italian restaurant I have ever eaten
at. I stayed for the day, then ate a meal late at night.
I can't believe how small the kitchen is, the standard of
food and the number of people they serve every night.'
—Benjamin Bayly

AZIZA

Recommended by
Jason Fox

5800 Geary Boulevard
Richmond
San Francisco
California 94121
+1 4157522222
www.aziza-sf.com

Opening hours	Closed Tuesday
Credit cards	Accepted
Price range	Affordable
Style	Casual
Cuisine	Moroccan
Recommended for	Local favourite

BAR AGRICOLE

Recommended by
Jason Fox,
Russell Moore

355 11th Street
SoMa
San Francisco
California 94103
+1 4153559400
www.baragricole.com

Opening hours	Closed Monday
Credit cards	Accepted
Price range	Affordable
Style	Casual
Cuisine	Modern American
Recommended for	Late night

'Late at night you don't want to take chances. You want
a perfect cocktail and a perfect terrine.'
—Russell Moore

BENU

22 Hawthorne Street
SoMa
San Francisco
California 94105
+1 4156854860
www.benusf.com

Opening hours	Closed Monday and Sunday
Credit cards	Accepted
Price range	Expensive
Style	Smart casual
Cuisine	Asian-American
Recommended for	Worth the travel

'Corey Lee's team of chefs, pastry chefs, and butchers are unmatched. Each time I visit Benu, I come away in awe of the food they're making. It's the best restaurant in the United States.'—David Chang

A bold monument to modernism, Benu was high-achiever Corey Lee's first restaurant after leaving The French Laundry fold. Complex and thought-provoking, Lee's dishes make light work of classic techniques, injecting Asian flavours into immaculate dishes. (Lee even designs the plates and bowls himself.) Gels and foams feature widely on the ambitious tasting menu, which changes daily but always begins with a thousand-year-old quail egg. Benu treads a fine line between high-concept cooking and customer satisfaction, yet Lee's contemporaries are resoundingly gushing in their praise. Needless to say, innovation and exceptional craftsmanship comes at a price – you've been warned.

SAISON

178 Townsend Street
SoMa
San Francisco
California 94107
+1 4158287990
www.saisonsf.com

Opening hours	Closed Monday and Sunday
Credit cards	Accepted
Price range	Expensive
Style	Smart casual
Cuisine	Modern American
Recommended for	High end

'Josh Skenes manages to bring an extreme focus of flavours to every course of his twenty- to thirty-plus-course tasting menus. Mostly vegetable and seafood based, simple and seasonal precision – in the style of Japanese *kaiseki*, but very much northern California. Excellent cocktails and epic wines too.' —Chad Robertson

Chef Joshua Skenes's high-minded restaurant Saison started life as a Mission District pop-up. It's changed somewhat since its Sundays-only 2009 incarnation. Saison now has a full-time forager, two Michelin stars, a reputation for selling the city's most expensive *prix fixe*, and an inspired new home in SoMA that cleverly (and beautifully) blends kitchen with dining room. Skenes chases the city's – nay, the world's – best ingredients like a chef possessed and targets their 'deepest point of flavour', be it abalone roasted over embers with sea lettuce, seawater-cured uni roe with caviar, sea robin from Hokkaido or sixty-day dry-aged beef. Expect great things from Skenes.

SIGHTGLASS

270 7th Street
SoMa
San Francisco
California 94103
+1 4158611313
www.sightglasscoffee.com

Opening hours	Open 7 days
Reservation policy	No
Credit cards	Accepted
Price range	Affordable
Style	Casual
Cuisine	Coffee Shop
Recommended for	Breakfast

UNA PIZZA NAPOLETANA

Recommended by
Matt Dillon

210 11th Street
SoMa
San Francisco
California 94103
+1 4158613444
www.unapizza.com

Opening hours	Closed Sunday to Tuesday
Reservation policy	No
Credit cards	Accepted
Price range	Affordable
Style	Casual
Cuisine	Pizza
Recommended for	Worth the travel

'Not just pizza… Anthony Mangieri is a highly knowledgeable and skilled baker. The dough. The dough. The dough. Unapologetically, the dough. So much life. So perfectly his. You feel like you are in Anthony's veins. On a field trip through his soul. I kept tearing into his dough to see into his mind. The aroma was mesmerizing.'—Matt Dillon

YANK SING

Recommended by
Chris Cosentino,
Michael Tusk

Rincon Center
101 Spear Street
SoMa
San Francisco
California 94105
+1 4157811111
www.yanksing.com

Opening hours	Open 7 days
Credit cards	Accepted
Price range	Affordable
Style	Casual
Cuisine	Chinese
Recommended for	Breakfast

'I don't normally go out for breakfast, but I really enjoy going to get dim sum on Sundays. Yank Sing is a perfect spot with so many great dishes to choose from. It's hard to go wrong. From braised chicken feet to barbeque pork buns and both baked and steamed, jellyfish salad – there isn't a dish to miss on the dim sum cart.'—Chris Cosentino

KINGDOM OF NOODLES

Recommended by
Chris Cosentino

1639 Irving Street
Sunset District
San Francisco
California 94122
+1 4155668318

Opening hours	Closed Wednesday
Reservation policy	No
Credit cards	Accepted
Price range	Budget
Style	Casual
Cuisine	Chinese
Recommended for	Bargain

'The hand-pulled noodles are the best, served in a delicate broth with wonton dumplings and pak choi (bok choy). It's the perfect quick lunch or dinner on a budget. I always like to get farmer's cucumbers and a few orders of the chive pancakes.'—Chris Cosentino

YUMMY YUMMY

Recommended by
Chris Cosentino

1015 Irving Street
Sunset District
San Francisco
California 94122
+1 4155664722

Opening hours	Closed Tuesday
Credit cards	Accepted
Price range	Budget
Style	Casual
Cuisine	Vietnamese
Recommended for	Regular neighbourhood

'When I first saw the name, I was very sceptical, but I was wrong. The food is so fresh, with clean flavours. The pho broth has the perfect balance of spice, not so much that it overpowers the meat. I always get the #1. It's close to home so I eat there once a week with my family. There is always something new that we find on the menu or the owner Nelson wants us to try. The food is very convivial, which is great for sharing new things, especially with my son.'—Chris Cosentino

ALTA CA

Recommended by
Evan Rich,
Chad Robertson

1420 Market Street
Tenderloin
San Francisco
California 94102
+1 4155902585
www.altaca.co

Opening hours	Open 7 days
Credit cards	Accepted
Price range	Affordable
Style	Casual
Cuisine	Modern American
Recommended for	Late night

'My friend Daniel Patterson's first casual restaurant in San Francisco proper, with Chef Yoni Levy cooking the food. Alta serves a modern, soulful style of California cuisine complemented by an ambitious cocktail menu, and lots of small house-produced wines.'
—Chad Robertson

LERS ROS THAI

Recommended by
Hiro Sone

730 Larkin Street
Tenderloin
San Francisco
California 94109
+1 4159316917
www.lersros.com

Opening hours	Open 7 days
Credit cards	Accepted
Price range	Budget
Style	Casual
Cuisine	Thai
Recommended for	Late night

'The very tasty fried garlic pork spare ribs are a must. *Larb phed yang* (duck salad) is my favourite. The baby eel with fresh green peppercorn is spice heaven. Friendly staff and open till midnight.'—Hiro Sone

Originally intended as a late-night haunt for local Thai residents working in the industry, Lers Ros (pronounced 'lerhh rohh') transcends its location in Tenderloin, San Francisco's most rough-and-ready neighbourhood. Set up in 2008 by chef-owner Tom Silargorn – who is usually seen dexterously manning the wok – it's all about the balance of flavours, with dishes like pad Thai and roast duck larb mercifully avoiding concessions to the saccharine Western palate. Silargorn's success has meant recent expansion into the hip areas of Hayes Valley and Mission – both nearby, but with entirely different demographics.

TURTLE TOWER

Recommended by
Thomas McNaughton,
Cal Peternell

645 Larkin Street
Tenderloin
San Francisco
California 94109
+1 4154093333
www.turtletowersf.com

Opening hours	Closed Thursday
Reservation policy	No
Credit cards	Not accepted
Price range	Budget
Style	Casual
Cuisine	Vietnamese
Recommended for	Bargain

'One-stop shop. Noodle goodness in every bite.'
—Thomas McNaughton

'IT'S A CHARLESTON ICON THAT IMPROVES WITH AGE.'

MIKE LATA P801

'This restaurant makes me happier than any other restaurant in the world.'

SEAN BROCK P803

USA EAST

'CLASSIC KANSAS CITY BARBEQUE.'

PATRICK RYAN P783

'The perfect place to celebrate or to enjoy being in Beantown.'

TIM CUSHMAN P776

'They have biscuits that are off-the-charts good.'

TORY MILLER P811

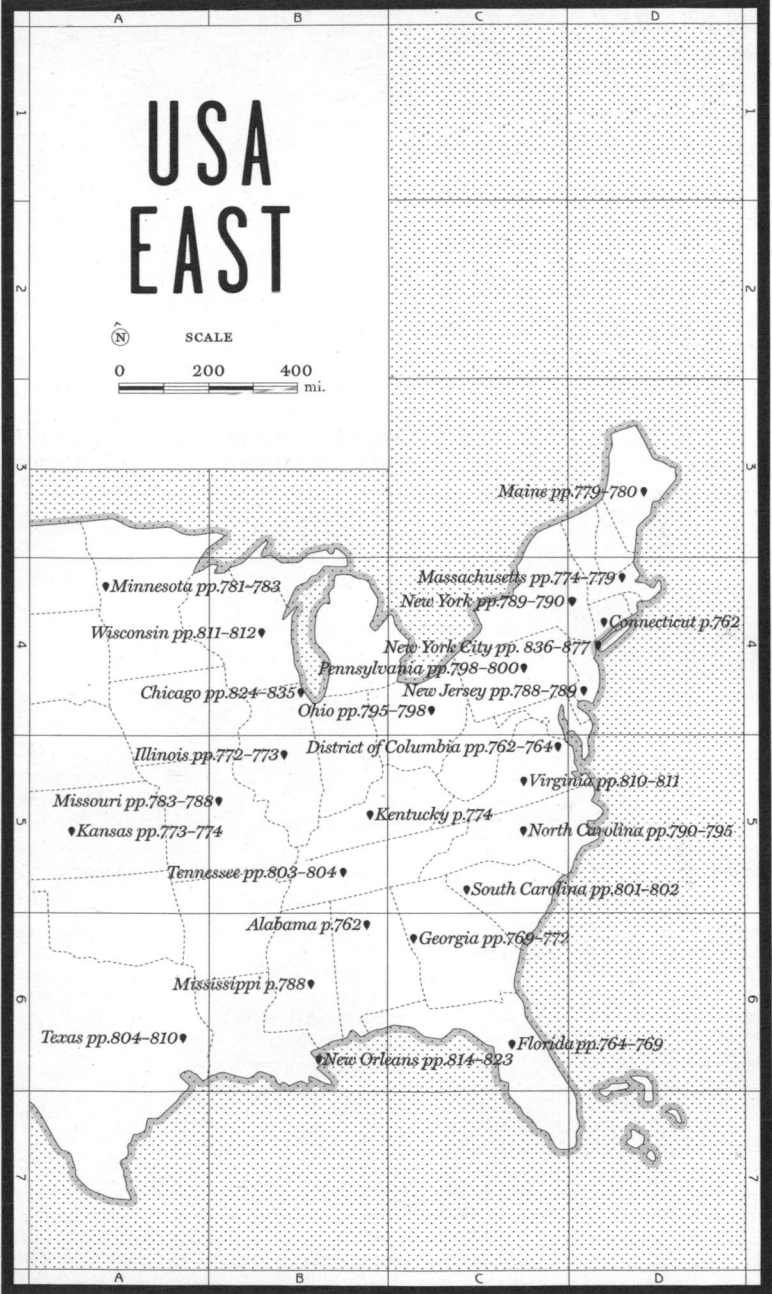

USA EAST

SCALE

0   200   400
mi.

Maine pp.779–780 ♦

Minnesota pp.781–783 ♦

Massachusetts pp.774–779 ♦
New York pp.789–790 ♦

Wisconsin pp.811–812 ♦

Connecticut p.762 ♦

New York City pp. 836–877 ♦
Pennsylvania pp.798–800 ♦

Chicago pp.824–835 ♦

New Jersey pp.788–789 ♦

Ohio pp.795–798 ♦

Illinois pp.772–773 ♦

District of Columbia pp.762–764 ♦

Virginia pp.810–811 ♦

Missouri pp.783–788 ♦

Kansas pp.773–774 ♦

Kentucky p.774 ♦

North Carolina pp.790–795 ♦

Tennessee pp.803–804 ♦

South Carolina pp.801–802 ♦

Alabama p.762 ♦

Georgia pp.769–772 ♦

Mississippi p.788 ♦

Texas pp.804–810 ♦

Florida pp.764–769 ♦

New Orleans pp.814–823 ♦

HIGHLANDS BAR AND GRILL

2011 11th Avenue South
Birmingham
Alabama 35205
+1 2059391400
www.highlandsbarandgrill.com

Opening hours................................Closed Monday and Sunday
Credit cards...Accepted
Price range..Affordable
Style..Formal
Cuisine...Southern American
Recommended for.................................Local favourite

'Frank has developed an institution for what it means
to dine in the South and helped lift pimento cheese to
a regional icon.'—Linton Hopkins

GLENVILLE PIZZA

243 Glenville Road
Greenwich
Connecticut 06831
+1 2035321691

Opening hours...Open 7 days
Reservation policy...No
Credit cards..Not accepted
Price range...Budget
Style...Casual
Cuisine..Pizza
Recommended for.................................Local favourite

'The owner, Vinny, has been making a very thin-crusted
pie for forty years. The best in town!'
—Rebecca Kirhoffer

LE PAIN QUOTIDIEN

382 Greenwich Avenue
Greenwich
Connecticut 06830
+1 2034047533
www.lepainquotidien.com

Opening hours...Open 7 days
Reservation policy...No
Credit cards...Accepted
Price range...Budget
Style...Casual
Cuisine...Café-Bakery
Recommended for...Bargain

'Great bread and I love the dipping eggs!'
—Rebecca Kirhoffer

LAKESIDE DINER

1050 Long Ridge Road
Stamford
Connecticut 06903
+1 2033222252

Opening hours...Open 7 days
Reservation policy...No
Credit cards..Not accepted
Price range...Budget
Style...Casual
Cuisine..Diner
Recommended for...Breakfast

They have the best home-made doughnuts. Be sure to
go early as they run out and they often limit how many
you can buy – they are that good! I love that it's the
same now as it was twenty-five years ago. Good food,
great setting and an amazing view.'—Rebecca Kirhoffer

COMMUNITY TABLE

223 Litchfield Turnpike
Washington
Connecticut 06777
+1 8608689354
www.communitytablect.com

Opening hours........................Closed Tuesday and Wednesday
Credit cards...Accepted
Price range..Affordable
Style..Smart casual
Cuisine...Modern American
Recommended for.............................Wish I'd opened

'The space is just so smart.'—Bjorn Somlo

2 AMYS

3715 Macomb Street Northwest
Washington
District of Columbia 20016
+1 2028855700
www.2amyspizza.com

Opening hours...Open 7 days
Reservation policy...No
Credit cards...Accepted
Price range...Budget
Style...Casual
Cuisine..Pizza
Recommended for...........................Regular neighbourhood

'This is the best pizza in town! My family and I have
been going here for years. My daughters love it and

sometimes I even get a bit jealous because they get more excited about going to 2 Amys than going to my own restaurants.'—José Andrés

CENTRAL MICHEL RICHARD

Recommended by
Cathal Armstrong

1001 Pennsylvania Avenue Northwest
Washington
District of Columbia 20004
+1 2026260015
www.centralmichelrichard.com

Opening hours	Closed Sunday
Credit cards	Accepted
Price range	Affordable
Style	Smart casual
Cuisine	International
Recommended for	Wish I'd opened

'Classic French bistro.'—Cathal Armstrong

DAIKAYA

Recommended by
José Andrés

705 6th Street Northwest
Washington
District of Columbia 20001
+1 2025891600
www.daikaya.com

Opening hours	Open 7 days
Credit cards	Accepted
Price range	Affordable
Style	Casual
Cuisine	Japanese
Recommended for	Regular neighbourhood

'It is amazing how a bowl of ramen can be so simple and complex at the same time. In D.C., I love what Katsuya Fukushima and his business partner Daisuke Utagawa are doing. On the ground level there's the ramen shop, which is fun and casual, and on the upper level there's the *izakaya* bar, serving small Japanese plates.'—José Andrés

JOHNNY'S HALF SHELL

Recommended by
Patrick O'Connell

400 North Capitol Street Northwest
Washington
District of Columbia 20001
+1 2027370400
www.johnnyshalfshell.net

Opening hours	Closed Sunday
Credit cards	Accepted
Price range	Affordable
Style	Smart casual
Cuisine	Seafood
Recommended for	Local favourite

LITTLE SEROW

Recommended by
Massimo Bottura

1511 17th Street Northwest
Washington
District of Columbia 20036
www.littleserow.com

Opening hours	Closed Monday and Sunday
Reservation policy	No
Credit cards	Accepted
Price range	Affordable
Style	Casual
Cuisine	Northern Thai
Recommended for	Bargain

'Frankly I love Asian food when it is cooked simply. Above all, it's really surprising to find such an authentic modern Asian place in D.C.'—Massimo Bottura

MAKOTO

Recommended by
José Andrés

4822 MacArthur Boulevard Northwest
Washington
District of Columbia 20007
+1 2022986866
www.makotorestaurantdc.com

Opening hours	Open 7 days
Credit cards	Accepted
Price range	Expensive
Style	Smart casual
Cuisine	Japanese
Recommended for	Regular neighbourhood

'It is one of the best sushi restaurants in town.'
—José Andrés

MINIBAR

Recommended by
Quique Dacosta

855 East Street Northwest
Washington
District of Columbia 20004
+1 2023930812
www.minibarbyjoseandres.com

Opening hours................................Closed Monday and Sunday
Credit cards..Accepted
Price range...Expensive
Style..Smart casual
Cuisine...Modern American
Recommended for...Wish I'd opened

'José Andrés has been able to build a gastronomic empire through effort, knowledge and perseverance, from Jaleo to Minibar in the United States, where he has flown the flag for Spanish cooking. I like them for this reason but also because of his philanthropic sensibilities.'—Quique Dacosta

RESTAURANT NORA

Recommended by
José Andrés

2132 Florida Avenue Northwest
Washington
District of Columbia 20008
+1 2024625143
www.noras.com

Opening hours..Closed Sunday
Credit cards..Accepted
Price range...Expensive
Style..Smart casual
Cuisine...Modern American
Recommended for..Local favourite

'Nora Pouillon is the queen of farm to table. Restaurant Nora has been in business for thirty years now and it was the first restaurant in the United States to be certified as organic at a time when a lot of people were not thinking about organic. What Nora created with her restaurant was amazing and she paved the way for a lot of chefs, as well as the farm-to-table movement.'—José Andrés

TOKI UNDERGROUND

Recommended by
José Andrés

1234 H Street Northeast
Washington
District of Columbia 20002
+1 2023883086
www.tokiunderground.com

Opening hours..Closed Sunday
Reservation policy..No
Credit cards..Accepted
Price range...Budget
Style...Casual
Cuisine...Taiwanese
Recommended for...............................Regular neighbourhood

'A great place for ramen.'—José Andrés

SUSHI ROCK CAFÉ

Recommended by
Patrick O'Connell

1515 East Las Olas Boulevard
Fort Lauderdale
Florida 33301
+1 9544625541

Opening hours...Open 7 days
Reservation policy..No
Credit cards..Accepted
Price range...Affordable
Style...Casual
Cuisine...Japanese
Recommended for..Bargain

BLACKBRICK CHINESE

Recommended by
Giorgio Rapicavoli

3451 Northeast 1st Avenue
Miami
Florida 33137
+1 3055738886
www.midtownchinese.com

Opening hours...Open 7 days
Reservation policy..No
Credit cards..Accepted
Price range...Affordable
Style...Casual
Cuisine...Chinese
Recommended for...Wish I'd opened

'I absolutely love what Richard has done at Blackbrick. He's making delicious food that he loves and is proud of. He is the restaurant's general contractor, painter, dishwasher, cook... He put his heart and soul into the place. I truly respect him for it.'—Giorgio Rapicavoli

THE CYPRESS ROOM

3620 Northeast 2nd Avenue
Miami
Florida 33137
+1 3055205197
www.thecypressroom.com

Opening hours	Closed Sunday
Credit cards	Accepted
Price range	Expensive
Style	Smart casual
Cuisine	Modern American
Recommended for	Wish I'd opened

'1920s fine dining with a warm log-cabin feel and delicate touches.'—Kevin Sbraga

DB BISTRO MODERNE

JW Marriot Marquis
255 Biscayne Boulevard Way
Miami
Florida 33131
+1 3054218800
www.dbbistro.com/miami

Opening hours	Closed Sunday
Credit cards	Accepted
Price range	Affordable
Style	Smart casual
Cuisine	French Bistro
Recommended for	High end

'It's perfection.'—José Mendin

ENRIQUETA'S SANDWICH SHOP

186 Northeast 29th Street
Miami
Florida 33137
+1 3055734681

Opening hours	Closed Sunday
Reservation policy	No
Credit cards	Accepted
Price range	Budget
Style	Casual
Cuisine	Cuban
Recommended for	Breakfast

'Even though it's a Cuban café, it reminds me of the cafés back home in Puerto Rico. I love the egg and bacon sandwich.'—José Mendin

HARRY'S PIZZERIA

3918 North Miami Avenue
Miami
Florida 33127
+1 7862754963
www.harryspizzeria.com

Opening hours	Open 7 days
Reservation policy	No
Credit cards	Accepted
Price range	Budget
Style	Casual
Cuisine	Pizza
Recommended for	Regular neighbourhood

'It has a small, seasonal menu with a special pie every day. I love their salads and brunch and it's Michael Schwartz, so of course, it's delicious!'—José Mendin

JAPANESE MARKET SUSHI DELI

1412 79th Street Causeway
Miami
Florida 33141
+1 3058610143

Opening hours	Closed Monday and Tuesday
Reservation policy	No
Credit cards	Accepted but not AMEX
Price range	Budget
Style	Casual
Cuisine	Japanese
Recommended for	Wish I'd opened

'They're just doing what they want to do with no bells and whistles. Just fresh fish and simple, traditional food.'—Michael Schwartz

MAKOTO

Bal Harbour Shops
9700 Collins Avenue
Miami
Florida 33154
+1 3058648600
www.makoto-restaurant.com

Opening hours	Open 7 days
Credit cards	Accepted
Price range	Affordable
Style	Smart casual
Cuisine	Japanese
Recommended for	Worth the travel

'It's worth flying to Miami just to eat there! Three words: fresh, innovative, incredible!'—Susur Lee

NAOE
661 Brickell Key Drive
Miami
Florida 33131
+1 3059476263
www.naoemiami.com

Recommended by
Michael Schwartz

Opening hours	Closed Sunday
Credit cards	Accepted
Price range	Expensive
Style	Smart casual
Cuisine	Japanese
Recommended for	High end

'In a word, special. This intimate Japanese restaurant is literally chef-to-table. Each night, what you eat is up to chef Kevin Cory. His *omakase* (chef's choice menu) service begins with a bento box of delicacies and family-produced sake, and concludes with a stream of incredible nigiri and other seafood and Japanese ingredients brought in from Japan. The small, dimly lit dining room is minimally appointed with nightly polished wood and set to classical music.'—Michael Schwartz

PUBBELLY
1418 20th Street
Miami
Florida 33139
+1 3055327555
www.pubbelly.com

Recommended by
David McMillan &
Frédéric Morin

Opening hours	Closed Monday
Reservation policy	No
Credit cards	Accepted
Price range	Affordable
Style	Casual
Cuisine	Bar-Bistro
Recommended for	Worth the travel

'We're fascinated by this group. They've opened four or five little, super-intelligent, delicious restaurants. Solid.'—David McMillan & Frédéric Morin

SAKAYA KITCHEN
3401 North Miami Avenue
Miami
Florida 33127
+1 3055768096
www.sakayakitchen.com

Recommended by
José Mendin

Opening hours	Open 7 days
Reservation policy	No
Credit cards	Accepted
Price range	Budget
Style	Casual
Cuisine	Korean
Recommended for	Bargain

'Fast, casual Asian food, great salads and sandwiches and wonderful flavours.'—José Mendin

SUGARCANE RAW BAR GRILL
3252 Northeast 1st Avenue
Miami
Florida 33137
+1 7863690353
www.sugarcanerawbargrill.com

Recommended by
Khalid Mohammed

Opening hours	Open 7 days
Credit cards	Accepted
Price range	Affordable
Style	Casual
Cuisine	Asian-Latin American
Recommended for	Worth the travel

EL TROPICO
8391 Northwest 12th Street
Miami
Florida 33126
+1 3054776222

Recommended by
Giorgio Rapicavoli

Opening hours	Open 7 days
Credit cards	Accepted
Price range	Budget
Style	Casual
Cuisine	Cuban
Recommended for	Breakfast

'They make a buttery tostada with "French bread" that's out of this world.'—Giorgio Rapicavoli

ZUMA MIAMI

270 Biscayne Boulevard Way
Miami
Florida 33131
+1 3055770277
www.zumarestaurant.com

Recommended by
José Mendin,
Giorgio Rapicavoli

Opening hours	Open 7 days
Credit cards	Accepted
Price range	Expensive
Style	Smart casual
Cuisine	Japanese
Recommended for	High end

'Zuma's tasting menu is full of crazy-delicious foods: foie gras, truffles, lobster, caviar, kobe beef and more. More importantly, chef Michael Lewis can cook the hell out of them.'—Giorgio Rapicavoli

CASA TUA

1700 James Avenue
Miami Beach
Florida 33139
+1 3056731010
www.casatualifestyle.com/miami

Recommended by
Bryn Williams

Opening hours	Open 7 days
Credit cards	Accepted
Price range	Expensive
Style	Smart casual
Cuisine	Italian
Recommended for	Worth the travel

'This is an exquisite Italian restaurant. I came across it while on holiday in Miami and the food was just sublime – I kept asking for more! To this day, I have never tasted gnocchi so good.'—Bryn Williams

THE BROKEN SHAKER

Freehand Miami Hotel
2727 Indian Creek Drive
Miami Beach
Florida 33140
+1 7863258974
www.thefreehand.com

Recommended by
Michael Schwartz

Opening hours	Open 7 days
Reservation policy	No
Credit cards	Accepted
Price range	Affordable
Style	Smart casual
Cuisine	Bar Snacks
Recommended for	Late night

'Best cocktail bar in Miami. The owner Elad Zvi is this crazy Israeli. The bar itself is tiny, tucked away in the Freehand Miami Hotel. Any given night of the week the crowd spills out onto the courtyard under a canopy of trees lit by string lights creating this amazing energy. Potted herbs and citrus trees (no joke!) are set to the back and picked for drinks (especially the nightly-changing punch bowls). It's like an exceptionally curated thrift store: great glassware, lots of cool period stuff scattered about like no one thought about it but you know they did and that's the magic of it. You go, have a great hand-crafted cocktail, relax with friends and meet some new ones. They do this spread of charcuterie, cheese, pickles... Just what I want to eat late at night. I make a habit of taking friends from out of town here. It's one of the obligatory stops. They've captured something really special here. It makes you want to go back again and again.'—Michael Schwartz

JOE'S STONE CRAB

11 Washington Avenue
Miami Beach
Florida 33139
+1 3056730365
www.joesstonecrab.com

Recommended by
José Mendin,
Giorgio Rapicavoli,
Michael Schwartz

Opening hours	Open 7 days
Reservation policy	No
Credit cards	Accepted
Price range	Affordable
Style	Smart casual
Cuisine	Seafood
Recommended for	Local favourite

'This place is a classic. It's like our Peter Luger's. Great seafood and even better fried chicken. The best part about it is skipping the queue (waiting line) and getting Joe's take away (take out).'—Giorgio Rapicavoli

JUGOFRESH

Recommended by
Michael Schwartz

1935 West Avenue
Miami Beach
Florida 33139
+1 7864722552
www.jugofresh.com

Opening hours	Open 7 days
Reservation policy	No
Credit cards	Accepted
Price range	Budget
Style	Casual
Cuisine	Juices and Smoothies
Recommended for	Breakfast

'Cold-pressed juices. For me it's all about being healthy in the morning.'—Michael Schwartz

LAS OLAS CAFE

Recommended by
Giorgio Rapicavoli

644 6th Street
Miami Beach
Florida 33139
+1 3055349333

Opening hours	Open 7 days
Reservation policy	No
Credit cards	Not accepted
Price range	Budget
Style	Casual
Cuisine	Cuban
Recommended for	Bargain

'Get the pan con bistec (steak sandwich) for $5 (£3) and have them put it on the sweet medianoche bread instead of Cuban. It's crunchy, salty, sweet and sour… the best.'—Giorgio Rapicavoli

MACCHIALINA

Recommended by
Michael Schwartz

820 Alton Road
Miami Beach
Florida 33139
+1 3055342124
www.macchialina.com

Opening hours	Open 7 days
Credit cards	Accepted
Price range	Affordable
Style	Smart casual
Cuisine	Italian
Recommended for	Regular neighbourhood

'It would be enough just to dine in the care of this husband-and-wife team of chef Michael Pirolo and Jen Chaefsky, but their thoughtful hospitality is only the beginning. There's a great Italian wine list, nightly specials that change with the seasons, house-made pastas and even a fresh spread of oysters shucked in front of you at the bar. Cosy, delicious and a place you want to return to time and time again.'
—Michael Schwartz

YAKKO-SAN

Recommended by
José Mendin,
Giorgio Rapicavoli

3881 Northeast 163rd North Street
Miami Beach
Florida 33160
+1 3059470064
www.yakko-san.com

Opening hours	Open 7 days
Credit cards	Accepted
Price range	Affordable
Style	Casual
Cuisine	Japanese
Recommended for	Regular neighbourhood

'Fantastic Japanese small plates. It's a terrific restaurant that serves authentic food at great prices and is extremely consistent.'—Giorgio Rapicavoli

BUCCAN

Recommended by
Paul Newman

350 South County Road
Palm Beach
Florida 33480
+1 5618333450
www.buccanpalmbeach.com

Opening hours	Open 7 days
Credit cards	Accepted
Price range	Affordable
Style	Smart casual
Cuisine	Modern American
Recommended for	Worth the travel

'Very innovative small plates. I like the wood-fired Brussels sprouts.'—Paul Newman

HMF

Recommended by
Paul Newman

The Breakers Hotel
1 South County Road
Palm Beach
Florida 33480
+1 8552373450
www.hmfpalmbeach.com

Opening hours	Open 7 days
Reservation policy	No
Credit cards	Accepted
Price range	Expensive
Style	Smart casual
Cuisine	International
Recommended for	Late night

'Professional, knowledgeable and a beautifully coiffed service team. High style and unapologetic decadence! HMF has brought back classic cocktail culture and paired it with their award-winning, full-on Breakers Hotel wine list. There's a great selection of small plates fashioned from the world's favourite food trucks for combining, sharing and experimenting.'
—Paul Newman

ANTICO PIZZA

Recommended by
Ford Fry

1093 Hemphill Avenue Northwest
Atlanta
Georgia 30318
+1 4047242333
www.anticoatl.com

Opening hours	Closed Sunday
Reservation policy	No
Credit cards	Accepted
Price range	Affordable
Style	Casual
Cuisine	Italian
Recommended for	Wish I'd opened

'I like the authenticity of it and how low-key it is. My favourite is the Diablo pizza.'—Ford Fry

BACCHANALIA

Recommended by
Justin Burdett, Ford Fry,
Steven Satterfield

1198 Howell Mill Road
Atlanta
Georgia 30318
+1 4043650410
www.starprovisions.com

Opening hours	Closed Sunday
Credit cards	Accepted
Price range	Expensive
Style	Smart casual
Cuisine	Modern American
Recommended for	High end

'The entire experience there from the service to the attention to detail of the food is incredible. Annie is super talented and she also uses some products from her own farm at the restaurant. It's been the number one in Atlanta for a while for good reason.'—Ford Fry

CARDAMOM HILL

Recommended by
Steven Satterfield

1700 Northside Drive
Atlanta
Georgia 30318
+1 4045497012
www.cardamomhill.net

Opening hours	Closed Sunday
Credit cards	Accepted
Price range	Affordable
Style	Smart casual
Cuisine	Southern Indian
Recommended for	Regular neighbourhood

'The most interesting Indian restaurant I've ever experienced. The chef and owner, Asha Gomez, hails from Kerala where they eat fish, fowl, pork and beef, and the flavours are intensely exotic. Her goat biryani and her fish-head curry are two of my favourites. I also really love this dish called "Kerala Railways Beef Curry". It's spicy curried beef wrapped in a banana leaf on a bed of cool yogurt and rice.'—Steven Satterfield

FOX BROS. BAR-B-Q

Recommended by
Ford Fry

1238 Dekalb Avenue Northeast
Atlanta
Georgia 30307
+1 4045774030
www.foxbrosbbq.com

Opening hours	Open 7 days
Reservation policy	No
Credit cards	Accepted
Price range	Budget
Style	Casual
Cuisine	Barbeque
Recommended for	Bargain

Identical twin Texan brothers Jonathan and Justin Fox began serving Lone Star State-style bar-b-q out of Smith's Olde Bar in Atlanta on a part-time basis back in 2004. Such was the response to their re-creation of the smoky, slow-roasted meats that they grew up on, that they opened their own place the following year in a converted gas station. Since then their parking lot has been full and there's been a mercifully quick-moving line out of the door for hefty portions of their reasonably priced, hickory-smoked brisket, pulled pork and chicken-fried ribs (smoked spare ribs in chicken-fried steak batter).

THE GENERAL MUIR

Recommended by
Steven Satterfield

Emory Point
Suite b-230 1540 Avenue Place
Atlanta
Georgia 30329
+1 6789279131
www.thegeneralmuir.com

Opening hours	Open 7 days
Credit cards	Accepted
Price range	Affordable
Style	Casual
Cuisine	Jewish-American
Recommended for	Breakfast

'The last time I had brunch here it blew me away. Chef Todd Ginsberg focuses on Jewish heritage cuisine. They make home-made bagels, house-cured corned beef, amazing pickles and the brunch menu is very inventive. The chopped liver is great and the chicken laffa, a sort of Jewish burrito, was deeply layered with pulled chicken, aubergine (eggplant), yogurt and hot pepper. And I love the corned beef hash plate with sunny-side-up eggs. They also make a great cocktail and the space is beautiful.'—Steven Satterfield

HOLEMAN & FINCH PUBLIC HOUSE

Recommended by
Andrea Reusing

2277 Peachtree Road Northwest
Atlanta
Georgia 30309
+1 4049481175
www.holeman-finch.com

Opening hours	Open 7 days
Reservation policy	No
Credit cards	Accepted
Price range	Affordable
Style	Casual
Cuisine	Southern American
Recommended for	Late night

NUEVO LAREDO CANTINA

Recommended by
Ford Fry

1495 Chattahoochee Avenue Northwest
Atlanta
Georgia 30318
+1 4043529009
www.nuevolaredocantina.com

Opening hours	Open 7 days
Reservation policy	No
Credit cards	Accepted
Price range	Budget
Style	Casual
Cuisine	Mexican
Recommended for	Regular neighbourhood

'I love Tex-Mex and they get that style of cooking more than anyone in town. It's good, cheesy Mexican.'
—Ford Fry

OCTOPUS BAR

Recommended by
Justin Burdett, Ford Fry,
Steven Satterfield

561 Gresham Avenue Southeast
Atlanta
Georgia 30316
+1 4046279911
www.octopusbaratl.com

Opening hours	Closed Sunday
Reservation policy	No
Credit cards	Accepted
Price range	Affordable
Style	Casual
Cuisine	Asian Fusion
Recommended for	Late night

'It's more of an industry scene, so it's a great place to catch up with people. The food has Asian influences, but the dishes are very unique.'—Ford Fry

RIA'S BLUEBIRD

Recommended by
Steven Satterfield

421 Memorial Drive Southeast
Atlanta
Georgia 30312
+1 4045213737
www.riasbluebird.com

Opening hours	Open 7 days
Reservation policy	No
Credit cards	Accepted
Price range	Budget
Style	Casual
Cuisine	Southern American
Recommended for	Local favourite

'It changed a neighbourhood, one breakfast at a time. Now this once-downtrodden strip of industrial buildings has become one of the hippest corridors in the city. And Ria's Bluebird was there first. Ria Pell unwaveringly served whatever *she* wanted to serve, with no substitutions, *ever*. Fluffy, award-winning pancakes, spicy beef brisket, *huevos rancheros*, or grits, biscuits and eggs. There's always a pot of hot coffee ready and fresh fruit jam (jelly) on the table. Ria's Bluebird is always packed and everyone leaves there happy. I was so saddened to say goodbye to Ria when she passed away in late 2013, but the legacy of her restaurant will be a part of Atlanta for a long, long time.'—Steven Satterfield

SOTTO SOTTO

Recommended by
Steven Satterfield

309 North Highland Avenue Northeast
Atlanta
Georgia 30307
+1 4045236678
www.urestaurants.net

Opening hours	Open 7 days
Credit cards	Accepted
Price range	Affordable
Style	Smart casual
Cuisine	Italian
Recommended for	Regular neighbourhood

'Sotto Sotto specialize in classic Italian pasta dishes and have an excellent Italian wine list. I usually get some kind of simple salad, a half-order of pasta, and then the roast chicken cooked in a wood-burning oven. Their Barolo list is out of control.'—Steven Satterfield

TAQUERIA DEL SOL

Recommended by
Steven Satterfield

1200 Howell Mill Road
Atlanta
Georgia 30318
+1 4043525811
www.taqueriadelsol.com

Opening hours	Closed Sunday
Reservation policy	No
Credit cards	Accepted
Price range	Budget
Style	Casual
Cuisine	Tex-Mex
Recommended for	Bargain

'This place is always fast, very consistent and really delicious. I'm kind of a predictable customer there. I usually get one *carnitas* (pulled pork) taco, one bean-and-cheese taco and a side of turnip greens. The tequila selection is amazing and they make a killer Margarita. Owners Mike Klank and Eddie Hernandez are real hitmakers. They have three locations in and around Atlanta for a quick fix anytime.'
—Steven Satterfield

WHITE HOUSE

Recommended by
Linton Hopkins

3172 Peachtree Road Northeast
Atlanta
Georgia 30305
+1 4042377601
www.whitehouserestaurant.net

Opening hours	Open 7 days
Reservation policy	No
Credit cards	Accepted
Price range	Budget
Style	Casual
Cuisine	Diner-Café
Recommended for	Breakfast

'They know how to poach eggs and make strong coffee.'
—Linton Hopkins

BLAKELY CHICKEN

Recommended by
Linton Hopkins

212 North Main Street
Blakely
Georgia 39823
+1 2297234201

Opening hours	Open 7 days
Reservation policy	No
Credit cards	Not accepted
Price range	Budget
Style	Casual
Cuisine	Southern American
Recommended for	Bargain

'I discovered Blakely Chicken by accident and they make the best fried chicken. I go for the fried chicken livers and hot sauce.'—Linton Hopkins

WAFFLE HOUSE

Recommended by
Justin Burdett

537 Highway 441 South
Clayton
Georgia 30525
+1 7062122033
www.wafflehouse.com

Opening hours	Open 7 days
Reservation policy	No
Credit cards	Accepted
Price range	Budget
Style	Casual
Cuisine	Diner
Recommended for	Breakfast

'I have eaten at Waffle House my entire life. I even remember my first cup of coffee there when I was five years old and having breakfast with my grandparents.'
—Justin Burdett

CAKES & ALE

Recommended by
Ford Fry

155 Sycamore Street
Decatur
Georgia 30030
+1 4043777994
www.cakesandalerestaurant.com

Opening hours	Closed Monday and Sunday
Credit cards	Accepted
Price range	Affordable
Style	Casual
Cuisine	Modern American
Recommended for	Local favourite

'Chef Billy Allin has got a great sense of flavour. He's very seasonally focused and he produces amazing flavour combinations using different ingredients and techniques.'—Ford Fry

COMMUNITY Q BBQ

Recommended by
Ford Fry

1361 Clairmont Road
Decatur
Georgia 30033
+1 4046332080
www.communityqbbq.com

Opening hours	Open 7 days
Reservation policy	No
Credit cards	Accepted
Price range	Budget
Style	Casual
Cuisine	Barbeque
Recommended for	Bargain

A temple to all things BBQ, Community Q guarantees to charm all comers with its honest grab-it-and-growl approach to cooking. Counter ordering and quick-fire service keep the customers rolling in and rolling out, stuffed with Flintstone-esque beef ribs, pulled pork and chicken, spicy BBQ beans and the legendary mac 'n' cheese. Hell, even the greens come with pieces of pork. Time your arrival carefully – queues (waiting lines) are longest after 5.30 p.m., and the kitchen regularly runs out of meat before closing – and you'll leave as thousands before you: with smoky hair, sticky fingers and a heaving doggy bag.

CLEVELAND-HEATH

Recommended by
Cassy Vires

106 North Main Street
Edwardsville
Illinois 62025
+1 6183074830
www.clevelandheath.com

Opening hours	Closed Sunday
Reservation policy	No
Credit cards	Accepted
Price range	Affordable
Style	Casual
Cuisine	Modern American
Recommended for	Worth the travel

'Ed and Jenny are doing a lot of really great things across the river. You can taste their passion in every bite you take. And even with all their acclaim, waiting lists and awards, they are still two of the humblest people I have ever met.'—Cassy Vires

PAGE'S RESTAURANT
Recommended by
Paul Virant
26 East Hinsdale Avenue
Hinsdale
Illinois 60521
+1 6303239058

Opening hours	Open 7 days
Reservation policy	No
Credit cards	Accepted but not AMEX
Price range	Budget
Style	Casual
Cuisine	Diner
Recommended for	Regular neighbourhood

'Great food – I love the meatloaf reuben.'—Paul Virant

RAMEN MISOYA
Recommended by
David Posey
1584 South Busse Road
Mount Prospect
Illinois 60056
+1 8474374590
www.misoya-usa.com

Opening hours	Open 7 days
Reservation policy	No
Credit cards	Accepted
Price range	Budget
Style	Casual
Cuisine	Ramen Noodles
Recommended for	Wish I'd opened

'The best ramen spot in the Chicago area. Phenomenal service and tasty cold brews.'—David Posey

YORK TAVERN
Recommended by
Paul Virant
3702 York Road
Oak Brook
Illinois 60523
+1 6303235090
www.yorktavernoakbrook.com

Opening hours	Open 7 days
Reservation policy	No
Credit cards	Accepted
Price range	Budget
Style	Casual
Cuisine	American
Recommended for	Bargain

'It used to be an old pony express stop in the 1800s, located right on Salt Creek. Really solid cheeseburger, great beers and an awesome selection of tunes on the jukebox.'—Paul Virant

WALKER BROTHERS
Recommended by
Carrie Nahabedian
153 Green Bay Road
Wilmette
Illinois 60091
+1 8472516000
www.walkerbros.net

Opening hours	Open 7 days
Reservation policy	No
Credit cards	Accepted
Price range	Budget
Style	Casual
Cuisine	American
Recommended for	Breakfast

'The best 49ers flapjacks, amazingly light Dutch baby German pancake, of course the famous apple pancake, which is more like a big warm gooey dessert. I don't drink coffee, but everyone says they make the best. Real whipped cream, butter, lots of fresh ingredients when other breakfast places use processed. There is a reason everyone loves it.'—Carrie Nahabedian

OKLAHOMA JOE'S BAR-B-QUE
Recommended by
Colby Garrelts
3002 West 47th Avenue
Kansas City
Kansas 66103
+1 9137223366
www.oklahomajoesbbq.com

Opening hours	Closed Sunday
Reservation policy	No
Credit cards	Accepted
Price range	Budget
Style	Casual
Cuisine	Barbeque
Recommended for	Wish I'd opened

'Best barbeque in Kansas City, hands down. You can't go wrong with anything. People seem to gravitate to the "Z-Man".'—Colby Garrelts

Given the number of awards that line the walls of this jumping gas-station grill joint, it's no surprise that Oklahoma Joe's has been declared the smokin' best of Kansas City's 100-plus barbeque restaurants. Owners and world-beating barbeque champs Jeff and Joy Stehney pack 'em in at lunchtime, but now that they've opened a second and a third restaurant, the queues (waiting lines) have eased. Diners rave about the Z-Man beef brisket sandwich and the pulled pork, but it's the ribs that reign supreme. You'll have to get in quick for the burnt ends, which have a near-religious following.

EL POLLO REY

Recommended by
Colby Garrelts

901 Kansas Avenue
Kansas City
Kansas 66105
+1 9133714243

Opening hours	Open 7 days
Reservation policy	No
Credit cards	Accepted
Price range	Budget
Style	Casual
Cuisine	Chicken
Recommended for	Bargain

'All they serve is marinated grilled chicken and they serve it with fresh home-made tortillas, avocados, limes, rice and beans... Enough for two and it's a whopping $7 (£4).'—Colby Garrelts

RYE

Recommended by
Patrick Ryan

10551 Mission Road
Leawood
Kansas 66206
+1 9136425800
www.ryekc.com

Opening hours	Open 7 days
Credit cards	Accepted
Price range	Affordable
Style	Smart casual
Cuisine	American
Recommended for	High end

'It's not necessarily a "special occasion" restaurant but they do have a reserve steak programme and the fourteen-day, 400 g (14 oz) dry-aged ribeye was the best I've ever had. This restaurant exemplifies Midwestern farm cooking.'—Patrick Ryan

JACK FRY'S

Recommended by
Edward Lee

1007 Bardstown Road
Louisville
Kentucky 40204
+1 5024529244
www.jackfrys.com

Opening hours	Open 7 days
Credit cards	Accepted
Price range	Affordable
Style	Smart casual
Cuisine	Modern American
Recommended for	Local favourite

'Jack Fry's is an institution and still serves great food. It's a place where you can feel the history of the city as soon as you walk in. A live piano player, which at other places seems tawdry, here feels right at home.'
—Edward Lee

This Louisville Highlands stalwart wears its history with pride. The days of back-room bootlegging and bookmaking are well gone, immortalized now in the black-and-white pictures that line the walls of the handsome dining room – these days, it's a more genteel affair. This is good old-fashioned fine dining: high-end, French-influenced dishes such as scallops with cauliflower mousse, balsamic beurre rouge, fingerling potato crisps and black truffle populate the menu, with the likes of shrimp and grits adding some Southern flavour. Don't expect hushed tones and starchy service though – locals love Jack Fry's for its relaxed atmosphere and live jazz.

WAFFLE HOUSE

Recommended by
Edward Lee

4320 Bishop Lane
Louisville
Kentucky 40218
+1 5024586434
www.wafflehouse.com

Opening hours	Open 7 days
Reservation policy	No
Credit cards	Accepted
Price range	Budget
Style	Casual
Cuisine	Diner
Recommended for	Bargain

'Jukebox, home fries and a hell of a greasy burger.'
—Edward Lee

CHARLIE'S SANDWICH SHOPPE

Recommended by
Tim Cushman

429 Columbus Avenue
Boston
Massachusetts 02116
+1 6175367669

Opening hours	Closed Sunday
Reservation policy	No
Credit cards	Not accepted
Price range	Budget
Style	Casual
Cuisine	Diner
Recommended for	Breakfast

'It has an exceptional diner menu with everything from pancakes to corn beef hash. I also appreciate the musical history of the restaurant. Opened in 1927, Charlie's was known for serving African American jazz musicians when hotels were segregated. Today, pictures of those musicians decorate the walls.'—Tim Cushman

GRILL 23
161 Berkeley Street
Boston
Massachusetts 02116
+1 6175422255
www.grill23.com

Recommended by
Tony Maws

Opening hours	Open 7 days
Credit cards	Accepted
Price range	Expensive
Style	Smart casual
Cuisine	Modern American
Recommended for	High end

'The best steak in town with a wine list that has some hidden gems.'—Tony Maws

MEI MEI
506 Park Drive
Boston
Massachusetts 02215
+1 8572504959
www.meimeiboston.com

Recommended by
Yotam Ottolenghi

Opening hours	Open 7 days
Reservation policy	No
Credit cards	Accepted
Price range	Budget
Style	Casual
Cuisine	Street Food
Recommended for	Worth the travel

'I love street food: it's the place of so much innovation and perfectionism. Standing out, eating with your hands, chatting with fellow eaters. Eating stunning food without the frills and fancy.'—Yotam Ottolenghi

Kickstarter-funded Mei Mei serves a superbly inventive range of Chinese-American dishes (Trotters & Waffles, beef heart tartare, parsnip and apple fritters), at prices not too far removed from their humble street-food origins. It's exactly the kind of imaginative and idiosyncratic menu (it changes weekly based on what they can find from local farms) that the street-food scene does so well — what's more impressive is how well it's translated to this bright and colourful bricks-and-mortar spot near Fenway. A bravely unique range of drinks too — try the Bird's Nest, with pine cream, poached egg and soda...

NEBO
520 Atlantic Avenue
Boston
Massachusetts 02210
+1 6177236326
www.neborestaurant.com

Recommended by
Tim Cushman

Opening hours	Closed Sunday
Credit cards	Accepted
Price range	Affordable
Style	Smart casual
Cuisine	Italian
Recommended for	Regular neighbourhood

'Owned by the Pallotta sisters, they use their family recipes and serve traditional and sincere Italian food. It's a great neighbourhood spot.'—Tim Cushman

NEPTUNE OYSTER
63 Salem Street
Boston
Massachusetts 02113
+1 6177423474
www.neptuneoyster.com

Recommended by
Matthew Gaudet,
Tony Maws

Opening hours	Open 7 days
Reservation policy	No
Credit cards	Accepted
Price range	Affordable
Style	Casual
Cuisine	Seafood
Recommended for	Local favourite

If you want to perch at the Neptune's marble counter you're going to have to get in line. It's strictly no reservations for its sixteen stools and handful of banquettes. The market-priced raw bar offers the best shellfish in season, from finest East and West Coast oysters to razor clams, crab claws, and littleneck and cherrystone clams. Michael Serpa's menu occasionally acknowledges North End neighbourhood's Italian heritage — a lobster spaghettini or a vitello tonnato sandwich — alongside more eclectic influences — *hamachi* ceviche made with kimchi. Their Maine lobster roll, served either hot with butter or cold with mayo, has a cult following.

NO. 9 PARK

9 Park Street
Boston
Massachusetts 02108
+1 6177429991
www.no9park.com

Opening hours	Open 7 days
Credit cards	Accepted
Price range	Expensive
Style	Smart casual
Cuisine	French-Italian
Recommended for	Local favourite

'Chef Barbara Lynch's flagship restaurant serves beautiful food in a spectacular Boston location. When you arrive you're at the foot of the State House and on the corner of Boston Common. The menu is innovative and fun, the service warm and consistent. The perfect place to celebrate or to enjoy being in Beantown.'
—Tim Cushman

PEACH FARM

4 Tyler Street
Boston
Massachusetts 02111
+1 6174823332
www.peachfarmboston.com

Opening hours	Open 7 days
Reservation policy	No
Credit cards	Accepted but not AMEX
Price range	Affordable
Style	Casual
Cuisine	Chinese
Recommended for	Late night

'Crazy fresh – sometimes brought to the table alive – seafood. Fun atmosphere. The delicious XO sauce is great to have with anything. It's the best in Boston.'
—Matthew Gaudet

PHO PASTEUR

682 Washington Street
Boston
Massachusetts 02111
+1 6174827467
www.phopasteurboston.net

Opening hours	Open 7 days
Credit cards	Acccpted
Price range	Budget
Style	Casual
Cuisine	Vietnamese
Recommended for	Bargain

'Their broths are delicious. They always hit the spot.'
—Matthew Gaudet

PHO VIET

Super 88 Market
1095 Commonwealth Avenue
Boston
Massachusetts 02215
+1 6175628828

Opening hours	Open 7 days
Reservation policy	No
Credit cards	Accepted
Price range	Budget
Style	Casual
Cuisine	Vietnamese
Recommended for	Bargain

'It's a stall in the Super 88 Market eatery that serves consistently great bowls of soup.'—Tony Maws

REGINA PIZZA

11 1/2 Thacher Street
Boston
Massachusetts 02113
+1 6172270765
www.reginapizza.com

Opening hours	Open 7 days
Reservation policy	No
Credit cards	Accepted
Price range	Budget
Style	Casual
Cuisine	Pizza
Recommended for	Bargain

'The original Regina Pizza is a North End landmark and delivers the best pies in the city. I always order mine with extra sauce and well done.'—Tim Cushman

SAM'S

Recommended by
Joanne Chang

60 Northern Avenue
Boston
Massachusetts 02210
+1 6172950191
www.samsatlouis.com

Opening hours	Open 7 days
Credit cards	Accepted
Price range	Affordable
Style	Casual
Cuisine	Modern American
Recommended for	Regular neighbourhood

'Amazing views, the best service, and I want to eat
everything on the menu.'—Joanne Chang

SORELLINA

Recommended by
Joanne Chang

1 Huntington Avenue
Boston
Massachusetts 02116
+1 6174124600
www.sorellinaboston.com

Opening hours	Open 7 days
Credit cards	Accepted
Price range	Expensive
Style	Formal
Cuisine	Modern Italian
Recommended for	Wish I'd opened

'The service is impeccable, it's the most beautiful and
elegant dining room in town, the food is always great
and it's always busy.'—Joanne Chang

TAIWAN CAFÉ

Recommended by
Joanne Chang

34 Oxford Street
Boston
Massachusetts 02111
+1 6174268181

Opening hours	Open 7 days
Credit cards	Not accepted
Price range	Budget
Style	Casual
Cuisine	Taiwanese
Recommended for	Bargain

'Their mápó tòfu (tofu in spicy sauce), pea tendrils and
Hakka-style aubergine (eggplant) are among my
favourite dishes in the world.'—Joanne Chang

WINSOR DIM SUM CAFÉ

Recommended by
Joanne Chang

10 Tyler Street
Boston
Massachusetts 02111
+1 6173381688
www.winsordimsumcafe.com

Opening hours	Open 7 days
Reservation policy	No
Credit cards	Accepted
Price range	Budget
Style	Casual
Cuisine	Dim Sum
Recommended for	Breakfast

'Dim sum made to order.'—Joanne Chang

O YA

Recommended by
Joanne Chang

9 East Street
Boston
Massachusetts 02111
+1 6176549900
www.oyarestaurantboston.com

Opening hours	Closed Monday and Sunday
Credit cards	Accepted
Price range	Expensive
Style	Smart casual
Cuisine	Japanese
Recommended for	High end

'Incredible sushi and Japanese small plates, extremely
creative, lovely decor and service.'—Joanne Chang

AREA FOUR

Recommended by
Matthew Gaudet,
Bjorn Somlo

500 Technology Square
Cambridge
Massachusetts 02139
+1 6177584444
www.areafour.com

Opening hours	Open 7 days
Reservation policy	No
Credit cards	Accepted
Price range	Affordable
Style	Casual
Cuisine	Pizza
Recommended for	Worth the travel

'It is very rare to get good pizza and the rest of the food
is so solid.'—Bjorn Somlo

BELLY WINE BAR
1 Kendall Square
Cambridge
Massachusetts 02139
+1 6174940968
www.bellywinebar.com

Opening hours	Open 7 days
Reservation policy	No
Credit cards	Accepted
Price range	Affordable
Style	Smart casual
Cuisine	Bar-Small plates
Recommended for	Wish I'd opened

'It's everything I want in a casual place: great wine and old-school, simple, well-prepared food.'—Tony Maws

OLEANA
134 Hampshire Street
Cambridge
Massachusetts 02139
+1 6176610505
www.oleanarestaurant.com

Opening hours	Open 7 days
Credit cards	Accepted
Price range	Affordable
Style	Casual
Cuisine	Middle Eastern-European
Recommended for	High end

'The food is thoughtful, the staff are warm and the restaurant is beautiful. I always head to Oleana to celebrate a special occasion.'—Tim Cushman

SOFRA
1 Belmont Street
Cambridge
Massachusetts 02138
+1 6176613161
www.sofrabakery.com

Opening hours	Open 7 days
Reservation policy	No
Credit cards	Accepted
Price range	Affordable
Style	Casual
Cuisine	Middle Eastern
Recommended for	Breakfast

'Interesting and tasty pastries. Fun hot dishes too.'
—Tony Maws

J. T. FARNHAMS
88 Eastern Avenue
Essex
Massachusetts 01929
+1 9787686643

Opening hours	Open 7 days
Reservation policy	No
Credit cards	Not accepted
Price range	Budget
Style	Casual
Cuisine	American Seafood
Recommended for	Local favourite

'An iconic example of New England seafood. Delicious lobster rolls and chowder but most of all, the freakin' fried clams! The best! The quintessential summer meal here.'—Matthew Gaudet

SPOON
26 Housatonic Street
Lenox
Massachusetts 01240
+1 4138814040
www.spoonlenox.com

Opening hours	Closed Monday
Reservation policy	No
Credit cards	Accepted
Price range	Budget
Style	Casual
Cuisine	Café
Recommended for	Breakfast

'They source high-quality ingredients and cook either healthy or glutinous food and somehow do both very well.'—Bjorn Somlo

CHILLI GARDEN
41 Riverside Avenue
Medford
Massachusetts 02155
+1 7813968488
www.chilligardenmedford.com

Opening hours	Open 7 days
Credit cards	Accepted
Price range	Budget
Style	Casual
Cuisine	Szechuan
Recommended for	Regular neighbourhood

'It's a less-than-no-frills Chinese joint in a very untrendy location serving knock-your-socks-off Szechuan food.'—Tony Maws

ANTONIO'S

Recommended by
Saul Bolton

267 Coggeshall Street
New Bedford
Massachusetts 02746
+1 5089903636
www.antoniosnewbedford.com

Opening hours	Open 7 days
Reservation policy	No
Credit cards	Accepted
Price range	Affordable
Style	Casual
Cuisine	Portuguese
Recommended for	Worth the travel

'Always filled with locals chowing down on local fried baby sardines with lemon. Rabbit stew, fish stew, it goes on and on... It's great and it's cheap. Antonio's is awesome.'—Saul Bolton

AYELADA

Recommended by
Bjorn Somlo

505 East Street
Pittsfield
Massachusetts 01201
+1 4133444126
www.ayelada.com

Opening hours	Open 7 days
Reservation policy	No
Credit cards	Accepted
Price range	Budget
Style	Casual
Cuisine	Frozen Yogurt
Recommended for	Bargain

'Mildy sour and lightly sweetened frozen yogurt that is so good.'—Bjorn Somlo

PHO 'N RICE

Recommended by
Matthew Gaudet

289 Beacon Street
Somerville
Massachusetts 02143
+1 6178648888
www.phonrice.com

Opening hours	Open 7 days
Credit cards	Accepted
Price range	Budget
Style	Casual
Cuisine	Vietnamese-Thai
Recommended for	Bargain

'It's just simple pho tai done well for little money.'
—Matthew Gaudet

BODA

Recommended by
Rob Evans

671 Congress Street
Portland
Maine 04101
+1 2073477557
www.bodamaine.com

Opening hours	Closed Monday
Reservation policy	No
Credit cards	Accepted
Price range	Budget
Style	Casual
Cuisine	Thai small plates
Recommended for	Late night

FORE STREET

Recommended by
Rob Evans

288 Fore Street
Portland
Maine 04101
+1 2077752717
www.forestreet.biz

Opening hours	Open 7 days
Credit cards	Accepted
Price range	Affordable
Style	Casual
Cuisine	Modern American
Recommended for	Local favourite

GORGEOUS GELATO

434 Fore Street
Portland
Maine 04101
+1 2076994309
www.gorgeousgelato.com

Opening hours	Open 7 days
Reservation policy	No
Credit cards	Accepted
Price range	Budget
Style	Casual
Cuisine	Ice cream
Recommended for	Wish I'd opened

HOT SUPPA!

703 Congress Street
Portland
Maine 04102
+1 2078715005
www.hotsuppa.com

Opening hours	Open 7 days
Reservation policy	No
Credit cards	Accepted
Price range	Affordable
Style	Casual
Cuisine	American
Recommended for	Breakfast

OTTO PIZZA

576 Congress Street
Portland
Maine 04101
+1 2077737099
www.ottoportland.com

Opening hours	Open 7 days
Reservation policy	No
Credit cards	Accepted
Price range	Budget
Style	Casual
Cuisine	Pizza
Recommended for	Bargain

PAI MEN MIYAKE

188 State Street
Portland
Maine 04101
+1 2075419204
www.miyakerestaurants.com

Opening hours	Open 7 days
Credit cards	Accepted
Price range	Budget
Style	Casual
Cuisine	Japanese
Recommended for	Regular neighbourhood

PICCOLO

111 Middle Street
Portland
Maine 04101
+1 2077475307
www.piccolomaine.com

Opening hours	Closed Monday and Tuesday
Credit cards	Accepted
Price range	Affordable
Style	Smart casual
Cuisine	Italian
Recommended for	High end

PRIMO

2 South Main Street
Rockland
Maine 04841
+1 2075960770
www.primorestaurant.com

Opening hours	Variable
Credit cards	Accepted
Price range	Affordable
Style	Casual
Cuisine	European
Recommended for	Wish I'd opened

THE BACHELOR FARMER

Recommended by
Jamie Malone

50 North 2nd Avenue
Minneapolis
Minnesota 55401
+1 6122063920
www.thebachelorfarmer.com

Opening hours	Open 7 days
Credit cards	Accepted
Price range	Affordable
Style	Casual
Cuisine	Modern American
Recommended for	Wish I'd opened

'There's a strong identity running through everything they do. I love the feel and boldness of the space. It's warm and inviting, the perfect place for a long dinner. You have to start with a cocktail at Marvel Bar, the cocktail lounge downstairs.'—Jamie Malone

LA BELLE VIE

Recommended by
Jamie Malone,
Jack Riebel

510 Groveland Avenue
Minneapolis
Minnesota 55403
+1 6128746440
www.labellevie.us

Opening hours	Open 7 days
Credit cards	Accepted
Price range	Expensive
Style	Formal
Cuisine	Modern European
Recommended for	High end

'Minnesota's best fine-dining experience from legendary local chef Tim McKee. Outstanding service.' —Jack Riebel

BRASA

Recommended by
Jack Riebel

600 East Hennepin Avenue
Minneapolis
Minnesota 55414
+1 6123793030
www.brasa.us

Opening hours	Closed Sunday
Reservation policy	No
Credit cards	Accepted
Price range	Affordable
Style	Casual
Cuisine	Caribbean
Recommended for	Wish I'd opened

'An excellent quick-service restaurant featuring local ingredients and a chef-driven menu.'—Jack Riebel

CHIMBORAZO

Recommended by
Jamie Malone

2851 Central Avenue
Minneapolis
Minnesota 55418
+1 6127881328
www.chimborazorestaurant.com

Opening hours	Open 7 days
Credit cards	Accepted
Price range	Budget
Style	Casual
Cuisine	Ecuadorian
Recommended for	Bargain

'Ecuadorian food that is stellar! I order *churrasco* (grilled meat) and the house-made passion fruit ice cream. Everything is made from scratch and really good.'—Jamie Malone

HONG KONG NOODLE

Recommended by
Jack Riebel

901 Washington Avenue Southeast
Minneapolis
Minnesota 55414
+1 6123799472
www.mnhongkongnoodle.com

Opening hours	Open 7 days
Reservation policy	No
Credit cards	Accepted
Price range	Budget
Style	Casual
Cuisine	Chinese
Recommended for	Regular neighbourhood

'My favourite Minneapolis Chinese and it's open late! A chef's dream.'—Jack Riebel

LEFT HANDED COOK
Recommended by
Jamie Malone

Midtown Global Market
2929 Chicago Avenue South
Minneapolis
Minnesota 55407
+1 6122364526
ww.thelefthandedcook.com

Opening hours	Closed Sunday
Reservation policy	No
Credit cards	Accepted
Price range	Budget
Style	Casual
Cuisine	Korean
Recommended for	Regular neighbourhood

'Bibimbap! It is so good, the perfect meal. It has everything: great rice with pickled and fermented vegetables, a perfect egg and insanely good short ribs.'
—Jamie Malone

MATT'S BAR
Recommended by
Jack Riebel

3500 Cedar Avenue South
Minneapolis
Minnesota 55407
+1 6127227072
www.mattsbar.com

Opening hours	Open 7 days
Reservation policy	No
Credit cards	Not accepted
Price range	Budget
Style	Casual
Cuisine	Burgers
Recommended for	Local favourite

'Home of the Minnesota original "Jucy Lucy Burger", which is a must have in Minneapolis.'—Jack Riebel

PICCOLO
Recommended by
Jamie Malone

4300 Bryant Avenue South
Minneapolis
Minnesota 55409
+1 6128278111
www.piccolompls.com

Opening hours	Closed Tuesday
Credit cards	Accepted
Price range	Affordable
Style	Smart casual
Cuisine	Modern American
Recommended for	High end

'Doug Flicker, the chef-owner, truly has a style of his own. His food is not made, it is crafted, and it's spectacular.'—Jamie Malone

TILIA
Recommended by
Jamie Malone

2726 West 43rd Street
Minneapolis
Minnesota 55410
+1 6123542806
www.tiliampls.com

Opening hours	Open 7 days
Reservation policy	No
Credit cards	Accepted but not AMEX
Price range	Affordable
Style	Casual
Cuisine	Modern American
Recommended for	Late night

'Steven Brown is the chef-owner. He kitted out the place himself and paid attention to every single detail. Even the restaurant's speakers are covered with cool vintage speaker covers. The kids menu comes on a little origami fortune teller! Everything has a story behind it; the place is beaming with evidence of an owner who cares deeply. Oh, and the food is awesome!'
—Jamie Malone

VICTOR'S 1959 CAFE
Recommended by
Jamie Malone

3756 Grand Avenue South
Minneapolis
Minnesota 55409
+1 6128278948
www.victors1959cafe.com

Opening hours	Open 7 days
Credit cards	Accepted but not AMEX
Price range	Affordable
Style	Casual
Cuisine	Cuban
Recommended for	Breakfast

'It's really tiny and a little run-down. There is graffiti all over everything, the tables, the walls, the front door. On weekends the queue (waiting line) goes out the door; people wait for hours. It's the perfect breakfast café with hot coffee and a ridiculously good potato omelette.'—Jamie Malone

HMONGTOWN MARKETPLACE
217 Como Avenue
St. Paul
Minnesota 55103
+1 6514873700
www.hmongtownmarketplace.com

Opening hours	Open 7 days
Reservation policy	No
Credit cards	Not accepted
Price range	Budget
Style	Casual
Cuisine	Hmong
Recommended for	Bargain

'Very cool and unique Hmong market with great food stalls serving authentic foods.'—Jack Riebel

KEYS CAFÉ & BAKERY
767 Raymond Avenue
St. Paul
Minnesota 55114
+1 6516465756
www.keyscafe.com

Opening hours	Open 7 days
Reservation policy	No
Credit cards	Accepted
Price range	Budget
Style	Casual
Cuisine	Bakery-Diner
Recommended for	Breakfast

'An old-school family-owned and -operated St. Paul joint. Solid home cooking.'—Jack Riebel

MICKEY'S DINER
36 7th Street West
St. Paul
Minnesota 55102
+1 6512225633
www.mickeysdiningcar.com

Opening hours	Open 7 days
Reservation policy	No
Credit cards	Accepted but not AMEX
Price range	Budget
Style	Casual
Cuisine	Diner
Recommended for	Late night

'A classic diner serving up excellent malts and twenty-four-hour breakfast.'—Jack Riebel

STONE SOUP COTTAGE
5809 Highway North
Cottleville
Missouri 63304
+1 6362442233
www.stonesoupcottage.com

Opening hours	Closed Sunday to Tuesday
Credit cards	Accepted
Price range	Expensive
Style	Smart casual
Cuisine	French
Recommended for	Wish I'd opened

'I have the utmost respect for chef Carl. What he has built is something I think every chef wishes to have done. He has 100 per cent control over every dish that leaves his kitchen and still has time to see his family. He can walk out his back door, pick a tomato, whip up a delicious dish and then tell his diners about it. It is so small and so incredibly beautiful.'—Cassy Vires

GATES BAR-B-Q
3205 Main Street
Kansas City
Missouri 64111
+1 8167530828
www.gatesbbq.com

Opening hours	Open 7 days
Reservation policy	No
Credit cards	Accepted
Price range	Budget
Style	Casual
Cuisine	Barbeque
Recommended for	Local favourite

'Gates Bar-B-Q is a place that everyone should go to if they are in Kansas City. They opened in 1946, have six locations and ship their sauce all over the world. Gates is classic Kansas City barbeque and I love that not much has changed over the years. The service is "aggressive" and the food is consistent. I like to go with a group and get the "President's plate" so people can sample a little of everything. Gates Extra Hot is the best barbeque sauce in the world, easily.'
—Patrick Ryan

GENESSEE ROYALE

Recommended by
Colby Garrelts,
Patrick Ryan

1531 Genessee Street
Kansas City
Missouri 64102
+1 8164747070
www.genesseeroyale.com

Opening hours	Closed Sunday
Reservation policy	No
Credit cards	Accepted
Price range	Budget
Style	Casual
Cuisine	Café-Bistro
Recommended for	Regular neighbourhood

'Great, creative, fairly straightforward, contemporary American breakfast. I really like their fried chicken and cream biscuit breakfast paired with a Bloody Mary.'
—Patrick Ryan

HAPPY GILLIS

Recommended by
Patrick Ryan

549 Gillis Street
Kansas City
Missouri 64106
+1 8164713663
www.happygillis.com

Opening hours	Closed Monday
Reservation policy	No
Credit cards	Accepted
Price range	Budget
Style	Casual
Cuisine	Café
Recommended for	Wish I'd opened

'Supreme attention to detail and quality in a homely atmosphere.'—Patrick Ryan

JOHNNY JO'S PIZZERIA

Recommended by
Patrick Ryan

1209 West 47th Street
Kansas City
Missouri 64112
+1 8164014483

Opening hours	Closed Sunday
Reservation policy	No
Credit cards	Accepted
Price range	Budget
Style	Casual
Cuisine	Pizza
Recommended for	Bargain

'The best pizza in the city and one of the only places that you can get New York-style pizza. It's got great Monday night cash-only deals and that's usually when I roll through. The pepperoni and jalapeño is my go-to.'
—Patrick Ryan

MICHAEL SMITH

Recommended by
Colby Garrelts

1900 Main Street
Kansas City
Missouri 64108
+1 8168422202
www.michaelsmithkc.com

Opening hours	Closed Monday and Sunday
Credit cards	Accepted
Price range	Affordable
Style	Smart casual
Cuisine	Modern American
Recommended for	High end

'Chef Smith is a James Beard-award-winning chef. He is responsible for kick-starting the restaurant scene in Kansas City that we all know now. His Crossroads restaurant serves flawless, smart fine dining in a beautiful room and his wife, Nancy, puts together a stunning wine list.'—Colby Garrelts

PORT FONDA

Recommended by
Colby Garrelts

4141 Pennsylvania Avenue
Kansas City
Missouri 64111
+1 8162166462
www.portfondakc.com

Opening hours	Open 7 days
Credit cards	Accepted
Price range	Budget
Style	Casual
Cuisine	Mexican
Recommended for	Late night

'Awesome vibe and loud music! Best urban/modern Mexican, large beers and the best mescal list in the city.'—Colby Garrelts

THE RIEGER GRILL & EXCHANGE

Recommended by
Patrick Ryan

The Rieger Hotel
1924 Main Street
Kansas City
Missouri 64108
+1 8164712177
www.theriegerkc.com

Opening hours	Closed Sunday
Credit cards	Accepted
Price range	Affordable
Style	Casual
Cuisine	Modern American
Recommended for	Regular neighbourhood

'They change their menu regularly and have the best pastas in the city. Chef Howard Hanna is really talented with using offal and implementing the fifth cuts (the toughest, least expensive cuts) into the menu. Most recently I had the francobolli ravioli with butternut squash, n'duja, Brussels sprouts, lemon brown butter and ricotta salata.'—Patrick Ryan

ROOM 39

Recommended by
Colby Garrelts

1719 West 39th Street
Kansas City
Missouri 64111
+1 8167533939
www.rm39.com

Opening hours	Closed Sunday
Credit cards	Accepted
Price range	Affordable
Style	Casual
Cuisine	Modern American
Recommended for	Breakfast

'The chefs Ted and Andy just do breakfast well. Their quiches are perfect, their daily specials are always spot on. Order anything with eggs.'—Colby Garrelts

TOWN TOPIC

Recommended by
Patrick Ryan

2021 Broadway
Kansas City
Missouri 64108
+1 8168422298
www.towntopic.com

Opening hours	Open 7 days
Reservation policy	No
Credit cards	Accepted but not AMEX
Price range	Budget
Style	Casual
Cuisine	Burgers
Recommended for	Late night

'Town Topic has been serving up greasy-spoon diner food since 1937 and it's open really late. It is the perfect place to end up after a long night of drinking. I like the double with everything, an order of onion rings, a side of chilli and a chocolate shake.'—Patrick Ryan

BLOOD AND SAND

Recommended by
Gerard Craft

1500 Saint Charles Street
St. Louis
Missouri 63103
+1 3142417263
www.bloodandsandstl.com

Opening hours	Closed Sunday
Credit cards	Accepted
Price range	Affordable
Style	Smart casual
Cuisine	Modern American
Recommended for	Late night

DIABLITOS CANTINA

Recommended by
Cassy Vires

3761 Laclede Avenue
St. Louis
Missouri 63108
+1 3146444430
www.diablitoscantina.com

Opening hours	Open 7 days
Credit cards	Accepted
Price range	Budget
Style	Casual
Cuisine	Mexican
Recommended for	Bargain

'$2 (£1.20) tacos, $2 (£1.20) wells – need I say more?'
—Cassy Vires

FIVE STAR BURGERS

8125 Maryland Avenue
St. Louis
Missouri 63105
+1 3147204350
www.5starburgersstl.com

Opening hours	Open 7 days
Reservation policy	No
Credit cards	Accepted
Price range	Budget
Style	Casual
Cuisine	Burgers
Recommended for	Bargain

'Great burger and great beer – you don't need more than that!'—Gerard Craft

Chef-owner Steve Gontram made his name by spending fourteen years at Harvest, one of St. Louis's first fine-dining restaurants. In 2012 he sold out to his senior chef to open Five Star, a bold attempt to bring carefully made, semi-gourmet burgers to the Midwest. Patties are hand-shaped, cooked to temperature to arrive with full table service: this ain't a fast-food joint. Chips (fries) come flavoured with maple, while craft beer is given a prominent role, with eighteen on draught. Try the Whole Hog, a minced pork burger with bacon and pulled pork. There are now two locations in the state, with more planned.

GRINGO

398 North Euclid Avenue
St. Louis
Missouri 63108
+1 3144491212
www.gringo-stl.com

Opening hours	Open 7 days
Reservation policy	No
Credit cards	Accepted
Price range	Budget
Style	Casual
Cuisine	Mexican
Recommended for	Regular neighbourhood

'A really affordable local spot with great food and you can bring the kids.'—Gerard Craft

HALF & HALF

8135 Maryland Avenue
St. Louis
Missouri 63105
+1 3147250719
www.halfandhalfstl.com

Opening hours	Closed Monday
Reservation policy	No
Credit cards	Accepted
Price range	Budget
Style	Casual
Cuisine	Café-Bistro
Recommended for	Breakfast

'I can go in and eat light with some coffee or really stuff myself with good, greasy bacon.'—Gerard Craft

Half & Half serves the kind of hearty food Midwesterners want for breakfast: cornbread with chorizo, two fried eggs and potatoes; or crispy balsamic-braised pork belly with more fried eggs, potatoes and peach compote. Lemon-flavoured doughnuts come dusted in icing sugar. The space is functional and clean: a tiled floor, largely bare walls – a solitary poster of Bob Dylan graces one corner – and blue seats. Coffee is sourced from specialist blenders. At night the restaurant changes its menu and staff to become Little Country Gentleman, an entirely separate venture.

MISSION TACO JOINT

6235 Delmar Boulevard
St. Louis
Missouri 63130
+1 3149325430
www.missiontacostl.com

Opening hours	Closed Monday
Reservation policy	No
Credit cards	Accepted
Price range	Budget
Style	Casual
Cuisine	Mexican
Recommended for	Regular neighbourhood

NICHE

Recommended by
Cassy Vires

7734 Forsyth Boulevard
St. Louis
Missouri 63105
+1 3147737755
www.nichestlouis.com

Opening hours...Closed Sunday
Credit cards...Accepted
Price range...Expensive
Style...Smart casual
Cuisine...Modern American
Recommended for..High end

'Chef Gerard Craft is a force to be reckoned with. His
tasting menus are like visiting a museum: beautiful,
thought provoking, inspiring and satisfying.'
—Cassy Vires

OLIO

Recommended by
Gerard Craft

1634 Tower Grove Avenue
St. Louis
Missouri 63110
+1 3149321088
www.oliostl.com

Opening hours...Open 7 days
Credit cards...Accepted
Price range...Affordable
Style...Casual
Cuisine..Mediterranean
Recommended for.............................Regular neighbourhood

PAPPY'S SMOKEHOUSE

Recommended by
Gerard Craft

3106 Olive Street
St. Louis
Missouri 63103
+1 3145354340
www.pappyssmokehouse.com

Opening hours...Open 7 days
Reservation policy..No
Credit cards...Accepted
Price range...Budget
Style...Casual
Cuisine..Barbeque
Recommended for..Wish I'd opened

'I wish I'd opened it except I could never throw down
like Skip Steele or Mike Emerson. The best barbeque
out there.'—Gerard Craft

SIDNEY STREET CAFE

Recommended by
Gerard Craft,
Cassy Vires

2000 Sidney Street
St. Louis
Missouri 63104
+1 3147715777
www.sidneystreetcafe.com

Opening hours...............................Closed Monday and Sunday
Credit cards...Accepted
Price range...Expensive
Style...Smart casual
Cuisine...Modern American
Recommended for..High end

'This place is a landmark in St. Louis and chef Kevin
Nashan gets the best fish this city has ever seen.'
—Gerard Craft

SOUTHWEST DINER

Recommended by
Gerard Craft,
Cassy Vires

6803 Southwest Avenue
St. Louis
Missouri 63143
+1 3142607244
www.southwestdinerstl.com

Opening hours...Open 7 days
Reservation policy..No
Credit cards...Accepted
Price range...Budget
Style...Casual
Cuisine..Mexican
Recommended for...Breakfast

'The cornmeal pancakes are delicious and they do
great chilli.'—Cassy Vires

TASTE BAR

Recommended by
Cassy Vires

4584 Laclede Avenue
St. Louis
Missouri 63108
+1 3143611200
www.tastebarstl.com

Opening hours	Open 7 days
Credit cards	Accepted
Price range	Affordable
Style	Casual
Cuisine	Bar-Small plates
Recommended for	Late night

'This place is a must visit in St. Louis. The cocktails are out of this world and it has a great underground feel to it. The kitchen is open until midnight and the food is some of the best in town. Their *barbacoa* is always on my order, plus chips (fries), curried lamb, smoked beetroot (beets), brick chicken, fried pickles…'
—Cassy Vires

TONY'S

Recommended by
Gerard Craft

410 Market Street
St. Louis
Missouri 63102
+1 3142317007
www.tonysstlouis.com

Opening hours	Closed Monday and Sunday
Credit cards	Accepted
Price range	Expensive
Style	Smart casual
Cuisine	Italian
Recommended for	Local favourite

'They don't get a ton of credit but it is super-old-school Italian fine dining that only exists in Rome these days.'
—Gerard Craft

TRIPEL

Recommended by
Cassy Vires

1801 Park Avenue
St. Louis
Missouri 63104
+1 3146787787
www.tripelstl.com

Opening hours	Closed Monday
Credit cards	Accepted
Price range	Affordable
Style	Casual
Cuisine	Belgian Brasserie
Recommended for	Regular neighbourhood

'Yummy food, delicious drinks and really cool vibe are all great reasons to go, but that's not why I go there… It's for the staff, especially the bar staff who are so vibrant and personable.'—Cassy Vires

BIG BAD BREAKFAST

Recommended by
Sean Brock

719 North Lamar Boulevard
Oxford
Mississippi 38655
+1 6622362666
www.bigbadbreakfast.com

Opening hours	Open 7 days
Reservation policy	No
Credit cards	Accepted
Price range	Budget
Style	Casual
Cuisine	Southern American
Recommended for	Breakfast

'Chef Currence is one hell of a guy and his personality really shows through in this amazing breakfast-driven restaurant. Any time I'm anywhere near Oxford I'm sure to make a detour. The bacon and biscuits alone are worth a three-hour drive.'—Sean Brock

DOZZINO

Recommended by
Kevin Pemoulie

534 Adams Street
Hoboken
New Jersey 07030
+1 2016566561
www.dozzino.com

Opening hours	Closed Monday
Reservation policy	No
Credit cards	Accepted
Price range	Budget
Style	Casual
Cuisine	Pizza
Recommended for	Local favourite

'They are doing their own version of artisanal pizza in wood-fired ovens.'—Kevin Pemoulie

RAZZA
Recommended by
Kevin Pemoulie
275 Grove Street
Jersey City
New Jersey 07302
+1 2013569348
www.razzanj.com

Opening hours	Closed Sunday
Reservation policy	No
Credit cards	Accepted
Price range	Affordable
Style	Casual
Cuisine	Pizza
Recommended for	Local favourite

'They use almost all local ingredients and they're very involved in our community.'—Kevin Pemoulie

TAQUERIA DOWNTOWN
Recommended by
Kevin Pemoulie
236 Grove Street
Jersey City
New Jersey 07302
+1 2013333220

Opening hours	Open 7 days
Reservation policy	No
Credit cards	Accepted
Price range	Budget
Style	Casual
Cuisine	Mexican
Recommended for	Bargain

'They serve great tacos for ridiculous prices. They also have a great Michelada (Mexican beer cocktail).' —Kevin Pemoulie

KENILWORTH DINER
Recommended by
Kevin Pemoulie
614 Boulevard
Kenilworth
New Jersey 07033
+1 9082456565

Opening hours	Open 7 days
Reservation policy	No
Credit cards	Accepted
Price range	Budget
Style	Casual
Cuisine	Diner
Recommended for	Breakfast

'I'm a sucker for Jersey diners and this is my favourite. It's a great, classic diner. They make a mean Taylor ham, egg and cheese sandwich.'—Kevin Pemoulie

THE BARN AT BEDFORD POST
Recommended by
Rebecca Kirhoffer
954 Old Post Road
Bedford
New York 10506
+1 9142347800
www.bedfordpostinn.com

Opening hours	Open 7 days
Credit cards	Accepted
Price range	Affordable
Style	Casual
Cuisine	Modern American
Recommended for	Regular neighbourhood

'It's a beautiful farmhouse in a rural setting so far removed from city living. They have an amazing Dutch pancake – who doesn't love pancakes and maple syrup?' —Rebecca Kirhoffer

CROSSROADS FOOD SHOP
Recommended by
Bjorn Somlo
2642 Route 23
Hillsdale
New York 12529
+1 5183251461
www.crossroadsfoodshop.com

Opening hours	Closed Monday and Tuesday
Credit cards	Accepted
Price range	Affordable
Style	Casual
Cuisine	Modern American
Recommended for	Regular neighbourhood

'Great clean and honest food. Very rare to find.' —Bjorn Somlo

BLUE HILL AT STONE BARNS
630 Bedford Road
Pocantico Hills
New York 10591
+1 9143669600
www.bluehillfarm.com

Recommended by
Massimo Bottura, Daniel
Boulud, Andrea Carlson,
Paul Cunningham, Brad
Farmerie, Neal Fraser, Tory
Miller, Khalid Mohammed,
Claus Meyer, Mads
Refslund, Masato
Shimizu, Tim Siadatan

Opening hours	Closed Monday and Tuesday
Credit cards	Accepted
Price range	Expensive
Style	Formal
Cuisine	Modern American
Recommended for	Worth the travel

'The epitome of a true farm-to-table experience. The grounds are as exquisite as the food.'—Daniel Boulud

At his ten-year-old 'farm-to-table' restaurant (the follow up to Blue Hill New York), Dan Barber sources ingredients solely within the Hudson Valley and mainly from the working farm and educational centre on which the restaurant is based. Talk about fresh: guests even 'cut their own' greens at the table. Barber's not called the 'high priest of locavorism' for nothing. Menus arrive in list form, as an inventory of the day's harvest that reveals itself in a succession of elegant vegetable-led small plates. As a gastronomic experience, it's uplifting, edifying and lengthy: clear at least four hours for your multi-course Farmers' Feast.

BEACON
8 West Water Street
Sag Harbor
New York 11963
+1 6317257088
www.beaconsagharbor.com

Recommended by
Harold Dieterle

Opening hours	Open 7 days
Reservation policy	No
Credit cards	Accepted
Price range	Affordable
Style	Casual
Cuisine	Modern American
Recommended for	Local favourite

Gazing out at the sunset from the Beacon it's hard not to feel lucky. The hour-plus wait for a table – no reservations even if you're a 'have-yacht' – was worth it after all. Hamptons' holidaymakers and locals eagerly anticipate the waterfront restaurant's annual reopening each May. There's no surer sign that summer is coming than when the Beacon mixes its first Margarita of the year. The lobster rigatoni, fish tacos and New York strip steak are house trademarks best enjoyed at a coveted patio or window table. Owners David Loewenberg and chef Sam McCleland also run the nearby Bell & Anchor.

THE ADMIRAL
400 Haywood Road
Asheville
North Carolina 28806
+1 8282522541
www.theadmiralnc.com

Recommended by
Justin Devillier

Opening hours	Open 7 days
Credit cards	Accepted but not AMEX
Price range	Affordable
Style	Smart casual
Cuisine	Modern American
Recommended for	Worth the travel

'It's a really laidback restaurant that feels old school, like a dark supper club. The design is industrial. They steam their mussels in PBR, and everything from the oysters to the tartare is totally on point.'
—Justin Devillier

CHAI PANI
22 Battery Park Avenue
Asheville
North Carolina 28801
+1 8282544003
www.chaipaniasheville.com

Recommended by
Katie Button

Opening hours	Open 7 days
Reservation policy	No
Credit cards	Accepted
Price range	Budget
Style	Casual
Cuisine	Indian Street Food
Recommended for	Bargain

'It's not the typical Indian food that you see everwhere; it has introduced me to what Indian food really is. The chef, Meherwan Irani, uses local ingredients and makes delicious authentic dishes that are extremely affordable and always consistent. Some of my favourites are the *uttapam* (thick pancake) and the chicken *pakoras* (fritters).'—Katie Button

CUCINA24

24 Wall Street
Asheville
North Carolina 28801
+1 8282546170
www.cucina24restaurant.com

Opening hours	Closed Monday
Credit cards	Accepted
Price range	Affordable
Style	Smart casual
Cuisine	Italian
Recommended for	High end

'The chef, Brian Canipelli, creates really interesting seasonal local versions of Italian food. Start the evening with a cocktail – their lead bartender whips up some of the best in town – then follow that with a couple of appetizers, a bottle of nice Italian wine (they have a really well-selected wine list) and a few dishes to share. And don't leave without dessert.'
—Katie Button

FIG BISTRO

18 Brook Street
Asheville
North Carolina 28803
+1 8282770889
www.figbistro.com

Opening hours	Open 7 days
Credit cards	Accepted
Price range	Affordable
Style	Casual
Cuisine	Modern American
Recommended for	Regular neighbourhood

'Fig has easily become my go-to spot for a nice long lunch. The food is always extremely consistent, they offer half glasses of wine, which for lunch is great because you can pair a half glass with each course. I typically order the pork belly or seasonal soup as an appetizer followed by their quiche which is so light and airy, it takes quiche into another universe. I just can't stay away.'—Katie Button

THE JUNCTION

348 Depot Street
Asheville
North Carolina 28801
+1 8282253497
www.thejunctionasheville.com

Opening hours	Closed Monday
Credit cards	Accepted
Price range	Affordable
Style	Casual
Cuisine	Modern American
Recommended for	Breakfast

'The Junction serves the best brunch in town. Their cocktails are delicious but it's the sticky bun with blue cheese and candied orange zest that has my heart.'
—Katie Button

KING JAMES PUBLIC HOUSE

94 Charlotte Street
Asheville
North Carolina 28801
+1 8282522412

Opening hours	Open 7 days
Reservation policy	No
Credit cards	Accepted
Price range	Affordable
Style	Casual
Cuisine	Gastropub
Recommended for	Wish I'd opened

'Steven Goff is doing some cool things in Asheville with the craft beer scene there.'—Justin Burdett

STORM RHUM BAR & BISTRO
125 South Lexington Avenue
Asheville
North Carolina 28801
+1 8285058560
www.stormrhumbar.com

Opening hours	Open 7 days
Credit cards	Accepted
Price range	Affordable
Style	Casual
Cuisine	Modern American
Recommended for	Late night

'A great spot for late-night eating. Their kitchen is always open until 1.00 a.m. and at that hour I'm looking for a beer and one of their delicious hot dogs or a hamburger. They make everything from scratch, including the ketchup and the buns.'—Katie Button

TABLE
48 College Street
Asheville
North Carolina 28801
+1 8282548980
www.tableasheville.com

Opening hours	Open 7 days
Credit cards	Accepted
Price range	Affordable
Style	Casual
Cuisine	Modern American
Recommended for	Local favourite

'Since Table opened in 2005, the farm-to-table food scene in Asheville has really taken off. They paved the way for all the restaurants that followed in their wake. They pay super-close attention to their ingredients, seeking out the best products, and they change their menu constantly. Their food is a true representation of the culture and products of the region.'—Katie Button

WICKED WEED BREWING
91 Biltmore Avenue
Asheville
North Carolina 28801
+1 8285759599
www.wickedweedbrewing.com

Opening hours	Open 7 days
Reservation policy	No
Credit cards	Accepted
Price range	Affordable
Style	Casual
Cuisine	Modern American
Recommended for	Wish I'd opened

'Raised the bar for breweries in Asheville. They opened an enormous space, an all-in-one brewery/restaurant/ tasting room, and they are clearly putting a lot of effort into making every aspect of their concept outstanding. It's packed almost every day, but the consistency of the food and the risks they take with the beer they produce are always outstanding.'—Katie Button

NEAL'S DELI
100 East Main Street
Carrboro
North Carolina 27510
+1 9199672185
www.nealsdeli.com

Opening hours	Closed Monday
Reservation policy	No
Credit cards	Accepted
Price range	Budget
Style	Casual
Cuisine	Deli-Café
Recommended for	Breakfast

ĀN
2800 Renaissance Park Place
Cary
North Carolina 27513
+1 9196779229
www.ancuisines.com

Opening hours	Closed Sunday
Credit cards	Accepted
Price range	Affordable
Style	Smart casual
Cuisine	Modern Asian
Recommended for	High end

'The food is brilliant and complex. It's billed as new world cuisine. The menu celebrates some of the freshest, most pristine fish I've ever experienced. I find the combinations and preparations intriguing and inspiring. The chef is Steven Greene, and he is a force... a true talent.'—Ashley Christensen

CROOK'S CORNER

Recommended by
Andrea Reusing

610 West Franklin Street
Chapel Hill
North Carolina 27516
+1 9199297643
www.crookscorner.com

Opening hours	Closed Monday
Credit cards	Accepted
Price range	Affordable
Style	Casual
Cuisine	Southern American
Recommended for	Regular neighbourhood

SCRATCH

Recommended by
Andrea Reusing

111 Orange Street
Durham
North Carolina 27701
+1 9199565200
www.piefantasy.com

Opening hours	Closed Monday
Reservation policy	No
Credit cards	Accepted
Price range	Budget
Style	Casual
Cuisine	Café-Bakery
Recommended for	Local favourite

TOAST

Recommended by
Andrea Reusing

345 West Main Street
Durham
North Carolina 27701
+1 9196832183
www.toast-fivepoints.com

Opening hours	Closed Sunday
Reservation policy	No
Credit cards	Accepted but not AMEX
Price range	Budget
Style	Casual
Cuisine	Italian Sandwiches
Recommended for	Bargain

THAI PARADISE

Recommended by
Justin Burdett

3078 Georgia Road
Franklin
North Carolina 28734
+1 8283490973

Opening hours	Closed Monday
Credit cards	Accepted but not AMEX
Price range	Budget
Style	Casual
Cuisine	Thai
Recommended for	Regular neighbourhood

'This is a family-run, authentic Thai place – I live for their *thom kha gai*.'—Justin Burdett

MADISON'S RESTAURANT

Recommended by
Justin Burdett

Old Edwards Inn
445 Main Street
Highlands
North Carolina 28741
+1 8287872525
www.oldedwardsinn.com

Opening hours	Open 7 days
Credit cards	Accepted
Price range	Affordable
Style	Smart casual
Cuisine	Modern American
Recommended for	Local favourite

'This is the pinnacle of Highlands dining with the luxurious back-drop of the Inn.'—Justin Burdett

PANCIUTO

Recommended by
Andrea Reusing

110 South Churton Street
Hillsborough
North Carolina 27278
+1 9197326261
www.panciuto.com

Opening hours	Closed Sunday to Tuesday
Credit cards	Accepted but not AMEX
Price range	Affordable
Style	Casual
Cuisine	Modern Italian
Recommended for	High end

JK'S RESTAURANT

Recommended by
Kevin McCaffery

1106 South Croatan Highway
Kill Devil Hills
North Carolina 27948
+1 2524419555
www.jksrestaurant.com

Opening hours	Open 7 days
Credit cards	Accepted
Price range	Expensive
Style	Casual
Cuisine	Steakhouse
Recommended for	Worth the travel

'Live wood grill – get the veal rib chop and quail salad with Roquefort dressing.'—Kevin McCaffery

BIDA MANDA

Recommended by
Ashley Christensen

222 South Blount Street
Raleigh
North Carolina 27601
+1 9198299999
www.bidamanda.com

Opening hours	Closed Sunday
Credit cards	Accepted
Price range	Affordable
Style	Smart casual
Cuisine	Laotian
Recommended for	Regular neighbourhood

'It's an authentic Laotian restaurant in a contemporary environment. The food is fresh, inventive and delicious. They have a beautiful bar programme. It is owned and run by a brother and sister who hail from Laos. Their family still lives in Laos and the restaurant is their love letter home.'—Ashley Christensen

CENTRO

Recommended by
Ashley Christensen

106 South Wilmington Street
Raleigh
North Carolina 27601
+1 9198353593
www.centroraleigh.com

Opening hours	Closed Sunday
Reservation policy	No
Credit cards	Accepted
Price range	Affordable
Style	Casual
Cuisine	Mexican
Recommended for	Bargain

'Serves bright, crisp combinations. The food is delicious and always makes me feel good. At lunch they offer a chicken soup with avocado and rice. It's filling, belly-warming, restorative, and only $6 (£3.50)! It's a great meal and such great value!'—Ashley Christensen

THE MECCA RESTAURANT

Recommended by
Ashley Christensen

13 East Martin Street
Raleigh
North Carolina 27601
+1 9198325714
www.mecca-restaurant.com

Opening hours	Closed Sunday
Reservation policy	No
Credit cards	Accepted
Price range	Budget
Style	Casual
Cuisine	Diner
Recommended for	Breakfast

'It is the oldest restaurant in downtown Raleigh, and it is still run by the family that started it. It's a soul food kind of joint, and the presiding godfather of the Raleigh restaurant scene.'—Ashley Christensen

THE PLAYERS' RETREAT

Recommended by
Ashley Christensen

105 Oberlin Road
Raleigh
North Carolina 27605
+1 9197559589
www.playersretreat.net

Opening hours	Open 7 days
Credit cards	Accepted
Price range	Budget
Style	Casual
Cuisine	American
Recommended for	Local favourite

'It is embedded in Raleigh history. Right across the street from North Carolina State University, it welcomes folks from all walks of life... students, professors, plumbers, politicians, you name it. It's down and dirty, and still offers killer food, an outstanding wine list and the biggest Scotch whisky list in the state. The walls are adorned with thousands of vintage beer cans. It's my kind of joint.'—Ashley Christensen

POOLE'S DINER

426 South McDowell Street
Raleigh
North Carolina 27601
+1 9198324477
www.poolesdowntowndiner.com

Opening hours	Open 7 days
Reservation policy	No
Credit cards	Accepted
Price range	Affordable
Style	Casual
Cuisine	Diner-Café
Recommended for	Worth the travel

'It's honest and fresh and super pleasant. It's Southern food but clean.'—Alexandra Raij

Launched in 2007 by chef Ashley Christensen, this downtown hotspot takes its name and diner aesthetic from the building's original occupant – a pie shop that was among the district's first eateries. Christensen, who honed her talents in the Triangle's top kitchens, is one of the Southeast's most hardworking young stars (she opened a number of new ventures in 2014, cementing her local mini-empire) and here she turns out an evolving blackboard (chalkboard) menu of unpretentious, high-flavour comfort food based on local seasonal ingredients. Snug red leather banquettes and a double horseshoe-shaped bar underscore the joint's appealing retro-chic vibe.

L'ALBATROS

11401 Bellflower Road
Cleveland
Ohio 44106
+1 2167917880
www.albatrosbrasserie.com

Opening hours	Closed Sunday
Credit cards	Accepted
Price range	Affordable
Style	Smart casual
Cuisine	French
Recommended for	Wish I'd opened

'No matter when you go the food execution is unreal! The same can be said for the front of house – always exceptional attention to detail and to the customer.' —Christopher Hodgson

BAR CENTO

1948 West 25th Street
Cleveland
Ohio 44113
+1 2162741010
www.barcento.com

Opening hours	Open 7 days
Credit cards	Accepted
Price range	Affordable
Style	Smart casual
Cuisine	Gastropub
Recommended for	Late night

'Bar Cento's late-night pizza is the best in town.' —Christopher Hodgson

DANTE

2247 Professor Avenue
Cleveland
Ohio 44113
+1 2162741200
www.restaurantdante.us

Opening hours	Closed Sunday
Credit cards	Accepted
Price range	Expensive
Style	Smart casual
Cuisine	Modern American-Italian
Recommended for	High end

'Dante is one of the best chefs I've ever known. His namesake restaurant is my go-to spot in Cleveland for an anniversary. Ginko (directly underneath) is hands down the best sushi in town. There has never been a moment when I doubted my decision to go to either restaurant. Inventive, great quality food and an elegant atmosphere. Dante is that guy who welcomes you in and is genuinely grateful that you are dining with them.'—Christopher Hodgson

EAT AT JOE'S

1475 South Green Road
Cleveland
Ohio 44121
+1 2163813101

Opening hours	Open 7 days
Reservation policy	No
Credit cards	Not accepted
Price range	Budget
Style	Casual
Cuisine	Diner
Recommended for	Breakfast

'By far the best hash browns in town.'
—Christopher Hodgson

EDWINS

13013 Shaker Square
Cleveland
Ohio 44120
+1 2169213333
www.edwinsrestaurant.org

Opening hours	Closed Sunday
Credit cards	Accepted
Price range	Affordable
Style	Smart casual
Cuisine	French
Recommended for	Regular neighbourhood

'Owner Brandon Chrostowski has a passion for food, wine and people in general like nobody I have ever met. I always feel like family when I pick my seven-cheese selection from the thirty-five he offers.'
—Christopher Hodgson

FIRE FOOD AND DRINK

13220 Shaker Square
Cleveland
Ohio 44120
+1 2169213473
www.firefoodanddrink.com

Opening hours	Closed Monday
Credit cards	Accepted
Price range	Affordable
Style	Smart casual
Cuisine	Modern American
Recommended for	Breakfast

'Their brunch is always the one that I consider missing church for.'—Christopher Hodgson

HAPPY DOG

5801 Detroit Avenue
Cleveland
Ohio 44102
+1 2166519474
www.happydogcleveland.com

Opening hours	Open 7 days
Reservation policy	No
Credit cards	Accepted
Price range	Budget
Style	Casual
Cuisine	Hot Dogs
Recommended for	Bargain

'It's the only place I know where you can put fried eggs on a hot dog and a hundred other ingredients if you feel like doing so. Not to mention a huge side of tater tots with as many dipping sauces as you desire.'
—Christopher Hodgson

LOLITA

900 Literary Road
Cleveland
Ohio 44113
+1 2167715652
www.lolitarestaurant.com

Opening hours	Closed Monday
Credit cards	Accepted
Price range	Affordable
Style	Smart casual
Cuisine	Modern American
Recommended for	Local favourite

'Even though Lolita has been around for ten years it's still constantly innovating its menu and bringing forth brand new ideas. Executive chef James Mowcomber, under the careful tutelage of chef Michael Symon, has been blasting out dishes from roasted bone marrow to picci pasta with octopus and mint.'—Jonathon Sawyer

LUCKY'S CAFE

Recommended by
Christopher Hodgson

777 Starkweather Avenue
Cleveland
Ohio 44113
+1 2166227773
www.luckyscafe.com

Opening hours	Open 7 days
Reservation policy	No
Credit cards	Accepted
Price range	Budget
Style	Casual
Cuisine	Café
Recommended for	Breakfast

'What Heather Haviland has done with mac and cheese at Lucky's Cafe is fit for the gods. Just make sure you add jalapeños.'—Christopher Hodgson

MIEGA KOREAN BARBEQUE

Recommended by
Jonathon Sawyer

3820 Superior Avenue
Cleveland
Ohio 44114
+1 2164329200
www.miegabbq.com

Opening hours	Closed Monday
Credit cards	Accepted
Price range	Affordable
Style	Casual
Cuisine	Korean
Recommended for	Bargain

'Besides the vast variety of authentic Korean cuisine, the price cannot be beat! From great hot pots filled with everything from vegetables to seafood that serve four people, to a $13 (£8) large spread of *banchan*, with all things sour, fermented and pickled in house. And on top of all that, take in the scenery in the Asiatown Plaza while watching hipsters display their art and martial arts classes taking place across the way.'—Jonathon Sawyer

THE TAVERN COMPANY

Recommended by
Christopher Hodgson

2260 Lee Road
Cleveland
Ohio 44118
+1 2163216001
www.thetaverncompany.com

Opening hours	Open 7 days
Credit cards	Accepted
Price range	Budget
Style	Casual
Cuisine	American
Recommended for	Late night

'The owner is just a great guy. I crave their chicken wings and hanger steak every time I drive by.'
—Christopher Hodgson

VERO PIZZA NAPOLETANA

Recommended by
Jonathon Sawyer

12421 Cedar Road
Cleveland
Ohio 44106
+1 2162298383
www.verocleveland.com

Opening hours	Closed Monday
Reservation policy	No
Credit cards	Accepted
Price range	Budget
Style	Casual
Cuisine	Pizza
Recommended for	Regular neighbourhood

'Best modern crust in Cleveland. The one-of-a-kind wood-burning oven churns out thin and crispy Neapolitan pizzas to order. With ingredients such as Protected Designation of Origin (PDO) cheeses, heirloom tomatoes and double zero flours, it's second to none. Chef-owner Marc-Aurele Buholzer is also a great ambassador for Cleveland Heights and is very involved with the community.'—Jonathon Sawyer

CAFÉ BRIOSO
Recommended by
Jonathon Sawyer
14 East Gay Street
Columbus
Ohio 43215
+1 6142288366
www.cafebrioso.com

Opening hours	Closed Sunday
Reservation policy	No
Credit cards	Accepted
Price range	Budget
Style	Casual
Cuisine	Café
Recommended for	Breakfast

'Simply the best place to nerd out on coffee. It's the only place around that serves triple-basket pours, single-origin pour-overs, the "perfect" espresso shot and so many more tasty drinks, all while you nosh on carefully crafted house-made bagels and sandwiches and watch insanely talented baristas. I love hanging out and talking shop about coffee, and I always manage to drink way too much!'—Jonathon Sawyer

FLOUR RESTAURANT
Recommended by
Christopher Hodgson
34205 Chagrin Boulevard
Moreland Hills
Ohio 44022
+1 2164643700
www.flourrestaurant.com

Opening hours	Open 7 days
Credit cards	Accepted
Price range	Affordable
Style	Smart casual
Cuisine	Italian
Recommended for	Regular neighbourhood

'They always have great specials and an incredible selection of cheese.'—Christopher Hodgson

CHEZ FRANÇOIS
Recommended by
Christopher Hodgson
555 Main Street
Vermilion
Ohio 44089
+1 4409670630
www.chezfrancois.com

Opening hours	Closed Monday
Credit cards	Accepted
Price range	Expensive
Style	Formal
Cuisine	French
Recommended for	High end

'Chez François is on another level for me. It was one of the top three dining experiences of my life, incredible service. Matt the owner makes everybody who walks through the doors feel like family. Sensational food, beautiful environment. Just an all-round awesome place.'—Christopher Hodgson

AVANCE
Recommended by
Kevin Sbraga
1523 Walnut Street
Philadelphia
Pennsylvania 19103
+1 2154050700
www.avancephiladelphia.com

Opening hours	Closed Monday
Credit cards	Accepted
Price range	Affordable
Style	Smart casual
Cuisine	Modern American
Recommended for	High end

'They are living up to the location's expectations and history (it once housed Le Bec-Fin, a dining icon in Philadelphia and the US).'—Kevin Sbraga

BROAD STREET DINER
Recommended by
Kevin Sbraga
1135 South Broad Street
Philadelphia
Pennsylvania 19147
+1 2158253636

Opening hours	Open 7 days
Reservation policy	No
Credit cards	Accepted
Price range	Budget
Style	Casual
Cuisine	Diner
Recommended for	Breakfast

'It is affordable, convenient and quick.'—Kevin Sbraga

CAFÉ SOHO
Recommended by
Michael Solomonov
468 West Cheltenham Avenue
Philadelphia
Pennsylvania 19126
+1 2152246800
www.mycafesoho.com

Opening hours	Open 7 days
Credit cards	Accepted
Price range	Affordable
Style	Casual
Cuisine	Korean-Japanese
Recommended for	Late night

'The best chicken wings around, hands down. Soy garlic sauce is a must.'—Michael Solomonov

THE FARM AND FISHERMAN
Recommended by
Michael Solomonov
1120 Pine Street
Philadelphia
Pennsylvania 19107
+1 2676871555
www.thefarmandfisherman.com

Opening hours	Closed Monday
Credit cards	Accepted but not AMEX
Price range	Affordable
Style	Smart casual
Cuisine	Modern American
Recommended for	Local favourite

'A thirty-seat gem in Center City. It's farm-to-table done right. The food is outstanding, and the chef Josh Lawler is committed to serving 100 per cent locally sourced products.'—Michael Solomonov

HIGH STREET ON MARKET
Recommended by
Kevin Sbraga,
Michael Solomonov
308 Market Street
Philadelphia
Pennsylvania 19106
+1 2156250988
www.highstreetonmarket.com

Opening hours	Open 7 days
Credit cards	Accepted
Price range	Affordable
Style	Casual
Cuisine	Modern American
Recommended for	Breakfast

'It's an up-and-comer in Old City that opened in September 2013. They bake the most amazing breads in the universe. Seriously. Their house-made seeded red onion bialys are out of this world.'
—Michael Solomonov

PHO 75
Recommended by
Michael Solomonov
1122 Washington Avenue
Philadelphia
Pennsylvania 19147
+1 2152715866

Opening hours	Open 7 days
Reservation policy	No
Credit cards	Not accepted
Price range	Budget
Style	Casual
Cuisine	Vietnamese
Recommended for	Regular neighbourhood

'I tend to gravitate towards Asian soup houses. Pho 75 do one thing and they do it very, very well. Honestly, it's the most consistent meal in Philly – and it's probably the least expensive, too.'—Michael Solomonov

PHO HA
Recommended by
Kevin Sbraga
610 Washington Avenue
Philadelphia
Pennsylvania 19147
+1 2155990264
www.phohaonline.com

Opening hours	Open 7 days
Reservation policy	No
Credit cards	Not accepted
Price range	Budget
Style	Casual
Cuisine	Vietnamese
Recommended for	Bargain

'You can always get a delicous, piping-hot bowl of soup for under $10 (£6).'—Kevin Sbraga

PIZZERIA STELLA
Recommended by
Kevin Sbraga
420 South Second Street
Philadelphia
Pennsylvania 19106
+1 2153208000
www.pizzeriastella.net

Opening hours	Open 7 days
Reservation policy	No
Credit cards	Accepted
Price range	Budget
Style	Casual
Cuisine	Pizza
Recommended for	Regular neighbourhood

'Always great service and great food.'—Kevin Sbraga

PUB & KITCHEN
Recommended by
Kevin Sbraga
1946 Lombard Street
Philadelphia
Pennsylvania 19146
+1 2155450350
www.thepubandkitchen.com

Opening hours	Open 7 days
Credit cards	Accepted
Price range	Affordable
Style	Casual
Cuisine	Gastropub
Recommended for	Late night

'Cool atmosphere, good food and good drinks. They serve a menu until 1.00 a.m., which is important to me because I'm usually working late.'—Kevin Sbraga

SANTUCCI'S ORIGINAL SQUARE PIZZA
Recommended by
Kevin Sbraga
901 South 10th Street
Philadelphia
Pennsylvania 19147
+1 2158255304
www.santuccispizza.com

Opening hours	Open 7 days
Reservation policy	No
Credit cards	Not accepted
Price range	Budget
Style	Casual
Cuisine	Pizza
Recommended for	Local favourite

'Their tomato pie is outstanding!'—Kevin Sbraga

SBRAGA
Recommended by
Michael Solomonov
440 South Broad Street
Philadelphia
Pennsylvania 19146
+1 2157351913
www.sbraga.com

Opening hours	Closed Sunday
Credit cards	Accepted
Price range	Affordable
Style	Smart casual
Cuisine	Modern American
Recommended for	Bargain

'The tasting menu. Chef Kevin Sbraga is one of the most inventive chefs in the city. The food is always delicious, satisfying and doles out just the right amount of refinement.'—Michael Solomonov

VETRI
Recommended by
Michael Solomonov
1312 Spruce Street
Philadelphia
Pennsylvania 19107
+1 2157323478
www.vetriristorante.com

Opening hours	Closed Sunday
Credit cards	Accepted
Price range	Expensive
Style	Smart casual
Cuisine	Italian
Recommended for	High end

'To put it simply, it feels like my home.'
—Michael Solomonov

BUTCHER & BEE

Recommended by
Mike Lata

654 King Street
Charleston
South Carolina 29403
+1 8436190202
www.butcherandbee.com

Opening hours	Open 7 days
Credit cards	Accepted
Price range	Budget
Style	Casual
Cuisine	Sandwiches
Recommended for	Late night

'Casual, quirky and consistently delicious. They always have something I'm craving... even before I know it.'
—Mike Lata

CHARLESTON GRILL

Recommended by
Mike Lata

224 King Street
Charleston
South Carolina 29401
+1 8435774522
www.charlestongrill.com

Opening hours	Open 7 days
Credit cards	Accepted
Price range	Expensive
Style	Smart casual
Cuisine	Modern American
Recommended for	High end

'A special occasion demands the presence of a true maître d'. Mickey Bakst can make you feel like a rock star and he's happy to do so.'—Mike Lata

FIG

Recommended by
Peter Hoffman

232 Meeting Street
Charleston
South Carolina 29401
+1 8438055900
www.eatatfig.com

Opening hours	Closed Sunday
Credit cards	Accepted
Price range	Affordable
Style	Casual
Cuisine	European Bistro
Recommended for	Worth the travel

'Great ingredients, delicious food and sensibility. Terrific wine list, comfortable ambience and well-trained staff.'—Peter Hoffman

HOMINY GRILL

Recommended by
Mike Lata

207 Rutledge Avenue
Charleston
South Carolina 29403
+1 8439370930
www.hominygrill.com

Opening hours	Open 7 days
Credit cards	Accepted
Price range	Affordable
Style	Casual
Cuisine	Southern American
Recommended for	Breakfast

'It's a Charleston icon that improves with age. I've been going for years and it has matured beautifully into the kind of restaurant you want to share with your friends. Freshest eggs in town and with a fast turnaround, it's almost quicker than making myself breakfast at home.'
—Mike Lata

HUSK

Recommended by
April Bloomfield

76 Queen Street
Charleston
South Carolina 29401
+1 8435772500
www.huskrestaurant.com

Opening hours	Open 7 days
Credit cards	Accepted
Price range	Affordable
Style	Casual
Cuisine	Southern American
Recommended for	Worth the travel

'I love Sean Brock's inspiration: using Low Country ingredients and refining those ingredients to make amazing, delicious food.'—April Bloomfield

Sean Brock's follow-up to McCrady's pursues the same farm-to-fork philosophy. The market-driven menu moves beyond South Carolina's larder (pantry) to make use of Kentucky honey, Tennessee steak and North Carolina catfish. But if it isn't a product of Southern pride, it doesn't make it near the wood-fired oven. The restored 1893 Queen Anne home with its columned porches has taken well to its new purpose: an open kitchen on the ground floor and a second-floor dining room that's as fetching as any in Dixie. The adjacent brick building houses a bar that touts craft bourbons and hand-carved Tennessee country hams.

MCCRADY'S

2 Unity Alley
Charleston
South Carolina 29401
+1 8435770025
www.mccradysrestaurant.com

Recommended by
Michael Anthony,
Matt McCallister

Opening hours	Open 7 days
Credit cards	Accepted
Price range	Expensive
Style	Casual
Cuisine	Modern Southern American
Recommended for	Worth the travel

'It's in the top five meals I've had in the country.
Definitely one of my favourite spots. I'll be going there
again!'—Matt McCallister

Housed in a handsomely restored eighteenth-century
tavern, McCrady's has been home to Sean Brock's
antebellum-inspired new Southern culinary vision
since 2006. Brock has established links with local
farmers to revive heirloom crops and champion
high-welfare breeds. His menus combine these raw
materials plus research from his vast collection of
nineteenth-century Southern cookbooks with the
latest high-tech techniques and more down-home
methods such as pickling. Make sure to stop in the
bar, which specializes in mixing pre-Prohibition
cocktails, before making your way to a dining room
that's a similarly smart concoction of exposed brick
and crisp linen.

THE ORDINARY

544 King Street
Charleston
South Carolina 29403
+1 8434147060
www.eattheordinary.com

Recommended by
Linton Hopkins,
Chris Shepherd

Opening hours	Closed Monday
Credit cards	Accepted
Price range	Affordable
Style	Smart casual
Cuisine	Modern Seafood
Recommended for	Wish I'd opened

'I love restaurants that show where they're from. Their
seafood and what they do with it is definitely indicative
of their Carolina waters.'—Chris Shepherd

TWO BOROUGHS LARDER

186 Coming Street
Charleston
South Carolina 29403
+1 8436373722
www.twoboroughslarder.com

Recommended by
Sean Brock,
Gabrielle Hamilton

Opening hours	Closed Monday and Sunday
Reservation policy	No
Credit cards	Accepted but not AMEX
Price range	Affordable
Style	Casual
Cuisine	Modern American
Recommended for	Regular neighbourhood

'Two Boroughs Larder is the most exciting restaurant to
open in Charleston in a long time. Every time I go there
I want to order the entire menu and usually end up
ordering almost everything. Josh creates food that
cooks like to eat and Heather always takes amazing
care of the guests in the dining room on a nightly basis.
The menu changes often and that keeps me coming
back for more.'—Sean Brock

EVO

1075 East Montague Avenue
North Charleston
South Carolina 29405
+1 8432251796
www.evopizza.com

Recommended by
Mike Lata

Opening hours	Closed Sunday
Reservation policy	No
Credit cards	Accepted
Price range	Budget
Style	Casual
Cuisine	Pizza
Recommended for	Bargain

'A cheap meal is synonymous with cheap product
unless you're talking about pizza. The owners of this
off-the-beaten-path restaurant have the best value
dollar for dollar in the city... and the food is some of
my favourite.'—Mike Lata

ANDREW MICHAEL ITALIAN KITCHEN
712 West Street
Brookhaven Circle
Memphis
Tennessee 38117
+1 9013473569
www.andrewmichaelitaliankitchen.com

Opening hours............................Closed Monday and Sunday
Credit cards..Accepted
Price range..Affordable
Style..Smart casual
Cuisine..Italian
Recommended for..Worth the travel

'They're smart cooks. They do well-presented food.'
—Chris Shepherd

GUS'S FRIED CHICKEN
310 South Front Street
Memphis
Tennessee 38103
+1 9015274877
www.gusfriedchicken.com

Opening hours..Open 7 days
Credit cards..Accepted
Price range..Budget
Style..Casual
Cuisine..Chicken
Recommended for..Worth the travel

EL AMIGO TAQUERIA
3901 Nolensville Pike
Nashville
Tennessee 37211
+1 6158336434

Opening hours..Open 7 days
Reservation policy..No
Credit cards..Accepted
Price range..Budget
Style..Casual
Cuisine..Mexican
Recommended for..Bargain

'Some of the best tacos I have ever eaten. They have an
enormous variety and every single one is as delicious
as the next. The kicker... the tacos are around $1.25
(75p) each.'—Sean Brock

ARNOLD'S COUNTRY KITCHEN
605 8th Avenue South
Nashville
Tennessee 37203
+1 6152564455

Opening hours............................Closed Saturday and Sunday
Reservation policy..No
Credit cards..Accepted
Price range..Budget
Style..Casual
Cuisine..Southern American
Recommended for..Local favourite

'This restaurant makes me happier than any other
restaurant in the world. It's such an iconic Southern
place. It's the perfect meat and three. Everyone
working there is family and they shop at the farmers'
market daily. The green beans are cooked forever and
melt in your mouth. One of the most flavourful things
I've eaten.'—Sean Brock

HERMITAGE CAFE
71 Hermitage Avenue
Nashville
Tennessee 37210
+1 6152548871

Opening hours..Open 7 days
Reservation policy..No
Credit cards..Not accepted
Price range..Budget
Style..Casual
Cuisine..Diner
Recommended for..Late night

'I adore this place. It feels like you are stepping back
in time. It's that classic American diner where you sit
at the counter and watch them cook your eggs and
cheeseburgers. I could sit there for hours and entertain
myself. Plus you never know who you are going to see
stumble in the door late at night in Nashville.'
—Sean Brock

HUSK
Recommended by
Dan Hong
37 Rutledge Street
Nashville
Tennessee 37210
+1 6152566565
www.husknashville.com

Opening hours	Open 7 days
Credit cards	Accepted
Price range	Affordable
Style	Casual
Cuisine	Southern American
Recommended for	Worth the travel

'Quite simply the finest meal I have had in the past year. Amazing Southern cuisine made with locally sourced ingredients. I ate there three times in three days.'—Dan Hong

PEG LEG PORKER
Recommended by
Edward Lee
903 Gleaves Street
Nashville
Tennessee 37203
+1 6158296023
www.peglegporker.com

Opening hours	Closed Sunday
Reservation policy	No
Credit cards	Accepted
Price range	Budget
Style	Casual
Cuisine	Barbeque
Recommended for	Wish I'd opened

'It's just no fuss, great barbeque. And they have a sliding ceiling-hook system for transporting pigs from the walk-in to the smoker that goes through the dining room. Genius.'—Edward Lee

ROLF AND DAUGHTERS
Recommended by
Sean Brock,
Jason Vincent
700 Taylor Street
Nashville
Tennessee 37208
+1 6158669897
www.rolfanddaughters.com

Opening hours	Open 7 days
Credit cards	Accepted
Price range	Affordable
Style	Casual
Cuisine	Modern American
Recommended for	Regular neighbourhood

'Rolf and Daughters may be one of my all-time favourite restaurants. The roast chicken is out of this world and, in my opinion, there isn't a soul in America making better pasta. Sometimes I'll eat there three nights in a row. I love a neighbourhood place like that.'
—Sean Brock

THE BARN
Recommended by
Sean Brock,
Susan Spicer
Blackberry Farm
1471 West Millers Cove Road
Walland
Tennessee 37886
+1 8652738513
www.blackberryfarm.com

Opening hours	Open 7 days
Credit cards	Accepted
Price range	Expensive
Style	Smart casual
Cuisine	Modern American
Recommended for	High end

'Hands down the most relaxing place I have ever been. Every member of the staff treats you like you are a billionaire. The property is breathtaking and so is the cuisine of Chef Joseph Lenn. Sam Beall has created and operates a truly magical experience that you can only find in the Smoky Mountains.'—Sean Brock

BARTLETT'S
Recommended by
Tyson Cole
2408 West Anderson Lane
Austin
Texas 78757
+1 5124517333
www.bartlettsaustin.com

Opening hours	Open 7 days
Credit cards	Accepted
Price range	Affordable
Style	Casual
Cuisine	Modern American
Recommended for	Regular neighbourhood

LA CONDESA

Recommended by
Susan Spicer

400 West 2nd Street
Austin
Texas 78701
+1 5124990300
www.lacondesa.com

Opening hours	Open 7 days
Credit cards	Accepted
Price range	Affordable
Style	Casual
Cuisine	Modern Mexican
Recommended for	Wish I'd opened

CONTIGO

Recommended by
Tyson Cole

2027 Anchor Lane
Austin
Texas 78723
+1 5126142260
www.contigotexas.com

Opening hours	Open 7 days
Credit cards	Accepted
Price range	Budget
Style	Casual
Cuisine	Modern American
Recommended for	Local favourite

ELIZABETH STREET CAFÉ

Recommended by
Kevin Naderi

1501 South First Street
Austin
Texas 78704
+1 5122912881
www.elizabethstreetcafe.com

Opening hours	Open 7 days
Reservation policy	No
Credit cards	Accepted
Price range	Budget
Style	Casual
Cuisine	French-Vietnamese
Recommended for	Worth the travel

FRANKLIN BARBECUE

Recommended by
Paul Qui

900 East 11th Street
Austin
Texas 78702
+44 5126531187
www.franklinbarbecue.com

Opening hours	Closed Monday
Reservation policy	No
Credit cards	Accepted but not AMEX
Price range	Budget
Style	Casual
Cuisine	Barbeque
Recommended for	Local favourite

'It represents Austin well: from a trailer to a restaurant, a hobby to the best barbeque in the country. It just shows how brave people in Austin can be.'—Paul Qui

Franklin Barbeque has been dubbed as putting the 'queue' in 'BBQ'. Open from 11.00 a.m., punters start lining up several hours before that, many with their own chairs. The Franklin is Aaron Franklin who, with his wife Stacy, began in 2009 by serving out of a trailer in an East Austin car park (parking lot). They moved to their current permanent premises in 2011. Only open for lunch, they stop serving when they've sold out of brisket, ribs, pulled pork, turkey and sausage. The sold-out sign sometimes appears before they've even opened the door, depending on the length of that queue (waiting line).

HOPDODDY BURGER BAR

Recommended by
Tyson Cole

1400 South Congress Avenue
Austin
Texas 78704
+1 5122437505
www.hopdoddy.com

Opening hours	Open 7 days
Reservation policy	No
Credit cards	Accepted
Price range	Budget
Style	Casual
Cuisine	Burgers
Recommended for	Wish I'd opened

JEFFREY'S

Recommended by
Kevin Naderi

1204 West Lynn Street
Austin
Texas 78703
+1 5124775584
www.jeffreysofaustin.com

Opening hours	Open 7 days
Credit cards	Accepted
Price range	Expensive
Style	Smart casual
Cuisine	French-American
Recommended for	Worth the travel

'I love all of Larry McGuire's Austin restaurants. They are all solid and very well executed. The decor at Jeffrey's is impeccable, the staff are experienced and helpful, the food is on point and fresh. I envy the way the train runs with one captain.'—Kevin Naderi

JOSEPHINE HOUSE

Recommended by
Kevin Naderi

1601 Waterston Avenue
Austin
Texas 78703
+1 5124775584
www.josephineofaustin.com

Opening hours	Open 7 days
Credit cards	Accepted
Price range	Budget
Style	Casual
Cuisine	Café-Bar
Recommended for	Worth the travel

JUICELAND

Recommended by
Paul Qui

2307 Lake Austin Boulevard
Austin
Texas 78703
+1 5126280782
www.juicelandaustin.com

Opening hours	Open 7 days
Reservation policy	No
Credit cards	Accepted
Price range	Budget
Style	Casual
Cuisine	Juices sand Smoothies
Recommended for	Breakfast

'A juice always hits the spot.'—Paul Qui

With seven locations spread across Austin, you're never far from a branch of JuiceLand. The original Barton Springs branch, formerly an outpost of Daily Juice, opened in 2011 and mixes its hippy-dippy vibe with a vast selection of juices, smoothies, *aguas frescas*, fruit cocktails and shots of the good stuff. From the 'Fresh & Easy' charms of the Valley Girl (grapefruit, lemon, lime, orange and pineapple) to the 'Next-Level' challenge of the Ninja Bachelor Party (pineapple, jalapeño, celery, kale, spinach and parsley), there's a healthy morning eye-opener to suit everyone.

LAMBERTS DOWNTOWN BARBECUE

Recommended by
Kevin Naderi

401 West 2nd Street
Austin
Texas 78701
+1 5124941500
www.lambertsaustin.com

Opening hours	Open 7 days
Credit cards	Accepted
Price range	Affordable
Style	Casual
Cuisine	Barbeque
Recommended for	Worth the travel

LAS TRANCAS

Recommended by
Paul Qui

1210 East Cesar Chavez Street
Austin
Texas 78702
+1 5127018287

Opening hours	Closed Monday
Reservation policy	No
Credit cards	Not accepted
Price range	Budget
Style	Casual
Cuisine	Mexican
Recommended for	Regular neighbourhood

'This tacos from this trailer are delicious.'—Paul Qui

PERLA'S

Recommended by
Kevin Naderi

1400 South Congress Avenue
Austin
Texas 78704
+1 5122917300
www.perlasaustin.com

Opening hours	Open 7 days
Credit cards	Accepted
Price range	Affordable
Style	Casual
Cuisine	Seafood
Recommended for	Worth the travel

BAGUETTE ET CHOCOLAT

Recommended by
Tyson Cole

12101 Farm to Market
2244
Bee Cave
Texas 78738
+1 5122638388
www.baguetteetchocolat.com

Opening hours	Closed Monday
Reservation policy	No
Credit cards	Accepted
Price range	Budget
Style	Casual
Cuisine	Café-Patisserie
Recommended for	Breakfast

CROSSROADS DINER

Recommended by
Matt McCallister

Suite 1100, 8121 Walnut Hill Lane
Dallas
Texas 75231
+1 2143463491
www.crossroads-diner.com

Opening hours	Closed Monday
Reservation policy	No
Credit cards	Accepted
Price range	Budget
Style	Casual
Cuisine	Diner-Café
Recommended for	Breakfast

'It is super consistent, really delicious, and executed by a classically trained chef. He was a huge chef in Dallas and then decided to open a breakfast joint. I'm an Eggs Benedict person so I usually get that. Their hashbrowns are also ridiculous, and they have great pancakes.' —Matt McCallister

GEMMA

Recommended by
Matt McCallister

Suite 109,
2323 North Henderson Avenue
Dallas
Texas 75206
+1 2143709426
www.gemmadallas.com

Opening hours	Closed Monday and Tuesday
Credit cards	Accepted
Price range	Affordable
Style	Smart casual
Cuisine	Modern American
Recommended for	Late night

'Gemma is a newer restaurant in Dallas. Last time I went there they did a chicken Milanese as the special: breaded, fried, topped with acidic rocket (arugula) salad. Really good.' —Matt McCallister

HOUSTON'S

Recommended by
Matt McCallister

5318 Belt Line Road
Dallas
Texas 75240
+1 9729601752
www.hillstone.com

Opening hours	Open 7 days
Credit cards	Accepted
Price range	Affordable
Style	Casual
Cuisine	American
Recommended for	Regular neighbourhood

'I've been going to a Houston's of some sort since I was fourteen years old and I always get the same thing: a French dipped sandwich and spinach-artichoke dip. It's always consistent. I don't have to think about my order one bit. It's not mind blowing but it's a solid option.' —Matt McCallister

LUCIA

Recommended by
Matt McCallister

Suite 101,
408 West Eighth Street
Dallas
Texas 75208
+1 2149484998
www.luciadallas.com

Opening hours	Closed Monday and Sunday
Credit cards	Accepted
Price range	Affordable
Style	Smart casual
Cuisine	Italian
Recommended for	Wish I'd opened

'The *best* Italian food in the city. Lucia consistently executes some of the best stuff. They have an amazing charcuterie programme, the pasta's spot on, and the chefs are really talented.' —Matt McCallister

MANSION RESTAURANT

Recommended by
Matt McCallister

Rosewood Mansion on Turtle Creek
2821 Turtle Creek Boulevard
Dallas
Texas 75219
+1 2144434747
www.rosewoodhotels.com

Opening hours	Open 7 days
Credit cards	Accepted
Price range	Expensive
Style	Smart casual
Cuisine	Modern American
Recommended for	High end

'Bruno is the only Michelin-starred chef in Dallas. He grew up working for Alain Ducasse and is super talented, super classic and has great technique.' —Matt McCallister

OFF-SITE KITCHEN

Recommended by
Matt McCallister

2226 Irving Boulevard
Dallas
Texas 75207
+1 2147412226

Opening hours	Closed Sunday
Reservation policy	No
Credit cards	Accepted
Price range	Budget
Style	Casual
Cuisine	Burgers
Recommended for	Bargain

'Their burgers are ridiculous. When out-of-town chefs come to Dallas, I send them there for a quick meal.' —Matt McCallister

BRENNAN'S OF HOUSTON

Recommended by
Kevin Naderi

3300 Smith Street
Houston
Texas 77006
+1 7135229711
www.brennanshouston.com

Opening hours	Open 7 days
Credit cards	Accepted
Price range	Affordable
Style	Formal
Cuisine	Cajun-Creole
Recommended for	High end

'I love going to the extreme institutions that have been around for ages and do classics very well. Brennan's of Houston is a restaurant with deep roots in this city. The waiters are in suits, they still have service captains and they also require diners to wear jackets. They do classic Louisiana and East Texas favourites with slight twists. They use fresh and local ingredients too.' —Kevin Naderi

BROTHERS TACO HOUSE

Recommended by
Chris Shepherd

1604 Dowling Street
Houston
Texas 77003
+1 7132230091
www.brotherstacohouse.com

Opening hours	Open 7 days
Reservation policy	No
Credit cards	Accepted
Price range	Budget
Style	Casual
Cuisine	Mexican
Recommended for	Breakfast

'I go for the quality of ingredients. Plus, it's quick, in and out.'—Chris Shepherd

CAFE TH

Recommended by
Chris Shepherd

2108 Pease Street
Houston
Texas 77003
+1 7132254766
www.cafeth.com

Opening hours	Closed Sunday
Credit cards	Accepted
Price range	Budget
Style	Casual
Cuisine	Vietnamese
Recommended for	Bargain

'The service is great. It's quick, easy, delicious and serves an excellent banh mi.'—Chris Shepherd

DARBAND SHISHKABOB

Recommended by
Kevin Naderi

5670 Hillcroft Avenue
Houston
Texas 77036
+1 7139758350
www.darbandshishkabob.com

Opening hours	Open 7 days
Reservation policy	No
Credit cards	Accepted
Price range	Budget
Style	Casual
Cuisine	Persian
Recommended for	Bargain

'Darband is an old-time hidden gem. It serves Persian food with no fuss or muss at very reasonable prices. It has been around for about twenty-five years and is consistently packed. They are known for their simple kebabs of beef, chicken or lamb with white or dill rice. Skewered tomatoes and onions add zest and a large plate of feta cheese with herbs, served with fresh house-made flatbread are huge winners. Average plates run around $10 (£6).'—Kevin Naderi

GOODE COMPANY TAQUERIA

Recommended by
Ford Fry

4902 Kirby Drive
Houston
Texas 77098
+1 7135209153
www.goodecompany.com

Opening hours	Open 7 days
Reservation policy	No
Credit cards	Accepted
Price range	Budget
Style	Casual
Cuisine	Tex-Mex
Recommended for	Breakfast

'It's got great traditional Mexican breakfast dishes. Some of my favourites are the marinated meats, hand-made tortillas and beer sausage.'—Ford Fry

HK DIM SUM

Recommended by
Chris Shepherd

Suite 110, 9889 Bellaire Boulevard
Houston
Texas 77036
+1 7137777029
www.hkdimsumcity.com

Opening hours	Open 7 days
Reservation policy	No
Credit cards	Accepted but not AMEX
Price range	Budget
Style	Casual
Cuisine	Chinese
Recommended for	Regular neighbourhood

'For the quality of ingredients, the textures and flavours.'—Chris Shepherd

THE PASS & PROVISIONS

Recommended by
Kevin Naderi,
Jesse Schenker

807 Taft Street
Houston
Texas 77019
+1 7136289020
www.passandprovisions.com

Opening hours	Closed Sunday
Credit cards	Accepted
Price range	Affordable
Style	Smart casual
Cuisine	Modern American
Recommended for	Worth the travel

'I like that you can go and get a casual pizza or sit down and have a gastronomic experience.'—Jesse Schenker

PHO BINH BY NIGHT

Recommended by
Chris Shepherd

Suite 101, 12148 Bellaire Boulevard
Houston
Texas 77072
+1 8323512464
www.phobinh.com

Opening hours	Closed Monday
Reservation policy	No
Credit cards	Accepted
Price range	Budget
Style	Casual
Cuisine	Pho
Recommended for	Late night

'The flavour of their broth is unparalleled. Combine that with the fresh herbs and you can't beat it.'
—Chris Shepherd

REEF

Recommended by
Chris Shepherd

2600 Travis Street
Houston
Texas 77006
+1 7135268282
www.reefhouston.com

Opening hours	Closed Sunday
Credit cards	Accepted
Price range	Affordable
Style	Casual
Cuisine	Seafood
Recommended for	Local favourite

'It shows what Gulf Coast seafood is all about.'
—Chris Shepherd

TAN TAN RESTAURANT

Recommended by
Paul Qui

6816 Ranchester Drive
Houston
Texas 77036
+1 7137711268
www.tantanrestaurant.com

Opening hours	Open 7 days
Credit cards	Accepted
Price range	Budget
Style	Casual
Cuisine	Asian
Recommended for	Bargain

'Super cheap.'—Paul Qui

PATINA GREEN

Recommended by
Matt McCallister

Suite 102
116 North Tennessee Street
McKinney
Texas 75069
+1 9725489141
www.patinagreenhomeandmarket.com

Opening hours	Closed Monday and Sunday
Reservation policy	No
Credit cards	Accepted
Price range	Budget
Style	Casual
Cuisine	Bakery-Café-Deli
Recommended for	Local favourite

'Patina Green is located on the square in McKinney, a
small town north of Dallas. It's a cool, cute little city.
They still have the town square festivals, 4th of July
parade, that kind of stuff. I'm good friends with the

chefs Robert and Kaci Lyford. They really epitomize
local food. Every single thing that they use comes from
around Texas. *Everything*.'—Matt McCallister

ELSIE'S MAGIC SKILLET

Recommended by
Cathal Armstrong

8166 Richmond Highway
Alexandria
Virginla 22309
+1 7033600220

Opening hours	Open 7 days
Reservation policy	No
Credit cards	Accepted
Price range	Budget
Style	Casual
Cuisine	Diner-Café
Recommended for	Breakfast

'It's an old school dive.'—Cathal Armstrong

LOTTE PLAZA

Recommended by
Cathal Armstrong

Suite 100
43930 Farmwell Hunt Plaza
Ashburn
Virginia 20147
+1 7038582780
www.lotteplaza.com

Opening hours	Open 7 days
Reservation policy	No
Credit cards	Accepted
Price range	Budget
Style	Casual
Cuisine	Asian
Recommended for	Bargain

'It's a Korean supermarket. In the back there are street
vendors that sell cheap but delicious Korean food.'
—Cathal Armstrong

CAPITAL GRILLE

Recommended by
Cathal Armstrong

1861 International Drive
McLean
Virginia 22102
+1 7034483900
www.thecapitalgrille.com

Opening hours	Open 7 days
Credit cards	Accepted
Price range	Affordable
Style	Smart casual
Cuisine	Steakhouse
Recommended for	Local favourite

'It's a classic American steakhouse.'—Cathal Armstrong

GAMASOT

Recommended by
Cathal Armstrong

6963 Hechinger Drive
Springfield
Virginia 22151
+1 7032560780

Opening hours	Closed Monday
Credit cards	Accepted
Price range	Budget
Style	Casual
Cuisine	Korean
Recommended for	Regular neighbourhood

'After a gruelling weekend service, my favourite go-to food is *yukgaejang*. It's a hearty Korean beef-and-vegetable soup that warms from the mouth to the toes. It's a one-pot soup that is fiery, bold and spicy. This is my favourite place to get it.'—Cathal Armstrong

THE INN AT LITTLE WASHINGTON

Recommended by
José Andrés

Middle and Main street
Washington
Virginia 22747
+1 5406753800
www.theinnatlittlewashington.com

Opening hours	Open 7 days
Credit cards	Accepted
Price range	Expensive
Style	Smart casual
Cuisine	Modern American
Recommended for	High end

'I have so much respect for Patrick O'Connell because, when you are able to be at the top of the game for so many years with a restaurant that is literally in the middle of nowhere, it is astonishing. He's been in the business for over thirty-five years and is so talented and brilliant. He is also able to enjoy success in the most unlikely location because this restaurant is a destination in the heart of America.'—José Andrés

4 & 20 BAKERY AND CAFE

Recommended by
Tory Miller

305 North 4th Street
Madison
Wisconsin 53704
+1 6088198893
www.4and20bakery.com

Opening hours	Open 7 days
Reservation policy	No
Credit cards	Accepted
Price range	Budget
Style	Casual
Cuisine	Café-Bakery
Recommended for	Breakfast

'They have biscuits that are off-the-charts good.'
—Tory Miller

CULVER'S

Recommended by
Tory Miller

2102 West Beltline Highway
Madison
Wisconsin 53713
+1 6082741221
www.culvers.com

Opening hours	Open 7 days
Reservation policy	No
Credit cards	Accepted
Price range	Budget
Style	Casual
Cuisine	Fast Food
Recommended for	Local favourite

'This place has all the Wisconsin classics you could want: frozen custard, cheese curds and butter burgers.'
—Tory Miller

FOREQUARTER

Recommended by
Tory Miller

708 1/4 East Johnson Street
Madison
Wisconsin 53703
+1 6086094717
www.forequartermadison.com

Opening hours	Open 7 days
Reservation policy	No
Credit cards	Accepted
Price range	Affordable
Style	Casual
Cuisine	Modern American
Recommended for	Late night

'Local foods and great drinks.'—Tory Miller

A six-strong cooking collective runs this former
music shop turned night-time no-reservations
restaurant (though an exception is made for Sundays).
Expect creative craft cocktails (French 75 or 'shandy:
bergamot, lemon, mint, vodka' daily) alongside an
originally authored, regularly changing menu.
Savouries might include Kitchen Sink Salad with
sunflower seeds and black-eyed beans (peas), or
Winds of Change — smoked mackerel, popped
amaranth. Finish with pudding of peppermint and
chocolate liquid nitrogen ice cream or croissant cake.
Low lighting with a communal vibe (only eighteen
seats), Forequarter attracts a younger, fashionable
crowd — and it's also a great place to take a date.

HA LONG BAY

Recommended by
Tory Miller

1353 Williamson Street
Madison
Wisconsin 53703
+1 6082552868
www.hlbmadison.com

Opening hours	Open 7 days
Credit cards	Accepted
Price range	Budget
Style	Casual
Cuisine	Asian
Recommended for	Regular neighbourhood

'It's kind of a Vietnamese "bistro" but I go there for the
pho and LS7 *nem khao tod* soul food.'—Tory Miller

'*A perfect New Orleans experience.*'
JOHN BESH P818

NEW ORLEANS

'IT'S LOUISIANA CUISINE UNLIKE ANY YOU'VE EVER HAD.'
ALON SHAYA P816

'**Really captures the romantic vision of New Orleans's French Quarter dining.**'
DONALD LINK P818

'YOU CAN GET A GREAT NEW ORLEANS-STYLE PIE — WILD SHRIMP, ANDOUILLE, SPICY TOMATOES – AS WELL AS KILLER SANDWICHES.'
TORY MCPHAIL P823

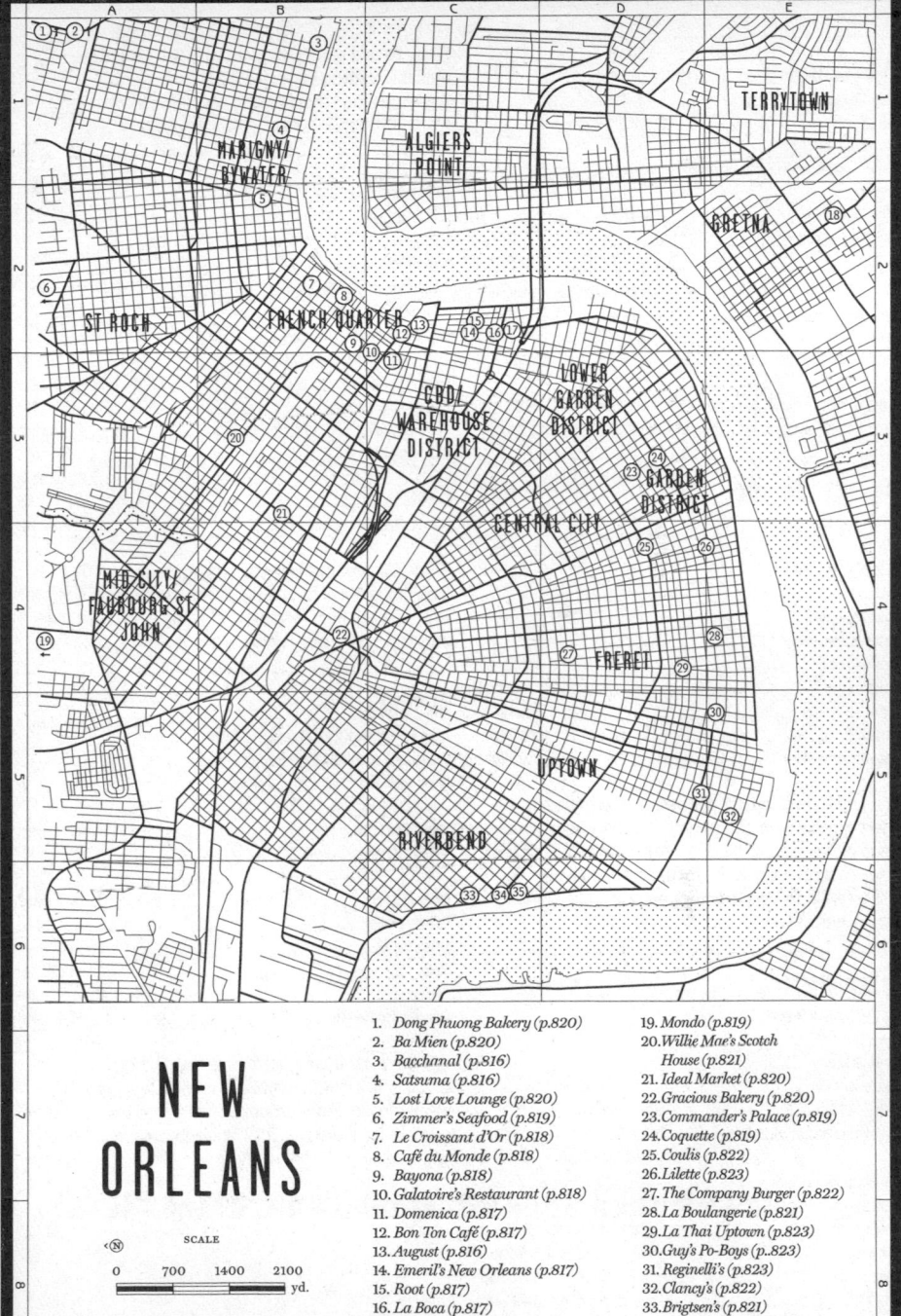

NEW ORLEANS

SCALE

0   700   1400   2100   yd.

N

LA COCINITA
Recommended by
Tory McPhail
New Orleans
Louisiana
+1 5043095344
www.lacocinitafoodtruck.com

Opening hours	Closed Sunday to Tuesday
Reservation policy	No
Credit cards	Accepted
Price range	Budget
Style	Casual
Cuisine	Taco Truck
Recommended for	Late night

'Really good Central American street food that reminds me of the flavours we have at SoBou.'—Tory McPhail

TACEAUX LOCEAUX
Recommended by
Donald Link
New Orleans
Louisiana
+1 5043074747

Opening hours	Variable
Reservation policy	No
Credit cards	Accepted
Price range	Budget
Style	Casual
Cuisine	Taco Truck
Recommended for	Late night

'It's simple. First off, it's the best taco in town but it's also *beyond* a taco. The flavours are big and bright and some of the most original I've had. I can't think of too many chefs or anyone else for that matter who would disagree. On Fridays they park outside my favourite bar.'—Donald Link

BACCHANAL
Recommended by
Alon Shaya
600 Poland Avenue
Bywater
New Orleans
Louisiana 70117
+1 5049489111
www.bacchanalwine.com

Opening hours	Open 7 days
Reservation policy	No
Credit cards	Accepted but not AMEX
Price range	Affordable
Style	Casual
Cuisine	Modern American
Recommended for	Late night

'They have a great courtyard with live music, an amazing wine list and they cook great Central American food that helps to keep your alcohol level from getting the best of you.'—Alon Shaya

SATSUMA
Recommended by
John Besh
3218 Dauphine Street
Bywater
New Orleans
Louisiana 70117
+1 5043045962
www.satsumacafe.com

Opening hours	Open 7 days
Reservation policy	No
Credit cards	Accepted
Price range	Budget
Style	Casual
Cuisine	Café
Recommended for	Breakfast

'Satsuma now has two great locations in New Orleans. One in the Bywater and the newest addition in Uptown. My favourite item for breakfast is the rocket (arugula) and egg-white sandwich.'—John Besh

AUGUST
Recommended by
Alon Shaya
301 Tchoupitoulas Street
Central Business District
New Orleans
Louisiana 70130
+1 5042999777
www.restaurantaugust.com

Opening hours	Open 7 days
Credit cards	Accepted
Price range	Expensive
Style	Smart casual
Cuisine	Modern American
Recommended for	High end

'It's the most innovative food in town where every detail is thought through. The service, wine list and after-dinner drinks cannot be compared to any other place in New Orleans. It's Louisiana cuisine unlike any you've ever had.'—Alon Shaya

LA BOCA

Recommended by
Stephen Stryjewski

870 Tchoupitoulas Street
Central Business District
New Orleans
Louisiana 70130
+1 5045258205
www.labocasteaks.com

Opening hours..Closed Sunday
Credit cards...Accepted
Price range...Affordable
Style..Smart casual
Cuisine...Argentinian Steakhouse
Recommended for...Late night

BON TON CAFÉ

Recommended by
John Besh

401 Magazine Street
Central Business District
New Orleans
Louisiana 70130
+1 5045243386
www.thebontoncafe.com

Opening hours..............................Closed Saturday and Sunday
Credit cards...Accepted
Price range...Affordable
Style..Smart casual
Cuisine..Cajun
Recommended for.....................................Local favourite

'Bon Ton Café has real Cajun and Creole classics done
the old-school way. This place reminds me of my
grandmother's cooking.'—John Besh

COCHON BUTCHER

Recommended by
Susan Spicer

930 Tchoupitoulas Street
Central Business District
New Orleans
Louisiana 70130
+1 5045887675
www.cochonbutcher.com

Opening hours..Open 7 days
Reservation policy...No
Credit cards...Accepted
Price range..Budget
Style..Casual
Cuisine..Sandwiches
Recommended for..Breakfast

DOMENICA

Recommended by
Susan Spicer

Roosevelt Hotel
123 Baronne Street
Central Business District
New Orleans
Louisiana 70112
+1 5046486020
www.domenicarestaurant.com

Opening hours..Open 7 days
Credit cards...Accepted
Price range...Affordable
Style..Casual
Cuisine...Italian
Recommended for.................................Regular neighbourhood

EMERIL'S NEW ORLEANS

Recommended by
Tory McPhail,
Alon Shaya

800 Tchoupitoulas Street
Central Business District
New Orleans
Louisiana 70130
+1 5045289393
www.emerilsrestaurants.com

Opening hours..Open 7 days
Credit cards...Accepted
Price range...Affordable
Style..Smart casual
Cuisine..Modern American
Recommended for.....................................Local favourite

'I love eating at the bar. Chef David Slater is cooking
amazing food there. The menu is very eclectic and
surprises you at every turn. Also, they have some great
New Orleans classics like barbeque prawns (shrimp)
with biscuits that never get old.'—Alon Shaya

ROOT

Recommended by
Stephen Stryjewski

200 Julia Street
Central Business District
New Orleans
Louisiana 70130
+1 5042529480
www.rootnola.com

Opening hours..Open 7 days
Credit cards...Accepted
Price range...Affordable
Style..Smart casual
Cuisine..Modern American
Recommended for...Late night

BAYONA

Recommended by
Donald Link

430 Dauphine Street
French Quarter
New Orleans
Louisiana 70112
+1 5045254455
www.bayona.com

Opening hours	Closed Sunday
Credit cards	Accepted
Price range	Affordable
Style	Smart casual
Cuisine	Modern American
Recommended for	High end

'I've always felt that Bayona really captures the romantic vision of New Orleans's French Quarter dining. It's elegant without being stuffy, the wine list is set up to let you go wild with people that know what they're selling. Not to mention that the food is unpretentious and always full of flavour and depth.' —Donald Link

CAFÉ DU MONDE

Recommended by
Tory McPhail

French Market
800 Decatur Street
French Quarter
New Orleans
Louisiana 70116
+1 5045254544
www.cafedumonde.com

Opening hours	Open 7 days
Reservation policy	No
Credit cards	Not accepted
Price range	Budget
Style	Casual
Cuisine	Café
Recommended for	Local favourite

'Everyone loves it. It's not expensive and you see chefs, celebrities, tourists and locals all hanging out together.' —Tory McPhail

LE CROISSANT D'OR

Recommended by
Alon Shaya

617 Ursulines Avenue
French Quarter
New Orleans
Louisiana 70116
+1 5045244663
www.croissantdornola.com

Opening hours	Closed Tuesday
Reservation policy	No
Credit cards	Accepted but not AMEX
Price range	Budget
Style	Casual
Cuisine	French Patisserie
Recommended for	Breakfast

'I like getting their warm blueberry croissant. It's the perfect little neighbourhood bakery and if you show up early enough, the croissants are still warm out of the oven.' —Alon Shaya

GALATOIRE'S RESTAURANT

Recommended by
John Besh

209 Bourbon Street
French Quarter
New Orleans
Louisiana 70130
+1 5045252021
www.galatoires.com

Opening hours	Closed Monday
Credit cards	Accepted
Price range	Affordable
Style	Formal
Cuisine	Creole
Recommended for	High end

'One of the dozen or so downtown restaurants that is more than 100 years old. In my opinion, it is the best of its class. Friday lunch at Galatoire's is a perfect New Orleans experience.' —John Besh

COMMANDER'S PALACE

1403 Washington Avenue
Garden District
New Orleans
Louisiana 70130
+1 5048998221
www.commanderspalace.com

Opening hours	Open 7 days
Credit cards	Accepted
Price range	Expensive
Style	Formal
Cuisine	Southern American-Creole
Recommended for	Local favourite

'I can't think of any restaurant more iconic than Commander's. The Brennan family, who run it, have set the standard for dining in New Orleans. My daughter and I go every year for her birthday. I hope my restaurants can maintain such a high standard as Commander's throughout the years.'—Donald Link

COQUETTE

2800 Magazine Street
Garden District
New Orleans
Louisiana 70115
+1 5042650421
www.coquette-nola.com

Opening hours	Closed Tuesday
Credit cards	Accepted
Price range	Affordable
Style	Smart casual
Cuisine	Modern Southern American
Recommended for	Wish I'd opened

'My favourite American cuisine is Creole-Cajun cooking and Coquette does that with a modern twist.' —Takashi Inoue

This vibrant Garden District bistro, opened in 2008, has a menu that's never short of surprises. Chef Michael Stoltzfus (formerly at the august August) woos his guests with Southern staples – (prawns) shrimp and grits, fried chicken biscuit, catfish – and then keeps them on their toes by incorporating non-trad touches. Stone-cut oats, sunny-side egg and spring (collard) greens are gilded with black truffle; gumbo is made with pig's trotter (feet) and devilled egg, while cornbread cavatelli with shitake mushrooms and city ham is pasta NOLA-style. Cocktails and desserts are no less eclectic. Chandeliers and exposed brick nail the smart-casual vibe.

ZIMMER'S SEAFOOD

4915 Saint Anthony Avenue
Gentilly
New Orleans
Louisiana 70122
+1 5042827150

Opening hours	Closed Monday and Sunday
Reservation policy	No
Credit cards	Accepted but not AMEX
Price range	Budget
Style	Casual
Cuisine	Cajun-Creole Sandwiches
Recommended for	Bargain

'For po-boys.'—Susan Spicer

TAN DINH

1705 Lafayette Street
Gretna
New Orleans
Louisiana 70053
+1 5043618008

Opening hours	Closed Tuesday
Reservation policy	No
Credit cards	Accepted but not AMEX
Price range	Budget
Style	Casual
Cuisine	Vietnamese
Recommended for	Regular neighbourhood

MONDO

900 Harrison Avenue
Lakeview
New Orleans
Louisiana 70124
+1 5042242633
www.mondoneworleans.com

Opening hours	Open 7 days
Credit cards	Accepted
Price range	Affordable
Style	Casual
Cuisine	Modern American
Recommended for	Wish I'd opened

'A great neighbourhood place that's all about world cuisine. You could put almost anything you wanted on the menu and it would work – no limitations.' —Tory McPhail

LOST LOVE LOUNGE

Recommended by
Susan Spicer

2529 Dauphine Street
Marigny
New Orleans
Louisiana 70117
+1 5049492009
www.lostlovelounge.com

Opening hours	Open 7 days
Reservation policy	No
Credit cards	Accepted
Price range	Budget
Style	Casual
Cuisine	Vietnamese
Recommended for	Late night

GRACIOUS BAKERY

Recommended by
Justin Devillier

Suite 100
1000 South Jefferson Davis Parkway
Mid-City
New Orleans
Louisiana 70125
+1 5043013709
www.graciousbakery.com

Opening hours	Open 7 days
Reservation policy	No
Credit cards	Accepted
Price range	Budget
Style	Casual
Cuisine	Café-Bakery
Recommended for	Breakfast

'Such high quality. The owner, Megan Forman, is always there – she's very well trained and technically oriented. I like the cheesy croissant sticks and the brownies that are wrapped in brioche and baked.'—Justin Devillier

IDEAL MARKET

Recommended by
Alon Shaya

250 South Broad Street
Mid-City
New Orleans
Louisiana 70119
+1 5048228861
www.laidealmarket.com

Opening hours	Open 7 days
Reservation policy	No
Credit cards	Accepted but not AMEX
Price range	Budget
Style	Casual
Cuisine	Central American
Recommended for	Bargain

'It's a Central American grocery that has a large hot-food section with amazing women cooking *barbacoa*, Spanish rice, jalapeño-and-onion-grilled chicken, hand-made tortillas, and much more all from scratch. For $8.99 (£5), you get dinner for two that will keep you full for the following day!'—Alon Shaya

BA MIEN

Recommended by
John Besh

13235 Chef Menteur Highway
New Orleans East
New Orleans
Louisiana 70129
+1 5042550500
www.bamien.com

Opening hours	Closed Monday
Credit cards	Accepted
Price range	Budget
Style	Casual
Cuisine	Vietnamese
Recommended for	Regular neighbourhood

'New Orleans has some amazing Vietnamese places. Ba Mien has so many great dishes like the *bahn coun* (rice noodle dumplings), lemongrass chicken and tiny Vietnamese egg rolls with piles of herbs and pickled vegetables.'—John Besh

DONG PHUONG BAKERY

Recommended by
Justin Devillier

14207 Chef Menteur Highway
New Orleans East
New Orleans
Louisiana 70129
+1 5042540214
www.dpbanhmi.com

Opening hours	Closed Tuesday
Reservation policy	No
Credit cards	Accepted
Price range	Budget
Style	Casual
Cuisine	Vietnamese Sandwiches
Recommended for	Bargain

'Their $3 (£2) banh mi are delicious. It's in a culturally rich Vietnamese neighbourhood. They make French bread in a New Orleans style. The sandwich line is make your own, so you can design your own sandwich.' —Justin Devillier

WILLIE MAE'S SCOTCH HOUSE

Recommended by
Alon Shaya

2401 Saint Ann Street
Treme-Lafitte
New Orleans
Louisiana 70119
+1 5048229503

Opening hours...Closed Sunday
Reservation policy...No
Credit cards..Accepted
Price range...Budget
Style..Casual
Cuisine...................................Southern American
Recommended for..............................Local favourite

'Run by a third-generation family member, Carrie
Seaton, they serve up the best fried chicken, red beans
and rice, and cornbread in town.'—Alon Shaya

LA BOULANGERIE

Recommended by
Donald Link

4600 Magazine Street
Uptown
New Orleans
Louisiana 70115
+1 5042693777

Opening hours...............................Closed Tuesday
Reservation policy...No
Credit cards........................Accepted but not AMEX
Price range...Budget
Style..Casual
Cuisine..Café-Bakery
Recommended for...Breakfast

'For the most part, my days of big greasy breakfasts are
behind me. I love them, just not all the time. If I were
in that mood I would head to Camellia Grill. Mostly
though I head to La Boulangerie bakery for excellent
croissants, quiche, and almost any pastry or bread that
they produce there.'—Donald Link

BRIGTSEN'S

Recommended by
Justin Devillier, Susan Spicer

723 Dante Street
Uptown
New Orleans
Louisiana 70118
+1 5048617610
www.brigtsens.com

Opening hours............................Closed Monday and Sunday
Credit cards..Accepted
Price range..Affordable
Style...Smart casual
Cuisine.................................Southern American-Creole
Recommended for...........................Local favourite

'It has remained consistently authentic and hasn't turned
into a tourist trap. It's a picture-perfect example of
Creole cuisine.'—Justin Devillier

CAMELLIA GRILL

Recommended by
John Besh, Bruce Bromberg

626 South Carrollton Avenue
Uptown
New Orleans
Louisiana 70118
+1 5043092679

Opening hours.................................Open 7 days
Reservation policy...No
Credit cards..Accepted
Price range...Budget
Style..Casual
Cuisine..Diner-Café
Recommended for......................................Late night

'When looking for a delicious late-night snack, Camellia
Grill's cheeseburger with a fried egg on top can't be
beat! Or if you're really hungry, the chef's special
omelette with chilli is so darn good. And don't forget
to order a freeze!'—John Besh

In the twenty months between the Camellia Grill (est.
1946) closing post-Katrina and reopening in 2007,
New Orleanians would pin notes of support on the
legendary diner's door, pining for a slice of grilled
pecan pie. Reopened under new ownership, it soon
got its groove back. The showmanship of the bow-tied
waiters remains undiminished; the omelettes are still
huge; and there's always a line for a stool at the
marble counter. With its nostalgic diner menu that
does everything from eggs any style to waffles, grits
and burgers, the Camellia Grill manages to please
the tourists and keep the locals happy.

CLANCY'S

Recommended by
Susan Spicer

6100 Annunciation Street
Uptown
New Orleans
Louisiana 70118
+1 5048951111
www.clancysneworleans.com

Opening hours	Closed Sunday
Credit cards	Accepted
Price range	Affordable
Style	Smart casual
Cuisine	Cajun-Creole
Recommended for	Local favourite

THE COMPANY BURGER

Recommended by
Donald Link,
Alon Shaya,
Stephen Stryjewski

4600 Freret Street
Uptown
New Orleans
Louisiana 70115
+1 5042670320
www.thecompanyburger.com

Opening hours	Closed Tuesday
Reservation policy	No
Credit cards	Accepted
Price range	Budget
Style	Casual
Cuisine	Burgers
Recommended for	Wish I'd opened

'For years I debated opening a hamburger place in New Orleans due to the severe lack of one. Then Adam Biderman opened his and relieved my yearnings. I find it shocking that it took so long to have such an outstanding burger place here. Luckily it's not too far from my house.'—Donald Link

COOTER BROWN'S

Recommended by
Justin Devillier

509 South Carrollton Avenue
Uptown
New Orleans
Louisiana 70118
+1 5048669104
www.cooterbrowns.com

Opening hours	Open 7 days
Reservation policy	No
Credit cards	Accepted
Price range	Budget
Style	Casual
Cuisine	Bar-Southern American
Recommended for	Late night

'They serve oysters until late – it's unpretentious and the oysters come on a plastic tray, for old-school prices. There are also an astonishing number of beers on tap.' —Justin Devillier

COULIS

Recommended by
Tory McPhail

3625 Prytania Street
Uptown
New Orleans
Louisiana 70115
+1 5043044265

Opening hours	Open 7 days
Reservation policy	No
Credit cards	Accepted but not AMEX
Price range	Budget
Style	Casual
Cuisine	Diner-Café
Recommended for	Breakfast

'It's on the way to work, it's good, local, great-quality food and I like to support the small restaurateurs.' —Tory McPhail

GUY'S PO-BOYS

5259 Magazine Street
Uptown
New Orleans
Louisiana 70115
+1 5048915025

Opening hours	Closed Sunday
Reservation policy	No
Credit cards	Not accepted
Price range	Budget
Style	Casual
Cuisine	Cajun-Creole Sandwiches
Recommended for	Bargain

'I don't know if cheap is the right word here, but by comparison it is inexpensive. In a town known for po-boys, everyone has their favourite and Guy's is definitely mine – the prawn (shrimp) and catfish in particular. Marvin has been there every time I have gone in and knows his customers by name. I moved away once for three years and he still remembered me when I came back. It's also one of the few places I will always take people from out of town.'—Donald Link

LILETTE

3637 Magazine Street
Uptown
New Orleans
Louisiana 70115
+1 5048951636
www.liletterestaurant.com

Opening hours	Closed Sunday
Credit cards	Accepted
Price range	Affordable
Style	Smart casual
Cuisine	French-American
Recommended for	Regular neighbourhood

'Lilette really captures the essence of what a good bistro is supposed to be. The food over the years has always been top notch and very consistent. I'm fond of the service style and the well-chosen wine list. It sits in Uptown New Orleans and has become one of, if not the best, example of what an Uptown bistro should be.'
—Donald Link

REGINELLI'S

5961 Magazine Street
Uptown
New Orleans
Louisiana 70115
+1 5048991414
www.reginellis.com

Opening hours	Open 7 days
Reservation policy	No
Credit cards	Accepted
Price range	Affordable
Style	Casual
Cuisine	Pizza
Recommended for	Bargain

'Everyone loves pizza, but here you can get a great New Orleans-style pie – wild prawns (shrimp), spicy tomatoes, andouille – as well as killer sandwiches.'
—Tory McPhail

LA THAI UPTOWN

4938 Prytania Street
Uptown
New Orleans
Louisiana 70115
+1 5048998886
www.lathaiuptown.com

Opening hours	Closed Monday
Credit cards	Accepted
Price range	Affordable
Style	Casual
Cuisine	Thai
Recommended for	Regular neighbourhood

'It is very approachable – I sit at the bar, watch a ball game and enjoy great small plates, but it all comes down to the amazing flavours in their dishes.'
—Tory McPhail

'It's rare to find a roast duck that tastes good at any hour in Chicago, let alone at 3.00 a.m.'
MATTHEW KIRKLEY P832

'ENOUGH TECHNIQUE TO APPEAL TO THE CHEF-NERD IN ME'
ANDREW ZIMMERMAN P827

'It is Midwestern and solid.'
JEAN JOHO P829

CHICAGO

'Delicious hot dogs are served all night long by ladies with attitude.'
EDWARD LEE P827

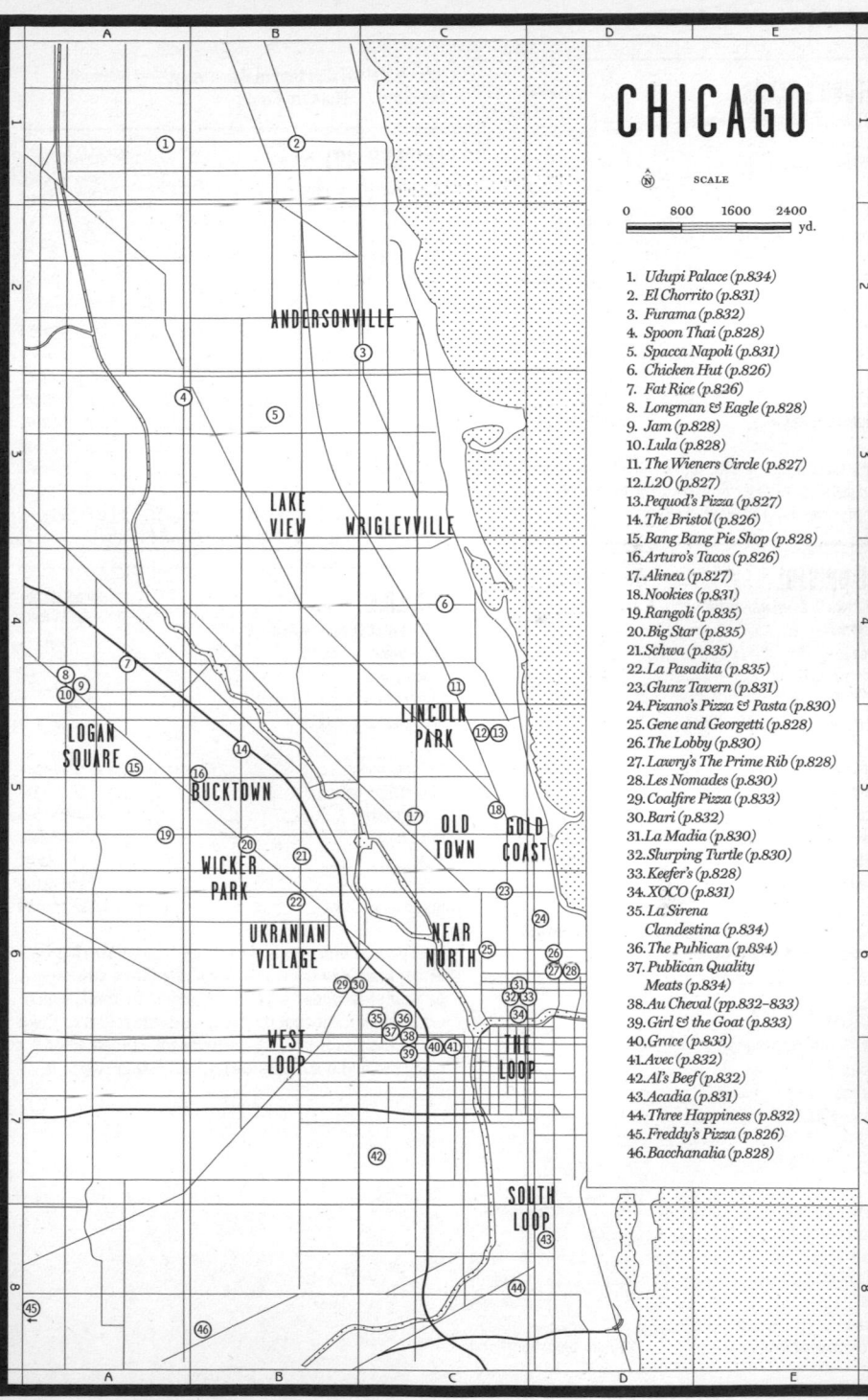

CHICAGO

SCALE

0   800   1600   2400
yd.

ARTURO'S TACOS

Recommended by
Mindy Segal

2001 North Western Avenue
Bucktown
Chicago
Illinois 60647
+1 7737724944
www.arturos-tacos.com

Opening hours	Open 7 days
Reservation policy	No
Credit cards	Accepted
Price range	Budget
Style	Casual
Cuisine	Mexican
Recommended for	Regular neighbourhood

'They have great service and I love their soups. They always have fresh tortillas and salsas. It's also open twenty-four hours!'—Mindy Segal

THE BRISTOL

Recommended by
Homaro Cantu

2152 North Damen Avenue
Bucktown
Chicago
Illinois 60647
+1 7738625555
www.thebristolchicago.com

Opening hours	Open 7 days
Credit cards	Accepted
Price range	Affordable
Style	Casual
Cuisine	Modern American
Recommended for	High end

'Good, honest, local food. Not overpriced. Always delicious.'—Homaro Cantu

FREDDY'S PIZZA

Recommended by
Homaro Cantu

1600 South 61st Avenue
Cicero
Chicago
Illinois 60804
+1 7088639289
www.freddyspizza.com

Opening hours	Closed Sunday
Reservation policy	No
Credit cards	Not accepted
Price range	Budget
Style	Casual
Cuisine	Italian
Recommended for	Regular neighbourhood

'It's an Italian deli that makes everything by hand. Delicious.'—Homaro Cantu

CHICKEN HUT

Recommended by
David Posey,
Mindy Segal

3200 North Broadway
Lake View
Chicago
Illinois 60657
+1 7738681755

Opening hours	Open 7 days
Reservation policy	No
Credit cards	Not accepted
Price range	Budget
Style	Casual
Cuisine	Fast Food
Recommended for	Bargain

'Nothing about Chicken Hut is fancy. The food is easy, not fussed over and delicious.'—David Posey

FAT RICE

Recommended by
Jason Vincent

2957 West Diversey Avenue
Lake View
Chicago
Illinois 60647
www.eatfatrice.com

Opening hours	Closed Monday and Sunday
Reservation policy	No
Credit cards	Accepted
Price range	Affordable
Style	Casual
Cuisine	Modern Asian
Recommended for	Regular neighbourhood

'The people who own and run it are hands down the nicest people in the world. They based their cuisine on that of an under appreciated region in China, which was a significant spot on the spice-trade route, so there are influences from both Portugal and Europe. Really crazy melting pot. Super delicious.' —Jason Vincent

ALINEA

1723 North Halsted Street
Lincoln Park
Chicago
Illinois 60614
+1 3128670110
www.alinea-restaurant.com

Recommended by
Juan Manuel Barrientos,
Alberto Chicote, Rolf Fliegauf,
Thrainn Freyr Vigfússon,
Georgianna Hiliadaki, Timothy
Johnson, Onno Kokmeijer,
Chong Chee Loong, Markus
Mraz, Jet Tila, Jordi Vilà,
Paul Virant

Opening hours............................Closed Monday and Tuesday
Credit cards..Accepted
Price range...Expensive
Style..Formal
Cuisine..Modern American
Recommended for.......................................Worth the travel

'The best gastronomic experience in the world – from the moment I entered until the very end. Not only the food but the service blew me away.'—Onno Kokmeijer

Alinea has been described as innovative, cutting-edge and futuristic, but such words don't begin to describe the experience of having a chef 'paint' one's dessert directly onto the table, of eating an edible balloon filled with helium and tasting of apple, of a lamb dish with some eighty-six different components. The undisputed genius behind the sophisticated Lincoln Park restaurant, awarded three Michelin stars in 2010, is French Laundry-trained Grant Achatz, poster boy for progressive American cooking. Securing a reservation can take months. Achatz and partner Nick Kokonas have built on Alinea's success with a unique 'ticketed' restaurant, Next, and cocktail bar, The Aviary.

L20

2300 North Lincoln Park West
Lincoln Park
Chicago
Illinois 60614
+1 7738680002
www.l2orestaurant.com

Recommended by
David Posey,
Andrew Zimmerman

Opening hours........................Closed Tuesday and Wednesday
Credit cards..Accepted
Price range...Expensive
Style..Formal
Cuisine..Modern Seafood
Recommended for...High end

'Chef Matthew Kirkley is a rare talent. Impeccable sourcing, pristine seafood, enough technique to appeal to the chef-nerd in me and enough restraint to let the produce remain the star.'—Andrew Zimmerman

PEQUOD'S PIZZA

2207 North Clybourn Avenue
Lincoln Park
Chicago
Illinois 60614
+1 7733271512
www.pequodspizza.com

Recommended by
Paul Virant

Opening hours...Open 7 days
Credit cards..Accepted
Price range...Budget
Style..Casual
Cuisine...Italian-American
Recommended for..Local favourite

'Really solid deep-dish pizza, baked in pans that allow the cheese to caramelize.'—Paul Virant

THE WIENERS CIRCLE

2622 North Clark Street
Lincoln Park
Chicago
Illinois 60614
+1 7734777444

Recommended by
Edward Lee,
Bruce Sherman

Opening hours...Open 7 days
Reservation policy..No
Credit cards...Not accepted
Price range...Budget
Style..Casual
Cuisine..Hot Dogs
Recommended for...Breakfast

'The only time I eat breakfast is when I have stayed out too late and there's no better breakfast than a hot dog from Wieners Circle in Chicago. Don't forget to get the chocolate milkshake. Delicious hot dogs are served all night long by ladies with attitude.'—Edward Lee

In a city where there's said to be more hot-dog stands than branches of all the big fast-food brands combined, Lincoln Park's Wieners Circle has found fame – much of it for the X-rated patter of the ladies that work the counter. That's not to say that if you order 'the works' – a grilled Vienna Beef on a warm poppy-seed bun, topped with mustard, onions, relish, dill pickle spears, tomato slices, peppers and celery salt – you'll be disappointed. Open until 5.00 a.m. on weekends, it's popular with weary bar-hoppers who prefer their dog with a side of small-hours verbal abuse.

SPOON THAI

4608 North Western Avenue
Lincoln Square
Chicago
Illinois 60625
+1 7737691173
www.spoonthai.com

Opening hours	Open 7 days
Credit cards	Accepted but not AMEX
Price range	Budget
Style	Casual
Cuisine	Thai
Recommended for	Bargain

BANG BANG PIE SHOP

2051 North California Avenue
Logan Square
Chicago
Illinois 60647
+1 7732768888
www.bangbangpie.com

Opening hours	Open 7 days
Reservation policy	No
Credit cards	Accepted
Price range	Budget
Style	Casual
Cuisine	Café
Recommended for	Breakfast

'They have great biscuits and sausage… and pie.'
—Andrew Zimmerman

JAM

3057 West Logan Boulevard
Logan Square
Chicago
Illinois 60647
+1 7732926011
www.jamrestaurant.com

Opening hours	Closed Wednesday
Reservation policy	No
Credit cards	Accepted
Price range	Affordable
Style	Casual
Cuisine	Modern American
Recommended for	Breakfast

'It's the best breakfast in the US in my opinion.
Delicious, fresh, creative.'—Homaro Cantu

LONGMAN & EAGLE

2657 North Kedzie Avenue
Logan Square
Chicago
Illinois 60647
+1 7732767110
www.longmanandeagle.com

Opening hours	Open 7 days
Reservation policy	No
Credit cards	Accepted
Price range	Affordable
Style	Casual
Cuisine	Bar-Bistro
Recommended for	Breakfast

'Their house-made sausage and eggs is always perfect.
The "PBR Breakfast" is my favourite. And they have
great coffee.'—Mindy Segal

LULA

2537 North Kedzie Boulevard
Logan Square
Chicago
Illinois 60647
+1 7734899554
www.lulacafe.com

Opening hours	Open 7 days
Credit cards	Accepted
Price range	Affordable
Style	Casual
Cuisine	Modern American
Recommended for	Local favourite

'The menu is hyper-seasonal, hyper-local and the food
is always very creative and delicious. Plus, they have
crazy, chef-accessible hours of operation.'
—David Posey

A pioneer of the farm-to-table movement in Chicago,
Lula sees itself as something of a renegade on the
city's dining scene. Simple sophistication is what's
on offer here. So brushed concrete and exposed
ducts meet modern art and elegant drapes in the
dining room, and colourful seasonal dishes are
peppered with unusual components: Slagel Family
Farm flank steak with root vegetables roasted in
coffee and black garlic, or steamed black cod with
green garlic, almond, white balsamic and kumquat.
To experience the chefs in full flow, pitch up for the
Monday night Farm Dinner, but even the brunch,
which runs 'til 2.30 p.m., is full of surprises. Save
room for dessert – it's the stuff of local legend.

BACCHANALIA

Recommended by
Carrie Nahabedian

2413 South Oakley Avenue
Lower West Side
Chicago
Illinois 60608
+1 7732546555
www.bacchanaliainchicago.com

Opening hours	Open 7 days
Credit cards	Not accepted
Price range	Affordable
Style	Smart casual
Cuisine	Italian
Recommended for	Regular neighbourhood

'More than forty-five years old, it's a small but old-school bar that serves home-style Italian food. I love their Chicken Vesuvio (watch out for the garlic!). It's a place where you dine early on Sundays. They let you bring in your own wine, the family loves chefs and a fair amount of Chicago's restaurateurs can be seen dining there regularly.'—Carrie Nahabedian

GENE AND GEORGETTI

Recommended by
Carrie Nahabedian

500 North Franklin Street
Near North
Chicago
Illinois 60654
+1 3125273718
www.geneandgeorgetti.com

Opening hours	Closed Sunday
Credit cards	Accepted
Price range	Expensive
Style	Smart casual
Cuisine	Steakhouse-Seafood
Recommended for	Local favourite

'The first place I went after my jaw was "unwired" (after the longest eight weeks living on liquids due to a broken jaw) was this place for a nice juicy ribeye. I can still taste the char-grilled meat and the flavour. That was over thirty years ago, but thankfully things have not changed a bit here.'—Carrie Nahabedian

KEEFER'S

Recommended by
Tony Mantuano

20 West Kinzie Street
Near North
Chicago
Illinois 60654
+1 3124679525
www.keefersrestaurant.com

Opening hours	Closed Sunday
Credit cards	Accepted
Price range	Expensive
Style	Smart casual
Cuisine	Steakhouse
Recommended for	Local favourite

'Great steaks, hearty tavern food, good beers – exactly what you expect from a Midwest type of meal. Great bar scene – dine at the bar.'—Tony Mantuano

LAWRY'S THE PRIME RIB

Recommended by
Jean Joho

100 East Ontario Street
Near North
Chicago
Illinois 60611
+1 3127875000
www.lawrysonline.com

Opening hours	Open 7 days
Credit cards	Accepted
Price range	Affordable
Style	Smart casual
Cuisine	Steakhouse
Recommended for	Local favourite

'An old-American style of restaurant. It is Midwestern and solid.'—Jean Joho

Chicago's loyalty to Lawry's knows no bounds. The upmarket chophouse, an offshoot of the Beverly Hills original, has been serving up roasted prime rib of beef to locals and visiting carnivores since 1984. The original was opened in 1938, which explains the time-warp feel of the place, from the mansion setting – you might have stepped into the White House circa 1950 – to the kitsch staff uniforms and table-side rituals, but when the meat is this good, who cares? It's carved into telephone-directory-thick slabs from silver carts, and served with lashings of mash, gravy and Yorkshire pudding.

THE LOBBY

Recommended by
Jean Joho

Peninsula Hotel
108 East Superior Street
Near North
Chicago
Illinois 60611
+1 3125736760
www.peninsula.com/chicago

Opening hours	Open 7 days
Credit cards	Accepted
Price range	Affordable
Style	Smart casual
Cuisine	Modern American
Recommended for	Breakfast

'It has a superior quality of food, amazing attention to detail and great service.'—Jean Joho

LA MADIA

Recommended by
Carrie Nahabedian

59 West Grand Avenue
Near North
Chicago
Illinois 60610
+1 3123290400
www.dinelamadia.com

Opening hours	Open 7 days
Credit cards	Accepted
Price range	Affordable
Style	Casual
Cuisine	Italian
Recommended for	Bargain

'La Madia is the work of Jonathan Fox, who put Maggiano's on the map. It has exceptional thin-crust artisanal pizzas, a good-looking space and more.' —Carrie Nahabedian

LES NOMADES

Recommended by
Carrie Nahabedian

222 East Ontario Street
Near North
Chicago
Illinois 60611
+1 3126499010
www.lesnomades.net

Opening hours	Closed Monday and Sunday
Credit cards	Accepted
Price range	Expensive
Style	Formal
Cuisine	Modern French
Recommended for	Wish I'd opened

'Since the first time I dined there as a guest of the late, great Jovan Tryboevic, I've loved it. Classic French cuisine in a sexy French brownstone off Michigan Avenue. There's an intimate bar that's perfect for an illicit drink poured into hand-etched crystal Martini glasses. They have a large selection of half bottles of all-French wine as well as beautiful oriental rugs adorning the floor of their second-floor private dining room. Its intimidating entrance is flawless, just so New York in Chicago.'—Carrie Nahabedian

PIZANO'S PIZZA & PASTA

Recommended by
Matthew Kirkley

864 North State Street
Near North
Chicago
Illinois 60610
+1 3127511766
www.pizanoschicago.com

Opening hours	Open 7 days
Credit cards	Accepted
Price range	Budget
Style	Casual
Cuisine	Pizza
Recommended for	Regular neighbourhood

'Over the past ten years of living in Chicago, Pizano's has been a constant haunt of mine. With a warm and almost quaint decor, this cosy, first-floor terraced (row) house space serves solid and consistent red-sauce Italian restaurant classics. You will always find friendly service, and with a kitchen that stays open until 1.00 a.m. every night of the week, you're bound to find many other restaurant folk such as me there.' —Matthew Kirkley

SLURPING TURTLE

Recommended by
Jean Joho

116 West Hubbard Street
Near North
Chicago
Illinois 60654
+1 3124640466
www.slurpingturtle.com

Opening hours	Open 7 days
Credit cards	Accepted
Price range	Budget
Style	Casual
Cuisine	Japanese
Recommended for	Late night

'I have great respect and admiration for chef Takashi's food and his ramen is very satisfying late in the evening.'—Jean Joho

XOCO
Recommended by
Carrie Nahabedian
449 North Clark Street
Near North
Chicago
Illinois 60654
www.rickbayless.com

Opening hours	Closed Monday and Sunday
Reservation policy	No
Credit cards	Accepted
Price range	Affordable
Style	Casual
Cuisine	Modern Mexican
Recommended for	Bargain

'XOCO is Rick Bayless's version of Mexican-style tortas, soups and more at a great price.'—Carrie Nahabedian

GLUNZ TAVERN
Recommended by
Tony Mantuano
1202 North Wells Street
Old Town
Chicago
Illinois 60610
+1 3126423000
www.glunztavern.com

Opening hours	Closed Monday
Reservation policy	No
Credit cards	Accepted
Price range	Affordable
Style	Casual
Cuisine	European
Recommended for	Regular neighbourhood

'Schnitzel and a beer. Run by one of the country's oldest wine-shop owners, it's a really fun place.'
—Tony Mantuano

NOOKIES
Recommended by
Tony Mantuano
1746 North Wells Street
Old Town
Chicago
Illinois 60614
+1 3123372454
www.nookiesrestaurants.net

Opening hours	Open 7 days
Reservation policy	No
Credit cards	Accepted but not AMEX
Price range	Budget
Style	Casual
Cuisine	Diner
Recommended for	Breakfast

'It's really old-school, always busy. I get the same every time: an egg-white omelette with bacon, spinach and feta.'—Tony Mantuano

SPACCA NAPOLI
Recommended by
Tony Mantuano
1769 West Sunnyside Avenue
Ravenswood
Chicago
Illinois 60640
+1 7738782420
www.spaccanapolipizzeria.com

Opening hours	Closed Monday
Credit cards	Accepted
Price range	Affordable
Style	Casual
Cuisine	Pizza
Recommended for	Regular neighbourhood

'Authentic Neapolitan pizzeria. Chef Jonathan Goldsmith is a great host.'—Tony Mantuano

EL CHORRITO
Recommended by
Bruce Sherman
6404 North Clark Street
Rogers Park
Chicago
Illinois 60626
+1 7733810902
www.elchorrito.com

Opening hours	Open 7 days
Reservation policy	No
Credit cards	Accepted
Price range	Budget
Style	Casual
Cuisine	Mexican
Recommended for	Late night

ACADIA
Recommended by
Jason Vincent
1639 South Wabash Avenue
South Loop
Chicago
Illinois 60616
+1 3123609500
www.acadiachicago.com

Opening hours	Closed Monday
Credit cards	Accepted
Price range	Expensive
Style	Smart casual
Cuisine	Modern American
Recommended for	High end

'They're not falling over you. My go-to.'—Jason Vincent

THREE HAPPINESS

209 West Cermak Road
South Loop
Chicago
Illinois 60616
+1 3128421964

Recommended by
Matthew Kirkley

Opening hours	Open 7 days
Reservation policy	No
Credit cards	Accepted
Price range	Budget
Style	Casual
Cuisine	Cantonese
Recommended for	Late night

'Don't let the rundown, eerie interiors of this tiny space fool you, it's good food. It is rare to find a roast duck that tastes good at any hour in Chicago, let alone at 3.00 a.m.'—Matthew Kirkley

FURAMA

4936 North Broadway Street
Uptown
Chicago
Illinois 60640
+1 7732711161
www.furamachicago.com

Recommended by
Bruce Sherman

Opening hours	Open 7 days
Credit cards	Accepted
Price range	Budget
Style	Casual
Cuisine	Dim Sum
Recommended for	Breakfast

AL'S BEEF

1079 West Taylor Street
West Loop
Chicago
Illinois 60607
+1 3122264017
www.alsbeef.com

Recommended by
Homaro Cantu

Opening hours	Closed Sunday
Reservation policy	No
Credit cards	Not accepted
Price range	Budget
Style	Casual
Cuisine	Italian sandwiches
Recommended for	Local favourite

'Only in Chicago can you find a line out the door to stand and eat a beef sandwich.'—Homaro Cantu

AVEC

615 West Randolph Street
West Loop
Chicago
Illinois 60661
+1 3123772002
www.avecrestaurant.com

Recommended by
Matthew Kirkley,
Tony Mantuano, David
Posey, Paul Virant

Opening hours	Open 7 days
Reservation policy	No
Credit cards	Accepted
Price range	Affordable
Style	Smart casual
Cuisine	Modern Mediterranean
Recommended for	Regular neighbourhood

'Chef Perry Hendrix delivers consistently solid fare and adds new and interesting dishes.'—David Posey

BARI

1120 West Grand Avenue
West Loop
Chicago
Illinois 60642
+1 3126660730
www.bariitaliansubs.com

Recommended by
Jason Vincent

Opening hours	Open 7 days
Reservation policy	No
Credit cards	Accepted
Price range	Budget
Style	Casual
Cuisine	Italian sandwiches
Recommended for	Bargain

'Italian grocery on Grand Avenue, where the mobs used to own everything. This is real Italian.'—Jason Vincent

AU CHEVAL

800 West Randolph Street
West Loop
Chicago
Illinois 60607
+1 3129294580
www.auchevalchicago.com

Recommended by
Brad McDonald,
David Posey,
Mindy Segal,
Andrew Zimmerman

Opening hours	Open 7 days
Reservation policy	No
Credit cards	Accepted
Price range	Affordable
Style	Casual
Cuisine	Modern American
Recommended for	Late night

'The burgers and fries are consistently good and it's a short walk from my restaurant, perfect for midnight dining.'—Andrew Zimmerman

A Mecca for the hip, the hungry and the downright gluttonous, Chicago's Au Cheval pulls none of its punches. Full-bore diner dishes might take their cues from Europe, but the presentation — loaded with cheese and eggs — and the unashamedly supersized portions are all American. Locals queue (wait in line) out the door for the city's best cheeseburger (a single packs two patties, a double three) and the beast of a bologna sandwich, delivered by staff that, like the cooking, are both laid-back and on point. The joint is at its jumping best in the early hours — slide into one of the studded leather booths for a ball-breaker of a cocktail and a man-sized pile of *chilaquiles*, only served after midnight.

COALFIRE PIZZA

Recommended by
Bruce Sherman

1321 West Grand Avenue
West Loop
Chicago
Illinois 60642
+1 3122262625
www.coalfirechicago.com

Opening hours	Closed Monday
Reservation policy	No
Credit cards	Accepted
Price range	Budget
Style	Casual
Cuisine	Pizza
Recommended for	Bargain

GIRL & THE GOAT

Recommended by
Tory Miller

809 West Randolph Street
West Loop
Chicago
Illinois 60607
+1 3124926262
www.girlandthegoat.com

Opening hours	Open 7 days
Credit cards	Accepted
Price range	Affordable
Style	Casual
Cuisine	Modern American
Recommended for	Worth the travel

'Great atmosphere and amazing food. Pretty busy all the time but worth it.'—Tory Miller

The girl in the name is Stephanie Izard ('izard' being a Pyrenean goat breed), the tousle-haired whirlwind and 2008 *Top Chef* winner. Izard opened the vast, rustic-style Girl & The Goat with Boka Restaurant Group in 2010 amid the kind of hype that would intimidate a lesser chef. Her original style paid off and The Goat is now permanently buzzing. Brace yourself for fearlessly global small plates and some audacious sweet-savoury pairings. Star dishes include wood-roasted pig face, *hamachi crudo* with pork belly, smoked goat pizza, and spicy green beans. A sibling, Little Goat, opened in 2012.

GRACE

Recommended by
Matthew Accarrino,
Carrie Nahabedian

652 West Randolph Street
West Loop
Chicago
Illinois 60661
+1 3122349494
www.grace-restaurant.com

Opening hours	Closed Monday and Sunday
Credit cards	Accepted
Price range	Expensive
Style	Smart casual
Cuisine	Modern American
Recommended for	Worth the travel

'Amazingly technical and very tasty food. Great service, a complete thought.'—Matthew Accarrino

Great things were expected of Curtis Duffy when, late in 2012, he opened Grace, his earnest – in the true sense of the word – contribution to the culinary arts in Chicago's West Loop. He hasn't disappointed. Duffy earned his stripes at Chicago's finest – Charlie Trotter's, Trio, Alinea, Avenues – and is now in the same league himself. Grace is grace itself: a serene space, seventeen linen-dressed tables, sixty-four soft white leather chairs, plush carpet and a contrastingly hard-edged, glass-walled kitchen. Choose between two elaborately presented, nine-course menus ($205; £123) that meld modern haute technique with inspiration from Japan: the vegetarian 'Flora' or the omnivorous 'Fauna'.

THE PUBLICAN

Recommended by
Andrew Zimmerman

837 West Fulton Market
West Loop
Chicago
Illinois 60607
+1 312/339555
www.thepublicanrestaurant.com

Opening hours	Open 7 days
Credit cards	Accepted
Price range	Affordable
Style	Casual
Cuisine	Bar-Bistro
Recommended for	Local favourite

'The Publican is built on the basic tenets of Chicago
food: pork, sausages, beer, local sourcing and
camaraderie.'—Andrew Zimmerman

Known in particular for its amazingly good brunches,
this stripped-back, beer-led restaurant is all about
immaculate produce served at its simplest and best.
It comes courtesy of the team behind Chicago's
much-loved, James Beard-nominated Blackbird
restaurant, but with a stark, hall-like interior – all
straight wooden lines and flagstone – farmhouse
fare and a vast beer list. The menus are split into
pork-heavy 'meat', 'fish', which includes five types of
oyster, and 'vegetable', with each section revealing
impeccably sourced ingredients, be it the steamer
clams from feminist novelist turned fishmonger Ingrid
Bengis in Maine, or the 'country rib' from the Slagel
Family Farm in Illinois.

PUBLICAN QUALITY MEATS

Recommended by
Homaro Cantu,
Brad Farmerie

825 West Fulton Market
West Loop
Chicago
Illinois 60607
+1 3124458977
www.publicanqualitymeats.com

Opening hours	Open 7 days
Reservation policy	No
Credit cards	Accepted
Price range	Budget
Style	Casual
Cuisine	Sandwiches
Recommended for	Bargain

'A sandwich shop, but a sandwich shop that cures its
own meat and bakes its own bread – it's where I want
to be eating.'—Brad Farmerie

Publican Quality Meats – located, appropriately
enough, in Chicago's meatpacking district – is One
Off Hospitality's 2012 follow-up to the European beer
hall-style of The Publican (est. 2009). PQM takes the
form of a chic butcher's shop, high-end market and
café whose focus is – you've got it – quality meats.
Chicago culinary powerhouse Paul Kahan (avec,
Blackbird) is executive chef and partner, and his
influence comes through in the strongly seasonal
menu and ethical sourcing. Every last scrap of meat
is used, be it beef tongue in the PQM Reuben, pig's
tails in the Bolognese or blood in the *cocido* (meat,
potato and chickpea stew).

LA SIRENA CLANDESTINA

Recommended by
Carrie Nahabedian

954 West Fulton Market
West Loop
Chicago
Illinois 60607
+1 3122265300
www.lasirenachicago.com

Opening hours	Open 7 days
Credit cards	Accepted
Price range	Affordable
Style	Casual
Cuisine	Latin American
Recommended for	Late night

'John Manion makes his restaurant feel like your
personal restaurant with his great style, love and, of
course, food and drinks. I eat whatever he tells me to.'
—Carrie Nahabedian

UDUPI PALACE

Recommended by
Andrew Zimmerman

2543 West Devon Avenue
West Ridge
Chicago
Illinois 60659
+1 7733382152
www.udupipalacechicago.net

Opening hours	Open 7 days
Credit cards	Accepted
Price range	Budget
Style	Casual
Cuisine	South Indian
Recommended for	Bargain

'For under $10 (£6) I can get a *masala dosa* as big
as my head... cheap but with loads of flavour.'
—Andrew Zimmerman

BIG STAR

1531 North Damen Avenue
Wicker Park
Chicago
Illinois 60622
+1 7732354039
www.bigstarchicago.com

Opening hours	Open 7 days
Reservation policy	No
Credit cards	Not accepted
Price range	Budget
Style	Casual
Cuisine	Mexican
Recommended for	Late night

'Besides the amazing array of fifty different bourbons and unique craft beers, Big Star has hands down the best tacos made by an American in America. Paul Kahan is one of a kind: all of his restaurants and concepts are so specialized and singular they can't be copied or replicated.'—Jonathon Sawyer

LA PASADITA

1140 North Ashland Avenue
Wicker Park
Chicago
Illinois 60622
+1 7732782130
www.pasadita.com

Opening hours	Open 7 days
Reservation policy	No
Credit cards	Accepted but not AMEX
Price range	Budget
Style	Casual
Cuisine	Mexican
Recommended for	Late night

'Best tacos in Chicago.'—Homaro Cantu

RANGOLI

2421 West North Avenue
Wicker Park
Chicago
Illinois 60647
+1 7736977114
www.rangolifeast.com

Opening hours	Closed Monday
Reservation policy	No
Credit cards	Accepted
Price range	Affordable
Style	Casual
Cuisine	Indian
Recommended for	Regular neighbourhood

'It is hard to resist a really good Indian restaurant that I can walk to. Incredible vindaloo… deathly hot but great flavour.'—Andrew Zimmerman

SCHWA

1466 North Ashland Avenue
Wicker Park
Chicago
Illinois 60622
+1 7732521466
www.schwarestaurant.com

Opening hours	Closed Monday and Sunday
Credit cards	Accepted
Price range	Expensive
Style	Smart casual
Cuisine	Modern American
Recommended for	Wish I'd opened

'Schwa is a chef's dream… small dining room, no rules but those imagined by the chef, and the food (which is brilliant) is the only thing that matters.'
—Andrew Zimmerman

'The atmosphere is like an oasis in the middle of Manhattan.'
DAVID CHANG P870

'IT HAS A CLASSIC, OLD NEW YORK FEEL — UNPRETENTIOUS AND DELICIOUS.'
TAKASHI INOUE P854

'THIS LITTLE BEAUTY IS A PURIST'S DELIGHT.'
GEOFF LINDSAY P852

'IT'S GANGSTER — A COOL, LOW-KEY SPOT WITH DELICIOUS FOOD AND KILLER COCKTAILS.'
JOSEF CENTENO P853

NEW YORK CITY

'Intense flavours and noisy, downtown atmosphere.'
MASSIMO BOTTURA P851

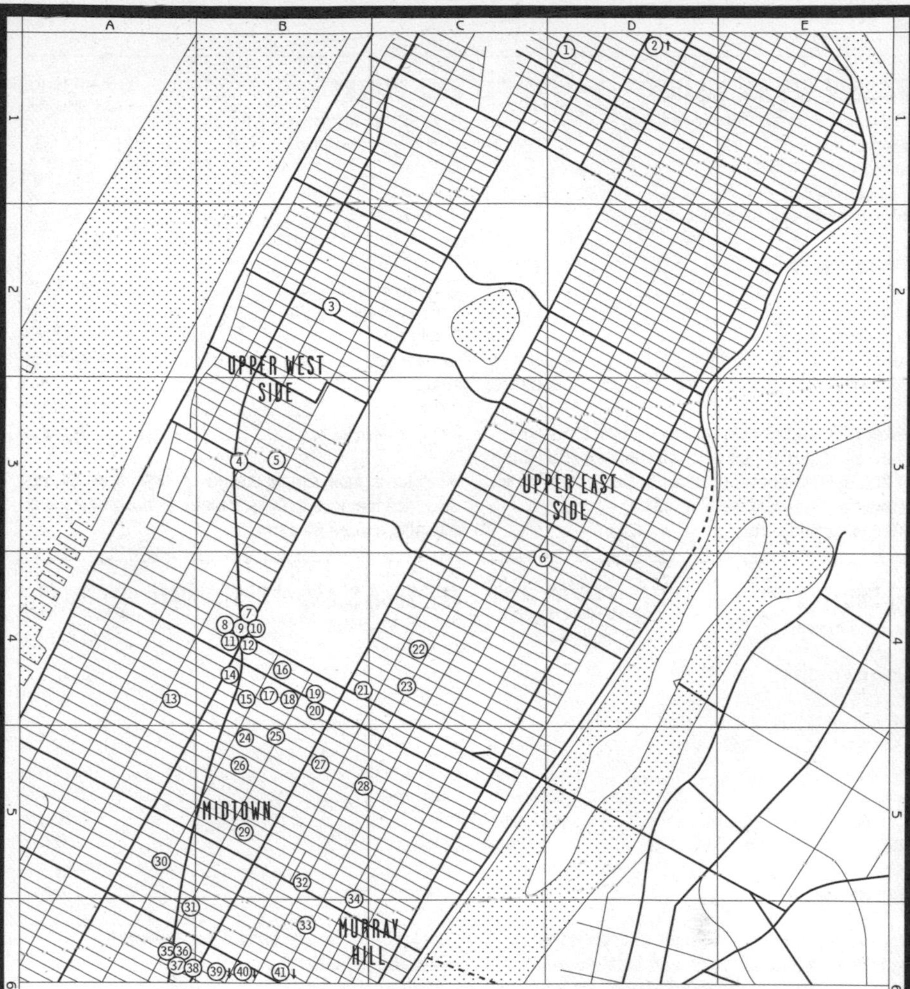

MANHATTAN

UPTOWN & MIDTOWN

UPPER WEST SIDE

UPPER EAST SIDE

MIDTOWN

MURRAY HILL

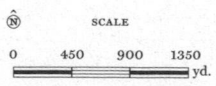

N

SCALE

0   450   900   1350
yd.

1. *Patisserie Des Ambassades (p.838)*
2. *Red Rooster (p.838)*
3. *Barney Greengrass (p.845)*
4. *Gray's Papaya (p.845)*
5. *Super Tacos (p.846)*
6. *Atlantic Grill (p.843)*
7. *Jean-Georges (p.845)*
8. *Masa (p.846)*
9. *Bar Masa (p.844)*
10. *Bouchon Bakery (p.845)*
11. *Per Se (p.846)*
12. *Marea (p.841)*
13. *Totto Ramen (p.842)*
14. *Yakitori Totto (p.842)*
15. *Carnegie Deli (p.840)*
16. *Petrossian (p.842)*
17. *Norma's (p.841)*
18. *The Burger Joint (p.840)*
19. *Betony (p.839)*
20. *Má Pêche (p.841)*
21. *Rotisserie Georgette (p.844)*
22. *Daniel (p.844)*
23. *The Regency Bar & Grill (p.844)*
24. *Le Bernardin (p.839)*
25. *53rd and 6th Halal Cart (p.839)*
26. *Sake Bar Hagi (p.842)*
27. *La Grenouille (p.839)*
28. *The Four Seasons Restaurant (p.838)*
29. *DB Bistro Moderne (p.840)*
30. *Bonchon Chicken (p.840)*
31. *Keens Steakhouse (p.841)*
32. *Grand Central Oyster Bar (p.838)*
33. *Kajitsu (p.843)*
34. *Sushi Yasuda (p.839)*
35. *Seoul Garden (p.842)*
36. *New Wonjo (p.841)*
37. *Gahm Mi Oak (p.840)*
38. *Kunjip (p.841)*
39. *The Breslin Bar & Dining Room (p.843)*
40. *NoMad (p.843)*
41. *Rose Bakery (p.838)*

PATISSERIE DES AMBASSADES
Recommended by
Marcus Samuelsson

2200 Frederick Douglass Boulevard
Harlem
Manhattan NY 10026
+1 2126660078
www.patisseriedesambassades.com

Opening hours	Open 7 days
Credit cards	Accepted
Price range	Budget
Style	Casual
Cuisine	Café-Bakery
Recommended for	Breakfast

'A West African patisserie serving the best croissants and the playlist is always fun: Bob Marley, Mariah Carey and Phil Collins. It never changes. Sussudio blasting in the morning is a great wake-up call.'
—Marcus Samuelsson

RED ROOSTER
Recommended by
Margot Henderson

310 Lenox Avenue
Harlem
Manhattan NY 10027
+1 2127929001
www.redroosterharlem.com

Opening hours	Open 7 days
Credit cards	Accepted but not Diners
Price range	Affordable
Style	Smart casual
Cuisine	Southern American
Recommended for	Worth the travel

It took an expat Ethiopian-Swede to open Harlem's first break-out success since gentrification began in the mid-1990s. Combining a sense of the area's African-American past with its diverse future and a touch of Scandinavian flair, Marcus Samuelsson's Red Rooster has been a hit since it opened in 2011. Sitting not far from the soul-food legend that is Sylvia's, it serves a brand of elevated home cooking that satisfies both Harlem's fashionable newcomers and its longstanding residents. On the menu, corn bread, prawns (shrimp) and dirty rice, and spring (collard) greens sit alongside Swedish meatballs and gravlax.

ROSE BAKERY
Recommended by
April Bloomfield

Dover Street Market
160 Lexington Avenue
Kips Bay
Manhattan NY 10016
+1 6468377754
www.newyork.doverstreetmarket.com

Opening hours	Open 7 days
Reservation policy	No
Credit cards	Accepted
Price range	Affordable
Style	Casual
Cuisine	Café-Bakery
Recommended for	Breakfast

'They have great, simple pastries, great coffee and they do a nice fry-up with eggs, tomatoes, mushrooms and sausage.'—April Bloomfield

THE FOUR SEASONS RESTAURANT
Recommended by
Rebecca Kirhoffer

99 East 52nd Street
Midtown East
Manhattan NY 10022
+1 2127549494
www.fourseasonsrestaurant.com

Opening hours	Closed Sunday
Credit cards	Accepted
Price range	Expensive
Style	Formal
Cuisine	Modern American
Recommended for	Wish I'd opened

'The location, the interior and the art work.'
—Rebecca Kirhoffer

GRAND CENTRAL OYSTER BAR
Recommended by
Peter Hoffman,
Ken Oringer

Grand Central Station
89 East 42nd Street
Midtown East
Manhattan NY 10017
+1 2124906650
www.oysterbarny.com

Opening hours	Closed Sunday
Credit cards	Accepted
Price range	Affordable
Style	Casual
Cuisine	Seafood
Recommended for	Local favourite

'I've taken more friends and out-of-town guests there than any other restaurant over thirty-five years. A great classic place – only eat oysters though and drink good wine.'—Peter Hoffman

LA GRENOUILLE
3 East 52nd Street
Midtown East
Manhattan NY 10022
+1 2127521495
www.la-grenouille.com

Recommended by
Daniel Boulud

Opening hours...............Closed Monday and Sunday
Credit cards..Accepted
Price range..Expensive
Style..Formal
Cuisine...French
Recommended for..............................Local favourite

'A fifty-year-old standard, not just for the food, but for the service, the crowd and the remarkable consistency.' —Daniel Boulud

SUSHI YASUDA
204 East 43rd Street
Midtown East
Manhattan NY 10017
+1 2129721001
www.sushiyasuda.com

Recommended by
Brad McDonald

Opening hours...................................Closed Sunday
Credit cards..Accepted
Price range..Affordable
Style..Smart casual
Cuisine..Sushi
Recommended for....................................High end

'The sushi here is better than I had in most of the three-star spots in Tokyo. They have a strict time limit to your seating, so you can always guarantee your guests are on time.'—Brad McDonald

53RD AND 6TH HALAL CART
53rd Street and 6th Avenue
Midtown West
Manhattan NY 10019
www.53rdand6th.com

Recommended by
Alex Young

Opening hours..............................Open 7 days
Reservation policy................................No
Credit cards............................Not accepted
Price range...................................Budget
Style..Casual
Cuisine............................Middle Eastern
Recommended for.......................Late night

LE BERNARDIN
155 West 51st Street
Midtown West
Manhattan NY 10019
+1 2125541515
www.le-bernardin.com

Recommended by
Andrew Carmellini, Justin Cogley, Justin Devillier, Jose Enrique, Renee Erickson, Michael Ferraro, Alexis Gauthier, Frederic Morineau, Paul Owens, Marcus Samuelsson, José Santaella, Sarah Pilner & Jasper Shen, Michael Toscano

Opening hours...............................Closed Sunday
Credit cards..Accepted
Price range..Expensive
Style..Formal
Cuisine...Seafood
Recommended for.....................................High end

'It deserves every award it wins. The dishes seem so simple on the menu, but when you see and taste them, you realize they are the result of super refinement and ultra precision. The big New York room and service that makes you feel like you go every week... amazing.' —Alexis Gauthier

BETONY
41 West 57th Street
Midtown West
Manhattan NY 10019
+1 2124652400
www.betony-nyc.com

Recommended by
Jason Franey, Tory McPhail

Opening hours..............................Open 7 days
Credit cards..Accepted
Price range..Affordable
Style..Smart casual
Cuisine..Modern American
Recommended for..............................Wish I'd opened

'The dining room is beautiful, the kitchen is state of the art and the food is gorgeous.'—Jason Franey

BONCHON CHICKEN
Recommended by
Paul Liebrandt
207 West 38th Street
Midtown West
Manhattan NY 10018
+1 2122713339
www.bonchon.com

Opening hours	Open 7 days
Reservation policy	No
Credit cards	Accepted
Price range	Affordable
Style	Casual
Cuisine	Korean
Recommended for	Bargain

'Spicy Korean chicken goodness!'—Paul Liebrandt

THE BURGER JOINT
Recommended by
Michael Smith
Le Parker Meridien Hotel
119 West 56th Street
Midtown West
Manhattan NY 10019
+1 2127081400
www.burgerjointny.com

Opening hours	Open 7 days
Reservation policy	No
Credit cards	Not accepted
Price range	Budget
Style	Casual
Cuisine	Burgers
Recommended for	Worth the travel

'Just the quirky set-up of having a low-key burger joint hidden behind a huge curtain in the foyer of a high-end hotel is memorable enough, but the burgers are really good too!'—Michael Smith

CARNEGIE DELI
Recommended by
Michael Toscano
854 7th Avenue
Midtown West
Manhattan NY 10019
+1 2127572245
www.carnegiedeli.com

Opening hours	Open 7 days
Reservation policy	No
Credit cards	Not accepted
Price range	Budget
Style	Casual
Cuisine	Deli
Recommended for	Local favourite

'Every chef who lives in New York has their favourite deli: Katz's, 2nd Avenue or Carnegie. Although I love them all, my favourite is Carnegie Deli. The size of the sandwich is enough for three meals, on the third day when I'm finishing off the last bite of my pastrami reuben, it's just as good as the first. The chopped liver, open-faced pastrami reuben and the tongue, egg and cheese sandwiches are my favourites.'
—Michael Toscano

DB BISTRO MODERNE
Recommended by
Michael Ferraro
55 West 44th Street
Midtown West
Manhattan NY 10036
+1 2123912400
www.dbbistro.com

Opening hours	Open 7 days
Credit cards	Accepted
Price range	Affordable
Style	Smart casual
Cuisine	French-American
Recommended for	High end

The name might be rather opaque ('DB' is chef and owner Daniel Boulud, who also heads a Michelin-star-studded worldwide restaurant empire, and a 'Bistro Moderne', which is – er, we'll get back to you on that) but there's nothing obscure about the appeal of this buzzing, beautifully designed, theatre district restaurant. The 'db Burger', filled with braised short ribs, foie gras and black truffle, has been much imitated but never equalled and sets the tone: familiar and approachable food that you want to eat again and again, but with enough thrilling luxury to ensure you won't get bored.

GAHM MI OAK
Recommended by
Andrew Carmellini
43 West 32nd Street
Midtown West
Manhattan NY 10001
+1 2126954113
www.gahmmioak.com

Opening hours	Open 7 days
Reservation policy	No
Credit cards	Accepted
Price range	Affordable
Style	Casual
Cuisine	Korean
Recommended for	Late night

KEENS STEAKHOUSE
72 West 36th Street
Midtown West
Manhattan NY 10018
+1 2129473636
www.keens.com

Recommended by
April Bloomfield,
Bruce Bromberg,
Brad Farmerie

Opening hours	Open 7 days
Credit cards	Accepted
Price range	Expensive
Style	Smart casual
Cuisine	Steakhouse
Recommended for	Local favourite

'A pretty legendary slice of history, and one of the original players in the world of steakhouses.'
—Brad Farmerie

KUNJIP
9 West 32nd Street
Midtown West
Manhattan NY 10001
+1 2122169487
www.kunjip.net

Recommended by
Masato Shimizu

Opening hours	Open 7 days
Credit cards	Accepted
Price range	Affordable
Style	Casual
Cuisine	Korean
Recommended for	Late night

MÁ PÊCHE
Chambers Hotel
15 West 56th Street
Midtown West
Manhattan NY 10019
+1 2127575878
www.momofuku.com

Recommended by
Massimo Bottura

Opening hours	Open 7 days
Credit cards	Accepted
Price range	Expensive
Style	Smart casual
Cuisine	Asian-American
Recommended for	Bargain

'Do you want to know what my favourite schedule for a morning in New York is? A visit to MoMA in the morning and lunch at Má Pêche. Otherwise you can just get breakfast before MoMA.'—Massimo Bottura

MAREA
240 Central Park South
Midtown West
Manhattan NY 10019
+1 2125825100
www.marea-nyc.com

Recommended by
Gabrielle Hamilton,
Rebecca Kirhoffer,
Mark Sullivan

Opening hours	Open 7 days
Credit cards	Accepted
Price range	Expensive
Style	Smart casual
Cuisine	Italian seafood
Recommended for	High end

'Stunning and creative seafood dishes. Unpretentious, elegant and grown-up.'—Mark Sullivan

NEW WONJO
23 West 32nd Street
Midtown West
Manhattan NY 10001
+1 2126955815
www.newwonjo.com

Recommended by
Edward Lee

Opening hours	Open 7 days
Credit cards	Accepted
Price range	Affordable
Style	Casual
Cuisine	Korean
Recommended for	Late night

'A full menu of Korean barbeque, kimchi, hot stews and an array of pickles will cure any hangover you might have had.'—Edward Lee

NORMA'S
Le Parker Meridien Hotel
119 West 56th Street
Midtown West
Manhattan NY 10019
+1 2127087460
www.parkermeridien.com

Recommended by
Steffen Hansen

Opening hours	Open 7 days
Credit cards	Accepted
Price range	Affordable
Style	Smart casual
Cuisine	American
Recommended for	Regular neighbourhood

'Hot-shot place for lunch. Huge portions and great service if you can get a table.'—Steffen Hansen

PETROSSIAN

Recommended by
Michael Mina

182 West 58th Street
Midtown West
Manhattan NY 10019
+1 2122452214
www.petrossian.com

Opening hours	Open 7 days
Credit cards	Accepted but not Diners
Price range	Expensive
Style	Smart casual
Cuisine	French-Russian
Recommended for	High end

'Whenever I'm looking to indulge, I go to Petrossian for caviar service.'—Michael Mina

SAKE BAR HAGI

Recommended by
Marcus Jernmark,
Brad McDonald,
Matthew Orlando,
David Pasternack,
Jesse Schenker

152 West 49th Street
Midtown West
Manhattan NY 10019
+1 2127648549
www.sakebarhagi.com

Opening hours	Open 7 days
Reservation policy	No
Credit cards	Accepted but not Diners
Price range	Budget
Style	Casual
Cuisine	Japanese
Recommended for	Late night

'This is chef's food at its best. Stripped down to two, three or four components, the umami-rich dishes are always satisfying. Fried chicken gizzards, grilled sardines with spicy cod roe, chicken skin yakitori and fish cakes. Also, they will hold a bottle of sake with your name on it for ninety days in their cooler.'
—Brad McDonald

SEOUL GARDEN

Recommended by
Masaharu Morimoto

34 West 32nd Street
Midtown West
Manhattan NY 10001
+1 2127369002
www.seoulgarden32.com

Opening hours	Open 7 days
Credit cards	Accepted
Price range	Affordable
Style	Casual
Cuisine	Korean
Recommended for	Late night

'I like their spicy tofu soup and beef dumplings. The first sip of hot soup makes me smile, especially during the cold winter in New York. They are open for twenty-four hours so it is a natural place to grab a bite after working late.'—Masaharu Morimoto

TOTTO RAMEN

Recommended by
Tory Miller,
Marcus Samuelsson

366 West 52nd Street
Midtown West
Manhattan NY 10019
+1 2125820052
www.tottoramen.com

Opening hours	Open 7 days
Reservation policy	No
Credit cards	Not accepted
Price range	Budget
Style	Casual
Cuisine	Japanese
Recommended for	Bargain

'Totto Ramen – it really can't get any better and it is always so consistently delicious.'—Marcus Samuelsson

YAKITORI TOTTO

Recommended by
Michael Anthony

251 West 55th Street
Midtown West
Manhattan NY 10019
+1 2122454555
www.tottonyc.com

Opening hours	Open 7 days
Credit cards	Accepted
Price range	Affordable
Style	Casual
Cuisine	Yakitori
Recommended for	Bargain

'No one pays as much attention to the details of cooking modest food as they do. Just watch the guy on the grill focus on his work – it's awesome.'
—Michael Anthony

KAJITSU

125 East 39th Street
Murray Hill
Manhattan NY 10016
+1 2122284873
www.kajitsunyc.com

Opening hours	Closed Monday
Credit cards	Accepted
Price range	Expensive
Style	Smart casual
Cuisine	Japanese Vegan
Recommended for	Worth the travel

This vegan-friendly, *kaiseki*-serving, East Village Japanese specializes in *shojin ryori*. Brought, in the thirteenth century, by Zen monks across China to Japan, where it was perfected – or rather led closer to perfection – *shojin ryori* is all about celebrating seasonal vegetables. In twenty-first-century Manhattan this translates to a very Zen, twenty-eight-seat space that's all wood, beige walls and stone floors, with colour and beauty provided by the tableware and the food itself. The multi-course menu changes every month, the only constant being a serving of soba noodles. A very enlightening experience regardless of whether you are vegan or not.

THE BRESLIN BAR & DINING ROOM

Ace Hotel
16 West 29th Street
NoMad
Manhattan NY 10001
+1 2126791939
www.thebreslin.com

Opening hours	Open 7 days
Reservation policy	No
Credit cards	Accepted
Price range	Affordable
Style	Smart casual
Cuisine	Bar-Bistro
Recommended for	Worth the travel

'My favourite restaurant outside London. One of those places that seems so effortless. Food of the gods without any fuss or pretence. Have a pint in the bar then grab a seat upstairs and stare longingly into the kitchen.'—Tom Adams

Attached to the New York branch of the hipper-than-thou but still heavily branded Ace Hotel group, The Breslin's kitchen is overseen by expat Brit April Bloomfield of The Spotted Pig fame, who is also responsible for The John Dory, the hotel's oyster bar. The Breslin's retro-tavern good looks, quality cocktails and gutsy cooking have won it a loyal following. Particularly for its breakfast and weekend brunch menus, which run from an authentic Full English, complete with black pudding (blood sausage), to much more familiar takes on US classics, such as pancakes with maple syrup, frittatas and fried peanut butter and banana sandwiches.

NOMAD

NoMad Hotel
1170 Broadway and 28th Street
NoMad
Manhattan NY 10001
+1 3474725660
www.thenomadhotel.com

Opening hours	Open 7 days
Credit cards	Accepted
Price range	Expensive
Style	Smart casual
Cuisine	Modern American
Recommended for	Worth the travel

'The last meal I ate there was one of the best in my life: everything was just breathtakingly perfect. Daniel Humm is one inspired and inspiring chef.'
—Sami Tamimi

ATLANTIC GRILL

1341 3rd Avenue
Upper East Side
Manhattan NY 10075
+1 2129889200
www.atlanticgrill.com

Opening hours	Open 7 days
Credit cards	Accepted
Price range	Affordable
Style	Smart casual
Cuisine	Seafood-Grill
Recommended for	Worth the travel

DANIEL

60 East 65th Street
Upper East Side
Manhattan NY 10065
+1 2122880033
www.danielnyc.com

Opening hours	Closed Sunday
Credit cards	Accepted
Price range	Expensive
Style	Formal
Cuisine	Modern French
Recommended for	High end

'Daniel's restaurant is named after him because it fully represents who he is. Refined, precise and pleasant. It's a place that would not disappoint anyone.'
—Massimo Bottura

Daniel Boulud's increased international focus has seen him open less formal cafés, bistros and bars around the world, but at his eponymous spot in the heart of Manhattan's Upper East Side he flexes his high-end muscles with refined yet imaginative cooking. The opulent dining room, refurbished by the same design agency behind Thomas Keller's Per Se, is the scene for dishes that are rooted in the French chef's native Lyon but which have a distinctive American twang thanks to the use of local ingredients. The result is a supremely slick operation that remains one of Manhattan's culinary hotspots among the city's high rollers.

THE REGENCY BAR & GRILL

Loews Regency Hotel
540 Park Avenue
Upper East Side
Manhattan NY 10065
+1 2123394050
www.regencybarandgrill.com

Opening hours	Open 7 days
Credit cards	Accepted
Price range	Affordable
Style	Smart casual
Cuisine	International
Recommended for	Breakfast

'It's business, social and travellers so the mix creates a wonderful morning ambience.'—Daniel Boulud

ROTISSERIE GEORGETTE

14 East 60th Street
Upper East Side
Manhattan NY 10022
+1 2123908060
www.rotisserieg.com

Opening hours	Closed Sunday
Credit cards	Accepted
Price range	Affordable
Style	Smart casual
Cuisine	French
Recommended for	Regular neighbourhood

'My favourite meat is chicken and this restaurant is homely with great energy and reminiscent of rotisseries in France.'—Daniel Boulud

BAR MASA

Time Warner Center
4F, 10 Columbus Circle
Upper West Side
Manhattan NY 10019
+1 2128239800
www.masanyc.com

Opening hours	Closed Sunday
Reservation policy	No
Credit cards	Accepted
Price range	Affordable
Style	Casual
Cuisine	Japanese
Recommended for	Wish I'd opened

'Serves sushi and sashimi in a less strict Japanese way than the three-star Masa. It's a mix of Californian and Southeast Asian flavours with Japanese, which crafts perfection. I love it!'—Tim Raue

BARNEY GREENGRASS

541 Amsterdam Avenue
Upper West Side
Manhattan NY 10024
+1 2127244707
www.barneygreengrass.com

Opening hours	Closed Monday
Reservation policy	No
Credit cards	Accepted
Price range	Affordable
Style	Casual
Cuisine	Deli-Café
Recommended for	Worth the travel

'It's a long way to go for breakfast, but it wouldn't be hard to persuade me. Scrambled eggs and smoked sturgeon salty lox. A slab of cream cheese and a bialy on the side. Wash it down with a Dr Brown's Cel-Ray soda.'—Tom Harris

BOUCHON BAKERY

Time Warner Center
3F, 10 Columbus Circle
Upper West Side
Manhattan NY 10019
+1 2128239366
www.bouchonbakery.com

Opening hours	Open 7 days
Reservation policy	No
Credit cards	Accepted
Price range	Affordable
Style	Casual
Cuisine	Café-Bakery
Recommended for	Breakfast

'Thomas Keller's refined bakery. For breakfast I head there for their excellent pain au chocolat, my favourite type of pastry, and coffee.'—Marcus Jernmark

GRAY'S PAPAYA

2090 Broadway
Upper West Side
Manhattan NY 10023
+1 2127990243
www.grayspapayanyc.com

Opening hours	Open 7 days
Reservation policy	No
Credit cards	Not accepted
Price range	Budget
Style	Casual
Cuisine	Hot Dogs
Recommended for	Bargain

'Hot dogs are a quintessential New York street food that definitely fall under the category of cheap eats. It's not often, but when I do crave this guilty pleasure Gray's Papaya is definitely above your typical street dog. Usually after travelling I feel the need for Gray's not-so-friendly fast service to get me back into the New York state of mind.'—Michael Ferraro

JEAN-GEORGES

1 Central Park West
Upper West Side
Manhattan NY 10023
+1 2122993900
www.jean-georges.com

Opening hours	Open 7 days
Credit cards	Accepted
Price range	Expensive
Style	Formal
Cuisine	French-Asian
Recommended for	Worth the travel

'Classic French with an Asian twist. The food and service is exactly like it should be. Very professional service.'—Steffen Hansen

Born in Alsace but now a long-term US citizen, there's nothing conventional about Jean Georges's rise up the culinary ladder, not least because his primarily Asian-influenced cuisine is a far cry from his Gallic roots. The JG empire has swelled to more than twenty establishments in recent years, serving all manner of styles of cuisine, but to taste him at his best go to his Central Park flagship, where classics such as peekytoe crab dumplings and yellow fin tuna ribbons make a regular appearance. Prices for the dinner menu can be quite hefty, but lunchtime offers a more affordable taste of what's offered.

MASA

Time Warner Center
4F, 10 Columbus Circle
Upper West Side
Manhattan NY 10019
+1 2128239800
www.masanyc.com

Opening hours	Closed Sunday
Credit cards	Accepted but not Diners
Price range	Expensive
Style	Smart casual
Cuisine	Modern Japanese
Recommended for	High end

'This is an exceptional restaurant, really worth booking for a special occasion. It's a whole experience in itself that will tickle your senses.'—Jean-François Piège

The best seats in the (Zen-like) house at Masayoshi Takayama's twenty-six-seat sushi restaurant are at the counter, under the watchful eye of Masa himself. Take a moment to caress the hinoki wood tabletop (sanded daily, apparently), before immersing yourself in the Masa *omakase* experience – one of the world's most expensive dining events. Forget you're in the Time Warner Center shopping mall, and concentrate on the luxury: tuna tartare with equal parts toro (flown in from Tokyo's Tsukiji Market) and osetra caviar; wagyu beef tataki with summer truffles; and truffle ice cream. Bar Masa next door (and in Vegas) offers luxury for less.

PER SE

Time Warner Center
4F, 10 Columbus Circle
Upper West Side
Manhattan NY 10019
+1 2128239335
www.perseny.com

Opening hours	Open 7 days
Credit cards	Accepted
Price range	Expensive
Style	Formal
Cuisine	Modern American
Recommended for	High end

'It's perfection, the complete package.'—Hadleigh Troy

Coming here is not about the money. It is excruciatingly expensive, but pleasure comes at a price, and chef-owner Thomas Keller is no artful dodger. Pleasure is Per Se's *raison d'être* – if the view of Central Park doesn't take your breath away, they'll sweat blood and tears to make sure the food does. A temple to sous vide, Keller's East Coast urban interpretation of the legendary French Laundry pulls out all the stops to make its food memorable. Chef de cuisine Eli Kaimeh has been running the kitchen since 2010 and his tasting menus change daily, although exquisite 'oysters and pearls' with caviar is a regular feature.

SUPER TACOS

97th Street
Upper West Side
Manhattan NY 10025
+1 9178370866

Opening hours	Open 7 days
Reservation policy	No
Credit cards	Not accepted
Price range	Budget
Style	Casual
Cuisine	Mexican Taco Truck
Recommended for	Bargain

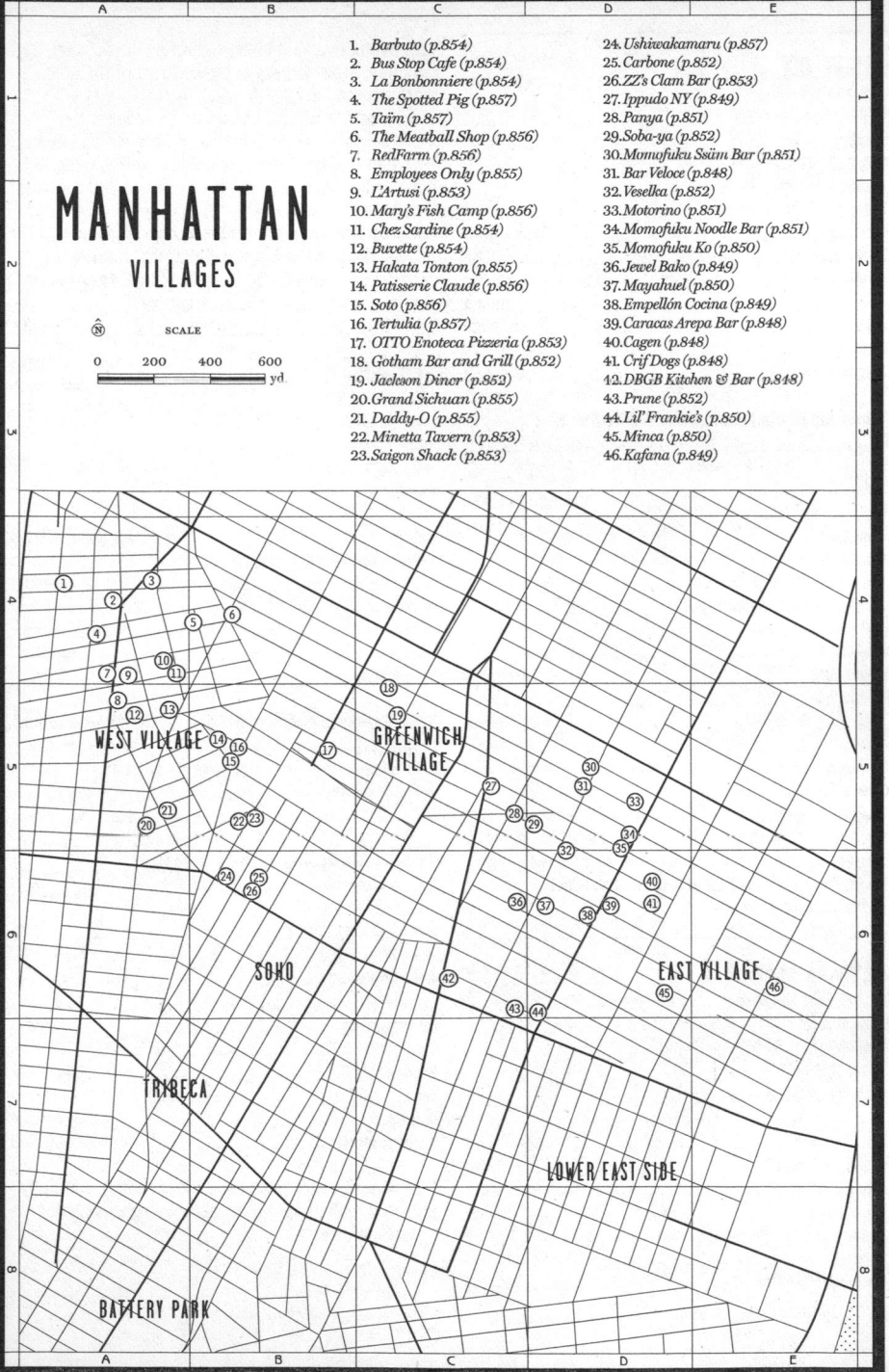

MANHATTAN

VILLAGES

N̂

SCALE

0   200   400   600
yd.

BAR VELOCE

175 2nd Avenue
East Village
Manhattan NY 10003
+1 2122603200
www.barveloce.com

Opening hours..Open 7 days
Reservation policy...No
Credit cards..Accepted
Price range..Budget
Style..Casual
Cuisine...Bar Snacks
Recommended for...Late night

'I love the mortadella panini.'—Wylie Dufresne

CAGEN

414 East 9th Street
East Village
Manhattan NY 10009
+1 2123588800
www.cagenrestaurant.com

Opening hours..Closed Monday
Credit cards..Accepted
Price range..Expensive
Style..Smart casual
Cuisine..Japanese
Recommended for.............................Regular neighbourhood

'Cagen is my friend chef Toshio Tomita's restaurant. He
used to work with me at Nobu. I like it because in the
perfect setting, with a chef's counter, he serves kappo
ryori: high-end traditional Japanese cuisine.'
—Masaharu Morimoto

CARACAS AREPA BAR

93 1/2 East 7th Street
East Village
Manhattan NY 10009
+1 2125292314
www.caracasarepabar.com

Opening hours..Open 7 days
Reservation policy...No
Credit cards.................................Accepted but not Diners
Price range..Budget
Style..Casual
Cuisine..Venezuelan
Recommended for...Bargain

This diminutive East Village joint has introduced
countless New Yorkers to the delights of the arepa
since opening in 2003. Thicker than a tortilla – it's
somewhere between a snack and a meal – the
Venezuelan corn staple is crisp on the outside and
soft in the middle, and here comes stuffed with all
manner of fillings from mashed chicken and avocado
(the authentic Reina Pepiada) to shredded beef and
Cheddar. Addictive sides include taro chips with
guacamole and fried green plaintains. A Brooklyn
branch launched in 2008, but the original HQ remains
just as packed as the arepas themselves.

CRIF DOGS

113 Saint Marks Place
East Village
Manhattan NY 10009
+1 2126142728
www.crifdogs.com

Opening hours..Open 7 days
Reservation policy...No
Credit cards..Accepted
Price range..Budget
Style..Casual
Cuisine..Hot Dogs
Recommended for...Bargain

'An amazing selection of hot dogs with unique and fun
toppings. I also love to pop in to PDT – the secret bar
with access from Crif Dogs – for a cocktail.'
—Daniel Boulud

DBGB KITCHEN & BAR

299 Bowery
East Village
Manhattan NY 10003
+1 2129335300
www.dbgb.com

Opening hours..Open 7 days
Credit cards..Accepted
Price range..Affordable
Style..Smart casual
Cuisine..French-American
Recommended for...Worth the travel

'The vibe, the atmosphere and the simple yet carefully
prepared food make this restaurant a special place.'
—Juan Gaffuri

EMPELLÓN COCINA

105 1st Avenue
East Village
Manhattan NY 10003
+1 2127800999
www.empellon.com

Opening hours	Closed Monday and Sunday
Credit cards	Accepted but not Diners
Price range	Affordable
Style	Casual
Cuisine	Modern Mexican
Recommended for	Worth the travel

Wd~50's and Alinea's former pastry chef Alex Stupak first decided to flex his sweet talent in a totally different direction in 2011 with the opening of Empellón Taqueria, in the West Village. This, the follow-up to that classy and creative taco joint, opened around a year later in the East Village and takes even more risks in its adventurous approach to Mexican food. Forget about cheap and cheerful, carb and dairy-heavy staples and think fresh and delicate tapas-style small plates that often make use of unexpected ingredients — sea urchin, shitake mushrooms, Brussels sprouts — while still maintaining a Mexican soul.

IPPUDO NY

65 4th Avenue
East Village
Manhattan NY 10003
+1 2123880088
www.ippudony.com

Opening hours	Open 7 days
Reservation policy	No
Credit cards	Accepted
Price range	Budget
Style	Casual
Cuisine	Ramen Noodles
Recommended for	Bargain

JEWEL BAKO

239 East 5th Street
East Village
Manhattan NY 10003
+1 2129791012
www.jewelbakosushi.com

Opening hours	Closed Sunday
Credit cards	Accepted
Price range	Expensive
Style	Smart casual
Cuisine	Japanese
Recommended for	High end

'The *omakase* (chef's choice menu) is one of the greatest high-end sushi deals in town.'—Anita Lo

KAFANA

116 Avenue C
East Village
Manhattan NY 10009
+1 2123538000
www.kafananyc.com

Opening hours	Open 7 days
Credit cards	Not accepted
Price range	Budget
Style	Casual
Cuisine	Serbian
Recommended for	Bargain

'Yugoslavian meats and salads, and a wine list made up almost exclusively of Serbian and Croatian labels. Cash only and hardly anyone in the room is speaking English.'—Gabrielle Hamilton

LIL' FRANKIE'S

Recommended by
Mads Refslund

19 1st Avenue
East Village
Manhattan NY 10003
+1 2124204900
www.lilfrankies.com

Opening hours	Open 7 days
Credit cards	Not accepted
Price range	Budget
Style	Casual
Cuisine	Italian
Recommended for	Bargain

'Consistent food, atmosphere and the value is great!'
—Mads Refslund

The quintessential New York-Italian joint, Lil' Frankie's occupies a small but atmospheric spot off Houston, where it serves hordes of hungry New Yorkers generous plates of pasta and wood-fired pizzas at prices that belie the care and attention that have gone into their making. In true NYC style, they don't take bookings for less than six at a time, and the queues (waiting lines) on busy nights can be off-putting. But you can put your name down and find a local bar to while away the wait, and before you know it you'll be enjoying your spaghetti *limone* and pizza *polpettine* (baby meatballs).

MAYAHUEL

Recommended by
Nick Anderer

304 East 6th Street
East Village
Manhattan NY 10003
+1 2122535888
www.mayahuelny.com

Opening hours	Open 7 days
Reservation policy	No
Credit cards	Accepted
Price range	Affordable
Style	Casual
Cuisine	Mexican
Recommended for	Regular neighbourhood

'They have the best *chilaquiles* and tamales in town.'
—Nick Anderer

MINCA

Recommended by
Brad McDonald

536 East 5th Street
East Village
Manhattan NY 10009
+1 2125058001
www.newyorkramen.com

Opening hours	Open 7 days
Reservation policy	No
Credit cards	Not accepted
Price range	Budget
Style	Casual
Cuisine	Ramen Noodles
Recommended for	Bargain

'This is some of my favourite ramen in the city. There is hardly ever a wait and the broth is just perfectly suited to my taste. I will go for kimchi ramen when I feel a cold coming.'—Brad McDonald

MOMOFUKU KO

Recommended by
Alberto Chicote, Angela
Hartnett, Vicky Ratnani

163 1st Avenue
East Village
Manhattan NY 10003
+1 2125000831
www.momofuku.com

Opening hours	Open 7 days
Credit cards	Accepted
Price range	Expensive
Style	Smart casual
Cuisine	Asian-American
Recommended for	Worth the travel

'Delicious, but we all know that.'—Angela Hartnett

You'll need patience and a computer to register for a Momofuku account even to have a chance of securing a reservation at David Chang's twelve-seat counter. To actually get one you either need luck, or a dedicated team of personal assistants, multiple accounts and more patience. You can book only a week in advance, the seats released online each morning at 10.00 a.m. seemingly gone seconds later. Assuming your luck's in, once you locate the low-key entrance, you'll find no waiters, no printed menu, and your no-choice ten courses (sixteen if you snag a lunch booking) served to you by the chefs behind the counter.

MOMOFUKU NOODLE BAR
171 1st Avenue
East Village
Manhattan NY 10003
+1 2127777773
www.momofuku.com

Recommended by
José Santaella,
Stephen Stryjewski,
Michel Troisgros

Opening hours	Open 7 days
Reservation policy	No
Credit cards	Accepted
Price range	Budget
Style	Casual
Cuisine	Asian-American
Recommended for	Wish I'd opened

'It's simple but sophisticated.'—José Santaella

MOMOFUKU SSÄM BAR
207 2nd Avenue
East Village
Manhattan NY 10003
+1 2122542296
www.momofuku.com

Recommended by
Michael Anthony, John Besh,
Massimo Bottura, Andreas
Dahlberg, Wylie Dufresne,
Ben Greeno

Opening hours	Open 7 days
Credit cards	Accepted but not Diners
Price range	Affordable
Style	Casual
Cuisine	Asian-American
Recommended for	Wish I'd opened

'One of my favourite places in the world. I always stop at David Chang's more R&R place to have a meal with my staff, my wife, my family or my friends. Intense flavours and a noisy, downtown atmosphere.'
—Massimo Bottura

David Chang's follow-up to his noodle bar, opened in 2006, is the restaurant that made him a superstar. Named after the Asian answer to the burrito that was originally to have been the mainstay on the menu, it has evolved to offer a menu that's heavy on meat – particularly pork – and that's not afraid to feature offal. At the back is Booker and Dax, a cocktail bar that offers a short menu of snacks from country hams to Chang's famous pork steamed buns of which everyone still can't seem to get enough.

MOTORINO
349 East 12th Street
East Village
Manhattan NY 10003
+1 2127772644
www.motorinopizza.com

Recommended by
Andrew Carmellini

Opening hours	Open 7 days
Reservation policy	No
Credit cards	Accepted
Price range	Budget
Style	Casual
Cuisine	Pizza
Recommended for	Bargain

Manhattanites have been known to travel to the outer boroughs in search of the perfect pizza, but since Mathieu Palombino's Williamsburg eatery (with branches in Hong Kong and Manila) made the reverse move in 2009, there's no longer any need to leave the city. Palombino inherited the space and its $40,000 pizza oven from previous occupants Una Pizza Napoletana, but relaxed the rules to include starters, pizza by the slice (takeaways [takeouts] are popular) and credit card payment. More importantly, the well-priced, puffy-lipped pies rank among the city's best, pairing light, bubble-filled dough with vibrant toppings such as Brussels sprouts and pancetta.

PANYA
8 Stuyvesant Street
East Village
Manhattan NY 10003
+1 2127771930

Recommended by
Masato Shimizu

Opening hours	Open 7 days
Reservation policy	No
Credit cards	Accepted
Price range	Budget
Style	Casual
Cuisine	Café-Bakery
Recommended for	Breakfast

PRUNE

Recommended by
Brad Farmerie,
Geoff Lindsay

54 East 1st Street
East Village
Manhattan NY 10003
+1 2126776221
www.prunerestaurant.com

Opening hours	Open 7 days
Credit cards	Accepted but not Diners
Price range	Affordable
Style	Casual
Cuisine	Modern American
Recommended for	Worth the travel

'Gabrielle Hamilton's tiny little restaurant is a true gem. Gabrielle's take on French provincial fare is deliciously quirky and thoroughly captivating. Flying in the face of modern trends in restaurants, this little beauty is a purist's delight.'—Geoff Lindsay

SOBA-YA

Recommended by
Peter Hoffman

229 East 9th Street
East Village
Manhattan NY 10003
+1 2125336966
www.sobaya-nyc.com

Opening hours	Open 7 days
Reservation policy	No
Credit cards	Accepted
Price range	Affordable
Style	Casual
Cuisine	Japanese
Recommended for	Regular neighbourhood

'House-made soba noodles, great broths and toppings, quality ingredients.'—Peter Hoffman

VESELKA

Recommended by
Brad McDonald,
Christina Tosi

144 2nd Avenue
East Village
Manhattan NY 10003
+1 2122289682
www.veselka.com

Opening hours	Open 7 days
Reservation policy	No
Credit cards	Accepted
Price range	Budget
Style	Casual
Cuisine	Ukrainian-American
Recommended for	Breakfast

'Buckwheat pancakes and bottomless cups of coffee. For breakfast you want to go someplace familiar. It's a neighbourhood institution so they remember regulars.'
—Brad McDonald

CARBONE

Recommended by
Justin Leboe, Benny Novak,
Ken Oringer

181 Thompson Street
Greenwich Village
Manhattan NY 10012
+1 2122543000
www.carbonenewyork.com

Opening hours	Open 7 days
Credit cards	Accepted
Price range	Expensive
Style	Smart casual
Cuisine	Italian
Recommended for	High end

'Carbone brings it back to the essence of an old-school fine dining experience, but keeps it fresh and fun. You've got to love the waiters in tuxedos, the tableside Caesar salad, the dessert trolley… they've just really nailed it.'—Ken Oringer

GOTHAM BAR AND GRILL

Recommended by
Paul Liebrandt

12 East 12th Street
Greenwich Village
Manhattan NY 10003
+1 2126204020
www.gothambarandgrill.com

Opening hours	Open 7 days
Credit cards	Accepted
Price range	Expensive
Style	Smart casual
Cuisine	Modern American
Recommended for	Local favourite

'Iconic food from chef Alfred Portale.'—Paul Liebrandt

JACKSON DINER

Recommended by
Dan Barber

72 University Place
Greenwich Village
Manhattan NY 10003
+1 2124660820
www.jacksondiner.com

Opening hours	Open 7 days
Credit cards	Accepted
Price range	Affordable
Style	Casual
Cuisine	Indian
Recommended for	Local favourite

MINETTA TAVERN
113 MacDougal Street
Greenwich Village
Manhattan NY 10012
+1 2124753850
www.minettatavernny.com

Opening hours...Open 7 days
Credit cards...Accepted
Price range..Expensive
Style...Smart casual
Cuisine..French
Recommended for...............................Local favourite

'The feel of the room and food is perfect New York.'
—Paul Liebrandt

A Greenwich Village fixture since 1937, Keith McNally
has breathed new life into the old joint, giving it the
same sort of upscale French brasserie polish that
served him so well at Balthazar. There was no bouncer
on the door back in the day when the Beats hung out
here, nor, I imagine, were banquettes trimmed in such
crisp crimson leather. But enough of the original
tavern's features remain for it to retain its character.
Add a menu that delivers gutsy Gallic comfort, such
as roasted bone marrow with confit shallots or crispy
pig's trotter with Dijon mustard and lentils, and it's
not hard to see why the retooled Minetta has been
such a hit.

OTTO ENOTECA PIZZERIA
1 5th Avenue
Greenwich Village
Manhattan NY 10003
+1 2129959559
www.ottopizzeria.com

Opening hours...Open 7 days
Credit cards...Accepted
Price range..Budget
Style..Casual
Cuisine...Pizza
Recommended for.....................Regular neighbourhood

SAIGON SHACK
114 MacDougal Street
Greenwich Village
Manhattan NY 10012
+1 2122280588
www.saigonshacknyc.com

Opening hours...Open 7 days
Reservation policy...No
Credit cards...Not accepted
Price range..Budget
Style..Casual
Cuisine...Vietnamese
Recommended for.................Regular neighbourhood

'The perfect bowl of pho. So flavourful, light, full of
vegetables and I could be out in less than thirty
minutes. My special escape.'—Michael Toscano

ZZ'S CLAM BAR
169 Thompson Street
Greenwich Village
Manhattan NY 10012
+1 2122543000
www.zzsclambar.com

Opening hours.......................................Closed Monday
Credit cards...Accepted
Price range..Expensive
Style...Smart casual
Cuisine..Modern Seafood
Recommended for.............................Wish I'd opened

'It's gangster – a cool, low-key spot with delicious food
and killer cocktails. Not as easy a combination to find
as you'd expect.'—Josef Centeno

L'ARTUSI
228 West 10th Street
West Village
Manhattan NY 10014
+1 2122555757
www.lartusi.com

Opening hours...Open 7 days
Credit cards...Accepted
Price range...Affordable
Style...Smart casual
Cuisine..Italian
Recommended for.....................Regular neighbourhood

'Chef Gabe Thompson makes soul-satisfying, seasonal
Italian food that I crave. And the staff are warm and
welcoming.'—Anita Lo

BARBUTO

775 Washington Street
West Village
Manhattan NY 10014
+1 2129249700
www.barbutonyc.com

Recommended by
Bruce Bromberg,
Gabrielle Hamilton,
Marcus Samuelsson,
Jesse Schenker

Opening hours	Open 7 days
Credit cards	Accepted
Price range	Affordable
Style	Smart casual
Cuisine	Italian
Recommended for	Local favourite

'Quintessentially New York.'—Marcus Samuelsson

LA BONBONNIERE

28 8th Avenue
West Village
Manhattan NY 10014
+1 2127419266

Recommended by
Takashi Inoue

Opening hours	Open 7 days
Reservation policy	No
Credit cards	Not accepted
Price range	Budget
Style	Casual
Cuisine	Diner-Café
Recommended for	Breakfast

'It has a classic, old New York feel, unpretentious and delicious.'—Takashi Inoue

From the outside La Bonbonniere looks like a forgettable greasy spoon, but the framed photographs of cheerful Hollywood stars who are its fans testify to the uniquely comforting offering of this classic diner. It's at its best at breakfast, with eggs over easy served with chips (fries), sage-flecked sausages and buttered toast; the burger, which comes with two slices of American cheese, is equally famous. Tin walls, padded vinyl stools and Formica counters make this a charming, timeless nugget of vanishing Greenwich Village, where it has stood for the past sixty years.

BUS STOP CAFE

597 Hudson Street
West Village
Manhattan NY 10014
+1 2122061100
www.busstopcafenyc.com

Recommended by
Jesse Schenker

Opening hours	Open 7 days
Reservation policy	No
Credit cards	Accepted
Price range	Budget
Style	Casual
Cuisine	Café
Recommended for	Breakfast

'It's extremely close to my restaurant. The food is consistent and they know me there.'—Jesse Schenker

BUVETTE

42 Grove Street
West Village
Manhattan NY 10014
+1 2122553590
www.ilovebuvette.com

Recommended by
Ken Oringer

Opening hours	Open 7 days
Reservation policy	No
Credit cards	Accepted
Price range	Budget
Style	Casual
Cuisine	French
Recommended for	Breakfast

'It's just like being in Paris. They have amazing egg dishes that they cook with the steamer of an espresso machine and amazing charcuterie.'—Ken Oringer

CHEZ SARDINE

183 West 10th Street
West Village
Manhattan NY 10014
+1 6463603705
www.chezsardine.com

Recommended by
Ségué Lepage

Opening hours	Open 7 days
Reservation policy	No
Credit cards	Accepted
Price range	Affordable
Style	Casual
Cuisine	Japanese-American
Recommended for	Worth the travel

'To get a table at Chez Sardine is, to me, a great privilege. Mehdi Brunet-Benkritly is by far the most talented chef I know. His cooking is highly evocative.'
—Ségué Lepage

An *izakaya* in the loosest possible sense, this tiny Greenwich Village corner spot greets customers with a portrait of Mr Miyagi and the promise of Japanese food seen with a hedonist's eye. Chef Mehdi Brunet-Benkritly, of next door's sister restaurant Fedora, is a French Canadian with history at Au Pied de Cochon, who applies his alma mater's spirit of excess to snacks such as a pork and *unagi* handroll, and caviar and *uni* toast. Pancakes are topped with salmon roe, soy and lime yogurt, while there's no little richness in crab-stuffed avocado tempura or miso-maple salmon head. Inventiveness continues to the cocktail list, although there's sake for those who want it.

DADDY-O

Recommended by
Harold Dieterle

44 Bedford Street
West Village
Manhattan NY 10014
+1 2124148884
www.daddyonyc.com

Opening hours	Open 7 days
Reservation policy	No
Credit cards	Accepted
Price range	Affordable
Style	Casual
Cuisine	Bar-Bistro
Recommended for	Late night

'They have a great burger, great tater tots and a great drinks list with speciality cocktails. It's a great chef hangout bar, so you always run into guys there.'
—Harold Dieterle

Styled like a classic neighbourhood bar, locals far outnumber the out-of-towners. Jocks come to shout at sports on the big screen and drink beer, others for the cocktails, the bar carrying a sizeable selection of single malts, rum and tequila. The kitchen, open until 4.00 a.m., serves a dependable menu of bar classics. A special mention must go to their sides of tater tots and The Plate – a tribute to Nick Tahou Hots's (Rochester, NY) cult classic Garbage Plate: two red or white hot dogs or two cheeseburgers, topped with hot sauce, mustard and onions, served over home fries and macaroni salad.

EMPLOYEES ONLY

Recommended by
José Santaella

510 Hudson Street
West Village
Manhattan NY 10014
+1 2122423021
www.employeesonlynyc.com

Opening hours	Open 7 days
Credit cards	Accepted
Price range	Affordable
Style	Casual
Cuisine	Modern American
Recommended for	Late night

'I don't tend to eat late at night, but when I do, I go here for the bar scene and the great comfort food.'
—José Santaella

GRAND SICHUAN

Recommended by
Harold Dieterle

15 7th Avenue South
West Village
Manhattan NY 10014
+1 2126450222
www.grandsichuannyc.com

Opening hours	Open 7 days
Credit cards	Accepted
Price range	Budget
Style	Casual
Cuisine	Szechuan
Recommended for	Bargain

'My favourite thing here is the soup dumplings – always hits the spot and consistent.'—Harold Dieterle

HAKATA TONTON

Recommended by
Edward Lee,
Tory Miller,
Carlo Mirarchi

61 Grove Street
West Village
Manhattan NY 10014
+1 2122423699
www.tontonnyc.com

Opening hours	Open 7 days
Credit cards	Accepted
Price range	Budget
Style	Casual
Cuisine	Japanese
Recommended for	Bargain

'Hot pot – simple, cheap and delicious.'—Tory Miller

MARY'S FISH CAMP
64 Charles Street
West Village
Manhattan NY 10014
+1 6464862185
www.marysfishcamp.com

Recommended by
Karam Sethi

Opening hours	Closed Sunday
Reservation policy	No
Credit cards	Accepted but not Diners
Price range	Affordable
Style	Casual
Cuisine	Seafood
Recommended for	Worth the travel

'For their lobster rolls and fried oysters.'—Karam Sethi

THE MEATBALL SHOP
64 Greenwich Avenue
West Village
Manhattan NY 10011
+1 2129827815
www.themeatballshop.com

Recommended by
Christina Tosi

Opening hours	Open 7 days
Reservation policy	No
Credit cards	Accepted
Price range	Budget
Style	Casual
Cuisine	Italian-American
Recommended for	Late night

PATISSERIE CLAUDE
187 West 4th Street
West Village
Manhattan NY 10014
+1 2122555911

Recommended by
Anita Lo

Opening hours	Open 7 days
Reservation policy	No
Credit cards	Not accepted
Price range	Budget
Style	Casual
Cuisine	Café-Bakery
Recommended for	Breakfast

'It has been there forever and the croissants are buttery and light.'—Anita Lo

REDFARM
529 Hudson Street
West Village
Manhattan NY 10014
+1 2127929700
www.redfarmnyc.com

Recommended by
John Besh,
Ken Oringer

Opening hours	Open 7 days
Reservation policy	No
Credit cards	Accepted but not Diners
Price range	Affordable
Style	Smart casual
Cuisine	Modern Chinese
Recommended for	Worth the travel

'I start thinking about RedFarm the second I board my plane to New York. I have gone to great lengths to get my hands on their crispy beef.'—John Besh

SOTO
357 6th Avenue
West Village
Manhattan NY 10014
+1 2124143088
www.sotonyc.com

Recommended by
Tyson Cole

Opening hours	Closed Sunday
Credit cards	Accepted
Price range	Affordable
Style	Smart casual
Cuisine	Japanese
Recommended for	Worth the travel

Named after the proprietor, Sotohiro Kosugi, this whitewashed room behind a door with no sign does a modest forty-two covers. A third-generation sushi chef, he performs his craft in front of expectant diners propped up at the blonde wood bar. Together with some exceptional raw fish, delicately cooked dishes also come out from the kitchen in impressive fashion. This is a very serious operation. Tables run in line along the side of the restaurant amid a very stark decor of spotlighting, slats and symbolic red circles. Pleasingly, there is also a lengthy list of speciality sakes.

THE SPOTTED PIG

314 West 11th Street
West Village
Manhattan NY 10014
+1 2126200393
www.thespottedpig.com

Opening hours	Open 7 days
Reservation policy	No
Credit cards	Accepted
Price range	Affordable
Style	Casual
Cuisine	Gastropub
Recommended for	Late night

'There is no better late-night food to be had in this city!'—Anita Lo

New York's original gastropub keeps rock 'n' roll hours – the kitchen's open until 2.00 a.m. every night – which seems fitting given its music biz credentials (Jay-Z and Bono are among the investors). Expat British chef April Bloomfield, also of The Breslin and John Dory Oyster Bar, has eschewed British pub grub in favour of Italian-infused comfort food with a strong emphasis on seasonal flavours. We're talking pan-seared bass with romanesco; pig's ear salad with lemon and capers; and trademark dishes such as sheep's milk ricotta *gnudi*, or the chargrilled Roquefort cheeseburger with shoestring fries. The Pig turned ten in 2014.

TAÏM

222 Waverly Place
West Village
Manhattan NY 10014
+1 2126911287
www.taimfalafel.com

Opening hours	Open 7 days
Reservation policy	No
Credit cards	Accepted
Price range	Budget
Style	Casual
Cuisine	Middle Eastern
Recommended for	Bargain

'Delicious falafel. Fast food that makes you feel healthy.'
—Anita Lo

TERTULIA

359 6th Avenue
West Village
Manhattan NY 10014
+1 6465599909
www.tertulianyc.com

Opening hours	Open 7 days
Credit cards	Accepted
Price range	Affordable
Style	Smart casual
Cuisine	Spanish Tapas
Recommended for	Regular neighbourhood

The conviviality of the *sidrerías* – local cider houses – in Asturias, northern Spain, was the inspiration for chef Seamus Mullen's West Village 'Spanish gastropub'. Set in raffish surrounds – rough brickwork, distressed wooden tables, a cider barrel behind the bar and an open wood-fired oven – in a former Prohibition-era speakeasy, it's heartwarming stuff, but certainly doesn't lack ambition. Deftly executed tapas classics – tortilla, Iberian ham croquettes, grilled prawns (shrimp) with garlic and Padrón peppers – are elevated by fine ingredients and judicious flourishes. Mullen stretches his legs with the sharing dishes and seasonal daily specials, chalked up on a blackboard above the kitchen.

USHIWAKAMARU

136 West Houston Street
West Village
Manhattan NY 10012
+1 2122284181
www.ushiwakamarunyc.com

Opening hours	Closed Sunday
Credit cards	Accepted but not Diners
Price range	Affordable
Style	Casual
Cuisine	Japanese
Recommended for	Regular neighbourhood

'It's a small dining room that fills up quickly most nights, so I try to get there on either the earlier or later side of the night. The quality of the fish is superb, and the technique and the flavour of the rice is what you would find at sushi restaurants at a much higher price point. I always start my meal with a Japanese draft beer, consistently super cold and crisp.'
—Michael Ferraro

MANHATTAN
DOWNTOWN

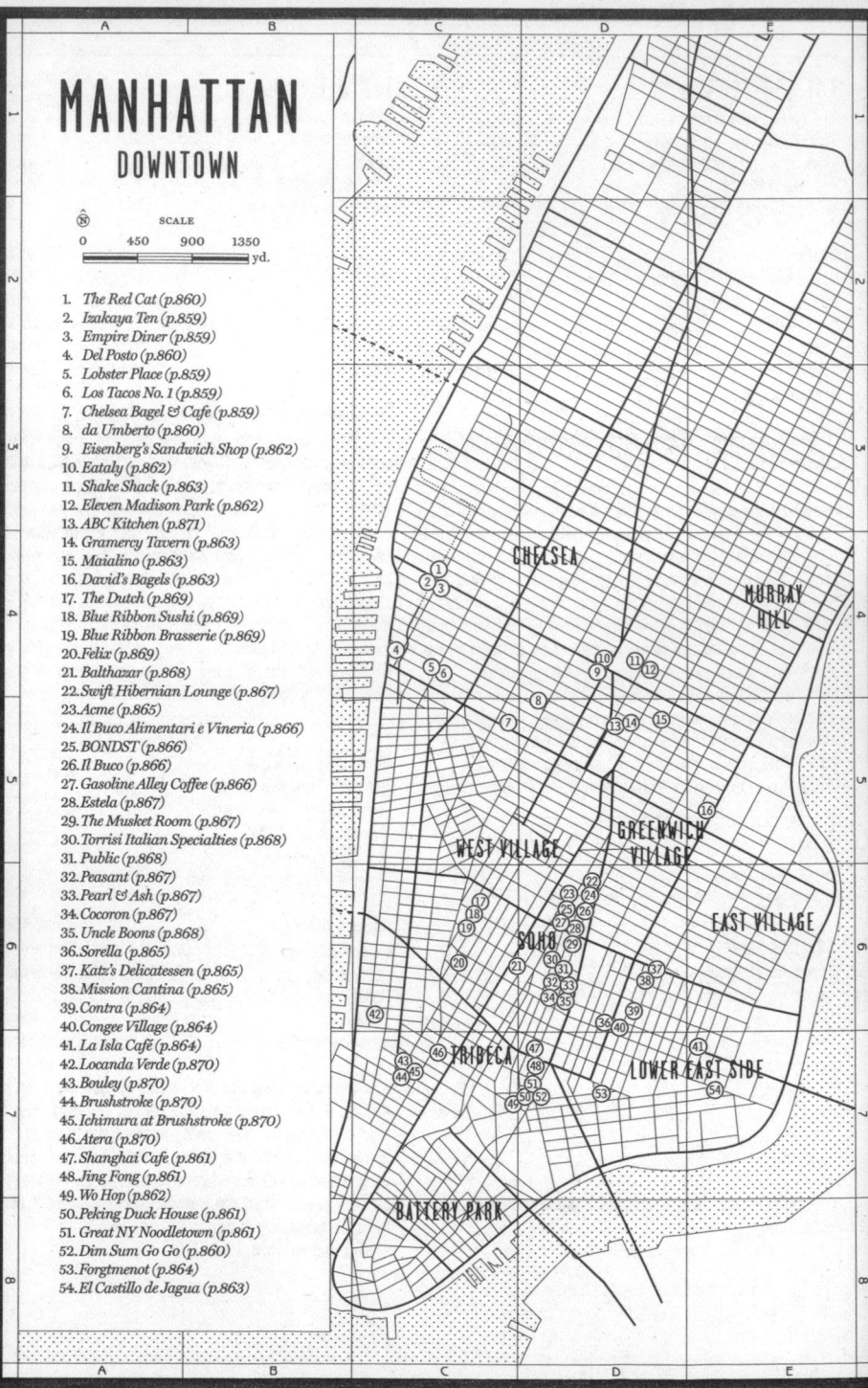

N SCALE
0   450   900   1350
yd.

CHELSEA BAGEL & CAFE

Recommended by
Harold Dieterle

139 West 14th Street
Chelsea
Manhattan NY 10011
+1 2124622435
www.chelseabagel.com

Opening hours	Open 7 days
Reservation policy	No
Credit cards	Accepted but not AMEX
Price range	Budget
Style	Casual
Cuisine	Bagels
Recommended for	Breakfast

'Their selection is always fast, easy and fresh.'
—Harold Dieterle

EMPIRE DINER

Recommended by
Marcus Samuelsson

210 10th Avenue
Chelsea
Manhattan NY 10011
+1 2125967523
www.empire-diner.com

Opening hours	Open 7 days
Reservation policy	No
Credit cards	Accepted
Price range	Affordable
Style	Casual
Cuisine	Diner
Recommended for	Late night

'I'm a diner type of guy. I love Empire Diner – classic.'
—Marcus Samuelsson

IZAKAYA TEN

Recommended by
Ken Oringer

207 10th Avenue
Chelsea
Manhattan NY 10011
+1 2126277777
www.izakayaten.com

Opening hours	Open 7 days
Credit cards	Accepted
Price range	Budget
Style	Casual
Cuisine	Japanese
Recommended for	Late night

'Izakaya Ten is super authentic. They've got incredible shochu and a great sake selection. It's quality "down and dirty" Japanese street food.'—Ken Oringer

LOBSTER PLACE

Recommended by
Ken Oringer

Chelsea Market
75 9th Avenue
Chelsea
Manhattan NY 10011
+1 2122555672
www.lobsterplace.com

Opening hours	Open 7 days
Reservation policy	No
Credit cards	Accepted
Price range	Affordable
Style	Casual
Cuisine	American Seafood
Recommended for	Regular neighbourhood

LOS TACOS NO. 1

Recommended by
Takashi Inoue,
Ken Oringer

Chelsea Market
75 9th Avenue
Chelsea
Manhattan NY 10011
+1 2122560343
www.lostacos1.com

Opening hours	Open 7 days
Reservation policy	No
Credit cards	Accepted but not AMEX
Price range	Budget
Style	Casual
Cuisine	Mexican
Recommended for	Regular neighbourhood

'This spot is close to work and has the best el pastor tacos in New York. Great for a quick lunch.'
—Ken Oringer

DEL POSTO

85 10th Avenue
Chelsea
Manhattan NY 10011
+1 2124978090
www.delposto.com

Recommended by
Massimo Bottura, David
Chang, Gabrielle Hamilton,
Luke Mangan, Ken Oringer,
Kevin Pemoulie, Andy Ricker,
Jon Shook, Christina Tosi,
Jason Vincent

Opening hours	Open 7 days
Credit cards	Accepted
Price range	Expensive
Style	Smart casual
Cuisine	Modern Italian
Recommended for	High end

'Mario Batali has narrated Italian cooking to the Americans for years in a simple, direct and fascinating way. More than any other, Del Posto, under the leadership of Mark Ladner and with its impeccable staff, is the monument to all that he narrates and communicates.'—Massimo Bottura

Delightfully over the top as ever, Del Posto seems to be hitting its stride and winning back New Yorkers a decade after opening. The polished mahogany and marble interior, live piano soundtrack and perfectly poised service pushes deep into occasion-dining territory, pitched more at Wall Street power lunchers than Meat-packing locals. The food, however, is for everyone. Don't miss the outstanding pastas – piquant crab, jalapeño and minced spring onion (scallion) spaghetti; unctuous lamb ragù and orecchiette topped with crisp rye crumbs. Be warned, the bill here comes on heavyweight stationery, but the $39 (£23) three-course prix fixe is one of Manhattan's best bargains.

THE RED CAT

227 10th Avenue
Chelsea
Manhattan NY 10011
+1 2122421122
www.theredcat.com

Recommended by
Marcus Samuelsson

Opening hours	Open 7 days
Credit cards	Accepted
Price range	Affordable
Style	Casual
Cuisine	European Bistro
Recommended for	Local favourite

DA UMBERTO

107 West 17th Street
Chelsea
Manhattan NY 10011
+1 2129890303
www.daumbertonyc.com

Recommended by
Harold Dieterle

Opening hours	Closed Sunday
Credit cards	Accepted
Price range	Affordable
Style	Smart casual
Cuisine	Italian
Recommended for	Regular neighbourhood

'It has a great, old-school, Italian feel and they treat their regular customers like family. They are very hospitable and the food is, of course, great.' —Harold Dieterle

DIM SUM GO GO

5 East Broadway
Chinatown
Manhattan NY 10038
+1 2127320797
www.dimsumgogo.com

Recommended by
Alexandra Raij

Opening hours	Open 7 days
Credit cards	Accepted
Price range	Affordable
Style	Smart casual
Cuisine	Chinese
Recommended for	Late night

'It has interesting dumplings and a chopped squab that is very tasty. I also love their noodles with dry scallop. The owner is always holding court and you can see the staff eating there.'—Alexandra Raij

GREAT NY NOODLETOWN

28 Bowery
Chinatown
Manhattan NY 10013
+1 2123490923
www.greatnynoodletown.com

Recommended by
Andrew Carmellini,
David Chang, Michael
Ferraro, Zakary Pelaccio,
Andy Ricker

Opening hours	Open 7 days
Reservation policy	No
Credit cards	Not accepted
Price range	Budget
Style	Casual
Cuisine	Chinese
Recommended for	Late night

'I've been giving this answer for years, but Great NY Noodletown is still one of the best places to go late at night. The food is consistently good. Dan-dan noodles and the whole duck are must-haves when eating here.'—David Chang

This Chinatown classic delivers on the far from empty promise of its name. It's true that service can be brisk – understandable since it's open until 4.00 a.m., making it a popular post-bar crawl, small-hours spot for the well oiled and the weary. But the lengthy menu – which covers all the bases from congee to barbeque meats, via various poultry and seafood dishes, to a lengthy list of noodle soups – is good enough to warrant inspection in the cold and sober light of day. Particularly worthy of investigation is their soft-shell crab, in season from around May until about October.

JING FONG

20 Elizabeth Street
Chinatown
Manhattan NY 10013
+1 2129645256
www.jingfongny.com

Recommended by
April Bloomfield,
Man-Sing Lee

Opening hours	Open 7 days
Reservation policy	No
Credit cards	Accepted
Price range	Affordable
Style	Casual
Cuisine	Dim Sum
Recommended for	Worth the travel

'Jing Fong serves very authentic Chinese cuisine. As a Chinese chef myself, I enjoy visiting the local Chinese restaurants wherever I travel to and I do set high standards for them. I was very surprised with Jing Fong's high-quality dishes when I was in New York recently.'—Man-Sing Lee

PEKING DUCK HOUSE

28 Mott Street
Chinatown
Manhattan NY 10013
+1 2122271810
www.pekingduckhousenyc.com

Recommended by
Carlo Mirarchi,
Christina Tosi

Opening hours	Open 7 days
Credit cards	Accepted
Price range	Affordable
Style	Casual
Cuisine	Chinese
Recommended for	Bargain

'You and your three closest friends can dine on Peking duck and cheap beer for less than $100 (£60).'—Christina Tosi

Peking Duck House has two Manhattan locations, in Midtown and Chinatown, both of which hide themselves behind unremarkable facades (and a red curtain). Unlike many restaurants of this type, there are no ducks hanging in the windows like a butcher's shop. Instead, the animals are treated with more respect, prospective diners having to cross the threshold to experience any part of the mallard magic that awaits them. The decor is more clean than comfy but people don't come to scrutinize the red carpet and bleached walls – they flock here for the legendary Peking duck and house-made pancakes.

SHANGHAI CAFE

100 Mott Street
Chinatown
Manhattan NY 10013
+1 2129663988
www.shanghaicafenyc.com

Recommended by
Ken Oringer

Opening hours	Open 7 days
Reservation policy	No
Credit cards	Not accepted
Price range	Budget
Style	Casual
Cuisine	Shanghaiese
Recommended for	Bargain

'A real Chinatown gem. They have a soft tofu with crab roe dish that is beyond addictive, and in my opinion the best soup dumplings in town.'—Ken Oringer

WO HOP

Recommended by
Bruce Bromberg

17 Mott Street
Chinatown
Manhattan NY 10013
+1 2129628617
www.wohopnyc.com

Opening hours	Open 7 days
Reservation policy	No
Credit cards	Not accepted
Price range	Budget
Style	Casual
Cuisine	Chinese
Recommended for	Late night

Descend the red staircase into Chinatown's Wo Hop, as generations of night owls and New York cops have been doing long before you, since 1938. If some of the dishes seem about as current as the celebrity photos plastered on the walls, embrace it: this frill-free Cantonese has classic status. Service is brusque, the portions are huge, and there's always a wait for a table. Order egg drop soup for old time's sake, and maybe roast duck *chow fun*, congee, and noodles with shrimp and lobster sauce. Wo Hop keeps pleasingly ungodly hours: 10.00 a.m. until 7.00 a.m., seven days a week.

EATALY

Recommended by
Kevin Thornton

200 5th Avenue
Flatiron
Manhattan NY 10010
+1 2122292560
www.eataly.com

Opening hours	Open 7 days
Credit cards	Accepted
Price range	Affordable
Style	Casual
Cuisine	Italian Bar-Bistro-Deli
Recommended for	Wish I'd opened

EISENBERG'S SANDWICH SHOP

Recommended by
Nick Anderer

174 5th Avenue
Flatiron
Manhattan NY 10010
+1 2126755096
www.eisenbergsnyc.com

Opening hours	Open 7 days
Reservation policy	No
Credit cards	Accepted
Price range	Budget
Style	Casual
Cuisine	Diner
Recommended for	Local favourite

'Quintessential New York City greasy spoon. Great BLT and fast service at all times of the day.'—Nick Anderer

ELEVEN MADISON PARK

Recommended by
April Bloomfield, Massimo
Bottura, Fisun Ercan, Steffen
Hansen, Edward Lee, William
Mahi, Reto Mathis, Patrick
O'Connell, Uwe Opocensky,
Peeter Pihel, Tim
Raue, Joan Roca

11 Madison Avenue
Flatiron
Manhattan NY 10010
+1 2128890905
www.elevenmadisonpark.com

Opening hours	Open 7 days
Credit cards	Accepted
Price range	Expensive
Style	Smart casual
Cuisine	Modern American-French
Recommended for	Worth the travel

'There is so much fun and they show it. Great team, great space and a great chef. Daniel Humm has really brought New York food to New York. It's a journey without ever leaving, and they do magic tricks at the end. How cool is that?'—Uwe Opocensky

Doing away with traditional à la carte dining has brought Eleven Madison Park dazzling accolades that would make any chef weep. Swiss-born chef-owner Daniel Humm joined the team in 2006 and has been widely credited for EMP's ascendancy. Housed in a theatrical Art Deco space above Madison Square Park, Humm's confident and contemporary French cooking is as opulent as that of his high-end Manhattan competitors and has won EMP three Michelin stars. To encourage dialogue between diner and chef, there is no conventional menu; instead, a grid of ingredients from which you pick four, and the kitchen does the rest. For grander budgets there's also a bespoke tasting menu.

GRAMERCY TAVERN

42 East 20th Street
Flatiron
Manhattan NY 10003
+1 2124770777
www.gramercytavern.com

Opening hours	Open 7 days
Credit cards	Accepted
Price range	Affordable
Style	Smart casual
Cuisine	Modern American
Recommended for	Wish I'd opened

'Not just because of its longevity and the famous chefs that are part of its history, but because it has created numerous talents that have gone on to smaller markets and connected the food conversation beyond New York City. Their impact on the food scene is astounding and admirable.'—Nikos Roussos

SHAKE SHACK

Madison Square Park
Flatiron
Manhattan NY 10010
+1 2128896600
www.shakeshack.com

Opening hours	Open 7 days
Reservation policy	No
Credit cards	Accepted
Price range	Budget
Style	Casual
Cuisine	Burgers
Recommended for	Bargain

The queue (line) is almost as famous as the food at the original Madison Square Park branch of super-restaurateur Danny Meyer's glossy burger chain, Shake Shack. Local office workers and tourists stand in line for up to an hour for their ShackBurger – a juicy made-to-order wonder comprising squidgy bun, American cheese, hand-formed beef patty and secret Shack Sauce – with crinkle-cut cheese chips (fries). Enjoy with an outrageous 'concrete' of fudge sauce and chocolate truffle cookie dough, a freshly squeezed lemonade or a Brooklyn Brewery Shackmeister Ale. Starting with one branch in 2004, Shake Shack now has thirty-nine, including outposts in Moscow and Istanbul.

DAVID'S BAGELS

273 1st Avenue
Gramercy Park
Manhattan NY 10003
+1 2127802308
www.davidsbagelsnyc.com

Opening hours	Open 7 days
Reservation policy	No
Credit cards	Accepted
Price range	Budget
Style	Casual
Cuisine	Bakery-Deli
Recommended for	Breakfast

'Everything bagel with whitefish salad.'—Nick Anderer

MAIALINO

Gramercy Park Hotel
2 Lexington Avenue
Gramercy Park
Manhattan NY 10010
+1 2127772410
www.maialinonyc.com

Opening hours	Open 7 days
Credit cards	Accepted
Price range	Expensive
Style	Smart casual
Cuisine	Italian
Recommended for	Regular neighbourhood

'I love all of the home-made pasta. My favourite dish is *malfatti al Maialino* – braised suckling pig and rocket (arugula) with pasta.'—April Bloomfield

EL CASTILLO DE JAGUA

521 Grand Street
Lower East Side
Manhattan NY 10002
+1 2129950244

Opening hours	Open 7 days
Reservation policy	No
Credit cards	Accepted
Price range	Budget
Style	Casual
Cuisine	Latin American
Recommended for	Breakfast

'The food is tasty and they make great Cuban sandwiches.'—Alexandra Raij

CONGEE VILLAGE

100 Allen Street
Lower East Side
Manhattan NY 10002
+1 2129411818
www.congeevillagerestaurants.com

Recommended by
Nick Anderer, Bruce
Bromberg, Takashi Inoue,
Masato Shimizu

Opening hours	Open 7 days
Credit cards	Accepted
Price range	Budget
Style	Casual
Cuisine	Chinese
Recommended for	Bargain

'No need for reservations or pre-planning, great for groups and awesome Chinese food, particularly the tofu and razor clams.'—Nick Anderer

CONTRA

138 Orchard Street
Lower East Side
Manhattan NY 10002
+1 2124664633
www.contranyc.com

Recommended by
Mads Refslund

Opening hours	Closed Monday and Sunday
Credit cards	Accepted
Price range	Affordable
Style	Smart casual
Cuisine	Modern American
Recommended for	Regular neighbourhood

'I believe in the concept – it's a locally sourced, seasonal, five-course tasting menu at an affordable price.'—Mads Refslund

Such is the pace of innovation in our world cities that tracking influence and counter-influence can be a bewildering task. Paris's 'bistronomy' movement (which took its cue from London's gastropubs) is apparently the inspiration behind Contra (with shades of Noma and Fäviken thrown in), where providing a daily-changing foraged-heavy menu for a very reasonable $55 (£33) keeps the young chefs on their toes. Occasional special evenings spotlighting guest chefs provide yet more variety – with no two nights the same, regular visitors are constantly rewarded. The wine list leans heavily – of course – towards natural, unfiltered kinds.

FORGTMENOT

138 Division Street
Lower East Side
Manhattan NY 10002
+1 2124318080

Recommended by
Marcus Samuelsson

Opening hours	Open 7 days
Reservation policy	No
Credit cards	Accepted
Price range	Budget
Style	Casual
Cuisine	American-Greek
Recommended for	Regular neighbourhood

'I go here with my soccer buddies after weekend games. It's the perfect pub; it's comfortable and relaxing.'—Marcus Samuelsson

LA ISLA CAFÉ

212 Delancey Street
Lower East Side
Manhattan NY 10002
+1 2125984752

Recommended by
Alexandra Raij

Opening hours	Open 7 days
Reservation policy	No
Credit cards	Not accepted
Price range	Budget
Style	Casual
Cuisine	Latin American
Recommended for	Bargain

'This is a van driver's dream! Awesome food for the money and nowhere to sit. I can't believe a place like this has survived and thrived enough to continue giving quality. It shows why being better than you need to be is the only way to really set yourself apart.'
—Alexandra Raij

You could easily walk past this tiny Dominican joint underneath a grey Manhattan building – but that would be a shame. It's a hole-in-the-wall masterpiece, offering take away (take out) only, popular with cops and construction workers on the Lower East Side. A few dollars buys you an enormous plate of chicken stew, seafood stew or roast pork, which comes with vegetables, including yucca and cabbage. Breakfast dishes include codfish with eggs or fried codfish cakes; fans also rave about mashed plantain and Dominican oatmeal. On high days and holidays they do a great paella.

KATZ'S DELICATESSEN

205 East Houston Street
Lower East Side
Manhattan NY 10002
+1 2122542246
www.katzsdelicatessen.com

Opening hours...Open 7 days
Reservation policy...No
Credit cards..Accepted
Price range...Budget
Style...Casual
Cuisine...Deli-Café
Recommended for............................Local favourite

'When I'm in New York I love to get up late and get down to Katz's Deli for a pastrami-on-rye sandwich. It sets me up for the whole day.'—Marc Fosh

MISSION CANTINA

172 Orchard Street
Lower East Side
Manhattan NY 10002
+1 2122542233
www.missioncantinanyc.com

Opening hours...Closed Monday
Credit cards..Accepted
Price range...Budget
Style...Casual
Cuisine..Modern Mexican
Recommended for............................Regular neighbourhood

'The atmosphere is laid back and the food is always on point. It's something fun and casual to do and I always have a good time.'—Kevin Pemoulie

SORELLA

95 Allen Street
Lower East Side
Manhattan NY 10002
+1 2122749595
www.sorellanyc.com

Opening hours...Closed Monday
Credit cards..Accepted
Price range..Affordable
Style...Casual
Cuisine..Italian
Recommended for..Late night

'Emma Hearst has created a cool, comfort-driven Italian downtown hangout.'—Daniel Boulud

Close to Chinatown, Sorella offers New Yorkers a portal to Piedmont. Start with a *gran selezione* of finely sliced prosciutto, speck and finocchiona. Then get serious with chef Molly Nickerson's bold cooking, which includes broccoli fritto with pickled hot pepper aioli, Grana Padano cheese and basil, or agnolotti crammed with celeriac (celery root) purée, braised oxtail and sage butter. Alongside, select from up to twenty-five wines by the glass from a list that is entirely Italian, except for grower Champagnes. Then savour an imaginative cocktail, such as the Ginsalata (Death's Door Gin, cucumber juice, fresh lime and basil syrup). Sorella stays open until 2.00 a.m. at weekends.

ACME

9 Great Jones Street
NoHo
Manhattan NY 10012
+1 2122032121
www.acmenyc.com

Opening hours...Open 7 days
Credit cards..Accepted
Price range..Affordable
Style...Smart casual
Cuisine...Modern Nordic
Recommended for..............................Worth the travel

'I love visiting New York, the number of superb local cuisines is astonishing. Acme is definitely worth a visit.'—Adam Aamann

BONDST

Recommended by
Mads Refslund

6 Bond Street
NoHo
Manhattan NY 10012
+1 2127772500
www.bondstrestaurant.com

Opening hours	Open 7 days
Credit cards	Accepted
Price range	Affordable
Style	Smart casual
Cuisine	Japanese
Recommended for	Local favourite

'I really admire Marc Spitzer's approach to Japanese cuisine. He's using super-fresh natural ingredients.'
—Mads Refslund

IL BUCO

Recommended by
Zakary Pelaccio, Bruce
Sherman, Masato Shimizu

47 Bond Street
NoHo
Manhattan NY 10012
+1 2125331932
www.ilbuco.com

Opening hours	Open 7 days
Credit cards	Accepted
Price range	Affordable
Style	Smart casual
Cuisine	Italian
Recommended for	Regular neighbourhood

This NoHo hotspot has long been a neighbourhood staple: even in its days as an antiques store, shoppers would stay on for a midday *pranzo* in the tiny kitchen. The space still has a cosy, rustic feel, but in its current incarnation it offers some of Manhattan's most superlative farm-to-table cuisine, attracting local designers, actors and foodies, who tend to come in groups and work their way through the entire Med-inspired menu. With a cellar hosting some 400 bottles from boutique European and New World producers, the wine list is equally impressive. (The owners also run a buzzing market/enoteca nearby).

IL BUCO ALIMENTARI E VINERIA

Recommended by
Peter Hoffman,
Zakary Pelaccio

53 Great Jones Street
NoHo
Manhattan NY 10012
+1 2128372622
www.ilbucovineria.com

Opening hours	Open 7 days
Credit cards	Accepted
Price range	Affordable
Style	Casual
Cuisine	Italian Bar-Bistro-Deli
Recommended for	Regular neighbourhood

'It's beautiful, brings together all the elements of house charcuterie, café, ice cream and fine dining – excellent execution all round.'—Peter Hoffman

GASOLINE ALLEY COFFEE

Recommended by
Mads Refslund

325 Lafayette Street
NoHo
Manhattan NY 10012
+1 2129330113
www.gasolinealleycoffee.com

Opening hours	Open 7 days
Reservation policy	No
Credit cards	Accepted
Price range	Budget
Style	Casual
Cuisine	Café
Recommended for	Breakfast

'Their coffee and pastries are really solid.'
—Mads Refslund

SWIFT HIBERNIAN LOUNGE

Recommended by
Nick Anderer

34 East 4th Street
NoHo
Manhattan NY 10003
+1 2122603600
www.swiftnycbar.com

Opening hours	Open 7 days
Credit cards	Accepted
Price range	Budget
Style	Casual
Cuisine	Bar Snacks
Recommended for	Late night

'I like the mini burgers with spicy English mustard. They are always open till 4.00 a.m. even if there's no one at the bar. Nice to have a reliable late-night spot.'
—Nick Anderer

COCORON

Recommended by
Peter Hoffman

37 Kenmare Street
NoLita
Manhattan NY 10012
+1 2129660800

Opening hours	Open 7 days
Reservation policy	No
Credit cards	Not accepted
Price range	Budget
Style	Casual
Cuisine	Japanese
Recommended for	Bargain

'Cheap soba noodles, quick service, tight tables and the toppings are always a bit slight but the flavours are good and the price is right.'—Peter Hoffman

ESTELA

Recommended by
Kevin Pemoulie,
Chad Robertson

47 East Houston Street
NoLita
Manhattan NY 10012
+1 2122197693
www.estelanyc.com

Opening hours	Open 7 days
Credit cards	Accepted
Price range	Affordable
Style	Smart casual
Cuisine	European small plates
Recommended for	Worth the travel

'A great chef making the food we want to eat, while still surprising us a bit by how he puts a few simple flavours together in a way we haven't tasted before.'
—Chad Robertson

THE MUSKET ROOM

Recommended by
Michael Meredith

265 Elizabeth Street
NoLita
Manhattan NY 10012
+1 2122190764
www.musketroom.com

Opening hours	Open 7 days
Credit cards	Accepted
Price range	Affordable
Style	Smart casual
Cuisine	Modern New Zealand
Recommended for	Worth the travel

PEARL & ASH

Recommended by
Ken Oringer

220 Bowery
NoLita
Manhattan NY 10012
+1 2128372370
www.pearlandash.com

Opening hours	Open 7 days
Credit cards	Accepted
Price range	Affordable
Style	Smart casual
Cuisine	Modern American
Recommended for	Wish I'd opened

'This spot on the Bowery is super fun and funky. They've got great food, an amazing wine list and just a great energy all round.'—Ken Oringer

PEASANT

Recommended by
David Pasternack

194 Elizabeth Street
NoLita
Manhattan NY 10012
+1 2129659511
www.peasantnyc.com

Opening hours	Closed Monday
Credit cards	Accepted but not Diners
Price range	Affordable
Style	Smart casual
Cuisine	Italian
Recommended for	Wish I'd opened

PUBLIC

210 Elizabeth Street
NoLita
Manhattan NY 10012
+1 2123437011
www.public-nyc.com

Opening hours	Open 7 days
Credit cards	Accepted
Price range	Affordable
Style	Smart casual
Cuisine	Modern International
Recommended for	Wish I'd opened

'A beautiful and elegant space serving spectacular food.'—Anna Hansen

TORRISI ITALIAN SPECIALTIES

250 Mulberry Street
NoLita
Manhattan NY 10012
+1 2129650955
www.torrisinyc.com

Opening hours	Open 7 days
Credit cards	Accepted
Price range	Expensive
Style	Smart casual
Cuisine	Italian-American
Recommended for	Local favourite

'I'm not really sure what exactly New York cuisine is, but Rich Torrisi and Mario Carbone have certainly captured it.'—David Chang

When this tiny twenty-seater in Nolita opened in the summer of 2010, styled as an old-school Italian grocers, it operated as a sandwich shop during the day. Now that Rich Torrisi and Mario Carbone (chefs and equal partners in the operation who liked the sound of 'Torrisi' best) have Parm next door (and at Yankee Stadium) doing the retro Italian sandwich thing, Torrisi's open kitchen is given over to a daily-changing nine-course set menu. Expect innovative takes on classic Italian dishes with enigmatic names such as 'clams casino' or 'rainbow'. Extended tasting menus are available on request.

UNCLE BOONS

7 Spring Street
NoLita
Manhattan NY 10012
+1 6463706650
www.uncleboons.com

Opening hours	Closed Monday
Credit cards	Accepted but not AMEX
Price range	Affordable
Style	Casual
Cuisine	Thai
Recommended for	Worth the travel

BALTHAZAR

80 Spring Street
SoHo
Manhattan NY 10012
+1 2129651414
www.balthazarny.com

Opening hours	Open 7 days
Credit cards	Accepted
Price range	Affordable
Style	Casual
Cuisine	French
Recommended for	Breakfast

'I have eaten breakfast through brunch, lunch and afternoon snacks, dinner and late night at Balthazar and I have never eaten a non-perfect element. That place is *irritatingly* good and wonderfully family friendly.'—Paul Cunningham

Keith McNally is among the most prolific restaurateurs in the Western Hemisphere. In the elegantly distressed warehouse-y district of SoHo, his restaurant Balthazar is a textbook Burgundy banquette-clad brasserie. The attention to detail by which it honours the French model is obsessive. The continuously bustling atmosphere is brought by the hordes of all-day diners who delight over Eggs Benedict and waffles in the morning and steak frites and confit duck in the evening. This is an institution not just within New York City but in the wider world of modern gastronomy.

BLUE RIBBON BRASSERIE

97 Sullivan Street
SoHo
Manhattan NY 10012
+1 2122740404
www.blueribbonrestaurants.com

Recommended by
Brad Farmerie,
Rebecca Kirhoffer,
Corey Lee,
Mads Refslund

Opening hours..Open 7 days
Credit cards..........................Accepted but not Diners
Price range...Affordable
Style..Casual
Cuisine...American
Recommended for....................................Late night

'Part of the magic is that Blue Ribbon fills up around midnight and is completely packed until 4.00 a.m. pretty much every night of the week. It's filled with an assortment of those in the food and booze industry, actors and rock bands sucking down oysters and eating bone marrow.'—Brad Farmerie

It's easy to forget that the original SoHo outpost of what's now an empire – a bakery brand, a Brooklyn bowling alley and a series of sushi bars, including one in Vegas – was once such a game changer. Now branded as the Blue Ribbon Brasserie, when it first opened back in 1992 it became a haven for restaurant industry types by insisting on keeping the same unsocial hours as they did. While the policy of only being able to book for tables of five or more frustrates a few, the seafood-heavy menu of classy comfort food is still the business.

BLUE RIBBON SUSHI

119 Sullivan Street
SoHo
Manhattan NY 10012
+1 2123430404
www.blueribbonrestaurants.com

Recommended by
Miles Kirby,
Paul Liebrandt

Opening hours..Open 7 days
Reservation policy...No
Credit cards...Accepted
Price range...Affordable
Style..Casual
Cuisine...Japanese
Recommended for....................Regular neighbourhood

'It's open late at night and the quality and consistency is fantastic.'—Paul Liebrandt

A soothing and accomplished SoHo presence since 1995, when it opened in a Sullivan Street basement on the same block as the original Blue Ribbon, the quality comfort food-touting restaurant that founded the Bromberg brothers' New York empire back in 1992. Open until the small hours, seven days a week, the lengthy menu – bolstered by daily specials based on whatever Pacific and Atlantic Ocean catches have come in – is overseen by Toshi Ueki. Well into its second decade, it remains, despite the hours it keeps, as fresh as is the fish in its nigiri and one of New York's finest sushi bars.

THE DUTCH

131 Sullivan St
SoHo
Manhattan NY 10012
+1 2126776200
www.thedutchnyc.com

Recommended by
Rebecca Kirhoffer

Opening hours..Open 7 days
Credit cards...Accepted
Price range...Affordable
Style..Smart casual
Cuisine...American
Recommended for....................................Late night

FELIX

340 West Broadway
SoHo
Manhattan NY 10013
+1 2124310021
www.felixnyc.com

Recommended by
Marcus Jernmark

Opening hours..Open 7 days
Credit cards..................Accepted but not Mastercard or Visa
Price range...Affordable
Style..Casual
Cuisine...French
Recommended for..........................Regular neighbourhood

'There are some restaurants that you go to because they feel like home, and for me one of them is Felix. The people who work there are a major reason why it's so special. They've worked there for a long time and are always interacting with guests – to me they feel like family. I tend to go mostly for their well-known Sunday brunch parties. It's a fun environment with good music playing and well-executed, comforting, French bistro fare.'—Marcus Jernmark

ATERA

77 Worth Street
Tribeca
Manhattan NY 10013
+1 2122261444
www.ateranyc.com

Recommended by
Konstantin Filippou, Ramón
Freixa, Steffen Hansen,
David Hawksworth, Takashi
Inoue, Marco Müller

Opening hours	Closed Monday and Sunday
Credit cards	Accepted
Price range	Expensive
Style	Smart casual
Cuisine	Modern American
Recommended for	Worth the travel

'Everything tastes fantastic. The drinks pairings are extremely well executed. My guess is they will have three stars soon'—Steffen Hansen

BOULEY

163 Duane Street
Tribeca
Manhattan NY 10013
+1 2129642525
www.davidbouley.com

Recommended by
Anita Lo

Opening hours	Closed Sunday
Credit cards	Accepted
Price range	Expensive
Style	Formal
Cuisine	Modern International
Recommended for	Local favourite

'Perfection. Still on the cutting edge. Intelligent and knowledgeable use of multicultural influences.'
—Anita Lo

BRUSHSTROKE

30 Hudson Street
Tribeca
Manhattan NY 10013
+1 2127913771
www.davidbouley.com

Recommended by
Takashi Inoue

Opening hours	Closed Sunday
Credit cards	Accepted
Price range	Expensive
Style	Smart casual
Cuisine	Japanese
Recommended for	High end

'It's a mixture of Japanese *kaiseki* and French cuisine, and they use high-end ingredients like foie gras and truffles.'—Takashi Inoue

ICHIMURA AT BRUSHSTROKE

30 Hudson Street
Tribeca
Manhattan NY 10013
+1 2127913771
www.davidbouley.com

Recommended by
Takashi Inoue

Opening hours	Closed Monday and Sunday
Credit cards	Accepted
Price range	Expensive
Style	Smart casual
Cuisine	Sushi
Recommended for	Regular neighbourhood

'It feels intimate at the Ichimura sushi bar and it's frequented by people who really know about sushi. Chef Ichimura is a master. I enjoy his skill as well as his hospitality.'—Takashi Inoue

LOCANDA VERDE

377 Greenwich Street
Tribeca
Manhattan NY 10013
+1 2129253797
www.locandaverdenyc.com

Recommended by
David Chang

Opening hours	Open 7 days
Credit cards	Accepted
Price range	Affordable
Style	Smart casual
Cuisine	Italian
Recommended for	Breakfast

'They serve the best lemon ricotta pancakes. The atmosphere is like an oasis in the middle of Manhattan. It's the perfect place to have a relaxed, well-cooked breakfast.'—David Chang

Styled as a fashionably casual neighbourhood Italian, Locanda Verde rapidly replaced the widely panned and damned Ago in 2009. Attached to The Greenwich Hotel, a luxurious eighty-eight-room operation co-owned by Robert De Niro – Hollywood icon, restaurateur extraordinaire and patron saint of Tribeca's revival – it's an in-demand Downtown breakfast destination. The kitchen is overseen by New York restaurant scene legend Andrew Carmellini (also currently of The Dutch and ex of A Voce and Café Boulud), whose morning menu includes ricotta with truffle honey and burned orange toast; oatmeal with grappa-stewed fruit; and toasted hazelnut French toast with sour cherries and mint.

ABC KITCHEN

Recommended by
Peter Hoffman,
Masato Shimizu

35 East 18th Street
Union Square
Manhattan NY 10003
+1 2124755829
www.abckitchennyc.com

Opening hours	Open 7 days
Credit cards	Accepted
Price range	Affordable
Style	Smart casual
Cuisine	Modern American
Recommended for	Wish I'd opened

'Solid farmers' market food, a high level of execution with stylish decor supported by the ABC store.'
—Peter Hoffman

A&A BAKE & DOUBLES SHOP

Recommended by
Zakary Pelaccio

481 Nostrand Avenue
Brooklyn
New York 11216

Opening hours	Closed Sunday
Reservation policy	No
Credit cards	Not accepted
Price range	Budget
Style	Casual
Cuisine	Caribbean Bakery-Café
Recommended for	Breakfast

ASKA

Recommended by
Gunnar Karl Gíslason,
Eduardo Moreno

90 Wythe Avenue
Brooklyn
New York 11249
+1 7183882969
www.askanyc.com

Opening hours	Closed Monday
Credit cards	Accepted
Price range	Expensive
Style	Smart casual
Cuisine	Modern Nordic
Recommended for	Worth the travel

'It's an eclectic place with a very purist type of cooking with well-defined Nordic flavours. Their execution and technique are very good and the extreme combination of ingredients creates a perfect balance.'
—Eduardo Moreno

THE BAGEL HOLE

Recommended by
Saul Bolton

400 7th Avenue
Brooklyn
New York 11215
+1 7187884014
www.bagelhole.net

Opening hours	Open 7 days
Reservation policy	No
Credit cards	Not accepted
Price range	Budget
Style	Casual
Cuisine	Bagels
Recommended for	Breakfast

'It's an old-school bagel shop with some of the best bagels in New York... maybe the best? I love good-crust, chewy bagels – they're very hard to find.'—Saul Bolton

BAR CORVO

Recommended by
Alexandra Raij

791 Washington Avenue
Brooklyn
New York 11238
+1 7182300940
www.barcorvo.com

Opening hours	Open 7 days
Reservation policy	No
Credit cards	Accepted but not AMEX
Price range	Affordable
Style	Casual
Cuisine	Italian
Recommended for	Breakfast

'Bar Corvo is friendly, has nice food and an outdoor space.'—Alexandra Raij

BATTERSBY

Recommended by
Nick Anderer,
Alexandra Raij

255 Smith Street
Brooklyn
New York 11231
+1 7188528321
www.battersbybrooklyn.com

Opening hours	Open 7 days
Credit cards	Accepted but not AMEX
Price range	Affordable
Style	Smart casual
Cuisine	Modern American
Recommended for	Wish I'd opened

'There's an intimacy between kitchen and dining room. You feel like the chefs are cooking just for you, like you're in their dining room at home.'—Nick Anderer

BLANCA

261 Moore Street
Brooklyn
New York 11206
+1 6467032715
www.blancanyc.com

Recommended by
Josef Centeno, Enrique
Olvera, Franck Pecol,
Jorge Vallejo

Opening hours	Closed Sunday to Tuesday
Credit cards	Accepted
Price range	Expensive
Style	Smart casual
Cuisine	Modern American
Recommended for	Worth the travel

'It is the place that has had the greatest impact on me recently. The food is perfect from start to finish and delicious. You have to go there!'—Jorge Vallejo

BROOKLYN FARE

200 Schermerhorn Street
Brooklyn
New York 11201
+1 7182430050
www.brooklynfare.com/chefs-table

Recommended by
Saul Bolton, Harold
Dieterle, Jose Enrique,
Marcus Jernmark, David
Kinch, Michael Mina

Opening hours	Closed Monday and Sunday
Credit cards	Accepted
Price range	Expensive
Style	Formal
Cuisine	Modern American
Recommended for	Wish I'd opened

'The quality of cooking, the ingredients, the respect for the food and the pure unadlerated deliciousness is unparellelled.'—David Kinch

The fanfare for Cesar Ramirez's eighteen-seater attached to a Brooklyn neighbourhood grocery store has inevitably brought some changes. They've finally got their liquor licence for one – which means that the previous BYO, no-corkage set-up may go and prices rise for his superb market-driven tasting menus that don't scrimp on luxury. Officially known as 'The Chef's Table at Brooklyn Fare', diners sit around a D-shaped stainless-steel counter, while Ramirez and brigade cook in front of them in a spotless state-of-the-art kitchen, gleaming copper pans hanging from the ceiling. A second Hell's Kitchen branch opened in 2014.

THE BROOKLYN STAR

593 Lorimer Street
Brooklyn
New York 11211
+1 7185999899
www.thebrooklynstar.com

Recommended by
Carlo Mirarchi,
Christina Tosi

Opening hours	Open 7 days
Reservation policy	No
Credit cards	Accepted
Price range	Affordable
Style	Casual
Cuisine	American
Recommended for	Late night

CAFÉ GRUMPY

383 7th Avenue
Brooklyn
New York 11215
+1 7184994404
www.cafegrumpy.com

Recommended by
Saul Bolton

Opening hours	Open 7 days
Reservation policy	No
Credit cards	Accepted
Price range	Budget
Style	Casual
Cuisine	Café-Bakery
Recommended for	Breakfast

'They have great beans and they roast them well. They know how to pull a good shot of espresso (which is not easy) then to top it off they use great local milk which is steamed to perfection.'—Saul Bolton

CLOVER CLUB

210 Smith Street
Brooklyn
New York 11201
+1 7188557939
www.cloverclubny.com

Recommended by
Peter Hoffman

Opening hours	Open 7 days
Credit cards	Accepted
Price range	Affordable
Style	Smart casual
Cuisine	Bar-Small plates
Recommended for	Late night

'Great cocktails, always expertly made and well balanced.'—Peter Hoffman

DI FARA PIZZA

Recommended by
Tim Cushman

1424 Avenue J
Brooklyn
New York 11230
+1 7182581367
www.difara.com

Opening hours	Closed Monday and Tuesday
Reservation policy	No
Credit cards	Not accepted
Price range	Affordable
Style	Casual
Cuisine	Pizza
Recommended for	Wish I'd opened

'Domenico DeMarco is a legend, owning and operating the restaurant since 1964. He is still there every day, making each pie by hand.'—Tim Cushman

AL DI LÀ TRATTORIA

Recommended by
Saul Bolton

248 5th Avenue
Brooklyn
New York 11215
+1 7187834565
www.aldilatrattoria.com

Opening hours	Open 7 days
Credit cards	Accepted but not AMEX
Price range	Affordable
Style	Smart casual
Cuisine	Northern Italian
Recommended for	Wish I'd opened

'It embodies what every chef wishes for in a restaurant: 1) it is a clear and positive expression of the owners' ideals of atmosphere, food and service; 2) it's been consistent over a long span of time in a world of "one and done"; and 3) it is always busy.'—Saul Bolton

DOVER

Recommended by
Nick Anderer

412 Court Street
Brooklyn
New York 11231
+1 3479873545
www.doverbrooklyn.com

Opening hours	Open 7 days
Credit cards	Accepted but not AMEX
Price range	Expensive
Style	Smart casual
Cuisine	Modern American
Recommended for	Wish I'd opened

THE ELM

Recommended by
Tom Aikens,
Geir Skeie

King & Grove Hotel
160 North 12th Street
Brooklyn
New York 11249
+1 7182181088
www.theelmnyc.com

Opening hours	Open 7 days
Credit cards	Accepted
Price range	Affordable
Style	Casual
Cuisine	Modern French
Recommended for	Wish I'd opened

'Very casual but perfectly prepared food. The rooftop bar has an exceptional view of Manhattan.'—Geir Skeie

Williamsburg appears to have gentrified all the way from 'edgy', through 'trendy', and is now something approaching 'smart'. Evidence comes in the form of a few unashamedly high-end restaurants that have opened in the last couple of years, not least of which is The Elm. Here patrons eat innovative, seasonal dishes such as Flavours of Bouillabaisse (spiked with fennel blossom) or the remarkable Summer Garden containing around fifty different fruits and vegetables, in a huge room decorated with a 9 m (30 ft) living wall and carved wood installations. Service, though, is true to the area's roots – informal but efficient.

FONDA

Recommended by
Saul Bolton

434 7th Avenue
Brooklyn
New York 11215
+1 7183693144
www.fondarestaurant.com

Opening hours	Open 7 days
Credit cards	Accepted
Price range	Affordable
Style	Casual
Cuisine	Mexican
Recommended for	Regular neighbourhood

'A bustling casual Mexican restaurant that uses great ingredients, makes fresh tortillas, great guacamole and has excellent Margaritas – all of which appeal to me on a regular basis.'—Saul Bolton

FRANNY'S

348 Flatbush Avenue
Brooklyn
New York 11238
+1 7182300221
www.frannysbrooklyn.com

Recommended by
Brad McDonald, Matthew
Orlando, Cal Peternell

Opening hours	Open 7 days
Reservation policy	No
Credit cards	Accepted
Price range	Budget
Style	Casual
Cuisine	Italian
Recommended for	Regular neighbourhood

'Hands down the most consistent and delicious food for a price you can actually afford every day. I've eaten there fifty-plus times and I've never been disappointed once. John Adler is a stickler for local ingredients and in-your-face flavours. It's amazing what he can do to elevate even the humble leek to something outrageous. If I have twenty-four hours in New York, I will always eat at Franny's.'—Matthew Orlando

GORILLA COFFEE

97 5th Avenue
Brooklyn
New York 11217
+1 7182303244
www.gorillacoffee.com

Recommended by
Saul Bolton

Opening hours	Open 7 days
Reservation policy	No
Credit cards	Accepted
Price range	Budget
Style	Casual
Cuisine	Coffee Shop
Recommended for	Breakfast

'I cannot help but mention Gorilla Coffee, whose crew has been turning out great coffee for the past twelve years on 5th Avenue in Brooklyn and have recently opened a crazy fresh state-of-the-art shop on Bergen and Flatbush in Brooklyn.'—Saul Bolton

GRIMALDI'S PIZZERIA

1 Front Street
Brooklyn
New York 11201
+1 7188584300
www.grimaldisnyc.com

Recommended by
Michael Ferraro

Opening hours	Open 7 days
Reservation policy	No
Credit cards	Not accepted
Price range	Budget
Style	Casual
Cuisine	Pizza
Recommended for	Local favourite

ISA

348 Wythe Avenue
Brooklyn
New York 11211
+1 3476893594
www.isa.gg

Recommended by
Christian Page,
Zakary Pelaccio

Opening hours	Open 7 days
Credit cards	Accepted
Price range	Affordable
Style	Casual
Cuisine	Mediterranean
Recommended for	Worth the travel

'Best-looking, best-tasting and best-feeling restaurant I have been to in a long while.'—Christian Page

MAISON PREMIERE

298 Bedford Avenue
Brooklyn
New York 11211
+1 3473350446
www.maisonpremiere.com

Recommended by
Ségué Lepage

Opening hours	Open 7 days
Credit cards	Accepted
Price range	Affordable
Style	Casual
Cuisine	Seafood
Recommended for	Bargain

'I love oysters, especially if there's a big plate of them at $1 (65p) apiece...! This is the best place to enjoy a nice, long happy hour.'—Ségué Lepage

PETER LUGER STEAKHOUSE

178 Broadway
Brooklyn
New York 11211
+1 7183877400
www.peterluger.com

Recommended by
Saul Bolton, Michael
Ferraro, Corey Lee,
Vicky Ratnani

Opening hours	Open 7 days
Credit cards	Not accepted
Price range	Expensive
Style	Smart casual
Cuisine	Steakhouse
Recommended for	Local favourite

'They're known worldwide for one thing and are the best at doing that – simple and timeless.'—Corey Lee

There's a brutal simplicity to the menu at Peter Luger's when it comes to ordering your main course. Of course you'll find a few other things on the menu but it's the USDA prime porterhouse, available for one, two, three or four, that most diners go for. After all, lamb chops can be found anywhere. Luger's is not perfect – the dining room, despite its kitsch charm, could do with an update – but the steaks, and for that matter, the extra thick rashers of bacon, are unbelievable.

PIES 'N' THIGHS

166 South 4th Street
Brooklyn
New York 11211
+1 3475296090
wwww.piesnthighs.com

Recommended by
Christina Tosi

Opening hours	Open 7 days
Reservation policy	No
Credit cards	Accepted
Price range	Budget
Style	Casual
Cuisine	Southern American
Recommended for	Wish I'd opened

'It's the ultimate chick restaurant, serving fried chicken and down-home baked goods, run by amazing chefs.'
—Christina Tosi

POK POK NY

117 Columbia Street
Brooklyn
New York 11231
+1 7189239322
www.pokpokny.com

Recommended by
Brad Farmerie,
Carlo Mirarchi

Opening hours	Open 7 days
Reservation policy	No
Credit cards	Accepted
Price range	Budget
Style	Casual
Cuisine	Thai
Recommended for	Bargain

'Andy Ricker's food is like a salty/spicy drug – taste it and you need more. Super authentic and soulful and delicious.'—Brad Farmerie

ROBERTA'S

261 Moore Street
Brooklyn
New York 11206
+1 7184171118
www.robertaspizza.com

Recommended by
Anton Bjuhr, Daniel
Boulud, Andreas Dahlberg,
Kobe Desramaults, Brad
Farmerie, Alexandre
Gauthier, Alexandra Raij,
Guy Savoy, Christina Tosi

Opening hours	Open 7 days
Reservation policy	No
Credit cards	Accepted
Price range	Budget
Style	Casual
Cuisine	Italian
Recommended for	Local favourite

'It's this amazing jumble of radio station meets farm meets pizzeria meets bar meets disco meets fabulous tasting-menu restaurant. There are no rules to the way they do things and that's why it's the quintessential modern-day Brooklyn restaurant.'—Christina Tosi

If when folk describe a place as 'very Brooklyn' you don't quite know what they mean, head to Roberta's in Williamsburg for a primer. The breeze-block frontage, concrete floors, tattooed waiting staff and obscure craft beers served in jam jars spell hipster heaven, as does this former garage's predilection for foraged ingredients and crops from its own urban farm. Launched by former musicians in 2008, Roberta's initially offered little more than its amusingly monikered, wood-fired pizzas such as Pearly Whites and Specktater, but brilliant, self-taught chef Carlo Mirarchi doesn't just sling dough – his limited-edition tasting menus are now much in demand.

SPEEDY ROMEO

Recommended by
Brad Farmerie

376 Classon Avenue
Brooklyn
New York 11238
+1 7182300061
www.speedyromeo.com

Opening hours	Open 7 days
Credit cards	Accepted
Price range	Affordable
Style	Smart casual
Cuisine	Italian-American
Recommended for	Regular neighbourhood

'This is a real-deal restaurant masquerading as an unassuming neighbourhood "pizza place". Yes, the pizza is amazing (they often have guest-chef pizzas by notable New York chefs) but when you get beyond the pizza and into the octopus, sweetbreads, smoked beetroot (beets), dry-aged beef and home-made mozzarella, that's when you see the real magic happen.'
—Brad Farmerie

Introducing Provel: a curious hybrid of provolone, Swiss and Cheddar cheeses beloved of the pizza eaters of St. Louis, Missouri. Until recently you wouldn't have encountered Provel outside the Midwest but now it's big in Brooklyn. How so? In 2012, old college buddies Todd Feldman (a casting director) and Justin Bazdarich (a Midwesterner and ex-Vongerichten chef) opened their long-mooted restaurant Speedy Romeo in Clinton Hill, majoring in wood-fired American-style pizza pies, grills and seafood. The Saint Louie, authentically 'party-cut' into squares and topped with Provel, is just one of the rehabilitated classics at this hip neighbourhood joint that's so 'Brooklyn' it's been in *Girls*.

ST. ANSELM

Recommended by
Tony Maws

355 Metropolitan Avenue
Brooklyn
New York 11211
+1 7183845054

Opening hours	Open 7 days
Reservation policy	No
Credit cards	Accepted
Price range	Affordable
Style	Casual
Cuisine	Modern American
Recommended for	Worth the travel

'Great grilled food and you want to use your hands.'
—Tony Maws

TACOS MATAMOROS

Recommended by
Saul Bolton

4508 5th Avenue
Brooklyn
New York 11220
+1 7188717627

Opening hours	Open 7 days
Credit cards	Accepted
Price range	Budget
Style	Casual
Cuisine	Mexican
Recommended for	Late night

'Fresh. Cheap. Delicious. Who says New York doesn't have great Mexican food? Great fried tripe tacos, a monkey bowl of radishes and roasted jalapeños, salsa verde, a bottle of cold beer – what else do you need?'—Saul Bolton

VINEGAR HILL HOUSE

Recommended by
Zakary Pelaccio

72 Hudson Avenue
Brooklyn
New York 11201
+1 7185221018
www.vinegarhillhouse.com

Opening hours	Open 7 days
Credit cards	Accepted
Price range	Affordable
Style	Casual
Cuisine	Modern American
Recommended for	Local favourite

M. WELLS DINETTE

Recommended by
Alexandra Raij

MoMa PS1
22–25 Jackson Avenue
Queens
New York 11101
+1 7187861800
www.magasinwells.com

Opening hours	Closed Tuesday and Wednesday
Credit cards	Accepted
Price range	Affordable
Style	Casual
Cuisine	Modern American
Recommended for	Regular neighbourhood

Quebec native Hugue Dufour trained at the legend-
arily pork-rich Au Pied de Cochon in Montreal. He has
brought much of that lard-laden generous approach
to M. Wells Dinette, the reincarnation of
a restaurant he ran, to great acclaim, in Long Island.
Attached to an outpost of MoMA, and located in a
former schoolhouse, the cafeteria-style dining room
includes blackboards on which the menus are chalked.
Horsemeat tartare has been dropped after a public
outcry, but you might still enjoy apple-flavoured blood
pudding with kraut, or meatloaf with stroganoff
gravy, Spätzle and foie gras. Block out the rest of
the afternoon for a lengthy nap.

PARK SIDE RESTAURANT

Recommended by
Harold Dieterle

107–01 Corona Avenue
Queens
New York 11368
+1 7182719871
www.parksiderestaurantny.com

Opening hours	Open 7 days
Credit cards	Accepted
Price range	Affordable
Style	Smart casual
Cuisine	Italian
Recommended for	Wish I'd opened

'This restaurant is an old-school Italian family joint that
always has amazing dishes. They even make their own
wine, which is fun.'—Harold Dieterle

TAQUERIA COATZINGO

Recommended by
Michael Toscano

7605 Roosevelt Avenue
Queens
New York 11372
+1 7187797930

Opening hours	Open 7 days
Reservation policy	No
Credit cards	Not accepted
Price range	Budget
Style	Casual
Cuisine	Mexican
Recommended for	Late night

'They serve my favourite *tacos al pastor* (spicy pork),
lengua (beef tongue) and *carnitas* (pulled pork). Also,
their *pancita de res* (beef tripe soup), *tortas*, *cemitas*
(meat, avocado and cheese sandwich) and *nachos
Texanos* are out of control. And they're open until
3.00 a.m.'—Michael Toscano

WHITE BEAR

Recommended by
Saul Bolton,
Tony Mantuano

135–02 Roosevelt Avenue
Queens
New York 11354
+1 7189612322

Opening hours	Closed Wednesday
Reservation policy	No
Credit cards	Not accepted
Price range	Budget
Style	Casual
Cuisine	Chinese
Recommended for	Bargain

'A hole in the wall with the best spicy wontons for $4
(£2) – yum.'—Saul Bolton

CENTRAL AMERICA & CARIBBEAN

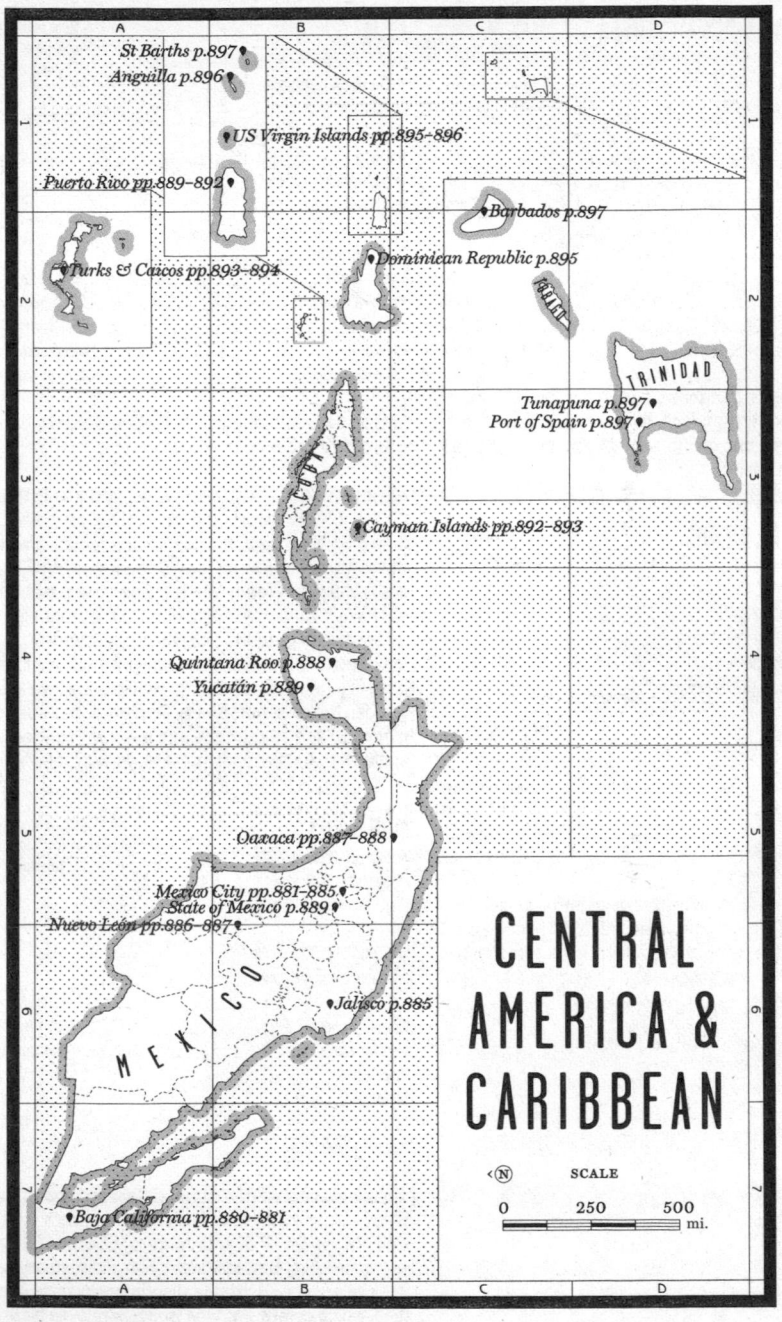

St Barths p.897 ♦
Anguilla p.896 ♦

US Virgin Islands pp.895–896 ♦

Puerto Rico pp.889–892 ♦

♦ Barbados p.897

Turks & Caicos pp.893–894 ♦

♦ Dominican Republic p.895

TRINIDAD

Tunapuna p.897 ♦
Port of Spain p.897 ♦

CUBA

♦ Cayman Islands pp.892–893

Quintana Roo p.888 ♦
Yucatán p.889 ♦

Oaxaca pp.887–888 ♦

Mexico City pp.881–885 ♦
State of Mexico p.889 ♦
Nuevo León pp.886–887 ♦

MEXICO

♦ Jalisco p.885

CENTRAL AMERICA & CARIBBEAN

‹Ⓝ›   SCALE

0   250   500
mi.

♦ Baja California pp.880–881

LA COCINA DE DOÑA ESTHELA

Recommended by
Steve Samson

San Marcos
Ensenada
Baja California 76372
Mexico
+52 6461568453

Opening hours	Open 7 days
Reservation policy	No
Credit cards	Not accepted
Price range	Affordable
Style	Casual
Cuisine	Mexican
Recommended for	Worth the travel

'This little place (the cook's house) has really great, freshly made Mexican food. It is awesome! Really good *gorditas* and *naranjada* (orangeade) that I still dream of...'—Steve Samson

CORAZÓN DE TIERRA

Recommended by
Jorge Vallejo

La Villa del Valle
Ensenada
Baja California 76372
Mexico
+52 6461568030
www.corazondetierra.com

Opening hours	Open 7 days
Credit cards	Accepted
Price range	Expensive
Style	Smart casual
Cuisine	Modern Mexican
Recommended for	Wish I'd opened

'One of the most honest offerings of Mexican food today. The place is magical. You eat in the middle of a vineyard, in the valley of Guadalupe, in an area that has everything.'—Jorge Vallejo

LAJA

Recommended by
Bruno Oteiza &
Mikel Alonso

Km. 83 Carretera Tecate-Ensenada
Valle de Guadalupe
Ensenada
Baja California 22750
Mexico
+52 6461552556
www.lajamexico.com

Opening hours	Open 7 days
Credit cards	Accepted
Price range	Affordable
Style	Smart casual
Cuisine	Modern Mexican
Recommended for	Worth the travel

'It is an oasis in the region of Valle de Guadalupe.'
—Bruno Oteiza & Mikel Alonso

Having worked in some esteemed kitchens in the US, chef Jair Téllez returned to his native Baja California with a vision of Laja, his destination restaurant 'in the middle of nowhere'. Since opening in 2001, he and his devoted team (many trained from the bottom up) have turned the dream into reality, planting orchards and gardens and using ingredients indigenous to the surrounding wine country. Laja itself is pure rustic simplicity: whitewashed walls and wooden tables set off breezy modern dishes such as mackerel and sea urchin, and quail with butternut squash cream. Seconds are always available.

MANZANILLA

Recommended by
Diego Hernández Baquedano,
Enrique Olvera

Teniente Azueta 139
Ensenada
Baja California 22800
Mexico
+52 6461757073
www.rmanzanilla.com

Opening hours	Open 7 days
Credit cards	Accepted but not AMEX
Price range	Affordable
Style	Casual
Cuisine	Mexican
Recommended for	Local favourite

'Creating a cuisine that's both simple and sophisticated is not easy to achieve. At Manzanilla they do it really well. The quality of their produce and Benito Molina's skill in handling the local area's fish and seafood makes this place special. I like the slightly smoky taste of his food, which comes from the wood-fired oven he uses to cook his dishes.'—Diego Hernández Baquedano

MARISCOS EL PIZÓN

Recommended by
Diego Hernández Baquedano

Avenida Dr Pedro Loyola
Calle Guaymas
Ensenada
Baja California 22890
Mexico
+52 6461487961

Opening hours	Closed Wednesday
Reservation policy	No
Credit cards	Not accepted
Price range	Budget
Style	Casual
Cuisine	Seafood
Recommended for	Bargain

'It's the best street stall in the area if you want to eat sea urchins. Alan Pasiano was a diver and worked catching sea urchins in Baja California – his skill led him to be quality-approved at Tsukiji Market in Japan. He now has a modest street stall where he sells freshly made dishes containing urchins, large clams, horse mackerel and other seafood from the local area. He only serves four people at a time at his stall so all the attention is focused on the person eating.'
—Diego Hernández Baquedano

ITANONI

Recommended by
Gabriela Cámara Bargellini,
Alejandro Ruiz

Belisario Domínguez 513
Oaxaca
Baja California 68050
Mexico
+52 9515139223
www.itanoni.com

Opening hours	Open 7 days
Reservation policy	No
Credit cards	Not accepted
Price range	Budget
Style	Casual
Cuisine	Mexican
Recommended for	Breakfast

'They offer breakfast based on a variety of Indian corn in stews, simply delicious.'—Alejandro Ruiz

LA CAZA CLUB

Recommended by
Diego Hernández Baquedano

Avenida Miguel Alemán Valdez
Tijuana
Baja California 22044
Mexico
+52 6646863361

Opening hours	Open 7 days
Credit cards	Accepted but not AMEX
Price range	Affordable
Style	Smart casual
Cuisine	Modern Mexican
Recommended for	Regular neighbourhood

'I really like chef Humberto Aviles's cooking, his flavours represent the area we are in, its atmosphere and its music. The drinks they serve and the friends you make keep you going back to this place.'
—Diego Hernández Baquedano

MARISCOS RUBEN

Recommended by
Ricardo Zarate

Corner of 8th and Quintana Roo
Tijuana
Baja California
Mexico

Opening hours	Open 7 days
Reservation policy	No
Credit cards	Not accepted
Price range	Budget
Style	Casual
Cuisine	Seafood
Recommended for	Worth the travel

ASIAN BAY

Recommended by
Pablo San Román

Avenida Tamaulipas 95
Mexico City
Federal District 06140
Mexico
+52 5555534582
www.asian-bay.com

Opening hours	Open 7 days
Credit cards	Accepted
Price range	Affordable
Style	Casual
Cuisine	Chinese
Recommended for	Regular neighbourhood

'Their cooking techniques are natural and the service amiable.'—Pablo San Román

AZUL HISTÓRICO

Recommended by
Enrique Olvera

Isabel la Católica 30
Mexico City
Federal District 06000
Mexico
+52 5555101316
www.azulrestaurantes.com

Opening hours	Open 7 days
Credit cards	Accepted
Price range	Affordable
Style	Casual
Cuisine	Modern Mexican
Recommended for	Local favourite

'If you want to understand Mexican cuisine, this must be your first stop.'—Enrique Olvera

The courtyard of Azul, with its striking living canopy of carefully trimmed tropical trees, is only the first thing that makes jaws drop at this impressive Centro Histórico hotel restaurant. Serving regional Mexican food (Oaxaca and the Yucatán are particularly well represented) with an unapologetically gourmet twist, dishes such as the famous *mole negro* or *cochinita pibil* (slow-roasted pork in pibil sauce) are presented with flair and imagination, and even the house margaritas are a cut above. However, perhaps the most telling sign of its success is its consistent popularity with locals – on an average night, every table is taken, with hardly a tourist in sight.

EL BAJÍO

Recommended by
Bruno Oteiza & Mikel Alonso,
José Andrés, Gabriela
Cámara Bargellini

Alejandro Dumas 7
Mexico City
Federal District 11550
Mexico
+52 5552818245
www.carnitaselbajio.com.mx

Opening hours	Open 7 days
Credit cards	Accepted
Price range	Affordable
Style	Smart casual
Cuisine	Mexican
Recommended for	Breakfast

'This is an amazing restaurant that has been around for over forty years and is run by Carmen and her family. What Carmen and her staff do is so inspiring and I have a deep respect for the craft that she and her family have been perfecting for so many years. For me, El Bajío is one of those places that perfectly embraces the spirit of Mexico.'—José Andrés

Mexico City's El Bajío restaurants (eleven outlets across the city) are synonymous with one person: Carmen 'Titita' Ramírez Degollado, an untrained cook now recognized as a leading authority on traditional Mexican food. Carmen's husband opened the original Azcapotzalco branch in 1972 but, after his death in 1981, it fell to Carmen to run the business. This she did, supplementing the menu of *carnitas* (pulled pork) and *barbacoa* with dishes from her Veracruz childhood, including *gorditas* with black beans and avocado leaf, and *pulacle papanteco tamal* with pumpkin seeds and courgettes (zucchini). Ferran Adrià has described El Bajío as the best Mexican restaurant in the world.

BIKO

Recommended by
Juan Mari & Elena Arzak,
Gabriela Cámara Bargellini

Avenida Masaryk 407
Mexico City
Federal District 11550
Mexico
+52 5552822064
www.biko.com.mx

Opening hours	Closed Sunday
Credit cards	Accepted
Price range	Expensive
Style	Smart casual
Cuisine	Basque-Mexican
Recommended for	High end

'I like going to Biko for a special occasion because the chefs are lovely and their speciality, aside from cooking extremely well, is making their guests feel really special.'—Gabriela Cámara Bargellini

Basque–Mexican fusion best describes joint chef-owners Bruno Oteiza and Mikel Alonso's style of cooking, but before you go running for the Sierra Madre mountains their restaurant Biko is not half as mad as it sounds. Two menus are offered – creative and traditional – meaning that if foie candy floss (cotton candy) isn't your bag you can opt for more obviously Mexican food, albeit with an avant-garde Spanish twist, such as pork jowl with tomato and *chicharrón* or grilled quail with clarified gazpacho. At around $75 (£45), the tasting menu's a snip, but you'll have to negotiate with the city's high rollers to get a table.

DUO SALADO Y DULCE
Recommended by
Gabriela Cámara Bargellini

Avenida Amsterdam 53
Mexico City
Federal District 06100
Mexico
+52 5552116727
www.duosaladoydulce.com

Opening hours	Open 7 days
Credit cards	Accepted
Price range	Budget
Style	Casual
Cuisine	Modern Mexican
Recommended for	Breakfast

'It is a modest, nice, comfortable place and the food selection is fantastic. The owners mix unexpected flavours in a lovely way. It's all of the highest quality and carefully put together.'—Gabriela Cámara Bargellini

ENO
Recommended by
Jorge Vallejo

Francisco Petrarca 258
Mexico City
Federal District 11570
Mexico
+52 5555318535
www.eno.com.mx

Opening hours	Open 7 days
Credit cards	Accepted
Price range	Affordable
Style	Casual
Cuisine	Mexican
Recommended for	Breakfast

'The café service is the best in the city. It has a variety of traditional dishes with really well-chosen products and the cakes are delicious.'—Jorge Vallejo

MAXIMO BISTROT
Recommended by
Enrique Olvera

Tonalá 133
Mexico City
Federal District 06700
Mexico
+52 5552644291
www.maximobistrot.com.mx

Opening hours	Open 7 days
Credit cards	Accepted
Price range	Affordable
Style	Casual
Cuisine	Modern Mexican
Recommended for	Bargain

'The value of its daily menu is unbeatable for quality and taste.'—Enrique Olvera

MEROTORO
Recommended by
Thomasina Miers

Amsterdam 204
Mexico City
Federal District 06140
Mexico
+52 5555647799
www.merotoro.com

Opening hours	Open 7 days
Credit cards	Accepted
Price range	Affordable
Style	Casual
Cuisine	Mexican
Recommended for	Worth the travel

NICOS
Recommended by
Enrique Olvera,
Jorge Vallejo

Avenida Cuitláhuac 3102
Mexico City
Federal District 02080
Mexico
+52 5553966510
www.nicosmexico.mx

Opening hours	Closed Sunday
Credit cards	Accepted
Price range	Affordable
Style	Casual
Cuisine	Mexican
Recommended for	Breakfast

'I love *huevos Azcapotzalco*: eggs with tortillas, salsa, black beans and cheese. And I love the *champurrado* (a corn and chocolate hot drink).'—Enrique Olvera

PATISSERIE DOMINIQUE
Recommended by
Bruno Oteiza &
Mikel Alonso

Chiapas 157
Mexico City
Federal District 06700
Mexico
+52 5555642010

Opening hours	Open 7 days
Reservation policy	No
Credit cards	Not accepted
Price range	Budget
Style	Casual
Cuisine	French Patisserie
Recommended for	Breakfast

'The best sweet bread and spectacular eggs *en cocotte*.'—Bruno Oteiza & Mikel Alonso

PUJOL

Francisco Petrarca 254
Mexico City
Federal District 11570
Mexico
+52 5555454111
www.pujol.com.mx

Recommended by
Massimo Bottura, Isaac
McHale, Jordi Roca,
Jorge Vallejo

Opening hours	Closed Sunday
Credit cards	Accepted
Price range	Expensive
Style	Smart casual
Cuisine	Modern Mexican
Recommended for	Worth the travel

'Enrique's critical and ironic slant on his country's traditional cooking is taking Mexican flavours onto the world's stage. From the remarkable taco to meats, it's a menu guiding us through the symbolic dishes of one of the world's most celebrated cuisines.'
—Massimo Bottura

Enrique Olvera's alta cocina outpost in the affluent Polanco district of Mexico City has established him as one of Mexico's most forward-thinking chefs. He graduated from the Culinary Institute of New York to open Pujol in 2000, when he was still only twenty-four. Inspired by the richness of Mexican street food and home cooking, Pujol successfully elevates simple national staples (most notably in a haute take on the humble taco), champions indigenous ingredients and artfully uses traditional techniques such as cooking in clay pots. All of which is delivered with a playful sense of fun and a pleasing lack of pretension.

QUINTONIL

Newton 55
Mexico City
Federal District 11560
Mexico
+52 5552801660
www.quintonil.com

Recommended by
Bruno Oteiza & Mikel
Alonso, Diego Hernández
Baquedano, Alejandro Ruiz

Opening hours	Closed Sunday
Credit cards	Accepted
Price range	Affordable
Style	Smart casual
Cuisine	Modern Mexican
Recommended for	Worth the travel

'I like this place more and more. Whenever I'm there dinner becomes a special occasion. Jorge Vallejo and Alejandra Flores always manage to surprise you with some new detail.'—Diego Hernández Baquedano

RESTAURANTE BAR MONTEJO

Benjamín Franklin 261
Mexico City
Federal District 06140
Mexico
+52 5552721981
www.restaurantebarmontejo.com

Recommended by
Gabriela Cámara
Bargellini

Opening hours	Closed Sunday
Credit cards	Accepted
Price range	Affordable
Style	Casual
Cuisine	Mexican
Recommended for	Regular neighbourhood

'Simple and very consistent, I go back with a lot of affection and anticipation for *tacos cachondos* filled with *cochinita pibil* (slow-roasted pork in pibil sauce).'—Gabriela Cámara Bargellini

ROSETTA

Colima 166
Mexico City
Federal District 06700
Mexico
+52 5555337804

Recommended by
Guillermo González
Beristáin, Enrique Olvera

Opening hours	Closed Sunday
Credit cards	Accepted but not AMEX
Price range	Affordable
Style	Casual
Cuisine	Italian
Recommended for	Regular neighbourhood

'It surprises me every time I go because of the really intelligent simplicity with which Elena Reygadas cooks, incorporating different ingredients that fit together perfectly. I had the best dessert I have ever tasted here called Dessert Salad.'—Guillermo González Beristáin

There's a certain irony that in this most patriotically foodie of cities, many people's favourite new restaurant is a superbly accomplished and authentic... Italian trattoria. Rosetta's first great asset is the building, a grand old house (formerly an art gallery) in Roma with painted walls and elaborate Art Deco fittings and flourishes. In this wonderful setting the food has room to shine – the house bread and pasta are as good as anything from Europe, and octopus carpaccio or burrata speak of a dynamic young chef (Elena Reygadas) with years of experience working in Italy. Smart staff and a strong Italian wine list seal the deal.

SUD 777

Boulevard de la Luz 777
Mexico City
Federal District 01900
Mexico
+52 5555684777
www.sud777.com.mx

Recommended by
Diego Hernández
Baquedano,
Jorge Vallejo

Opening hours	Open 7 days
Credit cards	Accepted but not AMEX
Price range	Affordable
Style	Casual
Cuisine	Mexican
Recommended for	Late night

'A relaxed restaurant where all the food is delicious, the service is very attentive and they focus on having a light menu that's delicious and fun, based on seasonal variation and what's available in the kitchen garden.' —Jorge Vallejo

TACOS HOLA

Avenida Amsterdam 135
Mexico City
Federal District 06100
Mexico

Recommended by
Gabriela Cámara Bargellini

Opening hours	Open 7 days
Reservation policy	No
Credit cards	Not accepted
Price range	Budget
Style	Casual
Cuisine	Mexican
Recommended for	Regular neighbourhood

'Have the Manzano pepper stuffed with curd cheese.' —Gabriela Cámara Bargellini

TAQUERÍA EL CALIFA

Atlata 22
Mexico City
Federal District 06170
Mexico
+52 5552762498
www.elcalifa.com.mx

Recommended by
Jorge Vallejo

Opening hours	Open 7 days
Reservation policy	No
Credit cards	Accepted
Price range	Affordable
Style	Casual
Cuisine	Mexican
Recommended for	Late night

'The best *tacos al pastor* (spicy pork) in Mexico, in my opinion. The sauces are excellent and the quality is always top notch.'—Jorge Vallejo

TORI TORI

Temístocles 61
Mexico City
Federal District 11550
Mexico
+52 5552818112
www.toritori.com.mx

Recommended by
Gabriela Cámara Bargellini

Opening hours	Open 7 days
Credit cards	Accepted
Price range	Affordable
Style	Smart casual
Cuisine	Japanese
Recommended for	Regular neighbourhood

'For the spicy tuna dish.'—Gabriela Cámara Bargellini

LA DOCENA

Avenida Américas 1491
Guadalajara
Jalisco 44630
Mexico
+52 3338172798

Recommended by
Fernando Trocca

Opening hours	Open 7 days
Credit cards	Accepted
Price range	Affordable
Style	Casual
Cuisine	Seafood
Recommended for	Bargain

'Great oyster bar and restaurant, at a good price.' —Fernando Trocca

RESTAURANT CAFE CAPRI

Recommended by
Guillermo González Beristáin

Venustiano Carranza 150
Allende
Nuevo León 67350
Mexico
+52 8262682976

Opening hours	Open 7 days
Reservation policy	No
Credit cards	Accepted but not AMEX
Price range	Budget
Style	Casual
Cuisine	Mexican
Recommended for	Breakfast

'I have to drive at least forty minutes to the south of the state to a small town called Allende. Besides having an extensive menu of northeastern food, they make the best *machacado con huevo* (dried beef with scrambled eggs). The difference in this place is that they dry the meat themselves, in the heat of the kitchen, not in the sun, then they fry it quickly with eggs that have hardly been scrambled. This is accompanied by freshly made flour tortillas.'—Guillermo González Beristáin

CHEF HERRERA

Recommended by
Guillermo González Beristáin

Rio Orinoco 114
Monterrey
Nuevo León 66230
Mexico
+52 8183366706
www.chefherrera.mx

Opening hours	Open 7 days
Credit cards	Accepted
Price range	Affordable
Style	Casual
Cuisine	Mexican
Recommended for	Late night

'Unique Mexican cuisine prepared by one of the most talented, and also irreverent, chefs in the country, Adrian Herrera. The *pipian negro* (black pipian sauce) with Asian touches is unmissable.'
—Guillermo González Beristáin

LA NACIONAL

Recommended by
Guillermo González Beristáin

Avenida Madero 1160
Monterrey
Nuevo León 64720
Mexico
+52 8183753890
www.lanacional.net

Opening hours	Open 7 days
Credit cards	Accepted
Price range	Affordable
Style	Casual
Cuisine	Mexican
Recommended for	Local favourite

'Top-quality, traditional, regional cooking from this consistent restaurant. A favourite among locals and foreigners.'—Guillermo González Beristáin

NEUQUEN

Recommended by
Guillermo González Beristáin

Río Amazonas 225
Monterrey
Nuevo León 66220
Mexico
+52 8181150493
www.neuquenrestaurante.com.mx

Opening hours	Open 7 days
Credit cards	Accepted
Price range	Affordable
Style	Casual
Cuisine	Argentinian-Italian
Recommended for	Bargain

'Argentinian chef Dante Ferrero makes the best empanadas I have ever tasted. The empanada stuffed with goat perfectly represents the fusion of his Argentinian roots with his new home, Monterrey. My favourite empanadas are those stuffed with nuts, celery and blue cheese. A bargain for the amount of flavour you get.'—Guillermo González Beristáin

THE RESTAURANT

Sollano 16
Centro San Miguel de Allende
Monterrey
Nuevo León 37700
Mexico
+52 4151547877
www.therestaurantsanmiguel.com

Opening hours	Closed Monday
Credit cards	Accepted
Price range	Expensive
Style	Smart casual
Cuisine	Modern Mexican
Recommended for	Regular neighbourhood

'Donnie Masterton is cooking great seasonal food in a great setting.'—Neal Fraser

Life is good in colonial San Miguel de Allende, sipping mescal martinis beside the fountain below The Restaurant's retractable roof. Chef Donnie Masterton cooks comfort food, organic in inclination, for up to a hundred diners at a time. His dishes include starter of kale and jicama (Mexican turnip) with grapefruit, radish, cucumber and mint; then herb-roasted mushrooms with soft polenta, house-made ricotta and a little white truffle oil; then pecan, bourbon and butterscotch bread pudding with vanilla ice cream. Incidentally, Thursday is burger night, including 'El fillet o fish', a wasabi-pricked salmon burger. In addition to the martini, there's a good range of Mexican wines.

ROMERO Y AZAHAR

Avenida de la Industria 300
Monterrey
Nuevo León 66279
Mexico
+52 8183352090

Opening hours	Open 7 days
Credit cards	Accepted
Price range	Affordable
Style	Casual
Cuisine	Modern Mexican
Recommended for	Regular neighbourhood

'Modern northeastern cooking with the best ingredients, but also unpretentious in a contemporary setting.'—Guillermo González Beristáin

YAMASAN RAMEN HOUSE

Avenida Vasconcelos 345
San Pedro Garza García
Nuevo León 66267
Mexico
+52 8183351779

Opening hours	Open 7 days
Credit cards	Accepted but not AMEX
Price range	Affordable
Style	Casual
Cuisine	Ramen Noodles
Recommended for	Wish I'd opened

'It is literally a hole in the wall with a bar and a few seats. It serves the best home-made ramen and udon noodles in the city. Chef and owner Nagata Oriundo serves you himself. My favourite dish is the Japanese-style beef curry.'—Guillermo González Beristáin

MEZQUITE

Manuel Garcia Vigil 601a
Oaxaca
Oaxaca 68000
Mexico
+52 9515142099

Opening hours	Open 7 days
Reservation policy	No
Credit cards	Accepted
Price range	Budget
Style	Casual
Cuisine	Mexican
Recommended for	Late night

'I like it there because it's a place where you can enjoy a drink, have some appetizers in a beautiful setting with the best view of the city. The appetizers are included with your drinks and they are great quality.'
—Alejandro Ruiz

ORIGEN

Recommended by
Thomasina Miers,
Alejandro Ruiz

Calle Hidalgo 820
Oaxaca
Oaxaca 68000
Mexico
+52 9515011764
www.origenoaxaca.com

Opening hours	Open 7 days
Credit cards	Accepted
Price range	Affordable
Style	Casual
Cuisine	Modern Mexican
Recommended for	Worth the travel

'Chef Rodolfo Castellanos offers a distinct menu based on high-quality seasonal ingredients and the decoration is inviting.'—Alejandro Ruiz

Of the handful of fine-dining restaurants in Oaxaca, Origen, in the historical heart of the city near the Basilica of Our Lady of Solitude, is by far the best. With white walls, high arches, stone floors and limestone columns, the building is traditionally Mexican, but the brightly coloured furniture and modern art bring it bang up to date. Rodolfo Castellanos does the same with Mexican food, using organic ingredients and contemporary techniques to show just how good Mexican food can be. Here you can have beef carpaccio with Mexican flavours, *mole* is used with restraint and, even though miles inland, beautifully fresh seafood is served.

PITIONA

Recommended by
Alejandro Ruiz,
Pablo San Román

Ignacio Allende 108
Oaxaca
Oaxaca 68000
Mexico
+52 9515140690
www.pitiona.com

Opening hours	Open 7 days
Credit cards	Accepted
Price range	Affordable
Style	Smart casual
Cuisine	Modern Mexican
Recommended for	High end

'One of the best restaurants in the city.'—Alejandro Ruiz

LE CHIQUE

Recommended by
Normand Laprise

Karisma Azul Hotel Sensatori Resort
Carretera Federal Cancun
Puerto Morelos
Quintana Roo 77580
Mexico
+52 9988728450
www.karismahotels.com

Opening hours	Variable
Credit cards	Accepted
Price range	Expensive
Style	Smart casual
Cuisine	International
Recommended for	Worth the travel

OJO DE AGUA

Recommended by
Pablo San Román

Hotel Ojo de Agua
Avenida Javier Rojo Gómez SM 2
Puerto Morelos
Quintana Roo 77580
Mexico
+52 9988710027
www.ojo-de-agua.com

Opening hours	Open 7 days
Credit cards	Accepted
Price range	Affordable
Style	Casual
Cuisine	Mexican
Recommended for	Breakfast

'They serve a variety of sandwiches and they have the most delicious croissants.'—Pablo San Román

HARTWOOD

Recommended by
Jeremy Charles

Km. 7.6 Tulum Beach Road
Tulum
Quintana Roo 77780
Mexico
www.hartwoodtulum.com

Opening hours	Closed Monday and Tuesday
Credit cards	Not accepted
Price range	Affordable
Style	Casual
Cuisine	Mexican
Recommended for	Wish I'd opened

'A passionate, risk-taking chef serving honest and true food'—Jeremy Charles

RAÍZ

Recommended by
Bruno Oteiza
& Mikel Alonso

Calz de Los Jinetes 102
Ciudad López Mateos
State of Mexico 52950
Mexico
+52 5553708191
www.raizrestaurante.com

Opening hours	Open 7 days
Credit cards	Accepted
Price range	Affordable
Style	Smart casual
Cuisine	Modern Mexican
Recommended for	Regular neighbourhood

'An elegant place that makes you feel at home.'
—Bruno Oteiza & Mikel Alonso

EL FAROLITO

Recommended by
Gabriela Cámara Bargellini,
Enrique Olvera

Avenida de las Fuentes 28
Naucalpan de Juárez
State of Mexico 53950
Mexico
www.tacoselfarolito.com.mx

Opening hours	Open 7 days
Reservation policy	No
Credit cards	Accepted
Price range	Budget
Style	Casual
Cuisine	Mexican
Recommended for	Late night

'Several locations, open late at night and smoky *tacos
al pastor* (spicy pork).'—Enrique Olvera

AMARANTA

Recommended by
Diego Hernández Baquedano

Francisco Murguía 402
Toluca de Lerdo
State of Mexico 50130
Mexico
+52 7222808265
www.amarantarestaurante.com

Opening hours	Open 7 days
Credit cards	Accepted but not AMEX
Price range	Affordable
Style	Casual
Cuisine	Mexican
Recommended for	Breakfast

'I like its honesty, which makes this place unique. The
use of Mexican ingredients and the warmth of the

Salas family make having breakfast a real experience.'
—Diego Hernández Baquedano

NÉCTAR

Recommended by
Gabriela Cámara Bargellini

Avenida Andres García Lavin 32
Mérida
Yucatán 97116
Mexico
+52 9999380838
www.nectarmerida.com.mx

Opening hours	Closed Monday
Credit cards	Accepted
Price range	Expensive
Style	Smart casual
Cuisine	Modern Yucatecan
Recommended for	Worth the travel

'Chef Roberto Solís has had a restaurant with this name
for many years, but at the end of 2013, a new Néctar
finally opened its doors to the public, in a different
location. In this new space, besides having a menu
based on fantastic local ingredients prepared with
innovative techniques and concepts, Néctar also has a
modern design which makes use of materials, colours
and textures from the local area. It's worth the trip to
see the result.'—Gabriela Cámara Bargellini

BLT STEAK

Recommended by
José Santaella

The Ritz-Carlton
Avenida Gobernadores 6961
Carolina
Carolina 00979
Puerto Rico
+1 7872531700
www.bltsteak.com

Opening hours	Open 7 days
Credit cards	Accepted
Price range	Expensive
Style	Smart casual
Cuisine	Steakhouse
Recommended for	Regular neighbourhood

'Good-quality food and great service.'—José Santaella

LA COMAY

PR-187 Km. 8, Piñones
Luíza
Carolina
Puerto Rico

Opening hours	Closed Monday to Thursday
Reservation policy	No
Credit cards	Not accepted
Price range	Affordable
Style	Casual
Cuisine	Creole
Recommended for	Bargain

'It's a shack in front of the beach. It's family run and the ambience is a true Puerto Rican experience. Their conch salad is so fresh and tender and their land crab stew is a must have.'—Jose Enrique

THE ENGLISH ROSE

Carretera Bo. Ensenada 413
Rincón
Mayagüez 00677
Puerto Rico
+1 7878234032
www.rinconpuertoricobedandbreakfast.com

Opening hours	Open 7 days
Credit cards	Accepted
Price range	Affordable
Style	Casual
Cuisine	Breakfast-Brunch
Recommended for	Breakfast

'Home-made bread and sausage with spectacular views of the mountains and the west coast of Puerto Rico.'—Raúl Correa

1919 RESTAURANT

Condado Vanderbilt Hotel
Avenida Ashford 1055
San Juan
San Juan 00907
Puerto Rico
+1 7877241919
www.1919restaurant.com

Opening hours	Closed Monday and Sunday
Credit cards	Accepted
Price range	Expensive
Style	Smart casual
Cuisine	Modern Italian
Recommended for	High end

'Its ambience is elegant and sophisticated. The food is prepared with fresh ingredients and innovative techniques. The service is excellent.'—Raúl Correa

BODEGAS COMPOSTELA

Avenida Condado 106
San Juan
San Juan 00907
Puerto Rico
+1 7877246088
www.bodegascompostela.com

Opening hours	Closed Sunday
Credit cards	Accepted
Price range	Expensive
Style	Casual
Cuisine	Spanish
Recommended for	High end

'This restaurant specializes in Spanish food and they also sell Spanish wine, which they import. I love it, not only for the way they handle their product, which is excellent, but for their wine pairings, which are amazing. They are so knowledgeable in what they do that it's an experience every time I go, not just having a great time but also being educated as well.'
—Jose Enrique

LA CASITA BLANCA

Calle Tapia 351
San Juan
San Juan 00933
Puerto Rico
+1 7877265501

Opening hours	Open 7 days
Credit cards	Accepted but not AMEX or Diners
Price range	Budget
Style	Casual
Cuisine	Puerto Rican
Recommended for	Local favourite

'Authentic Puerto Rican cuisine. It feels like home every time I'm there.'—Jose Enrique

EL COCO DE LUIS

La Plaza del Mercado Santurce 19
San Juan
San Juan 00907
Puerto Rico
+1 7877217595

Opening hours	Open 7 days
Reservation policy	No
Credit cards	Accepted
Price range	Budget
Style	Casual
Cuisine	Café-Bar
Recommended for	Bargain

'It's good, simple food and the soups are fantastic.'
—José Santaella

LA CUEVA DEL MAR

Calle Loiza 1904
San Juan
San Juan 00915
Puerto Rico
+1 7877268700
www.lacuevadelmar.com

Opening hours	Open 7 days
Credit cards	Accepted
Price range	Budget
Style	Casual
Cuisine	Seafood
Recommended for	Bargain

'There's nothing better than fresh local seafood. This is
a great place for a relaxed lunch with a cold beer.'
—Raúl Correa

EN BOGA

Avenida de Diego 308
San Juan
San Juan 00923
Puerto Rico
+1 7879672244

Opening hours	Closed Monday
Credit cards	Accepted
Price range	Affordable
Style	Casual
Cuisine	Puerto Rican
Recommended for	Regular neighbourhood

'Pedro Torres is a great young chef. I like his classic but
modernist style, brutal!'—Raúl Correa

LA JAQUITA BAYA

Avenida Fernandez Juncos 801
San Juan
San Juan 00927
Puerto Rico
+1 7879935359

Opening hours	Closed Sunday
Reservation policy	No
Credit cards	Accepted
Price range	Affordable
Style	Casual
Cuisine	Puerto Rican
Recommended for	Local favourite

'Chef Xavier Pacheco serves great Puerto Rican food
with fun presentation. The setting of the restaurant is
very authentic – it is a must if you are in town.'
—Raúl Correa

JOSE ENRIQUE

Calle Duffaut 176
San Juan
San Juan 00907
Puerto Rico
+1 7877253518
www.joseenriquepr.com

Opening hours	Closed Monday and Sunday
Reservation policy	No
Credit cards	Accepted
Price range	Affordable
Style	Smart casual
Cuisine	Puerto Rican
Recommended for	Wish I'd opened

'It's simple, local comfort food but with sophisticated
presentation. It's also San Juan's hottest restaurant
and one of my favourites. Get in as soon as the doors
open because the wait can be a long one!'
—Raúl Correa

KASALTA

Recommended by
Jose Enrique,
José Santaella

Avenida McLeary 1966
San Juan
San Juan 00911
Puerto Rico
+1 7877277340
www.kasalta.com

Opening hours	Open 7 days
Reservation policy	No
Credit cards	Accepted
Price range	Budget
Style	Casual
Cuisine	Café-Bakery
Recommended for	Breakfast

'Well, there's nothing like a Mallorca (an egg, ham and cheese sandwich) and an espresso.'—Jose Enrique

NEW TASTE OF CHINA

Recommended by
Jose Enrique

Avenida Ashford 1018
San Juan
San Juan 00907
Puerto Rico
+1 7877218111

Opening hours	Open 7 days
Credit cards	Accepted
Price range	Affordable
Style	Smart casual
Cuisine	Chinese
Recommended for	Late night

'I love the ambience and the variety of dishes is amazing: roasted duck to live lobster on the menu. The place has huge round tables – it's a blast.'
—Jose Enrique

PIZZERIA DE PIRILO

Recommended by
Raúl Correa

Calle Fortaleza 201
San Juan
San Juan 00901
Puerto Rico
+1 7877213322

Opening hours	Open 7 days
Reservation policy	No
Credit cards	Accepted
Price range	Affordable
Style	Casual
Cuisine	Pizza
Recommended for	Late night

'Nice draft beer selection and great rustic pizza with an old San Juan charm.'—Raúl Correa

GELATO & CO. CREMERIA ITALIANA

Recommended by
Frederic Morineau

94 Solaris Avenue
George Town
Grand Cayman KY1-1108
Cayman Islands
+1 3453244359
www.gelatoeco.com

Opening hours	Open 7 days
Reservation policy	No
Credit cards	Not accepted
Price range	Budget
Style	Casual
Cuisine	Ice cream
Recommended for	Wish I'd opened

'Great concept shop and the quality of the ice cream itself is first class.'—Frederic Morineau

ICOA FINE FOODS

Recommended by
Frederic Morineau

11 Seven Mile Shops
West Bay Road
George Town
Grand Cayman KY1-1208
Cayman Islands
+1 3459451915
www.icoacafe.com

Opening hours	Open 7 days
Credit cards	Accepted but not AMEX
Price range	Budget
Style	Casual
Cuisine	Bakery-Café-Deli
Recommended for	Breakfast

'Jurgen, the chef, is very creative and passionate about Southern Asian cuisine.'—Frederic Morineau

RAGAZZI

Recommended by
Frederic Morineau

Buckingham Square
West Bay Road
George Town
Grand Cayman KY1-1205
Cayman Islands
+1 3459453484
www.ragazzi.ky

Opening hours	Open 7 days
Credit cards	Accepted
Price range	Affordable
Style	Casual
Cuisine	Italian
Recommended for	Bargain

'Love the Austrian pizza!'—Frederic Morineau

CALYPSO GRILL

Recommended by
Frederic Morineau

Morgan's Harbour
West Bay
Grand Cayman KY1-1202
Cayman Islands
+1 3459493948
www.calypsogrillcayman.com

Opening hours	Closed Monday
Credit cards	Accepted
Price range	Affordable
Style	Casual
Cuisine	Seafood
Recommended for	Regular neighbourhood

'A friendly place with simple fresh food, consistently done well.'—Frederic Morineau

MORGAN'S HARBOUR RESTAURANT

Recommended by
Frederic Morineau

Morgan's Harbour
West Bay
Grand Cayman KY1-1204
Cayman Islands
+1 3459467049

Opening hours	Open 7 days
Credit cards	Accepted
Price range	Affordable
Style	Casual
Cuisine	Seafood
Recommended for	Local favourite

'They buy local fish direct from the fishermen and cook it right away. The food is served in a great outdoor area, very laid-back, Caribbean style.'—Frederic Morineau

DA CONCH SHACK

Recommended by
Paul Newman

Blue Hills Road
Providenciales TKCA 1ZZ
Turks and Caicos Islands
+1 6499468877
www.daconchshack.com

Opening hours	Open 7 days
Credit cards	Accepted
Price range	Budget
Style	Casual
Cuisine	Caribbean
Recommended for	Local favourite

'Simple and unpretentious. You dine at picnic benches in the sand while being served a fresh catch of lobster, fish and conch. Try the island favourites of cracked conch and lobster served with rice and peas, crunchy coleslaw, sweet plantain and home-made "blazing" scotch bonnet sauce. Wash it all down with buckets of Presidente beer or pitchers of rum punch.' —Paul Newman

FRESH CATCH

Recommended by
Paul Newman

5 Salt Mills Plaza
Providenciales TKCA 1ZZ
Turks and Caicos Islands
+1 6492433167

Opening hours	Open 7 days
Reservation policy	No
Credit cards	Accepted
Price range	Affordable
Style	Casual
Cuisine	Caribbean
Recommended for	Bargain

'Centrally located on the strip, this place is owned and operated by a very talented local saxophonist who gives impromptu concerts to his diners. Brilliant island fare and the best fish sandwich!'—Paul Newman

GARAM MASALA

Recommended by
Paul Newman

Regent Village
Providenciales TKCA 1ZZ
Turks and Caicos Islands
+1 6499413292

Opening hours	Closed Tuesday
Credit cards	Accepted
Price range	Affordable
Style	Casual
Cuisine	Indian-Pakistani
Recommended for	Late night

'The best naan bread ever.'—Paul Newman

LAS BRISAS

Recommended by
Paul Newman

Neptune Villas
Chalk Sound Drive
Providenciales TKCA 1ZZ
Turks and Caicos Islands
+1 6499465306
www.neptunevillastci.com

Opening hours	Closed Tuesday
Credit cards	Accepted
Price range	Affordable
Style	Casual
Cuisine	Spanish
Recommended for	Breakfast

'Popular with tourists and locals alike, the dining terrace is on the waterfront overlooking the spectacular clear turquoise waters of Chalk Sound. Very friendly service, fresh fruit smoothies and great Mimosas!'
—Paul Newman

THE RESTAURANT

Recommended by
Paul Newman

Amanyara Aman Resort
Malcolm's Beach
Providenciales TKCA 1ZZ
Turks and Caicos Islands
+1 6499418133
www.amanresorts.com

Opening hours	Open 7 days
Credit cards	Accepted
Price range	Expensive
Style	Smart casual
Cuisine	International
Recommended for	High end

'Michelin-standard food, visiting celebrity chef diners, tranquil Zen-like atmosphere with unhurried, seamless service. My team celebrates each end of season with a "bin-ends" wine luncheon where resident chef Fritz and his team offer the most tantalizing pairing of mainly Asian-inspired treats.'—Paul Newman

YOSHI'S SUSHI BAR

Recommended by
Paul Newman

Salt Mills Plaza
Grace Bay Road
Providenciales TKCA 1ZZ
Turks and Caicos Islands
+1 6499413374
www.yoshissushi.net

Opening hours	Closed Sunday
Credit cards	Accepted
Price range	Affordable
Style	Casual
Cuisine	Japanese
Recommended for	Regular neighbourhood

'Simply good sushi.'—Paul Newman

AROMA DE LA MONTAÑA

Jamaca de Dios
Palo Blanco
Jarabacoa
La Vega 41000
Dominican Republic
+1 8294526879
www.aromadelamontana.com

Opening hours	Open 7 days
Credit cards	Accepted
Price range	Affordable
Style	Casual
Cuisine	Indernational-Caribbean
Recommended for	Worth the travel

'It is a gorgeous mountain resort where you can enjoy a moment of peace and tranquillity in full contact with nature, a place where dreams touch the earth. An extraordinary dining experience with international and Dominican food. It is the only restaurant in the Caribbean with a rotating floor, which is utterly enchanting. The rotating cabin moves while you're eating so you can enjoy the scenery below – it is impressive. The owner and staff are very attentive.' —María Marte

ZOZO'S RISTORANTE

Sugar Mill
Caneel Bay Resort
St John 00831
US Virgin Islands
+1 3406939200
www.zozos.net

Opening hours	Open 7 days
Credit cards	Accepted but not AMEX
Price range	Expensive
Style	Smart casual
Cuisine	Italian
Recommended for	High end

'Take a ferry ride to St John, have a cocktail at the round bar before going to your table overlooking Cruz Bay, or bring friends and book the Wine Room Table just outside the wine room windows. Every bite is made in house: thick, house-aged chops, fresh pasta, daily seafood.'—Kevin McCaffery

BAD ASS COFFEE

5330 Yacht Haven Grande
Charlotte Amalie
St Thomas 00802
US Virgin Islands
+1 3403442744
www.badasscoffee.com

Opening hours	Open 7 days
Reservation policy	No
Credit cards	Accepted
Price range	Budget
Style	Casual
Cuisine	Café
Recommended for	Breakfast

BETSY'S BAR

Honduras
Charlotte Amalie
St Thomas 00803
US Virgin Islands
+1 3407749347
www.betsysbar.com

Opening hours	Open 7 days
Credit cards	Accepted but not AMEX
Price range	Affordable
Style	Casual
Cuisine	American-Caribbean
Recommended for	Late night

'Perfect eggs, thick-cut bacon, ham, sausage and triple-cheese triple decker.'—Kevin McCaffery

CUZZIN'S

7 Wimmelskafts Gade
Charlotte Amalie
St Thomas 00802
US Virgin Islands
+1 3407774711
www.cuzzinsvi.com

Opening hours	Closed Sunday
Credit cards	Accepted
Price range	Affordable
Style	Casual
Cuisine	Caribbean
Recommended for	Local favourite

'Try the "old wife (triggerfish) and fungi" and conch with butter sauce.'—Kevin McCaffery

GREENGO'S CARIBBEAN CANTINA

Recommended by
Kevin McCaffery

34–35 Dronningens Gade
Frenchtown
St Thomas 00801
US Virgin Islands
+1 3407148282
www.greengoscantina.com

Opening hours	Open 7 days
Reservation policy	No
Credit cards	Accepted but not AMEX
Price range	Affordable
Style	Casual
Cuisine	Mexican
Recommended for	Bargain

'Tex-Mex fusion. Great tacos, burritos, nachos, taquitos, quesadillas and ghost pepper salsa.'—Kevin McCaffery

HOOK LINE & SINKER

Recommended by
Kevin McCaffery

62 Honduras
Frenchtown
St Thomas 00803
US Virgin Islands
+1 3407769708
www.hooklineandsinkervi.com

Opening hours	Open 7 days
Credit cards	Accepted
Price range	Affordable
Style	Casual
Cuisine	European
Recommended for	Breakfast

'Best Eggs Benedict!'—Kevin McCaffery

PIE WHOLE

Recommended by
Kevin McCaffery

24a Honduras
Frenchtown
St Thomas 00802
US Virgin Islands
+1 3406425074
www.piewholepizza.com

Opening hours	Closed Sunday
Credit cards	Accepted but not AMEX
Price range	Affordable
Style	Casual
Cuisine	Italian
Recommended for	Wish I'd opened

'Earl and Laura built their own brick oven, tiled with fabulous artwork and colours. Crisp, thin pizza, fresh pasta, Italian and Belgian beer.'—Kevin McCaffery

THIRTEEN

Recommended by
Kevin McCaffery

13a Estate Dorothea
Northside
St Thomas 00802
US Virgin Islands
+1 3407746800

Opening hours	Closed Monday and Sunday
Credit cards	Accepted
Price range	Affordable
Style	Casual
Cuisine	Modern International
Recommended for	Regular neighbourhood

'The food is creative and it's a fun spot to meet up with friends.'—Kevin McCaffery

JACALA BEACH RESTAURANT

Recommended by
Paul Newman

Meads Bay
The Valley
Anguilla 2640
Anguilla
+1 2644985888

Opening hours	Closed Monday and Tuesday
Credit cards	Accepted
Price range	Affordable
Style	Casual
Cuisine	French-Caribbean
Recommended for	Wish I'd opened

'Stalwarts of Anguilla's famous Maliouhanna Resort are now operating their own restaurant on Meads Bay. The formidable team of Jacques Borderon and Alain Laurent with their personal style of service, make for a wonderful casual dining experience. It's something to be truly savoured and enjoyed. Hand-blended cocktails, Caribbean crayfish salads, grilled watermelon, stunning tuna "sandwich"... and when finished with your libations at lunchtime, take a beach chair and doze off in the sand, or in the evening lie back and look up at the stars.'—Paul Newman

ON THE ROCKS

Recommended by
Paul Owens

Relais & Châteaux Hotel
Eden Rock
St Jean Bay
F97133
Saint Barthélemy
+590 590297999
www.edenrockhotel.com

Opening hours	Open 7 days
Credit cards	Accepted
Price range	Expensive
Style	Smart casual
Cuisine	French-Caribbean
Recommended for	High end

MARSHALLS

Recommended by
Paul Owens

Holders Hill
Paynes Bay Beach
Saint James BB23001
Barbados
+1 2464322132

Opening hours	Closed Sunday
Credit cards	Not accepted
Price range	Affordable
Style	Casual
Cuisine	Caribbean
Recommended for	Bargain

'Local food.'—Paul Owens

THE BREAKFAST SHED

Recommended by
Khalid Mohammed

Audrey Jeffers Highway
Port of Spain
Trinidad and Tobago

Opening hours	Open 7 days
Reservation policy	No
Credit cards	Not accepted
Price range	Budget
Style	Casual
Cuisine	Creole
Recommended for	Breakfast

'For the fish broth or the fried fish and bake.'
—Khalid Mohammed

ME ASIA

Recommended by
Khalid Mohammed

48 Ariapita Avenue
Port of Spain
Trinidad and Tobago
+1 8686286888

Opening hours	Open 7 days
Credit cards	Accepted
Price range	Affordable
Style	Casual
Cuisine	Chinese
Recommended for	Late night

'Try their noodle soup.'—Khalid Mohammed

WINGS RESTAURANT & BAR

Recommended by
Khalid Mohammed

16 Mohammed Terrace
Tunapuna
Trinidad and Tobago
+1 8686456607

Opening hours	Closed Sunday
Credit cards	Not accepted
Price range	Budget
Style	Casual
Cuisine	Indian
Recommended for	Local favourite

'A rum-shop-turned-restaurant that does the best curries. It throws the idea of location, location, location out the window.'—Khalid Mohammed

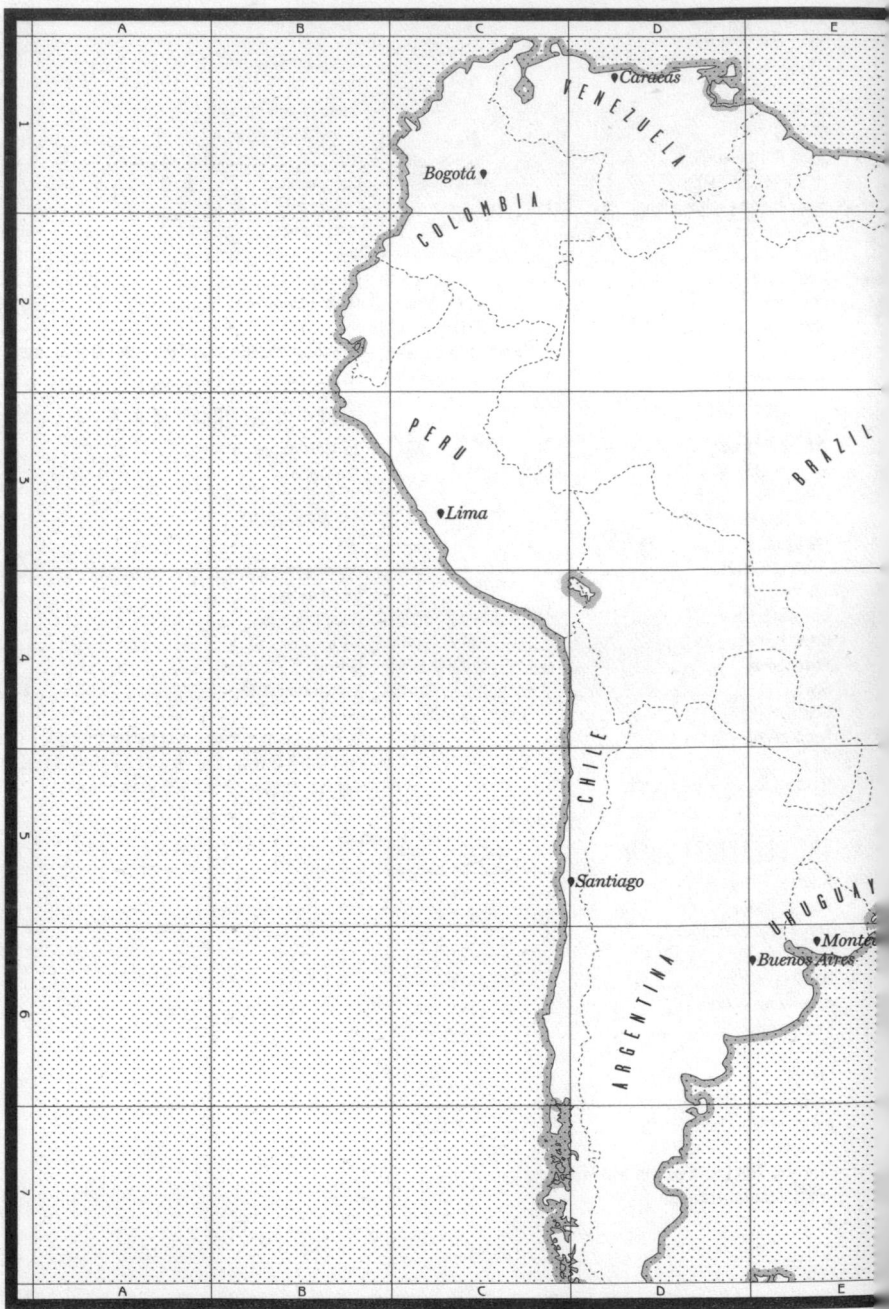

SOUTH AMERICA

N SCALE

0   300   600
mi.

Rio de Janeiro
Paulo

'PURE MAGICAL REALISM: THE BEST PARTY IN THE WORLD ACCOMPANIED BY EXCELLENT FOOD AND A UNIQUE SETTING.'
JORGE RAUSCH P905

'THIS IS WHERE THE REAL SOUL OF PERUVIAN FOOD IS.'
MARTIN MORALES P905

SOUTH AMERICA NORTH

'GREAT FOOD AND UTTERLY MAGICAL SURROUNDINGS.'
EDUARDO MORENO P903

'PROBABLY ONE OF THE BEST CUPS OF LOCAL COFFEE IN THE WORLD.'
VIRGILIO MARTÍNEZ P907

'It only closes when the fish runs out and the sun goes down.'
MARTÍN MOLTENI P908

Nueva Esparta p.903
Caracas pp.902–903
Vargas p.903
VENEZUELA

Antioquia p.904
Cundinamarca p.905
Bogotá pp.904–905

COLOMBIA

ECUADOR

PERU

Lima pp.906–909

Arequipa p.905

BOLIVIA

SOUTH
AMERICA
NORTH

N

SCALE

0   225   450 mi.

ALTO

Recommended by
Sumito Estévez

Transversal 3 y Avenida 1
Caracas
Federal District 1020
Venezuela
+58 2122843655

Opening hours	Closed Sunday
Credit cards	Accepted
Price range	Expensive
Style	Smart casual
Cuisine	European
Recommended for	High end

Carlos García is the name to drop in Caracas fine-dining circles. García is an experienced chef whose time at two of the world's most famous restaurants, elBulli and El Celler de Can Roca, is apparent on his modern Mediterranean meets Venezuelan menus. The intimate eight-table, gently luxurious restaurant opened in 2007 and soon found an audience eager to join García on his journey into Venezuela's culinary traditions. Expect a flamboyant take on black bean soup, goat in coconut milk, tuna 'ham' with goat's cheese snow, or suckling pig, and don't miss the Tierra de Cacao for chocolate seven ways.

EL ARANJUEZ

Recommended by
Eduardo Moreno

Calle Madrid
Caracas
Federal District 1060
Venezuela
+58 2129935679

Opening hours	Open 7 days
Reservation policy	No
Credit cards	Accepted
Price range	Affordable
Style	Casual
Cuisine	Venezuelan
Recommended for	Local favourite

'In my opinion, the restaurants that best reflect Venezuelan tastes are the ones that specialize in grilled meat. El Aranjuez is my favourite.'—Eduardo Moreno

AREPERA AMADANI

Recommended by
Eduardo Moreno

2da Avenida de Montecristo
Caracas
Federal District 1071
Venezuela

Opening hours	Closed Sunday
Reservation policy	No
Credit cards	Not accepted
Price range	Budget
Style	Casual
Cuisine	Bakery
Recommended for	Breakfast

'In Montecristo, a suburban area of Caracas, this arepera sells *arepas* (corn cakes) made with pork crackling. I love having breakfast here and having pork crackling *arepas* stuffed with chicken salad and yellow cheese.' —Eduardo Moreno

FUGU

Recommended by
Eduardo Moreno

Calle La Trinidad y Avenida Río de Janeiro
Caracas
Federal District 1060
Venezuela
+58 02129935647
www.sushifugu.com

Opening hours	Open 7 days
Reservation policy	No
Credit cards	Accepted
Price range	Affordable
Style	Casual
Cuisine	Japanese
Recommended for	Regular neighbourhood

'I have simple tastes when it comes to eating. I often go to this Japanese restaurant in a residential area of Caracas known as Las Mercedes. The food is always excellent.'—Eduardo Moreno

MEDITERRANEO

Recommended by
Eduardo Moreno

Gran Meliã Caracas Hotel
Avenida Casanova y Calle El Recreo
Caracas
Federal District 1050
Venezuela
+58 2127628111
www.melia.com

Opening hours	Open 7 days
Credit cards	Accepted
Price range	Affordable
Style	Casual
Cuisine	Mediterranean
Recommended for	Bargain

'The best-value meal I've found so far is the brunch served here. The variety of food makes it an excellent choice.'—Eduardo Moreno

MOKAMBO

Recommended by
Sumito Estévez Singh

Calle Madrid y Calle Monterrey
Caracas
Federal District 1060
Venezuela
+58 2129912577

Opening hours	Open 7 days
Credit cards	Accepted
Price range	Affordable
Style	Casual
Cuisine	European-Caribbean
Recommended for	Breakfast

'Serving the best breakfast in our country for ten years.'
—Sumito Estévez Singh

PERROS RULO

Recommended by
Eduardo Moreno

Calle Orinoco y Calle Nueva York
Caracas
Federal District 1061
Venezuela

Opening hours	Open 7 days
Reservation policy	No
Credit cards	Not accepted
Price range	Budget
Style	Casual
Cuisine	Hot Dogs
Recommended for	Late night

'Going out for dinner late at night in Caracas, where I live, is very risky due to the lack of security. The usual would be to have street food like hot dogs, meat rolls and *arepas* (corn cakes). Perros Rulo is my favourite hot dog stand.'—Eduardo Moreno

LA CASA DE RUBÉN

Recommended by
Sumito Estévez Singh

Next to Hotel Bella Vista
Avenida Santiago Mariño y Playa Bella Vista
Porlamar
Isla de Margarita
Nueva Esparta 6301
Venezuela
+58 2952611602

Opening hours	Closed Sunday
Credit cards	Not accepted
Price range	Affordable
Style	Casual
Cuisine	Venezuelan
Recommended for	Local favourite

'Chef Rubén has been cooking for forty years and his restaurant is an iconic and touristic place in Margarita.'
—Sumito Estévez Singh

RECOVECO

Recommended by
Eduardo Moreno

Calle La Soledad, Casa 955
Cerro El Ávila
Galipán
Vargas 1060
Venezuela
+58 4241446572
www.recoveco.com.ve

Opening hours	Closed Monday
Credit cards	Accepted
Price range	Expensive
Style	Smart casual
Cuisine	Venezuelan
Recommended for	High end

'In Caracas, there's a beautiful mountain overlooking the city and the sea called El Ávila. Somewhere between sky and sea is a wonderful restaurant called Recoveco. Great food and utterly magical surroundings.'
—Eduardo Moreno

DONDE JUANCHO
Recommended by
Juan Manuel Barrientos
Calle 10c 29c–20
Medellín
Antioquia
Colombia
+57 3110617
www.dondejuancho.com

Opening hours	Open 7 days
Reservation policy	No
Credit cards	Not accepted
Price range	Budget
Style	Casual
Cuisine	Burgers
Recommended for	Bargain

SANCHO PAISA
Recommended by
Juan Manuel Barrientos
Km. 16 Vía Las Palmas
Medellín
Antioquia
Colombia
+57 44440752
www.restaurantesanchopaisamedellin.com

Opening hours	Open 7 days
Credit cards	Accepted
Price range	Affordable
Style	Casual
Cuisine	Colombian
Recommended for	Regular neighbourhood

'It reminds me of my childhood. This place represents all that we Antioqueños are.'—Juan Manuel Barrientos

CLUB COLOMBIA
Recommended by
Jorge Rausch
Carrera 9 y Avenida 82
Bogotá
Cundinamarca
Colombia
+57 2495681

Opening hours	Open 7 days
Credit cards	Accepted
Price range	Affordable
Style	Casual
Cuisine	Colombian
Recommended for	Breakfast

'It has a wide variety of typical products such as *arepas* (corn cakes), *almojabanas* (cheese rolls) and *pan de yuca* (cassava bread). It also has a spectacular buffet of typical Colombian food.'—Jorge Rausch

CREPES & WAFFLES
Recommended by
Jorge Rausch
Carrera 5 70a–08
Bogotá
Cundinamarca
Colombia
+57 12552006
www.crepesywaffles.com.co

Opening hours	Open 7 days
Reservation policy	No
Credit cards	Accepted
Price range	Affordable
Style	Casual
Cuisine	International
Recommended for	Wish I'd opened

'It is now a very successful chain of restaurants which offers something unique because it is entirely original. They also take great care over the quality and freshness of their products.'—Jorge Rausch

GORDO BROOKLYN
Recommended by
Jorge Rausch
Carrera 4a 66–84
Bogotá
Cundinamarca
Colombia
+57 13455769
www.gordobar.com

Opening hours	Open 7 days
Credit cards	Accepted
Price range	Affordable
Style	Casual
Cuisine	American
Recommended for	Late night

'It's a good bar that serves hearty and delicious food and really well-prepared cocktails.'—Jorge Rausch

HARRY SASSON
Recommended by
Jorge Rausch
Carrera 9 75–70
Bogotá
Cundinamarca
Colombia
+57 13477155
www.harrysasson.com

Opening hours	Open 7 days
Credit cards	Accepted
Price range	Affordable
Style	Smart casual
Cuisine	Asian
Recommended for	High end

JULIA

Recommended by
Jorge Rausch

Carrera 5 69a–19
Bogotá
Cundinamarca
Colombia
+57 13482835
www.juliapizzeria.com

Opening hours	Open 7 days
Reservation policy	No
Credit cards	Accepted
Price range	Affordable
Style	Casual
Cuisine	Pizza
Recommended for	Bargain

'It's a small, rustic pizzeria with a good variety of Italian wines. It has a really good atmosphere and excellent prices.'—Jorge Rausch

SUSHIGOZEN

Recommended by
Jorge Rausch

Calle 94 14–11
Bogotá
Cundinamarca
Colombia
+57 12570282

Opening hours	Closed Sunday
Credit cards	Accepted
Price range	Affordable
Style	Casual
Cuisine	Sushi
Recommended for	Regular neighbourhood

'It's a little sushi restaurant where the dishes are simple and the quality of the fish is impeccable. Sushi is too complicated nowadays and they respect its essence here.'—Jorge Rausch

ANDRES CARNE DE RES

Recommended by
Jorge Rausch

Calle 3 11a–56
Chía
Cundinamarca
Colombia
+57 18612233
www.andrescarnederes.com

Opening hours	Closed Monday to Wednesday
Credit cards	Not accepted
Price range	Affordable
Style	Casual
Cuisine	Colombian
Recommended for	Local favourite

'It's one of the most beautiful restaurants I know, with food made from the best ingredients and simple but impeccable recipes. Pure magical realism. The best party in the world accompanied by excellent food and a unique setting.'—Jorge Rausch

LA NUEVA PALOMINO

Recommended by
Martin Morales

Leoncio Prado 122
Arequipa 054
Peru
+51 54252393

Opening hours	Open 7 days
Credit cards	Not accepted
Price range	Affordable
Style	Casual
Cuisine	Peruvian
Recommended for	Worth the travel

'For me, La Nueva Palomino is the best *picantería* in Peru. Here, tradition and passion are abundant. An incredible array of dishes and flavours are on offer, from grilled alpaca steaks to prawn chowder; from quinoa stews to pork *chicharrón* confit or trotter salad. A *picantería* is a family-run, traditional eatery found in the Andes and they have existed for many years. For me, this is where the real soul of Peruvian food is. All their ingredients are organic, local and cooked brilliantly with some dishes being new creations, while others are from recipes that are hundreds of years old. It's hosted beautifully too – a warm welcome is always given and the service is quick and communicative. I grew up eating at *picanterías* so it's great that this one exists and can set an example for others.'
—Martin Morales

ANTIGUA TABERNA QUEIROLO

Avenida San Martin 1090
Lima 15084
Peru
+51 14600441
www.antiguatabernaqueirolo.com

Recommended by
Mitsuharu Tsumura

Opening hours	Open 7 days
Credit cards	Accepted
Price range	Affordable
Style	Casual
Cuisine	Peruvian
Recommended for	Local favourite

'A magical place that's more than 100 years old with a rich history. The decor, ambience and customers make it truly unique. The bread with ham, the stuffed potatoes and the *cau cau* (traditional tripe stew) are not to be missed. Naturally, you can't leave a tavern without having a good *chilcano de pisco* (brandy cocktail)...'—Mitsuharu Tsumura

ASTRID & GASTÓN

Avenida Paz Soldan 290
Lima 27
Peru
www.astridygaston.com

Recommended by
Massimo Bottura, Sumito
Estévez, Takashi Inoue,
Virgilio Martínez, David
Pasternack, Martín
Rebaudino, Joan Roca

Opening hours	Closed Sunday
Credit cards	Accepted
Price range	Affordable
Style	Smart casual
Cuisine	Modern Peruvian
Recommended for	Worth the travel

'Gastón's ability to tell stories of Peru through his tasting menu is incredible. Every year, alongside magnificent dining-room service, I find new characters and interesting plotlines on this culinary tale that is unique in its genre.'—Massimo Bottura

After twenty years at his Miraflores HQ, during which Gastón Acurio established an empire, and helped to elevate Peruvian cuisine to haute status, his landmark restaurant relocated to an old San Isidro hacienda in March 2014. Casa Moreyra, which cost $2m (£1.2m) to renovate, is a vast complex with a main dining hall, private dining salons, sixty-seat gastrobar (for à la carte) and gardens dedicated to 'experimental' growing. Far from being glitzy, however, the minimal space leaves diners to focus on the food: a three-hour, multisensory tasting menu (Viru), which voyages across the sea, desert, Andes, Amazon and Altiplano.

CANTA RANA

Génova 101
Lima 04
Peru
+51 12477274

Recommended by
Virgilio Martínez,
Rafael Osterling

Opening hours	Open 7 days
Credit cards	Accepted
Price range	Budget
Style	Casual
Cuisine	Seafood
Recommended for	Bargain

'It's in a bohemian part of town, so the place is very relaxed and has a great vibe. Their ceviches are incredible.'—Virgilio Martínez

CENTRAL

Calle Santa Isabel 376
Lima 15074
Peru
+51 12428515
www.centralrestaurante.com.pe

Recommended by
Gastón Acurio, Massimo
Bottura, Nuno Mendes,
Fernando Rivarola, Jordi
Roca, Mitsuharu Tsumura

Opening hours	Closed Sunday
Credit cards	Accepted
Price range	Affordable
Style	Casual
Cuisine	Modern Peruvian
Recommended for	Worth the travel

'An amazing concept by super-talented chef Virgilio Martínez, focused on fiercely local Peruvian products and impressive technique. Beautiful, incredibly fresh and clean flavours paired with stunning, well-considered wines in a serene dining room. The open kitchen is beautiful and the passion for their project is evident in the efforts of their wonderful team.'—Nuno Mendes

EGGO

Calle Tahiti 175
Lima 15026
Peru
+51 3529915

Recommended by
Gastón Acurio,
Virgilio Martínez

Opening hours	Open 7 days
Reservation policy	No
Credit cards	Accepted
Price range	Budget
Style	Casual
Cuisine	Café-Bakery
Recommended for	Breakfast

'Probably one of the best cups of local coffee in the world. It's very casual and the food, the coffee, the eggs are all incredible. The level of freshness is simply unbelievable.'—Virgilio Martínez

Far away from the crowds of central Lima, in La Molina, tucked away on a quiet backstreet behind a supermarket, is brand-new artisan bakery and café EGGO, which in the few short months it's been open has wowed the residents of this upmarket suburb with a remarkably assured output of hot sandwiches, pastries, coffees and milkshakes. Proof they don't take themselves too seriously comes in the form of their take on the McDonald's Egg McMuffin – chorizo, egg and melted Gouda on brioche – but they pay attention where it counts. Ice creams are by Lima favourite, Anelare.

FIESTA

Avenida Reducto 1278
Lima 15074
Peru
+51 2429009
www.restaurantfiestagourmet.com

Recommended by
Mitsuharu Tsumura

Opening hours	Open 7 days
Credit cards	Accepted
Price range	Affordable
Style	Casual
Cuisine	Peruvian
Recommended for	Regular neighbourhood

'It's a restaurant with a unique quality that specializes in Chiclayana (Northern-style) cooking – one of my favourite types of Peruvian food. It manages to maintain traditional flavours while adding a great deal of technique, especially to the cooking process.'
—Mitsuharu Tsumura

LA GLORIA

Calle Atahualpa 201
Lima 15074
Peru
+51 14455705
www.lagloriarestaurant.com

Recommended by
Rafael Osterling

Opening hours	Closed Sunday
Credit cards	Accepted
Price range	Affordable
Style	Smart casual
Cuisine	Modern Peruvian
Recommended for	Late night

'I like it because I feel at home there.'—Rafael Osterling

LA LUCHA

Óvalo Gutiérrez
Lima 15073
Peru
www.lalucha.com.pe

Recommended by
Hernán Gipponi

Opening hours	Open 7 days
Reservation policy	No
Credit cards	Not accepted
Price range	Budget
Style	Casual
Cuisine	Sandwiches
Recommended for	Wish I'd opened

'I love the concept of high-quality sandwiches that you can enjoy with a beer or juice. I'd like to do something similar myself.'—Hernán Gipponi

MAIDO

Calle San Martín 399
Lima
15074
Peru
+51 5114462512
www.maido.pe

Recommended by
Gastón Acurio,
Virgilio Martínez

Opening hours	Open 7 days
Credit cards	Accepted
Price range	Affordable
Style	Smart casual
Cuisine	Japanese-Peruvian
Recommended for	Regular neighbourhood

'I love this restaurant because of the quality of the food prepared by the great Mitsuharu Tsumura. He stands at the counter serving Nikkei cuisine that's full of flavour and beautifully fresh.'—Virgilio Martínez

LA MAR

Avenue La Mar 770
Lima 15074
Peru
+51 4213365
www.lamarcebicheria.com

Recommended by
Andoni Luis Aduriz,
José Andrés, Virgilio
Martínez, Claus Meyer,
Martín Molteni,
Blaine Wetzel

Opening hours	Open 7 days
Reservation policy	No
Credit cards	Accepted
Price range	Affordable
Style	Casual
Cuisine	Seafood
Recommended for	Worth the travel

'Their style of cooking is fresh, simple, honest and enjoyable. It's the ideal place to enjoy seafood from the Pacific Ocean, as can only be done in the port of Chile and the ports of other countries that form this seafood-rich coastline. This restaurant's style is very informal and laid back and it closes only when the fish runs out and the sun goes down.'—Martín Molteni

EL MERCADO

Hipólito Unanue 203
Lima 15074
Peru
+51 2211322
www.rafaelosterling.com

Recommended by
Virgilio Martínez,
Ricardo Zarate

Opening hours	Closed Monday
Credit cards	Accepted
Price range	Affordable
Style	Casual
Cuisine	Seafood
Recommended for	Worth the travel

'I like it because of the vibe there. It's amazing to see how people come and go, drink Pisco Sour cocktails, eat too much... It's very varied. It's also one of the few restaurants where you can confidently order anything from the extensive menu because you know that it'll always be of a high quality.'—Virgilio Martínez

OSSO CARNICERÍA & SALUMERIA

Calle Tahiti 175
Lima 15026
Peru
+51 3681046

Recommended by
Gastón Acurio

Opening hours	Closed Monday
Credit cards	Accepted
Price range	Budget
Style	Casual
Cuisine	Butcher
Recommended for	Wish I'd opened

'Great tasting menu for just one table, inside a *boucherie*. One day I will do something like that. One table, amazing personal experience.'—Gastón Acurio

EL PAN DE LA CHOLA

Avenida Mariscal La Mar 918
Lima 15074
Peru

Recommended by
Rafael Osterling

Opening hours	Closed Sunday
Reservation policy	No
Credit cards	Accepted
Price range	Budget
Style	Casual
Cuisine	Café-Bakery
Recommended for	Breakfast

'It's an excellent bakery that offers freshly baked goods, very good sandwiches and local coffee. It also has a great atmosphere.'—Rafael Osterling

LA PAVA

Avenida Comandante Espinar 847
Lima 15074
Peru
+51 14475780

Recommended by
Mitsuharu Tsumura

Opening hours	Closed Sunday
Reservation policy	No
Credit cards	Accepted
Price range	Budget
Style	Casual
Cuisine	Peruvian
Recommended for	Late night

'I've been going there for years and they do an incredible roast pork sandwich. It's a small place that's always full of people. The service and the quality of the ingredients are both excellent.'—Mitsuharu Tsumura

LA PICANTERÍA

Calle Santa Rosa 388
Lima 15047
Peru
+51 12416676
www.picanteriasdelperu.com

Recommended by
Gastón Acurio,
Federico Fialayre,
Rafael Osterling

Opening hours	Closed Monday
Reservation policy	No
Credit cards	Accepted
Price range	Affordable
Style	Casual
Cuisine	Peruvian
Recommended for	Bargain

'Sharing plates in the middle of an emerging district: Surquillo. The cheap version of fiesta gourmet. Great traditional food by Hector Solis.'—Gastón Acurio

AL TOKE PEZ

Avenida Angamos 886
Lima 15074
Peru

Recommended by
Mitsuharu Tsumura

Opening hours	Closed Monday
Reservation policy	No
Credit cards	Not accepted
Price range	Budget
Style	Casual
Cuisine	Seafood
Recommended for	Bargain

'Tomas Matsufuji serves high-quality food at a very good price here. There's only one small counter, but the ceviche, pork crackling and rice dishes are spectacular!'
—Mitsuharu Tsumura

SOUTH AMERICA SOUTH

'IT LIES DEEP IN THE NATIVE WOODS, SURROUNDED BY AN ORGANIC ORCHARD'
MARTÍN MOLTENI P931

'FOOD FROM THE AMAZONIAN SOUL.'
ROBERTA SUDBRACK P912

Pará p.912 ♥

B R A Z I L

Pernambuco pp.912–913 ♥

♥ Bahia p.912

♥ Minas Gerais p.912

Rio de Janeiro pp.914–917 ♥
♥ São Paulo pp.918–929

C H I L E

A R G E N T I N A

U R U G U A Y

♥ Maldonado pp.929–930
♥ Santiago pp.944–945   ♥ Montevideo p.930
♥ Mendoza p.931   ♥ Buenos Aires pp.930–931, 932–944

♥ Río Negro p.931

♥ Tierra del Fuego p.931
♥ Magallanes p.944

SOUTH
AMERICA
SOUTH

N̂   SCALE

0   350   700
mi.

PARAÍSO TROPICAL

Recommended by
César Santos

Rua Edgard Loureiro 98b
Salvador
Bahia 40342-100
Brazil
+55 7133847464
www.restauranteparaisotropical.com.br

Opening hours	Open 7 days
Credit cards	Accepted but not AMEX
Price range	Affordable
Style	Casual
Cuisine	Modern Brazilian
Recommended for	Wish I'd opened

'The restaurant grows its own ingredients. A wide variety of fresh fruits and vegetables, and they prepare delicious dishes. Very similar to my cooking.'
—César Santos

VIRADA'S DO LARGO

Recommended by
Bel Coelho

Rua do Moinho 11
Tiradentes
Minas Gerais 36325-000
Brazil
+55 3233551111
www.viradasdolargo.com.br

Opening hours	Closed Tuesday
Credit cards	Not accepted
Price range	Affordable
Style	Casual
Cuisine	Brazilian
Recommended for	Worth the travel

'Chef Beth Beltrão's food is authentic and extremely flavoursome.'—Bel Coelho

REMANSO DO BOSQUE

Recommended by
Roberta Sudbrack

Travessa Perebebui 2350
Belém
Pará 66095-662
Brazil
+55 9133472829
www.restauranteremanso.com.br

Opening hours	Open 7 days
Credit cards	Accepted
Price range	Affordable
Style	Casual
Cuisine	Brazilian
Recommended for	Worth the travel

'Food from the Amazonian soul made with amazing ingredients and a touch of one of the most important families in Brazilian gastronomy.'—Roberta Sudbrack

MAISON DO BOMFIM

Recommended by
César Santos

Rua Bonfim 115
Olinda
Pernambuco 51120-130
Brazil
+55 8134291674

Opening hours	Closed Monday
Credit cards	Accepted but not AMEX
Price range	Affordable
Style	Casual
Cuisine	French Brasserie
Recommended for	Regular neighbourhood

'A very cosy restaurant where you can drink good wine and eat delicious food prepared by chef Jeff Colas.'
—César Santos

ANJO SOLTO CREPERIA & BAR

Recommended by
César Santos

Avenida Herculano Bandeira 513
Recife
Pernambuco 51110-131
Brazil
+55 51110131
www.anjosolto.com.br

Opening hours	Open 7 days
Reservation policy	No
Credit cards	Accepted but not AMEX
Price range	Budget
Style	Casual
Cuisine	Crêpes
Recommended for	Late night

'It's open late, they have a good selection of crêpes and I meet friends there.'—César Santos

GERALDO

Rua da Piedade 107
Recife
Pernambuco 54330-310
Brazil
+55 8132314177
www.restaurantedogeraldo.com.br

Opening hours	Closed Sunday
Credit cards	Accepted
Price range	Budget
Style	Casual
Cuisine	Brazilian
Recommended for	Bargain

'Good-quality, typical regional food.'—César Santos

LEITE

Praça Joaquim Nabuco 147
Recife
Pernambuco 50010-480
Brazil
+55 8132247977
www.restauranteleite.com.br

Opening hours	Closed Saturday
Credit cards	Accepted
Price range	Expensive
Style	Smart casual
Cuisine	Traditional Portuguese
Recommended for	Local favourite

'Located in the heart of the capital of Pernambuco, it's the oldest restaurant in Brazil and is frequented by influential people, with excellent Portuguese food adapted to Pernambucan tastes.'—César Santos

PARRAXAXÁ

Avenida Engenheiro Domingos Ferreira 1200
Recife
Pernambuco 51021-060
Brazil
+55 8134687374
www.parraxaxa.com.br

Opening hours	Open 7 days
Reservation policy	No
Credit cards	Accepted
Price range	Budget
Style	Casual
Cuisine	Brazilian
Recommended for	Breakfast

'I don't usually have breakfast out but when I do, it's at this restaurant. They serve typically northeastern food, which takes me back to my childhood.'—César Santos

QUINA DO FUTURO

Rua Xavier Marquês 134
Recife
Pernambuco 52050-230
Brazil
+55 8132419589
www.quinadofuturo.com.br

Opening hours	Closed Sunday
Credit cards	Accepted
Price range	Affordable
Style	Casual
Cuisine	Japanese
Recommended for	Worth the travel

'The chef, André Saburó, takes great care over the quality of his food, always choosing the best ingredients for his customers. He's very capable and creative.'—Mara Salles

WIELLA BISTRÔ

Avenida Engenheiro Domingos Ferreira 1274
Recife
Pernambuco 51011-051
Brazil
+55 8134633108
www.wiellabistro.com.br

Opening hours	Open 7 days
Credit cards	Accepted
Price range	Expensive
Style	Smart casual
Cuisine	French Bistro
Recommended for	High end

'It's a sophisticated restaurant where the chef, Claudemir Barros, produces beautiful dishes using Pernambucan ingredients and techniques from world cuisine.'—César Santos

POUSADA DA ALCOBAÇA

Recommended by
Roberta Sudbrack

Rua Agostinho Goulão 298
Petrópolis
Rio de Janeiro 25730-050
Brazil
+55 2422211240
www.pousadadaalcobaca.com.br

Opening hours	Open 7 days
Credit cards	Accepted
Price range	Affordable
Style	Casual
Cuisine	Brazilian
Recommended for	Regular neighbourhood

'Amazing food made in a wood oven. Almost all the ingredients come from the enormous garden outside. Authentic and delicious Brazilian cuisine made with lots of care and fresh ingredients.'—Roberta Sudbrack

Chef-owner Laura Góes's hotel, restaurant and gardens are found on the road to the Serra dos Órgãos National Park, 80 km (50 miles) from Rio. Built in 1914, the mansion, today festooned with flowers, has a large vegetable garden and orchard providing the kitchen with a good deal of produce. Góes's dishes include locally fished trout with almonds and capers, spicy bouillabaisse, and crushed cassava (yucca root) toasted on her wood-fired stove. Saturday is *feijoada* (black bean stew stirred with meat) day. For dessert, try *queijadão* (coconut and cheese pie) or lime meringue pie. The kitchen table, which seats up to twenty-four, offers a great view of culinary action.

ACONCHEGO CARIOCA

Recommended by
Felipe Bronze, Claude &
Thomas Troisgros

Rua Barão de Iguatemi 379
Rio de Janeiro
Rio de Janeiro 20270-060
Brazil
+55 2122731035

Opening hours	Open 7 days
Credit cards	Accepted
Price range	Affordable
Style	Casual
Cuisine	Brazilian
Recommended for	Regular neighbourhood

'Has a relaxed atmosphere, serves really well-made Brazilian food and *carioca* (from Rio de Janeiro) pub food. The beer menu is phenomenal.'
—Claude & Thomas Troisgros

AZUMI

Recommended by
Felipe Bronze

Rua Ministro Vivieros de Castro 127
Rio de Janeiro
Rio de Janeiro 22021-010
Brazil
+55 2125414294

Opening hours	Open 7 days
Credit cards	Accepted
Price range	Affordable
Style	Casual
Cuisine	Japanese
Recommended for	Late night

'They have the most traditional Japanese food in town, very good dishes and keep the Tokyo atmosphere. It's a humble place with exquisite food.'—Felipe Bronze

LA BICYCLETTE

Recommended by
Claude & Thomas Troisgros

Rua Jardim Botânico 1008
Rio de Janeiro
Rio de Janeiro 22460-030
Brazil
+55 2132569052
www.labicyclette.com.br

Opening hours	Open 7 days
Reservation policy	No
Credit cards	Accepted
Price range	Affordable
Style	Casual
Cuisine	Café-Bakery
Recommended for	Breakfast

'It's in the Botanical Gardens and you can have breakfast listening to the birds and enjoying all that nature has to offer. Their breads and sandwiches are amazing.'—Claude & Thomas Troisgros

BIRA DE GUARATIBA

Recommended by
Claude & Thomas Troisgros

Estrada da Vendinha 68a
Rio de Janeiro
Rio de Janeiro 23020-810
Brazil
+55 2124108304
www.restaurantedobira.com.br

Opening hours	Closed Monday to Wednesday
Credit cards	Not accepted
Price range	Affordable
Style	Casual
Cuisine	Brazilian
Recommended for	Local favourite

'It's a privileged place to sit outdoors where you can enjoy the view of the Marambaia restinga and the rainforest while eating top-quality Brazilian fish and seafood dishes.'—Claude & Thomas Troisgros

BRASEIRO DA GÁVEA

Recommended by
Roberta Sudbrack

Praça Santos Dumont 116
Rio de Janeiro
Rio de Janeiro 24050-060
Brazil
+55 2122397494
www.braseirodagavea.com.br

Opening hours	Open 7 days
Reservation policy	No
Credit cards	Accepted
Price range	Affordable
Style	Casual
Cuisine	Brazilian
Recommended for	Local favourite

'Delicious meat on the grill.'—Roberta Sudbrack

CERVANTES

Recommended by
Felipe Bronze

Rua Prado Júnior 335b
Rio de Janeiro
Rio de Janeiro 22011-001
Brazil
+55 2125429287
www.restaurantecervantes.com.br

Opening hours	Closed Monday
Reservation policy	No
Credit cards	Accepted
Price range	Budget
Style	Casual
Cuisine	Brazilian
Recommended for	Bargain

'They have this giant and delicious pork and pineapple sandwich – very iconic and fairly cheap.'
—Felipe Bronze

GEPETTO

Recommended by
Roberta Sudbrack

Estrada dos Bandeirantes 23417
Rio de Janeiro
Rio de Janeiro 22640-904
Brazil
+55 2124281100
www.restaurantegepetto.com.br

Opening hours	Open 7 days
Credit cards	Accepted
Price range	Budget
Style	Casual
Cuisine	Italian-Brazilian
Recommended for	Bargain

'Family ambience, great food and the best french fries in town.'—Roberta Sudbrack

IRAJÁ GASTRÔ

Recommended by
Felipe Bronze

Rua Conde de Irajá 109
Rio de Janeiro
Rio de Janeiro 22271-020
Brazil
+55 2122864249
www.irajagastro.com.br

Opening hours	Open 7 days
Credit cards	Accepted
Price range	Affordable
Style	Casual
Cuisine	Modern Brazilian
Recommended for	Wish I'd opened

'It's a very cool place, with a dynamic and delicious menu, executed well by chef Pedro de Artagão.'
—Felipe Bronze

JOBI

Recommended by
Roberta Sudbrack

Avenida Ataulfo de Paiva 1166
Rio de Janeiro
Rio de Janeiro 22440-035
Brazil
+55 2122740547

Opening hours	Open 7 days
Reservation policy	No
Credit cards	Accepted
Price range	Affordable
Style	Casual
Cuisine	Brazilian
Recommended for	Late night

'Great *carioca* (from Rio de Janeiro) ambience and
boteco food!'—Roberta Sudbrack

This one often stays open until the last customer
leaves – easily passing 4.00 a.m. – making it ideal
for chefs clocking off. The green-painted walls, red
chequered tablecloths and framed pictures lend this
fifty-year-old venue an easy-going lack of pretentiousness; big television screens help to draw the crowds
when the football is on. Jobi is most famous for its
Chopp, a super-chilled draft lager that is enormously
refreshing in the Brazilian heat; while its proximity to
the beach represents another way to cool off. Bar
snacks include empanadas and sandwiches. Many
say the best tables are on the upstairs balcony, which
offers great opportunities for people-watching.

OLYMPE

Recommended by
Felipe Bronze,
Roberta Sudbrack

Rua Custódio Serrão 62
Rio de Janeiro
Rio de Janeiro 22470-230
Brazil
+55 2125378582
www.olympe.com.br

Opening hours	Open 7 days
Credit cards	Accepted
Price range	Expensive
Style	Smart casual
Cuisine	French
Recommended for	High end

'Great French cuisine made by the Troisgros family.
Generations of good food and respect. Don't miss the
pupunha (peach palm fruit) and foie gras terrine!'
—Roberta Sudbrack

PADARIA BAR CONFEITARIA

Recommended by
Roberta Sudbrack

Avenue Ataulfo de Paiva 1030
Rio de Janeiro
Rio de Janeiro 22440-035
Brazil
+55 2122941597

Opening hours	Open 7 days
Reservation policy	No
Credit cards	Not accepted
Price range	Budget
Style	Casual
Cuisine	Café-Bakery
Recommended for	Breakfast

'Very simple place to have breakfast at the counter!
Very "*Carioca* way"! Best golden bread kneaded in
town.'—Roberta Sudbrack

QUIOSQUE DO PORTUGUÊS LAGOON

Recommended by
Claude &
Thomas Troisgros

Avenida Borges de Medeiros 1424
Rio de Janeiro
Rio de Janeiro 22430-042
Brazil
+55 2183081373

Opening hours	Open 7 days
Credit cards	Accepted
Price range	Affordable
Style	Casual
Cuisine	International
Recommended for	Late night

'They do the best caipirinhas in Rio.'
—Claude & Thomas Troisgros

ROBERTA SUDBRACK

Rua Lineu Paula Machado 916
Rio de Janeiro
Rio de Janeiro 22470-040
Brazil
+55 2138740139
www.robertasudbrack.com.br

Recommended by
Luca Gozzani, Rodrigo
Oliveira, Claude &
Thomas Troisgros

Opening hours	Closed Monday, Wednesday and Friday
Credit cards	Accepted
Price range	Expensive
Style	Smart casual
Cuisine	Modern Brazilian
Recommended for	Wish I'd opened

'Roberta knows how to use Brazilian ingredients with great skill and simplicity. There are always surprises on the menu.'—Claude & Thomas Troisgros

SATYRICON

Rua Barão da Torre 192
Rio de Janeiro
Rio de Janeiro 22411-000
Brazil
+55 2125210627
www.satyricon.com.br

Recommended by
Felipe Bronze

Opening hours	Open 7 days
Credit cards	Accepted
Price range	Expensive
Style	Smart casual
Cuisine	Italian seafood
Recommended for	Regular neighbourhood

'They have the very best and freshest seafood in town.'
—Felipe Bronze

TALHO CAPIXABA

Avenida Ataulfo de Paiva 1022
Rio de Janeiro
Rio de Janeiro 22440-035
Brazil
+55 2125128760
www.talhocapixaba.com.br

Recommended by
Felipe Bronze

Opening hours	Open 7 days
Reservation policy	No
Credit cards	Accepted
Price range	Budget
Style	Casual
Cuisine	Café
Recommended for	Breakfast

'It's a traditional neighbourhood place in Leblon. They have good made-to-order sandwiches with delicious and freshly baked breads.'—Felipe Bronze

What began decades ago as a butcher's shop has gradually morphed into a deli-bakery meets upmarket grocery store. Talho Capixaba, which sells take-away (take-out) pastries, salads and sandwiches (charged by their weight) to the well-heeled residents of Leblon, is a popular pit stop on the way to the beach. Breakfast at one of its in-demand outside tables or in the upstairs café, where freshly baked croissants and *empadas* (large empanadas) and freshly squeezed juices are a particular draw, is a Rio must-do. It's priced for the area, so don't go looking for a bargain — but do expect smart service and high quality.

'SÃO PAULO DESERVES THIS GEM.'

MARA SALLES P922

'*His fried pork crackling and tapioca bites are famous.*'

FERNANDO RIVAROLA P929

'A LITTLE BIT OF PARIS IN SÃO PAULO.'

EMMANUEL BASSOLEIL P922

'**The best spicy sausage in São Paulo!**'

BENNY NOVAK P927

SÃO PAULO

'IF BRAZILIAN COOKING IS ASSUMING AN IMPORTANT POSITION IN THE WORLD, IT'S THANKS TO ITS UNIQUE AND INCREDIBLE PRODUCE AND TO ALEX ATALA.'

MASSIMO BOTTURA P921

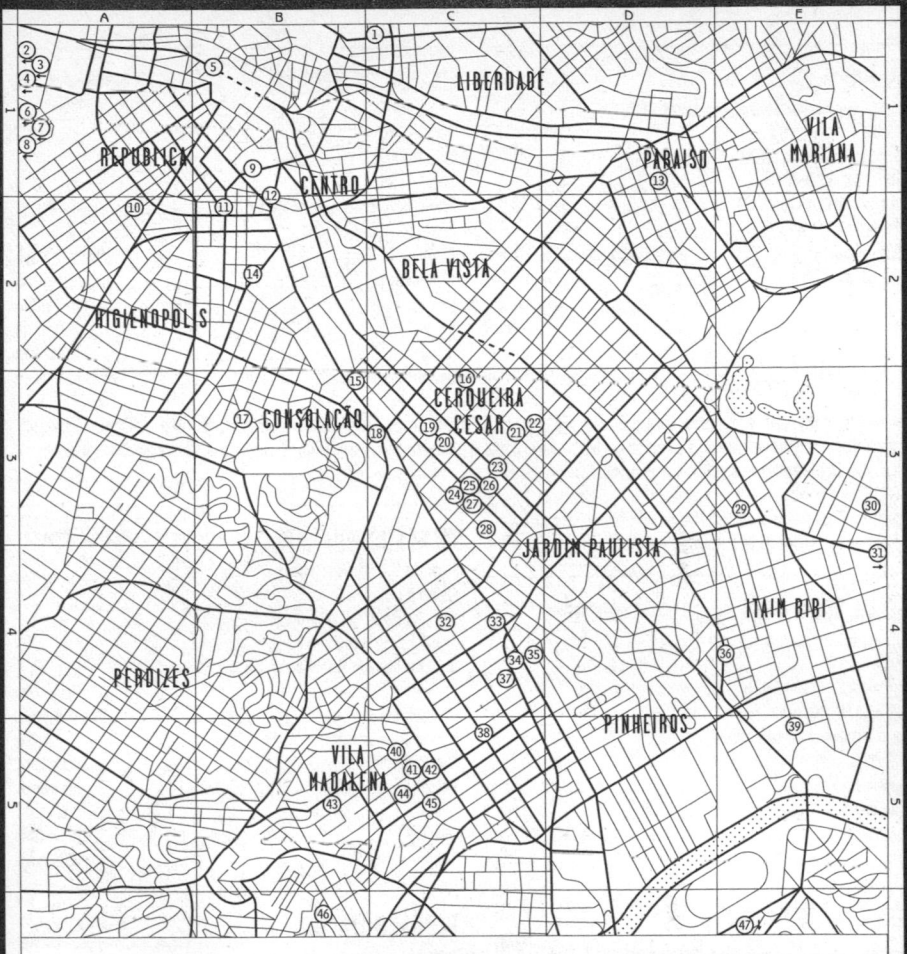

SÃO PAULO

‹Ⓝ›   SCALE

0   500   1000   1500
└────┴────┴────┘ yd.

1. *Jiynu Sushi (p.925)*
2. *Mocotó (p.929)*
3. *Padaria Jardim Brasil (p.928)*
4. *Carlinhos Restaurante (p.926)*
5. *Mercado Municipal (p.920)*

6. *Casa Garabed (p.927)*
7. *As Véia (p.925)*
8. *Sushi Hiroshi (p.927)*
9. *Terraço Itália (p.920)*
10. *Bar Número (p.923)*
11. *Churrascaria Boi na Brasa (p.927)*
12. *Bar da Dona Onça (p.920)*
13. *Shinzushi (p.926)*
14. *Jardim de Napoli (p.920)*
15. *Sujinho (p.922)*
16. *Deliqatê (p.923)*
17. *Barcelona Doces e Pães (p.921)*
18. *Riviera Bar (p.922)*
19. *Restaurante Amadeus (p.921)*
20. *Epice (p.923)*
21. *Spot (p.921)*
22. *Brasil a gosto (p.923)*
23. *Frevo (p.923)*
24. *Padaria Juliet (p.924)*
25. *Tordesilhas (p.924)*
26. *D.O.M. Restaurante (p.921)*

27. *Rex Restaurante (p.924)*
28. *Restaurante Marcel (p.924)*
29. *Tre Bicchieri (p.925)*
30. *Marie-Madeleine (p.922)*
31. *Kinoshita (p.925)*
32. *Arturito (p.926)*
33. *Jun Sakamoto (p.927)*
34. *Maní (p.925)*
35. *Mercearia do Conde (p.924)*
36. *Tian (p.922)*
37. *Goshala (p.926)*
38. *Chou (p.926)*
39. *Colher de Pau (p.922)*
40. *Lá da Venda (p.927)*
41. *Filial (p.927)*
42. *Peixaria Bar e Venda (p.928)*
43. *Tanuki (p.928)*
44. *Coffee Lab (p.926)*
45. *Martin Fierro (p.928)*
46. *Restaurante Vito (p.928)*
47. *Ton Hoi (p.920)*

TON HOI
Recommended by
Benny Novak

Avenida Professor Francisco Morato 1484
Butanta
São Paulo SP 05512-100
+55 1137213268
www.tonhoi.com.br

Opening hours	Closed Monday and Sunday
Credit cards	Accepted
Price range	Affordable
Style	Casual
Cuisine	Chinese
Recommended for	Regular neighbourhood

'Family-friendly Chinese restaurant, serving generous, very well-prepared portions. It used to be less expensive but it still provides good value for money. Simple and traditional Chinese canteen atmosphere. Almost impossible to get a table at the weekend as it's always so full, but it's worth the wait!'—Benny Novak

BAR DA DONA ONÇA
Recommended by
Bel Coelho

Avenida Ipiranga 200
Centro
São Paulo SP 01046-010
+55 1132572016
www.bardadonaonca.com.br

Opening hours	Open 7 days
Credit cards	Accepted
Price range	Budget
Style	Casual
Cuisine	Brazilian
Recommended for	Local favourite

'Jana prepares high-quality bohemian food. The bar is in one of the most iconic buildings in the city, the Copan building.'—Bel Coelho

JARDIM DE NAPOLI
Recommended by
Mara Salles

Rua Martinico Prado 463
Centro
São Paulo SP 01224-010
+55 1136663022
www.jardimdenapoli.com.br

Opening hours	Open 7 days
Credit cards	Accepted
Price range	Affordable
Style	Casual
Cuisine	Italian
Recommended for	Local favourite

'It serves food of a consistently high standard, tirelessly overseen by the long-standing owners and employees.'
—Mara Salles

MERCADO MUNICIPAL
Recommended by
Julien Duboué

Rua da Cantareira 306
Centro
São Paulo SP 01024-000
+55 1133133365
www.mercadomunicipal.com.br

Opening hours	Open 7 days
Reservation policy	No
Credit cards	Accepted
Price range	Budget
Style	Casual
Cuisine	Brazilian
Recommended for	Bargain

TERRAÇO ITÁLIA
Recommended by
Luca Gozzani

Avenida Ipiranga 344
Centro
São Paulo SP 01046-010
+55 1121892929
www.terracoitalia.com.br

Opening hours	Open 7 days
Credit cards	Accepted
Price range	Expensive
Style	Smart casual
Cuisine	Italian
Recommended for	High end

'Beautiful view of São Paulo, piano music, Italian food...'
—Luca Gozzani

D.O.M. RESTAURANTE

Rua Barão de Capanema 549
Cerqueira César
São Paulo SP 01411-011
+55 1130880761
www.domrestaurante.com.br

Recommended by
Emmanuel Bassoleil,
Akrame Benallal, Massimo
Bottura, Katie Button, Atul
Kochhar, Alberto Landgraf,
Davide Oldani, Daniel
Patterson, Peeter Pihel,
Fernando Rivarola, Helena
Rizzo, Mara Salles

Opening hours	Closed Sunday
Credit cards	Accepted
Price range	Expensive
Style	Smart casual
Cuisine	Modern Brazilian
Recommended for	Worth the travel

'If Brazilian cooking is assuming an important position in the world, it's thanks to its unique and incredible produce and to Alex Atala, who has been able to present it to the world with food that is both modern and old-style.'—Massimo Bottura

One-time painter and decorator and punk DJ Alex Atala has almost single-handedly put experimental, fine-dining Brazilian cuisine onto the world stage thanks to an ungodly amount of dedication and vision. At D.O.M. – *domus optimus maximus* (home is greatest and best) – Atala has turned scouring the Amazon rainforest for forgotten ingredients into an art form, as well as a pretty solid business model. Thanks to him, Brazilian food is no longer regarded as being merely homely and unsophisticated but as vibrant, interesting and, at times, downright cool. If you like eating ingredients that are unlikely to have ever left Brazil, D.O.M.'s the place to go.

RESTAURANTE AMADEUS

Rua Haddock Lobo 807
Cerqueira César
São Paulo SP 01420-002
+55 1130612859
www.restauranteamadeus.com

Recommended by
Vítor Sobral

Opening hours	Open 7 days
Credit cards	Accepted but only AMEX and VISA
Price range	Expensive
Style	Casual
Cuisine	Seafood
Recommended for	Local favourite

SPOT

Alameda Ministro Rocha Azevedo 72
Cerqueira César
São Paulo SP 01410-000
+55 1132830946
www.restaurantespot.com.br

Recommended by
Alex Atala

Opening hours	Open 7 days
Credit cards	Accepted
Price range	Affordable
Style	Casual
Cuisine	Modern Brazilian
Recommended for	Wish I'd opened

'Spot has been a trendy place since it opened its doors twenty years ago! Always packed with interesting people, it's always great fun!'—Alex Atala

BARCELONA DOCES E PÃES

Rua Armando Penteado 336
Consolação
São Paulo SP 01242-010
+55 1138264689
www.barcelonapaes.com.br

Recommended by
Benny Novak

Opening hours	Open 7 days
Reservation policy	No
Credit cards	Accepted
Price range	Budget
Style	Casual
Cuisine	Bakery-Café-Deli
Recommended for	Breakfast

'I usually have breakfast at home but when I go out at the weekend I go to Padaria Barcelona on Praça Vilaboim to enjoy a Minas cheese (typical Brazilian cheese from Minas Gerais) pasty or a cold sandwich.'—Benny Novak

RIVIERA BAR

Avenida Paulista 2584
Consolação
São Paulo SP 01310-300
+55 1132581268
www.rivierabar.com.br

Opening hours	Open 7 days
Credit cards	Accepted
Price range	Affordable
Style	Casual
Cuisine	International
Recommended for	Late night

'The old, much-loved Riviera of the 1970s has re-opened with renewed vigour and a total lack of pretentiousness. The comfy chairs on the upper level and the vibrant urban landscape complement the buzzing bar, which serves great drinks and good food in a no-nonsense setting. São Paulo deserves this gem.'—Mara Salles

SUJINHO

Rua da Consolação 2063
Consolação
São Paulo SP 01239-050
+55 8132315207
www.sujinho.com.br

Opening hours	Open 7 days
Credit cards	Accepted
Price range	Affordable
Style	Casual
Cuisine	Brazilian
Recommended for	Late night

'It serves the best barbequed spring chicken in the city, it's open until the early hours and it's an eclectic place.'—Mara Salles

For pricy São Paulo, this no-nonsense churrascaria is something approaching a bargain. But then with a name that roughly translates as 'slightly dirty', you'd hardly expect prohibitively priced fine dining. Never less than lively and with hours that cater for the night owl, they serve sizeable portions of grilled beef, chicken and hamburgers – all made for cold beer. The loyal band of bohos that are its regulars knows how to keep the party going. When it gets crowded – and it will – there's overspill into a second outpost just across the street. Popular former president Lula is among its high-profile fans.

COLHER DE PAU

Rua Doutor Mário Ferraz 563
Itaim Bibi
São Paulo SP 01453-011
+55 1131688068
www.colherdepau.com.br

Opening hours	Open 7 days
Credit cards	Accepted
Price range	Affordable
Style	Casual
Cuisine	Brazilian
Recommended for	Regular neighbourhood

'Typical Brazilian food from the state of Minas Gerais, beautiful place and bright surroundings.'
—Luca Gozzani

MARIE-MADELEINE

Rua Afonso Braz 511
Itaim Bibi
São Paulo SP 04511-011
+55 1123870019
www.marie-madeleine.com.br

Opening hours	Closed Monday
Reservation policy	No
Credit cards	Accepted
Price range	Affordable
Style	Casual
Cuisine	Café-Bakery
Recommended for	Breakfast

'A little bit of Paris in São Paulo.'—Emmanuel Bassoleil

TIAN

Rua Jerônimo da Veiga 36
Itaim Bibi
São Paulo SP 04536-000
+55 1123899399
www.tianrestaurante.com.br

Opening hours	Open 7 days
Credit cards	Accepted
Price range	Affordable
Style	Casual
Cuisine	Asian Fusion
Recommended for	Bargain

'The cheapest trip to Asia. Wonderful recipes and exotic seasonings.'—Emmanuel Bassoleil

BAR NÚMERO

Rua da Consolação 3585
Jardim Paulista
São Paulo SP 01416-001
+55 1130613995
www.barnumero.com.br

Recommended by
Rodrigo Oliveira

Opening hours	Closed Monday and Sunday
Credit cards	Accepted
Price range	Affordable
Style	Smart casual
Cuisine	Bar
Recommended for	Late night

BRASIL A GOSTO

Rua Professor Azevedo do Amaral 70
Jardim Paulista
São Paulo SP 01409-030
+55 1130863565
www.brasilagosto.com.br

Recommended by
Vítor Sobral

Opening hours	Closed Monday
Credit cards	Accepted
Price range	Affordable
Style	Casual
Cuisine	Brazilian
Recommended for	Local favourite

DELIQATÊ

Alameda Jaú 1191
Jardim Paulista
São Paulo SP 01420-001
+55 1130634988
www.deliqate.com

Recommended by
Benny Novak

Opening hours	Open 7 days
Reservation policy	No
Credit cards	Accepted
Price range	Budget
Style	Casual
Cuisine	Café-Bakery
Recommended for	Breakfast

'They cure and smoke their own bacon, serve great scrambled eggs and make very good cheese bread (with real cheese)!'—Benny Novak

EPICE

Rua Haddock Lobo 1002
Jardim Paulista
São Paulo SP 01414-000
+55 1130620866
www.epicerestaurante.com.br

Recommended by
Alex Atala,
Fernando Rivarola

Opening hours	Closed Monday
Credit cards	Accepted
Price range	Expensive
Style	Casual
Cuisine	Brazilian
Recommended for	Worth the travel

'I'm a huge enthusiast of the new generation of chefs in Brazil. They are doing great things for Brazilian gastronomy, which makes us very proud. The chefs from this restaurant are extremely creative and have beautiful technique.'—Alex Atala

Epice is a cool haven amid the high-end boutiques of the long, palm-fringed Rua Haddock Lobo and is the relative newcomer from the truly international chef Alberto Landgraf. With Japanese and German blood, Landgraf grew up in Southern Brazil, but learned to cook in London, working alongside Gordon Ramsay and Tom Aikens. The interior is suitably chic and precise, with abundant wood bathed in natural light. Landgraf's food is also finely formed, with the pig as star, as in the pig's trotter with foie gras mousseline and pickled carrots or the home-made charcuterie. As the restaurant's name suggests, spice is also a regular component, notably in the dessert of sautéed pear with pain d'épice and pear sorbet.

FREVO

Rua Oscar Freire 603
Jardim Paulista
São Paulo SP 01426-001
+55 1130823434
www.frevinho.com.br/en

Recommended by
Helena Rizzo

Opening hours	Open 7 days
Credit cards	Accepted
Price range	Budget
Style	Casual
Cuisine	Middle Eastern-European
Recommended for	Late night

'I love their Beirute Especial sandwich (Middle-Eastern flatbread with steak, cheese, salad and egg).'
—Helena Rizzo

MERCEARIA DO CONDE

Recommended by
Helena Rizzo

Rua Joaquim Antunes 217
Jardim Paulista
São Paulo SP 05415-010
+55 1130817204
www.merceariadoconde.com.br

Opening hours	Open 7 days
Credit cards	Accepted
Price range	Affordable
Style	Casual
Cuisine	Modern Brazilian
Recommended for	Regular neighbourhood

'They serve simple food using fresh ingredients. Very attentive service.'—Helena Rizzo

PADARIA JULIET

Recommended by
Mara Salles

Rua da Consolação 3156
Jardim Paulista
São Paulo SP 01302-001
+55 1130828562

Opening hours	Open 7 days
Reservation policy	No
Credit cards	Accepted
Price range	Budget
Style	Casual
Cuisine	Café-Bakery
Recommended for	Breakfast

'They take great care over little details and the service is always warm and attentive.'—Mara Salles

RESTAURANTE MARCEL

Recommended by
Vítor Sobral

Rua da Consolação 3555
Jardim Paulista
São Paulo SP 01416-001
+55 1130643089
www.restaurantemarcel.com.br

Opening hours	Open 7 days
Credit cards	Accepted
Price range	Affordable
Style	Casual
Cuisine	French
Recommended for	Local favourite

REX RESTAURANTE

Recommended by
Emmanuel Bassoleil

Rua da Consolação 3193
Jardim Paulista
São Paulo SP 01416-001
+55 1125067386
www.rexrestaurante.com.br

Opening hours	Closed Sunday
Credit cards	Accepted
Price range	Affordable
Style	Smart casual
Cuisine	International
Recommended for	Late night

'Restaurant frequented by cool people from São Paulo's night scene, enjoying drinks and food such as fettuccine, burgers, mussels and apple Tarte Tatin, all in a young atmosphere with dogs and more dogs, pictures, statues, paintings...'—Emmanuel Bassoleil

TORDESILHAS

Recommended by
Emmanuel Bassoleil,
Federico Fialayre,
Helena Rizzo

Alameda Tietê 489
Jardim Paulista
São Paulo SP 01417-020
+55 1131077444
www.tordesilhas.com

Opening hours	Closed Monday
Credit cards	Accepted
Price range	Affordable
Style	Casual
Cuisine	Brazilian
Recommended for	Local favourite

'A beautiful trip around Brazil through Mara Salles's recipes.'—Emmanuel Bassoleil

Mara Salles, doyenne of Brazilian cuisine, has been cooking at Tordesilhas since 1990. The restaurant upgraded to grander premises in the Jardins neighbourhood in 2013 but has retained its rustic charm. Inspired by what she learned as a child at her mother's side, Salles focuses on rural dishes and native ingredients. Diners will find her just as likely to modernize a regional classic as she is to create something completely new with Brazilian ingredients. Greatest hits include prawns (shrimp) in cassava (manioc) cream with coconut milk, meat and cheese pasties, and a trio of Amazonian ice creams. To drink: a selection of reserve *cachaças* (white rum made from sugar cane).

TRE BICCHIERI

Recommended by
Emmanuel Bassoleil

Rua General Mena Barreto 765
Jardim Paulista
São Paulo SP 01433-010
+55 1138854004
www.trebicchieri.com.br

Opening hours	Open 7 days
Credit cards	Accepted
Price range	Affordable
Style	Casual
Cuisine	Italian
Recommended for	Regular neighbourhood

'You can eat *buonissima* Tuscan food with excellent service at a good price.'—Emmanuel Bassoleil

MANÍ

Recommended by
Alex Atala, Emmanuel
Bassoleil, Bel Coelho,
Mauro Colagreco, Matías
Kyriazis, Alberto Landgraf,
Soledad Nardelli,
Benny Novak

Rua Joaquim Antunes 210
Jardim Paulistano
São Paulo SP 05415-010
+55 1130854148
www.manimanioca.com.br

Opening hours	Closed Monday
Credit cards	Accepted
Price range	Expensive
Style	Casual
Cuisine	Spanish-Brazilian
Recommended for	High end

'I was surprised by the creativity and the refinement of the food.'—Mauro Colagreco

JIYUU SUSHI

Recommended by
Mara Salles

Rua dos Estudantes 166
Liberdade
São Paulo SP 01505-000
+55 1132081159
www.jiyuusushi.com.br

Opening hours	Closed Sunday
Credit cards	Accepted
Price range	Affordable
Style	Casual
Cuisine	Japanese
Recommended for	Regular neighbourhood

'I feel at home here and the food is meticulously prepared and unpretentious.'—Mara Salles

KINOSHITA

Recommended by
Vítor Sobral

Rua Jacques Félix 405
Liberdade
São Paulo SP 04509-000
+55 1138496940
www.restaurantekinoshita.com.br

Opening hours	Closed Sunday
Credit cards	Accepted
Price range	Expensive
Style	Casual
Cuisine	Modern Japanese
Recommended for	Worth the travel

A sleek modernist cube bordered by rounded hedges, Kinoshita provides a sophisticated contrast to the tall, residential buildings of Vila Nova Conceição. It is the domain of chef Tsuyoshi 'Mura' Murakami who named the restaurant after his émigré father-in-law who launched the original version of Kinoshita. Murakami practises *kappo* cuisine, which combines aromas and textures to extremely sensual effect, 'like poetry,' he says. Such renditions may include cod-fish roe sushi with quail egg; tuna sashimi with foie gras and teriyaki; and sous-vide wild boar grilled with miso. Lucky diners may be offered a green tea bonbon made by Murakami's wife. Kinoshita boasts a sake sommelier and a brave cocktail list – the Midori-wasabi Martini is worth a try.

AS VÉIA

Recommended by
Rodrigo Oliveira

Estrada Santa Inês 3000
Mairiporã
São Paulo SP 07600-000
+55 1144852084
www.velhao.com.br

Opening hours	Open 7 days
Reservation policy	No
Credit cards	Not accepted
Price range	Budget
Style	Casual
Cuisine	Brazilian
Recommended for	Local favourite

SHINZUSHI

Recommended by
Alberto Landgraf

Rua Afonso De Freitas 169
Paraíso
São Paulo SP 04006-050
+55 1138898700
www.shin-zushi.com

Opening hours	Closed Monday
Credit cards	Accepted
Price range	Affordable
Style	Casual
Cuisine	Japanese
Recommended for	Regular neighbourhood

'My Sunday night hangout – great people and the best Japanese restaurant in Brazil!'—Alberto Landgraf

CARLINHOS RESTAURANTE

Recommended by
Rodrigo Oliveira

Rua Rio Bonito 1641
Pari
São Paulo SP 03023-000
+55 1133159474

Opening hours	Closed Sunday
Credit cards	Accepted
Price range	Budget
Style	Casual
Cuisine	Brazilian
Recommended for	Bargain

ARTURITO

Recommended by
Mara Salles

Rua Artur de Azevedo 542
Pinheiros
São Paulo SP 05404-011
+55 1130634951
www.arturito.com.br

Opening hours	Open 7 days
Credit cards	Accepted
Price range	Affordable
Style	Casual
Cuisine	Modern Mediterranean
Recommended for	Wish I'd opened

'It is characterful, serves good food and the chef is very hands-on.'—Mara Salles

CHOU

Recommended by
Helena Rizzo

Rua Mateus Grou 345
Pinheiros
São Paulo SP 05415-050
+55 1130836998
www.chou.com.br

Opening hours	Closed Monday and Sunday
Credit cards	Accepted
Price range	Affordable
Style	Casual
Cuisine	European
Recommended for	Wish I'd opened

'I like the simplicity, the chefs' use of a wood-fired oven and the choice of ingredients. I feel like I'm at a friend's house when I'm there.'—Helena Rizzo

COFFEE LAB

Recommended by
Bel Coelho,
Helena Rizzo

Rua Fradique Coutinho 1340
Pinheiros
São Paulo SP 05414-012
+55 1133757400
www.coffeelab.com.br

Opening hours	Closed Sunday
Reservation policy	No
Credit cards	Accepted
Price range	Affordable
Style	Casual
Cuisine	Café
Recommended for	Breakfast

'I always go there just for the coffee. Isabela is an excellent barista and toasts her own coffee on-site. The result is the best coffee in Brazil.'—Bel Coelho

GOSHALA

Recommended by
Helena Rizzo

Rua dos Pinheiros 267
Pinheiros
São Paulo SP 05422-010
+55 113060367
www.goshala.com.br

Opening hours	Open 7 days
Credit cards	Accepted
Price range	Budget
Style	Casual
Cuisine	Vegetarian
Recommended for	Bargain

'They have a R$24 (£6; $10) set-price menu that changes daily.'—Helena Rizzo

JUN SAKAMOTO
Recommended by
Rodrigo Oliveira
Rua Lisboa 55
Pinheiros
São Paulo SP 05413-000
+55 1130886019

Opening hours	Closed Sunday
Credit cards	Accepted
Price range	Expensive
Style	Casual
Cuisine	Japanese
Recommended for	High end

In a city that knows sushi – there are more Japanese restaurants in São Paulo than steakhouses – Jun Sakamoto's eponymous outpost is considered the very finest. Born and raised in Brazil, trained in New York, Sakamoto is famously fanatical about sourcing ingredients, as fastidious about his rice and wasabi root as he is about the foie gras he pairs with tuna tartare, or the *uni* (sea urchin) for his nigiri. The wood, glass and leather-trimmed interior, which has aged well in the fifteen years since opening, doesn't detract from the food. Aim for a counter seat and go for the *omakase* menu if budget allows.

CASA GARABED
Recommended by
Rodrigo Oliveira
Rua José Margarido 216
Santana
São Paulo SP 02021-020
+55 1129762750
www.casagarabed.com.br

Opening hours	Closed Monday
Reservation policy	No
Credit cards	Accepted
Price range	Budget
Style	Casual
Cuisine	Lebanese
Recommended for	Regular neighbourhood

SUSHI HIROSHI
Recommended by
Rodrigo Oliveira
Rua Capitão Manuel Novaes 189
Santana
São Paulo SP 02022-035
+55 1129796677
www.sushihiroshi.com.br

Opening hours	Open 7 days
Credit cards	Accepted
Price range	Budget
Style	Casual
Cuisine	Japanese
Recommended for	Regular neighbourhood

CHURRASCARIA BOI NA BRASA
Recommended by
Benny Novak
Rue Marquês de Itu 188
Vila Buarque
São Paulo SP 01223-000
+55 1132236162
www.churrascariaboinabrasa.com.br

Opening hours	Open 7 days
Credit cards	Accepted
Price range	Budget
Style	Casual
Cuisine	Barbeque
Recommended for	Bargain

'Old-style churrascaria. Meat on a spit, basic surroundings and unbeatable value for money. They serve the best grilled pork loin and spicy sausage in São Paulo!'—Benny Novak

FILIAL
Recommended by
Benny Novak
Rua Fidalga 254
Vila Madalena
São Paulo SP 05432-070
+55 1138139226
www.barfilial.com.br

Opening hours	Open 7 days
Reservation policy	No
Credit cards	Accepted
Price range	Affordable
Style	Casual
Cuisine	Brazilian
Recommended for	Late night

'A simple bar that serves excellent *coxinhas* (stuffed savoury snacks) and good fillet steak sandwiches with cheese.'—Benny Novak

LÁ DA VENDA

Recommended by
Alberto Landgraf

Rua Harmonia 161
Vila Madalena
São Paulo SP 05435-000
+55 1138131711
www.ladavenda.com.br

Opening hours	Closed Monday
Credit cards	Accepted
Price range	Affordable
Style	Casual
Cuisine	Brazilian
Recommended for	Breakfast

'Best Brazilian cheese bread and a huge variety of cakes. Great for coffee or a juice.'—Alberto Landgraf

MARTIN FIERRO

Recommended by
Bel Coelho

Rua Aspicuelta 683
Vila Madalena
São Paulo SP 05433-010
+55 1138146747
www.martinfierro.com.br

Opening hours	Open 7 days
Credit cards	Accepted
Price range	Budget
Style	Casual
Cuisine	Italian-Brazilian
Recommended for	Bargain

'Excellent meat and great salads at a good price. I also love their pasties.'—Bel Coelho

PEIXARIA BAR E VENDA

Recommended by
Luca Gozzani

Rua Inácio Pereira da Rocha 112
Vila Madalena
São Paulo SP 05432-010
+55 1125893963

Opening hours	Open 7 days
Credit cards	Accepted
Price range	Affordable
Style	Casual
Cuisine	Seafood
Recommended for	Local favourite

'I like the fish they serve and their products are all of a high quality. It attracts a diverse clientele and has a relaxed atmosphere.'—Luca Gozzani

RESTAURANTE VITO

Recommended by
Alex Atala,
Emmanuel Bassoleil

Rua Isabel de Castela 529
Vila Madalena
São Paulo SP 05445-010
+55 1130321469
www.vitorestaurante.com.br

Opening hours	Closed Monday and Sunday
Credit cards	Accepted
Price range	Affordable
Style	Casual
Cuisine	Italian-Brazilian
Recommended for	Regular neighbourhood

'Chef André Mifano does very creative Italian cuisine – it's inspiring. The restaurant has some of the best charcuterie I have ever tasted.'—Alex Atala

TANUKI

Recommended by
Bel Coelho,
Benny Novak

Rua Jericó 287
Vila Madalena
São Paulo SP 05435-040
+55 1138143760
www.tanukisushi.com.br

Opening hours	Open 7 days
Credit cards	Accepted
Price range	Affordable
Style	Casual
Cuisine	Sushi
Recommended for	Regular neighbourhood

'Exceptionally high-quality fish and the restaurant is very good value! Very good for a business lunch and it has a youthful, unpretentious atmosphere.'
—Benny Novak

PADARIA JARDIM BRASIL

Recommended by
Alex Atala,
Rodrigo Oliveira

Avenue Jardim Japão 1298
Vila Maria
São Paulo SP 02221-001
+55 1122019434
www.padariajardimbrasil.com.br

Opening hours	Open 7 days
Reservation policy	No
Credit cards	Accepted
Price range	Budget
Style	Casual
Cuisine	Café-Bakery
Recommended for	Breakfast

'*Padarías* in Brazil are special places where you can find all types of foods. There are so many different sandwiches and natural juices. Some of my favourites are papaya with orange juice, the traditional *pingado* (coffee and milk) and the *pão na chapa* (a fresh type of baguette smothered in butter and squashed on a hot grill).'—Alex Atala

MOCOTÓ

Avenida Nossa Senhora do Loreto 1100
Vila Medeiros
São Paulo SP 02219-001
+55 1129513056
www.mocoto.com.br

Recommended by
Alex Atala, Bo
Bech, Bel Coelho,
Julien Duboué,
Alberto Landgraf,
Fernando Rivarola

Opening hours	Open 7 days
Reservation policy	No
Credit cards	Accepted
Price range	Budget
Style	Casual
Cuisine	Brazilian
Recommended for	Bargain

'Rodrigo Oliveira heads up this *cachaçeria*, which specializes in the Brazilian *sertaneja* (country) style of cooking. His fried pork crackling and tapioca bites are famous across the country and each morsel of food, though simple at first sight, is superior in terms of flavour and preparation. It's amazing to see people waiting for almost two hours for a much-desired portion of food.'—Fernando Rivarola

You will find Mocotó at Vila Medeiros, a traditionally working-class district of São Paulo. It is run by Rodrigo Oliveira de Almeida, the son of an émigré who came to São Paulo seeking his fortune armed with little more than a couple of shirts, one pair of trousers (pants) and the shoes on his feet. Dishes – offered alongside some 350 sturdy *cachaças* (white rum made from sugar cane) – offer a lighter version of northeast Brazil's cuisine. These include *sarapatel* (pork offal), *feijão de corda* (string beans stewed with sausage, bacon, dried meat and butter [lima] beans) and *paleta de cordeiro do velho chico* (braised lamb feather blade). *Mocotó* (cow's foot broth) is the house classic.

GARZÓN

Hotel Garzón
Costa Jose Ignacio y La Canilla
Garzón
Maldonado 20402
Uruguay
+598 44102811
www.restaurantegarzon.com

Recommended by
Roberta Sudbrack

Opening hours	Open 7 days
Credit cards	Not accepted
Price range	Expensive
Style	Smart casual
Cuisine	International
Recommended for	Wish I'd opened

'A place to dream, to smell and eat unhurriedly. A place where the fire is the protagonist and king! There is no place like this in a world, it is unique.'
—Roberta Sudbrack

LUCIFER

Camino a la Estación Custiel
Garzón
Maldonado 20402
Uruguay
+598 99255249

Recommended by
Alejandro Morales

Opening hours	Closed Monday
Credit cards	Not accepted
Price range	Affordable
Style	Casual
Cuisine	Uruguayan
Recommended for	Regular neighbourhood

'I like the menu and the soft and feminine atmosphere here. It's a nice walk to Garzón to have lunch or dinner at Lucifer and then I like to walk around the village afterwards.'—Alejandro Morales

MARISMO

Km. 18 Ruta 10
José Ignacio
Maldonado 20402
Uruguay
+598 44862273

Recommended by
Julien Duboué

Opening hours	Open 7 days
Credit cards	Not accepted
Price range	Affordable
Style	Casual
Cuisine	Uruguayan
Recommended for	Worth the travel

PARADOR LA HUELLA

Recommended by
Stephen Stryjewski

Calle de Los Cisnes y Playa Brava
José Ignacio
Maldonado 20402
Uruguay
+598 44862279
www.paradorlahuella.com

Opening hours	Open 7 days
Credit cards	Accepted
Price range	Affordable
Style	Casual
Cuisine	Uruguayan
Recommended for	Worth the travel

SANTA TERESITA

Recommended by
Alejandro Morales

Calle Las Garzas y Calle Las Calandrias
José Ignacio
Maldonado 20402
Uruguay

Opening hours	Open 7 days
Credit cards	Not accepted
Price range	Budget
Style	Casual
Cuisine	International
Recommended for	Breakfast

'It's still not very well known but it has some very good things on offer: the cold-brewed iced coffee, the 'tostadas' (toasted bread dishes), the atmosphere and the old building.'—Alejandro Morales

SANTAS NEGRAS

Recommended by
Alejandro Morales

Camino Sainz Martinez y Los Lobos
José Ignacio
Maldonado 20402
Uruguay
+598 44862262

Opening hours	Open 7 days
Reservation policy	No
Credit cards	Not accepted
Price range	Affordable
Style	Casual
Cuisine	Uruguayan
Recommended for	Late night

'I like going there at night to eat a *chorizán* (chorizo sandwich).'—Alejandro Morales

ELMO RESTO BAR

Recommended by
Alejandro Morales

Los Bonitos y El Cinto
Manantiales
Maldonado 20002
Uruguay
+598 94069111
www.elmo.com.uy

Opening hours	Open 7 days
Credit cards	Not accepted
Price range	Budget
Style	Casual
Cuisine	Mediterranean
Recommended for	Bargain

'Good pizza, good pasta, excellent atmosphere and music.'—Alejandro Morales

MISTURA MANANTIALES

Recommended by
Alejandro Morales

18 de Julio
Manantiales
Maldonado 20002
Uruguay
+598 42775711
www.misturamanantiales.com

Opening hours	Variable
Credit cards	Accepted
Price range	Affordable
Style	Smart casual
Cuisine	Modern Uruguayan
Recommended for	High end

'I like the set-up – it's very homely.'—Alejandro Morales

CAFÉ MISTERIO

Recommended by
Alejandro Morales

Avenida General Fructuoso Rivera 1700
Montevideo
Montevideo 11500
Uruguay
+598 26018765
www.cafemisterio.com.uy

Opening hours	Closed Sunday
Credit cards	Accepted
Price range	Affordable
Style	Smart casual
Cuisine	Asian-European
Recommended for	Local favourite

'It's been going for twenty years and it just gets better and better.'—Alejandro Morales

ITALPAST

Recommended by
Emilio Garip,
Martín Rebaudino

Juan Dellepianne 1050
Campana
Buenos Aires B2804AEJ
Argentina
+54 3489425275
www.italpastdeli.com.ar

Opening hours	Closed Monday
Credit cards	Accepted
Price range	Affordable
Style	Casual
Cuisine	Italian
Recommended for	Regular neighbourhood

'Everything is delicious but I recommend trying the *porchetta*, the Sardinian gnocchi, the rabbit and the chef's recommendations.'—Emilio Garip

SOL DE MAYO

Recommended by
Estefania Di Benedetto

Avenida Mitre 1001
Campana
Buenos Aires B2804AQH
Argentina
+54 3489431306

Opening hours	Closed Monday
Credit cards	Accepted
Price range	Affordable
Style	Casual
Cuisine	Bakery-Café-Deli
Recommended for	Wish I'd opened

'It's a good bakery with a variety of sandwiches and daily specials. It also has open spaces that are very welcoming.'—Estefania Di Benedetto

LA CASONA DEL TOBOSO

Recommended by
Martín Rebaudino

Belgrano 349
La Cumbre
Córdoba 5178
+54 3548451436
www.lacasona-del-toboso.com.ar

Opening hours	Open 7 days
Credit Cards	Accepted
Price Range	Affordable
Style	Casual
Cuisine	Argentinian
Recommended for	Wish I'd opened

'My father opened this restaurant in my home town in 1966. It's still open and it's a town classic that has given us work and a lot of joy.'—Martín Rebaudino

LA CASA DEL TATA

Recommended by
Soledad Nardelli

Belgrano s/n
Maimará
Juyjuy 4622
+54 3884997389
www.lacasadeltata.com.ar

Opening hours	Open 7 days
Credit Cards	Accepted
Price Range	Affordable
Style	Casual
Cuisine	Argentinian
Recommended for	Wish I'd opened

BRINDILLAS
Recommended by
Gonzalo Aramburu

Guardia Vieja 2898
Luján de Cuyo
Mendoza M5509XAF
Argentina
+54 2614963650
www.brindillas.com

Opening hours	Closed Monday and Sunday
Credit cards	Accepted
Price range	Affordable
Style	Smart casual
Cuisine	Modern Argentinian
Recommended for	Worth the travel

'You feel totally pampered here. It's undoubtedly worth the trip just to experience the Mariano Gallego treatment. He is a great champion of this wonderful country's cuisine.'—Gonzalo Aramburu

CASSIS
Recommended by
Estefania Di Benedetto,
Martín Molteni,
Soledad Nardelli

Ruta 82, Lago Gutiérrez
San Carlos de Bariloche
Río Negro 8400
Argentina
+54 2944476167
www.cassis.com.ar

Opening hours	Variable
Credit cards	Accepted but only Visa
Price range	Affordable
Style	Smart casual
Cuisine	Modern Argentinian
Recommended for	Wish I'd opened

'It lies deep in the native woods, surrounded by an organic orchard, almost falling into Lake Gutierrez. You couldn't ask for more calm, beauty or unforgettable moments.'—Martín Molteni

LOBBY BAR
Recommended by
Emilio Garip

Llao Llao Hotel
Km. 25 Avenida Ezequiel Bustillo
San Carlos de Bariloche
Río Negro 8400
Argentina
+54 2944445700
www.llaollao.com

Opening hours	Open 7 days
Credit cards	Accepted
Price range	Affordable
Style	Casual
Cuisine	International
Recommended for	Breakfast

'It definitely serves the best breakfast in the country. Nothing beats eating delicious, perfectly cooked delicacies and wonderful baked goods at a spot overlooking the lake.'—Emilio Garip

CHEZ MANU
Recommended by
Soledad Nardelli

Avenida Fernando Luis Martial 2135
Ushuaia
Tierra del Fuego 9410
Argentina
+54 2901432253
www.chezmanu.com

Opening hours	Open 7 days
Credit cards	Accepted
Price range	Affordable
Style	Casual
Cuisine	French-Argentinian
Recommended for	Wish I'd opened

'Breathtaking landscapes, food cooked with fresh, seasonal ingredients grown by local farmers, excellent quality, and warm people.'—Soledad Nardelli

'WE ARGENTINIANS LOVE MEAT AND THE MEAT THERE IS SECOND TO NONE.'
MARA SALLESMARTÍN REBAUDINO PP938–939

'It's one of Buenos Aires' old riverside grills.'
MARTÍN MOLTENI P936

'SHOWCASES THE WIDE RANGE OF FLAVOURS THAT THE PORTEÑOS ARE USED TO.'
GONZALO ARAMBURU P944

BUENOS AIRES

'IT HAS SOMETHING OF THE FOOTBALL LOVER'S TAVERN ABOUT IT. THEIR RIBEYE CAP IS TO DIE FOR.'
JUAN GAFFURI P944

'Highlights the gastronomy of each of our country's regions.'
ESTEFANÍA DI BENEDETTO P936

'YOU CAN ENJOY THE BEST CUTS OF MEAT OUR COUNTRY HAS TO OFFER.'
HERNÁN GIPPONI P939

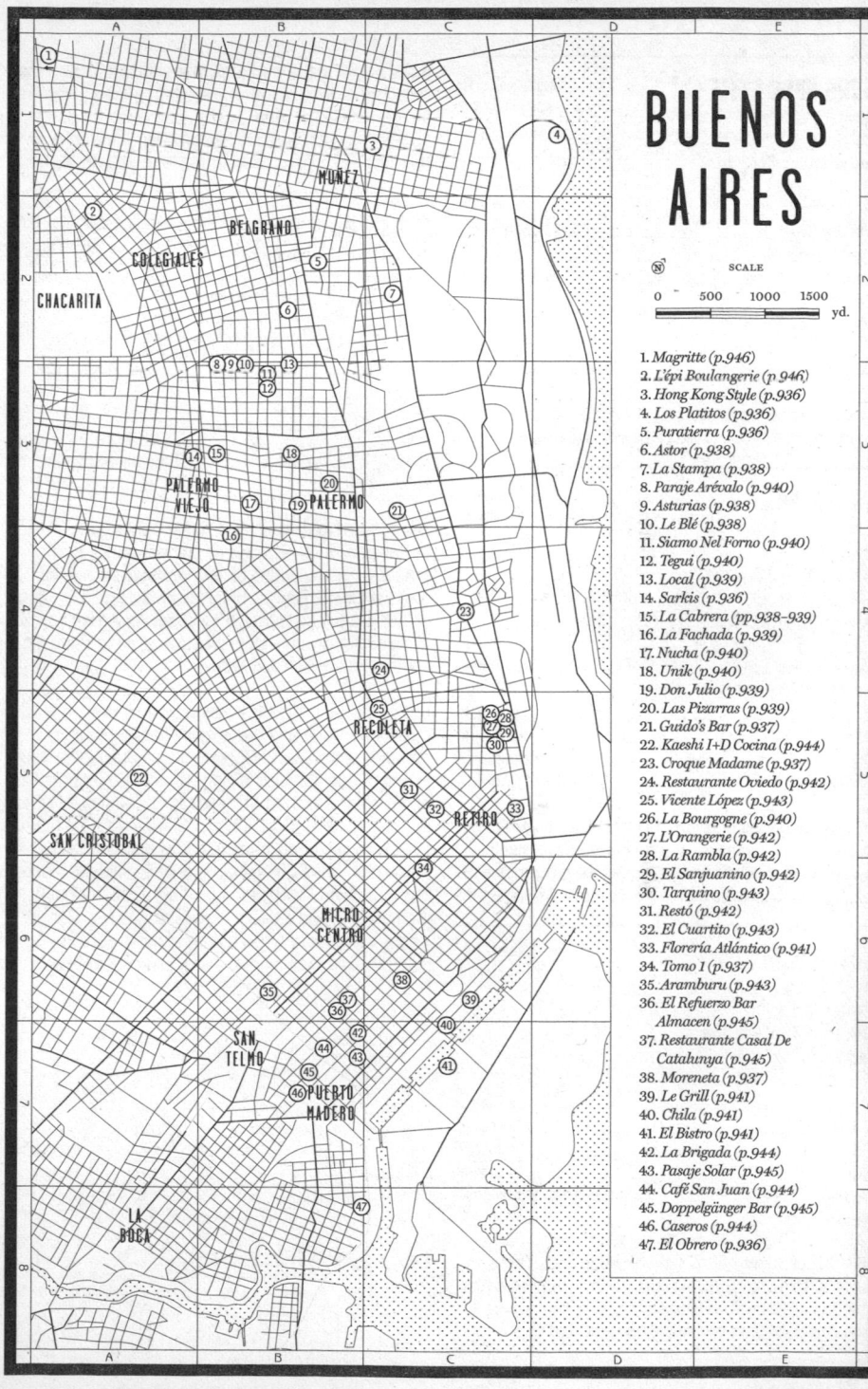

BUENOS AIRES

SCALE

0   500   1000   1500
yd.

HONG KONG STYLE

Montañeses 2149
Belgrano
Buenos Aires C1428DMT
+54 47863456

Opening hours	Closed Wednesday
Reservation policy	No
Credit cards	Not accepted
Price range	Budget
Style	Casual
Cuisine	Chinese
Recommended for	Regular neighbourhood

'It's a Chinese family restaurant with great home-made food. Lui, the owner, is the chef.'—Fernando Trocca

PURATIERRA

3 de Febrero 1167
Belgrano
Buenos Aires C1426BJI
+54 1148992007
www.puratierra.com.ar

Opening hours	Closed Sunday
Credit cards	Accepted
Price range	Expensive
Style	Smart casual
Cuisine	Modern Argentinian
Recommended for	Local favourite

'Signature Argentinian cuisine by chef Martín Molteni. It offers a wide-ranging and balanced menu, which values local products and highlights the gastronomy of each of our country's regions.'—Estefanía Di Benedetto

LOS PLATITOS

Avenida Rafael Obligado s/n Puesto 57
Costanera
Buenos Aires C1425XAB
+54 47811499

Opening hours	Open 7 days
Credit cards	Accepted
Price range	Budget
Style	Casual
Cuisine	Argentinian Steakhouse
Recommended for	Local favourite

'It's one of Buenos Aires's old riverside grills. There used to be many more, but they gradually closed down due to cut-backs. This is one of the survivors, where you can enjoy different cuts of meat served on a massive grill at the bar. It is perhaps the last survivor that reflects the old customs of our city. The meat is mature but grass-fed. The menu is simple: you can have sweetbreads, kidneys, chorizo and large cuts of boneless beef with *chimichurri* sauce.'—Martín Molteni

EL OBRERO

Agustín Caffarena 64
La Boca
Buenos Aires 1157
+54 1143629912

Opening hours	Closed Sunday
Credit cards	Not accepted
Price range	Affordable
Style	Casual
Cuisine	Argentinian Steakhouse
Recommended for	Local favourite

'It's a tavern that serves traditional dishes influenced by Italian and Spanish cuisine but with added local flavours, such as potato tortilla, *gramajo* scrambled eggs (scrambled eggs with chips, cooked ham, onions, oil and butter) and pasta. It's a simple place with a cheerful, lively atmosphere. A great place to share food with friends.'—Soledad Nardelli

Look past the gritty dockside neighbourhood, the shabby frontage and the window bars – instead, focus on the steak. El Obrero (the worker) in La Boca is one of Buenos Aires's longest established *parrillas* and is the restaurant of choice for touring celebrities and the stars of Boca Juniors (Maradona's old team). El Obrero has been in the hands of just one family since 1954 and little appears to have changed since. The bentwood chairs, the tiled floors, the football memorabilia and celebrity snaps are as reassuring as the blackboard (chalkboard) menu of tortilla, calamari and – of course – very fine cuts of beef.

MORENETA

Recommended by
Fernando Rivarola

Moreno 477
Microcentro
Buenos Aires C1091AA1
+54 1143311428
www.moreneta.com.ar

Opening hours	Closed Saturday and Sunday
Credit cards	Accepted but not AMEX
Price range	Affordable
Style	Casual
Cuisine	Bakery-Café-Deli
Recommended for	Breakfast

'It's owned by a couple, Luciana Conte and Sebastian Raggiante, who trained in Spain, France and Italy, and in 2010 they were awarded a Michelin star in Mallorca. They then came to Argentina to set up their own business. Their home-made bread is delicious and the place is very cosy and ideal for a daytime meal, like breakfast or lunch.'—Fernando Rivarola

TOMO 1

Recommended by
Emilio Garip

Panamericano Buenos Aires Hotel & Resort
Carlos Pellegrini 521
Microcentro
Buenos Aires C1009ABK
+54 1143266698
www.tomo1.com.ar

Opening hours	Closed Sunday
Credit cards	Accepted
Price range	Expensive
Style	Smart casual
Cuisine	Modern Argentinian
Recommended for	Local favourite

'This is my favourite place. It's one of those restaurants where, despite it being in the top three in the country, you can still order a simple dish or a traditional recipe and they'll cook it for you. It's a luxurious restaurant which is also very homely – a combination that makes for a great restaurant.'—Emilio Garip

CROQUE MADAME

Recommended by
Juan Gaffuri

National Museum of Decorative Arts
Avenida del Libertador 1902
Palermo
Buenos Aires C1425AAS
+54 48068639
www.croquemadame.com.ar

Opening hours	Open 7 days
Credit cards	Accepted
Price range	Affordable
Style	Casual
Cuisine	French Bistro
Recommended for	Breakfast

'It's a very relaxed place and there are some lovely outdoor areas which will get your day off to a good start.'—Juan Gaffuri

GUIDO'S BAR

Recommended by
Estefanía Di Benedetto,
Matías Kyriazis

República de la India 2843
Palermo
Buenos Aires C1425FAB
+54 48022391

Opening hours	Closed Sunday
Credit cards	Not accepted
Price range	Affordable
Style	Casual
Cuisine	Argentinian-Italian
Recommended for	Regular neighbourhood

'It's a typical Italian tavern run by Carlos Sosto that has been going for over thirty years – it's a benchmark of local cuisine. The place is ideal for a tasty and varied meal.'—Matías Kyriazis

LA STAMPA

Recommended by
Federico Fialayre

Migueletes 880
Palermo
Buenos Aires C1426BUJ
+54 1147762787
www.lastamparistorante.com

Opening hours	Open 7 days
Credit cards	Not accepted
Price range	Affordable
Style	Casual
Cuisine	Italian
Recommended for	Regular neighbourhood

'La Stampa is a family restaurant. I confess that I like the look and unpretentious feel of taverns and so La Stampa's slightly pretentious ambience bothers me a bit, but the pizza is to die for.'—Federico Fialayre

ASTOR

Recommended by
Gonzalo Aramburu,
Matías Kyriazis

Ciudad de la Paz 353
Palermo Viejo
Buenos Aires C1426AGE
+54 1145540802
www.astorbistro.com

Opening hours	Closed Saturday and Sunday
Credit cards	Accepted but not AMEX
Price range	Affordable
Style	Casual
Cuisine	Modern Argentinian
Recommended for	Bargain

'The best place to go if you don't want to spend a lot is Astor. It's a new bistro run by Antonio Soriano. I like it because you can see the kitchen at work and how the guys run around behind the scenes to get orders ready.'
—Gonzalo Aramburu

ASTURIAS

Recommended by
Matías Kyriazis

Gorriti 6002
Palermo Viejo
Buenos Aires C1414BKN
+54 1147761865

Opening hours	Open 7 days
Reservation policy	No
Credit cards	Not accepted
Price range	Budget
Style	Casual
Cuisine	Bakery-Café-Deli
Recommended for	Breakfast

'It's a classic local bakery. I like going there for its excellent butter croissants.'—Matías Kyriazis

LE BLÉ

Recommended by
Martín Molteni

Honduras 5999
Palermo Viejo
Buenos Aires C1414BNK
+54 47790272
www.leble.com.ar

Opening hours	Closed Monday
Reservation policy	No
Credit cards	Not accepted
Price range	Budget
Style	Casual
Cuisine	Bakery
Recommended for	Breakfast

'They prepare great classic French patisserie for breakfast, all of a very high quality. The place is in the Palermo neighbourhood and it's very simple and quiet. A place where you can forget about time for a while.'
—Martín Molteni

LA CABRERA

Recommended by
Hernán Gipponi,
Martín Rebaudino

José Antonio Cabrera 5127
Palermo Viejo
Buenos Aires C1414BGS
+54 48325754
www.parrillalacabrera.com.ar

Opening hours	Open 7 days
Credit cards	Accepted
Price range	Affordable
Style	Casual
Cuisine	Modern Argentinian
Recommended for	Local favourite

'I'd say that the restaurant that best represents my city today is La Cabrera. We Argentinians love meat and the meat there is second to none. They serve dry-aged beef, chorizo and sweetbreads, all accompanied by very good Argentinian-style side dishes.'
—Martín Rebaudino

DON JULIO

Recommended by
Hernán Gipponi

Guatemala 4699
Palermo Viejo
Buenos Aires C1425BUK
+54 1148326058

Opening hours	Open 7 days
Credit cards	Accepted
Price range	Affordable
Style	Casual
Cuisine	Argentinian Steakhouse
Recommended for	Local favourite

'You can enjoy the best cuts of meat our country has to offer.'—Hernán Gipponi

LA FACHADA

Recommended by
Hernán Gipponi

Aráoz 1283
Palermo Viejo
Buenos Aires C1414DPY
+54 1147746535
www.lafachada.com.ar

Opening hours	Open 7 days
Reservation policy	No
Credit cards	Not accepted
Price range	Budget
Style	Casual
Cuisine	Argentinian-Italian
Recommended for	Bargain

'It prepares what I think are the best local empanadas. My favourite is the Mendocina, stuffed with spicy meat. I like the fact that there are more pizzerias than grills in Buenos Aires and that, despite their low cost, they use good-quality ingredients and really care about their work.'—Hernán Gipponi

LAS PIZARRAS

Recommended by
Gonzalo Aramburu, Federico
Fialayre, Hernán Gipponi

Thames 2296
Palermo Viejo
Buenos Aires C1425FIF
+54 1147750625
www.laspizzarrasbistro.com

Opening hours	Closed Monday
Credit cards	Accepted
Price range	Affordable
Style	Casual
Cuisine	Bistro
Recommended for	Regular neighbourhood

'It's a small restaurant in Palermo run by chef Rodrigo Castilla, who specializes in market cuisine. He cooks with fresh ingredients that are sourced daily and his dishes are really tasty.'—Hernán Gipponi

LOCAL

Recommended by
Soledad Nardelli

Arévalo 2061
Palermo Viejo
Buenos Aires C1414CQO
+54 1147736119
www.localrestaurant.com.ar

Opening hours	Closed Monday
Credit cards	Accepted
Price range	Affordable
Style	Casual
Cuisine	Argentinian
Recommended for	Regular neighbourhood

'They serve home-made food cooked in a clay oven and they really make you feel at home. It's also run by the owner.'—Soledad Nardelli

NUCHA

Recommended by
Martín Rebaudino

Armenia 1540
Palermo Viejo
Buenos Aires C1414DKH
+54 1148339345
www.nucha.com.ar

Opening hours	Open 7 days
Credit cards	Accepted
Price range	Affordable
Style	Casual
Cuisine	Bakery-Café-Deli
Recommended for	Breakfast

'I like going here for breakfast. It's good for pastries.'
—Martín Rebaudino

PARAJE ARÉVALO

Recommended by
Gonzalo Aramburu,
Martín Molteni

Arévalo 1502
Palermo Viejo
Buenos Aires C1414CQF
+54 1147757759
www.parajearevalo.com

Opening hours	Closed Monday
Credit cards	Accepted
Price range	Expensive
Style	Smart casual
Cuisine	Modern International
Recommended for	High end

'It's a gourmet restaurant with a calm and relaxed atmosphere. The step-by-step tasting menu with accompanying wine is the only menu on offer, but Matías will ensure that you have a special night, thanks to his modern cooking style, which is both simple and complex at the same time.'—Martín Molteni

SIAMO NEL FORNO

Recommended by
Estefanía Di Benedetto

Costa Rica 5886
Palermo Viejo
Buenos Aires C1414BTJ
+54 1147750337

Opening hours	Closed Monday
Credit cards	Accepted
Price range	Budget
Style	Casual
Cuisine	Pizza
Recommended for	Bargain

'Neapolitan-style pizza cooked in a clay oven. They use only fresh ingredients and its owner, Nertor Gattorna, takes charge of the oven.'—Estefanía Di Benedetto

TEGUI

Recommended by
Estefanía Di Benedetto,
Federico Fialayre,
Hernán Gipponi

Costa Rica 5852
Palermo Viejo
Buenos Aires C1414BTJ
+54 1152913333
www.tegui.com.ar

Opening hours	Closed Monday and Sunday
Credit cards	Accepted
Price range	Expensive
Style	Smart casual
Cuisine	Modern Argentinian
Recommended for	High end

'It's a magical place, from the decor down to the food. You go through a door covered in graffiti and find yourself in this very cosy, characterful place. The food is incredible. Chef Germán Martitegui is very particular and quite obsessive when it comes to his work, and this is reflected in his faultless menu.'—Hernán Gipponi

UNIK

Recommended by
Juan Gaffuri,
Hernán Gipponi

Soler 5132
Palermo Viejo
Buenos Aires C1425BXN
+54 1147722230
www.unik.pro

Opening hours	Closed Sunday
Credit cards	Accepted
Price range	Expensive
Style	Smart casual
Cuisine	Modern Argentinian
Recommended for	High end

'Excellent food and great atmosphere.'—Juan Gaffuri

The creation of French-Argentine architect Marcelo Joulia, Unik is a bar, restaurant and design hub in the stylish Palermo barrio of Buenos Aires. A mismatched array of carefully selected furniture, such as design classics by Charles Eames, hotchpotch (hodgepodge) hanging lights and 1970s Formica tables makes for a setting as zeitgeisty as the menu. Starters include roasted beetroot (beets) with rye dust and a black tomato gazpacho. Keep room for their speciality main of Patagonian lamb cooked two ways. Finish off with pain perdu with cinnamon-caramel ice cream and wash down with one of many wines, including some serious Argentine Malbecs.

EL BISTRO

Faena Hotel
Martha Salotti 445
Puerto Madero
Buenos Aires C1107CMB
+54 1140109200
www.faena.com

Recommended by
Martín Molteni

Opening hours	Closed Sunday to Tuesday
Credit cards	Accepted
Price range	Expensive
Style	Smart casual
Cuisine	Modern Argentinian
Recommended for	High end

'This is a great white dining hall inside an eccentric hotel, where you sit down and admire Philippe Starck's wonderful decor with a good glass of wine in hand. It's a very different night out.'—Martín Molteni

CHILA

Alicia Moreau de Justo 1160
Puerto Madero
Buenos Aires C1107AAV
+54 1143436067
www.chilaweb.com.ar

Recommended by
Martín Berasategui,
Federico Fialayre, Emilio
Garip, Hernán Gipponi,
Matías Kyriazis

Opening hours	Open 7 days
Credit cards	Accepted
Price range	Expensive
Style	Smart casual
Cuisine	Modern Argentinian
Recommended for	High end

'An amazing restaurant with a superb chef, Soledad Nardelli. It's well worth a visit.'—Martín Berasategui

LE GRILL

Alicia Moreau de Justo 876
Puerto Madero
Buenos Aires C1107
+54 1143310454
www.legrill.com.ar

Recommended by
Hernán Gipponi,
Matías Kyriazis

Opening hours	Open 7 days
Credit cards	Accepted
Price range	Affordable
Style	Smart casual
Cuisine	Argentinian Steakhouse
Recommended for	Local favourite

'It's a grill-house that serves fine Argentinian beef and excellent cold meats and cheese. It has its own meat-ageing chamber. It's a modern place where owner Andrés Porcel offers great service.'
—Matías Kyriazis

LA BOURGOGNE

Alvear Palace Hotel
Avenida Alvear 1891
Recoleta
Buenos Aires C1129AAA
+54 1148082100
www.alvearpalace.com

Recommended by
Federico Fialayre,
Emilio Garip

Opening hours	Closed Sunday
Credit cards	Accepted
Price range	Expensive
Style	Smart casual
Cuisine	French
Recommended for	High end

'It serves the best French cuisine in the city. They have foie gras, veal with Béarnaise sauce, frog, the best bread in the city, French and Argentinian cheeses, a great wine cellar and a refined and civilized ambience.'
—Emilio Garip

FLORERÍA ATLÁNTICO

Arroyo 872
Recoleta
Buenos Aires C1007AAB
+54 1143136093

Recommended by
Federico Fialayre,
Emilio Garip

Opening hours	Closed Sunday
Credit cards	Accepted
Price range	Affordable
Style	Casual
Cuisine	Bar-Small plates
Recommended for	Late night

'Florería Atlántico is better known for its cocktails but their rustic flame-cooked dishes are much more sophisticated than even their customers give them credit for. It also has the advantage of staying open late, so I often end up there. And I like Hernán Gipponi's cooking.'—Emilio Garip

L'ORANGERIE

Recommended by
Alberto Chicote

Alvear Palace Hotel
Avenida Alvear 1891
Recoleta
Buenos Aires C1129AAA
+54 1148082949
www.alvearpalace.com

Opening hours	Open 7 days
Credit cards	Accepted
Price range	Expensive
Style	Smart casual
Cuisine	Café
Recommended for	Breakfast

LA RAMBLA

Recommended by
Juan Gaffuri

Posadas 1602
Recoleta
Buenos Aires C1112ADD
+54 1148046958

Opening hours	Open 7 days
Credit cards	Accepted
Price range	Budget
Style	Casual
Cuisine	Sandwiches
Recommended for	Bargain

'A classic restaurant and bar where they make an amazing meat *lomito* (Argentinian sirloin steak sandwich). The meat alone must weigh almost 300g (10 oz).'—Juan Gaffuri

RESTAURANTE OVIEDO

Recommended by
Juan Gaffuri

Antonio Beruti 2602
Recoleta
Buenos Aires C1425BBD
+54 1148213741
www.oviedoresto.com.ar

Opening hours	Closed Sunday
Credit cards	Accepted
Price range	Expensive
Style	Smart casual
Cuisine	Modern Seafood
Recommended for	Regular neighbourhood

'They serve local cuisine with a Spanish twist. Great food and service.'—Juan Gaffuri

RESTÓ

Recommended by
Martín Molteni,
Fernando Rivarola

Montevideo 938
Recoleta
Buenos Aires C1019ABT
+54 1148166711

Opening hours	Closed Saturday and Sunday
Credit cards	Not accepted
Price range	Affordable
Style	Casual
Cuisine	Argentinian
Recommended for	Bargain

'For the past sixteen years, Guido Tassi, owner, chef and disciple of Michel Bras, has been offering what might be one of the most accessible and delicious menus in the city. The restaurant always works with seasonal ingredients and has a limited but interesting menu, made up of dishes and ingredients that constantly change depending on the season and market availability. The place is small and the decor is subtle and considered. The restaurant is inside the building that used to be the Society of Architects' headquarters.' —Fernando Rivarola

EL SANJUANINO

Recommended by
Martín Rebaudino

Posadas 1515
Recoleta
Buenos Aires C1112ADA
+54 1148042909
www.elsanjuanino.co

Opening hours	Open 7 days
Credit cards	Accepted
Price range	Budget
Style	Casual
Cuisine	Argentinian
Recommended for	Late night

'After going out for dinner and a drink, I like to have some lovely empanadas with a good piece of goat's cheese and *cuaresmillo* (Argentinian peach) here.' —Martín Rebaudino

TARQUINO

Recommended by
Fernando Rivarola

Rodríguez Peña 1967
Recoleta
Buenos Aires C1014AAD
+54 1160912160

Opening hours	Closed Sunday
Credit cards	Accepted
Price range	Expensive
Style	Smart casual
Cuisine	Modern Argentinian
Recommended for	Local favourite

'Located in the lovely neighbourhood of Recoleta, two-year-old Tarquino is a restaurant that aims high when it comes to innovation. Its head chef, Dante Liporace, brilliantly transforms the flavours of local and contemporary cuisine. The restaurant is located within the small but luxurious Hub Porteño Hotel, and the dining room boasts lavish decor. During the day, it offers a lunch menu that is appealing and delicious. In the evenings, you can order innovative dishes à la carte or as part of a tasting menu.'—Fernando Rivarola

VICENTE LÓPEZ

Recommended by
Hernán Gipponi

Azcuénaga 1110
Recoleta
Buenos Aires C1115AAH
+54 1147967955
www.vicentelopezcafe.com.ar

Opening hours	Closed Monday
Credit cards	Accepted
Price range	Affordable
Style	Casual
Cuisine	Bakery-Café-Deli
Recommended for	Breakfast

'Actually, more than going to the coffee shop, I like to stop by the bakery, buy butter croissants and pastries – in my opinion, the best you can get – and then go to the riverside to drink some *mate* (a popular Argentinian drink similar to tea).'—Hernán Gipponi

ARAMBURU

Recommended by
Federico Fialayre, Hernán
Gipponi, Matías Kyriazis,
Soledad Nardelli

Salta 1050
San Cristobal
Buenos Aires C1074AAV
+54 1143050439
www.arambururesto.com.ar

Opening hours	Closed Sunday
Credit cards	Accepted
Price range	Expensive
Style	Smart casual
Cuisine	Modern Argentinian
Recommended for	High end

'It's one of the best places in Buenos Aires, run by chef Gonzalo Aramburu and it's famous for its modern cuisine based on local ingredients. Ideally, you should book the chef's table in his private studio.'
—Matías Kyriazis

EL CUARTITO

Recommended by
Juan Gaffuri,
Martín Molteni,
Fernando Trocca

Talcahuano 937
San Cristobal
Buenos Aires C1013AAS
+54 1148161758

Opening hours	Closed Monday
Credit cards	Not accepted
Price range	Budget
Style	Casual
Cuisine	Pizza
Recommended for	Late night

'Old-school pizza masters working non-stop at the counter prepare double *fugazzeta*, which is very typical of my childhood and culture.'—Martín Molteni

Argentina's national preference for thick-crust, cheesy pizza will never convince the Neapolitan purists, but El Cuartito's avid fans don't much care. They've been snaking out the door for a slice of this vintage pizza shop's superb Argentine variety since 1934. Popular orders are the *fugazzeta rellena* (cheese-stuffed, cheese-and-onion-topped pizza), empanadas, chickpea (garbanzo bean) flour flatbreads (NB: eaten with the pizza) and cold Quilmes beers. Porteños (inhabitants of Buenos Aires) of every stripe consider this scruffy, football-poster-lined joint their very own: office workers wolf down a slice at the bar and soigné opera fans sneak in from the Teatro Colón.

KAESHI I·D COCINA

Recommended by
Fernando Rivarola

Sánchez de Loría 641
San Cristobal
Buenos Aires C1220ADA
+54 1120750200

Opening hours	Closed Wednesday
Credit cards	Not accepted
Price range	Affordable
Style	Casual
Cuisine	Sushi
Recommended for	Late night

'I love Asian food and chef Leo Choi is an expert in that area of cuisine. He welcomes you as if he was inviting you into his own home and prepares the best sashimi I have ever tasted in Buenos Aires. He is very careful with the ingredients he uses and makes sure that everything is fresh and served at its best. It's also a family-run business and he works with his wife.'
—Fernando Rivarola

LA BRIGADA

Recommended by
Juan Gaffuri

Estados Unidos 456
San Telmo
Buenos Aires C1101AAI
+54 1143615557
www.parrillalabrigada.com.ar

Opening hours	Closed Monday
Credit cards	Accepted
Price range	Affordable
Style	Casual
Cuisine	Argentinian Steakhouse
Recommended for	Local favourite

'It's a very good grill-house that's highly representative of our culture. It has something of the football lover's tavern about it. Their ribeye cap is to die for.'
—Juan Gaffuri

CAFÉ SAN JUAN

Recommended by
Gonzalo Aramburu

Avenida San Juan 450
San Telmo
Buenos Aires B8000XAV
+54 1143001112

Opening hours	Closed Monday
Credit cards	Not accepted
Price range	Affordable
Style	Casual
Cuisine	Modern Argentinian
Recommended for	Local favourite

'Showcases the wide range of flavours that the Porteños (inhabitants of Buenos Aires) are used to. I go there a lot as it's always good to chat with the chef-owner Léle and to share a pure Fernet.'
—Gonzalo Aramburu

CASEROS

Recommended by
Gonzalo Aramburu

Avenida Caseros 486
San Telmo
Buenos Aires C1152AAN
+54 1143074729
www.caserosrestaurante.com.ar

Opening hours	Closed Sunday
Credit cards	Accepted
Price range	Affordable
Style	Casual
Cuisine	Argentinian-Italian
Recommended for	Wish I'd opened

'Located on one of the most beautiful boulevards in the city, the food at this place is fresh, simple and delicious. It doesn't disappoint and it's one of my favourite restaurants. The chef, Silvina Trouilh, is always there cooking and adding quality to each order.'
—Gonzalo Aramburu

DOPPELGÄNGER BAR

Recommended by
Estefanía Di Benedetto,
Matías Kyriazis

Avenida Juan de Garay 500
San Telmo
Buenos Aires C1154AAD
+54 1143000201
www.doppelganger.com.ar

Opening hours	Closed Monday and Sunday
Reservation policy	No
Credit cards	Accepted
Price range	Affordable
Style	Casual
Cuisine	International
Recommended for	Late night

'It's a bar that serves classic cocktails and the best Martinis in town, accompanied by good plates of food.'
—Estefanía Di Benedetto

PASAJE SOLAR

Recommended by
Fernando Rivarola

Balcarce 1022
San Telmo
Buenos Aires C1064AAV
+54 1143611549

Opening hours	Closed Monday
Credit cards	Not accepted
Price range	Affordable
Style	Casual
Cuisine	Argentinian-Italian
Recommended for	Regular neighbourhood

'The food is simple, fast and as tasty as a home-cooked meal. They offer a menu of daily specials, which represents a sensible cooking style. The service is personalized and the owners are always around. They serve really delicious chard fritters while you wait and they even give you the recipe so that you can try them at home. The restaurant is in an old refurbished house that has been turned into a small hotel. It has an open patio that's perfect for hot days.'—Fernando Rivarola

EL REFUERZO BAR ALMACEN

Recommended by
Gonzalo Aramburu

Chacabuco 872
San Telmo
Buenos Aires C1069AAR
+54 1143613013

Opening hours	Closed Monday
Credit cards	Not accepted
Price range	Budget
Style	Casual
Cuisine	Argentinian
Recommended for	Late night

'In the evening, I usually go to El Refuerzo. Alfredo Tourn is another colleague that puts everything into his dishes.'—Gonzalo Aramburu

RESTAURANTE CASAL DE CATALUNYA

Recommended by
Soledad Nardelli

Chacabuco 863
San Telmo
Buenos Aires C1069AAQ
+54 1143610191

Opening hours	Open 7 days
Credit cards	Accepted
Price range	Affordable
Style	Casual
Cuisine	Catalan
Recommended for	Regular neighbourhood

'The food is simple and cooked with fresh ingredients, and the restaurant is located in one of the city's historic sites – a magical old theatre with a very relaxed ambience.'—Soledad Nardelli

SARKIS

Recommended by
Martín Rebaudino

Thames 1101
Villa Crespo
Buenos Aires C1414DCW
+54 1147724911

Opening hours	Open 7 days
Credit cards	Not accepted
Price range	Budget
Style	Casual
Cuisine	Armenian
Recommended for	Bargain

'It's always full and the food is delicious and really fresh. I love good Armenian cooking.'
—Martín Rebaudino

L'ÉPI BOULANGERIE

Recommended by
Estefanía Di Benedetto

Roseti 1769
Villa Ortuzar
Buenos Aires C1427BWI
+54 1145526402
www.lepi.com.ar

Opening hours	Closed Monday
Reservation policy	No
Credit cards	Not accepted
Price range	Budget
Style	Casual
Cuisine	Bakery
Recommended for	Breakfast

'This French bakery is ideal for buying yeast-free breads during the day. In addition to the food, the bakery itself is a really lovely, enjoyable place, where you are served by the owners. Croissants and pains au chocolat are some of the things that I always order.'
—Estefanía Di Benedetto

MAGRITTE

Recommended by
Emilio Garip

Olazábal 5501
Villa Urquiza
Buenos Aires C1431CGL
+54 1145236316

Opening hours	Open 7 days
Credit cards	Accepted
Price range	Affordable
Style	Casual
Cuisine	Argentinian
Recommended for	Bargain

'The food is delicious, the portions are generous, everything is fresh, the wines are good and it's also inexpensive.'—Emilio Garip

THE SINGULAR RESTAURANT

Recommended by
Rodolfo Guzmán

The Singular Patagonia Hotel
Norte Km. 5
Puerto Natales
Magallanes 6160000
Chile
+56 612722030
www.thesingular.com

Opening hours	Open 7 days
Credit cards	Accepted
Price range	Expensive
Style	Smart casual
Cuisine	Chilean
Recommended for	High end

'I don't think the restaurant is very expensive but the hotel is in one of the most spectacular places on Earth, in wonderful surroundings. I think every person in the world should have the experience of staying there. The restaurant is very good but also very simple, and the ingredients they use are honest and sourced locally with great care. Eating in a place like this in Patagonia is a great privilege.'—Rodolfo Guzmán

RANCHO DOÑA MARÍA

Recommended by
Rodolfo Guzmán

Autopista Los Libertadores Km. 41
Colina
Santiago 9340000
Chile

Opening hours	Open 7 days
Credit cards	Not accepted
Price range	Budget
Style	Casual
Cuisine	Chilean
Recommended for	Regular neighbourhood

'I like this restaurant despite its dirt floor, the plastic chairs and the hens wandering around because the food is 100 per cent Chilean. Everything you taste is based on recipes that have been passed from generation to generation, which I find ridiculously delicious. María learnt from her mother who, in turn, learnt from her grandmother and so on. María cooks in a clay oven, just like rural Chileans did hundreds of years ago.'—Rodolfo Guzmán

AQUÍ ESTÁ COCO

Recommended by
Rodolfo Guzmán

La Concepción 236
Santiago
Santiago 7500014
Chile
+56 24106200
www.aquiestacoco.cl

Opening hours	Closed Sunday
Credit cards	Accepted
Price range	Affordable
Style	Smart casual
Cuisine	Seafood
Recommended for	Local favourite

'As well as being a restaurant that tourists in Santiago really shouldn't miss – not only because of what it represents but because of the quality of the seafood – it has been in business for over thirty-five years. The restaurant has recently undergone major refurbishment and the family's passion for their work is something that I rarely see in other places. I've really enjoyed it every time I've been there.'—Rodolfo Guzmán

EL QUILLAY

Recommended by
Rodolfo Guzmán

Camino San Jose de Maipo
Santiago
Santiago 05700
Chile
+56 004563333
www.brontob.wix.com/el-quillay

Opening hours	Open 7 days
Reservation policy	No
Credit cards	Not accepted
Price range	Budget
Style	Casual
Cuisine	Chilean
Recommended for	Bargain

'It serves inexpensive Chilean food and is famous for its empanadas stuffed with *pino* (a seasoned mixture of minced beef, onions, raisins, olives and hard-boiled eggs) and cheese. I actually like it because the cheese empanadas are spectacular. The buttermilk is separated from the cheese, which is made with local cow's milk. The empanadas de pino are baked in a clay oven and are among the best I've ever tasted and are really cheap. El Quillay is on the coastal road to Santiago and there's a big sign by the road but you have to be careful not to miss it!'—Rodolfo Guzmán

MESTIZO

Recommended by
Rodolfo Guzmán

Avenida Bicentenario 4050
Vitacura
Santiago 7630000
Chile
+56 974776093
www.mestizorestaurant.cl

Opening hours	Open 7 days
Credit cards	Accepted
Price range	Expensive
Style	Smart casual
Cuisine	Modern Chilean
Recommended for	Wish I'd opened

'You have to go to Mestizo. It's an urban restaurant in a privileged area of Santiago, serving food that retains Chilean flavours and which has greatly improved in the last year. It also has a delicious cocktail and juice bar. Thanks to the spectacular architecture, you can watch the sunset from inside the restaurant but feel as though you are outdoors. It's in a spectacular part of the city. The restaurant is beautiful and very close to nature and despite it being in a capital city, I don't think there are many projects like this anywhere else in the world. The food is good and it has great potential!'
—Rodolfo Guzmán

QUINOA

Recommended by
Rodolfo Guzmán

Avenida Luis Pasteur 5393
Vitacura
Santiago 7630186
Chile
+56 29540283
www.quinoarestaurante.cl

Opening hours	Closed Sunday
Credit cards	Accepted
Price range	Affordable
Style	Casual
Cuisine	Chilean
Recommended for	Breakfast

'It's a place where the bread – Chilean flatbread, based on the *tortilla al rescoldo* – is kneaded and baked daily. They have at least twenty different types of artisan tea, natural yogurt, cereal and home-made cakes and marmalades.'—Rodolfo Guzmán

INDEX BY RESTAURANT

INDEX BY TYPE

LATE NIGHT

WORTH THE TRAVEL

Phaidon Press Limited
Regent's Wharf
All Saints Street
London N1 9AP

Phaidon Press Inc.
65 Bleecker Street
New York, NY 10012

www.phaidon.com

First published in 2015
© 2015 Phaidon Press Limited

ISBN 978 0 7148 6866 0

A CIP catalogue record for this book
is available from the British Library.

As many restaurants are closed Sunday and/or
Monday, and some change their opening hours
in relation to the seasons or close for extended
periods at different times of the year, it is always
advisable to check opening hours before visiting.
All information is correct at the time of going to
print, but is subject to change.

Commissioning Editor: Emilia Terragni
Project Editor: Sophie Hodgkin
Contributing Editor: Joe Warwick
Production Controller: Steve Bryant

Designed by Kobi Benezri

The publisher would like to thank all the participating
chefs for their generosity, time and insightful
restaurant recommendations; Joe Warwick for his
commitment and enthusiasm; and Imogen Adams,
Hilary Armstrong, Douglas Blyde, Adam Brown,
Sophie Chatellier, Colin Christie, Sophie Dening,
Lena Hall, Corinna Hardgrave, Anne Heining, Anna
Kibbey, Clodagh Kinsella, Andy Lynes, Ana Minguez,
Laura Nickoll, Chris Pople, Nick Redgrove, Emma
Robertson, Emma Sturgess, Oliver Thring and Mari
Zizka for their contributions to the book.

Printed in Italy